THE

WAR OF THE REBELLION:

A COMPILATION OF THE

OFFICIAL RECORDS

OF THE

UNION AND CONFEDERATE ARMIES.

PREPARED, UNDER THE DIRECTION OF THE SECRETARY OF WAR,

BY

Lieut. Col. ROBERT N. SCOTT, Third U. S. Artillery,

AND

PUBLISHED PURSUANT TO ACT OF CONGRESS APPROVED JUNE 16, 1880.

SERIES I—VOLUME XVI—IN TWO PARTS.
PART I—REPORTS.

WASHINGTON:
GOVERNMENT PRINTING OFFICE.
1886.

PREFACE.

By an act approved June 23, 1874, Congress made an appropriation "to enable the Secretary of War to begin the publication of the Official Records of the War of the Rebellion, both of the Union and Confederate Armies," and directed him "to have copied for the Public Printer all reports, letters, telegrams, and general orders not heretofore copied or printed, and properly arranged in chronological order."

Appropriations for continuing such preparation have been made from time to time, and the act approved June 16, 1880, has provided "for the printing and binding, under direction of the Secretary of War, of 10,000 copies of a compilation of the Official Records (Union and Confederate) of the War of the Rebellion, so far as the same may be ready for publication, during the fiscal year"; and that " of said number, 7,000 copies shall be for the use of the House of Representatives, 2,000 copies for the use of the Senate, and 1,000 copies for the use of the Executive Departments."*

This compilation will be the first general publication of the military records of the war, and will embrace all official documents that can be obtained by the compiler, and that appear to be of any historical value.

---

*Volume I to V distributed under act approved June 16, 1880. The act approved August 7, 1882, provides that—

"The volumes of the official records of the war of the rebellion shall be distributed as follows: One thousand copies to the executive departments, as now provided by law. One thousand copies for distribution by the Secretary of War among officers of the Army and contributors to the work. Eight thousand three hundred copies shall be sent by the Secretary of War to such libraries, organizations, and individuals as may be designated by the Senators, Representatives, and Delegates of the Forty-seventh Congress. Each Senator shall designate not exceeding twenty-six, and each Representative and Delegate not exceeding twenty-one of such addresses, and the volumes shall be sent thereto from time to time as they are published, until the publication is completed. Senators, Representatives, and Delegates shall inform the Secretary of War in each case how many volumes of those heretofore published they have forwarded to such addresses. The remaining copies of the eleven thousand to be published, and all sets that may not be ordered to be distributed as provided herein, shall be sold by the Secretary of War for cost of publication with ten per cent. added thereto, and the proceeds of such sale shall be covered into the Treasury. If two or more sets of said volumes are ordered to the same address the Secretary of War shall inform the Senators, Representatives or Delegates, who have designated the same, who thereupon may designate other libraries, organizations, or individuals. The Secretary of War shall report to the first session of the Forty-eighth Congress what volumes of the series heretofore published have not been furnished to such libraries, organizations, and individuals. He shall also inform distributees at whose instance the volumes are sent."

The publication will present the records in the following order of arrangement:

The 1st Series will embrace the formal reports, both Union and Confederate, of the first seizures of United States property in the Southern States, and of all military operations in the field, with the correspondence, orders, and returns relating specially thereto, and, as proposed, is to be accompanied by an Atlas.

In this series the reports will be arranged according to the campaigns and several theaters of operations (in the chronological order of the events), and the Union reports of any event will, as a rule, be immediately followed by the Confederate accounts. The correspondence, &c., not embraced in the "reports" proper will follow (first Union and next Confederate) in chronological order.

The 2d Series will contain the correspondence, orders, reports, and returns, Union and Confederate, relating to prisoners of war, and (so far as the military authorities were concerned) to State or political prisoners.

The 3d Series will contain the correspondence, orders, reports, and returns of the Union authorities (embracing their correspondence with the Confederate officials) not relating specially to the subjects of the *first* and *second* series. It will set forth the annual and special reports of the Secretary of War, of the General-in-Chief, and of the chiefs of the several staff corps and departments; the calls for troops, and the correspondence between the National and the several State authorities.

The 4th Series will exhibit the correspondence, orders, reports, and returns of the Confederate authorities, similar to that indicated for the Union officials, as of the *third* series, but excluding the correspondence between the Union and confederate authorities given in that series.

ROBERT N. SCOTT,
Major, Third Art., and Bvt. Lieut. Col.

WAR DEPARTMENT, *August* 23, 1880.

Approved:

ALEX. RAMSEY,
Secretary of War.

CONTENTS.

CHAPTER XXVIII.

(V)

CONTENTS OF PRECEDING VOLUMES.

VOLUME I.

CHAPTER XXVIII.

OPERATIONS IN KENTUCKY, MIDDLE AND EAST TENNESSEE, NORTH ALABAMA, AND SOUTHWEST VIRGINIA.

June 10–October 31, 1862.

SUMMARY OF THE PRINCIPAL EVENTS.*

June   10, 1862.—Maj. Gens. U. S. Grant, D. C. Buell, and John Pope, U. S. Army, ordered to resume command of their separate army corps.†
Skirmish at Winchester, Tenn.
Skirmishes at Wilson's and Rogers' Gaps, Tenn. ‡

11, 1862.—Skirmish near Monterey, Ky.

11–13, 1862.—Skirmishes at Big Creek Gap, Ky. †

16, 1862.—Skirmish at Winchester, Tenn.

17, 1862.—General Braxton Bragg, C. S. Army, supersedes General G. T. Beauregard in command of Department No. 2, or the Western Department.

18, 1862.—Skirmish at Wilson's Gap and occupation of Cumberland Gap by the Union forces. ‡

20–23, 1862.—Affairs in Owen County, Ky., and skirmish near Lusby's Mill.

21, 1862.—Skirmish at Rankin's Ferry, near Jasper, Tenn.
Skirmish at Battle Creek, Tenn.

26, 1862.—Maj. Gen. John Pope, U. S. Army, assigned to command of the Army of Virginia.

28, 1862.—Skirmish at Sparta, Tenn.

30, 1862.—Affair at Powell River, Tenn.
Skirmish at Henderson, Ky.

July   2, 1862.—Skirmish at Huntsville, Ala.
Department No. 2 extended.

3, 1862.—Skirmish near Russellville, Ala.

4–28, 1862.—Morgan's first Kentucky raid.

5, 1862.—Maj. Gen. William J. Hardee, C. S. Army, temporarily commanding Army of the Mississippi.
Skirmish at Battle Creek, Tenn.

7–11, 1862.—Operations about Cumberland Gap, Tenn.

11, 1862.—Maj. Gen. Henry W. Halleck assigned to command of the Armies of the United States.

12–16, 1862.—Expedition from Decatur, Ala., and skirmish near Davis' Gap.

13, 1862.—Action at and surrender of Murfreesborough, Tenn.

15, 1862.—Skirmish at Wallace's Cross-Roads, Tenn.

---

* Of some of the minor conflicts noted in this "Summary" no circumstantial reports are on file.

† See Series I, Vol. X, Part II, p. 288.

‡ For reports, see Cumberland Gap Campaign, Series I, Vol. X, Part I, p. 51.

July	17, 1862.—Skirmish between Mount Pleasant and Columbia, Tenn.
	18, 1862.—Raid on Henderson, Ky., and Newburg, Ind.
	Department of East Tennessee (Confederate) extended.
	21, 1862.—Skirmishes around Nashville, Tenn.
	25, 1862.—Skirmish at Courtland, Ala.
	Skirmish at and near Trinity, Ala.
	Skirmish at Clinton Ferry, Tenn.
	26, 1862.—Action near Spangler's Mill, near Jonesborough, Ala.
	Skirmish at Tazewell, Tenn.
	27–30, 1862.—Expedition from Woodville to Guntersville, Ala., and skirmishes (July 28) at Guntersville and Law's Landing, and (July 29) at Old Deposit Ferry.
	28, 1862.—Skirmish at Stevenson, Ala.
	29, 1862.—Skirmish at Russellville, Ky.
Aug.	2– 6, 1862.—Operations at Cumberland Gap and skirmish (August 6) near Tazewell, Tenn.
	3, 1862.—Skirmish near Morganfield, Ky.
	4– 7, 1862.—Attack on Union pickets near Woodville, Ala. (August 4), and reconnaissance from Woodville to Guntersville, Ala. (August 5–7).
	5, 1862.—Skirmish at Sparta, Tenn.
	Skirmish near New Market, Ala.
	7, 1862.—Attack on convalescent train near Decatur, Ala.
	11, 1862.—Affair near Kinderhook, Tenn.
	Skirmish near Williamsport, Tenn.
	12–13, 1862.—Capture of Gallatin, Tenn., and destruction of bridges in that vicinity (August 12) and skirmish (August 13).
	13, 1862.—Skirmish at Huntsville, Scott County, Tenn.
	14, 1862.—Skirmish near Mount Pleasant, Tenn.
	15, 1862.—General Braxton Bragg, C. S. Army, resumes command of the Army of the Mississippi.
	16, 1862.—The Army of Kentucky (Confederate), under Maj. Gen. E. Kirby Smith, crosses the Cumberland Mountains into Kentucky.
	16–22, 1862.—Operations about Cumberland Gap, Tenn., including action at London, Ky., and skirmishes at Flat Lick, Ky., and Pine Mountain, Tenn. (August 17).
	17, 1862.—Skirmish near Mammoth Cave, Ky.
	18, 1862.—Surrender of Clarksville, Tenn.
	19, 1862.—The Department of the Ohio re-established.
	19–20, 1862.—Scout from Woodville to Guntersville, Ala., and vicinity.
	19–21, 1862.—Raid on Louisville and Nashville Railroad, skirmishes at Pilot Knob, Drake's Creek, and Manscoe Creek, near Edgefield Junction (August 20), and action (August 21) on the Hartsville Road, near Gallatin, Tenn.
	20, 1862.—Skirmish at Pilot Knob, Tenn.
	22, 1862.—Skirmish at Trinity, Ala.
	23, 1862.—Maj. Gen. Horatio G. Wright, U. S. Army, assumes command of the Department of the Ohio.
	Action at Big Hill, Ky.
	24, 1862.—Maj. Gen. J. P. McCown, C. S. Army, assigned temporarily to command of the Department of East Tennessee.
	25, 1862.—Skirmish at Red Bird Creek, Ky.
	Skirmish at Madisonville, Ky.
	26, 1862.—Skirmish at Cumberland Gap, Tenn.
	27, 1862.—Skirmish at Round Mountain, near Woodbury, Tenn.
	Skirmish at Bridgeport, Ala., and attack on Fort McCook, Battle Creek, Tenn.

Aug.   27, 1862.—Skirmish near Cumberland Gap, Tenn.

Skirmish near Murfreesborough, Tenn.

Skirmish on Richland Creek, near Pulaski, Tenn.

Skirmish near Reynolds' Station, Nashville and Decatur Railroad.

27–28, 1862.—Army of the Mississippi, under General Braxton Bragg, C. S. Army, crosses the Tennessee River.

27–Oct. 22, 1862.—Operations of Wheeler's Cavalry in Tennessee and Kentucky.

29, 1862.—Skirmish between Big Hill and Richmond, Ky.

29–30, 1862.—Skirmishes at Short Mountain Cross-Roads (August 29), and Little Pond (August 30), near McMinnville, Tenn.

30, 1862.—Battle of Richmond, Ky., or engagements at Mount Zion Church, White's Farm, and Richmond.

Skirmish near Larkinsville, Ala.

31, 1862.—Skirmish at Stevenson, Ala.

Skirmish on the Kentucky River, Ky.

Skirmish at Rogers' Gap, Tenn.

Sept.   1, 1862.—Maj. Gen. J. P. McCown, C. S. Army, assumes command of the Department of East Tennessee.

Skirmish at Uniontown, Ky.

Skirmish at Tait's Ferry, Kentucky River, Ky.

Skirmish at Morganfield, Ky.

Skirmish at Huntsville, Ala.

2, 1862.—Skirmish near Nashville, Tenn.

Lexington, Ky., occupied by the Confederate forces.

3, 1862.—Skirmish at Geiger's Lake, Ky.

4, 1862.—Skirmish at Shelbyville, Ky.

5, 1862.—Skirmish near Madisonville, Ky.

5–10, 1862.—Expedition from Fort Donelson to Clarksville, Tenn., and skirmishes (September 6) at New Providence and (September 7) at Riggin's Hill.

7, 1862.—Skirmish at Pine Mountain Gap, Tenn.

Skirmish near Murfreesborough, Tenn.

Surrender of outpost at Shepherdsville, Ky.

8, 1862.—Skirmish at Barboursville, Ky.

9, 1862.—Skirmishes on the Franklin and Scottsville Roads, Ky.

Skirmish at Columbia, Tenn.

10, 1862.—Operations at Rogers' and Big Creek Gaps, Tenn.

Skirmish at Columbia, Tenn.

Skirmish at Fort Mitchel, near Covington, Ky.

Skirmish at Woodburn, Ky.

12, 1862.—Skirmish at Brandenburg, Ky.

Glasgow, Ky., occupied by the Confederate forces.

14, 1862.—Skirmish at Henderson, Ky.

14–17, 1862.—Siege of Munfordville and Woodsonville, Ky.

17, 1862.—Skirmish near Falmouth, Ky.

17–Oct. 3, 1862.—Evacuation of Cumberland Gap, Tenn., and march of its garrison to Greenupsburg, Ky.

18, 1862.—Affair at Glasgow, Ky.

Skirmish near Florence, Ky.

Skirmish at Owensborough, Ky.

19, 1862.—West Virginia embraced in Department of the Ohio.

Skirmish at Southerland's Farm, Ky.

19–20, 1862.—Skirmishes at Brentwood, Tenn.

Sept. 23, 1862.—Department of the Tennessee constituted, under command of Maj.
           Gen. George H. Thomas, U. S. Army. (Inoperative.)

25, 1362.—Skirmish near Snow's Pond, Ky.
           Skirmish at Ashbysburg, Ky.

26, 1862.—Action at West Liberty, Ky.

27, 1862.—Maj. Gen. J. P. McCown, C. S. Army, assigned to command of the
           Department of East Tennessee, and Maj. Gen. Samuel Jones,
           C. S. Army, to command of the District of Middle Tennessee.

27–28, 1862.—Skirmishes at Augusta and Brookville, Ky.

29, 1862.—Capture of the Third Georgia Cavalry near New Haven, Ky.

30, 1862.—Skirmishes at Russellville and Glasgow, Ky.
           Skirmish near Louisville, Ky.
           Skirmish at Goodlettsville, Tenn.

Oct.   1, 1862.—Skirmish on the Bardstown Pike, near Mount Washington, Ky.
           Skirmish on Fern Creek, Louisville and Frankfort Road, Ky.
           Skirmish near Nashville, Tenn.
           Skirmish at Davis' Bridge, Tenn.

3, 1862.—Skirmish at Cedar Church, near Shepherdsville, Ky.

4, 1862.—Skirmish near Bardstown, Ky.
           Skirmish near Clay Village, Ky.

5, 1862.—Skirmish at Neely's Bend, Cumberland River, Tenn.
           Skirmish at Fort Riley, near Nashville, Tenn.

7, 1862.—Maj. Gen. Gordon Granger, U. S. Army, assigned to command of
           the Army of Kentucky.
           Skirmish near La Vergne, Tenn.

8, 1862.—Battle of Perryville, or Chaplin Hills, Ky.
           Skirmish at Lawrenceburg, Ky.

9, 1862.—Action at Dry Ridge, Dog Walk, or Chesser's Store, near Salt
           River, Ky.

10–22, 1862.—Pursuit of Confederate forces from Perryville to London, Ky.

11, 1862.—Skirmish at Lawrenceburg, Ky.

13, 1862.—Skirmish on the Lebanon Road, near Nashville, Tenn.

14, 1862.—Skirmish at Manchester, Ky.

15, 1862.—Skirmish at Neely's Bend, Cumberland River, Tenn.

15–20, 1862.—Operations against guerrillas in the counties of Henry, Owen, and
           Gallatin, Ky.

16–25, 1862.—Operations in Bath, Powell, Estill, Clark, Montgomery, and
           Bourbon Counties, Ky.

18, 1862.—Skirmish at Bloomfield, Ky.
           Action at Lexington, Ky.

19, 1862.—Skirmish at Bardstown, Ky.

20, 1862.—Skirmish on the Gallatin Pike, near Nashville, Tenn.
           Skirmish at Hermitage Ford, Tenn.

23, 1862.—Skirmishes near Waverly and Richland Creek, Tenn.

23–24, 1862.—Destruction of Goose Creek Salt-Works, near Manchester, Ky.

24, 1862.—The Department of the Cumberland re-established.
           Maj. Gen. Leonidas Polk, C. S. Army, temporarily in command of
           Department No. 2.

25, 1862.—Skirmish at Lawrenceburg, Ky.

27, 1862.—Maj. Gen. William S. Rosecrans, U. S. Army, assumes command
           of the Fourteenth Army Corps.

28, 1862.—Maj. Gen. John C. Breckinridge, C. S. Army, assumes command
           of the Army of Middle Tennessee.
           Skirmish near Waverly, Tenn.

30, 1862.—Major-General Rosecrans assumes command of the Department of
           the Cumberland, superseding Major-General Buell.

GENERAL REPORTS.

No. 1.—Extracts from Annual Report of Maj. Gen. Henry W. Halleck, General-in-
Chief U. S. Army.

No. 2.—Findings of the "Buell Commission" and accompanying documents.

No. 1.

*Extracts from Annual Report of Maj. Gen. Henry W. Halleck, General-
in-Chief U. S. Army.*

HEADQUARTERS OF THE ARMY,
Washington, November 25, 1862.

SIR : In compliance with your orders I have the honor to submit the
following report of military operations since the 23d of July last, when,
in compliance with the President's order of July 11, I assumed command of the Army as General-in-Chief :

*   *   *   *   *   *   *

When I left the Department of the Mississippi, in July last, the main
body of the army under Major-General Buell was between Huntsville
and Stevenson, moving toward Chattanooga, for which place they had
left Corinth about the 10th of June.

Major-General Curtis' forces were at Helena, Ark., and those under
Brigadier-General Schofield in Southwestern Missouri. The central
army, under Major-General Grant, occupying the line of West Tennessee and Northern Mississippi, extended from Memphis to Iuka, and
protected the railroads from Columbus, Ky., south, which were then
our only channels of supply.

These several armies, spread along a line of some 600 miles from the
western borders of Arkansas to Cumberland Gap, and occupying a
strip of country more than 150 miles in width, from which the enemy's
forces had recently been expelled, were rapidly decreasing in strength
from the large numbers of soldiers sent home on account of real or pretended disability. On the other hand, the enemy's armies were greatly
increased by an arbitrary and rigidly enforced conscription. With
their superiority in numbers and discipline they boldly determined to
reoccupy Arkansas, Missouri, Tennessee, and Kentucky, and, if possible, to invade the States of Ohio, Indiana, and Illinois, while our attention was distracted by the invasion of Maryland and Pennsylvania
and an extended Indian insurrection on the western frontiers.

This plan had very many chances of success, but the timely order of
the President of August 4, calling for additional forces, and the patriotic response of the people of the Northwest, thwarted the enemy's well-
formed calculations.

General Bragg suddenly transferred a large part of his army from
Tupelo, Miss., through the States of Alabama and Georgia, reached
Chattanooga in advance of General Buell, turned his left, and rapidly
crossing the State of Tennessee entered Kentucky by Munfordville
and Lebanon.

General Buell fell back upon Nashville without giving the enemy
battle; then followed or rather moved parallel with Bragg, who, after
capturing our garrison at Munfordville, turned off from the main road
to Louisville, along which General Buell passed, the latter reaching
Louisville without any engagement. Another column of the enemy

had moved from East Tennessee, after blockading Cumberland Gap, upon Lexington and threatened Cincinnati.

A small force of our raw troops, which had been pushed forward to Richmond, Ky., under Major-General Nelson, were met by the enemy and completely routed.

In the mean time every effort had been made to collect new troops at Cincinnati and Louisville and to fortify these places against a *coup de main*. To give confidence to the new levies a portion of General Grant's army was withdrawn from Mississippi and sent to Kentucky and Cincinnati. No attack was attempted by the enemy.

Major-General Buell left Louisville on the 1st of October with an army of about 100,000 men in pursuit of General Bragg. The latter engaged a part of General Buell's army at Perryville about 10 o'clock on the 8th of October. A general battle ensued and was continued till dark. It was mainly fought by Major-General McCook's division. The enemy retreated during the night. The losses were heavy on both sides, but no official reports of the numbers engaged or the losses on either side have been received.

After this battle the main army of the rebels retreated to East Tennessee. General Buell pursued it as far as Mount Vernon or London, then fell back to the line from Louisville to Nashville. Here Major-General Rosecrans superseded him in the command by order of the President.

As the Secretary of War has ordered a military commission to investigate the operations of General Buell in this campaign it would be obviously improper for me to express any opinion unless specially directed to do so.

*   *   *   *   *   *   *

Very respectfully, your obedient servant,

H. W. HALLECK,
General-in-Chief.

Hon. E. M. STANTON,
Secretary of War.

No. 2.

Findings of the "Buell Commission" and accompanying documents.

WAR DEPARTMENT,
Washington City, November 4, 1862.

General HALLECK:

GENERAL: You will please organize a Military Commission to inquire into and report upon the operations of the forces under command of Major-General Buell in the States of Tennessee and Kentucky, and particularly in reference to General Buell suffering the State of Kentucky to be invaded by the rebel forces under General Bragg, and in his failing to relieve Munfordville and suffering it to be captured; also in reference to the battle of Perryville and General Buell's conduct during that battle, and afterward suffering the rebel forces to escape from Kentucky without loss or capture; and also to inquire and report upon such other matters touching the military operations aforesaid as in the judgment of the Commission shall be beneficial to the service. The Commission will sit at the city of Cincinnati. General Buell will be ordered there and have permission to appear and produce and examine witnesses before the Commission.

Yours, truly,

EDWIN M. STANTON,
Secretary of War.

—

SPECIAL ORDERS, }   HEADQUARTERS OF THE ARMY,
No. 356.   } *Adjt. Gen.'s Office, Washington, November 20, 1862.*

I. A Military Commission will convene at Cincinnati, Ohio, on the 27th instant to investigate and report upon the operations of the army under the command of Maj. Gen. D. C. Buell, U. S. Volunteers, in Kentucky and Tennessee.

Detail for the Commission.—Maj. Gen. Lewis Wallace, U. S. Volunteers; Maj. Gen. Edward O. C. Ord, U. S. Volunteers; Brig. Gen. Albin Schoepf, U. S. Volunteers; Brig. Gen. N. J. T. Dana, U. S. Volunteers; Brig. Gen. Daniel Tyler, U. S. Volunteers; Maj. Donn Piatt, aide-de-camp, judge-advocate and recorder.

The Commission will adjourn from place to place as may be deemed advisable for the convenience of taking testimony and will report an opinion in the case.

*   *   *   *   *   *   *

By command of Major-General Halleck:

E. D. TOWNSEND,
Assistant Adjutant-General.

—

WAR DEPARTMENT, *April 13, 1872.*

The Secretary of War has the honor to report to the House of Representatives, in reply to a resolution of the 1st of March, calling for a copy of the proceedings of the Military Commission instituted by the War Department in the year 1862 to inquire into the military operations and conduct of Maj. Gen. Don Carlos Buell, including all letters, dispatches, opinions, and orders on file in that Department relative thereto, that a careful and exhaustive search among all the records and files in this Department fails to discover what disposition was made of the proceedings of the Commission and the papers annexed thereto, and that no record indicative of the nature of the report of the Board or the conclusions reached by it can be found, other than what is contained in the accompanying papers, which are as follows :

Copy of the original opinion of the Commission called to investigate the operations of the Army of the Ohio in Tennessee and Kentucky, under command of Major-General Buell, U. S. Volunteers, with the views of the General-in-Chief thereupon. [Inclosure No. 2.]

Copy of a communication from General Buell of April 10, 1864, addressed to the Adjutant-General of the Army, commenting upon the report of the Board. [Inclosure No. 5.]

Copy of an unsigned communication reviewing the proceedings of the Commission, which was referred to the Secretary of War by the Judge-Advocate-General, at the request of Lieutenant-Colonel Piatt, on the 23d of May, 1863. [Inclosure No. 3.]

Copy of a communication submitted by General Buell to the Commission May 2, 1863, a copy of which was furnished the War Department by him April 11, 1864. [Sub-inclosure No. 1.]

Copy of a communication from General Buell April 11, 1864, transmitting copy last above named, and also a copy of a statement prepared by him for submission to the Commission, reviewing the evidence taken before it, which is herewith. [Inclosure No. 4 and sub-inclosure No. 2.]

Copy of General Orders, No. 29a, Headquarters Army of the Ohio, July 11, 1862. [Inclosure No. 6.]

WM. W. BELKNAP,
Secretary of War.

[Inclosure No. 1.]

ADJUTANT-GENERAL'S OFFICE,
Washington, December 11, 1871.

General JOSEPH HOLT,
     Judge-Advocate-General, Washington, D. C.:

SIR: I have respectfully to inform you that the proceedings of the Military Commission convened by Special Orders, No. 365, War Department, Adjutant-General's Office, November 20, 1862, which investigated Maj. Gen. D. C. Buell's operations in Kentucky and Tennessee, have been submitted to the Secretary of War April 15, 1863.

The accompanying correspondence of General Buell in review of the evidence before the Military Commission is all that could be found on the files in this office.

     I am, sir, very respectfully, your obedient servant,

E. D. TOWNSEND,
Adjutant-General.

[Inclosure No. 2.]

Opinion of the Commission.

The order convening the Commission requires it " to investigate and report upon the operations of the army under the command of Maj. Gen. D. C. Buell in Kentucky and Tennessee." It further requires the Commission to " report an opinion in the case."

Very early in its sessions the Commission resolved to direct its investigations to the following points :

1st. The operations of Major-General Buell in Tennessee and Kentucky.

2d. Suffering Kentucky to be invaded by rebels under General Bragg.

3d. The failure to relieve Munfordville.

4th. The battle of Perryville and conduct there.

5th. Permitting the rebels to escape without loss from Kentucky.

6th. Inquire and report upon such other matters touching military operations above specified as in the judgment of the Commission shall be beneficial to the service.

The first point really comprehends all the rest; but convenience required such a division of the subject.

The sixth point, it will be perceived, is general, and was made to cover such subjects as—

1st. General Buell's loyalty, against which there is no evidence worthy of consideration.

2d. General Buell's policy toward the inhabitants of disaffected districts into which his operations extended. This we find to have been what is familiarly known as the conciliatory policy. Whether good or bad in its effects, General Buell deserves neither blame nor applause for it, because it was at that time understood to be the policy of the Government. At least he could violate no orders on the subject, because there were none.

2. SUFFERING KENTUCKY TO BE INVADED BY REBELS UNDER BRAGG.

We find that the rebels under Bragg concentrated at Chattanooga about the 22d of July, 1862, for the purpose of invading Kentucky. Prior to that, on the 11th day of June, General Buell, with his Army of the Ohio was ordered by General Halleck to march against Chattanooga, and take it, with the ulterior object of dislodging Kirby Smith and his rebel force from East Tennessee. We are of opinion that General Buell had force sufficient to accomplish the object if he could have marched promptly to Chattanooga. The plan of operation, however, prescribed by General Halleck compelled General Buell to repair the Memphis and Charleston Railroad from Corinth to Decatur and put it in running order, as a line of supply during the advance. While that road proved of comparatively little service, the work forced such delays that a prompt march upon Chattanooga was impossible. The delays thus occasioned gave Bragg time to send a numerous cavalry force to operate against General Buell's lines of supply, which were unnecessarily long. So successful were the incursions of the cavalry that no opportunity was found, after the Memphis and Charleston Railroad was completed to Decatur, to concentrate enough of the Army of the Ohio to capture Chattanooga and execute the ulterior purposes of the expedition.

The massing of the rebel force at Chattanooga compelled a relinquishment of the design against that place; after which General Buell was required to exert all his energies to prevent the recapture of Nashville and the invasion of Kentucky. This he could have done, in our opinion, by an early concentration of his army at Sparta, McMinnville, or Murfreesborough, with a view to active offensive operations against Bragg the moment he debouched from the Sequatchie Valley. Instead of that, he waited until the 5th of September before concentrating at Murfreesborough, from which he retired to Nashville, thereby allowing Bragg to cross the Cumberland River without interruption. The Commission cannot justify the falling back from Murfreesborough to Nashville, but is of opinion that it was General Buell's duty from that point to have attacked the rebel army before it crossed the Cumberland, and it is the belief that had that course been pursued Bragg would have been defeated.

3.—THE FAILURE TO RELIEVE MUNFORDVILLE.

In the relative movements of the armies of Generals Buell and Bragg Munfordville was important on account of its railroad bridge over Green River and its natural strength as a position for battle. Bragg moved upon it by way of Glasgow, and not anticipating great resistance, he dispatched a column in advance of his main body to take it. The column was repulsed by the garrison on the 14th of September. Bragg then moved his whole army against the post. On the 17th of September it was justifiably surrendered. The order to hold Munfordville proceeded from General Wright, commanding the Department of the Ohio, of which Kentucky formed a part. It was given in expectation that General Buell would reach the place in time to save it. General Wright seems to have had no certain information upon which to base his expectation; at the time the order was given he only knew that both Bragg and General Buell were advancing toward it. Nor was there any undertaking on General Buell's part to relieve the garrison or any preconcert of action whatever respecting it. We are of opinion therefore that the orders given the commander of the post should have left him discretion to fight or retire according to circumstances. As it was, the order was to hold it to the last. Had not Bragg moved so quickly on Munfordville he would have been attacked at Glasgow by General Buell, who was moving to the attack when the surrender took place. Defeat of the rebels at Glasgow would of course have saved Munfordville. While General Buell was on the march to Mufordville he heard of its surrender. Relief was then too late.

It is our opinion, therefore, that General Buell is not responsible for the capture of the town, except so far as his failure to attack Bragg south of the Cumberland River made him responsible for the consequences of that failure.

4.—BATTLE OF PERRYVILLE AND CONDUCT THERE.

General Buell left Louisville about the 1st of October with a force superior, in our judgment, not only to Bragg's army, but to the armies of Bragg and Kirby Smith united. His routes were well chosen and the advance of his columns admirably regulated. His immediate object was to attack the rebels and destroy them; failing in that, he was to drive them out of Kentucky.

Engagement was expected at Bardstown, but Bragg sullenly retired toward Perryville, at which place it would seem from his orders and instructions to corps commanders General Buell next intended to attack him on the 9th September [October]. Positions for the formation of the line of battle were defined in those orders.

Accordingly, on the morning of the 8th, Gilbert, with his corps, was in position in the center; McCook, with his corps (less Sill's division), arrived on the left about 9 o'clock, and Thomas, in command of the right wing (Crittenden's corps), reached his position and reported his arrival to General Buell about noon.

About 2 o'clock in the afternoon the enemy poured a heavy column of attack upon McCook, effecting, in our opinion, a partial surprise. The contest, however, was obstinate and bloody and ended by night-fall, at which time McCook's right had been turned and driven back with serious loss. The duration of the battle was about five hours.

There can be no question about its being the duty of somebody to assist McCook. As his right had been posted not exceeding 300 yards from Gilbert's left and as the severest fighting was on McCook's right we cannot see why Gilbert did not re-enforce him when so requested. He should have done it, if for no other reason than because McCook's discomfiture exposed his own flank. Nothing but positive orders fixing and holding him in his position can justify his failure. If such there were, they have not been heard of in the testimony. Moreover, it is clear that all General Buell's orders were in preparation for attacking the next morning, not in anticipation of being attacked that day. In this latter event therefore the exercise of discretion could not have been improper if the action taken had been promptly reported to headquarters, particularly as General Buell was not on the field for instant consultation. As it was, assistance did not reach McCook until about dark.

General Buell established his headquarters about 2½ miles from the front on the Springfield road. He was not on the field or along the line during the day, and had no intelligence of the attack on McCook until 4 o'clock in the evening. About 2 o'clock a heavy and furious cannonading was heard at his headquarters, and coming out of his tent he said, "There was a great waste of powder over there," and directed General Gilbert, who was with him at the time, to send an order to the front "to stop that useless waste of powder." It is clear to us that General Buell did not believe a battle was in progress, and that he supposed the firing heard was from some reconnaissance. On this point it is our opinion that he should either have been on the field in person ready for emergencies and advantages, or have taken and required to be taken every precaution for the instant transmission of intelligence to his headquarters. As he had an organized signal corps with his army, this failure was all the more culpable. And in this connection we are of opinion that General McCook's failure to send up instant notice of the attack upon him in force was equally culpable.

We find that during the greater part of the attack on McCook Gilbert's corps was unengaged, while Thomas' wing had not so much as a demonstration made against it. We have reason to believe also that all Bragg's army at Perryville at the time was flung upon McCook, and that his lines of retreat by way of Harrodsburg and Danville were so exposed that after 4 o'clock they could have been to a great degree, if not entirely, cut off if Crittenden's corps had been vigorously pushed forward for the purpose. In our judgment the opportunity slipped through General Buell's absence from the field or on account of his ignorance of the condition of the battle. We are very sure that if he could have ordered supports to McCook at an earlier hour than he did order them the attack would have been repulsed with less loss to himself and greater to the enemy.

5.—PERMITTING THE REBELS TO ESCAPE WITHOUT LOSS FROM KENTUCKY.

It cannot be said that the rebels escaped without loss from Kentucky. Besides their killed and wounded at Perryville they were compelled to destroy a large quantity of stores which had been collected at Camp Dick Robinson.

The morning after the battle it was very early discovered that Bragg had retreated from his positions near Perryville and that his army had for the most part gone in the direction of Harrodsburg. Leaving all his sick and wounded and some material at Harrodsburg, and being joined by Kirby Smith, he hastened across Dick's River to Camp Dick Robinson. There he destroyed and abandoned the stores mentioned and resumed his retreat. In these movements the march of his columns was hurried; that part of it from Perryville to the river was confused and disordered. Our opinion is that if General Buell had taken up a vigorous pursuit as soon in the morning of the 9th as the retreat was discovered the check received by the rebels at Perryville would have been turned into rout, with all its consequences. But the manner in which they were followed to Harrodsburg can hardly be called a pursuit. General Buell should have endeavored, by energetic movement of his whole army, to crush them somewhere between Perryville and Dick's River.

From Camp Dick Robinson Bragg had but two roads left him by which he could hope to escape from Kentucky. Dividing his forces at Crab Orchard, one portion of them could go out by way of Cumberland

Gap, the other by way of Somerset. Had General Buell intercepted him on these lines, as we think he could have done, from either Perryville or Danville, Bragg would have been compelled to give battle, with the same results, we doubt not, as if he had been defeated before crossing Dick's River.

The evidence establishes that General Buell received information on the night of the 11th that Bragg had crossed the river to Camp Dick Robinson; yet he made no determined movement with the main body of his army until 12 o'clock in the night of the 13th. From the morning of the 9th to the night of the 11th he waited to learn whether his enemy would cross the river; that being definitely known, he lost two days before taking any decisive action. Finally, on the night of the 13th, as stated, he started Crittenden's corps through Danville toward Crab Orchard. It was then too late; Bragg, with his column and all his train, had passed the point of interception. To this delay we are compelled to attribute the escape of the rebels from Kentucky.

LEWIS WALLACE,
Major-General and President of Commission.

DONN PIATT,
Lieutenant-Colonel, U. S. Volunteers, Judge-Advocate.

[Indorsement.]

HEADQUARTERS OF THE ARMY,
Washington, D. C., May 29, 1863.

As the Commission has reported no charges against Maj. Gen. D. C. Buell nor recommended any further proceedings I respectfully recommend that the Commission be dissolved, and its officers, as well as General Buell, be ordered on other duty.

So much of the report as states that General Buell's march on Chattanooga was delayed by the repairs of the Memphis and Charleston Railroad and that General Buell's lines of supply were unnecessarily long is incorrect. General Buell had no other line of supply than this road till he reached Decatur and connected with Nashville. General Buell was not delayed an hour beyond what he himself deemed necessary to secure his supplies. Moreover, his lines of supply were those which he himself selected. Indeed there were no others from which to select.

The fault here, as elsewhere, was having too large supply trains and in not living more upon the country. He was frequently urged to subsist his troops in this manner. Whether or not he could have done so is not reported by the Commission.

H. W. HALLECK,
General-in-Chief.

[Inclosure No. 3.]

The Commission called to investigate the operations of the Army of the Ohio in Kentucky and Tennessee has seen fit to include the march from Corinth toward Chattanooga of that army within its limit of investigation, although such inquiry is evidently not included in the letter of instructions from the War Department. The operations of the Army of the Ohio commenced with that march, and therefore it *is* considered properly the correct commencement.

When the rebels vacated Corinth in 1862, when they had accumulated large stores and an efficient force, there appeared no place upon which they could rally in time to oppose successfully the army under Major-General Halleck in the attempt to open the Mississippi and possess ourselves of East Tennessee. To accomplish the latter purpose, General Buell, in command of what has since been known as the Army of the Ohio, was sent in the direction of Chattanooga, with instructions to seize that place and through it East Tennessee. It has been proved on the part of the Government and not denied by the defense that the rebels were not in force at that time in either place, and had General Buell pushed on he would have taken the more important strategic points almost without resistance. Why this was not done General Buell assures us, as I gather from the character of evidence introduced and the direction of the examination, was owing to a lack of supplies and the attempt to repair and keep open long lines of railway through a hostile population, which lines it seems were continually being cut by rebel cavalry and by the inhabitants, organized into guerrilla bands for that purpose.

This explanation or defense the Government claims is not satisfactory. The lack of supplies cannot justify a delay of a month or six weeks for repairs when that time would have enabled the army to seize and occupy a country rich as was East Tennessee, and inhabited by a friendly, loyal population. Raids on lines of communication with outrages of a disloyal people would have ceased with the necessity that caused them. They were inaugurated and continued for the purpose of embarrassing the expedition into East Tennessee. They would have ended with its occupancy.

But the most extraordinary fact pressing in this connection upon the Commission is that the commander of the Army of the Ohio knew at the time that these lines would be useless for the lack of rolling stock, and although an attempt is made evidently to shield himself under the orders of Major-General Halleck, we find no earnest remonstrance that would justify this Commission in regarding such a defense as sufficient. The brief oral instructions claimed to have been received, followed by the yet briefer telegrams, evince a confidence in and a discretionary power given to Major-General Buell which should now bar any attempt at shifting the responsibility. The fact that he knew at the time the hopelessness and absurdity of these efforts is conclusive. If the army had supplies enough to justify the long delay for the purpose of reconstructing lines, which were cut almost as rapidly as they were connected, I hold that he had sufficient to seize and hold East Tennessee, and the better way to get Morgan and Forrest from his rear was to keep them busy at his front. The defenseless state of Chattanooga and East Tennessee would have called for every available rebel soldier, and General Buell's regiment of engineers could have repaired the roads unmolested.

While Major-General Buell was thus engaged the enemy had not only time to strengthen their exposed points but to elaborate the invasion, which changed our operations from offensive to defensive, and eventually forced the army from Battle Creek back to its base at Louisville.

Some time in the first part of August General Bragg crossed the Tennessee at Chattanooga with about 30,000 men. At that time General Buell had his lines extended some 40 miles. The returns found at headquarters (Nashville) give us effective men present for duty 50,000 as the Army of the Ohio, and of these 47,500 were south of the Cumberland, and, the Government claims, could have been massed so as to have forced Bragg to a fight before he left Tennessee.

The case then as claimed by the Government is this: General Buell, in command of a largely superior force of veteran soldiers, well disciplined and equipped, was forced to fall back in long, rapid marches, under great privations, suffering shameful disasters, and with every mark of defeat, from its advance on Battle Creek, in Tennessee, to its base of supplies on the Ohio River.

ARMY OF THE OHIO.

As to the efficient force under Major-General Buell at the time of the invasion I call the attention of the Commission to the testimony of Major Wright and Lieutenant-Colonel Darr, both of Major-General Buell's staff, and the returns found at headquarters in Nashville. From an examination of this evidence it will be found that of the Army of the Ohio General Buell had 47,500 men south of the Cumberland River at the time Bragg crossed the Tennessee. The returns and other evidence introduced by the Government make the force at least 10,000 men [more?]. But I prefer taking the testimony offered by the defense.

BRAGG'S FORCE.

Bragg crossed the Tennessee with about 30,000 men of all arms. For evidence of this fact I refer in the first place to the testimony of the spy Pratt. He was in the employ of General Buell, and had excellent opportunities of observation in the enemy's lines. He informs us that Bragg had of infantry from 22,000 to 24,000. No attempt is made to impeach this man. On the contrary, General Buell in his cross-examination makes him his own witness, and the Commission will find that in his statement he is fully sustained by circumstances and the testimony of other witnesses. Col. M. Shoemaker, a prisoner at the time, saw Bragg's forces cross the Cumberland on the 9th of September, and states that he had about 30,000 men. Colonel Wilder, the gallant commander at Munfordville, refused to surrender until he had seen the forces opposed to him, with liberty to report the number. He estimates Bragg's army at not over 36,000. Mr. G. R. Taylor, a Union citizen of Munfordville, who was within the enemy's lines, gives 30,000 as the outside of Bragg's army. Mr. F. A. Smith learned from one of Bragg's staff at Munfordville that they had sixty regiments, confirming what the spy Pratt had sworn to. I have called attention here to evidence of actual observation. The fact is known to the witnesses of their own knowledge and is free of doubt or speculation. It will be observed that these witnesses are unknown to each other, widely separate, and yet concur in the same statement. To this we may add the Forsyth letter, one of Bragg's staff, introduced by General Buell through the testimony of General Rousseau, that states the entire army in Kentucky, including of course Kirby Smith's, to be 40,000 men, and we may now add General Bragg's report of his operations in Tennessee and Kentucky, which gives his army that crossed as not exceeding 30,000.

Circumstantial evidence comes in to sustain this already well-established fact. General Bragg, after capturing Munfordville, a naturally strong position, which, held by him, would have forced Buell to a fight at great odds or a surrender of Bowling Green and Nashville, suddenly evacuated and fell back to Bardstown. It will not do to say that this resulted from a lack of supplies. Bragg's stores, collected by Kirby Smith, were at Bardstown, and available with their possession of the country at Munfordville. He retreated because he saw the approach

of an army nearly double his own. The opinion of officers of intelligence and position in the Army of the Ohio are introduced by the Government, not for the purpose of proving the force under Bragg, but to
show that something near his actual strength was known at the time,
and it is somewhat remarkable that General Buell was ignorant of a
fact patent to his army. General Thomas, for example, said that he
could never make out the strength of Bragg's army above 45.000, and
of this 10,000 were left to take care of the flank and rear and to threaten
Nashville. This force he says was not within supporting distance had
Bragg been compelled to fight between the Cumberland River and
Munfordville. General Thomas, although introduced by the Government, is made General Buell's witness, and his statements are to be regarded as beyond dispute. General Rousseau, a witness summoned by
the defense, says:

My impression is that the strength of General Bragg's army was overrated. I put
Bragg at from 35,000 to 45,000 at Munfordville.

Major-General McCook states:

On Monday at Bowling Green I understood the enemy was at Glasgow, his force
estimated at about 30,000 men. It was simply the talk among my brother generals.

Brigadier-General Wood:

I am satisfied by information received from various sources that Bragg's army led
into Kentucky did not exceed 35,000 men.

Brigadier-General Steedman says:

The opinion is firmly fixed in my mind by frequent conversation with officers at
various points on the march that the strength of the Confederate Army was in the
neighborhood of 35,000.

General Fry:

From all sources of information Bragg's army was estimated at 36,000. There were
rumors that he had 50,000 or 60,000. The most intelligent officers placed it at not
exceeding 36,000.

Colonel Streight states:

From facts I could gather they (the rebels) had from 30,000 to 35,000. At Gallatin
I learned from General Wood that he had placed them at about 33,000.

I could multiply these evidences of knowledge on the part of subordinate officers, but do not consider it necessary. True, other officers make
the estimate greater, but they are men whose opportunities would not
justify a positive opinion, such as Generals Granger and Boyle.

It is true that a man by the name of Rapier is introduced, who claims
to have counted the forces under General Bragg, and makes them over
100,000. But his story is so improbable and contradictory that it cannot claim reasonable credence. He flies in fear from his dwelling on the
approach of the rebels, and yet places himself in full view of their column on the road-side, when for two days from early in the morning until
late at night, without rest and without refreshment, he calmly counts and
notches upon a stick the regiments as they hurry past upon the double
quick. He makes the force over 100,000 and marches them upon one
road. He has no motive for this other than idle curiosity; and, again,
Captain Jones produces certain tables, showing that prisoners representing one hundred and sixty regiments had been taken during Bragg's
occupation of Kentucky. It would be quite impossible to ascertain
through such testimony the number of Bragg's army. It is certainly
worthless when brought forward to contradict that of witnesses who
speak from positive knowledge. However, General Buell himself saves

us further doubt upon the subject. In his telegram from Louisville to General Halleck, shortly before moving out against the enemy, he states their force to be 60,000. This estimate is subsequently asserted by wit-nesses both on the part of the Government and the defense. General Buell has proven that of this Kirby Smith's, Stevenson's, and Marshall's forces make 30,000, leaving to Bragg the 30,000 with which he drove the Army of Ohio from North Alabama to Louisville.

The Government considers this a subject of careful investigation on the part of the Commission. That an army of veterans, numbering, with the divisions added from General Grant, some 65,000—that, as claimed by the defense, no defeat could dishearten and no marches in retreat could demoralize—that such an army should fall back through shameful disasters, with long fatiguing marches and great privation, bearing every mark of defeat, before half its numbers, makes a new page in our history of shame, and calls for explanation or severest punishment.

SPARTA.

Bragg seems from the evidence to have anticipated that his crossing the Tennessee River would be disputed. Upon what his anticipation was based is difficult to determine. Long after his design, if not his plan, of invasion had been developed the Army of the Ohio was stationed along an extended line, devoted to guarding and repairing railways, in a manner that made it impossible to concentrate for the purpose of opposing his crossing. When, however, this crossing was effected the ablest military minds in the army, other than its commander, suggested a concentration where the rebels could be met as they passed from the Sequatchie Valley to the plains of Middle Tennessee.

Sparta or McMinnville is suggested, but especially Sparta, where they could have been fought with every prospect of success. That Bragg must pass by Sparta was reasonable to suppose at the time, and with the light before the Commission a necessity. Had he retained Chattanooga as his base he could not have passed to the right or the left of our army in position without having his line of communication cut and his army turned upon a line of country where General Buell has been at some pains to prove an army could not subsist. If, on the other hand, he burdened himself with little transportation and only carried subsistence for eight or ten days, thereby cutting loose from his base, which proved to be the fact, his road lay through the Sequatchie Valley out by Sparta, and on the almost direct line to Bardstown, along which route his supplies had been provided. The position at Sparta is, we are assured, naturally a strong one, and offers such advantages that 15,000 might have been intrusted to its defense against the 30,000 of the enemy; but while all seems doubtful on the part of our army, with hesitation in its movements and uncertainty in its future, Bragg acts as if his way were assured to him and success the certain result of his efforts. History of military campaigns affords no parallel to this of an army throwing aside its transportation, paying no regard to its supplies, but cutting loose from its base, marching 200 miles in the face of and really victorious over an army double its size.

SUBSISTENCE.

Why the Army of the Ohio was not massed at Sparta, or indeed at any other point in Tennessee, for the purpose of disputing the further progress of this confident enemy was owing, the defense assures us, to the fact that while our lines were successfully cut our supplies would not justify extended operations. The defense is not tenable. The defense shows us that the Army of the Ohio had twenty days' rations; this, on half rations, made forty days, and in less than forty days the campaign in Kentucky and Tennessee was at an end. But in addition to this we learn that the line of railway from Nashville to McMinnville was in operation, and that from Louisville to Nashville could have been opened in two weeks, with the exception of that through the burnt tunnels, which left a wagon road of about 20 miles.

THE INTENT.

General Buell made no effort to mass his army and meet Bragg, but fell back to Nashville. It is believed on the part of the Government that a key to this extraordinary conduct may be found in the fact that, threatened as he was in front by Bragg and in rear by Kirby Smith, with his supplies limited and his communications cut, General Buell deemed it necessary to abandon both Tennessee and Kentucky and continue or rather renew the contest on the banks of the Ohio. He certainly did not fall back upon Nashville for the purpose of defending that place. Had he believed Nashville threatened from its front McMinnville or Sparta would have been the point to concentrate for its defense. But the Government has shown that this could not have been Bragg's intent, and that General Buell had every reason to know it at the time. Bragg's objective when he crossed at Chattanooga must have been Bowling Green. The possession of Bowling Green gave him Nashville, while at the same time he was marching in the direction of his supplies. General Buell by massing his forces at some point on the Cumberland, Lebanon for example, could have disputed the crossing of the river and at the same time have carried Nashville. Had Bragg attempted to avoid him by crossing farther up he would have been thrown upon a country so destitute of subsistence that his march must have proved disastrous.

As to General Buell's intention, however, we are not left in doubt. That he fell back to Nashville to gather up his supplies and then evacuate his acts prove. But in addition to this we have the testimony of Governor Andrew Johnson as to what General Buell actually said.

Before calling attention to this deposition it is well to consider, however, the significance of the defense in relation to it. Long before such a charge was ever dreamed of General Buell had strengthened his case in response to it. As if conscious of something that might come up, he has indicated the charge by a defense in advance. But Governor Johnson says positively that General Buell informed him that he considered Nashville of no importance in a military point of view, and it would have been evacuated three months before had his advice been followed. That he became alarmed evidently at the attitude of Governor Johnson, and said subsequently to Generals Thomas and McCook that Nashville must be held at all hazard, is true; but he never changed his intention. And it will be observed that he takes and uses up Governor Johnson's opinion when he says that the place should be preserved on account of its political importance.

This evidence of Governor Johnson's is further sustained by a telegram from General Halleck, which was found lying loose and unrecorded at the Department Headquarters, General Buell informing me in open court at the time I presented it to him that he knew nothing of it, while the dispatch to which it is an answer cannot be found at all. The answer, however, carries the query that produced it. It reads :

WASHINGTON, *September* 7, 1862.

Major-General BUELL :
    March where you please, provided you will find the enemy and fight him.
                                    H. W. HALLECK.

There was little intent of this sort at a time when, as Colonel Fry testifies, there was a sense of relief or rejoicing when it was found that Bragg had really crossed the Cumberland, from the fact, I suppose, that Bragg had not directly sought his enemy and fought him. Had not the telegram read that was sent, " Where shall I march ? " And does such telegram indicate a settled purpose of any sort ? But, again, on the 14th of September, two days before the surrender of Munfordville, we find him telegraphing to General Halleck, "It has been apparent to me for some time that on purely military grounds the force in Middle Tennessee should fall back on its base ; " that is, Louisville. "The political effect of such a move, however, seemed to me so serious that I hesitated to execute it." He was hesitating then when Governor Johnson called and pressed this political view on him. This important dispatch closed with a prayer for instructions. Instructions for what ? Had not his course been determined upon ? Or was not the general seeking to shield his abandonment of these States under instructions from Washington ?

He fell back upon Nashville for its defense, and yet left open the only road by which Nashville could be assailed. He left Nashville on the 7th to get between the enemy and Louisville and keep open his line of communication, yet he delays his march so as to permit an inferior force to get between him and Louisville, and, by seizing Munfordville, make the discomfiture of our army complete by compelling the surrender or evacuation of all the important posts in its rear. Had Bragg have seen fit to make a stand at Munfordville, Buell would have been forced to abandon Bowling Green and Nashville and steal off the best route he could find to the Ohio.

Bragg, with his inferior force and lack of supplies, dared not to remain in Munfordville, and fell back to Bardstown, and six days after General Buell writes to General Nelson at Louisville. This extraordinary letter is so important as proving the real intent of General Buell that I quote it at length. It must be remembered that Munfordville had surrendered, and the paroled officers had sought General Buell and informed him of the exact strength of Bragg's army as being but 36,000 strong and suffering terribly for lack of food, and yet he fled with his brave army of 50,000 from this force, while a like number awaited his coming at Louisville. Under these circumstances this is the advice he gives General Nelson :

HEADQUARTERS ARMY OF THE OHIO,
September 22, 1862.

Major-General NELSON :
    I dispatched to you last evening from Horse Cave, but the courier did not leave until after I arrived here last night. I learn since, with tolerable certainty, that the enemy marched in force toward Elizabethtown. He may go rapidly through to attack Louisville, or if he thinks you too strong to be easily beaten he may go to Bardstown to effect a junction with Smith, or he may halt at Elizabethtown to complete the junction and fight me there. The latter I consider the more probable, considering I am so close at hand. If he marches on Louisville he will probably go by Shepherdsville, and it might be possible for him to reach there Thursday. In any event you

should be re-enforced to the last man without a moment's delay. My own movements depend so much on the movements of the enemy that I can hardly tell you what to do. If you have only the force you speak of it would not, I should say, be advisable for you to attempt a defense of Louisville, unless you are strongly intrenched. Under no circumstances should you make a fight with his whole or main force. The alternative would be to cross the river or march on this side to the mouth of Salt River and bridge it, so as to form a junction with me. But, as I tell you, so much depends upon circumstances that I must leave this question to your discretion. I only offer you my suggestions in regard to it. This much do at any rate : Send a million of rations down the river, say opposite Brandenburg, to make them safe, to be subject to my order, and have a boat bridge made to be thrown rapidly across the mouth of the Salt River for my use, if I require it. Lose no time. Steamers should be opposite Salt River subject to my orders.

Bear in mind in these arrangements that the enemy will probably have a small cavalry force at the mouth of Salt River. All steamers used for the service referred to should be kept constantly under steam and ready to escape if threatened. Communicate with me daily. I shall probably continue on the Louisville pike at least as far as Elizabethtown. I shall be at Bacon Creek to-night or beyond there if the enemy should be determined to stand at Elizabethtown. Your advance on the Louisville pike, with the means of crossing Salt River, would undoubtedly have an important effect and perhaps give you an opportunity of acting an important part.

I received your dispatch in answer to mine from Dripping Spring.

D. C. BUELL,
Major-General, Commanding.

Braxton Bragg defeated the design. He did not march on Louisville nor dare he risk an engagement with the superior Army of the Ohio. He marched off toward Bardstown, where his subsistence was accumulated, and thereby lost the conquest he set out to accomplish. General Buell marched into Louisville, incorporated into his army the raw recruits that had been gathered there, and set out vigorously in search of the enemy. His army from Tennessee, numbering over 45,000, was joined by an army of 48,000, while the enemy he went out to fight had not over 60,000 men. The doubt and hesitation which seemed to paralyze his movements on the retreat from North Alabama to Louisville vanished, and what the clear-headed, energetic general could do was done. Sending Sill's division to hold Kirby Smith in check near Frankfort, General Buell divided the Army of the Ohio on three different roads converging on Bardstown and set out in a vigorous pursuit of Bragg. Bragg retired from Bardstown to Perryville, closely pressed by Buell. At Perryville the rebel leader evidently expected to fall in with Kirby Smith. Kirby Smith was not there, and Bragg found it necessary to check the farther advance of our army until Kirby Smith could come to his assistance. Of this fact General Buell was evidently well acquainted. He warned his subordinate generals of the approaching struggle, and on the morning of the 8th we find the immense army in line of battle, prepared to advance upon the enemy.

And here he fell into the same state of doubt and confusion that marked the retreat from Nashville, and this continued until the rebel invaders were safe out of Kentucky. After getting his force into line by noon on the 8th why he delayed the attack until the 9th we have been unable to understand; nor has the Commission been favored with a reasonable explanation. It was evidently the policy to overwhelm Bragg before he could form his junction with Smith. This junction General Buell had feared from the first moment he began his retreat from Nashville. Here was the long-wished-for opportunity, and yet his army was to be kept in line, suffering for the water which the enemy held possession of, from noon of the 8th till morning of the 9th. What else could Bragg desire? The rebel general evidently misunderstood the design, for observing that McCook, in command of the left wing, had broken his line and was moving in column to the water the soldiers were suffering for, he suddenly threw the weight of half his army upon the one corps, drove it back a mile, killing 918 men and wounding some 5,000.

There are circumstances attending this brief but bloody engagement which baffle comprehension. General Buell, who had approached Perryville conscious of the presence there of the enemy in force, retired to headquarters, 2½ miles in the rear of his left wing, and, surrounded by a large and well-organized staff, was ignorant of the struggle until too late to render aid, although he heard the furious cannonade that gave token of a combat about 2 o'clock, pronouncing it a waste of ammunition and demanding that it should stop, took no steps, either through the signal corps then in operation or by his staff, to investigate the cause, or, if necessary, to apply a remedy.

What a golden opportunity to annihilate the rebel army then presented itself we now learn. Had the right wing of our army been swung around, the rebel force would have been captured or destroyed. General Mitchell, without orders, marched his brigade through Perryville, and, coming in the rear of the rebels, then attacking McCook's corps, actually took prisoners and captured the ammunition train of the battery playing upon the left wing. All this while Gilbert's corps remained idle spectators of the unequal contest, and not only failed to tender re-enforcements, but when such aid was solicited by subordinate officers and men positively refused.

At 4.30 General Buell learned of the battle and sent an aide to General Thomas ordering the forces under his command to re-enforce McCook. The aide lost two hours in the search of General Thomas, who was found at the front after night when the battle had ceased.

This blow seems to have paralyzed the Army of the Ohio. No further effort was made to find and attack the enemy from the 8th till the 12th. No advance was even ordered, for an army of 70,000 men that is confined in its maneuvers to a space of 10 miles cannot be said to advance. In the mean time the rebels retreated through Harrodsburg past our forces to Camp Dick Robinson. This was a third time a march of this kind was successful. A pursuit was then ordered that resulted in nothing.

After the fight before Perryville had our army been pushed through Danville to Camp Dick Robinson the retreat of Bragg and Smith would have been intercepted. The defense claims that other roads were open to them on which to escape. It is a singular fact that in the opinion of the defense a road is always open to the rebels, who need no transportation and are not dependent upon the ordinary laws of subsistence; while to us there seems to be but one road, and that is through disaster to our base.

The fact is the route through Camp Dick Robinson to Cumberland Gap was the only available one to Bragg. On this their supplies were collected, and from the nature of the country at Crab Orchard the pursuit would have to cease. Had Bragg have been forced back to the center of Kentucky, depending as he would have to on the country for supplies, the move must have been fatal to him. Already disheartened by the reception given them by the people of the State, had he been forced to open plunder of that people for support the effect in both a political and military point of view must have been disastrous. But as the road into Kentucky had been strangely left open to him, so was the road out of Kentucky made easy.

[Indorsement.]

JUDGE-ADVOCATE-GENERAL'S OFFICE,
May 23, 1863.

Respectfully referred to the Secretary of War by the request of Lieutenant-Colonel Piatt.

J. HOLT,
Judge-Advocate-General.

[Inclosure No. 4.]

BALTIMORE, MD., *April* 11, 1864.

General LORENZO THOMAS,
Adjutant-General U. S. Army :

SIR: I have the honor to inclose herewith a copy of the communication which I addressed to the Commission which investigated my military operations in Kentucky and Tennessee. As I received no information in regard to the action taken on the original, or the disposition made of it, I request that this copy may be filed with the record.

I inclose also a printed copy of the statement in review of the evidence which I prepared to submit to the Commission. I request that it also may be filed with the record.

Very respectfully, your obedient servant,

D. C. BUELL,
Major-General.

[Sub-inclosure No. 1.]

BURNET HOUSE, *Cincinnati, May* 2, 1863.

TO THE COMMISSION:

On examination I have found the record of the Commission to be deficient and inaccurate in several particulars of greater or less importance.

It will be remembered that at an early stage of the proceedings I proposed an examination of the record for the purpose of correcting such errors, but the Commission deemed it best to defer the examination until the investigation should be closed. I desire now to call attention to the most important of them.

While the first witness, Colonel Lytle, I think, was giving his evidence the Commission was cleared, at the motion of one of the members, for some purpose not stated at the time. After the Commission had been in secret session some time I was invited in, and the president directed or intimated to the judge-advocate to swear me to secrecy in regard to the proceedings of the Commission. I declined to be sworn, and the Commission was again cleared. The judge-advocate subsequently came out and informed me that it had been determined that the investigation should be continued without my presence. I objected to this decision, and the judge-advocate returned to the Commission, and I presume stated my objection. He subsequently returned to me again, and informed me that it had been concluded to admit me to the sessions of the Commission, but that it had been decided that I should not cross-examine witnesses, though I could introduce witnesses in the defense. I objected to this also. I returned to the Commission and stated in person my objections to its decisions. I was asked by the president whether I based my claim to be present and cross-examine witnesses on the privileges belonging to a party accused. I answered that undoubtedly the pending investigation implied some sort of accusation or imputation against me, but that I did not think it necessary to say whether I considered myself in the light of a party accused or not; that for the present I based my claim upon the instructions of the Secretary of War under which they were acting, which stated that I would "be permitted to appear and produce and examine witnesses before the Commission."

Without coming to any final decision on these questions the Commission adjourned.

The following morning I submitted a written statement of what I considered to be my right with reference to these several points, and that statement was sustained by the Commission. It is proper that these facts should appear on the record, and I request that they may be placed there.

It will be remembered that some discussion took place at the time with reference to the rights which I claimed. It is impossible for me now to repeat the precise words in which I presented them. If there should be any question in regard to these several points then I desire to establish them by evidence, in order that the record may be corrected.

The other errors, as far as I have observed them, I have noted in my copy, and they can be pointed out more conveniently by referring to the record.

D. C. BUELL,
Major-General.

BALTIMORE, MD., *April* 11, 1864.

The above is a true copy of a communication submitted to the Commission which investigated my military operations in Kentucky and Tennessee. I request that it may be filed with the record, because I have not been informed what action was taken upon or what disposition was made of the original.

D. C. BUELL,
Major-General.

[Sub-inclosure No. 2.]

Statement of Major-General Buell in review of the evidence before the Military Commission.

The investigations of this Commission have not gone further back than shortly after the evacuation of Corinth by the rebel army in May last, and it might perhaps be expected that this review of my command in Kentucky and Tennessee would not go beyond that period; but I have for more than a year remained silent under misrepresentations which have misled the public mind with reference to the administration of my command. I deem it proper, therefore, to sketch briefly the history of the army I recently commanded and of my connection with it for the period anterior to the time to which this investigation has extended. It is proper also as bearing on subjects that have been investigated, because many circumstances connected with it shaped or affected the subsequent operations under my command.

In the early part of November, 1861, the condition of affairs in Kentucky became the subject of the most anxious solicitude to the Government and throughout the country. One-third of the State was in the possession of the rebel forces, under whose protection a provisional government was inaugurated at Russellville. It was supposed that the Union element was confined for the most part to the old men; that the mass of the young men were on the eve of joining the rebel cause, and that nothing but extraordinary exertion and judicious management could rescue the State from the vortex toward which the excitement of revolution was rapidly carrying her. This was certainly an unjust reflection on the loyalty of the State, but there is no doubt that the presence of a large rebel force rendered the occasion critical.

It was unexpectedly announced to me about the 9th of November that I was to be charged with this weighty responsibility. I received general instructions from the general-in-chief, Major-General McClellan, on the night of the 12th, and on the 15th of November I assumed command at Louisville of the new Department of the Ohio, embracing the States of Ohio, Michigan, Indiana, that portion of Kentucky east of the Cumberland River, and the State of Tennessee.

The enemy, under the command of General Sidney Johnston, was in possession of Bowling Green, with, according to the best information, about 25,000 men, his advance guard extending to Munfordville. Including Hopkinsville and other points his force north of the Cumberland amounted probably to 35,000 men. He had a small force at Fort Henry, on the Tennessee River, and Fort Donelson, on the Cumberland; and he had railroad communication with Columbus, on the Mississippi, where he had a large force, and with Nashville and all points south and east. These facilities enabled him to concentrate at any point in a very short time all the force in the Confederacy not required for defense elsewhere. At that time he could hardly be said to be threatened in any quarter except in front of Washington. The coast expeditions had not been inaugurated, and our force in Missouri was not yet prepared to operate beyond the limits of that State. He had also a small force, not probably exceeding 2,500 men, under Humphrey Marshall, threatening the northeastern part of Kentucky through Pound Gap, and a considerable force, under General Zollicoffer, at Cumberland Gap and on the road north of it. These last had recently been compelled to fall back from an attempt to invade the central part of the State, but they were still in a position to renew the effort. In addition to this the population was in a state of great disquiet. Bands were constantly organizing to join the rebel ranks and intimidate the loyal people, and in some parts of the State the Union element scarcely dared to express itself.

Kentucky at this time was the point which offered to the enemy the best prospect of advantage. His intention to have possession of Louisville within a limited period was constantly avowed. The disloyal element confidently expected it, and if the Government force had not been speedily increased the attempt would no doubt have been made. As soon, however, as the re-enforcements began to arrive he commenced fortifying strongly at Bowling Green and other points.

In reality the effective Government force which I found in Kentucky consisted of two divisions, about 23,000 men, on the Cumberland Gap road and the Nashville road, and about 4,000 men on the Big Sandy, in the northeast part of the State; but there were besides some forty or more Kentucky regiments or fractions of regiments scattered over the State in recruiting districts that were more or less available for local service. Very many, in fact nearly all, of them were not yet mustered in; many without arms, equipments, or proper organization; some of them embracing various arms of service—artillery, cavalry, and infantry. In the whole force were included about eight field batteries and four regiments of cavalry. The latter were all without any suitable arms; some had pistols only and some muskets. There was not, I believe, a carbine in the hands of the troops. In the infantry arms of two or three different calibers could frequently be found in the same regiment, and many of these were of foreign make, and unfit for service from various defects which rendered them unsafe or unreliable. The troops were but little instructed some of them not at all, and four or five general and perhaps as many staff officers embraced the whole military experience in the department. Officers having no rank whatever were acting as generals and staff officers under conditioned promises of appointment, and the supplies and equipment were in many respects deficient and defective. There was not transportation enough not already employed to serve 20,000 men two days' march from a depot or line of railroad.

The first thing to be done was to organize, arm, equip, and mobilize this heterogeneous mass, and this was both a difficult and tedious work. The Kentucky troops had to be collected from remote quarters and the fractions consolidated and organized; a work which the Military Board of the State had commenced before my arrival. Supplies of every kind had to be procured; a difficult matter, owing to the quantity suddenly required to supply the enormous force the Government was calling into service. In a word, pretty much everything necessary to make an army of soldiers had to be done. But little assistance could be obtained from abroad. Experienced staff officers could not be obtained. I expected two regular batteries from Missouri. About the 1st of January two companies of artillery, without batteries, making together about 70 men, with one officer, reported to me. The expectation of a regiment of regular cavalry resulted even worse than that. After my arrival at Nashville two companies reported, with about 70 men. New regiments began to report occasionally very soon after my arrival, and from the 26th of November to the 1st of January several regiments that had seen some service joined from Western Virginia. About the last of December some fourteen raw regiments were received from Ohio and Indiana. The force was afterward further increased from time to time. In the mean time the enemy had also received considerable accessions to his strength.

The organization of the troops into brigades and divisions was effected without delay as fast as they arrived. It was made a rule in the organization not to group the regiments by States, but to represent as many States as possible in each brigade; an arrangement which was attended with the happiest results in the discipline and tone of the army.

The instructions which I received on leaving Washington pressed upon me the importance of sending a column into East Tennessee. While the organization of my army and the preparation of transportation to enable it to move were going on I studied the subject very carefully, and also suggested a plan of campaign against Nashville, and expressed my views very fully to the general-in-chief with reference to both. I said that the campaign to East Tennessee would give occupation to 30,000 men—20,000 to enter the State, with a reserve of 10,000 on the line of communications; and I stated what means would be required to supply the force at such a distance—200 miles by wagon transportation, a good part of the way through a barren, mountainous region. For a campaign against Nashville I proposed to march rapidly against that city, passing to the left of Bowling Green through Glasgow and Gallatin, while a force from Missouri should ascend the Cumberland River under the protection of gunboats. This was essential, because to make the movement successful it would be necessary to move very light and depend on receiving supplies by the Cumberland River after getting through. In organizing my troops I disposed them so that they could be directed upon either or both of these objects. By the last of December I had collected troops enough to organize four divisions—about 40,000 men. I had thrown one division forward to Munfordville, one to Bacon Creek, on the same road, one near Green River, on the New Haven turnpike, and had one at Lebanon. Many of the Kentucky troops were yet scattered and not mustered in, but in some cases two or more regiments had been brought together for local service, with as many regiments added from other States, as at Calhoun, where there were perhaps 6,000 men for the protection of the Green River country, and at Columbia perhaps 3,000. Other new regiments were rendezvousing at Bardstown for organization and preparation for service. As yet the most strenuous efforts had not succeeded in obtaining the necessary means of transportation for an advance.

About the middle of December Humphrey Marshall again invaded the State through Piketon with about 2,500 men, though his force was represented at 6,000 or 7,000. On the 17th I sent Colonel Garfield to take charge of a force of five regiments of infantry and about a regiment of cavalry and operate against him. Marshall was defeated in two sharp engagements on the Big Sandy, near Prestonburg, and by about the middle of February was driven out of the State.

Simultaneously with the advance of Marshall into Northeastern Kentucky General Zollicoffer made his appearance on the Cumberland River near Somerset. His force was represented at 12,000 men, but probably did not exceed 8,000. The force sent for that purpose and to observe his movements failed to prevent him from crossing. I had previously kept a regiment at Somerset, and ordered the erection of a small work, both to watch that route into the State and to prevent the shipment of coal to Nashville. Zollicoffer crossed at Mill Springs and intrenched himself on the north bank of the river. On the 27th of December I ordered General Thomas to march from Lebanon and attack him, in conjunction with the force already at Somerset, and at the same time sent two regiments of infantry and a battery of artillery to Jamestown to blockade the river, a steamer having already passed up with supplies for the enemy at Mill Springs.

Want of transportation delayed General Thomas' departure until the 1st of January. The weather had previously been tolerably good, but that very day the rainy season set in, and from that time until near the end of March the earth was thoroughly saturated and every stream was flooded. The season in that respect was remarkable. The difficulties of the march were so great that General Thomas only arrived at a position 12 miles from Mill Springs and about 75 miles from Lebanon on the 18th. The enemy came out and attacked him at daylight on the morning of the 19th. The result was a signal victory to our arms. The enemy was pursued to his intrenchments and during the night crossed the river. He lost a considerable number of men in killed, wounded, and prisoners, fourteen pieces of artillery, some 1,400 animals, and a large amount of other property and stores. General Zollicoffer was among the killed.

The battle of Mill Springs was at that time one of the most important that had occurred during the war, and the victory was, I believe, the first the Union arms achieved where the forces engaged were so large; but the lack of transportation and the condition of the roads rendered it impossible to follow it up.

Owing to the delay in procuring sufficient transportation for the expedition to East Tennessee I had regarded the campaign against Nashville as the one which it would be necessary to enter upon first in order to save time. I was waiting for the arrangement of the necessary concert between the forces on the Mississippi and my own to commence it, when, owing to the illness of the general-in-chief, and at the request of the President, I wrote on the 3d of January to Major-General Halleck, who was in command in Missouri, and proposed substantially the same plan I had submitted to the general-in-chief, and substantially the same as that which afterwards resulted in the capture of Fort Henry, Fort Donelson, and Nashville. It contemplated an advance upon Nashville through Kentucky, a strong demonstration, which might be converted into a real attack, against Columbus, if the enemy should weaken that point to strengthen others that were threatened, and an advance of 20,000 men up the Tennessee and Cumberland Rivers under the protection of gunboats. Such a force I deemed sufficient at that time, for the works at Forts Henry and Donelson had as yet no great strength and were but feebly armed and garrisoned. If the expeditions should be threatened by a superior force they were to unite, under the protection of the gunboats, and make themselves secure until released by my advance upon Nashville. At that time I expected that the expedition already commenced against the enemy at Mill Springs would be fully accomplished in ten days and General Thomas' troops in a position to be available for other service.

General Halleck replied to my proposition that he had not spare force enough to undertake it, and suggested the objection that the proposed operation was one upon outer lines, but he offered to make a demonstration from Paducah toward Columbus. These facts explain in part why I was not prepared to act as promptly as I could otherwise have done when General Halleck subsequently commenced his advance up the Tennessee River. He stated also that he hoped in a few weeks to be able to render me material assistance. A mere demonstration, not in sufficient force to take a decided part in the campaign, would have been of no avail, because either my advance must be rapid directly against Nashville by flanking Bowling Green—an essential condition of which would be that I should meet supplies transported up the Cumberland—or else it must be deliberate, and with heavy artillery, against Bowling Green, strengthened as that position was by fortifications on both sides of Barren River, and I had not then the means necessary for such an operation. Besides, I received about the same time communications from the President and the general-in-chief urging the expedition to East Tennessee as of primary importance. I therefore gave my attention to it, intending to start that expedition from Somerset with the troops that were moving against the enemy at Mill Springs. The preparation of transportation was urged forward, and a strong force was set to work to corduroy the road to render it practicable. Nevertheless it was barely possible to subsist the 10,000 men at Somerset. The experiment demonstrated the impracticability of sending an expedition to East Tennessee in such force as to insure success in the present condition of the roads, and on the 1st of February I so advised the general-in-chief in a letter, with full explanations, and expressed my purpose to proceed against Bowling Green.

I had had no communication with General Halleck since his reply to my letter of the 3d of January, but on the 30th I received a dispatch from him, saying, without giving particulars, that he had ordered an expedition against Fort Henry. The same day I had suggested to him by letter a rapid gunboat expedition up the Tennessee and Cumberland Rivers to destroy bridges over those streams. Although Forts Henry and Donelson had been considerably strengthened, I believed the gunboats could pass them without any great risk. On the 6th I ordered one brigade from the mouth of Green River and eight new regiments to re-enforce General Halleck's expedition. They did not, however, arrive until after the capture of that place, which occurred on the 6th, but took part in the subsequent operations against Fort Donelson.

General Halleck found great difficulty in the movement against Fort Donelson, although the distance from Fort Henry was only about 12 miles. The enemy had greatly strengthened the works and increased the garrison. Protected as Bowling Green was by fortifications, the formidable river in front, and by the condition of the roads, I apprehended that my operations against that place could not be rapid enough to prevent the enemy from re-enforcing Fort Donelson so strongly as to endanger the success of General Halleck's operations. Upon consulta tion with him, therefore, I commenced on the 13th the movement of three divisions to re-enforce him by water, which would not only make the reduction of the place certain, but give force enough to operate against Nashville on that line, while the rest of my force was threatening Bowling Green in front. The advance of General Mitchel's division arrived opposite Bowling Green on the morning of the 14th, and found the bridge in flames and the enemy evacuating the place. That officer was directed to cross rapidly and throw a force forward toward Nashville, and the advance on that line was strengthened by a division which was to have gone to the Cumberland.

The operation of passing the river at Bowling Green in its swollen condition was difficult and tedious. The advanced division, General Mitchel's, did not get entirely over for ten days, notwithstanding the energy of that officer. While this was going on the troops in rear were employed in repairing the railroad. On the 24th the river was so high that small steamers were taken over the broken dams and reached Bowling Green with supplies and to assist in ferrying. About the same time a pontoon-bridge was laid, and although the overflow of the banks seriously interfered, yet the troops were able to pass with comparative rapidity.

In the mean time I was informed about the 17th of the surrender of Fort Donelson. I arrived at Bowling Green on the 20th, and on the 21st learned that the enemy had evacuated Clarksville and fallen back on Nashville, and that he had burned the bridges at Nashville. On the morning of the 22d the troops that had crossed the river at Bowling Green, two brigades and a half, started for Nashville, without wagons, very few having yet been got across. With about 1,000 men on cars, which the enemy had not succeeded in carrying off or destroying, I expected to reach within 9 miles of Nashville that night; but a heavy rain destroyed the road in advance of us and I did not reach the river opposite Nashville until the night of the 24th. The remainder of the troops arrived at the same time by marching. I had telegraphed General Halleck, and sent a courier through to Clarksville giving information of my movements, and requesting that the gunboats should proceed at once up the river. I apprended that they would meet one battery on the way, but they arrived without molestation on the night of the 24th, convoying the transports with the troops of General Nelson and General Crittenden, three brigades; and on the morning of the 25th the troops entered Nashville, and took position beyond the city toward Murfrees'orough, the enemy having retired to that place.

The river was out of its banks and the work of crossing was tedious. General Mitchel's division passed over on the 25th and 26th and the other divisions as rapidly as possible, but the whole had not crossed until about the 5th of March. General Thomas' division arrived by water on the 2d. The troops moved by forced marches, without baggage, owing to the difficulty of getting their wagons over the streams. The trains did not, therefore, arrive for several days after. Those that could arrive more rapidly that way were transported by water up the Cumberland.

The strength of the enemy at Murfreesborough, after the evacuation of Nashville, was estimated at the time, and has since been stated by persons who had means of judging at about 30,000 men. This force included what was collected of the troops that were defeated at Mill Springs and the force that had been at Bowling Green and other points north of the Cumberland River, excepting what was captured at Fort Donelson. It commenced moving south from Murfreesborough in a very few days after my arrival at Nashville, and, as is well known, eventually formed a junction with the forces of General Beauregard at Corinth. A pursuit with the hope of overtaking it on its line of march would have been futile for that object even if the force had been up to commence it at once, for every stream was flooded and every bridge was destroyed as the enemy retired. The only alternative was to operate deliberately against some line or point which it was his object to defend, and the Memphis and Charleston Railroad presented such an object. It was the same for the forces that were operating up the Tennessee River, under the orders of Major-General Halleck, more particularly against the enemy's forces that by the recent operations had been compelled to evacuate the principal part of West Tennessee. It was necessary that our forces should act in concert against that object; better still that they should act under one direction; and the order of the War Department, which I received on the 12th of March, placing the whole force under General Halleck's command, was therefore eminently proper. On the 15th I commenced the movement toward the Tennessee River, in pursuance of the understanding which had voluntarily taken place between us before the orders of the War Department were received. General Halleck's dispatch of the 16th designated Savannah as the point where I was to form a junction with the force already assembling on the Tennessee River.

Before leaving Nashville I sent Brig. Gen. G. W. Morgan to take command of a column I had left on the Cumberland Gap road, which was increased to a division by scattered regiments that remained in Kentucky. He was instructed to pursue with energy and discretion the object of taking Cumberland Gap, and for his further progress to be governed by circumstances in East Tennessee or to hold the enemy in check in that quarter if his force should prove insufficient to advance. The operations of this column have been investigated partially by the Commission, and I shall allude to them again in that connection. I also moved General Mitchel's division forward to Fayetteville, 26 miles from Huntsville, for the purpose of seizing the Memphis and Charleston road. The enemy withdrew his troops from that line, excepting small guards, and General Mitchel, on the 12th of April, five days after the battle of Shiloh, entered Huntsville. Various other dispositions and instructions were made with reference to the troops that were to occupy Middle Tennessee during my absence with the main army. The latter numbered about 37,000 men, the former about 18,000.

The march toward the Tennessee River on the 15th of March commenced with one division, preceded by a rapid movement of cavalry, to get possession of the bridges as far as Columbia before the enemy could destroy them. It succeeded with all of the bridges excepting the one over Duck River at Columbia and one 4 miles north of that place. The work of preparing the means of crossing Duck River was urged forward by all possible means and was under the charge of zealous and energetic officers, but it was not completed until the 31st of March. The river, which, at first 40 feet deep, had been gradually receding, was watched day by day, and finally became fordable for cavalry the very day the bridges were completed. The army then moved forward steadily, the advance and myself reaching Savannah, about 90 miles from Columbia, on the evening of the 5th of April. The other divisions followed, with intervals of 6 miles from the head of one division to the head of the next.

The battle of Shiloh, which occurred on the 6th and 7th of April, has been justly considered one of the most remarkable of the war, in regard to the numbers engaged, the reverses of the first day, and the success of the second. The particulars, so far as my command was concerned, have been given in my official report of that battle, hereunto appended,* and it is not necessary to repeat them. I believe that report states in very moderate terms the part which my command took in the incidents of that field. It has been conceded that my army rescued our forces on the west bank of the Tennessee from certain destruction or capture, and the movement which preceded the battle was prompt and even rapid. I marched from Nashville not to rescue those forces, but to form a junction with them to operate against the enemy's position at Corinth; and it was desirable, and General Halleck's instructions required me, to effect the junction as promptly as possible. I was informed that I should find General Grant's army at Savannah, on the east side of the river, and I was surprised, and even concerned, when I heard during the march that it was on the west bank; but I was relieved from anxiety by the information that it was so protected by high water in the streams which interposed between it and the enemy, and nearly surrounded it, as to be perfectly secure.

It is not necessary to go into the particulars of the campaign against Corinth. My command formed the center in the advance on that place. By General Halleck's order one of my divisions—General Thomas'— served with General Grant's command in that advance, and did not again come under my supervision, or actually under my control, until about the last of July. The enemy's works were entered about daylight on the morning of the 30th of May, having been evacuated the previous night.

I come now to the period embraced in the investigations of the Commission, and proceed to a general review of the more material facts which have been developed in the evidence. I shall do this without pretending to offer at present a nice analysis of the testimony, or, as a general rule, even citing that which bears on the points which I claim to be established by it. No other course could well be pursued, because otherwise much time would be consumed in illustrating facts to which no importance might attach, as no specific charges or allegations have been submitted for trial. Such an analysis could only be made by me after knowing what points the Commission may give importance to. That I have no means of knowing now, a vast amount of evidence, oral and documentary, having been submitted without any explained

---

* See Series I, Vol. X, Part I, pp. 291-296.

purpose, and which may be important or not, according to the interpretation or bearing given to it. Nor shall I remark upon any of the incidents of this investigation.

The subjects submitted to the Commission by the War Department
are as follows:

First. In reference to General Buell suffering the State of Kentucky to be invaded
by the rebel forces under General Bragg.

Second. In his failing to relieve Munfordville and suffering it to be captured.

Third. In reference to the battle of Perryville and General Buell's conduct during
that battle and afterward suffering the rebel forces to escape from Kentucky without
loss or capture.

Fourth. Such other matters touching the military operations aforesaid as in the
judgment of the Commission shall be beneficial to the service.

On the 30th of May, after the evacuation of Corinth by the rebel
forces, I received a communication from Major-General Halleck, informing me that his first object was to open the lines of railroad cen-
tering at that point from our rear and flanks, and directing me to put
one of my divisions on that duty on the Memphis and Charleston road
east of Corinth. I accordingly detached the division of General Wood
on that service. The army of General Pope was following up the
retiring enemy in the direction of Baldwyn. On the 4th of June I received instructions to re-enforce General Pope, near Booneville, with
two divisions, in anticipation of an attack from the enemy. I accompanied those divisions myself. The enemy, however, continued his
retreat toward Okalona; and on the 9th I received intimation that a
part of the force under my command would return to Tennessee, and
that I could make my arrangements accordingly. At my request I was
authorized to start the two divisions (Nelson's and Crittenden's) that
were with me in that direction. General McCook's division, then at
Corinth, was to remain there until relieved by General Thomas' division, which had also been sent to re-enforce General Pope. General
Thomas' division originally formed part of my army, but had been
detached from my command since the commencement of the advance
upon Corinth. I was informed that it would probably rejoin me at a
future day for the movement toward Tennessee.

I stopped at General Halleck's headquarters on my return from
Booneville on the 10th, and visited them again on the 11th, and during
those visits received his oral instructions with reference to the campaign I was to enter upon. Its object was the occupation of East
Tennessee and certain important points on the railroad through that
region of country; Chattanooga, Dalton, and Knoxville were points
which it was considered important to occupy. I requested that I might
be allowed to choose my own route, and at that interview General
Halleck assented, though he had been in favor of moving directly on
Chattanooga through North Alabama; but on the 12th I received a
dispatch from him saying that, on further reflection, he deemed it best
that the route he had suggested should be pursued. My own idea had
been to strike a little farther north, through Middle Tennessee and
McMinnville.

General Halleck desired that the movement should be made as
promptly as possible, but it was a condition that the railroad from
Corinth east should be repaired, and it was his idea that I should draw
my supplies by that route. I did not concur in his views in regard to
the advantages of that route, and I immediately gave orders for repairing the roads from Nashville through Tennessee and for procuring
supplies in that way, but I placed the superintendence of the Memphis

and Charleston road under an energetic and experienced engineer, Brigadier-General Smith, put troops on the route, and gave orders for pushing the repairs as rapidly as possible. Subsequently I suggested the inexpediency of repairing the road. It was for 80 miles parallel with the enemy's front and peculiarly exposed to attack. This objection was realized in the end, and, in addition, it was found impossible to get stock enough on the road to make it of material use even while it was kept open, so that substantially we derived no advantage from it. It however occupied the troops until about the last of June in opening it and detained General Thomas' division a month longer in guarding it, so that that division did not reach Athens and Huntsville until the last of July.

As soon as my destination was pointed out to me instructions were given to my engineer officer, Captain Morton, to prepare the means of crossing the river at Florence, and similar instructions were given to General Mitchel, then commanding at Huntsville, for crossing a portion of my force at Decatur, so as to have the advantage of two roads and two crossings. A very efficient ferry was prepared at Florence and a very inefficient one at Decatur.

General McCook's division marched from Corinth on the 11th and reached Florence on the 15th of June. It was followed closely by Crittenden's division, which had come into the road at Iuka from Booneville. General Wood's was advanced to and beyond Tuscumbia to repair and guard the road, while General Nelson's took its place between Iuka and Tuscumbia. The few boats that were of light enough draught were employed in forwarding supplies by water to Florence, and in order to make up for the deficiency wagon trains were put on the road from Eastport to Iuka to connect with the single half-serviceable locomotive and the few cars that were available on the railroad. The boats were only able to carry from 30 to 40 tons over the shoals, and after a few trips could not run at all; after which wagon trains were started on the north side of the river between Florence and Waterloo, nearly opposite Eastport. The ferry at Florence was ready for use on the 22d of June and the crossing was commenced, but rumors of a movement of the enemy toward Iuka suspended the forward movement from the opposite side until the 25th. Wagon trains were first put across and dispatched to Reynolds' Station, where they connected with the railroad trains from Nashville, to convey supplies over the gap in the road to Athens. General Mitchel had previously been instructed to have supplies for a certain number of days, until the trains should be established, to meet the troops on their arrival at Athens and Decatur. The divisions moved forward in close succession by marches of about 14 miles a day—Nelson's and Wood's as soon as they were relieved from the road by other troops. Wood's division finished crossing at Decatur on the 6th of July. The other three divisions, crossing at Florence, commenced arriving at Athens on the 27th of June. The troops halted at these points momentarily, and their trains were thrown into the gap on the railroad to push forward supplies.

The problem of advancing into East Tennessee was now fairly before me. The force which I brought along numbered between 24,000 and 25,000 effective men, and there were besides about 16,000 more scattered through Middle Tennessee and North Alabama, that I had left behind for service in that region when I marched to form the junction with General Grant's army on the Tennessee River in April. That force, mainly under the command of General Mitchel, has been generally awarded praise for the service it performed and very justly, yet not more than 2,000 men ever appeared on the field of its operations to oppose it. It was not the numbers of the enemy that made its service difficult and creditable, but it was the large extent of country it occupied, the length of the lines it had to guard, and the difficulty of supplying it. Those lines had still to be held in a further advance and with no less force to make them secure, for the force which endangered them had been largely increased by the transfer of a large part of the enemy's cavalry to the north side of the Tennessee River after the evacuation of Corinth and by the organization of an additional force of guerrillas throughout Middle Tennessee and North Alabama and in the southwestern portion of Kentucky.

The limited force available for a further advance into the enemy's country was not, however, at the time of my arrival, the difficulty, for undoubtedly it was superior to the force which the enemy at that moment had in East Tennessee. Experience has shown what might have been deduced from reason, that if the movement could have been made without serious resistance while the enemy was yet inferior in force, it could have had no permanent result with no more troops than I had. The advance of 60,000 veteran rebel troops through a friendly population into Kentucky, where they undoubtedly met many friends, has been considered bold, and must have proved fatally disastrous to them but for their precipitate retreat. I know no reason why 25,000 or 30,000 men should be sufficient to advance with any greater prospect of a permanent advantage into an exhausted and comparatively barren country and in as close proximity to the whole power of the enemy. It was my error to believe at that time that the thing was practicable, and I did not represent it otherwise when I was assigned to the execution of it; but I must say also, in extenuation, that I did not anticipate that the enemy was to be left so unemployed at other points that he could devote his greatest effort against my enterprise. Besides, I regarded it as in the highest degree important and I supposed that no larger force could be spared for it.

However, at the time of my arrival with my army in North Alabama the immediate obstacle to the execution of the first step, the capture of Chattanooga, was that of supplies and the means of crossing the Tennessee River. The means to overcome these difficulties had to be created, for they did not exist. The lumber had to be sawed and a bridge built, and supplies for the troops had to be brought, for the country was destitute of them. The country between Decatur and Huntsville and extending up into Middle Tennessee is a cultivated and productive one; but as far north as the Tennessee line, and even including the southern tier of the counties of Tennessee, it is cultivated mainly in cotton. The planters never produce more than an ample supply of meat and corn for their own use and not always that. Farther north Tennessee produces considerable quantities of surplus provisions, but not enough to supply the demand farther south, as is shown by the fact that large quantities of produce from the Northwestern States have annually found a market at Nashville. The demand upon the surplus provisions of Tennessee had been increased by the rebellion, which cut off the supply from the Northwest, and by the armies, rebel and Union, which during the winter and spring of 1862 fed upon the country to a considerable extent. North Alabama particularly was left in a condition to need the necessaries of life, instead of affording subsistence for an army. East of Huntsville the spurs of the Cumberland Mountains run down nearly to the river, leaving only here and there a narrow valley or cove of arable land. The whole country is rough and almost barren, producing no more than is necessary for the support of a poor and sparse population. East of Stevenson, as far as Chattanooga, it may be said to be destitute both of population and supplies. Beyond Chattanooga the productive region of East Tennessee commences; but during last summer it was exhausted of supplies, and the people themselves were, as they are now, notwithstanding the new crop they have since gathered, suffering for food. These facts go to the extent of rendering it impossible for my army to have advanced and depend on the resources of the country. The alternative of drawing its supplies from its principal base, the Ohio River, was imperative, and my wagon transportation was not sufficient to cover breaks in the railroads north of Huntsville and to advance beyond Bridgeport at the same time.

The first essential, therefore, was the opening of the railroads from Nashville; and to that end the force which General Mitchel had been ordered to put at that work was increased by engineer and other troops to the whole force that could be employed. Hired mechanics, under the military superintendent of railroads, an able and efficient man at such work, were also employed, and orders were given to push forward the repairs with all possible dispatch. But the work was much more formidable than had been supposed, and the work which I had expected to see completed in ten or fifteen days was not finished until the 31st of July on the Nashville and Decatur road. The Nashville and Chattanooga road was completed on the 12th of July; the trains started through on the 13th, and were stopped by the attack and surrender at Murfreesborough, by which and by subsequent successful attacks the completion of that road was delayed until the 28th of July.

In order to conceal the object, or at least the progress, of my campaign as much as possible it was desirable not to concentrate my force at a point which immediately threatened the enemy's position until I was prepared to move against him. This was also expedient from the necessity of placing the troops in positions where they could be most conveniently subsisted, and where they could give the necessary assistance in repairing the roads and in guarding them until they should be securely established, and protected at the more vulnerable points by stockades or other defenses which would enable a small force to maintain itself against a larger one. Prior to my arrival in North Alabama, however, General Mitchel had entertained serious apprehensions of an attack on the positions which he occupied in that region, particularly at Battle Creek and along the Nashville and Chattanooga Railroad, and repeated dispatches from him urged the pressing importance of reenforcements to guard against the supposed danger. These reports of a probable attack at Battle Creek were repeated just after my arrival, and rendered it proper to increase the force at that point. McCook's and Crittenden's divisions were accordingly ordered there. They marched from Athens about the 4th and arrived at Battle Creek about the 14th of July. One brigade from the former was put at work on the road from Stevenson to Decherd. Nelson's division still remained at Athens, furnishing a strong working party on that road. Wood's division was stopped near Decatur, where it protected the ferry and the small garrison on the opposite side of the river, the idea not having been yet abandoned of making the Memphis and Chattanooga road west of that point available for supplying my troops and communicating with the forces about Corinth. With these dispositions, orders were given for establishing the regular road guards and for getting together again the fragments of brigades and regiments previously there, which were found scattered in very great confusion; a brigade was organized to move from Murfreesborough and Tullahoma and occupy McMinnville; intelligent and energetic officers were put in charge of the road guards and road repairs; mills were set to work to get out lumber for a pontoon bridge; horses were ordered for the cavalry, which had been left in Middle Tennessee, and was in bad condition; and various other preparations ordered to enable the troops to move promptly and effectively as soon as the roads were completed so that supplies could be provided.

The first raid of Morgan into Kentucky took place early in July. He threatened Bowling Green and Munfordville about the 8th of July, defeated three companies of cavalry at Burkesville about the same time, and then went to Lebanon, where he destroyed the depot and hospital buildings. Thence he proceeded north through Lexington as far as Paris. He was engaged at Paris and other points during his expedition, but with no important result. He finally recrossed the Cumberland River at or near Mill Springs about the 23d of July and made his way to Knoxville.

The force which made this incursion has been said not to have exceeded 1,000 men, though at the time it was estimated as high as 2,500 or 3,000. It produced a good deal of alarm in the State, and many apprehended that the force would receive large accessions to its ranks and that the sympathizing part of the population would become troublesome, but those apprehensions were not realized. The injury was confined mainly to the inconvenience and suffering inflicted on individuals, and I have no doubt that the effect on the population was to strengthen its adhesion to the Union.

A good deal of censure was cast on the troops and the military officers in the State that Morgan should have escaped without capture or greater loss, but not with much justice, when the circumstances are considered. The objects to be aimed at by my army, after the occupation of Nashville in February, made it necessary to carry forward, for further operations, nearly the whole of the force at my disposal; and, indeed, the high stage of water in the Cumberland River afforded security at that time against such invasions, even if the rebel force had not left that region of country to concentrate for the struggle on the south side of the Tennessee. For these reasons, except the column which was operating against Cumberland Gap, not more than about 4,000 troops, mostly infantry, were left behind, and these were scattered over the principal part of the State, more as a police force and to guard railroads than to prevent invasion.

The probable result of our operations against Corinth developed to my mind the advantage the enemy could derive from the employment of a large cavalry force in Middle Tennessee and Kentucky, and on the 12th of May I advised the Secretary of War of the necessity of having at least five more cavalry regiments in those two States. I was answered that there was not at the time any cavalry to spare for that service, but that an additional force was to be raised, and that a part of it would be sent to me. None came, though authority was given to the officer commanding in Kentucky to raise some cavalry regiments. These, however, were in no condition to render much service at the time of Morgan's first raid. Subsequent events have shown, what might have been evident enough without the experiment, that to prevent such incursions and carry on the operations in front which the progress of our arms had rendered necessary was physically impossible with the force that was available. I had a front extending from Corinth to Cumberland Gap, through a hostile population, a distance of 300 miles; in fact it extended to Piketon, in the northeast corner of Kentucky, 100 miles farther, with lines of communication varying from 200 to 300 miles in depth. To press successfully against the rebel armies along the line of the Memphis and Charleston Railroad it had been necessary to denude the lines and the whole country in my rear almost entirely of troops. The front from Battle Creek to Cumberland Gap it was not possible to occupy at all. Is it astonishing that 1,000 cavalry, familiar with every path, should be able to penetrate this vast extent of country and escape without capture?

Morgan had not yet disappeared from Kentucky, after his first inroad, when Forrest, with a large force, suddenly appeared at Murfreesborough on the 13th of July, surprised and captured the garrison, consisting of some 1,400 men—cavalry, artillery, and infantry—forming part of the force which was about to march from that place and Tullahoma to occupy McMinnville, and did serious damage to the railroad. Two other regiments which had been designed as a permanent garrison for Murfreesborough had been detached and sent into Kentucky on the occasion of Morgan's incursion. The consequence of this disaster was serious. The use of the railroad from Nashville, which had been completed the very day before and which I was depending on to throw supplies into Stevenson for a forward movement, was set back two weeks; the force of Forrest threatened Nashville itself and the whole line of railroad through Tennessee, and the occupation of McMinnville was delayed two weeks. It became necessary to move northward some of the troops in North Alabama to drive out the rebel force and guard against further embarrassment. Nelson's division was ordered by rapid marches to Murfreesborough, one brigade going by railroad through Nashville; two brigades of Wood's division were ordered from Decatur to Shelbyville by forced marches and subsequently to Decherd, to give greater security to Elk River Bridge and guard the important route from the mountains into North Alabama through Winchester. A little later the remaining brigade of Wood's division was ordered to Stevenson to erect defensive works for the depot which was to be established at that point for the movement against Chattanooga. The excitement caused by Morgan's raid into Kentucky had been so great and the call for troops so urgent that I apprehended I should be compelled to send a division there; but to do that was to put an advance into East Tennessee out of the question, and I determined to trust Kentucky to the few troops already there rather than abandon the object for which I had started.

The movement of General Nelson toward Nashville was delayed somewhat by injury to the Duck River Bridge by high water. He arrived at Murfreesborough on the 18th. The enemy left as he advanced, threw himself on the road between that place and Nashville, and captured a guard of about 80 men and destroyed two more bridges. The efforts of General Nelson to intercept him were unsuccessful. After throwing up some field works for a small force at Murfreesborough to protect the depot which it was necessary to establish there, General Nelson started on the 2d of August with two brigades and arrived at McMinnville on the 3d of August. One brigade remained at Murfreesborough, but on the arrival of the force which had been designated to occupy the place that brigade joined him at McMinnville.

The railroad from Nashville to Stevenson was completed on the 28th of July, that from Nashville to Decatur on the 31st, and preparations commenced for an advance. Supplies were pushed forward to the depot at Stevenson, the pontoon bridge was gotten ready to be laid, the wagon trains which had been in use on the Decatur road were thrown across to Decherd, from which point they could be moved rapidly to Stevenson, and the troops, including General Thomas' division, which arrived at Athens and Huntsville about the 31st of July, were moved so as to be in convenient positions for the same object. In the mean time the enemy continued his operations with large bodies of cavalry against our long lines of communication through Tennessee and Kentucky, seconded in Tennessee by the organization of guerrilla bands, which swarmed in every part of the country. These latter were frequently encountered and defeated by detachments of our small cavalry force; but the former, moving in superior force and striking at vulnerable points, were generally successful, and finally on the 10th of August severed effectually our communications between Nashville and Louisville. In addition to the destruction of our lines of communication the effect of these operations and of the formidable preparations which were reported and believed to be in progress for the invasion of Middle Tennessee and the capture of Nashville was to intimidate our friends and embolden our enemies among the people, who not only would not bring in supplies voluntarily, but used every means to prevent us from finding them, so that nothing could be obtained from the country except by means of our own trains under the protection of strong escorts. On the 6th of August I gave orders for fortifying Nashville, to make it secure with a small garrison against any attack from cavalry.

On the 10th of August Morgan again made his appearance at Gallatin, surprised and captured the garrison, amounting to 150 infantry; then moved toward Nashville, destroying several bridges and capturing the guards; then toward Bowling Green, destroying the tunnel 7 miles north of Gallatin and several trestle-works and small bridges in that region. He was, however, handsomely repulsed in some instances by the small force opposed to him in these attacks. Simultaneously with this Forrest, with a large force, moved toward the Cumberland River, to be in a position to support Morgan or threaten Nashville if it should diminish its garrison, which consisted of about 2,000 men. Immediately after the occurrence of the first raid I determined to withdraw my cavalry as much as possible from its service in detachments against the bands of guerrillas which infested the roads and concentrate it in large bodies. By supporting them with infantry, equipped to move lightly, I hoped to be able to drive the enemy's heavy cavalry force from the lines. One of these commands I designed should operate from Murfreesborough and another from McMinnville. An experienced cavalry officer was assigned to the command of the former, with general instructions which allowed him a good deal of discretion. The zeal of this officer caused him to move in pursuit of the enemy with about 700 men before the whole of his command had joined. On hearing of this, and knowing that he was outnumbered by the enemy, I dispatched instructions for re-enforcing him with infantry from McMinnville if he could be reached and to restrain him until he had sufficient strength. The instructions did not, however, reach him, nor could his whereabouts be ascertained so as to re-enforce him. Hearing that Morgan had again appeared in the neighborhood of Gallatin he crossed the river at Hartsville in pursuit, engaged Morgan's force not far from that place about the middle of August, was defeated, and himself and some 150 of his men taken prisoners. The remainder made their escape, in stragglers and small bodies, to Nashville. The strength of Morgan's band at this time was estimated at from 1,500 to 3,000.

Work was immediately commenced to repair again the road north of Nashville, but the continued presence of Morgan's force in that quarter made it impossible to carry it beyond Gallatin, except by withdrawing from the front so large a force as to preclude the idea of an advance, and I therefore determined to defer it until it could be protected by a force which I hoped might come from Louisville of the new troops that were being called out. On the 16th of August I ordered Major-General Nelson to Kentucky to command, and sent with him three generals and some other officers of experience and two batteries of artillery. The position required an officer of his rank, and I had great confidence in his energy and ability.

While the enemy was producing this serious embarrassment by the operations of his large cavalry force, regular and irregular, on our long lines of communication, he was collecting a large army at various points in Tennessee from Chattanooga eastward. For a considerable time the main point of concentration was doubtful and the railroad facilities which the enemy possessed enabled him to concentrate speedily at any point. General Bragg arrived in person at Chattanooga on the 28th of July, by which time his whole force was within easy reach of that point, and from that time reports were current of his intention to assume the offensive. Sometimes they were quite positive that he was already crossing the river at Chattanooga, Kingston, and other points.

The lowest estimate that could be made of the force with which the enemy was prepared to advance, according to the best sources of information, was 60,000 men. That has, I think, been more than confirmed by the evidence before the Commission. Eye-witnesses estimated the force as high as 100,000. My dispatch of the 7th of August to the General-in-Chief, Major-General Halleck, gave information on this subject somewhat in detail and not in a discouraging tone; for I was continuing my preparation to advance, and was, in my own mind, disposed to make perhaps more than due allowance for exaggeration in the information that reached me. I was the more confident when, on the 10th of August, General Halleck authorized me to call on General Grant for two divisions if I should find it absolutely necessary. On the 12th I requested General Grant to send the divisions, intending to use one of them to protect my communications with Louisville and bring the other to the front· but their movements were at first involved in some uncertainty. At a later period I could get no information of them at all, and feared that General Grant had not been able to spare them, as he was himself threatened. One of them reached Murfreesborough on the 1st and the other Nashville about the 12th of September.

Very soon the information of the enemy's intention took such shape as to leave no doubt that he was about to invade Middle Tennessee with a superior force, and to make it proper to suspend the accumulation of supplies at Stevenson and establish a depot at Decherd, as being most suitable for that disposition of my troops which the designs of the enemy, as far as they could be divined, rendered proper to oppose him. The information pointed to Nashville as his principal aim, and justified the conclusion that at least he believed he had force enough to accomplish his object. It was ascertained that the number of my troops was quite accurately known to him. The route which he would take was altogether a matter of conjecture, to be founded on probabilities. McMinnville was mentioned very often, in the information which reached me, as the first point of attack, and they were so frequent that I deemed it proper to strengthen the force in that quarter; but the difficulty of crossing the mountain weakened the probability of an advance in that direction, while an advance into North Alabama was not only spoken of in con nection with the enemy's plans, but offered many advantages. By crossing Walden's Ridge into the Sequatchie Valley he had a good, level road down that valley to Battle Creek, which was an indefensible position for us while he occupied the opposite side of the Tennessee River with his artillery. This would keep him in constant communica tion with his supplies at Chattanooga by means of the railroad on the opposite bank and the steamers which he had; his large cavalry force operating against Nashville and on my lines of communication would compel me to employ at least 20,000 men to protect them even that far, leaving about 25,000 men to oppose his advance in front. If the column from Kingston should advance on Nashville I should be compelled to fall back in the face of even an inferior force for the protection of that place; and thus both Alabama and the principal part of Middle Ten nessee could be reclaimed by the enemy without necessarily risking a battle. It is not too much to say that 50,000 men thus employed on this theater of operations, with the superior cavalry force which the enemy had, would be an overmatch for 60,000 operating upon lines of such depth in the midst of an unfriendly population.

Such were the inducements which an advance upon Battle Creek offered to the enemy, even supposing that I was entirely on the north side of the Cumberland ridge, say at Decherd; but in fact he was well aware that I still occupied North Alabama, with some 12,000 men at Battle Creek, while the rest of my force extended as far north and east as McMinnville. If he could reach Battle Creek before the force at that place should extricate itself by moving to the east it would have to go around by the way of Huntsville, and thus make a march of 120 miles to reach Decherd, the nearest point at which it could possibly form a junction with the forces north of the mountain, while he, by a march of 25 miles from Jasper, could reach the same point, and thus throw his whole force between my scattered troops. The position at Battle Creek is, for a force whose communications are on the north side of the mountain, one of the worst that can be imagined against an enemy coming from the Sequatchie Valley and holding the opposite bank of the Tennessee River. A spur of the Cumberland ridge comes to within 200 yards of the river; Battle Creek runs at the foot of this spur on the east side, emptying into the river near the point; the only position for troops is west of the spur; the road to Decherd, a distance of 25 miles, passes around the point of this spur and along its side up Battle Creek in full view from the opposite side of the river and the creek; and there is no other road to the north side of the mountain practicable for loaded wagons short of Huntsville, distant 75 miles.

For the double purpose of guarding against an attack in this faulty position and of observing the movements and checking the advance of the enemy in the Sequatchie Valley I issued the instructions of the 19th of August to Major-General McCook, my purpose then being to attack the enemy in the Sequatchie Valley if possible or to give him battle at the first point on his route where I could concentrate my troops. Those orders required General McCook, upon the first intelligence of an ad vance of the enemy toward the Sequatchie Valley, to move promptly up the valley to the Anderson and Therman road with the two bri gades of his division which were with him, to check the progress of the enemy and observe his movements. If pressed, he was to fall back on the Therman road deliberately until he should form a junction with the main force coming from the side of McMinnville. The other division which was with him at Battle Creek, General Crittenden's, was also to move up the valley to the Tracy City and Altamont road, which enters the valley 10 miles below the Therman road. He was to support General McCook in the valley, watching the old Nashville and Chattanooga stage road, which enters it from the Tennessee River at the point designated, and under like circumstances he was to fall back for a similar purpose on the Higginbottom road toward Tracy City and Altamont, where the junction would be formed.

On the 20th I learned that the enemy was certainly crossing at Chattanooga and other points, and I immediately directed General McCook to execute the orders already described. On the same day I left Huntsville, visited the posts at Stevenson and Battle Creek, and the following day went to Decherd to direct the movements for the proposed junction. I deemed it of the highest importance, for political as well as military reasons, to maintain my position in North Alabama, if possible, in connection with those movements, for which the instructions of the 19th of August, given to General Rousseau, the officer in command in North Alabama, in anticipation of my advance upon Chattanooga, were equally applicable ; but I reduced the force in that quarter somewhat, leaving a regiment in fortifications at Battle Creek, one at Stevenson, and two at Huntsville, besides the road guards and the force on the Nashville and Decatur line. The orders for the concentration at Altamont (see the instructions of the 23d of August to General Thomas) had reference to the plan of operations above referred to for opposing the movements of the enemy, except that the information rendered it apparently certain that the enemy would advance on the Therman road, and that Altamont was the point farthest to the front at which he could be met. On the first supposition I had expected to intercept him in the Sequatchie Valley.

In moving up the valley on the 20th General McCook received information from his spies and scouts which made him believe that the enemy would be in the Sequatchie Valley, and therefore in a position to intercept him before he could march to the Therman road, and he therefore returned down the valley to the Higginbottom road. That road was found to be impractible for his artillery, and he moved still nearer to Battle Creek, and put himself on the road which follows up Battle Creek and then crosses the mountain. I there sent him orders on the 23d to move to Pelham for the purpose of effecting the concentration at Altamont. The difficulties of the route prevented the concentration at the time appointed, and in the mean time information in regard to the movements of the enemy made it a matter of very great doubt whether it could be effected at that point at all before the enemy would anticipate it. The only alternative seemed to be to concentrate there or at Murfreesborough. I determined to attempt the former, and gave the orders accordingly. Those orders anticipated that, from the greater difficulties General McCook had to overcome, the troops moving from McMinnville under Major-General Thomas would reach Altamont first. The latter was instructed to attack the enemy's advance, if it should have reached there, and hold his position, if possible, until the other troops came up ; and in the event of being unable to do that the various columns were instructed as to the roads by which they should fall back to form a junction in rear. General Thomas marched to Altamont with a portion of his force at the time appointed. He found no enemy, and believing that he could not remain there for want of water, returned immediately to McMinnville. On his report and in consequence of his action I stopped the movement of all except General McCook's division, which remained at Altamont in observation until the final concentration at Murfreesborough.

The information which I received still pointed clearly to the Therman road as the one by which the enemy would advance, if at all. It is the best road across the mountain, and has the advantage of branching at Altamont into no less than four roads, which descend the mountain to an arc 40 miles long, from McMinnville on one flank to Decherd on the other. Still the movements of the enemy were less rapid than was expected, and placed him in a position to use that road or those farther east. Many officers doubted that he meant to cross out of the Sequatchie Valley at all, but supposed that his movements were only intended as demonstrations to cover the advance of his columns into Kentucky from Knoxville.

In the mean time our supplies were diminishing rapidly, with no prospect of renewal until a sufficient force was detached to restore our broken communications. This pressing necessity left no time either to advance or to await the arrival of an enemy who could choose his time and route, with the certainty that the necessity of subsistence would very soon compel me to fall back, in whole or in part, whether there was an enemy in front or not, as long as his cavalry continued its operations in rear. The news from Kentucky was unsatisfactory. The rebel force under Kirby Smith was coming into the State, there was nothing but new levies to oppose him, and it was not known what number of them had been collected. So far from being able to open the communication between Nashville and Louisville and from Cumberland Gap to Lexington, it was not improbable that those places themselves might soon be seized by the rebel forces. Under these circumstances I determined to concentrate my army at Murfreesborough and set to work to open the railroad north of Nashville. That object had already been delayed too long upon the hope of having it done by a force from Louisville. Orders were accordingly given on the 30th of August to the various commands and guards, distributed over an area of about 150 by 100 miles of territory and some 300 miles of railroad, so as to concentrate on the 5th of September. The routes and marches were prescribed, and the movement was executed simultaneously and with perfect precision. With the exception of the force on the Decatur road, which was ordered to Nashville, the whole army, coming from various quarters and different distances on four roads, concentrated at Murfreesborough on the 5th of September, bringing with it whatever supplies could be collected from the country. A small remnant of provisions, for which there was insufficient transportation, was destroyed at Huntsville, and with that exception not a pound of supplies was lost by the movement. After it was ordered I learned that a considerable quantity of cotton, belonging to persons who had purchased it in the country, was at Athens, awaiting transportation. In order to give them an opportunity to remove it I delayed the evacuation of that place perhaps a day or so.

On the 1st of September I learned that a large rebel force, under General Kirby Smith, had actually appeared in Central Kentucky, having defeated and routed the force under General Nelson at Richmond. This effectually cut off the division at Cumberland Gap from its base. I was anxious to rescue that force, and the shortest route by which it could be done was to direct a column from McMinnville, by the way of Somerset, upon the rear of Kirby Smith's army. I supposed that that might be done and still keep a front about McMinnville toward the army of General Bragg in the Sequatchie Valley, while the two divisions, one of which had arrived that day from Corinth, should open the communications between Nashville and Louisville. The forces at McMinnville and in that vicinity had not yet withdrawn from their position, and I accordingly suspended their movement, leaving its execution, however, to General Thomas, who was at McMinnville, and had the best opportunity to know any movements of the enemy in the Sequatchie Valley that would affect it. He answered, stating the advantages of a concentration at Murfreesborough, and advising me that he would march the following day, and so the concentration was executed as originally ordered.

I proceed now to notice certain theories and opinions that have been advanced concerning a plan of operations to oppose the movement of the rebel army across the mountain. As evidence they are of no more value than though they had been expressed in idle discussion around a camp-fire, and are only entitled to credit according as they are correct in their premises and rational in their conclusions. They were new to me until this investigation had made some progress, and it appears that one of them in particular was promulgated after the arrival of my army in Louisville, where it was used as a text for criticism by officers who have not appeared as friendly witnesses before this Commission.

Neither my own feelings nor any fact that I am aware of would justify me in assuming that General Thomas has entertained any other than the most friendly disposition toward me; but I was surprised at the opinion expressed by him before the Commission that Bragg's army might have been attacked at Sparta, and more astonished at the statement that he had urged upon me to concentrate at that place. My inquiries elicited the information that this proposition was communicated to me by telegraph on the 28th of August. At my request the dispatch was subsequently presented. It proved to have been written on the 22d instead of the 28th. It will be better understood after a brief review of the circumstances that gave rise to it.

General Thomas took command at McMinnville on the 19th of August. About that time I received very positive intelligence that the rebel forces were crossing the Tennessee River at three points at least—about 10,000 at Kingston, at least 10,000 at Harrison, and a force variously estimated at from 40,000 to 60,000 at Chattanooga. I telegraphed General Thomas and other officers on the 19th and 20th in regard to this information, and prepared them for the further movements the enemy might be expected to make. I told him to look to Sparta and Smithville, anticipating that the column from Kingston might advance on that route against McMinnville while we were threatened by a larger force elsewhere, or else toward Nashville to threaten our communications. This column he evidently kept in his mind, and it seemed to me that it was the only one he seriously regarded. The Chattanooga force proper, as he called it, he appeared either to doubt the existence of, or at least its purpose to cross the mountain. On the contrary I had reasons, which he probably did not know, to believe that it would advance by the Therman road. I therefore telegraphed General Thomas on the 22d of August as follows:

From McCook's information this morning it seems almost certain that Bragg is marching on McMinnville. His advance was at the top of Walden's Ridge last night. McCown is said to be crossing at Kingston and Withers at Harrison. Of course they will expect to unite. What sort of ground can we take by concentrating at McMinnville? How would it do at Altamont? Is the ground such as to give us the advantage of our artillery? How many days' rations have you? Are you provided with ammunition? Be ready to march in the morning. Answer immediately.

And again as follows:

Of course you will instantly recall your absent troops. I will probably bring the Second Kentucky by rail to march from here. We will advance to attack in the Sequatchie Valley. I can hardly think the enemy will attempt the march across to McMinnville—at least not immediately. It appears to me that he will rather endeavor to get into North Alabama, and perhaps strike across to Decherd. If we advance to Altamont we may thwart him in both and preserve our communications with Decherd and Nashville. If we concentrate at McMinnville we lose North Alabama and Decherd. What think you? The great difficulty is in moving in the mountains with our trains. Of course we must cut loose from everything but our ammunition trains and subsistence for about six days, most of it in haversacks.

His answer to the first is the dispatch dated the 22d, at McMinnville, referred to in his testimony, and is in these words:

By all means concentrate here. The enemy cannot reach Nashville by any other route across the mountains unless by Sparta. At Altamont I am positively informed the enemy would have an equal advantage with ourselves. Here we will have a most decided advantage; and by being here, should he march by Sparta, we can meet him either there or at Allen's Ford, across Caney Fork. He is obliged to pass this place or Sparta to reach Nashville. I have six days' rations and plenty of ammunition. Did you get my dispatch of to-day? I cannot think that Bragg is coming here either by the Hill or Therman road. My reconnoitering party went into Dunlap yesterday.

His answer, of the same date, to the second is as follows:

We can get neither forage nor water at Altamont. It will be as difficult for us to march across the mountains as the enemy to come either to Altamont or this place. I would not advise concentrating here except for battle or for an advance into East Tennessee. I think our communications with Nashville will be better preserved by holding Decherd with a division, to enable us to concentrate either there, if threatened, or at this place. I have also information that Tupelo has been abandoned, and the most of the enemy at that place have been sent to Chattanooga. I therefore do not apprehend an attempt to regain North Alabama.

Upon further information that the enemy was advancing rapidly on the Therman road I answered him on the 23d as follows:

There is no possibility of our concentrating at McMinnville. We must concentrate in advance and assume the offensive or fall back at last to Murfreesborough. I deem the former the wisest, and we will act accordingly. I wish you therefore to move by a forced march to Altamont, there to form a junction with McCook, Crittenden, and Schoepf. McCook and Crittenden started for Tracy City from Jasper yesterday. I presume they are now at Tracy City, though possibly not. Schoepf will march at once. The junction must be formed to-morrow, and any division meeting the head of the enemy's column first must at least hold it in check until a larger force arrives.
One battery to a division will, I think, be ample in the mountains. McCook and Crittenden have with them six batteries. Leave all of yours, therefore; at least don't take more than two. It will be necessary to leave some force with them, at least two regiments, and they should be covered with breastworks to-night without fail.
I shall order Schoepf's batteries here to be similarly disposed of. There must be no delay or failure. The enemy's advance was at the top of Walden's Ridge, 10 miles from Chattanooga, night before last, and talked of being at McMinnville to-morrow. That is hardly possible, but they must be met at the earliest possible moment. Communicate with McCook to-night by a trusty scout. The distance is 32 miles. He may possibly not be at Tracy City. If not, look for him on the road to Battle Creek. If you think best you may send your artillery to this place, which will release the force that would be required to protect them there; though if they will be safe there is some advantage in having a force at McMinnville. Take no wagons except what will be necessary to carry rations and cooking utensils. I shall probably leave here with Sill's brigade to-morrow for Tracy City to join you. Communicate always in cipher by telegraph to this place and by courier through Tracy City. Schoepf sends a report that Hardee is advancing on the Dunlap road. Answer, so that I may know exactly what you do. Your staff officers make mistakes in the use of the cipher.

I apprehend that further comment on this subject is unnecessary. The dispatch in question was in answer to my own inquiry, and had reference to the relative merits of McMinnville and Altamont as battle grounds. It is certain that General Thomas has not consciously laid claim to an idea which did not possess him; but I apprehend that developed facts have been so mingled in his mind with impressions coincident in some particulars, though essentially different in the material points, that his memory has failed to draw the exact distinction between them. It is, however, due to him to say that the idea may have been in his mind that Bragg might cross the mountain to Sparta, and that he did not distinctly express it to me, imagining that I also entertained it myself.

But I do not propose to draw any advantage from the question whether or not a proposition was made to me to concentrate at Sparta. If it had been made, I should have judged it according to its merits with the lights before me at the time, and I do not doubt that I should have rejected it on grounds which I will state.

Besides the road which crosses from Jasper to Decherd and the one which ascends the valley and thence goes to Crossville there are no less than three roads by which the enemy could ascend the mountain to debouch from the Sequatchie Valley: First, the Therman road, which passes through or near Altamont, and then branches into at least four roads that descend the mountain into the plains of Middle Tennessee between Decherd and McMinnville, a distance of about 40 miles; second, a road which ascends the mountain at Dunlap and passes to McMinnville; third, a road which ascends the mountain a short distance below Pikeville and branches on the mountain, the left-hand branch going to McMinnville and the right hand forking again some 20 miles from McMinnville, one fork going to the latter place and the other to Sparta. There is also a road on the top of the mountain connecting all these roads. These geographical features would enable the enemy to arrive within 20 miles of McMinnville by not less than two roads before determining whether he would move on that point or Sparta, and by covering his movements with his superior cavalry force he could easily arrive within 6 or 8 miles of either of those points before his destination could be known at all, and it is 22 miles at least from McMinnville to Sparta. If I had been at Sparta he could have been at McMinnville and in possession of my line of supplies before I could have known it. If I awaited at McMinnville the development of his plan he could have gone to Sparta and pursued his course as he did. If I had divided my force between McMinnville and Sparta, to anticipate him at both points, he could have advanced with reasonable probability of success against either of them; and if the fractions should have been so strongly fortified as not to warrant an attack, he could have avoided them, thrown himself between the two, and thus have forced them to retreat separately, or attempt the offensive against a concentrated force. General Thomas' own experience at McMinnville in obtaining information on which success would have depended confirms my answer to one phase of this proposition and is applicable to all of them.

On the 31st he reports:

The general impression is that the enemy is advancing, but I have yet to see the person who has seen any of the Chattanooga forces proper.

And on the 2d of September, in reply to the discretional instructions heretofore alluded to, he says:

I will start to-morrow. I have heard again that the enemy intends advancing on this place by the Therman, Dunlap, and Sparta roads. By concentrating at Murfreesborough we shall be within striking distance of this place. By convenient roads our main force can be thrown upon the enemy between this and Decherd or Hillsborough, overcome him, and drive him toward Sparta, his longest line of retreat. A large force of cavalry and light infantry can be pushed across the mountains by the Dunlap and Therman roads, attack him in rear, and completely rout his whole force. I have studied the roads, and am now convinced that this is our best plan of attack.

It was afterward ascertained that the rebel forces under General Bragg actually commenced to arrive at Sparta the day after the date of this dispatch.

The reasons which made the concentration at Murfreesborough necessary and proper may now be briefly summed up:

It had been supposed that for the lack of supplies on the route the enemy would make his march across the mountains rapidly. Several days had already elapsed since, from the best information that could be obtained of his movements, it was supposed he would have arrived within striking distance, and he was still not nearer than the Sequatchie Valley.

My supplies had been cut off for twenty days, and the expectation that the force in Kentucky would reopen the railroad, on which they were dependent, was frustrated by the invasion of the State by Kirby Smith, which, as the result proved, gave more than ample occupation to the raw troops that were there. I did not even know what force of that kind could be expected, for its organization had only very recently been commenced and the State had recently been organized into a separate department not under my command. I was already reduced to about ten days' supply—a little more than that of breadstuff and some minor articles and a good deal less of meat and other articles scarcely less essential. The quantity was increased at Nashville a little by the collection of flour and meat in the country. General Thomas reported on the 28th from McMinnville that no provisions could be procured in that region, and that for forage he could get fodder, but no corn; and his statement in regard to the scarcity in the country is confirmed by testimony before the Commission. Such straits did not admit of any further delay to await an enemy who could choose his own time for the meeting and who had already been eight days behind the time at which I had reason to expect him. An immediate concentration at a point nearer the source of supply, from which I was separated 260 miles, was clearly necessary. It promised the only means of opening the railroad and still holding Nashville, the possession of which was believed to be the enemy's first object.

But the concentration at Murfreesborough was expedient on other grounds. I could not have concentrated at any point as far in advance as McMinnville more than about 31,000 men, and that force was not sufficient to attack Bragg's army united at any point. If I could have taken any position in which I could force or induce him to attack without delay it would have been well, but such was not the case. In this uncertainty as to the time he might delay and as to the route on which he would strike in force, while perhaps threatening by other routes, screened as he was by a range of mountains, with our communications with Louisville completely severed, and our supplies already reduced to a narrow margin, perhaps to be entirely exhausted when the advance of the enemy would make rapid operations necessary, it was plainly necessary to concentrate at some point nearer our base, by which means my effective force would be increased so as to be sufficient to meet the enemy whenever he should come and still have enough to open our communications.

The plan of operations presented in the evidence of another witness of rank before the Commission was to concentrate the army at Murfreesborough as soon as the rebel army commenced its advance from

Chattanooga. This, except as to the time of the concentration, is the plan that was actually executed. The earlier execution of it would not have affected the result, but the distribution of my small cavalry force to guard the various passes across the mountains, from 40 to 60 miles distant—which was one feature of the plan—could only have resulted in the capture or dispersion of the whole of them whenever the enemy chose to effect it. As for the idea of first concentrating at Murfreesborough and then advancing to attack the enemy at Sparta, it must suppose that the enemy would wait seven or eight days at that place to be attacked, which he did not do. I do not, therefore, see any advantage in this variation of the plan that was adopted; and if it had been submitted to my judgment I should have rejected it.

Two witnesses of high rank, in answer to a question as to points north of the Cumberland River at which Bragg's army "could have been attacked with a prospect of success," expressed the opinion that it might have been done at Glasgow. This opinion was undoubtedly expressed without reflection, unless it referred to the advantage which the locality of Glasgow would have afforded for the attacking army in case of a collision there, and not to the possibility of intercepting Bragg's army at that point; for the testimony of these two witnesses shows and the map shows that until Bragg's army crossed the Cumberland River and took up its march northward it was impossible to know from its movements whether its plan was to go into Kentucky or turn to the west against Nashville; that it is 50 miles from the Cumberland River where Bragg crossed it to Glasgow, while it is 95 miles from Nashville, where my army was, to Glasgow; and from these facts the witnesses admit that it was not possible to have intercepted Bragg's army at that point unless he had tarried there. In point of fact the evidence shows that on the 7th of September I learned that a portion of Bragg's army had crossed the Cumberland River at Carthage and was moving northward, probably toward Bowling Green, where I had caused some supplies to be accumulated by the way of Green River, and that I immediately ordered a portion of my army to march for that point; that on the 10th I learned, what was before unknown, if not improbable, that another portion had crossed at Gainesborough, and had probably marched in the same direction, and that I ordered other divisions, making six, for the same point, accompanying them myself; that this movement was made rapidly, the last of the six divisions arriving at Bowling Green Monday morning, the 15th, which was the time at which the rear of Bragg's army passed Glasgow. Thus, after gaining intelligence of his passage over the Cumberland River, I moved my army 65 miles while he was moving 50, with the advantage of two roads, and I was still 30 miles in rear of him.

The same process of demonstration will show that even if I had known he was going by Munfordville, and if there had been nothing to delay me an hour at Bowling Green, I could not have intercepted him at Munfordville, because I had 105 miles to march, while he had but 68, the distance from Glasgow to Munfordville being 18 miles. In fact his advance actually attacked the latter place the day before my sixth division reached Bowling Green. But, furthermore, it was not yet to be assumed that his destination was Central Kentucky; on the contrary, Glasgow was an important position for him. It effectually commanded my line of communication with my base of supplies, while he had two lines open—one with the East Tennessee Railroad, which was his permanent base, and also with the valley of the Cumberland, and the other with Central Kentucky, where the occupation of Kirby Smith had established for him a second base.

Munfordville did not offer the same advantages, for, although a much stronger natural position, yet in taking it he gave up his communications with Tennessee, and rendered those with Kirby Smith less secure against a force operating from the Ohio River, supposing Louisville to be secure to us. At Munfordville his communication with Kirby Smith must have been along the Louisville turnpike and thence across to Bardstown, while at Glasgow it would be along the old Lexington road through Summersville and Lebanon, or through Columbia and Lebanon or Liberty, by all of which roads I have moved large bodies of troops. Besides, at Munfordville he would have been in a much less productive region than at Glasgow. These considerations, taken in connection with the risk he would run by advancing farther into Kentucky, made it at least reasonably doubtful whether he would not halt at Glasgow. The fact that his purpose was to penetrate still farther into Kentucky and that he had designs on Louisville was only known when it was ascertained that he had left Glasgow and through correspondence which was captured subsequent to that time. But supposing it had been reasonably certain that Bardstown was his destination, it was not to be assumed that he would go by the way of Munfordville; on the contrary, it is undoubtedly true that but for the bait which was offered to him in the garrison at that place he would not have gone there at all, for the simple reason that without any object whatever it would have taken him off the direct and excellent turnpike from Glasgow to Bardstown and thrown him on another road not so good and 12 miles longer. This brings me naturally to the question of the relief of Munfordville.

The foregoing explanations show that I could not have reached Munfordville in advance of the rebel force even if it had been desirable to leave it between me and Nashville. The first information received at Bowling Green that Munfordville was attacked or threatened was on the 14th, and the report was that it had been captured, though that was not certain. On the same day the last of five of my divisions arrived at Bowling Green, and on the same day, as was afterward ascertained, the main body of the rebel army marched from Glasgow, 18 miles from Munfordville, with the advantage of two roads. If I had moved forward at once I could not have reached Munfordville in less than four days, for, considering that I must march on one road, it would, for the rear of my column, have been equivalent in time to a march of 60 miles; and in the presence of an enemy whose position was not known the march could not well have been made more rapidly. As for re-enforcing the garrison by the first of my divisions which arrived at Bowling Green, even if the necessity of it could have been known it would have been out of the question, for those divisions would have been thrown into the midst of the whole rebel force; a folly which it appears the enemy actually anticipated, and prepared to reap the fruit of.

But I propose to inquire also what necessity there was for such relief, and on what grounds it could reasonably have been expected that I would furnish it. It is apparent from a study of the map, and the evidence shows, that the possession of Munfordville was not essential to Bragg's army in a strategical point of view. At least three other preferable routes were open to him, whether his object was to attack Louisville directly or to advance into Central Kentucky for other purposes: First, the shorter and better road from Glasgow to Bardstown and thence on to Louisville; second, the old Lexington road to Lebanon; third, the road through Columbia, Liberty, and Danville. He would not in any event take the road to the mouth of Salt River; because it threw him more away from the base of supplies which Kirby Smith's presence had established in Central Kentucky, because it made his junction with Kirby Smith more difficult and uncertain, and because it placed him in the angle between the Ohio and Salt Rivers, neither of which could he cross without ferrying or bridging. The same facts made the possession of Munfordville a matter of no strategical value to us. Its importance, therefore, was determined by the value of the bridge, which alone it was intended to protect as a link in the chain of communication between the troops farther south and Louisville, their base of supplies. The bridge, if destroyed, could be rebuilt in a week—was actually rebuilt in about ten days; and as the principal part of the force which drew supplies across the bridge was coming north, its preservation was not of immediate importance. I have been disposed to say, therefore, that the determination to hold the bridge was an error of judgment; but I will not now assert that it was so, seeing that doubt existed as to the probability of Bragg's coming that way and that the commander considered himself able to hold his position against the force which at first threatened him. If it was evident that Bragg would come against the place with his whole or any considerable part of his army, then it is certain that to attempt to hold it was an error, for no position could be less tenable for a small force against a very large one. · It must be apparent that the possession of Munfordville was of no importance that would justify the jeopardizing any considerable force to hold it, and the evidence shows that for two days and a half after the first attack the way was open for the withdrawal of the garrison. Its relief from the direction of Bowling Green was therefore unnecessary, if it had been possible. Let us see now how far the place was considered to be in jeopardy and on what ground it was reasonable to expect relief from Bowling Green.

It appears that on Saturday, the 13th, the commanding officer learned that a force, represented to be 7,000 strong, was advancing upon his post from the direction of Glasgow; that he reported the fact to his superiors at Louisville, saying:

If I had one more good regiment and a few more pieces of artillery that force could not take me. As it is I shall do my best to prevent it. Can you send me re-enforcements to-night? I shall send train to Salt River for them.

To which he received in reply, "I send you what you ask." The same day he also reports, "Some indications that the main rebel force are going toward Lebanon," and that his intrenchments would be finished that night. These reports were certainly not alarming, and did not indicate that he expected or required assistance from Bowling Green, however desirous he might be to see a force coming from that quarter. On the same day he sent scouts to Bowling Green with verbal messages. These scouts could not have carried word that he was in jeopardy and required help from there, for his superiors had given him all he thought necessary at that time and as yet no force had appeared in front of him. I now remember that the scout Miller came to me, but so little was there in his communications to me different from the information I derived from unauthorized persons, that I had forgotten, nor do I now remember, that he came as a messenger. He knew less about the enemy and scarcely if any more about the garrison than others, especially one who came from the vicinity of the fort the morning of the attack and reported quite confidently that the garrison had surrendeied. Those persons reported first to the commanding officer at Bowling Green, and he had no better recollection of the special object and importance of their mission than myself. Nor could it at any rate have altered the case. I must of necessity have operated against the rebel army which was already virtually between me and Munfordville. There was no communication between me and the commander in Kentucky, and, knowing that the rebel army was between me and Munfordville, he had no reasonable assurance that I could succor that place. It was not under my command, I really knew nothing of its condition, and I could not suppose that it would be needlessly exposed to so large a force.

All the information I had led to the supposition that Bragg's army was probably yet at Glasgow, and on Tuesday afternoon, the 16th, I marched with six divisions (one being still in the rear), in three columns, to attack the enemy if he should be at that place. The facts shown in evidence that the last of those six divisions had only arrived after a march of 15 miles the day before, with very rapid and fatiguing ones on previous days; that some time was necessarily required to make arrangements with reference to the garrison and trains that were to remain; that supplies had to be distributed, and that the supply of provisions was imperfect, making it necessary to collect breadstuffs from the country to supply the troops, will amply justify this short delay. The troops in three columns had to start upon the main turnpike road from Bowling Green to Munfordville, but successively turned upon roads which converge on Glasgow. The cavalry thrown in advance reported on Tuesday night that the enemy had left Glasgow, and the following day my army marched to Cave City and Horse Well, within 10 miles of Munfordville. During that day I heard of the surrender of Munfordville, and on the night of that day the commanding officer of the post reported to me at Prewitt's Knob with his troops on parole.

The position at Munfordville is one of great natural strength for a large force. I understand that it was the subject of dissatisfaction that the rebel army was not attacked in that position; but I have never heard that the feeling was concurred in by the officers of higher rank, several of whom, distinguished before and since for gallant conduct, have testified that such an attack would not have been judicious under the circumstances. The advantage of position in favor of the enemy must have made the result at least doubtful; and even a very serious check, in the exhausted condition of our supplies, would have been disastrous. I could have avoided the enemy by passing to either side of him, but I deemed it all-important to force him farther into the State, instead of allowing him to fall back upon Bowling Green and Nashville, and I matured a plan and determined to attack there rather than allow him that course. I believed that the condition of his supplies would compel him to abandon his position; and I was very well satisfied when that proved to be the case. He commenced to withdraw on the night of the 20th, and my advance drove out his rear guard, after some skirmishing, on the 21st. The march was continued, and skirmishing was kept up with his rear guard until he turned off toward Bardstown.

Many considerations rendered it proper to direct my march on Louisville instead of following his route. The want of supplies made it necessary, many of the troops being out by the time they reached the mouth of Salt River. This reason would have been insuperable if, as was not improbable, the enemy should concentrate his force and throw himself rapidly between me and Louisville. The junction of Bragg and Kirby Smith was not only possible but probable. It would have made their combined force greatly superior to me in strength, and such a disposition would have placed him between two inferior forces, which, from their positions, could not have acted in concert against him, and which, therefore, were liable to be beaten in detail. One of these forces, that occupying Louisville, was composed of perfectly raw, undisciplined, and in a measure unarmed troops, with but very little artillery and very few officers of rank or experience. It could not have withstood the veteran rebel army two hours, and the consequence of its defeat and the capture of Louisville would have been disastrous in the extreme. That force, however, mixed judiciously with my old troops, could be made to render good service, as the result proved.

These considerations determined me to concentrate rapidly at Louisville. The last division reached that point on the 29th of September. On the same day the incorporation of the new troops with the old, and other preparations which a long and fatiguing march of the old troops and the inefficiency of the new rendered necessary, were completed, and on the morning of the 30th the consolidated army was prepared to march against the rebel forces which occupied the principal part of Kentucky. The campaign which ensued, and which resulted in the expulsion of the enemy from the State, has been sketched in my official report of the 4th of November, herewith appended.* As far as the facts are concerned the investigations of this Commission have shown, perhaps, that I did not make allowance enough for the diminution of my force by absentees and stragglers from the new regiments, and that therefore I probably overestimated my own strength at and after the battle of Perryville, if I did not also underestimate the combined strength of the enemy. These investigations also give reason to believe that the aggregate loss of the enemy during the campaign was greater than I represented, and they have developed additional interesting incidents; but they point to no statement which I could now desire to alter. I shall limit myself, therefore, to the elucidation of certain particulars in which the wisdom of my acts would seem to have been called into question by the course of the investigation.

The battle of Perryville, although but a partial and by no means as fruitful a contest as I had expected, was not without important and gratifying results. I shall notice very briefly the causes which prevented it from being more so.

When, on the 5th of October, Bragg's army proper retired from Bardstown it was uncertain where it would unite with the force of Kirby Smith, though Danville was the point where I most expected to find them, and my corps were accordingly directed on Perryville and Harrodsburg. When, on the night of the 6th, I ascertained that Kirby Smith had crossed the Kentucky River at Salvisa, Harrodsburg or Perryville became the most probable point of concentration, and the destination of the corps which were marching on Harrodsburg had to be changed to Perryville. Information during the 7th that the enemy were turning toward Harrodsburg inclined me to suppose, though not confidently, that Harrodsburg, and not Perryville, would be the point. In the movement on that place the center corps, with which I was, marched by a shorter and better road, and therefore arrived within about 3 miles of Perryville on the evening of the 7th, while the other

---

* See battle of Perryville, or Chaplin Hills.

corps were expected to be still about 7 miles in rear, on their respective roads to the right and left.

Finding a sufficient force at Perryville on the evening of the 7th to stop our progress without a general engagement of the corps it was presumed that the enemy had determined to make his stand there, and the following instructions were sent to General McCook:

OCTOBER 7—8 p. m.

GENERAL: The Third Corps (Gilbert's) is within 3¼ miles of Perryville, the cavalry being nearer, probably within 2½ miles. From all the information gained to-day it seems probable that the enemy will resist our advance into the town. They are said to have a strong force in and near the place. There is no water here, and we will get but little, if any, until we get it at Perryville. We expect to attack and carry the place to-morrow. March at 3 o'clock precisely to-morrow morning without fail, and move up till the head of your column gets to within about 3 or 3½ miles of Perryville; that is to say, until you are abreast of the Third Corps. The left of this corps rests near Bottom's place. Perhaps Captain Williams, Jackson's cavalry, will know where it is. From the point of the road Gilbert is now on across direct to your road is about 2½ or 3 miles. When the head of your column gets to the vicinity designated (3 or 3½ miles from town) halt and form it in order of battle, and let the rear close well up; then let the men rest in position and be made as comfortable as possible, but do not permit them to scatter. Have the country on your front examined, a reconnaissance made, and collect all the information possible in regard to the enemy and the country and roads in your vicinity, and then report in person as quickly as practicable to these headquarters. If your men have an opportunity to get water of any kind they must fill their canteens, and the officers must caution them particularly to use it in the most sparing manner. Send to the rear every wagon and animal which is not required with your column. All the usual precautions must be taken and preparations made for action. Keep all teams back except ammunition and ambulances. Nothing has been heard from you to-day. Send orderlies by bearer to learn the locality of these headquarters. The general desires to see Captain Williams, Jackson's cavalry, by 7 o'clock in the morning at these headquarters.

Respectfully, &c.,

JAMES B. FRY,
Colonel and Chief of Staff.

Similar instructions, but suited to the locality on which he was to form for the attack, were given to General Thomas, who, as second in command, was with the right corps.

It was expected that these instructions would get these two corps into position for the attack by 7 or 8 o'clock in the morning; whereas, in consequence of delays which were more or less unavoidable, the heads of the columns did not come up until between 10 and 11 o'clock and the rear division of the right corps did not get into position until about 4 o'clock. This rendered it improbable that the attack could be made until next morning and was one of the causes which marred the success I confidently expected. Afterward the lateness of the hour at which I received intelligence of the condition of affairs on the left rendered it impossible to reap the fruit that would otherwise still have remained.

It has been a matter of surprise that so severe an engagement could have taken place within 2½ miles of my headquarters without my knowledge. The commander of an army covering a line 6 or 7 miles long, interspersed with woods and hills, must of necessity depend on the reports of his generals for information of what is transpiring on different parts of the field. After the failure to get into position as soon as I had expected I no longer anticipated a battle that day; but a good deal of artillery firing had been going on between the advance guards of the two armies since our arrival the evening before, excepting at night. The cause of this was well understood, and the greater or less rapidity of the firing at intervals was not a matter to attract particular attention, especially as it was to be expected that information of anything of serious import would be promptly conveyed to me. For that reason I received with astonishment the intelligence of the severe fighting that commenced at 2 o'clock. Not a musket-shot had been heard nor did the sound of artillery indicate anything like a battle. This was probably caused by the configuration of the ground, which broke the sound, and by the heavy wind, which it appears blew from the right to the left during the day, though the latter I had not thought of until it was established in evidence before the Commission. Be that as it may, many witnesses, without exception, have testified to the absence of all reason to suppose at my headquarters that a battle was raging, and the testimony of hundreds more could have been adduced to the same effect.

It has been asked why, after the battle of Perryville, I did not immediately follow the enemy to Harrodsburg, without waiting for Sill's division to come up. That the entire rebel army could have been brought to battle there I have no doubt. The forces were nearly equal on both sides—on one side nearly all veteran troops, under perfect discipline; on the other, a portion, the old "Army of the Ohio," equally good, but more than one-third of the whole raw and undisciplined.* The enemy would have had the advantage of the strong position which he selected. The result of a conflict under such circumstances is not to be predicted. I am not willing to admit that I might have failed, and yet no man can assert that the result ought certainly to have been otherwise under the circumstances. It was sufficient for me that I could make it reasonably certain by waiting for my troops to come up.

My studies have taught me that battles are only to be fought for some important object; that success must be rendered reasonably certain if possible—the more certain the better; that if the result is reasonably uncertain, battle is only to be sought when very serious disadvantage must result from a failure to fight or when the advantages of a possible victory far outweigh the consequences of probable defeat. These rules suppose that war has a higher object than that of mere bloodshed, and military history points for study and commendation to campaigns which have been conducted over a large field of operations with important results and without a single general engagement. In my judgment the commander merits condemnation who, from ambition or ignorance or a weak submission to the dictation of popular clamor and without necessity or profit, has squandered the lives of his soldiers. In this connection it is proper to review the circumstances which should have weight upon the question of hastening a battle at the particular juncture referred to.

There is not, I venture to say, a particle of evidence upon the records of this Commission which does not lead to the conclusion that the objects and intention of the rebel Government in the invasion of Kentucky last summer were to hold possession of the State by force of arms and secure it to the cause of the rebellion. The circumstances of the invasion and the formidable force employed in it, the advance of the smaller force under Kirby Smith, which established depots and collected supplies, that made comparatively easy and safe the subsequent advance of the main force under General Bragg to a point so remote from its original base; the further re-enforcement of this large force by the column under Breckinridge at the very time when, if a temporary raid

---

* To quotation from this paragraph in his letter of April 10, 1864, there omitted to avoid duplication, General Buell adds the following note:

"The evidence places the rebel army in Kentucky at not less than 60,000. It places my force at Perryville at less than 58,000 before the battle."

had been the object, the main force should have been rapidly withdraw-ing instead of re-enforcing; the deliberation and permanency with which the invading army maintained its position in the face of the force which was preparing to drive it out; the inauguration of a provisional State government under the authority of the Confederate Government; the enforcement of the conscription and other Confederate laws; the avowal of the Confederate authorities; the plan of campaign sketched in the letter of General Beauregard to his Government; the convictions of the people of Kentucky from what they saw and the assurance of the rebel authorities; the constant and confident declarations of all persons con-nected with the invading force; the disappointment and disapprobation which the whole Southern press expressed at the result—all go to show that the object of the invasion was permanent occupation. That object could only be secured by giving battle to and destroying or driving from the field the army which was opposed to it.

Such a plan and determination were also clearly indicated by the movements of the enemy after the commencement of my march from Louisville. If his object had been to retreat without a struggle as soon as I moved against him, the force of Kirby Smith, which was then at various points north of the Kentucky River, would at once have moved by the roads concentrating at Richmond and thence on to Cumberland Gap. It was for that force the shortest and best road and a better route for supplies than the one it pursued. The main force, under Bragg, would have moved on one or more of the roads which converge upon Glasgow, through New Haven, Lebanon, and other points. This line would have given him the advantage of marching by several of the best roads in the State, converging at convenient distances. It would have taken him through a region of country where supplies were com-paratively abundant; it would have enabled him to concentrate his army at Bowling Green and perhaps capture that place before he could be overtaken; or, if not, to move upon Murfreesborough, where he would have railroad communication with Chattanooga and good lines of retreat to the other side of the Tennessee River if necessary, or the opportunity of capturing Nashville if he should deem that feasible; or, if he desired to retreat through Cumberland Gap, he would go on through Danville and Stanford. Instead, however, of starting upon these natural lines of retreat toward Tennessee, Kirby Smith moved west, entirely off his line of retreat, and crossed the Kentucky River near Salvisa; and Bragg, after turning the angle at Perryville, moved northward, the very opposite of his direction of retreat. That the original object of this movement was to concentrate the whole rebel force at Harrodsburg instead of Camp Dick Robinson is evident from the fact that if the latter had been the object Kirby Smith would have moved directly to that point over the Hickman bridge, instead of ford-ing the river lower down to go out of his way, and Bragg would have marched through Danville to the same point. Thus the circumstances of the invasion indicated that there would be a formidable struggle for the possession of the State, and the movements of the rebel forces to meet the operations that were in progress against them pointed to a great battle at or near Harrodsburg.

The battle of Perryville, by every reasonable explanation, increased instead of weakening the probability of a great battle at Harrodsburg. It has been asserted that General Bragg fought the battle of Perryville with portions of three divisions, only about 15,000 men. It is certain that he fought it with only a part of his whole force. His motive there-fore may be supposed to have been either to check my advance to give time to take up a position with his main force beyond, or else because he hoped to gain some advantage by striking the head of my column, supposing I was moving on only one road, before I could get a superior force up to oppose him. In either case he could not have expected to accomplish much more than he did in this partial engagement. He was repulsed, it is true, but not until night protected him from very serious consequences, and there was nothing in the result that should have decided the fate of so important a campaign. His loss was probably much less than mine, from the fact that the attack was made when my troops were in column and to that extent unprepared.

That General Bragg moved to Camp Dick Robinson instead of awaiting an attack by my whole force at Harrodsburg is no evidence that he would not have been willing to give battle to the part of it which I had at Perryville. With an equal force he could safely risk a battle in the strong position he could have taken, and in fact did select, when the result would by no means be as certain there, against a superior force, as it would be in the still stronger position of Camp Dick Robinson, which had the further advantage of being a depot for his supplies. For these reasons, and on account of its inaccessibility and superior strength, neither did his withdrawal to Camp Dick Robinson indicate an intention to abandon the object of his campaign and retreat precipitately from the State. These reasons justified the conclusion that the rebel army was to be encountered in battle, notwithstanding critics after the fact may answer that the result contradicts the conclusion, and they justify every reasonable precaution to have made the success of such a struggle certain. They afford an interpretation to the movements of the army under my command subsequently to the battle of Perryville.

Pending the arrival of General Sill's division the left corps, General McCook's, laid near Dicksville, from which a road extends to Harrodsburg; the center, General Gilbert's, was abreast of the left, on the direct road from Perryville to Harrodsburg; and the right, General Crittenden's, was on Salt River, about 4 miles from Danville. Cavalry was in front on the Harrodsburg and Danville roads. A good deal of the ammunition of McCook's corps and some in the center corps had been expended in the battle of the 8th, and so much of the means of transportation had been required for provisions that wagons could not be spared for a sufficient supply of reserve ammunition on starting from Louisville. This was hurried forward and other matters attended to in the condition of the army which had resulted from the battle. These of themselves would not have delayed my movements, though they were important.

General Sill's division arrived on the evening of the 11th and the army was ordered to move on the 12th. Strong cavalry reconnaissances had been kept out every day, but on the evening of the 10th I ordered out three brigades of infantry with cavalry to move on the 11th to discover more of the position or movements of the enemy. One moved beyond Danville toward Camp Dick Robinson; one on the Danville and Harrodsburg road toward the latter point; and the third toward the same point on the Perryville and Harrodsburg road. About daylight an officer, just in from Harrodsburg, came to my tent and reported to me with great earnestness that the enemy was moving against us in force from Harrodsburg, distant about 8 miles. The troops were put in position to be prepared, if the report should prove true, and in the mean time the several reconnaissances proceeded as ordered. The one on the left discovered and reported the enemy apparently in force about

2 miles south of Harrodsburg early in the morning; but he withdrew during the day, and the two reconnaissances which were ordered toward Harrodsburg entered that place in the evening, capturing some property and a large number of sick, wounded, and some other prisoners.

It was probable that the enemy had retired to Camp Dick Robinson, but it was reported that some at least had gone in the direction of the Kentucky River, and it was necessary to ascertain the fact. It would require a day to do that by reconnaissance. If the reconnaissance were supported in force, we should be prepared to take advantage of the contingency of the enemy still being this side of Dick's River; and, in any event, no time would be lost in the movement to turn the position at Camp Dick Robinson, if it should be found that the enemy had actually retired to that place. On the 12th, therefore, the whole army swung around on Danville as a pivot, the right and center on the Danville and Harrodsburg road and the left near Harrodsburg on the Perryville and Harrodsburg road while a reconnaissance was pushed forward to gain the desired information. It ascertained that the enemy had crossed Dick's River.

If it should be said that these dispositions proved to have been unnecessary by the withdrawal of the enemy, it may be answered that such may be the case with nine out of ten of the dispositions that are made in every campaign; that battles occur only occasionally in the movements of opposing armies, but that preparation for battle may be necessary every day. Without such preparation battles may be multiplied, and so in most cases are defeats to the careless.

The enemy's position in rear of Dick's River being, from the character of that stream, impregnable in front, I moved on the 13th to turn it by the south. On the night of that day I heard that the enemy was retreating from Camp Dick Robinson toward the south and I immediately ordered pursuit. The leading division marched at 12 o'clock that night and the others following in rapid succession. Crittenden's and McCook's corps, the former leading, took the road to Stanford and Crab Orchard, while Gilbert's took the road to Lancaster and Crab Orchard. On both roads the enemy's rear guards were overtaken the next day and were pressed continually as far as London. No general battle occurred between the two armies, though the enemy was foiled in his object and driven from the State.

Anticipating a movement of the rebel army into Middle Tennessee, the Army of the Ohio moved promptly in that direction, and on the 31st of October had, under my orders, advanced as far as Bowling Green and Glasgow. It was my intention to have reached Murfreesborough by the 10th of November. On the 30th of October I turned over the command to Major-General Rosecrans, in obedience to orders from the general-in-chief.

A careful study of the topography of Central Kentucky shows it to be a region possessing remarkable strategical features for defensive operations, especially for a force whose line of retreat is toward the State of Tennessee. The Kentucky River, running across the State from east to west, with its cliffy banks, makes a strong line of defense, while its somewhat frequent fords, opposing but slight obstacles to the movements of an army when the river is low, yet easily defended from the opposite bank, make it an admirable line for a retreating army to take shelter behind, and a perfect curtain to cover ulterior movements Its advantages in this respect are very greatly increased by the character and position of Dick's River, which, coming from the south, empties into the Kentucky River where the latter makes a strong bend to the north.　Dick's River has the same characteristics of cliffy banks, and its fewer crossings make it a much stronger line of defense than the Kentucky River.

Together these streams make the position of Camp Dick Robinson, in the fork, almost impregnable for a large army, except from the southeast.　In that case the defensive army, with its right flank protected by Dick's River and its left by the broken ground to the east, may fall back easily and securely to the north side of the Kentucky, and by a short march either to the east or the west recross to the south side and fall upon good lines of retreat; and these movements can only be counteracted by considerable detours or by previous detachments, which would weaken the opposing army so much as to endanger the main attack, unless the army is very greatly superior in strength.　On the north side of the Kentucky River the country is traversable by good roads between the Lexington and Richmond road and any of the roads crossing the river lower down; but on the south side the country bordering the river between the mouth of Dick's River and the Lexington and Richmond road is destitute of practicable roads parallel with the river.　Besides the advantages already alluded to, the whole of that region of country abounds in strong positions commanding the only water for an army within several miles, so that the attacking force is forced to fight under all the disadvantage of exhauston for the want of it, as was the case at Perryville.

These details make it easy to answer the theories that have been advanced for the annihilation or capture of the entire rebel army under General Bragg.　One of those theories assumes that that army might have been destroyed in crossing Dick's River.

A defile, if it does not retard the march materially, is always a benefit to a retreating army, and the line of Dick's River is admirably adapted to such an object.　It is only necessary for the retreating army to make demonstrations of battle with a strong rear guard, which will require corresponding preparations and delay on the part of the pursuer.　In the mean time it throws its artillery across rapidly to take positions to sweep the opposite bank, and under such protection the remainder of the retiring army crosses with safety.

Great stress has been laid on the importance of Danville to cut off the retreat of the rebel army from Perryville.　My right rested after the battle within 4 or 5 miles of Danville and my cavalry watched and went beyond that place.　Danville controlled no line of retreat for the enemy except through that point and thence on toward Somerset or Columbia. That was as well covered by being 4 or 5 miles from Danville with a perfectly open and unobstructed country between as it would have been at Danville itself, and the enemy did not attempt to use it at all.　Danville is 8 miles at the nearest point from the road going from Camp Dick Robinson to Cumberland Gap, and the strong line of Dick's River between prevents Danville from having any command of that road.

The first point at which the enemy's retreat on the Cumberland Gap road could be intercepted is Lancaster, 10 miles from Danville.　If the Army of the Ohio moved to Lancaster in force in advance of the rebel army, it threw its communications into the hands of the enemy.　If, before being assured that the enemy had crossed Dick's River, it divided its force over the 20 miles from Perryville to Lancaster to protect its communications and intercept the retreat of the enemy through Lancaster, it rendered itself liable to be beaten in detail; and if, after being assured that the enemy had crossed Dick's River, it left small detachments sufficient to guard the passes over that river and then moved with the main body on Lancaster, there is no reason why the enemy should not have been able to hold it in check on the line of Dick's River long enough to secure his line through Lancaster if he was determined to retreat.

An army on ordinary marches, continued for many days, will average about 2 miles an hour; but in a forced march for 20, and at least for 10 miles, it can average 3 miles an hour. If the rebel army had 60,000 men, with artillery, and 1,500 wagons for baggage, supplies, &c., it would in marching occupy 39 miles along the road in one column or 19½ miles each in two columns. It would therefore require six hours and a half to clear its camp on two roads; the whole of it will have arrived at or passed a point 20 miles distant in fourteen hours or a point 10 miles distant in ten hours. Thus the rebel army, moving from Camp Dick Robinson in two columns, would clear its camp in six hours and a half, and arrive at Lancaster, 10 miles distant, in ten hours; or, if it continued on without stopping, would arrive at Crab Orchard, 20 miles distant, in fourteen hours.

It appears that the retreating army actually marched in three columns from its camp at Dick Robinson, the country along its route being open and practicable. From Lancaster it took two roads, the one to the left going by the way of Lowell and coming into the Cumberland Gap road at Big Hill, and the other going through Crab Orchard, Mount Vernon, and London. The latter is intersected at Crab Orchard, 20 miles from Danville, by the road from Danville through Stanford. The reasons which would render it injudicious to expose my communications and leave open a better line of retreat to the enemy, by anticipating his possible retreat through Lancaster, apply with greater force to Crab Orchard. If the rebel army would retreat without accepting battle, the topography of the country made it entirely possible for it to do so. Being once established on its line of retreat beyond any point where it could by any possibility be intercepted the rebel army made good its retreat, as other armies have done in this and other wars under less favorable circumstances.

There are few circumstances under which a disciplined and well-managed army can be forced to a general battle against its will, though the occasions are multiplied if the opposing army has a greatly superior force of good cavalry or is so greatly superior in strength that it can divide its force with reasonable prospects of success to each fraction. A disciplined army, moving on its line of communication, can always retreat more rapidly than it can be pursued. It meets or overtakes its supplies on the road, or finds them at temporary depots previously established, or it collects them from the country as much as possible on its line of march. The pursuing army, on the other hand, finds the country stripped; it has nothing in advance to rely on; it must carry everything along, with the hinderance of enormous trains, and the difficulties are increased with every day's march. The retreating army prepares a front of resistance more rapidly than the pursuer can prepare a front for attack. The strong positions are reconnoitered in advance, on which the requisite force forms as rapidly as on a drill ground; while the pursuer, ignorant of the ground and of the force that awaits him, must inform himself of both in order to develop a corresponding force, or else find the head of his column beaten back. In the mean time the main body of the retiring army has gained some hours' march; the rear guard watches the enemy's preparation, awaits his attack, and repulses it if it is made injudiciously or with insufficient force, or else at dark resumes its march, to repeat the same operation whenever it is necessary and the occasion is favorable. A single tree felled judiciously across the road will delay the pursuer perhaps fifteen minutes, four of them at intervals will delay him an hour, and thus the distance between him and his adversary is increased.

These advantages to defensive operations do not exist in the same degree in all descriptions of country. They are particularly marked in a broken and wooded country, where the movements and position and strength of an enemy are only to be ascertained by feeling him, and especially where there are no parallel roads by which the retreating army can be attacked in flank. The advantages alluded to make it wise frequently for a commander to fall back to a chosen ground when his adversary advances, and the battle of Perryville affords an illustration of this principle. The rebel army was moving for concentration at some point which could not be known to its adversary. A portion of it took advantage of the strong position at Perryville, commanding the only water within a distance of several miles, over which the Army of the Ohio must march to attack. That position afforded also the advantage of several lines of retreat. With these combined advantages, when it was discovered that a part of the rebel army was making a stand, it was as reasonable to expect to find its combined force there as at any other point, and dispositions had to be made accordingly. I believe that a sound and unprejudiced criticism will show that the movement of the Army of the Ohio was executed promptly and judiciously; that it arrived more simultaneously and in-better order than the enemy could have expected, considering that the point which he would choose for battle could not be foreseen; and that but for the lack of timely information of the condition of things on the afternoon of the 8th the main portion of the enemy's force at Perryville would have been captured.

Contests between unequal forces result sometimes, but very rarely, from the fact that the inferior has no alternative but to fight or surrender. In by far the greatest number of cases, however, the conflict results from a lack of ability on the part of the inferior to avail himself of the means of extricating his army; or from a contempt for or ignorance of the strength of his adversary; or from an advantage of position which in his opinion will outweigh that of superiority of numbers and a corresponding ignorance of that advantage or faulty dispositions on the part of the superior army; and these last are the cases in which most frequently the inferior army is victorious. When the armies are about equal, they maneuver so as to deceive and cause each other to make detachments or force each other to battle on ground unfavorable to the adversary. In all these cases the object is not merely to give battle for the sake of fighting, but to fight for victory, or at least safety, and with such advantages as will make success reasonably certain; and the more serious the consequences of defeat the greater the caution to be observed. Ignorance and error multiply battles far more than valor and generally with the penalty of disaster. If precaution and the observance of rule diminish the number of battles, and sometimes miss the accidental success which folly and recklessness might have gained, it is nevertheless true that in the end they usually triumph.

The operations of the column under the command of General G. W. Morgan at Cumberland Gap have been brought before the Commission. The deposition of Colonel De Courcy, an officer under General Morgan's command, introduced as evidence for the Government, alleges that after General Morgan commenced his advance upon Cumberland Gap in May last he was suddenly arrested by a telegraphic dispatch from me, ordering a retrograde movement and stopping all further proceedings on the Tennessee side against the Gap.

General Morgan commenced his advance against Cumberland Gap in pursuance of the orders which I gave him in March preceding about the 22d of May. He had repeatedly represented that he was operating against a superior force of the enemy, and on the 8th of June he telegraphed that the enemy had—

> Over 5,000 at Cumberland Gap, 8,000 at Big Creek Gap, with troops at Clinton and Knoxville. Should their force concentrate the enemy will outnumber us nearly three to one. What is General Negley doing?

Seeing no reason why I should expect him to advance by difficult mountain roads and defeat three to one of the enemy, and supposing that he may have regarded my orders for him to advance as more imperative than I meant them to be, without regard to the force opposed to him, I telegraphed him on the 9th as follows:

> General Negley is fully employed in Tennessee and can give you no direct assistance. The force now in Tennessee is so small that no operations against East Tennessee can be attempted. You must therefore depend mainly on your own resources.

And on the 10th I telegraphed him as follows:

> Considering your force and that opposed to you, it will probably not be safe for you to undertake any extended operations. Other operations will soon have an influence on your designs, and it is therefore better for you to run no risk at present.

These are the dispatches which caused the retrograde movement referred to. I leave them to speak for themselves, in connection with the dispatches which elicited them.

But, furthermore, on the same day, the 10th, I received a dispatch from General Morgan, giving a rumor that the Gap was evacuated, to which I replied the same day:

> If Cumberland Gap is evacuated you should seize and hold it, and take any other advantage that may present itself, but not advance to a point from which you would have to fall back.

About this time General Mitchel, considering himself in danger from an anticipated advance upon him, was urging the necessity of a stronger force in Middle Tennessee and I was about commencing my march from Corinth in that direction.

Cumberland Gap was occupied on the 18th of June. General Morgan had about 7,500 men. His dispatches report the strength of the enemy opposed to him at not less than 10,000 or 12,000, and I have no reason to doubt that he reported correctly. At no time did he represent that he was able to hold East Tennessee with the force he had or the wish to attempt it, nor do I believe that he could have done it. It is true that on the 20th he telegraphed:

> My telegraph orders from Major-General Buell of the 10th instant do not permit me to advance upon Knoxville, and I will not, until further instructions, advance farther than Tazewell.

And he also stated the preparation he had made to destroy bridges, but had countermanded in consequence of that dispatch. He was answered on the 22d, four days after his arrival at the Gap, as follows:

> It is impossible at present to send you any cavalry. The general has not intended his orders to prevent such expeditions for special purposes as you refer to in your dispatch of the 20th; on the contrary, he approves them. His wish is for you to make yourself secure in the Gap and accomplish all the results you can by rapid expeditions, but not to attempt a deliberate advance on Knoxville as long as it seems probable that you would not be able to maintain your position there. The general wishes

to make no actual advance which he cannot maintain. It brings our friends among the people into trouble and is injurious otherwise to our interests.

JAMES B. FRY,
Chief of Staff.

I have no doubt :hat General Morgan acted wisely, and that he had not force enough to attack the enemy in force. He certainly was not restrained from doing anything that duty and honor demanded.

The policy which I observed toward the people of the territory occupied by my army has been vehemently and bitterly assailed by a portion of the press, but I believe that reason and justice will sustain it on every score, whether of expediency or humanity. In entering on my command it was with an earnest willingness to devote my life to the object of restoring the Union, and I never doubted as to the course my duty required me to pursue. It was to defeat the rebels in arms whenever I could and to respect the Constitution and laws and the rights of the people under them as far as was possible consistently with a state of things which rendered military success a matter of primary importance for the restoration of the authority of the Government. This has been my rule of action from first to last. I did not undertake to punish men for opinion's sake or even for past acts, for Congress has prescribed the penalty for their offenses and the mode of proceeding against them. Men in arms I treated as enemies; persons not in arms I treated as citizens of the United States; but I allowed no man to preach or act treason after the progress of my army had brought him again under the protection as well as the authority of the Government.

I have, when necessary, given protection to the persons and property of peaceable citizens; and this I have done both to preserve the discipline of my troops and out of respect for the just rights of the people under the laws of war, if not under the civil law. When the public interest has required the use of private property for public purposes I have so used it, allowing just compensation for it as far as practicable; and this I did not only on the ground of justice, but as a measure of military expediency, for it enabled me to secure for my army necessaries which otherwise would have been concealed or destroyed.

The bearing of this question on the success of my military operations is something which I was bound to weigh well. It is recognized as one of great importance to the success of an invading army. Wars of invasion, always difficult, become tenfold so when the people of the invaded territory take an active part against the invading army. A system of plunder and outrage in such cases will produce the same effect of hatred and revenge that such treatment does under other circumstances among men, and the embarrassments resulting from them to the invading army become of the most serious nature.

These considerations are of such importance to success that there is no exception to the rule of securing the neutrality if not the friendship of the population as much as possible by just and mild treatment, and then, having given no good cause for hostility, to treat with kindness those who behave well and with severity those who misbehave.

Some months ago a statement appeared in the newspapers, on the reported authority of Gov. Andrew Johnson, that I had only been prevented by his resolute expostulations from abandoning Nashville when I moved north with my army in September last. He has since made the same assertion in a deposition. Whenever I have spoken on this subject I have denounced the statement as false and I now repeat that denunciation. I am very willing .to bear the responsibility of my own acts or intentions, and it gives me sincere pleasure at all times to acknowledge any assistance I may receive from others either in counsel or action. If I had determined to abandon Nashville it would have been upon my best judgment, and I should cheerfully have submitted to a verdict on the wisdom of my course. I assert that I never intimated to Governor Johnson an intention or wish to leave Nashville without a garrison; that there was no discussion between us *pro* and *con* on the subject, and that the determination to hold the place was my own, uninfluenced by him in any manner. I had not that confidence in his judgment or that distrust of my own which would have induced me to seek his counsel. On account of his official position I called on him first to inform him what I meant to do, and last to tell him what garrison I had concluded to leave. On both occasions, as far as my plans were concerned, I was the speaker and he the listener. My officers were far more likely to know my views than he, and they have stated that I said always that the political importance of the occupation far outweighed any purely military bearing of the question, and that I should hold the city.*

D. C. BUELL,
Major-General.

BURNET HOUSE, *May* 5, 1863.

[Inclosure No. 5.]

BALTIMORE, MD., *April* 10, 1864.

General LORENZO THOMAS,
    Adjutant-General U. S. Army:

SIR : I have heard that the Secretary of War intends to publish in general orders the result of the investigation of my military operations in Kentucky and Tennessee during the summer of 1862 by the Military Commission organized by Major-General Halleck. Supposing that the pressure of official business may thus far have prevented the Secretary from making a careful examination of the record, which is very voluminous, and believing that such an examination will essentially modify the effect of the manner in which the Commission has stated facts and refute many of its opinions, my object is to ask attention to some of the features of the report and to request that its publication may be accompanied by the official decision of the Department.

The report premises by saying that "very early in its sessions the Commission resolved to direct its investigations to the following points," and it specifies six "points." It would appear from this as though the

---

* The documents appended to the foregoing statement appear in this series as follows:

Major-General Buell's report of the battle of Shiloh, Vol. X, Part I, p. 291.
Major-General Buell's report of the battle of Perryville, Vol. XVI, Part I, p. 1022

General Orders, Department of the Ohio:

   No. 23, December 27, 1861, Vol. VII, p. 15.
   No. 4*a*, January 20, 1862, Vol. VII, p. 24.
   No. 4*b*, January 23, 1862, Vol. VII, p. 78.
   No. 13*a*, February 26, 1862, Vol. VII, p. 669.

General Orders, Army of the Ohio:

   No. 6, April 8, 1862, Vol. X, Part I, p. 297.
   No. 29*a*, July 11, 1862, Vol. XVI, Part I, p. 65.
   No. 47*b*, October 12, 1862, Vol. XVI, Part I, p. 1032.
   No. 50, October 30, 1862, Vol. XVI, Part II, p. 654.

first steps in the inquiry had developed ground for these six grave questions; the truth is that they had been submitted in the instructions under which the Commission acted. I do not consider this discrepancy unimportant.

The report then takes up in their order the several subjects referred to; the first, however, " The operations of General Buell in Kentucky and Tennessee," being disposed of as being included in the other five.

" SUFFERING KENTUCKY TO BE INVADED BY THE REBELS UNDER BRAGG."

But few facts are given on this subject, and those are vague and indefinite. What is meant by saying that my lines of supplies were *"unnecessarily long"?* It is true that I was more than 300 miles from my base, the Ohio River, with only a thread of railroad for communication; but how could the line be said to be unnecessarily long when it was impossible to make it shorter. On the more material points the report is silent. Nothing is said of the strength of the enemy, nor of some of the most important of his movements, nor of the strength of my army, nor of the state of my supplies; but the Commission contents itself with expressing the belief that—

By an early concentration of my army at Sparta, McMinnville, or Murfreesborough, with a view to active offensive operations against Bragg the moment he debouched from the Sequatchie Valley, he would have been defeated.

Subsequent events have confirmed what the evidence abundantly shows, that the force under my command was inadequate for the mission it had undertaken. The statement in which I reviewed the evidence before the Commission presents this subject more circumstantially and I extract from it here. After explaining the embarrassment under which I had labored in consequence of the enemy's large cavalry force operating on my communications the statement continues: *

*   *   *   *   *   *   *

I am conscious of having carried my statement into tedious details out of much anxiety to explain my acts and the reasons that dictated them. I will not extend it to show why it was that although the concentration of my army at Murfreesborough was necessary in consequence of the state of my supplies, and although it was suitable to meet any direct advance against Nashville, yet it was no longer suitable after it became probable, though uncertain, that Bragg, instead of moving directly on Nashville, was moving toward, in fact was probably already at, the Cumberland River by the time my army was concentrated. As it was, my movement from Murfreesborough to Nashville did not " allow Bragg to cross the Cumberland," which he had already nearly reached, but it enabled me the easier to take measures against his subsequent movements.

Undoubtedly a much earlier concentration of my army at Murfreesborough would have had certain advantages. It would have enabled me to re-establish my communications and made them much shorter, but I have explained that I hoped until the last that they would be reopened by the troops in Kentucky, and that I was unwilling to abandon the object with which I had started out and give up the advanced positions I occupied.

---

*General Buell here quotes from " the railroad from Nashville to Stevenson," &c., p. 35, to " should have rejected it," on p. 45.

"THE FAILURE TO RELIEVE MUNFORDVILLE."

The Commission is of opinion that General Buell is not responsible for the capture of the town, except so far as his failure to attack Bragg south of the Cumberland River made him responsible for that failure.

This implies that Bragg could have been and should have been attacked south of the Cumberland. I have discussed that point in the preceding pages of this communication.

"BATTLE OF PERRYVILLE AND CONDUCT THERE."

The facts under this head are imperfectly and inaccurately stated, and the opinions, to my mind, show a misconception of the subject. The strength, positions, and to a great extent the movements of the opposing armies, with many other facts essential for a proper understanding of the subject, are omitted.

The rebel forces occupied a line extending from Lexington to Bardstown, Kirby Smith's force being on the right and Bragg's army proper on the left. It was to be presumed that those forces would concentrate when I moved against them, and it was "intended" to attack them whenever they could be properly brought to battle. It cannot be said that "an engagement was expected at Bardstown," though it was thought to be possible. The statement that "I next intended to attack him (Bragg) on the 9th of October" conveys no correct explanation of my plans and movements. The evidence shows that after reaching Perryville, where the enemy appeared to have concentrated, my instructions, given on the night of the 7th, contemplated an attack on his position on the morning of the 8th. That purpose was frustrated by the lateness of the arrival of the right and left corps, and it was deemed necessary to defer the attack until the next morning. The evidence is not that McCook's corps arrived at 9 o'clock on the 8th; the head of it arived between 10 and 11. The evidence shows that General Thomas' staff officer about 1.30 o'clock reported the arrival of the head of the right corps; the rear division of it was not yet up. The staff officer took back to General Thomas more detailed instructions in regard to the disposition of that corps.

The camp of my headquarters was located the evening of the 7th at a proper distance in rear of the center corps, the disposition of which I personally directed, and it was not necessary or convenient to change my camp. The signal station for headquarters was somewhat in advance, on a high elevation, commanding a more extended view of the ground than any other.

The assertion that I—

should either have been on the field in person ready for emergencies and advantages, or have taken and required to be taken every precaution for the instant transmission of intelligence to my headquarters—

and that—

as I had an organized signal corps with my army, this failure was all the more culpable—

discloses a want of knowledge on the part of the commission of what was necessary to be done and misrepresentation of what was actually done. Had I considered my presence along the lines necessary I might as properly have been required on the right as on the left, in which case I should have been 5 miles from the left instead of 2½ miles. The evidence shows that the signal corps was in operation, and that signal stations had been established to communicate intelligence from different parts of the line to my headquarters. What further precautions could be required except the presence of commanders, whose duty to communicate with me was as well understood as though it had been prescribed in their commissions?

The evidence shows that Gilbert's corps was not "unengaged." It lost nearly 1,000 men that day, which proves that the "whole force of the enemy" was not "*flung*" upon McCook." It is not a very ingenuous representation of the matter to assert what could have been accomplished "if Crittenden's corps had been vigorously pushed forward," when all mention of the fact is omitted that orders to that effect were given as soon as I was advised of the attack on McCook and that they could not be executed because of the lateness of the hour.

"PERMITTING THE REBELS TO ESCAPE WITHOUT LOSS FROM KENTUCKY."

The same misconception and errors of statement run through the report of the Commission under this head as under the preceding one. It is right in one admission, that—

it cannot be said that the rebels escaped without loss from Kentucky.

The evidence does not justify the statement in any proper sense that—

the morning after the battle it was very early discovered that Bragg had retreated from the position near Perryville.

On the contrary, the fact was not ascertained until about 10.30 o'clock, between which time and the early morning my army was moving to attack; the opinion being general that the enemy would be found near Perryville and the battle renewed that morning. The evidence shows this conclusively, though it also shows that some of the most advanced troops discovered very early that *the portion of the enemy which they could see* was moving from the position which it held the previous night; but even that did not come to the knowledge of the corps commanders nor to my knowledge. There is no evidence to justify the broad statement nor is it substantially true that Bragg—

left *all* his sick and wounded and some artillery at Harrodsburg, and being joined by Kirby Smith, hastened across Dick's River—

and that that part of the movement—

from Perryville to the river was confused and disordered.

Still less is it proven or true that any portion of the statement was known by me or by my army at the time. On the contrary, it is shown that the advance of my cavalry toward Harrodsburg on the 9th was effectually resisted, and that on the morning of the 10th Kirby Smith's forces, and probably a large portion of Bragg's army proper, were actually in line of battle 2 miles south of the town. This fact justified the presumption that his whole force was there, and I have now no doubt that the whole of it would have been there in case of battle.

I have **never** called my movement to Harrodsburg nor from there to Danville "**a** pursuit." I meant and have described it as a movement to find and give battle to the rebel army. The pursuit I have described as commencing at Danville on the 13th, when the retreat from Camp Dick Robinson was first discovered.

The comments of the Commission on the retreat of the enemy would seem to indicate ignorance of the topography of the country and of the facts concerning the retreat. There is ground in the evidence for the belief that Bragg's retreat was decided upon on the 12th of October in opposition to the views of a majority of his commanders and the sentiment of his army. There is a mass of facts in evidence and of public notoriety to show that his determination to avoid battle and retire from the State was suddenly adopted. The failure of the Commission to give place to this material fact has the effect of giving a wrong impression as to the dispositions the circumstances required me to make. The subject is treated as though Bragg's army was a disorganized rabble, which it was only necessary to surround with a line of skirmishers to capture. The evidence does not—

establish that General Buell received information on the night of the 11th that Bragg had crossed the river at Camp Dick Robinson—

nor that "he made no determined movement with the main body of his army until the night of the 13th." The statement that from the morning of the 9th until the night of the 11th I waited to learn whether my enemy would cross the river is unfit to appear in an official report; and the further statement that, that fact being definitely known, I lost two days before taking any decisive action, is contrary to the evidence, as is also the statement that finally, on the night of the 13th, I started Crittenden's corps *through* Danville—for it was there already. This statement, taken in connection with other remarks, would convey the false impression that that corps, in fact the main body of my army, was still at Perryville.

It is thus that the Commission explains "the escape of the rebels from Kentucky."

In the review which I prepared of the evidence taken by the Commission I made a different statement and explanation of the incidents of that campaign. I hope it is a more intelligent one. I know it is more in accordance with the facts, and it may not be inappropriate to insert it here. After describing the operations about Munfordville and the close movement after Bragg's army until it turned off toward Bardstown the statement proceeds:*

*   *   *   *   *   *   *

The Commission states that it made its sixth "point" to cover the question of my "loyalty." I certainly made no defense of my loyalty, nor did I know that it was under investigation, though I did not fail to observe that evidence was elicited of the scandalous remarks that had been made concerning it by some persons, one of them a member of the Commission. I shall not cavil at the brief announcement that against my loyalty "there is no evidence worthy consideration."

My policy toward "the inhabitants of disaffected districts" was also brought under the sixth "point," and the Commission concludes that—

Whether good or bad in its effects, General Buell deserves neither blame nor applause for it, because it was at that time supposed to be the policy of the Government. At least he could violate no orders upon the subject, because there were none.

I am not disposed to take exception to this opinion, though I dissent from it. If an officer faithfully does what the policy of his Government makes a duty, in my opinion he deserves approbation; and if, without any such obligation, he elects to do what he is at liberty to do or omit, then he deserves approbation or blame accordingly as his acts are good

---

* General Buell here quotes from "many considerations rendered it proper," &c., p. 48, to "they usually triumph," on p. 57.

or bad in their effects. It might, I think, very properly be asked why the Commission introduced the subject at all.

I will not use this occasion, though I cannot think that it would be inappropriate, to comment on the irregularities which marked the proceedings of the Commission and the spirit manifested by a portion of its members. Just and thinking men will hesitate to declare in a judicial verdict, with reference to the conduct of operations of such magnitude, more particularly when an important result has been obtained, that the commander ought to have acted differently : First, because, under circumstances which make it frequently impossible to know exactly the true state of affairs, he must act on appearances and probabilities more than on positive knowledge; and, second, because it is seldom possible to say what would have been the consequences of a different action. In this case no such hesitation is apparent.

For want of time I was not able to present my review of the evidence until the Commission had prepared their report and adjourned. How far that review might have modified the report if it had been before them it is impossible for me to say.

I submit these remarks with the confident belief that the justice of the Secretary will see ample ground for them.

Very respectfully, your obedient servant,

D. C. BUELL,
Major-General.

[Inclosure No. 6.]

GENERAL ORDERS, } HEADQUARTERS ARMY OF THE OHIO,
No. 29a.   }   *In Camp, Huntsville, Ala., July* 11, 1862.

The general commanding the Army of the Ohio takes pleasure in announcing the success of an arduous and hazardous campaign by the Seventh Division, Brig. Gen. G. W. Morgan commanding, by which the enemy's fortified position at Cumberland Gap was turned and his force compelled to retreat as our troops advanced to attack.

The general thanks Brigadier-General Morgan and the troops of the Seventh Division for the ability displayed in the operations against this important stronghold, and for the energy, fortitude, and cheerfulness which they exhibited in their struggle with difficulties of the most formidable magnitude for an army.

By command of Major-General Buell :

JAMES B. FRY,
Colonel and Chief of Staff.

—

GENERAL ORDERS, } WAR DEPT., ADJT. GEN.'S OFFICE,
No. 45.   }   *Washington, June* 14, 1872.

The following act of Congress is published for the information and government of all concerned :

AN ACT to provide for the restoration of the records of the proceedings of the court of inquiry concerning the operations of the army under the command of General Don Carlos Buell, in Kentucky and Tennessee.

Whereas it appears in the matter of investigation made by the court of inquiry, in the years eighteen hundred and sixty-two and eighteen hundred and sixty-three, into the operations of the army under the command of General Don Carlos Buell, in Kentucky and Tennessee, that the records of the proceedings of said court are not to be found on the proper files in the War Department; and whereas it further appears that there is now in the possession of Benn Pitman, the phonographic reporter of said court, a full and complete report of the proceedings of said court of inquiry: Therefore,

Be it enacted by the Senate and House of Representatives of the United States of America in Congress assembled, That the Secretary of War be directed to employ at once Benn Pitman, the reporter for the court of inquiry in the said matter, to make a full and complete transcript of the phonographic notes taken by him during the said investigation, and to put the same on file among the records of the War Department, and to furnish a copy of the same to Congress.

Approved June 5, 1872.

By order of the Secretary of War:

E. D. TOWNSEND,
Adjutant-General.

—

AIRDREE, KY., *February* 12, 1873.

Hon. WILLIAM W. BELKNAP,
Secretary of War, Washington, D. C.:

SIR: Among the papers sent to the Military Committee from the War Department on the 13th of April last, in answer to the call of the House for the record of "The Buell Commission," as it is sometimes called, is one which comes to my knowledge in that way for the first time, and is described as "an unsigned communication, reviewing the proceedings of the Commission," &c.* The paper is, in fact, without date, address, or signature, but bears the following indorsement:

JUDGE-ADVOCATE-GENERAL'S OFFICE,
May 23, 1863.

Respectfully referred to the Secretary of War by request of Lieutenant-Colonel Piatt.

J. HOLT,
Judge-Advocate-General.

On the last day of the open session of the Military Commission the President inquired, "Does the judge-advocate propose to submit any paper?" To which the judge-advocate (Lieutenant-Colonel Piatt) replied:

From the nature of the Commission, or Board of Officers, as I understand it, called to investigate the operations of the Army of the Ohio, I am not required to sum up the evidence. Indeed so voluminous is the evidence that it would not be possible to do so within any reasonable time. Most of the questions under consideration are matters of opinion, and as military men the Board is better able to treat of them than I am. There is very little conflict of testimony coming within my peculiar province, and I therefore ask to be excused.

It is not necessary to remark here that by the rules governing the proceedings of military tribunals, as well as upon general principles of law, any argument of the case by the judge-advocate before the Commission should have been submitted in the hearing of the accused and the latter would have been entitled to answer. The paper referred to did not follow that rule. Indeed it seems only to have made its appearance after the Commission had concluded its labors and while its voluminous record awaited the action of the reviewing authority.

I do not ascribe this circumstance to a preconcerted plan; on the contrary, I believe that such a course had not entered the thoughts of the judge-advocate, and that, however suggested, the execution was the offspring of the moment. To my mind, nevertheless, the proceeding has the character of a surreptitious attempt to warp the ordinary course of

* See Inclosure No. 3 (p. 12) to Secretary of War's report to House of Representatives, April 17, 1872.

justice and is deserving of rebuke. It is for this reason mainly that I make this mention of it.

It is not my purpose to comment on the paper itself. I will not correct its representation of facts nor weigh its criticisms, though they are for the most part in conflict with themselves and with my review of the subject. Its most prominent feature is an effort to sustain a statement made by Gov. Andrew Johnson, which I had denounced, to the effect that I was prevented by his expostulations from abandoning Nashville in the fall of 1862. I shall leave that question where the evidence places it, without going into further personal statements.

I request that you will be good enough to let this communication accompany the records of the Commission, and I am, very respectfully, your obedient servant,

D. C. BUELL.

—

TRANSCRIPT FROM PHONOGRAPHIC NOTES OF THE BUELL COURT OF INQUIRY.

CINCINNATI, December 1, 1862.

Col. W. H. LYTLE (a witness for the Government), being duly sworn by the judge-advocate, testified as follows:

By the JUDGE-ADVOCATE:

Question. What is your position in the service of the United States, colonel?

I have been in the three-months' service, but was commissioned in the three-years' service on or about June 6, 1861.

Question. Will you state to the court what part of that time you were in service under command of Major-General Buell in Tennessee and Kentucky?

I reported for duty in the Department of the Ohio on or about January 2, 1862.

Question. You will please state to the court what you know of the operations of General Buell at the time of the invasion of the State of Kentucky by General Bragg.

I can only give the movements of that portion of the army with which I was connected. On the 31st of August, 1862, I was in command at Huntsville, Ala., and under orders from General Buell conducted on that day the evacuation of the town. My orders were to make Shelbyville inside of four days. I made the march inside of two days and a half. I camped 4 miles from Nashville on the evening of September 5, having halted nearly a day at Murfreesborough for orders. From thence we marched to Perryville via Louisville.

Question. During that time what division were you attached to?

I commanded the Seventeenth Brigade of General Rosecrans' division.

Question. State to the Commission what you know of General Bragg's position during the march of the rebels.

I was not specially informed as to his movements, my attention being directed generally to my own command. I had the general idea that Bragg was marching in a direction parallel, or nearly so, to that of our own army.

Question. Could you point out the parallel movement of General Bragg?

I am not able to do so; I had no opportunity at the time to observe.

Question. Do you know anything, colonel, about the surrender and failure at Munfordville?

I know nothing of it; I know only of the movements of my own command.

Question. You know of the surrender of that place?

Yes, sir.

Question. Can you state to the Commission as to the probability of its being relieved?

I do not know; I do not recollect the date of the surrender of Munfordville. My command reached Bowling Green September 11. We halted there several days, and did not arrive at Munfordville until after its surrender.

Question. What was the cause of your delay at Bowling Green?

I do not know.

Question. Do you recollect how many days you were there?

My impression is we were there three or four days. Of course I have no opportunity now to refer to any official document, but my recollection is that we were there three or four days.

Question. I understand you to say that Munfordville was surrendered before you arrived there?

The town, I think, was surrendered either during our halt at Bowling Green or during our march thence to Munfordville. The march from Bowling Green to Munfordville consumed (including the halt at Horse Well) six or seven days. We were at Horse Well about two days.

Question. What was the cause of the slow march you made between Bowling Green and Munfordville?

I do not know.

Question. Could you produce any reason for your delay?

At Horse Well we were drawn up in line of battle, fronting toward Munfordville.

Question. Had you any evidence of a large force in the neighborhood at the time?

I saw none. There was more or less skirmishing reported during our halt there. As general officer of the day I rode to the extreme outposts; the enemy's pickets could be seen.

Question. What position had General McCook's corps in the army?

It had at that time, I think, the advance on that road. My impression is that it was the first to arrive in Louisville.

Question. You stated that you do not know the reason of the delay at Bowling Green or why the march was so slow from Bowling Green to Munfordville.

I do not know.

Question. What was the rate of marching previous to arriving in Bowling Green?

I made rapid marches to Nashville with the command left at Huntsville. The march thence to Bowling Green, as was also the march from Munfordville to Louisville, was as rapid as possible.

Question. Were you engaged at the battle of Perryville?

I was.

Question. Will you state, as near as you can, the circumstances of the affair?

CINCINNATI, *December* 2, 1862.

Col. W. H. LYTLE'S examination continued.

(Map produced by the judge-advocate, that the movements and positions of the Union and rebel armies might be pointed out by the witness.)

The witness then proceeded and said:

Our column (McCook's army corps) moved by the way of Taylorsville, Fairfield, Bloomfield, and Chaplin, encamping the night before the fight at Mackville. There were but two divisions of the army corps at that point—Rousseau's and Jackson's. The Third Division (Sill's) was not with us. My original orders at Mackville were to move at 6 a. m. Before daylight, however, I received orders to move immediately. My own command was in motion in twenty minutes. I had no tents. My brigade had the right of Rousseau's division, which had the advance of the corps.

We arrived on the field of battle about 10.30 a. m., to the best of my recollection. As we reached the ground I saw a column of our troops on the Springfield road, which I ascertained subsequently was a portion of Gilbert's corps. [Witness points out Springfield road on map.]

Having been directed by General Rousseau to place a good skirmishing regiment in advance, the Tenth Ohio occupied that position, and on our arrival on the field was at once deployed as skirmishers.

General Rousseau's original line of battle was considerably in the rear of the line he actually occupied during the fight. Our march had been accelerated when we heard cannonading.

By the JUDGE-ADVOCATE:

Question. Where was that cannonading?

I do not know exactly; think it was from a battery on the right of my position during the fight. General Rousseau's original line was nearly at right angles with the road, his right resting near Russell's house.

I will remark here that my recollection of the topography of the field may not be accurate, as I saw it only during the fight and afterwards from an ambulance on my return from the enemy's lines.

On our arrival on the field at 10.30 a. m. a section or more of artillery was thrown forward and opened fire. No response having been elicited, General Rousseau directed me to move with my brigade toward Perryville. At this time the Tenth Ohio Infantry, thrown forward as skirmishers, had not returned, though I had sent a staff officer and several orderlies to recall it. My orders being imperative, however, to march, I sent an order to Lieutenant-Colonel Burke, commanding, to fall in in the rear of my brigade, and directed Colonel Beatty, with his regiment (Third Ohio Infantry), to take the advance.

Question. How far was your right from the next corps on your right?

I saw no line of battle on my right at all. My own command was composed of the Third and Tenth Ohio Infantry, Fifteenth Kentucky Infantry, Forty-second and Eighty-eighth Indiana Infantry, and Loomis' battery.

In compliance with orders about 12 o'clock I resumed the march, the Third Ohio having the right. The impression at this time seemed to be that the enemy had retired. My column was in motion, as directed, when my attention was directed to a scattering fire on the left of the road. It immediately struck me that it proceeded from the skirmishers of the Tenth Ohio, which, as I have said, had not yet reported. Riding up to the eminence where our artillery had been posted in the morning, commanding a ravine, an officer of my staff approached me and said he discovered the enemy on the opposite side of the ravine. With my glass I saw heavy masses of rebels apparently deploying into line of battle. The morning was bright and clear. General Rousseau directed me to form line of battle immediately. My column, then in motion and descending the hill into the ravine, was marched by the right-about, and the order was complied with. Cannot state the precise distance from the enemy.

My brigade had the right of Rousseau's division in line of battle. Harris' brigade was on my left. Jackson was on the left of Rousseau. We had then an artillery duel, which lasted perhaps two hours.

Question. Could you see the enemy's line at the time from that eminence?

They were screened by the timber. In the ravine which separated us from the enemy was the rocky bed of a creek. The men had suffered much from thirst. One of my regiments (the Forty-second Indiana) had been ordered to the ravine in the morning by General Rousseau to supply the men with water, but there was little or none there

After the fire of the artillery had been prolonged some time Captain Loomis reported that his long-range ammunition was nearly expended. I accompanied him and reported to General Rousseau. The general and Loomis rode off together, as I supposed either to have Loomis' ammunition replenished or another battery sent forward to take its place. I returned immediately to the front.

Question. During this time did you receive any orders from any other officer? Had General Rousseau received any orders from General McCook from 12 to 2 o'clock?

I received no orders during that time from any other officer. As to whether General Rousseau received any orders from General McCook or not during the time mentioned I cannot state. The position of my regiments was reported to General Rousseau when the fight opened, and my general instructions were to hold my ground there as long as practicable, and in case it became impracticable to hold it to retire in good order. Shortly after my return to the front I saw Loomis' battery being retired. I dispatched a staff officer or orderly to inquire whether, my artillery being withdrawn, the general desired any change in the position of my line. To this message I got no answer, nor can I say whether or not it ever reached the general. Shortly after 2 o'clock p. m. the fire of the rebel artillery slackened and his infantry advanced. The Third Ohio was immediately ordered from the slight depression of ground that partially screened it from the artillery fire to the crest of the hill. The Fifteenth Kentucky was ordered to support it. The Tenth Ohio was on the left of the Third Ohio, from which I had not felt at liberty to withdraw it. The Eighty-eighth Indiana was held in reserve.

We held our position for two hours or more after Loomis was retired, and finally, being without our battery and exposed to a severe fire of artillery as well as that of an infantry force greatly superior in number, the brigade fell back in good order and reformed, as I am informed, in the neighborhood of the original line selected in the morning near Russell's house.

Question. Did it appear from the sound of the cannon that the enemy was on the left?

The rattle of small-arms was so deafening that it would have been hard to tell. I could see only two regiments on my left, such was the conformation of the ground. While the fight was progressing I became satisfied, between 2 and 3 o'clock, that we were outnumbered.

My battery had been withdrawn, and the brigade was exposed not only to a severe fire from the enemy's infantry posted in the ravine, but from a heavy fire of his artillery, which swept the crest of the ridge. I accordingly sent back a staff officer for reenforcements. He returned with the message that I should hold the position as long as I could, and if it became impracticable, should retire; that Jackson was very hard pressed, and no re-enforcements could be spared. Between 3 and 4 p. m. I renewed my application for re-enforcements, but to this second application received no response.

Meanwhile my whole line, after a most obstinate and resolute struggle and severe loss, had been retired, with the exception of one regiment, the Tenth Ohio.

Question. How many rounds of ammunition had you?

Forty rounds. The ammunition train was, I think, in the woods near the Russell house, though of this I am not certain. Our line was so suddenly formed that I had no time to ascertain its location. I had finally sent back for the Eighty-eighth Indiana, being determined to hold our position if possible until re-enforcements came up. I could not believe but what they would finally arrive from some other corps, having seen the column on the Springfield road in the morning. Before the Eighty-eighth got up, however, the Tenth was nearly enveloped by the enemy and was obliged to fall back. A most destructive fire was poured on the regiment's front and from the flanks, and while endeavoring to cover its movement to the rear with skirmishers I was wounded and captured. These are the material points that came under my observation up to the time that I was taken prisoner.

It is my impression that after Harris was obliged to retire for want of ammunition the attack of eight or ten regiments of the enemy was concentrated on my brigade, or rather on the three regiments—the Third Ohio, Fifteenth Kentucky, and Tenth Ohio—which were the last to retire.

Question. Did you know the headquarters of General Buell?

I did not. I saw General McCook and General Rousseau. After the battle began General Rousseau's attention, as I gathered from his official report, was mainly directed to the left of the line. My loss was very heavy. The orders to the brigade were executed to the letter as I understood them. I am informed the loss of the brigade was between 700 and 800 killed and wounded. Have not yet seen official report.

Question. How far to the right was the army?

General Gilbert's corps, on the Springfield road, could be readily seen with the naked eye. I do not think the Springfield road was more than a mile from my position. There was a battery on my right, on a wooded eminence, probably a quarter of a mile distant, but there was no infantry between my right and the battery.

Question. Which way was the wind blowing?

I remember that when a barn near the right of the Third Ohio was fired by the enemy's shells the whole line was almost enveloped in smoke. The wind must have been, I think, a southerly wind; it blew from right to left of my line.

Question. Was it known that the enemy was in force at Perryville?

That I do not know. I remember meeting General McCook in the morning, and that the General remarked there would be fun before night or some remark to that effect.

Question. With the exception of Gilbert's column were you not aware of the positions of the other corps?

I was not.

Question. You had no knowledge of the force of the enemy?

Nothing definite.

Question. When you were taken prisoner could you form any estimate of the numbers of the enemy?

I could not.

Question. Did you know their line of retreat, what roads they went by, where their force lay, and where they arrived that night?

I have some delicacy in testifying to these points under the terms of my parole. I can state that I was very much surprised that we were not re-enforced that day, and also that no advance was made the next morning.

Question. What reason can you give that prevents you answering these questions?

My impression is that there is a provision in the terms of the parole "that I shall not reveal anything that I might have discovered within the line of the enemy." I therefore decline to testify on these points.

Question. How many days were you in the hands of the enemy?

The battle was fought on Wednesday, the first week of October. I was paroled the next day, and returned to our lines on Friday night and immediately reported at General Buell's headquarters.

Question. Where were General Buell's headquarters?

They were on the Harrodsburg pike, beyond the position we occupied, near the road. When I returned I was in a buggy; I returned by way of Danville.

Question. Where were you at the time you received your parole?

I was at Harrodsburg.

Question. For how long were the men provided with provisions?

They had provisions for three days.

Question. During the battle the men threw away their haversacks, sometimes their knapsacks. Had you noticed anything of the kind in your corps?

I did not observe that they did so; I noticed that they were very cool.

Question. When you were at headquarters did you see Gen. Bragg?

I was not at the headquarters of the enemy.

Here the court desired the witness to produce the parole, to which the witness assented.

The day following the colonel produced the parole.

Copy of the parole.

HDQRS. ARMY OF THE MISS., *Harrodsburg, Oct.* 9, 1862.

I, Wm. H. Lytle, Army of the United States, having been taken prisoner by the Confederate States Army and this day paroled, whereof this is witness, do swear that I will not bear arms against the Confederate States, nor will I in any way aid or abet its enemies, until I am regularly exchanged, under the penalty of death; nor will I disclose anything that I have seen or heard in said Confederate States Army to its prejudice.

WM. H. LYTLE,
Colonel, Commanding Seventeenth Brigade, Third Division.

Sworn to and subscribed before me October 9, 1862.

SAM'L K. HAYS,
Major, C. S. Army.

The Commission adjourned to meet December 4, at 10 o'clock a. m.

CINCINNATI, *December* 4, 1862—10 a. m.

Examination of Col. W. H. LYTLE continued.

Cross-examination by General BUELL:

Question. On leaving Huntsville did you receive orders to proceed directly to Nashville?

I did not. I received orders to proceed to Murfreesborough by way of Fayetteville and Shelbyville, my orders being to reach in four days.

Question. When did your division leave Nashville on the march toward Kentucky?

My brigade left its camp near Edgefield and joined the main column.
September 7, 1862, halted at Gee's Tavern.
September 8, marched to Tyree Springs.
September 9, marched to Sharp's Branch, near Franklin.
September 10, marched to Cave or Sinking Springs, near Bowling Green.
September 11, marched to Bowling Green.
September 16, march late; camp 3 miles from Barren River.
September 17, bivouac near Dripping Springs, 9 miles from Glasgow.
September 18, to Prewitt's Knob.
September 19, to Horse Well.
September 21, to point 3 miles from Munfordville.
September 22, march late; camp at Munfordville.
September 23, to Nolin.
September 24, Burlington (or Bloomington).
September 25, cross Salt River; halt; at 2 march resumed.
September 26, marched to Louisville.

Question. Do you know what the orders were under which your division marched?

I do not.

Question. Do you know what its immediate destination was?

I do not

Question. Did you know any circumstance which made it necessary for it to reach any particular place at any given time?

I was not personally informed of any.

Question. Did any division leave Nashville in advance of it?

I do not recollect.

Question. On what road did it march?

We marched on the Bowling Green road by way of Tyree Springs.

Question. Was your march continued from the time you left Nashville until you arrived at Bowling Green?

The march was continuous, making only the necessary halts.

Question. When did you arrive at Bowling Green?

On the 11th September.

Question. Was your division first to arrive at Bowling Green?

My impression is that our division was not the first to arrive. I think there were several before us.

[NOTE BY GENERAL BUELL.—"It was the first division that arrived."]

Question. When did you march from Bowling Green?

We marched from Bowling Green on the 16th, in the afternoon.

Question. How far did you march that afternoon and on what road?

We marched on the Dripping Springs road, and camped 3 miles from the Barren River.

Question. What time in the afternoon did you encamp?

I cannot remember.

Question. Before or after dark?

I cannot remember.

Question. On what road did you march the following day?

We marched to Dripping Springs; that was the termination of the second day's march from Bowling Green.

Question. Where did you encamp the second day?

Upon a high hill at Dripping Springs.

Question. Where did you encamp the third day?

At Prewitt's Knob.

Question. Where did you encamp the fourth day?

At Horse Well.

Question. Did you that day make the march you expected to make?

I have no reason to think we did not.

Question. Where did you arrive at the end of the fifth day's march?

At Bear Wallow, quite early in the forenoon.

Question. When did you leave Bear Wallow?

On the afternoon of the seventh day out from Bowling Green.

[NOTE BY GENERAL BUELL.—Marched from Bowling Green late on the "16th," and arrived at Munfordville on the 21st—*five* days instead of "seven."]

Question. Did you know the immediate destination of the army when leaving Bowling Green?

I did not.

Question. Where did you suppose Bragg's army was?

My impression was that it was moving in a line parallel with ours, but know nothing of his position.

Question. Who was in command of your column?

General Rousseau.

Question. Of what troops was it composed?

His own old division and General Smith's.

Question. Were there any detachments from your column at Bear Wallow?

There was a detachment moved in the direction of Glasgow to cut off a train, as I supposed.

Question. Did it return before the column left there?

It did not.

Question. For what point did you march?

We marched on the pike, turned to the left, and halted within 3 miles of Munfordville.

Question. On what day of the week and month?

I cannot give the day of the week; it was on the 21st of September.

Question. When did you reach Louisville?

On the 26th September.

Question. What is the distance between Louisville and Munfordville?

Between 70 and 80 miles.

Question. How many encampments did you make between Munfordville and Louisville?

I remember but four.

Question. Was there any unnecessary loss of time?

The marches were made promptly. We had good marches up to the time of arriving at Bowling Green.

Question. Do you know anything of the amount of supplies on hand at the time of leaving Bowling Green?

I do not.

Question. At what hour on the morning of the 8th of October did McCook's column leave Mackville?

I moved about 5 o'clock.

Question. Was the line of battle formed by McCook's corps a continuous line or did it consist of detached positions taken up at the moment?

I can make no statement except as to that portion attached to my command.

Question. Could you judge of the position of the line by the firing?

I could not.

Question. Was the engagement throughout the entire line during the principal part of the action?

I inferred it was a general one.

Question. Did you know where the headquarters of General McCook were during the engagement?

I did not.

Question. Did you know where the headquarters of General Rousseau were during the battle?

I had no express information where they were.

Question. In your evidence you express surprise at the enemy's not being pursued next day; did that surprise arise from the knowledge you obtained while a captive or from other circumstances?

Among other reasons, I had supposed no other division but ours had been engaged. I was surprised no attack was made the next day because I understood the enemy's attack had been repulsed by our corps. I decline to state anything I saw within the lines of the enemy.

Question. Was that attack made by the whole of the rebel army upon this one corps?

That I cannot state.

Question. Is it true that no other part of the lines was attacked except General McCook's corps?

I believe other portions of the army were engaged before the battle was over.

Question. Did you know that any division of the army was in the rear and on the march to join its corps?

I did not; I supposed there was a general concentration of the army at that point.

Question. Did you know what the strength of the army at Perryville was on the 8th?

I did not.

Question. What did you suppose it to be?

I supposed we had 60,000 or 70,000 men.

Question. Did you know what the condition of our army was?

I did not know its condition.

Question. Did you know what loss it sustained in the battle of the 8th?

I had no means of ascertaining.

Question. Had you formed any estimate of the loss.

No; it would have been impossible.

Question. What did you suppose to be the strength of the rebel army, independent of Kirby Smith's force?

I supposed General Bragg had 40,000 or 50,000.

Question. Was that the general estimate among persons who had opportunity of knowing?

I cannot say what opinion others had; estimates differ.

Question. What did you suppose to be the force under Kirby Smith's command; by that I mean the whole rebel force in Kentucky, not including Bragg's army, and including that of Humphrey Marshall?

I had no knowledge of any other corps except of that portion under command of Kirby Smith. I estimated that at from 15,000 to 20,000.

Question. Does that include the force under Humphrey Marshall?

It does not. Any force under him I know nothing of.

CINCINNATI, *December* 4, 1862.

Col. LEWIS D. CAMPBELL, having been duly sworn by the judge-advocate, testified as follows:

By the JUDGE-ADVOCATE:

Question. What is your position in the Army?

I am not in the service now.

Question. State what was your position while in the Army during service in Tennessee and Kentucky.

I was colonel of the Sixty-ninth Ohio Volunteer Infantry. I organized the regiment, and was ordered in April last, after it was mustered in the service, to report to General Buell in Nashville. It was in the later part of April that we marched to Nashville. I arrived there, and not finding his assistant adjutant [general] there I reported to General Dumont, who was in Nashville at the time. I was ordered by him to go into camp, and in the course of two or three days I received an order directing me to distribute my regiment on the line from Nashville to the Duck River, near Columbia, extending over some 40 miles, at five different posts, subsequently six posts, and make my headquarters at Franklin, Tenn. I had distributed my regiment in accordance with the order. Subsequently General Negley ordered a company to be taken and stationed at Duck River. General Dumont approved of it.

Question. Where were you at the time General Bragg invaded Kentucky and how long did you remain with the army after that?

I was with the army after the 9th of August. I was in Nashville on the 8th, when I resigned, intending to return within a week, but the railroad communications were cut off by the guerrillas in the neighborhood of Gallatin, and I was not able to go home without the risk of being captured. I remained in Nashville until the army came north. This was on the 7th of September.

Question. Can you state the position east of Nashville which Bragg's army occupied when he invaded Kentucky?

I cannot state it definitely. On Sunday, the 7th of September, General Crittenden and other officers came to my room, and in the course of conversation I expressed great anxiety to come home, but at the same time would like to have some opportunity of participating in what was then an expected battle. General Crittenden invited me to go with him, and I made arrangements with him on the march to act as his volunteer aide in the event of a battle. On that evening (Sunday, September 9), in company with General Crittenden and staff, we crossed the Cumberland at Nashville and came out within 4 or 5 miles on the Gallatin road, and remained there all night. I came through with Crittenden all the way until we came to Salt River, about 18 miles south of Louisville. As it was then, the general thought that there would be no engagement.

With the permission of General Crittenden I came with his brother to Louisville, and left the divisions of Generals Crittenden and Wood at West Point. I was not with the army after that.

Question. What time was it understood that Bragg had advanced into Kentucky east of Nashville?

I think the first I heard of it was about from the 1st to the 5th of September. I am not quite positive, but I think it was about that time. I cannot name the day within any certainty.

We heard that Bragg was crossing the Cumberland River and was up in the neighborhood of Hartsville or in that direction. That place had been regarded as the headquarters of the guerrillas at the time Colonel Boone was captured and at the time General Johnson had surrendered. Lieutenant Holliday was captured at Tyree Springs and taken to headquarters and then paroled. He represented that there was a formidable force of rebels at that point. My inducement to go with General Crittenden was the assurance which I had from him privately that to go with the army would be the safest way to return home. He expressed the opinion very strongly that there would be an engagement between the contending forces before many days. As I had gone into Tennessee with a view of assisting there I was anxious before I went home to participate in a fight.

Question. Did the subsequent information confirm you in the fact that the Confederate army had approached?

We heard of them on our march of their being on our right. I never heard of any considerable force being on our left. All the information I received was to the effect that they were to our right, perhaps a little farther advanced.

Question. Could you not trace out on the map the march of the rebel army at Hartsville?

I could not. I had not the means at the time. I felt a delicacy of exhibiting any improper inquisitivenesss. I was with General Crittenden almost constantly.

Question. What position did General Crittenden's army hold on that march?

I understood the divisions of Generals Wood and Rousseau were in advance of General Crittenden when we left Nashville and that they were to take the Gallatin road.

The Court. You must speak of your own knowledge.

The Witness. I saw on Monday, after we left Nashville, that we overtook a part of General Rousseau's forces. I saw his staff officers and conversed with them and subsequently joined them. We frequently halted on the march to Bowling Green. Near the city we were encamped a few days. We arrived at Bowling Green on Saturday, the 13th. It was the Saturday before the attack on Munfordville. Sunday we understood that Wilder had been attacked and had repulsed the enemy. On Tuesday following Wilder surrendered; that was on the 16th, I think. At that time we were in Bowling Green. We arrived there on Saturday, the afternoon, and remained until Tuesday evening. General Crittenden was encamped, and General McCook was down about 2 miles beyond Bowling Green, at the Cave. I don't exactly recollect the name of the place. General Crittenden marched on Tuesday evening and crossed the river and there remained over night. We heard on Sunday night or Monday morning that Munfordville had been attacked.

Question. At what rate had you been marching from Nashville to Bowling Green?

I should state here that I am not a soldier by education and profession and know little about what should be regarded a proper march. From Nashville to Bowling Green we were halted four times before we arrived at Bowling Green. We were eight days on the road. I think one day we did not march more than 2 or 3 miles. We left Bowling Green, as already stated, on Tuesday evening. On that day Colonel Wilder surrendered. I think the next day we made a pretty heavy march, that is, on Wednesday. On Tuesday evening we marched through Bowling Green across the river. We arrived at Cave City in the afternoon on Thursday. It was from there 10 to 12 miles to Munfordville. We crossed the Barren River at Bowling Green on the bridge, but the train, I think, forded it.

Question. What was the object of the delay at Bowling Green?

There was a baggage train sent in advance to Bowling Green. It was a heavy train.

Question. Did General Crittenden give you any reason for remaining so long in Bowling Green?

I think General Crittenden was very anxious to move. He had information that Frankfort was taken and he seemed rather impatient to move. The troops were also very anxious to move, particularly the Ohio and Indiana troops, of which our forces were principally composed.

Question. Do you know the reasons why Munfordville was not relieved?

I never heard of any reason why it was not relieved and no re-enforcements sent.

(General Buell objected to the question on the ground that the question assumes that Munfordville ought to have been relieved and that it should have been relieved by his army.)

Question. You left the army near Louisville and of course know nothing of its subsequent operations?

I do not.

Question. How long did you remain in Cave City?

We remained there from Thursday afternoon until Sunday afternoon and then came on to Munfordville. General Wood's corps was in advance of General Crittenden's that afternoon. I left Crittenden soon after we left Cave City. He said then that he was going to see General Buell. Being upon a hill at that time, I heard cannonading. I supposed the action had commenced. When I came to Munfordville I found General Wood on the other side of the river near Munfordville with his division. I learned that he had encountered the rear guard of the rebel army and had some light firing and shelling promiscuously. General Buell came up about dusk. We remained until about 10 o'clock the next day. All the information we could get was that the enemy had proceeded in the direction of Bardstown to the right, and had commenced leaving on Saturday morning and continued on Saturday night and Sunday. General Wood drove the last of them out.

Question. Do you know the direction by which Bragg retired?

I understood to the right, in the direction of Bardstown, On Monday, 22d, the following day, the advance guard of our army had some skirmishing north of Munfordville. We received some information in farm-houses where we found some citizens of secession proclivities and some others of Union sentiments. All confirmed the information that the enemy had gone to the right. I recollect I was much disappointed, as others were, when we received information that the march was directed to the Elizabethtown road, a different road from that which the enemy took. We went on to Elizabethtown and from there to West Point; it was a tolerably rapid march. The rate of our march increased when we were made to understand that the enemy was more to the right than before. At Elizabethtown we halted part of the day and marched 12 or 13 miles this side. There we remained all night, and the next day we struck the Salt River, and then I left General Crittenden.

Question. You left the army at Salt River?

Yes, sir. I would have remained with General Crittenden, but I supposed there would be no fighting, and as I had been a long time from home and sick I desired to go home.

Question. Do you know anything as to the operations of the army while you were with the army?

I do not know anything that would be pertinent to the subject of investigation.

The COURT. Confine yourself entirely to the invasion of Kentucky. Where were you when Munfordville was surrendered?

We were lying at Bowling Green, that is, within 2 miles south of Bowling Green, from Saturday until Tuesday morning, which covered that Sunday when Colonel Wilder repulsed the enemy at Munfordville. Wilder surrendered on the following Tuesday.

Question. Did you know on Tuesday that he surrendered?

We did not know that until perhaps we learned it on the march of Wednesday night. After we got to Cave City Colonel Wilder came in our camp on parole. The following morning I heard the circumstances under which he surrendered, and particularly the fact that a part of the terms were that he should be allowed to go around the lines of the enemy to see that their representations with regard to their strength were correct. He gave as his own opinion that Bragg's force there was from 22,000 to 25,000 men and that he had seventy pieces of artillery. I think it was on Wednesday afternoon when we heard the rumor. We did not know the facts, however, until Thursday night or Friday morning. Wilder came on Thursday night to Cave City, and, I believe, remained with us.

By the COURT:

Question. What is the distance from Cave City to Bowling Green?

I should judge 25 miles.

Question. How long did it take to march it?

It was five days from the time we left Bowling Green until we arrived in Cave City, two of which days only we were marching.

Question. Were there any other Federal troops on that march in advance of Crittenden?

I understood he had been sent to the right.

Question. State as near as you can.

There were troops in advance of General Crittenden when we crossed the river at Bowling Green.

Question. Do you know whose troops they were and their strength?

I had no information.

Question. Do you know where they went to?

I do not know, except from rumor.

Question. You know whose troops they were. Was it a heavy column of troops or a few?

It was a heavy column. I know that General Rousseau's force was there. After we left Bowling Green we were not delayed long. It was in the evening when we crossed the river and the next morning our orders were to march. It was about 3 o'clock a. m.

Question. What was the strength of General Crittenden's force at that time?

I could not give that with precision. There were some changes made in the march. My information would not be very reliable. I understood there were changes made in regard perhaps to his artillery. The whole artillery which we had at Cave City, according to the opinion I heard expressed by Generals Wood and Crittenden, was one hundred and twenty-six pieces. Colonel Wilder reported the enemy's at seventy pieces. I think General Thomas' division did not get up until Saturday night. General Crittenden's headquarters were right in the city, within a stone's throw of the railroad, near the reservoir. I understood General Buell was in the neighborhood at some place within a proper distance of communication. I was not personally conversant of the fact as to the precise point where General Buell had his headquarters.

Cross-examination by General BUELL:

Question. Your subsequent information confirmed your impression that the Confederate army was at Hartsville or that Bragg was there?

I did not understand that he had crossed at that point. That point I understood to be the headquarters of the rebel forces.

Question. Did your subsequent information confirm you in your opinion that he had crossed at that point?

Somewhere in that region. I do not know whether I had any information as to the precise point.

Question. Was the information positive?

No; it was like any other rumor. It was a rumor obtained in Hartsville.

Question. Do you know what force the enemy had at that point?

Only by rumor; but I never did put much reliance upon rumor.

Question. Do you know what the enemy's immediate destination was?

I do not. I understood that there had been some change. I did not know anything personally of their movements except what I gathered from common conversation.

Question. You have stated that there was a general impatience in the army as to its movement. Did the impatience proceed from a knowledge of the movements of the enemy or was it mere impulse?

I did not hear much of the impatience until after we had the information of the attack upon Colonel Wilder at Munfordville. We were at Bowling Green and halted three or four days. A spirit of impatience began to develop itself in Cave City when we came in striking distance of the enemy.

Question. Was the position of the enemy known at that time?

The information of Colonel Wilder's surrender was communicated by the colonel himself and all we know was through him.

Question. Had Colonel Wilder surrendered ?

Yes, sir.

Question. Did you know the strength of the enemy at that time ?

All I know, as I said before, came from Colonel Wilder.

Question. Did you know the strength of my army ?

From what I had seen I supposed you had probably in the neighborhood of 40,000 or 45,000 men and one hundred and twenty-six pieces of artillery.

Question. Did you know the precise position of the enemy at Munfordville ?

I did not know.

Question. Did you know anything of the circumstances that controlled the movement of my army ?

I knew nothing. I was informed that you had a full supply of provisions.

Question. For how long a time ?

I understood sufficient to take you through to Louisville.

Question. In what time ?

In the time that it would ordinarily take for a march. I do not know that I heard any one say as to the precise amount of rations. Besides I could not make the proper estimate as to what should be the necessary supply of the army.

Question. How many days' supply did you think I had?

I do not recollect the exact amount. I understood from the officers that there was a sufficient supply.

Question. Would the date of the arrival of Crittenden's army indicate the arrival of the whole army or only a portion ?

I do not think that the whole army arrived at one or the same time.

Question. What do you consider to be a good day's march for a body of troops ?

As I stated before, I have very little experience in these matters. I should state, from the little experience I have had, that in order to have men in good fighting condition they might make on the average from 12 to 15 miles per day and be in good condition. The march of which I spoke, which General Dumont made, was 45 miles in twenty-five hours, but was too exhaustive for the men.

Question. Did you know when the army left Bowling Green what its immediate destination was ?

I did not know. I think it was to overtake or catch Bragg. I had no information, direct or indirect, and to General Crittenden I propounded no question. It was presumed the intention was to find the enemy.

Question. Did you know to what point the army was marching ?

I supposed it marched upon Munfordville, and if the enemy could be found to engage them.

Question. Did you know that Bragg's army had left Glasgow at that time ?

I did not. I knew nothing of the movement of Bragg except what I learned upon the march. All I heard was from Colonel Wilder, from Thursday night to Friday morning.

Question. Was the army obliged to march to any one point or could it march upon various roads ?

I suppose it could have marched upon various roads.

Question. I want to know whether it was necessary for the army, in prosecuting its march, to pass through one point or could it move from the beginning upon different routes?

I never had an opportunity to examine the maps which had the routes marked on them. I understood that a portion of your army had marched off in the direction of Glasgow—to the right in that direction.

Question. I understand you to say after leaving Bowling Green a portion of the army had diverged from the main road?

I understood so.

Question. Upon how many roads?

They all started upon one route; the road to the right, which a portion took, lay in the direction of Glasgow. They united again at Cave City. It was said that the enemy was in Glasgow, but I did not hear anything as to the exact force which Bragg had there.

Question. You stated that you were disappointed that instead of pursuing Bragg's army on the road, they turned out in the opposite direction toward Elizabethtown; what was the immediate advantage you expected to gain by following that army on its march toward Bardstown?

I supposed we had forces enough to achieve a victory over them wherever they might be found; and as they made toward the Ohio River, I thought we could catch them in the same direction.

Question. Was that impression based upon the knowledge you had of Bragg's forces?

My impression was founded on the belief of the fact that ours was a superior force, better equipped, &c., and upon my general information which I received from the specimens of rebel soldiers I had seen. There were some taken upon the road by skirmishing; they were mounted soldiers.

Question. Do mounted men constitute the bulk of the rebel army?

Not exactly.

Question. What knowledge had you of the circumstances of the rebel army, respecting their efficiency, as compared with ours?

I had no opportunity but such as was common to everybody. It is the general impression that the troops of the rebels are inferior to ours. I think the general impression, as far as I had been able to ascertain from those who had the means to obtain information, is that they are better disciplined than ours, but not as well armed and equipped. That is the impression to my mind.

Question. Did you know of the existence or presence of any other rebel forces besides the army of Bragg in Kentucky?

I had no information except the representations that were made in regard to Kirby Smith's force.

Question. What force was General Smith supposed to have?

I do not know. My supposition was that Kirby Smith had 20,000 men.

Question. Did you know the position of Kirby Smith's forces at the time our army was following General Bragg's?

I noticed perhaps in a paper which we picked up on the road, which stated that the pickets did come within a few miles of Cincinnati, and this was perhaps in fact the cause of the impatience which seemed to prevail to engage Bragg and push on to the Ohio. I understood that General Dumont was off in that direction in Kentucky between the points of General Smith's and Bragg's forces, but that was only rumor again.

Question. You stated that General Dumont's force was interposed

6 R R—VOL XVI

between them; did you know the strength or efficiency of General Dumont's forces?

I did not know his strength or efficiency.

Question. Was the force with which I marched from Bowling Green sufficient to meet the rebels after the junction of Bragg and Smith?

I should have supposed that you would have sufficient assistance from the direction of Louisville in the event of the junction of the rebel army.

Question. Did you know of any such assistance?

I know there had been a very large force in Louisville of Ohio and Indiana troops

Question. Did you know the position of the enemy's forces?

I did not.

Question. Did you know their strength?

I did not.

Question. Did you know their movements?

I did not.

The commission adjourned to meet December 5, 10 a. m.

LOUISVILLE, *December* 5, 1862—10 a. m.

Commission met pursuant to adjournment. All the members present; also the judge-advocate and General Buell.

J. T. PRATT, being duly sworn, testified as follows:

By the JUDGE-ADVOCATE:

Question. State your name and occupation.

J. T. Pratt is my name. I am a school teacher by profession, in La Grange, Tenn.

Question. Have you been in the service of the United States; if so, when, where, &c.?

I came to Nashville and reported to General Schoepf; he gave me an introduction to General Thomas, also an introduction to General Fry, who had two sisters residing at La Grange. I had left General Bragg's army in the Sequatchie Valley. I made the following report to General Schoepf and General Buell, that I estimated the force of Bragg's army to be from 22,000 to 25,000 men. I drew my statement from this, that they had moved in the warmest of the weather from Tupelo, Miss., and had left many sick there. I would also state that after having laid there inactive some time they left a number of sick at Chattanooga. I said I had counted several regiments and taken an average from these. In stating now the average I must rely wholly upon my memory. I averaged them at between 200 and 300. I stated there were three and sometimes four regiments to a brigade. In my first statement I said there were three brigades to a division and six divisions in the army. I then stated the respective commanders. There were two corps, or wings, commanded respectively by Generals Polk and Hardee. That I think is the extent of my report to him.

Question. State, if you know, what course the rebels would take in invading Kentucky.

General Buell asked me if I thought they were directing their course to Nashville I stated I thought they were not.

Question. What opportunity had you of knowing their strength?

By observation and inquiry.

Question. Were you inside the enemy's lines?

I was.

Question. Where was General Buell when you made this report?

At Nashville, in a house on High street.

Question. Did you make any subsequent report to General Buell?

General Schoepf requested General Thomas to have me return to General Bragg's lines. I did so, finding him at Glasgow. I arrived at Glasgow on Sunday; I do not remember the day of the month. I there saw General Bragg's army strike their tents on that Sabbath, and then had an opportunity of counting several regiments and made several inquiries. I saw also the pike which they took in leaving Glasgow. I returned and reported in the first place to General Schoepf; he sent me to General Thomas and I reported to him. He sent me to General Buell in the morning. I confirmed my former statement as to the numerical strength of the enemy. I recollect in my second statement to General Buell I said I had found out that some divisions had four brigades. I stated to him the pike they took—the pike that runs due north.

Question. How many days elapsed between your time of leaving Glasgow and your report to General Buell?

I should think four or five days.

Question. In either of your reports did General Buell inquire regarding artillery?

As to that I should not like to say upon oath what the question or the answer was. I think I told him a battery to a brigade.

Question. Did General Buell question you as to the general condition of the army, as to supplies and transportation, &c.?

I think there were some questions asked in regard to a wagon train. I think I made the statement they were well armed. As to supplies, if I made a statement I do not recollect what it was. I think I said they had a small wagon train.

Question. At the time you made your second statement, at Prewitt's Knob, was it known generally that Munfordville was surrendered?

I think I heard of it at Bowling Green before I made the report.

Cross-examination by General Buell:

Question. What did you estimate the strength of the rebel army at Tupelo to be?

I don't think I made an estimate, but they left a number of sick.

Question. Can you answer how many?

I think I made the statement they had buried several thousand, but not as to number of sick who were left there. It would be very difficult to form an estimate of the number of sick General Bragg left in Mississippi. I made no estimate. I think "many" was the adjective I used.

Question. How long were you at Tupelo?

I merely passed through there, perhaps remaining ten or twenty hours. In speaking of the graves, I would say I came to Tupelo from Holly Springs; that in entering Tupelo by the road I came I passed through several camping grounds, or, more properly, by several camping grounds, from which the army had been withdrawn, and upon each camp ground I saw the graves where each several brigade had buried their dead. In most cases these were marked by a few rails piled up; in some cases a piece of board with an inscription. I rode to several of these plats and counted the graves, and in that way I arrived at the estimate of the dead (several thousand).

Question. Was the army with which General Bragg invaded Kentucky identically the same as that you saw at Tupelo?

As to that question I cannot make a distinct reply, as I arrived at Tupelo after a part of the army had left.

Question. When were you at Tupelo?

In the month of July, the latter part.

Question. Had the principal part of the army left at that time?

All had left, I think, excepting Price's division and the division of which General Walker is a brigadier-general.

Question. When did you arrive at Chattanooga?

I arrived in Chattanooga just as the rear of the army was passing the river. Saw General Bragg on the south side of the river. Cannot positively fix the date.

Question. Did you see the whole of the army at Chattanooga or near there?

I saw what I considered all the army after I crossed the river on the march.

Question. Had any portion of the army left the river when you arrived; and, if so, what portion of it?

A portion of it had, but what portion of it I could not state. A portion of it had marched 4 or 5 miles from the river and camped.

Question. Did the army cross Walden's Ridge by one or more than one road?

I should think they nearly all crossed by the old Anderson road.

Question. Did you accompany the army on the march; and, if so, what portion of it, how long, and up to what point?

When the army camped on the north side of the river, that night after dark I rode to General Wheeler's cavalry brigade; this was the advance of the army, I think, at that time, that went on the road I mentioned before, the old Anderson road. I think it passed over the next day. I passed with it. It went as far as a Mr. Bennett's house, about 3 or 4 miles from Dunlap, at the point where the road entered the Sequatchie Valley. It was there I saw the army cross the next day and there made my estimate of its strength. I arrived at my conclusion in regard to the strength by conversation with officers on the road from Tupelo to Chattanooga and by observation while with the army. I counted one or two regiments in Cheatham's division; most of his men are Tennesseeans. One or two in General Withers' division; General Withers' division I supposed to be chiefly Alabamians.

Question. Did the whole of the army cross at Chattanooga?

The portion I saw crossed at Chattanooga.

Question. Did it halt in Sequatchie Valley while you were there or continue its march?

I cannot state as to that; I left.

Question. Did you count the divisions as they came into the valley?

No, sir; I did not.

Question. What reason have you to believe that you saw the whole of the army at that time?

I heard it stated that the whole army was there. I also saw a great number of soldiers.

Question. Did the artillery cross by the same road? Did it cross with the troops or separately?

There was artillery that followed the cavalry and also infantry that was with the artillery.

Question. Can you state how much artillery crossed with the cavalry?

No, sir; I don't know how many pieces; a good many. I saw some infantry cross with the artillery, but that all the infantry crossed by that road I can't say.

Question. Did you see any artillery besides that that accompanied the cavalry?

I saw other artillery in the valley; I mean to say I saw more artillery in the valley than I thought I had seen cross the mountains.

Question. Did you count the number of pieces then?

I never counted the artillery, no more than that. As I said before, I saw in some cases four and some cases six guns to a battery. As to a general estimate of guns, I did not make that.

Question. Did your estimate of the strength of Bragg's army, which you say you reported to me, include cavalry?

I think I made a separate report of cavalry. My estimate of 25,000 includes everything.

Question. Did you know what route the army proposed to take and what destination it had in view?

I heard Pikeville and Sparta mentioned as places of destination, and judged from that they were going to Nashville.

Question. By what route did you reach Nashville after you left Bragg's army?

I struck from where we were through Dunlap. I was some time in going. I followed no particular road, but passed near Pikeville, leaving it to my right; then near a little town called Bunker Hill, leaving Sparta to my left; thence to Rome, a little place on the Cumberland River, leaving Carthage on the right; from Rome directly to Nashville, entering Nashville on the Lebanon pike. I arrived two or three weeks after leaving Chattanooga. This I state from recollection.

Question. Did you leave Dunlap in advance of the rebel army?

I left before the bulk of the army had arrived. A little cavalry was there when I reached there.

Question. How long was it after you left Nashville until you arrived at Glasgow?

Nearly two days.

Question. Did you see the whole army at Glasgow?

I saw what I considered the bulk of it.

Question. How many divisions did you see?

I did not see the army division by division, but I saw a large portion of General Buckner's division; I counted several regiments in this, as I have before stated. I also saw four brigades in one division. I saw Generals Cheatham's and Buckner's divisions, and counted the strength of some of the regiments; found them to be from 225 to 325, and drew an average of 280 to 290.

Question. Did you count the number of regiments in a brigade?

I counted the number in two brigades; in one three, in another four regiments.

Question. Did you count the number of brigades in a division?

In one instance I did—General Buckner's division; I found it to be four brigades.

Question. Under what circumstances did you leave the rebel army? Were you privileged to leave or did you leave without permission?

I left without a pass or permission. I had no conversation with any one about it.

Question. Had you any reasonable apprehension of being prevented from leaving; and, if so, what means did you resort to to avoid apprehension?

I was not regularly in the army; was not connected with it in any way; and I wasn't in any department; therefore I supposed that I would be conscripted if I remained or forced to take up arms in some way. I rode up out through Dunlap before they established pickets. I rode the same horse I rode around Tupelo.

Question. Did you have any intercourse with high officers in the rebel army?

No, sir; I did not. I conversed with Captain Alexander, from Louisville, Ky.; he was General Walker's assistant adjutant-general. I had conversation with him at Tupelo. Occasionally on the road from Tupelo I had conversation with others, but not lengthy on the road from Tupelo.

Question. How did you make your escape from the rebel army the second time?

As I stated before, I staid at Glasgow until General Bragg's army had left; then I left.

Question. Who were you staying with when you were in the army?

I was with a brother, in First Alabama, Allen commanding.

Question. Did you have to make any explanation upon your return?

I did not see any person that recognized me. I was arrested by a citizen where I staid all night for expressions that I made. He had a pistol and saw that I was unarmed; said that he was going to carry me back to the lines. But at last he relented, after he found the army had moved. That is all the interference I met with.

Question. Did you return to the rebel army after your interview with General Buell at Prewitt's Knob?

Yes, sir.

Question. State where you found it, how long you remained with it, and where you left it.

I found it at Bardstown, two days after I left General Buell. Remained there one day before I was arrested by a Captain Burton, from La Grange, as a Union man, and was placed in the guard-house with United States soldiers, among others Lieutenant Scott, Fourth Indiana Cavalry. After I had been there two days I was sent south of the lines with General Forrest, who left at this time with an escort to take charge, as I supposed, of the Army of the Tennessee. I came down with him through Springfield, Lebanon, Tompkinsville, from thence to Dixon's Springs. All this time I was under arrest. When I got at Dixon's Springs it was in the afternoon, 5 o'clock. General Forrest went to a private house and took me with him. The next morning he left early, as he said, for Lebanon, Tenn. He left three or four men with me to follow on after him. They were all privates. I went with them nearly to the river, where they crossed from Dixon's Springs to Lebanon road. Here I dismounted in a lane. The privates with whom I was left had all procured liquor and at this time were quite intoxicated. I dismounted, as I said before, and I made my escape and went to Nashville.

Question. Where have you been since?

I have been at Nashville, at Murfreesborough, and at Chattanooga.

Question. Did you go to Chattanooga on any duty for the Government?

Yes, sir; I went there for General Negley and arrived at this place yesterday.

Question. What did you come here for?

I was going to New York to see my father.

Question. How happened it that you were summoned before this Commission?

I recognized General Schoepf in the office and spoke to him. He asked me where I was going. I told him. He requested me to remain here, and I received an order to appear here at 12 o'clock.

Question. Have you received compensation from the Government for your secret service?

I received from you $150, and $30 from General Negley; that is all I received.

The Commission adjourned to meet December 8, at 10 a. m.

NASHVILLE, *December* 8, 1862—10 a. m.

Commission met pursuant to adjournment. All the members present; also the judge-advocate and General Buell.

Maj. Gen. A. McD. McCook (a witness for the Government), being duly sworn, testified as follows:

By the Judge-Advocate:

Question. State, if you please, your position in the Army of the United States.

I am a major-general of volunteers since the 17th of July, 1862.

Question. You will state, if you please, what part of that time you were under the command of Major-General Buell, and especially during the invasion of Kentucky by Bragg, and all you know about the expedition following.

I organized and commanded the Second Division of the Army of the Ohio at Camp Nevin; that was my command when General Buell assumed command of the Army of the Ohio. I marched with that division to Nashville with short delays on the road at different camps, and from Nashville to the battle-field of Shiloh; from thence to Corinth; thence to Battle Creek, Tenn., and there was placed in command of the Fifth Division in addition to my own. The Fifth was commanded by General Crittenden. I commanded these two divisions in front of Chattanooga, where the rebel army, under General Bragg, was supposed to be concentrating. I remained at Battle Creek until General Buell planned an advance against the enemy, part of which I was to carry out. My orders were to march up the Sequatchie Valley. I will state one brigade (the Fourth) was here detached and stationed along the Nashville and Chattanooga Railroad as far as Cowan. My instructions were on marching up Sequatchie Valley to leave Crittenden's division at the place where the Higginbottom pike leaves the Sequatchie Valley to ascend the Cumberland Mountains. With the rest of my command I was to move up to Anderson's house, and there prevent the enemy from crossing Sequatchie Valley and guard the Anderson road. When I reached to within 10 miles of the Anderson road I was on the march, and was met by two of my spies, whom I considered trusty men. One was a corporal in the Forty-ninth Ohio, the other a refugee from Chattanooga I had sent out. They presented me with a synopsis of what they had seen around Chattanooga. They approached me in different directions and had not seen each other. They informed me that Bragg was crossing at Chattanooga with seventy regiments and a great deal of artillery; that Withers was crossing at Harrison, 12 miles above, had already crossed eleven regiments; that McCown was crossing at Kingston (this was about the 10th of August), supposed to have 10,000 men. General Heth commanded a division under him. The most reliable of these spies, Corporal Kennedy, informed me that the army that crossed at Chattanooga were advancing rapidly toward Anderson road. That same morning I received information that 600 of the enemy's cavalry had reached Dunlap. I then had but two brigades and three batteries of artillery with me. Had been informed by a citizen of that vicinity, whom I considered loyal, that the enemy's pickets and advance were on the top of Walden's Ridge, 7 miles from where I was to go to take position. Knowing there were several roads crossing Walden's Ridge practicable for infantry and cavalry, I did not consider it safe for me to go to that place with a command of that size. My instructions from General Buell were to take position upon the Anderson road; to hold it if I could; if not, to retreat by a road to Tracy City; in case I could not reach Anderson road to ascend the mountain by Higginbottom turnpike to Tracy City, where I would be met by General Schoepf. I did not know what command General Schoepf had, but was merely informed that he would meet me there. I did not know he commanded the First Division.

I then returned to Higginbottom pike with my command; went to top of mountain myself; tried to carry a battery up, and found the road impracticable for military carriages. I then marched from that point with my own and Crittenden's division back to Battle Creek, and camped 6 miles from the mouth of the stream. From this point I could have marched by Sweeden's Cove road, which led to Tullahoma; by Battle Creek road to Pelham, or by Fiery Gizzard road.

While in this camp I received an order from General Buell (I would here add, the part of General Buell's plan on the Anderson road I alone am responsible for; I did not carry out his instructions) to march with my two divisions to Pelham; to reach Pelham by one day's march; to march from Pelham to Altamont, and then form a junction with General Thomas, and attack the enemy on Therman road in case he advanced that way.

On my march from Battle Creek to Pelham night overtook me 7 miles from Pelham. I there bivouacked with my two divisions and descended the mountain the next morning, and reached Pelham at 10 o'clock (5th of September). There found General Schoepf encamped with First Division of the army, and was joined by the other brigade of my division, which marched from Tullahoma. I sent couriers when on top of the mountain to Altamont. They returned and reported General Thomas had been there with about 600 cavalry, but had left. An order reached me at Pelham from General Buell that in case I had not descended the mountain to encamp at a place where Battle Creek road intersected the road which led from Tracy City down to Cowan.

I went into camp at Pelham and assumed command of all the troops there. Was there visited by General Buell in person, who ordered me to move with my own (Second) division up to Altamont. I remained there until I exhausted all forage and water, and then descended the mountain by Hickory Creek road and encamped at Hubbard's Cove. Our army had been on one-half rations for a month, except what the men had provided for themselves, such as green corn and fresh meat. Our supply of salt was very small. I will state General Buell sent me a synopsis of his plan of campaign while at Battle Creek, which was to attack the enemy as they debouched into the Sequatchie Valley and as he descended into the plains of Tennessee from the Cumberland Mountains, which was as perfectly planned as could be. This plan could not be carried out for want of supplies. The railroad was constantly kept cut, and my impression then was that we had but twenty days' rations for our army in Tennessee.

After reaching my camp in Hubbard's Cove, on Hickory Creek, I there received General Buell's plan of concentrating his army at Murfreesborough and my instruction what to do. This plan of concentration, in my opinion, was as perfect as it possibly could be. I then marched on Murfreesborough; had entire control of the rear of the army until I reached the city of Nashville.

The enemy in their movements could have but two objectives—Nashville and Kentucky. I considered a march to Kentucky a hazardous one for them, and, in case we were to fight in Tennessee, Murfreesborough or Nashville were the points we could concentrate at. By coming to Nashville, by assistance of troops from the Army of the Mississippi, we could place about 15,000 more men in line to fight than we could at Murfreesborough.

I was never satisfied with the manner in which General Buell's army was scattered along the Memphis and Charleston Railroad. But I believe others, higher in authority, are responsible for that altogether. I was never told so by General Buell, but still that was my impression.

General Buell has been censured by the public press for not arriving at the battle of Shiloh sooner. I commanded his advance, and had communication with General Grant, who was at Savannah. I built the bridges over Duck River. I don't believe he could have gotten his troops to the battle of Shiloh sooner without abandoning his transportation. Duck River was not fordable for 50 miles either way, there being 40 feet of water in it. A notification was also received from General Nelson stating we would not be needed before Tuesday. There was no information that warranted any rapid marches. I supposed General Buell's army was to co-operate in an offensive campaign, and that Savannah was the point to concentrate upon.

I do not remember the day I arrived in Nashville, with rear of General Buell's army, from Murfreesborough. I arrived at Mill Creek, 2½ miles from Nashville, with 750 wagons, about 3,000 cavalry, and my own division, at 11 o'clock at night; made the march in one day, 30 miles. I reported in person to General Buell that night about 12 o'clock. I returned to my camp that night; received an order early next morning to be ready to march. I was on the march and received an order, countermanding the former, to encamp at McEwing's house, about 11 miles from here, with my own old division. I remained here that day and until 5 o'clock on the evening of the next day.

During my stay that time near Nashville I visited General Buell some two or three times. On one occasion he asked me about how many men it would take to defend Nashville. I replied about 20,000 men. I believe he asked me if I thought 20,000 men would hold it. I told him I did not consider it a very defensible place. At that time I thought Price's army was marching into Middle Tennessee. I advised General Buell to abandon the place and to allow me to burn it. He replied Nashville must be held at all hazards, and was very glad he did not select me to defend it. My reasons for advising General Buell to burn Nashville, I believe it to be the most treasonable place in the Southern country, except the little place of Murfreesborough. I was in General Buell's quarters on the evening of the second day I arrived here, when he received a dispatch from General Jacob Ammen that his outpost at Edgefield Junction was in the presence of the advance of the enemy. General Buell then ordered me to proceed immediately to his assistance with my division. I reached Edgefield Junction about 2 o'clock in the morning. Ammen's division was ordered to move forward that morning on the road to Bowling Green. I was there joined that morning by General Buell and staff. General Buell then marched that morning with my division toward Bowling Green. We left that camp at 12 o'clock the same day we arrived and marched to Tyree Springs. The next march we made was within

14 miles of Bowling Green, at a creek which made its appearance there, and next morning my division reached a place, Cave Mills, 4 miles this side of Bowling Green. There we found General Crittenden encamped with his division. We encamped there that night. Next day I marched to a camp 1½ miles below Bowling Green, near Barren River. At Bowling Green the army was reorganized, as far as command was concerned. These divisions were called columns, consisting of two divisions each. We remained at Bowling Green two days. My command consisted of my own division and the division of General Robert [B.] Mitchell, of the Army of the Mississippi. I then received an order to march next morning. The rest of the army, Crittenden and Rousseau. I marched that day to Dripping Springs, 16 miles from Bowling Green, with my two divisions. We remained at Dripping Springs until next day, 1 o'clock. I then moved on and camped at Prewitt's Knob, a distance of 13 miles. Remained at Prewitt's Knob two days; then marched to a point near Munfordville, on Green River, a distance of about 14 miles; made the march at night. Next day I marched from Munfordville and camped at Bacon Creek, having to cross Green River. Next day I was marched from Bacon Creek to Elizabethtown, a distance of 24 miles. Next day's march was from Elizabethtown to mouth of Salt River, 23 miles. Next day's march was within 7 miles of Louisville, at a place called Greenwood, on the Ohio River, at 10 o'clock p. m. On reaching Greenwood, as the rear of my division was marching into camp, I received an order to march upon Louisville. The roads being very dusty and great scarcity of water and hard marching upon pike roads, my men were worn-out. I sent for my brigade commanders and inquired particularly as to the condition of my men. I then postponed marching until 3 o'clock a. m. At 3 o'clock a. m. I received a note from General Buell by hands of Lieutenant Anderson, ordering my division to halt where I was, General Buell supposing I had been on the march. I also received a note from General Crittenden, who had obeyed the order and marched on Louisville, not to hurry my command, as his men were standing in the streets and not assigned to any camp. I left my camp at Greenwood at 8 o'clock and marched to Louisville and camped near the Jeffersonville Ferry, where I remained until an advance was made against Bragg and Kirby Smith, then in Kentucky.

At Louisville the army was organized into corps, consisting of three divisions. I was placed in command of the First Corps, consisting of my own (Second) division, General Rousseau's division (Third), and General Jackson's division (Eleventh), consisting of raw levies. I don't exactly remember the number of days we were at Louisville in reorganizing, but we moved at the earliest possible moment supplies could be obtained, and as it was I marched with a deficiency of canteens and haversacks. We marched without baggage. I think one wagon to a regiment was allowed to carry officers' blankets and a few rations. Soldiers had mess-pans made and carried them on their persons. Regiments that were supplied with cooking utensils one wagon was allowed to carry them.

When we marched from Louisville my corps was divided. Sill's division was ordered to march on Shelbyville pike toward Frankfort. My other division marched 6 miles on Bardstown pike, then turned to the left on Taylorsville pike, and camped that night beyond Jeffersontown. I was ordered next day to march to a point, the junction of Shelbyville and Taylorsville and Louisville and Taylorsville pikes. It was absolutely impossible for me to encamp there, as the streams were dry. I marched that night 5 miles farther, to Taylorsville, on Salt River. I remained at Taylorsville next day; the day after marched to Bloomfield. I was kept in communication with General Buell, and he prescribed the day's march for each corps from day to day. The orders were for each corps to have four orderlies at his headquarters, so as to enable him to communicate with the different corps from day to day.

I remained at Bloomfield with my two divisions from Saturday until Monday morning. While at Bloomfield I received instructions from General Buell to be ready to march to the support of Sill in case he should fail at Frankfort or to be ready to march to the support of Sill to operate with the main body in an attack on Bragg. I then received an order to march from Bloomfield to Harrodsburg, there to form a junction with Sill at or near Harrodsburg. I sent that order to General Sill and told him to meet me on a certain day. This order was countermanded. Sill was ordered to march by way of Lawrenceburg and Chaplintown, and then follow my route, by way of Chaplintown, Willisburg, and Mackville, to the position assigned me at Perryville. General Buell sent me a guide, Capt. Beverly [D.] Williams, who bore an order. The order was an optional one to march by way of Willisburg and Mackville to Perryville, and if that was impracticable to march by way of Springfield. Captain Williams informed me he could carry me through by way of Willisburg and Mackville. I left Bloomfield Monday and marched to Chaplin River, 1½ miles beyond Chaplintown. On Tuesday I marched to Mackville—on the 7th of October. At 2 o'clock on the morning of the 8th I received a letter of instructions relating to my position in line at Perryville, ordering me to march at 3 o'clock a. m. I marched at 5 o'clock a. m., my division being separated about a mile on account of water. I reached a point designated for my line about 9 o'clock a. m. near Perryville. Was ordered to take position about 3 miles from Perryville.

When I arrived at the point designated General Rousseau went forward and reconnoitered the ground. I saw General Gilbert's line, his left skirmishing with the enemy, although no enemy were visible except a few in the woods and along the fence. The enemy were driven from the front. I sent my aide, Lieutenant Hosea, to see whose troops they were. He returned and reported they were Colonel Greusel's. I called General Rousseau's attention to the left of General Gilbert's line, and also Captain Loomis', who was Rousseau's chief of artillery, and marked the line of battle for them. I was a total stranger to the country. Captain B. D. Williams, who was my guide, was called off to General Buell's headquarters at 7 o'clock that a. m. I marked the line of battle of General Rousseau, and Captain Loomis replied they understood it perfectly. I commenced forming it, and selected the position for Loomis' battery myself. The right of my line was not over 350 yards from General Gilbert's left. The line was then being formed—Rousseau's division—the line being marked out for it. General Jackson's division had not yet arrived on the ground. On the march I picketed all the roads leading from Mackville leading to my rear. General Gay in the mean time was making a reconnaissance with cavalry.

Our march that day to Mackville had to be done carefully. I had flankers and skirmishers thrown out. Jackson's division, being composed of raw troops, understood their duties imperfectly, and consequently could not march rapidly. I ordered General Rousseau to reconnoiter my front with skirmishers. He ordered the Tenth Ohio, commanded by Lieutenant-Colonel Burke. I gave orders to Major Campbell, my assistant adjutant-general, to post General Jackson's division on a high piece of ground to the right of the Mackville road with regiments doubled on the center, with a view to move them in any direction. I then informed General Rousseau that my order was to report to General Buell in person and that I was about to leave the field (11 a. m.), but would return in a short time. I would state that previously I had a conversation with Captain Long, who was stationed in that part of the field as a picket. He told me he had been there and had only seen a little force of the enemy's cavalry; that General Gilbert's troops had been engaged with the enemy, but not in any force. General Buell's written instructions led me to believe he was going to attack the enemy at Perryville.

I left the field and reported to General Buell in person, whose headquarters were 2¼ miles from my line. I reached his headquarters about 12.30 o'clock; reported that my line was formed; my right was about 350 yards from Gilbert's left; also reported my men wanted water badly, the water the night before being scarce and bad at that. He ordered me to return to my line and make a reconnaissance down to the Chaplin River and obtain water for my men. I left his tent in company with his chief of staff, Colonel Fry. I asked Colonel Fry who was down in Perryville. He replied Hardee was there with two divisions. I then bade them good-by, and said I was going down to drink at the river and asked him to go. I returned to my line, and found that General Rousseau had placed a couple of batteries in position and replied to three batteries that had opened on him at long range. I rode up to where the batteries were, and not seeing any of the enemy's infantry, I ordered no more ammunition to be wasted. I was then informed by my guide, Captain Williams, and Colonel Harris, commanding Ninth Brigade, that if I would ride off to the left a few hundred yards on the Mackville road I would get a position that would command Chaplin River and could see the water. I went forward in person, examined the ground, and saw the water. Sent for Generals Jackson and Terrill, told them what I was ordered to do, showed them the water, marked out a line for them, which was a continuation of the left of Harris' brigade, Rousseau's division, right resting on a wood and line running along a high commanding ridge, and at the left of the line was a crochet to the rear, in order to hold the high ground. General Jackson replied to me, as did also General Terrill, that they understood the line. They had previously sent for the troops to place in that position, and were then on the march to this position. I also ordered General Terrill, as soon as his line was formed, to advance a line of skirmishers down to the water. He replied to me, " I'll do it, and that's my water." The only enemy in sight at that time was about 400 or 500 cavalry on the other side of Chaplin River (1 o'clock). Water was about 600 yards in front of my line. This cavalry was driven away by Stone's battery, Starkweather's brigade, that was put in position on a high ridge to the left of my line. I had previously ordered two companies Thirty-third Ohio into the woods as skirmishers to reconnoiter the woods. I ordered General Jackson to superintend this reconnaissance, and he replied that he would. I told him I would then ride down into these woods and see what they were about, as I heard nothing from them. General Jackson requested me not to go, saying that Providence had been kind to me, and that some lurking scoundrel might shoot me. I told him I would not go, and rode to the right in the rear of the skirmishers, and in a few minutes the firing commenced between the Second and Thirty-third Ohio skirmishers and the enemy.

About 2 o'clock an assault was made upon my entire line, the heaviest being on my left and center. In about half an hour after I left Jackson Williams reported to me

Jackson was killed. As soon as I found the assault was going to be a general one I dispatched an aide to General Sheridan to see to my right that it was not turned. About 3 o'clock, when I found the enemy were outnumbering me, I sent an aide to the nearest commander for assistance (Captain Fisher).   He met General Schoepf on the road marching to the battle-field.   Captain Fisher was referred to General Gilbert, who was with General Schoepf's command, and was referred by General Gilbert to General Buell.   At 3.30 o'clock I dispatched another aide, Captain Hoblitzell, to General Schoepf, to tell him my condition.   The same time I dispatched Major Bates, of my staff, to report to General Buell my condition.   In the mean time Terrill's brigade, of Jackson's division, which consisted of all raw troops, had given way, but Starkweather's brigade, being so admirably posted, drove the enemy back on the left. I remained in the left center of my line until the enemy were driven in confusion from the left center and center of my line and then galloped to the right, and arrived just in time to see my right turned by a heavy force of the enemy.   It was then and there most of my casualties occurred that day.   I ordered two regiments of Webster's brigade, which had been posted in the rear of the right center of Rousseau's line, to move to the right and repel the assault.   I galloped to Russell's house, where my headquarters had been during the morning, and ordered my chief of artillery to bring up a section of artillery and repel this advance of the enemy.   The section was opened, but they opened a battery about 600 yards from us and opened such a heavy fire upon that point that the battery was brought away.   Loomis' battery had exhausted all its long-range ammunition and had been retired 100 yards in rear of Russell's house. I rode to the battery, and ordered Captain Loomis, as soon as the enemy came close enough, to open upon them with canister.   He double-charged his Parrott guns and did it handsomely.   I then rode back to where the Mackville and Perryville and Springfield-Dicksville roads cross.

(Continued December 9, 1862.)

NASHVILLE, *December* 8, 1862.

Lieut. FRANK [J.] JONES (a witness for the Government), being duly sworn by the judge-advocate, testified as follows:

By JUDGE-ADVOCATE:

Question. What position have you in the service?

First lieutenant, Thirteenth Regiment Ohio Infantry, and acting assistant adjutant-general of Third Division.

Question. State whether or not you were in the battle of Perryville, whether you were taken prisoner there, and what you know of the number of the enemy.

I was in the battle of Perryville; was taken prisoner there just at night-fall, 8 or 9 o'clock, after the battle.   As regards the number of the enemy, I know nothing except what I heard from Captain Spence, assistant inspector-general Polk's staff, who stated they were 30,000 or 35,000 strong.

(Objected to by General Buell on account of its being hearsay evidence.   The room was cleared and the objection was sustained.)

Question. State what you know of the subsequent movements of the enemy.

Of that I know nothing, being taken to Harrodsburg by a circuitous route, avoiding their army.   I saw nothing except detached bodies near Harrodsburg; besides, I made no inquiries.

Question. How long were you at Harrodsburg after the battle when paroled?

Was paroled day after the battle, in provost-marshal's office in Harrodsburg,

Could you judge from the bodies you saw which way the enemy were moving?

No, sir; I could not.

Cross-examination by General BUELL:

Question. What time did you arrive at Harrodsburg?

Next day after the battle, 12 or 1 o'clock.

Question. State if you please, what route you took in going there.

After leaving General Polk's headquarters we went by a circuitous route, over a dirt road, until we met the main body of the rebels, which was on the march to Harrodsburg. At this point we left the road upon which they were marching and went through the woods to Harrodsburg.

Question. On what road is the residence of Mr. Bowman, at which you staid?

At the junction of two roads, one leading to Danville, the other came in on the right-hand side as you went near Harrodsburg.

Question. You are positive the left-hand road was the Danville road?

I am not positive it is the main road to Danville, but the road we went.

Question. Did you see any large bodies of rebel troops marching past Mr. Bowman's house while you were there?

No, sir; I did not.

Question. What do you mean by detached bodies of troops which you say you saw?

Smaller bodies of men than the whole column; a brigade or regiment away from the column.

Question. Where did you see them and in what way were they marching?

As far as the troops in the town are concerned, they appeared to have no apparent object; those leaving the town marched from the town on the opposite side from that where Mr. Bowman's house was situated.

Commission adjourned to meet December 9, at 10 a. m.

NASHVILLE, *December* 9, 1862—10 a. m.

Commission met pursuant to adjournment. All the members present; also the judge-advocate and General Buell.

General ROBERT B. MITCHELL (a witness for the Government), being duly sworn, testified as follows:

By the JUDGE-ADVOCATE:

Question. What is your position in the Army of the United States?

Brigadier-general.

Question. State, if you please, what service you have seen under General Buell in Tennessee and Kentucky as to time.

I marched from Iuka to Tennessee on the 28th July, 1862, in command of the Fourth Division in the Army of the Mississippi, for the purpose of joining General Buell's command at this point. I do not think it possible that I can recall the dates. I marched to Columbia, Tenn., under my written orders, and there I received orders by telegraph to join General Buell's army at Murfreesborough, Tenn., which I did, and reported to General Buell in person. From there I marched to this point, Nashville. After remaining here a few days, in the rear of General Buell's army, I marched in the direction of Louisville, under his directions. I do not remember where I overtook the main army. The army was at Bowling Green, Ky., marching to Louisville and from Louisville to Crab Orchard. At Louisville the army was reorganized. In consequence of the arrest of General Davis I was placed in command of the Ninth Division of the Army of the Ohio, and commanded it from Louisville to Crab Orchard.

Question. Do you know at what place the rebels under General Bragg invaded or crossed the Cumberland in their invasion of Kentucky?

I do not.

Question. Do you know anything of their line of march to Bardstown?

Only from report.   From Bardstown I followed close in their wake to Perryville   I commanded the advance of the central army corps from Bardstown to Perryville.

Question. Do you not know now, as you know any other historical fact, what was the course taken by the rebels?

I have an impression from observation and from hearsay.

Question. Will the knowledge which you have justify you in stating to the Commission at what points, previous to the capture of Munfordville, that army might have been attacked with the prospect of success?

Well, it would.   I commanded a division, without any knowledge, except from common report, where the enemy were.   You are well aware that all kinds of reports are flying along the line from morning to night.   We believed the enemy were marching very near us, but had no positive knowledge of the fact.

Question. What do you know of our failure to relieve Munfordville?

I have no personal knowledge.   I had no means of knowing about the distribution of troops or the necessities until two days before we arrived at Munfordville.   I was detached from the main army at this point; but I find it impossible to recollect the names of localities.

General BUELL. There is a map which shows exactly the movements of the column.   It would be very useful to the Commission.   It is a map I used myself, and on which the roads are traced.

(Judge-advocate directs the map to be obtained for the use of the Commission.)

Question. Where were you, general, at the time of the surrender of Munfordville?

My impression is that we were near Bowling Green.

Question. How long had you been there previous to the capture?

I lay there about a day and a half.   I was in the rear, and joined the main command, I think the last division before General Thomas.

General BUELL. It was the last but one.

General MITCHELL. I cannot remember the day of the capture, but I lay at Bowling Green a day and a half after the capture, and the first knowledge I had of Munfordville being in the hands of the enemy was two days before our arrival there. The knowledge I had was at the time we met the troops that had been paroled there.

Question. Your recollection of the date of that event is not sufficient to enable you to fix the day?   You cannot tell how long you were at Bowling Green before that place was captured?

I cannot; I can only give my impression.

Question. You proceeded with the army from Louisville to Crab Orchard and were present at the battle of Perryville?   What was your position there?

I occupied the right of General Gilbert's corps.

Question. State, if you please, if you took any part in that fight.

I did.   About 10 o'clock in the morning of the 8th of October I was ordered to the front.   Had been occupied for three previous days in front.   During the night General Sheridan, with a portion of his division, was ordered to pass me.   It was the night of the 7th.   He passed me some time in the night.   I was ordered about 10 o'clock to move forward with my entire division, and after marching probably 2 miles General Gilbert rode up to my line and directed me to take position with two brigades to the right of the road leading from Springfield to Perryville.   I was directed to place two brigades in position on that hill, leaving one brigade in the valley to the left of the road as a reserve.   I went up and formed my two brigades, which were in the advance on the hill, and was directed there to wait orders by General Gilbert.   I had no orders directly from General Buell, but after 7 in the evening I had orders to form two of my brigades in line of battle, and encamped in front of General Buell's headquarters, and received orders from him personally to advance one brigade as outpost and lay there that night. I placed my men in position about 12 o'clock on the right of the road in sight of the town of Perryville. This was on the 8th. I remained there for orders until Sheridan's line was attacked by the enemy. It was a pretty severe skirmish. An effort was made to take a battery that was in an advanced position and was repulsed by Sheridan, and a few moments after that time to Sheridan's right and my front there was a large force of the enemy, a full division, if not more, concentrated, and had commenced a movement on Sheridan's right. In the mean time Sheridan had sent a messenger saying that unless he was supported or re-enforced he would have to fall back. I directed the messenger to return and to say to Sheridan that I was watching the movements of the enemy and would strike them before they reached his right. In ten minutes I ordered Colonel Carlin, colonel Thirty-eighth Illinois, then in command of the Thirty-first Brigade, to advance under cover of the timber as far as possible, and directed him to break the enemy's lines there without firing a gun. He proceeded under the order until he had arrived within 150 yards of this concentration under cover of the timber and a kind of half-hedge fence. There were thorn bushes innumerable along the fence after he left the timber that covered his movements. In consequence of the timber and the brush he got to within 150 yards without being discovered, and under my direction ordered a double-quick at the charge of the bayonet and drove the enemy without firing a gun. As soon as they were repulsed they were driven into the town of Perryville, 1½ or 2 miles. That must have been about 3 o'clock or probably later, perhaps nearly 4. There is an elevation on the side of the town. On our arrival at that elevation there was a battery opened upon us, shooting across the town. I ordered up four pieces of Carlin's battery, two pieces having been detached for supporting General McCook, and two or three pieces of another battery in my division opened fire upon this battery, in the mean time throwing our skirmishers into Perryville. In twenty minutes we silenced the battery on the other side of the town and had driven the enemy out of the town of Perryville. I sent my aide-de-camp to direct the commanding officer of that regiment to change his direction to the left of the town and rather to the rear of the enemy and directed Colonel Carlin to support him. I rode back to the brigade that was following up for the purpose of supporting Carlin's brigade about 600 yards; it may have been more, but not exceeding 700 yards. This regiment that had changed their direction to the left of the town had captured thirteen wagon loads of ammunition, two ambulances, and two caissons, said to be of the Washington Battery, and brought them off the field.

Before I had changed my direction I was visited by General Gilbert's aide-de-camp and directed to hold back; that I was acting rashly and would not be sustained. I had not followed General Gilbert's aide-de-camp's directions, but preferred my own, and took possession of the hill, and I said if General Gilbert desires to give me orders I wanted them in writing; that I had received a great many orders from his staff officers that were not sustained by him, and if he desired me to fall back he must bring me a written order from General Gilbert. At the time of the capture of these wagons—perhaps a little before—I received an order in pencil, directing me to fall back on a line with General Sheridan, who commanded the left of our army corps in that fight. I told him I would obey the order, and fell back with one brigade in line with General Sheridan. With the other brigade I exercised my own discretion, and so far as Carlin's brigade was concerned I directed him to remain till we got further orders.

After falling back I occupied a commanding position, with artillery covering the town of Perryville and the Danville road. I directed him to remain until we had specific orders from headquarters. The other brigade fell back in line with General Sheridan's and within supporting distance, knowing that General Wood's advanced brigade was within striking distance. He had notified me through my aide-de-camp that he was there. I occupied that position all night.

I never saw anything of General Gilbert from the time the fight commenced till 3 the next morning, on the field. He came to where I was lying under a tree between 2 and 3 o'clock next morning. In the mean time I had visited General Buell and advised him of my position, and soon General Gilbert came, and that was the first time I saw him after he ordered me to take my position on the heights to the right of the road.

In justice to General Buell I should state that when I came in he said I had the only face that looked like victory since the commencement of the fight.

Question. What explanation did General Gilbert give of his conduct?

He never gave me any.

Question. Did he ever give you any?

Not of his conduct there. After the time I followed in pursuit of the rebel army, under the direction of General Gilbert he undertook to explain why he was not in the front to direct personally.

Question. What reason did he give?

He said I might think it strange his not coming some time to the front. His staff annoyed me from the time I went into the corps till I left it. They would come and order a brigade to do a certain thing as direct from General Gilbert, as they said, and when I talked to General Gilbert he denied authorizing such an order.

After I had engaged the enemy for about three hours in front of the town of Lancaster we advanced slowly and steadily, and he came up to me after he had ordered me to fall back within a mile of Lancaster. He came up, and I told him we had committed a great error by not taking possession of that road; that I had discovered a large number of wagons passing there, and I was satisfied the enemy were getting away in the rear with their transportation trains. Had he permitted me to advance to that road I could have cut off a large number of wagons. He said there was no water and that we could not make an encampment. Our men, I told him, had been without water, and could have stood it for one night. Said he, "You may think it strange that I was not in the front, but I remained in the rear for the purpose of supporting you." I replied that I preferred he would just let me alone and permit me to exercise my own judgment. I had lost all confidence in General Gilbert. I did not know whether he was captain or general. I only knew him from the fact that he wore two stars. He was commanding an army corps as a major-general.

Question by General TYLER. How was he placed there?

I don't know. I was ordered to report to Major-General Gilbert.

Question by the PRESIDENT. Was he not major-general?

I saw him subsequently at Louisville and he had only one star.

Question. Was he a brigadier-general?

I don't know. I saw in the papers that he was appointed brigadier.

Question by JUDGE-ADVOCATE. How long did the army remain at Perryville after the action there and what course did it take?

Two whole days. I marched the third day.

Question. In what direction did you march?

I started out and struck the Harrodsburg pike, marched on about three miles, and went on the road between the road to Harrodsburg and the road to Danville; there is a road between the two.

Question. You were there in pursuit of the rebels; they were marching in the direction of Harrodsburg?

I understood they had marched from Harrodsburg to Danville on the pike. We marched half way in the direction of Perryville to Harrodsburg and then struck in a direct [map produced] route to Danville between the two roads. After leaving Bowling Green I was ordered to take the Merry Oak road to Glasgow, and was ordered to proceed cautiously, by General Buell himself, to Wright's Store, to encamp that night, which I did. I went in pursuance of General Buell's direction, and met a brigade of cavalry, which came into camp some three hours after I had arrived there. I have a memorandum from you [addressing General Buell] saying unless I met the enemy I was to proceed the next morning to a certain point, Bell's Tavern, a railroad station, where there was a cavalry force said to be.

Question. Did you understand the object of Bragg's army in marching toward Harrodsburg after that action at Perryville?

I know no other reason than that they were cut off in the Danville road by a portion of my command. We covered with parts of two batteries the Danville road, and with the force on my right, had we been supported, we could have held the position against Bragg's whole army. I know another reason: the supposition was they were to make a junction with Kirby Smith, and I subsequently understood they did.

Question. How did it come that that position was not maintained?

It was. I have a diagram which will give you an idea of the country there. (Diagram produced.) The town of Perryville and the Danville road were covered by parts of two of my batteries. The road leading from Perryville to Harrodsburg was 10 miles, on which the enemy retreated, and I am told that from Harrodsburg to Dan ville is 10 miles.   My battery was on an elevation west of the town.   That is the position my batteries occupied, supported by Carlin's brigade, with six or seven guns in position there.

(Map produced as furnished by General Buell on the night of the 8th*.)

Question. What prevented you from holding Perryville?

I did hold it.   I advanced to Perryville.

Question. What was there to prevent the army moving forward to Danville?

I do not know of anything.   Next morning, on the 9th, I was ordered to proceed to Good-Night Springs, and found on the field 2,000 stand of small-arms—on the road up and at Good-Night Springs—which I collected and turned over to General Gilbert's ordnance officer.

Question. What would have been the effect of the army moving on to Danville instead of Harrodsburg?

We could have cut off the entire army by moving in that direction at the time I moved in the direction of Good-Night Springs.

By General TYLER:

Question. You supposed the enemy were whipped that night and had reatreated?

General McCook told me he thought he had been a little worsted, but I thought we had done all that could be required of us on the right.

By the JUDGE-ADVOCATE:

Question. Where were General Buell's headquarters during the action of the 8th?

It was back on this road, perhaps 2½ miles from the battle-field.   I could not tell definitely.

Question. Was there any severe fire of musketry?

Not very, till we got into Perryville, where we had a brisk skirmish; but the musketry was on General McCook's front.   From half past two for an hour and a half we heard musketry.   It was terrific.

Question. You marched to Perryville expecting to meet the enemy in force there?

I did.   I think I reported to General Buell on the night of the 7th that I could have taken possession of the town that night.   I do not recollect the remark he made, but the next night when I told him I occupied the town of Perryville he appeared surprised.

Question. Cannot you recollect the conversation that occurred between you and General Buell the evening before?

He said I was rash, intimating that I was exceedingly eager, but I could not recollect the exact words.   I recollect very distinctly telling him that we could have entered the town, but he laughed and turned it off in some way.   We had been skirmishing during the evening before the battle.

Question. Was General Buell at his headquarters during that engagement?

I do not know.   General Buell was thrown from his horse.

General BUELL. I authorize the witness to state that I was at my headquarters.

The WITNESS. General Buell was lame from the fall from his horse.

Question. To whom did you report the result of your fight?

To General Buell at least as late as 9 o'clock at night.   The fight was over about

_____

* Not found.

5. We fell back about 5, or perhaps before. I sent an aide-de-camp with a rough diagram, made on horseback, to General Gilbert, showing him the locality, but he came back and reported that he could not find him. I was unable to get any orders, except as I told you, through his aide-de-camp, and I refused to obey them, because they had deceived me before. I instructed the aide-de-camp to go to General Gilbert and say to him that we were in the rear of the enemy's batteries and I asked for instructions. That was after I was ordered back by the aide-de-camp of General Gilbert.

Question. What would have been the effect of your advancing at the time you received the order from General Gilbert?

Had I been supported I could have taken the Washington Battery. I had made a reconnaissance in person, and there was no infantry supporting the battery except those that were taken prisoners—about 170. Everything that I did discover was in advance of the batteries and fighting McCook; the battery was also shelling McCook.

Question. Were you present at a meeting of officers at Prewitt's Knob, in which the movements of the army were discussed and General Buell's conduct commented on?

I was at no council. I was never at a council of any kind during the time I was in the Army of the Ohio.

Question. Do you recollect any conversation at General McCook's headquarters at Prewitt's Knob?

I cannot call anything to mind.

Question. Were you present at any conversation at which it was suggested that General Buell should be put under arrest and General Thomas put in command?

I never heard any such talk.

The President. You have stated that General Gilbert was not in the front?

I would not state that he was not at the front, but I did not see him. I don't know where he was. After he ordered me to the right of the road I never saw General Gilbert till next morning. I frequently asked him for an explanation of the object of the movement and what he expected us to do, but he failed to give me any reply. General Schoepf was in command of one of the divisions. He was in the reserve.

By the President:

Question. What was the strength of Gilbert's corps?

I cannot come near it. My best impression is about 21,000. On reflection I think it was larger.

Question. How many batteries had he?

He had two full batteries and a four-gun battery, and my impression was that each of the other divisions in our corps had three batteries. It was reported to me, as General Wood advanced, Bragg was within a mile of Crittenden's corps on my right. That was about 4 o'clock in the evening, within sight of the Danville road. My division was 8,500 when at Louisville. I think Sheridan's division was not as strong as mine. General Schoepf had more regiments, but mine were fuller. I think we had that number of men.

(Diagram produced and the positions of Sheridan's and Mitchell's divisions marked.)

I have not studied the diagram sufficiently to fix the distance with exactness. My original line was 1¾ miles from Perryville. We could not see McCook's from our position. Sheridan was next on my left and then McCook.

The President. I would like to have you mark upon this map the line of your advance and how far you had got.

The distance was about 600 yards, entirely out of town.

The PRESIDENT. Had you plenty of ammunition?

An ammunition wagon to each regiment very close at hand. I had but little use for small-arms. The brigade that was taken from me by General Gilbert without no tifying me was exhausted of their ammunition, and the cartridge-boxes were filled on the morning of the 9th, when they were supplied with a full complement of ammunition. They lost something over 400 men, 2 field officers killed and 1 mortally wounded. I think there were 13 officers killed and wounded. General Gilbert came to me and asked me to send some officers of influence to reconcile that brigade, saying it was demoralized. I sent my acting assistant adjutant-general, and marched the regiments over in as good condition as I ever saw any command and as eager to go into the fight again, without any show of demoralization. Four officers were slightly wounded and the balance very severely.

Cross-examination by General BUELL:

Question. General, you stated in your direct testimony that you said to me that you could have gone into Perryville with your division on the evening of the 7th?

Yes, sir.

Question. Did you base that opinion on anything you saw?

Well, from the manner of the enemy—the manner in which they fell back, not showing a disposition to make a very stubborn stand. General Buell replied to me that I could not have done it with twice my number; and furthermore told me that if I could go in there with my division he would put another star on my shoulder.

Question. How closely were the enemy pursued in the town that day?

I think, to the best of my recollection now, it was not less than 2¼ miles by the road. Across the hills it might have been nearer, but by the way we went it was that distance.

Question. What time did your division advance on the morning of the 9th?

It was quite early; I could not tell; it could not have been much after 6 o'clock, probably before. We opened fire by 6 on the cavalry trying to pass the Danville road. I was in line of battle an hour before I had any orders to advance. General Gilbert sent an order after we had been in line of battle an hour. The firing was opened from our advanced brigade by Colonel Carlin.

Question. Did you see anything of the corps on your right as you were advancing on the morning of the 9th?

Yes, sir, I did; the advance brigade. It advanced about the same time I did in the morning to my right across the Danville road. I think the whole corps crossed there. I know the advance brigade went in the direction of Harrodsburg. I supposed at the time that the cavalry was driven up by that division from their extreme flank, where they had been the day before, but I could not tell. I know they appeared to be in a great hurry to get out of the way as fast as possible. We got ten or twelve shots at them from our artillery. This was part of Crittenden's corps. I met General Wood that morning, but cannot state exactly the time. He was commanding one of General Crittenden's divisions.

DECEMBER 9, 1862.

Testimony of General McCook continued (from December 8).

I then proceeded to the point where the Mackville and Perryville road crosses the Springfield and Dicksville road. There I met my aide-de-camp, Captain Hoblitzell. Colonel Gooding commanded the brigade. He reported to me, and I ordered him to his position with the regiments and told him what to do. Capt. O. F. Pinney, Fifth Wisconsin Battery [also reported], and I posted him in a position near the skirts of the wood near the crossing to the right of Mackville and Perryville road. The fight still continued fiercely. This was about 5 o'clock in the evening or half past 5; dark came on about 6. General James [B.] Steedman, who commands a brigade, also reported to me that he had his brigade ready for duty. I ordered his batteries into position to the right of pickets and posted his infantry to the right of these batteries. The brigade was formed in two lines, extending nearly to where Colonel McCook's brigade was in camp. About the time I got this brigade posted it was quite dark and the firing had ceased on both sides.

I remained in front of this line, watching the movements of the enemy, till half past nine. I established my headquarters about 70 yards in front of this line and about 150 yards in rear of Russell's house, where I had been in the morning. I remained on the right in front of this line because I thought the main attack would be made in that direction. The moon came up, a bright moon, and they could have fought as well as by day. Finding there was no motion or drum movements of the enemy that I could discover, I rode to the left of my line to see how it had retired. This was about half past nine at night. I went to the left, could not find General Rousseau, but found that he had retired his line from the position they had occupied in the evening and afternoon. The enemy's camp-fires were around the lines, almost surrounding his position, and our pickets were 40 yards from each other. They were talking. I there saw Colonel Starkweather, who commanded a brigade, and Colonel Harris, and Colonel Hall, One hundred and fifth Ohio. I asked them what kind of a position they were in. They said almost surrounded by the enemy; that the pickets were within 40 yards of each other; that the rebel cavalry threatened them on the left; that Bush's and Stone's batteries were in a position to be taken at any moment in case the enemy made a heavy assault.

I determined that the line should be changed, but from what I saw I did not think the enemy would attack till daylight. My reason for this was they came from Harrodsburg to give us battle. I immediately rode off to select a stronger line, to retire these batteries and Rousseau's infantry to a better position. I selected it. General Rousseau then rode up. He had been at General Buell's headquarters. I carried him with me to select the position for his line and marked it, with the left on Mackville road and the right resting on the point where Steedman's was posted on high ground. This was a good position. During the night I had succeeded in taking off all my ammunition and ambulances and hospital wagons. I succeeded in the night in getting off that road.

General Buell sent me word in the evening late that if I had to retreat to retreat by the Dicksville and Springfield road, which led to his headquarters; therefore the Mackville road was of no importance to me. This was about half past nine. I told General Rousseau that I considered this change of line was a very hazardous one, and, if the representations were correct, as soon as they heard the first gun there would be an attack made on them. I told him not to form the movement yet; that General Buell had sent for me; he wished to see me. I told him I would go to General Buell and ask for more assistance to keep a certain position to cover this change of line. Then we started off to General Buell's headquarters, and reached there about 12 o'clock at night. I found General Thomas at General Buell's headquarters. I reported to him in regard to my fight in the afternoon. I told him what the condition of affairs was and told him where the line was. He replied that I was cut off from him. I told him yes, from the Dicksville and Springfield road, where General Rousseau had retired the line. I asked him for two brigades for about two hours; that I wanted them to hold a certain position in order that I could change my line. I then asked him for one brigade. He positively declined giving me two brigades, and I then asked him for one. He told me I was cut off. When I was just coming off the ground General Rousseau's aide-de-camp told me the change had been made. The line of battle which had been formed by my two divisions was the best possible one that could have been selected in my opinion. I examined the ground, and I examined it six days after, when all the facts connected with the battle were known, and I am conscientiously satisfied that it was the best disposition that could have been made of those troops in order to have saved my communication on the Mackville road. The posting of Starkweather's brigade was admirable. He posted the brigade there himself. I did not see the posting of that brigade myself. General Rousseau deserved the credit of it.

The enemy were whipped on the left thoroughly; they were routed on my center, routed on my right. I was badly whipped. I believe re-enforcements could have been sent me without prejudice to the cause; and I have since said that had I my old division that I fought with at Shiloh I would have been responsible for Bragg's escape that night.

General BUELL. I object to this expression of feeling.

The WITNESS. I have no feeling in this matter toward General Buell, but have stood by him throughout his removal from the Army of the Ohio.

General BUELL. My objection is that it is an expression of opinion, or rather an expression of feeling with regard to the matter, based upon circumstances that developed themselves after the event. I do not wish it to be understood that it is an expression of prejudice or of feeling toward me.

The court was then cleared for deliberation.

Upon being opened the judge-advocate announced that the objection was not sustained; opinions of corps and division commanders being considered important to the Commission to enable it to come to a conclusion upon the matters before it.

The WITNESS. I will state, in reference to the conversation or report, that I believed the enemy would attack me at daylight, and General Buell disagreed with me in opinion. He didn't think so. Next morning I received an order to close my line to the right and ordered Steedman's brigade to return to its command to General Schoepf.

General BUELL. Was that a written order?

The WITNESS. Well, sir, I think it was a pencil written order, a note from Colonel Fry. That order reached me; and I closed my lines to the right, and Steedman's brigade went to join its proper division. I will also state that about the time Steedman's brigade was coming to my assistance I met Major Wright, who reported that his re-enforcements were there, and asked me how I was getting along. I replied to him that I was doing the best I could with the troops I had, and with these troops I thought I could hold my position there. That was about 5.30; it was nearly dark. The next day my corps was ordered to advance and take a position to the right of Dicksville.

I wish to state something in addition. At the time that the attack was made upon me at the battle of Chaplin Hills the co-operation of General Gilbert's corps, I believe, would have secured a complete victory. My right was turned almost within view of his troops. But what his orders were in regard to these movements I know nothing. Co-operation there would have secured a victory in my opinion. I don't think General Gilbert was in front during the battle. I don't know whether he was or not, but I have inquired of his officers and they say he was not. I thought it was his duty to co-operate with me on that day. It is the duty of a general to relieve a brother general, whatever his orders may be.

The day after the battle of Perryville my line was thrown forward about 1 mile. I cannot be positive; I think it was the second day after the battle my line was thrown forward. I think I got the order, a written note, from the chief of staff. Next day we moved forward to the Harrodsburg pike, about 2½ miles, my command resting on the Harrodsburg pike. Next day I marched to Harrodsburg; from there to Fry's Springs, 3 miles; next day 6 miles beyond Danville, and the next day 2½ miles beyond Crab Orchard, where I halted.

The JUDGE-ADVOCATE. Have you the orders sent you, the memorandum spoken of in your evidence, and the report of your proceedings?

I have a report of the battle of Chaplin Hills. I have a number of memoranda.

The JUDGE-ADVOCATE. You have given us a detailed account of the marching of our forces to Louisville and thence to Perryville. Can you trace upon the map the march of the rebels under Bragg from the invasion till they reached Bardstown?

From Dunlap they came over to Sparta; they did not come on the Therman road. Some came through Spencer and Pikeville. I had information when I was at Murfreesborough that General Sam. Jones had come to Sparta. One of General Buell's men told me so. Some of them crossed at Gainesborough and some at Carthage, others at Scottsville, and concentrated at Glasgow.

General BUELL. He should be particular; he might mislead you.

The WITNESS. That is my impression; I had no charge of the secret service.

General BUELL. They did not pass through Scottsville.

The WITNESS. Part of the army crossed at Munfordville.

The JUDGE-ADVOCATE. At what point in that invasion ought the enemy to have been attacked by General Buell's army?

General BUELL. May I make objection to that? It requires General McCook to give evidence upon the question of duty, in regard to which he could not know the circumstances that controlled it. He may know at what point an attack might have been favorable, but he could not know that the attack ought to have been made unless he had all the information which determines the conduct of the commander of the army. He may state to the Commission at what point it might have seemed convenient.

The JUDGE-ADVOCATE. At what point in that invasion might an attack have been made by General Buell's army with a prospect of success ?

The WITNESS. I will state that I knew nothing about the position of the enemy till I arrived at Bowling Green.

General BUELL. At what date ?

The WITNESS. I don't know the date. On Monday I heard the enemy was at Glasgow ; don't know where the information came from ; I think from General Buell's headquarters. I had a conversation with Mr. Hobson ; it was at Bowling Green. I understood the enemy was at Glasgow, about 20 miles from Bowling Green, the force estimated at about 35,000. It was simply talk among my brother generals, and I got from Mr. Hobson my impression that in addition to that troops were coming on from Nashville. We heard rumors of it. General Buell intended to attack the enemy at Glasgow, and if we had pushed on might have attacked him at Munfordville. But I was not in favor of the Munfordville attack, because I knew the advantage the enemy would have in position. I had a conversation with General Buell at Dripping Springs, and I knew that we should sacrifice a great many men if we attacked the enemy there. I think, after what has been said, if more haste had been made from Nashville and a forward movement made at Bowling Green we might possibly have reached the enemy at Glasgow. But it was a matter of speculation altogether, as I believe they were running the day that General Wood arrived at Munfordville. I believe the enemy had left it that day, at least the rear guard out of Munfordville, and it was reported they had some infantry. I presume if General Buell had marched on Bardstown he might have got a fight out of the enemy at Muldraugh's Hill. My idea was that Louisville was threatened; Cincinnati had also been threatened. Kirby Smith was in front of it, and the more haste was made in getting to Louisville the better. That was my impression. I will state that General Buell was traveling with me, and I did not take any means of acquainting myself with the position of the enemy. I considered it his business entirely. When I am marching alone I do. I would also state that when at Edgefield Junction I received a letter from General Wood, who was then encamped at Bowling Green, to make haste and hurry up, that the enemy were marching on Glasgow ; also some dispatches came down from General Crittenden to Buell, which I turned over.

The JUDGE-ADVOCATE. Was that your opinion at the time of the invasion or is it an opinion made up since from circumstances which have come to your knowledge?

It is the opinion I had at the time. I built some of the defenses of that place and knew exactly what it would take to take them.

The JUDGE-ADVOCATE. Do I understand you to say, General McCook, that those were the only two points where the enemy might have been attacked with a prospect of success ?

General BUELL. He has not stated that those points could have been attacked with a prospect of success.

The WITNESS. Unless General Buell had turned off from his course and marched to Hodgensville.

The JUDGE-ADVOCATE. It appears to me that the witness stated that an attack could have been made with a prospect of success at points which he has not yet mentioned. I have no anxiety or wish to make points; on the contrary, I permitted this evidence to take a wide range, that all the facts in reference to this case might come before the Commission. I have no prejudice of feeling in the case.

General BUELL. I beg to express my gratification at the disposition which the judge-advocate's remarks indicate and I withdraw my objection.

NASHVILLE, *December* 10, 1862.

Commission met pursuant to adjournment. All the members present; also the judge-advocate and General Buell.

Examination of General McCook continued.

By the JUDGE-ADVOCATE:

Question. In connection with your statement in regard to the Army of the Ohio being stretched out so much on the railroad, state, if you please, at what places the several portions were at the time Bragg commenced moving from Chattanooga.

At the time General Bragg commenced moving, my own division, and General Crittenden's, the Fifth Division, were on the march from Battle Creek to Pelham; General Schoepf's, the First Division of the Army of the Ohio, was stationed at Pelham; General Thomas, in command of the Fourth and Sixth Divisions, and General Nelson and Wood were at McMinnville; General Hazen, with one brigade of Nelson's division, was stationed at Murfreesborough; Rousseau's (Third) division was marching from Huntsville.

Question. Can you state what forces you had in all?

I think that our army when concentrated would have been about 45,000 men. The cavalry were posted at different points through the country and there were detached regiments stationed along the railroads to defend bridges. There were some few troops at Nashville, the number I do not know, under the command of General Dumont and Colonel Miller.

Question. Did you know the destination of our army at the time you crossed the Cumberland River?

I was under the impression I was going to Kentucky, because I was under the impression that Bragg had gone there. I will also state in connection with this that General Buell is the most uncommunicative general I have ever seen or heard of. I never knew from time to time where the other divisions of the army were posted, or when on the march from Louisville to the battle to attack Bragg at Perryville I never knew where my brother commanders were or could be found at any time.

Question. In reference to that Perryville fight, what was your force there.

My own force, including those guarding trains and everything, was about 13,000 men, but my actual force in battle was not more than about 10,000.

Question. You said in your narrative that you had a conversation with General Buell after the Perryville fight; did you give all that conversation?

I gave what I believed to be the substance of the conversation. I went to General Buell, and, picking up the map, explained the position of my lines. General Thomas was present, and also Capt. Beverly D. Williams, of my staff, who heard the conversation. I told General Buell I had had a very severe fight. He said he was surprised to hear of it and that he had not heard of it till 5 o'clock. He then talked with me at intervals. He was engaged in conversation with General Thomas as to whether we should attack the enemy in the morning or not. I explained to General Buell the position of my lines. I told him I had two batteries that had fought gallantly during the day in a very perilous situation. I told him the manner in which Rousseau had retired his line on the left; that the enemy had lit fires around him and in front of him; that the pickets were only about 40 yards apart; that there was a regiment of cavalry on the left threatening any movements that might be made, and that from appearances I believed I was surrounded. I asked General Buell for the loan of two brigades for two hours at furthest, to hold a certain position while I changed my lines to cover the movements. He told me I could not have them; he positively refused to give them to me. I then asked him if I could have one brigade. He told me I should not have another man. I was at that time very much vexed and provoked. I felt that I should have had the relief. I confidently believed that I should be attacked at daylight and I told General Buell so. It was evident to my mind that the enemy had come on to a chosen field to attack our army, and I supposed the battle would be renewed in the morning and attack if they were not attacked themselves. General Buell replied that he did not think he could be attacked.

Question. Did he give any reason for that belief?

He did not.

Question. Do you know now or did you know at the time the direction taken by the enemy after that fight? Do you know any reasons for the enemy's taking the route to Harrodsburg instead of falling back on Danville?

The matter is very simple. They were moving back to form a junction with Kirby Smith's force.

By General TYLER:

Question. Did Kirby Smith come to Harrodsburg to join them with his whole force?

Yes, sir.

By the JUDGE-ADVOCATE:

Question. Can you give any reason for the delay that occurred after that fight in pursuing the enemy?

No reason whatever. I believe they should have been vigorously pursued next morning at daylight. I will state that my troops, who had fought all day without water, could have occupied the part of a reserve very well; better soldiers I never saw.

Question. Had you pushed across to Danville instead of following the enemy around by Harrodsburg what would have been the effect?

That the retreat would have been cut off. It might possibly have driven the enemy toward Louisville.

By General TYLER:

Question. They would have had to fight a battle?

Yes, sir.

By the JUDGE-ADVOCATE:

Question. You stated in your evidence that General Buell's plan of defeating the enemy when they first crossed the Tennessee was defeated by a lack of commissary stores?

That is my impression. The railroad was certainly cut.

Question. Were not the provisions you had on hand sufficient to justify an attack there, as to following the enemy all the way from Louisville?

No, sir; they were not. At Bowling Green we had a million of rations. That amount of rations would not have been sufficient.

By General TYLER:

Question. How many days' rations had you?

The amount of provisions, I think, was equal to twenty days.

Question. Did the country furnish nothing to collect?

But little; cattle and green corn, but the corn was all quite hard, and our supply of salt was short.

Question. You stated in your examination that General Buell sent you orders that if you had to retreat to retreat on the line toward his headquarters?

Yes; to fall back from the Chaplin Hills.

Question. Did he explain to you any reason for retreating in that direction?

No, sir; it was the only one left. I should have exposed my plan to the enemy by any other.

Question. You stated in some part of your testimony that General Buell told you his whole plan for the concentration of the Army of the Ohio?

He gave me a synopsis of that plan.

Question. What was it?

Murfreesborough was the point, moving in converging lines, so that every division was in supporting distance of each other from day to day, which I think was the most perfect plan that could have been desired.

Question. You stated that you were not satisfied with the scattering of General Buell's army on the Memphis and Charleston Railroad?

Any man of judgment would say it would have taken 50,000 men to keep that railroad in running order. I never heard General Buell express his opinions about these things, but I never considered him responsible for that nor do I think his army ever did, and the facts so prove. General Buell's written instructions induced me to believe that he intended to attack the enemy at Perryville. His instructions were that on account of the want of water the enemy would oppose his entrance into that town.

The PRESIDENT. Were any special orders given you with respect to that attack?

None, except those I presented to the Commission, that I was to take my position there and ascertain what was in my front and not allow my troops to scatter and to form my line with my right resting on Gilbert near Bottom's house.

By General TYLER:

Question. You stated that the assault commenced at 2 o'clock?

Yes, sir; about 2.

Question. Was there any movement of the enemy that induced you to believe the attack would be made?

I rode to the farthest point and reconnoitered. The enemy were concealed in the dry channels of Chaplin River and in mass there, and it was difficult to see anything unless you went down to the bluff and looked over. These facts I learned afterward, of course, by dear experience.

Question. You say you reported the attack on your lines at half past three?

I sent an aide-de-camp. My aide returned to the field afterward, but brought no orders. My orders were communicated to me by Major Wright, I think it was, on General Buell's staff, who arrived on the field that evening about half an hour before dark.

Question. What were the orders?

That in case I was compelled to fall back to fall back on the Springfield road, in anticipation of support. When Major Wright was in conversation these brigades appeared. Captain Hoblitzell was marching at the head and reported that he had a brigade marching to my support.

By General DANA:

Question. What was the strength and position of the forces with which you marched toward the Anderson road?

Two brigades of infantry and three batteries of artillery. General Crittenden accompanied my command to the point where the Higginbottom turnpike ascends the mountain.

Question. About what strength?

About 4,000 would cover the entire force.

By the PRESIDENT:

Question. What was the strength and position of Bragg's forces marching toward that road?

I found that my spies had misinformed me in reference to the movements of Bragg's forces. The force that was reported was a very heavy one It was reported that Bragg had crossed with seventy regiments. Newton, in my employ as a spy, and who had proved entirely reliable, so informed me. He was a refugee from that place. Citizens also reported to me that their pickets were on the top of the hills just above my position and that their advance had reached the top of Walden's Ridge.

Question. What force was left at Nashville at the time General Buell had marched to the north ?

When General Buell and I left Nashville General Thomas was here in command of the First Division; there had been a detachment of a division under General Negley; General Robert [B.] Mitchel was also here; Negley's and Paine's divisions, about 16,000 men; but there were quite a number of convalescents who could fight, and it made the force about 18,000 men that could be put in line to fight.

Question. What was the strength of the force with which General Buell marched from Nashville north ?

His army was about 45,000 men after taking out the Nashville garrison; but I will not be positive.

Question. While at Bowling Green did you know anything of the garrison at Munfordville being in danger ?

While there I heard that it had been attacked and had been taken, but the intelligence was uncertain. I was very anxious to know the result of it, because I had built a portion of the defenses of that place myself and I thought the defenses there would tell their tale some day yet. I was therefore the more interested in the matter. On my return in the morning I heard that the attack had been made and Colonel Wilder had repulsed it.

General Tyler. Did serious apprehensions exist in the army for the safety of Munfordville ?

I did not think Bragg would be guilty of such imprudence as to go there, but that his march would be by Columbia. In the face of our army I consider it a piece of impudence, because if he went in that direction he hazarded his army. Bowling Green is 40 miles from Munfordville, and I thought he would march toward Columbia, and by that means endeavor to form a junction with Kirby Smith in Kentucky. I had no spies in that country, nor had I when General Buell was present ever interested myself in gaining information on the question. I was a general to obey his orders without questioning his plans.

By the President :

Question. Was there any time wasted after marching from Nashville before marching to Munfordville in halting or marching or any halts which were needlessly made, not absolutely necessary ?

If I knew my general's plans I would answer without question. I had a conversation with General Wood, who said we ought to march on to Munfordville, but I knew nothing of the force there.

Question. Was there a general feeling existing in the army after leaving Nashville that the march was too slow and time unnecessarily wasted on the road ? Did such a feeling exist among the superior officers ?

I never had any discussion with them. Some of my junior officers had discussed the matter, but I always shut them up, and would not allow such conversations in my presence. But I had no conversations with any general officers upon the subject. I will state frankly that I had confidence in my works that I had built there, and I for one was not in favor of giving battle there, because the enemy would have great advantages.

Question. That was after you knew of the surrender of the garrison there ?

Yes, sir; General Buell asked me what my opinion was. He said he wanted the opinion of a man that had faith. He considered me a man not afraid to fight whenever an opportunity offered. He also knew the character of the troops I commanded, and I very frankly told him what I believed would be the result of the attack at

Munfordville; that I believed we could whip them, but that it would be at a great sacrifice of life.

General TYLER. Had you been compelled by an overwhelming force to retreat toward General Buell's headquarters what would have been the condition of your army; would you have been sacrificed or fought your way back?

I would never have left with my troops alive. With the changes I had made during the night I could have retreated on the Springfield road.

The PRESIDENT. When General Bragg's army debouched from the Sequatchie Valley what was the position of General Buell's army in reference to the advance of his (Bragg's army); were you in advance or the rear and what distance from the point where the debouchment was made?

By that time I think most of the army was concentrated at or around Murfreesborough or on those converging lines marching toward Murfreesborough.

By General TYLER:

Question. Was our army in the advance or in the rear of Bragg's army?

I did not know where he was. My idea was that General Buell intended to attack him at some point near McMinnville debouching into the valley of the Tennessee, but his provisions did not admit of it, and had he gone and fought a battle he would not have had an opportunity of pursuing them and making it a decisive battle.

Question. Could he have made them retrograde through the valley and take up another line?

I have never been in that portion of Tennessee, and I cannot give you an intelligent answer to that question.

Question. Suppose he had been headed off, what would have been his course?

Gone back beyond the Tennessee River or he might have taken a position in the mountains themselves, but he could not have advanced or got supplies there. He might have got supplies from Chattanooga or Pikeville or that neighborhood of country. The Sequatchie Valley was a very rich one; any given amount of forage for an army as large as any general would wish to handle might be obtained there. I would state that I always had the most implicit confidence in General Buell as a general, but he was the most uncommunicative general I have ever seen or read of; that is, to his brother generals. He kept his own secrets and plans till there was an absolute necessity for them to be known. I believe that the department of the Army of the Ohio was the most important command in the Army, and without the army being greatly increased in strength no general could operate with any hope of success in Tennessee. It was my opinion then and it is my opinion now. It is the largest contract of the war that is on the table now.

By General ORD:

Question. On the march from Corinth was there much marauding or plundering?

No, sir; there was not. I never allowed it. Some time in August or September there was an order authorizing the appropriation of property for the use of the army received from Washington.

Question. Did that make any difference?

Yes, sir; it ruined the discipline of our army to a certain extent. It was the worst order that was ever published for a body of troops. General Pope's orders on the Potomac was the cause of it. Our soldiers read it and believed it. It will demoralize any army in the world. I never failed to give redress to those inhabitants who complained of depredations, and I arrested every field officer in one entire brigade for suffering their soldiers to burn rails to cook with. Of course there were more or less petty grievances that will occur in the march of an army through any country, but General Buell's orders were opposed to it.

Question. Did General Buell use vigorous efforts to correct this marauding after the publication of this order?

He always did. Not only on the marching of my division, but he has provoked me on many occasions by reprimanding my command when I thought he should have required me to do it. I have seen him do it personally and order men to be punished for it, and especially for straggling.

Question. Straggling is a necessary result of marauding, is it not?

No man did more to repress it than General Buell, and I am sorry to say that there are frightful causes of complaint now.

General BUELL. May I inquire if he has heard it charged against the Army of the Ohio that it was lawless?

No, sir.

By General ORD:

Question. Did this produce any feeling on the part of the officers toward General Buell?

I do not know whether it produced any feeling or not. The immediate commanders were responsible for these things and it was on them depended the execution of the orders; on them the fault-finding would fall. I believe that General Buell's army was the best ever put in the field, and I have heard General Rosecrans say it was the best organized army that ever was, and that is my belief this day. There was never a more untiring general than General Buell. I never knew when he slept. I have been at his headquarters at all hours, but never found him asleep. I have spoken to him many times about it.

Question. Did you get the newspapers in your camp during the months of August and September?

We did not get them very frequently during that time, for I think the railroad was cut.

Question. Was it apprehended among the army that General Buell's conduct would be criticised in the newspapers?

I was under the impression that it would be. I have been abused by the Abolition press North and I hope I shall continue to be.

Question. Do you think the remarks of the newspapers had any influence in producing insubordination in the Army?

In one case I do. There was a pest of a correspondent in my division that I was after all the time, but could never catch. I think it would have an effect upon soldiers. I remember once General Buell was called an ass, but I never could find out who the correspondent was. As a rule I expel correspondents; they are not judges of what to publish and what to suppress. I believe they are the worst enemies of our Army, for I have seen publications that have given information respecting my movements known only to my officers high in command—facts in relation to the organization of my division and its movements. I know that correspondents complained bitterly because General Buell never encouraged them. The same complaint was made against me. I had the correspondent of the Cincinnati Gazette arrested and put out of the army because he published things he had no business to. I will further state, in this country, above all others, it is a difficult thing to obtain anything like satisfactory evidence of the position of the enemy, for their front is always covered with cavalry, and it is very difficult to get spies into their lines. I have always found it so, and there are no citizens on whom you can rely. Those who have information and are disposed to tell it are afraid to do so.

By General BUELL:

Question. Will you please give the particulars of your march from Corinth to Battle Creek? Give the date of your departure from Corinth and your arrival at Florence; how you were employed there at the time of your march from Huntsville to Battle Creek. Give the distances, if you remember them.

After the evacuation of Corinth there was a portion of General Buell's army sent down in pursuit after Bragg's army. My division remained near Corinth, I think, three days. General Buell then returned and ordered me to march to Iuka, which is a distance of 45 miles. I remained at Iuka one day, when Generals Nelson and Crittenden joined the column. General (then Colonel) Jackson's cavalry were also here. Wood's divison was also in that vicinity; a portion of General Wood's divison, Hascall's brigade, was, I think, scattered along the railroad, building bridges and repairing that road. I marched with my division, remaining one day at Iuka. I then marched to Florence, Ala., a distance, I think, of about 40 miles. General Buell had previously sent his engineer to prepare boats and means of ferrying the army. The bridge at Florence had been destroyed by the rebels. At the earliest possible moment these boats were ready—I think the second day after our arrival. General Buell placed me in charge of ferrying my own division, Crittenden's division, and of the reserve artillery. This took, I think, two days and a half, working as late at night as we could. I also had to build a road down to Jackson's old ferry. I built it by General Buell's orders. I remained one day at Florence. I then marched on to within 6 miles of Huntsville, Ala., without interruption, making long marches, a distance, I think, of 70 miles. I there received an indulgence of ten days' leave of absence and went to Ohio. When I returned my division was at Stevenson. I joined it on the 17th of July. On the next day I marched to Battle Creek. My average marches were 16 miles a day. The weather was very dry, warm, and dusty. We did not lay a day longer than was necessary at Florence, except to repair the ferry and convey the troops over. I worked night and day, and knew more about this than even General Buell himself.

Question. Do you know of any measures taken while you were at Florence to have the supplies in readiness at points in North Alabama for the troops when they arrived?

I recollect there were trains sent from Eastport and every effort was made on the river to get supplies up. The water was low.

Question. To get supplies into North Alabama, Huntsville, and around there?

Every possible exertion was made in the repairing of the railroads to get supplies and every disposable wagon was ferried across as soon as it was prepared, and these wagons were sent up to Reynolds' Station and were hauling supplies to Athens, Ala. My own supply trains, General Crittenden's, and General Wood's were all at work, and every available team was used to throw supplies there.

Question. With all these trains was it possible to accumulate any supplies in advance?

It was not possible by using every means then in the power of the Army of the Ohio.

Question. Do you know whether the work on these railroads was prosecuted with all possible industry?

A. Yes, sir; with the utmost vigor.

Question. In your position of command at Battle Creek did you exert yourself to obtain information of the strength of the enemy at Chattanooga?

I used every means in my power. There was not a day in which I was not expecting some persons to return to me with information.

Question. Were there any of your informants that you had confidence in?

Yes, sir.

Question. State, if you please, what information they gave you in regard to the strength of the enemy at Chattanooga; that is, shortly before you marched or about that time.

The JUDGE-ADVOCATE. That is precisely what you objected to in my examination.

General BUELL. Precisely; and the objection you did not sustain; but the case is entirely different. I am endeavoring to draw out the information which it was necessary to obtain and on which every com mander regulates the movements of his army.

My impression was that the entire army that had been at Corinth was at Chattanooga. When I was in command at Battle Creek some of the enemy's camps were in sight of some of my signal stations. Our pickets were on opposite sides of the Tennessee River. As far as the eye could go the river was picketed and in force. General McCown was in command at Chattanooga when I first went there. He in a short time was superseded by General Bragg. They had their troops stationed at different points back of Chattanooga, near the Lookout Mountain, at the junction of the Will's Creek Railroad. They had troops stationed also in front of me, a division at Shell Mound, and scattered down the railroad toward Bridgeport, and carried information to their officers every hour. Cars went down, and were busy, particularly at night, going and coming, and they could have had no reason for running where they did except for the transportation of troops. They had all the railroad bridges guarded by brigades.

By General BUELL :

Question. Will you state what estimate was placed upon the strength of Bragg's army in round numbers?

From the best information, my impression is that he had about 75,000 men. I believed the entire army of Corinth was there. Soldiers from Alabama were there. I got this information from deserters.

Question. Did you report this information to me from time to time as you received it?

I had communication with you two or three times a day, sometimes oftener. Whenever I received information it was telegraphed to you at once.

Question. Were there any means of crossing the Tennessee River?

None whatever, except by making bridges. There were no boats, except one small boat at Battle Creek, which I found sunken, and which had capacity for carrying about 40 men. I will state, in addition, on the opposite side of the river was a line of rifle pits occupied by the enemy where it was approachable to ferry.

Question. Suppose the means of crossing the river provided, were the means of supplying the army such as to make it possible for the army to advance to the enemy's country?

No, sir; we were on half rations at the time and just drawing our rations from day to day. The country in that vicinity offered no supplies whatever, except a few cattle hid in the Cumberland Mountains, and the country east of us had been very thoroughly foraged by the enemy.

Question. Do you know what points in North Alabama and what line of road from there to Nashville were still occupied when you marched to Battle Creek?

I am not positive, but I think the Tennessee and Alabama Railroad was occupied. I think the bridge over Duck River was completed. The railroad from Stevenson to Murfreesborough was occupied. I am not certain whether the railroad from Huntsville to Stevenson was occupied or not. There was a small force there when I left the place.

Question. Do you know whether the abandonment of North Alabama and all points on the railroad leading from there were simultaneous with your movement; or was your movement independent of that, having in view the possession of that country and those lines?

That question I am not prepared to answer. One thing I will say: it was absolutely necessary to abandon that country, whether the enemy came to Middle Tennessee or Kentucky.

Question. Suppose it was my plan to hold Alabama and the line of road from there to Nashville, say Huntsville, Stevenson, and the road thence to Nashville, and supposing also I held McMinnville, please to state what was the importance of Altamont as a point of concentration or as a point through which the enemy could advance.

The enemy could have marched down to Murfreesborough or they could have marched directly on McMinnville. They had their option, if they held that place.

Question. Do you know anything of the character of Caney Creek, a stream which passes between McMinnville and Sparta?

I do not. I believe the country is rough, but nothing more.

Question. Did the interruption of the line of communication of the army with Louisville and the means which the enemy had of continuing that interruption make it necessary to them to throw at least a portion of the army into Kentucky independent of the presence of an enemy into Tennessee?

Absolutely necessary; and I was expecting and feared all the time that General Buell's army would have to abandon that country for supplies, if for nothing else.

NASHVILLE, *December* 11, 1862—10 a. m.

Commission met pursuant to adjournment. All the members present; also the judge-advocate and General Buell.

Examination of General McCOOK continued.

Cross-examination by General BUELL:

Question. Please state, from your observation, what you know of the practicability of maintaining the available part of the army at Altamont.

It was absolutely impossible to do it. I know of no place on the top of the Cumberland Mountains where a division of 10,000 men could have lived a week. I was stationed at Altamont myself till my animals ate up every available stack of fodder in reach of me on the mountain. When I left my position at Altamont all my supply of stock water was exhausted. We had but one spring, and that was up on a run, and the soldiers were clamoring about that run to get water for their canteens when I left there. There was a little water in a stream about 3½ miles from Altamont. The water was standing in pools, but was stagnant and not fit for use nor sufficient in quantity anywhere near. All supplies that possibly could reach that army would have had to be hauled from adjacent coves from 10 to 14 miles, and for anything like a supply you would have to go 20 miles, and nothing then could have been obtained but green blade fodder, and that would had to have been wagoned up the mountains over the worst roads I ever saw. It took my own division train, when I was traveling with reduced baggage, from 8 a. m. to 12 at night to pull up the mountains, and then only with the great assistance of my men. I had companies stationed along the road at distances of 100 yards apart to help the wagons up, and I think I had the reputation in the Army of the Ohio of having the best transportation in it, that is, the animals were in the best condition in it.

Question. Do you know any point at which an army concentrated could prevent an enemy from crossing the Cumberland Mountains into the plains of Tennessee?

No, sir; I do not know any point that could prevent them from crossing into the Tennessee Valley.

Question. What would you think of the plan of distributing the army which I commanded, say, from Decherd to Sparta, so as to guard the different passes by which an enemy could debouch into the plains of Tennessee?

I think it would have subjected the army to be whipped in detail, because the communication between Sparta and McMinnville is bad, and therefore it would have isolated the troops at Sparta, and therefore subjected them to capture or death. The troops at Pelham or McMinnville might have been concentrated in the rear somewhere.

Question. Supposing the stream which passes between McMinnville and Sparta and the character of the country between those points generally being such as to afford more than one or two practicable passes, would it or not be practicable for an enemy to cross from Pikeville to Sparta safely?

Yes, sir; I think it could be concentrated there.

(Army report, August 20, introduced by General Buell.

Question. Please examine the morning report for 20th August, here submitted for you, and state from it the actual available force that was operating against the army of General Bragg at that time.

The morning report of the divisions that were operating in front number as follows :

	Men.
General Schoepf, First Division	6,000
General McCook, Second Division	7,855
General Nelson, Fourth Division	6,888
General Crittenden, Fifth Division	3,377
General Wood, Sixth Division	5,640
McCook, Cavalry Brigade	640
Total	30,400

Question. With all the information you have obtained from first to last in regard to the strength of the rebel army under General Bragg, by information derived from spies and other information and by actual contact with that army, what credence would you attach to the statement that when it crossed the Cumberland Mountains it did not exceed 22,000 infantry and artillery?

Well, sir, I would not have believed it, and any man who would have come to me to give such information as that I would have suspected of treachery and would have been very apt to have taken charge of him. I knew who the division commanders were, and had the organization of the army, which proved to be correct.

Question. At what point on the march of Bragg's army from Sparta into Kentucky could it certainly have been known that Kentucky instead of Nashville was its destination?

I think when the enemy had arrived at Tomkinsville, Ky., for I was a little apprehensive that they were going to fall back and go in at Gallatin, Ky.

Question. What is the distance from Carthage and Gainesborough, the points at which the enemy crossed the Cumberland River, to Glasgow?

The distance from Gainesborough to Glasgow about 45 miles; from Carthage to Glasgow 50 miles.

Question. What is the distance from Nashville to Glasgow?

By Scottsville, about 85 miles; by Bowling Green, which is the best traveled road, 95 miles.

Question. Was it necessary for the army on the march from Nashville to go via Bowling Green?

It was absolutely necessary, because we were without supplies and we had a million of rations stored there in anticipation of the railroad being cut.

Question. Do you know when the rebel army reached Glasgow or when it marched from there?

I do not remember the precise date.

Question. Of what importance was Munfordville as a military post?

Munfordville was an important military post, because it guarded the bridge over Green River.

Question. Did it control the movements of an army from Glasgow going into Kentucky?

No, sir; because it was a better road to keep to the right.

Question. Its importance was then determined by the value of the bridge?

Yes, sir.

Question. How long would it take to rebuild that bridge?

With natural advantages, I should think it could be rebuilt in twelve days.

Question. Was it not actually rebuilt in less time?

I can't say positively as to that; I cannot answer that question.

Question. Would you have considered the object of the post at Mun-fordville of sufficient importance for a small garrison to attempt to hold it against a large army, under the circumstances, at the time?

Under the present circumstances I would not. No, sir; I would not.

Question. Supposing that I had had knowledge at the very moment of the crossing of the Cumberland River by the rebel army, would it have been possible for my army to have reached Glasgow as soon as the rebel army?

No, sir, it would not; not with a force sufficient to fight that army. No, sir, you could not have reached Glasgow.

Question. How much time do you suppose would have been lost in getting information of that movement after the enemy had crossed?

Well, sir, I could not give an estimate as to that. I can say that the first positive information that I had was from a note from General Wood at Edgefield Junction, on the morning General Buell arrived there, and this information was confirmed by a trusty preacher at Tyree Springs. I cannot fix the dates.

Question. When did you march for Bowling Green after that informa-tion was received?

I was ordered to march on the next morning at daylight, and I got off at 6 o'clock a. m. and made a long march; the delay was caused by General Buell changing my order of march. He required me then to place all my troops in front of my baggage trains and to be prepared for battle at any moment.

Question. Was it to be supposed that an army crossing the river at Carthage and designing to invade Kentucky might aim to strike first at Bowling Green?

Bowling Green was the first objective of the enemy when I left Nashville, and I had a conversation with General Buell on that subject, either in his quarters or on the road, in which he expressed a fear that they would get there in advance of him. My impression was that there was a million of rations stored there for our army and I was marching there to get my part of them, and if General Buell had not had Wood's and Rousseau's divisions there I believe the enemy would have gone in and taken possession of the fortifications.

Question. What was the immediate object when the army marched from Bowling Green?

To attack the enemy at Glasgow.

Question. Were the troops marched by certain roads with a view to that attack?

Yes, sir, they were; Rousseau's column was turned off to the right; I was furnished with a map and my route defined.

Question. When was it known at headquarters or in the army that the enemy had left Glasgow?

I first was satisfied of the fact at Dripping Springs, at the end of the first day's march.

Question. Where did you march the next day after the march to Dripping Springs?

The next day I marched to Prewitt's Knob.

Question. When there did you march from there for Munfordville?

I remained at Prewitt's Knob all next day and until 4 o'clock p. m. of the second day, two days, till I arrived within 1 mile of Munfordville from Bowling Green.

Question. Was there any point short of that at which the turnpike road comes into the Ohio River at the mouth of Salt River on which the army could depend for supplies after those which it had with it were exhausted?

No, sir; there was not.

Question. You have stated that the position at Munfordville was a very strong one for an army; now, taking into consideration all the circumstances, even with equal chances of success, would it have been desirable to attack the enemy at that point without necessity?

I have answered that question previously, that I was not in favor of attacking the enemy there. I do not think it would.

Question. Do you know of any intelligent man in the army who, with a knowledge of these circumstances, was in favor of attacking Bragg's army at Munfordville?

Not at that time; I never heard the matter discussed; I never talked with my equals in rank about the matter; I never suffered my juniors to criticise the commanding general's actions without hushing them up; that is, in my presence.

Question. Did you have occasion to silence the criticism of intelligent men on this subject?

I had occasion once to silence a colonel.

Question. Will you mention his name?

I should prefer not doing it unless compelled. It was Colonel Parrott, of the First Ohio Volunteers; Edward A. Parrott, I believe, is his name.

Question. Were you present at an assemblage of officers, or did you ever hear of an assemblage of officers, at which it was proposed to depose General Buell from the command of the army and to place General Thomas in command?

(Question objected to by judge-advocate.)

I never was present at any such meeting nor have I ever heard of it. It is information to me if it ever occurred.

Question. Is it a fact sufficiently notorious to be reasonably certain that the invasion of Kentucky by the force of General Bragg and Kirby Smith had for its object to seize the principal cities and hold the State?

I believe that was the intention. Kirby Smith's demonstrations in front of Cincinnati was a sufficient cause to make me think so, and with the anxiety expressed by the late General Nelson I was satisfied that Louisville was in great danger. I was not anxious about Louisville as much as Cincinnati, for I believed General Buell's army concentrated about Louisville could have whipped any given amount of men that could have been set up before them.

Question. In pursuing that object was it reasonable to suppose that the enemy counted the cost of it; that is, that he estimated the means of resistance he would have to meet?

I most certainly believe he did or he would have gone and taken the city.

Question. Was it to be supposed that he would abandon that object with a single partial engagement?

No, sir; I think it was the presence of General Buell's army in Kentucky that prevented him. I do not think that the repulse that the enemy got at Chaplin Hills, near Perryville, was sufficient to have driven him from the State.

Question. By what routes might the enemy have been expected to retreat from Kentucky if he had determined to retreat without further resistance ?

There were three roads left open for him. He could have gone off by Danville, Stanford, Mount Vernon, and Cumberland Gap, and could have gone the route through Stanford and Somerset, or he might have crossed the Kentucky River and escaped by Mount Sterling into Western Virginia.

Question. Did the concentration of the enemy at Harrodsburg, either previously or subsequently to the battle of Perryville indicate an intention to retreat from the State precipitately ?

It did not. The march to Harrodsburg did not indicate an abandonment of the State. My information led me to believe that they would fight at a place near Harrodsburg, and when they went to Camp Dick Robinson I confidently expected to have a fight there, their position being a very strong one.

Question. Supposing it had been assumed that the enemy designed to retreat after the battle of Perryville and that he designed to retreat by way of Cumberland Gap, please state what road or roads he must have taken from Camp Dick Robinson and what position an army should have taken to interrupt him.

Our army would either had to have gone via Crab Orchard to Mount Vernon to have intercepted him or the Lancaster route and to have cut them off on the Richmond route. I should have thought the army ought to have been near London.

Question. Suppose my army to have been directed on different points you have named, then, on the assumption that the enemy was retreating finally from the State, in what position would it have placed my line of communication, supposing the enemy to have been at Harrodsburg or in that region ?

It would have placed them in possession of the enemy.

Question. Did the enemy in moving from Harrodsburg go through Danville at all ?

No, sir; I don't think they did. I understand that a part of their cavalry did, but their army did not.

By General BUELL :

Question. General, will you please describe the character of the country bordering the Chaplin River, on both sides, north of Perryville, from there toward Harrodsburg, west of the Harrodsburg road, and of that region of country within a scope of, say, 10 miles west from the Harrodsburg road ?

The bed of Chaplin River is a very deep one. It was dry with the exception of water standing in pools. The country immediately north of Perryville was a rough one. All the country between the Mackville and Perryville road and the Harrodsburg and Perryville turnpike was rough. There were winding approaches down to the bed of the Chaplin River and approaches from the river which led toward the Harrodsburg pike. Between Perryville and Harrodsburg there was a very strong position for the enemy. The country is rugged and rough. I do not know of any good road that connects the Mackville and Perryville with the Harrodsburg road.

Question. Is it a country in which an army could operate conveniently or from which it could extricate itself if defeated ?

I do not think it is, because the road I marched on I consider a bad road, and the same character of country prevails till you get into the valley of the Salt River.

Question. Supposing an army giving battle in that position which the enemy occupied at Perryville and driven back on its left and compelled to fall back, what road would it be desirable for it to take; what would be the natural line of retreat ?

Their natural line of retreat would be by the Harrodsburg road.

Question. Suppose our army compelled to fall back by an attack on its left, by what roads could it have retreated?

By the Springfield road.

Question. Any other road?

Yes, sir; it might have fallen back on the Lebanon road.

Question. I contend there was no question as to the result of a contest between my army and the rebel army; but supposing the chances to have been equal, which risked most—the rebel army, by exposing itself to be driven from the Harrodsburg pike by an attack on its left, or my army, by supposing it to be driven from the Mackville road?

I think the rebel army would be the most exposed.

Question. Would not the rebel army have been driven into an impracticable country, in which it must have been destroyed?

Yes, sir; I do not think it could have existed there had it been driven into that rough country; that is, Chaplin Hills. It could not have existed there, I think.

Question. But suppose in such an attack the left of the rebel army had not been turned, by what roads could it then have retreated?

Harrodsburg and Danville.

Question. Do you think, then, it was judicious to endeavor to cut off the enemy from the Danville road by attacking its left strongly?

I think it would have been a good movement.

Question. What orders were given on the night of the 8th in reference to the movements of the enemy on the morning of the 9th; that is, was an attack ordered upon the enemy's position?

On the night of the 8th of October I was at General Buell's headquarters about 12 or 1 o'clock. I met General Thomas there. I understood there was to be an attack in the morning. General Buell asked me the question if I would be ready to attack. I replied that my men were very weary and exhausted, but that we could go to work, and I understood that an attack was to be made from an order given to General Thomas. I did not see General Gilbert there, who commanded the other corps. I was very tired at the time myself and very sleepy. I had slept but very little the night before—about an hour.

Question. What part were you to take in the operations of the following day?

I was to act as a reserve.

Question. At what hour was the attack to be made?

At 6 o'clock in the morning.

Question. When the advance the following morning discovered that the enemy had retired, what position was your corps to take?

My corps was to take a position, the left resting on the Dicksville road or near it, to join on to Gilbert's left.

Question. Can you state where that was to have been?

No, sir. I know nothing about it. I went forward and selected my own position and found out where his left was—the other side of Chaplin River.

Question. Did you take that position the next day?

That is a point in my mind which I do not exactly remember. I think it was the second day, on the morning of the 9th, General Gay made a reconnaissance in my front, the order for which I gave the judge-advocate.

Question. Do you remember anything that prevented you from taking that position?

Nothing prevented me from moving. I think it was late on that day we moved. I recollect posting my troops there and of going to ascertain the locality, but could not find General Gilbert, but I found General Mitchell, who was then on the left of General Gilbert's corps, and my troops and Rousseau's division joined on with Mitchell's.

Question. You have spoken in your direct evidence of a road which you call the Dicksville and Springfield road; where does that road come into the Perryville and Springfield road?

I do not know the exact point on the road. There are a great many lines leading back and forth, but my impression is that it comes out near the road where there is a hospital. A man named Bottom lives there, but I cannot state the exact point, because the fences were considerably torn down, and I always rode in a direct direction.

Question. Was the country between the Perryville and Mackville road and the Perryville and Springfield road more practicable than the country bordering on Chaplin River?

Yes; it was. It was a country over which we could have moved.

Question. Did the movement which you proposed to make on the night of the 8th actually take place while you were at my headquarters?

It actually took place when I was at your headquarters and while I was on my way back.

Question. Did you not think that perhaps what you considered my refusal to give you an additional force referred to the disposition of the troops for the following day?

I did not understand it so.

Question. If that movement was actually being made while you were requesting troops, what would have been the necessity for troops or could they have been on the ground in time?

Yes, sir. I dispatched an aide-de-camp from your headquarters.

By the PRESIDENT:

Question. I understand, then, that the movement was executed by your orders?

Yes, sir.

By General BUELL:

Question. Did the result prove that the additional forces were neces sary?

No, sir; because the enemy retreated.

Question. You have stated that I directed you to retreat by a certain road. Did you understand that I spoke of the retreat of the army or of your portion of it?

Only of my corps, if I was compelled to fall back on the Springfield road. I had no idea that the other portion of the army were going to fall back.

Question. Were you during the march from Louisville to Perryville kept in constant communication with the rest of the army and my headquarters?

Yes, sir; as constantly as it was possible to be. I dispatched couriers, who usually found you at your headquarters. On several occasions you wrote to me to have couriers at your headquarters, but I believe that every available and efficient order you gave reached me. My orderlies, when I directed them to your headquarters, would go to where they believed you were. Once they missed your headquarters when I was at Bloomfield.

Question. Do you know on what day of the week or month you arrived at Bowling Green with your division?

I recollect it was Sunday morning that I arrived within 3 miles of Bowling Green, but cannot state the day of the month

Question. Would it have been possible to march your corps from Nashville to Glasgow by the time it reached Bowling Green?

No, sir; we could not have done it.

Question. If the surrender of Munfordville actually took place on the Monday following your arrival at Bowling Green, would it have been possible, if you started from Nashville at the time you did, to reach Munfordville in time to prevent that surrender?

Yes, sir; I think it could.

Question. How many days elapsed from the date of your departure from Nashville and the Monday on which the surrender of Munfordville took place?

We arrived within 4 miles of Bowling Green Sunday morning, 6 o'clock. We marched 12 miles that morning.

Question. Could you have marched from Bowling Green, after having marched 12 miles on Sunday morning, and reached Munfordville in time to prevent the surrender of that place on Monday?

The JUDGE-ADVOCATE. Was it not on Wednesday? That is my recollection of it.

(Conversation between judge-advocate and General McCook, in which it was said that the latter day was correct.)

Question. Was it supposed that the enemy was at Glasgow when you arrived at Bowling Green?

Yes, sir; that was my impression from all I could pick up.

Question. Supposing you had marched by forced marches to the rescue of Munfordville with the rebel army at Glasgow, would you have exposed your re-enforcements to a flank attack from Glasgow?

Yes, sir; we should have had to march together and be prepared for battle.

Question. Could you then, under the circumstances, have made that distance with the rapidity which was necessary in order to reach Munfordville to rescue that place in presence of the rebel army?

My answer to that question is, no.

Question. Which would have been the most judicious determination, supposing it were possible to march by the rebel army at Glasgow, to make that march and leave the rebel army at liberty to fall in upon your rear, occupying Bowling Green, and so cutting off communication eventually between Nashville and Louisville, or even to have sacrificed Munfordville for the purpose of keeping the rebel army in advance and driving it into a position where it could have been operated against by greatly superior forces; which would you have selected?

I would have preferred the latter movement. The former certainly would not have allowed the army to come in on the rear, because had they got possession of Bowling Green it would have been a vital point. Nashville would necessarily have fallen, and they could have done it had we passed them at Glasgow.

Question. Did the rebel army make any stand after it left Munfordville until it arrived at Bardstown?

Not to my knowledge. I heard they had been drawn up in line of battle at Hodgensville for a fight, but I do not know it from my own knowledge.

Question. Did you understand that the whole army halted at Hodgensville?

No, sir; only the rear guard.

Question. Is it probable that that rear guard would have withstood the advance of my army?

I am very well satisfied they would not.

Question. Then would anything have been gained by turning off from the road which we were pursuing with an object?

No, sir; I do not see how you could have turned off for want of supplies.

Question. Was there anything in the nature of the country or the relative position of the forces that would have prevented the junction of Bragg's forces with those of Kirby Smith at Bardstown had they desired?

No, sir.

Question. Would it have been in the option of Bragg to give battle at Bardstown or avoid it for the purpose of forming such a junction?

Yes, sir.

Question. Was there anything in the position of our forces and the rebel forces to have prevented that junction from being formed at an earlier day had they desired?

No, sir; my impression was that that was what General Bragg was running for.

Redirect examination by the JUDGE-ADVOCATE:

Question. General, you stated in your examination in chief that the number of General Buell's army at the time of Bragg's invasion was 45,000?

I think about that number.

Question. You now state it to be about 34,500. Will you please state where the difference is?

The difference in that estimate existed in Rousseau's army, which was down in Alabama, and the troops in Nashville and adjoining that were guarding the communications of the army.

Question. At what date was the entire force of 45,000 available?

If the army had been concentrated at Nashville.

Question. You have stated that the army under Bragg numbered 60,000 or 70,000. Upon what did you base your calculations?

I did not state positively, but it was from the most reliable information that could be obtained from scouts.

Question. Can you give the name of any reliable scout from whom you received information and what that information was?

My scouts generally placed it at a higher figure. I would deduct a certain per cent. from their reports. One of my most reliable scouts was named Kennedy.

Question. What number of regiments did he give as moving from Chattanooga under Bragg?

He reported about seventy regiments. But from Newton, whom I sent to obtain information on the East Tennessee Railroad and to count every car load of soldiers that went up and down that road—and his estimate was that there were seventy-one regiments.

Question. How did the number of these regiments run?

He could not form any estimate of that. I was under the impression that the old regiments were much reduced in number, but their conscription had gone on, and I could not form any estimate of their number; they greatly varied.

Question. Has not experience taught you that if scouts and deserters state the number to be 60,000 or 70,000 it is probably half that number?

It is a natural impression; but I was satisfied that Bragg had the Corinth army with him, with a few detachments under Breckinridge.

Question. You proposed attacking the enemy at Glasgow. Did you suppose they had 60,000 or 70,000 men?

I did not suppose they had 60,000 men at Glasgow, but I naturally supposed that in the face of General Buell's army, of which the Confederates knew, they would not attempt to invade Kentucky except with a very large force.

Question. Was not your calculation and that of the officers generally based upon that fact—that he would not dare to invade Kentucky with that number?

I think not. My impression was that Bragg had crossed with seventy regiments and that Withers had crossed with larger forces.

Question. Do you remember saying to Lew. Campbell, of Ohio, at Bowling Green, that there were only 25,000 ragged rascals, and that you thought it time to go and whip them?

I think I never made such a remark.

Question. Is your recollection of that impression such as would justify such a remark?

It is not. With different people coming in with different stories the matter was discussed, but I never believed their army was as small as that.

Question. You say that you were impressed with the belief that Bragg would not invade Kentucky in the face of General Buell's army, and that he would not undertake it with less than 60,000 or 70,000 men?

That is my impression at that time.

Question. If General Bragg anticipated an uprising in Kentucky and assistance from Kirby Smith in that quarter, would it not have been more available for him to have taken 30,000 rather than 60,000 or 70,000; that is, in reference to his supplies?

Of course it would. He could then have moved with more celerity.

Question. If the enemy's number was as your estimate makes it, how do you account for the evacuation of so strong a place as Munfordville at your approach?

I do not know what the objects of the enemy were at that time. I merely formed my opinion from information gained since; but at that time I thought certainly that the enemy had as many men as General Buell had, and it was want of rations on their part that took them from Munfordville.

Question. In that connection can you account for the fact that an army of that size, after forming a junction with Kirby Smith, declined to fight at Harrodsburg or at Dick Robinson?

That is something I cannot understand why they did not fight there, where I expected them to fight; I cannot account for it; but General Buell's army was much increased in strength, and they may have known that we outnumbered them. I believe that with all the re-enforcements they got in Kentucky our army outnumbered them.

Question. What is your estimate, from all the information you obtained, of Kirby Smith's forces?

Including his entire force I think Kirby Smith had about 20,000 men, including the re-enforcements he got in Kentucky. I got that testimony from people in front of Cincinnati. I think he got about a thousand in Kentucky.

Question. At the time we occupied Munfordville after the enemy left do you know where Kirby Smith's army was?

We thought it was in front of Cincinnati or before Lexington or Franklin.

Question. You stated in your examination that Cincinnati was threatened, and not Louisville, by Kirby Smith?

By Smith, but not by the entire force. I do not know what there was in front of Cincinnati but raw recruits. I do not see why he did not take it.

Question. You said in your examination in chief that while encamp'd at Hubbard's Cove General Buell gave you his plan of operation.

His plan of concentration.

Question. What is the date of that, when he gave you a synoposis?

I think, sir, it was on the last day of August. I recollect I was about to move down to Altamont on the 1st, and I had already done it on the last day, if I remember, anticipating the order.

Commission adjourned to meet December 12, at 10 a. m.

NASHVILLE, *December* 12, 1862—10 a. m.

Commission met pursuant to adjournment. All the members present; also the judge-advocate and General Buell.

Examination of General McCook continued.

By the JUDGE-ADVOCATE:

Question. General McCook, the plan furnished you at Battle Creek had reference to the invasion of General Bragg, and that invasion must therefore have been known to General Buell in the latter part of August. Is this so?

I think the intention of General Bragg was known. We could of course only approximate to his intention. The army was concentrated at Chattanooga, and I think they intended to advance upon Nashville and go into Middle Tennessee. There was a letter found by my pickets, which led me to believe this, written by one Isham Harris, of this State, which proposed to give a synopsis of the plans of Bragg, that he intended to have his beloved capital, as he called it.

Question. Have you possession of it?

I have not. I gave it to General Buell. The plan proposed was not carried out, but I know that a portion came true; that is, in the posting of two brigades, which he said he had succeeded in getting to Chattanooga. In this letter it indicated that General Bragg would cross the army somewhere in the vicinity of Florence or Tuscumbia. The letter might have been a catch, but I think from everything it was original. As soon as it was found its contents were telegraphed to General Buell. Of course the army was not intended to remain at Chattanooga, but as soon as their army would be concentrated an attempt would be made, because at that time General Buell's forces were very much scattered along the road and through the country, and they proposed to break through the line before he could concentrate. That was expressed in the letter. I suppose General Buell was aware that they would, if possible, attempt to come into Tennessee. The letter was found about the 8th or 10th of August.

Question. Can you fix the date at which Bragg's army crossed the Tennessee and how long after that event it came to your knowledge?

I was satisfied that he had crossed the Tennessee River on the day that I halted in the Sequatchie Valley. It was somewhere between the 10th and 20th.

Question. At what point did General Buell's plan contemplate concentrating his forces to resist the invasion of General Bragg?

The point was not indicated to me. He was either to attack the enemy as he debouched into the valley or as he descended into the valley of Middle Tennessee. There was a condition in the plan, as I understood it.

Question. In that connection you say that a lack of supplies prevented that plan being caried out. Did this alone prevent the plan from being successful?

That was my impression. I was daily expecting an order to fall back on account of supplies. I just fed my men from day to day. I did expect that General Buell's army would be compelled to fall back from the position it occupied there for the purpose of supplies, if for nothing else. Every general knew how his troops had to suffer marching through that country, with little water and half rations.

Question. Could an army of 60,000 or 70,000 men, marching rapidly through Tennessee by way of Dunlap, Pikeville, Sparta, Carthage, and Munfordville, have subsisted upon the country along the route?

With the supplies they had concentrated at Chattanooga, the amount of transportation, and the manner they supplied their army I think they could. Every farmer who had an ounce of bread or bacon to spare hauled it as the army passed by. The rebels never carried an ounce of provisions, but the people fed them. And the people gave all they got to the last pound. They had a large train also. They made forced and rapid marches, but suffered a great deal.

Question. Could you give the Commission any idea of what proportion of supplies could be relied on in that way with that army of 60,000 or 70,000 men?

That would depend upon the nature of the inhabitants and of the country we marched through. I think half rations could have been procured for them.

The PRESIDENT. Am I to understand that Bragg's army amounted to 60,000 or 70,000 men?

No, sir; that was the impression I had when they crossed at Chattanooga.

By the JUDGE-ADVOCATE:

Question. You are acquainted with the works and strength of Munfordville. What force would have been sufficient to hold that place against Bragg's army?

Munfordville is a position that could not be turned very easily. I should think that one-half the number could have held the place against Bragg's army. The advantages of defense would have been one-half.

Question. Had Bragg made a stand at Munfordville could you have avoided fighting him there?

Not without his taking Bowling Green. Our hope was to fight him there and let him go. I consider Bowling Green a more important point than Nashville.

Question. Had he defeated you at Munfordville would it not have been the total destruction of your army and the loss of Kentucky?

Yes, sir; if the army had been pursued with the vigor I thought he would have shown.

Question. After the hurried retreat would not intelligent officers in the army have estimated their strength at 60,000 or 70,000?

I do not think so. When they left Munfordville my estimate was about 35,000 to 40,000. Dr. Gardner said, "They have as many troops as you have." He is a man of good judgment and fine reputation as a surgeon and a man that is not liable to be stampeded under any circumstances.

Question. At Munfordville for the first time you came to the knowledge of the fact that you had overestimated Bragg's army?

Yes, sir; the difficulty, too, of getting information in the country was so great that if the army had proved to be 10,000 or 15,000 larger or smaller either way it would not have surprised me.

Question. With Munfordville secured and Bowling Green in our possession what would have prevented General Buell throwing his army into the rear and cutting off supplies?

He would only have to go and find the enemy and whip them wherever he found them.

Question. Then he would not have marched to Louisville?

I think not.   General Buell had an army that could not be whipped.

Question. With an army under the command of Bragg less in number than that under General Buell, with a large force at Louisville, can you understand why Bragg was in no hurry to form a junction with Kirby Smith?

If I knew exactly the extent of Bragg's knowledge about our army and position I could understand it; not without.

Question. Was it possible that Bragg threw his army so boldly into Kentucky without knowing the number of the army in his rear?

That I do not know. Speculations can be made, and when the facts are known opinions can be formed; but I think Bragg was pretty well posted. His means of information were excellent.   I think it was a part of his plans that Price should come up to Tennessee, but he ran against Rosecrans at Iuka. That is what he should have done, but running against Rosecrans prevented it.

Question. Are the names of the rebel officers of General Bragg's captured at Prewitt's Knob known to you, and what time after they were captured were they released?

I know nothing of that circumstance but what I heard. One of them was named Forsyth, of Georgia. When they went or upon what conditions they were released. I do not know.

Question. I understand you now to say that after the Munfordville affair you came to a better knowledge of the number of Bragg's army and that it numbered 30,000 or 35,000?

I did not say it was 30,000 or 35,000. I got my impression from Dr. Gardner. My conclusion was that Bragg had crossed with 35,000 or 40,000.

Question. You estimated Kirby Smith's army, from all the information you could get, at about 20,000?

I so thought.

Question. Do you say that Kirby Smith and Bragg formed a junction at Harrodsburg?

I think they did. They could have done so and should have done so.

Question. Did not their refusal to meet you at a strong position at Harrodsburg and declining to fight you at Dick Robinson and making a hurried retreat from Kentucky satisfy you that you had overestimated their number there as you had at Munfordville?

No, sir; I have no reason to change it. I think they had about 60,000 men.

By General TYLER:

Question. You say there were a million of rations at Bowling Green; how long would they have lasted your army?

I say I was so informed, but the fact did not exist. I simply said I believed so; now I know there was not.

Question. Has any information come to you since yesterday?

No, sir; I will simply state facts I know. I was informed there was a million of rations of bread at Munfordville, but I do not think there was a million there, for when my commissary went in for bread he could not get it.

Question. Were there any Union forces except General Buell's which could by any possibility have relieved Munfordville?

I do not see why it should not have been relieved from Louisville.

Question. Do you know whether the army was massed at Bowling Green on Sunday morning when you arrived there?

Rousseau's and Wood's divisions were there; Colonel McCook in command of cavalry. My own division arrived at 6. Crittenden's division was there, encamped in the same place. On Monday the Fourth Division was there. Mitchell was 15 miles in the rear, got up on Monday; and Thomas' division, I understood General Buell to say, had been ordered from Nashville up to Bowling Green. General Thomas was a man I had great confidence in, and in battle I wanted to have him on the same line with me, and I was anxious for him to come up.

Question. How far is Bowling Green from Munfordville?

Forty miles.

Question. Had you forces enough massed at Bowling Green Sunday morning to have relieved Munfordville Wednesday morning?

On the flank of the enemy we had forces enough, but I do not think in the presence of the enemy we could have got there. It would have made 20 miles a day, which is rapid marching even for small detachments; but I do not think we could have got our army there in time.

By General ORD:

Question. Could troops have come from Louisville quicker than you could have sent them from Bowling Green?

They could have come from Louisville in five hours. It is about 70 miles from Munfordville to Louisville. Had they come 10 miles an hour, it would take them about seven hours. They had the telegraph, too, when we had to send through the enemy's country by courier.

Question. Did you have any information that Munfordville was beleaguered by an overwhelming force?

I knew on Monday morning and heard it was taken, and got on my horse and rode to General Buell's headquarters, and there heard that the attack on Munfordville had been repulsed, and there I learned that Colonel Wilder was in command. Previously I do not know who was there.

Question. You did not know then it required relief?

I knew Bragg was at Glasgow, 20 miles and 40 miles from there. It was therefore supposed that if Bragg could not take it with one brigade he would send more.

Question. Any applications from Munfordville for relief?

None that I ever heard of. I was present at General Buell's headquarters at Dripping Springs when a man named Miller said Munfordville had surrendered.

By the PRESIDENT:

Question. Do you know if there was any communication between the officer in command at Louisville, or General Wright, commanding the department, and General Buell?

I knew nothing of it at all if there was. It was beyond my sphere of knowledge, and it was something which I don't think General Buell's division commanders knew anything about. They had their lines marked out for them, and they generally marched on them and asked no questions.

Question. Do you know whether communication of that kind was possible at that time?

I think communication was possible. It could have been sent by telegraph to Munfordville and from thence worked around through the bushes. It is therefore possible.

Question. Have you information which will enable you to answer whether there was any co-operation between General Wright and General Buell?

I never knew anything at all about it. I used to inquire about my friend Nelson. I was delighted when I heard he had recovered from his wound; but I knew nothing but that General Nelson was in command and had 100,000 men. That was the news we got. General Buell never told me anything about it. I did not have an hour's conversation with General Buell from the time we left Dripping Springs till we got to Louisville.

By General BUELL:

Question. The judge-advocate has inquired whether if Munfordville had been made secure I could not have thrown my army upon the line of communication of the enemy. I should like you to state if Bragg had any line of communication on which his safety depended.

I do not think he had. General Buell would then have been free to have marched after Bragg as long as rations lasted.

Question. In order that that should have been the case, would it not have been necessary that Louisville should be secured?

Yes, sir; I think Louisville was the most important place; it was our base of supplies.

Question. How many divisions were yet in the rear when you arrived at Louisville?

Thomas' and Mitchell's divisions were in the rear.

General SCHOEPF. What do you know of the dissatisfaction of the officers and men and the petition sent with respect to the removal of General Buell after the battle of Perryville?

I was informed while on the march from Danville to Lebanon that there was such a paper in existence in General Gilbert's corps. Who was the originator of it I do not know. I never saw the paper. The first development of this feeling of dissatisfaction I discovered on the march from Nashville to Louisville. They complained of being marched to death and of being half fed. Another cause of this dissatisfaction was that General Buell was always very much engaged in his quarters and did not go around among his soldiers much. I have frequently felt that had he visited his camps more, reviewed his troops more, and shown himself more to his soldiers a different state of feeling would have existed. I always had confidence in General Buell as a general, and, thank God, I have yet.

By General BUELL:

Question. Do you know the names of the signers of the paper referred to?

I had a conversation with one of them outside the door here a few moments ago. I asked him about it, as to whether he ever heard of such a meeting of officers in the army wishing to depose General Buell and put General Thomas in command, and in this conversation with General Steedman he said he had signed a paper and had presided at a meeting of officers requesting the President to remove General Buell. I think General Steedman has confidence in General Buell, but was influenced by the junior officers and men in his command.

Question. Where was that meeting held?

I did not know, but somewhere on the Rolling Fork. I knew nothing for certain, but believe it was so. It was subsequent to the battle of Perryville; but their feeling was more particularly directed against General Gilbert.

Question. Did the paper state any reason?

I never saw the paper. It was merely mentioned on the way down, but it was by officers I had no control over. I knew of no other officers that signed it. General Steedman said it was a respectful petition to the President of the United States. He thought it the most direct road to the President.

Question. Did you ever hear of any similar proceedings on the part of officers of General Thomas' division, particularly in reference to their commanders?

Yes, sir; I did. Once, in front of Corinth, T. W. Sherman was put in command of General Thomas' division, which produced great dissatisfaction in the division, and the officers of the brigade and the colonels petitioned to have him removed. I know they were very much dissatisfied. They complained of his manner more than of his want of ability.

Question. Did you ever know of any other case?

Not that I recollect; that was the only instance.

Question. Was that division under my command at the time?

No, sir; it was assigned to the army of General Grant. I was requested by my deceased brother, General Robert [L.] McCook, to see General Buell and see if the change could be made; that the men were so angry with him that he might meet with violence from their hands. I spoke to General Buell about it, and it was one of his best divisions, and I know he as well as myself was much interested in their welfare.

Question. Do you know whether General Steedman's division was affected by the assignment of General Gilbert according to his supposed rank at that time?

Yes, sir; General Steedman ranks General Gilbert.

General SCHOEPF. Could it be known to General Steedman at the time that he was not a brigadier-general?

I believe Gilbert never had a commission as a major-general.

General BUELL. Has there been anything in the active operation of my troops, and in their scattered condition for a considerable time, that would have interfered with as frequent inspection of them as might otherwise have been made?

My answer to that is, yes.

By General BUELL:

Question. Did you have any doubt that Bragg would concentrate his forces at Harrodsburg for battle after the battle of the 8th?

I believed he would concentrate.

Question. What did you suppose his whole force would amount to?

At that time I had no positive way of ascertaining what his forces were, but I believe they would amount to about 55,000 men.

Question. Did you know the strength of our army after the battle of the 8th?

I did not, sir, except as far as my own forces were concerned.

Question. Did you know that the absent division of your corps was on the march to join you?

Yes, sir; I did.

Question. Was there anything on the retreat of the rebel forces from Perryville which indicated that the retreat was a disorderly one?

Not by the indications of their march. There was nothing left upon the road except what they could not carry away—gun-carriages and guns that were taken in battle—for they cut up the carriages and left them.

Question. Supposing that there was a reasonable probability that the enemy would give battle at Harrodsburg with a force not much, if any, inferior to your own and that you were in expectation of re-enforcements in a very short time, would it be considered judicious to wait for these re-enforcements to join or would you have considered the result of the battle so absolutely certain as to make it advisable to attack with what you had?

Yes, sir; I believe that the army we had there could have whipped them. That was my impression then and is my impression yet.

Question. Do you think it would necessarily have been so had the forces been nearly equal, considering the advantages the enemy would have in choice of position and the position being strong at Harrods-burg?

There would, of course, be a doubt about the matter. We had pursued Bragg a long distance, and if we could catch up with him I thought it would be the best policy.

Question. Did you consider the troops of which our army was composed at Perryville superior to the troops of the rebel army?

I believe the old troops I had were superior to the troops of the rebel army; my new troops were vastly inferior.

Question. What proportion of the whole army was composed of new troops?

There was one regiment of new troops to each brigade, and Jackson's division, consisting of two brigades, were all new troops. I suppose the army marching from Louisville was about 80,000 men.

Question. Supposing, then, that the two armies had been nearly equal and the advantages of position on the part of the enemy and that you were expecting re-enforcements, would it have been advisable to seek a battle under such circumstances?

If the armies had been nearly equal I would prefer to have waited. I will state that I never knew what the strength of our forces was on the advance till I saw General Buell's official report to-day, and I will say that they were much less than I thought they were. I was surprised and amazed to see it.

Question. Supposing the army after the battle of Perryville had taken position at Danville, would that necessarily have prevented the escape of the rebel army?

No, sir; they would have gone farther up the road; they would go out by Richmond.

Question. How far is Danville from the road which leads from Camp Dick Robinson to Lancaster?

Danville is about 8 miles from Camp Dick Robinson, and that is the nearest town on the road from Camp Dick Robinson to Lancaster; but Dick's River is the obstacle.

Question. Give the character of Dick's River.

Dick's River has precipitous bluffs and can be crossed only in one place.

Question. Would the occupation of Danville have prevented the enemy from retreating from Camp Dick Robinson by that road?

I think that the occupation of Danville would not, but we would have been in a position where the enemy could have been cut off from Lancaster. We should have been marching on his flank all the time had he attempted to move, but the enemy could not be reached on account of Dick's River till it was crossed, and we might have arrived simultaneously at Lancaster had we started at the same time.

Question. With such a stream as Dick's River between the armies would he have been in great danger?

Not in great danger till Dick's River was crossed by our army.

Question. Was it certain that the enemy would take a position at Camp Dick Robinson?

I thought so, but the thing was not developed till we left Harrodsburg.

Question. After it was ascertained that the enemy had gone to Camp Dick Robinson do you say that Danville was a proper position for our army to take?

Certainly it was. It was the only position left.

By General TYLER :

Question. You do not mean to say, general, that their army, man for man, was superior to ours?

The material of our army is as good or superior to that of the rebel.

Commission adjourned to meet on December 13, 1862, at 10 a. m.

NASHVILLE, *December* 13, 1862--10 a. m.

The Commission met pursuant to adjournment. All the members present; also the judge-advocate and General Buell.

Colonel SHOEMAKER (a witness for the Government), having been duly sworn by the judge-advocate, testified as follows :

By the JUDGE-ADVOCATE :

Question. What is your position in the service of the United States?

Colonel, commanding the Thirteenth Michigan Volunteers.

Question. State, if you please, to the court what you know of General Bragg crossing the Cumberland River at the point they crossed and all about it.

I was at Hartsville, at Dixon's Springs, on the night of the 8th of September; left there on the morning of the 9th; passed through Carthage; crossed the Cumberland River at that point; saw Generals Bragg and Hardee on the south bank of the Cumberland on the afternoon of the 9th; saw a portion of the army of General Bragg on the south side of the Cumberland on that day.

Question. What were they doing, colonel?

They were mostly bivouacking. I saw some marching. It was toward evening I saw most of them, and they had apparently just gone into camp; many of them were moving. I saw many of them next day, many troops and wagons, and I saw scattering parties through to Sparta, but no body of forces. I also saw at Dixon's Springs some cavalry, said to be the advance of General Cheatham.

Question. I propose, Mr. President, to ask a question over which we have had some discussion, and which I presume General Buell will again object to. What do you know of the size of the invading army at that point, as gathered from your own observation and what the rebel officers informed you?

General BUELL. I object to that portion of the question which proposes to take as evidence the statements of the officers of General Bragg's army in regard to its strength.

General Buell and Colonel Shoemaker retired, during which the Commission unanimously—

Resolved, While the Commission is not disposed to deny the position of General Buell as to the inadmissibility of purely hearsay evidence on a trial of an accused party it will not sustain the objection now offered, but will place the answers of the witness on its record and be governed in its opinions according to the weight which collateral testimony may give to such answers.

Colonel SHOEMAKER. I saw what I judged to be a division of General Bragg's army on the road as we were passing along.

General TYLER. Can you locate them?

They were within 6 miles of the river, on the south side of the Cumberland River. I also saw some cavalry at Dixon's Springs on the morning of the 9th of September, commanded by General Wheeler, and said to be the advance of General Cheatham's portion of the army.

The JUDGE-ADVOCATE. What is your opinion as to the size of that army?

General BUELL. That is, "what he heard."

Colonel SHOEMAKER. I formed the opinion at the time that the army of General Bragg did not exceed 30,000 men, and what I saw there and at Knoxville confirmed me in the opinion.

By the PRESIDENT:

Question. Just state what that was from which you formed your opinion.

It was from conversation with officers of the army and what I saw myself. I can state generally what I heard from the officers. General Cheatham was crossing with his force in the neighborhood of Hartsville, General Bragg at Carthage, General Polk at the town of Gainesborough, and from what I could learn I judged there were about 20,000 men. There was a great expectation among all the officers that there would be a general rising in Kentucky, and their hopes were based on that supposition. I saw General McCown. He stated to me that he had already shipped some 3,000 (I am not positive as to the number) of arms for the recruits raised by Morgan, and he thought they would be required to raise arms for 20,000.

Question. I would like to have this question answered if possible: State what you saw, colonel, that confirmed your opinion, formed from the statement of those officers, and who the officers were.

The officer with whom I had the most conversation was Lieutenant Kuhn. He was of the body guard of Bragg, and commanded the protection that went with me to Knoxville.

Question. What other officers do you recollect?

Major Scott and Lieutenant-Colonel Anderson. There were a number of officers that I talked with whose names I do not know. I saw General Bragg, and he said nothing to me nor I to him relative to the strength of forces on either side, but he refused to parole me, giving as his reason that I had seen too much—but I had seen but little—and he refused to parole me on that account rather than because I had seen more. It was my desire to be paroled, but he paroled me to go to Knoxville.

Question. What were the facts, from your own personal observation, that you saw to confirm any opinion of that kind?

I was taken prisoner on Sunday evening, and was till next Monday at noon going through and at Knoxville, and my opinion was made up from what I saw and heard generally. I do not know any more particular points that I could state.

Cross-examination by General BUELL:

Question. Did the opinion which you formed then from observation and hearsay agree with the opinion you had previously formed of the rebel army?

I think it did.

Question. Did I understand when you left Nashville you estimated the rebel army under Bragg to be 30,000 and no more?

That was my opinion. I do not know that I placed it particularly at 30,000 and that that opinion was formed at Nashville, but my opinion of the strength of General Bragg's army was not much changed by what I saw and heard.

Question. Your opinion of the strength of Bragg's army continued the same?

Yes.

Question. Do you know how many divisions there were in Bragg's army?

I do not.

Question. Do you know the organization of the divisions?

I do not. I know nothing further than what I stated in my direct examination.

Question. Did you count the number of men in any regiment?

I did not.

Question. Did you by actual observation make an estimate of the strength of any regiment?

No, sir; I did not. I saw a body of troops in camp bivouacked, and as we passed them estimated, as I naturally would, what the number there might be. I supposed there would be, as I stated before, a division. I passed directly through and took no particular account of them.

Question. Either of the number of men or regiments?

Neither.

Question. Did you think it a large division or a small one?

Rather a small one.

Question. What number of men do you suppose there were in that body of troops?

I should estimate them at from 6,000 to 8,000.

Question. Why do you suppose it to be such a body of troops as we call a division?

From the number of men and the extent of ground they occupied.

Question. Might it not have been more or less?

I think it might have been less, but I don't think it could have been more.

Question. State definitely, if you please, colonel, the conversation you had with those rebel officers which gave you this opinion in regard to their strength.

I do not know that I can do so. The opinion I was asked to give was formed from conversations I had at different times; but without impressing any particular conversation upon my mind I can only give the conclusions I arrived at. The particular conversation held with any particular officer I could not state. But I rode with that lieutenant to whom I have referred five days. He was the only commissioned officer of the body guard, but he was a very pleasant gentleman and appeared to be sociable, and we talked a great deal in relation to the war; but it would be impossible to give definitely the conversation with him or any other officer. My opinion was based upon conversations generally and my own observations.

Question. In any of these conversations was it stated definitely or approximately that the army of General Bragg was about 30,000 strong?

I do not know that I could state positively at what figure any particular officer placed that army. I recollect a conversation in reference to the battle of Shiloh, in which this question was brought up, that we had overestimated the strength of their army in our battles; that we had overestimated their men at Shiloh, at which they said they had but 28,000 men, and that a great many overestimated the number of men in General Bragg's army, but what was the exact number they stated I could not say. I arrived at that opinion as the general result of the conversations I had with the different officers, and perhaps without basing it upon any fixed number that any officer might have stated.

Question. I understand you to say that the officers from whom you derived your opinion in regard to the strength of Bragg's army represented the strength of the rebel army at Shiloh at 28,000?

One officer with whom I conversed made such a statement.

Question. In making this estimate, then, you had no method of computation as to the number of regiments and divisions and the strength of regiments in arriving at your conclusion?

Not at all. I knew nothing of the exact number of regiments or divisions, but it was a general conclusion I arrived at from different sources of information.

Question. Is it probable that an officer, an intelligent officer, in the rebel service would give you a correct impression as to the strength of the rebel army when that was the subject of conversation?

Ordinarily I should say not, but I was a prisoner and going south, and they conversed with perhaps a little more freedom than they would have done under other circumstances.

Question. They might possibly have overestimated or underestimated?

Yes, sir.

Question. Upon what data had you previously arrived at the conclusion that the rebel army under General Bragg was not more than 60,000 strong?

I was stationed at Stevenson, Ala., up to, I think, the 30th of August, and of course it was a subject very much discussed there and upon the march to Nashville. I had formed that opinion from no particular facts perhaps, but as every officer in the Army forms an opinion in relation to the movements of his own army or that of the enemy. But there was no precise knowledge that led me to know what their precise forces were. It was a mere matter of opinion, and formed from such general information as I was likely to obtain from my position in the Army.

NASHVILLE, *December* 13, 1862.

General J. B. STEEDMAN (a witness for the Government), having been duly sworn, testified as follows:

By the JUDGE-ADVOCATE:

Question. State, if you please, your position in the United States Army.

I am brigadier-general.

Question. State whether you were in the service under General Buell when the army moved up in pursuit of Bragg in the invasion of Kentucky.

I was.

Question. Will you state, if you please, to the Commission what estimate the intelligent officers of the army placed upon the number of Bragg's army in the march from Nashville to Munfordville?

General BUELL. This amounts to nothing more than collecting the rumors of the camp; it is no evidence whatever. The answer to such a question can be of no value as evidence.

The judge-advocate argued the legality of the question.

General BUELL. The investigation of rumors was commenced by the prosecution. I have not in my cross-examination asked for any such evidence as the question of the judge-advocate tends to elicit from the witness.

Generals Buell and Steedman retired, when the Commission unanimously—

Resolved, The Commission is disposed to give the investigation the widest scope. Whether the opinion, estimates, or impressions of a witness are to be of weight when the Commission make up their opinion will be for future consideration, and the Commission will be governed by the laws of evidence and equity.

The question will be put.

General BUELL. If it please the Commission, I should like to be informed whether my objections were made matter of argument by the judge-advocate in secret session.

The PRESIDENT. I can assure General Buell that nothing is done to his prejudice inconsistent with law.

General BUELL. I do not wish to inquire into anything that properly belongs to the Commission in secret session, but if the prosecution introduces arguments upon my objections I claim that I ought to be privileged to hear them and I think they should be recorded. I wish to inquire if that rule is being observed.

The court was then cleared, and the Commission affirmed the reply and the assurance of the president.

General STEEDMAN. The opinion of officers of our army who interested themselves in obtaining information as to the strength of the enemy, so far as I became acquainted with their opinions, fixed Bragg's strength at from 25,000 to 35,000 after his army emerged from the Sequatchie Valley at or near Pikeville. The largest estimate I ever heard made by those who pretended to know about the strength of the enemy was made here at the quarters of General Schoepf by a young man who professed to be in the employ of the Federal officers; whether he was or not I am unable positively to state. I know, however, he communicated with my superior officers on the subject; fixed Bragg's strength at between 37,000 and 38,000, exclusive of artillery; 27 brigades—9 divisions of 3 brigades each. The strength of their regiments was estimated at 350, making about 37,800. The strength of Bragg's army was a matter of discussion very frequently among the officers of our army at various points on the march when they had an opportunity to meet to discuss these things. I heard a great deal of discussion about it near Cave City. The impression was very firmly fixed upon my mind from opinions expressed by officers generally with whom I talked on the subject that the strength of the Confederate army was in the neighborhood of 35,000.

Question. Aside from any reliable information, would not the opinions of intelligent officers be very much influenced as to the number of Bragg's army by the fact that he threw an army from Chattanooga into Kentucky in the face of General Buell's forces, which was a bold undertaking and requiring a large army?

It would make the impression, perhaps, upon the minds of officers and anybody who thought upon the subject that the army was larger than it really was; at least I would add that it would make the impression upon the minds of the officers generally that the army was a very large one.

By the JUDGE-ADVOCATE:

Question. You will state, if you please, whether you accompanied the march from Nashville to Munfordville, what you know of the surrender of that place, and the failure on the part of General Buell's army to relieve it.

I accompanied the march of the rear division from Nashville to Bowling Green. I know nothing of the surrender of Munfordville, except what I read in the newspapers and heard from the paroled officers and soldiers on their march from Munfordville to Bowling Green. That our army failed to reach there in time to prevent the capture of the garrison I know, but whether General Buell was responsible for it or not I do not know. The advance of the army was at Bowling Green some time before my division reached there.

Question. I would ask you, general, what time the rear division reached Bowling Green?

I think it was on Wednesday, September 17, but I do not undertake to be positive. I think also that was the day of the surrender of Munfordville.

Question. Had the enemy made a stand at Munfordville would General Buell's army have been forced to fight? Could you have avoided a battle there?

General Buell's army would have fought had it been permitted to, and my impression is that we would have had to fight.

Question. What, in your opinion, would have been the effect of a defeat of our army at Munfordville upon our fortunes in Kentucky and Tennessee?

I have never thought of that.

Question. You can state, if you know, whether Munfordville is a strong position or not.

I have never examined the position occupied by the troops there. I never was at the fortifications and know but little about them. I simply crossed the river with my command.

Question. Did not the estimate made of Bragg's army of 30,000 or 35,000 come to be a certainty after you left Munfordville in the opinion of the officers?

I think the opinion was so strong that it became a conviction, but I am not prepared to say it was a certainty.

Question. Was it not the general opinion among the officers that the enemy would make a stand at Munfordville?

There was a diversity of opinion among the officers on that subject. Some were of the opinion that the enemy were in force at Munfordville and intended to stand, while others thought they were merely checking us with a small force of cavalry and artillery to enable them to get up into the heart of Kentucky to secure supplies.

Question. Were you present at the battle of Perryville? If so, without giving us a detailed account of that battle, state where your position was.

I was present on the field at the close of the action and was near the battle with my command when it commenced. I was on the Springfield and Perryville road, encamped within 3 miles of the battle-field the night previous, and was ordered to move up about the time the firing commenced. I moved up on the Springfield and Perryville road to a point within three-fourths of a mile from the right of Rousseau's division, where my command was halted for a considerable length of time, within sound of the artillery and musketry; and at about 4 o'clock in the afternoon, but having no time-piece cannot state positively as to the hour, General Schoepf, who was in command of the First Division, sent me an order to move up with my brigade, and while moving he informed me that he had received orders to send two brigades to the support of General McCook, and that he had designated the Second and Third Brigades, commanded by General Fry and myself, and ordered me immediately forward. I moved up under his orders as quickly as possible; found General McCook standing by Loomis' battery; reported to him in person; got my brigade into position on the right of that battery, which was on the extreme right of Rousseau's division; took position between Rousseau's division and General Sheridan's. Fry's brigade, as I understood subsequently, was ordered back. The officers and men of the First Division during the firing in front and while they were halted in sound of it were very anxious to go forward. Why they did not go forward at an earlier hour I am unable to say. We were perhaps two hours occupying the last position the division was ordered to occupy, perhaps longer.

Question. How far back upon the Springfield pike were you at the commencement of that fight?

Perhaps 3 miles. I have a more distinct recollection of the camp than I have of the distance. It was a hard place to get water. The only water there General Gilbert kept for his own use, his staff, and escort, while the soldiers were perishing for it. He had a guard over it and would not let them have a drink.

Question. Could you hear the sound of firing at that point you designated 3 miles back?

Very distinctly the sound of artillery, but could not hear the musketry.

Question. Did the firing indicate a severe engagement?

I did not suppose there was a severe engagement till we advanced from that camp up to the position from which I have already stated my brigade was ordered forward to the support of General McCook's troops. While we were halted there the officers of the division generally were satisfied that there was a severe engagement going on in front.

Question. Do you know at what point Kirby Smith's army made a junction with Bragg's after that engagement?

I do not know of my own knowledge, but from reports I have an opinion that the junction was made at or near Harrodsburg.

Question. How long after that engagement was it that the junction was made?

My impression is that, if made at all, it was made the next day.

Question. You can state, general, whether Major-General Buell enjoyed the confidence of his officers and men during the operations of the army under his command in Tennessee and Kentucky after he took up the line of march after Bragg?

That is a very difficult question. I will state, however, that I think until about the time the army was ordered back to Nashville that no officer ever enjoyed to a more eminent degree the confidence of his officers and soldiers than General Buell. I know very well that I was proud to state that I belonged to Buell's army; but from the time the retrograde movement was commenced I am compelled to say I think the confidence in General Buell began to wane in the army; whether just or unjust, there was a great lack of confidence in him during the march from Nashville to Louisville. I have heard a great deal of murmuring among officers and men. The impression became general, so far as my opportunities for knowing the sentiments of the army enabled me to judge, that General Buell did not want to fight Bragg; that he was unwilling to risk an engagement, while the men, the officers, and troops generally were anxious to fight, conscious of our ability to whip Bragg's army at any place at which we could catch up with it to engage it. I might add that there was a great deal of dissatisfaction manifested at Cave City. I heard more there than at any other point on the march. There were more troops there than at any other point. The army was tolerably well massed there, and we halted there between forty and fifty hours, I think, while the feeling in the army was very strong that we ought to advance and attack the enemy. What the halt was for I am unable to state.

Question. Have you stated, as far as you know, the origin of the lack of confidence? Did it not originate from forced marches and half rations given to the soldiers?

I have stated that my opinion was that the lack of confidence resulted from a feeling in the army, whether just or unjust, that General Buell did not wish his army to fight Bragg. I heard no complaint against General Buell on account of the severity of the marches or the scarcity of rations. The feeling in the army was strong that our mission to Mississippi and Alabama was a failure; that very little had been accomplished; that we were obliged to go back and do the work over again. And I heard officers higher in position than myself express the opinion that we ought to check Bragg's army between McMinnville and Pikeville; that we ought at once to advance upon him; that General Buell ought to throw his whole force upon Bragg and prevent his going to Kentucky at all. My judgment is that the only feeling against General Buell originated in his failure to bring on an engagement between Bragg's forces and his own at some point in Tennessee.

Question. How far was that feeling affected by General Buell's failing to review and appear frequently among his troops?

I never heard any complaint of General Buell's failing to appear among his troops. There was a little feeling in the army that he was rather too exclusive; that he did not avail himself of the judgment and experience of the officers in the field who commanded his troops quite as much as he should. I have heard that feeling frequently expressed, but I never heard a complaint against him for not reviewing his troops. After the battle of Shiloh, when my command was marching, General Buell passed it, and, without any officer having anything to do with it, the men recognized him and raised a shout as he passed. It was very difficult then to suppress cheers as General Buell passed the men. I know he was very popular at that time in my command.

Question. What were the manifestations, after the army was withdrawn toward Nashville, when General Buell made his appearance among troops.

I cannot state beyond my command. I never saw any manifestations in my command of enthusiasm when General Buell appeared. After the commencement of the retrograde movement I will state in plain terms that he was decidedly unpopular.

Question. You have mentioned, general, that several superior officers expressed the opinion that the enemy ought to have been attacked at certain points as they invaded Kentucky. Can you give us the names of these officers?

Maj. Gen. Alexander McDowell McCook, General Schoepf, General Mitchell, and General Fry. From the colonels with whom I talked I never heard a dissenting voice.

Question. State to the Commission, if you please, what expression of opinion you heard from Major-General McCook upon the movements of General Buell's army and General Buell's capacity as a commander.

While the troops were at Pelham I had a conversation with General McCook in relation to the movements then going on. I remember his words. He was sitting beside me in General Schoepf's quarters, and he brought his hand down with considerable force on my knee. "Don Carlos won't do," said he; "he won't do." Said I, "General, there is considerable feeling in the army on the subject." "O," said he, "George Thomas is the man, and we must have him." I think General Buell was in the same building at the time, in the other part of the house, having a conversation with General Crittenden. I remember that conversation with more distinctness from the peculiarity of the language used by General McCook.

By General TYLER:

Question. You say General Bragg's army passed out of the Cumberland Mountains at Pikeville; was it in General Buell's power to have concentrated forces enough at or near that point to have resisted successfully Bragg's advance or to have whipped him?

From what I have heard of the topography of the country and the scarcity of water I do not think that General Buell could have massed his troops near that point and given Bragg battle without a great deal of suffering on account of the scarcity of water. My impression is that he could have concentrated all the forces under his command between that point and McMinnville or Sparta and given General Bragg battle.

Question. Did not Bragg with his whole army pass over that ground and find a supply of water?

I have no doubt but what he did, though his army was stretched out very much. The understanding in our army was that there was a great scarcity of water; in fact I was informed by some general officer who once made a little campaign up there that it was almost impossible to subsist troops there and to keep them there for any length of time on account of the scarcity of water. There was no water to be had. A portion of our troops who attempted to go up there were withdrawn on account of the scarcity of water.

By General DANA:

Question. What was the name of the young man who gave the information at General Schoepf's quarters in Nashville as to the strength of the rebel army when they debouched from the Sequatchie Valley at or near Pikeville and who fixed it at 37,000 or 38,000?

His name was Pratt.

Question. What was supposed in the army to be the reason why General Buell did not wish his army to fight that of the rebel Bragg?

Various reasons were assigned. Some ascribed it to timidity, some to prudence. There were all sorts of reasons; some went so far as to impugn the loyalty of General Buell. For myself I never doubted his loyalty, though I have heard considerable said on that point—that General Buell did not desire to whip Bragg.

Question. On account of his disloyalty?

Yes; I have heard charges of disloyalty against him.

Question. Were these charges of disloyalty made against General Buell by officers in high rank?

I have heard officers of the rank of brigadier-general, colonels, and lieutenant-colonels charge General Buell with disloyalty.

Question. Did you ever hear these officers make such charges in the presence or hearing of their inferiors in rank ?

I have.

Question. State the names of the officers making these charges and in whose presence they were made.

I decline to do that unless positively required so to do.

Question. You are not required to give any testimony which would implicate yourself.

The reason I decline was under the rule which shields the court, the jury, and the witnesses. If I am required to state I will, with the declaration in advance that I have heard a member of the court say so.

The court decided that the question be put.

I have heard General Schoepf, in my presence, declare General Buell's disloyalty ; I have heard the colonel of the Fourteenth Ohio, George P. Este, in the presence of several officers of his regiment, doubt the loyalty of General Buell; I have heard the lieutenant-colonel commanding (I think) the Eighth Kansas Regiment charge General Buell with disloyalty in the presence of superiors There were quite a number of officers present, but I think no inferiors. I am unable to recollect all the officers by name. I frequently heard officers express doubts of General Buell's loyalty.

By General DANA :

Question. Did you ever hear these declarations made by officers of any rank in the presence or hearing of enlisted men ?

No, sir ; I do not think I did. I have no recollection of having so heard.

Question. Who were the superior officers before whom the lieutenant-colonel of the Eighth Kansas Volunteers made allegations against the commanding general as to his loyalty ?

(General Steedman declined to answer the question unless so ordered by the Commission.)

The PRESIDENT. Was it at a public meeting ?

It was a meeting held in the camp at Rolling Fork, 6 or 7 miles from Lebanon, Ky., at the house of a citizen, and it was generally understood among the officers of the several commands that they were to assemble at that time and place. It was held with closed doors, to exclude its proceedings from the enlisted men of the army.

The PRESIDENT. It is the opinion of the court that, without criminating yourself, you can answer the question.

I do not feel that it would be criminating myself to state all I know about it. I did not think there was anything criminal in the meeting at the time nor do I now. We were present for the purpose of conferring with each other as to the condition of the army, and interchange of opinions as to the feeling toward the commander-in-chief of the Army of the Ohio ; and after it assembled there was a great deal of discussion as to the best manner of expressing our opinions in relation to General Buell. The result was a dispatch to the President was agreed upon, asking him to relieve General Buell from the command of the army, for the reason that, in the opinion of the signers, he had lost its confidence. That dispatch was signed by all the officers who were present. It was during the discussion upon the several propositions made before the meeting that that officer, in the course of his remarks, expressed his doubt as to the loyalty of General Buell. I do not remember his name, but my understanding was that he was the lieutenant-colonel commanding the Eighth Kansas Regiment. I never saw him before and have never seen him since. I think all the colonels commanding regiments in the First Division were present at that meeting. There may have been one or two absent, but my recollection is that they were all there. The brigade commanders of the First Division were all there, and one division commander, General Fry. There were a number of colonels from either General Mitchell's or General Sheridan's division, I am not positive which, but the officers commanding regiments 'n Col. Daniel McCook's brigade were present. Colonel Post, commanding a brigade, was present; I think he was of General Mitchell's division. The last time I saw that dispatch to the President it was in the hands of Col. John M. Harlan, commanding the Second Brigade in the First Division, and my recollection now is that there were either twenty-one or thirty-one, I am not positive which, commanders of regiments' names to it. I am positive there were twenty-one.

By General DANA:

Question. State what you know of General Gilbert's rank at the battle of Perryville.

He wore shoulder-straps, indicating he was a major-general. My understanding since then is that he was not a major-general, but that he was an unconfirmed brigadier-general.

Question. Do you know whether he was appointed brigadier-general prior to or since the battle of Perryville?

I do not know.

Question. By what authority was he placed as a major-general in command of an army corps?

My understanding was that he was assigned the command by General Buell.

Question. Were the division and brigade commanders in the corps to which General Gilbert was assigned as commander impressed with the idea that he was their junior or their senior?

The division and brigade commanders of the rank of brigadier-general were of opinion that General Gilbert was their junior after the battle of Perryville; at least I never heard any question about General Gilbert's rank till my command reached Crab Orchard. I was there told by General Robert [B.] Mitchell that General Gilbert was an uncommissioned brigadier-general, and that all the brigadiers in the corps ranked him.

Question. Was there any dissatisfaction felt or expressed in the army about the assignment of this officer to a command when he had not the right to exercise it?

There was a great deal of dissatisfaction in the First Division with General Gilbert prior to the battle of Perryville, and a great deal of feeling among all the officers of the corps that I ever heard say anything about it, after it was ascertained that he had not the right to exercise that command. There was a feeling that he was somebody's pet, and put where he had no right and for which he was not qualified. He quarreled with nearly all the officers of the First Division about very unimportant and trifling things, and there was a general opinion that he gave his attention entirely to small things instead of attending to the important duties of his position.

Question. Where was General Gilbert during the progress of the battle at Perryville and what do you know of his behavior at that battle?

He was with the Reserve, as it was called. He was not on the battle-field, I think, at all; if he was I had no knowledge of it. He remained with the troops that were in reserve awaiting orders. I saw very little of him, merely noticed him passing once or twice, but did not hear him say anything, and therefore I cannot speak as to his conduct.

Question. Was any portion of his command, and, if so, what portion, in front, in the immediate presence of the enemy, during the battle, and was he at any time with that portion of his command?

I am only enabled to speak of my brigade except from official report. My brigade belonged to General Gilbert's command, and was in front, in presence of the enemy; General Gilbert was not with us. I did not hear during the battle nor since, from any person, that General Gilbert was on the battle-field at all; that he was any nearer to it than I described in my testimony this morning, that is, within half to three-quarters of a mile from our lines, while we were engaged. General Gilbert may have been there, but I did not hear of his being in front.

Question. If General Gilbert had ordered a support to General McCook at the time you took your last position what would have been the probable result?

In my opinion if General Gilbert had ordered the First Division to support General McCook at 3 o'clock in the afternoon, while we were halted within half to three-quarters of a mile of the engagement, the enemy would have been routed and driven from his position. He would have been utterly defeated had a single division been added to the strength already engaged. At the time my brigade was ordered forward and took its position on the right of Loomis' battery it was too late to render any important aid. It was nearly night. There were but a few rounds fired after I was in position. The battery of my brigade opened fire and continued to fire probably for twenty-five minutes, when the firing ceased all along the lines. My infantry were not engaged at all.

Question. How long was the Reserve Division halted at the last position it took near the battle-field, from which you were ordered to support General McCook?

I think about two hours and a half.

Question. What orders did you receive from General McCook on your arrival to his support?

I rode forward in advance of my brigade and found General McCook near Loomis' battery. He recognized me at once, and approaching me remarked that he had never been so glad to see me in his life; asked me where my brigade was, and I told him it was immediately in my rear. I asked him to assign me a position. He left me hurriedly, with the remark, "You remain here for a short time and watch the front, and if you see anything going wrong take care of it." I think he said, "Give any order you think necessary in my name." He was retiring from me at the time, and said he, "I will return in a few minutes and give you orders." That was about twenty minutes past four; perhaps near half-past four. I never saw General McCook again until the fight was over. I remained there for some time. A very severe engagement was going on in front of the battery to the left, where I understood subsequently Lytle's brigade was engaged. I witnessed that, and saw the enemy advancing from the right. They had advanced near a deep ravine in front of the battery near to where a barn had been burned by our shells, and I remarked to our commissary, who was with me, that I could not wait any longer for General McCook; that the enemy were advancing and I must get my troops into position, as the battery was entirely exposed. It was not supported at all. There was no infantry on either side. When returning where I expected to find my brigade, as I had ordered it to halt in the rear of the battery at the school-house, I met the troops of my command in motion passing through a corn field. I rode rapidly up and inquired of Major Townsend, commanding the Eighteenth Infantry, who had ordered him to move; he said General McCook had passed the brigade, and ordered him to take a position with his regiment on the right of Loomis' battery. I moved the whole brigade on to the right of Loomis' battery, and got my artillery into position on the right of that battery and opened on the enemy's lines. I saw no more of General McCook until after dark. I heard his voice on the right of the Eighteenth Infantry, conversing with some officers there of the Eighteenth Regulars and the Ninth Volunteers. He asked me to send one of my aides to find General Rousseau and ascertain for him the result of his command, as far as he was able to get it. I sent one of my aides, in accordance with his request, and he was captured by the enemy within their lines.

Question. State, if you know, who was the commander of the division of cavalry during the campaign which ended with the battle of Perryville and what number of regiments or squadrons composed the command.

I understood during the advance from Louisville that Captain Gay had command of all the cavalry attached to our corps; that is, the Third Corps, commanded by General Gilbert, but what regiments or the number comprising the command I do not know. I know little about the cavalry. I heard the colonel of one of the cavalry regiments which was assigned to the command of Captain Gay complaining of the course taken in assigning Captain Gay to the command, and heard him remark that he would decline to receive commands from Captain Gay.

Question. Will you state that officer's name?

It was Colonel Milliken, of the First Ohio Cavalry.

Question. Did any irregularities arise from his exercising command over his superiors in rank?

I am not aware of any arising from that reason.

The JUDGE-ADVOCATE. You have, General Steedman, spoken of a member of the court having expressed his opinion that Major-General Buell was not a loyal man.   Please state the circumstances under which it was said and all the conversation you recollect.

It was in a private conversation between General Schoepf and myself, during which a great deal of what had transpired from the time General Buell assumed the command of the army up to the time at which we were talking was discussed.   I remember relating a conversation that I had with a citizen near this place in March last to General Schoepf, the substance of which was that the citizens here had expressed a great deal of admiration for General Buell.   I was on picket with my regiment some 4 miles from this place, when a citizen came to me and engaged in conversation about our officers and their disposition relative to the feelings of the Southern people.   He asked me if I knew General Buell personally.   I told him I did not; I only knew him as the commander of the army.   He said if all our officers were like General Buell we would not have any trouble with the people.   He proceeded to tell me a story, which was new to me, that General Buell had an aunt living near Nashville with whom he said he was acquainted, and I think he said, too, with whom General Buell had lived in early life.   He said he was intimately acquainted with the lady and had seen her since General Buell had been at Nashville, and she had assured him that everything was right; that special protection would be given to the peculiar institution, and that he had no apprehension on that score, while he lauded the general very highly.   It was all news to me that General Buell had relations here.   I did not know then nor do I know now whether he has relations here or not.   General Schoepf also told me something about a story he heard of the feelings of the rebels at Huntsville; that the rebels about that place were very much attached to General Buell, and understood they regarded him with great favor.   General Schoepf remarked, "This can't be so, that General Buell sympathizes with the rebels.   He cannot be on both sides.   If they admire him so much he must sympathize with them some at any rate."   Said he, "If all these stories are true I would not like to trust him a great deal, and I have not the utmost confidence in him anyhow."   That was the substance of the conversation, without pretending to recollect and repeat all the conversation that took place between us.

Cross-examination by General BUELL:

Question. You have stated, general, that the general estimated strength of Bragg's army when it crossed the Tennessee River was from 25,000 to 35,000.   Was that estimate based upon any method of computation or was it surmised as to the aggregate force?

The estimate as to the strength of Bragg's army was based upon information such as one army generally gets of the strength of another—upon the statements that were made as to the number of regiments and the number of effective men in each regiment; the aggregate was arrived at by computing the number of regiments reported and the average strength of the regiments reported, and, I may add, from the statements made by persons who said they had seen portions of Bragg's army and some of them who said they had seen all.   It was from all these sources of information that the estimate of the strength of Bragg's army was made up among our own people generally.

Question. Can you name any persons from whom this information was derived as to the number and strength of the regiments?

Yes, sir; I named a person in my direct examination.   I can describe another, state where I saw him and when, and also who saw him and heard his statements.   I do not know whether he can be found.   It was at Manchester that a citizen came to General Schoepf and myself and reported himself as, I think, General McCook's spy.   He said that three of them had gone out for the purpose of getting information for some one of our generals—I think General McCook; that he thought the other two who went out with him had been captured; and he went on to tell his whole story, which was very clear and plausible.   He appeared satisfied he was telling the truth.   He had the pass of one of our officers, whom he said he had secreted, and his representation as to the strength of Bragg's army was very nearly the same as the young man Pratt gave.   He represented that he had been in the Sequatchie Valley and had seen the whole army, and he stated it at rather less than the young man Pratt did, namely, at about eighty regiments, as near as my recollection serves me; but of the aggregate strength of the army I am not mistaken.   He said it was from 30,000 to 35,000 exclusive of the artillery.   This man came with our troops from Manchester, and my recollection is that he rode a horse with General Schoepf's escort a part of the time.   This estimate includes the cavalry, everything but the artillery, at the time they emerged from the

Sequatchie Valley. He represented that the main body of the army was on this side of the mountain. They were going, he thought, in the direction of McMinnville, and represented them to be on the plain, about 8 or 10 miles from what he called the foot of the ridge.

Question. You say he was one of General McCook's scouts?

He so represented himself, I stated; and we were satisfied from his statements and the papers he had on his person that his representations were correct.

Question. Do you know if he reported his information to General McCook?

I do not.

Question. Do you suppose that the impression which prevailed in the army as to the strength of Bragg's army may have been influenced by a knowledge of our own strength and by the natural desire of troops to engage an enemy, and thence convincing themselves that the enemy did not much, if any, exceed them in strength?

It is possible that the general disposition of the troops to underrate the strength of an enemy may have influenced the opinion of our army as to the strength of the enemy, though I do not know that it did.

Question. Do you not think that men anxious to meet an enemy would be more likely to underrate than overrate their strength?

I think it is the general disposition of men to underrate an adversary.

Question. I will speak now of your own opinion in regard to the propriety or expediency of moving upon Nashville. You have stated in your testimony that you thought the enemy might have been met and driven back at some point beyond McMinnville. Are you well enough acquainted with the country and the roads now to be able to pronounce a deliberate judgment in regard to the expediency of such operations against the enemy?

I stated in my direct examination that I knew very little about the topography of the country between McMinnville and the mountains or the facilities for getting water at that time, but that my understanding was that it was very difficult to get water for any considerable number of troops. I also stated that it was the opinion of the officers of the army that the enemy ought to have been met at or near McMinnville. I know but little about the character of the roads, nothing except of those I saw and of which I heard representations from such scouts as I conversed with; but, with the limited experience I have in the matter of war, I think our army was able to whip Bragg's at any place between the mountains and Kentucky. That was my belief at the time and nothing has occurred since to change that opinion. I thought then and think now that General Buell's forces were equal, if not superior, to Bragg's. Without pretending to give any opinion as to strategy, I believe our army was able to whip the rebel army any day after it crossed the mountains. The army felt so, and the confidence of the army in its ability to meet Bragg would have given it success.

Question. Do you know what available forces could have been concentrated about McMinnville?

I suppose that General Buell could have concentrated 40,000 men at McMinnville.

Question. Do you know anything of the circumstances which would necessarily have controlled the movements of my army in that country at that time, such as the amount of supplies particularly?

Of course I have no official information as to the number of rations at the disposal of General Buell at points between Nashville and Huntsville or Nashville and Decherd, along the line of the road, that were available; but I am confident that, for the short time that it would have been necessary to subsist the army anywhere in Tennessee to have whipped Bragg the army could have lived on the country.

Question. In what way could you manage to subsist an army from that country while it was engaged in actual operations?

I would draw the supplies for the support of the army through the same officers through whom we draw them from the Government, and precisely as we did it then, while we were supplied with half rations when marching from Decherd to Nashville.

Question. In what condition did those supplies exist in the country; that is, were they scattered over the country in the hands of the producers or were they collected in large bodies?

Generally on the farms of the producers.

Question. Can a large army operate actively in the presence of an enemy and depend upon supplies to be procured in that way?

Bragg's army, supplied in that way, generally kept us at bay through Tennessee.

Question. That does not answer the question.

That is my answer, general. I do not think that an army engaged in an important campaign could be subsisted for any very great length of time by drawing supplies in that irregular manner from the country; but the rebel army did go to Kentucky and back to Tennessee, making quite a successful campaign, and drawing their supplies from the country in the manner I have suggested.

Question. In procuring its supplies in that way from the country through which it marched did the rebel army have the assistance of the population? Did they bring in supplies freely to the army on its line of march?

The rebels undoubtedly had the sympathy of the population, but to what extent the people engaged in transporting supplies for them I have no means of knowing. I have heard, however, that in a portion of Tennessee the people did haul supplies in very considerable quantities to the rebel camps.

Question. Could we receive any such assistance?

Not without compelling.

Question. In what manner would you do that?

I would send a quartermaster out, with all the transportation of his regiment or of the brigade, to get supplies; direct him to order the negroes of the rebel citizens to hitch up their wagons—the same wagons they hitched up for the rebels—and haul such provisions as they had to the camp. I would compel them to do it if they refused. In other words, I would coerce them to do precisely for us what they had done voluntarily for the rebels.

Question. To what extent upon either side of the road do you suppose an army of 30,000 would have to go to procure supplies for its subsistence through such a country as that between McMinnville and Nashville?

Judging from that portion of it I passed through, an army of 30,000 could subsist in marching by going, at the farthest, 3 or 4 miles from the road. We subsisted half that number with half rations by going a very short distance. We only drew half rations from the Government, and supplied the balance from the country without going a mile from the road. The country was well supplied with cattle. There would have been no difficulty in finding beef. The commissaries had a pretty good supply of beef when we got here drawn from the country. It would depend, of course, a great deal upon the country, the seasons, and the crops.

Question. Could that be done in the presence of an enemy?

Unless the enemy lived on the road all the way. You would have to take the risk of getting a foraging party captured occasionally, just as they are doing now in front of Nashville, and we would have had the same opportunity to capture their foraging parties as they would ours. They were subsisted on the country.

Question. Is it true that you would have the same facilities in this country as the enemy has for gaining such advantages?

It is not true that we have such facilities for getting information. The enemy have greatly the advantage in that respect.

Question. Suppose both armies living in this manner from the coun-

GENERAL REPORTS.

try, what would the relative success of the two armies depend upon with such a system of supplying them?

Energy and pluck.

Question. In anything else?

That would be the main dependence, living in that way.

Question. Would it depend upon the strength and efficiency of their cavalry force at all?

It would depend upon the strength and efficiency of all the army, cavalry as well as infantry; but I would depend mainly upon the infantry if I were doing the foraging.

Question. Would it depend upon the disposition of the people?

I do not think they would have a great deal to say about it.

Question. Would their disposition have any effect upon the ease with which supplies could be obtained in that way?

The disposition of the people to favor the Confederate army would, of course, embarrass sending out foraging parties by our army, on account of the rebels getting information of our movements of that character more readily and frequently than we could of their movements.

Question. Do you suppose that such a system of supplying an army might have been a matter of so much more difficulty for one than for the other as to determine the success of the campaign, other things being equal?

I have already stated that the disposition of the people of the disloyal States would favor the Confederate cause, would throw obstacles in the way of our foraging, on account of their giving information to the enemy whenever we attempted to send out any such parties. Of course, if all other things were equal, that would be an advantage to the rebels which might, if they were exactly equal in all other respects, give them success in a campaign. I will add that I am not in favor of subsisting an army in that way, on account of the demoralizing effect on our own troops. I would only do it in an emergency, when I think a great advantage would accrue to our cause from doing it, when I could deal the enemy a deadly blow.

Question. What would be the consequence of defeat to an army depending upon such a system for subsistence?

Well, I can only speak from what I understood to be the effect upon the Confederate army when they were defeated; they would run away and reorganize at some other point.

Question. Is it true the rebel army ever has been defeated and driven from its supplies and thrown from day to day upon what it could gather upon its line of march?

Yes, it is true that some portions of the rebel army have been in that situation. That was especially the case at Mill Springs. They lost everything they had there.

Question. What was the strength of the army that was defeated at Mill Springs?

It was supposed to be about 10,000.

Question. Would the consequences to that army have been the same had it been 40,000 defeated under the same circumstances?

There would perhaps have been rather more suffering had the army been larger. It was at a very inclement season, in the midst of rain and mud. The roads were almost impassable, and they were certainly in a much worse condition than our army would have been had it been defeated at McMinnville, where the roads were good.

Question. In retreating from Mill Springs did not the rebel army fall back along the rear of its line of supplies?

My understanding was at the time, and has been since, that it had no supplies on the road, and that it retreated over about as bad a road as there was at that time in Tennessee. I traveled over a portion of it in Kentucky, and it was nearly impassable. A large portion of the supplies received at Mill Springs were transported by water.

Question. In what condition did that army retreat.

In rather an irregular manner, I understood.

Question. Was it not completely disorganized and dispersed, or nearly so?

It was badly whipped, terribly frightened, and retreated, it was understood, very rapidly; but most of the troops that were there escaped and have been engaged with our army at other points since. Several of the regiments that were there are still in the Confederate service.

Question. Did it not retreat as a disorganized mob?

It is said to have retreated in confusion.

Question. Was not the condition of the roads a security to that army instead of a hinderance?

Its pursuit was never attempted south of the Cumberland River. Its principal security was the Cumberland River.

Question. Suppose there had been no such obstacle in the way, would not the condition of the roads have contributed to the security of that retreating army?

The condition of the roads would have unquestionably embarrassed the pursuit more than the retreat under such circumstances.

Question. You say that the roads from McMinnville toward Nashville would have presented no such difficulty either to the retreating or the pursuing army; is it so, general?

The roads from McMinnville would have offered none other obstructions that would have prevented a rapid pursuit at the time of the defeat of the Confederate army at Mill Springs. The suffering of an army defeated at the time and under the circumstances that the rebels were defeated at Mill Springs was much greater than if defeated at the season of the year and under the circumstances we were placed in when Bragg was at McMinnville.

Question. I meant the suffering of the defeated soldiers from exposure. The suffering in one case would mainly have been from natural causes, would it not, such as the condition of the weather?

Yes; resulting from the defeat.

Question. What would have been the probable cause of suffering in the other case, supposing the weather to be good, the roads good, and every facility for rapid pursuit?

Heat, dust, want of water, apprehension of being captured, and all the difficulty that would embarrass a retreating army under such circumstances.

Question. Suppose, in addition to such causes of suffering, the army should be compelled to retard its march as much as would be necessary to collect supplies in the manner you suggest, what must have been the result of the pursuit by an efficient enemy?

If I were to judge of the manner in which the rebel army got from us in Kentucky I would say not very disastrous; but I think if the army were pursued rapidly, vigorously, not to permit itself to be checked by little squads of cavalry and a couple of pieces of artillery on every road, that it would succeed in cutting it up very badly and capturing a large portion of the retreating forces that had been in the fight.

Question. Do you suppose the rebel army, if it had defeated the Army of the Ohio at McMinnville, would probably have conducted the pursuit in that way?

I am unable to say what they would have done.

Question. Did the rebel army in retreating from Kentucky have to delay its march and collect supplies along the road?

I think not. I think they had collected from the country a sufficient amount of supplies to subsist upon while they were retreating.

Question. Are you well enough acquainted with the particulars of the retreat of the rebel army from Kentucky and of the pursuit to be able to say whether that army suffered as much in its retreat as it ought to have done?

Of my own knowledge of course I know but very little about the manner in which the rebel army conducted its retreat. My opinion was at the time that the pursuit was not as rapid as I felt it ought to have been, though I am free to say very frequently officers not charged with the responsibility are more willing to take risk than those who are. I think in the advance on the enemy in Kentucky, both before and after the battle of Perryville, our forces were frequently held in check when they ought not to have been.

Question. I want to know upon what knowledge you have based your disapprobation?

I was in command of a brigade in the advance on the road from Springfield to Perryville, and an attempt was made to check or attempt to check my command with a small force of cavalry and a couple of pieces of artillery, but I advanced upon them rapidly and drove them from their position three times. General Gilbert sent word by an orderly three times that day directing me to halt until he could overtake the right of the column. General Schoepf, who was with the head of the column and directing its movements, informed me also that General Gilbert had sent an orderly to him to halt the command about 2 o'clock in the afternoon of that day. General Gilbert overtook the head of the column the day we marched from Springfield, that is, the sixth, ordered a halt, and expressing a great deal of dissatisfaction with the rapidity of our movements, telling us all we were in danger of being cut off. I think if the column on that road in which my brigade lay had been permitted to move as rapidly as its division and brigade commanders desired it to move that the enemy would have been punished more than he was. He would have been driven from all his positions, and I felt at the time that the army he had on the road and the artillery would have been captured had the pursuit have been made as rapidly as it ought to have been.

Question. That was before the battle?

I am undertaking to show by my testimony that the corps commander placed by General Buell over three divisions of that army would not allow it to move as rapidly as it desired to move upon the enemy, and was very much afraid it would get cut off if it attempted to cut off a small body of cavalry and a couple of pieces of artillery that were impeding it on the road. After the battle the pursuit on one of the roads was something of the same character; that several times during the pursuit our advance was checked and held back by small bodies of cavalry with artillery. This information with regard to matters after the battle I got from officers who were engaged.

Question. On what road was the pursuit you refer to and what officer commanded the advance?

It was on the road to Crab Orchard, by way of Lancaster. There was quite a skirmish quite close to the town of Lancaster; on both sides of the town there were skirmishes, in which small bodies of cavalry were engaged with part of the enemy with a couple of pieces of artillery.

Question. Do you know the officer who commanded the advance and who was responsible for this slow pursuit?

I do not recollect which division commander it was. I heard a great deal of discussion about it, and the impression was made upon my mind from the amount of discussion I heard and the opinions expressed that the pursuit was a very slow one, and that we allowed the enemy to hold us in check by this system of occupying the roads in their rear with small bodies of cavalry and with a section of artillery.

Question. Has General Mitchell the reputation of being a pretty energetic officer?

Yes, sir; he has such a reputation. It was a portion of the cavalry under Captain Gay that was in advance. I remember one day after the battle of Perryville Captain Gay's cavalry was in advance on that road, as I understood, and was checked by the enemy at the crossing of the stream near Lancaster, and held in check until the infantry of Mitchell's division advanced with some artillery and dislodged them. From all the circustances which I have related my opinion is that the enemy was not punished as severely on the retreat from Kentucky as he might have been.

Question. Have you heard any condemnation of the pursuit expressed beyond Crab Orchard ?

No, sir. On the contrary, I have heard it spoken of as being vigorously carried on.

Question. Is it known that Bragg carried supplies with him in his advance from Chattanooga across the mountains ?

I cannot speak as to the extent of his supplies. It was understood in our army, however, that Bragg's army drew upon the country pretty largely for supplies in their march through Tennessee.

Question. Had supplies been collected in depots in Kentucky, in advance of his arrival, by the forces of Kirby Smith ?

It was the understanding in our army that supplies were collected by Kirby Smith in Kentucky; whether at depots on the route traveled by Bragg's army I am unable to say. I will add that I understand there were supplies collected for Bragg's army in Tennessee by citizens. I heard some one, I cannot tell who now, but it was one of the scouts employed by officers in our army, say that at some point in Tennessee the citizens had hauled in a considerable quantity of supplies for Bragg's army at the time the enemy reached the point where the supplies had been collected; I cannot remember the point, but it was not far from McMinnville; it was on his march somewhere between the mountain and Sparta.

By General TYLER:

Question. Could you give the court any information as to the time Bragg's army crossed at Chattanooga at or near Pikeville and the Tennessee River at or near Carthage ?

I have no memorandum to which I can refer to refresh my recollections as to dates, but my impression is that Bragg's army left Chattanooga about the middle of August and crossed the Cumberland Mountains at or near Pikeville about the 22d of August. We crossed at Carthage about the first week in September, as near as I can recollect. The command to which I was attached left Decherd on the 18th of August for Pelham, and that is the only date about which I can feel at all certain.

Question. When Bragg crossed the mountains at Pikeville what force had we collected at McMinnville, and what is the distance from McMinnville to Pikeville ?

I understood at that time that two divisions of our army, of about 15,000 men, with a small body of cavalry, were at or near McMinnville, under the command of General Thomas. I cannot state the distance.

By the JUDGE-ADVOCATE:

Question. You have been examined in reference to the sympathy of the inhabitants for the rebels as facilitating their procuring supplies. What would have been the effect of a kind, conciliatory policy toward the negroes in this connection by your army ?

I think nineteen out of twenty of the slaves of the disloyal States are friendly to the Union cause. What would have been the effect in aiding us to procure supplies from the country if a different policy had been pursued toward them than that enforced by the commanding officers of our army I am unable to say; it would be a mere matter of opinion. I will state, however, in this connection, that most of the information we received while the army was in Mississippi, Alabama, and Tennessee came from the negroes. They were always reliable on our side. When I say reliable, I do not mean to say that they were always truthful. Very frequently their anxiety to get with the army induced them to misrepresent the position of their masters and owners. The information was generally correct as to the locality and movements of the enemy, though I never considered it reliable as to the political status of their masters. They would invariably say their masters were rebels of the strongest kind. I think, however, they might have been made more useful to the Union army than they have been.

Question. What has been the policy of Major-General Buell in this respect?

His policy has been generally to exclude them from the camp and in favor of returning them to their owners.

Question. What, from your observation, is the effect of a kind, conciliatory policy toward the rebel inhabitants?

I think it has emboldened them and intensified their treason. They have regarded it as an evidence of our weakness.

By General BUELL:

Question. You have not given the dates at which the rebel army passed certain points in its march to Kentucky, particularly the date at which it passed Pikeville. Is that date fixed in your mind?

It is not, and I so stated—that I could not pretend to accuracy at all in the statements I made in reference to dates.

Question. Did you really know anything of the movements of the rebel army in crossing the mountains about the time of their marching?

All I know as to their movements was the received opinion in our army, the generally understood opinion of the army at the time—the officers of that portion of the army with which I was connected.

Question. Was it really the opinion that the rebel army crossed the mountains or was between Pikeville and McMinnville before our troops commenced their concentration at Murfreesborough?

The opinion was general in that portion of the army that was at Pelham, which included the divisions of General Schoepf, General Crittenden, and General McCook, that the advance of Bragg's army was across the mountain before the troops left Pelham. When the First Division reached Manchester on its march to Murfreesborough information that was regarded as reliable was received that Bragg had crossed the mountain with nearly his entire force. As I stated in my examination, that information was received through a scout who was in the employ, I think, of General McCook, who received it at General Schoepf's quarters, and communicated the information to General Schoepf and myself. It is proper I should state that the information received while the troops I have spoken of were at Pelham was not considered of that certain character upon which an army would base its movements.

Question. Had the army commenced its concentration when you received this information at Manchester?

It had.

Question. While you were lying at Pelham was it expected that the enemy might advance over the Therman road?

The route that the enemy would take from Pikeville was understood there to be a matter of very great uncertainty.

Question. Was the enemy known to be at Pikeville when you were at Pelham?

Not positively.

Question. Did the rebel army march through McMinnville in invading Kentucky?

My understanding is that a part of it did. It is understood that a portion of the cavalry passed through there. Whether any infantry did or not I am unable to state.

Question. While you were lying at Pelham were you in expectation of the enemy at that point or on roads near there?

It was understood that General Buell anticipated an attack there, but the officers and troops at that point did not, so far as I have heard an opinion expressed.

Question. Do you mean to express what was your opinion or what was the understanding of the troops generally?

I mean the understanding of the troops to which I was attached, especially of my own brigade, which was in the advance at Pelham until the divisions of General McCook and General Crittenden arrived.

Question. Did the disposition of the army while you were at Pelham indicate that General Buell expected an attack at that point particularly?

It indicated that General Buell thought an attack somewhere in that vicinity probable.

Question. On what ground did you think it improbable?

Upon the ground that I supposed the rebel army would avoid ours if possible.

Question. Upon what ground was that belief based?

Upon the ground that they would never hazard a battle with us unless they thought they outnumbered us and had the advantage.

By General DANA:

Question. Do you know of any instance where any officer of the Army of the Ohio, by his official position or acts, has influenced the return of a slave to servitude since the publication of the enactment of the late article of war on the subject?

I have never been officially informed that the amendment to the article of war alluded to in the question was a part of the Articles of War. My understanding, however, was that the amendment had been made, and provided that if any officer of the Army engaged in returning a slave to a rebel owner that officer should be cashiered. I have never seen an official copy of it, and do not know to this day what it is, and do not know officially whether any amendment to the Articles of War had been made; but after I understood that such an amendment had been made I received orders, while a colonel commanding a regiment, to permit persons whom I was satisfied were disloyal to search my camp for slaves. I received an order from General Fry, Iuka, to permit citizens who were named in the order to search my camp for runaway negroes.

Question. Please state the date.

It was about the 25th of June. I conversed with the citizen who bore me the order and to whom the authority was given to search my camp, and I was satisfied they were disloyal. I took the order and wrote upon the back of it that I declined to permit any citizen of a disloyal State to search my camp for slaves unless the officer in command of the department positively ordered the search and signed it officially. I then handed it back to the citizen. At Pulaski, in Tennessee, somewhere about the first week in August, I received a verbal order from General Fry himself to deliver up two negroes from my camp to a citizen of that town, which I declined to do. I did not know at the time, however, that the negroes were in my camp. The general rode up to my camp and told me he was informed there were two negroes belonging to a citizen whose wife he said he knew. She was a Rhodes. I replied to the general that I did not care what her name was, and that I would not permit a she rebel to enter my camp to get slaves any quicker than I would a he one, and he said he would take the responsibility of returning the negroes. I then informed him what I understood to be the law and that I should stand on it, and advised him not to trouble himself any further about negroes, but to leave that question to the colonels of the regiments and the claimants. Those are the only instances I know of.

Question. Have you a copy of the written order that was served on you at Iuka?

I have not. I did not retain the original order.

Commission adjourned to meet December 14, a. m.

NASHVILLE, *December* 14, 1862—10 a. m.

Commission met pursuant to adjournment. All the members present; also the judge-advocate and General Buell.

Colonel STREIGHT (a witness for the Government), being duly sworn by the judge-advocate, testified as follows:

By the JUDGE-ADVOCATE:

Question. State your name and position in the service of the United States.

A. D. Streight, colonel, commanding the Fifty-first Indiana Volunteers.

Question. State, if you please, where you were in the service during the invasion of Bragg from Chattanooga to Kentucky.

I started from Stevenson on the 20th or 21st of September with the Twentieth Brigade, and joined Crittenden's division at Bridgeport; marched with Crittenden to this point, where we joined with Wood's division, and from here we marched with Wood's division.

Question. What position had Wood's divison in the army in the march from Nashville to Bowling Green and Munfordville?

We marched in the advance from here to Gallatin; then we crossed to Mitchellsville. What force went up the other road I am unable to state. We joined other troops at Mitchellsville. Who had the advance that day I cannot say, but we arrived in the advance at Bowling Green. We went in the advance, I am certain, on our route as far as Mitchellsville, and we arrived in the advance at Bowling Green. Whether there were not some other troops marching in the advance some other day I am unable to say.

Question. What time, colonel, did it take you to march from Nashville to Munfordville; what time did you leave Nashville and what time did you arrive at Munfordville?

I have no dates; I cannot therefore give the exact days. Our first stay was at Gallatin, where we remained one day; we then moved rapidly to Bowling Green. One day and night we marched, I think, 36 miles.

Question. What time were you marching from Nashville to Bowling Green; how many days, and how long did you remain at Bowling Green?

We remained at Bowling Green five or six days, but the number of days we were marching I cannot recollect so well. I remember we were very impatient at lying idle, but it strikes me that we were on the road but three days from here to Bowling Green, and from there we did not move so fast, though we marched most of one night, and next day we moved up to within a few miles of Cave City, then to Cave City, which would make five days' marching. This would include all the marching from here to Cave City, where we halted. When we moved up it took all day to go to Munfordville. We were five or six days at Bowling Green and about five days at Cave City.

Question. Where were you at the time Munfordville surrendered and upon what day did it surrender?

I disremember, but we were on the march from Bowling Green to Cave City. The day after we arrived at Cave City the prisoners came down, and I think they surrendered the day before. It was not far from the time that we left Bowling Green; it was on the next day. I may be wrong as to the date, but not more than a day.

Question. What was the estimate placed upon the number of the invading army by intelligent officers during that march?

Well, sir, it was variously estimated at from 30,000 to 40,000. I do not think anybody estimated it above 40,000; some as low as 25,000. From facts I could gather they might have had from 30,000 to 35,000. There were various rumors, but all very indefinite. We were not in a position to know very definitely facts relative to it. I, at Gallatin, learned from General Wood that he had sent a party out who reported it at 33,000. That is my remembrance of it, which from that time led me to believe that my estimate was pretty correct.

Question. State, if you please, whether you were at the battle of Perryville, and what you know of the movements of the enemy subsequent to that fight.

Our division arrived about 4 o'clock on the day of the fight at Perryville. The evening before we went over what is called Rolling Fork, about 12 miles from Perryville. Although our division had orders early in the morning, we did not move until about 11; arrived about 4 the day of the Perryville fight. We took position on the right of Gilbert's force. That evening there was some little skirmishing, but very unimportant. We advanced about half a mile and bivouacked for the night. We were on the left of Crittenden, on the right of Gilbert, and about opposite to Perryville, and from appearances on the night of the fight we were at the extreme left of the enemy. They were trying when we came up to flank General Gilbert, which indicated that that was the extreme left. I saw no other troops farther left than about opposite Crittenden's right. The next morning, however, it appeared that they had moved somewhat to the left from where they were the night before.

At daylight next morning we advanced a few rods, more led by curiosity than by anything else, and, as I understood, without orders, to where we could overlook the town and somewhat overlook the position of the enemy. After daylight I saw them putting a battery into position a little to the right and the rear of Perryville; I also saw a considerable quantity of cavalry and infantry. I saw but one battery of artillery in the morning belonging to the enemy. When Wagner opened his battery they were driven from that point. That was the last seen of the artillery. The sun was half an hour high when we first saw the enemy moving off. They had evidently been moving previously. They continued to move for an hour and a half or two hours from the time I first saw them, perhaps longer. The cavalry moved across the field back of the town, which caused both parties to be moving off at the same time. The cavalry continued to pass till after the infantry had all gone and were passing when we left. There was a large body of them; they came out of the ravine and gully and passed over the ridge; passed down and accompanied another regiment, which hid them from our view. We could see them for perhaps a mile from the position we occupied on the eminence at the back of Perryville. They seemed moving off in the direction of Harrodsburg. They were moving with baggage trains, infantry, and cavalry. Of artillery I only saw one battery. I went down in person to where the enemy had previously planted a battery, and I was within 80 rods of the enemy; could see very distinctly; could distinguish countenances with a glass. I think they were passing off by their right till about 10 or 11 o'clock, when we fell back from the position we occupied perhaps 1½ or 2 miles to the rear and right, which took us out of sight. When we left the enemy were still moving off with the majority of their cavalry. I think I saw 3,000 infantry and a large force of cavalry. They were passing off, not rapidly, but moderately; no disorder about it. We fell back a little between 10 and 11 o'clock by orders of General Wood. Captain Lennard came and gave orders for the whole of Wood's division to fall back and retire to the right and rear of their position. We lay there till about 2, when we passed through Perryville, and went to the spring below and remained there for the night.

Question. State whether you reported the information you gained from observation to your superior officers.

I reported immediately to the brigade commander, Colonel Harker, and it is my impression that he sent an orderly to General Wood, but I have no recollection of that particularly.

Cross-examination by General BUELL:

Question. You have spoken about the impatience of the troops of your division at Bowling Green; what were they impatient to do, colonel?

They were very anxious to move on and relieve the Munfordville force. In fact there had been a general impatience at not being allowed to attack the enemy. It amounted almost to indignation, among both officers and men, at that time more particularly. The impatience had extended from the time we moved up with General McCook toward Chattanooga or about Jasper. We then fell back and came over the mountain, and from this point there had been more or less impatience expressed all the way through. But from the time we left Gallatin there was a decided impatience in moving away from the enemy and allowing them to move along on the line partially of our own march without attacking them. From the time we left Gallatin to when we arrived at Bowling Green it increased very much. We knew that

Munfordville was threatened, and while at Bowling Green we heard that Colonel Wilder had succeeded in repulsing the enemy. From that time there was clearly indignation among both officers and men. It was because we were not allowed to attack the enemy. From the time we fell back that feeling exhibited itself more particularly, but when we left Gallatin and proceeded toward Mitchellsville it increased, and then again at Bowling Green, knowing that Colonel Wilder was threatened, and hearing he was attacked the feeling further increased.

Question. Was your division anxious to move alone to the relief of Munfordville?

I never heard any remark that I know of relative to it. My remarks relative to relieving Munfordville applied to the general feeling in camp. There was nothing said as to whether one division should go or not. It seems to me that that would be somewhat inconsistent. To send one division would not have been very good judgment. I never heard an officer remark as to whether one division should move up or not. My impression is that the desire was not that one division should move up.

Question. Was there any judgment at all in this impatience; any knowledge of the position of the enemy, or of his strength, or of the force available to operate against him, or of the movements of other divisions of the army, or of the circumstances that controlled those movements?

I think it had become generally known and satisfactorily understood that the enemy had a force of about 30,000 to 35,000; that their position was on the northward, nearly opposite our forces; and it was generally known that Colonel Wilder or a force was at Munfordville, and also that the route taken by the enemy was in that direction. As to the movements of other divisions of the army, as to how they should move, I do not think it was known whether they could be spared or not. I do not think it was known what was detaining them. For my own part I did not, though I endeavored to keep myself pretty well posted. The facts that would make up the feeling in camp either for or against certain movements are not generally founded upon close calculation, though it is impossible for officers in a subordinate position to know why certain movements are made or why they are not.

Question. Toward whom was the impatience felt when General McCook returned after his expedition up the Sequatchie Valley?

The conversation and feeling turned upon the party responsible. It is very customary for conversations and observations to be made in the army without being directed against any individual. It was generally remarked and believed that the enemy were not in sufficient force to warrant our returning without at least an attempt to feel his position. It was not generally believed that the artillery could not be taken over the mountain, and that was the reason assigned for our not advancing farther there—that the artillery could not be taken over the mountain.

Question. Whose opinion was that supposed to be and who was supposed to be responsible for the attempt not being made?

The conclusion that I came to from what I heard was that the responsibility was thrown upon General McCook. I heard some remark that he had been ordered back. The opinion was rather divided and not definitely understood.

Commission adjourned to meet December 15, at 10 o'clock a. m.

NASHVILLE, *December* 15, 1862.

Commission met pursuant to adjournment. All the members present; also the judge-advocate and General Buell.

General THOMAS J. WOOD (a witness for the Government), being duly sworn, testified as follows:

By the JUDGE-ADVOCATE:

Question. Please state your name and position in the United States Army.

My name is Thomas J. Wood. I am colonel of the Second Regular Artillery and brigadier-general of volunteer forces.

Question. Please state if you were with the army in its pursuit of Bragg when he invaded Kentucky and what you know of the force of the rebels previous to your arrival at Munfordville.

I was with the Army of the Ohio in pursuit of the army led by Bragg when he invaded Kentucky, and all the information which I obtained from various sources satisfied me that the army led by General Bragg into Kentucky did not exceed 35,000 men.

Question. Previous to your arrival at Nashville, general, tell the Commission where and what was the situation about the time Bragg left Chattanooga, if you know.

For some ten or twelve days previous to the date of the commencement of the concentration of the army at Nashville I was stationed in the vicinity of McMinnville. I do not know the date of Bragg's leaving Chattanooga.

Question. State, if you please, whether at that time the railway from McMinnville to Tullahoma and from Tullahoma to Nashville was in operation.

It was during the greater part of the time; there were occasional interruptions.

Question. What is the character of the road and what was its condition at the time from Murfreesborough to Woodbury and from Woodbury to McMinnville?

I did not travel the usually followed road, but I know from reports that troops were constantly passing over from McMinnville to Woodbury, and the inference is that the road was good. There is an ordinary turnpike road from Woodbury to Murfreesborough, which I traveled over. I have no positive knowledge of the road from McMinnville to Woodbury.

Question. Do you know what the character of the road is from McMinnville to Spencer and from Spencer to Pikeville?

I do not know; I never marched over that road.

Question. What is your opinion, as a military man, as to the proposition to attack Bragg's army as he debouched from the Sequatchie Valley and descended from the Cumberland Mountains with the prospect of success?

Had the proposition been left to me I never would have attacked General Bragg in the Sequatchie Valley.

Question. Where would the proper place to attack him have been?

That would turn a great deal upon the condition of supplies. I have always entertained the opinion that if the supplies had warranted it it might have been judicious, had Bragg crossed the Cumberland River at all, in the neighborhood of Sparta; that would turn, however, upon the extent of supplies, which it is important for a military man to consider among the elements entering into such a movement. If the state of supplies had warranted it, after the army was concentrated at Murfreesborough, I believe General Bragg's army could have been beaten in the neighborhood of Sparta.

Question. Did you know, general, whether the army of General Buell was concentrated for a purpose of that sort and why it was not carried out?

I do not know that it was so concentrated or that such an arrangement or movement entered into General Buell's combinations. I had not seen General Buell from about the 15th of July, when I separated from him at Huntsville, till I met him in Nashville on the 6th of September. Had it been his intention he did not communicate it to me, for I had no personal, only telegraphic, communications and ordinary dispatches; even had I been with him I do not know that he would have communicated such a design to me.

Question. Upon what other points, in marching from McMinnville to Nashville and to Munfordville, would your judgment indicate General

Buell's army could have attacked Bragg's army with a prospect of success?

I think it might have been done after General Bragg crossed the Cumberland River, by a rapid concentration of the Army of the Ohio on the line that he was pursuing into Kentucky by the way of Glasgow. As is known, there is a turnpike road leading from this city to Gallatin and from there into Kentucky by the way of Scottsville and Glasgow. On the evening of the 6th of September I received an order from General Buell to commence crossing the Cumberland River with my division at daylight next morning and after the division had crossed to report to him in person. I did so. He then instructed me to march my division as far as what is called the Edgefield Junction, there to leave all the baggage in charge of the quartermaster, and take wagons enough to transport six days' rations for the troops and cooking utensils for the men. After making this arrangement to move with my division promptly in the direction of Gallatin, it was furthermore stated that it would be followed up by other divisions of the army on the same road; that he would probably be up at Gallatin the next morning by the time I got there. He also charged me to be very alert and gain all the information of the movements of the enemy that was possible. By following out what seemed to be General Buell's plan, so far as I could infer it from his orders to me in the disposition of the troops he was then making, I think it would have been possible to have concentrated his army at Glasgow before General Bragg concentrated his army there. It was not known at that time certainly, but only believed, that Bragg had crossed the Cumberland River. I certainly did not know anything of it, though I did shortly afterward.

Question. What was the practicability of General Buell's army reenforcing Munfordville previous to its being attacked by Bragg?

I think that while it might have been a hazardous movement to the Army of the Ohio in some respects, it could have been done.

Question. What would have been the effect of a stand being made by the rebel army of 50,000 or 60,000 men at Munfordville upon the Army of the Ohio?

It would have been very dangerous for the Army of the Ohio to have attacked 50,000 or 60,000 men at Munfordville. According to the best of my recollection, and I think I gained my information from entirely reliable sources, I do not think the Army of the Ohio could have been brought to attack at Munfordville from 42,000 to 45,000 men. The position which an enemy of any intelligence would have occupied for a battle in that vicinity is not at the town of Munfordville, but about 2 miles south of Green River. The position consists of a very strong, rocky, woody ridge, stretching nearly at right angles with the line of approach by which the attacking forces would have been compelled to advance, and my opinion is that that position would have given the party holding it an advantage of at least 10,000 men. It is true, in my opinion, that the position might be turned by the right if the forces attacking it form the southern side. It would not have been absolutely necessary to attack the rebels in this position. There is a road across the country, broken and bad, but, from my knowledge of the country, barely practicable, from Bowling Green, by the way of Brownsville, Litchfield, &c., to Elizabethtown and Louisville.

Question. What would have been the effect of such a movement upon Bowling Green and Nashville?

To some extent certainly it would have uncovered both places and left them open to an attack of the enemy.

Question. Can you state how far and well the Army of the Ohio was provided with transportation while at Nashville, before it commenced that march toward Kentucky, when the army was concentrated at Nashville?

My own division had an ample supply of transportation, and so far as I know from contact with other divisions they had sufficient transportation. My answer was based upon the impression that the question referred to transportation for that movement. What was sufficient for one movement might not have been sufficient for another.

Question. State whether you accompanied the army in its march from Louisville to Perryville; and, if so, what you know of the movements of the enemy the day subsequent to that battle.

I did accompany the Army of the Ohio in its march from Louisville to Perryville. In the morning of the day following the battle of Chaplin Hills, two brigades of my division advanced to the edge of the town of Perryville and sent me back a report that the enemy had evacuated it. We were then ordered to advance to the town and to encamp at the springs beyond it, nearly on the Harrodsburg road. In this movement we saw nothing of the enemy, but learned from citizens that he had fallen back toward Harrodsburg. The object of that answer is to intimate that I saw nothing of the enemy personally that day. After receiving the report from these two brigades I rode into the town of Perryville myself, preceding the commencement of the movement of the troops toward that town.

Question. When it became known that the enemy had fallen back from Harrodsburg, was it understood what was the object of that movement on their part at the time?

I do not know that it was understood what was the object of the movement. I presume most of the officers who are acquainted with the movement had their own opinions about it.

Question. What was the opinion among intelligent officers as to the object of the movement?

There was some variety of opinions entertained on the subject, so far as I heard opinions given; but the weight of opinion, so far as I had any information, was that the object in falling back to Harrodsburg was to form a junction with Kirby Smith's force and make a stand there, or at the crossing of Dick's River, or at Camp Dick Robinson; but various opinions were entertained as to where they would make a stand, as would be the case in all circumstances.

Question. What was Kirby Smith's forces estimated at?

I have heard them variously estimated at from 12,000 to 25,000. Among intelligent officers generally the force was never estimated at over 15,000 men.

Question. You can state whether the retreat of the enemy from Bardstown to Perryville and from Perryville to Harrodsburg toward Cumberland Gap was conducted in an orderly manner, or did it partake in any degree of the character of a rout?

As I did not see a great deal of the enemy's forces while it was in retreat, it is almost impossible to say whether it was conducted in an orderly manner, except from results and inferences, and, so far as I could judge from the indications along the line of march, my opinion is that it was conducted in an orderly manner, and did not partake in any degree of the character of a rout. This opinion is based upon the fact that had there been a general rout we should have captured more prisoners, more supplies, and munitions of war. I think the retreat was a rapid one, but well conducted for so large a force and with such large supplies.

Question. Can you give the reason for the delay that occurred after the fight at Perryville in pursuing the enemy?

No, sir; I do not know the reason.

Cross-examination:

Question. Had you any opportunity of gaining information in regard to the strength of the enemy at Chattanooga or the strength with which he crossed the mountains to invade Kentucky?

I received information from an expedition which I sent to Altamont from the neighborhood of McMinnville about the 22d of August that General Bragg had crossed the Tennessee River in the neighborhood of Chattanooga between the 16th and 20th of August with four divisions. The information I received about that time led me to suppose these divisions comprised some forty-eight or fifty regiments. But the information was varied. There was some contradiction in regard to the strength of these regiments. Some reports received said the regiments were weak; others that they had been filled up. Some of these statements put the regiments at from 300 to 400; others carried them up to 600. This information I got from my own operations in that country. About the 28th or 29th of August, as well as I remember, a person who reported himself to be a spy in the employ of General Buell came to McMinnville and was put in communication with me by General Thomas. This person represented himself as having passed some time in Chattanooga and as having left there only a short time before. He stated the enemy's force generally to be somewhere in the neighborhood of 60,000 men. He said that there were four divisions at Chattanooga, and that they had about 15,000 men in each division. He went into the minutiæ, giving names of commanders of divisions and commanders of corps, strength of regiments and strength of companies. His name, I believe, was Thatcher.

Question. According to all the information derived, what estimate did you at that time place upon the strength of Bragg's army in crossing the mountains?

My opinion at the time General Bragg's force was crossing the mountains and moving up the Sequatchie Valley, by weighing all the information I had been able to receive, was that it amounted to from 40,000 to 45,000 men. The opinions which I received from my own operations would not have led me to put so high an estimate as that upon the force; but the information obtained through the spy referred to led me to estimate it very much higher than the number I have given; but by comparing all the information, and making allowances and taking the mean between them, I entertained the opinion at that time that the force was about 45,000 men. This does not include Kirby Smith's.

Question. Had you as good an opportunity of acquiring information as to the strength and movements of the enemy as any colonel in your command?

I should think a great deal better.

Question. Did you ever hear the strength of the enemy estimated by any intelligent officer who had peculiar facilities for acquiring information as low as 25,000 men?

I never heard an estimate which placed it as low as 25,000 men.

Question. Do you believe now that Bragg entered Kentucky with no more than 25,000 men?

No, sir.

Question. Have you a pretty good knowledge of the country from the Nashville and Chattanooga Railroad northwest for a distance, say, of 50 or 60 miles?

A portion of my division, myself with it, was stationed three weeks at Decherd, on the Nashville and Chattanooga Railroad; subsequently it moved to Manchester; then to Morrison's Station, on the Tullahoma and McMinnville road; then to within 2 miles of McMinnville. This extended from the 20th of July to the 3d of September. During that time I was deeply interested in knowing as much as possible of the movements of the enemy—by what routes he could approach my own position. This led me to study the maps of the country as far as I could, and to gain all the information I could from the citizens in regard to the various roads through the mountains, more especially from Chattanooga to the various positions occupied by my division.

Question. What might be the various objects of an enemy crossing the Tennessee River near Chattanooga and descending into the Sequatchie Valley, having reference to the country we then occupied?

I suppose there might be a variety of objects. At that time the Army of the Ohio occupied a line extending from Nashville by the way of the Columbia and the Pulaski Railroad to Athens; thence eastward by way of Huntsville to Stevenson and Battle Creek; also troops were posted from Nashville along the line of the Nashville and Chattanooga Railroad and extending eastward as far as McMinnville. It might have been an object of the enemy to cross the mountains from the Sequatchie Valley and attack any of these forces in reserve along the line of the railroad to Athens eastward and crush them and afterward move rapidly on Nashville, or he might have crossed the mountains by the way of Altamont down on to McMinnville and fallen on the force there. The ultimate object of such a movement, I presume, would have been to clear the obstacles out of the way as soon as possible and move on Nashville. The object of such a movement would be Nashville. I cannot see that he would have crossed the mountains to stop at the foot of them.

Question. Could he have had it in view to descend the Sequatchie Valley and attack our forces in North Alabama, supposing that he was in a condition to assume the offensive?

My opinion is that it was in the range of his power. For such a movement as that I think he would have passed by way of Decherd, from my knowledge of the routes and roads. Whether it would have been within the objects proposed to himself or not is more than I can answer.

Question. State, if you please, the different routes by which the army could emerge from the Sequatchie Valley across the mountains.

Commencing at the most westerly route of the Sequatchie Valley of which I have any knowledge, it would have been possible to have passed a force by the way of Pelham, and from Pelham to Manchester, from Manchester to Woodbury, Murfreesborough, and so on. Then there is a road leading from the Sequatchie Valley, south of Dunlap, direct to Altamont (that is my recollection from the information I got), by which the enemy could have crossed the mountains. There is also a road leading from Dunlap to Altamont; a road also leading from Dunlap directly to McMinnville, crossing the mountains, and then down the valley of Caney Fork to McMinnville. There is also a road leading from Dunlap to Pikeville and from Pikeville to McMinnville, I think passing by way of Spencer. Also by continuing from Pikeville on toward Sparta the enemy could have turned the spur of the mountains and moved westward into the plains of Middle Tennessee. There is also a road, entirely west of any that I have described, leading from Decherd across the mountains to Stevenson.

Question. What is the nature of the ordinary road from Stevenson to Jasper and Battle Creek?

I do not know. I believe I have described all the routes of which I have any recollection, and while I have stated that all these roads were entirely practicable for the enemy, those portions lying in the mountains are not very good roads.

Question. Which of those roads is the most practicable?

Judging from my own knowledge of all the roads across the mountains directly, I consider the road from Dunlap to McMinnville the most practicable one.

Question. Do you know anything of what is called the Therman or Anderson road?

Not of my own knowledge. My information led me to believe that it is not a good road; rather a rough road; but a very good one for carriages.

Question. Does that road pass through Altamont?

No, sir; I do not think it does; it passes west of Altamont; but I may be mistaken. From that road it would be practicable to go by way of Altamont.

Question. Is Altamont in the mountains?

Yes, sir; it is.

Question. Describe, if you please, the different roads by which you can pass from Altamont into the plains northwest of the mountains.

There is a road leading from Altamont down the mountains into the plains to Winchester or Decherd. There is a road from Altamont by way of Tracy City and Hawkinsville by way of Decherd. There is another route from Altamont by way of Pelham, which also passes by Hawkinsville. There is a road from Altamont to Hillsborough, and by that way into the plain. There is also a road from Altamont by the way of Hickory Creek to Manchester; a branch leads off from this road to McMinnville; and there is also a road leading from Altamont over into the road leading from Dunlap direct to McMinnville. I would say, general, that there are quite a number of roads from Altamont by which troops could be marched down into the plains.

Question. Is there any one point which would command all those roads which diverged from the Therman or Anderson road?

I think a sufficient force occupying Altamont would be able to command the roads referred to in the question.

Commission adjourned to meet December 16, at 10 a. m.

DECEMBER 16, 1862.

Commission met pursuant to adjournment. All the members present; also the judge-advocate and General Buell.

Examination of General T. J. WOOD continued:

By General BUELL:

Question. Did you endeavor to ascend the mountains to Altamont with any portion of your command while you were in that region?

I did.

Question. Please state, then, the practicability of such a movement.

The road by which the ascent was attempted, and in part effected, is a very difficult one. The operation was a slow one, very slow indeed. Two brigades were marched up and one battery, I think, to the summit of the mountains, some 5 or 6 miles from Altamont. The ascent was commenced by another battery, but the operation was not completed; it was stopped by order of General Thomas, who was present and who was the ranking officer. It was quite a difficult operation and necessarily a slow one. No wagons, so far as I can recollect, were taken up the mountains at all. While it is what would be called a wagon road, it is a very bad one indeed, but could not be called an entirely impracticable one. The march up the ascent of the two brigades and part of another occupied pretty much one entire day.

Question. Did you understand that that movement was ordered in consequence of the information that the enemy was advancing on Altamont?

That was my impression at the time.

Question. Did you understand that it was a movement in which other corps of the army participated and to have for its object the concentration of the army at Altamont?

I had no information but to concentrate. I was informed by General Thomas, who was in command in that region of country at the time we were making the movement from McMinnville and that neighborhood toward Altamont, that General McCook and General Schoepf's divisions, according to the best of my recollection, would be concentrated at Altamont, and would probably reach there shortly after it was expected that the two divisions with which I was associated would be there.

Question. Supposing the information in possession of the commanding general to indicate that Bragg was in the act of crossing Walden's Ridge with the purpose of crossing the Cumberland Mountains by the Therman road, what would you think of the expediency and propriety of throwing a force of, say, 5,000 men in front of him on that road with instructions to fall back and unite with the army, forming a junction at Altamont, supposing such a junction to be practicable in other respects?

The judiciousness of such an arrangement would depend somewhat upon the distance in advance of Altamont a force of 5,000 men would be placed.

Question. Supposing this force of 5,000 men to be in the Sequatchie Valley and probably within reach of the Anderson road before the advance of the enemy could reach the valley?

I should consider it a very good arrangement for observing the enemy's movements, its rear being secured and the line of communication for falling back safe, always understanding, of course, that officers did their duty and never allowed themselves to be surprised in their communications.

Question. Can you state, from observation or official report, of the practicability of maintaining the army at Altamont, considering the want of water and other necessary supplies?

It would have been exceedingly difficult, if not absolutely impossible, to maintain any considerable force at Altamont for any length of time or even a few days. At the time I was at Altamont water was exceedingly scarce, and the road by which supplies would have been drawn I have already described. It is a very poor country indeed; land thin, little cultivation, and almost impossible to obtain any forage for animals in that locality for any length of time.

Question. Do you know anything about the Anderson or Therman road where it ascends the mountain from the Sequatchie Valley—whether it is good or bad?

I have no personal knowledge of that road. All I could state would be from information reported to me at the time. I was never farther than Altamont on that road.

Question. Did you learn while you were in that region that the enemy had worked upon that road and were the enemy's cavalry on that road about the time of your being there?

It was reported to me that the enemy was improving that road by parties I sent as far out as Altamont and scouting parties I sent out who encountered the enemy on that road. The opinion in regard to the improvement of the road was derived from citizens of the country.

Question. Could an army advance across the mountains by that road and descend into the plains by any roads you have described without difficulty?

I think they could, sir. We found it a great deal easier to get down than to get up.

Question. What is the distance from Jasper, the extreme road on one flank by which an enemy could march from the Sequatchie Valley, and Sparta, the point on the other extreme by which he could march from that valley?

Following the outlines of the mountains from Jasper around by the way of Decherd, McMinnville, and Sparta, in regard to guarding all the issues from the mountains, would cover a distance of over 100 miles.

Question. What force in proportion to the force of the enemy do you think would be necessary to guard such a line as that, the enemy in the Sequatchie Valley screened by the mountains and having the option of emerging from the valley by any of the various routes you have described considering all the possibilities of concentration?

I should think it would require a force from one-third to one-half larger than that of the enemy to do this effectually and to save the detachments from being overwhelmed before concentration had taken place.

Question. State, if you please, general, the disposition of the people of Middle Tennessee toward the Government and the army of the whole country in which we were operating.

The disposition of the people at that time, amounting almost to unanimity, was exceedingly hostile. The people of the districts I passed through were, with few exceptions, all rebels. The only locality I have ever been in in Tennessee in which I met with any evidence of genuine loyalty was Shelbyville. Of course here and there I met with an isolated individual who was loyal and had maintained his devotion to the Government, and I made it a point to learn of such persons with a view of getting information from them.

Question. Do you suppose it possible to conceal the movements of an army from the enemy in the midst of such a population?

I do not, sir.

Question. Is it possible to procure supplies for an army in the midst of such a population otherwise than by using force, supposing there are supplies?

I have always found it necessary to guard all my trains and protect all my operations for gathering supplies in Tennessee, and I do not think it would be possible to supply an army without covering its foraging parties in such a country with strong guards.

Question. Wil you state, if you please, general, what the condition of the country was at that time in regard to supplies? Were the supplies abundant and were they in the hands of producers, or were they collected in large quantities in different places?

The supplies necessary for an army were not at that time very abundant in the country, and, so far as my observation extended, were in the hands of producers, and not collected together in large quantities, and I always had to gather them by my own exertions.

Question. What were the supplies that the country afforded?

With rare exceptions only corn and beef; occasionally I succeeded in capturing a little flour.

Question. In what condition was the corn at that time?

For a period of twenty days before the Army of the Ohio commenced to evacuate Tennessee the corn could be used for the subsistence of animals by being cautious. Part of the twenty days I do not think it was in a condition for grinding, and could not therefore have been used as a reliance for breadstuffs for the men. A little of it was grated, I believe, by the soldiers themselves for making corn bread and mush, but that would be no dependence for feeding an army.

Question. Had the supplies of the men not been exhausted by the rebel forces before their retreat?

I think they had, sir, in a very considerable measure. In the country I was in some corn was left, but not a very great deal, and that was pretty much exhausted by us before the new crop came in.

Question. Can you state in a general way what the movements of the rebels were in the months of July and August in the organization of guerrilla bands and the use of a cavalry force in the country occupied by the enemy?

In the months of July and August last the rebels were active in organizing guerrilla bands to prowl through the country, and their cavalry force was actively employed in efforts to cut our lines of communication in rear of us, and this was frequently done.

Question. How did the cavalry of our army and that of the enemy compare in strength and efficiency, as far as you had an opportunity of judging.

I am not able to give an opinion worth anything in regard to the relative strength of our cavalry and that of the rebels, but I regret to say that I think the rebel cavalry generally showed much more efficiency and activity than ours did.

Question. Was there anything in the condition of our service which made it necessary to disperse our cavalry a great deal in small detachments, such as the occupation of a wide extent of country?

Our troops were very much scattered at that time, having long lines of communication and defenses to guard, and as a matter of course, for the protection of such small garrisons as many of them were, it was generally necessary to disperse the cavalry or divide it very much, with the view of furnishing all these garrisons the means of obtaining information of the designs and movements of the enemy.

Question. Do you know upon what point the army in Tennessee was dependent as a base of supplies?

I always understood Nashville to be the point. I never heard any other mentioned. The supplies were not furnished by Nashville, but brought to it from other points; and while it was also a base of our operations, in regard to our supplies it was merely a depot.

Question. What I mean to inquire is what was the source of supplies and the line of communication of the army with that source?

The supplies, as I always understood, were furnished outside of Tennessee. A great many, I believe, came from Louisville, by way of the Louisville and Nashville Railroad. While the Cumberland River was navigable, my understanding was that some of the supplies were brought up the Cumberland by boats. Where these supplies came from, whether from Louisville or other points, I do not know, nor can I say what time the Cumberland River ceased to be navigable for us. But during the latter period of our occupation of Tennessee we were wholly dependent on the line of Louisville and Nashville Railroad for our supplies. Occasionally some small supplies were found, as I mentioned, in the country.

Question. Do you know anything of the interruption of the railroad between Nashville and Louisville, by which the army was cut off from its source of supplies?

It was a matter of notoriety to everybody in the Army of the Ohio that the line of communication between Louisville and Nashville, as well as between Nashville and points farther south occupied by the army, was interrupted, by which the army was cut off from its supplies. We were frequently for a number of days, but I cannot state how many, without mail communication, and the reason always assigned, and which I believe was true, was the interruption of communication. At one period while I was at Decherd I found it necessary, on account of the interruption of communication and the importance arising therefrom of getting supplies, to take possession of all the mills in the neighborhood to obtain breadstuff for the men by grinding corn; but this was a difficult operation, and could not have been depended upon for a long period, nor could a large body of men have been subsisted by such means.

Question. What was the extreme length of the line of communication of the army from Louisville to points which it occupied in Alabama?

I should say that the average extended over 300 miles.

Question. Considering the scarcity of supplies in the country and the numbers and efficiency of the rebel cavalry, regular and irregular, what do you think of the practicability of depending upon the country for supplies for the army and carrying on at the same time active operations in a mountainous region, beyond the sphere in which these supplies were to be obtained, if at all?

I do not think it would be practicable, sir.

Question. Is it an axiom in military science that the army on the defensive in mountain warfare has the advantage?

Yes, sir. I should regard it as a military axiom that the party holding the mountain and living upon it can with a much smaller force maintain their position than the attacking party. I think the history of all mountain wars will bear out the statement.

Question. Was it at the option of General Bragg in invading Middle Tennessee to assume the offensive or defensive?

Yes, sir. I have already described a number of routes by which General Bragg could have crossed the mountains and descended into the plains of Middle Tennessee. By these routes offensive operations were of course open to him. On the other hand, he could have occupied a position in the mountains from which he might have threatened different points in Middle Tennessee. At the same time he could with his cavalry have carried on active operations, as was done, without occupying these positions in the mountains in our rear. Had General Bragg occupied such a position in the mountains his general war, in reference to any operations against him by the Army of the Ohio, would necessarily have been a defensive war.

Question. Supposing it had been certainly known that General Bragg designed to pass through Pikeville for the purpose of taking either the road to Sparta or McMinnville at his option, would it have been possible for my army to occupy a position in the mountains which would have had more than the effect to delay his movements, considering the condition of supplies, considering also the circumstances we had in view, and would it or would it not have been necessary at length to fall back?

From my knowledge of the position in the mountains, I do not think there is any point the occupation of which would have prevented General Bragg from moving by the route passing through Pikeville, considering, of course, the state of our supplies and the facilities which would then have existed for occupying such a position for obtaining supplies for the army. It is furthermore my opinion that had such a position been occupied on the hypothesis that General Bragg would not attempt to cross the mountains or pass up the Sequatchie Valley around the spur of mountains by Sparta, it would have been necessary to fall back and concentrate at some point in the plains of Middle Tennessee. This opinion is based upon my knowledge of the difficulty of getting supplies through the mountain, the badness of the roads, and also my judgment that the occupation of a point in the mountains merely could not have so seriously threatened the enemy's movements up the Sequatchie Valley, and would have rendered it necessary he should have cleared the position in the mountains.

Question. Was it generally understood, about the time of the enemy's advance from Chattanooga, that Nashville was the enemy's objective point?

My recollection of the weight of opinion of officers with whom I conversed about the time of the advance of General Bragg from Chattanooga is that Nashville was the objective point. Up to that time no demonstrations had been made which could lead to entertaining any other opinion.

Question. If it was improper under the circumstances to oppose the advance of Bragg's army into Middle Tennessee in or near the mountains, what, considering the character of the country and the position of the roads, was the natural and necessary point for concentrating the army to oppose his advance upon Nashville?

I think Murfreesborough was the most eligible point in the case stated, considering also the position and disposition at the time of our own troops.

Question. At what point in the line of march from Sparta on toward Kentucky could it first be certainly assumed that Kentucky was his destination?

After the enemy had passed above the spur of the mountains north of Sparta, and the information of his movements not indicating that he had turned westward with the bulk of his forces, but was perhaps continuing his movements northward, it would leave ground for conjecture that he had another object than Nashville. My information would go to show that parties were detached from about Sparta in the direction of Smithfield and Lebanon about the time the enemy was in that region of country. What was the extent of these parties I do not know. This occurred about the 5th or 6th of September. I tried myself to gain all the information I could of the movements of the enemy, and I confess I was not satisfied fully in my own mind up to that time whether his object was Nashville or Kentucky. I arrived in this city with my division on the 6th of September. Upon thinking over all the information I had been able to gain up to that time I began seriously to believe, from the movements of the enemy, that he had another object than Nashville, and of course that was Kentucky. I do not wish it understood that it was a positively entertained conviction. In consequence of beginning to entertain this conviction seriously and to be prepared for either alternative, according to my judgment and the exigencies of the case, I suggested, in an interview which General Buell did me the honor to have with me that day, that it would be proper to pass his army or a portion of it to the north side of the Cumberland river. This arrangement was proposed for a double purpose, both in reference to the invasion of Kentucky or an advance upon Nashville from the northern side of the river.

Question. When was it certainly ascertained that Bragg's army was advancing into Kentucky? And state how it was ascertained.

In a previous answer I have already stated that I crossed the Cumberland River at Nashville with my division early in the day of the 7th of September. I also gave in that answer the instructions I had from General Buell in regard to certain movements indicated in my answer. On reaching Gallatin, on the morning of the 8th, I received a telegraphic dispatch from General Buell directing me to halt within two or three miles of Gallatin, on the Nashville side, and to remain there until I received further orders from him. He furthermore directed me to send out the cavalry attached to my division, and to try by all means to get information of the position, designs, and movements of the enemy. I conformed with these instructions. I sent out the cavalry during the day and kept them out till a considerable time after nightfall on Monday, September 8. On the return of the cavalry it was reported to me that they had met at various points in various directions a hostile cavalry force, but in no instance had they seen any infantry. It was, however, reported to me, from a pretty reliable source, that Cheatham's division of the enemy was advancing toward Gallatin. With the view of arriving at the information that I desired to get in the most specific and reliable manner I employed a person, of whose loyalty I became entirely satisfied, to go eastward from Gallatin, following up the course of the Cumberland River, till he could obtain accurate and reliable information of the strength, position, movements, and designs of the enemy.

This person left me at sundown Monday, the 8th. During the night of the 8th I received an order from General Buell to move with my division from Gallatin, by way of Mitchellsville, to Bowling Green. I marched early Tuesday morning, and encamped that night in the neighborhood of Mitchellsville; next morning the march was resumed, and I advanced 8 miles beyond Franklin, Ky., when, having made about 22 miles that day, I went into camp. While in camp, about 2 o'clock Wednesday, the spy I had dispatched from the neighborhood of Gallatin joined me. He brought me information, which I then believed to be reliable and subsequent events have to a considerable extent verified it, that the enemy had crossed the Cumberland River at two or three different points, but his information to me was that the bulk of the force had crossed at Gainesborough. He furthermore informed me that all the information he could gain induced him to believe that the enemy's force was about 35,000 strong. He was quite an intelligent person, showing it by his manners and description of things. He furthermore informed me that the line of march of the enemy, as he had learned from soldiers, would be Tompkinsville, Glasgow, and Munfordville. He then added, "Beyond this point, general, I cannot certainly tell you where they will go; but it is generally said in their army that Louisville is their destination."

Believing this information to be very important, although the man represented to me that he had ridden 150 miles since he had left me at sundown Monday evening, I told him he must go immediately with the information to General Buell, whom I supposed was then in Nashville. I gave him a fresh horse and started him off at once, and told him he must see General Buell by daylight next morning. I was then about 56 miles from Nashville and about 12 from Bowling Green. I sent the messenger himself because I did not wish to trust to writing, but wished him to see General Buell himself, that he might tell his own narrative. I do not know certainly what time the next day this person reported to him; but that General Buell saw him I know, because he told me subsequently at Bowling Green that a person had reported to him and gave him the information (whether it was the first time such information was communicated to General Buell I do not know) that the enemy had crossed the Cumberland into Kentucky. It was the first information I had which put the matter beyond all question and set at rest the doubts as to what was the object of the enemy. I wrote a note then to General Rousseau, whose division was ahead of mine in the direction of Bowling Green, communicating the information I had obtained from the spy. I furthermore dispatched the information by couriers to the rear to General Crittenden, who was the next in my rear, to General McCook, and requested him to see that General Mitchell, who was in command of a division, got it also. I broke up my camp near night-fall and marched to Bowling Green that night, namely, the 10th of September.

AFTERNOON SESSION.

Examination of Brig. Gen. T. J. WOOD continued.

By General BUELL:

Question. Did you, general, know any reason for the movement of your division toward Bowling Green in advance of your information that the whole rebel army was moving upon Glasgow?

I did not have any positive information; in fact I did not have any. The dispatch I received directing that movement did not contain, so far as I recollect, any reason for it.

Question. Was it known while you were at Gallatin, with more or less certainty, that a portion of the rebel army had crossed the Cumberland River at Carthage and was moving northward?

I cannot say it was known by myself or by any person under my command or with whom I had communication at that time that any portion of the rebel army had crossed at Carthage and was moving northward. I heard a report either Saturday, the 6th, or Sunday, the 7th, and I think in General Buell's quarters, that some portion of the rebel forces had crossed the Cumberland River at Carthage, but how much reliance was to be placed upon the report I do not know; but I am certain I did not hear it stated then when I heard this report that any movement had taken place toward Kentucky; and my understanding of the movement toward Gallatin of my division, and what I understood was to be followed up by other divisions, was induced in part by this report. While at Gallatin, as I have already stated, reports came in that the rebel force that had crossed at Carthage would probably come to Gallatin. It was understood to be Cheatham's division. This information came from a well-known loyal man, and it was this opinion which induced me to employ the spy I have referred to in my preceding answer. The information I have referred to above as having been heard in General Buell's quarters came in directly through some lady who had been in that part of the country and had, I believe, brought the information to her husband.

Question. Supposing it to have been known that the rebel force which had crossed at Carthage was moving northward, was it probable that Bowling Green would be its destination, without having any positive information as to its destination?

Yes, sir; there is nothing in the topography of the country, nothing in the nature of the roads or communication, which would preclude the idea that Bowling Green would be its destination.

Question. Was there anything to entice the enemy to that point as a subordinate or minor operation?

Yes, sir; there was an important bridge over Barren River at Bowling Green which is one of the most important links in the line of railway between Louisville and Nashville. There had been at Bowling Green, at that time, to the best of my recollection, but a small garrison, which could not have made much resistance against a considerable force.

Question. Were there any supplies at that point which would have been important to the Army of the Ohio?

I was informed by General Buell in Nashville on the 6th and 7th of September that there were about a million of rations at Bowling Green. With the exception of one article, breadstuffs, there was a large quantity of supplies.

Question. What is the distance from Carthage and Gainesborough to Glasgow?

I think the distance to be about 50 miles and from Carthage to Glasgow about 50.

Question. With the information that the whole rebel army was moving upon Glasgow, would it have been judicious to bring a portion of the Army of the Ohio upon that point?

No, sir; I do not think it would have been a safe movement for half of the Army of the Ohio.

Question. What is the distance from Nashville to Glasgow by the way of Bowling Green?

It is 95 miles, according to my best recollection of the distance.

Question. After information of the fact that Bragg's army had marched over the Cumberland River toward Glasgow was it possible to concentrate the Army of the Ohio at that point in advance of them?

I do not think it was possible.

Question. Do you know when the division preceding the rear division of the Army of the Ohio arrived at Bowling Green?

My recollection is that it was on Sunday, the 14th of September, or Monday, the 15th, but on this point I cannot now be positive.

Question. What was about the strength of the Army of the Ohio at that time and at that point?

There were six divisions concentrated at Bowling Green about that time. I have no positive knowledge of the amount of cavalry force there, but I suppose the infantry force would have been somewhere in the neighborhood of 35,000 men. This estimate might be slightly under or slightly over the actual number.

Question. With what we know now of the strength of the rebel army, would it have been judicious or not to attack it without necessity with a less force than that when an additional force was coming up?

No, sir; it would not.

Question. Do you know when the rebel army marched from Glasgow?

From the information I received at the time of the movement from Bowling Green to Munfordville, the advance of the main rebel army left Glasgow on Monday, the 15th of September, and by Wednesday morning, the 17th, there was no rebel force at Glasgow. There might have been a few stragglers. Such was the information I received on the afternoon of the 17th of September from persons who represented themselves as citizens of Glasgow.

Question. Where was the rebel army supposed to be when the Army of the Ohio marched from Bowling Green?

The bulk of it was believed to be at Glasgow, and I think it was known that there was a brigade or more at Bell's or Glasgow Junction, and perhaps some parties thrown out on the roads leading from Glasgow to Bowling Green, of which there were two or three. Such was my impression, and I know more of the country and its topography than any other officer in the Army of the Ohio.

Question. Do you know whether it was a matter of newspaper information that a portion of Kirby Smith's force had been at Lebanon, and was it reported at Bowling Green that that force had moved toward Munfordville?

There were reports in the newspapers at that time that a force estimated at about 4,000 had been at Lebanon, and it was intimated that it belonged to a part of Kirby Smith's force; it was furthermore reported at Bowling Green, when the first attack was made on Munfordville, on Sunday, the 14th, that a part of Kirby Smith's or the force that was reported to be at Lebanon was concerned in it. The true facts of the case did not come out till two or three days afterward, when it became known that it was Chalmers' brigade that made the attack on Sunday.

Question. Was there even then any contradiction of the report that this portion of Kirby Smith's force was there?

No, sir; there was not.

Question. Was the report probable?

I cannot say it was, but I can say distinctly that there was no impossibility in it, and perhaps no improbability. There was nothing in the nature of the country or in the positions that could have prevented it. The country from the Kentucky River to Glasgow at that time was open to the movements of the rebel troops.

Question. Do you know with what immediate purpose my army marched from Bowling Green?

I believe I do, sir. I think I got it from the commanding general of the Army of the Ohio himself. It was with the intention of attacking General Bragg at Glasgow. Such at least was my understanding of it, and certainly I marched with my division from Bowling Green with that understanding. I talked with General Buell more than once upon that subject, and I think I knew his views. I remember distinctly that I gave it as my opinion that it would be a safe operation for us. I may be mistaken, but that is my recollection. The manner in which the army moved and the roads on which they moved all indicate that independently of any other information. Of course we all understood that information derived after leaving Bowling Green might change or modify the plan of operations. The army commenced to move from Bowling Green in the afternoon of Tuesday, the 16th of September, and my own division moved at 3 o'clock.

Question. How long were you precisely in marching from Bowling Green to Munfordville?

My division marched from Bowling Green Tuesday, the 16th of September. My division encamped in Woodsonville, on the south side of Green River, on Sunday, the 21st of September, making five days and a piece.

Question. Was there variation in the rate of marching during that time?

During the days that the troops marched, considering the number of the troops moving, the marches were about as usual. It was necessary to conform our marches to some extent to the places where water could be found. The country from Bowling Green to Green River is an exceedingly dry and badly watered one. There are scarcely any running streams, very few springs, and the dependence is upon ponds or surface water, and the season previous to and at that time was exceedingly dry.

Question. What is the distance from Bowling Green to Munfordville?

Forty miles.

Question. Do you think that movement an extraordinarily slow one. to have been made by an army of 40,000 men almost in the presence of an enemy whose position had to be ascertained step by step?

No, sir; I do not consider it an extraordinarily slow one.

Question. It has been observed by some witness in this investigation that the marches were long when the enemy was distant and much shorter when they were near. Do you think that extraordinary?

No, sir; I do not. In approaching an enemy whose position and strength are not fully known, and from whom battle is expected, common prudence would require that he should be approached cautiously until sufficient informa'ion had been obtained to warrant a change of such movements with safety.

Question. When an army moves upon a single road is not the movement of the head of the column necessarily slackened to bring the forces simultaneously upon the ground when it is expected to meet the enemy?

It must be done, unless the commander would run the hazard of attacking with his force in detail or separately.

Question. Were there any other routes except that by Munfordville by which Bragg's army could have marched into Central Kentucky from Glasgow?

Yes; there are two or three certainly. He could have avoided Munfordville, passing entirely to the eastward of it.

Question. Was it to be supposed that a force of 1,500 men at Munfordville, with no other object than to guard the railroad bridge, which could be replaced in a week, would attempt to oppose the advance of a large army such as Bragg commanded?

No, sir; I do not think it would.

Question. To leave it there was it not merely offering a bait to the enemy?

Yes, sir; I think it was. My opinion is that the force was sacrificed by being ordered to remain there, when it could have been withdrawn had the commander been allowed to use his discretion.

Question. Do you know whether I had any control over that force or any communication with it?

My understanding at the time we were at Bowling Green was that the force at Munfordville and the post belonged entirely to the command of General Wright and his, and so far as I know there was no official communication between that post and Bowling Green. The only information we got of the position of affairs was from citizens who came from the country and who brought rumors more or less reliable. The orders given to the garrison at that post came from the authorities I have mentioned. Such was my understanding.

Question. Will you state, if you please, the more important particulars of your movements from Corinth to North Alabama and the cause of the delay on that march and the manner in which your command was employed?

On Monday, the 1st of June, 1862, my division left Corinth, left under an order to proceed to Iuka, Tuscumbia, and Decatur, the object of the movement being to aid in repairing and to protect the working parties engaged in the repair of the Memphis and Charleston Railroad. A regiment of mechanics and engineers was sent along to aid in the work. The engineering department was committed chiefly to General Smith, while the military conduct of the whole matter was committed to me. My orders were to put the road in working order from Corinth to Decatur, to repair all the burnt bridges, and to make good any other destructions that had been committed on the road. Several important bridges were entirely rebuilt, tracks repaired and newly laid down—a great deal of such work, as would naturally occur to me as necessary to be performed. The most of the labor was performed by the troops of my division. The work was found to be much heavier than was orginally expected, and much delay occurred in the completion of it for the want of locomotives and cars, which could have been usefully employed in transporting material used in repairing the road. The greatest diligence was exercised on my part and the troops under my command to get through this work. It was not an agreeable duty, and the great separation of my forces necessary to carry on different parts of the work at the same time made it a very dangerous one, as it exposed us to be attacked by the enemy when we were very much scattered. For these reasons it was my desire to prosecute the work as rapidly as possible and to complete it at the earliest day. It was not, however, entirely completed till about the close of June, when I marched with the last of my [command] from Tuscumbia to Decatur, the bulk of the division having preceded me to Decatur, and repaired the road between Tuscumbia and Decatur and put it in working order.

Question. When did your division cross the river at Decatur?

I crossed with the rear of it on Sunday, July 6, 1862. The facilities for crossing the Tennessee were the poorest and of the most inconvenient character.

Question. Will you give the subsequent movements of your division up to about the time when the army was being concentrated around Altamont?

About midday, Sunday, July 13, I received an order to move with two brigades of my division to Stevenson, Ala. I marched that afternoon in obedience to that order. On reaching Huntsville, early Monday morning, the 14th, I received information of the raid on and of the taking of Murfreesborough. I went immediately to General Buell, in advance of my two brigades, to report their approach; was instructed by him to move as rapidly as possible to Shelbyville by the way of Fayetteville, Middle Tenn. I moved on with my command in the afternoon of the same day, continued the march the same day to Fayetteville and the day following to Shelbyville, making the entire distance of 87 miles in a small fraction over three days.

I remained two days at Shelbyville, when I received an order from General Buell to proceed immediately to Winchester, and take position in that vicinity in such a way as most effectually to protect and cover the railroad in that region, as well as generally to prevent the irruption of rebel troops into Middle Tennessee and Northern Alabama. I remained three weeks in the vicinity of Decherd. While stationed there the troops of my command were employed in guarding the railroad of Middle Tennessee from Wartrace to Decherd. Of course a great deal of time was occupied in scouting and exploring the country, getting information as to the position and designs of the enemy, as well as all information in regard to roads. Also while there, after the arrival of General Thomas, I aided in commencing and carrying out to a certain extent the fortifications designed to protect Decherd, the intention being at that time to make it a depot for the supplies of the troops in that part of the country.

About the 14th of August I left Decherd under orders to aid in putting the railroad from Tullahoma to McMinnville in working order. I marched from Decherd on August 14, from there to Manchester, from Manchester to Morrison Station, on the railroad, and remained there till the road was open entirely to McMinnville. This brought us up to about the 22d of August. About this time came in the reports of the crossing of the rebels at Chattanooga, and then commenced the movements which subsequently followed with a view of concentrating the troops at Altamont.

Question. Will you state what you know of the character and extent of the cavalry operations of the enemy about this time?

Their operations were very active, and according to all the information I obtained extended from Central Kentucky to Middle Tennessee. The rebel cavalry seemed to be on the alert during the whole of this time and ready to fall on any exposed place.

Information was derived by our scouting parties of their presence at various points throughout the country; in fact you could not miss, in going out, hearing of them and their movements. It was my understanding that Nashville was seriously threatened by them. It was reported that they had made their appearance in the vicinity of Nashville, and I never heard the report discredited. I was informed that the people were alarmed for the safety of the place.

Question. Were these movements of the enemy in large or small bodies or both?

From the reports I received the movements were sometimes made in considerable force; at other times in smaller parties. I heard of them moving in bodies of from 1,500 to 2,000; at other times in bodies from 100 to 300. I think perhaps I heard forces estimated as high as 2,500, but I think I never heard a higher estimate placed upon a single body.

Question. Had your march to Shelbyville any reference to these movements?

So I understood it and such were my instructions. It was feared that after taking Murfreesborough the enemy would move westward rapidly and perhaps cut our communication at Columbia, and it was with a view to be in position to prevent such a movement as this that I understood I was ordered to Shelbyville. I might add further, on receiving my orders to go to Shelbyville General Buell, who gave them to me in person, thought it might be necessary for me to go on to Murfreesborough; that, however, was to be regulated by circumstances, to be determined when I reached Shelbyville.

The night I passed at Fayetteville, which was the day before arriving at Shelbyville, I heard that the enemy was still at Murfreesborough. It was my intention, and I sent back a report to General Buell that if I should find this report confirmed on arriving at Shelbyville I would move promptly to Murfreesborough, for the purpose of attacking and clearing up any enemy that might be there. On arriving at Shelbyville I learned that the enemy had retreated to McMinnville after the capture of the force at Murfreesborough.

Question. Do you know anything of a simultaneous movement of another force from the vicinity of Athens toward Nashville with reference to the same movement of the enemy upon Murfreesborough and Nashville?

When General Buell gave me my instructions to go to Shelbyville he told me he had ordered General Nelson to proceed by rail with a force from Athens by way of Nashville to Murfreesborough. That General Nelson did go I was assured by the fact of frequent correspondence and communication with him while I was at Shelbyville and Decherd.

Question. Did the movements of the enemy seem to make these dispositions necessary at that time?

Yes, sir; I think they did. Some such arrangements were necessary to keep open our communications.

Question. Did it appear to you during the months of July and a part of August, before the concentration of the army commenced, that the troops were idle or that they were uselessly employed?

No, sir; it did not occur to me that they were idle or uselessly employed. I speak from the information I received at that time of the service they were performing. I know that many marches were made, and that the troops were generally, as far as my information extended, actively employed.

Question. Will you state, if you please, if you know anything of the condition of the railroads and of the difficulties of transporting supplies from Nashville into North Alabama during the months of July and August?

My opinion and observation combined led me to the conclusion that the two lines of communication by rail by which the troops in Middle Tennessee and Northern Alabama was supplied with provisions had been badly injured and torn up by the rebels in their retreat out of Middle Tennessee in the spring of 1862; that it required much labor to put these roads in working order again, and furthermore it required **great** vigilance and attention to keep them so.

EVENING SESSION.

General WOOD'S examination continued.

By General BUELL:

Question. State, if you please, what you think is likely to be the justice of criticisms upon the details of complicate military operations after the facts have all developed themselves, and the many circumstances, whether real or supposed, which necessarily influence the judgment and acts of the commander are not at all in view.

My opinion is that such criticisms are in a large majority of cases unjust and erroneous.

Question. Did you ever hear that it was my purpose to abandon Nashville in following the rebel army into Kentucky, and have you any reason to believe that the very reverse was my determination and nobody else's?

The day that I arrived in Nashville and prior to meeting General Buell, as I described in a former answer, I heard a report or rumor, from what scource I do not now remember, that General Buell had entertained some thoughts of abandoning Nashville. The report went further, to say that there had been some heated conversation and disagreement between General Buell and Governor Johnson on this point. This was during the morning of the 6th of September, 1862. I met General Buell, by his order, to report to him, about 1 p. m. of that day. I had a good deal of conversation with General Buell, at his request, in regard to the campaign probably ahead of us and in regard to what might possibly be the movements and design of the enemy, his supposed position from the best information at that time that we could gain of it, and of what means should be adopted on our part to meet the movements of the enemy. As I have said, the conversation was had at the request of General Buell, who spread out his maps for my examination. During the whole conversation, in which General Buell, with more than usual freedom and communicativeness with me, discussed his plans, there was not the slightest intimation of his intention to abandon Nashville, but, on the contrary, a statement of his intention to retain Nashville if possible. On the following day I had another conversation with General Thomas and General Buell at General Buell's headquarters, when the subject of the maintenance and defense of Nashville was discussed. I was present when General Buell informed General Thomas that he would leave him (General Thomas) in command at Nashville, and heard him give General Thomas various suggestions as to the defenses, &c. There was no intimation at that time of an intention to abandon Nashville, but every evidence given to induce me to believe that it was General Buell's fixed determination to hold it. I heard General Buell tell General Thomas what forces would be at his command to help him to defend Nashville, and that in his opinion this force would be sufficient to hold it against double the number; and it was further my understanding of the conversation in which I participated, as I have said, that General Buell considered that he was making sufficient provision for the defense of Nashville. I recollect an instance of that conversation, that General Thomas, after being satisfied that he was to remain at Nashville, said that he desired his own division to stay with him, and General Buell told him he could have it. So far as I know this opinion and intention of General Buell was not influenced by any other person.

Question. Do you remember how or from whom you heard this report of a disagreement between Governor Johnson and myself on this question?

I do not remember how or from whom I heard it. It came in so uncertain and vague a form that I attached no importance to it, and considered it one of the thousand idle rumors that float through camps and cannot be traced to any responsible scource.

Question. Was it the opinion in the army on the evening or night of the 8th of October that the engagement of that day had resulted in the defeat of the rebel army, or merely the repulse of an attack made upon a part of the Army of the Ohio?

I cannot state what was the opinion of the army, as I had very little intercourse on the night of the 8th with any person that pretended to be informed as to the events that transpired that afternoon, but so far as I heard an expression of opinion there was no belief entertained that there had been a defeat of the rebel army, and an impression seemed to prevail, so far as I had any means of arriving at a knowledge of it, that there would be fighting on the following day.

Question. Was it the expectation that there would be a battle between the two armies?

The impression prevailed among all persons with whom I had any conversation on the night of the 8th that there would be a battle on the following day.

Question. Do you know whether orders were given for attacking the enemy the next evening [morning]?

I cannot say that I know that orders were given, but I received an order myself to be prepared to advance to attack at daylight in the morning; this order was communicated to me from General Crittenden, who commanded the corps that I was attached to, with an intimation that a subsequent order would be given for the movement. This statement is made to show that I did not get my orders from the general commanding the army, and hence do not know what orders he issued himself. I did, however, receive a message by one of my aids from General Buell to be prepared for work on the following day, from which I understood that we would have a battle and severe fighting the following day, and I made all my preparations accordingly.

Commission adjourned to meet December 17, at 10 o'clock a. m.

NASHVILLE, *Wednesday, December* 17, 1862.

Commission met pursuant to adjournment. All the members present; also the judge-advocate and General Buell.

General WOOD'S examination continued.

Redirect examination by the JUDGE-ADVOCATE:

Question. Do you know that Bragg's army depended for supplies upon the country through which it passed?

I cannot say that I know it of my own knowledge. I always understood that a considerable part of the supplies used by Bragg's army was drawn from the country through which it passed. I also understood that a great many supplies were collected at Chattanooga, and these we heard were taken along with him. It was understood that a considerable part of his dependence was upon the country through which he passed. I cannot say that I have any positive knowledge of this, as I was not exactly with Bragg's army nor behind until after he got into Kentucky some distance.

Question. What, in view of his dependence for supplies, would have been the consequence of a check to Bragg's army?

In my opinion it would have depended to a considerable extent upon the check he might have received. It would perhaps have compelled him to hazard everything on the cost of a battle, with a view of getting us out of his way entirely. On the other hand, it might have compelled him to change his line of operations very much farther to the eastward, which of course would have delayed his movements to a considerable extent, or possibly it might have compelled him to give up his intention of invading Kentucky and to abandon the enterprise. This of course would depend in a great measure upon his ability to get supplies independent of the country through which he passed by carrying them with him.

Question. Had General Buell made a stand in the mountains, which army would have had the advantage in the matter of supplies, one drawing from McMinnville and Nashville and the other from Chattanooga?

Of course my answer will be entirely a matter of opinion, and as I have already said in former answers that I had no personal knowledge of the nature of the roads on the southeastern slope of the mountains across the Sequatchie Valley and over Walden's Ridge, I cannot give a very positive opinion; nevertheless, I should think that with the aid of railroad facilities (although we were much annoyed and threatened) and with the understanding that our army is better equipped in the matter of transportation than the rebel army, we would have had the advantage in drawing supplies.

Question. Had General Buell selected a point in the mountain to oppose Bragg after Bragg was crossing at Chattanooga which party would have been acting on the defensive?

In the case supposed our army, I presume, would have been on the defensive, as we should have taken that position to resist the advance of General Bragg, and it was my understanding when the matter of concentration of the troops at Altamont was being considered that it was with a view to resist such an advance across the mountains.

Question. Had a stand been made by General Buell at any point on the plains to meet Bragg as he descended from the Cumberland Mountains, would he (General Buell) have had supplies to carry out his purpose?

It is difficult for me to give an opinion on this subject, as I am not well informed as to the question of provisions at General Buell's command at that time. It would be a matter of inference to some extent. From the quantity of provisions which I think was issued to the divisions of the Army of the Ohio on their arrival at Nashville I should think that by putting the troops on half rations there would probably have been enough for the purpose indicated. My recollection is that we drew six days' rations. My division did when it arrived in Nashville. We had frequently need half rations and made them do at the time.

Question. Did you not and was it not known at the time that Bragg was co-operating with Kirby Smith?

I cannot say that I knew it or that of my knowledge it was known. I know that it was discussed as a possible or probable intention of General Bragg that it might be within the range of his operations. We did not feel perfectly satisfied that his immediate intention was to co-operate with Kirby Smith at all until after his movements indicated that his object was first Kentucky and not Nashville. Then, of course, it became evident beyond doubt that his first operation was with the rebel forces in Kentucky. It was frequently suggested during the earlier operations that co-operation with rebel forces in Kentucky might be the immediate object of General Bragg. Nashville was equally discussed with other places as being the first point of attack of Bragg's army, which in regard to certainty left the matter very much in doubt with that part of the army with which I had immediate connection at that time. The troops were very much scattered. Among other reasons suggested among the troops I served with was that General Bragg's army was destined immediately for Kentucky, because there was a great deal of political discontent in Kentucky, and it was to give a chance for this feeling to show itself in a rising.

Question. Was not an attack upon Nashville a co-operation, in fact, with Kirby Smith?

Whether in strict military parlance it would be considered a co-operation with Kirby Smith would be a matter of opinion among military men; but I should undoubtedly consider it a powerful auxiliary to General Smith's movements in Kentucky.

Question. What would have become of Kirby Smith and his army had General Buell been left free to co-operate with General Wright in attacking it?

I do not think there would have been much of it left.

Question. State at what time you became acquainted with Bragg's crossing the Tennessee and what you did with the information.

On the 22d of August, 1862, I sent a regiment of infantry from my camp, which was then at a little place called Vervilla, about 9 miles from McMinnville, to Altamont. I had learned previously that there were a few reliable loyal men in the neighborhood of Altamont from whom information might probably be obtained as to the movements, designs, and position of the enemy at Chattanooga. I instructed one of the officers of the regiment to put himself in communication with those persons. I had heard that there was frequent communication with the rebels themselves between Altamont and Chattanooga. This officer to whom I had committed the obtaining of information reported to me on his return, on the 23d, that he had heard from the loyal men in question that it had been reported about Altamont, through rebel couriers and other persons coming from the direction of Chattanooga, that the army of General

Bragg had commenced crossing the Tennessee River as early as the 16th of August—that is my recollection; that by the 20th there were four divisions across. He furthermore reported that it seemed to be the understanding among the citizens around Altamont that General Bragg's army, or a part of it, would cross the mountains, passing through that place.

Having no telegraphic communication myself immediately with General Buell, and General Thomas being in immediate command of all the troops in that region of country, I, on the afternoon of the same day, 23d of August, sent him a distinct report of this information, and my recollection is that he requested me to send it immediately to General Buell—he was at the time in telegraphic communication with General Buell—from the telegraphic station at McMinnville.

General BUELL. This testimony is unnecessary. I admit that ⁻ had information of General Bragg's crossing the river earlier than that given by General Wood.

Question. If at the time of General Buell's receiving this information of crossing he had concentrated his forces at Murfreesborough for the purpose of operating against Bragg what probably would have been the result?

It is difficult to say what might have been the result. I can suggest what in my judgment might have been the influence of such concentration, more particularly if that concentration had been followed up by other movements. I think it very likely that a concentration of the troops immediately at Murfreesborough would have had for the first result, if General Bragg had persisted in his designs of invading Kentucky, to throw his line of march much farther to the eastward than it was; perhaps, turning off at Pikeville, he would have been compelled, in order to avoid the movement upon his flank by the army concentrated at Murfreesborough, to avoid Sparta, to go much farther toward the east than the line of march he pursued. This would have thrown him more into the mountains of Tennessee and perhaps Kentucky, or he would then have been compelled to turn westward, making a considerable detour. If, on the other hand, he had continued his line of march through Sparta and toward the point at which he crossed the Cumberland River, in my opinion the early concentration of the Army of the Ohio at Murfreesborough would have put us in a condition to have moved eastward and brought the enemy to battle somewhere in that region of country.

Question. What effect would this change of line to the mountains have had upon General Bragg as to supplies?

I think it would have diminished his facilities and means of obtaining supplies.

Question. Was this your opinion in reference to the concentration at Murfreesborough at the time of the invasion, or is not your opinion now helped by facts that have come to your knowledge?

I am sure I entertained the opinion at the time I gained that information that our troops ought to be concentrated and so expressed that opinion to others. Of course that opinion has been strengthened by subsequent events. I rather think in the dispatch I described as having been written by myself to General Thomas I suggested that there should be an immediate concentration of our troops. I did not of course mean to designate any particular point, for I had not the necessary knowledge of other parts of the army, even had I sufficient rank to warrant giving advice on that point.

Question. That not having been done, and it was yet a matter of doubt whether Bragg had designs upon Nashville or crossing the Cumberland, what would have been the effect of a concentration of the forces at Lebanon?

The general effect would have been the same as that produced by the concentration at Murfreesborough. I think it would have made the crossing of the Cumberland by the enemy much more dangerous and hazardous to them, and, as a consequence of that, compelled them to make their crossing higher up the Cumberland. My understanding of the country farther eastward is that it is more broken, and would have lessened the facilities for the enemy's getting supplies and otherwise have trammeled his movements; but as to the extent of this I cannot of course give a positive opinion.

Question. Is the lack of supplies complained of on our part a sufficient reason for the failure to do anything of this sort?

I do not know to what extent it is charged that there was a want of supplies. I have said that on arriving at Nashville my division drew six days' subsistence; if the other divisions of the army obtained a like amount of subsistence on arriving at Nashville by putting the troops on half rations, as I have said they were frequently, in my judgment there would have been supplies enough to have attempted the concentration of the troops at Lebanon.

Question. I understand you to say that while at Nashville it came to your knowledge that the enemy was crossing the Cumberland and that you urged General Buell to advance up the Cumberland and dispute their passage?

No, sir; I did not say that. I have previously described at some length how I obtained the first certain information that the enemy had crossed the Cumberland River and of his movement in Kentucky. I have also in a previous answer said that while in General Buell's quarters at Nashville I heard a report made to him, as coming through some person who had information from above, that a part of the enemy's force had crossed the Cumberland River. I am free to say that, not understanding the report very distinctly, I could not of course attach any great importance to it, but that in view of all the circumstances and, as indicated in a former answer, beginning to be strongly impressed myself at that time with the opinion that the object of the enemy was an invasion of Kentucky, I did not take the liberty of suggesting to General Buell that it would be a safe, indeed the best, operation to put the bulk of his army on the north side of the Cumberland River. This arrangement would have put the Army of the Ohio in a position to operate against the enemy in his invasion of Kentucky, or, if we should be deceived as to that, we should still be in a position to protect Nashville against a decided movement by the rebel army under Bragg. I recollect I said to General Buell on that occasion, although I had made a considerable march that day, that if he deemed it desirable that the passage of the river should be commenced at once my division could go on. This conversation was on Saturday, September 6.

General DANA. I think it is the duty of the court to object to such questions. I make an objection to the question, inasmuch as there is danger in asking a witness a question such as that, wherein the question states him to have given testimony which does not appear on the record; and in future I shall object to questions being put in that way. The question started out with the assertion that the witness has given testimony which he has not given, nor is there anything like it on the record. The witness might be misled by such questions.

The JUDGE-ADVOCATE. General Dana is correct in his objection; but I was under the impression that such evidence had been given.

By the JUDGE-ADVOCATE:

Question. General, the two armies left the Cumberland and marched as far as Bowling Green and Glasgow nearly parallel. Did you understand at the time what the object of that march was on the part of our army?

General BUELL. I object to the question, inasmuch as it assumes as truth what is not true—that the armies were marching on parallel lines; whereas the fact is that they started from points from 40 to 60 miles distant and converged upon a point not more than 50 miles from the point of departure of one of them. In making the objection I do not consider that there is any question of law involved in it at all, and under ordinary circumstances I should not have thought of making an objection; but it has been the popular criticism upon the military operations under my direction that Bragg's army and my army have moved side by side of each other without an attempt on my part to molest him, whereas in fact they were moving from 60 miles to a less distance as they approached each other, with a country almost impracticable between them.

Question. Please state, general, while your army was moving from Nashville to Bowling Green at about the same time that Bragg's army was moving from the Cumberland to Glasgow whether you understood the object of our march at that time.

It is with me a matter of inference what might have been the intention of the commanding general of the Army of the Ohio in that movement. My own impression of the movement itself was that it was to bring about a concentration of the troops at Bowling Green for the defense and fortification of that place against any efforts of the enemy to capture its garrison and its supplies, and, the army being concentrated, subsequently to take such movements as circumstances and events might indicate as proper.

Question. As we did not attack the enemy at Glasgow, did not Munfordville become as important a point to us as Bowling Green?

General BUELL. I object to that question, inasmuch as it assumes that there was a neglect to attack the enemy at Glasgow, whereas the evidence shows that he could not have been attacked there.

The court is cleared for secret session.

The WITNESS. It is somewhat difficult to weigh with accuracy the relative importance of Munfordville and Bowling Green to us. I can say generally that I consider both places very important; in some respects the elements influencing the question of importance were about identical; and of course it was much to be desired that the enemy should not get possession of Munfordville.

Question. Are not the rules of prudence, caution, and so forth, as applicable to an enemy invading a country and moving in the same direction as the opposing force of superior numbers; and was not the success of the inferior invading army to be attributed to the wholesale disregard of those rules?

My answer to the first part of the question is, certainly, that all the rules of caution, prudence, watchfulness, &c., are equally applicable to the invading force as to its antagonist. But how far in this particular case the success of the enemy might have been due to the disregard of these rules I am not prepared to give an opinion. Of course a certain degree of audacity combined with a prudent degree of caution will generally lead to favorable results.

Question. Did General Buell give any reason for defending Nashville at the time he left General Thomas in command?

My recollection is that General Buell remarked in the course of his conversation to which I have previously referred that by abandoning Nashville we should almost entirely, if not completely, relinquish our hold on Tennessee; that in case Nashville should be strongly occupied by the enemy and we should be successful in driving the rebels out of Kentucky, it might and would probably cost us a great deal to retake Nashville, more particularly if the river should not rise at an early day, and especially if the enemy fortify the river in a way to oppose our ascent in case it did rise. And he furthermore expressed the opinion that the abandonment of Nashville would not only have a bad influence on our cause, more particularly in Tennessee, but throughout the country generally.

Question. Do you remember what gave rise to those remarks on the part of General Buell?

I do not now remember distinctly how that particular branch of the subject was introduced, but my best recollection is that the subject came under discussion in considering the difficulties of keeping Nashville supplied with provisions in case we should have a long campaign in Kentucky, and also in regard to leaving a sufficient garrison in Nashville for maintaining it with any reasonable degree of security. This latter consideration came up in connection with some conversation as to the probability of an advance from Northern Mississippi of a force under Price, Van Dorn, and Breckinridge, and other rebel leaders, it being reported in the newspapers and otherwise circulated at that time that such an invasion would be made.

Question. Was this conversation subsequent to the report that General Buell and Governor Johnson had words upon the subject?

It was subsequent to the time that I heard the rumor of such a conversation between General Buell and Governor Johnson. I heard this report when I first reached Nashville, on the 6th of September, which was about the middle of the day or before. I did not meet General Buell till about 1 o'clock that day or a little later.

Question. Do you know, general, the number of the army that marched out of Louisville under command of General Buell to attack Bragg at Bardstown?

No, sir; I do not know accurately the strength of that army. I made some estimate in regard to the strength of it myself, based upon information that I did possess.

Question. State what that estimate was.

I usually considered it, in round numbers, to be somewhere in the neighborhood of 80,000 men, artillery, cavalry, and infantry, all combined. My estimate was made by taking the strength of my own and other divisions I had some knowledge of and by averaging the whole number of divisions as nearly as I could consider their number. It might have fallen a little below or a little above. The approximation could not necessarily have been a very accurate one.

NASHVILLE, *Wednesday Afternoon, December* 17, 1862.

General T. J. WOOD's examination continued.

By General DANA:

Question. Had General Buell taken a defensive position in the mountains beyond Altamont, with the purpose of resisting Bragg's advance into the plains of Tennessee, was it or was it not possible for him then and there to have subsisted his army; and, if so, for how long a time?

I think this would have been a possible operation, upon the hypothesis, of course, that the troops in the rear charged with guarding the railway and line of communication had done their duty properly, and kept open our communication with the source of supply; but I do not think it would have been possible for a greater period than a few days, for the reason that the mountainous country itself affords very little that is useful in supplying an army and all the supplies for men and animals would have to be drawn entirely from our rear. Of course the transportation of forage for a considerable distance, which would have been a necessary result of this arrangement of troops, would in a short time have become a work of great magnitude and extent, and to this would have to be added the transportation of supplies from the line of railroad into the mountains.

Question. Was or was not the disposable force at General Buell's command at that time sufficient to enable him to place a sufficient force to defend his position in the mountains and at the same time place a sufficient force on his line of communication to guard them against any probable contingency?

The answer must be somewhat a matter of opinion, as I do not know the actual numerical strength of the force at General Buell's command at that time, but my opinion is that he had a sufficient force at his command to meet the case put in the question.

Question. At the time you subsisted your troops in Lower Tennessee on half rations what proportion of the other half rations was procured by them in the country to help out the short supply?

I can answer generally a very considerable portion; and without going into an estimate of the quantity, which would perhaps be very inaccurate, I can say generally that the troops of my command lived very well when they were on half rations. Certainly there was no suffering.

Question. What kind of supplies were gathered by the troops at these times to help out their short rations?

By my own particular command, which I can take as a test of others, some flour was found in the country. I caused corn to be ground into meal to be issued to the troops, collected beef cattle from the country, and at that period we were generally able to get a pretty good supply of fresh vegetables.

Question. Supposing none of these supplies could have been obtained, how long could the army have subsisted on half rations brought from the rear and have continued effective?

I should think, sir, for ⸰ long time. I do not think a soldier would become wholly ineffective for the want of provisions so long as he was supplied with half rations.

Question. At the time the rebel army was marching up the Sequatchie Valley were these supplies such as you have stated above procurable beyond Altamont or in that vicinity, supposing General Buell had taken up the defensive position alluded to?

I have already described that region of country as a very poor one. I do not think that that region of country would have afforded the supplies we drew from the more fertile and cultivated plains of Middle Tennessee.

Question. Was there between Altamont and the Sequatchie Valley any position where an army could post itself and at the same time be supplied with water?

I do not know, sir; I never was farther in the direction than Altamont; but I can answer generally, from my own observation and the information I received from others, that that whole district was at that time very badly watered.

Question. How many years have you devoted to the study of the military profession and what campaigns and tours of active service have you been engaged in?

It is now more than twenty-one years since I first went to West Point, and my studies and reading since that time have been chiefly directed to the military profession. I joined the Army of Occupation, as it was called, commanded by General Taylor, at Corpus Christi, in the month of September, 1845. I continued to serve with that army, and participated in all its chief operations, movements, and battles, up to the time that General Taylor relinquished the command of it, in the month of November, 1847. I was then relieved from duty in that army and ordered to the city of Mexico. I joined the army in the city of Mexico as soon as I could, and remained with that army till it evacuated Mexico and returned to the United States, in July, 1848. I was then ordered to Texas, and remained on duty in that department till the summer of 1854.

During the time I was in Texas I performed a good deal of staff duty and was engaged in various Indian campaigns and enterprises. In the spring of 1855 I was appointed a captain of cavalry in one of the regiments, and from early in the autumn of 1855, after my regiment was organized and when it took the field, I was almost constantly on duty with it, engaged in various expeditions on the Western plains, till the month of September, 1859. I then left my regiment and took advantage of a leave of absence to travel in Europe. I returned from Europe in April, 1861, and was ordered to Indiana to muster volunteers into service; remained there till October, when I was appointed brigadier-general, and ordered to join the troops in Kentucky. I have since that time been almost continuously on duty with what was lately termed the Army of the Ohio, and is now called the Fourteenth Army Corps and sometimes the Army of the Cumberland.

When I first took the field in Kentucky I commanded a brigade for a short time. After performing some other duties, such as commanding a camp of instruction and organization at Bardstown and performing some other work in the way of road-making in the mountains of Eastern Kentucky, the division which I now command was organized in the month of February, 1862, and I have remained in command of it ever since. This division has participated in all the material operations, movements, and campaigns of the late Army of the Ohio.

Question. Supposing yourself in the position of General Buell while commanding the Army of the Ohio at the time he received information of the crossing of the Tennessee River by the rebel forces and being possessed of such information as he was then probably possessed of, what would probably have been your plans and dispositions in order to have performed your duties so as in the best possible manner to have subserved the interests of your Government and to have inflicted the most damage on the enemy, while at the same time guarding to the best of your ability the interests of the States of Tennessee and Kentucky; that is, supposing those States loyal?

Had I been in command of the Army of the Ohio at the time I received satisfactory information that the rebel forces were crossing the Tennessee River at and in the vicinity of Chattanooga, being satisfied from my knowledge of the mountainous country that in all probability the enemy would never attempt to lead a strong force through the mountains into the plains of Middle Tennessee, I should have made my arrangements for concentrating the troops at an early day at the most eligible point in Middle Tennessee. I should of course have had the mountain passes well watched and observed by means of cavalry through the agency of spies. I think it important to remark in this discussion on the utter improbability of the enemy's leading a strong force through the mountains. This is simply my opinion, but I was well satisfied the first time I ever made an examination of that country that it would never be done and so stated it to General Thomas, and it was in consequence of this opinion, which he entertained as well as myself, that the two divisions I have spoken of as starting from McMinnville to go to Altamont were withdrawn, that is, by direction of General Thomas. By concentrating the troops in Middle Tennessee, even if the opinion that the enemy would not invade the country through the mountains was not correct, we should still have been in position to fall upon him as soon as he came out of the mountains, and at the same time be prepared to meet any movement up the Sequatchie Valley around the spur of the mountains into Middle Tennessee or to guard against the movement northward along that line into Kentucky. The fact that the enemy would have got possession of the country between the foot of the mountains and Murfreesborough which might have been selected as the point of concentration I do not consider a matter of material importance. Had we beaten his army, of course the country would soon again have fallen into our possession.

On the other hand, he could not have dared to pass us with a view of attacking Nashville, and would have been compelled, of course supposing Nashville to have been his chief object, to have beaten the concentrated Army of the Ohio in position first. By concentration at Murfreesborough or some such point we should more effectually have protected our communications to the rear than was possible by concentrating in the mountains. We should have greatly lessened the difficulties of obtaining the supplies that were drawn outside the limits of Tennessee, as well as increased our facilities for obtaining those which we did get in Tennessee. By this arrangement the commander would better have had his forces in hand and been prepared to meet any exigency that the events of the campaign might develop. As I have already described in various answers the number of roads by which it was absolutely practicable, though highly improbable, that the enemy could move across the mountains, consequently the simple occupation of any single position by our troops would not have effectually prevented such a passage; hence the necessity of early concentration at Murfreesborough or some other point in Middle Tennessee.

Question. Continuing now the hypothesis in the preceding question, and supposing your forces concentrated, as you have stated, at or near Murfreesborough, and supposing that you have received reliable information that the enemy has passed to the north of Sparta, please to consider that you have the information which General Buell was probably possessed of from day to day. After that please continue your plan of campaign up as far as Munfordville, supposing the enemy to have pursued the line of march which he actually did pursue.

In the first place I will remark, in regard to the operations of the army after being concentrated at Murfreesborough, that by an early concentration of the army at Murfreesborough, with proper preparations,—it is problematical of course,—but I entertain the opinion that if this had been done early enough the rebel army under Bragg might have been prevented passing much farther north than Sparta. But under the supposition that he had evaded the army concentrated at Murfreesborough and got so far advanced that he could not be stopped before getting across the Cumberland River, which the question seems to indicate, I should have crossed my army over the Cumberland River at Nashville as being the most eligible point, and have tried, by a rapid movement of it along the line of turnpike from Nashville to Gallatin, Scottsville, Glasgow, and into Kentucky, to have brought the enemy to battle if he persisted in marching on that road or compelled him to abandon that line of march and conduct his operations farther to the east.

Supposing the enemy to have been brought to battle and a victory to have been attained, of course it would have protected Bowling Green, Nashville, Munfordville, Louisville, &c. But if he had avoided battle and had moved farther to the eastward, Bowling Green and Munfordville would both have been effectually protected.

Question. After it was known at Nashville that the enemy had crossed the Cumberland River was it possible to conduct the Army of the Ohio to Glasgow by the route you have stated in force before the arrival of the enemy there?

It is impossible for n.e to answer that question, because I do not know when it was known at Nashville that the enemy had crossed the river.

Question. Please answer the question under the supposition that it was known at Nashville the following day after the enemy crossed the river, supposing the Army of the Ohio to be concentrated at Nashville.

No, sir; under the supposition given I do not think the Army of the Ohio could have concentrated at Glasgow before the enemy concentrated his troops there. The supposition is, as I understand it, that the Army of the Ohio is concentrated at Nashville. The other hypothesis is that the information of the crossing of the enemy is not received at Nashville till one day after the passage had been effected. According to my information the bulk of the enemy's forces crossed the Cumberland River at Gainesborough. The distance from Gainesborough to Glasgow is about 50 miles; the distance from Nashville to Glasgow is about 85 miles. Of course from this data every one can make up his own opinion.

Question. Suppose the rebel army to have crossed the Cumberland River in its march to the North and the commander of the Army of the Ohio not to have been able to learn the exact whereabouts of the main force of the enemy on any particular day prior to his arrival at Glasgow, would it have been prudent, taking into view the danger of a flank attack and the number of roads by which such an attack might be made, to have pursued his course from Gallatin to Glasgow?

Under the hypothesis of ignorance of the enemy's position and the other considerations suggested in it, the danger of a flank attack, &c., and the hypothesis of there being a number of roads favoring such an operation, it would not have been considered among military men, in my judgment, a prudent movement. I think it would have been a bold and audacious one. I think, however, that with proper observation in regard to the movements of the enemy the very audacity might have made it successful, of course supposing it to have been carried out very rapidly and vigorously. It would not, very clearly, been a prudent one.

By General Tyler:

Question. For what length of time was your division engaged in the repairing of railroads after you left Corinth?

For one month, namely, the month of June, 1862, repairing the Charleston and Memphis road from Corinth to Decatur. Subsequently, that is in the month of August, 1862, it was engaged for about a week in opening and repairing the railroad leading from Tullahoma to McMinnville.

Question. Were other divisions of the army engaged in repairing these roads and to what extent?

So far as I have any information only one other division of the Army of the Ohio did any work in repairing railroads. This division was commanded by the late General Nelson, whose division relieved mine in the vicinity of Iuka and finished the bridge over Bear Creek, which had been about completed by my division, and also the bridge over Buzzard's Creek, in the same neighborhood. It was common notoriety, and I believe true, that other troops belonging to the Army of the Ohio were engaged during the summer in opening railroads in Middle Tennessee.

Question. To what extent and for what military purposes were these railroads used afterward?

I think the part of the Memphis and Charleston road I have described as being repaired by my division was used to a very small extent in transporting provisions and troops. I do not think it ever amounted to a great deal; very few troops and few provisions were ever carried over that part of it. The roads of Middle Tennessee were used during the summer and early part of autumn in transporting supplies of every kind for the use of the Army of the Ohio and for transporting troops. I mean the roads of Middle Tennessee; the road leading from Nashville by the way of Columbia, Pulaski, and Athens to Huntsville; also the road leading from Nashville by way of Murfreesborough and Decherd to Stevenson. There is a branch from this road commencing at Tullahoma and leading to McMinnville.

Question. Did the repairing of the Memphis and Charleston road delay the movement of General Buell's troops to Stevenson or facilitate it?

I think, sir, it delayed it.

Question. What time did you arrive at Stevenson?

I never was there.

Question. What time did the troops arrive there and how near is that to Chattanooga?

I do not certainly know when Stevenson was first occupied by our troops. There were troops there, I am quite sure, about the end of June or the beginning of July. In round numbers I think Stevenson to be about 35 or 40 miles from Chattanooga.

Question. How long a time, general, would the moving of the Army of the Ohio from Corinth to Stevenson require, ignoring the road entirely, or in what time would you probably have reached there with the transportation you had when in use of the road?

I suppose it might have been done in from twenty to twenty-five days. I give a margin for difficulties and troubles. The Charleston and Memphis road was of no advantage in the movements and operations of the Army of the Ohio. The route I should have taken in moving from Corinth would be across the Tennessee River at or near the mouth of Bear Creek; I should then have moved eastward in the direction of Athens and Huntsville to Stevenson. That this is certainly the most direct route my recollection is, without being positively certain.

Question. Was General Buell's army ever within striking distance of Bragg before the rebel army crossed the Tennessee River?

I do not think the Army of the Ohio was ever concentrated in a position previous to the passage of Bragg's army across the Tennessee River to strike it.

Question. Do you think it was practicable to have concentrated the army at some point to have struck the rebel army at Chattanooga before it crossed the river?

In the early part of the month of July, when I got as far as Decatur and Huntsville, I considered it certainly within the range of the capability and power of the Army of the Ohio to have taken Chattanooga; moreover, I supposed the object of our movement in that direction was for that purpose. This was simply a deduction of my own from our movements. I did not obtain information from any one competent to give me exact information. It might have been possible at a later date, but from my own particular employment later in the summer I had not an opportunity of giving such attention to the subject as I previously had.

Question. Supposing within a week or ten days after the evacuation of Corinth by the enemy the Army of the Ohio had as rapidly as possible, considering the necessity of supplies and the transportation furnished that army, pushed on to Chattanooga by the route you have specified, what in your opinion would have been the result?

I think we could have taken Chattanooga.

Question. Have you ever been higher up the Tennessee River than Chattanooga?

I have never been quite so high as Chattanooga. Stevenson is the highest point to which I have been.

Question. From the information you obtained last summer, if Chattanooga could have been taken do you suppose it would have been practicable for the army to have continued on to Knoxville?

I do not think it would have been a practicable movement without a very considerable addition to the force of the Army of the Ohio. This will become apparent from the greatly increased line of communication we would have had to keep open and of course the greater exposure of our lines of communication to be cut. At the same time the occupation of Chattanooga itself would have been very much of a protection to operations in East Tennessee.

Question. Did Bragg's army after it passed the Tennessee River receive any reinforcements from Kirby Smith?

My information led me to the conclusion then, and I now entertain the same conviction, that General Bragg did not receive any material re-enforcements to the army he led across the Tennessee River and into Kentucky by the way of Tompkinsville till he formed a junction in Central Kentucky with Marshall's, Smith's, and Stevenson's forces.

Question. I have alluded to your testimony that you stated Bragg's army was at Glasgow on Monday, 15th.

I stated in answer to the question that the advance of Bragg's army left or commenced to leave.

Question. What proportion of General Buell's army was engaged with the enemy at the battle of Perryville?

It is difficult to say what proportion was engaged. I know about the force that was upon the ground and I have some knowledge of how that force was employed. Two divisions of General McCook's corps, as it was called, were most actively engaged in the battle of Chaplin Hills, and, according to my understanding, did the principal part of the fighting. As I have always understood, one brigade from General Gilbert's corps was detached to re-enforce General McCook. A considerable part of General Gilbert's corps were engaged in one way and another in the battle, but I do not think any serious work was done by it. Certainly it could not be said it was hotly engaged, and its casualties, as compared with the whole number of the division, would indicate this opinion to be correct. I am quite sure that only one brigade of Crittenden's corps, as it was called, fired a shot, and that was a brigade of my own division.

Question. Did you know or hear of any movement made by General Buell's army on the night of the battle or the next morning or during the next day to renew the battle or to find the enemy?

I cannot say I knew or heard of any movement taking place either that night, next morning, or the next day that could properly be called an effort to renew the battle on the part of the Army of the Ohio. Some movements were ordered in the corps to which my division was attached for an advance toward Perryville during the morning of the 9th, but such advance did not take place until after it was known that the enemy had evacuated the position in and around Perryville, and in fact till I had been in the suburbs of the place myself. But in all this I wish to be understood as speaking of what I saw and heard, and could not of course pretend to give evidence of the movements of the whole body of troops assembled in the vicinity of Perryville.

By General DANA:

Question. State as nearly as you can the disposal General Buell had made of his army about the time Bragg crossed the Tennessee to invade Kentucky. What point of occupation marked his left and what his right and how long prior to the movement of Bragg had his army held such a position?

The principal part of the troops of the Army of the Ohio were disposed, according to my recollection, at the time suggested in the question, from Nashville along the line of railway which leads from Nashville to Columbia and south as far as Athens, from Athens eastward by way of Huntsville and Stevenson to Battle Creek. The troops of this army were also stationed along the line of railway leading from Nashville to Stevenson; also along the road leading from Tullahoma to McMinnville, and some of them in the mountains and along the foot of the mountains from Decherd eastward as far as McMinnville. I think also about this time an expedition was made from the troops stationed at Battle Creek some distance up the Sequatchie Valley, but how far I never was informed. The troops at McMinnville would be considered the farthest east, and those at Athens, Northern Alabama, farthest west.

Question. By whose order did General Buell march from Corinth toward Chattanooga, what was the object of the movement, and do you know whether the operation was left to his own discretion or prescribed by the order?

I do not know that I was ever informed by any official functionary, but my understanding was that the movements were made in obedience to an order from General Halleck; but I never understood what was the specific object set forth in the order directing the movement, nor have I any knowledge as to whether discretion was allowed to General Buell in the execution of the order.

Commission adjourned to meet December 18, at 10 o'clock a. m.

NASHVILLE, *Thursday Morning, December* 18, 1862.

The Commission met pursuant to adjournment. All the members present; also the judge-advocate and General Buell.

General T. J. WOOD's examination continued.

Recross-examination by General BUELL:

Question. Do you know any reason why the army could not have advanced on Chattanooga as soon as it arrived in North Alabama?

I have already explained that my division of the Army of the Ohio was engaged for nearly a month after it came into North Alabama in repairing the Memphis and Charleston Railroad. After the completion of this work, and when my division was encamped within one day's march of Huntsville and a considerable portion of the army encamped in the neighborhood of Athens and Huntsville there was a considerable want of supplies, as I understood. There was a serious break in the railroad from Nashville by the way of Columbia, &c., which had to be repaired before it could be depended upon for getting supplies. I cannot now remember whether the road from Nashville to Stevenson was in working order throughout all its parts or not at this time. This was about July 7, 1862.

On 13th July, 1862, according to my best recollection, the garrison at Murfreesborough was captured and the road in several places in that vicinity broken up and bridges destroyed; so I was informed and so believed. It was a matter of common notoriety from that time, or for a month or more, up to the time we began our march out of Tennessee. Various efforts were made by bodies of the enemy to destroy our communications on this road, and it required great watchfulness and care to prevent it. I think, if I am not mistaken, that there were occasional interruptions of communications on the road at the period referred to, but they were of no great duration, according to my present recollection. I can state that from the time the garrison at Murfreesborough was captured up to the time the army commenced to concentrate at Nashville my own division was never supplied with subsistence further ahead than from five to seven days, and it was during this period, while the communications were so very much interrupted, that I was compelled at Decherd to resort to the means described in a previous answer to subsist my division. Whether the causes I have described were the real reasons for not advancing on Chattanooga I cannot say, as I was not in command of the army and not in very close communication with the commander; but they would seem to constitute difficulties in the way, and may have been reasons why no advance was made in that direction.

Question. Of what importance is Chattanooga as a military position and as a strategic point?

It is somewhat difficult to say of what strategic importance Chattanooga alone is, but I should think that a military force occupying Chattanooga, and with sufficient strength to maintain itself there, and also with its military connections to keep its communications open to the rear, would be able to command what is called the East Tennessee Railroad and some of the rail communications farther south. The simple occupation, if *per se*, in a strategic point of view, and without the ability to command the country for a certain distance west and east and south and east, would probably not be of any great advantage; but as far as I have ever thought of the propriety of occupying Chattanooga, it would have been with the hope at least that the Government might have been able to put there a force that would have been able to extend its operations sufficiently far into East Tennessee, and, if not to occupy the country, to destroy the rail communitions there.

Question. As a position in itself is it strong or weak?

I have never been at Chattanooga myself, and cannot give an opinion of its strength.

Question. Do or do not the railroads converging upon it from the east and south make it an exposed point for our troops?

I should say so, unquestionably.

Question. Would a force that might be sufficient to hold Chattanooga and cover its communications be sufficient to advance toward Cleveland, Dalton also, and especially to advance farther toward the south and east.

No, sir; I do not think it would.

Question. From your general knowledge of the force that the rebel Government could probably bring to bear upon Dalton or Cleveland, and supposing the communications of our army reasonably secure, what force do you think would be necessary to hold either of those points so as to cut the communications between Virginia and Georgia effectually by that route?

As I understand the matter, the occupation of Chattanooga, Cleveland, or Dalton, or any point in that region of country, would be with a view not only of preventing communication by what is called the East Tennessee Railroad in Virginia, but also to extend its operations far enough south and by the position it might occupy to cut off communication between the eastern part of the territory occupied by the rebel forces and the southwestern, or at least to impair those communications as much as possible. This would require such a force to extend its operations at least as far as Atlanta, Ga. Considering the importance of such communications to the rebels, and the isolated position which such a force would be in as regards its re-enforcements, I do not think it would be safe to occupy that region of country with any view to permanency with certainly less than 40,000 men, and probably 50,000 would be found necessary to accomplish effectually the purpose I have indicated above. This estimate of force would depend somewhat upon the vigilance and activity with which the commander handled his troops.

Question. Suppose the Army of the Ohio had marched to Chattanooga without meeting a man last summer, how long do you think it could have remained there with an enemy not more than 30,000 strong operating on its communications?

I should think only a few days; perhaps long enough to have broken up some important links in the railroad communications in the way of bridges, and then it would, in my opinion, with 30,000 men acting on its communications, have been compelled to fall back.

Question. Do you think in the long run such a result would have benefited the cause of the Government or have injured it?

I do not think it would have improved our cause in the long run. In considering myself the importance of occupying Chattanooga and that region of country I always did it with the expectation and understanding, and certainly that would be necessary in order that we should gain the full benefit of it, that we should be able to maintain that occupation; and with a view of making our forces, as far as I could exercise any influence with it, able to do that work, I constantly, during the past summer, in my correspondence with persons concerned in raising the military forces, insisted that our regiments should be filled up to the legal organization, they having fallen in the course of service much below it.

Question. Is there not, general, a good, level wagon road out of the Sequatchie Valley into North Alabama?

According to my best recollection there is such a road. I would not undertake to state positively how good a road it is, but I learned during my operations in Northern Alabama that there is a wagon road or route of the kind described. My knowledge of the road does not extend much farther than the east of Alabama.

Question. Is there not an old stage road crossing the mountains from Pelham and going on to Chattanooga called the Nashville and Chattanooga State road?

Yes, sir, I believe there is.

Question. Is there not a road from Jasper to Winchester by the way of Cowan or Decherd?

I was so informed while I was at Decherd during the summer. I never marched over the road.

Question. Did not our troops pass over these roads with their trains; at least two divisions of them?

I believe they did, sir; such is my understanding at least.

Question. What would have made you suppose that troops could not cross the mountains out of the Sequatchie Valley except by the way of Pikeville and Sparta?

I have not at any time, according to my recollection of my testimony, said that they could not have. I have habitually said that the roads through the mountains were practicable so far as I have any knowledge of them, but that they were not good, but on the contrary bad; and after learning something of these roads by personal observation and more of the other roads from information derived from others it was my opinion that they would not be used by the enemy.

Question. What makes the road from Pikeville to Sparta better than what is known as the Therman road? Is there anything in the character of the country, as you understand it, that would make it better?

According to my understanding of it there is. It is not so broken a country, and that part of the road in the mountains from Pikeville to Sparta is not so long as that in the mountains of what is known as the Anderson or Therman road. This opinion is derived from information which I picked up by inquiring in the country, and therefore may be an erroneous one.

Question. Is not the truth exactly the reverse in regard to the length of the mountain road? Is not the road from Pikeville to Sparta longer than the road from the Sequatchie Valley to McMinnville?

According to my understanding, supposing the enemy simply to wish to get over the mountains, the road from Chattanooga commonly called the Anderson or Therman road is shorter than the whole road by way of Pikeville to Sparta. But my understanding is that that part of the road by the Pikeville and Sparta route which lies in the mountains, and which is a great obstacle in either case, is shorter than the mountainous portion of the Anderson or Therman road. These are matters of opinion derived from information, and which may possibly be all wrong.

Question. Do you know of a good stage road from McMinnville to Altamont?

There are two or three roads leading from McMinnville to Altamont. I have traveled one such entirely between the two places, which is a practicable road for carriages and wagons except the ascent of the mountains, which is very difficult and bad. There is another advantage, I believe, in what is called the stage road from McMinnville to Altamont. I have traveled in part, namely, that part which is in the valley of Caney Fork, but I never ascended the mountain on that road or went as far as Altamont; consequently I can only give an opinion of that part of the road I passed over. I know nothing of the difficulties of the ascent of the mountain on that road.

On motion of General Tyler the court was cleared.

Question. You have spoken in your evidence of passing round the spur of the mountains by the way of Sparta.

According to my information the country north of Sparta and northeast for some distance is not so broken as that south and west of Sparta, and the mountains, as I believe from the information I gained in that part, "make off" into table-land in that direction.

Question. Are the ascent and descent the same?

Of course the elevated land would be crossed over, which makes both an ascent and a descent; but if the idea I have of the country from such information I was able to gain be correct, the ascent and descent would not be so difficult, and would probably give a better route for the passage of troops.

Question. Is it true, general, that the rules of prudence and caution are necessarily equally applicable to opposing armies or to the same army under different circumstances? On the contrary, is it not true that circumstances may force upon one general risks which the other would not be justified in assuming?

It is not true that the rules of prudence and caution are necessarily equally applicable to two armies always, and there may be reasons, such as the desperate nature of the enterprise the army is engaged in, why one such army might violate the ordinary rules of caution which in a general way are equally applicabl eto all military bodies, but which the antagonist of the first army might not be justified in disregarding.

Question. What was the strength of your division when you left Louisville on the march to Perryville?

My recollection now is, without being refreshed by reference to papers, that it was about 8,000; I think a shade over.

Question. What was it on the 8th of October, according to your returns?

I do not recollect what the returns would show for that particular day. I had left, by order of General Buell, one regiment at Bardstown, which of course would be subtracted from the strength I have given as marching from Louisville. That was all the loss of force by detail or order which my division suffered from the time it left Louisville to its arrival at Perryville; but there had been a great deal of straggling in the troops from Louisville to Perryville on account of the difficulties of the marches, the difficulty of obtaining water on the road, and other such causes, and it would be difficult to show accurately what diminution of strength any division might have suffered in that way. I do not remember what was about the strength of my division as shown by returns on or about the 8th of October, 1862, not having occasion to refer to that information since that time.

Question. Can you get that information by referring to your papers?

I am not sure that I can. I think it is doubtful. My division has marched a great deal since that time under circumstances calculated to hazard the safety of baggage and papers. I have been absent myself for a short period since the return of my division to Tennessee, during which time the records and papers were in the hands of other persons. I have not made an examination of them since with a view of determining whether such records have been preserved. By close investigation it might be determined pretty accurately from other data what it was.

Question. What time did your division advance on the morning of the 9th, after the battle of Perryville?

According to my recollection it was nearly midday. About 9 o'clock in the morning of the 9th I received orders from General Thomas, who was at that time second in command of the army and who more particularly marched with and supervised the corps of General Crittenden, to withdraw my division from its position in the general line of battle and which it had taken up during the afternoon of the 8th on its arrival in the neighborhood of Perryville, and place it in reserve in the rear of the divisions of Smith and Van Cleve. I obeyed this order, and subsequently, when the divisions of Smith and Van Cleve moved forward toward Perryville, my division followed them into the town and a little way beyond to the spring, where it encamped for the night.

Question. Was General Thomas aware that two brigades of your division were well advanced toward the town at that time?

I think he was informed of it, sir.

Question. Was it reported to you on the morning of the 9th that the enemy was marching off in sight of your advanced brigades?

Not until later in the morning than 9 o'clock, and after I had sent an order by the aide-de-camp for the two advanced brigades to fall back and take up a position in the rear of the divisions of Smith and Van Cleve.

Question. Do you know whether the enemy had retired at that time?

I cannot state of my own knowledge that I know it, but the reports made to me subsequently indicated that fact to be true.

Question. Did you report this information to your immediate commanding general?

I did, immediately. The report was made to me by my aide-de-camp, who had gone out to the front to order back the two advanced brigades, and as there seemed some little uncertainty and doubt as to whether it was so or not I rode forward myself, as mentioned in a previous answer, toward the town of Perryville, with a view to verifying the matter, and then returned and met Generals Crittenden and Thomas again and told them that nothing was to be seen of the enemy.

Question. Do you know any reason why this information of the movements of the enemy did not reach you earlier, if it was sent?

I do not, sir. I have described the manner in which it came to me and about the hour. During the whole of the morning of the 9th up to that time I was with my division and never probably more than 100 yards from it, and in a position to receive any information that was sent to me, as well as to supervise any movements of the division that might become necessary.

By General TYLER:

Question. Is not the Tennessee River navigable from Muscle Shoals and Knoxville during the summer for light-draught boats?

Without pretending to any very accurate information on the subject, I do not think it is navigable for most of the season from Muscle Shoals to Knoxville. I believe it is navigable during part of the year. I would not say for the greater part of the year.

Question. Is not Chattanooga the only Southern railroad connection between these two points; if not, what other Southern connection is there?

Chattanooga is on the line of the most direct railroad communication between Knoxville and the head of Muscle Shoals. But there is another way of going from one point to another without going to Chattanooga, but it is a very circuitous one and passes very far south.

GEORGE H. THOMAS (a witness for the Government), being duly sworn by the judge-advocate, testified as follows:

By the JUDGE-ADVOCATE:

Question. State, if you please, general, your name and position in the service.

George H. Thomas; major-general of the United States Volunteers.

Question. You will state, if you please, whether there was time between the 22d of August and the 2d of September to have concentrated the army under General Buell at Murfreesborough; and, if so, what effect that would have had on the invading forces under Bragg.

• As far as I can remember now I think there was sufficient time to have concentrated the army at Murfreesborough. I do not think that would have prevented Bragg from taking the road he did take.

Question. What point, in your judgment, would have been a better one to have operated from against the invasion?

I should have concentrated the army sufficiently to have fought at Sparta and urged General Buell to do so. His reply to me was that we had not subsistence enough at Murfreesborough to enable us to do so.

Question. You can state what your opinion was and is upon the sufficiency of that reason.

I believe now that the supplies were very limited at Murfreesborough. I did not know at that time anything about the state of supplies, as I was far away on the flank of the army.

Question. You can state whether, depending upon the supplies we had and what we could have gathered from the country, that proposition of yours was practicable.

Well, I think it was practicable; I think we had supplies enough to have enabled us to have met the enemy, fought, and whipped him; but that is simply my opinion, for I do not know the state of supplies.

Question. State to the Commission, general, why you selected Sparta in preference to Altamont.

There was an ample supply of water for our troops at Sparta, greater abundance of forage on the Caney Fork, and the position, in addition to that, was a very strong one. The enemy could not possibly have passed Sparta without fighting. He would have arrived in an exhausted condition, both from fatigue and want of supplies, and in my opinion could not have fought more than one day.

Question. With the army concentrated at Sparta would it have been necessary to have watched the passes at Spencer, Altamont, and other points by which he might have gone into the plains of Tennessee?

Yes; it would have been necessary until we ascertained positively that the enemy was on the road to Sparta.

Question. Had the Army of the Ohio sufficient force to have accomplished that?

That is a difficult question to answer, because we cannot always tell what movements an enemy may make. If the enemy had turned either of the roads in force it might have compelled us to withdraw from some of those roads to meet him. If he had not attempted any of those roads in force it would not have been necessary to use so large an observing force. I cannot say positively whether the army had a sufficiently strong force to have accomplished that thoroughly.

Question. After the army was concentrated at Nashville what would have been the effect upon the invading force had our army moved to Lebanon, upon the Cumberland?

The enemy being at Sparta and having their flank protected by Caney Fork, it would have been affected but little by the removal of the army to Lebanon, because they could have thrown out flank guards sufficiently strong to have prevented us from making any decided attack upon them until they had prepared themselves.

Question. What point upon the Cumberland would your better judgment suggest as being sufficient to affect the invading force and at the same time cover Nashville?

Lebanon would be an excellent place to cover Nashville while the enemy were marching from Sparta to the Cumberland, and as soon as they arrived at the Cumberland it would have been necessary to cross our forces to prevent the enemy from approaching Nashville from the north side of the river. Therefore if I had been in command of the forces while the enemy were marching from Sparta and Gainesborough I should have thought the best plan to throw a portion of the forces into Lebanon and concentrate the remainder at Gallatin, so as to be as near supporting distance to the troops at Lebanon as possible.

Question. When General Buell and forces marched out of Nashville toward Gallatin and Bowling Green did you understand the object of their march?

I understood it generally to be to watch the enemy and if possible to get into Bowling Green before he could arrive, so marching, however, as to prevent him from striking at the railroad from Nashville to Bowling Green. I do not think that General Buell wished to engage the enemy before reaching Bowling Green himself.

Question. Having secured Bowling Green, did you understand what next was the object?

As far as I know his next object was to offer battle to the enemy, that is, if he could succeed by reaching Bowling Green in putting his troops between Louisville and the enemy.

Question. Having secured Bowling Green, what other point on the railroad became one of importance to our army?

Munfordville and the crossing of Salt River. Those were the two most important points.

Question. Had the enemy made a stand at Munfordville what would have been the effect on our army? Could we have passed that place without a battle, and if defeated what would have been the result?

If the enemy had made a stand at Munfordville it would have been necessary for us to have fought him, and if defeated it would have been disastrous, as it was a difficult position for us to get out of.

Question. You can state, general, what effort was made on the part of General Buell to possess himself of that point before the enemy came up.

So far as I know, without ever having conversed with General Buell on the subject, I think he made very strenuous efforts to get possession of Munfordville before the enemy reached there. I was not with the main army at the time and cannot speak from positive knowledge.

Question. Can you state to the Commission how General Buell regarded Munfordville; whether it was an important point or not?

In a conversation I had with him at Prewitt's Knob, when I arrived, I came to the conclusion that he regarded it as a very important point, so much so that he believed the enemy would resist him, they being in Munfordville when I arrived at Prewitt's Knob, and he immediately after my arrival made all necessary preparations for a battle at Munfordville.

Question. State if you know the number of the army that marched out of Louisville under General Buell to attack Bragg at Bardstown.

I do not know how many, but I should estimate that there were about 54,000.

Question. What was the object in view when that army left Louisville?

The object was to overtake the enemy, fight, and destroy him if possible, either by a disastrous defeat or by cutting off his retreat if he succeeded in getting off in considerable force from the battle-field.

Question. How was that object affected by Kirby Smith's forces?

It became necessary for General Buell to divide his main army and leave two divisions watching Smith, marching against Bragg with his remaining divisions.

Question. Where was Kirby Smith at that time?

A portion of his force was at Frankfort, but his main force was believed to be at Lexington.

Question. Was it known what point Kirby Smith had been threatening and in what direction he was moving at that time?

It was generally believed he was threatening Louisville. I do not remember that his forces moved about that time. They had remained stationary for some days.

Question. Looking at the positions of the two armies under Bragg and Kirby Smith, what roads would they follow and at what point would they form a junction and by what roads was it reasonable to suppose they would leave Kentucky?

After the battle of Perryville, when it became necessary for them to leave Kentucky, there were but two roads that offered them any security to get to Tennessee direct; the one by Somerset and the other by Mount Vernon and London. They might have retreated through Mount Sterling and into Western Virginia.

Question. With what expectation did General Buell's army approach Perryville in reference to the enemy?

We expected to be resisted by the enemy at Perryville.

Question. What reason had you for such expectation?

We had met with resistance all the way from Louisville, and the resistance became stronger and stronger every day. At Bardstown there was quite a skirmish.; there was also a skirmish between Bardstown and Springfield as our troops advanced; and there being a very scant supply of water between Springfield and Perryville and a good supply at Perryville, I think that all thought the enemy would take and hold possession of the water and give us battle there.

Question. What, in your judgment, should have been the course of our army immediately following that battle?

I think as soon as we could determine whether the enemy was going to retreat across Dick's River we ought to have marched upon Danville or Lancaster or Stanford, whichever we could have effected.

Question. What would have been the effect, in your opinion, of such a movement?

I think, sir, we should have had, in all probability, another battle, depending entirely upon the good management of our army whether it would have been a complete disaster to the enemy or not.

Question. You can state whether that was your opinion at the time and what suggestions you made upon it.

As well as I can remember now I suggested to General Buell on the evening of the 9th that Crittenden's corps should be advanced as far as Danville; that future movements should depend upon what was developed by that movement.

By General DANA:

Question. Had you posted a portion of your force at Lebanon and the remainder of it at Gallatin while Bragg was approaching Gainesborough was it not at the option of the enemy to avoid you and march toward Munfordville?

Yes, sir.

Question. Why did not General Buell wish to engage Bragg's forces before reaching Bowling Green?

He wished to get his army between Louisville and the enemy and secure his supplies; for, his supplies secured, he could then attack him.

Question. At the time you were at McMinnville what number, from your best recollection, did you estimate the aggregate of Bragg's forces to be?

I never could make out more than 45,000, but the information I received at McMinnville was not very definite. The people who gave me information were generally ignorant and did not know how to estimate numbers. I therefore did not know how to estimate them.

Question. Taking into consideration all the information you then possessed, with what force would you then have felt justified to give battle to Bragg on his descending into the plains of Tennessee?

I think if I could have got 45,000 men at Sparta I would have given battle to him.

Question. Were Bragg's forces materially increased or diminished from that time prior to their reaching Munfordville?

I do not remember to have heard of any additional force joining him. I understood that he was marching by way of Sparta and concentrating his troops as he passed along. My estimate of his forces was based upon what I could learn—what passed through Sparta by the various roads. A force was left to watch his flank and rear and threaten Nashville. I do not think, however, that that force was more than 10,000.

Question. In the event of his having been compelled to accept battle on his line of march from the Cumberland to Munfordville was this force within supporting distance?

I think not. I believe that the greater part of it was south of the Cumberland, though I am not positive as to where the whole was.

Question. After General Buell became aware that Bragg probably did not intend to take Nashville, but would cross or had crossed the Cumberland, could General Buell then have safely reached Glasgow in sufficient force to have compelled Bragg either to retreat or accept battle?

I do not think he could.

Question. What was the earliest moment after the battle of Perryville at which it was known that the enemy would cross Dick's River?

I do not think that it was decided before 12 o'clock on the 11th. It was strongly suspected, however, on the night of the 10th. Colonel Harker's brigade, in Wood's division, had quite a skirmish with their rear guard on the morning of the 11th.

Question. Could any earlier information have been reasonably gained on this subject?

We were compelled, of course, to depend for our information on persons who were friendly to the Federal cause. We had to feel our way entirely from Perryville to the crossing of Dick's River. The information we received from some of those loyal persons was that they were retreating across Dick's River; but of course we had to ascertain that positively ourselves, and it was necessary to be sufficiently strong to resist any attack on their part.

Question. What was your position on the 8th of October?

I was in command of the right wing.

Question. What was the position of the right wing in reference to the town of Perryville?

The extreme right was about 3 miles southwest of Perryville, on the hills bordering the stream that runs by Perryville (Chaplin River I think it is called). The troops were facing toward the east.

Question. Where were your headquarters or personal position on the night of the 8th?

Half a mile in rear of the center of the right wing.

Question. On the morning of the 9th did you receive any report from any source as to the enemy being in view in retreat near the town of Perryville; and, if so, from what source and at what hour?

I did not receive any such report.

Question. Did you receive any report on the morning of the 9th of the fact of any officer in your command having been in the suburbs of the town of Perryville?

I did not.

Question. Where was General Buell during the day of the 8th of October?

He was at night, when I saw him, at his headquarters, immediately on the road between Springfield and Perryville. I do not know the exact distance, but I believe his headquarters were about half a mile beyond the line. I passed the camp of one division in going to his headquarters, which was but a short distance in front of this camp. During the day of the 8th I did not leave the right wing, and therefore do not know where General Buell was during the day.

Question. Was General Buell ill during that day?

Yes, sir; he was lame from the effects of a fall from his horse or the falling of his horse upon him.

Question. Was your personal whereabouts on the forenoon of the 9th probably known to the corps, division, and brigade commanders under your command?

It should have been. I sent word to all of them on the day of the 8th where I could be found, and it was understood that I should return to the same place on the morning of the 9th. After the troops commenced moving I could easily have been found by any one, as I was on the road all the time from the position the troops occupied in the morning until they reached the camp near Perryville, where they encamped that night.

Question. General, from the habits of the sub-commanders under your orders is it at all likely that any one of them on the morning of the 9th made any reports to the headquarters of the army which were not made through your headquarters?

I do not think they would have done it. They usually reported through me. I am not aware of an instance of their having reported direct to headquarters.

Question. On the morning of the 9th did you hear of any baggage trains of the enemy being seen in retreat?

I do not remember any such report being made.

Question. On the night of the 8th, after the battle was ended, what was your belief as to the relative condition of the two armies as affected by the work of the day?

The only information I received was after reaching headquarters (General Buell's) on the night of the 8th, that is, regarding the battle on the left, and the impression made on my mind then was that General McCook's corps had been very much cut up and could do but little fighting the next day, but General Gilbert's corps and the right wing were in as good condition as before the battle. I believed from what I had heard that the rebel army would resist us the next day; that they considered they had achieved a victory on the left and would resist us the next day.

Question. At what time on the day of the 8th did you become aware that the left wing was engaged with the enemy?

I did not know that a battle had been fought on the left until after night-fall, when, as I was riding to my tent, Lieutenant Fitzhugh, of General Buell's staff, over took me and told me. This must have been about 7 o'clock.

Question. Did you hear any firing on that day; and, if so, what was the character of it?

I heard cannonading about the time that the head of Crittenden's corps reached the position it was to take up, and I directed Captain Mack, my chief of artillery, to report to General Buell that I had arrived in position and with the head of the column, and would superintend the placing of troops in position, and requested the general to send me any orders by Captain Mack. Captain Mack returned about 12, with a plan of the ground and directions from the general to dispose the troops in a certain manner preparatory to an attack the next morning at Perryville; but the arrangement was not positive; it left the arrangement of the troops somewhat to my discretion if I thought it was necessary, I asked Captain Mack if he knew what that firing was we heard on the left in front; his reply was that the report came to headquarters that it was Captain Gay, chief of cavalry, reconnoitering, and the enemy were firing upon him with artillery. About 3 o'clock in the afternoon I again heard very heavy cannonading, and directed General Crittenden to send a staff officer to General Gilbert to know what that firing was. The sun was probably half an hour high when he returned. General Gilbert replied to General Crittenden by a short note, stating that he had met with some little resistance himself, but was then camping his troops for the night; that General Rousseau had been engaged—I think he said had been driven back slightly, but had regained his ground. The firing continued at intervals from about half past two till about an hour of sundown, but I am not positive.

Question. Would such firing as that which you describe proceed from the resistance of a reconnaissance?

I do not think so; and for that reason I sent to General Gilbert to know why there was such firing.

Question. Taking into consideration the relative distance of yours and General Buell's headquarters from the scene of this conflict and the direction of the wind, would the sound of artillery or small-arms be more readily heard at General Buell's headquarters than at yours?

I think that with as high a wind blowing as there was that day the cannonading was not more distinctly heard at his headquarters than where I was. The wind was blowing very heavily.

Question. Was the wind blowing from his headquarters toward the firing or from the firing to his headquarters ?

I think the direction of the wind was to his left from the direction of the firing.

Question. At the hour that General Gilbert sent his report in answer to General Crittenden's inquiry as to what the firing was, what was the actual condition of things in reference to his own and McCook's command ?

With reference to his own, he reported that he was putting his troops in camp for the night. In reference to Crittenden's command, it had been in position for several hours and the troops were quiet in camp, with the exception of Smith's division, a portion of which was skirmishing with the enemy in front. Smith's division was moving up gradually to gain the hills which overlooked the creek and was skirmishing with the enemy till dark. The other two divisions of Crittenden's corps were in position and quite in supporting distance of one another. I cannot state what the condition of McCook's command was, because I had no knowledge of it at that time.

Question. The last question is intended to get the information as to whether the reply of General Gilbert at that time gave the correct information which was desired of him, or whether, from your subsequent knowledge, you do not know that his statement was incorrect.

I learned at General Buell's headquarters that night that the information received from General Gilbert was not a true statement of the case, but at the same time I believe General Gilbert reported all he knew at the time.

Question. Is General Gilbert's ignorance of the actual condition of things at that time a sufficient proof that he was not at those parts of the field where the presence of a commander is most called for while his troops are engaged ?

No; I do not think it is. General Gilbert had the superintendence of three divisions, and while superintending those three divisions he could not reasonably be expected to know what was going on at a distant point from his command. There was no unusual delay in the reception of his reply to General Crittenden's note; therefore I think he must have been with his corps.

Question. How many years is it since you first commenced the study of the military profession ; how and in what scenes of service have you been engaged since that time ?

About twenty-nine years. I have served in the Florida war, in the Mexican war, and in this rebellion.

Question. Placing yourself in the position of General Buell, in command of the Army of the Ohio, at the time he commenced his retrograde movement toward Nashville from Northern Alabama, and being possessed of such information as he was then probably possessed of, what at that time would probably have been your plans and dispositions in reference to performing your duties in the best possible manner so as to have subserved the best interests of your Government, to have inflicted the most damage on the enemy, and to have properly guarded, to the best of your ability, the States of Tennessee and Kentucky ? Keep in view in answering this question the information which General Buell probably got from day to day during the whole course of the movement.

I think it very likely that I should have pursued the same course that he pursued, although I believe now, from the information I had myself, that he should have met the enemy at Sparta and fought him there. The information I had, however, at that time was probably very different from that General Buell had. It is my opinion that could we have fought the enemy at Sparta we could have destroyed his army there.

Question. Were you second in command of the Army of the Ohio?

I was the second officer in rank.

Question. During the term of the campaign was General Buell as communicative to you as regards his plans as was proper for a commander to be and as was necessary to be in the event of an accident befalling him?

Whenever we met General Buell was always communicative, and after our arrival at Louisville I think that he explained to me his plan of the campaign as fully as was necessary. Previous to that we were not a great deal together, and although I did not know what his intentions were on all occasions, I believe he would have communicated with me freely if we could have been together so that we could converse with safety. He did not like to risk his plans to the hands of a courier or any other means.

Question. Do you know whether a failure to relieve the garrison at Munfordville is in any way to be attributed to the commander of the Army of the Ohio?

I do not know.

By General ORD:

Question. When you suggested to the commander of the army, General Buell, the propriety of concentrating a sufficient force at Sparta to meet the enemy, had you any reliable information of the enemy's position? If so, what was it?

I had information from the citizens of the Sequatchie Valley, the neighborhood of Kingston and Crossville, also from scouts sent out by myself, that the enemy was crossing that portion of the country, and said it was their intention to pass through Sparta, and some said attack McMinnville; others said Murfreesborough, others said Nashville, and again others said the army was marching by that road as the most direct to Kentucky.

Question. Did the position of the enemy, as located by this information, afford General Buell ample time, considering the roads and the condition of his men, to concentrate a sufficient force at Sparta to have met them?

I think it did.

Question. After arriving at Sparta, in case the enemy had delayed in the valley or taken another route, was the condition of our supplies such that we could have remained some time at Sparta as the best position for an army of observation?

We could not have remained for any length of time at Sparta with the amount of supplies we had at that time.

Question. Were there at that time other practicable roads leading toward Kentucky which would have enabled the enemy's army to have avoided the army at Sparta?

There is a road from Kingston to Montgomery and Livingston which they could have used. There was also a road from Knoxville, Clinton, Jacksborough, and Monticello which they could have used, and there are intermediate country roads, of which I have been told, on which troops could have moved, but they are very difficult.

Cross-examination by General BUELL:

Question. At what date would you have concentrated your army at Sparta to have resisted Bragg?

I would have concentrated at Sparta about the time that the army concentrated at Murfreesborough. Instead of moving the troops to Murfreesborough I would have placed them in such a position as to concentrate at Sparta the day it became necessary to fight; that I think was about the 2d or 3d of September.

Question. Where would the enemy have been at that time?

I believe the main body of the enemy would have been between Spencer and Sparta at that time.

Question. How long would it have taken you to move your army from McMinnville to Sparta?

The troops that were at McMinnville could have been removed to Sparta in two days from where they were and placed in position. The other troops could have been started in sufficient time to have arrived immediately afterward. The one division would probably require four days, the other two divisions would have reached in five days, as well as I remember the position of the troops now.

Question. You suppose, do you not, that the enemy would be apprised of your movement?

Yes.

Question. How close could the enemy come to McMinnville before deciding whether to go to Sparta or McMinnville?

They could come within about 24 miles.

Question. Not any nearer?

They might come nearer, but with a force at McMinnville, if they designed going to Sparta, they would turn off before getting so near.

Question. Is there not a road following the general direction of the mountain on its top nearly midway between McMinnville and Pikeville or McMinnville and Dunlap and running into the Sparta road; and, if so, how close would that have brought the enemy to McMinnville before he must necessarily determine whether to go to Sparta or McMinnville?

That is the road I had in view in answering the first question—about 24 miles. According to my recollection that road runs about midway of one edge of the mountain to another; it is nearer to Dunlap than it is to McMinnville.

Question. What is the distance from McMinnville to Dunlap?

The citizens there always represented it to me as being 40 miles. It is about 30 according to the military map and 25 by another map.

Question. Does your estimate of the distance from McMinnville to where the road turns off to go to Sparta remain the same?

The road, as I understood it, was on the top of the mountain, and ran along the mountain near the top of the ridge. It must be 20 miles at least from McMinnville.

Question. How far is it from McMinnville to the foot of the mountain, according to your recollection?

It is 12 miles by one road and 14 by another; there are two roads.

Question. How far is it from McMinnville to Sparta?

According to my best recollection now it is about 22 miles, and a little over 20 in a direct course. By the military map, reckoning the winding of the roads, I presume it would be almost 22.

Question. With your army at Sparta, the enemy concealing his movements by cavalry and other means which are possible, which do you think would reach McMinnville first, if he were suddenly to determine to march on that point?

I think I could march there first with my forces.

Question. Will you explain why?

Because the road is better.

Question. How much time would you allow yourself to get knowledge of his movements before commencing your movement?

That is a matter of uncertainty; but in concentrating my forces at Sparta I should not have left McMinnville unoccupied. I should have left a force sufficiently strong to have checked him in any attempt to take possession of the town, and as far as possible made him determine to take one road or the other decidedly; that is, either the road to McMinnville or the road to Sparta.

Question. Would you not in that way divide your force and render yourself liable to be beaten in detail?

I do not think I would have done so there. As a general rule the forces should not be divided, but the physical features of the ground at McMinnville and between there and Sparta are such as to enable an officer to divide his troops, in my opinion.

Commission adjourned to meet December 19, at 10 o'clock a. m.

NASHVILLE, *Friday Morning, December* 19, 1862.

The Commission met pursuant to adjournment. All the members present; also the judge-advocate and General Buell.

General THOMAS' examination continued.

Cross-examination continued by General BUELL:

Question. Would the enemy in descending from the mountains upon McMinnville have been able to use more than one road?

They would not have been able to use but one road direct from Dunlap. They would approach McMinnville by one road. They could, however, have approached McMinnville by turning off after reaching the road from McMinnville to Pikeville or they might pass from Dunlap to Manchester and descend the mountains toward Altamont.

Question. Or farther away toward Winchester?

Yes; they might descend into the highlands of Tennessee toward Winchester or Pelham.

Question. Or directly from Altamont to McMinnville by a good road?

That would be if they approached direct from Altamont. To reach McMinnville from Altamont they had to strike the road from Dunlap to Altamont in the valley of Rock River some distance from McMinnville. It is, as near as I remember, 8 or 10 miles from McMinnville where the road turns off.

Question. Would an army in descending upon McMinnville by these different roads meet with any greater difficulties than you would have in crossing Caney Fork between Sparta and McMinnville?

I think it would, for the reason that the roads I saw on the side of the mountain were very rocky and difficult. The only great obstacle on the road between McMinnville and Sparta is the crossing of Caney Fork at Rock Island.

Question. Is that a formidable obstacle?

It is; but an army could pass that easier than down those hill-sides.

Question. Did you travel over the road from McMinnville to Altamont by the way of Beersheba Springs, and is it not a good mountain stage road?

I did not pass over that road, but I have always heard that it was a good mountain stage road, and the only one that is good from the mountains to the highlands.

Question. When you were at McMinnville did you ever have any information which indicated that the enemy might cross or was crossing the mountains by the way of Altamont?

I did not get that information myself. The information I received from my scouts indicated that the enemy were passing toward Pikeville and Sparta, but I think, from the message which I received from General Buell, it was reported to him that the enemy were passing or might pass across the mountains through Altamont.

Question. Did your cavalry report the enemy on the Altamont road?

They reported a portion of the enemy on the top of the ridge, but marching toward Spencer, as far as they could learn.

Question. At what time did you propose a concentration of the Army of the Ohio at Sparta and in what manner?

As well as I can remember the dates, it was somewhere about the 28th of August, and I proposed to have the troops in readiness near McMinnville to either sustain the troops that were under my command there if attacked, or if the enemy turned in the direction of Sparta decidedly to take position there.

Question. How was this recommendation made?

I do not remember whether it was sent by a messenger or by telegraph in cipher.

Question. Have you a copy of the recommendation?

I have with my papers, but not here.

General BUELL. I request that it may be presented to the Commission.

Question. Have you ever heard that I proposed to abandon Nashville in marching the Army of the Ohio into Kentucky and what do you know of my determination upon that matter?

General Buell, in conversation with me after the army was concentrated in Nashville, frequently said that it would be perfectly disastrous to abandon Nashville; that we would lose more than we could gain in twelve months, or perhaps more than we could gain at all in Tennessee or in this part of the country. That was the substance of his remarks. I never had an idea that he thought of abandoning Nashville. When he left me to take command of Nashville in his absence he wished me to designate the number of troops I wanted to defend the place, and said that if he could possibly spare them I should have them. And I remember about the last conversation I had with him the subject was again spoken of in the same terms, and I replied that if I had to abandon Nashville I would leave it a heap of ashes.

Question. Have you any reason to suppose that my determination upon that question was influenced by or was the result of any consultation with Governor Johnson?

I have no reason to suppose so.

Question. Did you see while at Prewitt's Knob a man by the name of Pratt, who came into camp and represented himself as having information from the rebel army?

I do remember him, sir. He came to my tent the evening before the army marched, and I sent him to General Buell.

Question. What statement did he make to you?

I was very busy at the time; just returned from the picket line, and did not have a great deal of conversation with him, and cannot say positively what information he did give me. I thought it of more importance that he should see General Buell, and therefore sent him to him immediately.

Question. Did you deem his information very important, if you remember it?

That was the reason why I sent him to General Buell. He told me in general terms that he was just from the rebel army and could give important information, and knowing he had gone out for the purpose of procuring it and his story being a very connected one I sent him at once to General Buell, thinking it was of very great importance that he should know what information this young man could give.

Question. Did he then or at any other time represent that he had counted the rebel forces, and that they did not exceed 22,000, infantry and artillery?

It appears to me that he stated he had counted the rebel forces, but I do not remember what statement he made as to the number.

Question. Whatever his statement may have been, have you at any time entertained a doubt as to his honesty?

I thought it a little singular that he should have appeared so suddenly at that time.

Since then the members of my staff have spoken of him, and without having any positive ground to base an opinion on I myself have doubted his loyalty and I think they have too.

Question. Were you present when General McCook came to my head-quarters on the night after the battle of Perryville?

I was.

Question. Did you hear the conversation which passed between us?

I heard the greater part of it.

Question. Did you hear General McCook make application for re-enforcements to enable him to withdraw his corps from the position which it occupied, and did you from that conversation think that the re-enforcements were necessary to enable him to do it safely?

I do not remember that General McCook made any direct application for re-enforcements. It seems to me that General Buell was questioning him as to whether he had made certain dispositions of his troops, and General McCook replied that the dispositions were being made or that they were about completed, but represented that some portion of his troops were in bad condition and ought to be sustained, and I think that General Buell replied that if he could make this disposition he did not think support was necessary, but that he would give him support if he possibly could. I do not remember the particular words of this conversation, but think this was the purport of it, as my attention was particularly called to the dispositions of the troops on the right of the army for the attack in the morning that we were to make. I was thinking of these dispositions more than of the other.

Question. Was any such impression made on your mind as that General McCook asked assistance which was necessary for the safety of his command and that I peremptorily refused it?

No such impression was made on my mind.

Question. Will you state, if you please, what the orders were for the following day?

The orders for Crittenden's corps were to form in column so as to be able to deploy into line of battle immediately and march upon Perryville and attack the enemy if he was there in the morning, and it was the impression that we would have a battle the next day.

Question. At what hour was the advance to be made?

At 4 o'clock in the morning.

Question. Were those orders executed?

They were not executed at the time. The troops did not get fairly in motion, I presume, before half past six. I was detained at General Buell's headquarters till nearly 4 o'clock myself, but sent a message by signal to General Crittenden to commence the movement, and when I reached the ground, about half past six, I found the troops were just about to move. I believe the cause of their not moving was the result of General Crittenden's misconstruing the order. The impression was that he was to be ready to move at 4 o'clock.

Question. Will you give the particulars of the movements of that day, as far as they are important, stating where you stopped?

After the right wing entered Perryville I sent word to General Buell that the troops were in Perryville and that the enemy seemed to have retired toward Harrodsburg—this must have been about half past ten or eleven o'clock—and then asked for orders. The orders for Crittenden's corps were to go on to the spring beyond Perryville and encamp for the day. There was a considerable delay in getting this order, as it took some time for messengers to go to General Buell's headquarters and back. I do not know where General Gilbert's corps encamped that night nor McCook's. In advancing to the position in which I was to encamp the right wing, I was told to be particular in guarding against any demonstration of the enemy to attack us. One division was placed on the road between Perryville and Danville.

Question. Will you explain, if you please, general, why the right corps did not get into Perryville before the time you mentioned and what delayed its movements?

The division of General Smith had some skirmishing on the morning of the 9th with the enemy's cavalry. That was the only delay of which I know. After this cavalry was driven off the troops then marched into Perryville as rapidly as the ground would permit. A portion of the troops marched by the road and the other across the fields and pasture.

Question. How much of the time was occupied with this skirmishing?

The troops must have been engaged skirmishing through the woods from half past six till probably 9. I do not remember to have noted the time particularly, but the troops moved as soon as I arrived there.

Question. Did you know of a portion of General Wood's division being very near the town early in the morning?

I did not know of it.

Question. Did you know of their being recalled and why?

No, I did not.

Question. At what time and on what occasion did you recommend that the army should take position at Danville?

That was on the 10th, I think; the day after we left Perryville and marched to Mr. Harlan's farm, I think on the Salt River or a branch of it. My recollection is that I suggested that Crittenden's corps should be sent to Danville and that the whole army should be sent, its after movements to be regulated by what we might discover the enemy to be about.

Question. How far, in fact, was Crittenden's corps from Danville?

I think about 5 miles, as well as I can remember.

Question. Was one division encamped at Fry's Spring?

Yes, sir.

Question. Was it known then what the position of the enemy was certainly?

It was not certainly known.

Question. Was it known until the evening of the 12th that the enemy had certainly crossed Dick's River, and in moving from Harrodsburg might he not have gone toward the Kentucky River without his destination being certainly known until it was traced up?

I do not think it was certainly known that he had crossed Dick's River until the 12th, but from the information which we got from the citizens of the country I was under the impression that he would cross there, and that was the reason why I recommended to General Buell to place Crittenden's corps in Danville. He could have crossed the Kentucky River from Harrodsburg and either have gone to Camp Dick Robinson or to Lexington. I presume that that was one reason why General Buell was influenced not to send Crittenden's corps to Danville on the 11th.

Question. Considering the character of the enterprise the enemy had undertaken, do you think it unreasonable to suppose that he might go into the interior of Kentucky or that he might move on the Frankfort road and thence across to Louisville?

I don't think it is unreasonable to suppose that he might have gone to Central Kentucky, thence to cross Dick's River, and attempt to hold that part of the State, at least long enough for them to have completed preparations to get out of the State, but I do not think that he would attempt to march on Louisville without retiring from Perryville.

Question. Was there anything in the condition of Bragg's army or in its relative strength to justify the assumption that he was fleeing ignominiously, and that no enterprising service was to be expected from him?

Nothing but the fact of his having retired from Perryville; for, as far as I could learn, he had retired in good order. As I said before, I did not think that he would attempt to go to Louisville because he had retired before us from Perryville. There is no reason to suppose that he might not have attempted to hold Central Kentucky, and having selected a strong position, remain there and await a good opportunity to undertake some new enterprise or to resist us as we attacked him.

Question. Was not the attack which he made at Perryville made by a portion of his forces, and was it not calculated to inspire respect rather than contempt for him as an adversary?

As far as I could learn the attack at Perryville was made by a portion of the forces, and the character of the battle was such and the result such that it would have been imprudent to have marched against him without proper precautions.

Question. Is it to be assumed that he had no other design, and that he had no alternative except to retreat by Lancaster and Crab Orchard from Camp Dick Robinson?

No; it cannot be assumed that he had no other design.

Question. Suppose my army had been put in the way of his retreat by that route, what line of conduct was he at liberty to pursue by a study of the map?

If he should choose to run the risk of battle, and, if successful, he might have retired through Danville toward the south by Hustonville and Liberty and Jamestown or by the roads south, or he might have passed through Stanford and Somerset if he felt obliged to leave Kentucky. If successful against us, of course then he could have remained in Kentucky. If we had fought him and he had been defeated, he still might have been strong enough to have marched by way of Richmond toward the eastern part of Kentucky, but I do not think he could have retreated through Mount Vernon and the Rockcastle Hills or by Somerset if we had had a battle and had whipped him.

Question. Suppose he had crossed the Kentucky River at Camp Dick Robinson toward Lexington, what would you have done?

I would have secured all the ferries and fords on the river with a sufficient force to have held him there and then march against him by way of Frankfort, that route being the best for the security of our supplies.

Question. What force would be required, do you suppose, for these different crossings to prevent him from making use of any one of them at his option?

I believe a brigade of infantry and one battery of artillery could hold the Hickman Bridge against any force that could be brought against it. The crossing at the mouth of Dick's River, as well as I understood it, could be held by probably the same amount of troops; and I am also of opinion that a brigade could hold the crossing at Clay's Ferry.

Question. What force would have been sufficient to prevent you from crossing the river at Frankfort?

We had possession of Frankfort at that time, so I was informed.

Question. Was that possession in sufficient force to withstand Bragg's army, considering the character and the number of the troops?

I do not suppose it was sufficient to withstand it entirely.

Question. Suppose he had designed to pursue this course, crossing the river on the Lexington and Richmond road, which would have been likely to procure possession of that crossing first?

The enemy would, of course.

Question. What would prevent the enemy, then, while you were marching to Frankfort, from actually marching out of Kentucky by the Cumberland Gap?

If he secured the ferry, of course he could take that road to the Cumberland Gap.

Question. Is not the river fordable near that point at a low stage?

It is seldom, if ever, fordable there; so I am informed by the citizens.

Question. Are there many fords lower down on the river?

There is one about half way between Clay's Ferry and Hickman Bridge which is fordable at a very low stage of water, but it is a difficult crossing. That is the only ford I know of.

Question. Is it your impression that the river is generally not fordable; that is, only passable by ferries and bridges?

Yes, sir.

Question. State, if you please, the more important particulars of your march from Corinth into Middle Tennessee last summer—the date of your orders, and the occasion of any delay you met with in the march, and the route you took, &c.

I do not remember now the date that I left Corinth, because I do not fix those things in my mind. It would have been in the latter half of the month of June. I left under orders to distribute my division along the railroads from Iuka to Decatur. The troops commenced moving the second or third day after I received the order. It was as soon as they could move and get rations. We reached Iuka the second day. As soon as I arrived there General Nelson marched, and I sent a cavalry force to distribute along the road for the purpose of relieving the bridge guards and allow General Nelson's troops to concentrate at Tuscumbia. I think it was about four days after General Nelson left that the troops again moved forward to Tuscumbia, leaving infantry guards at different bridges as far as that town. At Tuscumbia details were made to relieve the bridge guards which had been posted by General Wood from Tuscumbia to Decatur; the remainder of the divisions remained at Tuscumbia. It took some little time to make these different arrangements, but I do not think there was any unnecessary delay.

About the last of July I received information that my division would be relieved from duty on the railroad, and General Buell ordered me to concentrate as soon as possible and march to Huntsville, I believe. Before that was commenced, however, General Fry's brigade was ordered to cross the river and go to Reynolds' Station, on the Nashville and Decatur Railroad, I believe it is called, for the purpose of guarding a provision train from Reynolds' Station to Pulaski. The railroad not being completed at that time, General Schoepf's brigade was ordered to march by way of Athens, and the third brigade was ordered to cross at Florence and Eastport and march to Huntsville by way of Athens. There was also some delay in effecting all these movements, because it was necessary to wait for the arrival of the division which was to relieve my troops, and also the difficulty of crossing the Tennessee River. The troops were occupied in crossing the Tennessee River probably two days. After the delay of about ten days from the time the order was given to the time the division was relieved from guarding that road there was no delay from Corinth to the point where the troops were finally ordered, namely, Decherd, after the crossing of the Tennessee River was effected. As well as I remember now the division was concentrated in Decherd about the 10th of August.

Question. Were there any rumors, about the time of your arrival at Decherd of an advance of the enemy into Middle Tennessee from Chattanooga and other points?

Yes; there were rumors that Forrest and Morgan were reported to be at Sparta.

Question. Do you know anything of any difficulty in supplying the troops in North Alabama in consequence of roads being out of order?

I suppose I may say I know officially, as I was informed by Captain Darr, that it was a very difficult matter to get supplies for the troops. This, however, was in ordinary conversation between officers. I may have been told by General Buell himself when I met him in Huntsville, though I am not positive; but I know that Captain Darr informed me.

FRIDAY AFTERNOON, *December* 19, 1862.

General THOMAS' examination continued.

Cross-examination by General BUELL:

Question. Did you know of any petition having been gotten up and signed by officers within your own division for the removal of one of your brigade commanders? If you do, please state what you know about it and how that matter came to my notice?

There was such a petition, signed by a good many officers of the brigade, and it was handed to me with this officer's resignation. I tried to persuade him not to resign, but he insisted on doing so, and requested also to forward this application with his resignation. I permitted him to do so without approving of his resignation in the Army, and I presume that was the way in which the information reached General Buell.

Question. State, if you please, what I did in reference to that matter.

I think General Buell saw this officer, and after conversation with him his resignation was withdrawn and the application of those officers with it. I do not remember that any other action was taken in the matter. I sent for some officers and spoke to them myself about it, and I believe that the greater part of them apologized to the brigade commander for having signed any such paper; but I do not know whether General Buell saw any of these officers or not.

Question. Do you remember whether that paper was referred to you for official information with reference to official action?

That paper was referred to me, as I remember now, for a report of how it came to my headquarters, and I explained on the indorsement that was sent back with the resignation how it came to my headquarters. It came to my headquarters, and I sent it back to the officer concerned, the brigade commander. The officer concerned heard of it and tendered his resignation, and requested me to permit him to hand that paper with his resignation. I tried to dissuade him from doing so, but he still desired it and I permitted him to do it, but disapproved of the acceptance of his resignation, and that was the explanation I gave to General Buell when the paper was sent back.

Question. Do you know any reason why I could not at that time take any further steps with reference to such a breach of discipline?

I think about the next day after my division was transferred from the Army of the Ohio to the Army of the Tennessee.

Question. Who commanded that division immediately after the battle of Perryville and who were the brigade commanders in it, as well as you remember?

General Schoepf commanded the division up to the day of the battle of Perryville; and I was informed by some person a few days afterward that he had obtained a leave of absence about that time, probably the day after the battle, and that General Fry, being the senior brigadier-general in the division, commanded the division. General Steedman commanded the Third Brigade; Colonel Walker, of the Thirty-first Ohio, commanded the First Brigade, and Colonel Harlan, of the Tenth Kentucky, commanded the Second Brigade. Up to the battle of Perryville I presume General Fry commanded the Second Brigade.

Redirect examination by the JUDGE-ADVOCATE:

Question. General, did you hear General Buell express any discontent or administer any rebuke to General McCook for his conduct on the 8th at Perryville?

I do not think I heard him administer any rebuke, but I heard him say to General McCook that he had no idea that a battle was being fought till it was all over. I inferred from the remark of General Buell that he thought that General McCook ought to have been certain of his being informed of the necessity of sending some re-enforcements, though I might have been mistaken. The conversation was friendly—no harshness on the part of General Buell at all.

Question. General Buell is remarkable, is he not, for the manner in which he holds subordinate officers to what he considers their duty?

I regard General Buell as an excellent disciplinarian. I do not know that he is more remarkable than any other good disciplinarian in enforcing discipline.

Question. Can you state whether the signal corps was at work on that afternoon?

Yes, sir; part of it was.

Question. Do you know whether any information was sent regarding that fight in the afternoon by the signal corps?

None was received by me. The first information I ever received was through Lieutenant Fitzhugh.

Question. Do you know whether General Buell or any part of the army not immediately engaged did receive through the signal corps any information of that fight?

I do not know.

Question. Had we any higher respect or regard for the enemy after that fight than we had before?

I should think not.

Question. Was the attack there of such a nature as to throw us on the defensive?

It was not. General Buell made his dispositions to attack the enemy in the morning.

Question. Had the enemy attempted to hold Central Kentucky what position would he have selected and from whence would he have drawn his supplies?

If I had been placed in his position and should have attempted to hold Central Kentucky I should have taken a position somewhere near Lexington, where I could have drawn all my supplies. Of course every one has his idea as to the proper position to hold any territory.

Question. The enemy then would have had to draw his supplies from the country around Lexington?

Yes, sir.

By General DANA:

Question. Besides the instance you have mentioned of the officers of a brigade signing a petition for the removal of their brigade commander, do you know of any other instance in the Army of the Ohio of a similar petition being signed for the removal of a division commander? And, if so, state the time and circumstance.

I merely know from report that such a petition was signed by the majority of the officers of the division. Some of the officers of rank in that division refused to sign it. The paper never came to me, although the petition was forwarded, and I believe returned to the officers.

Question. What division was that, and did any of the brigade commanders refuse to sign it?

It was then the Seventh Division of the Army of the Tennessee, now the First Division of the Army of the Ohio. One brigade commander I heard of who refused to sign it—Brigadier-General Schoepf.

Question. Had General Schoepf any conversation with you and did he state any reasons for refusing to sign this petition?

He did have some conversation with me upon the subject, and stated that he refused to sign it because he did not think there was any reason for signing it; and in addition to that he regarded it as an act of insubordination, to say the least, and might be construed into a combination. If they were dissatisfied they should prefer charges against the officers; and he would have nothing to do with it. I think that was the only time that the subject was mentioned, when General Schoepf told me what he had done and asked me if I had heard of this petition being sent in.

By General ORD:

Question. In the retreat of General Bragg's army, after the battle of Perryville, did the enemy's cavalry sufficiently outnumber ours to require that our infantry or artillery should deploy at times in order to dislodge them ?

Yes.

Question. Did this involve the necessity of halts or delays on the part of our columns, that our infantry might form and take the road again ?

It did on two occasions, once at Stanford and the second time on the road beyond Crab Orchard. There were two other halts until our advance could dislodge the enemy's rear guard of cavalry. We did not halt for the night until 9 o'clock.

Question. Did these maneuvers of the cavalry in the rear of their infantry make corresponding halts necessary to the enemy's infantry on the retreat ?

No ; not at all.

Question. In the pursuit of an enemy by the roads taken by General Bragg's army after the battle of Perryville did the country afford facilities especially for defensive positions ?

The country did afford facilities for defensive positions at intervals of 3 or 4 miles. Strong defensive positions could have been taken after leaving Crab Orchard.

Question. Did the enemy make use of these ?

Yes.

Question. Did this involve further necessity for slow and cautious pursuit ?

It did ; that is, it involved the necessity for cautious pursuit. The pursuit was as rapid as we could make it under the circumstances.

Question. After the battle of Perryville do you think there were reasons why the enemy were not pursued farther than they were?

The difficulty of obtaining forage was one cause ; the difficulty of getting subsistence for the men over one narrow and bad road another cause ; and the obstruction thrown in the road by felling trees to so great an extent that by the time the road was cleared the enemy had effected his escape.

Question. As the pursuit advanced did the country become more difficult for the pursuing army to form and more susceptible of defense ?

It did. It became more difficult and more susceptible of defense until we reached the neighborhood of London ; there the country became open again. Before we could reach London the enemy had been enabled by the obstructions placed in the road to escape.

Question. Had we had as efficient and as large a force of cavalry as the enemy could we not have forced them to form the columns of infantry and give us battle on some ground favorable to ourselves ?

Not unless we could have anticipated their line of retreat before they reached Crab Orchard. We might, however, if we had had a very large force of cavalry, have attacked them at London as their column was passing through while their rear was involved in the hills of Rockcastle and have thrown them into confusion.

Question. Supposing the marching qualities of both retreating and pursuing armies the same, is plenty of good cavalry necessary to force a battle from a retreating army ?

I should think it was.

Question. Did the enemy's large force of cavalry and our deficiency, on the other hand, give them any great advantage in the way of enabling their infantry to form and select their own ground upon which to fight did they not feel disposed to continue their retreat ?

Yes, sir; I think it did.

Question. Which army can march the fastest, a large army or a small one?

A small one.

Question. Was our army larger or smaller than the enemy's after the battle of Perryville?

I think our army was the largest.

Question. Do you think the new troops which joined from Louisville in order to enable our army to pursue Bragg were able to march as fast as old troops or as fast as the enemy's troops? Were they any clog to our movements in rapid pursuit?

The new troops would have impeded our rapid march; they could not endure the fatigue of marching as well as the old soldiers.

By General TYLER:

Question. Was it a military probability that Bragg could pass his army and baggage over the mountain at Altamont, and was not the route by Perryville and Sparta in fact the only practicable military route up into the Tennessee Valley after he had passed forward into the Sequatchie Valley?

I think so.

Question. Crittenden was ordered to move on the enemy at 4 o'clock on the 9th of October, and moved at 6.30 o'clock, and Smith's corps engaged the enemy until 9 o'clock; during the whole of this time what kind of forces did General Smith engage? Did it or did it not indicate that the enemy was in force in his front?

He was under the impression that the enemy was in force in his front until he had cleared those skirmishers from the woods. The skirmishing had been quite heavy at times. There were some few dismounted men, whether cavalry or not I do not know; the largest portion was cavalry.

Question. Did General Buell's army ever get hold of Bragg's army before he fought the battle of Perryville?

We had several sharp skirmishes after the battle of Perryville between portions of our troops and the enemy's. I think it more than likely that portions of the two armies were opposed to each other at the battle of Shiloh. There were skirmishes in Alabama, but they occurred with General McCook's and General Crittenden's troops, not as army against army.

Question. The battle of Perryville was fought on the 8th; you testify that on the 11th was the first time you knew that Bragg's army had crossed Dick's River; between what places were the enemy's forces during this interval and what area of country did they go over?

We knew by 12 o'clock on the 11th that they had crossed, but we received information from the citizens that they were crossing before. Their rear guard crossed on the morning of the 11th either at King's Mill or at the mouth of the river. A portion of them were pursued by Harker to the crossing at King's Mill.

Question. What was the distance from Perryville to where Bragg crossed Dick's River?

I think about 16 miles; I am not positive.

Question. Where was the bulk of General Buell's army when the enemy crossed Dick's River; how far to the rear?

I believe the whole army was in the vicinity of Harrodsburg by 12 o'clock of the 11th, 6 or 8 miles from the crossing at King's Mill.

Question. If Bragg had been hardly pursued would not the crossing of Dick's River have been a serious obstacle to him?

It would, I think; though he would have crossed a portion of his forces at the mouth of the river.

Question. Assuming that Kirby Smith had occupied and plundered Lexington and had abandoned it, what possible military inducement could Bragg, after the battle of Perryville, have had in moving on Lexington?

He could have had none, except the desire to hold Kentucky or draw his supplies from the surrounding country.

Question. General, did or did not the battle of Perryville make it almost a military necessity that Bragg's army should commence its retreat, coupled with the abandonment of Lexington and that part of Kentucky, and that the intention was, if possible, to join the two armies and get out of Kentucky?

I thought so.

Question. We have heard of large trains of transportation, plunder, &c., which Bragg took out of Kentucky. What disposition did he make of those trains in the retreat and what was their position at the battle of Perryville, if you know?

I do not know what their position was at the battle of Perryville, but I believe they were assembled at Camp Dick Robinson, for we had heard before that they were assembling all their trains of transportation at Camp Dick Robinson; and after the retreat was decided upon these trains must have been sent in front, as we came across very few wagons on the road.

Question. Would you not consider it a very great military success for a small army, hampered with a large transportation train, retreating, to make its escape out of any country in the face of a superior army?

Yes; I should consider it a great military success.

Question. Is not the transportation train to an army a great hinderance to rapid military movement?

Yes.

Question. Were you encumbered by any of that kind of train except artillery in following up the enemy?

We were encumbered by the necessary subsistence train; nothing more.

Question. Where was Bragg's base of operations and supplies from the time he crossed the Tennessee River at Chattanooga or the vicinity?

I think he obtained his supplies from the country until he got to Bardstown; then he commenced collecting supplies from different points in Kentucky, with the intention of making a permanent depot at Camp Dick Robinson.

Question. What distance did Bragg march his army from the time he crossed the Tennessee River until he commenced what is now known to have been his retreat?

It was probably about 200 miles.

Question. During this whole march how did Bragg get his supplies?

I think he took ten days' supplies from Chattanooga; after that he drew his supplies from the country—Tennessee and Kentucky.

Question. What number of days did Bragg's military movement in Tennessee and Kentucky cover from the time he crossed the Tennessee River at Chattanooga until he was out of the reach of the army of General Buell beyond London?

I do not know precisely the date of his crossing the Tennessee River, but I suppose that it was about fifty days from the time he got fairly across the river to the time he got safel y beyond London.

Question. During this time did General Bragg's army, with the exception of the ten days' provisions be brought from Chattanooga, necessarily subsist on the country ?

Yes.

Question. Would not a country that would furnish provisions to a rebel army no more loyal than the States of Tennessee and Kentucky, under a proper military management, furnish at least half rations for an army of the same size as that of Bragg's ?

Yes, I suppose it would.

Question. Have the military rules that an army occupying a section of country possessed by the rules of war [has the right] to draw provisions from the country, been efficiently exacted by General Buell during his command of the Army of the Ohio ?

I do not know that any supplies have been drawn from the country occupied by General Buell's army except cattle, occasionally flour, and forage for the animals; the animals have generally been foraged on the country.

Question. And has not the result been that General Bragg, marching through the same country, has been consequently enabled to subsist his army ?

General BUELL. I beg leave to suggest to the Commission that one of their members is proceeding to condemnation, when their business is consideration. I must say for myself that I am astonished it should be asked; I am very glad that it has been asked.

The court was cleared. On being reopened the witness proceeded.

The WITNESS. General Bragg has not marched over the same ground, except in Kentucky from Bardstown as far as London and from Chattanooga up to Murfreesborough. I presume he had drawn some of his supplies in the vicinity of the railroad from Chattanooga to Murfreesborough.

By the PRESIDENT :

Question. From the time he concentrated his army at Murfreesborough to the time he reached Louisville was General Buell acting on the defensive or offensive ?

I should consider it as acting on the defensive; that is, first defending Nashville and then Louisville, with the railroad to Louisville.

Question. In your judgment what circumstance, if any, required such a policy from General Buell ?

The fact of the injury to the railroad making it necessary for him to keep between the enemy and Louisville, taken in connection with the fact that Kirby Smith had invaded and already had got possession of Central Kentucky.

Question. Do you mean to say that those circumstances required that policy from him from the time Bragg marched through the Sequatchie Valley until General Buell with his army reached Nashville ?

I believe that General Buell thought so.

Question. I am not asking that; I am asking your judgment.

I have said already that I desired to concentrate the army and meet Bragg at Sparta and fight him, because I thought we had supplies enough to enable us to do it.

Question. How am I to understand your answer, general ?

According to my judgment there was not a sufficient reason for falling back from Murfreesborough to Nashville.

By General BUELL :

Question. What force would you have required to meet the enemy at Sparta as you proposed ?

I believe that four divisions would have been sufficient.

Question. What number of men ?

Four divisions of 6,000 men; 24,000.

Question. And by that estimate what force do you suppose the enemy to have ?

I supposed, from all I knew, that the enemy had marched into Tennessee with 45,000 men, but I do not believe he could have brought that many men into an engagement at Sparta.

Question. About how many ?

I do not suppose that he could have brought into an engagement more than 30,000 men.

Question. You think, then, that with 24,000 men you could have kept Bragg out of Tennessee?

If I could have brought him to a battle at Sparta.

Question. Do you not regard that as a matter of certainty ?

I believe he could have been brought to battle at Sparta.

Question. How many days' rations would you require to make that result certain ?

Twenty days' would have been sufficient.

Question. Suppose that at the end of twenty days the enemy failed to give you battle at Sparta.

Then I should have been compelled to subsist upon the country.

Question. Could you have done that and maintain your position at Sparta ?   If so, explain how.

I think we could have maintained our position at Sparta ten days longer by subsisting on the country; that is, thirty days.

Question. Do you give that opinion from your knowledge of the supplies the country affords ?

Not from positive knowledge, but from reliable information.

Question. Do I understand you that you made a deliberate proposition to concentrate the army at Sparta and meet the enemy there ?

I did.

Question. And you have a copy of that communication ?

Yes, sir.

Question. Did you specify the force you thought necessary ?

I think that I proposed arranging the whole army so that it could be concentrated at Sparta.

Question. Did you give the details of your plan ?

Nothing further than the proposition to hold McMinnville, so as to compel the enemy to march by Sparta, and then concentrate the army at Sparta to meet him when he was compelled to march by Sparta on his way to Kentucky.

Question. Do you know what trains or supplies Bragg carried with him from Chattanooga ?

I do not know.

Question. How long was the principal part of Kentucky in posses sion of the rebel forces before Bragg's arrival there?

I do not remember; I expect a couple of months or so.

Question. Did the mass of the people make any active resistance to that occupation do you suppose?

They did not seem to make any active opposition.

Question. Was it very well known during that time that Kirby Smith was collecting supplies of various sorts necessary for the army; that he was making shot and shell and preparing other necessary supplies?

I heard after my arrival in Louisville that he had been very actively engaged in collecting supplies, and also had been preparing ammunition at Lexington, and one man also told me he had seen a train of twenty-five or thirty wagons going from Lexington to Camp Dick Robinson loaded with ammunition.

Question. As a source of supplies for an army, what comparison is there between Middle Tennessee in July and August last and the blue-grass region of Kentucky in September and October?

The resources of the blue-grass region of Kentucky were far greater than those of Middle Tennessee; there was an abundant supply in Kentucky. The supply in Middle Tennessee was not so great by half at least.

Question. Was it by seven-eighths?

The supply of some things in Tennessee was quite abundant—green corn, and there is some cattle; not a great deal of wheat, as far as I could learn; but a very abundant supply of all these in Kentucky.

Question. Have you any reason to suppose that in retreating from Kentucky Bragg took with his army any greater train than was necessary to carry the subsistence for it on the march; if so, how do you know it?

I could not learn positively of any train larger than was seen to carry supplies for his army. We heard from citizens that he had sent before his army large quantities of dry goods and things of that sort.

Question. Has it ever, that you know of, been stated that the rebel army plundered Lexington?

I think I heard some reports of that sort from citizens, but I do not think it has ever been known that they plundered Lexington; that is, that they stripped it of everything. They may have taken some things from Lexington.

Commission adjourned to meet December 20, at 10 o'clock a. m.

NASHVILLE, *Saturday Morning, December* 20, 1862.

Commission met pursuant to adjournment. All the members present; also the judge-advocate and General Buell.

Col. JOHN T. WILDER (a witness for the Government), being duly sworn by the judge-advocate, testified as follows:

By the JUDGE-ADVOCATE:

Question. State your name and position in the service and all you know about the surrender of Munfordville and the failure on our part to relieve it.

John T. Wilder; colonel Seventeenth Indiana Volunteers. I was ordered to Munfordville from Louisville by General Wright, on, I think, the 6th of September, to take command of the post. Shortly after I got there—I think it was the 7th of September—a party of guerrillas burned the bridge on the Salt River, 18 miles from Louisville, cutting off communication with Louisville. We had no rations, and telegraphed to Colonel Bruce at Bowling Green to send me some. He telegraphed back to me to be sparing of my rations, as General Buell's whole army was coming. He, however, sent me some hard bread. I collected the balance of my provisions from the country. On the 11th of September some deserters, reported to be from Buckner's division of Bragg's army, reached me. I questioned them as to the whereabouts of the rebel army. They stated that Buckner was 7 miles on the way toward Munfordville from Sparta, Tenn., and that Bragg's army was in the immediate vicinity. I telegraphed this information to General Buell at Nashville. Whether he received it or not I cannot say. I have understood since he had left Nashville. Here is a copy of the original dispatch:

Dispatch No. 1.

"MUNFORDVILLE, KY., *September* 11, 1862.

"Col. J. B. FRY,
    "*Assistant Adjutant-General and Chief of Staff, Nashville, Tenn.:*

"SIR: Two deserters, Irishmen, from Buckner's division of Bragg's army, came in here this morning, and report Buckner, with 10,000 men and Forrest's cavalry, 7 miles this side of Sparta, Tenn., on Sunday last; have two batteries. These men came across the country on mules about 160 miles. I think they tell the truth. Bragg was in the vicinity. I am building fortifications here with two raw regiments. Deserters say that Bowling Green is their point (the enemy's) for concentration.
                                                "J. T. WILDER,
            "*Colonel Seventeenth Indiana, Commanding at Green River.*"

A number of Kentuckian deserters from the army came and reported that Bragg's whole army was on its way to take, first, Bowling Green, and then Munfordville. That is what is meant in that last clause in that dispatch. On Thursday night, September 11, I learned that the advance of General Buell's army had reached Bowling Green. Trains ran through to Louisville from Bowling Green, I think, on Friday. On Friday night, the 12th, the rebels took possession of the railroad from Bowling Green to Munfordville. The advance division of infantry arrived in Glasgow the evening before.

Dispatch No. 2.

"MUNFORDVILLE, KY., *September* 12, 1862—3 a. m

"J. EDWARD STACY,
    "*Chief of Staff, Louisville, Ky.:*

"SIR: S. T. Purcell and R. Huggins have just come in from Glasgow, saying that Bragg's army arrived there at sundown last evening. Cheatham is reported in command. I have a force here of 2,600 raw men, with four pieces of artillery and provisions for eight days. What shall I do; fight them or fall back if attacked? They are reported to be from 22,000 to 50,000 strong. I am posted on south bank of river.
                                                "J. T. WILDER,
                    "*Colonel, Commanding at Green River.*"

"Brigadier-General DUMONT, *Lebanon Junction,*
"Capt. A. D. BRUCE, *Bowling Green, Ky.:*

"Rebels under Bragg are reported at Glasgow last night, 22,000 to 50,000 strong, their infantry command arriving last night.
                                                "J. T. WILDER,
                    "*Colonel, Commanding at Green River.*"

I was under the command of General Gilbert at the time; in fact all the time I was there I was under orders from Louisville. This dispatch was directed to Louisville.

Dispatch No. 3.

"MUNFORDVILLE, KY., *September* 12, 1862.

"J. EDWARD STACY,
    "*Assistant Adjutant-General and Chief of Staff, Louisville, Ky.:*

"Parties who left Glasgow late last night say they counted twelve regiments infantry and one of cavalry. Regiments small. Cheatham in command of advance of General Polk's division. Buckner reported not far off. My scouts left vicinity of Glasgow since noon; report no further advance of rebels to that time. Rebels say they are expecting division to-night.
                                                "J. T. WILDER,
                " *Colonel, Commanding Force at Green River.*"

Dispatch No. 4.

"MUNFORDVILLE, KY., *September* 12, 1862.

"Brigadier-General BOYLE, *Louisville, Ky.:*

"Lacey, one of my scouts, left the vicinity of Glasgow since noon. The rebels are there enforcing conscription. Lacey thinks they will go toward Columbia.

"J. T. WILDER,
"*Colonel, Commanding.*"

Dispatch No. 5.

"MUNFORDVILLE, KY., *September* 13, 1862.

"J. EDWARD STACY,
"*Assistant Adjutant General and Chief of Staff, Louisville, Ky.:*

"Scouts and numbers of citizens coming in state that the enemy are advancing 7,000 strong, and that a force has come in between here and Bowling Green to prevent re-enforcements from joining us. If I had one more good regiment and a few pieces of artillery that force could not take me. As it is I shall do my best to prevent it. Can you send me re-enforcements to-night? I shall send trains to Salt River for them.

"J. T. WILDER,
"*Colonel, Commanding at Green River.*"

Copy of return dispatch.

"Col. J. T. WILDER:

"I send you what you ask.

"J. EDWARD STACY,
"*Assistant Adjutant-General and Chief of Staff.*"

These are not all the dispatches I sent. The original copies formerly in my possession I committed to an officer, with instructions to destroy them in case we were taken. He did so. The dispatches here submitted I got from the telegraph office while I was prisoner.

Dispatch No. 6.

"MUNFORDVILLE, KY., *September* 15, 1862—9 p. m.

"Brigadier-General BOYLE, *Louisville, Ky.:*

"No advice from Bowling Green. Rebels at Cave City, under Bragg, in force. See J. E. Stacy, assistant adjutant-general; have telegraphed him all to-day. Rebels on north side of river coming down 2,000 strong.

"J. T. WILDER,
"*Colonel, Commanding at Green River.*"

Dispatch No. 7.

"MUNFORDVILLE, KY., *September* 13, 1862.

"J. EDWARD STACY,
"*Assistant Adjutant-General and Chief of Staff, Louisville, Ky.:*

"SIR: I have construction train and light cars here. Citizens state that about 300 rebel cavalry are at Bills and 200 at Cave City; also that Rousseau's advance fell back yesterday. I have started scouts to try and reach Bowling Green. Some indications that main rebel force are going toward Lebanon.

"J. T. WILDER,
"*Colonel, Commanding.*"

Dispatch No. 8.

"MUNFORDVILLE, KY., *September* 13, 1862.

"J. EDWARD STACY,
"*Assistant Adjutant-General and Chief of Staff, Louisville, Ky.:*

"Mr. Retter, one of the most loyal men in the county, keeper of the Woodland House, 10 miles south of here, sends his colored man, saying that Bragg is at Cave City with 20,000 men and that Buckner will join him to-morrow. His pickets are within 5 miles of here we know. The rebels boast of having taken off a dispatch from Louisville and exult over it. I believe half of this.

"J. T. WILDER,
"*Colonel, Commanding at Green River.*"

General DANA. I do not see the use of reading all these dispatches. The colonel is not brought here to justify himself in the surrender of Munfordville. He was an officer acting under another general. He was not under the immediate command of General Buell, but under the command of General Wright. If the colonel has any testimony to give as to communications between himself and General Buell or bearing on the movements of General Buell's army, so far it is proper to have the testimony introduced; but I see no use in entering on the record this volume of dispatches, which go to the rear.

The JUDGE-ADVOCATE. These dispatches are introduced to show the position of the enemy at the time General Buell was marching to or occupying Bowling Green. I wish to show that General Buell had sufficient time to relieve Munfordville.

Dispatch No. 9.

"MUNFORDVILLE, KY., September 15, 1862.
'J. EDWARD STACY,
    "<i>Assistant Adjutant-General and Chief of Staff, Louisville, Ky.</i>:

"SIR: I received the following dispatch this moment:

"'ELIZABETHTOWN, KY, September 13, 1862.
"'Colonel WILDER:

"'My men must be relieved immediately; their time is out and they will serve no longer and we can't make them. They will go if not relieved; they will not remain.
"'L. G. KNOX,
"'Lieutenant-Colonel, Commanding Fifty-fourth Indiana.'

"I cannot relieve them from here. Scouts say that no forces have left Bowling Green for this place. Rebels were last night camped 2 miles this side of Glasgow, at Beaver Creek. Artillery ammunition has not come. My intrenchments will be completed to-day.

"I just learn that rebel pickets are at Woodland, on railroad, 8 miles south of here, in considerable force.
"J. T. WILDER,
"Colonel, Commanding at Green River."

On the 13th of September I learned that the rebels were with their main force encamped on Beaver Creek, 2 or 3 miles north of Glasgow, with their line extending down near to Cave City; also that a force of 2,000 were coming down on the north side of Green River, which proved afterward to be Scott's cavalry, of Kirby Smith's forces. On Saturday night, 13th of September, he summoned me to surrender. On Sunday morning before daylight they attacked me on the north side of the river; also by an infantry force on the south side, commanded by General Chalmers. I repulsed them after about five hours' fighting, and that evening, the 14th, I drove them back 3 or 4 miles in all directions around the town, and the next morning got up a telegraphic communication to Louisville again. On Sunday evening, after the fight, I was re-enforced by 400 men, under Colonel Dunham, of the Fiftieth Indiana, who remained in command till Tuesday, the 16th, until about 5 o'clock in the evening, when he was placed under arrest in order to report to General Gilbert. We had been fighting them nearly all day on Tuesday. Colonel Dunham had been summoned to surrender, and I was summoned to surrender on Tuesday evening by General Bragg. I refused to do so till I knew the force he had. We parleyed about the matter considerably, and finally they consented to let me see the batteries. I went out to examine their guns, and surrendered the whole force on Wednesday morning, the 17th. The reason why I wished to see their force was I believed they would have the major part of it to hold General Buell in check. I did not believe they had their whole force there to take me, although my information all the time was that they were coming up with their main force.

By the JUDGE-ADVOCATE:

Question. During that time, colonel, what efforts, if any, were made to communicate with General Buell?

I had railroad communication to Bowling Green till Friday noon. I then sent out scouts. I sent one scout on Saturday, 13th—Mr. Wash. Miller, and two or three others.

I did not send written communications, only verbal ones, to the commanding officer at Bowling Green (I did not know if General Buell got them), stating that I must receive assistance, as a large force was coming in to take Munfordville. Mr. Miller got through to Bowling Green. Whether the others did or not I do not know. I have never seen them since. Mr. Miller staid there till Monday, the 15th, 3 o'clock, and then started back for Munfordville, and got back Tuesday night at dark, and told me I could expect no assistance from Bowling Green; that no troops had started to relieve me at the time he left. Up to that time I intended to fight them, be their force what it might, expecting, from the dispatch I had received from General Gilbert, that I would receive assistance from Bowling Green. At the time Mr. Miller came in Polk's right wing of Bragg's army had crossed the river 8 miles above and come down on the north side, completely surrounding me. I knew that no force could relieve me from Bowling Green, except a large one, after Friday, the 13th, and that after the fight on Sunday a large force was between Bowling Green and Munfordville, and lay there apparently quiet, I think, two days. I afterward asked Colonel Walter, of Bragg's staff, what was their object in lying still, and why they did not come up in force and take me instead of having a small force so cut up as Chalmers' force was on Sunday. He said they had a cavalry force on the north side of the river to prevent my retreating, and that they lay there expecting a force would come from Bowling Green to relieve me, in which case they meant to fall upon it and cut it to pieces, but that when they found General Buell moving up with his whole army, they then moved forward to take Munfordville and hold Green River against General Buell's army.

When I was a prisoner by some accident they did not parole me. When I got into General Buell's lines I went to his headquarters and told all I knew about their forces, their means of subsistence, &c. This was on the night of the 18th, about 9 or 10 o'clock. His headquarters were at Prewitt's Knob. General Buell questioned me closely about their numbers and position. I told him they had from 35,000 to 40,000 men; that they had no provisions that would sustain them three days; that if their whole force fought as they had fought me, no reasonable force could drive them away from Green River; but if their supplies were cut off from the east they could not live there three days; they would either be compelled to come out and fight or fall back from there, which afterward proved to be the case. In the terms of surrender I obtained four days' rations for my men, leaving only one day's for their forces there. They seemed much disappointed at not getting more provisions.

On Wednesday and Thursday, 17th and 18th, they gave me liberty to go anywhere I pleased throughout their camp, and I went about as I pleased. I saw no trains of provisions. I noticed some wagons with ammunition. I examined a number of haversacks of the dead killed on Sunday, and found that their provisions consisted almost entirely of green corn. I never saw an army in a more perfect state of discipline. They were terribly ragged and dirty and apparently tired out. I was present with General Buell when the information reached him that the enemy had reached Munfordville. That was on Sunday, 21st, then about 7 miles from Munfordville. We were then moving forward in line of battle apparently. General Buell had immediately on my arrival in his lines ordered my exchange. I supposed I was on duty. I was also with him explaining the road and the character of the country when he received notice that Kirby Smith's and Bragg's forces had formed a junction, which proved afterward to be false. I then came through with the army to Louisville, and was there notified that my exchange was not consented to by General Bragg.

Question. What number of men, munitions, and other stores were surrendered at Munfordville?

There were 3,546 men, according to the parole list, ten pieces of artillery, tents for about one and one-half regiments, and one day's rations for the men.

Question. What sort of a man is this scout you speak of?

A very reliable man; at least, so I found him.

Question. State in what manner you made up your estimate of Bragg's army.

I received information on the 15th by way of Glasgow that Bragg's army consisted of one hundred and four regiments, including cavalry and artillery. I received information from another source, from a Mr. Simpson, of Glasgow, and by citizens and scouts, that Bragg had eighty-four regiments of infantry, that he had twelve batteries of artillery, and that his cavalry force numbered from 6,000 to 10,000; that the regiments would number about 350, some said 400, some not over 325; but from my own observation I think they averaged 350 men. One hundred and four regiments of 350 men would be 36,400; twelve batteries of 130 men each would be 1,560, making in the aggregate one hundred and four regiments, 37,960 men. If the regiments numbered

400 each, it would make an aggregate of 43,160. He had six divisions—one under Buckner, sixteen regiments; one under Anderson, sixteen regiments; one under Bushrod Johnson, twelve regiments; Cheatham had sixteen regiments; Withers twelve regiments, and a man named Jones with twelve regiments (I have never heard of him since). That would make eighty-four regiments of infantry. That they had six divisions I am satisfied. I was introduced to officers while a prisoner, and know that they were divided in that shape, and were divided into two wings. Hardee commanded one and Polk the other.

Question. At the time of giving this information to General Buell was he satisfied of its correctness?

I do not know.

Question. How did he express himself?

I am not certain. He simply asked questions and I answered them.

Question. Made any comments on them?

No; in asking about the position of Munfordville, and stated that he had in person examined the semicircle of hills about the river with a view of using them himself, and knew it to be one of the strongest positions for a large force he ever saw.

Question. What comments, if any, did General Buell make upon the surrender of Munfordville?

None at all.

Question. At the time you sent this scout Miller to General Buell where was General Buell's army, and can you state where at that time the main body of Bragg's force was?

The advance of General Buell's army was at Bowling Green, I think, in three divisions; this was my opinion. The main body of Bragg's army was in the vicinity of Glasgow. His advance forces held the railroads and the turnpike between Munfordville and Bowling Green.

Question. You can state to the Commission whether it was possible, from the position of the force of both armies, for General Buell to have relieved you at that time?

I do not know. I think he could not have relieved me unless he had thrown a very large force forward to relieve me; a small force would undoubtedly have been cut up.

By General ORD:

Question. You say that when you were summoned to surrender by General Bragg on the 16th, Tuesday evening, the words are: "I refused to do so until I knew what force he had." What was the literal meaning of those words; that as soon as you could learn what force he had you would surrender?

General Bragg summoned me to surrender, stating he had over 25,000 troops and over sixty pieces of artillery then in position. My answer was, as near as I can recollect, that Colonel Dunham had held a council of the officers commanding the regiments, and that they had unanimously agreed that if the force was as great as was represented it would be folly to hold out longer, and that if we could have evidence that his force was such as he had represented I would surrender, otherwise I would not. His answer was the only evidence he could give of his force would be the use of it. I then sent out another person to the bearer of the flag of truce, told him that we had been summoned to surrender four times before by a force incompetent to compel it, and that unless we had evidence that was indisputable to us that he had a force there sufficient to reduce us in a short time we would not surrender. They then gave me an hour. I told the bearer of the flag, Colonel Walter, of General Bragg's staff, that it was useless to parley; that I would not surrender until I knew what force they had. I did not believe that the bulk of Bragg's army was there, but that a part of it was held back to hold General Buell in check, and that against a part of their army I would fight. He said it would be useless bloodshed, and went back to take my message to General Bragg. I asked then to see General Bragg in person. He took me up to his headquarters. We parleyed about it for an hour backward and forward. I told General Buckner that I did not think they could take me by assault of infantry; they had been trying that twice on that day, Tuesday. Buckner said he had attempted twice to take us by assault, but when they came through the strip of woods they could not form in line, and that they had determined to shell us out by concentrating a fire in which we could not live for an hour. I told them if they had that force there it would be useless for me to contend against them, but if they had that force there was no reason why I should not see it, and that I would undoubtedly surrender if I saw it; that I did not suppose they could afford to waste as much ammunition as would be required to reduce me upon a mere quibble. General Buckner then went with me to see the batteries. Lieutenant Bullitt, acting adjutant of the post, went on the north side and I on the south side. I counted forty-six guns on the south side; he counted twenty-six on the north side, so he reported to me; fifty-four of which were in position. This was Tuesday, about midnight. It was 2 o'clock when the articles of surrender were signed.

Question. How much of the time during the defense of Munfordville did your men live on half rations?

I think only two days.

Question. Supposing you had put your men on the smallest amount of food possible how long would your provisions have lasted?

Probably fifteen days. It was not a lack of provisions that compelled the surrender.

Question. About what time Tuesday evening or afternoon did the council and yourself come to the conclusion that if their force was an overwhelming one you must surrender?

About 4 o'clock. This was while Colonel Dunham was in command that that council was held; before he was put under arrest.

Question. About what time were you satisfied that the time had come to surrender, from the overwhelming force around you?

About midnight. From all I could see of the force surrounding us and the nature of it I was satisfied before sundown that unless re-enforcements reached us I could not hold out. But for fear there was any mistake about the force there I determined I would know something more about it; and not to be deceived I would draw their fire, and sustain their whole fire before I would risk being deceived in the matter. I had fully determined I would not surrender except to an overwhelming force.

Question. About what time did you tell their flag-of-truce bearer you would not surrender except to an overwhelming force and that you would inspect it yourself?

That was about 7 o'clock in the evening. It was at 5 o'clock I received a summons from General Bragg, and the parleying was continued all the evening.

Question. About what time did the scout Miller bring you the information that you could expect no help from General Buell?

It was about half past five, a short time after I received a summons to surrender; not more than half an hour.

Question. Was there a strong disposition to surrender among the officers when they held the council in the afternoon in case the force was overwheming.

I was present, and for fear there might be a disposition of that kind among them I suggested that I would not surrender under any circumstances and to no force unless I knew what it was, and it was adopted by all the officers present unanimously. This was about 4 o'clock in the afternoon.

Question. Did you apprehend that it is no longer the duty of an officer to hold a garrison when he finds that he is surrounded by an overwhelming force and that the prospects of relief are remote?

I think that when everything looks as though there was no chance of success it would be folly to murder the men. This is the way I looked upon it at the time. The rebels had positions commanding us on every side, and my information as regards relief was such that I could not expect any in time to save us.

By the Judge-Advocate:

Question. Had you received assurances from your scout of relief would you have made an effort to hold out and how much longer?

I do not know how much longer, but I should have held out till I was overpowered.

Question. Reference is made in one of those dispatches to conscripting. Do you know how much they added to their force by that process?

I do not know.

Question. Do you know whether they received any additions in the way of volunteers?

They did some; there was quite a number left the vicinity of Munfordville and joined them, their friends giving as the reason that they preferred fighting on that side to being drafted to go into the Federal Army. This was about the time they were preparing to force a draft for troops in Kentucky.

Questions. What actions, if any, have you been in; what service have you seen?

I was in the campaign in Western Virginia under General Rosecrans; under General Reynolds in the Cheat Mountain Division; I was in probably half a dozen small fights about Cheat Mountain and in one considerable fight at Greenbrier River under General Reynolds; I was in General Buell's army when that marched from Louisville to Corinth, and was in a number of skirmishes about Corinth.

By General Ord:

Question. Were you aware at the time of the surrender that in a position not easily taken by assault shelling out is a very slow business?

I have never been subjected to a very severe fire of shells. The rebels had positions within 600 yards around us; that on the north side especially commanded us. The ground in the main work sloped toward the north, exposing the men in the works to a fire from the north side.

Question. Were your guns under cover?

They were behind breastworks.

Question. Were the enemy's guns under cover?

They were not (except one battery), excepting the cover afforded by the woods and behind ridges.

Question. What small-arms had your men?

Mostly rifles. The men were chiefly raw recruits. Those engaged in the fight on Sunday had none of them been in service over three weeks. None of them had ever seen a battle before. A good many of them had not a complete outfit; some of them had no cartridge-boxes; quite a number of these men had no arms; a detachment of 102 had not a single gun; they were convalescents.

Question. After you made the statement you did to the council about not surrendering except to an overwhelming force, did the officers all concur that the force was too overwhelming and that it was time to surrender?

They all agreed about that, but I consulted none of them after having seen the fortifications of the enemy.

By General Dana:

Question. How many months have you been in service?

I have been in service over a year and a half. I enlisted April 21, 1861; have been in active service in the field since July, 1861. I have not always been in the capacity of a commander of a regiment. I started a private, and was at length elected captain of artillery. The battery was afterward put in the infantry service, and I was made lieutenant-colonel of the regiment, afterward made colonel. I have been in command of the regiment most of the time since July 1, 1861.

Question. Was the information brought by the scout Miller that you need expect no aid from Bowling Green founded on his own opinion or on information he received from General Buell?

He received none from General Buell whatever, he told me. He said General Buell asked him especially about the crossing of Green River, and about the road leading from Bowling Green to Elizabethtown leaving Munfordville to the right, but he sent no word to me whatever; that while he was present word was brought to General Buell that I had surrendered. The impression Mr. Miller had was that General Buell would try to reach Elizabethtown and get ahead of Bragg's forces by that short route to Elizabethtown. I was astonished that we got no information; no word sent by anybody. I had directed Mr. Miller to see General Wood and General Hascall, my brigade and division commanders, as soon as he could get there; that if General Buell was not there they would undoubtedly tell him what I might expect, as General Wood knew Mr. Miller personally and knew him to be reliable.

Question. At what time and in what manner were you placed under command of General Gilbert?

I had been in Indiana obtaining recruits for my regiment and came to Louisville; waited there a week for transportation, trying to join my regiment in Buell's army. The railroad was destroyed, communication cut off, and I was sent with my recruits, 214, to Munfordville; was then ordered back to Louisville by a telegraphic dispatch from General Boyle in person. I went to Louisville, there met General Wright, General Boyle, and Governor Morton. They were talking about the position of things in Munfordville. General Boyle was going to bring me to Louisville to take command of a brigade of new troops there; he wanted some one to drill them. General Wright opposed this; said I must go back to Munfordville and take command. I said I could not, as General Ward was the general in command of Munfordville at the time, and Colonel Dunham was also there; both of those officers ranked me, so I could not take command, but both of these officers were ordered away, and I was sent there to take command; having the Sixty-seventh and Eighty-ninth Indiana, both new regiments, the recruits of my own regiment, and two companies of the Seventy-fourth Indiana, and some scattered fragments of men, and about 400 convalescents without arms. The whole force was 2,600. I had 2,122 with arms. The principal parts of the works I built. Part of those built by General McCook I destroyed. His works were built for infantry; I wanted works for artillery. I tried to arrange the works to employ a small force, from 200 up to 1,000. There was a stockade built at the end of the bridge, which 1,200 men could have held against almost any infantry force. I was ordered to direct all my efforts to maintain Green River Bridge. About the 11th of September I was ordered by telegraph to send my reports and dispatches to General Gilbert. I was notified that he was in command of that part of Kentucky. Up to that time I had reported to General Boyle.

Question. Was it possible for these unarmed men to have procured arms at Louisville on their way down?

Three hundred of them belonged to the Thirty-third Kentucky, then organizing at Munfordville, and had not yet got arms; I had made efforts to have them drawn; and over a hundred were convalescents, joining their regiments without arms, who came there on Saturday, the 13th, in charge of Lieutenant Nichols, of a Wisconsin regiment.

Question. When you sent Miller and other scouts to General Buell at Bowling Green did you give distinct information as to the length of time you would be enabled to hold your position if not relieved?

I told him to say what force I had and that I had provisions for ten days. I did not say how long I could hold my position, not knowing what force was coming against me. I left that for them to infer. I simply sent a statement of my condition, the position I held, and the forces at my command, &c.

Question. Did you send information to General Buell that you were in a strait—that you must have relief; and did you inform General Buell that you had no reasonable expectation of relief from your rear?

I did not know General Buell was at Bowling Green when I sent my scouts. I sent to the officer commanding at Bowling Green that the rebels were in force between Munfordville and Bowling Green. I sent more to know what I might expect from there after giving a statement of my own condition than anything else.

Question. Did you give these scouts or messengers any official information for General Buell, or did they bear about any proofs by which General Buell could recognize them as messengers from you?

I gave them no official communication, nothing but verbal ones, but sent the men I knew could prove beyond doubt their reliability. I knew they had to pass the enemy's lines and would be thoroughly searched if taken, and I did not wish to inform the enemy of my position at Munfordville.

Question. Did these men, when they left your camp, know that you were in danger of surrendering to the enemy, and did they know that you were not to be relieved from the rear?

Neither did they know it nor I.

Question. Have you any reason to suppose that these men gave assurances to General Buell that your garrison would not receive relief from Louisville or from your rear?

I do not think they did, as they had no directions to do so. I myself had no doubt, after informing my superior officers of the state of things, that I would be taken care of some way; to the last I believed I would be re-enforced.

Question. Have you any reason to believe that General Buell clearly understood, prior to your surrendering, that you would not receive relief from your rear?

I had no means of knowing what General Buell's opinion of the matter was; I really did not know myself what I might expect, but was confident I should get relief from some source.

By the PRESIDENT:

Question. What time did you receive this dispatch which you have before referred to as coming from General Gilbert, telling you you would be aided or assisted from Bowling Green?

I think it was on the 12th September.

Question. How did you construe that dispatch; what meaning did you give it?

I supposed from that dispatch that General Buell's army would come to relieve me before Bragg could get there.

By General DANA:

Question. Did you ever send to General Buell or in the direction of General Buell an intimation that you had ever received such a dispatch as that?

I do not remember. I think I told Mr. Miller of it, that I had expected relief from Bowling Green. At the time I sent the rebels were in force between Munfordville and Bowling Green. I could not expect relief from Bowling Green except the rebels were driven out first.

Question. Do you now distinctly remember whether you gave Mr. Miller special instructions to inform General Buell that you had received an intimation from Louisville that he was expected to relieve you at Munfordville?

I do not remember that I did. I supposed, as a matter of course, that General Gilbert had information from General Buell that I had not, and was puzzled to know why he had not informed me more fully.

Question. Have you reason now to suppose that General Buell at that time knew that if he did not relieve you at Munfordville you could get no relief from your rear and would therefore be obliged to surrender?

I do not know.

Question. Do you or do you not now believe that the reason for your expecting relief from General Buell was owing to circumstances which might not probably have been known to him, inasmuch as you were depending for your supplies and support on your own commander?

My expectation was that General Gilbert would see that I was taken care of. I was under his command, and supposed he knew what relief I would get. I did not know what General Buell knew about it or what expectations General Gilbert had from General Buell except that dispatch. All the information I got of General Buell's forces, or from General Gilbert in regard to General Buell's forces, was this single dispatch in which Colonel Bruce telegraphed me that General Buell's whole army was coming, and that left me almost entirely in the dark. I supposed General Buell's army was moving north, but when I found General Bragg had got in his rear I supposed General Buell would drive him out of the way and relieve me. When I found he could not do so I telegraphed to General Gilbert. When the head of Polk's column was coming down the north side of the river I telegraphed back to General Gilbert that I had not force enough to hold the position, and that I was not alone in the opinion. This was on the 16th, after dark, that I got his answer. I do not know whether General Buell knew I expected relief from him or from Louisville. I believe I told Mr. Miller that I had been promised relief from Bowling Green.

Question. Have you learned since whether Mr. Miller distinctly told this to General Buell, that you had been promised relief from there?

I asked Mr. Miller some time this week in Nashville, and in fact when he came to Munfordville from Bowling Green, if he had conveyed my message; he said he had. This message was directed to the commander of the forces in Bowling Green. When Mr. Miller left I did not know that General Buell had got to Bowling Green.

Question. Do you know whether the commanding officer at Louisville or Cincinnati had any means of communicating direct with General Buell which was not known to you at that time?

I did not suppose but that the commanders of two departments, with such armies under their control, must certainly have communication with each other; I expect they had.

Question. Was there any other line of communication with that army except from Munfordville?

None that I know of. The cars had been running through Munfordville up to Friday, the 12th. I supposed, of course, there would be a concert of action between the commanders of the two armies.

By General TYLER:

Question. Your expectation that Miller would receive credence at headquarters was founded on the fact that he was personally known to General Wood?

I knew Mr. Miller had been employed in the secret service by General McCook, and he told me he was known to General Wood, and would have no difficulty in establishing his reliability. General McCook had had him in his employ in the same kind of service the winter before.

By General DANA:

Question. Does anything else now occur to you bearing upon this investigation which you have not stated in your testimony?

I heard General Buell say that General Gilbert had evidently placed too great a value on the possession of Munfordville. I could have got away from Munfordville with my whole force up to 5 o'clock on Tuesday if I had been allowed to, crossing the river on the north side, following the road down to the river through a woody, hilly country, and come around and joined General Buell's forces at Cave City or below there.

By General TYLER:

Question. Why did you not leave the position?

I had been ordered to hold out as long as possible and telegraphed the whole statement of facts to General Gilbert, expecting him to order me to get away if I could, which he did not.

SATURDAY AFTERNOON, *December* 20, 1862.

Colonel WILDER'S examination continued.

Cross-examination by General BUELL

Question. At what hour Tuesday were you summoned to surrender?

At 5 o'clock in the evening.

Question. Was the rebel force in position around your post before that hour? -

On the south side of the river they were, and just coming around on the north side. They had not got all their artillery in position then; probably not more than four batteries.

Question. When you sent your messenger to me did you know of the position and strength of the force of the rebel army that was threatening you?

At that time I was pretty well aware that the whole force of the rebels was on their way, but did not believe that more than 7,000 were threatening me then; the balance was back, coming on, and were between Munfordville and Glasgow; part of them were not yet arrived at Glasgow.

Question. In what way did your informant arrive at the strength of the regiments of Bragg's army?

I was informed by a great many persons. Some of them arrived at it by counting the regiments in some of the divisions and learned from men belonging to them what the force was. There was one man who had a relative in the advanced cavalry who told him what the force was; and there had been parties of rebel cavalry scouting the country for two weeks before, some of whom represented the force to be as high as 60,000; but taking all the information I could get I think it was about 40,000. The community about Munfordville are largely loyal, and have a good many relatives in the Southern army, who would come in from a distance to within 10 or 12 miles to see their friends, and from these I obtained information of the strength of the rebel army. I also obtained it from deserters.

Question. Which of these sources of information would represent the minimum strength?

Those who counted. Reports went through the country that they had as high as 75,000, but I gave no credence to them.

Question. Would what is called the effective strength of the forces according to returns be represented by the number of men found in the ranks?

My experience is that the paper showing is always in excess of that you can get in line for action.

Question. And particularly is it not in excess of the number that would appear in the ranks on the march, where this kind of information would be obtained?

The ranks in a regiment on the march would count for generally much smaller than when in camp. There are always stragglers and details for wagon guards in every army.

Question. So is it not likely that the information of those who have actually counted the strength of a corps on the march would fall short of its actual strength?

Very much so.

MORROW P. ARMSTRONG (a witness for the Government), being duly sworn by the judge-advocate, testified as follows:

By the JUDGE-ADVOCATE:

Question. State, if you please, your name and position in the service, -

and what yo i know of the number of the army under General Bragg at the capture of Munfordville, how you came by that knowledge, and all about it.

My name is Morrow P. Armstrong. My position in the Army is that of chaplain to the Thirty-sixth Indiana Volunteers. As near as I could form a judgment in reference to the numbers of Bragg's army they would be: Infantry ninety regiments, averaging 325 to a regiment, making 29,250; cavalry, I estimated at 7,000; batteries, twelve, which I averaged at 130; giving a total of 37,810. My information I obtained partly by sight and partly by conversation with officers in that army. I saw, I believe, all or the greatest part of Bragg's army I was with except Buckner's; two divisions of that were across the river. I was not across the river after the capture; did not pass through that part of Bragg's army.

Question. State, if you please, how you obtained those facilities for estimating the size of the army.

I was with the forces at Munfordville when they were captured and remained with them until they arrived within our lines; then I joined my regiment. I was unrestricted; I was privileged to go where I pleased. No person interfered with my movements. In fact, they told me they did not care where I went so that I did not go toward Louisville. The officers that I had most conversation with were a colonel on General Bragg's staff, a Tennessee captain, and a captain of the Mississippi Tenth; his name was [R. A.] Bell.

Question. State what you did with this information; whether you communicated it to any superior officers or not and whether it went to General Buell.

I told first General Wood, after entering our lines, all that I knew with reference to their numbers and of their position; secondly, I told General Smith; thirdly, General Rousseau; and, lastly, General Buell. General Smith and General Rousseau sent me to General Buell. If I mistake not it was on the 19th of September; at least it was on the Friday night after the night we were captured at Munfordville. I got to General Buell's headquarters somewhere near 11 o'clock at night.

Question. Do you know whether the rebel army had been increased after the invasion by recruits or volunteers?

I do not.

Question. Did you observe the condition of the rebel troops and can you state how they were off for provisions; whether they had any train accompanying them or not?

They had wagon trains accompanying them, but I think that their stock of provisions was scarce; at least they stated to us on Thursday morning that the reason why they did not give us more subsistence was they had it not to spare; that they had given us more than their men had. My share of that was about one hard cracker and a very small piece of fat bacon a day. This is what the officer who had that matter in charge said. A number of officers in that army told me that their men had to subsist on burnt corn and peaches, such as they could gather up. My observation among them was that they had little to eat.

By General DANA:

Question. Do you know whether the force you saw and estimated around Munfordville was the whole of Bragg's force?

From the information I had I am inclined to believe it was; of course I go on information I received, in making up my judgment, from the number of generals present and their rank; this must be the case. From them I learned pretty well the arrangement of their army under their commanders. I was informed that Polk and Hardee commanded wings. They had as division generals Buckner, Cheatham, Withers, Jones, Anderson, and Johnson; at least I got these names as division commanders. I saw most of these generals.

Cross-examination by General BUELL:

Question. How did you arrive at the strength of the regiments?

I arrived at the strength of a majority of those regiments by a comparison of them with regiments of our own with which I had been associated, carefully considering their length, estimating their numbers by the numbers of our own regiments, and hence I averaged those regiments at 325; some of them were quite small, others pretty large.

Question. Explain the process of this estimate.

I have been associated with a regiment of our own nearly nine months as a line officer of the regiment, and accustomed to measure with the eye the distance that a regiment would occupy drawn up in line of battle. Knowing what was the number of that regiment all along, at least during the nine months, I then with the eye measured the distance that those regiments occupied, and then endeavored to strike an average.

Question. What was the strength of the regiments that you compared these with ?

My own more particularly.

Question. What was the strength of that regiment ?

I made the comparison with my regiment, and the strength of that when I was last associated with it as a line officer was about 475.

Question. How was that regiment formed when you estimated the length of line it occupied ?

On dress parade.

Question. What was the length of line it occupied when so formed ?

It would be difficult to give it by feet.

Question. By yards ?

That would be difficult too.

Question. By any kind of measure you choose ?

The manner in which I have been accustomed to measure was by appointing a distance. It would be something near the length of this capitol.

Question. From that can you arrive at some standard of measurement ?

I have no idea myself how long this capitol is. I do not know the number of feet.

Question. Did you ever see a regiment of Bragg's army on parade ?

I saw them draw up in line and I saw them on the march.

Question. Did you estimate the length of the line occupied by any of them and how many of them ?

I estimated the length of their lines in my mind thus: When I saw a regiment drawn up in dress parade or line I looked along that line carefully, made up my judgment, and compared it in my mind with my own regiment. I did that with a number, and the majority of their regiments that I estimated were not as large as my regiment; some of them were larger, in my judgment.

Question. Did you count any of them ?

No, sir; I did not. I was afraid to do that, because I purposed, if I was not placed under pledge of honor, to reveal everything I knew in reference to them.

Redirect examination by the JUDGE-ADVOCATE:

Question. You say in reply to General Buell's question that you never measured by yards or feet the distance occupied by your regiment on dress parade ?

I have never stepped it; I have only measured it with my eye.

Question. You did not count the number in the rebel regiment or measure by yards or feet the distance they occupied ?

I did not

Question. You arrived at the conclusion by comparing the length of one of their regiments with your own?

Yes, sir.

Commission adjourned to meet December 22, 1862, at 10 o'clock a. m.

NASHVILLE, TENN., *Monday Morning, December* 22, 1862.

The Commission met pursuant to adjournment. All the members present; also the judge-advocate and General Buell.

General SPEED S. FRY (a witness for the Government), being duly sworn by the judge-advocate, testified as follows:

By the JUDGE-ADVOCATE:

Question. State, if you please, your name and position in the service of the United States.

Speed S. Fry; I am brigadier-general of the volunteer service.

Question. Did you accompany the march of the Army of the Ohio in the pursuit of Bragg after he crossed the Tennessee?

I did, sir.

Question. What was the condition of the Army of the Ohio as to discipline?

It was considerably demoralized.

Question. State, if you please, the cause of that demoralization, as far as you know.

There were two or three causes tending to demoralize the army. One was the want of supplies and the necessity of foraging upon a destitute country. Another was the idea that Bragg would be permitted with a large army to invade Kentucky. There seemed to be an intense feeling throughout the whole army on the subject of permitting the rebel army again to invade Kentucky. Officers and men felt that Bragg could have been checked before reaching Kentucky if proper diligence had been used.

Question. What estimate was placed upon the number of the invading army by intelligent officers, from all their sources of information, previous to reaching Munfordville?

From all the information obtained upon that subject the force of Bragg was estimated at 36,000. There were rumors, however, in the camp and throughout the country that Bragg had an army of from 50,000 to 60,000 men. The most intelligent officers with whom I conversed believed that Bragg's army did not exceed 36,000.

Question. You can state whether it was known at that time, that is, previous to your arrival at Munfordville, that Kirby Smith had invaded Kentucky, and what the object of Kirby Smith and Bragg was.

It was known before that that Kirby Smith had invaded Kentucky, and from all I could gather in regard to their object in this invasion it was to hold Kentucky as a part of the Southern Confederacy.

Question. You can state whether it was known at the time how Bragg was situated in reference to supplies and what expectation he had of forming a junction with Kirby Smith.

From the best information I could obtain Bragg was poorly supplied with provisions at the time of the invasion by his army. I could not ascertain certainly at what point they expected to form a junction; but, judging from events since that time, they must have expected to unite at Perryville or Harrodsburg.

Question. I ask you, general, in reference to the information or opinion held by the army at the time; that is, previous to the capture of

Munfordville.   I wish to know at what point it was expected that Bragg could get supplies for his army that he was then marching without.

I do not think he could have obtained supplies short of Bardstown, Lebanon, and through that region of country.   Of course he could have obtained some supplies soon after reaching Kentucky; not I think to a very great extent.

Question. State, if you please, whether you were at the battle of Perryville; what you know of the number of the enemy, and of their movements on the night after the battle and the day subsequent.

I was at the battle of Perryville.   I had no certain means of ascertaining the number of the enemy at Perryville during the fight.   My only information was obtained from citizens living in and around the place.   From that information I came to the conclusion that Bragg and Kirby Smith formed a junction at Perryville, and Kirby Smith, with the whole or a portion of his army, was there.   The day after the battle the evacuation took place, and they moved in the direction of Harrodsburg, as I learn, with the larger portion of their army.   A portion of it, I learned, moved in the direction of Danville.

Question. State, if you please, whether you are acquainted with that region of country and how you came to a knowledge of it.

I am very well acquainted with that part of the country.   I was born and raised within 8 miles of the place and have traveled a great deal over it.

Question. What was your position, general, on the day of the battle of Perryville and the day succeeding the battle; that is, what field were you in and what were you doing?

I was made the officer for the day of the center of the army the night previous to the battle.   About 11 o'clock at night I passed out with one regiment of my brigade to the house of Mr. Jardine Peter.   I there filed a regiment off to the left of the Springfield pike, and ordered them to take a position not far in the rear of the ridge upon which the battle commenced in the morning.   General Gilbert, after some reflection, concluded to send a strong picket out.   He ordered out Colonel McCook with his brigade, from, I believe, General Sheridan's division.   I directed Colonel McCook, with four regiments, I think, of his brigade, to take a position upon the right of the road and upon this ridge.   I took one regiment from his brigade and placed it upon the left of the road and the left regiment which I had already stationed there.   From the Tenth Indiana Regiment I directed one company to advance as near to the front as the officer might deem safe.   They advanced a little beyond this ridge of which I have already spoken to a house situated on the west side of another ridge nearer the town.   There they found the pickets of the enemy.   A few shots were exchanged, and, according to the directions I had given, my pickets fell back out of reach of their guns in order to prevent any alarm.   Colonel McCook, with his brigade, came upon the enemy just before day and had a considerable engagement, at least with the pickets.   I immediately went out to where the two regiments were on the left and advanced them at least half a mile.   I remained there some time watching the movements of the enemy, and felt satisfied from what I saw and from my knowledge of the position of the ground that just in front of me and to my left the enemy would make the most decided stand.   In the course of an hour after I had advanced those two regiments two pieces of artillery, together with some two or three regiments of cavalry, came to this point.   I inquired of Colonel Gay, who was in command of the cavalry, if there was any enemy just in front of that battery and of our forces.   He said the enemy had taken their position, he believed, just on the point of the first ridge of the two of which I have spoken, and deemed it advisable that I should go there and drive them away.   I followed his advice and succeeded in doing what he desired.   The fight was still going on immediately to my right by General Sheridan's division.   These two regiments remained there some time, but were finally ordered back; the Tenth Indiana to the rear to join its brigade, and the other, the Eighty-sixth Illinois, to join Colonel McCook.   I was not in the fight after that during the day.

Question. What was the conduct of General Gilbert immediately previous to the fight, pending the fight, and subsequent to it?

General Gilbert's conduct toward me was generally courteous and polite.   I had no reason to complain of him personally.   I heard a great deal of complaint from subordinate officers in regard to his conduct toward the men.   They spoke of it as being very unofficerlike and ungentlemanly.   I, however, saw nothing of it myself.   I saw very little of General Gilbert during the day of the fight.   I cannot therefore say what part he took in the engagement.

Question. I ask you, general, in reference to what he did; whether he did his duty; whether it was done with ability as a general, if you know.

The two divisions besides my own under his command were in the fight and behaved well, and I suppose that they were under the immediate control and direction of General Gilbert. So far as I could learn in regard to the management of those two divisions General Gilbert behaved well, though I know nothing of the part he took in it personally. He gave me no directions as to what I should do during the day. All the directions I obtained from him were as to what I should do the night previous to the battle as officer of the day, and what I did on the day of the fight was done, I must say, upon my own responsibility. I do not think I saw General Gilbert any time during the day of the fight. What directions he gave to his other divisions I am unable to say, and cannot therefore say whether he displayed great military skill or not.

Question. Had General Gilbert's entire force been engaged in that fight what effect would it have had upon the fortunes of the day, in your opinion?

My opinion is that the fortunes of the day would have turned a great deal more in our favor than they did.

Question. At the time you were approaching Perryville was it known to the army what the movements of Kirby Smith were—in what direction he was marching?

I learned that information had been obtained to the effect that Kirby Smith was marching in the direction of Harrodsburg from the north of Harrodsburg; that a portion of his army and General Sill's division had a slight engagement near Hardensville, I think in Shelby County, and perhaps another slight engagement near Lawrenceburg, 20 miles north of Harrodsburg.

Question. At what time on the morning of the 9th was it known to your army that Bragg was moving toward Harrodsburg and was the object of that movement understood?

I do not know at what time it was reported at headquarters. I learned it between 7 and 8 o'clock in the morning. I do not know what was the object of the movement. I suppose what was the object, but do not know certainly. I was satisfied myself that they were anxious to get out of our way.

Question. Had our army moved from Perryville on the morning of the 9th to Danville, or in that direction, what would have been the effect, instead of going to Harrodsburg?

I think the effect would have been to have checked them at Camp Dick Robinson, provided our army had continued to move in the proper direction beyond Danville. There was but one way of escape, in my opinion, for them from Camp Dick Robinson, and that way was left entirely open.

Question. By your moving toward Harrodsburg instead of Danville?

Yes, sir.

By General DANA:

Question. What was your rank and the character of your command in the Army of the Ohio from the time Bragg crossed the Tennessee River during the retrograde movement of the Army of the Ohio?

I was brigadier-general of the volunteer forces, and in command of a brigade comprising four regiments and one battery. From October the 9th, the day after the battle, I was in command of the First Division, and have been up to this time.

Question. Do you know anything, during one or two days prior to the battle of Perryville, of General Gilbert taking possession of a spring of water for the exclusive use of himself and his staff?

I knew nothing of it personally; I only heard that such was the fact. General Gilbert ordered me the night before the battle to place a guard over a pool of water for the use of the men.

Question. Do you know anything of the size and quantity of water in the spring you heard he took possession of?

I do not, sir. I did not know there was a spring there. All the water I drank, except on one occasion, was from the pool before spoken of.

Question. At this time were the men suffering from the want of water?

They were suffering very much.

By General ORD:

Question. Before the battle of Perryville did General Buell place over you any officer with whose right and capacity to command you were dissatisfied?

I cannot say that I was wholly dissatisfied myself, that is, on my own account. I was dissatisfied, however, on account of the treatment of that officer placed over me by General Buell toward officers under my immediate command. As to his right to command, I know nothing about it except what I have heard since. I have learned that he had no right to command me; indeed, I may say I heard it prior to his being relieved of his command, but made no complaint. I obeyed his orders as cheerfully as though he had been my superior in rank.

Question. State the name of this officer.

C. C. Gilbert.

Question. You say the Army of the Ohio was demoralized at that time; do you know positively the state of discipline in other divisions besides your own at that time?

I was thrown a great deal among other divisions, and found them as much, if not more, demoralized than my own.

Question. Do you know of any petition to remove General Buell from the command of the Army of the Ohio either before or after the battle of Perryville?

I know of only one and that was never presented.

Question. What was this petition based upon?

Simply upon the idea that those signing it did not believe General Buell was commanding the army in such a manner as to secure success for our arms.

Question. Did it make any specific charges against General Buell?

None that I recollect except that.

Question. About how many colonels of regiments signed this petition?

I did not count the number. Eight or ten, I suppose; perhaps more; not less, I am satisfied.

Question. Did you consider at the time that this petition was right and well founded?

I thought it was well founded at the time.

This question being objected to by the judge-advocate, the court was cleared.

Question. Do you know the names of any officers of the rank of colonel or above that rank who signed this petition?

Yes, sir.

Question. Will you state those names?

General James B. Steedman, Third Brigade of the First Division; Col. J. M. Harlan, commanding Second Brigade of the First Division; Colonel George, commanding Second Minnesota Regiment; Col. J. M. Connell, commanding Seventeenth Ohio; Col. M. B. Walker, commanding First Brigade, First Division; Col. John T. Croxton, commanding Fourth Kentucky; Maj. D. Ward, of the Seventeenth Ohio; Lieut. Col. F. W. Lister, of the Thirty-first Ohio, and several others whose names I cannot now call to mind.

Question. Did you sign this petition?

I decline to answer that question, sir.

Question. To whom do you consider that a general is responsible for the performance of his official duties—to his superior who places him in position or to his subordinates under his command?

I think he is responsible to his superior and to the people of his country, the subordinate officers included.

Question. Do you think this responsibility extends to the propriety of any move he may make?

In some instances I should think it did.

Question. How do you suppose a general should go to work to obtain the opinion of the subordinates under his command in regard to the propriety of any movement he was about to make?

I know no other means than by consultation.

Question. To what limit do you consider the responsibility to his subordinate officers extends, going down?

Under ordinary circumstances it is the duty of a general commanding an army to consult more especially general officers as low down as the commanders of divisions, and through them he could obtain the opinions of intelligent and well-informed officers of a lower grade. Under extraordinary circumstances there are many instances in which a general commanding an army would be greatly benefited in his movements by the consultation of officers of even the very lowest grades; and I think during the movements of our army in Kentucky there were many instances in which it would have been advisable that General Buell should have consulted the officers who were familiar with the country, and who, in my opinion, would have been of great service to him.

Question. Would it not be necessary, if the general had pursued the course you speak of in obtaining the opinions of officers of a lower grade, after consultation with higher officers, to postpone the movement until the officers of the lower grades might be consulted upon the special move about which they had no previous information?

If it were necessary to consult a great many officers, as a matter of course the movement would have been postponed to some extent; but generally speaking it would not be necessary to consult a great many officers; and the information necessary to be obtained from those officers who were acquainted with the character of the country and the strength of any particular position could be obtained very readily and very quickly.

Question. Is there any method or manner you know of by which the commanding officer can make these subordinate officers, to whom you think he is more or less responsible, responsible for the disasters which may ensue from following their advice?

General DANA. I object to that question as irrelevant.

The court was then cleared. On being reopened the witness proceeded.

The WITNESS. If an officer was called upon by his commanding general for information on any particular subject connected with the movements of the army, and that officer, having it in his power to give such information, should make a misrepresentation of facts, I do not see why he should not be court-martialed; but as a general thing, as I said before, I do not suppose there would be any way of reaching this officer for any disaster which might occur from following his advice.

Question. In your opinion do you consider that want of confidence which you state existed in General Buell was somewhat due to his not consulting the officers under his command enough?

I do, sir. There seemed to be a general complaint on that subject even with the officers who in the opinion of every one should have been consulted.

By General DANA:

Question. Within the precincts of whose corps and division was the meeting held to which you have testified?

It was at a house not within any officer's command.

MONDAY AFTERNOON, *December* 22, 1862.

General FRY'S examination continued.

Cross-examined by General BUELL:

Question. How long had this scarcity of provisions lasted which you say tended in a measure to demoralize the troops?

Our supplies were cut off some time in the month of August. While my division was stationed at Decherd we were on half rations—from that time until we reached Louisville or Bowling Green, I do not recollect which; Louisville I think.

Question. Are you able to say, general, how far this interruption of our communications was my fault?

I cannot say how far General Buell was in fault in regard to the cutting off of supplies; but our forces were very much scattered, and at points where there was no protection to the railroads.

Question. Will you specify the positions of the troops by way of illustration on this point?

So far as my recollection now serves me a portion of our troops were at Huntsville, a portion on the road between Huntsville and Decherd, and some few of them at Pulaski. My brigade and Colonel Walker's brigade were for a time at Decherd and Winchester, which is close by. A short time after we reached Decherd the First and Second Brigades were sent to Pelham, 16 miles southeast, I think, of Decherd. General McCook was, if I recollect rightly, at Stevenson or near there. General Wood's division and the division commanded by General Ammen were sent to McMinnville. I do not know what troops there were between this place and Decherd. I do not recollect the particular locality of any of the rest of the command.

Question. When did the interruption occur in the communications of the army during the time the troops were occupying these positions?

I think the principal interruption was at the tunnel some 7 or 8 miles beyond Gallatin. There were some other slight interruptions. I do not now recollect the exact point.

Question. Were they south of Nashville or north?

They were north.

Question. What force do you think would have been necessary to keep open the communications of the army between Nashville and Louisville?

I cannot tell what force it would take; at some points it would take a considerable force, at other points a less force.

Question. Do you know, or did you know, the object of the concentration of the troops on the line from McMinnville to Decherd?

I supposed the object was to meet the enemy, as I at first understood they were coming in that direction, but afterward satisfied myself that the enemy was rapidly making its way toward Kentucky, and so informed General Buell.

Question. When did you first become convinced that Bragg was marching for Kentucky, and not for Nashville, Tenn.?

I became thoroughly convinced while I was at Decherd, though I was fully of the opinion that that was his purpose while I was stationed at Tuscumbia, Ala., and so expressed it to officers of the army and by letter to my friends in Kentucky.

Question. On what was that opinion based?

It was based on information received from reliable persons who were conversant with the movements of the rebel army, and who told me they had conversed with citizens and with officers of the rebel army.

Question. Did that opinion have reference to the movements of the army under General Bragg or to those of the army under Kirby Smith?

It had reference to the movements of the army under General Bragg. When I became thoroughly satisfied that Bragg was moving toward Kentucky, Kirby Smith was already there with his army.

Question. What time?

I cannot specify the day of the month, but it was some time in the month of August.

Question. It was after the time, however, when you were first satisfied that an invasion of Kentucky would be made?

Yes, sir; it was.

Question. Was this opinion of such a character as to admit of no doubt?

I thought so, sir, and it turned out correct.

Question. Was it equally convincing to others as to yourself?

I believed it was universally believed that Bragg was moving toward Kentucky with the view of invading it.

Question. Did you believe that he had no intermediate object in the movement, particularly the capture of Nashville?

That idea was held out by some, and it may have been his purpose to have attacked Nashville; but from the direction in which his army went I did not believe myself that he contemplated any attack upon Nashville, knowing that he could do our army here as much injury by getting in its rear as he could by taking Nashville, and if his object in going to Kentucky would have been secured he would have gained more than by taking Nashville.

Question. In what way could he have derived advantage from getting into the rear of the Army of the Ohio in Kentucky?

He would have cut them off entirely from all supplies, and have had more and better opportunities of securing Kentucky to the rebel cause.

Question. Did you in your mind trace the route he would pursue in this invasion?

I traced it from information I received from others as to the direction in which he was going.

Question. I mean before the route was actually known by his own movements.

I cannot say that I traced it exactly, and had to be governed by information received from others as to the route he intended to take, but knew that there were routes by which he could very safely pass into Kentucky.

Question. What course would you have adopted in order to thwart him; and I ask, first, did you at the time form any definite plan with reference to it?

I thought we ought, under all the circumstances, to have attacked him at some point before he reached the Cumberland River, but not knowing well the geography of the country did not select any particular spot myself at which he ought to have been attacked. I gathered from well-informed officers that Sparta—I think that was the place—was the point at which he might easily have been attacked and driven back.

Question. From what officers did you get this information?

My impression now is that General Thomas gave it as his opinion that that was the point at which he might have been successfully attacked, though I would not say certainly that this was the point, but some point was designated.

Question. When was that opinion expressed?

I do not know that I heard General Thomas express it prior to the time of General Bragg's passing the point, but I understand that he had some time previously given it as his opinion and had urged the necessity of it.

Question. When did you hear that he had expressed that opinion?

I cannot specify the exact time, sir; I did not keep a memorandum of it; but it was while the army was at Louisville, I think.

Question. Do you know where the army of Bragg was when that advice was given?

I do not know exactly where General Bragg's army was, but I understood the opinion was expressed while General Thomas was at McMinnville. General Bragg's army was constantly moving in the direction of Kentucky, as I understood.

Question. Was the impression made on your mind that when this advice was given Bragg was actually in a position to be attacked at Sparta?

It was that Bragg was moving in that direction, and that there was an eligible point to concentrate our forces and prevent his passage into Kentucky.

Question. Are you well enough acquainted with the country to say now that Bragg could not have pursued any other route?

I suppose there are other routes he might have followed, but it would have thrown him, in my opinion, a great deal out of his way. His army would, in my opinion, have been checked.

Question. What routes do you think of now?

I do not know that I can exactly specify the route he might have followed, unless he had taken some other route higher up the Cumberland River and entered Kentucky somewhere near Birchville; that is, I understand there is a road in that direction through which he could have gone.

Question. Do you think that Bragg would have attacked your army in position?

I think it is very doubtful, sir.

Question. How strong a force would it have required to attack him in position?

It would have depended entirely upon whether he was fortified or not. If not fortified, I think we would have had force enough to have attacked him anywhere almost. He was not fortified anywhere on the road, as I understood.

Question. Do you not recognize that there are natural positions, particularly in mountainous regions, which have many, if not all, the advantages of artificial works?

Yes, sir; there are strong positions in the mountains and on rivers where there are bluffs through which the enemy would not venture to go; but, as I understood the region of country around the direction in which Bragg's army was at the time, we would have had as great an advantage as the enemy if we had pushed on and taken a position equally as good as we had at Murfreesborough, where our army was concentrated, as I understood, for the express purpose of meeting the enemy.

Question. Do you mean that the enemy could not have taken a position at Sparta which would not have given him greatly the advantage, numbers being equal?

I do not pretend to say so, if he had gotten there before we did.

Question. Suppose you had got there first and taken a position too strong for him to attack, could not he have changed his route and avoided you?

I have already stated that he might.

Question. In your plan for meeting the enemy at Sparta or thereabouts what force did you suppose he would have and what force did you suppose yourself to have?

My information was that the enemy had 36,000 men. I did not see the reports of our army, but understood we had nearly 50,000 men. I think that would have been sufficient to have met him.

Question. Suppose you could have interposed but 24,000, would you have thought it judicious to interpose yourself in that position when you could have increased the force by taking a position nearer your base?

I do not think so, unless the position taken was of such a strength as to have given us the advantage.

Question. Do you not think that in opposing yourself to an enemy that might choose his route, that might attack you or avoid at his option, it would be necessary for you to have a sufficient force to act on the offensive in order certainly to defeat his purpose?

It might be necessary and it might not; I cannot say. It is a very general sort of a question, and I do not suppose any man can answer it entirely satisfactorily.

Question. If an enemy may pursue various routes you can only put yourself on the defensive with reference to one of them; since while you are preparing yourself on one he may suddenly take advantage of the other and deprive you of the benefit of the position and thus compel you to attack him or let him alone. Perhaps you can answer the question with that explanation more definitely.

If he failed to attack me and I became satisfied that an attack on me would be disastrous I would let him pass. If I felt satisfied that I had an equal chance of securing a victory I should most unquestionably pursue him and attack him wherever I could catch him.

Question. Do you not think that under such circumstances, in order to defeat the purpose of your enemy, you ought to have a sufficient force to assume the offensive; that is, to pursue and attack him wherever you find him, notwithstanding some advantage of position he may have?

Of course it would be necessary to pursue him if you wished to attack him. It would not be advisable to attack 20,000 with 5,000 or 40,000 with 10,000.

Question. Would it always be advisable to attack 10,000 with 10,000 or 10,000 with 15,000?

Not always, sir. There are many instances in which it would be advisable and many in which it would not be advisable. I do not know, however, that this was an instance in which it would not be advisable.

Question. Has your condemnation of the campaign in Tennessee last summer been based on the supposition that we had an army of 50,000, or nearly that, which could be brought to bear upon any point, which could have been opposed to Bragg's army as it passed through the State?

I so understood it, sir; that when our army was concentrated—I mean that army with which General Buell left Corinth—we had something near 50,000 men, and perhaps more.

Question. Can you not see why Murfreesborough might have had some advantage over a more remote point for concentration and battle, supposing the enemy wished to advance upon you? Did the fact of its being nearer your base give it any advantage?

I had very little opportunity of examining the ground, and cannot say certainly that the advantages of Murfreesborough were greatly superior to those of other points. I had no objection to concentrating the forces there, under the idea that Bragg was moving on that point. I thought we could fight there as well as anywhere else in an open field fight. There was one advantage I might mention: it was a rich country, and we could supply our army better there than we could perhaps beyond there. There might also be an advantage in being nearer Nasville.

Question. How does the condition of Middle Tennessee compare now general, with what it was in July or August in regard to supplies?

When our army reached here last fall I suppose, so far as forage was concerned, it was better than when we left here early in September. As to provisions for an army and for feeding the men I suppose it is not so good now as then, both armies having drawn supplies to a certain extent from Middle Tennessee. The last year's crop added some supplies to a country previously pretty well exhausted. In other portions, however, through which I passed there was a large amount of supplies prior to the coming in of the present year's crop.

Question. Has the crop of last summer increased that supply or not, do you think?

I suppose it did increase it; but in some localities the supply must now be as low as it was prior to the coming in of the last year's crop by being drawn upon by both armies.

Question. Was the crop of last year really available when we left here?

We made it so; we used it very freely.

Question. Had not the crop of 1861 been drawn upon by both armies and to a greater extent than the crop of this year is now?

In some localities I suppose it was; in other localities it was not. In the immediate vicinity of Nashville, Murfreesborough, and Gallatin I suppose the crop for this year (1862) has been well-nigh exhausted; whereas the crop of 1861, in a very large region of country in Middle Tennessee, when I passed through that country, was scarcely touched, except now and then by a brigade passing along the road. The crops in the southern part of Middle Tennessee this year were very fine, at least corn. The rebels may since that time have taken all the forage in that region of country.

Question. What crop were we fed from last summer; the crop of 1861 or 1862? The crop of 1862 is the one just gathered.

In some places we were obliged to forage upon the crops of 1862, owing to the scarcity of the crop of 1861. In many places, however, we found the greatest abundance of corn, and sometimes hay, sometimes oats, of the crop of 1861.

Question. Suppose the Army of the Cumberland to be cut off from Louisville now, would it or would it not be in a condition to assume offensive operations?

It would not be in a position to assume offensive operations, as I understand it; not for the want of supplies and provisions for the men, but for the lack of forage.

Question. You mean that the supply of provisions for the men—for the army—is greater than the supply of forage?

I understand so, sir; for they have to forage upon the country here and have to fight for a great deal they get.

Question. Suppose the communication with Louisville to be effectually severed and that this army was opposed by one which could fight it or not at its option, how long could it stay here, supposing it to have on hand now supplies for ten days?

If we were compelled to fight the enemy and were overcome its stay would be but short; if, however, it succeeded in driving the enemy back and scattering its forces, it might be able to stay some time; I cannot say how long.

Question. Suppose the enemy did not give it battle but simply hovered about to prevent it from foraging?

If the communication between this and Louisville was effectually cut off I should think that our army here would be most effectually ruined, unless they had provisions enough on hand to take them to a point where they could secure supplies from the westward or elsewhere.

Question. Besides the necessity which existed last summer for foraging on the country to some extent, do you think there was a prevalent tendency among the troops to plunder and maraud upon the community through which they passed?

Yes, sir; I do.

Question. Was that due to the neglect of the officers, do you think, general?

I cannot say that it was due to the neglect of the officers altogether; there might have been some instances, and no doubt there were, in which it was due to the neglect of officers; but there seemed to be, outside of the necessity of foraging and seizing food from the country, a disposition on the part of the men to pillage, arising, I think, out of the fact that they were not allowed to strike a blow at some point upon the enemy. I heard this among the men themselves, and used as much influence and power as I possessed to prevent these depredations from being committed.

Question. Would you believe in the honor and courage of a man who pretended that he pillaged his unarmed friend because he had not an opportunity to fight a manly and armed foe?

There are some instances in which I would have great confidence in men who would even be guilty of pilfering under such circumstances as those; but, generally speaking, men who are disposed to pilfer, and who pilfer under any and all circumstances, are not to be relied upon. Men, however, in an army act very differently from what they do under ordinary circumstances, when at home, under the influences of peace. I believe there is such a thing as making men who are generally considered honest and upright at home thieves in an army, and I think this can be done by inefficiency and neglect on the part of officers. I have twice in my life been connected with the Army of the United States, and I have found this rule to prevail in both instances.

Question. When did this disposition to pilfer first evince itself?

This general system of pilfering was more clearly evinced after we left Decherd to march to Pelham in the month of August.

Question. Do you not think that this disposition was in fact due to the encouragement which it had received from the popular sentiment through the country and the idea of carrying on a war of vengeance instead of one for the preservation of the Union?

I do not think it was, sir. That may have had something to do with it with some.

Question. You have stated in your direct testimony that Bragg was moving into Kentucky with the purpose of forming a junction with Kirby Smith at Harrodsburg. Was it probable that after forming that junction he would suddenly determine to abandon his purpose in Kentucky without a decisive battle?

My opinion is that Bragg and Smith had a double object in view in invading Kentucky. One was to provide their army with such provisions and clothing as they could take from the citizens there; another was, if it was in their power, to hold Kentucky by power of arms and make it part and parcel of the Southern Confederacy. They gathered together all the provisions and clothing they could find in that portion of the State through which they passed, but finding that they were unable to hold the State against the army that was pursuing them they determined to evacuate it.

Question. When do you think that determination was formed?

My opinion is it was formed after the battle of Perryville, if the statements of the people of Kentucky are to be relied on at all.

Question. Was there anything at the time to indicate that the battle of Perryville had been of a decisive character or of such a character as to determine the result of an important campaign?

I think they became satisfied that if our whole force had moved upon them at Perryville they would have been very badly beaten and were afraid to venture another battle.

Question. Is your opinion based upon the assumption that Bragg's army and Kirby Smith's—the whole rebel force in Kentucky—were concentrated at Perryville?

Not entirely. I understood that Kirby Smith, with a portion of his army, would form a junction with Bragg at Perryville; whether true or not I am not able to say; but I believe, whether they formed it there or not, they did afterward unite their arms somewhere between that point and Lancaster.

Question. Was there anything to prevent that junction from being formed at Perryville?

Nothing, sir, that I know of; and I think it was partly accomplished.

Question. Suppose it proved that it was not accomplished at Perryville and that the enemy deliberately planned to form a junction at Harrodsburg, would that indicate an intention to retreat from the State without another battle?

I do not think that would indicate an intention to retreat from the State without a battle, but I think they were satisfied that they were not able to cope with our army, and that if our army had been hurled upon them at Perryville they would either have been captured or scattered to the winds. That determined the abandonment of the main object of the invasion of the State by the rebel army.

Question. Was there anything in the movements of the enemy immediately after the battle to indicate that he intended to retreat from the State?

Their leaving their position which they held there at Perryville and moving toward Harrodsburg indicated to some extent to my mind a determination to leave the State.

Question. Why should they have moved toward Harrodsburg, supposing them to be concentrated at Perryville?

Some of them moved toward Danville, as I understand; some toward Harrodsburg; and I suppose their object was to concentrate their forces and get them together, if possible, at Camp Dick Robinson, and move them off from there with all the provisions they had collected together. They moved in different directions to expedite their retreat as much as possible.

Question. What portion moved by Danville?

I cannot say; I only learned that some of them did.

Question. Are you satisfied that any portion of the army marched that way?

I have the same evidence for that which I have for the other; that is, from citizens.

Question. Were they cavalry or infantry?

I cannot say for certain which.

Question. Would your opinion of their plans be affected by the question whether a portion of them actually moved off by Danville or whether they formed a junction with the whole force at Harrodsburg; is that a matter which would be likely to affect your opinion of their plans?

My opinion was that at the time they left Perryville, whatever direction they went, their intention was to leave the State, and it so turned out.

Question. Do you not think that opinion is rather confirmed by the result than founded in reason at the time?

I think there were good reasons for it. One is that if they had felt satisfied of being enabled to drive us back and hold a position which they did hold at Perryville they would never have left it, for there is no point between Louisville and the farthest point to which our army went beyond Perryville at which they could have successfully met us. Perryville was the point, and I learn that General Bragg so expressed himself.

Question. Do you know of their having selected a battle ground at Harrodsburg?

I heard such a thing, but the fact of their abandonment shows very conclusively to my mind that they did not consider the place tenable against an army.

Question. Which army suffered most in the battle of Perryville do you think?

From the best information I could get and from an examination of the matter the suffering was almost equal.

Question. Have you ever heard the enemy's loss estimated at 4,000 and upward in that fight?

I have seen it stated that it is about equal to ours. I heard various rumors as to the numbers killed, wounded, and missing on both sides, and they all seemed to corroborate the statement that the sufferings of the two armies were about equal.

Question. Do you know when the rebel army commenced their retreat from Camp Dick Robinson?

Not exactly, save from what citizens told us. They were leaving there for some two or three days. From accounts I received I understood they commenced leaving there about the 10th or 11th of October.

Question. How far was our army, or a large portion of it, from Danville on the 10th of October?

I think I left Perryville on the 10th. I cannot tell how far the army was away, as I was not with it.

Question. How far is the spring which bears your name from Danville?

It is estimated at 5 miles by the pike.

Question. What extent of ground, in miles, would the army we had at Perryville occupy?

Judging from what I was told by those who were on the extreme right and left of our army and my knowledge of the ground it must have extended over the space of 8 to 10 miles; perhaps farther. I speak of the ground over which the enemy would have extended on the day of the battle.

Question. What extent of ground would necessarily have been required for it in camp?

If the ground were level the army could be encamped, I suppose, in a space of half that length. If the ground were rough and uneven it would have occupied more space.

Question. Suppose it had been known that the enemy had designed to retreat by the way of Crab Orchard and that before he could do that our army was placed across his route, what course could he have pursued?

He might possibly have pursued the course of Kentucky River Bridge. I do not know of any other way he could have got out of Camp Dick Robinson. I stated this morning that there was only one way to get out of Camp Dick Robinson, and that way was left open. He could, as I have stated, have succeeded in getting across the Kentucky River Bridge, unless pursued too hotly.

Commission adjourned to meet December 23, 1862, at 10 o'clock a. m.

NASHVILLE, *Tuesday Morning, December* 23, 1862.

The Commission met pursuant to adjournment. All the members present; also the judge-advocate and General Buell.

General FRY'S cross-examination continued.

By General BUELL:

Question. Who were the principal movers in the meeting which had for its object to prepare a petition for the removal of General Buell from the command of the Army of the Ohio ?

I believe I have said on that subject all that is proper to say.

The court was here cleared.

I cannot say who first moved in it. I gave yesterday the names of some of the principal parties concerned, and that is as far as I know.

Question. Was the object of that meeting made the subject of discussion by officers within your knowledge ?

I have heard the matter discussed by those whom I have mentioned and others.

Question. Were these discussions attended by a knowledge of the facts which affect the question and had these discussions for their object to arrive at a correct understanding of it, or did they merely consist in expressions of dissatisfaction ?

I do not know what knowledge they had of the facts affecting the question. There were expressions of dissatisfaction, based on the idea that the Army of the Ohio was not properly managed.

Question. Were these discussions in public or in private ?

In one sense they might be called public and in another sense private.

Question. Were they in the presence and hearing of subordinate officers and soldiers ?

I have in some instances heard expressions of dissatisfaction in the presence of subordinate officers and soldiers, and I have heard expressions of dissatisfaction among the soldiers, without having any reference to anything said by officers.

Question. Were these murmurings concurred in or discountenanced by officers senior to those who signed the petition ?

I think that they were generally discountenanced.

Question. I put a question to you yesterday in regard to the causes of the demoralization of the troops in a form which did not express my meaning nor the idea which I wish to present to you. I now ask whether the disposition to plunder and pillage on the part of the troops was not encouraged by the popular idea, which at that time was heralded through the country, of living upon the enemy, as it is called, and regarding that as constituting a vigorous prosecution of the war ?

I cannot say that I have heard that officers endeavored to advance the idea that it was proper on the part of a soldier to plunder and pillage ; on the contrary, nearly all with whom I had anything to do seemed to discountenance it.

Redirect examination by the JUDGE-ADVOCATE :

Question. You have said in response to questions asked by the Commission that a general commanding is answerable to his subordinates as he is to the people. Am I to understand from this that he is to be controlled or directed by his subordinates or that by consulting them he can in any case escape the responsibility imposed upon him by his position ?

Not at all.

Question. Do you know whether these propositions to remove officers by subordinates have been common in our army or not ?

I understand it has, sir. I know of only one instance personally ; that was in the case of T. W. Sherman, when he commanded the First Division. A large number of officers waited upon General Buell and requested him in person to have us transferred to his army and to aid us in getting General Sherman removed from the command of the division, and my impression now is that General Buell told us the proper way to come at the matter was by a written petition in respectful terms. We afterward, on the same day, waited upon General Halleck, and he gave us clearly to understand that General Sherman should be removed; that he knew our troubles and difficulties, and that he would remedy them as soon as possible, having for some days had the matter under consideration. General Sherman was in a short time relieved from the command.

Question. You have been asked, general, what confidence you would have in the honor and courage of a man who pretended that he pillaged his unarmed friends because he had not an opportunity to fight a manly and armed foe. How would your confidence in that soldier be affected by the fact of marching through a country where the inhabitants were hostile and the entire army subject to continued insult and abuse from the inhabitants?

My confidence in a soldier who was constantly insulted by the inhabitants of the country through which we were marching and who would commit depredations upon such citizens would not be greatly impaired. Although I discountenance pillage under any plea, I believe it is common with the best armies in the world.

Question. Do you not know that it is quite common in this war for the inhabitants of the country to be in arms against the forces of the United States as this force approached and then return to their usual avocations as farmers as the army goes through?

Yes, sir; I believe it has been very common.

Question. What has been the effect upon our army, so far as demoralizing it is concerned, by giving protection and guards to rebel property?

It has been, in my opinion, somewhat deleterious; I might say considerably so.

Question. Has not the jealous care of rebel property impressed upon our forces that our generals were really sympathizing with that side?

I think it has to a considerable extent, sir.

Question. You have been asked in reference to the lines of supplies. Do you know up to what time the trains were run upon the railroad between Bowling Green and Louisville?

I think they were running to within a short time before we reached Bowling Green, or about the time we reached there, in September.

Question. Do you recollect what interruption there was upon that line between Bowling Green and Nashville?

The tunnel was blown up; one bridge between the tunnel and Gallatin was destroyed; there were also some bridges destroyed between Gallatin and Nashville after we were on our return to Tennessee.

Question. Are you acquainted personally with the country about that tunnel that was destroyed?

I have only passed through it once and am not very well acquainted with it, but I know that it is quite a rough, hilly country.

By General DANA:

Question. Did you know or hear, at the time when General Buell was in command of the Army of the Ohio, of any proposition or attempt on the part of officers of his command, other than that already testified to, to depose him from the command and put General Thomas in his place?

I know of no attempt being made to place General Thomas in command. I have heard there was an attempt, but know nothing of the truth of it.

Question. Where and at what time did you hear that this proposition was made?

I heard it at Louisville, when we were marching back from Tennessee through Kentucky.

Question. Do you remember how you got this information?

From rumor, sir.

By General TYLER:

Question. General, I understand that you were born in the neighbor-hood where the battle of Perryville was fought and that you are ac-quainted with that section of country thoroughly. Suppose a vigorous advance had been made early on the morning of the 9th by General Buell's army upon General Bragg's force, would not obstacles of Dick's River render it almost impossible for Bragg to pass it under the cir-cumstances?

I was born in that region of country and am pretty well acquainted with it. I cannot say that it would have been altogether prudent in the early part of the action to have made a vigorous attack upon General Bragg, as I understood that General Crittenden's corps had not yet gotten into position. After General Crittenden had gotten into position my opinion is that a vigorous attack ought to have been made and would have resulted in the route of Bragg's army; and that in the event of its being routed it would have been almost impossible for him to have succeeded in crossing Dick's River at the point at which I understood he had crossed. It is a rough, broken, bluffy country, and my impression is that the passage across the river at that point at which he crossed is very narrow. I mean if the victory had been followed up rapidly.

Question. At what time, general, was General Crittenden's division [corps] in position?

I think I heard General Crittenden himself say that he was in position somewhere in the middle of the day; between 10 and 12 o'clock on the day of the battle.

By General ORD:

Question. General, you stated that the divisions of General Gilbert's corps, as far as you know, were not mismanaged at the battle of Perry-ville; do you know whether the divisions of Crittenden's corps were mis-managed?

I remarked that the divisions of Generals Sheridan and Mitchell, of General Gilbert's corps, so far as I know or observed, were well managed. The First Division I thought was very badly managed, from the fact that it was kept lying still during the greater part of the day and while the heaviest portion of the fight was going on. I cannot say, for I do not know, whether General Crittenden's corps was badly managed or not. I understood that when that corps was in position General Thomas and General Crit-tenden were both very anxious to advance and engage the enemy, and they seemed to be satisfied with the position of that corps. General Crittenden expressed himself in my presence as being highly delighted with the position of his corps, and said that all he desired at that time was to be allowed to advance upon the enemy.

Question. What position did your division occupy in the corps rela-tive to the corps of General McCook; about how far from it and in what direction?

During the greater part of the day my division was lying within a short distance of and in front of General Buell's headquarters, and I suppose it must have been 2 miles to the rear and to the right of General McCook's corps. I understand that in the evening General Steedman's brigade was ordered to the support of General Mc-Cook, but learned that it was not allowed to go into action. This I heard from Gen-eral Steedman himself. I understood from General Steedman that the battery con-nected with his brigade fired a few rounds.

Question. Do you know anything about the position of the enemy in front of General McCook's corps?

I know the ground pretty well, and from what I learned they occupied a pretty strong position, where they had the advantage in the ground.

Recross-examination by General BUELL:

Question. When the officers of the First Division called upon Gen-eral Buell at Corinth was he their commander or in a position with reference to them that would have justified him in admonishing or rebuking them ?

He was not the commander of the First Division ; it was not in his corps; but I suppose, being a superior officer, he would have the right, if we were guilty of any violation of military etiquette, to admonish or rebuke us.

Question. Was not the visit rather a social and complimentary one, though having for its object that which the witness has stated ?

The visit was not intended merely as a social visit ; it might be in one sense a complimentary one. We went to General Buell believing that he would give us such aid and such advice in the premises as were necessary, and he gave us the advice, according to my recollection, stated in a previous answer.

Question. Did he not decline to apply for a transfer of the division to his command, while at the same time expressing himself much gratified that they should desire to return to it?

He did decline to use his influence to have us transferred to his command, but gave us all the advice we wanted in regard to the particular object of our visit.

Question. Did he not advise you delicately, but as pointedly as would be becoming under the circumstances, that as far as your proceeding had for its object the removal of your commander it was improper ; that the same course might with equal propriety be pursued by your subordinates in reference to any and all of you ; and in parting with you personally did he not say to you that he would be very much gratified to have you back again, but that you must not, as he expressed himself pleasantly, be insubordinate ?

He did express a desire to have us back in his command, and warned us not to be insubordinate, and told us that our manner of proceeding, he thought, was a little improper, and that subordinate officers might act in the same way toward us; but, as I have before stated, advised us as to the proper mode of getting our removal. We assured General Buell that there was no disposition on the part of any of us to be at all insubordinate ; that what we did or what we should do in the premises should be done in the most respectful and officerlike manner.

Question. Have you ever of your own accord given protection to the property of citizens in the vicinity of your command and without troubling yourself about inquiring as to whether they were loyal or disloyal ?

I have scarcely ever been called upon by citizens for protection until my arrival at Gallatin. I there, under the direction of General Thomas, gave protection to citizens, both loyal and disloyal; but in most instances it was done when we had taken from them all the forage and such other articles as were necessary for us, leaving only enough for the support of the family and stock during the winter. In some few instances I may have given protection when the parties had been foraged upon to the extent authorized.

Question. Will you please state, general, who they were who proposed to depose General Buell from his command and from whom you acquired the information in regard to such a purpose ?

I do not know who they were, sir ; I had nothing to do with it.

Question. Can you not remember the names of those who mentioned it to you?

No, sir.

Question. Whom did General Steedman complain of as having prevented him from going into action on the evening of the 8th, after he was detached from his division ?

I do not recollect that he named any particular person.

Question. In your answer to the question by the judge-advocate did you mean to convey the idea that General Thomas and General Crittenden complained during the day that they were not permitted to engage the enemy ?

I do not know that they complained during the day, for I was not with them but I thought from General Crittenden's conversation that he felt a little aggrieved because he was not allowed to engage the enemy, though he did not say so in so many words. I heard General Thomas say that it was very late when he heard the fight was going on, and wondered why he had not been informed of it. He heard the artillery, and my impression now is that he said that upon inquiring as to what it meant the reply came that Colonel Gay was amusing himself with the rebel cavalry.

The judge-advocate proposes, in view of the movement of the Army of the Cumberland, to arrest for the present the case of the Government, reserving to himself the right hereafter to introduce further evidence, for the purpose of summoning the witnesses General Buell wishes to have examined.

Col. G. D. WAGNER (a witness for the Government), being duly sworn by the judge-advocate, testified as follows:

By the JUDGE-ADVOCATE:

Question. State, if you please, your name and position in the United States service.

G. D. Wagner; colonel of the Fifteenth Indiana Volunteers.

Question. State whether you were at the battle of Perryville; whether you took any part in that fight, and what you saw of the enemy on the night of the 8th, and what you know of his subsequent movements on the morning of the 9th.

I was at the battle of Perryville and took part in that fight. On the night of the 8th I saw very little of the enemy except his fires, or moving of troops except stragglers and unorganized bodies around the fires. These were on the left—about a mile on the left and half a mile to the front—till about daylight or a little before. Some time before daylight I heard considerable moving of wheels, which I supposed to be artillery. It was retiring. I did not see any troops at the time, but at break of day I rode some distance to the front of my command, gained an eminence from which I could look into the town of Perryville, and saw the enemy, as I thought, retiring by the Danville road. This was so early that I could just see a black line, but could not tell whether it was infantry or cavalry. When it became a little lighter I heard this column passing up the creek toward the right of our army, and the thought struck me that they were changing position of their forces from the left of Perryville to the right of our army—about an hour and a half after sunup—a body of cavalry— I should think a thousand—from the front on the right of our army. These I supposed to be the troops I saw going in that direction early in the morning. When I became convinced that they were retiring I immediately ordered forward my brigade and Cox's battery and commenced shelling them. Colonel Carlin, who was at my right, also advanced. Colonel Connor,[?] commanding a brigade of the division belonging to General Gilbert's corps, made a similar advance. The skirmishers of my command entered the town and took possession of it, capturing a few prisoners. They entered the town about sunup, or it might have been half an hour later. It was as quick as it could be done after daylight. I made another small advance to gain a better position for the battery; another body of rebel troops then appeared coming out of the woods to the left of the town near the springs, with the evident intention of gaining the Danville road, by which they retired. There were scattering troops seen in front, but after a few minutes there was no body of troops in sight. This was after shelling the first column. These troops marched down the road, and we had our battery in such a position as to enfilade the road. The enemy had two guns, which were put in position just at daylight back of the town, and they remained there till the last troops came. Captain Cox's battery again opened upon this body of troops and scattered them. A portion of the troops went up the road very orderly. Immediately after these troops passed the cavalry I have referred to retired from the right of the army in the range of my guns, and I ordered my battery to open upon them, but two or three colonels and officers standing by insisted that they were our cavalry advancing. They came out cautiously from the wood and formed in line, but did not act like an enemy advancing, so we did not open fire on them. I think that cavalry was the body of troops going, as I supposed, toward the right in the morning just at daybreak, as when they passed half a mile from the town to the right there was some timber which obscured them from view, and I could not see their position until they again retired across the open space of ground over which they had to pass.

AFTERNOON SESSION.

Colonel WAGNER's examination continued.

Cross-examination by General BUELL:

Question. Do you know any reason why you were not ordered to attack the enemy when he was so near you, or could any other attack have been judiciously made than that which you made without the concurrent action of other troops?

The reason that I did not advance farther that morning into the town and beyond it and undertake to cut off those troops that were retreating was because I was then much farther advanced than I was ordered to go. I had gone about as far as I thought I dared go without being ordered. After I had at dark ordered the troops to lay upon their arms, not even allowing them to go for water, a staff officer of General Gilbert came to me, with the request that I would advance up to the edge or into the town with my brigade. Colonel Carlin was at the edge of the town, and did not think it safe to remain in that position without support. I declined to do so, saying that he could get support from the rear from General Wood or General Crittenden to protect the right. This was for the reason that I was informed during the day that there was a large force in front of General Crittenden's main body, which, if I had advanced to that position, would have left them in my rear. I went with the aide-de-camp back to General Wood's headquarters, reporting the position of affairs in front, and joined with him in asking for support so as to enable us to hold the town during the night. General Wood sent one of his officers with the aide of General Gilbert to General Crittenden. I returned to my command. We received no further orders. Colonel Carlin took position on my left. When I went to the rear at this time I heard from officers a confirmation of the report referred to, that there was a large force in front of General Smith's division, on the extreme right of the army. This information, it is but just to say, was said to be reported by General Smith.

Redirect examination by the JUDGE-ADVOCATE:

Question. At what time did you arrive on the battle ground on the afternoon of the 8th?

I arrived in the rear line about half past two, as near as I can remember.

Question. How did this arrival of yours place Crittenden's corps on the battle ground at that time?

His forces were upon either side of the pike leading from Perryville to Lebanon, or about 2 miles from Perryville.

Question. How was that position in reference to that held by General McCook?

I do not know what General McCook's position was. I know only the position of General Gilbert.

Question. How was it in reference to General Gilbert?

My orders were on arriving in the rear of the line to form in line of battle on the left of General Van Cleve, who was the left of General Crittenden's line, prolonging the line in the direction of General Gilbert's right; therefore the general direction of these two lines was parallel to each other or nearly so.

Question. What was done for the next two or three hours after your arrival upon the battle-field?

Before I had quite formed my brigade in line of battle General Wood gave me an order to march immediately to the support of General Sheridan's right, which he said was being turned; this I immediately did. That was about half a mile directly to my left. On arriving within 600 yards of General Sheridan's forces I came in contact with a brigade of the enemy advancing upon General Sheridan's right, which I immediately attacked; but the mere appearance of my force upon their flank caused them immediately to about-face and retire, we advancing and they retiring until night.

Question. Can you say, colonel, from your knowledge of the ground, how far you were in the afternoon from General McCook's corps?

I could see the troops that were engaged with him off to our left; I should think it was about a mile; but I never rode over the ground, and it is only by looking from one point to another that I form this judgment.

Question. What did the movement of troops and firing that afternoon indicate to you?

Very little, if anything, of a fight, and it was remarkable and perfectly astounding to me and many other officers when we heard that there had been a great fight and there was heard so little firing; that was a common remark of the officers. Four miles before I arrived in the rear of the line of battle General Wood ordered me forward as fast as possible; to leave all transportation. He said it was reported that a fight was going on. He and I rode up the road till we got within 2 miles of Perryville, he frequently remarking, "How is it possible that there is a fight going on when we can scarcely hear firing at all?"

Question. How was that firing after you arrived there?

After I arrived in line for some time my own firing drowned that of everything else. I have no distinct recollection about the firing after that. But when I was within a mile of General Gilbert's corps I scarcely heard any firing worth talking about. I thought there was a skirmishing going on, but did not think there was a battle raging.

Question. About what time of day was it that General Wood ordered you hurriedly forward?

It was about 1 o'clock.

Question. Was the information you obtained given to your superior officers?

I made my report from time to time to General Wood, my division commander. All the time from daylight or soon after daylight there was quite a dust upon the Harrodsburg road, the road leading from Perryville to Harrodsburg, as though there was a movement of troops taking place. The road was hidden from view by timber. I supposed this to be the retiring of troops.

Question. How late in the day did you observe this, colonel?

That was about two hours after daylight. It went on at the same time that the movement took place on the Danville road, and continued, I should say, till about 8 o'clock.

Question. You say you were not engaged in the contest that day but slightly?

My brigade was engaged in Wood's division the first day.

Recross-examination by General BUELL:

Question. Do you know what time the corps to which you belonged advanced that morning?

I think the command began to move at about 7 and left about 9. Two divisions preceded me; two brigades followed me. This refers to the march from camp on the morning of the 8th.

Question. Do you know at what time your corps advanced toward the position of the enemy on the morning of the 9th?

I do not know the exact time, but can tell pretty nearly from certain facts. At about 9 to 9.30 o'clock, my brigade being at that time near the town of Perryville, with no enemy in view, I received an order to report to the rear of General Crittenden's corps. The explanation was that General Crittenden was going to advance upon the town of Perryville with his corps. General Wood's division, of which my brigade was a part, was to form a reserve in that advance. I pointed down to the town and told the aide-de-camp who brought the order that I had had possession of it from about sunup, and that there had not been a rebel near it, at least in sight, for an hour, and the last I saw of the enemy's cavalry they were retiring from the front of General Smith. At that time they were entirely out of sight, and I could see from the town in the direction of their retiring at least a mile.

Question. Did you report this information, and was any change made in the disposition of your brigade in consequence of it?

I can only state that from the information of others. I remarked to the aide-de-camp that he should go and inform the general of the fact, and that I could not consent to march my troops 2 miles to the rear and back again for nothing, as I supposed from the order it was known at headquarters that the rebel troops had retired. I retired my brigade some half mile to the rear, where I soon received orders to await further orders before I made any movement. I supposed that order to be the result of the information that I sent back by the aide-de-camp.

Question. Did you understand that these details with reference to the movement of the right corps were directed specially by myself or that they were under the direction of the corps commander, General Thomas?

I certainly supposed, sir, that all our orders came from ———. I had no knowledge as a brigade commander that you specially directed our movements. My intention was to send information to General Thomas and General Crittenden. I knew—at least I heard—that you were not on that portion of the line by one of your own staff.

Col. D. McCook (a witness for the defense), being duly sworn by the judge-advocate, testified as follows:

By General Buell:

Question. Colonel, will you state to the Commission, if you please, what you know of the operations in front of Perryville on the evening of the 7th and on the 8th? Confine yourself, if you please, to important incidents, so as not to occupy more time than is necessary for yourself and the Commission. Also please state your name and position in the service of the United States.

My name is Daniel McCook, colonel of the Fifty-second Ohio Volunteer Infantry, at that time commanding the Thirty-sixth Brigade and still commanding it, forming a part of the Tenth Division of the Third Army Corps of the Army of the Ohio. On the night of the 7th of October, 1862, my brigade went into camp within about 4 miles of Perryville, on the Springfield pike. We encamped on the right of the road, three-quarters of a mile from it, in line of battle. The Eighty-fifth Illinois, one of the regiments composing my brigade, was detailed for picket at 2 o'clock that night. I had just got my troops into position when I received an order from Maj. J. M. Wright, one of General Buell's assistant adjutants-general, ordering Major-General Gilbert to throw forward one of his brigades and seize the ground in front of Doctor's Fork, which our corps was depending upon for water, and also to consult Captain Gay as to the position and conformation of the country. This order was properly referred to General Sheridan by General Gilbert, and General Sheridan ordered my brigade to execute the duty. I immediately got on my horse, wakened up my men as quietly as possible, left orders for them to file into the Springfield road and there await further commands, while I went to find Captain Gay. During my meanderings to find Captain Gay I stumbled into General Buell's camp, and asked the sentinel if he could tell me where Captain Gay was. General Buell, I suppose recognizing my voice, requested me to come in. I found Captain Gay, got the information desired from him, put my column in motion for the high ground, which I subsequently learned to be called Peters' Hill. On the advice of General Buell I had dispatched a staff officer to get a battery from General Sheridan. He sent me Captain Barnett's Illinois battery. As soon as I got to the outpost Colonel Greusel pointed to me the enemy's picket line, which was on the crest of Peters' Hill. I formed the Eighty-fifth Illinois on the right of the Springfield pike, the Fifty-second Ohio (my own regiment) on the left of the Springfield pike, throwing forward well to the front and flanks two companies of each regiment as skirmishers. I formed the One hundred and twenty-fifth Illinois, another regiment composing my brigade, the right wing on the left side of the road and the left wing on the right side. My skirmishers had scarcely taken intervals, it being a bright moonlight night (between 3 and 4 o'clock in the morning), when the enemy opened upon me with a heavy musketry fire. My skirmishers advanced steadily up the hill on the left of the road, it being open ground; but being wood on the right of the road, the principal force of the enemy was concentrated there, and the Eighty-fifth Illinois made very slow progress. As soon as I discovered that their progress was so slow I ordered my skirmishers to change direction to the right, followed by the battalion, attack the rebels in flank, and drive them from the woods, thereby gaining the crest of Peters' Hill. In carrying this position I lost 6 men killed and 27 wounded. I threw my skirmishers 1,000 yards to the front, far enough to keep my main line from being annoyed, and ordered my men to lay down on the crest of the hill, well covered by it. By this time Barnett's battery had arrived. I put four guns into position on the left of the road, commanding the open country and valley, upon which part of General Rousseau's division subsequently formed; two guns I put off to the right of the road, commanding another open plain stretching off toward Perryville.

By this time it had got daylight. I dispatched staff officers to General Buell and to General Sheridan, informing them that I had carried the position and would await further orders. I hardly had the right section in position when the rebels came down the Springfield road from Perryville with a battery and what seemed to be two brigades of infantry. They put their battery in position on the hill at the back of the Bottom house and began shelling the woods. As soon as I saw them go into position I ordered the right wing of the Eighty-fifth Illinois onto the crest of the hill to the right of the section of the battery, as a support to it, which I had before ordered to the right of the road. I then ordered my men to lay down. The rebels shelled the woods for an hour and a quarter. Supposing from the quietness which I required my men to keep that they had run us out of the woods they deployed in the open ground to attack us. I restrained the impatience of the men till they got within 200 yards of me, and they only waited for one volley, which was delivered by the Eighty-fifth Illinois and the right wing of the One hundred and twenty-fifth Illinois and the section of artillery.

About this time two regiments of rebel cavalry showed themselves on the left of my position on the Mackville road, their infantry pickets being scattered through the field. The cavalry was heading from Perryville out toward Mackville. I opened on that cavalry with the two James guns which I had left on the left of the road and drove it back. About this time I became apprehensive from clouds of dust which I saw on my right hand and dust also which I saw to my extreme left along the bottom of Chaplin Creek that they were turning my position and surrounding me, and sent back to General Sheridan or General Gilbert, I do not remember which, for re-enforcements. General Gilbert came out, preceded a few minutes by General Sheridan, and examined my position, and told me not to advance any farther and that he would go back and report to General Buell. That was about 6 o'clock in the morning. Two brigades of General Sheridan's division were immediately dispatched to my assistance.

About this time there seemed to be a lull in the firing; occasionally a sharpshooter would annoy the line; my skirmishers would reply. Immediately on the left of the Springfield road was a grove of timber. Buckner came up with two brigades, slipping along the dry bed of Doctor's Fork, and got into those woods about 250 yards in my front. As soon as this was discovered the Second Missouri, supported by the Forty-fourth Illinois, with a section of artillery, was ordered to dislodge them. A few minutes before Captain Gay came out with his cavalry. He desired me to throw forward my skirmishers and clear the wood, which I declined to do. He then reported to General Gilbert, from whom I received a note telling me to hold my position—not to advance. This was between 6 and 7 o'clock in the morning. Captain Gay started his cavalry into the woods, and they came back very rapidly ; then he dismounted a portion of his command, and the Second Missouri and Forty-fourth Illinois, with Gay's cavalry dismounted, drove the rebels from that piece of woods, which movement was hastened by General Fry opportunely ordering forward the Eighty-sixth Illinois Regiment, which was on picket, to charge the left of the piece of woods over the open fields. The Second Missouri followed up their advantage, following the rebels over the open-country clearing beyond Sam. Bottom's house up through his orchard, and seized the line of heights, over which they could see Chaplin River very plainly, being the same line of heights and the same orchard occupied at a later period of the day by eighteen guns of the enemy. By some person's orders this regiment was ordered to fall back to the wood from which we had cleared the rebels. About this time all firing and appearance of the enemy ceased in our front. This happened between 7 and 8 o'clock.

Between 9 and 10 o'clock I received a note from General Gilbert informing me that General McCook was coming up immediately to my left, and that I must not be alarmed at any appearance of forces in that direction. About 10 o'clock I saw the head of Rousseau's column coming up to the Russell house on the Mackville and Perryville road ; they went beyond the house a short distance and seemed to be halted there awaiting orders. Between 11 and 12 o'clock the same day General Gilbert, I think, ordered forward Hescock's battery and Sheridan's division to occupy the same woods from which he had driven General Buckner. We went into those woods and formed a line of battle, our right resting over the Springfield pike. About this time Captain Gay, finding that he could not get down the Springfield road to Perryville, made a detour off to the left, and went down through the open fields to the left of Peters' Hill, and an artillery fire opened. A short time after this the rebels began to make their appearance with their artillery on Bottom's Hill and in the mouth of Doctor's Fork with their masses of infantry. Captain Hescock, whenever he saw them appear on this hill with their artillery, would open upon them or enfilade their position, and whenever the rebel masses would show themselves in the mouth of this Doctor's Fork he would drive them back. Between 12 and 1 o'clock everything was quiet except these occasional escapades of artillery, happening about every half hour; between 1 and 2 o'clock General Rousseau put Loomis' battery into position, which soon opened, and formed his line of battle, the right of it resting on a barn, which was subsequently burned by the rebel artillery, and his left stretching off obliquely in the direction of Chaplin Fork. His line was a continuation of General Gilbert's line. With the aid of Hescock, Loomis soon silenced this battery on Bottom's Hill, part of it in Bottom's orchard, and for some time the battle seemed to be over.

About 2 o'clock General Gilbert ordered us to fall back from our position in the woods. General Gilbert's line was separated from General Rousseau's by the rocky and dry bed of what I learned to be Doctor's Fork and about 150 paces distant. About 2 o'clock we were ordered back on this hill, our troops being raw. The regiments fell back individually in good order, but the brigades became so mixed up that I halted mine and would not move a step till the other brigades passed me. We fell back, forming a circular line on Peters' Hill, and with our left flank to the woods above referred to and the original line. I pointed out to General Gilbert the danger of our left flank and requested him to permit me to fill the woods we had just left with skirmishers, which request he granted; and in order to prevent a flank movement, under the cover of the woods I put the Eighty-sixth Illinois behind a picket fence, faced it by the rear rank, and told it to open on any troops it saw coming through the woods. We had scarcely got into this new position when eighteen pieces of the enemy's artillery galloped up to Bottom's Hill and opened on General Rousseau's right. This position had been enfiladed, and no doubt by Captain Hescock's battery. Two brigades of rebels formed in front of the new line of General Sheridan and attacked us. They came within 100 yards of our batteries, when the whole line charged bayonets on them and they ran. Our whole division was laying there, about four regiments deep, not covering more than a brigade and a half in front. The rebels reformed under the crest of the hill and attacked us again. By this time some troops on our right attacked them in flank and they fell back and left us; this was about 3 o'clock. The two attacks of battle lasted an hour.

After we drove them off the excitement which attends such little affairs as this subsided. I turned around and saw the barn on General Rousseau's right in flames, and saw the rebels in three lines in line of battle, with two regiments doubled on the center, their left flank coming up Doctor's Fork. They changed direction slightly to the right; these two regiments doubled on the center made a right partial wheel. They were so near I could see the daylight through their ranks with my glass. I saw them envelop and drive back Lytle's right flank. At that time our division, with two batteries, was lying idle. I begged General Sheridan to at least allow us to open on them with artillery, for from the fierceness of the engagement on our left and the weak attacks on our right I felt satisfied that the rebels were concentrating their whole force against our left wing. The answer I received to this earnest entreaty was that it might concentrate the fire of the enemy's artillery upon our troops. This came to me from General Gilbert through General Sheridan. I suggested that the troops could be moved over on the other slope of the hill, which was a backbone, and would be perfectly safe.

The rebels, after they had pulverized Rousseau's right with their eighteen guns, moved a portion of their artillery from Bottom's Hill to the clump of trees on the left of the Mackville road as you go toward Perryville. At the time I made the request to turn our batteries on them we could see them going into battery in this new position spoken of. We at last did, by General Sheridan, get permission for these batteries to open on the rebel battery and rebel column as we saw them on our left. We then opened a concentric fire upon them, crossing our fire in the enemy's battery. At the second discharge I saw one of their caissons blow up, and in one of those regiments doubled on the center that I spoke of before I saw the standard go down three times, caused by the execution of our artillery. This seemed to check them, which check we afterward learned was assisted by the arrival of Gooding's brigade on the field. By marching my regiment 250 yards over an open-plain corn field I could have taken the rebels in rear and flank and had them between Lytle's battery and my own.

About this time or shortly afterward darkness fell upon the scene, and we bivouacked on the hill I had originally carried in the morning. There was a strong wind blowing in the direction of General McCook's army corps from the direction of General Buell's headquarters; it was so high that at times I could distinguish musketry a half mile from me. It is my impression that I was informed by one of the signal officers on our hill, about fifteen minutes after 2 o'clock, that General Rousseau had telegraphed he was attacked along his entire front by infantry, cavalry, and artillery. I am not positive that the signal officer informed me that General Rousseau sent that dispatch, but I am satisfied that such a dispatch went through the signal office, and that this conversation was extorted by a burst of indignation of mine, coupled with a few oaths, demanding of General Sheridan why we had been ordered out of those woods.

Commission adjourned to meet December 24, 1862, at 10 o'clock a. m.

NASHVILLE, *Wednesday Morning, December* 24, 1862.

The Commission met pursuant to adjournment. All the members present; also the judge-advocate and General Buell.

Col. C. G. HARKER (a witness for the defense), being duly sworn by the judge-advocate, testified as follows:

By General BUELL:

Question. Will you state your name, rank, and position in the service of the United States?

C. G. Harker; colonel of the Sixty-fifth Regiment Ohio Volunteers; commanding Twentieth Brigade, Sixth Division.

Question. State, if you please, colonel, what march you made on the 7th of October last, as the army was approaching Perryville; where you encamped, and at what hour you marched the next morning.

We left camp in the vicinity of Springfield, Ky., on the morning of the 7th. After marching slowly all day and all night of the 7th we arrived at camp on the stream known as Rolling Fork about daybreak on the morning of the 8th. We took up the line of march about 11 o'clock or somewhat after, and started in the direction of Perryville. The march was retarded by the trains and troops in front causing delay.

Question. Was your camp on the night of the 7th on the direct route to Perryville?

It was not, sir; we turned off the direct route in order to get water; we were informed there was no water on the direct route suitable for the troops and animals.

Question. Do you know where you were expected to have encamped that night?

We were expecting to encamp 2½ miles from Haysville, at a point about 6 or 7 miles from Perryville.

Question. How much did your march to get water on the 7th take you out of your direct route? What distance was lost in your march of the following day?

I have learned from 3 to 4 miles.

Question. State, if you please, what position you took when you arrived near Perryville and what your command did, what you saw and what your command did on the evening of the 8th and morning of the 9th, and what you saw of the movements of the enemy on the morning of the 9th.

About half past two o'clock on the day of the 8th we received orders from General Crittenden, through General Wood, to go forward with my brigade, and arrived at a point on the right of Colonel Wagner at a late hour in the afternoon. We had previously received orders from General Wood to form in line of battle on the right of Colonel Wagner's brigade. At that time there was some artillery firing on the left. No enemy could be seen in our front and my troops were not engaged. After having formed in line of battle we received orders to advance to the front, which we did; perhaps we advanced three-quarters of a mile from the position where we first formed in line of battle; we still saw no enemy in our front. It then being about dark, we received orders from General Wood to fall back in some timber and bivouac for the night, which was done. Some time during the night orders came from General Wood to be in readiness to march at daylight. I believe he said "march;" he may have said "attack." The order was a verbal one. My command was under arms as per order, but received no further instructions from General Wood or any higher authority until a late hour in the morning, perhaps between 9 and 10 o'clock. We, however, heardfiring a little after sunrise; there was skirmishing upon our right; there were also one or two rounds of artillery, but from the conformation of the ground I could not tell the direction of the artillery. The position I then had not being a good one I advanced to the front without orders, taking a commanding position, from which I had a good view of the surrounding country. From this position bodies of cavalry could be seen to the front; we could not see whether they were our own troops or those of the enemy. By my glass I could see that they had on a blue uniform similar to our own. Not knowing what troops they were, I sent word to the rear for information and orders. These troops, after halting a short time in front of us, filed off to the right toward the direction of Harrodsburg. We could distinguish no infantry to a certainty, but a body of troops on the left could be seen, which were supposed to be infantry, and which also filed off in the direction of Harrodsburg. I sent back to General Wood to the place where he was expected to be found and reported all these circumstances. The messenger returned, stating that he could not be found at that point. This was about one hour after sunrise.

Some time after this Captain Lennard, aide to General Wood, came to the front, stating that the Sixth Division was ordered back to the reserve. I reported to him what we had seen. He replied that we were too far in the advance; that we had exceeded our orders; and that it was General Wood's orders to fall back, taking a position in the rear of the division on our right to the left of the Fifteenth Brigade, resting upon the Perryville and Lebanon road. We fell back as ordered, having troops resting on our right. We were halted about 2½ miles from Perryville and awaited further orders. Some time in the afternoon we received orders to proceed to the springs near Perryville; took up the line of march, and arrived there late in the afternoon and encamped. The springs were but a short distance, about half a mile, beyond Perryville, near the road leading from Perryville to Harrodsburg.

Question. Did you see any infantry on the morning of the 9th?

In my answer to the preceding question I stated that we could distinguish a body of troops that were supposed to be infantry, but could not tell for a certainty.

Question. Did any infantry move off on the Danville road or any troops you supposed to be infantry?

No, sir.

Question. Did your brigade form a part of the right corps?

Yes, sir.

Question. What part of the line of that corps did it occupy?

The Sixth Division formed the left of the line. My own brigade had a central position in the division.

Question. What time did you get into camp on the night of the 9th?

I stated at a late hour in the afternoon; some time before sunset.

Question. What movement did you make on the following day?

The Sixth Division moved off to the right of the Perryville and Harrodsburg road and halted at a place known as Cecil Farm, about equidistant from the towns of Danville, Perryville, and Harrodsburg.

Question. Did you make any movement on the 11th?

My brigade was ordered to make a reconnaissance in the direction of Harrodsburg. I proceeded in that direction, leaving camp between 8 and 9 o'clock. My orders were to approach as near Harrodsburg as I could with safety; the enemy was supposed to be in force at that place. I reached a point on the Danville and Harrodsburg road about 2½ miles from Harrodsburg about 11 o'clock; proceeded down this road cautiously to the town of Harrodsburg, skirmishing slightly with the enemy's cavalry all the way from about a mile from where we encamped in the morning until we reached Harrodsburg, the rear of the enemy's cavalry having left the town on our approach. It was after 1 o'clock that I reached the town. I received positive orders from General Thomas not to bring on an engagement, as he thought the enemy was there in force.

Question. Were the instructions of General Thomas distinct and impressive with respect to the presence of the enemy in force at Harrodsburg?

They were decidedly so.

Question. Did you ascertain certainly on the 11th what route the enemy took and whether he had crossed Dick's River at all?

I learned that he had taken the Bryantsville road in the direction of Dick's River, but did not learn positively that he had crossed. There was a strong force of cavalry reported to be a short distance from Harrodsburg, near Cave Run. It was not deemed safe to push the reconnaissance beyond Harrodsburg from the best information I could get.

Question. Did you report the result of your reconnaissance to General Thomas, and what further instructions did you receive, if any?

I sent him verbal messages of my reconnaissance, and received orders to take up a strong position near the town of Harrodsburg and await further orders.

Question. When did you receive further orders and what were they and what action did you take upon them?

I received orders on the morning of the 12th from General Wood to proceed on the Bryantsville road until I came to the crossing of Cave Run and there await further instructions. I proceeded as ordered, and after some skirmishing with the enemy's cavalry arrived at the crossing of Cave Run about 12 o'clock. I was there joined by a body of cavalry, in the command of Colonel McCook, who proceeded to the front with his troops. Learning that General Wood, with the balance of his command, was on my right and a little to my front, I pushed forward my own brigade to a point about 3 miles from Dick's River. I remained there in position till between 2 and 3 o'clock in the afternoon, when I received orders from General Wood to fall back and join the division, which was about to go into camp at a point about a mile from the Danville and Harrodsburg road and 4 miles from Harrodsburg.

Question, What time did you get into camp that day?

About dark.

Question. Did you see General Thomas at that time; did you know where he was?

I did not see him. I made my reports to General Wood in person. I learned that he was in camp near General Crittenden's headquarters; it was so reported. He was encamped on the Danville and Harrodsburg road.

Question. Did you find any of the enemy's property in Harrodsburg when you arrived there on the 11th and any of his sick?

I found about 70 head of cattle, some 200 barrels of pork, and 1,000 to 1,200 sick and wounded. This latter was reported by one of our officers, from the best information he could get and visiting the hospitals. We had taken quite a number of prisoners, stragglers, on the way and also in the town. As these cattle were in good condition to be driven, I imagine the enemy left very hurriedly.

Question. Will you state the particulars of your service in North Alabama during the months of July and August last, the date of your arrival there from Corinth, the position you took, and the service you were engaged in?

I was sent to the town of Stevenson, Ala., about the middle of July with my brigade. This was at the time a depot for supplies for the army serving in Alabama. I was ordered to fortify the place, and for that purpose was ordered to impress the services of the slaves in that vicinity and any private property that might be necessary—to make use of every means in my power to fortify and strengthen the place. I constructed a large earthwork, making use of some 400 negroes for that purpose. I also constructed a series of stockades to secure the place from an attack of the enemy or a dash of cavalry. I remained there until the troops left Battle Creek under General McCook, when I was ordered to join General Crittenden with three regiments of my brigade and a battery of artillery, leaving a regiment of infantry in the works at Stevenson.

Question. What garrison were the works at Stevenson designed to accommodate?

The earthwork was designed for about 500 infantry, a battery of four pieces of artillery, the larger stockade for about 60 infantry.

Question. Did you understand that these works had for their object to make the place secure as a depot for supplies for the army?

Not as a permanent depot, but as a depot of reception; the other troops were supplied from this point. That was my impression.

By General TYLER:

Question. On your arrival at Harrodsburg did you see any signs of burning up camp equipments, wagons, &c., on the part of Bragg's army?

They had undertaken to burn up the stores that were left there. I received no report as to the camp equipage.

Question. Did you find any amount of tents, wagons, &c., left behind?

There were none reported to me.

By General BUELL:

Question. What is your opinion in regard to the supply of camp equipage which the rebel forces had with them in Kentucky?

All the information that I received went to show that they had but little camp equipage; they were without tents.

By the JUDGE-ADVOCATE:

Question. Do you know anything about their destruction of property, their stores and wagons, subsequent to their leaving Harrodsburg, on their route to Cumberland Gap?

I know nothing about it, for the reason that our division was left back in the reserve.

Question. You accompanied the army through Danville?

Yes, sir; to a point some distance from Crab Orchard.

Capt. J. H. GILMAN (a witness for the defense), being duly sworn by the judge-advocate, testified as follows:

By General BUELL:

Question. Will you please state your name and position in the service of the United States?

J. H. Gilman; captain Nineteenth Regiment United States Infantry, and inspector of artillery in the Army of the Ohio.

Question. What was your position in the service during the recent campaign in Kentucky?

Inspector of artillery on the staff of General Buell.

Question. Did you inspect the ground in front of Perryville on the 8th of October last, with a view to posting the troops for battle?

I inspected a portion of it.

Question. Explain, if you please, what portion of it you inspected, what time you went on, and what time you left it.

I left camp about half past 8 on the morning of the 8th, returned about 11; inspected that portion of the ground near that occupied by General Sheridan's command along the road leading from Springfield to Perryville and on the right of the road.

Question. Were you in front of the troops at that time or did your inspection extend to the front of them?

We commenced near the road, just a short distance in the rear of the skirmishers. In passing toward the right about one-fourth of a mile from the road we got between our lines and the enemy's. The ground from which we selected our positions was in the rear of our line at the time, for the ground was occupied by them; they were partly on the ground.

Question. Were there any movements of the enemy in front, while you were there, that indicated preparation for an attack?

Firing was going on all the time we were there, but not very heavy. There was nothing there at that time that would indicate an immediate and strong attack. When we passed between the enemy's line and our own there was no firing between the two until we discovered we were between the two lines by the enemy's rising up in a small number, apparently not more than 200 or 300.

Question. Were the enemy to be seen in force anywhere?

Not from where we were. We went on the top of the high hills and we could not see the enemy in any large force.

Question. Was a reconnaissance being made by the cavalry while you were there?

It was; Captain Gay was there in charge of cavalry. Just as we left the Perryville road to go off to the right Captain Gay went off to the left with a heavy cavalry force, and I think with a section of artillery.

Question. Where were you during the balance of the day?

At or near General Buell's headquarters.

Question. How far was that from the ground on which General McCook's corps fought that day?

I think about 3 miles.

Question. Did you hear any firing which indicated to your mind that a battle was going on any time during the day?

We heard artillery fire, but not very heavy; nothing to indicate that anything more than skirmishing was taking place; about the same as occurred the day previous, when Captain Gay was engaged with the enemy near the same place.

Question. Did you hear any musketry?

I do not remember hearing any musketry after I returned to camp.

Question. At what hour in the day did you first become aware that a serious fight had taken place on the left?

I think between 4 and 5 o'clock I received the first intimation of it.

Question. Did you go to the scene of the fight that night; if so, with what orders and for what purpose and what did you see there?

I went to the ground occupied by our left on that day about 9 or 10 o'clock. The same night I had orders to collect what I could of General Jackson's division, find out who the senior officer was that was left in that division, and get them into position. I found a very small part of this division; got together what I could under Colonel Hall. I went there with General Rousseau; found General McCook there just in the rear of the line. He spoke to me about moving two batteries back which were apparently very near the enemy. There was a large fire just in front of these guns, at which place it was reported to General McCook that the enemy were putting up a heavy battery to enfilade this battery of his. I asked him if he felt sure that the enemy was putting up a battery there. He said there was very little doubt about it. He said he thought they had better be moving back, and asked if it was not my opinion, and I said it was. He then told General Rousseau that he had better move back. General McCook then went to General Buell's headquarters (this was between 11 and 12), word having been brought to General McCook that General Buell wished to see him. Soon afterward this line was moved back. The left of the line was moved very little and the right was thrown back some 300 or 400 yards. In going and returning I noticed that there was a large gap between General McCook's right and General Gilbert's left not occupied by troops. The troops before this movement were in front of the Perryville and Mackville road; afterward they were thrown to the rear.

Question. Did General Rousseau proceed to make this change without further orders from General McCook?

So far as I know he did. He may have received other orders, but not to my knowledge.

Question. Was there anything in the condition of things as they appeared to you to make it necessary to re-enforce General McCook in order to effect this change safely?

There was not. I thought it probable they might be fired upon in withdrawing the guns, but did not think it probable that the enemy would follow.

Cross-examination by the JUDGE-ADVOCATE:

Question. You moved down toward Perryville expecting to find the enemy there in force, did you not?

I supposed we were to meet the enemy in force at some place or other, but I did not know whether it would be exactly at Perryville, but supposed it would be near there; as soon as we could overtake them.

Question. Upon what was the expectation founded?

Upon the fact that we knew the enemy were not very far off; their rear guard was often in sight of our advance guard, and there had been several skirmishes between them.

Question. Was it not known that Kirby Smith was moving in the direction of Perryville and that a junction would be formed at or near that place?

I do not know.

Question. What report did you make to General Buell, on returning from a survey of the battle-field, as to what you saw, and what conclusions did you draw?

I do not know that I made any report to General Buell personally. I spoke to Colonel Fry, chief of staff. I reported to him that there was some skirmishing going on and that there seemed to be too much firing of artillery, and that they were evidently wasting their ammunition, as I could see no enemy in large force.

Question. What time of day was that?

About 11 o'clock in the forenoon.

Question. Did that firing continue from the time of your survey up to 5 or 6 o'clock in the evening?

It did not seem to be continuous, but we heard occasional firing of artillery and sometimes quite heavy. I think about 5 o'clock we heard it quite heavy.

Question. Was it continuous between 3 and 5 o'clock?

I do not think we heard it continuously during that time.

Question. Do you mean to say that it was not continuous or that you were so situated that you could not hear it?

I mean to say that we did not hear it. I have understood since that the firing was continuous.

Question. Do you mean to say that the firing on the 8th was as heavy or not heavier than it was on the 7th, only that it was more continuous; that it was of the same character as that on the day before?

No; I mean to say that it sounded where we were not like a severe battle. We did not hear the musketry.

Question. Were you about headquarters all that afternoon?

I think I was there all the time during the afternoon.

Question. Whom did you see there during the afternoon; that is, officers arriving from the direction of the battle-field, or did you see any one?

I do not think I saw any one until about dark arriving from the battle-field. I then saw Lieutenant Parsons and another officer.

Question. Did you not see Colonel Harlan there that afternoon?

I do not remember seeing him.

Question. What was said about headquarters in reference to that firing at that time?

Most of the remarks made in regard to the firing were that they were probably shelling the woods or firing at skirmishers and that the enemy probably intended to make a stand. The firing seemed to remain pretty much in the same place; it did not appear to advance or recede.

Question. Do you say that General Buell's headquarters were about 3 miles from the ground occupied by General McCook; was it not in fact 3 miles from Perryville?

I think his headquarters were fully 3 miles from Perryville. The ground occupied by General McCook was, I think, much farther to the left than Perryville. I rode over the ground but twice from where General McCook fought to General Buell's headquarters, and that was at night. I should think the distance was about 3 miles.

By General TYLER:

Question. You say the enemy's rear guard were often in sight of our advance guard and that skirmishing in consequence took place; do you suppose from this that Bragg's army was in retreat before General Buell's army?

I supposed that General Bragg was either retreating before the army or was going to select his own ground to fight upon.

Question. In throwing back General Rousseau's line was the particular ground he was to occupy pointed out and ordered by Major-General McCook?

I think not, from the fact that General Rousseau spent some time after General McCook left in reconnoitering the ground. The movement did not take place immediately on General McCook's leaving.

Question. You stated that General McCook's command would not be attacked in changing his line because it was in the night; was this the only reason? If not, what other reasons had you for supposing he would not attack?

I have stated in my answer that I thought it probable they would be fired on in withdrawing the guns, but that it would not be followed up by the enemy in the night-time, as I supposed it would be considered a dangerous thing, they at the same time knowing that there was a higher good position in the rear, where they would naturally suppose we would have a force posted to check them in case they followed.

Col. W. P. INNES (a witness for the defense), being duly sworn by the judge-advocate, testified as follows:

By General BUELL:

Question. Will you please state your name and position in the service?

W. P. Innes; colonel First Regiment Michigan Engineers and Mechanics.

Question. Were you in command of your regiment during last summer?

Yes, sir.

Question. Please state the manner in which your regiment was employed from about the time that it left Corinth in June until the army marched into Kentucky in September.

It was employed in the month of June with eight companies rebuilding the Memphis and Charleston Railroad; two companies were employed during the same month between Huntsville and Stevenson rebuilding the bridges and assisting to operate the road. In July we were engaged on the Tennessee and Alabama road and on the

Nashville and Chattanooga road. We were also engaged in bu.lding pontoon boats. We were then ordered, with part of my regiment, in the latter part of August, to come up here and repair the Louisville and Nashville road. We were employed building the bridges on this road when we were desired to take up the line of march for Kentucky.

Question. Please explain the extent of the work, particularly on the Tennessee and Alabama road and the Nashville and Chattanooga road ; whether your troops were constantly and industriously engaged upon the work and when it was completed so that the roads were in use throughout.

We built one bridge on the Tennessee and Alabama road across what is called Elk River. It was 700 feet long and 58 feet high, in about 20 feet of water. That was the heaviest bridge built. Four companies were employed on that work, with a large infantry detail. At that time we worked incessantly at it, rain or shine. At the same time I had three companies at work at what was called Richland Creek No. 1, which is a bridge 375 feet long, I think, 28 feet high, and in about 6 feet of water. I had two companies at the same time engaged on what is called the heavy trestle near the tunnel ; we rebuilt 1,050 feet of it; that was about 64 feet high. I had then another set of men working at Richland Creek No. 2 ; that is a bridge about 300 feet long and 30 feet high. We also relaid about 2 miles of track and cleared out the tunnel on the same road. We also built a bridge across Mill Creek at Millville ; came up to Columbia with two companies and repaired the bridge across Duck Creek that had been washed away by the high water. The companies that were at work on Elk River Bridge joined me about the middle of August on the Nashville and Chattanooga road. While this work was going on I rebuilt Crow Creek Bridge No. 3, as it was called ; also cleared out the tunnel and built the bridge at Cowan.

Question. At what time were these works completed so that the roads were in use to Stevenson ?

About the 28th of August.

Question. Are you an engineer ?

I have engineered for about eighteen years.

Question. Were these works prosecuted with industry and energy ; was any time wasted ?

They were. I took some pride in it. I think there was more work done during the time, considering the force, within a short time, as has ever been completed by the same amount of men. I could say also that I had a double incentive, for I was continually being urged on verbally and by telegraph that everything depended on the opening of these roads.

Question. Were these roads essential for supplying the troops with a view to advance the army ?

I should consider them very essential. I hardly see how the army could be supplied without them.

Question. You have spoken of being engaged in the construction of boats for a pontoon bridge. Will you explain the object of that bridge as far as you know it and what progress you made in the construction of them ?

I understood the object of the boats was to cross the Tennessee River in the vicinity of Bridgeport, for the purpose, I understood, of marching to Chattanooga or some other place. The boats were completed before I left them, except putting the bottoms together, which I decided had better not be done until they were ready to be launched, probably half a day's work on the whole of them. The tackle, anchors, and everything were on hand ready to launch them. The boats were finished about the 20th of August, except putting the bottoms together. They would have been finished long before if we could have got the timber. There was but one mill on the road that could saw the long timber required for the bridges, and I ran that mill day and night, not only with the force belonging to the mill, but with the detail from my own regiment. We used, I think, every means that we could to get it out in as short time as possible.

Question. Do you know anything of the construction of works at Stevenson for the protection of a depot of supples for the army ?

Yes, sir.

Question. Did you understand that depot was with a view to advance the army ?

Yes, sir, I so understood it; for the purpose of protecting the supplies.

Question. State, if you please, colonel, of what value the Memphis and Charleston Railroad was to the Army of the Ohio as a means of supplying it; that is, west of Decatur.

The Memphis and Charleston Railroad from Decatur to Huntsville and from there to Stevenson was of incalculable advantage to the army as a means of transportation. It was the only possible means except by land carriage.

Question. State whether that portion west of Decatur was of any value to the army.

I think not, sir.

Question. State its condition with regard to rolling stock from Decatur west.

It was very poorly supplied with stock. When I first went there there were a number of engines that could have been made available by a small amount of work.

Question. Do you know whether those engines were used or any serviceable amount of rolling stock was put in use between Corinth and Decatur ?

I think not, sir; the road was very poorly managed; that was my impression at the time. I know I was three days making the trip from Decatur to Corinth.

Question. Who had the control of that road ?

General J. B. McPherson. I was desired to report to him while constructing the bridges there. I think he was styled military superintendent.

Question. Was it under my immediate control in any manner ?

I think not, sir. I should have had control if it had been.

Question. Did you go directly from the work on that road to the work which you have described in your previous answer ?

Yes, sir; in less than twenty-four hours from my arrival in Huntsville, when I was ordered with a detachment of my regiment on to the Tennessee and Alabama road.

Question. Explain, if you please, how and when you were employed on the Louisville and Nashville road.

It was on the 25th of August I commenced building what is called Therman Cove Creek Bridge and completed it as soon as possible; it is a bridge 300 feet long, 64 feet high, and a very difficult bridge to construct on account of the quicksand foundation. I then proceeded to the Pilot Knob Bridge; that is a bridge 350 feet long and 20 feet high; and then to the Alexander Creek Bridge, which is a bridge about the same size as Pilot Knob Bridge. I was engaged upon that when we had orders to march to Kentucky. That was about the 7th or 10th of September.

Question. Were hired workmen employed on the road at any point about that time ?

I think not, sir. I understood they were getting out some timber for these bridges, but at the time I was working at Pilot Knob Bridge there were parties working at Saundersville. I think there were parties working beyond the tunnel, at Gallatin, but they did not come under my observation.

Question. Will you state what the condition of that road was at that time as a means of transportation for the army and what was the cause of its condition ?

I consider the road was perfectly useless from Gallatin to this point from my own knowledge, made so by the destruction of the bridges and the filling up of the tunnels by the rebels.

Question. Do you know how long it had been in that condition ?

I could not state the exact time. I heard when I was at Stevenson that the road was destroyed before I started to come here.

Question. Do you know anything of the condition of the Edgefield and Kentucky road at that time ?

I understood, sir, that that was perfectly destroyed. With respect to that road I should say it was hardly competent to supply the army, on account of its heavy grades.

Question. Do you know anything of the Cumberland River as a means of transportation at that time ?

My knowledge of the river now is that it was useless at that time, as it now is.

Question. Did you perform any work on the march to Louisville and from Louisville toward Bardstown ; and state, if you please, what ?

Yes, sir ; we rebuilt the pontoon bridge at Barren River on our way up ; also planked the railroad bridge for transporting troops over. We also did some work on the fortifications at Bowling Green ; made platforms for ten guns. We rebuilt the bridge on the march from Louisville to Bardstown across what is called Floyd's Fork, and got out a large part of the timber for the bridge across Salt River. We may have done other little pieces of work, such as repairing roads, but none of any great consequence.

Question. Was the army on its march from Louisville depending on wagon transportation ?

Entirely so.

Cross-examination by the JUDGE-ADVOCATE :

Question. Was the railroad from McMinnville to Tullahoma and from thence to Nashville in running order on the 22d of August, 1862 ?

If so, it must have been just completed and that was all, for I find I was ordered by telegraph to go to McMinnville and put the road in immediate order. I also had a personal interview with General Buell at that time.

Question. What was the date of that order and when did you have that personal interview ?

It was Tuesday, August 19.

Question. How soon thereafter can you say positively that that road was in working order ; that is, the two roads from Nashville to Tullahoma and from Tullahoma to McMinnville ?

As far as the road from Tullahoma to McMinnville is concerned, I do not know when that was from my personal knowledge, though I heard on my way there that the road was in order on the 23d.

Question. What bridges were destroyed between Nashville and Bowling Green at that time ?

Therman, Cave Creek, Saundersville Trestle, Pilot Knob Bridge, Alexander Creek, and two other bridges between there and Gallatin and two small bridges having no name.

Question. What time did it take you to repair those bridges ?

We were about fourteen days.

Question. How long has it taken to open that tunnel that was destroyed ?

I cannot say of my own knowledge. It was under the charge of General S eedman. It was some ten days after those other bridges were built and longer ihan it took us to rebuild those bridges.

Question. Where is that tunnel?

It is about 7 miles from Gallatin.

Question. What sort of a road is there around this tunnel?

Very bad indeed; impracticable for teams.

Question. How long would it require to make it practicable?

You could not do it, on account of the elevation to be overcome.

Question. What time did you arrive in Nashville?

From the 23d to the 25th of August.

By General BUELL:

Question. How long has it taken to put this road in order since the return of the army to Tennessee?

I think about thirty days.

Question. What force do you suppose has been employed on it or present along it during that time?

I think that between Gallatin and this point, on our way back to repair the bridges, there were four brigades besides General Wood's force; that I understood was in the vicinity of Gallatin. These were all the troops I had knowledge of, but I never went off the railroad and therefore had no means of knowing.

By General TYLER:

Question. Was the railroad from Corinth to Stevenson after its repair of any practicable use to General Buell's army in the transportation of provisions and men?

I think not, sir. There was great complaint that we could get neither men nor provisions over the road.

Question. And why not?

Because I think the road was not well managed.

Question. You spoke of some road with heavy grade that was of no use.

The Edgefield and Kentucky road.

Question. Why do heavy grades make a road useless?

Because of its requiring greater motive-power to transport the same amount of tonnage.

Question. What do you suppose would be the requirement for the daily transportation (in tons) for an army of 50,000 men?

I could not say, sir, without calculation. It would depend entirely upon the amount of transportation allowed to each regiment, and the amount of forage depending upon the number of horses they had.

Question. What was the capacity of this road; what would an engine of 25 tons carry?

Over that grade three or four cars would be considered a load for a 25-ton engine.

Question. Is the grade uniform over the entire road, so that a 25-ton engine will take only three cars?

No, sir; there are portions of the road where a larger train than that could be taken; probably ten or twelve cars.

Question. What is the maximum grade per mile on that road?

I understand, going over the mountain, the grade is over 200 feet to the mile.

Question. Do you mean to say that a 25-ton engine would not take more than three loaded cars over a grade of 200 feet to the mile, supposing the grade did not extend over one mile?

I think, sir, if the track was wet it would be about as much as a 25-ton engine could do.

The Commission adjourned to meet December 25, 1862, at 10 o'clock a. m.

NASHVILLE, *December* 25, 1862.

The Commission met pursuant to adjournment, all the members being present; also the judge-advocate and General Buell.

Major SIDELL (a witness for the defense), being duly sworn, testified as follows:

By General BUELL:

Question. State your name and position in the service, if you please, and the special duty upon which you have been engaged for some months past as far back as the month of July.

W. H. Sidell; major of the Fifteenth U. S. Infantry. I have been engaged on special duty as assistant adjutant-general since July 20 at Nashville.

Question. Give, if you please, major, a concise statement of the operations of the enemy in the vicinity of Nashville during the last summer, and of the effect of these operations and the measures adopted to counteract them.

The operations here were irregular and generally of small significance. At the time that I arrived Morgan, with his force, entered Kentucky, and I was detained in Louisville by General Boyle with reference to that condition of things. When I arrived here I found a small garrison of perhaps 1,200 effective men, with a body of convalescents, who were considered available to a certain extent, under the command of Col. J. F. Miller, Twenty-ninth Indiana Volunteers, who commanded the post. Immediately on my arrival the aggressions of these parties or forces, under various leaders and sometimes without leaders, began in cutting off couriers and interfering with forage and general trains of the army and interrupting the communication between this place and the various corps of the army in the vicinity. We had to be on the alert all the time in order to counteract these operations as they occurred, the general meaning of which is that the country was alive with these irregular forces. Among their operations they made an attack on Gallatin, or rather they entered there, for there was no great force, and there were two expeditions to go upon the road and endeavor to drive them away, which was effected by Colonel Miller. Subsequently to that a third movement was made by Lieutenant-Colonel Heffren, of the Fiftieth Indiana, who went to Gallatin and went into the tunnel, which was burning, 3 miles beyond Gallatin, and to prevent its falling in was lined with wood. The burning out of the interior was of very serious detriment. It is only now just repaired. This Lieutenant-Colonel Heffren, going without proper precaution, met with a disaster, that Colonel Miller was careful enough to avoid, in having his communications cut off in the rear. This so encouraged the enemy that nearly all the communications were destroyed between here and Gallatin. All this occurred toward the end of July and the beginning of August. Some cavalry were sent, under command of R. W. Johnson, brigadier-general, to Gallatin, going by the way of Lebanon, in this State, for the purpose of driving away such of these forces as were concentrated (a force of four companies at Gallatin, under Colonel Boone, a Kentucky regiment, had been taken by surprise, without any firing, and were captured). General Johnson met the rebels at Gallatin and was repulsed. Stragglers began to arrive in this city by way of Lebanon about 8 or 9 o'clock in the evening, giving us information.

This movement of Colonel Heffren and this repulse of General Johnson was the *finale* to the communication between this city and Louisville. This was early in August. In the other direction from Nashville, south, there were no large conflicts, but a continued series of annoyances, sometimes taking, in one instance 80, prisoners, who went out with wagon trains; at other times squads of from 8 to 10, who were sent in here for parole, as they called it. There was no knowledge that the enemy were always in an organized condition; in fact it was fair to be inferred that they were countrymen, without any organization.

When affairs had arrived at this point, as the forces here were not adequate to any large movement, it was thought proper to organize a light brigade; that is, a brigade so organized as to move with the facility of cavalry. Men were mounted as cavalry or artillery or infantry with the means of a mount, and provided with the means of transportation in wagons, the intention being to follow the enemy and to be self-supporting. This was under the command of Colonel Miller, and was organized, I think, about the 20th or 25th of August. Before, however, there had been any efficient action of this brigade the army returned from the South, and it was no longer necessary. Previously, as testified, the garrison here was very small and could spare a very indifferent force, but subsequently sufficient was spared to organize this light brigade, which would have answered a good purpose had the general army remained in the south. It was considered expedient also to throw up works of defense about the city, and I received an order from General Buell to reconnoiter for that object. At the same time he informed me that an engineering officer would be sent here to carry into effect whatever measures might be considered good in that relation. This officer was Captain Morton, of the Corps of Engineers of the U. S. Army, who planned his works with reference to their speedy completion, but with the capability of being indefinitely extended; and essentially the same works exist now with the strength added. About the 1st of September the army came here from below, and within the first ten days had gone north, leaving a garrison of about 20,000 effective men, or rather it was strengthened to that point by the arrival of the Army of the Mississippi. It was originally about 10,000 men of all grades. This was under the command of Brigadier-General Negley. General Negley was ordered to exercise vigilance and to defend the place to the last extremity, and accordingly did everything that occurred to him as a vigilant officer to do, particularly strengthening the works, sending out expeditions to the country, preparing a boat bridge on the river, laying in supplies, such as could be obtained in the country, with reference to a protracted siege, and building the bridge and defending themselves when attacked. The city was thereby held until the arrival of this army, and I think could have been held with the supplies we had some two or three weeks without getting further supplies.

When Colonel Miller was in command here, with his small garrison, he was ordered to defend the three railroads which go from this place, one north, the Louisville road, as far as the Tennessee line, and the two south, about 15 or 20 miles. The remaining portion of the road south also had a defense organized, without our having much information with regard to their particular means here in Nashville; we knew simply that there was a sufficient force on those roads to protect them. I believe General W. S. Smith was charged with that duty.

Question. Were those operations of the enemy at any time of so formidable a character as to give ground of apprehension for the safety of Nashville?

At one time, when there was a small garrison and no works of defense, and an illy-disposed population, as there has always been, it was possible that a dash could be made by such forces as those cavalry leaders of the enemy could have brought. On one or two occasions when this was apprehended measures were taken by barricading the streets with wagons, &c., and blocking up the main entrances to the city. At a later date, when we had a larger garrison, there were threatenings and sufficient apprehension to keep us at least on the alert. The day before the arrival of the army from Louisville, under General Rosecrans, an attempt had been made to destroy the bridges across the Cumberland and feel our works by a considerable force. They made an attack on the city on all the roads leading south at the same time and simultaneously an attack on the other side of the river, an attack of cavalry, the object being to get to the bridges to destroy them. I do not think they could have taken the city by regular siege with such a force as we then had in the city and vicinity. In addition to the strengthening of the works by operations of engineering were those of mounting all the pieces of artillery left by the enemy, making cartridges, &c.

Question. Do you know anything of the capture of Murfreesborough and of the inconvenience that resulted from that misfortune?

No, sir; I have no specific information on that subject, because it occurred before I came here.

Question. Did any portion of the army with which Bragg crossed the Tennessee River to invade Kentucky turn upon this place and take part in the siege?

I am not informed on that subject.

Question. What was the character of the force that was acting against the city during the absence of the army in September and October and what was its strength?

It was mostly cavalry. The last instance I was speaking of, before the arrival of the army, was infantry and artillery. The force I have no means of knowing, excepting that that portion which was on the other side the river consisted of cavalry, said to be 700 or 750.

Question. Was there any infantry with it in the beginning?

I think there was no infantry. This answer does not refer to that last day spoken of, but to their operations generally.

Question. Do you know who the commander was?

It was said to be Breckinridge.

Question. Do you know whether orders were given for fortifying positions occupied by bridge guards along the roads?

Yes, sir; I knew that such orders were given to fortify these positions by stockade or other means, and I am aware that it was generally done.

Question. What force do you think would have been necessary to keep open the communications between here and Louisville against cavalry operations of the enemy?

It ought to be stated that the cavalry operations of the enemy could always count on the assistance of the inhabitants. There is good reason to believe that in each one of the outrages committed in this vicinity the citizens, acting temporarily as soldiers, were engaged in it. I do not know how less than from 15,000 to 20,000 men could have made the communications secure.

Question. Were the difficulties of less magnitude in defending the roads south of Nashville?

There were some physical features on the Louisville and Nashville road giving peculiar facilities to an enemy; otherwise the difficulties were the same in defending the roads south of this point.

Cross-examination by the JUDGE-ADVOCATE:

Question. What time do you say you arrived here?

On the 18th or 20th of July. I was in Louisville, and received one or two telegrams, and arrived on the 18th.

Question. What time after your arrival was communication cut off between Bowling Green and Nashville?

I think there was no communication within ten days after my arrival.

Question. Am I to understand that there was a force of no magnitude or an organized force at all threatening Nashville and its communications while General Buell's army was in Tennessee?

No more than those forces of partisan leaders, Morgan and Forrest; there was no further organized force that I was cognizant of.

Question. Do you know that Morgan or Forrest was in the neighborhood of Nashville at that time?

The most precise information of the presence of Morgan refers to the time when General Johnson met him at Gallatin. This was about the middle of August. Previously to that I had no other information than a common report that sometimes Forrest's, sometimes Starnes' or Woodward's or Morgan's forces were there, but I have no absolute knowledge of the presence of any one of them.

Question. While you were being alarmed or excited in Nashville by these reports did you not frequently hear of Morgan being in two places at the same time?

I have no doubt that rumors of his presence often were erroneous; but, strictly speaking, I cannot recall any instance in which I heard of his being in two places at the same time.

Question. Do you not know that these attacks upon railroads and lines of communication were made by the inhabitants and attributed to Morgan or Forrest as a cover for their rascality?

I have fair reasons to suppose that the citizens did sometimes commit these acts and attribute them to the forces of the enemy. I judge, however, that they generally acted in concert with some forces present or in the vicinity.

Question. Up to what time were the trains running from Louisville to Bowling Green?

I cannot answer. The fact that communication was interrupted from Bowling Green here prevents absolute knowledge of that fact.

Question. What force, in your opinion, would have been requisite to have kept the railroad open from Bowling Green to Nashville?

To have kept it open beyond peradventure I think that not less than from 10,000 to 12,000 men would have been necessary.

Question. How is it necessary to distribute 10,000 to 12,000 men along that road to keep it open?

Well, I do not know how I could definitely state where the forces should be posted, but I think they should be distributed along the road in such a manner as to be always near any point which might be subject to attack in sufficient force to repel the attack. I take into consideration the disposition of the people, their capacity to injure, and the character of the force that was thrown against it. If this force could be counted on to be expected at any one place they could be met by a similar force, but in order to make this secure for an army it should be such that at any one point sufficient force could be had to meet an attack.

Question. Can you designate the points along the road where it would be necessary to have a force stationed?

The first principle would be to have them distributed with reasonable equality; then, in regard to the selection of places, I would have a force between Goodlettsville and Gallatin, between Mitchellsville and Gallatin two forces, and between Franklin and Bowling Green. When I say these places I do not mean the towns, but at such works in the vicinity as are peculiarly important in relation to the country roads in the vicinity.

Question. What forces would you station at Goodlettsville?

I am not prepared to answer that question as to the exact disposition of these forces at the various points. If I were obliged to do the work it would be with the topography of the country before me and such information as I could collect for doing it.

Question. Why, then, do you say it would require from 10,000 to 12,000 to keep that road open?

The answer was given on the general idea of the exposure of the road and the necessity for defending all points.

Question. Is it customary in guarding a road to place a guard at any other points than to take care of the tunnels and bridges on the road?

That question depends, of course, upon the amount of force there to spare for the purpose; such a force as could be no doubt would be disposed of at the most vulnerable points.

Question. Has it not been the practice to guard railroad bridges and tunnels from the fact that to destroy the one is a serious injury to the road, the other a permanent one, while the track is easily and quickly relaid?

Yes, sir.

Question. The largest force you mentioned as numbering 700 cavalry; how many infantry at any one point would you think necessary to repel an attack of 700 cavalry?

This number of cavalry mentioned was referring to the attack that was made previous to the entrance of General Rosecrans' army; a larger force was assembled at the time of the battle with General Johnson. The question resolves itself into the character and circumstances of the attack. If a regular advance is made upon a particular point of road a regiment of infantry would repel them; but as the attack may be made unexpectedly and at unexpected points, the force necessary to repel them would be indefinite.

Question. Major, were the inhabitants along the road of such a character as that between Bowling Green and Nashville at the time you mention? Is it possible for any amount of men to keep a road open by being stationed along it to repel attacks?

It is not absolutely possible.

Question. Would not that road have been protected between Bowling Green and Nashville under those circumstances if the inhabitants had been notified that for every interruption their country would be laid waste right and left?

That question involves so many considerations that I do not know how I can answer it categorically. It is not possible to decide what effect the declaration of such a policy would have throughout the State of Kentucky.

Question. Would it preserve the road?

I think it would have a conservative effect on the road.

Question. Do you not know of railroad lines and telegraph lines being preserved through disaffected regions in that way?

I have heard of the operations of the policy in Missouri.

By General TYLER:

Question. Did you not state in your testimony that the garrison of Nashville would require 20,000 men; would you regard 17,000 or 20,000 men necessary for the protection of Nashville against the guerrilla parties?

No, sir.

Question. Was Nashville at the time this garrison was left here threatened by anything but guerrilla parties and small bodies of cavalry?

We heard on several different occasions of the concentration of troops in the vicinity south; we heard also of the possible arrival of the army defeated at Corinth; and probably on two or three occasions we received information from the inhabitants which indicated the coming of regular forces.

Question. Did these rumors prove true or false; was there ever any large concentration of forces against Nashville?

I think there was never a positive concentration until it began to gather a short time before the arrival of General Rosecrans' army. I presume the beginning of that force was there a long time since. They had a general meeting at Murfreesborough, in which there were very strong persuasions used by Governor Harris with reference to the collection of forces there to attack Nashville and without a word of difference of opinion existing in regard to that subject.

Redirect examination by General BUELL:

Question. Is there any difference in the character of the military operations in Missouri and those of the Army of the Cumberland now?

I think there is, consisting of this, that in Missouri the object seemed to be to keep the State itself in a loyal condition as nearly as practicable, to suppress treasonable acts, and bring the State back to a tranquil condition; whereas here the object is the movement of a large army for strategic purposes.

Question. Is there any more effective way that you know of certain of counteracting the objects of this large army than by operating on its communications?

I know of no better way.

Question. Suppose the country on either side the railway should be laid waste by fire and sword, do you think it would be less an object with the enemy to destroy the road and interrupt communication by it?

I do not think it would be less an object; but I think it would interfere with the means, and I think that the threat of it might suppress the disposition on the part of the inhabitants.

Question. Do you really think that the inhabitants have acted very powerfully in interrupting the communications between here and Louisville in destroying the road as a means of transportation?

I do not think that the inhabitants, announcing themselves as such, have done much harm, but that they have acted clandestinely and in concert with the organized enemy. That question, of course, is one of opinion, depending on such rumors or information as we received from time to time in regard to the probable alliance between the inhabitants and the enemy, and the opinion is to be taken with much allowance.

Question. Is not the presence of large bodies of cavalry under Forrest, Morgan, and other rebel generals, operating upon the line of communication of the army during the past summer, as much a matter of fact as the presence of Kirby Smith's army in Kentucky?

I have no doubt that these forces were regularly operating against the communications of the army. I have no doubt, not only from the facts of their actual interruption, but also from the information brought by spies and others who obtained it, that such were their plans.

Question. There is no question of the fact, I suppose, that a considerable force of our troops was captured by a large body of the enemy's cavalry at Murfreesborough in July last, and does not that establish the fact of the presence of such large bodies in the country?

I was not in Nashville at the time of the battle of Murfreesborough but immediately subsequent, and became acquainted with the fact of a large number of persons having been taken in the battle and of the successful attack of the enemy at Murfreesborough. The business of my office brought that information constantly before me.

General NEGLEY (a witness for the defendant), being duly sworn, testified as follows:

By General BUELL:

Question. State, if you please, general, your name and position in the service of the United States.

James S. Negley, brigadier-general in the United States service.

Question. Give, if you please, a concise statement of your services during the past summer and up to the time of the return of the army to this place recently. State what the enemy's operations were in your vicinity and what measures were adopted to counteract them.

I was in command of the post at Columbia from the 1st of July. My command occupied the railroad from Franklin to the Tennessee River, on the Alabama and Tennessee Railroad. The enemy were quite numerous throughout the country. They were raising guerrilla parties in the vicinity of all the interior towns. Biffle was raising a regiment in the vicinity of Waynesborough, west of Columbia; Napier was raising another regiment in the vicinity of Charlotte and Centreville, nearly west of Columbia; and Major Hawkins was raising a regiment in the vicinity of Hillsborough, over toward Chapel Hill. There was a battalion raising between Columbia and Pulaski, in the neighborhood of Culleoka, a point on the railroad. There was a battalion, afterward a regiment, of guerrillas organizing on the edge of Atlanta, commanded by John T. Morgan. This force numbered in all between 2,500 and 3,000 men. Forrest at the same time was operating east of the line of railroad between Nashville and Tullahoma. He was operating between Manchester and extending toward Carthage and Sparta. The rapidity with which these guerrillas could organize at any one given point required a great deal of vigilance and watchfulness, for the troops would move from point to point in order to cut off the line of communication to the south. Scarcely a day would pass in which they did not commit some depredations on the road, stopping trains and pulling up the rails. They were very annoying in the vicinity of Columbia, their forces generally outnumbering the forces at the post. They threw the cars off the track three times and interrupted the travel for several days at different periods. At the time of the withdrawal of the troops they succeeded on one occasion in burning the bridges on each side of one of the trains that was bringing up troops.

At the beginning of September I withdrew my forces, by the order of General Buell, from the line of railroad. They were concentrated at Nashville. I took command of the forces at Nashville on the 14th of September. General Thomas was left in command of tho post, with three divisions that General Buell left—his own division, General Palmer's division of the Army of the Mississippi, and the Eighth Division, which I command. General Thomas, by order of General Buell, marched to Kentucky; took with him his own division, leaving with me two divisions. Shortly after the army had proceeded to Kentucky the unorganized party concentrated their forces in the vicinity of the city, at a place called La Vergne, under the command of Major-General Anderson. About that time General Forrest was sent from Kentucky to take command and organize the detached forces in Tennessee. He brought with him a portion of his own command to do so. He reached Murfreesborough while General Anderson, with over 3,000 men, was at La Vergne. Before he could carry his orders into execution we pursued the forces of General Anderson and captured a number, one of their pieces of artillery, and demoralized their forces entirely. This led to the disbanding of two regiments of cavalry and the withdrawal of General Anderson from that portion of the command. General Forrest then assumed command of all the forces and retained it until General Breckinridge arrived. This was between the 4th and 24th of October.

The enemy used every effort to prevent our obtaining supplies and forage. We were without supplies here for fifty days except what we procured from the country. We were obliged to go about 20 miles into the country. The enemy would drive off their cattle to some secluded point, which we had to ascertain and then follow them there. They were then concentrating their forces in the neighborhood of Gallatin and Goodlettsville for the purpose of surprising our forage trains, and before we could send out our small force we had to disperse the bands concentrated there. Some ten days previous to the arrival of re-enforcements to General Rosecrans' army General Breckinridge had organized a force in the neighborhood of 25,000 men. Of that force 6,000 were cavalry. He had twenty-eight pieces of artillery, three of which were siege guns. Their advance post was moved to La Vergne, then to the asylum, 8 miles distant, on the Murfreesborough road. From that point they would make sallies on our picket lines and forage parties. The day previous to the arrival of General McCook's command they made an attack upon the east and north side of the defenses at the same time, with the intention of destroying the bridge, I presume. The forces on the north side of the river, numbering 3,000, with two pieces of artillery, were commanded by General Morgan. They had only about 1,500 of those in action. The attack was made about 3 o'clock in the morning. It commenced on the eastern side of the Murfreesborough road, by the enemy, numbering about 3,000, with three pieces of artillery, driving in our pickets. They were speedily driven off without success on the north side. We constructed banquettes along the railroad, which they were only enabled to approach before they were driven back. On the eastern side they fired some fifteen or twenty shots from their artillery. We then opened on them two of the heavy guns at the fort, which obliged them to shift their position. They then moved over to the Franklin road and brought up Hanson's brigade, three batteries of artillery, stationing it between the Nolensville pike and the Murfreesborough pike, on a cross-road which runs diagonally from the asylum to the Franklin road. Their cavalry, about 3,000, with six pieces of artillery, moved down near the Franklin road on the intermediate, which runs parallel with the Franklin dirt road. A small force from this command approached the picket line on the Franklin road. Believing it possible that we could punish that party that came up the Franklin road, I sent a brigade on the Murfreesborough road to cover the real movements on the Franklin road, to engage them apparently on the Murfreesborough road while I took the regiments of infantry and some cavalry, with four pieces of artillery, and preceded the forces on the Franklin road. They retreated, making a stand upon every rising piece of ground, until they reached a distance of 3 miles from the city. I then endeavored to draw them upon our artillery by sending our cavalry forward, with directions to charge upon the rear of the enemy and then retreat, turning into the woods on the right, in hopes of bringing them on an ambuscade. My cavalry were so inexperienced that they followed a small portion of the enemy that remained on the Franklin road to within 5 miles of Franklin, and obliged me to move forward with my infantry force 5 miles farther to support them, taking us about 8 miles from the city. Before I could get the cavalry back the enemy had formed in considerable force on my left, with seven pieces of artillery, and we moved up toward the Franklin road to cut off their retreat. I left a regiment of infantry to protect the cavalry, and fell back opposite the position they assumed, and succeeded in placing two guns in position and opening fire simultaneously with their artillery. This enabled me to withdraw my cavalry and get in the rear in time to make preparations for a charge of cavalry which they had formed upon the Franklin road. They shifted three of their guns, and began to move up the reserve toward the Franklin road while trying to get into our rear, at the same time forming a line, which I presume was a regiment and a half, across the Franklin road, about 900 or 1,000 yards distant. I placed a regiment of infantry behind a fence close by the road to conceal them from view, and threw out two companies of cavalry as a decoy, with orders to open fire upon the enemy at a long range and then retreat. The enemy accepted the challenge, charging very handsomely over the rolling piece of ground that lay between the regiment and the line they had formed. Simultaneously with that I placed the three pieces of artillery to cover their retreat, which was extending to my rear. They charged up to within a hundred yards of the line of infantry—the fence that was on the Franklin road—when they discharged their pieces, halting temporarily to do so, and then charged forward, still not seeing our concealed regiment of infantry, and within about 40 yards they received the volley of the entire regiment, which drove them back in confusion, causing considerable loss. I took advantage of their retreat and the confusion they were in to withdraw my force to a better position in the rear, and in time to meet the movement from what I presume was their reserve, and moved toward the Franklin road about 2 miles from the city. They would perhaps have succeeded in getting into my rear but for a section of artillery which I had ordered from the city upon a rising piece of ground overlooking the ground upon which they were marching. The enemy then withdrew their force to La Vergne, where they remained till the arrival of General Rosecrans' army.

The troops that occupied the city of Nashville numbered about 10,000 effective men. There were 3,000 convalescents, organized into regiments, that remained in the city, and we were unable to send them out. During the siege we procured 3,500 loads of forage and provisions within a radius of 20-odd miles. The troops marched 540 or 550 miles in procuring supplies. We captured about 350 Confederate prisoners, had three engagements with the enemy, and about twenty skirmishes. Our whole loss was about 5 killed, 40 wounded, and about 60 persons captured. We lost no wagons or animals by the acts of the enemy, and the garrison was maintained in very good order and condition.

Question. Were your troops actually employed during the summer and did you succeed in inflicting punishment on those guerrilla bands that you have spoken of?

Yes, sir.

Question. Did General Bragg, in marching through Tennessee, leave any of his force to operate against Nashville?

He left General Breckinridge's division, which had been ordered into Kentucky, and had reached Knoxville on its way to Kentucky when General Breckinridge and his command were ordered to Murfreesborough.

Question. Your answer implies that they did not form part of the force with which Bragg left Chattanooga?

Yes, sir; he left none of his forces that he marched from Chattanooga with.

Question. Do you know anything of the road from McMinnville to the Sequatchie Valley by way of Altamont?

Yes, sir.

Question. Is it a practicable mountain road?

It is in the summer-time; the great difficulty is a deficiency of water.

Question. Is there not the same difficulty with all the mountain roads; that is, scarcity of water?

Yes, sir; there is but one stream of water between McMinnville and the Sequatchie Valley, and that is in the neighborhood of Altamont.

Question. Did you march with your troops to the Tennessee River opposite Chattanooga?

Yes, sir.

Question. State, if you please, what route you took.

I concentrated my forces at Pulaski; This was about the 30th of May; marched from Pulaski to Fayetteville, and found the enemy we were after had gone towards Sweeden's Cove, which is on the road to Jasper. We took the Fayetteville and Winchester road to Winchester; from Winchester, by way of Cowan, across the ridge of the Cumberland Mountains, into Sweeden's Cove to the west of Battle Creek. Then we took the Jasper road. Four miles beyond Jasper I divided my forces, sending a portion of the infantry across Walden's Ridge by a path 16 miles to the ferry opposite Chattanooga. We marched the artillery and transportation 22 miles up the valley to the Anderson and Therman road, crossing the ridge by the Therman or Anderson road to the ferry opposite Chattanooga. I returned by the same road to the Anderson cross-road in the Sequatchie Valley, sending one portion to Battle Creek to sustain a small force I had left there to engage the enemy's attention, and with that force to march to Stevenson, while with the other portion, commanded personally, I took the Therman road to Altamont, with the intention of attacking Starnes' cavalry, that were encamped at Altamont when I was crossing the mountains from Chattanooga. Before I arrived there Starnes moved to Pikeville, and I received intelligence that the enemy were proposing to cross the river and attack our forces at Fayetteville. I marched from Altamont through Hubbard's Cove to Manchester; from Manchester to Wartrace and Shelbyville. I then left a portion there to sustain that line, and marched the remainder by the Shelbyville road to Columbia. The time occupied in marching from Columbia to Chattanooga and returning was fourteen days; the distance we traveled was nearly 300 miles.

Question. How long were you in crossing the mountains from the Sequatchie Valley to Altamont?

Two days.

Question. How does that road compare with the Manchester and Jasper road?

It is a better road; that is, ascending from the eastern side; it is equally as bad ascending from the western side.

Question. Is there any difficulty about it at all more than with other mountain roads in that region?

No, sir; the roads are all very rough.

Question. Is there a good wagon road down the Sequatchie Valley and on to Stevenson?

In the summer-time very good—a level, smooth road; with the exception of Sequatchie River and Battle Creek it is a very good one. One has to be forded and the other has a bridge over.

Question. Is it, beyond all comparison, better than any other road out of the Sequatchie Valley?

Yes, sir.

Question. Do you know any roads crossing the mountain out of the Sequatchie Valley east of the Therman road?

Yes, sir; it is what is called the Dunlap or Grassy Cove road. It intersects the Grassy Cove road to Chattanooga and Knoxville to Dunlap. That is a very good road in summer-time. Where it crosses Caney Fork it is well supplied with water.

Question. How far is that from McMinnville?

Between 20 and 30 miles.

Question. Do you know anything of the road from Dunlap to Sparta?

Yes, sir; the road runs on the ridge for a considerable distance.

Question. Is there a road from Harrison into the Sequatchie Valley?

Yes, sir; it passes to the right of Therman road 44 miles in turning the mountain.

Question. Do you know of a road following the main ridge of the Cumberland, crossing these different roads, by which you can turn off to the left from the Dunlap and McMinnville road and come into the Therman road near Altamont?

There is a ridge road that runs to Alexandria—strikes the Carthage and McMinnville road at Alexandria. Where the Therman road strikes the Tracy City at Altamont there are cross-roads by which you could proceed to Pikeville. Spencer, Alexandria, McMinnville, or Hubbard's Cove and Manchester, and also one that leads by Tracy City to Cowan.

Cross-examination by the JUDGE-ADVOCATE:

Question. Do you say you were shut off from supplies in Nashville some fifty days? Did your forces suffer any during that time?

Only inconvenience; they suffered no want.

Question. The organization of these guerrilla bands that you speak of was subsequent to the invasion of Kentucky by Bragg?

Yes, sir.

Question. At what time was it that Breckinridge came over to take the command you speak of?

I cannot give you the exact date, but it was between the 4th and 21st of October. The Governor had offered opportunities to the people throughout Tennessee to enlist and select their own companies and organizations, and large numbers enrolled themselves. General Bragg refused to recognize the authority of the Governor or the propriety of the order, and ordered the troops to be organized into organizations already existing, except such regiments as were full. They disbanded all the forces here except two regiments.

Question. At what time did Bragg cross from Chattanooga and Harrison with his invading army?

In the middle of August.

Question. Where were you at the time?

At Columbia.

Question. Bragg marched up the Sequatchie Valley through Dunlap and Pikeville to Sparta. Was it known at the time he crossed that that would be the line he would take?

When he marched to Sparta he had not determined whether he would attack Nashville or march into Kentucky. He was contending against the programme laid out for him by Governor Harris. He approached Nashville in consequence of the pressure brought on him by Governor Harris. The governor was opposed to his marching into Kentucky, and had induced President Davis to send Bragg into Tennessee to retake Nashville. That is one reason why General Bragg threw a portion of his forces along the line of the Chattanooga and Nashville Railroad.

Question. What I asked you was whether it was known to you or to the more intelligent officers at the time of crossing the Tennessee River that Bragg would take that line up through Dunlap, Pikeville, and Sparta, and whether it was anticipated that that would be his line of march?

It was not known to me. I was aware of his crossing the river and the force he had, and it was presumed that he would go to Pikeville, from the fact that a portion of his cavalry came so low down the Sequatchie Valley.

Question. Did not his condition as to supplies and transportation, &c., force him up the Sequatchie Valley through Pikeville and Sparta?

That must have had an influence upon his march, but at the same time he had placed himself in a condition where there was no water—between Sparta and Alexandria. His forces were almost demoralized by the hardships of the march.

By General DANA:

Question. With what force did Bragg cross the Tennessee River?

Sixty thousand.

Question. Do you know anything of the condition of Bragg's army as to supplies when he crossed?

Yes, sir.

Question. What was his actual condition as to supplies?

He had no more than three days' provisions; he had not more than three wagons to every brigade; that is, for supplies.

Question. With the quantity of supplies with which he crossed the Tennessee and with the train of artillery and baggage he had with his army was it or was it not at his option, with equal chances, to go down into the plains of Tennessee by the different cross-roads you have described in the vicinity of Altamont or to go to Sparta?

No, sir; there was not a sufficiency of forage between Altamont and McMinnville to feed his cavalry one meal.

Question. Do you consider, then, that he was compelled on account of lack of supplies to go by the road to Sparta?

Yes, sir.

Question. And that he could not go by the Anderson or Therman road or by any other cross-road down into the plains of Tennessee?

He could not go with the supplies he had with him. He would have had sufficient supplies to maintain him three or four days.

Question. Was it known at the time that Bragg was in the Sequatchie Valley that the lack of supplies under which he was suffering prevented him from going by any other road than the Sparta road?

I am unable to say, sir.

Question. At the time that the Army of the Ohio occupied its position in the vicinity of Altamont and McMinnville by which road did you expect Bragg to come into the plains of Tennessee?

By the Alexandria road to Lebanon by the way to Dunlap. That opinion I did not form until I knew he was ascending the mountain. When he was in the Sequatchie Valley I was unable to tell where he would ascend the mountain, but presumed he would go to Pikeville or Sparta.

Question. At the time you entertained the opinion that he would come out by the road to Dunlap with what portion of the Army of the Ohio were you stationed?

I was at Columbia with 110 [?] men. There was one brigade extending along the railroad to the Tennessee River; another portion of General Buell's command was on the line of the Chattanooga and Nashville road to Nashville. There was a portion of General McCook's command near Altamont, so I understood; but I was not fully aware of the disposition of the forces of General Buell on that line.

Question. What was the programme Governor Harris laid down for Bragg's operations?

It was intended that Bragg should concentrate his forces at Chattanooga and march by way of Sparta, thus turning General Buell's left, retake Nashville, compel General Buell's army to fall back and cross the Tennessee, while the forces north of the Cumberland should be compelled to fall back to Louisville, thus obtaining possession of the railroad north of Bowling Green to Huntsville. Governor Harris was so well satisfied that that plan would succeed that he had urged appropriations in the Confederate Congress to establish defenses on the Cumberland and Tennessee Rivers.

Question. Was this programme of Governor Harris generally understood at that time among the officers of high rank in the Army of the Ohio?

No, sir.

Question. At the time General McCook lay at Altamont and General Thomas at McMinnville where was it generally expected among officers of high rank in the Army of the Ohio that Bragg would debouch from the Sequatchie Valley into the plains of Tennessee and by what road?

I am unable to say, because I had no consultation with them at the time. My communication was so cut off that I had no opportunity of exchanging opinions with them.

Question. When Bragg crossed the Tennessee River did you know at that time that he had but three days' supply ?

Not till some days afterward.

Question. Do you remember about how long afterward you obtained the information ?

Five or six days.

Question. Do you know anything of the letter of Governor Harris detailing the programme having been intercepted by our forces ?

I never heard of such a thing.

Question. How did you arrive at the estimate of 60,000 men of Bragg's forces crossing the Tennessee River ?

By a man who counted them as they passed along the Grassy Cove road, and also by a statement of the assistant ferry-man at Chattanooga.

Question. What data did your informant give you by which you made the estimate of 60,000 ?

He counted the regiments, gave me the number of regiments and number of brigades and divisions, and gave me the strength of several regiments of the different States.

Question. What did he state as the number of regiments and the average number of men to the regiment ?

I am unable to tell you the number of regiments in detail; he did not give me a memorandum in writing, but the strength of the regiments. Those from Virginia, from Tennessee, Louisiana, Mississippi, and Alabama averaged from 300 to 350 men; some from Tennessee were as low as 200; some brigades were composed of five regiments. The regiments from Georgia would sometimes exceed 700; they ranged from 500 to 700 and 800. There were several Florida regiments that were very strong.

Question. What was the name of your informant ?

Carter.

Question. At the time Bragg was in the Sequatchie Valley by which road did you consider it certain that he would debouch from the valley ?

I am unable, sir, to answer that question. I presumed that he would march by way of Pikeville to Sparta, because it was a better road for his artillery and transportation.

Question. Are the Anderson and Therman road and the Grassy Cove road equally practicable for an army as the road by way of Pikeville and Sparta ?

Yes, sir.

Question. At the time that General McCook lay at Altamont and General Thomas at McMinnville, suppose the Army of the Ohio had been concentrated in the vicinity of Sparta to oppose Bragg, which road would he then have traveled ? Would he have given battle to this army in position or traveled by some other road ?

He would have traveled by some other road.

Question. Which road would he have taken ?

That would depend upon where he wished to go. When he left Sparta he had not decided where he would go. It was not until he reached that point Governor Harris understood from him that he determined to cross into Kentucky. Till he reached Sparta or the vicinity Governor Harris was under the impression that he would go to Nashville, and he frequently asserted that it was understood that he marched on to Nashville.

Question. Had General Buell's army taken up the position before spoken of would it have held Bragg under the necessity of either giving him battle in the vicinity of Sparta or of retreating by the line by which he came?

Yes, sir.

Question. Could he not have gone by any other road?

He would have been compelled to cross so as to reach Kentucky by the way of Pikeville to obtain supplies; if he crossed the Cumberland farther east he would have been unable to sustain his army.

Question. Could General Bragg have avoided General Buell at Sparta and continued on his march?

I think not, with success.

Question. Please state to the Commission how you obtained the information that Governor Harris' plan of taking Nashville was not modified until after Bragg's army reached Sparta.

By having a person present at an interview between Governor Harris, Breckinridge, and Ex-Governor Foote, General Forrest, and Andrew Ewing.

Question. At what date did you first consider it certain that Bragg would not take Nashville?

Not until I heard he was near Rome.

Redirect examination:

Question. What is the distance from Dunlap to Sparta?

I think it is 40 miles; but I am not positive of the exact distance.

Question. How far is it from Dunlap to McMinnville?

By the nearest road I should judge it was about 40 miles.

Question. Do you know how far it is from McMinnville before you strike the mountain in going over to Dunlap?

About 10 or 12 miles.

Question. Is it a productive region about there?

No, sir; not until you come into the neighborhood of McMinnville.

Question. How far does this productive region extend toward Dunlap?

Not more than 8 or 10 miles.

Question. Is Sparta in the mountains or on the ridge of the mountains?

It is on the northern slope of the mountains.

Question. What is the character of the country between Dunlap and Sparta?

Very thinly settled; very little cultivated.

Question. Is it like the mountain region on the road from Dunlap across to McMinnville?

It is similar to it till you get near Sparta.

Question. You say Sparta is on the slope of the mountains; how close to Sparta do you get before you come to the productive region in that direction?

I understand, sir, not until you approach within 10 or 12 miles of Sparta.

Question. Would not that take you on the mountains 10 or 12 miles from Sparta?

Yes, sir; those slopes are all cultivated; they form parts of the Cove, and are all cultivated.

Question. Which is the most productive region, that about Sparta or that by McMinnville?

That south of McMinnville; the advantage is in favor of McMinnville.

Question. When you say in your testimony that those guerrilla bands were organized subsequent to the marching of the Army of the Ohio, do you mean that they had no effective organization at all or that they were not consolidated?

I mean that they were not consolidated.

Question. Were they effective as an offensive force?

Yes, sir; from the manner in which they operated in interfering with our communications.

Question. Have you been at McMinnville, Dunlap, or Sparta yourself?

No, sir; I know them only by examinations made by my couriers and by persons whom I sent to those points.

General R. W. JOHNSON (a witness for defendent), being duly sworn by the judge-advocate, testified as follows:

By General BUELL:

Question. Give your name and position in the service, if you please, general?

Richard W. Johnson; brigadier-general of volunteers.

Question. Were you on duty with the Army of the Ohio in Tennessee in the months of July and August last?

I was; up to August 21.

Question. State, if you please, concisely, the operations of the enemy's cavalry in Middle Tennessee prior to that time and the measures adopted to counteract them, as far as you were concerned.

The enemy's cavalry were all the time during the months of July and August attempting to break up our communications by railroad, in which they succeeded in several instances, and it became necessary to transport supplies by wagons, and these were often threatened by cavalry. At one time it was reported that the enemy's cavalry in large force were marching in the direction of Pulaski, Tenn. The commanding officer of the Army of the Ohio telegraphed to me, then in Battle Creek, to report to him at once in Huntsville. On my arrival in Huntsville he showed me several maps, told me what the enemy's cavalry were doing, and asked me if with the cavalry in the department I could stop the depredations of Morgan and his cavalry. I received orders from General Buell to go to a place known as Reynolds' Station, on the Tennessee and Alabama Railroad, and there assume command of all the cavalry in that neighborhood, and to march against any enemy's cavalry found near that and Murfreesborough. I assumed command on my arrival, and within two days marched by Fayetteville and Shelbyville in the direction where the cavalry were said to be. I found that if any had been there in an organized form they had left, but I found that citizens in the absence of the Federal forces would arm themselves and take advantage of any small force left to guard the bridges on the railroad. These parties would dismount on the approach of the Federal troops, secrete their arms, and be considered as citizens and be loyal for the time.

I marched to Murfreesborough, and on my arrival I reported to General Nelson, in obedience to General Buell's orders. From this point I was sent to a town called Liberty, and from Liberty to Smithfield, Smithfield to McMinnville, and in fact throughout the entire portion of country there, but was not able to find the enemy in any considerable force. I then marched from McMinnville, with 640 men, to a place known as Cookville; here I intercepted a message from Morgan himself, and found that he had left on the 19th, marching in the direction of Gallatin, Tenn. Marched on Gallatin, and met him in that place and had an engagement with him on the 21st. I would state that all the cavalry in that portion of Tennessee was placed under my command by instructions from General Buell. When I reported to General Nelson he divided up the command, leaving me only 640 men. While at Huntsville

General Buell indicated on the map the line he wished to take up, and in order to successfully occupy that line it was necessary to drive the rebel cavalry from between two roads and beyond the line that he wished to take up. This, I suppose, was the object of my going there in advance—to render the road safe for the transportation of supplies. There was at the time I started out a break in that road of about 50 miles by the destruction of bridges, which the mechanics were then employed in repairing. On my arrival at Reynolds' Station I found the cavalry posted along the railroad for its protection at bridges and to guard the wagon trains with provisions. The gathering up of these detachments required the two days' delay referred to in the testimony.

Cross-examination by the JUDGE-ADVOCATE:

Question. What number of men would it require between Bowling Green and Nashville to protect it, supposing the inhabitants to be disaffected along the line of railroad?

Fifty thousand men.

Question. An attempt, then, to guard the railroad under those circumstances is simply an absurdity?

No, I do not think it is. I can take 50,000 and guard it perfectly, according to my opinion, though I cannot operate outside the railroad. My operations must be confined to it alone.

Question. Would the road then do more than supply the army you had to guard it?

That would depend upon the quantity of rolling stock on that road.

Question. Were these depredations to be feared from the inhabitants alone or from the inhabitants assisted by a few guerrillas, and is there no other mode of protecting the road?

I know of no other.

Question. What would be the effect of a notice to the inhabitants along that road that the country would be laid waste on either side if they interfered with it?

Many of the persons who depredated upon these railroads have no interest in the property lying contiguous to it, and a threat of that kind would have no effect upon them. That plan has been pursued in Missouri and was unsuccessful there.

Question. Was the threat in Missouri carried out where it was made?

I am not prepared to say, but I think it was, part of the time, under General Pope, in his early operations in Missouri.

Question. Do you know of that mode of protecting railroad and telegraph lines having been adopted in Virginia?

I do not.

Question. At the time you speak of, when you were sent to take command of the cavalry, was there a force in and about that region of country you speak of?

It was variously estimated. General Buell exhibited to me some dispatches he received, I think from General Negley, in which General Negley stated that 500 rebel cavalry were then marching on Pulaski. General Buell told me, to prevent the possibility of that detachment taking a train which was to have left that day, that he had telegraphed for the train not to start till it was ascertained whether the force was there along the road at different points. I found the officers in command of detachments variously estimated that force, and some I believe that the whole or a great portion of the rebel army was there.

Question. Five hundred, then, is the largest body you know of?

In answer to a previous question I stated it was variously estimated; 500 were reported by General Negley, but of their actual existence I have reason to doubt. The officers and people along the line thought that that force was there.

Question. Is it possible or is it probable that any large organized force could have been in and about these railroads from Nashville at that time with General Buell's army situated as it was?

They might have been there for a short time, but could not remain there very long.

Question. Do you not know, general, and was it not supposed at the time, that these depredations upon the railroads were done by the inhabitants in a great measure?

I do not know it, but I believe the inhabitants assisted the guerrilla force when they came into the country, and when an opportunity offered they would act on their own responsibility.

Question. Now, if a general of General Buell's known determined and inflexible character had given notice to those along those roads that he would hold the inhabitants responsible, would those depredations have been committed?

I do not think General Buell's order would have had any effect upon those people or any other general's orders. There is a large idle floating population in these Southern States, and such characters as those would not be governed by any order that General Buell might issue. Just such characters General Mitchel had to deal with on the railroad running from Huntsville to Stevenson. He threatened to burn their villages if they fired upon the trains, and several villages or railroad stations were burned, and yet the trains were fired into afterward.

Question. If you had no other than an idle, irresponsible population to deal with a lesser guard would be necessary to take care of the road, would it not?

I think not; on the contrary, a still larger guard.

Question. Why so?

These men having no habitation, they are here to-day and in another place to-morrow.

Question. If the responsible settled inhabitants along the railroad knew that their property was in danger, would they not be guardians of the railroad property as of their own?

Individuals might be, yet individuals might be overpowered by this idle floating population, who would not be influenced by the opinions of some few of the owners along the railroad.

Question. If the settled owners along the railroad were friends instead of enemies, who would give you information of the approach of these guerrillas and who would assist you in putting them down, your trouble would be less, would it not?

I think so.

Question. You speak of its having been tried by General Pope in Missouri and failed; do you know this of your own knowledge or have you heard it?

I have only heard so from the common reports in the newspapers.

Colonel MILLER (a witness for the defendant), being duly sworn by the judge-advocate, testified as follows:

By General BUELL:

Question. State your name and position in the service, if you please.

My name is J. F. Miller; colonel of the Twenty-ninth Indiana Volunteers.

Question. Were you on duty in Nashville in the months of July and August and September last?

In the months of July and August I was on duty here, commanding the post.

Question. State, if you please, what the operations of the enemy were in your vicinity during that period, and, as well as you can, what forces he employed and with what effect.

Our troubles commenced here about the 8th of July, when the communication between here and Louisville was threatened. The enemy menaced the force at Bowling Green about that time, under John Morgan; perhaps 1,500 strong were reported near Bowling Green. I sent up fifteen companies of infantry and a section of artillery from this place, which, with the troops sent by General Boyle, drove off the enemy and saved those bridges at Bowling Green and Green River. The next trouble was at Murfreesborough. The enemy had attacked Murfreesborough July 13 by a force 2,000 strong, under Colonel Forrest. Colonel Lester was in command at Murfreesborough up to the 12th July. He had the Third Minnesota, the Ninth Michigan, and Hewett's battery of four pieces. On the 12th General Crittenden took command there; on the 13th the attack was made and the forces taken prisoners. The first reports we got here were that the enemy were 7,000 strong, and to look out for this place and to be prepared to defend it. I had at that time at Lebanon four companies of infantry and two of cavalry. Lebanon is north of Murfreesborough. On hearing of the attack on Murfreesborough Lebanon was evacuated and the troops brought here, and I had two regiments of infantry and four companies, three companies of cavalry, and ten field pieces of artillery. It was uncertain at that time where the enemy would strike after taking that place. We had a small force at Gallatin and along the railroad between here and the Kentucky line. I think there were ten or twelve companies.

I brought down three companies from Gallatin to re-enforce the garrison here, but no attack was made and they were sent back. July 16 we had information that there were a thousand of the enemy at Lebanon, and we expected they would strike the road to Gallatin or beyond there; but on the 17th General Nelson came here with a force of five or six regiments, and he assumed command with these troops. On the 18th he marched to Murfreesborough. About the same time General Boyle asked for re-enforcements in Kentucky, reporting the enemy along the line in considerable force. As General Nelson had not increased the garrison materially no troops were sent him.

On the 19th General Nelson informed me that the enemy were in considerable force near Murfreesborough and sent here for re-enforcements. He had taken nearly all the force he brought here with him. But the enemy did not attack him there. Forrest, with about 1,800 or 2,000 men (cavalry) came in his rear and menaced this place. They drove in the pickets here, but made no attack. They went out to the railroad and attacked the force General Nelson had left to guard the bridges, taking about 80 men at the Mill Creek Bridge and burned the bridge, and then went off in the direction of Lebanon and got away. General Nelson did not get them.

Nothing occurred till about the 27th or 28th of July, when Colonel Boone, who was in command at Gallatin, and I think seven or eight companies along the rear at a place called Pilot Knob, became alarmed and desired re-enforcements. The Thirty-first Indiana was sent to re-enforce him at that place. That was about the 30th July. On the 4th or 5th of August those troops were taken away, General Nelson deeming the force under Colonel Boone amply sufficient, as he said to me. About 10th of August Colonel Boone was attacked by what from the best information I should suppose would be a force of 600 to 700. He was surprised at daylight and captured. It was as complete a surprise as that at Murfreesborough. I went up with parts of two regiments after that to Gallatin and that region, but could not get a fight. Colonel Heffren was in command of four companies of the Fiftieth Indiana, which were posted at the different bridges between here and Gallatin in the stockades which had been erected by General Buell's orders. About the 20th he had from 50 to 60 men in each stockade. About the 20th of August he took his men out of the stockades, leaving about 8 or 10 in each, and went off on an expedition to Gallatin. On his return he was attacked by Morgan with probably 600 or 700 men, and the enemy succeeded in burning three of the bridges; and, the men being along the road, quite a number of them were taken prisoners. The bridges were all burned but one, where a party of 18 got into the stockades and held it against the whole force. If he had left his men in the stockades none of these bridges would have been injured at all in my opinion. Colonel Boone neglected to build the stockades which he was ordered to build by General Buell, and at the time he was captured at Gallatin the tunnel was destroyed and one of the bridges this side of Gallatin. The force along the road was deemed sufficient, and would have been, if the stockades had been built and the men kept in them, as they ought to have been. It was not long after this that the fight at Gallatin occurred between General Johnson and Morgan, the particulars of which I suppose have been stated here before.

Question. State, if you please, the result of it.

General Johnson was captured, with probably 100 to 150 men. They nearly all got away and retreated back to th s place. The force General Johnson had was 650 men. I do not know the force the enemy had, but probably more than he had. We were continually troubled here by guerrilla parties who hovered about the country and along the lines, but with no serious results, except those I have mentioned, in the vicinity. I always considered the force I had here sufficient to hold the city, and I think I never asked General Buell for re-enforcements.

Question. Did these large bodies of cavalry have artillery with them ?

I think not till after they took the four pieces at Murfreesborough.

Question. Did they do any harm to the railroad after the capture of Murfreesborough ?

Yes, sir; they burned those three Mill Creek bridges after General Nelson had gone out to Murfreesborough.

Question. But before his arrival there did they not destroy some bridges in the vicinity of Murfreesborough ?

They destroyed a bridge and the depot at Murfreesborough at the time they had the fight there. I do not know what they did beyond Murfreesborough on the road.

Question. Were these principal depredations you have mentioned committed by organized troops in the rebel service and without reference to the inhabitants along the road ?

I do not know whether they were organized troops or not; I know they were in the Confederate service; they were understood to be guerrillas. The Texas Rangers were about, too; we knew them to be forces under Morgan, Forrest, and Starnes.

Question. Are those commands not understood to be composed of troops belonging as much to the rebel army as other troops; are they not of the character of regular troops ?

Yes, sir; I suppose they are. They have always been treated the same as other Confederate troops and appear to be organized into regiments and companies, and I have no doubt are in the Confederate service the same as any other troops; that is their reputation. Colonel Morgan has been promoted by the Confederate authorities the same as other officers and so has Colonel Forrest.

Question. You did not understand that they were made up of the inhabitants of the country along those railroads on which they had been depredating ?

O, no; sometimes the citizens have joined them perhaps, but they acted in bodies as other invading troops, and seemed to understand their business as if acting under orders.

Question. Do you think if in consequence of these depredations you were to lay the country waste with fire and sword on either side of the railroad the depredations of these troops would be prevented ?

I do not think it would have any effect one way or the other. I think they are sent out for the express purpose of destroying the lines of communication and supply lines. They are organized for that business; they go mounted, and the troops are better adapted for that kind of work than perhaps any other. As a reason for this opinion I will state that in this part of the country the depredations they have committed have been committed against the desire of the people, so far as I know, and I know the people are complaining very bitterly of this kind of conduct, for they said, "If our lines are cut and destroyed the army in the State will subsist off the people, off the country; whereas if the lines are left open they will get their supplies from the North." I have heard this argument frequently by people who were not Union people. Further, this railroad line from Louisville here was not troubled by the people. There was a time last spring, in the early part of the summer, when General Dumont was in command, when the bridges were not guarded at all and no depredations were committed.

Question. Is this a very unusual method of operating against an enemy ?

I think it is very common in the history of all wars. It is one of the means of crippling an enemy, cutting off his supplies or cutting off his line of retreat, and I should think a very good plan of operation.

Question. Is it usual among civilized nations to hold the inhabitants of the country responsible for it?

Not that I know of. I think non-combatants are respected in their rights of property among civilized people.

Cross-examination by the JUDGE-ADVOCATE:

Question. What force did the rebels have when they captured Crittenden at Murfreesborough?

They had, from the best information I could get, five regiments, that would average perhaps 300 or 400. I suppose from 1,500 to 1,800 men made the attack there.

Question. Was there any artillery?

No, sir.

Question. What number of men had we there?

Between 800 and 900, I think.

Question. Were not the transactions upon the railroad between Bowling Green and Nashville very much of the same character?

I think that as far as Heffren's defense of these bridges is concerned it was very bad. There might be a question in regard to Colonel Boone's management.

Question. Would it have been possible for us to send 1,800 men to break up the line of communication between, say, Cleveland and Knoxville on that railroad or upon any other railroad running through the enemy's country?

Of course it would be possible, but it would be hazardous.

Question. What is the difference between a line of railroad running between this city and Louisville and any railroad running through the rebel country?

The railroad is the same thing in the enemy's country that it is in ours, perhaps as easily destroyed in one as in the other, provided there are no natural obstructions in the way; but it would be easier to get in the rear of the army where there were no defiles to pass or large streams than it would if there were no high mountains and large streams to cross; it would take a longer time and be in greater danger of being intercepted and cut off.

Question. I understand you to say, then, that the character and disposition of the inhabitants make no difference in the hazard of that undertaking?

I was presuming that the question implied that the character of the inhabitants would be the same in both cases; that they would be hostile to the attempting force in either case.

Question. Is there any difference between the character of the inhabitants along this line that has been broken up and that of any other line running through rebel territory?

I cannot answer that question; I really do not know.

Question. You say that a notice to the inhabitants along this line of railroad that they would be held responsible for its interruption and be punished if it were injured or destroyed would made no difference?

General BUELL. In order to save the Commission, the witness, and myself, I am willing to withdraw the questions and evidence as to whether threats to the inhabitants of the country bordering the railroads would or would not interfere with the operations of the army.

The WITNESS. I do not think it would make any difference. I do not think they could prevent it if they were to try.

By General TYLER:

Question. Do you think these parties of guerrillas, as you term them, had any direct assistance from the people along the line of railroad by giving information as to the condition of our troops?

General BUELL. I object to this term "guerrillas" as applied to these troops. They are as much troops as any in the rebel service. I think there is a difference between the cavalry of Morgan, Forrest, and Starnes and what we understand by "guerrillas." I know of no reason for giving them a character which does not belong to them, for they are not "guerrillas" in the proper sense of that term.

General TYLER. There is a letter from Beauregard in which he says he appointed this man (Morgan) for this very purpose, and calls them "guerrillas," and says, "You will hear from them."

The PRESIDENT. They are called "Partisan Rangers," I think, by the Southerners.

General BUELL. These troops are not of that character.

The WITNESS. I think it is possible that some persons may have given them information.

The Commission adjourned to meet on December 26, 1862, at 10 o'clock a. m.

NASHVILLE, *December* 26, 1862.

The Commission met pursuant to adjournment. All the members present; also the judge-advocate and General Buell.

Colonel HAZEN (a witness for the defense), being duly sworn, testified as follows:

By General BUELL:

Question. State your name and position in the service, if you please.

My name is W. B. Hazen, colonel of the Forty-first Ohio Volunteers. I have commanded a brigade in the Army of the Cumberland since January 1, 1862.

Question. With what part of the army were you in the recent campaign in Kentucky starting from Louisville?

I was in the division commanded by General W. S. Smith, in the Second Corps; it had position in the line of battle upon the right.

Question. Was your brigade sent on a reconnaissance under your command on the 11th of October, after the battle of Perryville?

It was with the advance of a regiment of cavalry and a battery of artillery.

Question. State, if you please, where you went and what you saw.

I went upon the road toward Danville. When within 1 mile of Danville I found a line of rebel cavalry with two pieces of artillery opposed to me. The cavalry were dismounted, and they made stout resistance to our progress. I pushed forward my command, and after skirmishing for half an hour they gave way and passed through the town of Danville, skirmishing all the way. I pursued them about a mile beyond Danville on the Camp Dick Robinson road, when, having executed my commission, I returned to camp. I learned by citizens, and by the report of one of my aides who saw the troops in person, that John Morgan, with from 200 to 300 cavalry, were drawn up in line of battle 1½ miles on the left of Danville, crossing the Harrodsburg road. I saw the principal people of Danville, the most influential people, and learned all I could of them as to their position and force. They all agreed in stating that the rebel forces were then concentrated at Camp Dick Robinson, and there would give us fight. I took great pains in being correct in regard to this information, and went back to camp thoroughly impressed with this belief, and reported the same to General Crittenden, commander of the corps I would further say that the people of Danville were very enthusiastic in our reception and endeavored to give me as correct information as possible. The people with whom I conversed were thoroughly our friends.

Question. Did you discover any indication that the enemy designed to retreat from Camp Dick Robinson?

None at all that I could discover; no one told me anything about it.

Question. What time did you return to camp to your division?

The same day, about 4 o'clock in the afternoon.

Question. When did you report to General Crittenden?

I reported immediately afterward, in company with General Smith, commander of the division.

Question. Do you know where the headquarters of the army were at that time?

I do not know positively. I was never at the general headquarters.

Cross-examination by the JUDGE-ADVOCATE:

Question. That movement was made on the 11th, you say; what time did the army move afterward?

The entire army moved on the 13th and 14th. Our division, and I think our entire corps, moved next day.

Question. How far did you march next day and where did you encamp?

We marched to the vicinity of Dick's River and turned to the vicinity of Danville, upon the Danville and Harrodsburg pike, and encamped there, a distance of 10 or 12 miles.

Question. Do you recollect whether it was on the Nicholasville road or not from Danville?

We marched across the country.

Question. At the time you entered Danville in that reconnaissance did you learn the number of the enemy?

Not positively. I had the same means that we always had—that is, reports and rumors—giving the number of the enemy from 40,000 to 100,000.

Question. After returning from Dick's River how long did you remain in camp before you moved again?

We moved a short distance the next day; the second day the army marched all day in the direction of Crab Orchard; that was on the 14th of October.

Question. Do you know what stores or other property the rebels destroyed at Camp Dick Robinson or do you know if they destroyed anything at all?

I know nothing of it.

Question. When did you learn that the enemy did not make a stay at Camp Dick Robinson?

I think the day after was the first on which I believed they had not made a stand there, but I had no positive information about it at all.

Question. The day you marched to Dick's River did you see anything of them at all?

We saw a few pickets, who fired upon the right flank of our skirmishers; that was all.

By General TYLER:

Question. Did you know the location of Camp Dick Robinson, and what part of the camp did the bulk of Bragg's army occupy?

I never was at Camp Dick Robinson, and know nothing in regard to the position of Bragg's army.

Question. How near do you suppose you were to Camp Dick Robinson on the 11th?

Six or seven miles. Danville was the nearest place.

Question. Were you nearer Camp Dick Robinson on the 12th than you were on the 11th?

We were. I supposed at the time we were about 2 miles from there.

Question. When you supposed you were within 2 miles of Camp Dick Robinson what enemy's force did you find in your front?

I would state that between us and what we supposed was Camp Dick Robinson was Dick's River. We saw no enemy except the pickets that I have previously spoken of. We did not cross the river. There was no force of the enemy on the side of the river we were except the pickets I have mentioned.

Question. Did you at that time drive the enemy's pickets across Dick's River?

We did not attempt to; we paid no attention to their pickets.

Question. By driving in those pickets and advancing to the banks of Dick's River would you not probably have obtained valuable information as to the position of the enemy on the other side?

I do not think we could have obtained any more than we did. The banks of the river were precipitous and covered with woods.

Question. What military information as to the force and position of the enemy did you obtain that day?

I obtained none at all. My position was a subordinate one, and I knew nothing of the object of the reconnaissance nor obtained any information than that I have given.

Question. Who commanded the reconnaissance on that day?

I do not know that it was a reconnaissance nor the object of the movement. I would say that General Smith commanded the troops that I was with. There were other movements of the troops. I think the entire corps moved there.

Redirect examination by General BUELL:

Question. Do you recognize, colonel, that the movement of a fraction of a large army in the presence of an enemy does not indicate the movement of the army itself or the character of the movement or the extent of it?

I do.

Question. Is the position of an army of 60,000 men to be indicated by a point?

It is not. It usually extends over a line of from 3 to 10 or 12 miles.

Question. How much ground would an army of 60,000 men occupy in order of battle?

I would say, without making a calculation, that it would extend over from 4 to 5 miles.

Question. Do you know anything of the character of Dick's River and the ground between you and the position which the enemy were supposed to occupy opposite to you?

I never saw Dick's River, but from the character of the ravines leading into it and from the representations of the inhabitants I should believe it to be impracticable for troops to cross.

Question. Do you know under whose supervision the movements of that part of the army to which you belonged were on the 12th and 13th?

Under Major-General Crittenden's, directed by his assistant adjutant-general, Lyne Starling; he acted more as a guide than a director.

Question. Do you know whether General Thomas moved with that part of the army?

General Thomas moved with that part of the army nearly all the time. He gave his personal supervision to the movements of the troops. I do not know where General Thomas was on that particular day.

Question. Do you know whether the other corps of the army did not move on the 12th, that the whole army did not swing around upon its right, changing its front?

It was my impression that the whole army did move. I had no positive knowledge except of the corps to which I belonged.

Question. What division led your corps in the advance on the night of the 13th toward Crab Orchard?

I think the Fifth Division, commanded by General Van Cleve. I may, however, be mistaken in the date.

Question. Whatever division it may have been, do you know the hour at which it started?

I do not know what division. It may have been General Wood's, which started on the night of the 13th.

Recross-examination by General Tyler:

Question. You say it was impracticable for troops to cross Dick's River. Did not almost the entire of Bragg's army cross over Dick's River after the battle of Perryville?

It is probable they did.

Question. At what distance from Dick's River was the bulk of General Buell's army at the time they probably crossed?

Probably from 12 to 18 miles.

Question. If General Buell's army had made a vigorous forward movement could Bragg have passed his army over Dick's River under offensive operations on the part of General Buell?

I do not know; my opinion is that he could have passed the greater part of his army over.

Question. Do you entertain that opinion in the face of the expression you used that it was "impracticable" for troops to pass over Dick's River?

There is a difference in an army passing over and having nothing to impede its progress, and in an army crossing over having a powerful foe to impede its progress on the other side. I conceive very readily how an army could cross over any ravine in the world. I can conceive that the passage of such a ravine as that, with a strong army to contest its passage, might be made absolutely impossible. There is another fact in connection with this: the order of opposing troops in retreat may be very different to opposing troops in an attack in the face of an enemy; it would make it a great obstacle in one case and very slight in another.

By General Buell:

Question. Suppose a line like that of Dick's River, absolutely impregnable against assault except at one or two points, with high commanding bluffs on the side toward which the enemy is retreating, is there anything more simple and certain than the passage of an army in retreat in the face of almost any enemy, supposing him to get a certain initiative and supposing him to have time to establish batteries and move them into position?

I would consider it a very easy military problem and have always supposed it to be an easy matter.

By General TYLER:

Question. Has not the passage of rivers and obstacles such as Dick's River presented by an inferior army in the face of a superior always been considered one of the most difficult military problems?

General BUELL. I would suggest that Dick's River is not a river, though it has the name; it is a defile merely. It is not the water that makes it difficult.

The WITNESS. It depends vastly upon the amount of bridging to be done and the amount of preparations necessary. I should consider that a retreating foe crossing a ravine of that kind, where there was no bridging and nothing to do but move over as soon as it arrived, if they had time to plant their guns to cover the face of their crossing with artillery of sufficient strength I should consider the crossing was certain.

Capt. O. A. MACK (a witness for the defendant), being duly sworn by the judge-advocate, testified as follows:

By General BUELL:

Question. Captain, state your name and position in the service, if you please, and what position you occupied during the recent campaign in Kentucky starting from Louisville.

Capt. O. A. Mack, Thirteenth Infantry, attached to the staff of Major-General Thomas as inspector of artillery, and have served in that capacity in the campaign referred to to the present time.

Question. With what portion of the army did you move during the few days previous to the battle of Perryville and subsequently?

After the first day from Louisville I moved with Major-General Crittenden's corps.

Question. What was the position of that corps relatively in the advance upon Perryville?

After leaving Bardstown that corps was on the right; previous to that time it had been in the center.

Question. Did you visit General Buell's headquarters on the morning of the 8th of October, the day of the battle of Perryville? If so, please state at what hour you arrived there and with what object you came.

On the 8th of October I was sent by Major-General Thomas to take a message to General Buell, to inform him that two divisions of General Crittenden's corps were in position about 2½ miles from Perryville; that the Third Division was about 2 miles in the rear, still on the march. I left General Thomas about 12 o'clock, perhaps a little later. I did not know where General Buell's headquarters were, and I think it was about half past 1 when I reached there, although the distance was only about 3 miles. I delivered the verbal message to General Buell, and remained at his headquarters for some time.

Question. What time did you leave headquarters?

I think it was a little before 3 o'clock.

Question. Did you return with instructions to General Thomas? And, if so, please state what they were.

I took instructions to General Thomas. General Buell gave me a small map of the positions around Perryville, with the positions of the other two corps marked on this map in pencil, explaining to him their position; also indicating the general position which he wished General Crittenden's corps to occupy that night. The positions for General Crittenden's corps were: two divisions to be on the direct route to Perryville, a little to the right of the road; the Third Division, the division which I had reported in the rear, to take the right-hand road to Mitchellsville, and a brigade of cavalry to precede it. General Buell instructed me to say to General Thomas that he did not propose to attack that evening, but that if he could obtain water by advancing he might proceed cautiously to the front. That is the general purport of my instructions, which I communicated to General Thomas.

Question. When you were at General Buell's headquarters did you see or hear anything of a severe battle raging on the left of the army?

While I was going to General Buell's headquarters and while I remained there I heard heavy firing, and I supposed there was an action going on until I reached his headquarters, and was there informed that it was the cavalry under command of Captain Gay and the rebels, with artillery on both sides. I also met General Gilbert, and was told by him in answer to my question that that was the cause of the firing.

Question. At what time was this that the firing made this impression upon you?

I heard the artillery during most of the time that I was making the passage from General Thomas' headquarters to General Buell's, and also while at General Buell's. It was during my trip across the country that my impression was that an action was going on.

Question. Which you say was between 12 and 1 o'clock?

My impression is that I arrived at General Buell's headquarters at about half past 1.

Question. Did you hear any musketry firing while you were there?

No; I did not while I was at General Buell's headquarters.

Question. Or anywhere in that vicinity?

Previously to my starting for General Buell's headquarters I thought I distinguished a volley-fire of musketry on several occasions when the wind was blowing strong, but I do not know; I could not say positively that I did; that was my impression.

Question. At what hour was that?

I should say that was between 11 and 12 o'clock.

Question. When did you first hear that there had been severe fighting on the left?

I think the first intimation I received was about half past six o'clock in the evening; I should say it was after sundown. Lieutenant Fitzhugh came over with a verbal message to General Thomas. I recollect that we were on the way back to the place where we expected to encamp that night; it must have been fully as late as half past 6. I would also state that I did not understand that there had been any general engagement. It was still later, after I had gone to bed, that I heard of the death of General Jackson, and that there had been a general engagement by General McCook's troops.

Question. Have you a pretty clear understanding, from observation or otherwise, of the character of Dick's River for a distance of 12, 14, or 15 miles from its mouth?

I have no personal knowledge of it.

Question. Supposing it to be a stream almost dry, so as to not require bridging at all, with high cliffy banks, passable only at one or two points, and supposing yourself in command of an army desiring to retreat over such an obstacle, and that you have high bluffs on the side toward which you wish to retreat commanding the country on the opposite side, and that you have a certain time to get your artillery into position on the opposite side, would you think it a very delicate matter to effect your passage in the face of almost any force?

No; I should not think that the case supposed would be a very difficult operation, the artillery being placed in position to cover the passage of the troops.

Question. Would not the river, in fact, be a security to the retreating forces, instead of an embarrassment?

After the artillery was over I should think it would.

Cross-examination by the JUDGE-ADVOCATE:

Question. Was the firing that you heard during the day of the 8th of such a character as to indicate a cavalry reconnaissance and would you suppose it to be such if you had not been told so?

No, I should not; it was much heavier than was necessary, in my opinion, for a cavalry reconnaissance.

By General DANA:

Question. When you met General Gilbert on your way to the head-quarters of General Buell where was he and how was he occupied?

He was just riding out of the headquarters of General Buell.

Question. Did he state where he got his information of the firing of which he gave an account?

No, he did not; he simply told me that it was Captain Gay operating upon the rebels.

Question. Do you know whether he carried that information to General Buell's headquarters himself?

I do not.

By General TYLER:

Question. Who told you at General Buell's headquarters that it was the cavalry under Captain Gay, with artillery, that was engaged with the rebels?

Colonel Fry, I think. The conversation was in General Buell's tent.

Question. What opinion did you entertain when you arrived at head-quarters of the nature of the action going on?

Before I arrived at headquarters I had no knowledge of the remaining disposition of the corps. My impression was that it was a sharp action going on on the left.

Question. Supposing a river with high bluffs and little water, with only one or two practicable routes to pass it, had to be passed by a retreating army of, say, 40,000 men, with artillery, baggage, &c., with a superior army of, say, 50,000 men in their front, what would be the fate of the rear of the retreating army if it should be vigorously attacked?

I cannot tell.

Question. What chance do you think it would have of passing over passages such as those described and under the circumstances stated in the previous question?

There are so many circumstances entering into an operation of that kind one can hardly give an opinion on the supposed case; but I should say that, supposing the troops to be equal on both sides and the commanders equally able, the retreating force labored under a disadvantage; but if he effected the crossing of the stream at all he would be able to cover his rear by the batteries established on the opposite side.

Question. How long a line would a retreating army of 40,000 men occupy, supposing it was operating or retreating on two roads?

A great deal would depend on the character of the roads and the country. I should suppose that on ordinary turnpikes a column of 15,000 men, properly closed up, would not occupy more than 5 or 6 miles, with their trains; they ought not to.

Question. At what distance would these batteries established on the opposite side of the river cover these troops?

With the field batteries in general use now, from three-quarters to one mile; with rifled guns, still farther than that.

By General ORD:

Question. Do you remember whether there was much wind at the battle of Perryville when you rode over to General Buell's headquarters?

Yes, sir; the wind blew heavily, but not steadily; it blew in gusts.

Question. Was the wind blowing from such a quarter that you could hear the sound of the cannonading you spoke of better or worse when you arrived at General Buell's headquarters than when you started or while you were on the way?

While going to General Buell's headquarters I passed over considerable high land, and on those elevated positions I was sensible of the difference the wind made in the sound of the artillery. When I reached headquarters I do not recollect noticing anything about the wind there; the cannonading was more distinct than at General Thomas', being considerably nearer.

Question. Were your opportunities of judging of the nature of this cannonading while on the road better than they would have been at General Buell's headquarters?

I do not think they were. There was no firing in front of General Crittenden's corps, but all the firing I heard appeared considerably to the left.

Question. Did you mention your impression of the nature of this firing to Colonel Fry?

I do not recollect whether I did or not. I think I said to General Gilbert that I thought there was a battle going on.

By General SCHOEPF:

Question. Was not the signal corps in full operation on the day of the battle?

Not on General Crittenden's front. The communication was opened with General Gilbert's corps in the evening. I recollect that during the day some of the officers reported that a signal was discovered on a house far off to the left, and the impression was that it was one of the signal corps, but it was subsequently ascertained that it was not; and no communications were received until after we had gone back to camp. During the night of the 8th and 9th, after the communications were opened, they continued to operate.

Question. Did you see General McCook at General Buell's headquarters before you left?

I did not. I was told that General McCook had been there and had gone back to his corps.

By General BUELL:

Question. According to the history of that day, as it is now known, at what time did the battle begin on the left, and what was in fact the character of the engagement up to the time when you arrived at my headquarters?

My recollection of General McCook's report is that the heavy attack on his front did not commence until about 1 o'clock; but that the firing that I heard previous to my arrival at General Buell's headquarters was principally from the skirmishing and the artillery that was with the cavalry.

Capt. JOHN G. CHANDLER (a witness for the defendant), being duly sworn by the judge-advocate, testified as follows:

By General BUELL:

Question. State your name and position in the service, if you please, and the position you occupied in the Army of the Ohio last summer.

John G. Chandler, captain, quartermaster's department. I was on duty as chief quartermaster in the field of the Army of the Ohio from about July 26 till about 30th October. I was connected with the army before that in the early part of the season.

but was detached about three months. I reported at Louisville about the 15th of February, was with the army about a month, and was then detached from it and served on the Tennessee River.

Question. State, in a general way, if you please, the position of the army in the months of July and August last and the means by which it was supplied.

The army was located from Tuscumbia, Ala., along the railroad running from that point to Chattanooga—from Battle Creek near Chattanooga; then from Decatur to Nashville, on the Decatur and Nashville road; and from Battle Creek in the direction of the Nashville and Chattanooga road and along that road. From the time the army crossed the Tennessee River the supplies were drawn from Nashville; both roads were used in the transportation of supplies from Nashville.

Question. State, if you please, what means were used to supply the troops in the positions which they occupied and to get supplies forward to the point from which they would start to advance against Chattanooga, that being the object.

After the troops crossed the Tennessee River to march toward Chattanooga they were supplied from Louisville as the principal depot and Nashville as an intermediate depot, and from Nashville by two railroads, one the Nashville and Decatur and the other the Nashville and Chattanooga road. This was for about a month, for the Nashville and Decatur road was soon abandoned, as the troops concentrated toward Chattanooga, and then there was but one line of communication from Louisville to the depot nearest to the position of the troops, which was Stevenson. The line was about 350 miles. About fifteen days' supplies were kept on hand at Nashville, and about 100,000 half rations, barely two days' supplies, at Stevenson; and this by using every means of transportation that the railroads could furnish, and to do this cars were purchased by Government and put upon the roads. In this state of affairs the army was on nearly half rations from the middle of July till the army arrived in Louisville. The supplies were carried to the camps at Battle Creek by means of wagons, of which there was a very limited supply, as the bulk of the transportation of the army was employed in carrying supplies to points where the railroads had been previously cut; in other words, the wagons were on the railroad far above the army while it was in the vicinity of Battle Creek.

Question. Were these means used to the fullest extent to push forward supplies to the depot at Stevenson?

Yes, sir.

Question. Do you know what efforts were made by orders and dispatches to have supplies thrown into Nashville rapidly?

Generally I do. I know that I was kept pushed all the time to be more energetic, to see that others were more energetic, and to push everybody that I could in my position to hurry forward supplies; that was the cry, as it were. The military superintendent of the road was also at work day and night endeavoring to conduct the road so that the greatest amount of work could be got from it with the limited amount of rolling stock and its poor condition generally.

Question. Were the Cumberland and Green Rivers made use of as long as they were available to throw supplies into Nashville?

The Cumberland was, I am enabled to state. Green River was not used while I was attached to the army?

Question. In what condition did you find the country in regard to supplies; to what extent did you avail yourself of its resources?

Forage was procured in the country. There was none brought by the railroad. There was but a limited supply of forage up to the 20th of August, when the new crop of corn came in, when there was plenty of forage. As far as I was able to learn there was but very little forage in our advance toward Chattanooga after leaving Stevenson. There were no other supplies for the quartermaster's department in the country. There was a small supply of forage brought through from Nashville about the 1st of August, but no accumulated supply.

Question. What was the force at Huntsville during the time you were there?

I should say about 3,000 men at Huntsville and within a mile or two.

Question. Is the country about Huntsville productive?

Yes, sir.

Question. To what distance did you usually have to send for forage for the small force that was there?

From 1 to 18 miles, about.

Question. Do you know what the character of the country is on the other side of the river from Bridgeport to Chattanooga?

I never visited that country, but it has always been represented to me as a sterile mountainous, unproductive country, with bad roads and creeks, and sparsely settled,

Question. Could an army have found anything to subsist on in that region?

I should think not.

Question. With the railroads broken, as you have stated, and the limited supplies, is it your opinion that it would have been possible for the army to advance to Chattanooga prior to the movement of the rebel army toward Nashville?

The difficulties of supplying an army were so great when they were 40 or 50 miles away from that point that I think it would have been almost impossible to move successfully against Chattanooga and supply the troops.

Question. Do you know whether the Memphis and Charleston Railroad from Decatur to Corinth was made use of to any extent; and, if not, why it was not?

It was not made use of to any extent in transporting supplies. There were but few supplies to be drawn from that quarter. That is one reason why it was not more used. There might have been other reasons that I am not aware of.

Question. Do you know anything about the amount of rolling stock and motive-power on that point of the road?

There was but very little of either that was available for our army.

Question. Were you at my headquarters on the 8th of October last, near Perryville?

Yes, sir.

Question. Did you hear the firing of musketry during that day?

No, sir.

Question. Was it the supposition of any person about the headquarters that a severe battle was raging on the left?

No, sir.

Question. When did you first learn that there had been a severe fight there; at about what hour of the day?

About 4 o'clock in the afternoon of that day.

Question. And how did you learn it then?

I learned it by the arrival at the camp of the headquarters of three or four of General McCook's staff officers, very much disconcerted, who reported that they were hunting their general; that a severe fight had occurred, and that they had not seen their general for some time.

Cross-examination by the JUDGE-ADVOCATE:

Question. At the time you mention that the army was on half rations did it suffer?

No, sir; I should think not; they complained, however.

Question. Do they not complain at all times?

Very apt to complain of their rations; new troops particularly.

Question. There was sufficient in the country, with a little exertion, to take the place of what was lacking, was there not?

There was sufficient green corn and a few vegetables, with which they got along of other supplies for the men there was little or none.

Question. What did you suppose that firing indicated at Perryville on the 8th, when you heard it at headquarters?

I supposed that our cavalry or some part of our army had become engaged with the enemy.

Question. Was that the supposition at headquarters?

It must have been the impression, I should think.

Question. Do you recollect whether it was talked about at headquarters? If so, state what was said and what the speculations of the officers were.

It was talked about. For three or four days previous to this Perryville fight on the 8th our cavalry, in command of Captain Gay, had been engaged with the enemy, and on every occasion and different times of the day firing had been heard on our front, and when this firing on the 8th first commenced it was supposed and talked of as being Gay's cavalry having met some of the cavalry of the enemy up to about the middle of the day, when it was reported about the camp of the headquarters that the troops on our left had been ordered to move forward to some creek, and it was supposed by members of the staff at headquarters that in moving down there they had met some force of the enemy; that is, when this rapid firing occurred. I myself knew nothing of the orders given from headquarters. It was merely camp talk.

Question. On any day previous after leaving Bardstown, when you came up to the enemy's rear, had you heard from Captain Gay a continuous firing extending over seven or eight hours in one spot?

No, sir.

By General ORD:

Question. Did the heavy firing on the left last seven or eight hours in one spot?

No, sir; I think not.

Question. Do you remember whether there was a strong wind blowing on that day or not?

I don't remember.

By General TYLER:

Question. What were the means of transportation that you found with the quartermaster on taking charge at Huntsville?

When I joined the army the infantry regiments were supplied with 12 wagons each; cavalry regiments, about 25; artillery, 5 wagons to a company; division trains, an average of about 75 serviceable wagons. These division trains were concentrated on the Nashville and Decatur road, to transport provisions around the break in the road at Athens.

Question. Suppose that you had had to draw all your supplies from one base of operations, how far, over fair roads, would the transportation have enabled the army to remove from its base?

An army five days' march from its depot of supplies could be supplied with this amount of transportation.

Question. Were you to collect the supplies from the country about where the army was operating, would you not consider this transportation abundantly able to supply the army?

No, sir; that is, with the army moving

Question. Do you think that Middle Tennessee was competent in the month of October to supply from the country the army we had operating there ?

I think it could have supplied an army of our strength, particularly a friendly army, or an army not in a hostile country, where everything is concealed and information cannot be obtained as to where the supply is.

By General DANA :

Question. What time of day did General McCook come to General Buell's headquarters on the 8th of October ?

I cannot say, sir; I think it was between 12 and 1 o'clock.

Question. About how long did he remain there ?

I do not know, sir.

Question. Do you know whether firing was going on in the direction of his corps at the time he was there ?

I think not, sir.

Question. Do you know whether he made any report when he arrived at headquarters that day ?

I do not, sir.

Question. About what time did General McCook's aides come to General Buell's headquarters looking after him ?

I think it was after 4 o'clock.

Question. Do you know whether they found him ?

I do not know, sir; they did not know whether he was alive. They seemed to express great fears that he was not alive or that he had been taken prisoner. They were in a very great state of excitement themselves, and acted as though they were lost, and he and everybody else.

Question. Did General Gilbert come to headquarters on that day ; and, if so, at what time ?

I cannot say positively; I think he did in the afternoon.

By General SCHOEPF :

Question. You stated that you had fifteen days' rations at Nashville; were they full or half rations ?

Full rations. We had a million rations at Nashville.

Question. Was that about the time the army concentrated at Nashville ?

Previous to that. We were able to get that start of rations by means of the river; we could not have done it with the railroad ; but when the troops were put on half rations this supply sufficed.

By the JUDGE-ADVOCATE :

Question. At the time you say you had these rations at Nashville had you any at any other place ?

Stevenson was the sub-depot for the troops. The army drew from Stevenson. The depot at Stevenson was furnished from Nashville and that from Louisville.

Question. That was the only place besides Nashville at which you had any store on hand ?

We had some at Huntsville, but only for a few days. We drew partly from Stevenson. We brought down some on the Nashville and Decatur road, but Stevenson was for a good part of the time considered an immediate depot.

Question. When you fell back did you bring those supplies with you ?

There were some supplies destroyed at Huntsville or left there, but I do not know for a certainty. I was not there at the time.

Question. You do not know what amount was brought back?

No, sir.

By General SCHOEPF

Question. Have you any knowledge of the fact that General Gilbert had a perfect line of communication from his headquarters to the front by means of his signal corps on the day of the battle of Perryville?

I do not know. The signal corps were operating from our headquarters to some station in front, but I do not know whose station it was. I saw our own flag and that flag communicate; that is all I know of the circumstance.

The Commission adjourned to meet on December 27, 1862, at 10 o'clock a. m.

NASHVILLE, *December* 27, 1862.

Commission met pursuant to adjournment. All the members present, also the judge-advocate and General Buell.

Capt. GEORGE S. ROPER (a witness for the Government), being duly sworn by the judge-advocate, testified as follows:

By the JUDGE-ADVOCATE:

Question. State your name and position in the United States service.

George S. Roper, captain, subsistence department.

Question. State, if you please, what took place in General Gilbert's command from 3 to 5 o'clock on the 8th of October, the day of the battle of Perryville.

General Gilbert's command, consisting of General Sheridan's, General Mitchell's, and General Schoepf's divisions, were in line of battle, the two first in the advance, General Schoepf in the rear, General Sheridan and General Mitchell being about 2 miles from the town of Perryville. That was the position they occupied from early in the morning of the battle. My impression was that the battle was on the 6th. It was after 4 o'clock before any of those troops were engaged. General Sheridan was attacked first, and was supported by two brigades of General Mitchell's command on his right. General Gilbert was in the rear of these two divisions in plain sight. At the time that the enemy attacked General Sheridan's command we were in plain view of the battle so far as our own troops were concerned. The enemy could not be seen from our position. After some twenty or thirty minutes of firing General Gilbert noticed through his glass a movement of the troops on the opposite hill which he did not appear to understand. Turning to me (I was the only staff officer present) he said, "What does that mean; what are they doing over there; can you see?" I answered that they appeared to be changing front. He said he did not understand the movement, and looking around him said, "Who can I send?" I volunteered to go, no orderly being at hand. He ordered me to go. I went to General Sheridan, and, with the respects of General Gilbert, asked the state of the case and the meaning of the present movement. General Sheridan's answer was that he had driven the enemy from before him, and "whipped them like hell!" was added; that General Mitchell had flanked them on the left and was then pursuing them toward Perryville; and that he was changing front to assist General McCook, and was going to open on that battery, pointing to a battery of the enemy which was firing upon General McCook's troops, and that he would silence it in five minutes. He fired the first gun at the battery while I was talking to him.

I returned immediately to General Gilbert with the report of General Sheridan, and he appeared very much gratified at the time, and used the expression, "Now we've got them; now we've got them; now is the time to push everything." Major Wright, of General Buell's staff, arrived then at the position where General Gilbert was stationed almost at the same time, and General Gilbert repeated the message that he had received from General Sheridan and directed him to report to General Buell, with the injunction to push everything. He also sent by a citizen who was employed in the commissary department of General Crittenden's command, Captain Kniffin's clerk, whose name I think is Harry Olds—he sent by him the same report to General Crittenden, with the request that he would hurry up his command.

Question. What did Major Wright say in reply to that, and do you know if he carried that message?

I cannot recall any reply, and I do not know if he carried the message.

Question. Were you at General Buell's headquarters·that morning? If so, state what occurred.

I think we were there twice during the morning of the day of the battle.

Question. What do you mean by "we"?

General Gilbert and his staff.

Question. What occurred while you were there?

I do not remember anything occurring in the morning, except Captain Michler and Captain Gilman returning from the front, and the report they made of having run on to a body of the enemy and having drawn their fire.

Question. Was that at your first visit?

Yes, sir.

Question. What occurred the second time when you were there?

The second time that we went back to General Buell's headquarters I think it must have been very nearly 12 o'clock. We remained there a considerable time. I should think we were there nearly two hours. It was while we were there at that time that we heard a heavy and furious cannonading commenced in front. General Buell and General Gilbert, when that heavy cannonading commenced, came from the tents, and General Buell remarked to General Gilbert that there was a great waste of powder there, and directed him to send an order to the front to stop that useless waste of powder. "Stop that firing," that was his expression. General Gilbert called his adjutant-general, Captain Stacy, who wrote a pencil order, which was sent to the front, I supposed in accordance with General Buell's orders to him. It was sent to the front by an orderly while we were there. I think at that time General Gilbert expressed a wish to go forward and General Buell asked him to remain to dinner, which was nearly ready. He did remain and dined with General Buell, but left almost immediately afterward for his command.

Question. State what you know of the signal corps being at work that day.

I noticed a flag station on the hill opposite General Buell's headquarters; there was another on the hill to the right, where General Gilbert was stationed, which was on the right of the pike that runs from Perryville. I saw another station away to the left of our position and in the rear of where Captain Gay had been figuring all the morning with his command, just on the edge of the wood, on the right of General McCook's position.

Question. How often were you at General Buell's headquarters that day?

My impression now is that we were there four times.

Question. State, if you can, at what other times during the day you were there besides those you have mentioned.

We were there later in the evening twice after those I have referred to; probably it might have been 8 or 9 o'clock in the evening; it was some time after dark.

Question. What officers besides General Gilbert did you see there?

I did not see any general officer there that I remember.

Question. Do you recollect seeing General McCook that day?

No, sir; I did not.

Question. What was the command at headquarters about that firing while you were there?

I do not remember anything further than that I have already stated.

Question. Where were the headquarters situated?

Facing the battle-field. They were on the left hand of the pike, I should think from 3½ to 4 miles from Perryville.

Question. Can you state whether General Buell was there all day?

No, sir; General Buell was at his quarters every time we were there.

Question. Were you in the service in Tennessee?

Yes, sir.

Question. State what you know of the supplies, character and quantity, obtained by the army from the country.

During the time that we were making the retrograde movement from Stevenson I was left at Decherd a few days by General Thomas (I was then with General Thomas). General Thomas went from there to McMinnville. I was not immediately connected with them, and did not handle any supplies during that time. I joined General Thomas again at this place.

By General DANA:

Question. What time of the day was it that General Gilbert sent a message by Major Wright to General Buell?

I think it must have been as late as 5 or half past 5 o'clock in the afternoon.

By General SCHOEPF:

Question. At what date did the army leave Louisville?

I believe it was the 1st day of October.

Question. Are you not certain with regard to the date on which the battle was fought at Perryville?

No, sir; I am not. It has always been my impression that it was fought on the 6th.

By General DANA:

Question. What time of the day was it that General Gilbert sent you with a message to General Sheridan?

It was as late as half past 4 o'clock.

General BUELL. I have no questions to ask the witness, but I desire to express my gratification at his evidence. It is manly and direct, and goes to show, to some extent, that General Gilbert, who in my opinion has been very much scandalized before this Commission, was not altogether negligent and out of place at the battle of Perryville. I have no particular interest in General Gilbert at all. I assigned him to a command because I thought his rank entitled him to it, because I believed he was at the time a major-general, and when the contrary became certainly known I removed him from that command. It was not done immediately, because the movement of the troops made it very inconvenient for the service, if not absolutely impracticable.

The Commission adjourned to meet December 28, 1862, at 10 a. m.

NASHVILLE, *December* 28, 1862.

Commission met pursuant to adjournment. All the members present; also the judge-advocate and General Buell.

Lieut. CHARLES ALLEN (a witness for the Government), being duly sworn by the judge-advocate, testified as follows:

By the JUDGE-ADVOCATE:

Question. Please to state your name and position in the United States service.

Charles Allen; first lieutenant, Third Ohio Vols., acting commissary subsistence.

Question. Examine this abstract of provision returns and state whether they are correct or not.

The one signed by myself is correct, and the recapitulation, including the one signed by Captain Little, is correct.

Question. State to the Commission whether that exhibits all the stores then in Nashville.

It shows on hand 31st August 51 barrels 185 pounds 12 ounces pork, 23,605 pounds 12 ounces bacon, 1,086 pounds 8 ounces of ham.

Question. You can state whether this includes the provisions collected from about the country here at that time.

My own statement includes what was actually in my hands at the dates mentioned, and Captain Little's statement purports to do the same with regard to what was in his hands, and the recapitulation includes both.

Question. What I want to know is whether that includes any part of the provisions gathered up about the country?

No provisions gathered up about the country came into my hands directly. Those foraging parties returned nothing into my hands directly.

General BUELL. Make a calculation from these returns, if you please, and state how many rations of meat and bread were on hand on the 31st of August.

(Lieutenant Allen is directed by the Commission to prepare these calculations from the provision returns and furnish them to the Commission).

By General BUELL:

Question. At what time did General Buell's army come to Nashville from Murfreesborough?

I do not recollect, sir.

By the PRESIDENT:

Question. When that army arrived do you remember whether rations were issued to it or not?

I issued rations to a portion of it myself.

Question. Have you anything to show how much you issued?

Yes, sir; I have an abstract of issues to the troops. It mentions the dates for which they drew rations and shows the regiments they were issued to.

Question. The several divisions of General Buell's army there had supply trains, had they not?

They usually had them, but I cannot answer positively with regard to that.

Question. I want to know whether rations were delivered to be taken with the army besides those that were actually issued to the several commands?

I issued provisions to General Thomas' division for the purpose of moving.

Question. Have you the papers to show the issues?

I issued on one Sunday to, I think, twelve regiments or more.

Question. I would like you to bring up the papers to show what you issued to the several commands in General Buell's army.

I only issued on provision returns, not in bulk.

Question. Who issued in bulk?

Capt. S. J. Little. Capt. R. Macfeely is the chief of the subsistence department, and he is the proper person to furnish the returns the Commission requires.

The Commission adjourned to meet at Louisville, January 3, 1863, or as soon thereafter as practicable.

LOUISVILLE, *January* 10, 1863.

Commission met pursuant to adjournment. All the members present; also the judge-advocate and General Buell.

Examination of Lieut. CHARLES ALLEN continued.

By the JUDGE-ADVOCATE:

Question. When you were being examined before, in Nashville, the returns showing the stores in Nashville at a certain time were given you to make out the quantity of rations; have you done so?

Here are the papers given me, and a statement of the number of rations.

The JUDGE-ADVOCATE. I move that these returns be accepted by the Commission.

(Lieutenant Allen's estimate of rations was delivered to the Commission.)

Cross-examination by General BUELL:

Question. Explain, if you please, how it happened that you and Captain Little had separate store-houses in Nashville.

I was assigned to duty for the purpose of issuing on provision returns in the city, and had a store-house for that purpose. Captain Little received all stores at the depot, as depot commissary, for which purpose he had several store-houses.

Question. Did all provisions that came into the city pass first through the hands of Captain Little as depot commissary?

Yes, sir; I believe all did.

Question. Your statement shows some accumulation of certain articles of provisions during the month of September. Are you able to explain this accumulation and show what quantities were procured in the country or city?

With one exception all the stores received by me during the month of September came through the hands of Captain Little. I cannot explain how he received additions or what they were during that time.

Question. Do you know the number of rations required in Nashville per day to supply the army at the date, say, of the 30th of August, or prior to that date?

No, sir; I do not.

Question. Are you able to state whether supplies were collected from the country?

During September, October, and the early part of November large foraging parties went out from Nashville for the purpose of collecting provisions; they usually brought in as much as they could carry. They were not regular subsistence stores, except bacon, flour, and wheat.

Redirect examination by General TYLER:

Question. Do you know how many days' rations were taken by General Buell's army when they marched to Bowling Green?

I do not of my own knowledge; only from hearsay.

Question. Who issued the commissary stores at that time?

They were issued in bulk by Captain Little.

By General DANA:

Question. There are issues on returns to citizens; what citizens were they made to?

The issues on the provision returns referred to are to citizens employed by the quartermaster's department and the subsistence department, or any department in the army which employs citizens and draws rations for either.

Question. Do you know whether any issues were made to citizens by Captain Little?

I do not, positively. It is not a part of his duty to make issues to citizens at Nashville.

Question. Do you know of any expenditure of subsistence stores for the aid or benefit of any citizens who were not employed by the United States, or contrabands who were under the protection of the United States?

Yes, sir. Issues were made to contrabands employed in the department and at work on the fortifications at Nashville.

Question. Were any sales of provisions made by any officers of the Government to any persons except to officers, to your knowledge?

No, sir; not to my knowledge.

Question. During the time that the Cumberland River was navigable was it possible to have amassed more subsistence on hand at Nashville than was actually amassed at that time?

In my opinion it would have been possible to have amassed more stores.

Question. Do you know of any instance of wastage of provisions by carelessness or exposure or from any other reason?

I do not.

Recross-examination by General BUELL:

Question. In expressing the opinion that it was possible to accumulate more stores at Nashville, does your mind recur to any case of neglect to make the best use of that means of accumulating supplies?

No, sir; it does not.

Question. Do you know whether orders were given for using all possible means, both by railroad and rivers (Cumberland and Green Rivers), to accumulate stores rapidly in Nashville?

I understand that such orders were given.

Question. Please read from your statement the number of rations on hand at the dates for which they were made.

Rations on hand August 31, 1862.

Rations of pork	13,981
Rations of bacon	31,474¼
Rations of salt beef	19,360
Rations of fresh beef (including 25 head beef cattle, estimated 800 pounds each net)	21,622⅕
Total number of rations of meat	86,437 $\frac{8}{15}$
Rations of flour	190,355½⅖
Rations of hard bread	332,797
Rations of corn meal	4,054
Total number of bread rations	527,786½⅖

Rations of beans... 132,080
Rations of pease... 22,111
Rations of rice.. 137,029
Total number of rations of beans and mixed vegetables...... 1,217,888

Rations of coffee.. 41,952$\frac{56}{100}$
Rations of tea... 56,354

Total number of rations of tea and coffee................. 98,306$\frac{56}{100}$

Rations of sugar (brown).................................. 106,039
Rations of vinegar.. 30,750
Rations of adamantine candles............................. 1,199,275
Rations of soap... 326,111
Rations of salt... 1,847,132
Rations of molasses....................................... 223,144
Rations of mixed vegetables............................... 1,085,808
Rations of onions... 6,666$\frac{2}{3}$
Total number of rations of pease, rice, and onions........ 165,806$\frac{3}{4}$
Articles kept on hand for sale to officers, and for extra and special issues
  to hospitals and troops:
    White sugar (pounds)................................. 5,734
    Whisky (gallons).................................... 1,414$\frac{1}{2}$
    Ham (pounds) .... 1,086$\frac{1}{2}$

Rations on hand September 30, 1862.

Rations of pork... 10,358$\frac{1}{2}$
Rations of bacon.. 2,258$\frac{3}{4}$
Rations of fresh beef..................................... 11,220

Total number of rations of meat........................... 23,837

Rations of flour.. 354,573$\frac{8}{11}$
Rations of hard bread..................................... 463,150
Rations of corn-meal...................................... 9,073

Total number of bread rations............................. 826,796$\frac{8}{11}$

Rations of beans.. 45,311
Rations of pease.. 12,800
Rations of rice... 73,980
Total number of rations of beans and mixed vegetables..... 1,245,144

Rations of coffee (green)................................. 2,630
Rations of coffee (roasted)............................... 33,026
Rations of tea.. 13,500

Total number of tea and coffee rations.................... 49,156

Rations of brown sugar.................................... 33,001
Rations of vinegar.. 114,900

Rations of adamantine candles............................. 7,073$\frac{1}{12}$
Rations of tallow candles................................. 14,777$\frac{5}{8}$

Total number of rations of candles........................ 21,851$\frac{47}{60}$

Rations of soap... None.
Rations of salt... 33,207
Rations of molasses....................................... 73,100
Rations of mixed vegetables............................... 1,169,833
Rations of onions... 933
Total number of rations of pease, rice, and onions........ 87,713
Articles kept on hand for sale to officers, and for extra and special
  issues to hospitals and troops:
    White sugar (pounds)................................ 4,952$\frac{1}{2}$
    Whisky (gallons) 804

Not included in the bread rations: 199 bushels of wheat.

F. A. SMITH (a witness for the Government), being duly sworn by the judge-advocate, testified as follows:

By the JUDGE-ADVOCATE:

Question. State your name and residence.

My name is F. A. Smith; residence, Munfordville, Ky.

Question. State if you were there at the time of the surrender by Colonel Wilder. If so, what was the number of General Bragg's army?

I was in the vicinity. The surrender, I believe, was at night. I was in town next morning about 9 or 10 o'clock. The number of men I do not know only from some officers on General Bragg's staff; they told me they had sixty regiments. I traveled over the encampment a great deal, and from the best estimate I could make in seeing the regiments, having counted many before, I estimated them as averaging from 200 to 700. My estimate was about 400 on the average for each regiment. I came in on the turnpike road; traveled with one regiment of cavalry and met another, which was said to be under command of General Forrest and some other general whose name I do not know. I did not estimate them at more than 800 each. In all the interviews I had with General Bragg I never heard him say what his force was. This statement of their having sixty regiments of men was made to me by Colonel Shultz, of New Orleans.

Question. You can state how your own estimate tallied with the statements of officers on General Bragg's staff.

No one told me how many men they had. I learned that they had sixty regiments. I heard Bragg say himself that they had seventy-two pieces of artillery.

Question. State what you know of Breckinridge's force at that time and where it was.

I know nothing of it whatever only from what General Bragg stated. He stated that Breckinridge was in the rear of General Buell with about 40,000, in his pursuit.

Question. Give the conversation, as you recollect it, between General Bragg and yourself.

I asked General Bragg if he was not placing himself in rather a precarious situation, between two great armies, or was it not a very ugly position to be in. He said it was, and that was just the condition of General Buell, being between his own army and General Breckinridge's, and the only way that General Buell would ever get to Louisville would be to turn off to the left and cross the river and come up on the Indiana side. He also stated that General Buell was a very smart man and knew it himself, and never would attempt to get to Louisville in any other way.

Question. Did you have any communications with General Buell on this subject; if so, what passed between you?

I did, sir. I called to see General Buell at Woodsonville, at night—the same night of the skirmishing of Bragg's rear guard and the approach of General Buell's army at Green River. I told him my purpose in calling to see him was to give him all the information I could in regard to Bragg's movements, for which General Buell thanked me very kindly. I told General Buell everything I knew that would result with interest to the Federal army. I gave General Buell my views in regard to the course, route, and destination of General Bragg's army. My views were made up on that subject from being called on frequently by Bragg's engineers to give them information as to routes and watering places. I told General Buell I thought there would be no doubt that the destination of General Bragg would be Bardstown and that his route would be by way of Hodgensville. I gave him the number of General Bragg's forces about as I have here.

Question. State what comment General Buell made when you informed him of the number of General Bragg's army.

General Buell, in all my information to him, seemed to be very quiet and calm; he listened very attentively and with interest to all I had to say; made little comment on anything. General Buell asked me many questions in regard to the route, water-courses, &c., and showed me his maps. We both looked over them. His maps were good—brought many roads to my mind which I had forgotten. General Buell at that time seemed to be anxious to get couriers to go to Louisville.

Question. Were you present at Munfordville at the time Colonel Wilder repulsed the rebels ? If so, state what the nature of that contest was, and, if you know, the loss of the rebels.

I was in hearing of the guns, perhaps a mile and a half off; was in the fortifications in the evening. The fight was commenced at 5 and ceased at 8 in the morning. The loss was variously estimated. A great many who were on the field directly after the fight told me there were a great many dead upon the field. The rebels estimated their loss to be in killed about 150. The citizens estimated the killed to be 400 to 500. Colonel Wilder estimated the killed to be about 350, making the killed and wounded about 700. The estimate made of the force by the rebels themselves was three regiments of infantry, while they had about two regiments of cavalry. I met one regiment of cavalry myself, but did not take time to count them. The fight was certainly very severe; seemed to be an incessant roar of musketry and cannon during the entire three hours. The citizens who saw the fight witnessed it from the cupola, from which they had a fair view of the whole ground. They say the rebels made three charges, and charged at one time within 30 feet of the breastworks. The rebels, it was said, retreated under a flag of truce. The officers in the fort said they acted very manly with the exception of that. I was with Colonel Wilder frequently before the fight. I never saw a man who was more diligent and worked harder to prepare for the contemplated attack. It is my opinion the fort was very well defended.

Cross-examination by General Buell :

Question. What was the strength of the force that attacked Munfordville estimated to be ?

I do not know.

Question. What was it estimated to be by the citizens who witnessed it or had knowledge of it ?

All the citizens that I heard speak of it lived on this side of the river, and what they saw was at a distance; and if they told me I do not remember what the number of regiments was estimated to be.

Question. Was the attack characterized by great determination and gallantry on the part of the rebel troops ?

From all I learned I thought it was. General Bragg, however, condemned it; he said, in effect, the attack was not authorized.

Question. Did his disapprobation extend to the conduct of his troops or to the judgment of the commander ?

The remark of General Bragg was that he thought the attack was very unwise on the part of the general who commanded; he remarked that the attack was unauthorized.

Question. How soon after the surrender did General Bragg commence to move his army across the river and put it in march for its destination, whatever that might be ?

The surrender was made, as I learned, at night, and the army commenced to cross next day. General Bragg moved his headquarters over in the evening.

Question. When did the army actually march from Munfordville ?

They commenced leaving in the morning, the day before the approach of General Buell's army, and were all gone by 3 o'clock. I walked to the depot myself and was upon the field when they were moving and saw a large number of the troops going off. I staid for an hour or two looking at them and talked with many of them, and when the army seemed to be entirely gone I noticed about 20 officers going off in the rear; they were all said to be generals. Among them I saw General Bragg and his staff and General Buckner, whom I knew. Many troops moved a day or two before. Every day there were troops going out, but my information was that they returned until that day, when they all moved off. General Bragg and his staff reported that they were going the day before they did go. Their headquarters were at my house and they packed up their things to go the day before, but something turned up which prevented their going until their final departure. It was frequently reported that in all probability they would have a fight there, as General Buell's army was very close—

rapidly approaching them. To screen my family from danger I asked General Bragg to let me know if there would be a general fight. On one or two occasions he sa_ there would not, that General Buell was not coming that way.

Question. Did General Bragg appear anxious to avoid a fight at th_ place ?

I thought that his movements indicated some trouble upon his mind; he was qui_ restless.

Question. Your estimate of the strength of the regiments was base_ upon your own observation, was it not ?

Yes, sir. I did not count any of the regiments, but having counted many of ou_ own regiments enabled me to form an estimate of what theirs was. I could not pr_ tend to say that I saw all of them coming into town, but I saw a great many; I al_ saw some of them drilling. I made the remark to one of the most prominent souther_ rights brethren in the place that I estimated his force to be about 24,000. He to_ me that I had overestimated it; that it was about 22,000.

Question. Was this estimate of yours based upon the informatio_ you have stated in the course of your testimony ?

My estimate was based upon what I saw and upon what I heard.

Question. Do you know anything of the organization of Gener_ Bragg's army ?

I heard a great deal, but know nothing positively. The discipline of the arm_ seemed to be very fine—great diligence; there seemed to be no idle officers at al_ they all seemed to be very busily engaged. They all demeaned themselves very we_ and the order seemed to be very strict.

Question. Did they have many wagons ?

I do not think they had for the number of men; nothing to compare to the numb_ we used in our regiments. Their wagons were of a character that would not attra_ attention like ours, all being small, light two-horse wagons, though frequently draw_ by four or six mules. Some were with covers; others with none, or mere sheets throw_ over them.

Question. Was this Colonel Shultz an officer of General Bragg's staf_

He was represented as such. He came to me with some major to procure hea_ quarters for General Bragg, saying he was on General Bragg's staff, and he was the_ with him all the while and seemed to superintend everything. I think his name w_ Shultz, but I may be mistaken. He told me he was from New Orleans and had be_ a cotton-broker. He must have lived there or he could not have answered ma_ questions I put to him.

Question. Were the circumstances of your communication with ea_ other such as to impose upon Colonel Shultz the obligation to state you accurately the force under General Bragg, or to give you the rig_ to expect he had stated it accurately ?

I would suppose that none in the army would hold themselves under any obligati_ to tell me anything correctly, they all knowing I was a Union man and again_ them. Those who did not ask me my politics I told, lest they might be mistake_ I asked Colonel Shultz directly what was the strength of General Bragg's army. _ told me sixty regiments. I did not press the question further. General Bragg to_ me that he would not consider it more than a breakfast spell to take General Buel_ army, if he would attack him, and that his army could eat Buell's up alive.

Question. Is there a good turnpike road leading from Glasgow Bardstown, crossing Green River east of Munfordville ?

There is a turnpike road running from Glasgow to Bardstown, and thence on_ Louisville, crossing Green River 10 miles above Munfordville.

Question. Is, then, the position at Munfordville any obstacle to t_ advance of an army from Glasgow in the direction of Louisville ?

I regard the position at Munfordville as being a natural fortification and a ve_ strong position, yet it is very much out of the way to go to Bardstown from Glasgo_

Redirect examination by General TYLER:

Question. How much nearer can you get from Glasgow to Bardstown by a good, practicable road, suitable for artillery, than by the way of Munfordville?

The turnpike road I would suppose to be nearer. It is about 20 miles from Glasgow to Munfordville, and from Munfordville to Bardstown about 50 miles by the way of Hodgensville. It is 108 miles from Louisville to Glasgow by the turnpike road.

Question. What distance is Munfordville from where the road from Glasgow to New Haven crosses Green River?

It is about 10 miles below it.

Question. Was General Bragg's army well supplied with provisions when at Munfordville?

Mr. Wintersmith, an old school-mate of mine, who was the general commissary, came to me to know if I had some bacon to sell. I told him I had some, but I thought his money would not suit me; and besides I desired to keep it for my neighbors, and if he possibly could I hoped he would excuse me. He said he would do so; that he had provisions there plenty to last him till he got to Hardin County; there he had 150,000 pounds of bacon already engaged. They made many inquiries of me for flour, and seemed to be in want of breadstuffs, and sent wagons out. Their men complained very much of hunger. Many of them told me they had not eaten a mouthful for three days.

Question. On what principle was Bragg's army supplied with provisions at that point?

I do not know, sir, only from what they asked me as to where they could get flour. I had bought some flour from William Carter, 10 miles above, and Bragg's army sent up and got it.

Question. Did or did not Bragg's army rely upon the country through which they passed for their provisions?

I think they did, sir; I do not know positively of my own knowledge.

Question. Have you any reason to suppose General Bragg did not start with a certain supply of provisions from Chattanooga sufficient to carry him into the productive regions of Tennessee and Kentucky?

I do not know, nor do I know anything of the country, never having been over that portion of Tennessee.

Capt. P. P. OLDERSHAW (a witness for the defendant), being duly sworn by the judge-advocate, testified as follows:

By General BUELL:

Question. Captain, state your name and position in the service, if you please; if you were present at the battle of Perryville, and the position you occupied there.

My name is Percival P. Oldershaw. My position is assistant adjutant-general. I was present at the battle of Perryville as assistant adjutant-general to Brig. Gen. James S. Jackson, commander of the Tenth Division of the First Corps of the Army of the Ohio, commanded by Maj. Gen. A. McDowell McCook.

Question. What was the position of General Jackson in the army at that time?

He was commanding the Tenth Division of the Army of the Ohio.

Question. From what point did you march on the morning of the 8th of October last, and at what hour did you march?

We started early in the morning, at a point distant about 2 miles from Mackville (it is about 9 miles farther from Perryville than Mackville), and arrived at Mackville about 7 a. m. Here we were detained by the delay of one of General Rousseau's brigades, which was receiving commissary stores, and did not leave there till 8 that morning or a little after, General Rousseau having the advance.

Question. State, if you please, the order in which your corps marched on that day and the hour at which your division arrived at the battle ground.

The division, I think the Third, under General Rousseau, had the advance; our division, the Tenth, followed. There were but two divisions in General McCook's command that day. I suppose that it was about midday or later when a body of our division arrived at Chaplin Hills.

Question. Did the whole of General Rousseau's division march in the advance?

No, sir. Colonel Starkweather's brigade having been delayed, as I understood, drawing supplies, General Jackson waited for him till 8 in the morning or later; finding him not coming up, General Jackson moved his division up, and as we approached the battle-field Colonel Starkweather, commanding the brigade, was in our rear.

Question. Did you hear the firing of artillery as you approached the battle-field?

I did, sir; at intervals.

Question. At what hour did the battle begin that day? I mean by that the severe engagement between General McCook's command and the enemy.

I think it was about 1 or a little later—probably half past 1—when we saw the rebel infantry line. I myself was in the front, near to General Jackson, and when we first saw them they were not more than 90 yards from us, in the woods. Previous to seeing them we were firing at long range from two batteries without seeing any enemy, and it was a great surprise to General Jackson and myself, as expressed by General Jackson, that the enemy was near to us. We had time to turn the cannons around a little and fire a few rounds of grape at this short range of not more than 90 yards. Almost in returning the first round of grape General Jackson fell by a bullet.

Question. Was the corps formed in line of battle at this time and prepared for the attack?

A portion of our division was not. I cannot answer for General Rousseau's.

Question. What precautions had been taken to guard against this surprise as you approached the enemy?

I know of none, sir, except from what I heard from Captain Wickliffe, of a Kentucky cavalry regiment, who told me he had a short skirmish in the woods, the same woods we first saw the enemy coming through when our division caught up with the rear of General Rousseau's, which was about half past 11, I presume. Most of General Rousseau's infantry were in the road, with their arms stacked, preventing our farther progress. General Jackson and myself then rode up to what appeared to be headquarters. It was a devastated house, destroyed by the rebels previously. Here we were all discussing matters, not touching upon a general engagement that day, and looking on at the artillery duel going on between General Rousseau and the enemy at long range, the enemy not being in sight.

Question. Was there anything indicating that a general battle was imminent at that time?

Nothing that I saw. General Jackson certainly was not looking for a general engagement. The only thing in the day's proceedings that indicated a probable fight was a stopping of the wagons at Mackville and sending them to Springfield, instead of following the army.

Question. How long after your arrival was it before the corps was formed in order of battle?

It was about an hour and a half. We staid some time at this temporary head quarters. Afterward, I went down the road to bring up the last brigade, which occu pied considerable time, and this last brigade was never in any perfect line of battle during that fight.

Cross-examination by General DANA:

Question. Who formed your line of battle that day; who marked it out?

General McCook's adjutant, Captain Campbell, met General Jackson and myself while on the road, and said he was ordered by General McCook to show us our position. He showed us our position for two brigades—the one was on one side of the road and the other on the other—not putting us in any line of battle, but ordering us to rest. After getting to this point, and during my absence to bring up the last brigade, the brigade that had been put at rest on the right of the road was moved forward to the left of the road and its battery opened. Who formed that line I do not know. The line of the other brigade was not perfect. The ground was very rolling, and General Jackson was killed before it all got up.

Question. Did you see General McCook on that morning?

I did, sir.

Question. About what time?

I saw him on the hill on which Parsons' battery was established. He was then looking on and admiring some artillery practice to our left by Starkweather's battery, up a large open ravine, that was firing on some cavalry. It was there I first saw General McCook that day. He ordered Parsons' battery to be placed on this hill, which was done; but I am not aware of his giving other orders concerning the position of the infantry.

Question. Were you present at an interview between General McCook, General Jackson, and General Terrill on that morning?

I was, sir.

Question. Did you hear any instructions given to those two generals by General McCook?

The instructions given were not in any special interview between these generals, but in the presence of some 15 or 20 officers. I remember distinctly the orders being given for the battery to be brought up, and I also remember General Jackson sending Captain Starling and one of his aides to bring up the infantry, but I remember no order from General McCook.

Question. Did General McCook point out or indicate the line of battle to these generals?

Not to my knowledge, sir. During my absence down the road Harris' battery was placed on the right of our line, and between that battery and Parsons' the line was formed, consisting of two brigades, but by whose orders I do not know.

Question. Did General Jackson or General Terrill, or either of them, state to General McCook that they understood the positions they were to occupy and the direction of the line of battle?

I cannot say, sir.

Question. Did General McCook leave the ground only that time that you know of?

He left almost immediately after I heard him give the instructions for the placing of his battery, with his staff.

Question. Did you hear him make any remarks that would indicate where he was going and for what purpose?

None that I remember now.

Question. Do you know whether General McCook sent any message to headquarters, during the time the engagement was going on, notifying General Buell of the condition of things on the left?

I do not, sir.

Question. Do you know of any reason why General McCook should not have sent any message with that information?

I do not, sir.

Question. Did you at the time or have you since acquired any information going to show that General McCook had any special purpose in fighting this action on his own account?

I have not, sir.

By General TYLER:

Question. Was Jackson's division ever in line of battle on that day?

Not in perfect order, sir. The ground was very broken, as stated before, and there was one regiment that had not got up when the rebel infantry advanced.

Question. What was the loss of that division?

I made a report of the loss. I think our total was 5,600, and our loss was over 20 per cent., making about 1,200 men in killed and missing.

Question. What influence did General Jackson's death have on the division; did it break immediately after or keep on fighting?

I do not think his death had any influence on the troops. The troops were all new to him at the time. He was killed early in the engagement, almost the first shot, and was not in a position to be seen by his troops, standing as he was at the moment on the left of the battery. The troops near him were lying on their bellies.

Question. Did this division participate in the change of position that General McCook made in the night by his whole *corps d'armée?*

I cannot say, sir. At night, when the battle was over, I went to the rear, some three-quarters of a mile or more, to find Brigadier-General Terrill, who was reported to be dangerously wounded. I found him so, scarcely able to breathe, and near his quarters I laid down that night and slept. The next day, not finding our army where it was when I left it at night, and not finding any rebel army on the ground we were fighting over, I proceeded with some orderlies to secure the body of General Jackson, and I did not rejoin General McCook or see him until I had been to Louisville and returned to the army.

By General DANA:

Question. Was there any neglect of the ordinary precautions of sending forward skirmishers or of trying to feel for the position of the enemy?

I cannot answer, as on the day of the fight and the day previous General Rousseau's division was in the advance.

The Commission adjourned to meet January 12, 1863, at 10 a. m.

LOUISVILLE, *January* 12, 1863.

Commission met pursuant to adjournment. All the members present; also the judge-advocate and General Buell.

Col. HENRY DENT (a witness for the defendant), being duly sworn by the judge-advocate, testified as follows:

By General BUELL:

Question. State, if you please, your name and the position you hold in the service of the United States.

Henry Dent; colonel of the Thirty-fourth Kentucky Volunteers. I am provost-marshal of the State of Kentucky.

Question. Colonel, state, if you please, what the feeling was in Louisville and Kentucky generally, as far as you know it, about the time of the invasion of Kentucky by General Bragg last summer and fall, in regard to the danger that this city was in from that invasion, and the feeling that was entertained among officers and soldiers in reference to the arrival of the Army of the Ohio, under my command.

The feeling in this city was very intense, both with officers and citizens; much anxiety was felt for the city. At one time we lost sight of the Army of the Ohio;

for about two or three days we could not hear of it. We could hear of General Bragg's approach, but could not hear of the position occupied by the Army of the Ohio. Our forces here were supposed to be green, and that we could not defend the city. I recollect General Nelson sent for me and said he must get a message through to General Buell—he must know where he was and must communicate with him; and he apprehended great danger unless the communication could get through. I found a suitable person; he got through the lines and communicated to General Buell and returned. General Nelson expressed himself as being then safe. Nobody here expected to save Louisville unless General Buell could arrive in time to check General Bragg's army. Our people had many of them left the State; they were warned to do so for the safety of their families. I never in my life saw a people apparently so grateful as they were when they ascertained that General Buell was within reach and that he was their only safety.

Question. Was Louisville at any time conceived to be in danger from the presence of Kirby Smith's force here in Kentucky?

I never heard any expressions from officers or citizens of danger from Kirby Smith's forces.

Cross-examination by General DANA:

Question. Was the communication sent by General Nelson to General Buell prior to the surrender of Munfordville or afterward?

It was subsequent to the surrender of Munfordville.

By General BUELL:

Question. Will the colonel state where that communication found General Buell?

I was informed, sir, by the messenger on his return that he found General Buell at Elizabethtown.

JOHN B. ANDERSON (a witness for the defendant), being duly sworn by the judge-advocate, testified as follows:

By General BUELL:

Question. State your name, if you please, and the position you have in the service of the United States.

My name is John B. Anderson; I am holding the position of superintendent of railroads for the Department of the Cumberland.

Question. Did you occupy the same position with reference to the Army of the Ohio during the past summer and autumn?

I did.

Question. State what work you performed on the different railroads in Middle Tennessee last summer to render them fit for the transportation of supplies.

I arrived in Nashville about the close of February or the first week in March; I am unable to fix the precise date. Made an examination of the Memphis Branch of the Louisville and Clarksville Railroad, between the State line and Clarksville, and then returned to Nashville. About the time the army moved from Nashville southward I organized a repairing force, who were engaged first in repairing bridges on the Tennessee and Alabama road as far as Franklin, Tenn. This work done, in connection with General Smith, then in charge of affairs, they afterward commenced on the Nashville and Chattanooga road, rebuilt three bridges over Mill Creek, repaired track and trestles between Antioch and La Vergne, and completed the repairs of Stone River Bridge north of Murfreesborough. The repairing force was then taken to the Tennessee and Alabama road; repaired Duck River Bridge, 600 feet long and 65 feet high; the spans were of 100, 200, 200, and 100 feet in length. The force then proceeded down the Tennessee and Alabama road, repairing the track and culvert at Hurricane, 5 miles below Columbia; the high trestle at Culleoka, 1,100 feet long, averaging 30 feet high, 10 miles below Columbia; then proceeded and rebuilt the bridges over Richland Creek and Robertson's Fork as far as Reynolds' Station, 68 miles south of Nashville, I believe. The force then returned to the Nashville and Chattanooga road and proceeded to erect a bridge at Garrison's Fork, 57 miles southeast from Nashville; commenced a trestle work at Normandy; I do not know the amount of repairs made there without reference to the record; then to Duck River and Elk River. When this work was finished the road was opened to Stevenson. The work at Elk River was finished on the 12th July. The force was then ordered to the McMinnville road, but before much repairs were done were recalled to rebuild bridges in the neighborhood of Murfreesborough, which were burned on the 13th and 14th of July by a force said to be under Forrest. I should have stated that no train was gotten through on the Chattanooga road previous to the burning of these bridges at Murfreesborough. The train advanced as far as Murfreesborough and was stopped by an engagement.

During the following week the bridges over Mill Creek were damaged, not entirely destroyed; they were rebuilt and the road opened July 24. From that date up to the 13th of August the Nashville and Chattanooga road was opened to Stevenson. There were further repairs made on the Nashville and Decatur road in order to bring away trains that were stopped between two destroyed bridges. This work was done about the close of August. That is about all the work we did in Middle Tennessee. Between the completion of the line through to Stevenson and the reconstruction of the bridges on the Decatur road, the McMinnville road was completed and put in operation.

Question. Was this work done under the authority of the commander of the Army of the Ohio?

It was.

Question. After the roads were opened were supplies pushed forward to Stevenson and other towns as rapidly as possible, for the use of the army?

They were.

Question. Was the work performed with industry and energy?

It was.

Question. Was there any delay that was avoidable?

None at all, I think.

Question. Was the work performed under your direction separate from that which was performed under the direction or the supervision of military officers, by engineer and other troops?

The work performed under my supervision was entirely distinct from that done by the military. I sent to the bridge at Harpeth River, near Franklin, the first party of carpenters who arrived, who worked on that bridge under the direction of General Smith; then they returned to me. All other work done by my party was independent of military officers and engineers.

Question. At what date were the repairs on the McMinnville road completed?

I think the first train reached McMinnville on the 23d of August.

Question. Did you perform any work on the Louisville and Nashville road?

I did.

Question. Explain what it was, and, as far as you know them, the circumstances which made it necessary.

On or about the 12th of August the bridge over Station Camp Creek, south of Gallatin, was destroyed by the enemy. I sent a portion of my force, who commenced the reconstruction of that bridge, but were driven away. Within the next few days the long bridge at Saundersville, the bridge at Pilot Knob, and the bridge at Manscoe Creek were destroyed. My force rebuilt the bridge at Saundersville with the exception of the track, and prepared the material of Station Camp Bridge. Either before or after the work at Saundersville they repaired the bridge partially burned over Red River, on the Edgefield and Kentucky road, connecting the Louisville and Nashville road (main stem) with the Memphis Branch of that road at the State line. That, I think, was all the work done previous to the army leaving Nashville northward.

Question. Do you know whether energetic efforts were used to get forward supplies from Louisville while these roads were in operation, and by the rivers also while they were navigable?

I think there were. I was in Tennessee, and could not know personally all that was done at Louisville, though I visited Louisville at different times during the summer. The Louisville and Nashville Railroad Company assured me they were doing all they possibly could to forward Government supplies, and that to the exclusion of other business. So far as I know, supplies were also forwarded by the Cumberland River while it remained navigable.

Question. Do you know whether efforts were made by the commander of the Army of the Ohio, by repeated instructions and injunctions, to further this object; that is, the accumulation of supplies at Nashville?

I know that the commander of the Army of the Ohio did, by repeated instructions, urge forward supplies to the entire capacity of all lines of transportation in use, and that I received from him almost daily dispatches urging the forwarding of supplies over the Government roads southward from Nashville.

Cross-examination by the JUDGE-ADVOCATE:

Question. Were you with the Army of the Ohio when it fell back from Middle Tennessee to Nashville?

I was not strictly with the army; I was either at Nashville, Murfreesborough, or Decherd, or some other point on the railroad, during the time the army fell back from Middle Tennessee to Nashville. I was engaged in managing trains used in removing baggage and sick and convalescent soldiers.

Question. Do you know what became of the various improvements and repairs that you made on these lines of railroads in Tennessee after the army fell back?

I do not know certainly. The bridges over Mill Creek, on the Nashville and Chattanooga road, were destroyed, but I do not know at what period. I have no definite information from the Nashville and Decatur Railroad.

Question. By whom or by whose orders were these bridges destroyed?

I am not aware that they were destroyed by the order of any one. The Mill Creek bridges, I presume, were destroyed by the enemy.

Question. At what time did you receive those urgent solicitations from General Buell to forward supplies from Nashville into Tennessee?

I cannot fix the date precisely at which these dispatches came, but it was from the time the road was opened through to Columbia; and during all the period that supplies were sent while the army occupied the country south of Columbia it was supplied over those routes to the full capacity of rolling-stock we had. The supplies were carried to Reynolds' Station, thence by wagons to Elk River, and by rail from that to Athens, Decatur, and Huntsville.

Question. At what point and in what quantities did you accumulate stores at that time?

It would be impossible to state the amount without reference to the manifest books.

General TYLER. It would be advisable to have those books which give the amount of Government freight during the whole time the road was opened.

(The witness was directed to bring them before the Commission for examination.)

By the JUDGE-ADVOCATE:

Question. What became of those stores when the army fell back from Nashville?

I presume there was no considerable portion which had not been issued. The commissary stores were brought back, to some extent, from Huntsville, Bridgeport, and Stevenson.

Question. At what period did the Cumberland cease to be navigable at that season ?

I do not know.

Question. Can you state the quantity of stores taken up the Cumberland previous to its closing that season ?

I cannot. I know that a number of boats were in the trade, but what business they did I do not know.

Question. What force had you engaged in repairing the road from Bowling Green to Nashville ?

I do not know without reference to the pay roll. I presume about 30 or 40 workmen.

Question. Was that your entire force ?

My force at the time we left Nashville was, I think, about 90 men, carpenters and laborers. The main portion of the force came on to the Louisville and Nashville road, some on the Nashville and Decatur road, and some on the Northwest road. At this period I was at Decherd most of the time, or at some other point on the Nashville and Chattanooga Railroad, and I am not positive as to the dates or the numbers employed on these various works.

Question. What time would it have taken your entire force to repair the roads between Bowling Green and Nashville ?

On the road between Bowling Green and Nashville, 12 miles south of the State line, a tunnel through the Cumberland Ridge had been destroyed, on which work could not be done at that period, for it did not become sufficiently cool for parties to pass through it for several weeks, at least so I was informed by parties residing there. It required ultimately a night and day force some fifteen or sixteen days to clear the tunnel. The bridges were all repaired between Bowling Green and Nashville in about twenty days.

Question. Leaving out the tunnel, do I understand you to say that it took twenty days with a force of 90 men to repair these bridges ?

Leaving out the tunnel, the entire amount of damage done on that road could not have been repaired by 90 men in twenty days.

Question. What was the measure in linear feet of all the bridges destroyed previous to General Buell's falling back from Nashville, and were they replaced by trestle work or by bridges ?

I do not know that all these bridges were destroyed previous to General Buell's army falling back, but the whole amount of repairs was equal to nearly 1,500 linear feet, varying in height from 10 to 40 feet, and were all trestles.

Question. State as nearly as you can what bridges were destroyed previous to General Buell's falling back from Nashville.

The bridge over Manscoe Creek destroyed, and rebuilt by the Michigan Engineers and Mechanics ; Saundersville trestle rebuilt by my force ; the bridge over Station Camp Creek at Pilot Knob rebuilt by the Michigan Engineers and Mechanics ; the bridge over Station Camp Creek No. 2, south of Gallatin, rebuilt in part by my force ; and the bridge over Station Camp Creek, north of Gallatin (not rebuilt until after the army returned). There was a trestle on the grade south of the tunnel and five bridges over North Drake's Creek, but I do not know whether they were destroyed before or after the army fell back.

Question. What number of these bridges were destroyed between Richland and Gallatin ?

Five bridges over North Drake's Creek, and the first crossing of the Station Camp Creek, and the trestle on the grade between the tunnel and Gallatin.

Question. Do you know anything of the turnpike road from Richland to Gallatin ?

I do not know, sir. There is, I think, no turnpike road from Richland. The railroad and turnpike roads separate north of Mitchellsville, between Mitchellsville and Franklin.

By General TYLER:

Question. At whose nomination do you hold your appointment?

I was appointed by General Sherman on the 2d November, 1861. The order was reannounced by General Buell after he took command. I have been appointed, by order bearing date November 2, 1862, by General Rosecrans and am now acting under his orders.

Question. Are the expenses of these repairs borne by the General Government or are they borne in part by the roads?

From the organization of my party last spring all expenses of repairs, labor, and material were defrayed from moneys earned on the roads and for freight not carried for the Government and for passengers, except the last pay roll before leaving Nashville. Since that time the expenses have been paid by the quartermaster's department, and I was ordered to charge to the Louisville and Nashville Company the amount of money expended on their road and branches, to be accounted for by them in the settlement of the transportation account with the Government. That order was from General Buell.

Question. Do you make regular statements of the earnings and expenses of the quartermaster's department the same as you would do to a regular company?

I have not made any reports of earnings or expenses to the quartermaster's department, but have submitted vouchers and pay rolls for expenses. Since September 1 I have kept regular railroad books of all earnings and expenditures.

Question. Why have you not made a report of regular earnings as you have expenses?

I have not made any earnings since my expenses have been reported to the quartermaster's department.

Question. What is the gauge on these Southern roads?

Five feet.

Questions. Are all the roads concentrating in Chattanooga of a uniform gauge of 5 feet?

They are.

Question. What became of the rolling stock belonging to the roads meeting at Chattanooga before our army advanced into Tennessee?

I do not know. I presume it was all taken South. We found at Nashville no engine in working order. Only one engine in good condition was found on the Nashville and Northern road, but I do not know at what point. All the engines found at Nashville were so damaged as to render it impossible to take them away.

Question. After the roads concentrating at Chattanooga as far as Stevenson were repaired at the cost of the Government had they sufficient rolling stock to operate those roads to any possible advantage?

There was a sufficient amount of stock to work the roads until the connection was made through to Decatur and Stevenson. By using the stock of the Louisville and Nashville Railroad Company, together with the Government stock, we were able to operate the roads successfully, but were not able to perform as much labor as could have been done with a larger stock.

Question. Had the Nashville and Louisville road as much rolling stock at this time as they have now?

I think not. They have been building cars and have purchased some additional engines. Their stock was inadequate at that time to carry the whole supplies of the army.

Question. Taking a month before Morgan's last raid, what would be the amount of tonnage the Nashville and Louisville road could have been able to transport daily over their road for the Government with this increased rolling stock?

I think not more than forty cars per day through to Nashville, in addition to the supplies for troops on the line.

Question. Is it or is it not your opinion that the public service would have been benefited by the permanent destruction (instead of repairing) of every yard of railroad from Corinth to Nashville that our armies passed over?

I think not. I do not know how the army could have been supplied by wagon trains from Nashville or from any other point on the Tennessee River without those railroads.

Question. Is it not a military fact that from the moment the enemy repossessed themselves of these railroads they had the rolling stock ready to operate them successfully?

So far as I am informed, no. When the Federal army fell back, all the rolling stock was brought northward to Nashville, with the exception perhaps of three or four wrecked cars and one engine, so badly disabled that it could not be repaired. The rolling stock to work these railroads for the enemy would necessarily have to be ferried across the Tennessee River at Bridgeport, and, so far as I have heard—mere rumor—they never did get across that river more than a few engines and cars.

Question. Was Bragg's army supplied at Murfreesborough by railroad or wagon?

I cannot answer the question. My impression has been that his supplies were obtained mainly from the surrounding country, but I have no positive information on the subject.

Question. Are you well acquainted with the country about Murfreesborough?

Not aside from the railroads, sir.

Question. From what you know do you suppose it capable of sustaining an army of 40,000 or 50,000 men?

I think so, but I cannot tell for how long a time. It is a good agricultural region, so far as I have been informed.

Redirect examination by General BUELL:

Question. You have stated, I believe, that while you were engaged repairing the Louisville and Nashville road with your hired party the engineer and other troops were also engaged on some other work, have you not?

They were; having, as I stated, built a bridge over Manscoe Creek and over Station Camp Creek at Pilot Knob, while my force was engaged on other bridges.

Question. State, if you please, what work you did on the different railroads leading from Louisville after the return of the Army of the Ohio from Kentucky in anticipation of its return to Tennessee again.

My force was ordered by General Buell to repair first the track of the Lebanon branch of the Louisville and Nashville road, and then proceed as rapidly as possible to reconstruct the bridges on the main stem toward Nashville. The work on the Lebanon branch was completed and the force moved at once to the bridges south of Bowling Green, and continued that work until the line was opened to Nashville.

Capt. STEPHEN E. JONES (a witness for the defendant), being duly sworn by the judge-advocate, testified as follows:

By General BUELL:

Question. Captain, state your name, if you please, your position in the service, and the duty on which you are now engaged.

My name is Stephen E. Jones, captain and additional aide-de-camp. I am acting upon the staff of Brigadier-General Boyle; stationed at Louisville.

Question. Have you official knowledge of the numbers and description of the prisoners of war that have passed through this place since October 1?

I have, sir, since my appointment upon the staff of Brigadier-General Boyle, from the second day after the death of General Nelson.

Question. Examine this paper, if you please, and state to the Commission what it purports to be and whether it is correct.

I recognize in this paper a report made to General Boyle of the prisoners received into the military prison from the 1st of October, 1862, to the 14th of December of the same year. It is correct as far as I know.

Question. Do you understand those prisoners to have been from the armies under the command of General Bragg and Kirby Smith, which occupied Kentucky until their recent retreat from the State?

I was going to state, if it was intended to embrace a letter which accompanied this report to General Boyle, that they were the prisoners of the army of Kirby Smith and General Bragg, of the Confederate forces, exclusive of the command of General Marshall in the State of Kentucky at the time; that it is not exclusively of any command, as far as I know, but perhaps inclusive of a few individuals in the command of Marshall, exclusive of any regiment, unless possibly a company known as Jessee's company, which I believed and have since ascertained did belong to the command of Humphrey Marshall. I make this explanation before answering the question, because of a remark which accompanied the report to General Boyle that it was exclusive of Humphrey Marshall's command. I call it exclusive of it, with the exception of that company, for this reason: that the prisoners of that command that reached the military prison of this State were unable to give their descriptive rolls, but simply stated that they were from Marshall's command, most of them being new recruits, and not knowing in many instances the companies to which they belonged.

Question. Do I understand you, then, that that report represents regiments from Bragg's army proper and from the force of Kirby Smith proper and not the regiments under the command of Marshall?

Yes, sir. It also includes regiments under the command of Morgan; whether they were attached to Kirby Smith's command or not I do not know; they were with him, but whether directly under his command or not I do not know.

Question. Please read from this, for the information of the Commission, the total number of prisoners of different grades, the number of regiments, battalions, squadrons, and batteries of the different arms of the service.

There were received in the military prison, and forwarded to Vicksburg to be exchanged, during the period mentioned, 4 colonels, 4 lieutenant-colonels, 5 majors, 42 captains, 120 lieutenants, 415 non-commissioned officers, 2,914 privates, making a total of 3,504. These represented 168 infantry regiments and 19 infantry battalions, 38 cavalry regiments and 20 cavalry battalions, 32 batteries, 2 regiments known by the name of legions (cavalry), I believe, 13 detached companies, or companies that were unattached, these being principally companies raised in full or in part in Kentucky during the present year; there not being time to form them into regiments was the explanation given by the prisoners.

Question. Have any prisoners of war been received since the date of that report?

Yes, sir.

Question. Can you state the number now?

I cannot without reference to my book in which I keep a record of it.

Question. Will you please get that, captain? Had you any information of prisoners of war scattered through the country that never presented themselves or were never delivered at this post?

I have heard of such prisoners through the country from various parties, but no definite or positive information, except through a friend of mine, who during the advance from Bowling Green to this place a portion of the time led the advance and had charge of the paroling of the prisoners.

The Commission adjourned to meet January 13, 1863, at 10 o'clock a. m.

LOUISVILLE, *January* 13, 1863.

The Commission met pursuant to adjournment. All the members present; also the judge-advocate and General Buell.

Capt. STEPHEN E. JONES re-examined.

By General BUELL:

Question. Have you now the report of the prisoners received since the former report which you have presented?

I have not, sir; that is, not made out in the form of a report, but so that I can give it verbally. Between the 14th and the 29th of December there were received 67 prisoners, of whom 64 were sent to Vicksburg, 3 not being well enough, and there are now in the military prison from the hospitals in the central portion of the State and captured in the month of October and paroled 136 prisoners; making in all, since the report of the 14th of December, 203, of whom 4 were captains, 6 lieutenants, and 21 non-commissioned officers. This is exclusive of quite a number of other prisoners now in the military prison that were captured principally, if not exclusively, from Morgan's command during his recent raid in the State. The number of these I did not attempt to ascertain.

Question. What, then, would be the total number of prisoners received here from first to last?

Three thousand seven hundred and seven.

Question. Are you able to form an estimate of the number of prisoners that have been informally paroled and that never came to this place?

I have no sufficient data for forming any approximate estimate of that. From the report of the party to whom I alluded in answer to a previous question, of the prisoners paroled between Bowling Green and Louisville, I suppose that, taking his statement exclusively, there were about 1,000. He told me he was a party to paroling about 300.

Cross-examination by the JUDGE-ADVOCATE:

Question. Captain, at what time was this report made out?

As it states there upon the back of the report, the 14th of December. The last prisoners embraced in it were sent to Vicksburg upon the 13th of December.

Question. At what time did you commence a statement of this sort and at what time did you terminate it?

I commenced no statement until the time mentioned there. I commenced the record of them from the day that I was first assigned to take charge of them by General Boyle, which was the 1st of October, they having previously been under the charge of Colonel Dent, the provost-marshal of the State.

Question. What was the object you had in view in making out this statement?

The object in making the record was to have an authentic record of the number of prisoners received, for the purpose of securing the exchange of our own men. The object in making that report was first to gratify my own curiosity, and secondly to furnish information through the papers to the curious at large.

Question. What information did you purpose furnishing by a report of this sort?

The information contained in the report itself of the number of regiments, battalions, detached companies that were represented by the prisoners in the military prison as having been in the Army of Occupation, I believe they called it, of the Confederate forces in Kentucky.

Question. You have given here the different regiments, but have not given the separate commands under which they served. Why is that?

From the fact that the descriptive roll of prisoners, as used when I was first assigned to the duty of receiving and forwarding the military prisoners from the place, does not embrace that. That form was furnished by Col. William Hoffman, Commissary-General of Prisoners, as I understood. I can show that to you by exhibiting a form of descriptive roll used and sent to Vicksburg with the prisoners, to be receipted and forwarded, one copy to the Adjutant-General's Office, one copy to General Rosecrans, and one to be left with the prisoners. I have one of these rolls with me.

Question. You got the information detailed in this from the descriptive rolls, and not from direct information from the prisoners?

On the reception of the prisoners in the military prison each one is called up, and his descriptive roll, his name, and as full a description as the form allowed is taken; of that three copies are made; and it is also recorded in a book I keep for the purpose, namely, a book of record.

(The Commission directs that all the rolls from which the abstracts presented are made be brought before them.)

The WITNESS. If the call is for rolls similar to this, that is impossible to get short of Washington City or General Rosecrans. Of the three rolls made out in a form like this, one is sent to Washington, one to General Rosecrans, and one to Vicksburg, and a copy I have in my book. The book I can produce. I have these rolls on hand from the fact that the prisoners there named are in the military prison; but when they go the rolls go with them. I have only the book, and from it the report is made.

By General TYLER:

Question. Can you not from your books and papers trace these prisoners to Kirby Smith's or Bragg's army or Breckinridge's army corps?

I could not answer that question positively without the book before me. My impression is that I only trace them to Bragg's and Kirby Smith's, and, as I stated yesterday, to the command of Morgan, which from the best information I could receive is not exactly attached to either.

By General SCHOEPF:

Question. How many of these prisoners were captured in the battle of Perryville?

This roll shows, as the court will see upon examination of it, when and where each prisoner was captured. It does not show that any prisoner was captured in any fight; it only shows the place, when, and where.

Question. It appears from your reply that all those prisoners that were captured were stragglers?

I would suppose from the form of the roll that it could not show anything in regard to that, whether they were captured in one way or another. The form furnished me was to show when and where; how captured, is not shown in any of the rolls.

By the PRESIDENT:

Question. Does it show by whom captured?

No, sir.

By the JUDGE-ADVOCATE:

Question. You will furnish for the benefit of the Commission a copy similar to this. I observe some things upon your report which I do not understand; probably you can explain. For example, the Tennessee regiments, as reported here, run up to One hundred and fifty-four; can you give any explanation of that fact?

I can give the explanation given by a number of prisoners to me in answer to a similar interrogatory put to them. It is this: Upon the formation of the regiments in Tennessee there arose a dispute as to which should be called First. One regiment claiming to be the First was assigned to some lower number, but refused to accept it, and perhaps petitioned for the privilege of being called by the number of its militia organization in the State. In that way a regiment appears upon all the records as One hundred and fifty-fourth, and, for a reason I can scarcely [understand] myself, a number of prisoners have asserted that there were two, and some three, of those regiments known as One hundred and fifty-fourth; a number giving on the rolls One hundred and fifty-fourth Senior and One hundred and fifty-fourth Junior; but they stated that the regiments did not run from one up to that number.

By General DANA:

Question. Are we to understand that One hundred and fifty-four, wherever it occurs upon your roll, is not necessarily the same regiment after all, but may, on the contrary, represent two or three regiments?

It is indicated upon the report two regiments; indicated by the number, one junior and one senior, as given me by the prisoners.

By the JUDGE-ADVOCATE:

Question. Did you not learn from the same source, captain, that the militia regiments of Tennessee and Kentucky after being consolidated by General Bragg or Kirby Smith would still retain their original militia numbers?

My impression is that this was an exceptional case.

Question. Do you claim that there is nothing in this report that would indicate the force under Bragg and Kirby Smith?

No, sir; I do not claim that it contains any further information than that which it bears upon the face of it; that is, the different regiments, &c., from which one or more numbers have been in the military prison here in the city.

Redirect examination by General BUELL:

Question. Have you any reason to doubt, captain, that the regiments represented on that report actually formed part of the rebel force that was in Kentucky in the months of September and October last?

I have not. I have supposed from their appearing in the military prison and from conversations among the prisoners at different times when I have been among them that they were all from regiments that were actually represented in the State.

Question. Is it not quite possible, if not probable, that there may have been regiments in that force not represented in that report?

I would suppose, from the fact that there was but a single engagement in the State in which, as I understood from various sources, both from reports on the other side as well as our own, the entire force of the Confederates was not represented in that action, it would be likely that there would be regiments from whom no prisoners came into our possession. Of that, of course, I know nothing; it is mere supposition.

Question. Are any of the peculiarities of the information embraced in the rolls which you have presented to the Commission—its completeness or incompleteness—due to the forms which have been furnished for your special observance in furnishing this information?

The variety is largely owing to the forms of the rolls, somewhat to the fact that no idea was ever entertained of the rolls being called for or required for any purpose but identifying any party that was once paroled taking up arms without having been duly discharged.

Question. I speak of the form of the information generally, such as the company and regiment of the prisoner and the time and place where he was captured. I do not refer to exceptional cases where even this information is not given.

If I understand General Buell's question aright, that is, why the information is not more complete, why it does not embrace the brigade, division, and corps of the prisoner, then it is entirely owing to the fact that this was never embraced in any form for making out descriptive rolls of prisoners.

Question. Was a copy of that report furnished to General Rosecrans?

That I cannot answer. I furnished them to General Boyle, and I know only of the disposition made of three of them. There were perhaps six or seven made out, but what disposition he made of the others I cannot tell.

Question. Can you get that information; and, if so, be enabled to inform the Commission with what view that report was furnished to General Rosecrans?

I presume General Boyle can give the information, and also the object he had in view in forwarding them to the different parties.

Recross-examination by the JUDGE-ADVOCATE:

Question. Captain, in a march of two months after an army short of provisions and distressed by fatiguing marches was it not likely that our army would pick up as stragglers or sick or take as prisoners representatives of nearly every regiment in the army?

In reply to that I would state that, from information received both from Confederate officers and privates and from citizens of the country through which General Bragg's army passed, such a thing as a straggler was not known. That is the concurrent testimony as far as I have received it from those three sources; that men were mercilessly shot that did not keep within the ranks. and sometimes, as their surgeons have reported to me, it was cruelly and mercilessly done when they were not able to keep up with the column. This was with respect to Bragg's army. In regard to General Smith's, I can only say I know nothing in regard to it beyond the statement of all the citizens of the country through which they passed that the discipline of the army was exceedingly exact, and that the men were kept in all that pertained to discipline very rigidly together. These things were made matters of complaint among officers and soldiers, and particularly among the surgeons of Bragg's army.

Question. Did you gather from that that General Bragg had no sick or wounded; of if he had that he shot them?

My answer had no reference to sick, but to stragglers on the march. Of the sick, I know not what disposition was made of them, whether they were transported or left in hospitals. As to the army itself, there was no straggling. As regards what would be picked up in the march of the two armies, of those who were sick and unable to keep up, I could not form a definite opinion unless I had some definite information as to the lines of march of the two armies; whether one followed immediately after or preceded or passed parallel at some distance from the other. The army following in the same line of march would of course pick up all the stragglers, if there were any and all the sick that were left behind; if they marched parallel and at some distance apart, few, if any, would fall into the possession of the other army. The first prisoners that we received came from a Georgia regiment; they were captured at New Haven. No prisoners that I know of were received or came afterward to this place that were captured below or south of New Haven; and in regard to those that were left in the hospitals or picked up in the march through Central Kentucky, I suppose there would be a large number; but whether they would represent all the regiments I could not perhaps form so good an idea as the court itself.

By General SCHOEPF:

Question. Captain, what was your position during the invasion of General Bragg?

At the time of Kirby Smith's invasion of Kentucky, which preceded somewhat that of Bragg, I was in the vicinity of Lexington upon sick furlough. Immediately upon hearing of the approaching invasion I reported to General Wallace, and was by him ordered upon the staff of Maj. Gen. C. [M.] Clay. I went with him to Richmond. When General Nelson relieved General Wallace and came to Richmond he relieved me of duty upon the staff of General Clay and ordered me to report to himself. I was upon his staff until the time of his death; after the battle of Richmond, and after his being wounded, acting under General Gilbert up to the time of General Nelson's return from Cincinnati, where he went after being wounded, when I reported to him and was upon his staff to the time of his death.

Question. What was the strength of Kirby Smith's force at that time?

I could give no definite information. It was variously estimated at from 12,000 to 20,000; perhaps as high as 30,000.

Question. What estimate did General Nelson place upon it?

I am not sure that I can give that. My impression is that it was in the neighborhood of 20,000 to 25,000. I think, perhaps, that some of the official papers of General Nelson's would show what estimate he placed upon it. I think there are official papers published in reference to the battle that give his estimate.

Question. What orders did General Nelson give in regard to the removal of the women and children from Louisville during the invasion by Bragg?

General Nelson gave orders for the women and children to be removed from Louisville within the space of twenty-four or forty-eight hours. If they were not removed within that time they were not to be allowed to go.

Question. Did the women and children comply with that order?

Large numbers of them did; but what proportion of the women and children in the city complied I could not tell. Large numbers went and large numbers remained.

Question. Was there any panic or scare among the military men here for the safety of Louisville during the invasion of Bragg?

I do not think there was a panic among the military men, but there was serious apprehension. There was a very great panic among the citizens, and of course some officers and some soldiers participated in the panic, but not, I think, generally. A deep-settled apprehension rested upon them, but not in the form of a panic.

Commission adjourned to meet January 14, at 10 o'clock a. m.

LOUISVILLE, *January* 24,[?] 1863.

Captain JONES' examination continued, as follows:

By the JUDGE-ADVOCATE:

Question. Captain, have you been able to comply with the order of the Commission with reference to the amending of your report?

I have not been able to comply with it fully, as that is impossible. I have made a sort of supplementary report, that will show, as nearly as the records will furnish, the data for what I supposed to be the object of the order. I have made a report of the place and date of capture as far as I could from the data I have had before me in my books of record, and when it was not possible to give the date of capture, the date of the shipment of prisoners from this point, beginning with those shipped previous to the 12th of November and then those between the 12th and 18th of November, and so on up to the 14th of January, including some forty-one counties.

Question. State, if you please, what number of prisoners out of those you report were captured subsequent to the battle of Perryville.

I could not do that with certainty. This report shows those that were sent from this point subsequent to the battle of Perryville, but I could not state from the records the exact number; I could only give my own impressions as to the proportion of those who were captured subsequent to the battle of Perryville. By an examination of the first book of record that I attempted to keep on taking charge of the prisoners, the mode in which it was kept and the objects which I had in view, the reasons will appear why I have not been able to comply with the order. To the 12th of November the record simply shows the company and regiment and the time of shipment. I received the attestation—to make it somewhat official and binding upon the Confederate authorities—of the Confederate officers of the regiments, where it was possible to obtain it, to which the prisoners belonged; and where they had no officer of the regiment, then a commissioned officer of the State in which the prisoners volunteered; in some few instances the signature of the party himself. For instance, beginning with the first, as I stated to the court, the Third Georgia Regiment, captured at New Haven. I have the attestation of the parole of Colonel Crawford, who commanded the regiment. That was previous to the battle of Perryville. Some 270 or 280, an entire regiment, was captured at New Haven.

Question. The places are always given where those prisoners were captured, are they not?

Those captured previous to the 12th of November are not given; but I suppose I have all the evidence that was requisite to secure an exchange and to secure detection of any one attempting to re-enter the service without having been formally exchanged. The rolls made were forwarded, one to Washington and one to Vicksburg, and no copy kept. Subsequent to the 12th of November the place and date of capture are exhibited.

Question. State as nearly as you can, from such data as you possess, what proportion of those prisoners reported to us were taken previous to the Perryville fight.

My impression is that there were not over 400 taken previous to the Perryville fight.

Question. Do you know, officially or otherwise, the number of prisoners taken in this late fight at Murfreesborough and the regiments they represented?

Only through what I have seen in the newspapers.

By General TYLER:

Question. Does the report which you furnish to the Commission show the prisoners taken by General Buell's army proper, by General Morgan at Cumberland Gap or those at Clarksville, General Granger near Lexington, and General Rosecrans' army in Tennessee; does it embrace all these commands?

My impression is, though I cannot state positively, that there are none embraced in the report that were captured by General Morgan at Cumberland Gap, from the fact that there were no means of forwarding such prisoners to this place. There might possibly have been some few captured by him on his retreat from the Gap to the Ohio River, when followed by John Morgan, in command of the Confederate forces, but I am not positive whether there were any or not. Those on the east and north of Lexington were probably captured by General Granger's forces, or by the colonel in command of the Eastern District of Kentucky, or in some cases by Home Guards, and in some cases the prisoners gave themselves up, and a large number of these were released on parole. Most of these are not probably recorded here, from the fact that by General Boyle's orders Colonel Dent was ordered to administer the oath to them and release them. My impression is that those captured north and east of Lexington were captured by forces not connected with General Buell's army. Those captured in the counties of Woodford, Franklin, Jessamine, Madison, Garrard, Lincoln, and the counties between that and the Cumberland Gap, as far, perhaps, as London on one road and Goose Creek Works road on the other, were captured by forces acting under General Buell's orders. Whether those captured in the county of Scott were captured by General Buell's forces or by those of General Granger I could not state, because I do not know whether any of General Buell's forces went beyond Lexington in that direction. My belief, from the best of my information is that all those captured in Lexington and in Fayette County were captured by the cavalry of General Buell's forces, that I understood visited Lexington at some time before the arrival of General Granger's forces there. There were also prisoners received, after the Army of the Ohio marched back into Tennessee, from Colonel Bruce and from perhaps one or two other officers; some perhaps from Colonel Foster. With the knowledge that the court must have of the line of march pursued by General Buell's forces in Kentucky they can, by an examination of this report, seeing the places from which the prisoners came and by whom taken, draw as correct an inference as I can give them. The prisoners I referred to were captured at Corinth, Fort Donelson, Mill Springs, and other places. Some four or five of them, that I think of, were forwarded from this place subsequent to the time that General Buell's army left Louisville and most of them very recently. Those were prisoners captured previous to the agreement for exchange between the United States and the Confederate authorities. At the time of that movement they were unable, from disease or from the effects of their wounds, to be sent back, and have therefore remained in our lines up to the present time. One that I remember that was captured at Mill Springs was not able to be moved from that place until some three or four weeks since.

By General SCHOEPF:

Question. The report here furnished to the Commission shows a certain

number of prisoners, as stated in your previous testimony, but here are
six pages, embracing about 400 prisoners, without any marks showing
from what regiments they are.   Where do you get your report from?

If you will look at the bottom of those blank pages and see by whom the parole of
those prisoners is attested that will show where I got it.   When it is not indicated in
the regiment column what regiment they belonged to they are the prisoners of the
Third Georgia Cavalry, and at the bottom is the attestation of Martin J. Crawford,
colonel Third Georgia Cavalry, that upon a certain day they were paroled:

"——— ——— is paroled by me this 15th Oct., 1862.

"STEPHEN E. JONES,
" *Captain, Louisville, Ky.*

"Attestation:

"MARTIN J. CRAWFORD,
"Colonel Third Georgia Cavalry."

By General BUELL:

Question. How many of the prisoners included in your report were
captured at Fort Donelson and Corinth, and do those prisoners belong
to regiments which are not otherwise represented as part of the force
which invaded Kentucky last summer?

There appear here to be 3 prisoners forwarded from this place that were captured
at Corinth, and 1 I remember, as I stated, was captured at Mill Springs, and 1 at Fort
Donelson.   The 1 captured at Mill Springs belonged, I think, to the First Tennessee
Regiment, represented by quite a number of prisoners.   Of the 3 captured at Corinth
I cannot now state what regiments they belong to or whether these regiments
are represented at all.   I can ascertain by looking over the parole-book whether
those regiments to which they belong are otherwise represented here.   Although
it is not strictly in answer to the question of General Buell, it is a statement
which I ought to make in explanation of the present report, namely, that it
embraces more than the report previously made, that is, in point of numbers; it
embraces several hundred prisoners that had been shipped from this place subsequent to the time the last report was made out and have been recorded since.
Of those I have not attempted to find out the regiments represented by them, but I
know from having counted them hurriedly this morning that some 35 of the privates
and from 6 to 8 of the officers have come down from the hospitals at Perryville, counting Harrodsburg, Danville, and Perryville—places lying 10 miles distant from each
other, and the hospitals being in common.   There are 45 from those three places that
did not appear in the other report, and altogether there is an increase of several hundred.   I do not know the exact number between this last report and the former for
the reasons I have explained.   The discrepancy would appear singular to the court
without explanation, and I make it in justice to myself and the accuracy of the report.

Question. Do you mean to say that there were 5 prisoners, 3 from
Corinth, 1 from Fort Donelson, and 1 from Mill Springs included in
your original report as presented to the Commission?

Yes, sir; these 5 went into the number of the former report.

Question. Can you ascertain now whether those 5 prisoners belonged
to the regiments which are not represented as belonging to the force
which invaded Kentucky last summer?

I do not know what State the 3 from Corinth are from; the 1 from Mill Springs and
the 1 from Fort Donelson were from Tennessee regiments.   I remember that fact from
having known one of them previously and the other remained in the city some time
before he was sent off.   It would take me some time to ascertain and answer correctly.
I find (examining the report) that one of the regiments represented as not invading
Kentucky is represented by other prisoners.

General BUELL. I wish you to get that information for the Commission, captain.

Question. Are the prisoners that you say came from Clarksville, from
Colonel Foster's command, and perhaps from other parts of General
Rosecrans' force included in your original report?

Some of them are and some of them are not.   My impression is that there are not a
great number of them.   In addition to this report which I now offer to the court I w

their direction I made out a list of the regiments represented at some four or five of the principal points—that is, where the largest number of prisoners were taken—which I left in my book here in this room when I came up some two days since expecting to be examined. That I do not find, and I have with me only a list of those regiments represented by the 952 prisoners who appear in this report under the head of "Place and date of capture not recorded."

Question. Can you ascertain how many of them and whether they belonged to regiments which are otherwise represented as a part of the force which invaded Kentucky last summer?

The nearest answer to that question would be to make out a report of the regiments represented at each of the various places mentioned in this report. It would require considerable time to do that; more than it has required to make out this other report, but it can be done.

Question. What is necessary to obtain an answer is to ascertain the number of those prisoners by referring to your reports, to observe the regiment to which they belong, then to refer to your previous report of prisoners captured in Kentucky belonging to regiments which formed part of the invading force, and thus ascertain whether there are regiments in the one class which are not represented in the other. Will that take long?

I could not tell how long; I will attempt to do it if the court wishes it.

If you please, get that information, captain.

The JUDGE-ADVOCATE. You may present it in a written statement.

General BUELL. State, if you please, what you understand the order of the Commission to have been with reference to the information you had to furnish on this occasion, captain, and state in what particulars the information you have furnished falls short of that which was required.

The JUDGE-ADVOCATE. I object to that question.

General BUELL. On what ground?

The JUDGE-ADVOCATE. I beg to state, Mr. President, that we have worked our recorder till he is fatigued and I suggest an adjournment.

CINCINNATI, OHIO, *February*[?] 14, 1863.

Capt. S. E. JONES' examination continued.

General DANA. If I remember aright, when Captain Jones was last examined the court was adjourned on an objection. I move that the record be referred to and read.

(The portion of the record referred to was read.)

The JUDGE-ADVOCATE. I withdraw my objection to that question if General Buell wishes to put it.

General DANA. I move that the last question be read to Captain Jones.

(The question was read.)

General SCHOEPF. I object to General Buell's reading a private letter while the whole Commission is waiting for the transaction of business. The question was read, and I want to have it answered, now that the witness is waiting.

General BUELL. Out of deference to the Commission as a body I will state in answer to the objection that I am reading a paper connected with the investigation and the testimony of the witness now before the Commission.

General SCHOEPF. The question was read to the witness, who has nothing else to do but to answer it, and if General Buell is not prepared to listen to the answer let him state so before the Commission.

General BUELL. I shall be prepared in a very few minutes. (After a pause.) You may proceed.

Captain JONES. I suppose the object of the question——

General TYLER. I wish the court may be cleared.

(The court was cleared.)

Captain JONES. I understood the object of the question to be to ascertain as far as possible the number of prisoners captured by the army under the command of General Buell from the time General Bragg crossed the Tennessee River at Chattanooga and from General Smith's army from the time it crossed the Cumberland Mountains till it went out of Kentucky and to separate the prisoners belonging to one corps from those belonging to another. The report falls short of that in not being able to distinguish the respective commands to which the different prisoners belong, I being not guided in my inference in that respect by the time and position of the prisoners when captured, and, as I stated in my examination, I was compelled to leave the court to draw their own inferences from the same sources.

General BUELL. Has the witness correctly explained what was required of him?

The JUDGE-ADVOCATE. Yes, sir.

General BUELL. A part of the witness' answer to a previous question by the judge-advocate, which made my question appropriate and necessary, has not been recorded. The witness commenced with saying that if he remembered the instructions given, and he believed he did, though he had no copy of the instructions—and it will be remembered also that none could be found for him to refer to—then he could answer so and so. It was that which made it necessary that it should be explained wherein his evidence fell short of what might have been required of him. I now present to the Commission in evidence the statement which was furnished by Captain Jones subsequent to his last examination with reference to the number of regiments that are represented by the prisoners of war that have been brought into Louisville and sent off for exchange.

The PRESIDENT. (To the witness.) Is that paper introduced by you in accordance with the direction of the court?

Captain JONES. It is a paper forwarded by me to the president of the court as a portion of the papers intended to form the report that I was ordered to make when I was last before the Commission.

(Report referred to marked A of Captain Jones' papers.)

General BUELL. In this report (marked B) you have designated certain regiments as not being represented by prisoners captured in Kentucky. Please to examine that statement, captain, and see whether one at least of these regiments is not actually represented on the same report by prisoners captured.

Captain JONES. I find here the Forty-ninth Tennessee, which I have reported as not represented as among the regiments captured in Kentucky, represented by the prisoners from regiments captured in Nelson County; but whether that is a mistake in having it represented as among those not captured in Kentucky or whether it is a mistake in having it represented as among those captured in Nelson County I cannot tell, not having that evidence before me. In looking over it as hurriedly as I am compelled to do before the court that is the only instance of the kind I notice.

By General BUELL:

Question. State when those prisoners were captured which belonged to regiments supposed not to be represented by prisoners captured in Kentucky and how many at each place.

There were 3 captured in Mississippi; Fort Donelson, 1 or 2 (I speak only from recollection); Mill Springs, Ky., 1. The balance of those not captured in Kentucky were captured in Tennessee, principally at Gallatin and in the vicinity, I think, of Nashville. The whole number reported here captured out of the State is 215; of these 57, possibly more, were brought in subsequent to the report that was first made of prisoners captured and subsequent to my first examination by the court.

Question. When were the others brought in?

Nineteen were brought in previous to the 12th November and subsequent to the 1st of October, the time at which my report of prisoners begins; 18 between the 12th of November and the 18th of November; 36 between the 18th and 29th of November; 14 between the 29th of November and the 5th of December; 53 between the 5th of December and the 13th of the same month; 15 between the 13th December and the 29th of the same month; and 57 between the 29th of December and the 14th of January; making, I think, 72 subsequent to my first examination by the court. That is exclusive of 3 that were captured in Mississippi, which came in previous to the 12th of November and subsequent to the 1st of October, and 1 between the 5th December and the 13th of the same month.

Question. Now, can you identify more precisely the place, with the date of capture, of these several batches; I mean those represented as not having been captured in Kentucky?

I could with the aid of my parole-book. I did not suppose it was necessary in making out the report, as there is a large number of names of insignificant places which I could not find on the map but only know they were in Tennessee; and the majority of the prisoners being in the vicinity of the two places I did mention I did not copy in the report any of the names of places at which the prisoners were captured in Tennessee.

Question. Mention, if you please, in the vicinity of what places the majority of the prisoners were taken—as many as you remember?

The majority of the prisoners, according to my recollection, were taken in the vicinity of Nashville and Gallatin. There were also prisoners from Franklin, from Murfreesborough, perhaps from Shelbyville. Those, I believe, were all the places whose names I now remember.

Question. Were they generally cavalry or infantry regiments?

That I could not answer. My attention was not called to it and my memory is not therefore charged with it.

Question. Is there anything that would indicate to your mind that they belonged to cavalry regiments and which operated upon the borders of Kentucky at the time of the invasion of the State by Bragg?

I do not think I could answer your question, sir.

Question. How does this last report of yours affect the statement made in the first as to the number of regiments, battalions, squadrons, batteries, and companies that belonged to the force which invaded Kentucky last summer and fall?

Excluding the Forty-ninth Tennessee, about which I am uncertain, it appearing both among those captured out of and among those captured in the State, there are five less infantry regiments represented in the State than those embraced in the first report; one cavalry battalion less and one cavalry regiment more; batteries the same; one infantry battalion more.

Question. What reasons have you heard given by persons connected with the rebel army for the limited number of sick persons belonging to that army that were left on the line of march from Chattanooga?

I conversed with a number of rebel officers and soldiers, and particularly with surgeons, in regard to that fact, it being a matter of curiosity to me, and was told by them that it was owing to the fact that when Bragg started from Chattanooga he had twenty days' rations, and that as fast as his wagons which carried the rations were emptied they were turned over to the hospital department. These wagons were used to relieve those who were wearied or sick upon the road, and by continually changing them, allowing them to ride a portion of the way and then give place to others, the health of the army was much kept up. Besides that their army was more healthy during the whole march, and the discipline did not allow any man to imagine himself sick who was not really so. They established hospitals at Tompkinsville and Glasgow, to which those who were not able to be transported were sent back, and from that place there were no hospitals till they reached Bardstown, and the sick were transported from north of those two places to Bardstown.

Question. How many wagons would be required to carry twenty days' rations for, say, 40,000 men, estimating only the essential parts of the rations, bread and meat?

Never having had anything to do with the quartermaster or commissary departments, I have not the remotest idea. I know that they varied, according to circumstances, in our army from two to thirteen to a regiment, besides brigade and division headquarters transportation; but I have no knowledge of the necessary transportation for the subsistence of an army.

Question. It is a matter of calculation—the number of days, the number of men, the weight of rations, and the average weight that can be carried by the wagons.

I should have to obtain the use of a copy of the Regulations and should need some little time to figure it out. I suppose with that I could answer.

Question. It is not worth while now, captain. Do you know anything about the release of prisoners of war at Louisville, in consequence of their acknowledging their allegiance to the Government, who were not included in any of the reports which you have submitted to the Commission?

According to the order of General Buell I had charge and supervision only of prisoners of war; deserters were under the control of Colonel Dent, Provost-Marshal-General of the State. Only by a special order which once or twice I received had I anything to do with them, unless their names got upon the rolls of the prisoners of war, strictly speaking, by mistake. I was informed by Colonel Dent that he had released between 800 and 1,000.

Question. Did these deserters come under the control of the provost-marshal within the period embraced in your report of prisoners of war, and did they belong to the represented force that was in Kentucky in August, September, and October last?

That was my understanding of Colonel Dent's statement.

Question. Have you any official or personal knowledge of the capture of property or stores belonging to the rebel army about the time of its retreat in any part of Kentucky?

I have no official knowledge. I heard the statement made by officers of the army and saw it published in the newspapers, but had no official information of stores captured at Camp Dick Robinson and Nicholasville.

The JUDGE-ADVOCATE. You are dismissed, captain.

General BUELL. I would like for Captain Jones to be retained by the judge-advocate.

General TYLER. Is the examination of General Smith concluded?

The JUDGE-ADVOCATE. I detained General Smith at the request of General Buell, who said he might probably wish to recall him, and I told him to remain.

The PRESIDENT. I would like the judge-advocate to be ready to state at the next session what has been the mode of examination that has been pursued with reference to these witnesses.

The JUDGE-ADVOCATE. We adjourned before Captain Jones' examination was concluded, and he was ordered to appear here to complete his testimony.

LOUISVILLE, *January* 14, [?] 1863.

Commission met pursuant to adjournment.   All the members present; also the judge-advocate and General Buell.

General BUELL. After the adjournment of the Commission yesterday I received this letter from the judge-advocate. He informs me that the Commission was kept in waiting half an hour for me, and he then goes on to admonish me that in future the Commission expects from me a more prompt attendance. I am as anxious as the Commission that this investigation should be closed as promptly as possible, and for the sake of personal as well as official courtesy I should be sorry to keep the Commission in waiting; but I desire to say that I am here by the permission of the Secretary of War and not by his requirement. It might be presumed that I could, if necessary, give an explanation that would satisfy any gentleman for failing to be present at the hour appointed. I request that the letter may be recorded.

A. G. CRADDOCK (a witness for the Government), being duly sworn by the judge-advocate, testified as follows :

By the JUDGE-ADVOCATE :

Question. State your name and residence.

My name is A. G. Craddock ; I reside near Munfordville, Hart County, Ky.

Question. Can you state whether you were near Munfordville when it was attacked by General Bragg's army or previous to that attack, and whether you carried a message from Colonel Wilder to General Buell's army ?

When Munfordville was attacked I was at Bowling Green, 40 miles from there. I carried a message from Colonel Wilder to General Rousseau on the Saturday night before it was attacked on Sunday morning, and delivered it to General Rousseau about sunup Sunday morning, the 14th of September.

Question. Did you know the nature of that message and whether it reached General Buell ?

The nature of it was for re-enforcements. In about half an hour after I got to the hotel General Buell came to General Rousseau's headquarters and sent for me. He asked me then the situation in and about Munfordville, and said that Colonel Wilder had better evacuate that post. That, as well as I recollect, was about the purport of his remarks to me. I started back on Sunday after that and never reached Munfordville till Tuesday morning, and when I got there Bragg's forces were at Munfordville.

W. B. CRADDOCK (a witness for the Government), being duly sworn by the judge-advocate, testified as follows:

By the JUDGE-ADVOCATE:

Question. State your name and residence, and whether you were at Munfordville at the time Bragg's army arrived there and attacked that place.

My residence is Munfordville, Ky.

Question. Were you there at the time the place was attacked by Bragg ?

I was not there at the time the fortress was surrendered ; I was about 2¼ miles from the place.

Question. State whether you saw any or all of Bragg's army and whether you counted any of his regiments.

I cannot state if I saw them all. I saw a number of them. I counted as well as I could two regiments of them.

Question. What did you make their number to be?

If my recollection serves me aright, one numbered 360, the other 250.

Question. Did you see any other regiments besides those two you counted?

Yes, sir; I saw a number.

Question. How did they compare with the two you counted?

The reason why I counted the two regiments was I saw on their colors the word "Shiloh." They were marching near where I was boarding, and I supposed they had been in the battle there, and I counted them to see how they numbered. I know that the two regiments I counted were from Arkansas, but I cannot say I noticed how many the other regiments numbered.

Question. Did you notice the other regiments close enough to say as to how they compared in size?

I could not say, sir.

Cross-examination by General BUELL:

Question. You counted the number of men in these two regiments while they were on the march, did you, Mr. Craddock?

Yes, sir.

Question. Did you suppose, from the fact of their having been in battle, that they had sustained heavy losses, and that therefore you would expect to find the ranks very greatly reduced?

I did.

Question. Did the strength of these regiments as you found them realize the expectations you had formed with reference to their diminished strength?

Their colors seemed to be very much shattered and torn with bullets, and I just supposed from that that they had lost severely.

The Commission adjourned to meet January 15, 1863, at 11 o'clock, a. m.

LOUISVILLE, *January* 15, 1863.

Commission met pursuant to adjournment. All the members present; also the judge-advocate and General Buell.

W. B. CRADDOCK's testimony continued, as follows:

The JUDGE-ADVOCATE. After the close of yesterday's session I discovered a fact within the knowledge of Mr. Craddock, the second witness examined, that seemed of importance to the investigation, and as he is sheriff of the county in which he resides and was anxious to return, I wrote down the question and his answer last night, and if there is no objection I propose to add them to his previous testimony:

Question. State, if you please, whether Breckinridge and his forces were at Munfordville while Bragg was there.

I heard Bragg say on Thursday night, after he came in on Wednesday, that he had received a dispatch from Breckinridge, in which Breckinridge said he hoped there was no misunderstanding. General Bragg added that Breckinridge was entering West Tennessee when he should have been at Glasgow.

(Admission of the testimony objected to by General Ord.)

General BUELL. The evidence is palpably false in its peculiar features. We know that Breckinridge did not enter West Tennessee. That is a matter of certainty. I have no objection to the evidence appearing on the record.   I admit the fact that General Breckinridge was not at Munfordvilie.

The court was cleared.

After discussion a vote was taken and the question and answer decided to be admissible.

General BUELL. I desire to say that I am not satisfied with that method of obtaining information, that is, by private consultation of the judge-advocate with the witness, as a general rule. I care nothing about this particular instance. I am not satisfied that the judge-advocate should himself be willing to pursue that course.

The JUDGE-ADVOCATE. It was only because this man was sheriff of the county and anxious to return and because I wished to avoid putting the Government to the expense of recalling him that the question was put to him last night.

General BUELL. The matter and points of this investigation have only come to my knowledge as they were presented in the testimony, and I have responded to them at the moment without time or opportunity for much reflection.   It has frequently happened that questions have occurred to me which would have been pertinent, but I have let them pass, desiring not to delay the proceedings of the Commission or cause the inconvenience which would result from recalling the witness.

GEORGE R. TAYLOR (a witness for the Government), being duly sworn by the judge-advocate, testified as follows:

By the JUDGE-ADVOCATE:

Question. State your name and residence.

My name is George R. Taylor; I reside at Munfordville, Ky.

Question. Were you in Munfordville at the time of its surrender and can you state anything as to the size of General Bragg's army?

General BUELL. I request that the testimony upon this point may be determined somewhere now, because it will extend our investigations indefinitely if it is to continue.   The process of calling up witnesses merely for the purpose of multiplying evidence will prolong your investigations to an indefinite extent.

The PRESIDENT. Do I understand you to object to the testimony?

General BUELL. No, sir; but I desire to present this view of the matter to the Commission.   There must be some time when the prosecution will cease; it ought to have ceased before the defense commenced.   This indefinite calling of witnesses to give evidence on a question upon which there can be no end of testimony is useless.   The first evidence introduced before the Commission was to establish the strength of General Bragg's army, and it has been continued up to this moment, and as I introduce witnesses other witnesses are introduced on the other side.   It is an interminable way of conducting the business before the Commission, and I notify the Commission now that it will be necessary for me to summon other witnesses who were then on the line of march of the enemy to establish a truthful view of this question.   The attempt to represent Bragg's army as a handful of men is not only unfair, it is absurd.   I have no disposition to magnify it, but I am sorry to see a disposition manifested to bring it below what is really the truth.

The JUDGE-ADVOCATE. The view taken by General Buell is true, but it was an irregularity that was unavoidable from the nature of the investigation and the trouble we had to obtain witnesses at the time we wanted them. So far as establishing the fact is concerned, I seek simply to bring out the fact; it is an important one, and so long as I can find a witness and the court is open I shall certainly introduce him to show what the size of General Bragg's army was. I have no wish to place it down below what it really was. I wish to bring out the fact of what was the size of General Bragg's army.

By the JUDGE-ADVOCATE:

Question. Were you in Munfordville at the time of its surrender and can you state anything as to the size of General Bragg's army?

Yes, sir; I was there at the time of Colonel Wilder's surrender. In regard to General Bragg's army, the information I have I got mostly from the officers. General Bragg came in there in such a manner that I could not get a good opinion of the number of men he had, from the fact that he came in from below, across the railroad bridge, and from above, fording the river. I was informed by a number of the officers that the number of their regiments was sixty, and the regiments, I judge, would not average over 500. I think I made the statement to General Buell that there were not over 30,000 men.

Question. At what time did you make that statement to General Buell and what comment did he make upon it?

I made this statement to General Buell at the time his army was passing through there—the night he stopped at Woodsonville. I do not remember his making any comment upon it.

Cross-examination by General BUELL:

Question. Did you see all of the regiments?

No, sir; I do not think I did.

Question. You have stated, I believe, that your opinion of the number of regiments was formed from statements made to you by officers?

Yes, sir.

Question. Are you positive that the number you have stated was intended to embrace the whole army?

I understood it so.

Question. What officers made this representation to you as to the number of regiments?

I could not give you the names; I talked to several colonels and some other officers.

Question. At what particular time was the statement made to you—what day of the week or month or with reference to some known event?

It was at various times while General Bragg's army was there.

Question. Do you know any reason why these officers should have exposed to you the strength of Bragg's army?

No, sir. In giving the number of regiments that they had they did not give me the number of men. The idea they wished to convey was that they had more men than would be supposed from the number of their regiments; they wished to give the idea that there were more men in each regiment than they actually had.

Question. Did you think that sixty was a very large number of regiments?

No, sir; I should think they would have more men from the number of generals they had.

Question. Do you know how many men were engaged in the attack on Munfordville on the 14th of September, that is, the first attack made?

I heard Colonel Wilder give the number of regiments and brigades, but I could not state precisely. I should judge from the number he gave that there were at least two and a half men to one in the fort.

Question. How many generals were engaged in that attack, did you hear?

The commander was General Chalmers; that is the only general I know of that was engaged.

Question. Did you witness the attack?

I was in Munfordville at the time the attack commenced, but left the town and was not there during the fight.

Question. What was the loss of the enemy in killed and wounded?

Colonel Wilder told me 714.

Question. Do you think it was necessary that those officers should tell you truly in regard to their strength if there could be any possible advantage in concealing it?

No, sir; I do not.

Question. Have you heard their strength estimated to be more than that by persons who had a good opportunity of judging?

Yes, sir.

Question. Have you ever heard of their representing their strength at more than that?

No, sir; I never have. In speaking of the number of men being estimated at more than that, I speak of the number of men, not of the regiments.

Question. Have you ever heard of their claiming to have a greater number of regiments than sixty?

No, sir; I do not think I have.

Question. Did you ever see a single brigade of Bragg's army on the march or in camp?

Yes, sir; I have seen them on the march.

Question. Did you count the number of regiments in it?

No, sir; I did not.

Question. Did it have as many as four, do you think?

I could not say whether there were as many as four regiments in any I saw or not. I did not count them. I saw them as they passed.

Question. Did you ever hear how many regiments they had in their brigades generally?

No, sir.

Question. Did you ever hear how many divisions they had in the army?

Yes, sir; there were either six or seven.

Question. Do you know how many brigades they had in a division?

No, sir.

Question. Did you understand that sixty covered the whole number of regiments, cavalry and infantry?

Yes, sir; that was my understanding, although I did not make particular inquiry in regard to cavalry.

Question. Are you able to fix the length of time that was required for the army to pass any given point on the road in hours?

No, sir.

M. A. RAPIER (a witness for the defendant), being duly sworn by the judge-advocate, testified as follows:

By General BUELL:

Question. Will you state your name and residence, if you please?

M. A. Rapier, of La Rue County, Kentucky.

Question. Are you a member of the Legislature of Kentucky?

I am, sir.

Question. Had you an opportunity of observing the army of General Bragg on its passage into Kentucky last fall; and, if so, under what circumstances, and state what you know of the strength of that army, the number of regiments, &c.?

I had an opportunity of observing the army of General Bragg. The circumstances were these: I live directly upon what is known to be the Green River and Nashville turnpike road, near the foot of Muldraugh's Hill. The turnpike leads around the hill 1¼ miles and is about 25 feet wide. It was impossible for any army to pass except upon that road of 25 feet. I became somewhat alarmed and did not remain at my house, but got upon the hill, where I could see the army pass. I endeavored to estimate the army by regiments. I numbered 142 or 143 regiments, the regiments running from 200 to 600. I numbered the wagons as they passed, about 2,000, with from 6 to 8 men to a wagon. As well as I recollect there were 180 pieces of artillery. I think that includes the caissons, or wagons for hauling the ammunition. I counted until dark and they were still passing; but how many passed or whether any more passed after I left my position I cannot say, but I left them passing.

Question. Your estimate of the artillery includes not only the cannon, but the caissons, battery wagons, and all the carriages belonging to a battery, does it?

Yes, sir.

Cross-examination by the JUDGE-ADVOCATE:

Question. By what means did you count these regiments; how did you separate them into regiments?

I counted and separated them in this way, sir: There seemed to be a rear guard behind each regiment. They were in very great hurry; seemed to be on the double-quick; and between the spaces and that which seemed to me to be a guard I numbered as regiments.

Question. At what time did you take your position on the hill that day?

About an hour after sunup in the morning.

Question. You say they were moving on the double-quick. Do you mean by that that they were walking rapidly or running or what was their pace?

Some of them were walking very fast and some running.

Question. Was that pace continued during the day?

Yes, sir; it was.

Question. How many of these regiments did you count as to the number of men in each regiment?

One hundred and forty-two or one hundred and forty-three, sir. I counted various times during the day, and they invariably ran from 200 to 600; some 300; some 250; none higher than 600. I do not remember the number of times I counted the number of men in each regiment, but I counted various times during the day and found them running from 200 to 600.

Question. Do you recollect what you made the average number of the regiments?

My recollection now is that I then averaged them at 400.

Question. What was passing at the time you left?

Infantry.

Question. How long before you left had the wagons ceased passing?

The main body of the wagons had ceased passing about 12 o'clock, though occasionally wagons were passing during the whole time I was there

Question. Have you ever seen any other army pass besides this of General Bragg?

I have seen divisions of armies.

Question. Did you ever before make an estimate as to the number that passed?

I did not, sir.

By General DANA:

Question. In which direction was this army moving?

Northeast direction, sir.

Question. Did you see any cavalry in the army?

I did, sir.

Question. What part of the column did it occupy?

The greatest portion of the cavalry occupied the rear and front.

Question. Was this cavalry included in the one hundred and forty-three regiments that you counted?

It was not.

Question. How many regiments of cavalry did you see?

I did not count the regiments of cavalry.

Question. What was your estimate of the quantity of cavalry they had with them?

My impression now is that there were 1,000 or 1,500 in advance and about 1,000 in the rear.

Question. Do you know whether Breckinridge's division was in that column?

I do not, sir.

Question. Have you heard since where Breckinridge's division was about that time?

I have heard only by rumors and have no correct information on the subject.

Question. From all you have heard, state your opinion as to where Breckinridge was at that time.

From my information I think he was in Tennessee, sir.

Question. Can you state about the day of the week or month and the number of miles to the north of Munfordville that you made this count?

It was on Monday, sir. I do not recollect the day of the month, but I have it registered at home, but it was in September. It was about 35 miles northeast of Munfordville.

Question. Can you state about how many days after the surrender of Munfordville?

I think the surrender was on Wednesday or Tuesday, and it was the Monday following.

Question. What appeared to be the contents of the two thousand wagons that you saw?

A portion of them seemed to be hauling ammunition, a portion provisions, and a portion of them seemed to be entirely empty.

Question. Was the quantity of provisions large or small?

I thought small.

Question. At what time in the day did the rear guard of cavalry pass that you speak of?

A portion of the cavalry was stationed and planted cannons upon the top of Muldraugh's Hill for some three or four days; the larger portion of them, with their cannons, then went to New Haven, and there were some 300 or 400 of them captured. The capture was on Monday morning.

By the JUDGE-ADVOCATE:

Question. Please look at the map and point out the place where you made your observations.

It was 5 miles from New Haven, on the road from Glasgow to Bardstown.

Question. Please state how far you were from the road when you counted the troops.

About 50 yards.

By General SCHOEPF:

Question. Please state the length of time that it occupied the whole rebel army to pass through.

The main portion were passing from Sunday, 10 o'clock in the morning, and passed until Monday night, when I quit counting; but were passing more or less until the Monday morning following.

Question. Did you stand there all the time during the march?

I did not, sir; I was not there of nights at all.

Question. Were you there during the whole time of Sunday and Monday?

I was there from 10 o'clock Sunday morning until dark Sunday night. I was there from after sunup in the morning on Monday till dark, and the greater portion of the days up to Monday morning following.

Question. What object had you in counting the troops? Did your memory serve you in counting them or did you keep a written account of the different troops?

Fearing that I would be captured by the army, and by some threats made to my family as to my whereabouts, I was induced to secrete myself for safety; to leave my home and get upon the hill, where I had a view of 4 miles of the road, and in full view of my house and family, feeling as all men feel banished from home and possession of my house and premises taken by the army. I sat there secreted, and notched upon an old stake—cut a notch for every regiment, or that which I supposed to be a regiment; the notches are there still. I had no view in counting the regiments except as I was banished from home and had some anxiety to know the strength of the army.

By General TYLER:

Question. Were you in sight, where you could be seen by the enemy as they passed?

I was seen once, sir. On seeing me they observed there was "a damned Yankee," and to "come down from there." I made a move as if to leave, and they replied that if I attempted to run they would shoot me.

Question. Did you come down in answer to their demand?

I did not, sir; I remained still till that regiment passed and then got more out of sight.

Question. Whose regiment was that?

I do not know, sir; I do not know any regiment.

Question. What number of men were there in this regiment?

I did not count that regiment, sir.

By the JUDGE-ADVOCATE:

Question. Upon which day did you make that count of the one hundred and forty-three regiments, Sunday or Monday?

I made the count of the one hundred and forty-two or one hundred and forty-three regiments on Monday. The advance cavalry and a portion of the wagons were passing on Sunday; but no infantry passed on Sunday.

Question. What time on Sunday did the wagons and cavalry pass?

They were passing from 10 o'clock Sunday morning until dark, when I left.

Question. Where did you remain Sunday night?

The greater portion of the night in the woods; the balance I was in a neighbor's house, 4 miles from the road.

Question. When you resumed your position on Monday morning on the hill were infantry or cavalry or any portion of the forces passing?

The infantry were passing.

Question. Had they been passing before you arrived there?

I do not know, sir; they were passing when I got back to my position, but I do not know when they commenced passing.

Question. Could you see down the road any distance?

I could see some 3 or 4 miles in the direction of New Haven; that is, the direction in which they were marching.

Question. At the time you observed them passing how much of this 3 or 4 miles you could see was occupied by the troops?

It seemed to me that the entire distance of 3 or 4 miles was entirely occupied.

Question. Am I correct, then, in saying that you began counting at that time, when you resumed your position there, and counted one hundred and forty-three regiments?

General BUELL. Permit the witness to explain.

The WITNESS. It was about 10 o'clock when I thought the road was entirely filled with troops. I do not know how much of the road was occupied when I began counting.

By the JUDGE-ADVOCATE:

Question. Did you look down that road and count the regiments that had passed at the time you resumed your position?

I did not. The regiments I counted as they passed me and notched them.

Question. You have no idea, then, how many regiments had passed before you resumed your position there to count?

I have not, sir.

Question. Could you see New Haven from your position on the hill?

I could see the steeple of the church very distinctly.

Question. Do you know where Bragg's forces came from on Sunday?

I do not, sir; only by rumor.

By General SCHOEPF:

Question. How long was the whole wagon train?

The wagon train commenced passing between 10 and 11 o'clock Sunday morning, and passed as thick as they could get along till Sunday night, dark, when I left.   On Monday there were also a great many wagons passed.

Question. Were they closed up or were there intervals between the wagons?

On Sunday they were closed up pretty much; on Monday they were at intervals.

Redirect examination by General BUELL:

Question. From what point on Green River did you understand this army came?

I understood from a soldier of their ranks, against whom I accidentally ran about midnight, that he was starved, and had marched from Red Mills that day, 17 miles.

Question. I did not refer to the length of march, but at what point was it rumored that the army crossed Green River?

Near Munfordville.

Question. When you were hailed in this position and ordered to come down, was it by an individual soldier in the regiment which happened to be passing?

It was, sir.

Question. When you speak of the rear guard of cavalry do you speak of what you saw that Monday or what you know from observation about the rear guard of the army?

I did not see them upon Monday. I speak of the cavalry left upon the hill and at New Haven after the main body had left some two days.

Question. You will observe, Mr. Rapier, that the tendency of certain questions that have been asked you is to make you appear to have said that the road for 4 miles was absolutely crowded with troops, when you subsequently counted one hundred and forty-two regiments.   Please to state whether you observed the column that had passed when you took your position on the hill on Monday morning; whether you made any computation or not; whether you carefully observed the column that had passed; if it was large or small when you took your position on Monday morning.

I made no observation on the road on the morning when I took my position and commenced notching the regiments. Some time in the evening I did make observations of the road, and it seemed to me that the wagons and horses and men that were along the road seemed to occupy a great portion of it. I made no observation and no count of the troops down the road, but had taken count of the regiments as they passed opposite of me.

Recross-examination by the JUDGE-ADVOCATE:

Question. You began this counting when the sun was about an hour up; at what time did the army leave its camp and commence moving that morning?

I do not know, sir.

Question. You say that at the time you saw them and other times during the day they were moving on the double-quick; is that correct?

I mean to say that they seemed to be in a hurry; some were walking fast and some at times would run.

Question. What did you make the number of that army to be?

From my observation and calculations I made it something near 70,000, by putting the regiments at 400 and 8 men to a wagon.

Question. Does this include cavalry and artillery?

That includes all.

By General BUELL:

Question. Do you know where this army encamped Sunday night, and from where it marched Monday morning?

I do not know, sir; only by rumor.

Question. How far from the position you occupied was it said to have encamped that night?

The advance guard of infantry was said to have been encamped about 3½ miles from my position.

Question. Where did the main body encamp, according to report?

Near Hodgensville.

Question. How far from that were you?

From my position about 6½ miles.

By General SCHOEPF:

Question. Please state to the Commission if you are an unconditional Union man.

General BUELL. I object. My objection is this: That while I have the assurance and belief that Mr. Rapier is an unconditional Union man, I do not know. We all know there are a great many opinions in Kentucky, at this time particularly, and I do not think it necessary or proper that Mr. Rapier should be examined upon that question, inasmuch as it has no bearing upon the subject of investigation or the reliability of his testimony. My supposition is that Mr. Rapier would answer it affirmatively, but I do not know, as I never before saw him in my life.

The question being objected to by General Ord also, the court was cleared, when, after discussion, General Schoepf withdrew his question.

Commission adjourned to meet Friday, January 16, 1863.

LOUISVILLE, *January* 16, 1863.

Commission met pursuant to adjournment. All the members present; also the judge-advocate and General Buell.

Col. E. M. McCOOK (a witness for the defendant), being duly sworn, testified as follows:

By General BUELL:

Question. State your name and position in the service of the United States, if you please.

E. M. McCook; colonel Second Indiana Cavalry, commanding First Cavalry Brigade.

Question. Were you with your regiment on duty with the Army of the Ohio last summer during its march from Corinth to North Alabama and Middle Tennessee?

I was.

Question. Give a concise statement, if you please, of the services upon which you were engaged from the time you left Florence until you left Reynolds' Station.

I was ordered from Florence with a supply train of, I think, some four hundred and fifty wagons or probably more—I do not recollect exactly—to establish a depot at Reynolds' Station, the terminus of the railroad there. I do not recollect the dates, but it was when our army crossed the river at Florence. I was engaged while at Reynolds' Station in forwarding supplies to the Army of the Ohio at Athens.

Question. Did you leave Florence in advance of the army ?

I think, sir, I did. None of the army had passed over the road that I did.

Question. By what means were supplies forwarded from Reynolds' Station to Athens ?

By wagons.

Question. What is the distance by wagon road ?

I think 45 miles.

Question. Do you know whether all possible energy and industry were used in the transmission of supplies by this means ?

Very frequently wagons had to wait there for the want of supplies coming on the railroad. Supplies did not arrive fast enough at one time to furnish loads for the wagons; at other times two hundred and forty or two hundred and fifty wagons a day were sent off with supplies when they were there to load into the wagons.

Question. Do you know anything of the cause of this delay and how long it lasted ?

My impression is that this delay took place on several occasions. The cause was some difficulty on the railroad; what the origin of that difficulty was I do not remember. On one occasion I remember that the trestle work was burned.

Question. What was it that made it necessary to use wagon transportation between Reynolds' Station and Athens ?

Several large bridges and pieces of trestle work were destroyed on the railroad.

Question. Were the troops and bridge parties engaged in repairing these injuries ?

They were.

Question. Were they constantly and, as far as you know, industriously engaged in this way ?

They were.

Question. What was the condition of the country about Reynolds' Station in regard to supplies, both of forage and provisions for men ?

There was no forage there at all, and I think no provisions; but I know nothing positively about that.

Question. How did you get your forage for your animals ?

From Louisville or from Nashville; it came on the railroad; sacks of corn and bales of hay.

Question. Were the supplies about there so scarce as to make it absolutely necessary that this means should be resorted to to forage your animals ?

Yes, sir.

Question. Is Reynolds' Station considered to be within the limits of the most productive region of Tennessee ?

Giles County, the county it is in, is said by the citizens there to be one of the richest counties in the State.

Question. What troops did you employ in escorting these wagon trains between the points you have mentioned ?

The Second Indiana Cavalry and part of the time the Third Kentucky Cavalry.

Question. Did the movements of the enemy's cavalry make it necessary that you should employ these troops in protecting the supplies ?

I thought it necessary and prudent that all the trains should have a strong escort ?

Question. Were you at McMinnville during the summer?

I was.

Question. What was the condition of the country there in regard to supplies, both of forage and provisions?

Forage was very scarce this side of McMinnville. When I sent out some of my men to find provisions I got 20 pounds of bacon; that was all I could get; the people there said that was all they could give me.

Question. How far did you have to send to get forage for your animals usually?

From 7 to 13 miles.

Question. What force was there at this time?

General Nelson's division, Second Indiana, Fifth Kentucky, and Second Kentucky Cavalry.

Question. Did this command draw all the supplies it could from the country about there?

My own command depended entirely upon the country for forage and I think the rest of the command did. Our rations we drew from Murfreesborough.

Question. What do you know generally about the operations of the enemy's cavalry during last summer in Middle Tennessee and of the embarrassment which was caused to the service by them?

The enemy's cavalry were very active, and I always believed that all the citizens in that section of the country were engaged in annoying our trains. I know that some of them burned our railroad bridges. We never had a sufficient cavalry force down there to guard all that line; the force was smaller then than it is now.

Question. Was our cavalry force actively employed at that time?

It was employed to such an extent that both men and horses were worn-out.

Question. What was the service upon which it was employed and was that service necessary and judicious?

After the battle of Shiloh—I only speak for my own regiment then—the picket duty was so severe my men were on duty twenty-four hours and twenty-four hours off. Our troops were generally employed in picket duty and escorting trains. I believe that this service was rendered necessary from the fact that all the two or three other cavalry regiments there were entirely new and had done no military duty.

Question. What particular time do you refer to?

Immediately after the battle of Shiloh, between that time and the taking of Corinth; after that also while we were in the vicinity of Corinth. I believe, sir, it was usefully employed.

Question. The question refers more particularly to the time last summer while you were in Middle Tennessee.

There were two regiments of cavalry under my immediate supervision; they were both of them actively employed and certainly usefully employed; they were escorting supplies for the army.

Question. At what time did you discontinue the transmission of supplies from Reynolds' Station to Athens?

I think, sir, the date was the 29th of July.

Question. And for what reason?

General Jackson took command of the cavalry and started after Morgan.

Question. Were supplies still forwarded from Reynolds' Station by wagon when you left there?

I do not know; before I left they were. The first bridge was not completed when I left there; no cars had run any farther than Reynolds' Station at the time I left.

Question. While you were there did you send a train of wagons with escort to Florence for sick, do you remember?

I did; seventy-five wagons.

Question. Where were they taken to?

Brought to Reynolds' Station.

Question. And from there?

I do not know.

Cross-examination by the JUDGE-ADVOCATE:

Question. Colonel, what was the cause of the scarcity in Giles County that you speak of?

The old crop was exhausted; the new one not ripe.

Question. Cannot you recollect what time that was; somewhat near the date?

It was in the month of July.

Question. What was the force that you supplied by wagon train from Reynolds' Station to Athens.

I do not know sir; I suppose it was General Buell's army and General Mitchel's.

By General TYLER:

Question. What time is the wheat crop ripe in Giles County?

Indeed, I do not know. I have never done anything but soldiering in that part of the country.

Question. Is not the wheat crop ripe in the month of July and harvested?

I do not know. To the best of my recollection I never saw a blade of wheat growing in the county. I never observed it. I was only interested in what my horses ate.

Question. Did you see any wheat growing in the adjacent counties?

Yes, sir; I did.

Question. What counties?

I cannot say.

Question. At what time would that wheat that you saw be ready for harvesting?

I am almost ashamed to confess my ignorance, but I do not think I ever saw a crop of wheat gathered in my life. I know nothing about it.

Question. What was the condition of the corn crop last July in that part of Tennessee where you were?

Well, sir, the corn was small. I know when we marched out of Tennessee in September I tried to burn the fields, but I could not do so, it was so green; when we marched north we had no roasting-ears; in July it was very small.

Question. How early was the corn fit to be used as roasting-ears in Tennessee?

I think some time in August was the first I got.

Question. At what place was it that you attempted to burn the corn fields and at what time was it?

It was after we left Murfreesborough, at that place where one of the soldiers had been shot in a field. He had unbuttoned his pantaloons and sat down to relieve himself, when he was shot out of a house. I found his body lying there. I tried to burn the fields. Every person ran away from there; there were none but women left, no men.

I cannot fix the place, general; it was where we had to leave the pike. The bridge had been burned down, so we had to go off the road, and I found the man; he had not been shot more than five minutes. It was in September.

Question. And was this man shot when you were encamped?

We were on the march; he was one of the soldiers who were in advance and had left the colu.nn.

Question. You say in one of your answers you have no doubt the citizens burned the railroad bridges and assisted in annoying the trains. Were there any attempts at punishing them for these offenses; and, if so, what were they?

I was ordered by General Buell to hang one of them. I placed him in charge of a guard of the Seventeenth Kentucky Infantry and he escaped from them.

Question. Do you know whether any punishments were made for those offenses? If so, state what they were.

If I recollect the language of the telegraphic order I received from headquarters correctly, the instructions were that when men were caught in the act of burning railroad bridges, or tearing up the track, or committing offenses of that character, punishment should be prompt and inflicted immediately. I did not witness any punishment of that kind; but I think from reports received from my officers that punishment of that kind was inflicted on persons whom they caught there; I think they killed several men there. I am satisfied from unofficial sources they did, although I did not see it done and they made no official report to me.

Question. At what point were you stationed when it was necessary to forage from 7 to 13 miles?

At McMinnville.

Question. How far from McMinnville was it that this man was shot in the corn field?

To the best of my recollection it must be 45 or 50 miles. It was after we marched from Murfreesborough that this man was shot. At McMinnville it was a matter of nightly occurrence to have pickets shot at within two or three miles of the town.

Question. Do you wish the Commission to infer that after organizing a party for the collection of forage, provisions, &c., sent out under proper officers, that such a party could obtain only 20 pounds of bacon as the result of the expedition?

I ordered the acting quartermaster of the Seventh Pennsylvania Cavalry to take with him some of the men of the Third Kentucky, and some of his own men that had no rations except coffee, to go through the country within a safe distance and see if he could procure some rations, something to eat—flour, bacon, anything he could find. He came back and reported to me that he had procured 20 pounds of bacon—I think that was the amount—and a little corn meal, and that was all he could get. This was when we were marching either from McMinnville to Smithville or from Smithville to McMinnville. I do not remember which. It was, however, in that vicinity.

Question. What kind of an agricultural country was that?

Very poor, sir, to the best of my recollection.

Question. What were its productions?

I cannot say, sir. I do not think they raised any cotton there or very little. I have only considered an agricultural country a good one that raised something good for horses to eat. I have not noticed the other products of the country. I have been looking out for forage and felt a good deal of anxiety about it.

Question. You say you were on the march when this acting quartermaster was ordered to bring in this 20 pounds of bacon?

I was.

Question. How long was he absent in collecting this amount of supplies?

We were not in a permanent camp; we halted in the evening about dusk. I do not know how long he was absent; probably two hours.

By General SCHOEPF:

Question. Had you not while at McMinnville sufficient corn blades and corn for your animals?

With the exception of one day we had rations; how full they were I do not know. One day the teams came back without anything. There was a skirmish on the road on which they started.

Question. Could you not have subsisted your animals on green corn at that time?

As to the quantity I cannot say, but I do not think the corn was sufficiently ripe to have fed the horses entirely on it. It might have done to have mixed it with the old corn or the old corn blades.

Question. Were you with the army on the march from Nashville to Louisville?

As far as Elizabethtown.

Question. Did you not during that march capture part of the enemy's train and at what place?

Yes, sir; at Horse Well or Horse Cave. I sent Colonel Wolford over there to attack the train. He brought back three wagons loaded with flour, and said he had cut the mules out of three more and disabled them.

Question. Why was not the enemy pressed more at that time?

He sent back for re-enforcements—about getting dark—which I sent. When the attack was first made they made a very spirited resistance; some 113 infantry prisoners were taken of the escort to the train and a good many killed. It became dark before the re-enforcements arrived. Colonel Wolford reported to me that he discontinued the attack because it was dark, partly, and partly because he was afraid he would be attacked by a superior force, which he heard was still farther in the rear of the train.

Question. Did you join General Buell's command at Louisville?

No, sir. I never went any farther than Elizabethtown, and rejoined his command at Springfield, Ky.

Question. Who commanded the whole cavalry?

Colonel Kennett.

Question. Where was he; on the march from Perryville with you?

He never went to Louisville; he was at Elizabethtown. He marched from Elizabethtown to Bardstown with part of his command and remained at Bardstown till after the Perryville fight.

Question. Did you not capture some officers of Bragg's staff at Prewitt's Knob?

One battalion belonging to my brigade did.

Question. Do you know their names and where they were sent to?

I have heard their names, but forget them. Major Wynkoop informed me they were paroled. I captured one who belonged to General Polk's or General Bragg's staff, I do not recollect which. He was paroled. I took him to General Crittenden, who paroled him.

Question. Can you state the time that elapsed between the capture and release of these officers?

I cannot. The officer I spoke of was released on the third day after his capture.

By General DANA:

Question. While at McMinnville how far on the road in the direction of Dunlap did you forage?

I cannot say. Foraging was done, as a general thing, off the main roads.

Question. Can you state how far in the direction of Chattanooga from McMinnville you foraged?

I cannot say. I very seldom accompanied the foraging parties. I went out once and came back by some by-road onto the road to Chattanooga, about 8 miles from McMinnville.

Question. From what you know of the country and from reports you have received how much of a belt of country in the direction of Chattanooga from McMinnville do you suppose would be capable of supporting a considerable body of cavalry with forage?

I have never been more than 15 miles, probably, south of that. My lieutenant-colonel went, as he reported, within 20 miles of Chattanooga with cavalry, came back, and said it was the most God-forsaken country he ever saw; there was no forage nor anything else.

Question. Have you ever been in the vicinity of Sparta?

I have been within a few miles, 7 or 8, of it.

Question. How does the country from Sparta in the direction of the Sequatchie Valley compare with the country from McMinnville in the direction of the Sequatchie Valley for forage?

I know nothing about it, and therefore make no comparison.

By General SCHOEPF:

Question. On what occasion was it that your lieutenant-colonel went toward Chattanooga; was it not while General Thomas went in that direction in person?

No, sir; he went there alone. He was ordered there by General Nelson to make a reconnaissance before General Thomas came there.

By the JUDGE-ADVOCATE:

Question. At the time the Army of the Ohio fell back to Nashville from Tennessee were you in the advance or in the rear?

I think, sir, that until we arrived at Nashville we were in the rear.

Question. State, if you know, what became of the bridges and other improvements that were put on those railroads to have them in running order when you fell back.

I cannot say. I see the judge-advocate probably misunderstands where I started from. I came from McMinnville to Murfreesborough, and when the army commenced to fall back I started from Murfreesborough. I never was on the line farther south than Reynolds' Station, except as I went with my trains.

Question. Was not that officer that you captured Colonel Forsyth?

No, sir; he was captured by a major of one of my battalions.

Question. Who took the parole of those officers?

I do not know, sir; I never saw them.

Question. What was the name of the officer that captured Colonel Forsyth?

Major Wynkoop, Pennsylvania cavalry, so he informed me.

Question. Do you say that General Crittenden paroled the officer that you took?

Yes, sir.

Question. What command had Captain Gay in that march toward Perryville?

I can only reply from hearsay that he had several regiments.

Redirect examination by General BUELL:

Question. Do you know the name of any officer or officers who have knowledge of the capture and paroling of any officers of General Bragg's army while the Army of the Ohio was on the march from Bowling Green to Munfordville? If so, please give the names of those officers.

I have no knowledge of the capture and paroling. The prisoners were paroled while the army was laying at Cave City—one a Lieutenant Lay; the other a major, whose name I do not know; and then there were some 15 or 20 wounded officers whom I paroled myself.

Question. Can you name other officers who have such knowledge?

Maj. Samuel Hill, Second Indiana Cavalry, took the prisoners back. Major Starling paroled them, I believe, or General Crittenden. I had no knowledge of it.

Question. State, if you please, all the particulars of the capturing and paroling of those prisoners that you have any knowledge of yourself.

Lieutenant Lay was captured at the tunnel below Mr. Proctor's, Bell's Tavern—he and, I think, 5 men, as they were riding south. This major was captured with two or three others when that party went out to attack the train captured and brought in by Colonel Wolford. My impression is that he was reported to me first, but I turned him over to General Crittenden; but I am not positive.

Question. Was there anything peculiar in the circumstances of the capture or paroling of these prisoners?

No, sir; nothing that I am aware of, either in the capture or parole.

General BUELL. I do not understand what the purpose of the investigation on this point is, but I desire to give the Commission and the judge-advocate every possible opportunity to get any information they may wish, and I shall be very glad if the examination will be continued on that point in reference to anything that may not be understood.

The JUDGE-ADVOCATE. A Major or Colonel Forsyth, I understand, was taken prisoner at some point near Munfordville and paroled, and that he immediately returned to the army and resumed his duty there as officer. I have seen his correspondence, and I gather from that that he paid no attention to his parole.

General BUELL. How do you know he paid no attention to his parole?

The JUDGE-ADVOCATE. I gather so from his own correspondence. He writes as though he had taken part with the army in its subsequent campaign. A case of that kind occurred in the Harper's Ferry affair, and when it was complained of to General Hill he knew nothing about it and treated it with perfect contempt. If every officer paroles his captured prisoners we shall lose prisoners by not getting them properly exchanged. That is my reason for asking the question.

The WITNESS. I paroled none of those prisoners at all.

General SCHOEPF. I understood the cartel was in full operation before we marched from Nashville. If, therefore, every officer paroled prisoners according to his pleasure it would not be right. They ought to be reported to headquarters and a list taken of all the prisoners captured, because we lose 'f every officer captures and paroles " on his own hook."

General BUELL. Is there anything in the evidence to show that officers paroled men at their pleasure?

By General TYLER:

Question. What prisoners were they that you captured?

The prisoners I paroled on that march were sick and wounded. Those able to move I sent to the rear.   I also forwarded a list of all that I paroled to headquarters. The arm of the service to which I belong compels an officer to parole prisoners when he cannot communicate with his superior officers.

By the PRESIDENT:

Question. Have you no authority on that subject derived from general orders particularly applicable to you when on such expeditions?

I have never seen any such orders.

By General BUELL:

Question. Is it not frequently necessary either to parole prisoners captured in that way or to let them go?

I have seen instances where it would be impossible to carry them with you.

Question. In stating that on one occasion you endeavored to burn the corn field, do you or do you not wish it understood that you intended that as a punishment for the murder which you supposed had been committed upon the soldier by the owners of the property or do you mean that you were in the habit of doing it?

I never burnt a blade of corn in my life that I am aware of. I attempted to burn this corn field because I was sure the man had been shot at out of that house, and had it not been for the women and children I should have burned the house. I should have done it as a just punishment, for the negroes about the house told me that their master had shot the man.

LOUISVILLE, *January* 16, 1863.

Capt. ROBERT MACFEELY (a witness for the Government), being duly sworn by the judge-advocate, testified as follows:

By the JUDGE-ADVOCATE:

Question. State your name and position in the United States service, if you please.

My name is Robert Macfeely; captain, commissary of subsistence of the United States Army.

Question. State what service you were engaged in during the months of July, August, and September of last summer, and what efforts, that you know of, were made to supply the Army of the Ohio with subsistence?

I was senior commissary of subsistence in the District of the Ohio, and on General Buell's staff, stationed in the city of Nashville, in charge of the depot at Nashville and the affairs of the subsistence department generally in the District of the Ohio. Efforts were made by me to obtain subsistence through Captain Symonds, depot commissary in Louisville, and by purchases by myself, as far as I could obtain them advantageously to the Government, in Nashville; also in the latter part of August I received directions through Colonel Fry, chief of staff to General Buell, to seize all subsistence stores in Nashville and the vicinity.

Question. At what points in Tennessee during its occupation by the Army of the Ohio were you instructed to furnish subsistence?

To all points on the railroads in Tennessee occupied by our troops, namely, Franklin, Tenn.; Columbia, Huntsville, Athens, Ala.; Decatur, Stevenson, Decherd Station, Murfreesborough; occasionally at Gallatin and at Clarksville so long as it was occupied by our troops, and probably other points occupied temporarily.

Question. How far were you successful in getting subsistence at these points?

I believe we were successful until the road was cut in the first place, I think some time in July, when there was no river communication to Nashville, at which time General Buell deemed it advisable, in consequence of the limited supplies on hand, to reduce the troops to half rations. On the resumption of communication by rail, stores came through regularly, and I believe, at least so it was said by the agents of the railroad company, as fast as they could carry them, until it was cut again in August.

Question. What time that summer did the Cumberland cease to be navigable?

My impression is that it was about the middle of July. I received stores by, I think, three or four steamers, which were left at Clarksville by the boats that brought them from Louisville, they being unable to get to Nashville in consequence of the insufficiency of water on the shoals. Most of these stores were brought up by light-draught boats from Clarksville; some of them were taken possession of when Clarksville fell.

Question. What became of the subsistence at these various points you have enumerated when the Army of the Ohio fell back to Nashville?

They were brought to Nashville on the cars and turned over to Captain Little, in charge of the depot store-house.

Question. Are you certain that none of them were destroyed?

No, sir; I am not. I know that some of them were brought away and turned over to Captain Little, and I was informed officially by Captain Darr, commissary of subsistence, attached to General Buell's headquarters in the field, that he brought all the stores from Stevenson, Decherd, and other points.

Question. Can you state to the Commission the amount of stores brought back in that way to Nashville?

I cannot state from memory. Captain Darr or Captain Little's provision returns for the months of August and September would show the amount received from the commissaries in those places.

Question. How far were you successful in purchasing or seizing stores about Nashville for the benefit of the army?

I purchased in open market in all 8,000 or 10,000 barrels of flour, which was all I purchased. Captain Little, under my directions, seized all the salt meat, flour, and other subsistence stores in the hands of the wholesale merchants in Nashville and in the country as far as we could obtain them. His reports will show the amounts.

Question. How many days' rations did the army take when it marched from Nashville to Bowling Green?

My impression is that they were ordered to take five days' rations, sufficient for subsistence to Bowling Green.

Question. How many rations had you at Bowling Green at that time?

I do not know, sir. I was not in communication with Bowling Green; but I heard unofficially that there was a considerable amount of stores there, I think a million of rations, which were intended for Nashville, but were stopped after the railroad was cut.

Question. Can you give the Commission any information as to the condition of the country about Nashville in August as to subsistence of this sort?

I made frequent inquiries, as it was my duty to do, as to the resources of the country in the vicinity of Nashville for supplying the army with subsistence. From citizens of Nashville and in the country around I was informed that nearly all the hogs and beef cattle in that part of Tennessee had been killed the winter previous by the rebels and salted in Nashville, and that most of the flour was also used by the Confederate army previous to our arrival there.

Question. What do you know of your own personal knowledge of these facts?

I have no means of knowing except through inquiry. I have not been over the country, never 5 miles from Nashville, from the time I was stationed there. From the quality of cattle which was seized by the army that remained in Nashville after the departure of General Buell I think that the statement as far as regards the cattle is correct. As the cattle seized and killed by us were generally yearlings, milch cows, and bulls; not one out of 20 cattle killed was such as would have been received from regular army contractors, and not fit for beef. The average weight was about 300 to 350 pounds of the cattle seized.

Question. Did the army suffer any while they were on half rations and while they were depending principally on the seizures in the neighborhood?

I will state that for a few days after the departure of General Buell, there being but a limited supply of small rations on hand—sugar, coffee, rice, &c., and having a large amount of hard bread and flour—I reported to General Thomas and requested that he would order the issue of full rations of flour and beef, as I thought there was sufficient to last his army until General Buell would return or for a month or six weeks. I submitted a statement of the amount on hand to General Thomas, and he authorized me to issue full rations of flour and meat. I saw no suffering of the men while they were on half rations and I heard no complaints.

Question. Were you with the army while stationed at these various points you have enumerated in Tennessee?

No, sir; I speak in my answer of what I saw and heard. I was not out of Nashville.

Cross-examination by General BUELL:

Question. Could the effect of half rations upon troops that were stationary in garrisons like those at Nashville be any criterion for judging of the sufficiency of such an allowance for troops that were engaged in active service in the field?

It would not. Troops on active duty and marching require more sustenance than those who are leading an inactive life.

Question. Is there not also a much greater wastage of provisions in the hands of troops when they are engaged in active service than when they are stationary?

There is probably twice as much wasted.

Question. Do you know, by the reports of officers of your department or otherwise, that instead of destroying its supplies when it was moving upon Nashville the army collected all the supplies it could from the country and brought them along with it?

Captain Darr, commissary of General Buell's staff, informs me that he had directed the commissaries at all the stations on the Chattanooga Railroad to seize all the cattle and other stores that they could and requested me to give the same directions to the commissary at Columbia and Franklin. I know that these orders were complied with, as beef cattle and flour were brought into Nashville with the army and turned over to the depot. At the time General Buell's army left Nashville, after taking the beef required by them, there were some 600 or 800 head of cattle remaining in Nashville in the hands of the officers of the subsistence department. These cattle were mostly seized by the different commissaries; a few were contract cattle.

Question. Do you know whether the supplies brought in in this way were taken up on the returns of the depot commissaries and issued regularly like other supplies?

I believe all the stores and cattle seized by the different commissaries previous to General Buell's departure from Nashville were turned into the depot and taken up on the returns of Captain Little, and issued regularly as other supplies were issued. After General Buell's departure there were very few supplies, with the exception of beef cattle, turned into the depot. If any were taken by the different foraging parties sent out at various times they were not turned into the depot there, but were issued irregularly, if issued at all.

Question. What is your observation of the system of supplying troops by foraging parties, both as regards the discipline of the troops and the economical use of the supplies?

From my observation of foraging, as carried on at Nashville, I consider it very ruinous to the discipline of the army. I saw numerous foraging parties at various times on their return to Nashville—men straggling, coming in without any order, every man for himself; some carrying chickens and other fowls, others pigs, bacon, candle-molds, chairs, brooms, and almost every article of household furniture.

These articles were not turned in, as required by General Halleck's order in reference to foraging parties, to the depot commissary, but were consumed by the individuals who took them or were disposed of in the stores in the city. There was only one exception that I saw, and that was a regiment commanded by Colonel Roberts, who brought his regiment in in fine condition, and it was a general remark among the officers as to the contrast between them and others.

Question. Is there any known process by which an officer at the head of the subsistence department of any army, like yourself, can gain information of the statistics and resources of the county about him except by the reports of others?

I believe not. I know of no other way except from his own personal observation in traveling over the country himself and examining it; I mean in regard to a country occupied by troops of both armies and the supplies consumed in the country ordinarily in times of peace. He may gain information from census reports and other reports made by State and county officers, but this would be no guide to the supplies in a country during a time of war.

Question. Would it be possible for an officer in that position to gain that information by personal observation and attend to his other duties at the same time? In other words, is there but one known way by which such information can be obtained, and that from the report of others?

General SCHOEPF. I object to this question. We are not here to examine officers in regard to their capacity or ability as to what they could have done, but we are here to establish facts as to what has been done.

The court was cleared, when, after discussion, it was decided that the question be put.

The WITNESS. It would not be possible for an officer to attend to his other duties and obtain this information by personal observation; he must depend entirely upon the reports of others who are familiar with the resources of the country.

Commission adjourned to meet Saturday, January 17, 1863.

LOUISVILLE, *January* 17, 1863.

Commission met pursuant to adjournment. All the members present; also the judge-advocate and General Buell.

Captain MACFEELY'S testimony continued, as follows:

Redirect examination by General SCHOEPF:

Question. You stated yesterday the different stations at which you had provisions; had you any at McMinnville and Winchester?

I stated yesterday some of the stations—all that I could recollect at the time—but said that there were probably other stations which were occupied temporarily by the troops. McMinnville and Winchester were supplied from Murfreesborough and from Tullahoma; but Murfreesborough and Tullahoma received their supplies direct from the depot at Nashville.

By General TYLER:

Question. Under whose order was this foraging carried on in the vicinity of Nashville?

I believe it was under the orders of General Negley, the commanding officer of the post.

Question. Were you there at the time this foraging was made?

I was, sir.

Question You stated in your testimony that Colonel Roberts brought in his regiment in fine condition; what amount of forage and provisions did he bring in?

He brought in no subsistence stores, at least none that were turned over to me at the depot. He had a number of wagon loads of hay and corn. I do not know whether this forage was turned into the depot or not. I meant that Colonel Roberts came in in good condition, and my reference to him was as to the manner in which the men marched—in close order and in a soldier-like manner, and as contrasting with the straggling parties that I had seen before, and that the men did not carry anything on their persons but their arms and accouterments.

Question. You stated in your testimony that "the men came straggling in, without any order, every man for himself, some carrying chickens and other fowls, others pigs, bacon, candle-molds, chairs, brooms, and almost every article of household furniture. These articles were not turned in, as required by General Halleck's order with reference to foraging parties, to the depot commissary, but were consumed by the individuals who took them or disposed of in the stores of the city;" and that Colonel Roberts' regiment was the only exception that you saw. Did you report these facts to your commanding general?

I did not.

Question. Why, as an officer of the staff, did you not report these facts to your commanding general?

These facts were so common as to have been the public talk in the town among officers, and the immediate officers of the staff of General Negley must have been cognizant of them and it was their duty to report them.

Question. Knowing these facts, as a staff officer of General Buell would you not consider it your duty to report to him?

I would had I been in communication with General Buell's headquarters.

Question. Were you not in communication with General Buell's headquarters; did you not receive requisitions from there?

I was not in communication with General Buell's headquarters. General Buell's headquarters at the time were in Kentucky. All communication was cut off between the army of Kentucky and Nashville. I received no requisitions from his headquarters for supplies at that time and they drew their supplies from other sources.

Question. Please fix the dates, as nearly as you can, between which these irregularities in collecting forage and subsistence occurred.

From about the middle of September until the end of October; it may have been a few days more or less.

Question. Between those dates were your communications cut off from General Buell's headquarters?

Yes, sir; all regular communications. I knew of no couriers or express or mail leaving for General Buell's headquarters during that period that I can recollect.

By General DANA:

Question. To whom is the neglect attributable for these irregularities that you have enumerated?

I do not know. I merely state the irregularities I saw without fixing the responsibility upon any person, as by doing so it would be a mere matter of opinion.

Question. Who was commanding officer at Nashville during that time?

General Negley.

Question. Who was inspector-general at Nashville at that time and had he any assistants; and, if so, who were they?

I know no person who occupied the position of inspector-general.

Question. Name the provost-marshal and his assistant at that time.

Colonel Gillem, Tenth Tennessee, was provost-marshal. I do not know that he had any assistant.

Question. What officer of General Negley's staff was performing the duty generally incumbent on the inspector?

I do not know of any officer performing that duty.

Question. Who was chief of General Negley's staff at that time?

I do not think he had any chief of staff; at that time Captain Lowrie was his assistant adjutant-general on his staff.

By the JUDGE-ADVOCATE:

Question. This pillage under the name of foraging broke out about that time, did it not; it was not known to the army before?

I do not know whether it was known to the army before. It first came to my knowledge in Nashville about that time.

Question. Had not General Buell been very strict in that respect, prohibiting such acts upon the part of his soldiers and protecting property generally?

I believe he had been very strict in prohibiting it. I have no personal knowledge except of what occurred at General Buell's headquarters when he was in the vicinity of Nashville and of the army that was left there.

Question. Did you not know that it was a matter of complaint among the officers, when they were sent out on these foraging expeditions, that they were embarrassed by safeguards distributed over the country?

I do not. I would also say that about the time that I received orders from General Buell to seize the subsistence stores in Nashville and in the vicinity we also received an order stating that all safeguards heretofore given by him would not be considered as protecting provisions and forage.

Question. Do you recollect the date of that?

I think it was somewhere about the 1st of September or the latter part of August.

Recross-examination by General BUELL:

Question. Is it not an admitted fact that such irregularities as you have yourself witnessed are more or less inseparable from the system of supplying an army by foraging, and is it or is it not your opinion that they are particularly unavoidable in an army where the means of discipline are as insufficient as they are with ours?

I think it is a fact generally conceded that a system of foraging carried on promiscuously has the effect to ruin the discipline of an army; that it is unavoidable in an army where the punishment is so inadequate for grave offenses as it has been in ours.

General BUELL. There is one witness I would like the judge-advocate to call for himself, not for me. His testimony, I think, is necessary at any rate to give value to testimony that has already been given, and that is the man Miller, who has been said to have brought a message from Colonel Wilder to the commanding officer at Bowling Green. It is not to me a matter of any consequence whether the message was sent, as stated by Colonel Wilder, or whether it was delivered; but as a matter of curiosity, and as having its connections which may be of interest, if not of consequence, I should be glad to have him before the Commission.

The PRESIDENT. That is a matter which I feel should to a great extent be left to the judgment of the judge-advocate. I hardly think it is proper for the Commission to assume to manage his examination for him.

General BUELL. Then, if it is more proper, I beg to make the suggestion to the judge-advocate himself.

Commission adjourned to meet Monday morning, January 19, 1863.

LOUISVILLE, *January* 19, 1863.

Commission met pursuant to adjournment. All the members present; also the judge-advocate and General Buell.

Capt. H. C. SYMONDS (a witness for the Government), being duly sworn by the judge-advocate, testified as follows:

By the JUDGE-ADVOCATE:

Question. State your name and position in the United States service

H. C. Symonds, captain, commissary of subsistence.

Question. Were you engaged as commissary of subsistence—if s., where—during the summer of Bragg's invasion of Kentucky?

I have been in the commissary department here in Louisville since September, 1861.

Question. You can state whether you were engaged in forwarding subsistence to the Army of the Ohio previous to and during the invasion of Kentucky.

I furnished all the subsistence for that army that was regularly furnished by the subsistence department.

Question. What lines of communication did you use in forwarding subsistence?

Principally the Louisville and Nashville Railroad.

Question. Did you use the Cumberland River, and was it used to its full capacity previous to its ceasing to be navigable and when did it close that summer?

About the last of April it was considered that the Cumberland was not very available as a means of transportation. There was low water, and nothing but light-draught boats could get up from about the last of April. I was not called upon to furnish all the supplies for Nashville during the whole month of May, only limited quantities, and not for the whole army there. I think the first shipment I made for the whole army, when it drew its whole supplies from Nashville, began about the 14th of June.

Question. Can you state what amount you did send to Nashville by way of the river?

I sent to Nashville by railroad between the 14th of June and the 11th of August very nearly 4,000,000 of rations: Coffee, 3,900,000 rations; sugar, 3,800,000 rations; salt meat, 2,800,000; hard bread, 3,400,000. In order to hurry them up we used boats. They could only go up to the Shoals, and from there they were lightered up by small boats. There were three or four boats employed by the quartermaster for this purpose, but none of them could go beyond the Shoals; some of them could go no farther than Clarksville. We sent up between July 10 and July 23 (after which there was so much difficulty in getting supplies up by the river that it was the opinion of the quartermaster that we had better rely wholly upon the railroad) what would amount to about 300,000 rations. We sent 700,000 rations of salt meat, 650,000 rations hard bread, 300,000 coffee and sugar. I preferred to send the coffee and sugar by railroad; they were the most valuable parts of the rations and the least in bulk. The total amount sent to Nashville between July 14 and August 11 (when shipments were stopped), the receipts of which were acknowledged, was: Salt meat, 3,000,000 rations; hard bread, 4,000,000 rations; coffee, 4,200,000 rations; rice, 1,400,000 rations; beans, 1,990,000 rations; sugar, 4,200,000 rations; candles, 4,400,000 rations; soap, 3,800,000 rations; salt, 5,000,000 rations; and nearly the full amount of the remaining portion of the rations.

Question. What amount was accumulated at Bowling Green from

Louisville after the railroad was cut between Bowling Green and Nashville?

There was shipped between the 18th and 27th of August for Bowling Green and received there 300,000 rations salt meat, 80,000 rations of hard bread, 1,900,000 rations beans, 200,000 rations rice, 1,280,000 rations coffee, 1,129,000 rations sugar, 780,000 rations soap. That was all that reached there.

Question. What do you know, captain, of subsistence reaching the Army of the Ohio, while it was occupying Tennessee and part of Alabama, by the way of the Tennessee River?

A part of the time that the army was on the Tennessee in the vicinity of Pittsburg Landing and Bridgeport I furnished the supplies. The first shipment was made on the 15th of May, and I sent up to that army while they were there 1,200,000 rations of salt meat. In round numbers the average number of rations I sent up the Tennessee River was 1,800,000 to the 13th of June, when I was ordered to send no more up.

Question. What is the weight of a single ration?

Gross weight about 3¼ pounds.

Cross-examination by General BUELL:

Question. Do the quantities stated in your testimony represent what was receipted for to you or what was actually received at Nashville?

What was receipted for to me.

Question. How is it in reference to quantities you have assigned to Bowling Green in that respect?

The same way. I have receipts for that amount. There was a large amount sent out to the depot which was never shipped and afterward returned to me from the railroad depot, and that particular part that was returned was probably the most essential to the movements of an army, namely, salt meat and bread.

Question. Is that included in the quantity represented as having been sent to Bowling Green?

No, sir.

Question. Were you frequently reminded last summer by communications from my headquarters of the importance of accumulating supplies at Nashville?

I was.

Question. Did you use all possible industry and energy for that object?

I did. While I was receiving those dispatches I went so far as to give some advice, to which I did not get a very satisfactory answer.

Question. If you regard that advice as of interest or importance to this investigation state what it was and what answer you received.

I found that by using all the energy and industry that I could I could not get forward the amount of full rations that seemed to be desired at Nashville, and I telegraphed to Colonel Fry that if they would not use more than half rations of salt meat, and would use less hard bread and more flour and procure their flour as far as possible in the country, I could easily supply the army; otherwise I could not see my way clear. He asked me in his answer what I meant by "not seeing my way clear." If I could procure the supplies here there would be no difficulty about transportation; that the quartermaster could furnish plenty, and the agents of the railroad assured him there was plenty of transportation if I would furnish supplies. That was the substance of it, though not perhaps the exact words.

Question. Have you those dispatches?

I do not know whether I have Colonel Fry's dispatch to me or not. I kept it in my pocket for a time and did not put it on the file. I have my first dispatch to him which called forth that answer.

Question. Present both of them to the Commission or whatever you have.

I have merely my own dispatch. I have been hunting for his reply. Mine was in answer to a dispatch from him asking how many rations I had on the way to Nashville and was as follows:

"JULY 15.

"I have now 800,000 full rations on the way to Nashville, half by boat and half by rail. Have shipped to Nashville since July 1 over 1,000,000 rations; shipped from the middle to the end of June 1,000,000 rations. Captain Macfeely calls for 2,000,000 a month. You must use much less hard bread, only half salt meat, or the stores cannot be transmitted. If you make the troops use flour and buy it where you are I can easily feed the army, but at present rates of hard bread and salt meat I cannot see my way clear."

Question. What proportion of the rations does that dispatch propose should be procured in the country?

I think it would take out fully one-third, possibly two-fifths, in the gross weight of the rations if it had been arranged for the rations to be drawn in that manner.

Question. Make the calculation, if you please, according to the suggestion in your dispatch. Does that make about $1\frac{3}{4}$ to be procured there?

It leaves about $1\frac{7}{10}$ to be procured there.

Question. Did you know what the resources of the country were when you made this suggestion, and was it only a suggestion or was it advice?

I did not know. I gave the suggestion as advice.

Question. Why would you advise what you did not know to be practicable?

Because I was convinced it would be impossible to meet all the demands made for provisions from Nashville.

Question. And suppose they could not be met there, would you still advise that they should be met there?

I had no advice to give beyond that. I merely gave it as advice. I saw the difficulties at this end of the line and I thought I appreciated them, and I thought I would advise them to do as much as they could in procuring supplies. I did not know what the capacities of the country were. Captain Macfeely was almost daily writing and telegraphing to furnish supplies to him, but I could not get them down.

Question. Do you know whether any supplies were issued to troops along the line from the stock that was sent to Bowling Green for the army in Tennessee?

I do not. I continued to send supplies until the railroad was cut this side of Bowling Green. I do not know what use was made of these rations sent to Bowling Green after the railroad was cut.

Question. Do you know why the use of the Green River was discontinued as a means of throwing supplies into Bowling Green?

I do not recollect that it was used at all for that purpose.

Question. Where do you procure provisions, particularly the bread and meat, that you send for the use of the army in Tennessee?

Principally in Cincinnati, Chicago, Saint Louis, Louisville, and the towns along the Ohio River.

Question. Do you procure large quantities in Kentucky?

No, sir; the greater part comes from beyond Kentucky.

Question. Is it because the supplies are not to be had in sufficient quantity that you procure them beyond the limits of Kentucky?

I do not know that the kind I require could be procured in Kentucky in such large quantities as I required to use them; certainly not of hard bread.

Question. Do you know what was the estimated daily consumption of rations by the army in Tennessee last summer (including wastage) of all authorized issues, both to troops and employés?

I had a great many letters from Captain Macfeely, and he repeatedly said he required 2,000,000 of rations a month. One time he called for 2,100,000, but his letters invariably referred to 2,000,000 a month that I must send to Nashville. Just before the railroad was cut between Nashville and Bowling Green he called for about 2,500,000 rations to be forwarded immediately and that they must arrive there before the 15th of August, as that amount would be necessary to fill up the depots, as ordered by General Buell.

Question. Could you procure in that part of Kentucky, that is, conveniently within your reach, flour enough to supply the army in Tennessee?

I could.

Question. Where would you get it from?

I could get large quantities in the vicinity of Bowling Green, and also in the vicinity of Louisville.

Question. Do you get any considerable quantities from those regions?

Nearly all the flour I use I procure here in Louisville. All the flour that is used in and around Bowling Green is procured by the commissary from that part of the country and has been for some time.

Question. Is what you procure in Louisville the product of this State or does it come from abroad?

I think it is the product of this State. The mills are here in town.

Question. Do you know whether flour and meat were shipped to Nashville last spring and all the time after the occupation of that place for a market when the routes by river and railroad were open?

I have no knowledge of anything of the kind.

By the JUDGE-ADVOCATE:

Question. Were not the troops along the line between this and Bowling Green supplied from here as usual after the road was cut between Bowling Green and Nashville?

I suppose so. I should have to go to my books to see if I shipped to points along the line.

Question. Please do so.

By General TYLER:

Question. Did you attempt to make any purchases of any part of your rations at Bowling Green or anywhere along the line of railroad between here and Nashville?

All my purchases I made in answer to advertisements, and I do not think anybody from Bowling Green ever bid; but I received letters from parties at Bowling Green offering to sell flour or bacon, but I wrote to the commissary there to attend to that himself; if there was flour to be bought, to procure all he needed at Bowling Green, to send his account to me, and I would pay him. I never bought any myself there.

Question. Were any purchases made under these instructions that you recollect; and, if so, to what extent?

There were some purchases made of flour under these instructions, but how much I cannot say.

Commission adjourned to meet Tuesday, January 20, 1863.

LOUISVILLE, *January* 20 1863.
Commission met pursuant to adjournment. All the members present; also the judge-advocate and General Buell.

General LOVELL H. ROUSSEAU (a witness for the Government), being duly sworn by the judge-advocate, testified as follows:

By the JUDGE-ADVOCATE:

Question. State, if you please, your name and position in the United States service.

Lovell H. Rousseau, major-general of volunteers.

Question. You will state, general, whether you were present at the battle of Perryville; and, if so, who marked out your line of battle upon that day.

At the battle of Perryville, or Chaplin Hills as it was called by our commander, I made my line of battle myself. Some changes were made by General McCook by consultation between us and some by him without consultation. General McCook was not on the ground when I first formed the line of battle.

Question. At what time did you arrive there and how long after was it that you saw General McCook?

It is hard to tell what time we reached the ground. I suppose it must have been about 10 or 11 o'clock; but I am not positive. General McCook was with me on the march and up to the time that we fell in with General or Captain Gay (whatever he may be), commander of cavalry. We heard firing of cannon for some hours as we approached the ground upon which the battle was fought. On the march I think General McCook received a note from General Buell, or else he had received it that morning, stating to him that he should approach Perryville with caution. That, I think, was the substance of the note. When we got to where we could see a portion of the enemy in the woods, who seemed to be scouts, watching, General McCook directed me to send forward a reconnaissance, leaving my artillery in the rear on the road—that the enemy were in the vicinity of Perryville, and would probably resist our approach in that direction. I did so, and they reported the enemy in view when they arrived in sight of the battle ground. I sent word back to General McCook that the enemy were in view. He came up to the front, and we rode up and looked over the ground and selected the line of battle, which was in rear of where it was actually fought. The enemy, however, seemed to be giving way and Gay seemed to be pursuing. He had two pieces of artillery and, I think, nearly all the cavalry. He wrote me a note to send him a regiment to support his pieces; that he had been driving them nearly all the morning. I sent him the regiment, which went to the front where his pieces were.

I made a mistake in my report of the battle in saying it was Captain Harris, when it should have been Captain Hotchkiss, who commanded the section. I did not catch the correct name in the confusion incident to the firing. We saw but few of the enemy, who soon disappeared from view and left toward Perryville. Hotchkiss' pieces were of short range, and I sent back for others to shell where we thought the enemy were. They finally disappeared, and I concluded, and so I supposed did McCook, that they would not fight at or near that point. He then rode off to see General Buell. I did not see him as he left. The enemy disappeared, and after waiting perhaps an hour—I do not remember the exact time—and my men having had no water for a long time and being near the Chaplin Creek and as we were halted by the enemy, I supposed I would be substantially obeying orders by moving on toward the water. I put the column in motion. As the head of the column was approaching to where Hotchkiss' pieces were my attention was called—I do not know by whom—to the fact that the enemy were in view again. I rode up to where these pieces were and got Hotchkiss' glass, and just as I was putting it to my eye they opened some two or three batteries and there was a very rapid and accurate firing of shells. I directed Captain Loomis to bring up the balance of his battery and Captain Simonson to bring up his. They did so, and the enemy soon ceased their rapid firing, but separated their pieces and kept up firing at intervals. I think the enemy had two or three batteries massed at that point. After that shelling they advanced their infantry and I galloped back to the balance of my troops to get them in position so as to front in that direction. The line I selected was almost at right angles with the line of the main army, which was fronting toward Perryville. I had formed, I believe, two brigades, Colonel Harris' brigade and Colonel Lytle's, or rather I directed Colonel

Lytle to form his own and I showed Colonel Harris where to form his, and after sending several messages to Colonel Starkweather, who was separated from my command by General Jackson cutting him off, he arrived and reported to me, and I formed his brigade on the left. General McCook, however, returned before I had placed Starkweather in line, and by his orders Generals Jackson and Terrill moved a battery and some of their troops to support it through my lines to the front.

The following note, produced at the president's direction from among the orders of General Buell to General McCook, is identified by General Rousseau as the note referred to in the testimony, and made part of the record at the request of General Buell:

> HEADQUARTERS OF GENERAL BUELL,
> *October 7, 1862—8 p. m.*
>
> GENERAL: The Third Army Corps (Gilbert's) is within 3½ miles of Perryville, the cavalry being nearer, probably within 2¼ miles. From all the information gained to-day it seems probable that the enemy will resist our advance into the town. They are said to have a strong force in and near the place. There is no water here and we will get but little, if any at all, until we get it at Perryville. We expect to attack and carry the place to-morrow.
>
> March at 3 o'clock precisely to-morrow morning without fail, and move up until the head of your column gets to within 3 or 3½ miles of Perryville; that is to say, until you are abreast of the Third Corps, the rest of the corps resting near Bottom's place.* Perhaps Captain Williams, Jackson's cavalry, will know where it is. From the point of the road Gilbert is now on across direct to your road is about 2½ or 3 miles. When the head of your column gets to the vicinity designated (3 or 3½ miles from town), halt and form it in order of battle and let the rear close well up, then let the men rest in position and be made as comfortable as possible, but do not permit them to scatter. Have the country on your front examined, a reconnaissance made, and collect all the information possible in regard to the enemy, the country, and the roads in your vicinity, and then report in person as quickly as practicable to these headquarters. If your men have an opportunity to get water of any kind they must fill their canteens and the officers must caution them particularly to use it in the most sparing manner. Send to the rear every wagon and animal which is not required with your column. All the usual precautions must be taken and preparation made for action. Keep all teams back except ammunition and ambulances.
>
> Nothing has been heard from you to-day. Send orderlies by bearer to learn the locality of these headquarters. The general desires to see Captain Williams, Jackson's cavalry, by 7 o'clock in the morning at these headquarters.
>
> Very respectfully, yours, &c.
>
> JAMES B. FRY,
> *Colonel and Chief of Staff.*
>
> A true copy.
>
> J. M. WRIGHT,
> *Assistant Adjutant-General.*
>
> Addressed to General McCook.

The WITNESS. I do not recollect having seen that note but once, and then only for a moment on the march; that was the next day after it was written. I received orders from General McCook at about 3.30 o'clock, I think, on the morning after the note was written, to march at 5 o'clock. I grumbled a little at the short notice, rode down to his headquarters, and he remarked to me that he had received it at a very late hour himself. I saw another note or two, perhaps, from General Buell, which were received, I think, on the march. I do not remember their substance, though I think I read them. The note just read and placed on the record is the note I previously referred to in my testimony.

Question. How long after the enemy began shelling you was it before you saw General McCook?

I cannot tell. It was not very long, but I do not recollect the exact time. General McCook came and aided in forming the line of battle, as previously stated.

Question. Did you see him during the action, and what orders did you receive from him?

He and I were in different parts of the field, I suppose. I was on the left of the line

---

* See Buell's copy of this dispatch, p. 50.

and in the center and kept so busy that I did not leave the lines. General McCook
sent word to me by an aide to see him at Russell's house, I think it was; it was just
in the center of the rear of our lines. That was late in the afternoon, and as we approached the house two or three batteries opened upon us from a point between us and
Perryville with shell, and it was the most rapid firing I have ever yet seen or heard.
I do not know whether the shells struck the house or not, but the air seemed full of
them. I think I saw as many as four or five burst at a time. When I got near the
house I was informed that General McCook had just left and was gone over toward
the left center of the line. There I found the Fifteenth Kentucky falling back and
a brigade of the enemy which had turned my right approaching from beyond the
house. My time for the next three-quarters of an hour was taken up in repelling
that attack, and I could not leave to hunt up General McCook, the attack was so
fierce and the result of the enemy's success would have been so disastrous to me; so
I did not see General McCook; that night he was on the ground; I could hear of him,
but could not get to leave my men to see him until after dark. The enemy pressed
us so hard that I had not a moment's time to go anywhere. Not having seen General
McCook I rode up to see General Buell, hoping to see General McCook there. Being
late in the evening, I supposed he had left and gone to General Buell, with whom I
had an interview and told him the result of the day. I told General Buell we would
require re-enforcements if the enemy renewed their attack in the morning. I remember when I said to him that they might renew their attack in the morning he
said, "We will not wait for them to attack; I will attack them at daybreak."
I went back then to General McCook and told him General Buell wanted to see
him, as all the commanders of corps were going to meet at General Buell's headquarters. He left about 11 o'clock at night to see General Buell, and directed me to
contract my lines and take another position on some hills there, which I did about
half past three in the morning.
I understood from General Buell, in substance, that he was prepared to make an
attack, and did not want to fustrate his plans by sending troops to the left unless
absolutely necessary, and that that necessity could be avoided by an early and vigorous attack at or near Perryville, and I was satisfied myself that if they were attacked there they could not fight us on the left, as that swept around by a sort of left
half wheel and would have placed the enemy rather in the rear of the main army
when they advanced and they could not have staid there. The general instructions
were to get my men so close together that I could hold my position there so as to let
the army attack with the force designed for that purpose.
On my return from General Buell's headquarters I found that General McCook had
not left the ground at all, but had called at my headquarters several times to see me,
and I found him there on my return. He then went with me and we selected a new
line of battle, which he desired me to take while he went to see General Buell. I
received during the day several orders from General McCook to advance bodies of
troops. I do not remember all the orders now. I received orders at the beginning
of the fight, I remember very distinctly, to advance certain regiments to the front,
which I did, to support the troops of Jackson and Terrill.

Question. At about what time was it, general, that this heavy firing
occurred near the Russell house that you spoke of?

About three-quarters of an hour before night.

Question. When you visited General Buell's headquarters do you
know whether you were the first to inform him of the action ?

I was not the first. I told the general about the fight. I thought it had been an
exceedingly hard one, but the general was pretty cool about it. I told him that I
thought he did not appreciate the fight we had had, and that it was the hardest fight
I had ever seen. He said he did appreciate it; that late in the afternoon he had heard
of the battle; and my impression was that it was between 3 and 4 o'clock that he got
the information, as he said, from an aide of General McCook that a battle was going
on and re-enforcements were needed, and that he had ordered re-enforcements as soon
as he got the information that they were required. His remark as to re-enforcements
was called forth by a remark of my own that we had much needed them during the
day. I recollect telling him about the enemy's constantly pressing forward without
caring whether they were killed or not; and he remarked to me that there seemed to
be no advance of the other side, or words to that effect, and I told him that we had a
little more than we could do to hold our own. It was very clear to my mind, from all
that occurred there between General Buell and myself, that he did not fully appreciate the fight we had had, though as the news came in from various persons he
learned the true state of affairs. It was clear to my mind that the information he had
received about the matter did not exhibit to him the true state of affairs on the left.
Some of General Buell's aides had been over on the battle ground while the fight was

progressing late in the afternoon, I understood. The general said there had been cannonading as the army advanced, sometimes more rapidly than others, but he had no information that there was a general engagement till late in the afternoon of that day. General Buell's headquarters were about 3 miles from where the battle was fought. I traveled in the night, however, and could not give an accurate judgment as to the distance.

Question. How was General Gilbert situated in reference to your forces that day?

I did not see General Gilbert during the whole day. I saw the left of his forces, or what I supposed were his, in line of battle not far from my right, perhaps not more than 400 to 600 yards.

Question. They were near enough to render you assistance when your right was turned, were they not?

Almost any part of the army might have been sent to re-enforce us. Gilbert's line, however, had been withdrawn when my right was turned. I think it had fallen back; but I speak of this from hearsay. I did not notice that the line was withdrawn. He was certainly near enough to render us assistance had he been inclined to do it. When I say "any part of the army might have come to our assistance," I do not mean to speak of the propriety of its doing so, but that it was near enough to do so.

Question. What command had Captain Gay that day?

I understood he had the command of all the cavalry.

By General DANA:

Question. What was your opinion on the evening of the 8th, about the time you left the field to go to General Buell's headquarters, regarding the enemy, as to whether they had been defeated or had gained a victory?

It was very certain they had gained no victory. They had gained some advantages on our left, but were finally repulsed and held and during the night they fell back, leaving their dead for us to bury.

Question. At the time you left the field that night to go to General Buell's headquarters was it your opinion that the enemy would stand and fight there next day or that he was retreating?

My impression was when I saw General Buell that he would stand and fight next morning, but when I returned to the field about 10.30 o'clock at night I saw indications that there would be no fight next morning. I saw large fires built in every direction and their cavalry were up to within 200 yards of our pickets; in fact they talked to each other that night. But the enemy were as tired of it as we were, and there seemed a disposition to wait as if by mutual consent. The moonlight was as bright as day almost. I gave orders once to turn one of my batteries on the cavalry, having learned where it was from a doctor who was down there; but I felt a little compunction about doing so and refrained, for I had some apprehension that they would renew the engagement, which I did not want without re-enforcements.

Question. At what time were you convinced that the rebel army was in retreat?

Next morning, when they were not to be found on the battle ground. I believed they were retreating during the night, but I was not certain of it. We heard wagons moving off to their rear.

Question. At what time did you first report that the enemy had retreated?

I did not report at all. General McCook was on the ground, and it was his business to report to General Buell, and I supposed he did so.

Question. At daylight on the morning of the 9th could you see in which direction the enemy was retreating?

No, sir; I could not. Some of the cavalry saw the rear of the enemy move over the hills, the road they came to attack us, as I understood. I am satisfied that a large body of the enemy left during the night; perhaps all the infantry.

Question. Had you any reason to believe at daylight next morning that the enemy was not in force in the immediate vicinity of Perryville and just beyond your view?

None in the world. I did not know anything about it, but I supposed, as the balance of the army did, that Bragg had a large army there, and that we would have a fight. That, I believe, was the universal impression.

Question. What was your impression as to the strength of Bragg's army at that time?

I always thought Bragg's army was overrated, though the information was that Bragg and Kirby Smith and Stevenson would make about 68,000 or 69,000 men. I put Bragg's force down in my own estimation, correct or incorrect, I cannot tell, at 35,000 to 40,000 when they were at Munfordville. I never rated it higher than 40,000. Kirby Smith had about 15,500 troops he brought into the State, so I was informed, and had got about 4,000 to 5,000 since of raw troops. Stevenson, they said, had about 15,000—7,500 I supposed.

I had the impression, as they themselves stated and as Bragg and the provisional governor had assured the people, that they would remain in the State and fight it out. I therefore thought they would concentrate their forces and give us battle up in that vicinity, and I was more impressed with this view from the fact that Kirby Smith had joined Bragg, as I understood, on the night of the battle. General Buell's information was, as I had from a very intelligent spy, that Bragg's army probably was over 60,000 men. In fact he said they had sixty regiments, many of them composed of 1,200 to a regiment. That was General Buell's information while he was considering whether Bragg's troops were going to Kentucky or were still in Tennessee. They certainly formed a line of battle between us and Harrodsburg, for I saw two very extended lines, each 2 miles long, one in the rear of the other, with their flanks well protected, showing that they had a very considerable force.

By the PRESIDENT:

Question. Is it your opinion, general, that the whole of Bragg's army or only a part of it was engaged in the action which you have described as taking place against McCook's corps?

Certainly; only a part of it, and as Bragg himself said in his report it was the divisions of Cheatham, Anderson, and Buckner.

Question. Is it not possible that the main body of Bragg's army at the time of that action was in retreat upon Harrodsburg while this portion that was engaged in the attack was only a corps, left behind to stop pursuit?

I have no idea, sir, that there was any retreat going on then. My information since from general report is that they were not retreating. Bragg himself said in his report that the two armies stood face to face in line of battle. The people told me at Harrodsburg that many of the troops that attacked us had gone up and through Harrodsburg and come down the other road to conceal their movements from us, and I have no doubt it was so.

By General DANA:

Question. In stating that on the morning of the 9th of October you had formed a definite opinion that the enemy had retreated, do you wish it to be understood that your opinion was that he had taken up a line of retreat for some distant point or did you wish it understood that he had fallen back to take up a new position for battle?

I have no "opinion" about their having retreated. It was a fact before my eyes that they were gone, and that was all I knew about it. I had an impression from the repeated assurances of Bragg and the boasts of the secessionists of the State, as well as from the numbers that were joining him, that he did not intend to leave the State without a general battle. I felt that we might come upon General Bragg any day between Bardstown and the mountains just where he might choose to select his line of battle; and I felt another thing, too, that approaching Bragg was like hunting a "lion in a jungle." He had the best army for its numbers that I ever saw.

Commission adjourned to meet Wednesday, January 21, 1863.

LOUISVILLE, *January* 21, 1863.

Commission met pursuant to adjournment. All the members present; also the judge-advocate and General Buell.

General ROUSSEAU'S testimony continued, as follows:

By General TYLER:

Question. General, in speaking yesterday of General Bragg's army you said "He had the best army for its numbers that I ever saw." Did you consider General Bragg's army at that time superior in its discipline and numbers to General Buell's army?

Yes, sir; I did consider it superior in discipline. I understand that he had a man shot every few days by his own orders. The principal reason why I think he had better discipline than we had in any of our armies was because I think he was seconded by his officers in a way perhaps that our generals were not and are not; I mean the subalterns. I did not consider it superior in numbers. That, however, is a mere guess of mine.

Question. General, give me your reasons for the fact that General Buell's army could not be brought to the same state of discipline that Bragg's army was?

In the first place, I understand all the officers who knew Bragg in the Army thought he was perhaps the best disciplinarian in the United States Army or among the very best. That is the universal opinion as far as I have heard, and I have conversed with a great many of the old Regular Army officers. In addition to that, I think the rebel officers, from the highest to the lowest, are more strict in the discharge of their duties than the subaltern officers of our Army, and that, I think, essential to the very existence of the Army in the rebellion, as it has been. I think that the want of discipline in our Army arises from the failure of subalterns to enforce it and to have breaches of discipline properly punished; and that is an evil that every sensible man who knows anything about the fact appreciates.

Question. General, whom do you consider directly responsible for the discipline of a regiment?

Of course the commanding officer.

Question. Who is responsible for the discipline of a company?

Of course the commanding officer, as far as his power and responsibility went, under the commanding officer of the regiment.

Question. Were you with General Buell's army at Corinth?

I was.

Question. Was the discipline of the army at or about the time of the battle of Perryville as good as it was at Corinth?

The discipline of General Buell's army proper was as good as it was at Corinth, and I am satisfied that the discipline of Buell's army was far better than that of any army I have ever seen, better drilled and better disciplined. When I speak of Buell's army proper I mean the troops under his immediate command at Corinth. General Mitchel's division was added to his army and a portion of it was at Chaplin Hills.

Question. What portion of General Buell's army at Perryville was drawn from Mitchel's army and what was the discipline of that portion of the army?

I cannot now tell exactly what troops of Mitchel's division were at Perryville. I had a part of the Third Division there, with a brigade added to it at Nashville and three raw regiments at this place. I think several regiments of Mitchel's command were left at or in the vicinity of Nashville. In the main the discipline is what we would call good, though of some regiments the discipline was not good. Mitchel's division had been stationed in Alabama, and a good deal of feeling had been gotten up between citizens there and the men. Many of the men belonging to it were shot down by bushwhackers, or persons represented to be such, and, as we felt, murdered, and of course that tended to exasperate the soldiers and to cause breaches of discipline;

and that want of discipline continued in some regiments in Kentucky, and many grievous outrages were committed here in this State.

Question. Did this want of discipline, as you are pleased to term it, affect the efficiency of these regiments on the field?

Any want of discipline of course affects the efficiency of soldiers, but those men fought well. Soldiers of regiments under the best discipline fought better and were more reliable.

Question. General, you spoke yesterday of Stevenson's division, 15,500; where did that division come from?

I do not know. I never heard of it myself until about the time of that battle, and then I got it from some of the citizens of the country; and all I have said about the numbers of Bragg's army has been a mere guess, from hearsay and from such information as we could pick up. I would not pretend to oppose my opinion to that of the commanding officer, whose means of knowledge were so much superior to my own.

Question. Was this division of Stevenson's a part of Bragg's army that crossed the Tennessee River at Chattanooga and the Cumberland at Carthage?

I do not know anything in the world about Stevenson. I do not know whether there was such a man or whether he had such an army. I believe there was such a man, and my understanding was that he was not with Bragg's army, and had not come from Chattanooga with Bragg's army, whichever way they came. I received a letter from a very intimate and loyal friend, after the battle of Perryville, stating the rebel force in Kentucky, and Stevenson was set down as reputed to have 15,000 men; this friend said 7,000 or 8,000 in fact, and that they were at Danville at the time this letter was written. The letter was written before the battle by a person who passed through Richmond after the battle there to this place around by Lexington.

Question. What was the position of your command with respect to that of the enemy on the night of the battle of Perryville a little after sundown, say about 8 o'clock?

The right of my line had fallen back some distance; the line, in fact, was turned, pressed back; the left fell back perhaps 200 or 300 yards, the center more, to about the original line of battle selected that morning. The enemy, it is true, were near us; their cavalry were within 200 or 300 yards of our pickets; but we had a front to the enemy, and were ready to renew the fight had there been any effort to drive us from our position. The artillery on the left fired guns, under my immediate orders, till after dark, and the infantry were there to support the guns.

Question. Was your line of battle or any part of it changed between 8 o'clock on the night of the battle and daybreak the next morning?

Yes; I have already stated that, and that it was done under the immediate direction of General McCook, who ordered the change and directed where it should be, and then went to call upon General Buell.

Question. Do you know anything of General Mitchell's command having possession of the village of Perryville on the afternoon of the battle and what that possession amounted to?

I suppose it was between 10 and 11 o'clock on the night of the battle. As I was leaving General Buell's headquarters I met General Mitchell, and he informed me, according to my recollection, that he had approached near the town with his forces, and had himself, with his escort, rode into the town and got a glass of water, and was just from there. I do not know whether he had possession of the town or not.

Cross-examination by General BUELL:

Question. Has the removal of the death-penalty from the authority of our army commanders had any effect upon the discipline of our armies, do you suppose, general?

I have no doubt of it, and no one with whom I have ever conversed on the subject doubts it.

Question. Judging from the experience of all armies and from your own observation do you suppose it is possible to have thorough discipline in an army without it ?

I suppose such a thing would be possible, but I am sure it is not practicable, and I am sure that it would tend greatly to induce discipline.

Question. Was our army at Perryville composed to a considerable extent of raw regiments, that had only been in service a very short time ?

Yes, sir; there were a good many raw regiments in that army, who marched badly and fought worse.

Question. Were those regiments under my command or discipline in any manner prior to their ingraftment upon the old army ?

General Buell personally could have had nothing to do with them. I had no knowledge as to whether they were even in his department or not up to the time they were added to the army.

Question. Do you suppose, general, that a lavish provision for troops in the way of clothing, provisions, and other comforts, and the occasional deprivation of those comforts unavoidably would have the tendency to produce a worse state of discipline than though they were habitually limited to what was absolutely necessary for them ?

Of course it would.

Question. Will you state, if you please, whether that difference exists between the army of the Government and the rebel army probably in the most marked degree ?

My information from rebel prisoners and others who pretended to know is that the rebels have never indulged the soldiers in lavish supplies. I suppose that that difference between the two armies does exist. Our army, when it receives its regular rations, has a lavish supply.

Question. Were you stationed in North Alabama last summer, general ?

I was; at Huntsville.

Question. Do you know anything of the policy that had been observed by our troops in that section of country toward the inhabitants? If so, please state what that policy was, or at least what the effect of this treatment was upon the temper of the people.

I know something of the practices of the soldiers there. General Mitchel had left before I reached Huntsville a few days. I can only say that between some of the regiments of General Mitchel's army and the people there was a very bitter feeling existing, and, as I before said, it was partly induced by the shooting of the soldiers by bushwhackers, and they in turn handled the people very roughly. I heard many well-authenticated incidents well calculated to excite a feeling among the inhabitants. I believe that many of the soldiers had been very much in the habit of taking everything they wanted and many things they did not want, such as men and women's and children's clothing, &c. I was informed by a loyal man there—and there were not many of them, in my judgment—that the course previously pursued had done great injury to the cause of the Government, and I have no doubt it was true. The people did not complain so much on account of what was taken from them as they did of the manner and the persons who did it. They seemed to give very freely to the officials, when it was demanded, whatever the Government required. The complaint was soldiers and officers entered private residences and took out of them whatever they wanted—silver plate, money, and anything else—and the manner of doing it, and of the wanton destruction of the furniture of the houses.

Question. State, if you please, what you know in regard to my policy with reference to the treatment of the people among whom we were and with reference to their property.

I had many conversations with General Buell as to the proper course to be pursued. His policy was one I cordially approved myself, and that was that whatever the Government needed its officials should take peaceably and peacefully, and that all private marauding, stealing, and robbing, which tended to the destruction of discipline and the efficiency of the army, should be repressed, and I have had occasion at various times to see that policy enforced in person by General Buell, and I believe that on all proper occasions that policy was enforced. That has been the policy of General Buell, as far as I have understood it, during the time that he commanded this department. As his army marched to Shiloh this policy was pretty faithfully carried out, but as the army returned in September last there was a great want of discipline exhibited; yet as it returned comparatively few grievances were complained of or outrages committed, and that is something I have never understood. I do not think that the want of discipline arose from any fault of General Buell, for I consider him one of the best disciplinarians I know.

Question. Do you know any instance of my failure to make use of the supplies of the country through which we were marching when they were necessary for the efficiency of the army?

No, sir; quite to the contrary. On all occasions when the army needed supplies and they could be obtained they were freely taken and used. I have never known a United States officer in this war that would fail to take supplies when the army needed them and he could obtain them.

Question. My policy with reference to slaves in the country through which we have marched has been made a subject of inquiry before the Commission. Will you please state what you know in regard to it?

The question is somewhat indefinite. I can say this much of General Buell's policy, that he desired to have as little to do with the slaves as might be. When they were needed as teamsters or to work on the fortifications I understood it to be his wish to use them freely as teamsters when belonging to secessionists and to take them all alike when they were needed on the fortifications. I recollect he objected to having slaves in camp, on the ground that whatever might be the political principles of the owners their presence there tended to the demoralization of the army; that they consumed the supplies intended for the army or else were driven to steal and maraud to get something to eat. I believe his policy was to turn all slaves whom you might call "surplus" out of camp up to the time that the law was changed on that subject. I believe he was opposed, as distinctly as I was, to aiding in any possible way a secessionist in obtaining possession of his slaves, but desired that loyal men should have their negroes. With General Buell's concurrence I used several hundred negroes at Huntsville and Nashville in erecting fortifications, and he knew that I had a great number of able-bodied negroes as teamsters in my command, as I think I informed him several times and as he could see himself. He objected to negroes going with the army in large numbers and waiting on the soldiers, as was practiced in the troops of General Mitchel and perhaps in others.

Question. Do you know any instance of my availing myself of the information of negroes, particularly when we were in Northern Alabama, and of my making certain disposition of my troops in consequence of their reports?

Yes, I know of several such instances occurring in which negroes gave information and bodies of troops were used on that information.

Question. Was that information generally of much value?

Generally not of the least, and on the occasion I refer to the stories told by the negroes were either entirely untrue or so exaggerated that the information amounted to nothing except to fatigue and weary our soldiers to no purpose. The negroes are far more useful to the rebels than to us, although nearly all of them are friendly to our Government, and for the reason, among others, that they are so useful to the rebels I am opposed to their owning any.

Question. State, if you please, what you know in regard to the scarcity or abundance of supplies in North Alabama and other parts of the country through which we marched last summer.

Supplies were very scarce on the whole line of march; in fact I think the inhabitants had not enough for their own purpose, though in some neighborhoods we could procure forage and now and then other supplies for the army. It was this scarcity that created the difficulty of keeping up very strict discipline, as one cannot very well punish a soldier who gets something to eat on the plea that he is suffering with hunger. We were a good deal of time on half rations from Huntsville up to Kentucky.

Question. Do you know whether the people about Huntsville were in very considerable want for the necessaries of life when we were there last summer; whether such articles did not demand very high prices among them, and whether they were introduced from the North?

Yes; many of the people of Huntsville and about Nashville I found to be in want of the necessaries of life, especially about Huntsville. Old Governor Clay's lady—a very strong secessionist old lady—told me that her family had very little to eat and that the soldiers had taken their bacon. I told her I would divide with her after her supply was exhausted, and she accordingly called upon me when her store was out. They are worth some hundreds of thousands of dollars; her husband was probably worth half a million. I told Captain Paul to issue rations for the Governor and his wife as indigent persons. The old lady said she would not have them in that way, and was disposed to take offense. I told her that was the only way in which she could get supplies, and she declined to take them as "poor persons." Many of the wealthy people there were hard pressed for the necessaries of life. Such articles already commanded high prices, of course, and persons were allowed to introduce what was prudently thought to be a simple supply to the citizens in and about Huntsville. I was in command there myself, and under General Buell's policy I allowed the bringing of supplies from Nashville and Louisville to that place, but always in limited quantities. The supplies designed to be taken there were always named and set down on paper and permission given to bring only such supplies as were therein named.

Question. Do you remember whether some such supplies were actually taken possession of for the subsistence of the troops subsequently?

Yes, sir; I remember especially some considerable quantities of bacon were taken possession of, and other articles which I do not now remember, and used by the army. In fact it was spoken of, when this policy was settled, that any provisions brought there in the way spoken of should be taken and used, if they were needed, before they were sold.

Question. When you were lying at Horse Well last summer, on the march from Nashville to Louisville, did you send off any detachment? If so, please state on what occasion and with what object and what result.

I do not think I sent any detachment. I went myself with a brigade and some cavalry to Glasgow to get some hundreds of barrels of flour that were said to be below the town. I did not get any; they had been taken away by the rebels, so I was informed. I asked General Buell's permission to go down there myself with that view and he gave it.

Question. Do you know anything of the capture and paroling of rebel prisoners of war while you were in that vicinity?

I captured a good many prisoners there.

Question. How long did your division remain in Louisville on your arrival here last September?

I do not recollect exactly; it was a few days. I think we left here on the 1st of October; that is my recollection. I suppose we remained here four to six days, but I am not certain. I have not thought of it.

Question. Will you state how the time was occupied in preparing the army for future operations; whether you were busy yourself and the rest of the army as far as you know and what was necessary in order to make the army efficient?

The army was much in need of clothing, shoes, &c., and I believe every commander here exerted himself to get supplies, and it was with great difficulty that we obtained them. The clothing, as I understood, had been removed, under General Nelson's orders, to Jeffersonville, Ind., in the expectation that General Bragg would help himself to it if it remained here, and it was with difficulty we could get hold of it. I had myself a great deal of trouble to get supplies, and I know that General McCook and others were also much troubled in getting theirs. I was not when I arrived here under the command of General McCook. I commanded the two divisions composing the right wing of the army below Munfordville. Ours were separate commands until the night before we started toward Perryville, as far as my knowledge of the fact goes. My division finally left without having obtained the supply of clothing and shoes needed.

Question. Was the army during that time provided in whole or in part with an outfit of light cooking utensils? If so, please state whether you consider it was necessary to enable the army to move with the limited transportation with which it did move.

By an order it was required that the troops should be supplied with so many coffee-pots, mess pans, &c., to be always carried by the men in the army, and the transportation was reduced. I thought then, and I am sure now, that the arrangement was a very excellent one, as the men were always prepared to make coffee and cook meat whether the train was with them or not. I think that was necessary to enable the army to move with facility, and I look upon the wagon trains of the United States Army as a great impediment to its movements and a nuisance.

Question. Considering the work that was done, paying, feeding, and supplying the troops with these various essentials, and the ingrafting of a large number of raw troops into the army, amounting almost to a reorganization of the whole, do you think that any time was wasted before the army marched from Louisville against the rebel army in Kentucky?

I know there was none, for I was myself at work as hard as I could to obtain the necessary supplies, and thus had an opportunity of knowing that no time was lost.

Commission adjourned to meet Thursday, January 22, 1863.

LOUISVILLE, *January* 22, 1863.

Commission met pursuant to adjournment. All the members present; also the judge-advocate and General Buell.

General ROUSSEAU'S testimony continued, as follows:

By General BUELL:

Question. Were you in command at Bowling Green on the 13th and 14th of September last?

I was senior officer there for two or three days about that time. General Smith had been placed in command of the post and was supposed to be acquainted with the routine of matters, and I thought it best not to change the command, though all matters of importance requiring action were referred to me, I believe, as commander of the forces there.

Question. Do you remember the arrival of any persons at that place on the days mentioned with information from Munfordville? If so, please state who they were and all the information they gave you.

While I was there several persons came from Munfordville or the vicinity with information of the state of matters at Munfordville. I do not recollect the name of any person except a Mr. Miller, who formerly kept a saw-mill at Munfordville. Somebody from that vicinity had seen me before I saw Miller; I think two or three had called on me from the neighborhood of Munfordville to give me information. I recollect that my information first was that Munfordville was taken. I do not recollect who gave that information now, but I told General Buell on the morning of his arrival at my headquarters, to which he came directly on reaching Bowling Green. I perhaps gave him that information and referred him to the person or persons who gave it. My recollection on those points, however, is not clear; rather indistinct. I am sure that I got the information that Munfordville was taken. Afterward that report was contradicted by Mr. Miller, as I recollect it, but I do not know how long after.

Question. If those persons had come to you with any pressing and important message do you thing the impression would remain on your mind? I will thank you, general, to refresh your memory as well as you can, and state to the Commission anything in connection with the arrival of those messengers or scouts that made an impression upon you which you can now recollect.

I recollect the information given much better than I do the parties who gave it,

Loyal men from several directions were coming in to give me information. About the same time I received information of the approach of Bragg's army, which was at that time occupying much of our attention. My recollection is that my informants were from the neighborhood of Munfordville; from a countryman living there. There were a good many of them, and I think I turned some of them who had important information over to General Buell in my tent and he conversed with them. That is my recollection of it now. One of those men said that he was between Munfordville and Bowling Green (I think he said he lived there), and that he inferred Munfordville was taken because he heard very rapid firing of cannon and musketry at the place and which lasted some time. I think that was his evidence for believing Munfordville was taken. He thought there was force enough of the enemy there to have taken Munfordville. It turned out that that was General Chalmers' attack, which was repulsed. I think General Buell obtained from the person or persons who brought that information the true state of the case—the evidence and conclusions that the informants had—and of course drew his own conclusions from the premises

Question. Do you mean by that that I obtained myself the ground upon which they came to the conclusion that Munfordville had been taken ; or, if not, what do you mean by " the true state of the case "?

When I say that General Buell had the ground and conclusions, he had the information and conclusions of the informants. Of course I mean that he could draw his own conclusions from the facts detailed.

Question. Is the impression left on your mind that these messengers, or any of them, came with pressing information from the commanding officer at Munfordville?

I am sure they did not. They brought no information from him at all—those I saw and to whom I now refer. When the information came to us, after the attack on Munfordville was repulsed, I felt no apprehension of its being very soon renewed. I thought from the information I had that Bragg's army was much worn down, and could not gather itself up and get to Munfordville as soon as it did.

Redirect examination by the JUDGE-ADVOCATE :

Question. General, you were speaking yesterday of the discipline of our army; was not the Army of the Ohio while falling back to Nashville and from Nashville to Louisville very much demoralized?

No; I do not think it was. There was more marauding than I had seen and a good deal of straggling. The marches, however, were pretty rapid, and we were pretty short of rations. These things, and, as I remarked yesterday, other matters I did not understand, had caused a laxity of discipline on coming up that did not exist as the army went back. I sometimes thought that the marauding and want of discipline on coming up resulted, perhaps, from the opinion of the soldiers that they would not go back again. That, however, was a conjecture. After our arrival at this point we lost a great many men by desertion, who went home to see their families; but I think the army at Munfordville, at least the two divisions I commanded, were in the best condition of any United States troops I have ever seen, and would have fought a battle better than they would before or since. They were well rested at Horse Well and pretty well supplied with rations and every way in fine condition for a battle; better than at Chaplin Hills by far. It is very probable that the retrograde movement had its bad influence on the discipline of the army, but I am not prepared to say to what extent.

Question. Is it not an admitted fact that the superior discipline and drill of the rebel army gives it an advantage over our forces?

I am sure that the rebel army is not better drilled than ours, and I believe not near so well drilled ; but I think discipline will always tell, and the discipline of the rebel army under the command of Bragg gave them an advantage over troops that are not so well disciplined. In speaking of the difference in discipline of the two armies I must not be understood as underrating the discipline of the Army of the Ohio or the Cumberland. That army has never lacked discipline in any great degree, in my judgment. Its discipline was, perhaps, as good as we could have with the sort of punishment we were allowed to inflict, and the failure of the subaltern officers in a great many instances to discharge their duties faithfully has also resulted finally in a lack of punishment both with officers and men. My opinion is that the soldiers of our army are the best in the world, and all that they want to exhibit that on all occasions is that the officers should be as good as the soldiers. But punishments are very rarely inflicted upon officers and about as rarely upon soldiers. My judgment is that more than one-half of the army is now absent from the field. Some regiments that I have commanded, I was informed, had in one or two instances but little over one-third of the men that were in the service in the field; and it has been impossible to get the subaltern officers to either report or punish the straggling of soldiers as a general rule—a practice, I think, which would ruin any army in the world. The subaltern officers did not want intelligence or courage, but the disposition to strictly enforce the necessary discipline. By subalterns I mean captains, lieutenants, &c.

Question. Do you attribute this lack of one-third of our forces at the present moment to absence without leave?

No, sir; but to leaves obtained on every possible kind of pretext; and that evil may in a great degree be traced to the same source I have been speaking of.

Question. Have not the rebel forces exhibited a superior steadiness under fire to our army and are they not easier handled in battle?

In attacking it seems almost impossible to repel the rebels; their dash is very hard to resist, and I have rarely seen it resisted when their troops were fresh. But one dash with the same troops is about as much as you get well done. I think our troops, if ordered to attack and well led, would probably attack as well as they do and I think may be handled as well. Individually I think the rebel soldiers are generally superior to our own, and that they understand as well as we do, and hence they never fight us in open ground where they can help it. They always skirmish where they can, that the individuality of the soldier may tell. In the battles I have seen them fight they always fought in the woods or on uneven ground if they could get it. That may in a great measure result from the desperate position they occupy and from the invincible hatred toward the Federal forces that has been inculcated by their leaders, and I think it is so. I saw them resisted for hours at Perryville, or Chaplin Hills, by the Third Division and driven back; and I must say that I do not consider any rebel command superior to that division in discipline or drill, or that could, in my judgment, whip it with equal numbers.

Question. What became of the slaves that were used on the fortifications after you were through with their labor?

In truth I never got through. I left Huntsville before the fortifications were completed and I left Nashville also before they were finished there. I think, however, I may safely say that very few of them have found their way back to their owners, even to loyal men. There were very few loyal owners about Huntsville, but a considerable number about Nashville.

Question. What do you know, general, about supplies having been furnished the army from the Tennessee River while you were at Huntsville?

I never heard of any coming from that direction.

Question. Do you know anything about the capture of Colonel Forsyth and another rebel officer, whose name I do not know, near Horse Well or in that neighborhood?

Yes, sir; I know all about it. Colonel Forsyth was, I think, on Bragg's staff. There was a Major Sheppard taken at the same time—he was on Hardee's staff; and a captain or a major on Governor Harris' staff, and I think three other commissioned officers. I think there were six taken in all. They were brought to my headquarters at night at Horse Well. We were just up from the supper table, and I inquired if they would take supper, and they said they would. They complained a good deal of fatigue, and I gave them some Bourbon and supper, and sent them under escort to General Buell's headquarters. I went to bed, and some time afterward these men were sent back to our picket lines, and I received a note at that time from Colonel Fry, chief of staff to General Buell, saying that I must send no more prisoners to headquarters, but to have them paroled, and that it was much to be regretted that those prisoners were allowed to come into the lines or to go to General Buell's headquarters, and that prisoners must not be sent there any more, and that I must send those prisoners out of the lines before day. This I endeavored to do, directing the officer in command of them, a major, I think, of the Seventh Pennsylvania Cavalry, to parole them. He was an intelligent gentleman, and told me that he understood it and would do it. They were accordingly taken away under escort, and sent away as ordered, and that was the last I saw of them. I sent no more prisoners to General Buell's headquarters. This is the substance of the order as I now recollect it, but I am not aware that I have thought of the circumstance since it occurred.

Question. Do you know whether their parole was properly taken or not?

I do not. I talked with the major on the subject and told him what I thought about the parole, and he said he understood it in the same way, and paroled them.

Question. Do you know whether Colonel Forsyth and the officers considered themselves under parole or whether they resumed their duties subsequently?

I have no information on that subject, except that Forsyth resumed his duties on Bragg's staff on the ground that he was a citizen and not a soldier, which fact he did not intimate to me when I had him in custody. He said he was a colonel and on Bragg's staff, and I treated him, of course, as an officer of the army, and never had a suspicion that he was anything else. Major Flynt, on General Thomas' staff, told me that Forsyth had resumed his duties on Bragg's staff on the ground stated. I only heard that down in the neighborhood of Nashville lately.

Question. Do you recollect the officer's name who paroled them?

I do not, but I am sure I could learn who he was.

Question. Do you not consider the paroling of these officers at that time and under the circumstances very imprudent?

It did not occur to me that it was so. I almost thought it was a very good thing they came into our lines. I was not of opinion that we could attack and drive Bragg from his position at Munfordville without the loss perhaps of half our army; and I did not agree with the implied censure of Colonel Fry for sending them into camp. Our troops were all along the road and had fires, and exhibited evidences of a very large force—very large; and I am of opinion to-day that it was the information gotten by Bragg from these men that started him from Munfordville, though that is a mere guess of mine. If Forsyth was really a citizen, which fact he concealed from us, and broke his parole, I suppose he gave whatever information he had. I do not think we had anything to lose one way or another by it. They seemed, however, to be very honorable gentlemen all of them, and I did not doubt they would keep the parole given. When speaking of "our troops," I mean the two divisions under my command. I do not know how the others were encamped, but believe the larger portion of them were not, perhaps, seen by these officers, as they were beyond General Buell's headquarters and up toward Cave City. My own camp-fires made a great show, and I allude to them in what I have said.

Question. Did not your advance, general, at Chaplin Hills, from the position assigned you by General Buell, really bring upon you that attack?

I cannot say that it did. We were not much in advance of where we first halted and where I supposed General McCook believed he was directed to go. We were attacked while on the march, before the column had barely been put in motion. It had not gone 200 yards, and in fact had not passed the position occupied by Hotchkiss' guns, under the command of Gay. My impression was then that the enemy had planned that attack. I thought so from the fact that the rebel scouts before referred to carried the information and soon after the attack was begun, though of course I cannot tell what induced the attack. It was not announced by General McCook that we would halt permanently there, and at the time I felt that the march was merely interrupted by the appearance of the enemy. I did not know and was not informed how much farther we would have to go to get to the point or position designed by General Buell; hence I thought it was right to advance and get water, though before the advance had progressed more than 200 or 300 yards, as before stated, the shelling by the enemy began and the attack by the infantry followed.

Question. Your men were suffering for want of water at that time were they not?

A good deal.

Question. When this movement was made in the direction of the water was there not some confusion naturally arising from the anxiety of the men to get there?

Not in the least. I should have felt that they had very little discipline if it had been so. The men stood up and fought all day afterward in the heat without water and without grumbling.

Question. Had you remained where you halted would you not have been in a better position to meet that attack than where it found you?

No; but the original line of battle selected was far better than the ground we fought on, I suppose. There were more undulations there, and the enemy's advance, I think, would have been more difficult; but both positions had their advantages and disadvantages. The troops were originally halted in the rear of the line of battle selected by General McCook and myself on approaching the field, as stated in the early part of this deposition. I do not now refer to the ground upon which the line of battle was finally formed.

Question. These people from Munfordville came to Bowling Green in search of General Buell, did they not?

No; I think they were stampeded off from up there and were hunting up the military authorities. They were not aware that General Buell was at Bowling Green; and, in fact, he did not reach there till after they had been there for some time, and he found them, as before stated, at my headquarters. I introduced them to General Buell on his arrival, and referred them to him to give such information as they had.

Question. Your impression is that they brought no message from Colonel Wilder; may you not be in error about this?

Well, I think not, with respect to the men I have referred to. It strikes me that while we were staying at Bowling Green some messenger came from Wilder with the news that he had repulsed the enemy. That is my recollection of it. I remember feeling a good deal of exultation and pride in Wilder for his spunk and confidence exhibited in reference to matters at Munfordville, and I think it was the news coming directly from Wilder by somebody that prompted the belief that he would not be again attacked, having repulsed the enemy with great loss in a considerable fight, in addition to the other reason that Bragg's army was much worn down by coming through the mountains. I am not sure that the person came as a messenger from Wilder. It may have been that he merely saw Wilder and received that information from him, though I am inclined to believe that he was from Wilder to the commanding officer at Bowling Green.

Question. What regiments are those that you were informed had not over one-third of their number?

My recollection is that the Thirty-eighth Indiana is one of them, and that portion of it that is now in the field is among the best regiments in the army. I do not recollect now what the other regiments were, but I think I may say that half the regiments have about one-half or two-thirds of their number in the field. That is my best impression.

By General DANA:

Question. General, in reference to the opinion that the rebel army is individually superior to our army, is this superiority to be attributed to a greater physical development on their part or to greater intelligence and courage?

I do not consider their physical development superior to that of our soldiers. It is certainly true, however, that men who love strife and fighting for its own sake have very generally joined the Confederate Army in the South. Even men from the free States who love mischief and blood have joined that Army. I think that consideration adds to their vim. Then, as I have before stated, they generally cherish a hatred and bitterness toward what they call the Yankees that our army does not entertain for them. I certainly do not consider them more intelligent, generally less intelligent, than our own soldiers.

Question. Do you not think a perfect self-reliance on their superior courage would naturally lead them, in equal numbers, to seek a fight in open field, in plain daylight, in preference to hiding in woods?

No; I have never seen a rebel lose a chance yet of winning an advantage with certainty if he understood it; and in the battles we have had they have been very well acquainted with the woods and the ground, and of course, even with equal courage, had a very great advantage in availing themselves of covers. Besides, I do not think their armies have generally been equal to ours in numbers, and that was a fact that was better conceded by fighting us in the way they have. There is another consideration: our troops are generally very well drilled, and fight in large bodies in the open field far better than they fight in any other way. They are better drilled as heavy infantry than they are as skirmishers, infinitely. This, I think, the rebels understand. Many prisoners I have taken have intimated the fact to me in talking to me about the progress of battles.

By General TYLER:

Question. In your testimony yesterday you said that the necessaries of life about Huntsville were brought from the North at the time you were there; what do you understand by the necessaries of life? Please enumerate the articles that were brought from the North.

I understand by the necessaries of life sugar, coffee, bread, meat, rice, &c.

Question. Was there not great want of fresh provisions—beef (cattle on the hoof), pork, &c.?

I think there was. North Alabama is not a cattle country, and when our supplies got low there I sent out and brought in all the cattle for many miles around, under the orders of General Buell—milch-cows and yearlings and everything I could scrape up.

Question. Over what extent of country?

Some 6 to 10 miles, I suppose, in every direction. When I say all, I do not mean every one. The order to the commissary was to get all he could. They were, however, very inferior cattle, small and thin. I think we left without using all the cattle while there. Several hundred, I think, were sent up to the troops at Stevenson on the cars. I don't think the supply of beef was worth talking about. I cannot tell whether it was reduced by supplying the army under General Mitchel before I got there, which I think probable. Whenever his communications with his base of supplies was interrupted he supplied himself from the country, as I was informed, and so did we under like circumstances. There was, I believe, very little pork in the country. I think it is a very poor hog country; poor probably for the reasons already stated and because attention was not turned in that direction.

Question. What was the condition of the summer crops—corn, wheat, &c.—so far as they could be made useful to the army, at the time you were passing down?

I did not go from Huntsville to Stevenson, but the corn crop seemed to be pretty good around the country about Huntsville, and I saw more corn than I expected to find in portions of Tennessee and Alabama. An order came from Captain Chandler, quartermaster to General Buell, directing us, when our supplies got short there, to have all the corn stripped by the farmers, so as to make it fit for the use of the army. It was not sufficiently cured without stripping it. The work was begun, and we sent out and procured a good deal of corn, but shortly afterward we evacuated the place and I do not know what else was done.

Question. You spoke yesterday in your testimony of the discipline of the army having been weakened by the ingrafting on it of new regiments. How many new regiments were put into each brigade?

I am not sure that I know; but I had three in my own division, one regiment added to each brigade, and I think that was the number added to each brigade in the army.

Question. What proportion, then, of your division consisted of new soldiers?

It is difficult to say. The Ninety-fourth Ohio had lost 200 or 300 near Lexington, Ky., taken by Kirby Smith's forces, and I do not recollect the number of the other regiments. I suppose 1,600 to 1,800 raw troops were added to my division, and I suppose my division amounted to between 7,000 and 8,000, artillery, cavalry, and all included. Considerable numbers of the raw troops of the army gave out on the road or straggled and did not go into battle at all, the hot weather, want of water, and hard marching rendering it almost impossible to keep them up.

Recross-examination by General BUELL:

Question. Do you know of any division or of any brigades in the other divisions that were composed entirely of raw troops; Sheridan's division, for example?

I think so. It must have been so, for we had a great many more raw troops than could have gone into the army a regiment to a brigade, as I understood it.

Question. Do you know anything about the composition of Jackson's division and of Colonel McCook's brigade in Sheridan's division? If so, please state how they were composed, whether of raw troops or of old troops.

The division of Jackson was entirely composed of raw troops, I believe. Col. Dan. McCook's brigade consisted of raw troops, and although Jackson's division was composed of excellent and brave men, I think they were very inefficient in battle, because they were raw and inexperienced.

Question. Has there been anything decided in my policy in reference to the absence of officers and soldiers from their regiments? Have my orders and my practice on that point been loose or decidedly the reverse?

The policy of General Buell as to those matters was more strict—a great deal more strict—than that of any commanding officer I know. In fact, it has been the cause of great complaint and much dislike in the army. To my certain knowledge a great many good men and good officers have taken great offense against General Buell on that account.

Question. Do you remember what day of the month it was that Colonel Forsyth and the other rebel officers you have referred to were captured and was it in the day or night, and if in the night were they sent off the same night?

I do not remember the day of the month. They were captured in the afternoon, about 9 miles from my headquarters, as I understood from Colonel Forsyth himself, over on what is called the Goose Neck road, or some such name. They were brought to my headquarters after dark. As soon as they had supper they were sent on to General Buell's headquarters, and returned between that time and 12 o'clock at night, and on the same night were sent out of our lines.

Question. Without inquiring at all what ground there may have been for the delays, supposing that my orders to General McCook had been exactly and promptly executed, that similar orders to General Thomas, who should have been within 7 miles of Perryville on the night of the 7th of October, had also been promptly and exactly executed, what effect do you suppose they would have had upon our fortunes at Perryville and the result of our operations there?

I do not think I can say what failure there was in obeying the orders of General Buell. I do not know how near we had arrived at Perryville to this day. I never was there, and I do not know whether the battle that we fought there was beyond where General McCook was expected by General Buell to go or not. I can however say this: that if our army had been in position when the enemy attacked us I think we should have obtained a very decided victory. It might have cost us a great deal, but that we expected and were willing to submit to. I thought General Bragg had a good army, but I also thought that we could whip it if we could get to it and have a fair fight. In fact I did not doubt it. The order to General Thomas I have not seen, and do not know what his specific orders were, and, as I before stated, I cannot say certainly whether General McCook was in or out of the position that General Buell designed he should take. After reaching the battle ground there was no reconnaissance made to the front by infantry or artillery. There was some of the Second Kentucky Cavalry sent off to our left front, and they watched the motions of the enemy. It may be that this order required, and it seems it did, that a reconnaissance should be made and the roads understood before General McCook reported to General Buell in person. Of course I cannot say that General McCook did not understand as much as General Buell required that he should by this order of the roads and the neighborhood before he reported to General Buell. I do not know what he knew on the subject. A reconnaissance was made, as I before stated, before we reached the battle ground, but it was directly on the road on which we were marching. I am unwilling to give a general answer as to whether this order was obeyed or not, or to say what would have been the result had a different course been pursued. I do not know the distance from the battle-field of Chaplin Hills to the town of Perryville. I was told it was a mile and a half and others said it was 3 miles. I can say that if a reconnaissance had been made to the front from the point where General McCook left us to report to General Buell the enemy would certainly have been discovered in force.

General BUELL. I wish to say myself to the Commission that I do not mean by the question to make any defense by reflecting on General McCook or General Thomas; that I am satisfied that some of the delays were unavoidable, and I do not know but that all of them were. It is simply meant to inquire what would have been the result if everything had worked as I expected it would and as my orders expressed.

Commission adjourned to meet January 23, 1863.

LOUISVILLE, *January* 23, 1863.

Commission met pursuant to adjournment. All the members present; also the judge-advocate and General Buell.

Col. GUSTAVUS A. WOOD (a witness for the defendant), being duly sworn by the judge-advocate, testified as follows:

By General BUELL:

Question. Colonel, state your name and position in the United States service.

Gustavus A. Wood; lieutenant-colonel of the Fifteenth Indiana Volunteers.

Question. Were you with the troops at McMinnville in August last?

I was in command of my regiment at Vervilla, from 7 to 10 miles from McMinnville.

Question. Were you sent to Altamont during that month by the general in command at McMinnville? If so, please to state with what object.

I was sent in command of the regiment on the 23d of August, receiving my instructions from General Wood, the division commander, which were to report as to the nature of the road to Altamont, and as to the forage and supplies that might be obtained in the vicinity, the facilities for camping, and also to gain such information with reference to the movements of the enemy as could be gathered during the expedition. The additional instructions as to my encampment were that I was to fall back and not to stop at Altamont and encamp a mile this side. Those were orders that I could not obey, so I fell back some 8 miles.

Question. Did you understand that your instructions emanated in the first place from General Thomas?

I understood them to originate in authority higher than General Wood, but was under the impression that the expedition was directed generally by General Buell. I was not advised as to whom the orders were from, but supposed it was carrying out some order of General Buell.

Question. Was your division under the command of General Thomas at that time, in common with the troops in the vicinity of McMinnville?

I supposed it was, although I was informed that in one instance orders were sent direct by General Buell to General Wood.

Question. State what the orders were in that instance, if you please, colonel.

It was an order for our division, in connection with others, to move to Altamont, designating the road the division was to take. We had received orders from General Thomas on the morning of the same day, the 25th or 26th of August, to move to McMinnville, and when in sight our direction was changed, and we moved down the Decherd road until coming to what was called the Hickory Creek road, when we were turned in the direction of Altamont. I was caused to make inquiries on account of the extra march made by the regiment, and learned the fact as above stated as to the issuing of orders. This is the only order that I know of General Buell delivering or sending directly to General Wood at that camp.

Question. •You were informed that this order was given by me directly to General Wood, were you?

Yes, sir; I think I saw the order.

Question. Are you positive that that order was addressed to General Wood by me directly ?

I am not; I did not notice the direction.

Question. What information did you gain while you were at Altamont or in that vicinity in regard to the movements of the army ?

I was informed generally by the citizens, who were mainly rebel, and by a Mr. Tipton, recognized as a loyal citizen, that it was their expectation that we would soon be attacked at McMinnville, and Vervilla particularly. I also got from the person of a prisoner I arrested a letter in pencil, dated August 19, on the north side of the Tennessee River, informing his cousin, the prisoner, that he was not at liberty to state the force they had there, but their officers were very confident they would soon clear the Yankees out of Tennessee, and containing also this expression: "I shall in a few days come through or near Altamont, at which time I shall be able to see you." The letter purported to have been written by the son of the county clerk of Grundy County, in the infantry service of the enemy. I reported also as to the nature of the road, that it was very difficult and rough, but possible for the transportation of light guns; that there was water for the camp at Altamont; that there were about 200 cattle in the various coves in the neighborhood of Altamont; that there was hay, but no corn, and no provisions except potatoes. I think I referred to a Michigan man who had potatoes, but no provisions to any amount. There was not much water or facilities for a large camp. I understood it meant only the establishing of an outpost at Altamont or a temporary camp. With that view I reported water there, where there was but little.

Question. Was the information, such as you received, positive that the enemy were advancing by Altamont ?

It was, and was deemed of so much importance that I was directed by General Wood to hurry up a report of the results of the expedition, which I did in his office, addressed to him, in which I gave it as my very decided opinion that the enemy was approaching by the Sequatchie Valley and Altamont and would attack this line, and that speedily. Appended to the report above referred to was the date, viz, 24th of August.

Question. Do you know whether your report was forwarded by General Wood to higher authority ?

I do not, sir. I only know that General Wood urged as a reason for my hurrying up the report that he desired to forward it immediately.

Question. May you not be mistaken in regard to the date of your report ?

I may be mistaken one day in the date of that report. I am confident that it was about the 24th, but it may have been the 23d or the 25th. I am also confident that the letter above referred to was dated the 19th, and I think it could not have been over four days old when I got it. I reported the next day.

Question. Were you with the troops that subsequently moved toward Altamont for the purpose of concentration ?

I was.

Question. Was it your understanding that you were advanced to meet the enemy on that occasion for the purpose of battle ?

It was.

Question. Do you know anything about the destruction of public property at McMinnville when that advance was made ?

Only from information; and I do not know now that I can state from whom I got that information.

Question. Was it reported among the troops that public property had been destroyed at McMinnville when they left that point for the purpose of advancing to Altamont ?

It was very generally reported

Question. Do you know or did you hear by whose orders that property was destroyed?

I think Colonel Ammen was mentioned in connection with the destruction of a portion of it, but about that I am not positive. A portion of the enlisted men and subordinates mentioned General Thomas in connection with it. Some enlisted men of General Wood's division, stragglers, passed through McMinnville that day; the command generally did not.

Question. Did this fact or report of the destruction of property at McMinnville have a bad effect upon the temper of the troops, do you think?

I think not, sir; at least not upon our branch. I do not know the effect it might have had upon General Thomas' immediate command of the troops at McMinnville.

Question. State, if you please, colonel, what property was said to have been destroyed.

Camp equipage and some ammunition.

Question. Did you ever hear any explanation of the act subsequently?

I heard it stated that the property was destroyed for want of sufficient transportation; that all the troops were to be concentrated at Altamont for the purpose of battle without being able to leave a sufficient guard at McMinnville to protect it. I understood that the troops at McMinnville had been directed to send their surplus baggage to Murfreesborough, and a portion of the transportation may have been engaged in this or may have been on the road hauling provisions from the railroad to McMinnville.

Question. In what way were your supplies transported at this time to McMinnville?

My impression is by wagon from Murfreesborough; some may have been transported over the Tullahoma branch, but I think at this time they relied upon the railroad at Murfreesborough and by wagoning from the railroad at Murfreesborough to McMinnville. The Tullahoma branch was cut a few days after the second Altamont expedition.

Cross-examination by the JUDGE-ADVOCATE:

Question. Colonel, this information that you received of the approach of the enemy at Altamont is based, I understand you to say, upon that letter you spoke of?

Not entirely. I only looked upon the letter, bearing the impress of having been written by an intelligent man, as confirmatory of the universal opinion of all the rebels outside of our lines at Altamont and on the road from our camp to that place. I looked upon their opinion, they having uninterrupted communication with their camp, as of value.

Question. Are the rebels in a habit, when meditating so important an expedition as this was, to advertise the route along which they intend to move?

I should think they would not generally. I suppose they were confident, however, in this respect from being so far from any camp of our troops.

Question. On the contrary, has not your observation taught you that they are secret and sudden in the performance of those things?

They have moved with celerity at times, but I cannot say that they have been generally very secret. In fact, before the end of the month cavalry did pursue that route, as I was informed, and destroyed our communications.

Question. Is your knowledge of the destruction of property at McMinnville of such a character as to justify you to say who was responsible, the extent of the destruction, and the result of it?

It is not, sir.

By General TYLER :

Question. How, when, and where did the enemy's cavalry destroy our communications?

By cutting the railroad, about the 28th of August, between McMinnville and Tullahoma.

Question. Did that cavalry pass over by Altamont?

I was informed that they had passed near Altamont.

Question. How, when, and where?

I was informed they had passed over the mountains by some road not generally traveled. I am not acquainted with the roads in that neighborhood, other than those leading into Altamont, and I cannot say by what exact route they crossed. From what I saw of the range I should judge the cavalry could cross in a great many places.

Question. At what point was the Tullahoma and McMinnville Railroad cut?

I cannot be positive. I was informed, if I am not mistaken, that it was between McMinnville and Manchester.

Question. What is the distance between McMinnville and Manchester?

I never traveled the route but once and did not pay particular attention to the distance, but I should think it would be from 15 to 20 miles.

Question. Do you know anything personally of the country between Tullahoma and McMinnville, and also do you know personally of any route by which those cavalry could come over and cut the communications?

I only know from traveling the road from Tullahoma to Manchester three times and from McMinnville to Manchester once. As to crossing the mountains other than by some three roads on the west, and one or two on the east, entering at Altamont, as before stated, I have no positive information, and relied upon the representations of the people of the country.

Question. Do you know by which of these three roads the cavalry came over and cut those communications?

I do not. My impression is that they did not come up either of these three roads— roads used for wagons, more or less—and was informed, as before stated, that the cavalry used a less public route, avoiding Altamont.

Question. What did you do with the letter written by the son of the clerk of Grundy County?

I appended it to the report of the expedition made to General Wood.

Question. You stated that there were some 200 head of cattle in the coves about Altamont; were these cattle collected for the use of our army?

Not to my knowledge.

Question. Was the army then in a condition to require fresh meat?

I believe we were at that time on full rations, though meat might have been used to great advantage. We were very shortly thereafter limited in rations.

Question. At what time were you at Altamont and what was the condition of the crops while you were there?

I was at Altamont about the 23d of August. In the immediate vicinity of Altamont there were no crops worth mentioning, it being an exceedingly sterile country.

Question. Was there any green or dry forage there?

A few farmers had a very little, but not enough to pay for gathering up. In the coves at the foot of the mountain the farmers had a very fair yield of corn, but very little dry corn or old forage, many farmers having none.

Question. State what kind of positive information it was you received that the army was marching on to Altamont to attack the enemy.

I was so informed by General Wood, my division commander. I saw, as before stated, some orders that to my mind indicated nothing less than an expected fight.

Question. Who were those orders sent by?

One was sent by General Buell and one by General Thomas.

Question. What was the purport of these orders?

General Thomas' order was one directing us to concentrate at McMinnville. General Buell's, as before stated, was directing us on the same day to concentrate at Altamont; at least it was executed the same day we attempted to execute General Thomas' order.

Question. Who was in command at McMinnville at the time the property was destroyed there?

I only know from information. I saw General Thomas with the troops and saw orders from him.

Question. How came you to see General Buell's order for concentration; was it published?

On the march, having marched from Vervilla to within 7 miles of McMinnville, and then down the Decherd road to a point opposite our camp 2½ miles distant, and then from that by way of Hickory Creek road toward Altamont, and being a very hot day, our troops were much exhausted and were straggling very much. There was some intimation that it was desired to execute the movement speedily, so as to arrive at Altamont that night. Having before passed over the road, and knowing it was a very difficult one up the mountain, it was thought best by Colonel Wagner for me to ride ahead and see General Wood and make proper representations as to the road and the degree of fatigue of our troops, so that, if it were possible and consistent with orders, to have the command stopped for the night at the foot of the mountains, 8 miles distant from Altamont. I rode ahead, met General Wood at the head of the column, and stated the facts of the case. He examined his orders in my presence, and not only stated what they were, but showed them to me, and finally concluded to remain there. I am not aware of General Wood showing them to anybody else. There was some dissatisfaction manifested by our portion of the troops in the expedition at the un-necessary march of 10 or 12 miles under a very hot sun, and it was not deemed improper that it should be known that it was not originally intended, but grew out of a change of orders.

Question. You say that General Wood showed an order from General Buell for this concentration at Altamont?

Yes, sir; for our troops to go there. It may have been an order directed to General Thomas, but handed to General Wood from the fact that he was on the road in advance and General Thomas' troops were not yet ready to start, and contained instructions as to the route to be pursued. I did not notice the direction.

Question. Do you suppose it was possible General Wood would open a communication addressed to General Thomas?

By no means; but it might be quite probable that under the circumstances General Thomas would hand the original letter to General Wood.

Redirect examination by General BUELL:

Question. Colonel, in giving information to General Wood, to which he attached such importance, of the result of your reconnaissance at Altamont, did you state to him the ground upon which the enemy was expected to advance by that route?

I stated to him fully and at length the information I had obtained, inclosing the original note referred to in my examination in support of my opinion that they were undoubtedly contemplating an early advance. I took into camp some 12 prisoners from Altamont, some of whom, I believe, were examined by the direction of General Wood. I also informed him verbally, if not in the communication, that a detachment of the enemy's cavalry had been at Altamont the day before the expedition.

Question. Did this marching and counter-marching of the troops to

McMinnville in such hot weather and then back again for the purpose of going to Altamont produce dissatisfaction among them?

Nothing of a permanent nature. They became very much fatigued, and were, as soldiers are apt to be, quite impatient, but after a night's rest there was nothing further heard of it. Twice afterward during the same month they went through fatiguing marches with their usual cheerfulness.

Question. Did they or did they not look upon it as evidence of confusion of plans?

They did, sir.

Question. Are you able to say how far they ascribed this apparent indecision and confusion to the commander of the army?

I cannot say in that instance. My opinion is that they generally charge it upon the highest officer in the army. It is the usual custom of the soldier, and I am not aware that it was generally known that the movement was the result of two orders.

By General SCHOEPF :

Question. You stated, colonel, that the troops were disheartened by the marching and counter-marching from McMinnville to Altamont. What was the feeling of the troops after their march to Kentucky and back again without any result?

I did not use so strong a term as disheartened. I stated that they were temporarily discouraged. So far as the Kentucky expedition is concerned, they looked upon it as barren of results in the way of destroying the enemy, and, of course, regretted the necessity of returning to Tennessee.

By General BUELL :

Question. Can you point to any instance in this war or to any instances in any war within the recollection of your reading where a large army in an open field has been destroyed by another?

General SCHOEPF. I object to that question, Mr. President, as it is to be supposed that every general is sufficiently conversant with military history to know all about it. This investigation is for our information in regard to the operations of the army in the Kentucky and Tennessee campaign, and the question has no bearing upon the investigation before the Commission.

The court was cleared, when, after discussion, it was decided that the question should be put.

The WITNESS. None in this war; very few in modern history. I believe the Romans claimed almost universally to have destroyed their enemy's armies, and in turn had armies destroyed at Cannæ by Hannibal; but within reliable history the instances are few, as far as I have read.

Question. Have you any doubt that the rebel army invaded Kentucky for the purpose of controlling it and bringing it to the support of the rebellion or for the purpose of defeating the armies of the Government that might be found in Kentucky?

I have not; although I am not yet satisfied that they attempted to carry out their plans as first intended.

Question. The question of one of the members of the Commission assumes that the march from Tennessee to Kentucky by the Army of the Ohio was barren of results; in view of the fact that the rebel army was foiled in the purpose which you have stated in your last answer are you prepared to say that the campaign was barren of results?

I am not, and did not so mean to be understood when I stated that the troops looked upon the expedition as barren of results in the way of destroying the enemy's army and regretted the necessity of their return to Tennessee. I look upon the campaign as successful, saving our army and defeating the enemy's plans upon Kentucky.

Question. Has the opinion prevailed among the troops of the Army of the Ohio that our force was vastly superior to the enemy in that campaign, and has that circumstance tended to increase their disappointment, if there has been any?

It was believed, up to about the time that we arrived between Munfordville and Elizabethtown, that our force was greatly superior to the enemy. About the time I refer to, the opinion of the army, so far as I know, underwent a change, and we looked upon the enemy as at least equal to us in numbers and effectiveness. The opinion that we largely surpassed them in numbers did not contribute to the dissatisfaction of the soldiers.

Question. How was it on that point with reference to the subsequent operations of the army against the combined forces of the enemy in Kentucky; I mean what was the prevailing opinion as to the relative strength of the armies?

It was thought by the soldiers after we left Louisville that we largely excelled them in numbers, and dissatisfaction was expressed by them in not engaging the enemy. This occurred mainly immediately after the battle of Perryville.

Question. In the impatience which troops naturally and always feel before engaging an enemy that they consider not superior to them do they take much account of the advantage which an adversary may derive from strength of position or of other circumstances which may determine the question of the battle?

Soldiers who express impatience do not and generally are not qualified to take such facts into consideration.

Recross-examination by the JUDGE-ADVOCATE:

Question. Colonel, have you read Bragg's report, Colonel Forsyth's and Hawes' letters, and Benjamin's dispatch, and other documents from rebel sources relative to this campaign in Kentucky?

I have read General Bragg's report and Benjamin's dispatch; I believe I have not seen the other communications referred to.

Question. Did not that expedition originate in an expectation that the people of Kentucky would respond by a general rising, and was not the disappointment in that in fact the cause of the hasty retreat of the combined forces out of Kentucky?

I suppose that General Bragg contemplated larger accessions to his army than he received, but I am not prepared to say that the disappointment in that was alone the cause of his evacuation, for the reason that he probably could not have the means of arming the people of Kentucky generally had they welcomed him heartily, and his effective force would not have been much greater than it was. He doubtless hastened his evacuation partly on account of such disappointment.

Question. Did he not depend upon the country he invaded for supplies?

I believe he did, sir.

Question. Would not his position then become hazardous on finding a country of enemies instead of friends?

Yes, sir.

General BUELL. Although Bragg did not receive that encouragement which he expected, did he actually find himself in the midst of enemies such as the Army of the Ohio was surrounded by in Tennessee?

No, sir; he must have received a great moral support from persons who failed to enlist in his army, judging from the expressions of the people along the march.

Commission adjourned to meet January 24, 1863.

LOUISVILLE, *January* 24, 1863.

Commission met pursuant to adjournment. All the members present; also the judge-advocate and General Buell.

HARRY I. TODD (a witness for the defendant), being duly sworn by the judge-advocate, testified as follows:

By General BUELL:

Question. Please state your name and place of residence.

Harry I. Todd; Frankfort, Ky.

Question. Are you well acquainted with the Kentucky River? If so, please state at the same time what opportunities you have had of acquiring a knowledge of it.

I am thoroughly acquainted with it. I commanded a steamboat for seven years which ran from the mouth of Dick's River most of the time to the mouth of the Kentucky River (though Louisville was the end of our trip), and for ten years I ran coalboats from the forks of the Kentucky River to Frankfort. I have crossed all the principal fords and ferries between Franklin and Boonesborough very often at low water.

Question. How far are the forks you speak of above Clay's Ferry or the point at which the Lexington and Richmond road crosses the Kentucky River?

It is 85 or 90 miles.

Question. Mention, if you please, the various points at which the river can be forded at low water—at which it could have been forded in the months of September and October last. You may limit your answer to the distance between Frankfort and 10 or 15 miles above Clay's Ferry.

There are nearly if not quite fifty places at which it could be forded between those places from July to the middle of December.

Question. Name the principal of those fords, if you please.

You can ford it immediately at Frankfort; within 4 miles above Frankfort; 8 miles above Frankfort; 13 miles above Frankfort, at which there is a turnpike road crosses from Versailles to Lawrenceburg; 17 miles above Frankfort, at which there is another turnpike road; 21 miles above Frankfort; 26 miles above Frankfort, at which there is another turnpike on both sides of the river, leading from Versailles to Harrodsburg; 30 miles above Frankfort, at which there is a turnpike leading on one side of the river to Harrodsburg; 45 miles above Frankfort, where there is another turnpike road from Versailles to Harrodsburg; 50 miles above Frankfort, where there is a turnpike road from Lexington to Harrodsburg; 55 miles above Frankfort; half a mile below the mouth of Dick's River there is a turnpike road on the south side of the river; 75 miles above Frankfort, where there is a road from Lexington to Danville; 80 miles above Frankfort, at the mouth of Sugar Creek, leading from Jessamine County into Garrard; 85 miles above Frankfort; 90 miles above Frankfort; 95 miles above Frankfort; 102 miles above Frankfort; 110 miles to Clay's Ferry, where there is a road from Lexington to Richmond; 115 miles to the next ferry above that; 120 miles to Boonesborough, where the road from Winchester to Richmond crosses; 125 miles to the next; 131 miles to the next; 138 miles to the next; 145 miles to the next; 155 miles to the next, and 165 miles to the next. That is up to within 35 miles of the fork, and covers all the principal ferries where there are main roads leading to them.

Question. Do you mean to say that there are good practicable fords at all these points, captain?

Yes, sir.

Question. What is the character of the ford at Clay's Ferry?

It is a very good ford, sir. The road for getting to the ford is not so good as that for getting to the ferry, but it was passable for wagons and stock and everything of that sort at the time you speak of or has been this last season.

Question. Are you acquainted with the country on the south side of the Kentucky River between the Lexington and Richmond road, the Lexington and Danville road, and the Lancaster and Richmond road?

I know the country between Lexington and Richmond, that is, immediately along the turnpike road, very well.

Question. I mean the country embraced by those lines I have named.

No, sir; not very well.

Question. That is, on the south side of the river, between the Lexington and Danville road, the Lancaster and Richmond road, and the Lexington and Richmond road—that angular tract of country in there?

I am not acquainted with the road between Lancaster and Richmond at all.

Question. Do you know anything of the character of the country generally?

I have not been in that particular locality. I know all about the country between Lexington and Danville toward Crab Orchard, leaving Lancaster to the left, or between Danville and Crab Orchard. I know all about the country between Richmond and Lancaster and beyond that, away into those mountains there, but have no knowledge of the road from Richmond to Lancaster. I never was on that road.

Question. Were you in Frankfort about the time of the battle of Perryville?

Yes, sir; I was there at that time.

Question. State under what circumstances, if you please.

I had been a fugitive from home about five weeks, and went there with General Sill's division as a sort of guide.

Question. Was there any apprehension among the people of Central Kentucky that Bragg's army would fall back into that region after leaving Perryville?

Yes, sir; a good deal.

Question. Was it the opinion of the people that that army had invaded Kentucky for the purpose of holding it?

Yes, sir; many of our best people were firmly of the opinion that they had found "the last ditch" up there, and would make a desperate fight there. That army took a great deal of property from some of our citizens; among other things about $80,000 worth of jeans and linseys. The parties to whom they belonged went from Lexington to Camp Dick Robinson, and from there to Danville, at which points they expected to see General Bragg or General Smith, or some of the prominent men, to get some evidence of the indebtedness. Failing in that, they came back, believing that there was to be a most desperate battle there or in the neighborhood of Camp Dick Robinson, and they would whip the Federal army, or if the Federal army whipped them they would fall back and take everything between Lexington and this place (Louisville), and this if they chose. Gentlemen who were there—friends of mine, and very intelligent men—satisfied me so well that they intended to make a determined fight there that I moved my family from Frankfort to this place, so that I could get across the river in case the war was transferred to that locality or its coming here. A great many people in my part of the State were induced to unite themselves with the rebel army because they were made to believe they would never have to leave the State. Other misrepresentations that were made in regard to the course that the Union army were pursuing as they came up induced a great many to run off and join the rebel army for protection. Among other things they told was that the Union army were taking up old men who had not joined their army and were making breastworks of them. There were similar reports of the same sort.

Cross-examination by the JUDGE-ADVOCATE:

Question. These fords that you speak of on the Kentucky River are ordinary ferries, are they not?

No, sir; there is a ferry at all the principal crossings, and at others a ford that is used at all seasons of the year when the water is down.

Question. Were they not made so numerous and practicable by the low stage of water at that time?

They are nearly always fordable at that season of the year and at divers other points; at almost every considerable little branch that runs into the river it can be forded.

Commission adjourned to meet January 28, 1863.

CINCINNATI, *January* 28, 1863.

Commission met pursuant to adjournment. All the members present; also the judge-advocate and General Buell.

General J. T. BOYLE (a witness for the defendant), being duly sworn by the judge-advocate, testified as follows:

By General BUELL:

Question. Will you please give your name and position in the United States service?

J. T. Boyle; brigadier-general in the volunteer service. I am commanding at Louisville, District of Western Kentucky.

Question. Are you well acquainted with the Kentucky River and its various crossings from Frankfort up some 20 miles east of the Lexington and Richmond road?

I am tolerably well acquainted with the geography and topography of that part of the country. I was born there and have lived there all my life.

Question. Mention the principal fords within the distance alluded to, as far as you know.

There are so many fords that I do not know that I can recall all of them at this moment. Ascending the river, there is Schryock, one of the main crossings between Lawrenceburg and Versailles into Woodford County. There is McCowan's Ferry, where there is a crossing to Versailles and Lexington, from which there are diverging roads to these places; a crossing at Munday's Landing; at Oregon; at Brooklyn, which is on the turnpike road from Harrodsburg and Shakertown to Lexington. There is a crossing at Lewis' Ferry, on the direct road to Shakertown and Lexington. There is a crossing immediately at the mouth of Dick's River, which is only a few hundred yards above this. The next main crossing is at the mouth of Hickman Creek, on the Lexington and Danville pike. There is a crossing at the mouth of Sugar Creek; another at the mouth of Paint Lick Creek; another at Tait's Ferry. The next main crossing is at Clay's Ferry, on the Richmond road. There are several small crossings that I do not now remember the names of, used mainly for neighborhood communications between the two sides of the river.

Question. Are these that you mention good fords at a low stage of water?

Yes, sir; most of them are very good.

Question. And were they so in the month of October last?

I presume they were, from the low stage of water in the streams at that time.

Question. Will you give the topography of the country on the south side of the Kentucky River—the country between the Kentucky River and the Lancaster and Richmond road—bounded on the north by the Kentucky River and on the other side by the road from Hickman around to Lancaster and Richmond and then on toward Clay's Ferry?

The country is undulating; parts of it very much broken. There are a variety of streams running into the Kentucky River from the south—Silver Creek, Paint Lick, Deep Creek, Scott's Fork of Sugar Creek, Sugar Creek, another fork of Sugar Creek of which I do not remember the name, besides other small streams. The country is broken by these streams and is hilly, but on these ridges there are very considerable tracts of fine level country, but elevated above the beds of these creeks. The road mentioned in the question passes above the source of most of these streams or crosses most of them high up. The roads that run to the Kentucky River from the turnpike pass on the ridges and sometimes down the valleys of these streams. One of them is a turnpike road from Lancaster to the Paint Lick Creek on the road to Richmond. I believe there is a turnpike partially made to the mouth of Sugar Creek from Lancaster; but of that I am not certain. The land near the Kentucky River, except in the bottoms formed by these creeks and in other bottoms of the river is rugged and broken. The cliffs of the river in same places are precipitous. The land is very rich, and it is a country very well settled. They have as good roads as can be made in a country as broken as this is.

Question. Are there very good roads passing along the river on the south side of it; is the country up and down the river considered to be practicable for wagons, and are there any roads by which an army can move with facility?

All the roads up and down the river are at right angles with these streams, which break and cut up the country. There are country roads passing up near the river that are made for the purpose of traveling up the river so far as to fall into the roads that lead to the county seat of Lancaster. There is no public road that I remember running parallel with the river or nearly so that is near to the river. The road from Lancaster to Richmond by the mouth of Paint Lick Creek is a good road, but it does not run exactly parallel with the river, though its general direction is in a line with that of the river. It would be very difficult for an army to pass up near the river with all the equipage of an army on those roads.

Question. What is the character of the Tait's Ferry road?

It is a very good road. At that season of the year it is a very eligible road for traveling. I think it is very much traveled to Richmond and to Madison County at that season of the year.

Question. Do you know whether a portion of Kirby Smith's force used that road in invading the State last summer?

I know it only as it was communicated to me officially. I have no personal knowledge of it. I have no doubt that they did use it, from information received by me.

Question. That is a road leading from Richmond to Lexington, is it not?

Yes, sir.

Question. How far below the Clay's Ferry road does that cross the Kentucky River?

I really cannot say with any certainty. I think it must be 10 or 12 miles.

Question. According to the best information you were able to obtain what do you consider to be the force with which Kirby Smith entered Kentucky in August last?

I have no accurate knowledge about the matter; of course any estimate that I would give would be but an approximation.

Question. What I want is the estimate you made about that time.

I believed at the time, and felt no doubt about it, that his force was from 15,000 to 20,000 strong. I believed afterward that his force was even greater than that; probably 25,000.

Question. Does this estimate include the troops commanded by Humphrey Marshall and the force that subsequently came in under the command of Stevenson?

I do not mean to embrace the force of Marshall or Stevenson either. They both came in some time after Kirby Smith entered the State—after the battle of Richmond.

Question. Under all the circumstances of that invasion, was it fair to believe, and is that your opinion, that it had for its object to hold the State to secure it to the Southern Confederacy?

I think that was a very reasonable and natural inference. I think that was their object and they felt the fullest confidence in the success of it, and the great body of the people of the State had serious apprehension that it would be the result and feared it greatly. I was so strongly impressed with that opinion myself that I was urgent that steps might be taken to prevent their permanent holding of it, but I was afraid the State would go. I believe I telegraphed to that effect to the President and probably to the Secretary of War. I think, however, that I communicated the fears I had on the subject before Kirby Smith had actually entered the State from the information I derived from General Morgan at Cumberland Gap and from spies I had in the country. I believe I also communicated the same thing to General Buell. I am sure I telegraphed to General Buell (I could tell when were I at Louisville) that it would be absolutely essential for him to come back to Kentucky to save it. There are some other matters that I telegraphed to the President, but I do not feel sure enough to speak of them without examining my papers.

Question. Has your reading of history and your observation of war brought you to the conclusion that there is no success in military operations short of the extermination of your enemy or his capture bodily, supposing the armies to be nearly equal and in an open field ?

Most certainly it has not; either my knowledge of history or my observation of war, which is limited. I think, so far as I know, that few contending armies ever exterminated each other, and I have never known or heard of an instance in which a retreating army of any considerable force was ever captured by the pursuing army. If there is such a case I have no recollection of it, unless it was in the history of the Jews, where God might have intervened and allowed them to take their enemy bodily. I remember no other case.

Question. Under all the circumstances, considering the strength of the rebel army which invaded Kentucky, the circumstances and object of that invasion, would you consider that the march of the Army of the Ohio through Tennessee to Kentucky, and the subsequent operating against the rebel forces in Kentucky, barren of results ?

I do not, sir; I think it absolutely necessary to have brought the army there for the purpose of saving the State. That was my opinion first, before it moved, when it was moving, and after it had reached Kentucky and moved in its operations against the rebel army, and is my opinion now.

Question. What effect do you suppose its movements had upon the object for which the State was invaded by the rebel forces ?

I think it had the effect of defeating their object; that is, if their object was to make their invasion successful by holding the State, which I believe was their object and purpose. I believe that they could and would have held the larger portion of the State if the army had not been moved from Tennessee. I think that we could have held a portion of the border of Kentucky on the Ohio against them, but that they would have held the greater portion of the State, including its capital. I believe that they would have derived great assistance from the people if they had held it sufficiently long to have inspired them with confidence that it was going to be a permanent result.

Question. About what force and what description of troops had you to oppose this invasion in the first instance, and so on up to about the time of the arrival of the Army of the Ohio ?

I cannot speak with positiveness and accuracy as to the amount of force that I had in Kentucky when I first ascertained that Kirby Smith was entering the passes of the mountains. I think I had about 2,000 men. I called for more troops from everybody; and Governor Morton and the president of this court, General Wallace, hastened up movements in Indiana so as to throw over several thousand troops by the time Kirby Smith had reached London. I think I had in the State some twelve regiments, probably not that many. General Wallace came to Louisville in command of a regiment and tendered his services to me. I requested him to go to Lexington, where I had thrown the great body of the forces I had, and I think when he reached there there were seven regiments. Probably two arrived afterward, making nine, which I requested him to take command of and to reconnoiter the country in the direction of Richmond, Big Hill, and of London, and that I would send him forces as fast as I could get them. I had besides those nine regiments some three or four regiments that were stationed at Munfordville and along the road and at Louisville. But all the forces that could be spared from guarding the road were directly afterward thrown toward Lexington. More troops were sent into Lexington, but not until General Wallace had been relieved by General Nelson. The battle of Richmond occurred directly afterward. The remnant of the forces up there that were not killed or captured retreated to Louisville. There were then massed at Louisville new troops from Indiana, Ohio, and Illinois. The new Department of the Ohio was created and General Wright assigned to the command. Other officers superior to me in rank—indeed an officer who was not superior to me in rank, by my consent and at my request, had the command, feeling he was better qualified than I was myself. The number of troops that were brought in from these States at that time, new regiments, I cannot state with accuracy, because reports were not made to me. General Nelson came down as soon as his wounds would permit to Louisville and assumed command. Such returns as were made of the troops were made to him. Regiments arriving and reporting to me, supposing I was in command, I notified him of, and required the officers to report to him. I knew generally about the number of regiments and the approximate strength of the force, but I do not believe anybody knew it with any degree of certainty, or with that degree of certainty that such a fact ought to have been known at the time, owing to the great confusion, excitement, and alarm. I believe that the forces in Kentucky, exclusive of those who were at Covington and Newport and concentrated at Louisville, amounted to from 45,000 to 50,000. Probably there were 51,000 or 52,000, estimating the regiments and batteries as full, including between 4,500 to 5,000 that were at Munfordville and that were captured, leaving probably 44,000 to 46,000. My estimate of the force is founded upon the number of regiments and batteries, as I now recollect them, that were there. There was a very small artillery force—two or three batteries and two or three that we improvised for the occasion. Such reports and returns that were made were, I presume, made to General Buell and to General Gilbert. Those returns would show approximately the force, though I doubt very much whether any such reports were made, or could have been made, as ought to have been made at that time, and especially after General Nelson got back, when he increased the excitement and alarm very much.

Question. Do you understand your estimate to cover the aggregate force; and, if so, about what would have been the effective force?

It is the aggregate force. I do not know what the effective force would have been of such a concern as that was. The men marched from camp, on the edge of the city, to the town, for the purpose of review and to learn how to march and to handle their guns. Large numbers of them broke down and one man was killed by sunstroke. I believe they were all raw regiments. I could not say what would have been the effective force.

Question. Do you remember the date of the arrival of the last division of General Thomas, of the Army of the Ohio, at Louisville?

I do not. I cannot remember the date with any degree of accuracy. I think that General Buell arrived there on the 26th or 27th of September, but I am not certain. I am merely stating the recollection I have of it now. General Thomas arrived there several days afterward.

Question. Did your position give you an opportunity of judging of the labor that was required to prepare the old army for further service and to complete the organization of that with the new force? If so, please state what your observation was with reference to it and whether it was done sluggishly or expeditiously.

I was left in command and continued in command at Louisville all the while when it arrived there and while it was there, with the exception of six or eight hours, when I was assigned to the command of a division, but was afterward ordered to remain at Louisville. I saw a good many of the troops. I knew probably most of the general officers of the army; I had served with it myself in the campaign to Shiloh and Corinth. I went to the camps of a portion of the force and to a brigade that I commanded at Shiloh. I heard a good deal of the condition of the men from the officers, and from all I heard and saw I thought the army was in rather a bad condition in some respects; it needed shoeing, clothing, and paying—inspiriting them by paying. They seemed to me to pretty much need everything that recruits just mustered in need. I think some of them were rearmed there.

I think the work of arming, shoeing, clothing, paying, and supplying them in every respect; combining the new with the old and organizing them into brigades and divisions and army corps; preparing them to march against the enemy; preparing all the provisions and supplies of subsistence and ammunition, and actually moving them, showed what struck me as wonderful energy, industry, and ability. I have never seen, known, heard, or read of anything evincing more in the same length of time. I saw no sluggishness, delay, want of energy, or want of anything for a preparation to meet and fight the enemy; on the contrary, everything was brought into requisition, it seemed to me, that any man or set of men could have exercised for the purpose of moving against the enemy and driving him out.

Question. On what day was the battle of Richmond fought, general?

I do not know positively.

Cross-examination by the JUDGE-ADVOCATE:

Question. At what season of the year and for how long a time, general, is the Kentucky River fordable at the places you have located?

That depends entirely upon the dryness of the season. As a general thing it is fordable from the latter part of June or the 1st of July to November, unless we have heavy fall rains to raise the streams. Sometimes it is even beyond that time, commencing earlier and extending later into the season in cases of extreme drought.

Question. Are not the banks of the river high and steep and the fords therefore difficult to approach at the places you speak of?

At those main crossings the roads are good and the approaches comparatively easy; on the turnpike road they are uncommonly good. There are many other crossings besides those I have mentioned that are not so generally used, where the approaches to them are more difficult to travel, not being worked so much. The cliffs of the river are precipitous on one side or the other nearly all the way up and at all the crossings, requiring much labor to make the crossings from the one side to the other practicable. They are less so on the other side.

Question. Enumerate those crossings, if you please, that you say are of easy access.

Schryock, which is on the road from Lawrenceburg to Woodford County; McCowan's Ferry—that is on the road from Salvisa, and I believe a road from Lawrenceburg runs into it, crossing over toward Woodford County; Oregon—there is a turnpike road running to Oregon on the south side; Munday's Landing—there is a dirt road, I think, not a turnpike—from Harrodsburg to Woodford County and to Jessamine via Shakertown to Lexington—that is a very fine pike on both sides of the river; Lewis's Ferry—that is on the direct road to Shakertown from Lexington and Nicholasville—a very good road to the ferry. The main road from Danville to the mouth of Dick's River crosses several hundred yards above that. It is a fair dirt road, considering that it is not worked much. It has been somewhat injured by a railroad crossing the river there, over which there was to have been a suspension bridge. The crossing at the mouth of the river is approached by the best turnpike in the State; it is one of the best I ever saw. The crossing on the Tait's Creek road I know more about from information than from personal knowledge. It must be an excellent one from what I understand of it. The cliffs are not so high or precipitous as below the crossing at Sugar Creek. Most of the crossings I mention have pretty good roads at that season of the year. The turnpike crossing is good at all seasons.

Question. Are not these crossings of such a character that a comparatively small force could dispute the passage of an army over them?

Yes, sir; I think so. An inconsiderable force at almost any of the crossings eligibly situated could impede and prevent the passage of a larger force. There are a great many minor crossings, besides those I have mentioned, at which infantry and cavalry could cross, but not in such force; but at any of them an opposing force in proper position could prevent it. The cliffs of the river are so precipitous and of such generally difficult crossing that they could be crossed only at these places, and a force in position on either side, whichever force had possession of it, could hold it. It is a strong natural defense.

Question. When did Kirby Smith's army enter Kentucky, general?

I cannot state the exact date, just as I cannot state the date of the battle of Richmond. He entered the State about eight or ten days before the battle of Richmond; perhaps it was ten days.

Question. At what point did he enter Kentucky?

The forces entered Kentucky at different points. The main force of Kirby Smith's entered by Deep Creek Gap, I believe. Scott's force of cavalry or some other cavalry must have entered at Kirby Smith's left at a considerable distance, and must have crossed through Jamestown, Tenn., into Clinton County, Kentucky, and came up by Mill Springs to Somerset, from Somerset to London, and joined a force which had come in with Kirby Smith, as I understand.

Question. From London through what places did they march?

I do not know certainly, as there was nothing at all to hinder their marching in that region of the State. I have believed that a force for the sake of subsistence and forage passed over different roads, concentrating at London or Big Hill. I think it likely that the main force came through Whitley County to London. Some of the force likely passed much nearer Cumberland Gap, and may have crossed at the Cumberland Ford and passed to Barboursville and London. I do not know the exact point at which he struck the Wilderness or Cumberland Gap road; that is, the main road. It diverges at London, one road running in the direction of Lexington and the other in the direction of Crab Orchard.

Question. From London he marched to Lexington and Frankfort, did he not?

Yes, sir. I do not know that he was ever in Frankfort; part of his army was at Frankfort; but from some telegraphic dispatches we captured I think he was never there.

Question. Was he not engaged after that invasion in gathering up supplies and did he not propose making Camp Dick Robinson a permanent place to gather them in?

I have no doubt he was extensively engaged in gathering up supplies of all kinds; there was nothing on the earth to hinder him from doing so, and I am sure from what I have learned that the necessities of his army demanded it. I do not know that he was concentrating his supplies at Camp Dick Robinson. A proclamation was issued by General Bragg at Danville, in which he announced that Camp Dick Robinson would be held as a recruiting point. I presume supplies were concentrated there for that purpose and that General Buckner was to have command there, and all the Kentucky troops that were to be raised were to report to him at that place. I received that proclamation two or three days after it was printed at Danville. They did accumulate at Camp Dick Robinson considerable supplies. A considerable portion of them were seized there after they left that were not destroyed, as I learned from the officer who had seized them and from the people from whom they had been taken, who appealed to me for the purpose of having them restored to them—property that they could identify, several thousand barrels probably of pork and other things. I think they had large supplies at Nicholasville and at Lexington, and that they were apparently gathering up supplies to last the army all the time, as if they were going to make a permanent occupation of the State. It may have been done for the purpose of impressing upon the people that that was their purpose; it certainly had that effect, and it looked as if it was intended as a permanent occupation from the amount of troops and the accumulation of supplies.

Question. Was he not engaged in sending these supplies out of Kentucky previous to the return of the Army of the Ohio?

I do not know. I think not, from anything I have heard. The only things that I heard of being sent were some jeans and linseys that it was reported he had sent out in the direction of Knoxville, but of that I have no reliable information. I do not think any considerable supplies were sent at all, excepting those which were sent just in advance of the retreating army.

Question. What became of the supplies that you understand were gathered at Lexington and Nicholasville as Kirby Smith fell back?

Some of them were destroyed; some of them were left, not destroyed, and were captured by our forces; others, I think, were sent off in the direction of Knoxville just before the retreat, and, as I believed, for the purpose of covering them and being protected by the army. I think they carried off considerable supplies. It would take a great deal to subsist them through the barren regions of country through which they passed.

Question. Was not the retreat of this invading army really caused by their disappointment in not being sustained by Kentucky?

It is conjectural entirely as to the extent of their disappointment; I could not say what effect that had upon it; but I have never for a moment thought that that was the cause of their retreat. I had believed it was because of the movement of our army upon them much earlier than they had any conception it would be prepared to move and from the fact that they had an exaggerated idea of our forces. I have believed that if they had known the force they would not have retreated, and that they could, considering the discipline of their troops and the length of time they had been in the service, successfully cope with our army. I had most serious apprehensions of it at that time. I felt that the retreat, from all that I had learned in regard to its character, was cowardly, and that the whole result was a grand triumph on the part of the Government.

Question. Their information of our forces, position, &c., is generally very accurate, is it not ?

I cannot say what is the degree of accuracy of their knowledge in that respect, but I have supposed generally that they had much more accurate knowledge of our forces than we had of theirs. I think in this case that the universal impression of the people of the magnitude of our forces had impressed them with the idea that it was greater, and the information that they had received through all the agencies that they usually employ and the advantages they had in Kentucky were overcome by the universality of that impression of our own people, including those that were ready to join them, for I know there was an impression that there was an immense army at Louisville and an immense army here in Cincinnati.

Commission adjourned to meet Thursday, January 29, 1863.

CINCINNATI, *January* 29, 1863.

Commission met pursuant to adjournment. All the members present; also the judge-advocate and General Buell.

General J. T. BOYLE's testimony continued, as follows :

By the JUDGE-ADVOCATE :

Question. You saw Bragg's report, did you not, of that expedition into Kentucky and the letters and comments of the rebel press upon it shortly after it occurred ?

I do not think I saw it; if I did, I did not read it. I saw the substance, probably, of an article of Provisional Governor Hawes, of Kentucky, and one of Mr. Forsyth, of Mobile. I do not think I ever read General Bragg's report.

Question. You cannot state, then, what estimate the rebels placed upon our forces immediately after the expedition ?

Only from information which I received from domestic rebels and citizens of Kentucky.

Question. I understand from your answer that you saw nothing of an official character at that time from Bragg or any of his officers ?

None at all, sir; excepting I might state that a great many prisoners, privates and officers, made statements to me in regard to the matter, but no official statement was made.

Question. Do you know anything of a communication addressed by General Buell to General Nelson upon the subject of holding or evacuating Louisville ?

I do not, sir.

Question. You spoke of an officer having been put in command over you that had no right to that place ; who was that officer ?

I did not speak of an officer put in command over me except by my consent. That officer was General Gilbert; it was done by General Wright. General Gilbert was placed in command at Lexington to withdraw the forces that were there, and not at Richmond, as well as the remnant that escaped from Richmond, and ordered, as I understood, to retreat or withdraw them from Lexington to Louisville or Cincinnati. Finding the route to Louisville the most desirable, he fell back by the road from Lexington to Frankfort and from Frankfort to Louisville. He was in command of that retreating column of General Cruft; General Jackson was with him. Both of them were brigadier-generals, and General Gilbert was not a brigadier-general. He was placed in that position at their written request by General Wright. When he reached Louisville, occupying that position, knowing him to be a man of talent in his profession, and believing him to have skill and ability, I readily acquiesced in his occupying the position. He continued in command until General Nelson arrived. There was but one officer, I believe, who was of the rank of brigadier-general objecting; he was not left there.

Question. What rank was given to General Gilbert?

I do not know. The forces that were there when he arrived and the column with which he retreated at that time amounted to fully the command of a division. There must have been more than 20,000 there and on the road; they were thrown in rapidly from the States.

Question. Did he not assume the title and wear the uniform of a major-general?

I never saw him with the uniform. I never knew him to claim the title, though I had the impression that his report was signed as major-general; but of that I am not at all certain.

Question. Were these circumstances explained to General Buell when he assumed command at Louisville?

Not that I know of. I did not communicate them to him, though I gave him such information as I had with regard to matters and affairs there. I speak now of the position and relation of General Gilbert to the troops. I told him about the battle and the retreat of the column. General Buell made diligent inquiry in regard to all the matters connected with the battle of Richmond and the retreat and condition of the forces—as to their arms and equipments of every kind. I never made any allusion to the position General Gilbert held at all that I remember.

Question. What was probably General Gilbert's rank in the army about that time?

I think he was a captain in the Regular Army.

Question. Do you know anything about Captain Gay having been given command as a general in that expedition?

I think General Wright or General Gilbert placed him in command of a brigade of cavalry. I think he continued in that position on the march. Whether he held the command as a general commanding the brigade or whether he was issuing and delivering orders as a staff officer I do not know; I was not with the expedition.

Question. And where are the books connected with General Nelson's command at that time?

I do not know where they are; I do not know if they were preserved. If he had any books there I did not know it. His orders to me of every kind were informal. I made and kept a record of them myself.

By General SCHOEPF:

Question. Who was that general you referred to that refused to be commanded by General Gilbert?

General Green Clay Smith.

Question. Was that the reason of his being sent away or was any other reason assigned?

General Wright did not state to me that that was the reason; I suppose it was, and thought he ought to have been sent away, for he was not fit to have taken the command of that retreating column in the condition it was. General Gilbert, in my opinion, and General Wright was of a similar opinion, was the best fitted man for the position; and that was the opinion of every brigadier-general that was there. It was apparently a military necessity.

Question. Please state the names of all the generals who were there unfit to command.

I have not formed opinions in regard to the qualifications of men such as ought to be expressed. General Smith, I suppose, could have commanded a brigade under ordinary circumstances very well; but these were not ordinary circumstances, and so it was felt by everybody at the time.

Question. You stated in a previous reply that the generals applied for Gilbert to be put in command; who were those generals?

General Jackson and General Cruft. I understood from General Jackson that he and General Cruft, and probably colonels of regiments, had requested of General Wright that it should be done. I do not remember any other brigadiers who were there except those three.

By General TYLER:

Question. General, you say that General Smith was unfit for this command that General Gilbert took; in what did that unfitness consist? Was it in habits or want of military experience or knowledge or what?

General Smith's habits, as far as I know, were excellent. He had no military knowledge or experience, or very little. I think he had not the steadiness of purpose and power of controlling men to have conducted the retreating column. General Jackson had much more experience, but was a very modest man, and felt his want of capacity for the position.

Question. At the time of the capture of Munfordville in what military district was it?

I do not know in what district Kentucky was for some considerable length of time. I was assigned to the command of the State of Kentucky on the 27th or 29th of May, and ordered to report to the Secretary of War and afterward ordered to report to General Halleck. I did not understand the matter, and reported to General Buell and General Halleck both. I think on the 19th of August the new Department of the Ohio was created. This battle of Munfordville occurred some time after that.

Question. Do I understand by your answer that you were commanding the State of Kentucky at the time Munfordville was taken or not?

No, sir. If I understand it, when Munfordville was taken it was in the new Department of the Ohio, which was created some time before. General Wright was in command of the Department of Kentucky up to that time. General Gilbert was in command of those forces, under General Wright, at the time.

Question. On what day were you relieved from the command of the District of Kentucky and by what order?

I think it was on the 23d of August, by the order of General Wright, assuming command of the new Department of the Ohio, which was created some days before, of which I had received notification from the Secretary of War and had communicated it to General Buell.

Question. What was your military position after the Department of the Ohio was created?

I was left in command of Louisville and the forces in the vicinity of Louisville and upon the lines of the road until General Gilbert was placed in command. I then commanded the forces in and immediately around the city until General Nelson arrived, when I commanded the forces in the city—two regiments and the convalescents.

Question. Who was in the immediate command of the troops along the line of railroad when Munfordville was taken?

My understanding is that General Gilbert was in command.

Question. Where was General Gilbert's headquarters?

At Louisville.

Question. Were your headquarters there at that time?

Yes, sir.

Question. You spoke yesterday, general, of Clay's Ferry route, from Richmond to Lexington; are you sure that Kirby Smith's army passed over that route?

I have no doubt that a portion of them passed there; a portion of them crossed at other ferries or fords.

Question. Are you acquainted with that route personally ?

Yes, sir.

Question. Are not 2 or 3 miles of that Clay road, the other side of the river, almost impassable for artillery ?

Not unless it has become so within the last year or so.   It is a turnpike road.

Question. Are you sure it is a turnpike road the whole distance over that ferry ?

I have not been over it for a long time, but it was a turnpike when I went over it.

Question. Is there not a dirt road connected with the turnpike ?

There is a dirt road passing from the ferry up to the ford.   Where the river becomes fordable it is a dirt road, but I would suppose perfectly passable as a turnpike road at that season of the year, for it was a season when such roads are good.

Question. What is the character of the country on the south side of the bank of the Kentucky River, along the face of those ferries, 2 or 3 miles back from the river ?

For a mile or two it is hilly and broken in most places; the lands then are undulating and rolling and among the best lands in Kentucky at most of those crossings. At some of the points where the cliffs of the river are entirely precipitous the level land commences within a few hundred yards of the top of the precipices, and it has the general level of the country.   Some of the richest lands of the State run within a hundred or two yards of the precipitous cliffs of the Kentucky River, but generally for a mile or two off it is rugged, and where these roads go down in the valleys it is more rugged, because it is broken by those streams, and at most of the crossings I have spoken of it is rugged and broken for 2 or 3 miles.

Question. Are the banks of the Kentucky River, as you have described them in your last answer, fit for encamping a large army ?

I suppose at most of the places within half a mile to a mile of the river, extending back, you will find camping ground for considerable armies.   At the mouth of Hick man, I suppose, within a mile of the bridge over the Kentucky River and on a direct line not more than half a mile or a little more and extending back indefinitely for any distance to Nicholasville, would be as fine a quality of camping ground as could be found in Kentucky.   It is the same at Tait's Ferry.   At the crossing on the road to Harrodsburg it is much farther off from the river.

Question. Which crossing is that ?

That is the crossing by Brooklyn, the turnpike road from Lexington to Harrodsburg; it is farther off where the camp could be accommodated.   At the crossing on the direct road to Shakertown camps could be formed up to the tops of the precipitous cliffs where the towers of the suspension bridge are built.   There would be some want of water, but it could be obtained by drawing it from the river or from a stream or creek which is a mile or two back.

Question. Do you think that at the place where the towers of the suspension bridge are built there is camping ground on the south bank of the river ?

I think, sir, you could commence within 50 yards of the towers and extend back to Lexington.   The width of the ground as you approach the river becomes narrow, but it opens as you go back.   Bradshaw's whole farm, which is in the immediate vicinity, would answer for camping purposes.

Question. Have you any reason to believe that General Bragg expected a large accession to his army from a general rising of the people of Kentucky to his assistance ?

I do not know that I could say that I have any well-founded reasons, though I have a belief that they expected a considerable rising in Kentucky in their favor.   I believe that the Kentuckians who were with him and the domestic rebels at home had made extravagant and exaggerated representations in regard to the matter.   How far Bragg was possessed of such a belief and how far such representations influenced him I have no knowledge, but I would presume naturally that he was to some extent influenced by them.

Question. From what you know of General Bragg's campaign do you or do you not believe that his retreat out of Kentucky was caused entirely by his disappointment in not being recruited from Kentucky as he expected?

From what I know of General Bragg's campaign I do not believe that his not receiving recruits in Kentucky or his disappointment of a general uprising had anything, or if anything very little, to do with his retreat from the State.

Question. What military reasons do you think General Bragg had for his retreat from Kentucky?

I do not know that he had any good reason for retreating, but I have stated that I supposed it was because of the exaggerated estimate of the force that General Buell was represented to have had and to the fact that he supposed his force was not able to cope with them. The facts that General Buell's army was prepared for motion and put in motion and moved against him much sooner than he could reasonably have expected were, I think, the reasons for his retreating. He was not prepared to receive General Buell, as I presume he thought at the time. I do not think he would have retreated if he had known the strength of our forces or if the movement had been delayed ten days on the part of our forces. I have no knowledge of any good military reason for his retreat except as indicated in this and other answers.

Question. Then, general, you believe that Bragg was able to contend with General Buell's forces with the probability of success?

I believe that his force was nearly as large as the effective force which General Buell could have brought against him. I believe Bragg's force was so large that, taking the largest number that he could have brought into action and handled effectively, it would have left him a strong reserve to have enabled him to have made the contest doubtful. I do not think that the disparity of numbers, of 8,000 or 10,000 where the armies reach over 50,000, is a reason to create a belief in the certainty of victory to the side having the larger force. As far as my knowledge of history extends and my personal observation such disparity is not much in favor or disfavor of either party. I have believed and still believe that in a fair fight, with any good general commanding on either side, the contest between those forces would have been doubtful. The superiority of numbers on our side was compensated for by the length of service, discipline, and drill that we might reasonably conclude the enemy had.

Question. Were not the two armies recently engaged at Murfreesborough substantially the same two armies that were opposed to each other last summer?

I do not know, but think not exactly, from the best information I have, which I think is pretty reliable. There must have been withdrawn from the rebel army, from the information that I have, a division, the strength of which I do not know, under Kirby Smith. Bragg lost in Kentucky in his retreat and in battle I think from 6,000 to 8,000 men; besides, he must have lost many from the effects of his campaign that we know nothing of after their arrival in Tennessee. Bragg received an accession before the battle of Murfreesborough of Breckinridge's command of not less than 5,000 men; he received some recruits and conscripts from Tennessee and some few troops, two or three thousand, from Georgia and Alabama, as I have been informed. But the army on our side had from 8,000 to 12,000, I do not know how many, of old, disciplined troops that General Rosecrans had. I should think there would be probably 10,000 of them; there may have been more, possibly less. I think the forces engaged in the contest were generally the same as were in Kentucky, with the exceptions I have named. I derived this information and the belief resulting from it from General Rosecrans, and the accounts of spies sent by him into the enemy's lines, whose reports I saw (one was delivered to me because it could not reach General Rosecrans), and from the statements of officers who were at Murfreesborough. I do not think there was any great inequality of force at Murfreesborough. I think that was a doubtful contest, and rather demonstrates the view I have taken of the issue of things in Kentucky had there been a battle there.

Question. Did you consider Bragg's army acting on the offensive in the campaign of Kentucky or not?

I considered it so at first. I think he was put on the defensive, though, much sooner than he expected to be.

Question. At what point of his march do you consider General Bragg put on the defensive in the campaign in Kentucky?

I do not know but what he may have been considered to be on the defensive the whole while; yet his demonstrations were unquestionably offensive at Munfordville and threateningly so at Bardstown. The other forces, under Smith, were part of Bragg's army, and were on the offensive from the time they entered the State, and were continually so advancing toward Cincinnati, having taken Lexington, marched upon the capital of the State and taken that also, marched to Shelbyville, to within 32 miles of Louisville, and a portion of them advanced to Floyd's Fork, within 16 or 17 miles of Louisville. Bragg did not advance farther toward Louisville than Bardstown with the main body of his army; some of them may have advanced as far as Salt River, which is within 20 miles of Louisville. They took the defensive then, I think, and maintained it for some time, falling back and massing on Chaplin River, in Mercer and Boyle Counties. They waited there the advance of General Buell's army. I suppose they may be said to have been on the defensive from the time General Buell reached Elizabethtown. Certainly their offensive demonstrations were less, if they did not cease, about that time; I mean that they fell back from the advanced positions near Louisville and Cincinnati and concentrated their forces. They were not offensive in their demonstrations except in the sense they seemed determined to give battle. I never expected them to retreat from the State without a battle. I think they were made to retreat by the expeditiousness with which the army moved against them and for other reasons before given.

Question. Do you consider General Buell's army to have been acting on the offensive or defensive from the time Bragg crossed the Tennessee River until the battle of Perryville?

In answer to a question from Mr. Lincoln by telegraph as to where Bragg was, I stated to him that he was in Tennessee, moving northward on a line parallel with the line on which General Buell was moving and east of General Buell, but how far from that line I did not know; but I thought he was harassing or would harass General Buell in his retrograde movement, or that he would diverge, crossing the Cumberland east of Nashville, at Carthage or Gainesborough or Burkesville and enter Kentucky, and I was fearful would penetrate the State before General Buell could possibly reach it. I believed then that General Buell was on the defensive, and I suppose that he continued so up to the point at which he could have received support from the forces at Louisville or, say, Elizabethtown. Which army was in point of fact on the defensive I cannot state, except as to the opinion I have formed from the movements of the armies and the results of those movements.

By the PRESIDENT.

Question. You spoke yesterday about the forces under Marshall and Stevenson having joined Kirby Smith; would you have us infer that they were with Kirby Smith when he made a junction with Bragg?

My belief is, from the information I have, that Stevenson moved to Danville and not to Lexington, and that he formed a junction with Bragg before Kirby Smith did. Marshall came to Lexington, and was in camp for some days in the immediate vicinity of Harrodsburg with his forces and before a portion of Kirby Smith's forces had crossed the Kentucky River. I do not believe that Marshall's forces had formed a junction until Kirby Smith came up that side of the river; they were resting back of Harrodsburg at the time of the battle. I think Stevenson's forces marched down the road toward Frankfort as far as Lawrenceburg and probably farther. I think they fell back in the direction of Harrodsburg and formed a junction when General Sill moved in that direction.

Question. You have a good knowledge of the country, have you not?

Yes, sir; I have lived in the immediate vicinity all my life.

Question. In your opinion would it form much of an obstruction in the way of General Buell's advance if he had intended to make an attack upon the other side of that river or to get into the way of Bragg's retreat from Camp Dick Robinson southwest?

Dick's River is very much like the Kentucky River in its banks and cliffs; they are precipitous, perpendicular cliffs, one or two hundred feet. There are a number of places, as on the Kentucky River, where there are crossings more or less eligible—at every crossing of turnpike or country roads or neighborhood roads. Those cliffs as they extend up to the vicinity of Crab Orchard become less precipitous and less high as they go up. A very small force on the south side of Dick's River could have held it against a large force attempting to cross. I think the natural defenses formed by the river and its cliffs are about as good as any artificial ones I ever saw. General Buell could not have crossed the river with an opposing force of any strength, such as a reasonable man would have thought of placing there, unless he had made a flank movement in the direction of Crab Orchard and crossed the river where the cliffs drop off and the banks are not high, as in the vicinity of Crab Orchard.

Redirect examination by General BUELL :

Question. Do you mean the Commission to understand, general, that all the rebel forces were on the south side of the Kentucky River and were within concentrating distance of the vicinity of Harrodsburg about the time of the battle of Perryville; I mean Kirby Smith's original force—Marshall, Stevenson, and Bragg's army proper ?

That is my information and belief. A portion of Smith's forces may not have reached Harrodsburg until the day of the battle. They had small forces holding the different points of the country.

Question. Have you seen it stated in the official report of the general-in-chief that I had 100,000 men under my command while I was operating against General Bragg in Kentucky ?

I have never seen anything of the kind.

Question. In the various criticisms of the Southern press upon Bragg's campaign and the various apologies made by his friends have you ever seen his retreat excused on the ground that his force was inferior to mine ?

I have not; but I have read very few of those criticisms. I do not remember to have read but two articles, I believe, of all of them. I have read some comments in our papers on the controversy between Forsyth and Governor Dick Hawes.

Question. Do you consider that the statement of General Forsyth in the article you refer to, that Kentucky was backed by an army of 40,000 men, was any indication of the actual strength of Bragg's army ?

I do not consider it as an indication of the actual strength, for I feel absolutely certain, as far as I can be sure from human testimony and the most reliable information, that there was a much larger force.

Question. Do you understand, general, that in all military operations the sphere of offensive movements is limited by certain circumstances, such as the amount of supplies and the distance to which you can carry supplies with the means available, and perhaps by other considerations also ?

I certainly understood that these circumstances mentioned—the amount, condition of supplies, means of transportation, and distance to be transported—and everything entering essentially into the time and expedition at which offensive movements can be made.

Question. Does it not follow, then, that an army may be on the defensive for everything beyond the sphere which is limited by these circumstances, and that within that sphere it may assume the offensive if an enemy should come within its reach ?

I suppose there can be no question that the offensive movements of an army must be limited by its means of subsistence and the means of transporting its subsistence; that an army may be on the offensive at one time and on the defensive at another, as they may have the means of supporting themselves in any offensive movement and in transporting subsistence.

Question. Is it not true that an army acting on the offensive within the sphere of its operations may be consequently checked in its offensive movements by the enemy's taking a position which it would be unwise to assail ?

I think so, certainly.

Question. So that for various reasons an army may be on the offensive one day as far as its movements are concerned and on the defensive
another day; is it not so?

Yes. I have stated in my former answers that an army might at one time be on the
offensive and at another on the defensive; limited in its movements, offensive or
defensive, by its means of subsistence, means of transportation of subsistence, by the
advantage of position of the enemy, and by other considerations. Having the advantage of supplies within the reach of depots of supplies, its operations might be made
offensive. I would suppose that the relative positions of armies as to whether they
are acting on the offensive or defensive would depend entirely upon these considerations, or at least mainly upon these considerations.

Commission adjourned to meet January 30, 1863.

CINCINNATI, *January* 30, 1863.

Commission met pursuant to adjournment. All the members present; also the judge-advocate and General Buell.

General BOYLE'S testimony continued, as follows:

By General BUELL:

Question. Can you state whether Major-General Nelson served under
the command of his junior in Kentucky about the time of the invasion
of that State by the rebel forces?

He did, sir. I was present when he met General Wright, and he stated to him, as
General Wallace had to me, that he was ready to serve in any capacity that he could
for his country's service; that rank should make no difference and should not be
regarded. He did receive orders from General Wright.

Recross-examination by the JUDGE-ADVOCATE:

Question. General, please look at the paragraph marked there (a
strip of newspaper was handed to the witness by the judge-advocate)
and state to the Commission whether that is what you referred to yesterday in speaking of Colonel Forsyth's estimate of the forces in Kentucky?

(Objected to by General Buell. Objection overruled.)

The WITNESS. No, sir; I never saw that notice before.

Question. In your cross-examination of yesterday this question was
asked you: " Do you consider that the statement of General Forsyth
in the article you referred to, that Kentucky was backed by an army of
40,000 men, is any indication of the actual strength of Bragg's army?"

General BUELL. This may be a proper time to urge the objection I
made to the question.

The JUDGE-ADVOCATE. What is the ground of your objection?

General BUELL The objection is that the question assumes that an
estimate was made by Mr. Forsyth in this article as to the strength of
Bragg's army, whereas neither my question nor the answer to that
question implies that any specific estimate was made by Mr. Forsyth
in the article alluded to. I only alluded to it myself because the statement is one that might by an ingenious critic be put forward as an estimate by Mr. Forsyth of the strength of that army.

By the JUDGE-ADVOCATE:

Question. I now ask you if this is the article to which you referred?

No, sir; I had no reference to this article, which is one I never saw before in all
my life. The article which I saw was many times less in length than this. We had
a condensed statement in some paper of the controversy alluded to, but I never saw
this before. I understood from the paper that I did read that the controversy was

as to the extent of rebel feeling in Kentucky and the number of men that would be likely to join the Confederates on their entering the State, and the numbers spoken of were not intended to represent the strength of the army, but the amount was stated as an argument by Forsyth to show that even with a great number the feeling did not exist in Kentucky which had been represented. The article representing the controversy which I saw, and which was a very condensed statement, made very little impression on me anyway.

Question. I would ask you whether the following sentence impressed itself upon your memory to such extent as that you can recollect it : " This is not a supposable case, seeing that Governor Hawes stands as the advocate of the loyalty of the State, which has just refused to take up arms for its own redemption with a Confederate army of 40,000 brave men at its back "?

I have just stated that I never saw the article, and of course it could not have impressed itself upon my memory, as implied by the question, nor do I remember the numbers stated in the article that I did see. I supposed, as I stated before, that it was fixed at an amount sufficiently large for the purpose of the argument, but I do not remember if it was 40,000 or 50,000 or 30,000. I certainly had no idea that it pretended to state the exact number of the rebel army that was in the State.

Question. You wish, then, to correct the impression made yesterday in your explanation to General Buell, that you had seen no such statement as to the number of men under General Bragg in Kentucky made by Mr. Forsyth ?

No, sir ; I wish to make no correction at all. I do not see that it is at all necessary.

By General SCHOEPF :

Question. In connection with your testimony that General Nelson agreed to serve under his junior in rank, do you know that Congress has vested the President only with that power, and was not General Buell, in assigning a senior to serve under General Wright, assuming a power not delegated to him ?

General Buell never did any such thing. I never intimated that he had done any such thing any more than he assigned General Wallace to serve under me. General Nelson and General Wallace both volunteered as a duty of patriotism, as I understood, to serve under those who were their juniors. General Nelson was ordered to Kentucky before the new Department of the Ohio was created, which took Kentucky out of General Buell's command. When General Nelson reached Nashville I advised him by telegraph of it. He continued, however, on his route to Louisville. When he arrived there I showed him the order of the Secretary of War to me creating the department and assigning General Wright to its command. A day or two after his arrival General Wright came, and having seen the first general orders of General Wright, I can state that he assumed command on the 23d day of September. It was voluntary entirely on the part of General Nelson that he took command under General Wright, just as it was with General Wallace taking command under me.

Question. You stated that Bragg lost during his invasion of Kentucky 8,000 men ; will you please enumerate those losses ?

I cannot answer the question with very great accuracy, not having the papers and records of my headquarters with me. My recollection and present estimate is that there were about 4,300 to 4,500 prisoners taken, and sent to Louisville and paroled there. I think the number altogether would be about 4,800. I think the killed were from 800 to 1,100 ; I cannot state the exact number. I think there were, from all the information I have, from 2,000 to 2,500 that were paroled, and made their way through the country home ; some of them, I have no doubt, joined the army notwithstanding the parole. My estimate is that there were from 6,000 to 8,000, as I stated in my answer. I have no doubt that the final effects of the campaign of Bragg's army diminished it even more than that, if we knew the results upon it after it arrived in Tennessee, but about which I have meager information and upon which it would not do to form an estimate.

Question. Did not our losses in prisoners, killed, and wounded at Perryville exceed those of the enemy during his invasion of Kentucky ?

No, sir ; I would not suppose it was to be compared, though I do not know so much of our loss as I do of the enemy's, the other branch of it having come under my notice from the administration of my own duties.

By General TYLER:

Question. Were you engaged in such military operations during the invasion of Kentucky as to place you in contact with Bragg's and Kirby Smith's armies, or is the information you have given the Commission as to the force, operations, and losses such as you have obtained from reports and from reading the public press?

I was in command of Kentucky when Kirby Smith entered the State. I had communication with General George W. Morgan at Cumberland Gap by telegraph daily. I had scouts in the country, spies in the country, to ascertain the position and force of the enemy. After Kirby Smith was in the State I had persons who entered his lines and who could form estimates of his force. I heard expressions of opinion from General Wallace, General Nelson, General Cruft, General Jackson, and other officers as to his force, according to the information that they had derived, having received it through spies and scouts, and from their observation. I acquired my knowledge and information of Bragg's forces in the same manner. I do not remember to have seen any newspaper statements or estimates; they would have formed no basis of opinion for me at all. I have seen numbers of officers and privates of intelligence that belonged to Bragg's and Kirby Smith's armies, some of whom I knew, and from information they gave me, and from the various sources, such as I presume are relied upon by prudent and discreet men placed in the position in which I was, I drew my opinions and formed my estimates. I supposed my position, commanding in Kentucky, required me to take all necessary steps for the purpose of ascertaining both the force, position, and amount of the armies of the rebels, and that I did, I thought, with industry and care; and I suppose that my information and knowledge upon the subject are as accurate, or ought to be more accurate, than that of most persons, if not of any one.

Question. What points of time does your command in Kentucky, referred to in the last part of your answer, cover?

I assumed command in Kentucky on the 4th of June. I remained in command until the 23d of August, when General Wright assumed command. I still remained at Louisville after he assumed command, and after General Buell's arrival I was left in command at Louisville of the forces that were left there.

Question. After General Buell's arrival at Louisville to the close of the campaign was your command confined to Louisville?

I had the command of the troops that were outside of Louisville. Some of them were at Shepherdsville.

Question. Please name the points where the troops under your command were stationed.

At Louisville and immediately around it, at Shepherdsville, at Jeffersonville, and of troops that were coming in. Some of them came in after General Buell left there, I believe. I took command of such troops as I sent to escort the trains as far as Bardstown. Some of the troops were those that arrived after General Buell left there or were on the north side of the river.

By General BUELL:

Question. Apart from the limits of your command, do you consider that your interest in the state of Kentucky and your acquaintance with its people would have given you peculiar facilities for gaining information in regard to the enemy that was invading it?

I think so, sir. I think I had as much facility and opportunity as almost any other native citizen of the State could have had, having a considerable acquaintance in every section and county in the State.

The JUDGE-ADVOCATE. Before the witness is dismissed I wish to say I did not call his attention to the correspondence between Forsyth and Hawes for the purpose of introducing it before the Commission, because that was done by General Buell yesterday; but having procured that correspondence and having found a positive statement as to the number of Bragg's army in Kentucky, I wished to call the attention of the witness to it, to see whether his memory was exact in that, and how far he could explain the comment made upon it yesterday; that was all.

General BUELL. My impression is that the controversy referred to was made the subject of testimony by the judge-advocate himself, and I should like to have the record examined to determine whether that is so or not.

The JUDGE-ADVOCATE. In every instance the witness has said he knew nothing about it. I have alluded to it several times and the witness has said he did not know anything about it.

General BUELL. I repeat my request that the record be examined as to whether the subject was introduced by the judge-advocate. The questions which I refer to are in the first part of the cross-examination by the judge-advocate. The first question is (General Buell reading from the record of January 29):

You saw Bragg's report, did you not, of that expedition into Kentucky and the letters and comments of the rebel press upon it shortly after it occurred?

The second question is:

You cannot, then, state what estimate the rebels placed upon our forces immediately after the expedition?

And I wish to say here that my impression is that the question is not properly recorded, and I submit to the judge-advocate whether it is or not. You may judge from memory or from the context as to whether it should read "our forces" or "their forces." I had myself seen no article in which the strength of the rebel army was alluded to in any manner in figures, unless the article of Mr. Forsyth should be considered as pretending to make an estimate of its strength, and therefore I alluded to that article in particular; so that I consider the subject was introduced by the cross-examination, and it was for that reason that I took it up in the further examination of the witness. I present the question to the Commission and the judge-advocate as to whether that question is correctly recorded in that one word, as to whether it should be "our" or "their" forces. It can be determined by the context better than by the recollection as to which word was used.

The JUDGE-ADVOCATE. My recollection is that it is correctly recorded. General Boyle had stated in his examination-in-chief that Bragg and his officers overestimated the force under General Buell, and hence his hurried retreat from Kentucky. In the cross-examination I asked this question, as it is recorded:

You cannot state, then, what estimate the rebels placed upon our forces?

General Buell does not seem to appreciate the statement that I made in reference to this criticism. I have referred to it repeatedly, but never for the purpose of bringing it before the Commission, but for the purpose of testing the information of the witness who happened to be upon the stand. Yesterday General Buell referred to this criticism and quoted a portion of it, and I therefore claim that he introduced this correspondence that I examined the witness upon this morning.

General BUELL. Then, Mr. President, I may answer that the frequent reference to this correspondence by the judge-advocate in his examination justified me in fortifying myself against any use he may design to make of that correspondence in the first place, and I may say also that I can give the same reason that he gave for examining the witness with reference to the substance of that correspondence; and I do not think the question I have raised as to the accuracy of the record is of very great importance. I will add, with reference to my views, that I remember asking the witness whether he had ever seen any defense made of Bragg's retreat from Kentucky on the ground that his force was insufficient to cope with *mine*.

(The recorder, having referred to his notes by the order of the President, stated at the next session the word reported and read to the court was "*our*.")

General W. S. SMITH (a witness for the defendant), being duly sworn by the judge-advocate, testified as follows:

By General BUELL:

Question. Will you state your name and position in the service, if you please?

William Sooy Smith, brigadier-general of volunteers.

Question. Were you in command at Bowling Green from the 10th to the 16th of September last?

I was.

Question. Did you receive any messages during your command from the commanding officer at Munfordville calling for re-enforcements and giving reasons why he should have them?

I did not.

Question. Do you remember to have seen any scouts or messengers who represented themselves as having been sent from the commanding officer at Munfordville for any purpose?

No, sir; I did not. I saw a citizen, who reported that he had come from that vicinity, but not by command of the commanding officer. I think it was on Monday morning succeeding the attack.

Question. Who was that citizen?

I do not recollect his name.

Question. Do you remember what information he brought?

He brought information of an attack upon Munfordville, but particulars he did not know.

Question. What information did he give in regard to the attack; do you remember?

He simply stated that an attack had been made; that he heard firing; and said he had been within 3 miles of Munfordville and heard very heavy firing, which continued at the time that he left.

Question. Did you about that time hear of the arrival of any messenger from the commanding officer at Munfordville with such information as I have alluded to in the previous question?

No, I did not. Col. Bruce had been in command there and might have received such a messenger. No such messenger was reported to me and I knew of no such.

Question. If any such messengers had gone to Colonel Bruce on the supposition that he was still in command would it have been his duty to send them to you and is it probable that he would have done it?

It would have been his duty and I think he would have done so.

Question. Were you at the headquarters of the Army of the Ohio at Decherd, Tenn., about the 22d or 23d of August last, for several days about that time?

I was at the headquarters of the Army of the Ohio at Decherd for several days during the month of August last, but what part of the month I do not distinctly remember.

Question. Have you any recollection that during that time information was received of the advance of the rebel forces from Chattanooga and other points? If so, please state what that information was, as far as you recollect it, and what movements were ordered in anticipation of it by the commander of the Army of the Ohio.

Information was received that General Bragg was concentrating a large force at Chattanooga, a force also at Kingston, and a small force below Chattanooga, on the Tennessee River, intending to cross the Tennessee River and the mountains lying between the Tennessee River and our position in Middle Tennessee. That force was variously estimated at from 40,000 to 100,000. It was understood that one hundred and twenty regiments had crossed or were about to cross the Tennessee River near Chattanooga. In consequence of that information the troops of the Army of the Ohio were ordered from Northern Alabama and several positions in Middle Tennessee in the direction of Decherd, Tullahoma, and McMinnville. Of the movements that were made farther back I know nothing. A force was afterward sent to Altamont and a small force was at Cowan.

Question. Can you state about the date of the orders for the concentration at Altamont?

No, sir; I cannot.

Question. Do you remember such orders distinctly?

I do.

Question. Can you state whether the information upon which those orders were issued appeared to make it certain that the enemy was advancing by way of Altamont and that he would arrive at that point very speedily?

I cannot say that the information rendered that certain. So far as the information reached me, I can only say that it was the general impression that that was their first objective point. It seemed to me that it was in his power to advance by that line or by one of several others leading through the mountains. It was a general impression that at least a portion of his force would certainly come that way.

Question. Was there anything in the information received about that time which indicated any other as the road by which he was to be expected to pass into Middle Tennessee?

There was information received, which was deemed reliable, that a force was advancing upon the Therman road, but I think that that information was later. I do not think any information had reached us of any movements farther north than the Altamont road; none certainly reached me.

Question. Do you understand the Therman road to be, for a considerable distance from the Sequatchie Valley, the same as the road leading to Altamont?

Yes, sir. I do.

Question. Do you remember the distance from Altamont at which the road forks, the Therman road going to the right to McMinnville and the other fork going to Altamont?

No, sir. I do not.

Question. Is your information with regard to the geography of that country sufficient to enable you to explain what made Altamont an important point for concentrating the Army of the Ohio in anticipation of the advance of Bragg's army by the Therman road?

The only information I possess in regard to the geography of the country is gained from maps of that region and conversations with the inhabitants of that part of the country, and the impression in my mind made by such knowledge was that it commanded at least two of the best routes through the mountains that were known;

two, at least, of the direct routes from the Sequatchie Valley into the valley of Middle Tennessee. It commands the route direct through Altamont, also the route through McMinnville, being within striking distance of the forks of the road.

Question. Can you state whether the impression existed at headquarters at the time the orders for concentration at Altamont were given that the enemy had made such progress that it was even a matter of doubt whether the concentration could be effected at that point before the enemy could arrive there?

Such was the impression, and I recollect distinctly hearing the commanding general express the desire that such a concentration should be effected, but said that there was not time to get sufficient force into position at that point.

Question. Do you know whether the troops actually moved to form such a junction?

I know that troops did move to Altamont and other troops moved in that direction to within supporting distance—as many troops as could be made available at the time.

Question. What was your position and command at the time you allude to?

I was in command of the post at Decherd, commanding all the troops stationed there.

Question. What was the strength of your command and what was the object of having troops at that point?

There were about 4,000 men. The object of holding a force at that point was to watch the approach of the enemy by the road which debouches from the mountains near Cowan and to perform this duty in conjunction with the force at Cowan; also to guard our railroad communications with the rear, then threatened by a cavalry force of the enemy.

Question. Was Decherd also a depot for the troops along that line at that time?

It was the depot for supplies.

Question. Can you state what there is in the topography of that country which made Decherd an important point with reference to any movement of the enemy to get in rear of the positions we held in North Alabama at that time?

There is a good road, which, debouching from the mountains, passes through Decherd, and, running in a southwesterly direction, leads directly to the rear of the position of our forces in North Alabama.

Question. What is the character of the country between the Chattanooga Railroad and the road leading from Decherd to Huntsville which you have just described, and in what position would the peculiar features of that country place a force at Huntsville taken in rear by a force coming from Decherd as you have supposed?

The country is very rugged and mountainous and not traveled by any practicable roads to my knowledge; so that it would be impossible for a force to escape from Northern Alabama and make its way to our positions in what we suppose the neighborhood of McMinnville by turning the enemy's force to its left; in other words, they would be cut off from a junction with the remainder of our forces.

General DANA here moved—

"That as the body of General Sill, lately killed at the battle of Murfreesborough, has arrived in Cincinnati, the Commission adjourn to enable the members to pay proper respect to his memory and the occasion."

Carried.

The Commission adjourned to meet January 31, 1863, at 10 a. m.

CINCINNATI, *January* 31, 1863.

Commission met pursuant to adjournment. All the members present; also the judge-advocate and General Buell.

General W. S. SMITH's testimony continued, as follows:

By General BUELL:

Question. Do you know enough of the country between Huntsville and Chattanooga, or any portion of that district of country, to be enabled to speak in regard to its resources—its supplies of forage and provisions?

I have passed through the country lying between Huntsville and Stevenson, with the exception of a very limited section. There are little valleys somewhat productive, but generally it is a very sterile country, and it could not be relied upon for supplies of provisions and forage to any very considerable extent.

Question. Can you describe the natural features of the country between Decatur and Stevenson so as to indicate to the Commission its agricultural advantages? Describe the breadth of the Tennessee Valley at these different points relatively, the positions of the mountains, and so forth.

From Decatur to a point a few miles beyond Huntsville in the direction of Stevenson there is a level country. We there reach the western line of the mountain ranges, which, running in a southwesterly direction, pass near Huntsville, and so on nearly to the Tennessee River. From that point to the northeastward is a mountainous region all the way to Stevenson, with the river running nearly parallel with the railroad, and is, as I have been told, a very narrow valley, scarcely producing anything. But what the breadth of the valley is I do not know, having never been there myself. It is a very flat country west of Huntsville, extending up into Middle Tennessee, and is very fertile.

Question. Do the mountains close in upon the river abruptly near Stevenson or a short distance above there?

At Stevenson they are but about 2 miles from the river. The direction of the range would seem to bring them into the river above.

Question. Do you know anything of the character of the country on the south side of the Tennessee River above Stevenson either from observation or from any other means by which a knowledge of the geography of the country is to be obtained?

I have heard that the mountains on the south side of the river between Stevenson and Chattanooga come right up to the river and that the mountainous country extends to a great distance to the south. I am familiar with the country from Chattanooga to Atlanta and farther south, and know that the whole country between Chattanooga and Atlanta is a mountainous country.

Question. Can you say anything in regard to the resources of the country between Chattanooga and Bridgeport or within a distance of 20 miles of that line?

The country within a distance of 20 miles of that line to the southward I suppose to be very barren. To the northward there would be a strip of country in the Sequatchie Valley within that distance of the line mentioned which is productive. The valley I understood to be of a width varying from 1 to 5 miles. With that exception I know of no fertile country within the limits mentioned, except perhaps a limited region lying immediately along the Tennessee River on the north side, above the point at which it is struck by Walden's Ridge, lying between the Sequatchie Valley and the Tennessee River and Chattanooga.

Question. Would the Sequatchie Valley be within 20 miles of Chattanooga?

It would not. A portion of it would be within 20 miles of the line connecting Chattanooga with Stevenson, the Sequatchie Valley running obliquely to the line.

Question. Do you know anything in regard to the amount of supplies procurable in the valley of the Tennessee, as far as you had any opportunity of observing; had the previous occupation of that country by our troops and other causes effectually drained it of supplies?

I know that it was exceedingly difficult to procure supplies or forage. I think no provisions of any amount could be collected between Decatur and Stevenson. That region of country had been occupied by our troops under General Mitchel for some months previous to the arrival there of the remainder of the Army of the Ohio, and must have been dependent on that region to a great extent for their supplies, inasmuch as railroad communication with Nashville had not been restored. The inhabitants of Huntsville were actually in want during my command of that post immediately after my arrival there.

Question. State, if you please, what time you were at Huntsville and what position you occupied there.

I was there in June and July. I was assigned to the command of the Third Division, and being the ranking officer, was in command of the post.

Question. State, if you please, what you know of the resources of the country at other points where you were stationed during the months of July and August, particularly along the Chattanooga Railroad north of Stevenson in the direction of Nashville.

From Stevenson to Cowan it is a barren, mountainous country. We there reach the valley of Middle Tennessee. That portion of it immediately adjacent to the mountains is fertile. Passing a belt of 4 or 5 miles we come to a glade country, the soil of which is thin and not very productive; it extends in the direction of Nashville to a point about 3 miles to the northwestward of Tullahoma. We there reach a hilly country that is but moderately productive, which extends to within about 10 miles of Murfreesborough. The country from that to Nashville is mostly level and fertile. A belt of fertile country next to the mountains follows the directions of the mountains, I believe, as far as McMinnville.

Question. How was that part of the country that you were in off for supplies last summer and were the supplies made use of for the public service as far as possible?

Supplies could not be collected to any very considerable extent. I received an order to collect all within my reach, and in compliance with that order succeeded in getting a thousand barrels of flour at Manchester, and perhaps two hundred barrels in all near Tullahoma at McQuiddy's mills. I also got beef cattle and sheep enough to supply my troops, who were part of the time on half rations.

Question. Did these supplies that you collected from the country go into the hands of the commissaries to be issued as regular supplies or were they consumed by the troops in addition to the half rations which were authorized to be issued?

They were turned over to the commissary to be issued regularly.

Question. Were you employed after the evacuation of Corinth in superintending repairs on the Memphis and Charleston Railroad between Corinth and Decatur? If so, please state, as circumstantially as you can, the work that was performed and the time occupied in that way and whether the work was executed with industry and energy.

I was so employed. The road had been greatly damaged by the destruction of its bridges and trestle work, both by our own troops and the troops of the enemy. There were placed under my command for the execution of the work an entire regiment of Michigan Engineers and Mechanics, with the exception of a detachment of two companies which were then serving with General Mitchel. In addition to that force I was authorized by order of General Buell to call upon division commanders whose troops were on the line for such additional force as I might require. I employed all the force that could be worked at the various points requiring repairs and pressed forward those repairs with all diligence, constructing 1,200 feet of bridges and trestle work, some of it to the height of 40 feet, and consumed in repairing the road about three weeks. Troops were ordered forward for the special purpose of assisting in the work and guarding the working parties.

Question. What was the ostensible object in repairing that road, and by whose orders, if you know, were those repairs made?

I understood that the road was to be opened for the purpose of transferring that portion of the Army of the Ohio that was then at Corinth over to Decatur, and also that the road might serve as a line of communication afterward between the Army of the Ohio and the Union forces in Northern Mississippi and West Tennessee. I also understood that the road was to be repaired by order of General Halleck.

The JUDGE-ADVOCATE. You need not state that unless it be of your own knowledge; the original order can be produced, if any such exists.

The WITNESS. I was told so by General Buell; that is all the knowledge I have of it.

By General BUELL:

Question. Do you know anything about the amount of rolling stock that was on the road and as to what practical use it was to the Army of the Ohio? If so, please state what you know about it.

There were seven locomotives captured to the westward of Corinth, immediately after the evacuation of Corinth by the enemy, in a damaged condition; besides those there were perhaps half a dozen locomotives in and about Corinth, also in bad condition, but still in running order. Almost every one that was sent upon that part of the line under my charge broke down and became utterly worthless; scarcely any use could be made of them on our line. There was a very limited number of cars available, and not over a dozen were employed at any time on the line between Corinth and Decatur during my superintendence there.

Question. Who had the immediate control of this working stock?

General McPherson.

Question. Who was responsible for the limited amount of it that was employed in the service of the Army of the Ohio?

That was a result to some extent of the necessities of the case. I applied constantly to General McPherson for additional rolling stock, which he failed to furnish; whether he could have done so or not I do not know.

Question. Have you any professional knowledge and have you had any experience in railroad engineering?

I am a civil engineer by profession, and was actively engaged in the duties of my profession for six years previous to my entering the service. Bridge building was a specialty in my practice.

Question. Have you, by reading or other means of information, any knowledge of the country between Somerset, Ky., and the Tennessee River, along the line running through Jackson, Tenn.?

In conversation with those familiar with that region of country I have learned that it is a rough and barren country.

Question. Do you know anything of the character of the road from the mouth of the South Fork of the Cumberland River to Jacksborough and so on toward Knoxville?

The JUDGE-ADVOCATE. General Smith's answer to the previous question is objectionable; hereafter the general will confine himself to his personal knowledge.

General BUELL. I desire to say, in reference to the injunction of the judge-advocate, that the information to be derived in regard to the geography of a country from personal knowledge is very limited. The subject of geography is one that is within the reach of every man who can read, write, talk, and hear, and the knowledge derived in that way of such subjects is as legitimate and reliable as can be expected, or as is necessary either for evidence or for practical purposes.

General ORD. I beg to remark that we should bring this question to a vote. The judge-advocate has no business to direct what the witness shall or shall not say.

The JUDGE-ADVOCATE. I was instructed by the Commission to warn witnesses to say only that which they knew of their own personal knowledge.

General TYLER. If the judge-advocate is to be lectured, I vote that the court be cleared.

The court was cleared, when, after discussion, the judge-advocate withdrew the remark.

The WITNESS. I do not.

Cross-examination by the JUDGE-ADVOCATE:

Question. General, what was done with the fortifications about Decherd when the Army of the Ohio fell back to Nashville?

Nothing, to my knowledge.

Question. What became of the various improvements made by yourself and others upon the various lines of railroad when you fell back to Nashville?

I burned a number of bridges that were situated between Decherd and Murfreesborough; also one of the stockades.

Question. Will you state what number of bridges were destroyed?

I think three; two of the most important.

Question. Were not all the lines of railway, that had been put in order with so much labor, destroyed when the army fell back?

I do not know what was done upon any other line than the one from Stevenson to Nashville.

General BUELL. I will save the judge-advocate time and trouble upon the subject, if he desires, by saying to the Commission that they were destroyed or ought to have been; that I gave directions to General Smith to destroy the bridges, as he moved along the road, as far as Murfreesborough.

The PRESIDENT. Then it becomes important for us to know whether your order was executed; and, if so, how far.

General BUELL. My directions were confined to the destruction of the bridges, I believe.

By the JUDGE-ADVOCATE:

Question. How much of that order was executed that was referred to by General Buell?

As already stated, three of the bridges were destroyed; two of them were the most important, one over Elk River and the other over Duck River. There were a number of small bridges—I do not exactly recollect how many—that were not destroyed.

Question. You may state why they were not destroyed.

Some of them were situated at some distance from my line of march, and I thought that the small ones would be easily repaired, at any rate, while the larger ones were being rebuilt, and, if so, their destruction would cause the enemy no additional inconvenience or loss of time.

Question. At what time did you become aware of the fact that Bragg was crossing the Tennessee River at Chattanooga?

The first information that I deemed reliable of his crossing I received while at Decherd, but at what precise date I do not remember.

Question. Was it in the forepart of August?

I think it was in the latter part of August.

Question. What did you estimate his number at ?

From 45,000 to 60,000 men.

Question. Was not your information of such a character that you could come to a nearer estimate than these two extremes ?

It was not. The number of regiments was stated at one hundred and twenty; their average strength I could not exactly ascertain, but I reckoned it at 400 to 500.

Question. If the principal officers of the Army of the Ohio, with fair means to make their estimate, fixed that army at 35,000 to 40,000, is your information of such a character that you could contradict them ?

General BUELL. I object to the question in its present shape. The principal officers of the Army of the Ohio have not estimated the strength of the rebel army at 35,000 to 40,000.

The JUDGE-ADVOCATE. I have not said that the principal officers of the Army of the Ohio had done so. I put a supposable case for the purpose of ascertaining the reliability of the witness' estimate. It is not allowable to tell the witness what previous witnesses have stated. I did not do it. General Buell has no right to do it.

General BUELL. I withdraw my objection.

The JUDGE-ADVOCATE. The mischief is done; it has taken my supposable case out of my hands. I move that the court adjourn.

Commission adjourned to meet Monday, February 2, 1863.

CINCINNATI, *February* 2, 1863.

Commission met pursuant to adjournment. All the members present; also the judge-advocate and General Buell.

Gen. W. S. SMITH's testimony continued, as follows :

General BUELL. I desire, Mr. President, to say, with reference to the objection I made on Saturday, that I desire now to repeat the objection and insist upon it. The question (of the judge-advocate) does not positively assert that a certain statement has been made in the testimony before the Commission, but it implies as much. Whatever may have been the design of the question, the tendency of it is to mislead the witness, and in a certain way to intimidate him also, by showing his opinion in contrast to that of officers of higher rank than himself, and whose opportunities for obtaining the information referred to he might naturally suppose to be better than his own. The question does virtually assume or assert that the evidence upon which it is founded has been established before this Commission in this investigation. I have no doubt that the rules of evidence would exclude the question, and that perhaps should be the only ground upon which I should urge my objection : but I might also say that if by a strict interpretation of the rules of evidence the question should be permitted to slip through, yet I see no reason why that sort of investigation should be pursued before a body of army officers and in the examination of an army officer.

The JUDGE-ADVOCATE. That the question was asked for the purpose of putting General Smith upon his guard is certainly a fact; whether you would call it intimidating or not is merely a choice of terms. It is an important question, one of the most important in this investigation, and I was anxious that General Smith should give us as clearly as he could the foundation upon which he fixed the number of that army at the time it crossed the Tennessee River, and that he should also state to us how far that was a conviction in his mind. For that purpose I put a supposable case, that could not, by any manner of means, be con strued into an assertion of the fact—If the principal officers of the Army of the Ohio stated so and so, is your information of such a character that you can venture to contradict them ?—a thing I had an entire right to do and which it was my duty to do.   I hold that it is one of the more important points of this investigation.   If that army of Bragg's was inferior to the Army of the Ohio in numbers, as in everything else, from the commander down to the humblest private in its ranks, it is a thing the Commission ought to know ; and it is very necessary for the Commission to have the evidence on which the conviction of each witness, especially a witness as intelligent as General Smith, is founded.   For that purpose I put a supposable case, and the urgency was sufficiently strong to justify me in insisting upon it in such a circumstance as this. I made no statement of fact, and only put a supposable case, which I hold was strictly correct—as to whether we were in the presence of an army inferior to our own or not—and I find no reason for not insisting upon its being put.   On the contrary, when General Buell came in with his objection and stated as a fact that which is not a fact—and I have no hesitation in saying it is not a fact—General Buell was himself guilty of transgressing the rules of an investigation of this sort.   The question, I maintain, is a legitimate and proper one.

General BUELL. I have nothing more to say, except that the question does imply that a certain supposition, an assumed fact, has been established in evidence before the Commission.   I will say also that the question at this time has no reference to the actual strength of Bragg's army, but to the strength it was supposed to have at that time.   The judge-advocate has framed his answer in an ingenious method, which I do not think it necessary to dissect or comment upon, and am quite content to leave the decision to the Commission.

The JUDGE-ADVOCATE. I would remark that after the statement made by General Buell my whole supposable case is taken from me.   I would withdraw the question; I have no motive in asking it.

General BUELL. So I understood the judge-advocate on Saturday.   It is not for that reason alone that I urge the objection, but it is for the sake of a principle and the establishment of a rule.

The court being cleared, General TYLER moved—

"That the question put by the judge-advocate, as follows : 'If the principal officers of the Army of the Ohio, with fair means to make their estimate, fixed that army at 35,000 to 40,000, is your information of such a character that you could contradict them ?' and objected to by General Buell, is correct, and that the objection made to it by General Buell in connection therewith was a violation of his duty to this Commission."

General ORD moved as an amendment—

"That, the question of the judge-advocate having been withdrawn, the Commission does not deem it necessary to take any further action upon the subject."

Carried.

By the JUDGE-ADVOCATE :

Question. Were you in command at Bowling Green previous to Colonel Bruce taking command there ?

No, sir; not previous.

Question. What time ?

From about the 10th to the 16th of September.

Question. It was known there at that time what force was at Munfordville, was it not?

I do not know precisely; it was supposed there was about one brigade there.

Question. Was it not known that one brigade depended upon the Army of the Ohio for support and assistance?

No, sir; I supposed it would be re-enforced from above.

Question. At what point above?

From any forces that were stationed between Munfordville and Elizabethtown or at Louisville, railroad communication being opened.

Question. At what time was it known at Bowling Green that the enemy had moved out of Glasgow toward Munfordville?

I do not recollect the precise date. The first intimation that I had that any portion of the rebel force had moved out of Glasgow was that brought by the messenger referred to, that an attack had been made at Munfordville.

Question. Do you recollect the messenger's name?

I do not.

Question. Was it Washington Miller?

I do not recollect.

Question. After the fall of Munfordville did not the estimate made of the force of the enemy change into a certainty as to their number?

I was told by Colonel Wilder, who had been in command at Munfordville, that he had seen pretty much their entire force, but could not state definitely their number. I think he said that he estimated them at from 35,000 to 45,000. He stated the number of pieces of their artillery at from ninety to one hundred. That is the nearest approach to certainty that I was able to make.

Question. Did not Colonel Wilder tell you that he refused to surrender until he knew positively the force of the enemy?

He said that before surrendering he had been shown the enemy's force in position, and then it was apparent to him that further resistance would be hopeless and would only result in useless slaughter; he therefore surrendered. He did not tell me that he knew their force positively.

Question. Did he not say to you at that time that from the best estimates he could make they did not exceed 36,000?

My recollection is that he said he estimated them at from 35,000 to 45,000.

Question. Did not the prisoners and the citizens give you some information subsequent to the capture of Munfordville upon which you could come to a positive knowledge as to the enemy's force?

They did not. I never conversed with any prisoner except Colonel Wilder, and with no citizen who could make any definite statement as to the enemy's force.

Question. Did you have any conversation with General McCook on that subject?

I never did.

By General TYLER:

Question. Is Chattanooga a strong and defensible position?

I regard it so.

Question. Do you think the army under the command of General Buell could have taken Chattanooga when Bragg occupied it?

I do not.

Question. How many men would you have required to hold that position against the same strength as the Army of the Ohio was at that time?

I think I could have held it with 25,000 men.

By General SCHOEPF:

Question. Do you know the strength of General Buell's army at that time?

Its strength was about 50,000.

Question. Supposing General Buell had marched his army directly from Corinth to and occupied Chattanooga and Knoxville, with Cumberland Gap in our possession and East Tennessee loyal to the Union, what would have been the strategic and moral effect?

The occupancy of those positions by our troops would have been an advantage scarcely to be estimated.

Question. You stated in your reply that you could have held Chattanooga with 25,000 men; would not the remaining 25,000 men have been sufficient to defend Nashville?

Supposing General Grant's army to occupy positions then held by it and the positions already named taken by the troops of the Army of the Ohio, Nashville would have been in a very retired position and I think safe without any considerable garrison. The remainder of the troops of the Army of the Ohio would have been more than sufficient for that purpose.

Question. Please state to the Commission if you have received a military education; and, if so, where?

I am a graduate of the West Point Military Academy; served one year in the regular service, and have been in the volunteer service from almost the commencement of the present war.

By General TYLER:

Question. On what day did the advance of General Buell's army reach Bowling Green?

I do not know the precise day. I found one brigade of it at Bowling Green on my arrival there about the 10th of September.

Question. Can you not fix the exact date?

I cannot. I ordered my adjutant to keep an accurate journal of all our movements and so never treasured those dates in my own mind, and I have not access to that journal now and have not had since I was summoned before the Commission.

Question. Can you give the position of General Buell's army on the 17th of September, the day that Munfordville was capitulated?

No, sir; I cannot.

Question. Can you give the position of some parts of it, those about Bowling Green for example?

I cannot on that precise day; as I said before, I do not treasure those dates in my mind.

Question. How long did General Buell's army remain at Bowling Green from the time its advance arrived there until a forward movement was made?

From the time that the first detached brigade reached Bowling Green to the time that the advance of the whole army moved from that point I should think was about ten days, though the place was held by this detached brigade for several days before the arrival of any of the rest of the troops. There was scarcely any delay at Bowling Green after the main body of the army came up. That delay was understood to have been caused in order to await the arrival of the troops in our rear

Question. What amount of General Buell's army was concentrated at Bowling Green on the 15th of September?

I cannot say how many troops were concentrated on that particular day. I understood that the whole force finally concentrated there amounted to 35,000 or 40,000 men.

Question. At what date?

I do not know the exact date; it was immediately previous to the advance of the army.

Question. Between what dates were you at Bowling Green?

From about the 10th and the 16th.

Question. What amount of General Buell's army was concentrated at Bowling Green between the 10th and 16th?

They did not report to me, General Buell himself being present, and the precise number concentrated before I relinquished command of the post I cannot state.

Question. On what day did you relinquish command of Bowling Green?

I think about the 16th. I cannot say that that was the exact day.

Question. Can you make an approximate estimate of the number of troops that arrived and reported between the 10th and the 16th?

I cannot; they did not report to me.

Question. And still you were in command?

Yes, sir; in command of the post.

General BUELL. I would suggest it was not the duty of the Army of the Ohio to report to Brigadier-General Smith, in command of the post. Brigadier-General Smith commanded a brigade, and was not the superior officer of the Army of the Ohio. The Army of the Ohio did not arrive immediately at Bowling Green as a military post; it came to Bowling Green and encamped in the vicinity, and the commander of the post had no more to do with it than the commander of any brigade in the army had to do with its management and position.

General TYLER. Do you object to the question?

General BUELL. No, sir. I thought I could save the trouble of putting questions that lead to nothing.

By General TYLER:

Question. Can you give the position of General Buell's army on the 16th, when Bragg's army crossed the Tennessee at or near Chattanooga?

No, sir; I cannot.

Question. What was the position of General Buell's army about the 23d of August, when you were at General Buell's headquarters at Decherd?

There was a portion of his troops, I think one brigade, at Huntsville, Ala.; there was perhaps one regiment between that and Stevenson; and I think one brigade—perhaps not so large a force—at Battle Creek. There was perhaps a brigade stationed between Stevenson and Decherd, a considerable portion of it being at Cowan. There was my force at Decherd of about 4,000 men. There was a force of one or two divisions I think at Altamont, one at Hillsborough, a small force at McMinnville, and some small forces at Manchester. Those are the only positions of troops at that time with which I am familiar.

Question. What was probably the aggregate number of men included in these forces that you have recapitulated?

I should think about 30,000 men.

Question. Was this the position of these different forces when it was your opinion that General Buell could not concentrate his forces at Altamont in time to meet Bragg?

It was.

Question. What force or corps occupied Altamont and how long did they remain there?

That I cannot answer.

Question. Was Altamont ever occupied by any considerable force even for twenty-four hours?

I understood that we had a force there of one or two divisions, but whether the town itself or whether any position in that vicinity was held for any long time I do not know. I know that the forces were moved from point to point with a good deal of activity about that time in accordance with the information that was received.

Question. But you do not know positively that any particular force occupied Altamont even for twenty-four hours?

No, sir; I do not know

Question. You say in your testimony that it was in Bragg's power to advance by way of Altamont or one of several other lines leading through the mountains; please name those several other lines.

He could proceed up the Sequatchie Valley to Dunlap and from that point through to McMinnville; that is one of the lines to which I refer. There is another road that I understood was practicable farther north still, leading from the Sequatchie Valley over to Sparta and so on up toward Gainesborough. I know of no other practicable routes.

Question. You say that the only information you possess in regard to the geography of the country about Altamont is derived from conversations with the inhabitants and consulting the maps; would not an officer stationed at McMinnville and in that vicinity and who had passed over the country in and about Altamont have far better opportunities to judge of the geography of the country than yourself?

As far as his personal observation extended he would.

Question. Did not the line into Middle Tennessee by way of Pikeville and Sparta present itself to you as one that Bragg would or might adopt?

It appeared to me that Bragg might use that road for at least a portion of his forces.

Question. Will you give the date at which such progress was made by Bragg when it was doubtful that General Buell could concentrate his forces at Altamont in time to meet him?

I cannot give the exact date; it was while I was at Decherd, as already stated.

Question. Cannot you give the date at which Bragg passed out of the Sequatchie Valley at Pikeville?

I have not treasured any of these dates, and cannot therefore give them.

Question. What reason did General Buell give you that he could not concentrate sufficient force at Altamont to meet Bragg?

He said that there were not troops within reach of that point to exceed the number of 25,000 within the time at which Bragg was expected to arrive at that point, positive information having reached us of the enemy's arrival in force at Dunlap.

Question. Where were you or General Buell when this information reached you that Bragg's army had arrived at Dunlap?

At Decherd.

Question. General, can you not by some event fix the date?

I cannot. I do not treasure any of these dates in my mind. Either from some mental peculiarity or habit the relation of events I can recollect, but dates I do not.

Question. What troops were moved to Altamont and how long did they remain there and what troops were moved into a supporting position?

I do not recollect what particular commands were moved either to Altamont or to Hillsborough, which is a supporting position. I only recollect that troops were thus moved on the supposition that the enemy were advancing upon Altamont.

Question. General, please name the road "that debouches from the mountains leading in a southwestwardly direction to the rear of our forces in North Alabama" and what forces were those.

I do not know the name of the road. The forces were those already mentioned as stationed at Huntsville and along the line from Huntsville to Stevenson, being about one brigade at Huntsville and about one regiment between that and Stevenson. There was also another brigade en route to Decherd from Huntsville.

Question. How far on each side of the line of railroad did you personally examine the country between Huntsville and Chattanooga? I mean in reference to its supplies.

I made no examination on either side of the road personally. I was instructed to order the troops under my command stationed along that line to collect supplies, and the knowledge that I gained of the resources of the country was from the replies of commanding officers that scarcely any supplies could be obtained and that the country surrounding them at the various positions for a considerable distance was barren.

Question. Was not that part of the Memphis and Charleston road between Huntsville and Chattanooga well supported from its local business—previous to the rebellion, I mean?

Of that I have no knowledge. I think it impossible, however, unless it drew business from a very great distance.

Question. Do you mean to say that the country from Huntsville between the railroad and the Tennessee River to Chattanooga is a barren and sterile country?

That is my information.

Question. You say you are familiar with the country between Chattanooga and Atlanta?

Along the railroad line connecting those two places I am.

Question. Do you mean to say that this is a barren, sterile country?

Nearly that entire line leads through a mountainous, rough country.

Question. Is it not the railroad from Chattanooga to Atlanta?

Yes, sir.

Question. Have you ever been over it?

Yes, sir.

Question. Is there any grade in that more than 45 feet to the mile? I ask you as an engineer.

That I cannot answer. The road follows the ravines and abounds in sharp curves, by means of which such a direction is given to the line of the road as to avoid, as far as possible, any heavy grades.

Question. What is the distance from Chattanooga to Atlanta; do you know?

I do not know the precise distance.

Question. Does not that tract of country from Chattanooga to Atlanta embrace the whole land ceded by the Cherokees to the State of Georgia and is it not considered the most productive part of the whole State, and in fact the granary from which the lower counties obtain their corn, wheat, pork, and other agricultural supplies for the support of their people?

I know nothing of that grant nor do I know anything of the country lying off the line of the railroad already mentioned from personal observation. I know I saw no fertile territory on the whole line, except perhaps a very limited region in the immediate vicinity of Atlanta.

Question. What is the distance from Chattanooga to the entrance to the Sequatchie Valley?

I should judge about 30 to 40 miles; I am not positive.

General BUELL. I would suggest that the record be not loaded with inaccurate information; if that information is needed it can be obtained; and for that purpose I would suggest that the witness' answers be confined to what he knows.

The JUDGE-ADVOCATE. That is just what I wished.

Question. To what extent did General Mitchel exhaust the supplies in the neighborhood of Stevenson and what kind of supplies were the inhabitants of Huntsville destitute of?

I cannot say to what precise extent General Mitchel's troops had exhausted the supplies of the country. The supplies which the inhabitants of Huntsville were destitute of were breadstuffs in particular. I do not think they lacked meat.

Question. While you were in command at Huntsville did you or did you not derive any supplies from the surrounding country?

We derived supplies of forage; not of provisions.

Question. Did you attempt to collect any provisions from the country; and, if so, in what manner?

I transmitted orders to the commanding officer under me, in obedience to instructions from General Buell, to collect supplies. At the post at Huntsville I collected none in the way of provisions; the commanding officer referred to succeeded in getting but little.

Question. At what point did you obtain the 1,200 barrels of flour you spoke of in your testimony?

One thousand barrels at Manchester and about 200 at McQuiddy's Mill, near Tullahoma.

Question. What were the circumstances attending the offer of those thousand barrels to you and how came so much to be collected there?

There was a fine mill near Manchester, owned by Mr. Huggins, at which I understood the flour had been manufactured. This Mr. Huggins came to me while I was in command at Tullahoma, accompanied by a staunch Union man, Mr. Rathbone, of Manchester, and tendered the flour for the use of the Government, stating that he feared it would be disturbed or taken away by the rebels. I immediately telegraphed to Major Darr, chief of the commissary department, and asked if I should purchase the flour. He replied that I should, and the flour was accordingly taken in accordance with these instructions, and an order received about the same time to collect all the supplies within our reach.

Question. Did you know that that quantity of flour was at the mill before it was offered to you by the owner?

No, sir; I did not.

Question. General, do you not believe from this fact of 1,000 barrels of flour having been offered to you that if proper exertions had been made a very large amount of flour might have been collected in that vicinity, or do you believe that was all the flour they had?

I do not think that any very large quantity could have been collected. I did collect all I could hear of in any amount, and the 1,000 barrels and that got at McQuiddy's Mill was all that I could procure. The grain of the country for a great distance surrounding those mills seemed to be taken to them for manufacture.

Question. To what extent could beef cattle, sheep, &c., have been collected there at that time?

I had great difficulty in collecting enough beef and sheep to supply the troops of my own command, part of the time being compelled to issue but half rations.

Question. You did supply your command with beef and fresh meat, did you?

Not fully. There was a small quantity of bacon delivered to us from day to day at Tullahoma and Manchester.

Question. Have you reason to believe that other corps and division commanders labored under greater difficulties in obtaining supplies of flour, fresh meat, &c., than you did?

I think they did, from the fact that their commands were larger and most of them were in a more barren region.

Question. Were you in charge of the repairs of the Memphis and Charleston road after the evacuation of Corinth?

I was; of that portion of the line between Corinth and Decatur.

Question. What was the length of that part?

I do not recollect its length.

Question. Did you report to General Buell the quantity and condition of the rolling stock which you stated in your direct testimony to be very imperfect?

I made no formal or complete report. I did complain that it was insufficient in quantity and in such bad condition as to be almost useless.

Question. Did you not as an engineer see that the repair of that road would be nearly useless with the rolling-stock you had on hand?

Yes, sir; I did.

Question. Did you report that fact to any superior officer?

I suggested to General Buell that the repair of the road would be useless, both on that account and because, lying parallel to the enemy's supposed front, it would be vulnerable at every point and liable to constant interruption. This he seemed to appreciate fully, and said that the repairs were being made against his own wishes.

Question. Did you say that in your march from Decherd to Murfreesborough you destroyed the bridges, &c., on the Nashville and Chattanooga road; how far distant from the railroad did you march, and did you destroy all the bridges and mechanical work between Decherd and Murfreesborough?

I have stated that I destroyed three bridges, two of them being the most important, and one stockade. My line of march was generally nearly parallel with the line of railroad and from 2 to 5 miles distant from it.

Question. Did those bridges include all the mechanical work?

No, sir; they did not. There were unimportant bridges and trestle works which I did not destroy, for the reason stated in my direct testimony. There were stockades which, having been constructed of green timber, I could not burn, and had not time to destroy them in any other way. The one destroyed had been built of seasoned timber. That I burned.

Question. How far had we possession of the Memphis and Charleston Railroad at that time ?

At the time I commenced the repairs, immediately after the evacuation, our forces had just commenced to advance on that line toward Decatur in sufficient numbers only to furnish the necessary protection to the working parties for the execution of that work. The road was not actually occupied by our troops. As the repairs proceeded we advanced along the line until we finally held possession from Corinth to Decatur, this possession being disputed by the rebels, who attacked the line at various points almost from day to day. On the north side of the Tennessee River I think the line was held from Decatur to Stevenson by the forces under General Mitchel.

Question. What is the military advantage of Chattanooga to the rebels ?

It is a salient point in their line of communication between Atlanta and Knoxville, and is itself a very strong position, which, held by them, enables them to cover that line for a great distance. It is far more important to them than it would be to us, inasmuch as it is not upon the direct line from Atlanta to Knoxville. The road leading from Dalton to Cleveland serving the rebels as a cut-off, this road could be used by them even if Chattanooga were held by us.

Question. How far is Chattanooga from Dalton ?

I do not recollect the distance.

Question. Is it 30 miles, should you think ?

I should think it was as much as that.

Question. If we held Chattanooga in force would not the junction at Dalton be under our control ?

Not if that junction were held by the rebels in force.

Question. Suppose we held that intersection at Dalton, what would be the possibility of getting from Georgia to Alabama by railroad ?

There would be but two lines left open, one by the way of Augusta up through Raleigh; the other line, lying near the coast, running from Savannah, Charleston, Wilmington, Petersburg, &c.

Question. From what section of country did Bragg draw supplies for his army while he lay at Chattanooga before he crossed the Tennessee River ?

The line south to Atlanta opens the line of communication for him to all their depots of supplies and from Atlanta southward. The road north would bring him supplies from the valley of East Tennessee. I suppose he drew his supplies mainly from those two lines and from all the region of country reached by that and other connections.

Commission adjourned to meet February 9, 1863.

CINCINNATI, *February* 9, 1863.

Commission met pursuant to adjournment. All the members present; also the judge-advocate and General Buell.

Gen. W. S. SMITH's examination continued.

General BUELL. In looking over your record, Mr. President, I observe something in the remarks of the judge-advocate in reference to my objection to a question of his which I did not distinctly hear and certainly very much misunderstood, or I should have asked the Commission to inquire upon what ground the judge-advocate contradicted my statement in the objection alluded to. I think it proper now to call your attention to the evidence, which substantiates the statement I made in my objection. I will premise that the question of the actual strength of the rebel army is one of interest.

The JUDGE-ADVOCATE. If we are going into a discussion it is scarcely proper to detail in the presence of one witness what has taken place in the presence of another.

(The witness retired, and General Buell continued :)

Of course, and for ulterior purposes, it is one of importance also; but as far as the object of this investigation is concerned it is the apparent strength of the rebel force that we are most concerned in, as justifying the measures that were adopted by the commander of the army with reference to the movements of the rebel army. That apparent force is something which will of course vary from time to time according to the information we obtain in regard to it. With reference to that there are three points of time at which the question of the strength of the rebel army becomes one of importance to this investigation. First, about the time of the crossing of the Tennessee River and the advance into Tennessee; the next is perhaps about the time that the rebel force was at Glasgow and Munfordville; and the next is about the time of the battle of Perryville. The question of the judge-advocate had reference to the strength of the rebel army at the first period I have mentioned, and you will remember that it was with reference to the estimate that was made of the strength of Bragg's army at that time. You may remember also the question and the objection I made to it. I stated that the principal officers of the army had not testified that Bragg's force was estimated at that time at from 35,000 to 40,000. The judge-advocate, I discover, contradicted that statement very positively, and it is to that point I desire to call your attention. For my own part I may say I should be very unwilling to contradict the statement of any gentleman without being well assured I had sufficient ground for doing it. I find by referring to the record that General McCook estimated the strength of the rebel army, according to the information he had of it, at from 60,000 to 70,000; General Wood at 45,000; General Thomas estimated it at 45,000; General Negley estimated it at 50,000 or 60,000, I am not positive which. These are the principal officers of the Army of the Ohio who have given evidence upon this question. Other officers, such as Colonel Shoemaker, General Steedman, and General Fry, estimated it from 30,000 to 36,000. These are not the principal officers of the Army of the Ohio, either by their rank or by the command which they exercised or the opportunities they had for obtaining information. I simply submit this statement of facts, which I certainly should have submitted at the time had I understood the remarks of the judge-advocate as they now appear upon the record.

The JUDGE-ADVOCATE. I do not know how my remarks appear on the record, as they were not read to me after they were delivered. The question in discussion I apprehend was a supposition made for the purpose of testing the accuracy of General Smith's estimate, and which was totally defeated by the interference of General Buell. The discussion that arose upon that point was simply as to the propriety of informing a witness of what had been sworn to by a previous witness, and which I had abstained from doing. Nor do I propose now discussing what was the actual strength, or the estimate at the time made by officers of the Army of the Ohio, of the force under Bragg at the time of crossing the Tennessee River, or indeed at any other time. It is all a matter of evidence, and the record is under the inspection of the Commission. The discussion we had at the time was as to the course pursued by General Buell, which I held to be improper. As to what the principal officers of the Army of the Ohio may have testified, my impression is that with the exception of General McCook and General Negley the weight of testimony of the principal officers was that the rebel army was estimated at from 35,000 to 40,000. But this is simply a matter of fact within the province of the Commission. It was only in reference to the conduct of General Buell that I made the remarks that I did.

General BUELL. The judge-advocate still persists in the contradiction, notwithstanding I have stated to you that the evidence is so and so. It is a matter very easy for you to determine. I simply inform you that I obtain these facts from the record. It is not a matter of opinion and not a debatable point.

The JUDGE-ADVOCATE. I thought it was improper and think so still, and shall continue to do so, to tell a witness what has been sworn to previously.

General BUELL. The judge-advocate committed that error himself when he virtually stated that the principal officers of the Army of the Ohio had testified so and so. I shall not interfere with the performance of the duty of the judge-advocate when he performs it legitimately and properly. He is represented as denying my statement, and it is to that point that I now address my remarks. It is not with reference to the strength of the rebel army, but merely to call attention to the contradiction made to my statement at the time, and for which, if my statement on record is correct, there was no sort of justification or excuse.

The PRESIDENT. I must be allowed to say that in my opinion it is a point that will have to be settled by the Commission from the testimony. There is considerable contradiction on the part of witnesses, and whenever there may be contradiction on the part of witnesses as to the strength of the rebel army the question must remain to be settled, and it is to that extent debatable.

General TYLER. I understood that the judge-advocate put a certain question, "Supposing so and so to be the case, would you put your opinions against the other officers whose means of obtaining information were as good as yours?" and the judge-advocate says, "My question is lost by General Buell saying there had been no such testimony before the Commission." The proper course would have been for General Buell to have objected to the question, and then had the court cleared to decide whether the question should be put or not.

General BUELL. It is very possible that I might, in my want of practical experience in proceedings of this kind, have overstepped the strict rules of such investigations; but that is not the question, nor is it the question as to what was actually the strength of Bragg's army at that particular time. The point is this: I stated that the principal officers of the Army of the Ohio had not testified that the strength of Bragg's army was from 35,000 to 40,000; it is the judge-advocate's flat contradiction of that statement that I object to, and that is the point I make now; and in answer to his contradiction I simply state to you what the record shows. I do not pretend to sum up and strike the balance between the evidence of the principal and subordinate officers of the army for your guidance. I simply show the evidence that substantiates the statement, which statement the judge-advocate contradicted. I am not considering the strength of the rebel army as you may decide. So far from understanding the judge-advocate to have contradicted my statement, I understood him to have admitted it; otherwise I should not have allowed those remarks to pass without calling your attention to them, because I am not in the habit of making statements that can be contradicted truthfully; I may do so accidentally.

By General BUELL:

Question. Do you know why the brigade which preceded you to Bowling Green was ordered to that point?

I do not know positively, but supposed that it was ordered there to strengthen the garrison of that place, in anticipation of a movement of the rebel forces in that direction.

Question. Do you understand it to have been independent of a movement of the Army of the Ohio toward Kentucky and was it considerably in advance of that movement?

It was considerably in advance of that movement, and I supposed it to be part of the distribution of that army, with a view to meeting the rebel force that was then understood to be advancing northward; but at that time I had no knowledge of any intended movement of the Army of the Ohio into Kentucky; I supposed its movements to be entirely controlled by those of the enemy.

Question. Were your instructions to you orally or in writing?

They were given to me orally, except the order to proceed to Bowling Green and there assume command.

Question. How long did the troops which were ordered to that point precede you?

I think four or five days, but am not sure.

Question. Is it proper to say that the Army of the Ohio remained at Bowling Green from the time of the arrival of this detachment for this special service up to the time of the departure of the army from that point in its advance toward Glasgow or Munfordville?

I should think not.

Question. What was the estimated strength of the rebel force at Corinth about the time of the evacuation of that point?

I should think an average of the estimates I heard to be about 100,000.

Question. What is supposed to have been the distribution of that force after its abandonment of Corinth?

I have very limited means of information on that point. I heard that the main body retreated southward, and that a portion of it was thrown, by rail most of the way, into the vicinity of Chattanooga, and thought there would be a race between the two armies for that point.

Question. Of what detached armies or large bodies of troops that have been generally recognized as taking part in the military operations of the rebels was that army composed?

I do not know that I could mention them all. The army that retreated before us from Shiloh, commanded first by Sidney Johnston and then by Beauregard, constituted one portion of it, and I understood the armies of Price and Van Dorn were present at Corinth. It was also understood that Bragg's force had arrived from Mobile.

Question. Can you name the principal commanders belonging to that consolidated force that had previously exercised independent commands?

Price, Van Dorn, Bragg, Polk, Beauregard, who commanded that army proper, and was then understood to be in command of the whole force. There might have been others, but those names were most frequently mentioned in the information that we received from within the rebel lines.

Question. Do you consider that the presence of certain high commanders would generally indicate the organization of any particular army; that is, would it generally indicate that the force to which they have habitually belonged will form part of that particular army?

I think their presence would indicate the presence also of commands appropriate to their rank. Whether the particular commands to which they have been attached previously would be supposed to be present I think would depend upon the relative positions of the consolidated army and their independent commands. If the independent commands were very distant, it is hardly to be presumed that they would form a part of the concentration, though they might.

Question. Suppose, in the distribution of a large force like that which the rebels had at Corinth, you should find in the several detachments general officers belonging to that force, would you usually expect to find in the detachments the commands to which they had been attached in the consolidated army?

I would.

Question. Do you know what part of that force remained in front of Corinth after other parts of it had been sent to other quarters?

I do not. I only know that the names of Price and Van Dorn were mentioned in connection with that force constantly for some time after the evacuation.

Question. Is it generally understood that the force that remained under Price and Van Dorn was identically the same as that they brought there, with the exception of re-enforcements of new regiments and conscripts; and have you ever heard of any officers or any body of troops belonging to that force which had previously belonged to the other principal armies or bodies of troops with which the rebels were operating?

I do not know what the understanding was with regard to that force. I was so situated as not to be brought into contact with the information that may have reached the headquarters of my superiors. All the information I had was derived from conversations with officers who were passing from Corinth along the line of railway on which I was occupied and from newspapers.

Question. Can you recognize in the organization of the rebel force that invaded Kentucky last summer the general officers that belonged to the army of Sidney Johnston, the army that occupied Columbus and West Tennessee, the force that came from Pensacola and Mobile, and the force that occupied East Tennessee?

I can most of them, as far as they were known to me.

Question. Can you mention any officer that belonged to either of those several commands that was to be found in any other command about the time of the invasion of Kentucky by Bragg?

Hindman is the only one I can think of. I supposed he was beyond the Mississippi. He had had command in Sidney Johnston's army, a brigade or division—I do not know.

Question. Was he in the consolidated army at Corinth, do you know?

I do not know. I know he was present at Shiloh; at least I was told so by the rebel prisoners.

Question. Do you know whether he was supposed to have taken any portion of the force from the consolidated army when he went to Arkansas; and, if so, what portion of it?

I do not know, sir, whether the supposition was that he took a force from the east or the west side of the Mississippi, or whether he was supposed to have raised a new force in Arkansas.

Question. Do you know what force he is supposed to have had since, according to the best information?

I have heard his force estimated at 15,000 men.

Question. What, according to the best information, is the force that Price and Van Dorn are supposed to have had after the evacuation of Corinth and the distribution of the consolidated force that was there?

I have heard their force estimated at from 30,000 to 40,000. I have no very reliable means of judging. This estimate, I think, was made subsequent to the time at which it was understood that Lovell's force had arrived to re-enforce them. I understood that Price and Van Dorn left Corinth each in command of a division.

Question. Where was the rebel army at the time of the distribution of the consolidated army of the Government [?] of Corinth ?

I supposed it to be undergoing redistribution as well as our own; a portion of it retreated south and a portion of it being thrown around toward Chattanooga and perhaps a portion thrown over to the Mississippi and possibly beyond it.

Question. Supposing in this distribution of the opposing armies that the portion which went from each in the direction of East Tennessee had undertaken to proceed by land marches to their destination; supposing Chattanooga to be that point, how much farther would the rebel fraction have had to march to reach its destination than the fraction of the Government army?

The difference of distance would have been very greatly in our favor, but just what the difference would have been I cannot say; but I suppose any practicable line of march for the rebels from Corinth to Chattanooga to be from 150 to 200 miles longer than the direct line which was in our possession. The difference may be even greater than that.

Question. Do you know that the rebel army could have marched across from Okalona or Tupelo, or any point near there, to Chattanooga by a direct line ?

I do not know that there was any direct line practicable for the march of a large army from either of the points named to Chattanooga, and if there should be a line, from Corinth to Chattanooga would still be very much shorter than the one by Okalona or Tupelo to Chattanooga.

Question. Was the rebel army supposed to be at Tupelo or in that vicinity when the Army of the Ohio was ordered from Corinth into North Alabama and in the direction of Chattanooga ?

I do not know that it was understood to be there. Our forces, I understood, had advanced to a short distance, say 15 or 20 miles, from Corinth southward when I left Corinth to repair the railroad from that point to Decatur.

Question. I beg you to refer to the map, general, and verify your information in regard to the distance from Tupelo to Chattanooga and from Corinth to Chattanooga.

The difference in distance from Corinth to Chattanooga and from Okalona to Chattanooga on air lines, according to the map, is about 30 miles; the distance from Corinth to Okalona according to the same map, is about 60 miles; this added to the difference would make the distance to Chattanooga by way of Okalona greater than the direct line from Corinth to Chattanooga by 90 miles.

Question. Is it a fact that part of the rebel army actually marched from Okalona by way of Tuscaloosa and Elyton to Chattanooga after the distribution of the rebel force in front of Corinth ?

I do not know.

Question. How long do you suppose it would take to prepare ferry-boats or bridges, whichever would be most expeditious, and cross the Army of the Ohio, as it marched from Corinth, over the Tennessee River twice, first between Corinth and Decatur and again at some point east of Huntsville, in order to reach Chattanooga ?

I should say that each crossing would require three weeks.

Question. Can you state the time that was actually employed in preparing boats and crossing a portion of the army at Florence ?

I cannot state the precise time, but I think it required from ten days to two weeks to cross McCook's and Crittenden's divisions after the arrival of the steamboats and barges that were used for that purpose.

Question. Did Nelson's division also cross at that time and place ?

I believe it did, and I should have included that in the estimate of time given in the previous answer.

Question. Had the rebels opened communication by the railroad between Tupelo and Chattanooga at that time ?

We had various accounts on that point, some to the effect that the railroad communications between those points was completed; others that it was not quite finished, but that there was a gap of a few miles.

Question. Do you refer now to the railroad from Meridian to Montgomery?

I do. There was, of course, railroad communication by way of Mobile before the completion of the road from Meridian to Montgomery.

Question. You say you know nothing of the wagon road from Okalona to Chattanooga through Tuscaloosa and Elyton ?

The JUDGE-ADVOCATE. It is with reluctance, Mr. President, that I rise to object to this mode of examination. A very wide latitude has been given the defense, but it seems to increase every day. Here is a witness who has been examined in chief, cross-examined by the judge-advocate, examined at length by the Commission, and then taken up again by General Buell upon new matter entirely. The way the investigation is proceeding we shall never come to a termination. I shall object to any mode of proceeding which is not legal and proper before a tribunal of this character.

General BUELL. I desire to say that this is a very singular time to commence the application of strict rules to an investigation of this kind. I desire also to say that I am not questioning the witness upon new matter at all, but with reference to matter which was introduced in the cross-examination; that is, with reference to the rapid movements of the Army of the Ohio from Corinth to Chattanooga. That is all I desire to say in reference to the objection of the judge-advocate.

The JUDGE-ADVOCATE. The latitude that has been allowed has been for the benefit of General Buell. I never asked it for myself, and as far as I am aware have never exercised it. I have permitted General Buell to proceed in his own way, but I think the proceedings should be as brief as possible, for the purpose of carrying on the investigation without unnecessary delay. With regard to this new matter introduced by General Buell, I remember nothing that was brought out in the cross-examination that would justify this part of it. I may be mistaken about it, and if I am General Buell has a right to go on.

General BUELL. Perhaps. I can save the Commission the trouble of an examination of the record by calling their attention to the questions put by General Tyler or by General Schoepf with reference to a rapid movement of the Army of the Ohio upon Chattanooga from Corinth. The object of that examination is to compare the relative facilities of the two armies for such a movement upon that point.

General SCHOEPF. I desire, Mr. President, in order that this examination may be conducted more intelligently, that General Buell be asked for the orders he received from General Halleck. I have asked for that letter several times and have not been able to get it, and I think the Commission should order General Buell to produce the letter or orders of General Halleck.

The PRESIDENT. I have not heard, for my part, that there is any such letter in existence.

General DANA. The record snows that if there is such a letter the judge-advocate be instructed to produce it in court.   I suppose it could be got from Washington.

General BUELL. In order that I may not appear in the light of withholding anything from the Commission I will state here that my impression is that General Halleck's instructions to me in the first place were oral.   I remember, however, one dispatch which had reference to the route which he deemed it best that I should pursue.   As far as I am concerned I would just as lief present any instructions I have from General Halleck now as at any other time, though I had designed to bring them in with my documentary evidence, and if such instructions are not found upon the books that I have submitted to the Commission I do not believe that they can be found.

The JUDGE-ADVOCATE. Will you let us have all the books you have?
General BUELL. I have given them to you.

The PRESIDENT. No reference has been made, so far as I know, to any letter from General Halleck to General Buell.

General SCHOEPF. Here is a letter (referring to General Buell's letter-book) showing just the contrary, and I would like the letter of General Halleck to be produced.

General BUELL. I did not understand that the remarks of General Schoepf were with reference to instructions as to repairing the railroad. I thought they had reference to the instructions on which I moved from Corinth to East Tennessee.   The dispatches are recorded in the books that are here under your inspection.

Commission adjourned to meet February 10, 1863.

CINCINNATI, *February* 10, 1863.

Commission met pursuant to adjournment.   All the members present; also the judge-advocate and General Buell.

General W. S. SMITH's examination continued.

By General BUELL:

Question. With the amount of rolling stock the rebels are understood to have on all their railroad communications how long ought it to take to transfer 25,000 men from Tupelo to Chattanooga?

I should think it would have taken from ten days to two weeks.

Question. Is the possession of East Tennessee and the line of railroad running through from Virginia to Georgia admitted to be of very great importance to the rebel authorities?

I think that it is.

Question. Considering the importance of that possession to them, and the superior facilities they possessed for transferring troops from the vicinity of Corinth to Chattanooga and other points in East Tennessee, what reasonable probability was there of being able to march the United States forces from Corinth to Chattanooga before such a movement would be anticipated and guarded against by all the means they could use for that purpose?

Without a more accurate knowledge than I possess of their facilities for rapid movement of troops, and also the necessities that existed for the presence of their forces at other points, it would be exceedingly difficult for me to say just what such a probability would be.   I think, however, the advantages in the race for any point on that line of communication between the rebel forces and the Government forces would have been decidedly in favor of the rebels; and considering the immense importance of that line of communication to them, I think it is but reasonable to suppose that they would have exerted themselves to the utmost to have thrown upon it the forces necessary for its protection.

Question. Are you aware that General Thomas' division did not arrive in North Alabama from Corinth until the last of July?

I do not know at what time it arrived there.

Question. Did you know that that division was considerably in rear of the rest of the Army of the Ohio that marched from Corinth?

I was advised of it, but do not know.

Question. In speaking of the strength of the Army of the Ohio in Middle Tennessee and North Alabama and setting it at 50,000, did you mean to give that only as an approximate estimate founded on your opinion or as an accurate statement?

I think it was a very near approximation, but I did not give it as an accurate statement. It was based upon what I supposed to be the average strength of the several divisions composing it.

Question. In the cross-examination by the court this question was put to you by General Schoepf: "Suppose General Buell had marched his army directly to and occupied Chattanooga and Knoxville, with Cumberland Gap in our possession and East Tennessee loyal to the Union, what would have been the strategic and moral effect?" Your answer to that question is: "The occupancy of those positions by our troops would have been an advantage scarcely to be estimated." In that answer do you mean to express an opinion as to the practicability of doing that thing any more than though Richmond and Gordonsville had been substituted for Chattanooga and Knoxville, Washington for Cumberland Gap, and Virginia for East Tennessee?

I did not mean to express any opinion as to the practicability of taking possession of the points named. A supposed case was presented. I simply took the hypothesis as granted, and answered, as I was asked, what the strategic and moral effect would have been in my opinion.

Question. In the examination by the court you expressed the opinion that Chattanooga could be held by 25,000 against 50,000. You also expressed the opinion that 25,000 men would be sufficient to defend Nashville, which, supposing the force in Middle Tennessee to be 50,000, would leave 25,000 for other service. What force now do you suppose would be sufficient to hold Chattanooga against those 25,000, supposing them to have been directed against that point?

I think 12,000 men could resist and prevent the crossing of 25,000 over the Tennessee River at any point in the vicinity of Chattanooga, and if Chattanooga itself were intrenched with reference to a defense of the place by 10,000 men they could hold it against an attack of 25,000.

Question. In the examination by the court this question was put by General Schoepf: "You stated in your reply that you could have held Chattanooga with 25,000 men; would not the remaining 25,000 have been sufficient to defend Nashville?" and you answered, "Supposing General Grant's army to occupy the positions then held by it and the position already named taken by the troops of the Army of the Ohio, Nashville would have been in a very retired position and I think safe without any considerable garrison. The remainder of the troops of the Army of the Ohio would have been more than sufficient for that purpose." In your answer did you mean to be understood as expressing the opinion that 25,000 men would be sufficient to occupy and hold East Tennessee and the railroad communication between Georgia and Virginia to East Tennessee?

I did not mean to express the opinion that 25,000 men would have been sufficient, on the supposition made, to hold Chattanooga and the line of communication through

East Tennessee. I meant simply to express the opinion that 25,000 men might have held Chattanooga against a force equal to the estimated strength of the Army of the Ohio, the other positions named being securely held by a sufficient force of Union troops. In the word "remainder," contained in the answer to question, I referred to the number 25,000 stated in the question as being more than sufficient to garrison Nashville under the circumstances presented.

Question. Are we then to understand your answer in this way: that Chattanooga and other points in East Tennessee and on the line of railroad through East Tennessee held by a sufficient force—whatever that might be—and General Grant occupying the position which he held, then 25,000 would be sufficient to make Nashville and other points in the rear of the army secure?

The idea I intended to convey was that the line from Memphis to Decatur being held by General Grant's army after the march of the Army of the Ohio to the north side of the Tennessee River and Chattanooga and the other points mentioned in East Tennessee being held by a sufficient force of Union troops 25,000 men would have been more than sufficient for the garrison of Nashville. I did not refer to the detachments that might have been necessary for guarding the various lines of communication to the rear of the line occupied by our troops.

Question. While you were stationed at Decherd and other points on the Nashville and Chattanooga Railroad were you exercising an independent command?

I had been placed in command of all the troops stationed to guard that line; likewise the line from Stevenson to Decatur and Decatur to Nashville.

Question. Would this independent command have made it more your duty and have afforded you greater facilities to obtain information of the strength of the enemy than a colonel commanding a regiment or a brigadier-general commanding a brigade under the command of a senior?

The JUDGE-ADVOCATE. I desire, Mr. President, to call your attention to this mode of examination as being very objectionable. A leading question is asked by General Buell that I did not object to at all, "Had you an independent command?" and General Smith answers it in such a manner as to leave us in doubt whether his was an independent command or not. General Buell assumes it was an independent command, and then proceeds with the examination. It is very easy for an intelligent witness like General Smith to give a direct answer—yes or no.

General BUELL. I was satisfied, because I thought the explanation of his command implied its independence. I wish him to be as definite as possible, and I will thank the witness to make it more definite if he can.

It was an independent command.

By General BUELL:

Question. It will be permissible now, I suppose, for the witness to answer the last question.

It would, unless such colonel or brigadier-general should be thrown to the front and so detached, in which case his facilities might have been as great as my own for procuring information such as that referred to.

Question. Suppose when the army concentrated at Murfreesborough the rebel army had thrown itself down upon the Nashville and Chattanooga Railroad, would that railroad, in working order, have been of advantage to the rebel force?

It would, the moment they could either transfer the rolling stock from the other side of the river or build any temporary crossing over the river, which would have enabled them to run through from Chattanooga; otherwise it would not have been used by them, as we were careful to move the rolling stock that was in our possession from that portion of the road.

Question. Did the rebels actually repair that road subsequent to the withdrawal of the Army of the Ohio from it?

They did. I was informed by scouts sent through Murfreesborough and in that vicinity that trains were constantly running through from Bridgeport to Murfreesborough. Deserters from the rebel army also gave me the same information, and stated that a bridge of some kind had been built over the Tennessee River, over which they were crossing their trains.

Question. Is it or is it not a notorious fact that that road was used by the rebels while they were at Murfreesborough?

It is.

General SCHOEPF. Suppose General Morgan at Cumberland Gap had been ordered to destroy the railroad, and had done so as effectively as General Carter did, do you think that under those circumstances the rebels would have anticipated General Buell's army at Chattanooga from Richmond?

I do not know the extent of the damages done to that railroad line by General Carter. If but a single bridge were destroyed, or if two or more bridges within a short distance from each other were destroyed, and a practicable country road connecting the two extremes of the road were perfect, the detention would not have been serious if the rebels had rolling stock abundant on both sides of the break. The detention depending so much upon these circumstances, it would be impossible for me to say what the probabilities in the case presented would have been.

General BUELL. If it is not too late I would object to that question, for the purpose of avoiding a protraction of your investigation. It amounts in reality to the introduction of new matter, upon which, I suppose, beyond all doubt, I should be privileged to cross-examine again, whether it is introduced by the judge-advocate or any member of the Commission. The practicability of destroying this road by the force at Cumberland Gap would depend upon what rebel force was opposed to it in East Tennessee, and it would be necessary to elucidate that question in order that you may understand the matter well.

General SCHOEPF. The privilege was given yesterday to General Buell to cross-examine General Smith as much as he pleased. I do not consider that it is introducing new matter. No military man would consider that the occupation of Chattanooga and Knoxville would have left the railroad uninjured.

The JUDGE-ADVOCATE. By the rules governing a tribunal of this sort the court has a right to ask any question it may see fit, and such questions do not form grounds for cross-examination either for the Government or defense. That, I believe, is the rule, whether it be enforced by the Commission or not. But General Buell is under a misapprehension in supposing that any question put by a member of the Commission would form any ground for cross-examination.

General BUELL. The judge-advocate is right as far as concerns questions that have for their object to throw additional light upon matter that has been the subject of investigation either by the prosecution or defense, but he is not right where entirely new matter is introduced the object or tendency of which is to fix responsibility or blame upon the party who is virtually upon his defense before the Commission or before any other tribunal.

General SCHOEPF. There is no new matter introduced.

General BUELL. It is new matter distinctly. It distinctly proposes a new operation, which has not been the subject of investigation before the Commission, and depends upon the conditions I have explained to you. The question assumes that there was nothing for the force at Cumberland Gap to do but to move down to the railroad and destroy it. That depends upon the force that was opposed to it.

General DANA. I wish emphatically to deny the right of the court to introduce new matter (after the examination-in-chief). I wish to make the assertion that the court has no right to question on any new matter and at the same time to shut off the judge-advocate or the other party interested before the court from cross-questioning on such new matter.

The JUDGE-ADVOCATE. I would suggest to General Dana that the court cannot put itself in antagonism to the defense, and it is supposed that all the questions it asks is for the purpose of enlightening itself; that is all. The word "cross-examination" is a term that places it in the position of being a prosecutor and against the defense. It is not supposed that a question would be asked introducing entirely new matter without that question having been written out and handed to the prosecutor, so as to give the defense an opportunity to examine upon it. If the rule is strictly followed it is simply this: that the court or commission has a right at any stage of the proceedings to ask any question it may see fit for the purpose of enlightening itself, and that does not form the ground for cross-examination.

General BUELL. I should like to say, with reference to the remarks of the judge-advocate, Mr. President, that he is right in assuming that the position of any member of this Commission or any other court implies impartiality; but the position does not screen a member of this Commission or any other court from the responsibility or fact of assuming the function of a prosecutor. If he pursues a course by his examination which is virtually a prosecution he is a prosecutor. The matter, whatever it may be, is something that the defendant has a right to defend himself against, whether it be introduced by the judge-advocate or any other accuser. The question which General Schoepf has put, as I have stated before, distinctly introduces new matter. The tendency of it is to throw blame on some person who had control of the forces at Cumberland Gap, and I am that person, for not doing a certain thing. That will involve the propriety and the right to explain why that certain thing was not done, and from that will flow the further investigation which I have intimated.

General SCHOEPF. We are not here to pronounce sentence upon General Buell. It is not a prosecution. It is for the purpose of investigating the facts connected with the Army of the Ohio in its Kentucky and Tennessee campaign, and all the facts we can educe we are bound to obtain in justice to General Buell as well as to the Commission. It is no prosecution.

The PRESIDENT. I understand the question is withdrawn.

General SCHOEPF. The question is answered.

The PRESIDENT. Do you (General Schoepf) withdraw your question?

General SCHOEPF. It is no use.

The PRESIDENT. I do not understand that under the rule adopted any member of this Commission by asking a question, whether based upon the examination-in-chief or upon the cross-examination, puts himself in the attitude of an accuser, and for the reason, as I understand, that we are not engaged in the investigation of any specific charges against any officer of the Army, but in the investigation of certain general operations of the army in the Kentucky and Tennessee campaign. That investigation is a duty imposed upon us by order of the President, and if the judge-advocate or General Buell should omit to ask a question in their examination proper or in the cross-examination touching any point that any member of this Commission should feel it his duty to inquire into, I think that is a question asked by him simply in the line of his duty, no more and no less, and that he has a right to ask such question at any time in this examination. If I should see fit and proper to ask a question on a subject not referred to by the judge-advocate or General Buell, I hold that I do not put myself by so doing in the attitude of an accuser; by no means.

General BUELL. I wish to be distinctly understood as not denying the right of any member of the Commission to cross-examination. I wish to be distinctly understood as not meaning to charge that the exercise of this right by any member of this commission, which is undoubted, puts him in the attitude of an accuser or anything of the sort. It is perfectly in accordance with the rules practiced in courts-martial or courts of inquiry, and I do not deny it at all. It is simply the manner or matter of investigation which determines whether it is in the nature of a prosecution or accusation, and whether the questioner puts himself in the attitude of an accuser or prosecutor.

General SCHOEPF. That statement is not in accordance with General Buell's practice. He stated that a member of the Commission had placed himself in the attitude of an accuser and now he states directly the opposite.

The court being cleared, the Commission decided that General Buell's objection be sustained and that the objection to the question was not too late.

By the JUDGE-ADVOCATE:

Question. You stated in your testimony that after the battle of Corinth a portion of the enemy's army was sent by rail to the vicinity of Chattanooga. Please state by what railroad and how you came by this information.

I stated that it was supposed that a portion of the rebel force had been so moved, the supposition being that they went by way of Mobile; that a portion of them were also marched across the gap, if any existed, in the road from Meridian to Selma (I think that is the name of the other terminus), and were transported around from that point to Chattanooga. Those reports I got from officers with whom I conversed. I had no other sources of information.

Question. What officers were these?

I talked frequently with Colonel Fry, chief of staff to General Buell, and with a great many officers of the Army of the Ohio whom I met from day to day.

Question. Has not your experience in the army since this war began taught you that, taking the best information that you could obtain as to the enemy's force, you had to make an allowance of a very heavy percentage as to their number?

It has; and such an allowance I have made in all the estimates I have given of the enemy's supposed strength.

Question. What were your means of obtaining information when you had an independent command?

I had the reports made to me by scouts that I sent as far to the front as possible; I also heard the reports of scouts made to General Buell at his headquarters while I was in camp near him at Decherd. I also received information from refugees that were constantly arriving from within rebel lines.

Question. State, as nearly as your memory will permit, the names of such scouts and refugees as gave you information upon which you relied.

There was Mr. Flemming, whom I employed frequently as a scout, and now a captain in the First Tennessee Cavalry. There was also an old man who lived in Wartrace, whose name I do not remember, and who rendered very valuable service to me as a scout. I have not treasured the names of several other scouts who served me or of the refugees who arrived. I could, however, ascertain by reference to the account of what I paid them for their services.

Question. Have you any written reports or memoranda made at that time—made by those scouts and refugees?

I think I have among my papers copies of dispatches that I sent to General Buell embodying the information that I received before his arrival at Decherd and also while I was in command at Manchester.

Question. Am I to understand from your statement with reference to the force being sent from Corinth that up to the evacuation of Corinth Chattanooga had been left undefended by the rebels?

I do not suppose that it had been left entirely so, but suppose that it was held by but a small force of the enemy.

Question. With Chattanooga naturally so strong that 25,000 men could hold it against 50,000 men and the rebels at Richmond in distress for lack of troops which place would your better judgment dictate the troops went to from Corinth?

General BUELL. I object to the question, Mr. President, because I think it opens a wide latitude to the investigation.

The JUDGE-ADVOCATE. I withdraw the question.

General BUELL. It assumes certain conditions that might be answered very well, but it is impossible for the witness to know that there was greater necessity for the troops at Chattanooga than at Richmond.

By General TYLER:

Question. You said you could move 25,000 men from Tupelo to Chattanooga in ten days or two weeks. By what railroad route could they have been moved?

A portion of them I should have moved by way of Tupelo to Mobile and from Mobile up the road to Atlanta and from Atlanta to Chattanooga, and a portion I should have moved across from Meridian to Selma, marching across any gap that might have existed in the railroad line between those two points, which was understood to be very inconsiderable if there was any at all, and from Selma on to Chattanooga by railroad, which intersects the same road as the one leading from Mobile up to Atlanta. I know that railroad connection exists between Selma and Chattanooga.

Question. What is the distance from Tupelo to Chattanooga by way of Mobile, Montgomery, and Atlanta?

I should think from 700 to 800 miles.

General BUELL. I request that the general may refer to the maps.

General TYLER. It is 714 by the railroad map. The general is right. You mean, of course, 25,000 men, with their artillery, baggage, provisions, and including the baggage train?

I would not include a baggage train.

By General TYLER:

Question. Would you consider an army in the field efficient without a baggage train?

That would depend upon the extent of its field of operations. In the case supposed I would consider it perfectly efficient for the garrisoning of Chattanooga without its baggage train and for any operations in that immediate vicinity.

Question. To move this army in two weeks would be about 2,000 men a day. How many cars and engines would you require to move 2,000 men, with their baggage, &c., in a single day?

I would require from 60 to 80 cars and from 8 to 12 engines.

Question. And with that amount of rolling stock you would require every day for ten days to two weeks to move an army of 25,000 men?

I would require double that amount of rolling stock—perhaps treble—to keep rains running simultaneously.

Question. How many cars and engines do you estimate would be needed to take 25,000 men over a line of 700 to 800 miles in length?

Allowing for all accidents and contingencies, I estimate that each train would make two trips within the time stated. The trains necessary to transport half the number would consist of about 360 cars and from 16 to 20 engines, and that rolling stock could be passed over the round trip twice. I should deem that sufficient for the entire work. The estimate that I made in my first answer was upon a different basis from this. I find that upon further consideration of the subject, making the estimate as I have in my last answer, it would require more rolling stock—more than double or treble the amount named in the answer to the previous question.

Question. Taking baggage, men, artillery, and the necessary forage and provisions, how many men on the average would you apportion to each car?

I would make my average about 30.

Question. Have you ever seen any trains with troops, carrying the necessary provisions, baggage, horses, &c., with 20 men to a car?

I have frequently moved troops that would average 60, 70, and even 80 men, with their baggage, to each car—loading them inside and outside. I think 30 to a car a very low and perfectly safe estimate.

Question. Have you ever seen men moved 800 miles with 60 to 80 men in a car?

I have not seen troops moved that distance with that number to a car.

Commission adjourned to meet February 11, 1863.

CINCINNATI, *February* 11, 1863.

Commission met pursuant to adjournment. All the members present; also the judge-advocate and General Buell.

General W. S. SMITH'S examination continued.

By General BUELL:

Question. Do you perceive any similitude between the circumstances of the occupation of Cumberland Gap by General Morgan's forces, previous to its withdrawal from that point in the months of June and July last, and the recent expedition of General Carter against the East Tennessee Railroad?

I do not. The mere occupation of a position could scarcely resemble in any respect an expedition of a force that should make a march of some hundreds of miles.

Question. Do you know anything about the particulars of Carter's expedition except what you have derived from his official report and the newspaper accounts?

I do not.

Question. According to those sources of information about what force was there in the range of his expedition to oppose the expedition of General Carter?

I have not even an approximate idea of that force. The understanding that I have gained in the accounts of the expedition I have read is that General Carter encountered but little resistance and met with but few rebel troops.

Question. Was the force which invaded Kentucky under Kirby Smith virtually the same as that which occupied East Tennessee and was opposed to our troops at Cumberland Gap last summer?

I have always supposed that the troops that Kirby Smith brought into Kentucky with him constituted a portion of the command that had been in front of General Morgan at Cumberland Gap, but supposed that other troops were still left there after Kirby Smith's departure on his Kentucky expedition.

Question. Do you know, in general terms, about the relative strength of that force and the force which occupied Cumberland Gap under General Morgan?

I have always estimated General Morgan's command at Cumberland Gap at about 10,000 men. I supposed that East Tennessee was held by about 20,000 rebel troops, and about 15,000 of that force I supposed Kirby Smith brought with him into Kentucky.

Question. Have you given any evidence before this Commission which implies that the security of the rebels' hold upon East Tennessee against any advance of the Army of the Ohio would have depended upon re-enforcements from Richmond?

I have not intended to convey any such idea. I do not believe that they were dependent on re-enforcements from Richmond at any time to hold East Tennessee.

General BUELL. I desire to ask the judge-advocate whether the additional testimony he proposes to introduce is to be confined to rebutting the evidence I introduced or to strengthening the evidence that he has introduced in the prosecution? I conceive there is a decided difference.

The JUDGE-ADVOCATE. The Government having rested in this investigation, the evidence introduced on the part of the judge-advocate can be only of a rebutting character. What the effect of that may be I do not pretend to say; it may strengthen my case or it may not; but it is purely within the rule of the law governing evidence introduced in that way.

General BUELL. I now inquire of the judge-advocate what information he has of the various witnesses that have been summoned from different places to appear before this Commission on the part of the defense? I remember Captain Merrill and Lieutenant Sheridan, of the signal corps, who are now in the Army of the Cumberland; Major Cotter, of some Ohio regiment, who is also with that army; Captain Bingham, assistant quartermaster, who is also with that army; Colonel Ralston, a citizen of Tennessee; Mr. Carter and Mr. Smith, who are also citizens of Tennessee. There may be others whose names I do not remember at this time.

The JUDGE-ADVOCATE. I had a dispatch from General Rosecrans, informing me that those gentlemen connected with the signal corps could not be spared from the active operations of the army, and suggesting that queries be put to them in writing, to be asked under oath, by the judge-advocate of the army, Major Skinner, which I submitted to General Buell yesterday, and I understood that that course could be pursued in reference to them. It is the first information I received in response to my summons for those gentlemen to appear before the Commission. This morning I received the following communication:

CAMP NEAR LA VERGNE, *December* 28, 1862—9 p. m.

(Post-marked Nashville, December 30, and signed by the late Colonel Garesché.)

MAJOR: We have just returned from a ride to the front and found your letter enclosing the summons for Lieutenant-Colonel Wood and Major Cotter. I laid it before the general for his orders, but he says he cannot spare either of them at this time. He regrets to disappoint the Commission, but deems it his duty to retain these officers with their command.

JULIUS P. GARESCHÉ.

Captain Bingham was summoned at the same time Captain Macfeely was, but seems to have paid no attention to the summons. Colonel Ralston was summoned at Nashville to appear before the Commission at Nashville, and when the Commission adjourned to Louisville received an order to accompany the Commission, which I reiterated at Bowling Green, to none of which he paid any attention or indeed made any response in any shape. Mr. Carter and Mr. Smith, citizens of Tennessee, were not found.

General BUELL. Is Captain Jones expected to appear here?

The JUDGE-ADVOCATE. I submitted his report to the Commission, and supposed from that that his written report would be as clear as his oral evidence would be. If you wish him to appear he shall be summoned.

General BUELL. I wish him to appear. I should like to know whether the judge-advocate took any measure to secure the attendance of Mr. Miller.

The JUDGE-ADVOCATE. No, sir; I did not.

General BUELL. Was he at Nashville at the time the Commission was there?

The JUDGE-ADVOCATE. Yes, sir; I issued a summons for him to appear while we were at Nashville.

General BUELL. I have seen a letter purporting to have been written by the father of Major-General McCook. I do not know but that I may desire to bring forward some testimony with reference to that letter, Mr. President. I have not determined about it. I noticed in yesterday's papers that Colonel Lytle, who is spoken of in that letter, is about to start this morning.

The PRESIDENT. He left this morning.

General BUELL. I should like to have him summoned.

(The judge-advocate directs that Colonel Lytle be summoned.)

General TYLER. The judge-advocate is the proper person to close this investigation. We have no right to say when it shall close, unless we take upon ourselves the duty of prosecuting; and as far as I am concerned I am not going to take that responsibility

The PRESIDENT. After the conversation that took place yesterday before the Commission I am of opinion that General Buell might consider any such interference at this time, after the notice we have given him, as a manifestation of the spirit of a prosecutor.

General DANA. I objected to it all the time.

The PRESIDENT. For my part I think we have a duty to perform, and on the other hand the judge-advocate has his duty to perform. We look for him to summon all witnesses and to conduct the examination; that is a part of his business; but if he tells us he will have a witness before us, it is for him to judge as to what time it would be most proper to have that witness introduced. If he desires to have General Wright, it is a duty we owe to the judge-advocate to allow him to use his own judgment in this matter, inasmuch as General Wright is his witness.

General DANA. Supposing we want General Wright on new matter.

General BUELL. I repeat my wish that the judge-advocate should proceed with the testimony, either oral or documentary. The inconvenience to the public service in delaying the Commission and the injury to myself which results from this sort of proceeding in the mixing up of witnesses on different sides is apparent to me, if not to the Commission. A good deal of matter in the course of subsequent examination of witnesses by the judge-advocate has appeared which I should have desired to explain or elucidate by witnesses which I have been required to call up in the intervals between these witnesses. I can hardly undertake to do that now; it would perhaps take as much time as you have occupied in the whole investigation. It therefore works injuriously to me and perhaps more so to the public interest.

The JUDGE-ADVOCATE. I have said before that the Government rests where we are. I have no other evidence to introduce and no new matter to bring before the Commission. So far as documentary evidence is concerned, I have laid it before the Commission as far as I have it. I wish all the books of the Department of the Ohio to be brought before the Commission. There is scarcely a telegram or a letter but has some bearing upon the case. I have some 80 to 100 pages copied for the purpose of throwing light upon the campaign of Kentucky and Tennessee, and as soon as possible will proceed to arrange them to be read before the Commission.

The PRESIDENT. As we are required to make up our opinion as to what is evidence before the court, it might be contended, and some members of the court might with great plausibility, if not with truth, contend, that if a document was not read before this Commission—whatever its importance might be—it ought not to be received as testimony. It should be read for another reason, and that is in justice to General Buell—it should be read with a view to notify him that such a document was considered as evidence. He might object to it, and it might become of importance to offer some explanations concerning it. I call to mind a letter addressed to General Nelson while he was in command at Louisville, the purport of which was, as I understood, to evacuate the city of Louisville, dropping down and taking a position the other side of Salt River. I regard that letter as of considerable importance, and if General Buell ordered it he may wish to explain it, and I should be much gratified to hear it.

General TYLER. In looking over the books submitted to the Commission I cannot find even the order on which General Buell acted in the campaign of Kentucky and Tennessee.

General BUELL. I think I have explained to the Commission that the instructions that were originally given to me were given orally by General Halleck.

The PRESIDENT. If that is the case it may become necessary for us to have General Halleck before us, inasmuch as under the present arrangement General Buell is not himself a witness.

General BUELL. The meaning and intent of those instructions were that my army should advance into East Tennessee, occupy first Chattanooga, and prospectively other points. I proposed to General Halleck that I should have the privilege of directing those operations by whichever route I might think proper. General Halleck first assented to that, but he subsequently notified me by telegraphic dispatch that upon further consideration he thought the best plan would be to proceed directly to Chattanooga, and I believe that dispatch is the only documentary evidence of those instructions I have.

The PRESIDENT. Is that on the record?

General BUELL. I think it is. The tendency and object of those instructions were to direct my army against Chattanooga, that being deemed the first important point.

The PRESIDENT. Before it is settled by the Commission that the Government rests its case I beg the judge-advocate to examine the books introduced by General Buell, and take therefrom such letters, dispatches, &c., as he thinks necessary and important for the elucidation of any question before the court and submit them to the court by a reading.

General BUELL. I wish to urge the propriety and justice of the introduction by the judge-advocate and the reading to the Commission of everything in the shape of documentary evidence that he proposes to introduce at all, and for the reasons I have given you, that it may be as important to me as the evidence of witnesses examined here. There is one other matter which I desire to bring formally to the notice of the Commission. I believe it is necessary for the interest of the Government and is due to myself that Governor Johnson should appear before this Commission, and that he should be introduced by the judge-advocate and not by myself. I think it is due also that General Wright should be introduced in the same way. As the object of this investigation is to give to the Government information and do justice everywhere, I can see no objection to the introduction of these gentlemen for the prosecution. I cannot insist upon it except as a matter of justice, and I believe that the ends of justice would be answered by it.

(General Buell desired the judge-advocate to detain General W. S. Smith, as further testimony might be required of him.)

Commission adjourned to meet February 13.

CINCINNATI, *February* 13, 1863.

Commission met pursuant to adjournment. All the members present; also the judge-advocate and General Buell.

(Reading documentary evidence.)

The JUDGE-ADVOCATE. Mr. President, in accordance with the resolution passed, by the Commission some weeks ago I addressed a note to General Buell calling upon him for all books, papers, telegrams, letters, and orders sent and received in his department having any bearing on this investigation, for the purpose of using the same before the Commission. In response to that Geneal Buell furnishes me with all the evidence connected with the department that has a bearing upon the investigation. In accordance with the instructions given me at Nashville it was agreed that an authentication should be dispensed with where General Buell and myself concurred. I now introduce these books before the Commission as so much evidence. I have also, in accordance with the resolution passed yesterday, made an abstract of the letters, telegrams, returns, &c., that I propose to use in this investigation. I will submit them to General Buell, and if he has no objection they will be considered as before the Commission.

General DANA. I move that the resolution referred to in the remarks of the judge-advocate as passed at Nashville be read to the Commission.

The JUDGE-ADVOCATE. I have not been able to find it; it does not appear to have been entered upon the minutes. The instructions were a matter of course, because when the Government and General Buell agree upon a document further authentication is unnecessary. The question that agitates the Commission is as to the mode of authentication; that is, whether these documents are before the Commission.

The PRESIDENT. I understand there is no such question agitating this Commission, because there is a positive direction to the judge-advocate to introduce such documentary evidence and read it to the Commission.

The JUDGE-ADVOCATE. I am ready at any moment to proceed to read what I propose to use.

General BUELL. There has been no consultation between the judge-advocate and myself as to what should or should not be admitted as evidence before the Commission. I presented the records that I had to him for his inspection and any use he might choose to make of them, and to anything he chooses to present I have no objection to offer now; the proper time will be when it is read to the Commission, and I shall not object to anything that has any bearing upon the matter under investigation.

The JUDGE-ADVOCATE. I have made selections from this evidence and will proceed to read them if the Commission so desire. It will be necessary to read all the documentary evidence I propose to introduce.

(Telegrams read by judge-advocate.)

General BUELL. I should like to inquire what interpretation the judge-advocate proposes to put upon the statements that are made in this documentary evidence as to the strength of the enemy; for instance, whether he expects that it would be admitted as evidence of that strength or only showing what it really expresses, namely, the rumored or reported strength of the enemy? What I wish to know is what effect the judge-advocate means that statements of this kind in documentary evidence, as to the strength of the enemy, for example, shall have; whether it is to be recognized as conclusive as to the strength of the enemy or only as setting forth the information that was received from time to time?

The PRESIDENT. Allow me to ask you, general, that it may be clearly understood, if you hold the position that it is your right to hear the construction which the judge-advocate puts upon these documents submitted to the Commission, and also to have him to distinctly avow for what purposes he proposes to use them—not merely those relating to the strength of the enemy, but all others he may submit to the Commission?

General BUELL. That is the substance of my wish.

The JUDGE-ADVOCATE. I cannot perceive why I should be called upon to put a construction upon these telegrams or letters any more than that I should put a construction upon the evidence of General Mc-Cook or state in advance what I expect to prove by the evidence of General McCook. I think I have proved enough when I have introduced his testimony. There are facts bearing upon this investigation which must carry simply what appears upon the face of them and no more. I do not propose to make arguments or draw conclusions from these documents; that is the business of the members of the Commission, not mine. If General Buell finds anything introduced that has no bearing upon the conduct of the Army of the Ohio in this investigation, he has, of course, a right to make objection to it; but so long as the Commission finds it has a bearing it will be presented, and I have no construction to put upon the evidence. When facts are introduced, argument will be left to the proper time for argument to be made.

General BUELL. Perhaps it may be well to state what are my views as to what should be the rule with reference to evidence introduced before this Commission. The instructions of the Secretary of War specify certain distinct ma.ters which are to be the subject of investigation. All these specifications are distinct except the last, which is somewhat general, and is in these words: "And also to inquire and report upon such other matters touching the military operations aforesaid as in the judgment of the Commission shall be beneficial to the service." It appears to me now that under this last and general specification the investigation should be with reference to the propriety or impropriety of some of my official acts. If anything is presented as evidence which shows upon its face something that requires explanation or investigation, that may be sufficient with reference to that; but with reference to evidence, documentary or otherwise, which may set forth official acts that may be proper or improper according to the interpretation that is put upon them, the judge-advocate should be required to state what bearing he understands this evidence to have upon some particular question as to the propriety or impropriety of my official acts. For example, if the propriety or expediency of some arrangement of troops for some particular object should be in question, the judge-advocate would properly introduce as evidence anything bearing upon that general arrangement. But if he should introduce a document that merely sets forth that I ordered a division or brigade or a regiment to a particular place, without having set forth the general purpose of his investigation, I hold that he should state distinctly the object he has in view in introducing that particular document. I hold that it is proper he should explain what he means to show by this particular document that is introduced, and whether he claims that there was any fault in the official act which it sets forth or not; and, if so, what that fault is.

The court was cleared for deliberation, when, after discussion, the following was resolved upon as the opinion of the court:

"That the document is to go on record as it stands, without explanation from the judge-advocate, and it is for General Buell to treat and explain it in his defense as he may think proper."

General BUELL. Is this a general rule or a rule having reference to this particular document? The first question I submitted to the Commission is not answered in that resolution; that is, as to whether the statements there as to the strength of the rebel force is to be considered as evidence of that strength or whether it only stands there as one of the various reports or rumors current in regard to that subject. I believe that question is before you, sir.

The PRESIDENT. I think, general, the resolution covers that point.

General BUELL. I think not, sir.

The PRESIDENT. I will, with your permission, general, take the sense of the Commission upon it.

The court was cleared, when, after discussion, it was resolved—

"That the above rule should be considered as applicable to all documentary evidence introduced."

General BUELL. That there may be no misunderstanding in reference to this, I wish it understood that if I make any exception to a document it is not that I object to the document as it actually is. It will require the authentication of my staff officers to secure my final assent to it as evidence before the Commission. I make this explanation because it is very possible there may be verbal errors that can be corrected by referring to the original papers, and I wish it therefore understood that my assenting to a document that is read here does not imply that I assent to it as it is read, but to the document as it ought to be.

General SCHOEPF. I move that all the documentary evidence that is to be introduced be read by General Buell before it is read to the Commission and that he then certify to its correctness.

General BUELL. That is what I propose to do with reference to the documentary evidence I introduce myself and that I think it will be best to do in all cases.

The PRESIDENT. My opinion on that matter is that any written papers or documents presented to this Commission and appearing as from the official records of General Buell, properly dated, sent by him or to him when he was in command of the Department of the Ohio, would be, *prima facie,* correct, and if not correct it would be for General Buell to point out the errors and that it would not be for the judge-advocate in any manner to correct them, and to amend them the original papers would have to be produced in court and all corrections made upon the face of the documents from the originals. *Prima facie* the documents that appear in the official books of the general commanding the Department of the Ohio would be received, in my judgment, as correct, though unsigned by the chief of the staff or the assistant adjutant-general.

General BUELL. I do not object to the rule; I simply made the remark so that I might not be understood as assenting to what might upon its face appear to be correct.

(Telegrams read by judge-advocate.)

General BUELL. You have read enough already to show the necessity and propriety of a proper examination of these official papers and of a proper authentication of them. These records were made out for my own use, and, as you see, have never been carefully examined and authenticated, and were written, as is apparent, by a careless clerk. The originals are on file, and time would be saved by a proper authentication before the papers are presented to the Commission. The rule the president has stated is a sufficient protection for me and I have no objection to proceed in that way, but it will involve a re-examination of all these papers and a comparison of them with the originals.

The PRESIDENT. There is no objection to General Buell correcting any errors in these records by a reference to the originals.

(Telegrams read by judge-advocate.)

Commission adjourned to meet February 14.

CINCINNATI, *February* 14, 1863.
Commission met pursuant to adjournment. All the members present; also the judge-advocate and General Buell.

(Telegrams read by judge-advocate.)

The JUDGE-ADVOCATE. Mr. President, I now introduce the consolidated reports exhibiting the strength of the Army of the Ohio for June 1,* June 10,* July 20,* August 1, and September 1,* 1862. I believe these exhibit the entire force of the army at those several periods, with the exception of two divisions (General Mitchel's and General Paine's, I think) that were subsequently or pending that time added to the Army of the Ohio.

(Telegrams read by judge-advocate.)

The JUDGE-ADVOCATE. I find among the telegrams an estimate of the army at Chattanooga without date or signature. I think, however, it is in the handwriting of General McCook; but till it is authenticated it should not be accepted by the Commission. I submit it for what it

---

*Not found.

is worth. I have now presented all the documentary evidence that I have to submit to the Commission.

General ORD. I do not object to this paper being submitted as testimony, though I object to its being read, because before anything is brought before the Commission it should be considered whether it is valid or not.

General TYLER. Has General Thomas responded to the request of the judge-advocate for his papers?

The JUDGE-ADVOCATE. Yes, sir.

General SCHOEPF. These consolidated reports are not correct. The First Division, my own division, is not entered on either of the reports.

General BUELL. (To the judge-advocate.) Do you propose to present this memorandum?

The JUDGE-ADVOCATE. No, sir.

General BUELL. It is, I believe, a memorandum submitted by Colonel Wilder when he was giving his testimony, and it became mixed up in the papers presented by him. I think you will have all the benefit from it that you desire in his testimony.

Commission adjourned to meet February 16, 1863, at 10 o'clock a. m.

CINCINNATI, *February* 16, 1863.

Commission met pursuant to adjournment. All the members present; also the judge-advocate and General Buell.

General TYLER. Mr. President, I have a resolution to offer on which I wish to make a few remarks and request that both may go on the record.

So far as I recollect, the judge-advocate has never retained a witness before the court after his examination was finished nor has a single witness as yet been recalled by the judge-advocate. By referring to our record it will be seen that General Smith and Captain Jones, after occupying the court four or six days in giving testimony, are now retained from their appropriate duties—General Smith being under orders to report to General Grant, now conducting the most important operations of the army—notwithstanding the order of the court passed on Tuesday, the 9th instant, which seems to me to preclude either the Government or the defense from recalling a witness. I now move that the judge-advocate and Major-General Buell both be instructed that after a witness has been once examined he cannot be recalled except for reasons stated and deemed satisfactory at the time, and that this Commission will not exercise its authority to retain any witness belonging to the Army of the United States whose examination has been concluded as per order of the 9th instant, and whose presence is undoubtedly required with his command.

General BUELL. I wish to enter my formal protest against this order. It comes in after the prosecution has been closed; it does not therefore affect the cause of the Government; it affects me seriously. A mass of documentary evidence has been introduced by the judge-advocate, the object of which he does not explain and the object of which I can only guess at myself. The witnesses that have been detained at my request have been detained in anticipation of what has occurred; that is, that matter would be introduced before the Commission which it would be necessary for me to explain by my witnesses, without knowing in advance what that matter was.

I object to the order, also, that it violates a rule of investigation before all tribunals, I believe, which gives either party the privilege of recalling any witness at any time while his side of the investigation is yet open. He may be dismissed for the occasion and called up again as if he had never been called to give evidence. I think the possible tendency of the resolution is to debar me from that justice I have a right to expect. The proceedings thus far have been conducted with that deliberation and in that manner which the judge-advocate has deemed best for himself and the Government, no restriction having been placed upon him in any way, and I do not understand why these cramps should be put upon the case upon the side of the defense. I will state that the object of this protest is to ask a reconsideration of the order and a revocation of it. I do not propose myself to subject the Government or the Commission to any greater inconvenience than may be absolutely necessary for the ends of justice.

The JUDGE-ADVOCATE. I believe, as I have stated before, that it is customary in all tribunals to retain witnesses till the trial is through, that they may be recalled at any time. I have nothing to say upon the rule offered by the Commission except this: that having closed the case for the Government I cannot introduce any new matter, and therefore one reason why the witness should be retained for the purpose of questioning on anything that may be introduced on the part of the Government is removed. So far as the judge-advocate is concerned the line of inquiry to be pursued is marked out by the Government. We are called upon to investigate certain facts connected with the operations of the Army of the Ohio in Kentucky and Tennessee, and I do not consider it my duty, nor do I think it would be proper, nor have I, to introduce any witness with the preamble as to what I expected to prove by that witness, nor have I made any comments on the facts brought forward. That is for the Commission to weigh and determine for themselves. I have called witnesses who have been supposed to know something about the facts of the case, and most of these witnesses have been summoned upon a consultation with General Buell himself, and having called them I have permitted them to state what they knew about the matter. It will be further observed that in a majority of instances General Buell has made the witnesses his own by the introduction of new matter while cross-examining.

General ORD. I move that we reconsider the resolution.

The court was cleared, when, after discussion, it was resolved not to reconsider the resolution.

The court being opened—

The PRESIDENT. There being nothing in the rule to prevent the detention of General Smith upon a sufficient reason or necessity shown by General Buell I will ask the general to state to the Commission his reasons for desiring to recall him.

General BUELL. I do not wish to detain Captain Jones any longer. I wish General Smith to appear before the Commission upon matter which has been introduced in the documentary evidence submitted by the judge-advocate since General Smith's examination. Will you summon General Smith?

The JUDGE-ADVOCATE. Yes, sir.

General SCHOEPF. Is not General Smith in Cincinnati?

The JUDGE-ADVOCATE. No, sir; I gave him permission to leave, as he could be summoned by telegraph at any time and be here in a few hours.

The court was cleared, when, after discussion, the Commission decided that General Smith would not be recalled, as the Commission was of opinion that sufficient reason for his recall had not been given under this rule.

The court being opened—

General BUELL. I would like to inquire if some particular reason would be deemed sufficient?

The PRESIDENT. I endeavored to state to General Buell that if a satisfactory reason were given for the recall of General Smith the Commission would recall him.

General BUELL. What I remember now particularly is embraced in a dispatch from General Mitchel to me, setting forth the facilities for the movement of the army rapidly from Chattanooga, particularly the facilities for crossing the river. I wish to show by General Smith what those facilities really were and how far they fell short of what is claimed for them in the dispatches of General Mitchel.

The PRESIDENT. Upon this additional statement, general, I understand you to renew your request for General Smith to reappear?

General BUELL. Yes, sir.

The court was cleared, with an apology from the President to General Buell for the inconvenience to which he was put in again being requested to retire.

On the court being opened—

The PRESIDENT. It has been decided to be unnecessary to recall General Smith upon the point made by you, general.

Maj. Gen. GORDON GRANGER (a witness for the defendant), being duly sworn by the judge-advocate, testified as follows:

By General BUELL:

Question. State your name and position in the service of the United States, if you please.

Gordon Granger; captain in the Regular Army and major-general of Volunteers.

Question. Were you on duty in the Department of the Ohio in the months of September, October, and November last; if so, at what place and what command had you?

I arrived in the Department of the Ohio from Corinth, Miss., on or about September 13, 1862, the command then consisting of four regiments of infantry, one of cavalry, and two batteries of light artillery. My first duty after my arrival was at Covington, where this command was augmented to some eight or nine regiments more. I remained there on duty until the siege of Cincinnati was raised, and then proceeded to Louisville with this command, and also took charge of about, I think, fifteen or sixteen or seventeen regiments—I do not remember more—of which I had the superintendence of the shipping by river and by rail. Arrived at Louisville I think about the 21st of September, and remained there on duty as second in command to General Nelson, afterward under General Buell, until about the 1st of October, when I was relieved and ordered to report to General Wright at this place. I was then assigned to the command of the troops about Covington and Newport, some twenty-six regiments, I believe. Under orders from General Wright I proceeded with this command to Lexington, Ky., where I arrived on the 25th of October; remained there in command of what is known as the Central District of Kentucky, with a force varying from 18,000 to 26,000. Was again relieved from that district on or about the 1st of February, 1863. I proceeded to Louisville and thence to the South with some 15,000 men.

Question. What was the cause of the transfer of your command from Covington to Louisville, as you have stated?

It was because of the approach of General Bragg's army, threatening that place—with a view to its defense.

Question. Did your official position during this period make it your duty to inform yourself in regard to the strength, effectiveness, and objects of the rebel forces which invaded Kentucky in August and September? If so, state what you know with reference to these several points. You may in this connection, if you please, state by what routes the enemy invaded Kentucky, and what points he occupied and what points he threatened.

My official position did require me to inform myself on the points enumerated, and in addition I received on one or two occasions verbal instructions from Major-General Wright to assist General Nelson by advice, counsel, head work, and hard work, and in fact everything I could do.

It would be better for me to state first that there was a rebel force already in Kentucky, under the command of Maj. Gen. Kirby Smith. That force entered Kentucky, from the best information that could be obtained, on or about the 20th of August, perhaps a little later, coming in from the south through the Big Creek Gap and Walker's Gap, about 40 miles west of Cumberland Gap, passing these two gaps with a force of about 18,000 strong. After clearing the gaps in this direction a rebel force under General Stevenson united with Kirby Smith's, of 6,000 strong. A portion of this force reached the city of Lexington, I think, about the 2d or 3d of September; remained in the State, occupying a position part of the time in front of Cincinnati, Cynthiana, Lexington, Mount Sterling, Frankfort, with some small posts, such as Nicholasville and Georgetown. The force which subsequently came into Kentucky, I learn, was under the command of General Bragg; it left some point on Battle Creek; the date I do not remember well enough to state, but my recollection is that it was about the 1st of September. It struck almost directly for the town of Glasgow; thence to Munfordville; from Munfordville it moved on to Bardstown. After leaving Munfordville General Nelson and myself were sending spies and obtaining information from all possible sources—from deserters that came in. The force by these parties was represented to be varying from 65,000 to 80,000; but from everything we could gather, the opinion of General Nelson, General Wright, and several others and myself, was that Bragg's force numbered from 50,000 to 55,000 men. That was the estimate put upon it by those best informed. I think I was the only one who put it at a little lower. My estimate was from 45,000 to 50,000. I have since learned that our estimate of 50,000 to 55,000 was very nearly correct.

These, then, were the two rebel forces in Kentucky on or about the 25th of September. Kirby Smith commenced about this time, or a few days previous, concentrating his forces at Frankfort, so that on or about the 25th of September Bragg was at Bardstown or near there—his main force was there—with some 55,000 men. Kirby Smith had lost by desertion and had left a great many sick (I found 1,500 at Lexington), which reduced his force to from 18,000 to 20,000 men. This was the strength and position of the two rebel armies from the best information we could get, and was the opinion of other general officers, about the 25th of September, 1862. Smith's army concentrated at Frankfort; it was lying about at Lexington. Some 6,000 or 7,000 came over under Heth (as near as I could ascertain) in front of Cincinnati.

The PRESIDENT. You mean to say that Bragg was at Bardstown and Kirby Smith at Frankfort at the same date?

The WITNESS. Yes, sir; about the same time. Bragg in person was at Frankfort, but the bulk of his force was at Bardstown. The objects of these forces, Bragg's and Smith's, in my opinion and that of others, as we supposed at the time, was a union and the attempted overthrow and defeat of General Buell's army at such a point as they could meet it with advantage. I learned that the object of Kirby Smith's advance was to get into Kentucky as early as possible in advance of Bragg, for the purpose of securing supplies of provisions, clothing, animals—in fact everything they stood in need of—and for establishing depots at convenient points for the use and benefit of Bragg's army on his arrival. Another object that I understood at the time, and have heard it a thousand times since, was that they expected a very large re-enforcement—that Kentucky would rise. I have heard officers assert that they expected a re-enforcement of about 50,000 men in Kentucky. With this they believed themselves enabled to defeat any force we had and then march to the Ohio. At the time it was my impression, from the best information I could get, that they meditated an attack upon Louisville, but I have since become satisfied that they regarded Louisville as of little or no importance to them.

By General BUELL:

Question. Was there in Louisville about this time a large amount of public and private property such as an army would require?

There was up to about the 25th of September, or perhaps a little earlier, a good deal of clothing and provisions, by which time most of it was removed to the opposite side of the river.

Question. What at this time were the limits of the Department of the Ohio and who was in command?

The southern limit was the southern boundary of Kentucky; southern and eastern limits the southern and eastern boundaries of Kentucky, embracing Western Virginia. The number of States in it I cannot mention distinctly. I know that Ohio, Illinois, Indiana, Michigan, and Wisconsin were in it. Whether Iowa was or not I do not know. I know that those mentioned were in it from the fact that a requisition was made upon the Governors of those States for troops and they came, and I saw orders addressed to those States. My impression is that Iowa was included, though I am not certain. The remainder of the boundary of the department was the western boundary of Kentucky adjacent to Tennessee. Maj. Gen. H. G. Wright was in command.

Question. Can you state the date of his entry upon command?

I believe it was about the 25th of August, but I am not positive.

Question. Considering the position and resources of Louisville, was it fair to presume that that was one main point the enemy aimed for?

That was my opinion at the time, as stated before; so much so, that every effort was made, by working night and day, to intrench and fortify and to make every species of defense to protect it. I furthermore judge so from some intercepted correspondence from General Beauregard to General Bragg which I had in my possession for some time.

Question. What United States forces were there at Louisville at the time of Bragg's invasion, prior to the arrival of the Army of the Ohio and what was their effectiveness?

About two days previous to the arrival of the Army of the Ohio I was told by General Nelson that his whole organized force there was about 36,000 to 37,000. I made the circuit of the trenches (I had charge of a portion of them), and from what I saw I believe that statement was correct. In addition to this we had citizens, squirrel hunters, and people picked up for the occasion, which swelled this force to 41,000 or 42,000. All this force, with the exception of four regiments of infantry, one of cavalry, and two batteries, I believe, was entirely new. The 36,000 or 37,000 mentioned were regularly organized into regiments, very well armed and very well equipped, but had had no instruction or drill. Four or five thousand of irregulars of every kind were but partially armed, some with shot-guns some without, some with ammunition and some without, but most of them with spades and picks.

Question. How much artillery was there and what was its effective condition?

To the best of my recollection there were seven batteries; two of them were good batteries, the others were of but very little account. I had something to do to get the guns and harness into condition, and the men were so ignorant that they did not know how to unlimber or limber up.

Question. Was there anything in the position and strength of the United States forces to prevent a junction between Bragg and Kirby Smith if they desired it or in the condition of the country and roads?

Nothing whatever that I am aware of. In fact I know there was nothing.

Question. What would probably have been the result of an engagement between these two rebel forces combined, or even of the main force under Bragg alone, and the United States force that was left at Louisville, supposing the latter not to have been strongly protected by intrenchments prior to the arrival of the Army of the Ohio?

The result, in my opinion, would have been an almost immediate defeat and utter rout. We were in hopes, in case we were attacked, to hold on to the trenches and suburbs if possible, to enable General Buell's army to come up and attack them in their rear, and it was seriously contemplated by General Nelson to burn the city as fast as they drove him from it. For the purpose of saving the army we constructed two pontoon bridges, one in front of the center of the city and one at the lower extremity of the city, in case of attack.

Question. Do you know the country and the roads by which the

Army of the Ohio would advance to Louisville about the time of the advance of Bragg's army to Bardstown from Green River?

I have a geographical knowledge of it. I have studied it for my own interest in connection with the movements of the rebel army and your own, but I have never been over it.

Question. Do you know the road by which the Army of the Ohio did advance from Munfordville to Louisville?

Yes, sir; from Munfordville to Elizabethtown; thence to Salt River; thence to Louisville; this is the inner road, nearest to the bank of the river. I sent some cavalry to Elizabethtown, which caused me to inquire into the condition of the road and the nature of the country. I also had something to do with constructing a bridge or ferry, I do not remember which—perhaps both—at this point, to have it in readiness for the crossing of General Buell's army. The distance to Elizabethtown, as near as I remember, is from 45 to 50 miles from Louisville, because we were one day and one night making the march, and there must have been a halt. The cavalry complained of scarcity of water, of the hard road, and the terrible dust and drought. Elizabethtown is about half way between Munfordville and Louisville.

Question. If the strength of the United States force at Louisville and their condition as to effectiveness would have made their defeat almost certain or have very greatly jeopardized them in the event of an attack by the rebel army under Bragg what do you think would have been a judicious disposition of that force, considering that the Army of the Ohio was advancing toward Louisville by the road you have just described?

My advice to General Nelson, and therefore my opinion at the time, was to give an order early in the morning of the day we are speaking of for the evacuation of the place and the crossing of the river (we had on hand some 800 wagons—to load these down with provisions; we had already loaded some steamers to proceed to Brandenburg with a million and a half of rations), to have all the troops formed and the wagons drawn out at sunset, move down the river in the direction of the Portland pontoon bridge so as to reach in front of it a little after dark; then, instead of crossing the river, to make a forced march by West Point with these wagons and our entire force to Elizabethtown or to such a point as where we should meet the advance of the Army of the Ohio, there to unite with General Buell, distribute our rations to his army, fall upon the rear of Bragg in case he turned toward Louisville, and there destroy him; in case we should drive him up in the angle between the Ohio and Kentucky Rivers, defeat and capture him entirely if possible. That was my opinion and advice at the time, which I notified General Wright and General Buell of as soon as they arrived in Louisville. I believed it to be a certain movement and would have secured the entire rebel army.

Cross-examination by General Tʏʟᴇʀ:

Question. Was General Wright there at that time?

No, sir; I notified him that I had given this advice as soon as I saw him. I begged Nelson very hard by talking to him several hours and one time I felt sure he would do it. I felt the movement would be a successful one. The rebels had commenced their deviation in the direction of Bardstown. Our spies at Shepherdsville and in the direction of Lebanon Junction had informed us that they were striking off toward Bardstown. We had some considerable cavalry that I advised should be pushed out on the Shepherdsville and Bardstown roads as a curtain to cover our real movement. There would have been scarcely any hazard or risk and it would have been impossible for them to have reached us. I was in hopes by this movement to entice Bragg to move directly upon Louisville. Had he done so he would have found nothing in Louisville for his army. We had already shipped everything of value, and (the order not being understood by any one but myself and the commanding generals) he would have found nothing, for the families had all day to remove their valuables. I believe Bragg would have regarded the order as a *bona-fide* order to evacuate the place and cross the river. In that event I could see no good reason for his not approaching Louisville. At any rate it occurred to me that it would be some days before he would understand the movement and be enabled to develop it, and that would give us time to complete our junction and make such organization as might be necessary, move up by New Haven, and cut him off from any possible retreat in the direction of Harrodsburg or Danville. These are the dispositions and movements I should have made had I been in command. We had planted upon the opposite bank of the river some heavy guns. We also had some few gunboats, with two or four 11-inch guns, and with these the city could have been made perfectly untenable to any troops that attempted to occupy it.

Question. In anticipation of such a movement as you have described, or of a possible reverse, if it had been determined to await the attack of Bragg's army at Louisville, and considering that the Army of the Ohio was out of supplies, was it judicious or not to order supplies to Brandenburg for its use if necessary?

I deemed it of vital importance.

Question. Is or is not the country between the road which you would have followed from Louisville to the mouth of Salt River and the road on which the enemy was moving of such a character as would have enabled you to make that movement with perfect safety?

I deemed it so. The object of throwing the cavalry out was not to fight a battle or to head off a column, but to intercept information carried by spies, of which there were thousands in our midst giving information every hour. My order was to intercept everything they found going in any direction. I never deemed the enemy could reach us till we arrived in the vicinity of Elizabethtown, and then it would be a very hazardous movement for them, one that I would rather court; for General Buell could have taken them in flank and have cut them in two. The country is a rough, tumbled-up country. The spurs of Muldraugh's Hill run off and form cuts and ravines that are almost impassable.

Question. Is there any road at all by which an army could pass from Bardstown directly to the mouth of Salt River?

No, sir; not to my knowledge.

Before the adjournment General Granger expressed a wish that his examination before the Commission might be conducted with as little delay as possible, as the exigencies of the service in his department and the necessity for his presence made it very desirable that he should be with his command.

Commission adjourned to meet February 17.

CINCINNATI, *February* 17, 1863.

Commission met pursuant to adjournment. All the members present; also the judge-advocate and General Buell.

General GRANGER'S examination continued.

By General BUELL:

Question. Up to the 25th September last what progress had been made in fortifying the city of Louisville against an attack of the rebel army?

At that date very little had been done. The work was commenced, I think, the day previous, and was carried on till, I think, about the 28th, when the trenches were completed.

Question. Can you state about what portion of the front remained uncovered by intrenchments?

On our extreme right, between our intrenchments and the river, there was a space left open of about one mile. I did not measure it, but that is my recollection. I think General Robert [S.] Granger, who was standing on the ground, thought that was about the distance. There was an opening also in about the center, near where General Gilbert had his troops posted. What that was I do not know or whether trenches were thrown up afterward when he arrived there, but for two or three days I know there was nothing done there. Again, on the extreme left was an open space of, I should think, half a mile, as near as I remember; it might have been a little more or a little less.

Question. You have stated the number of batteries that were at Louisville at this period; how many pieces would they embrace?

I think they were all six-gun batteries excepting one, which was a four rifled gun battery; that would make forty pieces.

Question. Do you know anything about the topography of the ground about Munfordville, whether as a military position it is very strong or otherwise?

I understand it to be a very strong position, particularly on this side of the stream.

Question. Do you recognize that in battles the strength of the position occupied by the army which acts on the defensive has a great deal to do with the result of the engagement?

Yes, sir; the army standing on the defensive and taking up its position of course must have many advantages over the one acting on the offensive, supposing their numbers anything like equal. The strength of the position may be such as to counterbalance the effect of the superior numbers making the attack.

Question. Is it recognized as a principle in military operations that, with equal prospects of success, circumstances may make it improper to risk a battle in one case when it would be advisable or even necessary to do so in another?

Yes, sir; I can suppose cases of that nature. In the first place it would be improper under those circumstances to risk a battle where you would jeopardize your communications, and again it would be wise to risk a battle where they were comparatively safe. It might also be wise to risk a battle if you had re-enforcements near at hand that could save you in case of a disaster, and very unwise and imprudent where there were no re-enforcements or assistance that could be brought to bear. A general might be forced to fight a battle under such circumstances perhaps to save his army from starving; it might be the last alternative. It might be imprudent again to fight a battle under those circumstances where in case of a defeat the whole country would be left open to the invading army, whereas by falling back they might defend themselves point by point until such dispositions might be made as to cope successfully in a better and stronger position and force the enemy to fight to disadvantage.

Question. Do you know anything about the condition of the Army of the Ohio as to supplies when it was following the rebel army toward Louisville and about the time that the rebel army was at Munfordville, in September?

Only by hearsay. I heard several general officers of that command in Louisville, previous to the arrival of the army there, and some that were with it, say that they had been for a portion of the time on half rations; that a part of the way they had been compelled to make forced marches on that account. Generals Crittenden, Wood, McCook, and Nelson, I know, told me they were very short of rations. I know that a requisition came from General Buell, for I saw it, that he wished four millions of rations to be sent by steamer to Brandenburg. The dispatch came when he was somewhere above Bowling Green.

Question. Do you know of supplies having been ordered to the mouth of Salt River to meet the army on its arrival there; and was it understood that that was necessary for the subsistence of the army?

Yes, sir. It had slipped my memory for the moment.

Question. With the supplies exhausted and the rebel army between it and its base what must have been the probable consequence of a repulse, or even a very serious check, of the Army of the Ohio in an attack upon the rebel army at Munfordville?

It must have produced a dissolution, breaking up, and capture of the Army of the Ohio.

Question. Suppose the Army of the Ohio to have been destroyed or disabled in this way, what would have been the consequence to the cause of the Government in Kentucky?

It would have been the loss of the State for six or twelve months to come; in fact it is hardly possible to foresee or foretell what would have been the real consequences. I do not see anything to have prevented the rebel army from crossing the Ohio River

Question. With a small garrison at Munfordville, the Army of the Ohio at Bowling Green, and the rebel army equal, or nearly equal, between these two points, and within 10 miles of the only road between them, and supposing it possible to throw a portion of the Army of the Ohio into Munfordville for the purpose of strengthening the garrison there against an attack by the rebel army or any portion of it, would such a disposition have been judicious or injudicious?

Does it suppose that the rebel army is concentrated?

Question. Yes, sir; concentrated or with the means of concentrating within twenty-four hours.

I should have regarded the movement or attempt to have thrown a partial force there as extremely hazardous; it would be a violation of one of the great principles of war to separate one's forces, which I have always fought against since this war commenced. I hardly see how it would be possible, supposing the two forces to occupy the position described, to have thrown a force into Munfordville, the rebel army occupying the road from Glasgow which runs nearly parallel with the pike. It would have been exposed in flank and liable to capture or to be cut to pieces at any point of the road. To have thrown it in by a detour would have made the distance so great that the rebel force would have reached there before it could.

Question. With the force that was being thrown into Kentucky by the Government about the time of Bragg's invasion, which would have been the most judicious and advantageous arrangement for the commander of the Army of the Ohio, coming from Tennessee—to have forced the rebel army still farther into Kentucky or to have passed it and left it in possession of Middle Tennessee and Southern Kentucky?

I do not understand whether you intend to hold Nashville, Bowling Green, &c., or to give them up.

Question. I leave those points garrisoned, but only with such garrisons as could be spared and yet preserve the Army of the Ohio with such force that it would be able to cope with the opposing army.

My opinion would be to oppose this army and not drive it into Kentucky, where they could get supplies, stores, and recruits. We see the consequence of a portion of this army getting into Kentucky, where they destroyed the railroad bridges, took a great deal of property, got some recruits, and furnished themselves with stores and supplies to get out of the State again. Another reason for passing this force would be that unless it was done they would be between the Army of the Ohio and its base of supplies, and they must be driven from the base or it must be reached in some other way. The movement made by Bragg is one almost without a parallel. Cutting loose from his base of supplies and skedaddling all over the country is something to which history scarcely affords a parallel, and it might well puzzle a general wishing to attack him to ferret out his movements. The supposition was that when he was cut off from his base of supplies we had him; but it seems he never lived so well as he did after he arrived in Kentucky.

Question. Would or would not the rebel army be in greater jeopardy in Kentucky, opposed by the forces that were being concentrated there to meet it, than in Middle Tennessee, where it was only opposed by a portion of that force?

Yes, sir; it would. Yet such is the nature of the country, that if the rebel army did not choose to stay in Kentucky there were several routes by which it could extricate itself, notwithstanding the Army of the Ohio and the forces already concentrated; that is, if they did not choose to stand and give battle.

Question. Mention those routes, if you please.

In the first place, if Bragg had crossed the Kentucky River he could then have united with Kirby Smith and passed out of the State by Pound Gap with safety. There is another route by which he did go out, and that I have never yet seen any means of preventing, and that is by Cumberland, Big Creek, and Walker's Gaps. By maneuvering adroitly I believe it was possible for him to have passed out not far from Lebanon Junction, perhaps taking Saloma and Campbellsville. At that season of the year, although they are dirt roads, most of them are tolerably good. He might even have gone out by the New Haven turnpike, he occupying a central position, in case the Army of the Ohio had been thrown farther to the right flank into the mountains and hills to his rear and left. The best three roads in the country were then in his possession. Had he come into Kentucky, however, and made a stand I regarded his destruction as certain.

Question. Did the previous arrival of Kirby Smith in Kentucky very much simplify and facilitate the subsequent movement of the rebel army under Bragg into the State, giving him in fact the advantages of two bases, the one from which he started and the one at the point of destination ?

Yes, sir; it facilitated him in more ways than one. In the first place, Kirby Smith held at bay all the forces that were concentrated here, preventing them from taking up a position on the verge of the blue-grass region or of uniting with or re-enforcing the Army of the Ohio. In the second place, Smith's army had already provided and placed in depot large supplies for Bragg's army on its arrival and was enabled to guard and keep them safe. The cavalry also of Smith's force destroyed and broke up a good deal of the Louisville and Nashville Railroad at the time of his entrance into the State. Had Smith's forces not preceded the advance of Bragg it would have been possible for us, with perhaps 35,000 to 45,000 men then concentrating in Kentucky, to have taken up a strong position below the fertile portions of the State, where supplies could be obtained, in a mountainous district, well adapted for defense, and might perhaps have held Bragg's advance till his forces were either half starved or till such time as General Buell could fall upon his rear. I do not believe that Bragg would have moved into Kentucky if Kirby Smith had not reached the State some weeks in advance. I do not think it would have been possible; at least it would have been one of the most fool-hardy and destructive movements he could have made. The movement of Smith, further, forced the evacuation of Cumberland Gap, making the route through it a safe one for his retreat.

Question. Have you studied the military topography of the country on either side of Dick's River and between Dick's River and the Kentucky River ? And, if so, please describe the character of Dick's River and the Kentucky River and the ground on either side.

I have some knowledge of it, sir. Dick's River is a small river, running nearly north, emptying into the Kentucky River about 40 miles above Frankfort. The stream is much like a gash through the country, with ragged, rough, precipitous banks, and the country extending back from it from 1 to 1½ miles is almost of an impracticable nature. There are only three crossings over it that I recollect. The lower crossing is on a line of road running from Harrodsburg through Dicksville and Bryantsville, crossing this stream between Bryantsville and Dicksville. The next crossing, ascending it, is what is known as the Danville and Lancaster Crossing. There is a crossing a little higher up, the name of which I have forgotten. The country after crossing Dick's River at the Harrodsburg crossing, and between there and the Kentucky River, is very rough, hilly, and full of ravines. There is some plateau land where Camp Dick Robinson was located. The only water that I recollect there is at Bryantsville, where there is a well or spring, but it is bad water, and obtained from Dick's River, I believe.

Question. Does that stream afford very safe protection to one army against an opposing army on the opposite side ?

Very strong on both sides; it is much stronger on the right bank than on the opposite side. It would be almost impossible to dislodge an army taking a position there, owing to the difficulty of crossing the stream. The bluffs and points where batteries could be planted would sweep the opposite approaches, and in high water it would be impassable. The river is subject to great rises during freshets of from 30 to 40 feet.

Question. With a stream like that of Dick's River, impassable except at very few points, as you have described it, and not requiring to be bridged on account of the water, is it in reality a hinderance to a retreating army or is it a protection and advantage to that army; that is, to an army in condition to maneuver and fight when necessary ?

This stream, from the nature of its banks and crossings, would afford great facili ties for a retreating army. It would only have to put out a strong rear guard to check the advance of the pursuing force, rush its artillery and train over, plant its batteries upon the most eligible points covering the crossings and approaches, move over its infantry and take position; it would be perfectly safe against three or four times its numbers. In a forward movement again it would be only necessary to leave a rear guard of moderate size to hold the crossing until the retreating army had made perhaps two or three days, while the pursuing one would be compelled to close up his troops, get them into position, and when his dispositions were completed the rear guard could pack up and move off safely, leaving the pursuing army two or three days' march in its rear. There is no point that I am aware of, either above or below for a long distance, where it would be possible to turn either flank of a retreating army.

Question. Suppose the rebel army at Camp Dick Robinson, and its retreat by either Somerset road or by the various roads through Lebanon and Glasgow cut off by the position of the Army of the Ohio at Danville and Perryville, what lines of retreat were then open to the rebel army?

There were two lines of retreat left open. From Camp Dick Robinson there is a good road leading first to Lancaster. From Lancaster there are two roads, one striking the Richmond and Cumberland Gap turnpike a little distance above Big Hill; the other struck this pike some 8 miles above that point, if I recollect aright. By taking this road to Bryantsville and availing themselves of the other two from this point it brings them on to the Richmond and Cumberland Gap turnpike. There is still another line left open: 8 miles, I think, in rear of Bryantsville is Hickman's Bridge, across the Kentucky River, a fine, large bridge In low water there is a ford a few hundred yards from it where infantry can cross. This places them on the route then into Central Kentucky. On the Nicholasville and Bryantsville turnpike, after crossing the Kentucky River, they can pass out by Lexington, Winchester, Mount Sterling, Owensville, and West Liberty, and so on through Pound Gap, getting over the Kentucky River. They can also cross at Tait's Ferry and Clay's Ferry and avail themselves of all the crossings, and then converge toward Mount Sterling and Winchester. These are the only two roads that are left open of which the enemy could avail themselves from Camp Dick Robinson in retreating from the Federal forces as described.

Question. Having crossed to the north side of the Kentucky River, could they also throw themselves upon the Tait's Ferry road and the Lexington and Richmond road, and in that way get on to the Richmond and Cumberland Gap road?

Yes, sir.

Question. With Dick's River, such as you have described it, running between Danville and the road from Camp Dick Robinson to Lancaster and thence on to Cumberland Gap, would the position of the Army of the Ohio at Danville have prevented or very seriously interfered with the retreat of the rebel army from Camp Dick Robinson toward Cumberland Gap by the way of Lancaster, supposing it to be employed to the best advantage to prevent that movement?

I do not see how it could (such is the nature of this stream) very seriously interfere with it, and my memory is that an army obliquing across the country in the direction of Richmond and Camp Dick Robinson is confined to one road, while the rebel army from Bryantsville has two, and I think three, roads. This stream is a barrier and a protection of the right flank of the rebel army in its movement. There are but a few miles of country there suitable or available for operations. I think about 25 miles would strike the rugged mountainous districts, where pursuit would be almost useless, and the stream of Dick's River heads very near to these mountains. Furthermore, the bridge in the vicinity of Crab Orchard I know was burned previous to that time. It was burned by Morgan in his first raid.

Question. Supposing the retreat of the rebel army by the road from Camp Dick Robinson to Lancaster and thence on to Cumberland Gap was certain to have been foreseen, what point would it have been necessary to occupy with the Army of the Ohio to intercept the rebel army in its movement, the Army of the Ohio moving from Perryville?

I should have posted it at Stanford, or even in advance at Lancaster would have been better; but I regard that as an impossibility. I think it would have been possible to have intercepted it and cut it off had the Army of the Ohio been posted at Stanford or 2 miles in advance to the east, where there is some water.

Question. Could it not still have crossed over from the Lancaster to the Richmond and Cumberland Gap road?

It could. I do not know what communications there are between these roads or what means there are of getting on this road from Stanford; my recollection is that there is a country road only. Supposing there is a good road from Stanford to Big Hill or some point above it, I think the distance the two armies would have had to march about that time would have been about equal, and a battle must have ensued for the road. If, however, there is no communication such as an army could move on, the rebel army retreating directly on the pike would be safe. I doubt, however, if the Army of the Ohio had been at Stanford or in advance of it whether Bragg would have attempted to retreat in that direction.

Question. Supposing the Army of the Ohio had taken a position at Stamford, so as to intercept the rebel army in its retreat through Lancaster and thence on to Crab Orchard and so on to Cumberland Gap, what would it still be at the option of the rebel army to do?

Cut off its communications and isolate it from its base.

Question. Could it also have retreated by the route through Central Kentucky and on the Lexington and Richmond road?

Yes, sir. The routes were still open.

Question. Have you had occasion in your official position to study the problem of throwing a force into East Tennessee from Central Kentucky?

Yes, sir. It is a matter to which I have given a good deal of study and reflection and abandoned it as impracticable.

Question. In the course of your investigations what have you learned to be the character of the country and its agricultural resources between Somerset and East Tennessee directly across the mountains?

The character of the country is altogether mountainous.

By General Tyler:

Question. Do you speak from personal observation?

No, sir.

Question. You have no personal knowledge?

No, sir. I speak from such information as I have obtained from officers who have been there and citizens who have resided there and from such facts as I gather from the geographical maps furnished us by the War Department. I have not explored or reconnoitered it in person. I learn the nature of the country to be altogether mountainous, rugged, broken, and generally sterile, producing but little. My knowledge of the roads is that they are almost impracticable for an army, and altogether so for four or five months of the year, owing to the high water of the Cumberland and its tributaries and to the soft, miry, clayey soil. I had occasion to examine it and study it very closely, as it was General Wright's wish to push in a force of some 15,000 men after the cavalry raid was made, in case the winter was open and it was found possible. General Carter (after his return from East Tennessee), Major-General Wright, and myself examined the subject with great care, and without a dissenting voice the project was abandoned as not being feasible. The reasons were that it was impossible, even if we could reach there with a force, to subsist it, and it was deemed very hazardous to place it on the other side of the Tennessee and Kentucky Rivers at that season of the year, when those streams were swollen. I do not think there are any pikes between, say, the point in Tennessee about Clinton (I think this is the first point at which we strike anything like a pike, and that, I *m told, is only a dirt road thrown up and drained on either side) from Somerset, Burboursville, Boston, and those points, which are starting points. There are no good wagon roads whatever at any season of the year. There are roads which wagons do travel, but the country is so very much cut up, so rocky and precipitous, as to render military operations there out of the question.

By General BUELL:

Question. Is personal observation usually considered essential for a knowledge of geography and are your sources of information those which are usually employed and considered satisfactory in the direction of military operations?

I have never heard or supposed that it was possible or necessary for a general commanding an army to make a personal observation of all the country his army might be called to pass over. The means employed are those I have mentioned, those that are laid down in military works, as obtained from maps, from residents, staff officers that may be sent upon such duties, spies &c. Such information by military men is considered—in fact it is the only information and is the best that can be obtained. I can imagine that upon a battle-field, or in selecting one, either for offense or defense, it is important for a general to see as much of the ground on which he has to place his troops as possible; but even then a commander has to rely upon the same sources of information I have referred to, and it is upon information obtained in this way that a general bases all his plans of march, campaign, and battle.

Question. Mention, if you please, all the general officers that belonged to the force that occupied Kentucky under Kirby Smith, as far as you have been enabled to learn?

I obtained a list from Dr. Irwin, medical director to General Nelson, who was taken prisoner at Richmond, and remained with our wounded some three weeks at Richmond and Lexington, but I have either lost or misplaced it. Those I can call to mind are Major-General Heth; McCown, brigadier; Cleburne, brigadier; Reynolds, brigadier; Gracie, brigadier; O'Bannon, brigadier; Boggs, brigadier; Morgan, brigadier; Marshall, brigadier; Buford, brigadier; Stevenson, I understand, is a major-general. I do not know that this list is complete. I think there were some four or five more, but these were those he met.

Question. Will the number of general officers, supposing it to be correctly ascertained, afford some criterion for judging of the minimum of the force; that is, the number of brigades and divisions?

Yes, sir; it should do so.

Question. Does it at all determine the maximum strength judging by the organization of our own forces? Are not brigades frequently commanded by colonels?

It would not be safe to base the maximum strength upon a calculation of that kind. In our own army, that I have served with, I suppose quite one-half of the brigades are commanded by colonels.

Question. I wish you, if you please, general, to make some calculation, upon certain established data, and place the result in evidence before the Commission. Suppose an army of 40,000 men, organized into seven divisions, each division with three brigades, and three batteries, averaging about five pieces to the battery, and each brigade containing four regiments of infantry—taking no account of cavalry at all—supposing each division to have a wagon train of 100 wagons, what length of road would it occupy in column, not on the march but in position to take up a march, and the intervals all closed—the smallest space that it can possibly occupy? Please answer the question in detail, general, giving the spaces occupied by a given number of men and the space occupied by the various kind of carriages and the space taken up by the prescribed intervals.

Commission adjourned to meet February 18.

CINCINNATI, *February* 18, 1863.
Commission met pursuant to adjournment.   All the members present; also the judge-advocate and General Buell.

General GORDON GRANGER'S examination continued.

To the concluding question on the record of Tuesday, February 17, General Granger replied as follows:

The question was as to the length of the column in marching order, consisting of 40,000 men, organized as follows: Seven divisions of infantry, twenty-one batteries, averaging five guns each, the divisions consisting of three brigades, each brigade consisting of four regiments, the number of men to each battery averaging 120; each division was to have 100 wagons. The total length of this column placed in marching order is 16 statute miles.

By General BUELL:

Question. Give, if you please, the data upon which you make this calculation.

The data upon which this calculation is made are these: Deducting first the number of artillerists gives the whole number of infantry. I have supposed that each man in his position preparatory to marching occupies a space of 22 inches; that each piece of artillery, with the artillery carriage, caissons, and forge, occupies a space of 14 yards; the same for each wagon; the intervals between regiments would be 22 paces, equal to yards; the intervals between batteries and battalions of infantry the same; the intervals between each piece about 2 yards. This is all reduced to yards and then converted into miles.

Question. Are these data prescribed by regulations and tactics in our service, and does the whole distance represent the smallest space upon which such a column could be formed for marching?

These are the exact data laid down, with one exception: the regulation fixes 20 inches; I have it 22, knowing that to be too small.

Question. Would it be possible for such a column to execute a march upon any ordinary road and preserve these intervals so as to occupy no more space in the aggregate than you have stated? If not, please state what would be the least average space that such a column in motion would occupy.

It would be impossible to move this column a half a mile preserving the intervals laid down as I stated. Upon an ordinary march and over an average road this column in the space of 10 miles would, in my opinion and with the best of troops, be extended from one-half to double its present length.

Question. What is the rate of travel per hour which results from the pace prescribed in tactics for infantry, and on a day's march what about will be the average rate of travel per hour of as large a column as we have under consideration?

The rate, as nearly as I recollect, laid down in tactics was 90 paces, consisting of 28 inches each, to the minute; the present rate is 110; also 160. At the rate of 90 steps a minute this will carry the soldier 2¼ miles per hour. At the rate of 110 it will carry him 3 miles per hour. With the movement of a column of 40,000 men, organized as the one we have under consideration, in my opinion it would require the best of management to move it at the rate of 2 miles per hour, and that with excellent roads. Over roads with breaks or ravines, where carriages might be detained, with so heavy a column, 1½ miles per hour for ten, or say eight hours, I should consider excellent marching.

Question. In the distribution of the 100 wagons per division I have supposed 3 to each regiment of infantry and 1 to each battery of artillery for hospital purposes (including ambulances); 2 to each regiment of infantry for ammunition, to make up, with what the soldier carries, 100 rounds per man. This makes 81 wagons to each division, leaving 19 wagons to each division for division, brigade, and regimental headquarters and for the troops.   Would it be possible for troops to move upon the battle-field even with a less allowance?

This allowance occurs to me to be the very smallest limits the troops should move upon the battle-field with.

Question. Would it be proper ordinarily for an army of this size, in anticipation of battle, to move from its depots with as limited an allowance of ammunition as 100 rounds?

No, sir; my rule has been to move with 300; General Halleck required 500 in front of Corinth, and our orders were that everything should be left before the ammunition wagons. I do not know whether this extended through General Halleck's army; it extended through the Army of the Mississippi.

Question. Supposing an army to be moved even a distance of 30 or 40 miles from its depots, about how many days' rations should it have with it to guard against the ordinary interruptions in its communications by accident or the operations of the enemy?

I would answer not less than from ten to fifteen. There are so many considerations to enter into as to what should guide a commander under such circumstances that it is hardly possible to give an answer that would be definite, as the nature of the roads, the nature of the country, the exposed or not exposed position of your lines of communication; but under ordinary circumstances the estimate I have made would be the correct one. Again, an army may be moving through a country where there is beef and other supplies which the troops may obtain.

Question. Even supposing that the army is moving through a country from which it can supply itself with forage, will it ordinarily be necessary to carry a certain supply along on every day's march, or at least carry the transportation that will be necessary to bring it into camp at the termination of the march?

It is usual and necessary to carry always from one to three days' rations, inasmuch as it is impossible to tell where your camp may be. I always endeavor to carry two or three days'; it facilitates the march very much and enables you to encamp where you please; whereas if you have no forage you may be compelled to make half a march or a double one.

Question. Will or will not these various requirements unavoidably increase very considerably the train of the army beyond that which we have given in this supposed case?

Yes, sir; it will nearly or quite double it.

Question. But supposing this minimum allowance for a wagon train, that is, the allowance that an army would unavoidably carry with it upon the battle-field, and supposing the minimum increase in the space which the column will occupy on the march beyond that which results from theory, that is, an increase of one-half, making the length of the column on the march about 24 miles, how many hours would it take to move this column from one point to another point 12 miles distant; in other words, supposing the advance of the army to march at 5 o'clock in the morning, at what time will the rear of the column get into camp 12 miles distant? You may suppose also that the column moves at an average rate of 2 miles an hour.

Is it supposed that this column moves on one road?

Question. On one road.

My estimate must be an approximation; it is that the column would get into camp about eighteen hours after the advance started. I had occasion once to time a column, on a pretty good road and marching well, of 7,000 men. This column had no wagons, but had——

General TYLER. Mr. President, I object to the general's explanation, as he has already answered the question, and this explanation is an after-thought, commenced some two or three minutes after the question is answered.

General BUELL. I request that the witness be allowed to continue and give the result of his experience.

After some conversation General Buell continued: If the investigation is to be interrupted in this manner I must request that the objection be placed on the record. I will venture to say that the question as it is put is pertinent, and the answer which the witness proposes to give is one from which every one present may derive information, if not benefit. I have no hesitation in saying that it would be proper to refer to experience derived from campaigns in this country, to the Italian campaign, or any other if necessary. I can derive information from it, and I have no doubt General Tyler himself might also.

(Conversation between members of the Commission, during which General Tyler withdrew his objection.)

The PRESIDENT. The question and any objection made to it ought as a matter of course to be entered upon the record, but where the objection is withdrawn I see no necessity for it.

General ORD. I wish to call your attention to one fact, namely, that these frequent interruptions of the witness by calling upon the recorder to read what he has written takes up more time than the answer would. This question has been read over five times, three times at the request of General Tyler himself.

The PRESIDENT. Any remarks of this kind should be made in secret session.

(Some conversation here ensued as to the precise point at which General Tyler withdrew his objection, during which General Buell arose to retire, previous to which he remarked:)

General BUELL. General Tyler objected to the testimony that General Granger was giving, when I requested, as I have stated, that he might be allowed to proceed and state to the Commission the results of his experience, but General Tyler continued his objection, and said that we might as well investigate the campaign of Italy and he may have referred to other campaigns. I then made the remarks that are on the record, but the general persisted in his objection. If these interruptions are continued I will ask the gentlemen of the Commission to say whether I have stated the matter correctly or not.

The court was cleared, and a discussion having ensued, it was finally decided that—

" The record following the answer of the witness is confused, owing to the recorder not having taken all the conversations which occurred, and the Commission is unable to agree on the words that were spoken, and therefore leave the record unexplained as it stands."

On the court being opened General BUELL said: Mr. President, I regret very much to delay your proceedings with personal matters, but they have not been of my seeking on this occasion; indeed, they are not on any occasion. In the explanation which I made to you before the court was cleared I made a statement of what occurred in connection with the objection of General Tyler to the answer which the witness was giving. I stated that General Tyler had objected to anything more than a categorical answer to the question which was put. I stated then that I gave reasons why the answer which the witness was giving was pertinent and proper. I stated then that I requested that the witness might be allowed to continue his answer. I stated also that General Tyler continued his objection to the answer. General Tyler then contradicted positively my statement that he had continued his objection. I believe he used the words "It is not true." I submit to you, sir, that it is not becoming the dignity of this Commission or of any member of this Commission that such scenes should occur, and I request that your record may be made distinct and positive on this point. I request that you may inquire whether my statement was correct; that you may consider among yourselves, and if you cannot agree, then that you may take the evidence of persons who were present as to whether the statement I made was correct or not. I am aware that this investigation is a tedious one; I am satisfied it is wearisome to every member of the Commission; it is unavoidably so to all of us. I have no desire to make it more so than is necessary. I consider the testimony which the witness was giving was proper and necessary in this investigation, and I have desired to bring nothing upon your record which I did not think proper and necessary.

General TYLER. I made the objection to the further answering of that question put by General Buell to General Granger, and the objection was noted, I believe, on the record. After General Buell made some observations to the court explaining the reason why he thought the question was a proper and pertinent one——

General BUELL. Allow me to interrupt. I do not desire any discussion between General Tyler and myself.

The PRESIDENT. (To General Tyler.) General, I must be allowed to say that, the record having been read before the Commission and fully canvassed in secret session, any remarks upon it are improper. If General Buell, to whom we are willing to extend the utmost courtesy, has been allowed to make a speech, if it may be so called, it is nothing but fair that General Tyler be allowed to make a reply; but for my own part I would suggest that at this point the court may be cleared, that it may decide on the question raised by the remarks of General Buell.

General BUELL. I would suggest that this is the proper course. If there are any remarks to be made by General Tyler I do not wish to hear them.

The PRESIDENT. If these remarks are to stand upon the record General Tyler has certainly a right to reply in open court.

General Buell here retired, and the court being cleared, General Tyler continued his remarks.

General TYLER. I withdrew my objection. General Buell, as I understood, subsequently asserted that I continued my objection after I had withdrawn it.

The following resolution was then adopted:

"The Commission are of opinion that the particular investigations requested by General Buell are foreign to the subjects legitimately before it.

"The examination of Major-General Granger will therefore continue."

On the court being opened—

General BUELL. I should like to hear all the record on this subject read from the time the witness was interrupted in his answer to the last question.

The PRESIDENT. The Commission have ordered that the examination should continue without further comment.

General BUELL. I wish nothing more than to verify the record of the remarks made by myself.

The PRESIDENT. At this time the object of the Commission is to proceed without further comment upon what has taken place this morning, and with that view I beg that you will permit the examination to lie over till you read the record from your own copy.

General BUELL. I am unwilling to be committed to a record made in that way; but if it is the decision of the Commission I have nothing more to say.

The PRESIDENT. That is the decision of the Commission.

General Granger continued:

some twelve or fifteen ambulances and two four-gun batteries, and taking a position about 2 miles from camp there awaited the approach of the column. The time in passing from the front to the rear was exactly two hours. It is upon this that I have in a measure made my estimate. At this ratio I have allowed twelve hours for the infantry and batteries to pass and six hours with a train. This answer is not given as a practical answer; it is given as a deduction from theory, from the fact that as the column is increased in numbers and its train in proportion it becomes more unwieldy and difficult to move. I do not know that any relative proportion where you increase the numbers and the consequent delay owing to this increase could be properly and accurately established.

Question. The calculation upon the data given shows that the army would make the distance in exactly the time stated. Do armies under ordinary circumstances march in this order when they are in the presence of an enemy, and how do you explain that under some circumstances they do make much greater distance in the aggregate?

In the movement of a heavy column in the vicinity of an enemy, to facilitate it in procuring water, camping grounds, fuel, forage, and also to avoid roads that are cut up by excessive travel, a commander would avail himself of all the roads lying parallel or nearly so or converging toward some common point of destination. If there was but one road, for convenience to his troops, facilities for camping, &c., he would divide it into two, three, or four bodies, moving them perhaps upon consecutive days. Thus divided upon the different roads or upon the same road, it is usual for these diminished columns to make the same distance or even greater distance in a much shorter period of time. This dispersion of troops, however, in the near vicinity of an enemy would be very injudicious. It would be necessary to keep them concentrated to prevent the enemy from falling upon them and defeat them in detail.

Question. Supposing the position of the enemy to be known, how close could the head of the column or army, moving on one road as we have supposed, properly approach that position before closing up its rear and putting itself somewhat in order of battle?

It will be necessary for me to suppose a case in order to give an answer to the question. If the country affords no cover, such as mountains, forests, streams, to conceal the approach of the army, and, again, should the enemy be on the alert, which the commander is supposed to know, keeping their front well reconnoitered and picketed, it would be extremely hazardous to move this column in the order described to within a less distance than 8 or 10 miles. At a point in this proximity it would be necessary at once to close up this column, and as fast as closed to form in order of battle, or at least to take position for a strong resistance until such time as the commander can close up his troops and make the necessary dispositions for battle. The nature of the country, the strength of the adversary, and his vigilance must always guide a commander in approaching an enemy in position. If he is satisfied that they have taken up their line of defense or line of battle and intend to give battle at that point, he may bring the head of his columns much nearer before deploying them. Should the country afford facilities to enable him to amuse or divert them by a powerful advance guard, he might bring them up to about two or three miles, and there close up and make his final arrangements for battle. Another fact that has much to do with this is points where water can be procured for the purpose of filling the men's canteens before going into action. In some instances it may be necessary to go near the enemy before deploying. The nature of the streams or springs may be such that but few men can procure water at the same time. A thousand considerations must influence the commander in movements and dispositions of this kind.

Question. Would the absence of water in sufficient quantity to suffice for an army any considerable time, say two or three days, sometimes prevent a commander from taking up a position which might have great strategic advantages and occupying that position for considerable time, during which the enemy may at his option give or avoid battle at that point?

If water could only be found sufficient for the use of the army at a distance of, say, half a day's march, it would be almost impossible in hot, dry weather to bring the troops in position in front of the enemy in a condition to fight a battle successfully. The absence of water might derange and perhaps destroy the best matured plan for battle, and at the same time afford corresponding advantages to the enemy. The advantages spoken of are that we can either give or refuse battle to the enemy.

Question. Suppose the army which we have taken as an example move toward an enemy whose position is not certainly known, who may be within 15 or 30 or 40 miles, and who is supposed to be at all times ready for battle, would it or would it not ordinarily be proper or necessary to move the army by short marches and in the compact manner you have supposed in answering the previous question?

It would be necessary to keep the troops well massed and in hand, in order to be ready at any hour for any emergency. It would also be necessary to see that they were not exhausted or worn-out by long and fatiguing marches.

Question. Would or would not a march of 12 miles, continued for several days in this manner, be a very serious tax upon the physical endurance of the troops?

Very great indeed. The rear of the column, amounting to nearly one-half, would find but little time for rest or repose. In a march of this nature, with the number of men supposed, the advance of the column would be in camp several hours before the rear would have moved; this would bring it in late at night or next morning or some time next day, according to the nature of the road and the country. The result would be, for the rear of the column, that night would be turned into day, and in a very few days, with all the changes by alternating divisions, placing one in front one day and then another and then another, after a march of one week the commander would find it necessary and important for the rest of his troops to lay by from one to three days.

Question. State, if you please, if you have received a military education, and what experience you have had in military service, especially in the movement of large bodies of troops.

I am a graduate of West Point; graduated in 1845, and have been in the Army since that time; have been brigadier-general nearly twelve months and major-general about six months. Served through the campaign of General Scott in Vera Cruz and the termination of the Mexican war; had a command for the last year varying from 5,000 to 25,000; served with a large army at the siege of New Madrid and Island No. 10, with an army, I believe, of some 30,000, as near as I recollect, and commanded a division at that place. Was also at the siege of Corinth, under Major-General Halleck, with an army of about 120,000; subsequently commanded two divisions until I came to the Department of the Ohio; most of that time have commanded the forces in Kentucky of 18,000 to 26,000. During this service enumerated, with the exception of a few months in Kentucky, have been on active duty in presence of or near the enemy.

Cross-examination by the JUDGE-ADVOCATE:

Question. Would not the officers connected with the Army of the Ohio who accompanied that army from Chattanooga to Louisville have better opportunities for estimating the strength of Bragg's forces than the officers in Louisville?

Yes, sir; up to a certain time they would.

Question. If a majority of those officers having a better opportunity of making an estimate, some of them actually within the enemy's lines, fix that force at from 35,000 to 40,000, are your sources of information of such a character that you could venture to contradict them?

General BUELL. I object to the question, sir, for the reasons which I gave when a similar question was put to Brigadier-General Smith.

(The court was cleared; after discussion it was decided that the question be put.)

The WITNESS. I do not regard my estimate as to the strength of General Bragg's army as any contradiction whatever. Their opinions were based upon the best sources of information to be obtained; so are mine also. Instead of a contradiction it is but an honest difference of opinion.

Question. Were your sources of information such that you can inform the Commission what officers commanded Bragg's right wing at Munfordville?

I cannot now positively call to mind, though I knew at the time perfectly well; my recollection is that General Polk commanded, but I am not positive.

Question. Do you know or do you recollect the officers commanding his left wing?

I did know at the time. I suppose that with a little thought it will all come back to me. It is a question of memory upon names which I am unable to recall.

Question. Were Hardee, Buckner, Anderson, Johnson, Polk, Cheatham, Withers, and Jones the officers having command under Bragg?

I recollect Hardee being mentioned as commanding one of the wings, I think the right; but, as I said before, I cannot be positive. I recollect the names of Polk, Buckner, and Cheatham very well, but as to Jones and Anderson being in connection with this army I am not so positive.

Question. Supposing the general officers under Bragg should number eight, what number would you estimate Bragg's army at upon the same principle that you fixed the number of Kirby Smith's in your examination-in-chief?

I do not think I enunciated any principle with respect to Kirby Smith's force. The question arose about general officers who were there. I think I stated distinctly that my information came from prisoners, officers, soldiers, and citizens. I also obtained that information from officers of General George [W.] Morgan at Cumberland Gap about that time. With reference to the strength of Bragg's forces, it was obtained in the same way, and in addition to this from men who were captured belonging to different regiments. We had in our possession prisoners and sick from one hundred and seventy-seven regiments of infantry; the number of cavalry I do not recollect, but it was a large cavalry force. I also had information from that army from very intelligent deserters—officers who had deserted. Putting all those things together, you have the data upon which my answer is founded.

Question. If you had representatives from one hundred and seventy-seven regiments of Bragg's army, upon what principle did you fix that number at 55,000?

That does not necessarily fix the number at 55,000; it is only corroborative, as I regard it, of my estimated strength, after having it enumerated by those and by others who had opportunities of judging. And again it strengthens my assertion of my estimate very much; having representatives from so many regiments, it is almost positive proof that they had that number of regiments or skeletons of them; they were represented in his force.

Question. With that fact alone, of your having representatives from one hundred and seventy-seven regiments, what estimate could you make of the force under Bragg?

A very fair way to arrive at it would be to ascertain how long, or about how long, these regiments had been in service, their strength at the time of entering into service, and my own experience of the decimation of the original number, of what it would be up to a certain date, taking always our own forces as a standard, in the way they are thinned out by battle, sickness, disease, &c. Those who are experienced in the military service are capable of forming something like an approximate estimate not varying very materially from the truth.

Question. In making that estimate you calculate upon the fact that you have representatives from every regiment in Bragg's army?

No, sir; not necessarily. We may have prisoners from one-quarter, one-half, or four-fifths; it is fair to suppose that we would have representatives from nearly all. After their hard marching, the battle of Perryville, and the haste with which they got out of the country, more or less men would be left behind, broken down and sick, perhaps from every regiment.

Question. Were those representatives of the regiments taken previous to or subsequent to the battle of Perryville?

Both previous to, subsequently, and at it.

Question. Your estimate, then, is of the entire force in Kentucky, and not that directly under Bragg between Bardstown and Chattanooga?

My estimate was of the force that Bragg entered Kentucky with and had in front of Louisville.

Question. What was the number of the Army of the Ohio at the time it was concentrated at Bowling Green?

I only know what I have been told by officers of that army, and my recollection of it at the time is it was about 42,000; but I have not thought of it or spoken of it since particularly

Question. Can you understand why with the forces such as you state them General Bragg gave up so strong a position as Munfordville and hurried off to Bardstown?

The only reason I have ever heard given was that he was out of subsistence and none could be procured there; that he moved up to meet trains sent by Smith to supply him.

Question. Did he not meet these supplies at Bardstown?

I do not know; from the fact that he tarried there I gather that he did.

Question. Was it not as possible to get those supplies from Bardstown to Munfordville as to march the army from Munfordville to Bardstown?

It was not so safe to do it; in fact there was a force at Shepherdstown and also at Salt River; our cavalry was also scouting in that direction. He would have run great risk of their being cut off. The bulk of Smith's army, I think, was on the other side of Kentucky River; perhaps a small guard with those trains.

Commission adjourned to meet February 19.

CINCINNATI, *February* 19, 1863.

Commission met pursuant to adjournment. All the members present; also the judge-advocate and General Buell.

General G. GRANGER'S examination continued.

By the JUDGE-ADVOCATE:

Question. What was the number of regiments under Bragg at Munfordville and what did those regiments average?

I have already stated what I know in regard to the number of regiments; as to what they averaged it is impossible for me to tell. In order to do it I should have to know the number of batteries and the amount of cavalry he had. My recollection is that he had some thirty-eight regiments of cavalry.

Question. The regiments you spoke of were those of the combined forces of Kirby Smith and Bragg, were they not?

No, sir.

Question. Is the Commission then to understand from your statement that Bragg had one hundred and seventy-seven regiments?

I do not know that I could be clearer on that point. It may be necessary to explain in brief that I obtained this information from the provost-marshal at Louisville and from General Boyle and others; but whether they stated that they were Bragg's regiments exclusively or Bragg's and Kirby Smith's combined I do not remember at this time. It was spoken of in a rambling conversation, and it may have been that they meant so. I have heard others speak of it, but I do not know that that point was ever settled.

Question. Are not the rebel regiments as a general thing more reduced by sickness than our own?

I believe they are, sir. This is the experience of those I have seen, such as prisoners captured, &c. At Island No. 10, where we took about 7,000 prisoners, which I helped to load, I remember the regiments were very small in consequence of sickness, desertion, and other causes.

Question. In the extraordinary movement made by Bragg, cutting loose from his base of supplies and not only living upon the country he invaded but marching into that country in the face of a well-organized and efficient army, do you not recognize that an army of 30,000 would be still more efficient than an army of 60,000 for such a purpose; and if with 25,000 or 30,000 he could accomplish so daring a movement, would it not be impossible with twice that force?

The supposition of this question, to my mind, is clearly erroneous. In the first place Bragg had two bases. The best information that I have is that he left Chattanooga with twenty days' rations at or near Chattanooga. After leaving that base of supplies he marched with the evident intention of reaching his new base of supplies already established in Kentucky by Kirby Smith, where he had every reason to believe abundant supplies would be found on his arrival there. The greater the number of men Bragg moved with in the face of a well-appointed army the greater his security, the more audacious his movements and the more able he would be to harass and annoy this well-appointed force; and unless the Federal force was handled with great care he could keep it in constant jeopardy, while with this smaller force of 20,000 men he could be pushed before it in all directions either by the whole force or by a fraction of it. The larger force would enable him to offer battle and with fair prospects of success, while under but few, if any, circumstances would it be wise or judicious to risk a battle with one-third of the number supposed.

Question. In what respect does my supposition differ from that of yours in answer to a question put to you on the 17th, which reads as follows: "The movement made by Bragg is almost without a parallel. Cutting loose from his base of supplies and skedaddling all over the country is something of which history scarcely affords a parallel; and it might well puzzle a general wishing to attack him to ferret out his movements. The supposition was that when he was cut off from his base of supplies we had him, but it seems that he never lived so well as he did after his arrival in Kentucky"?

The difference that I observe is this: Bragg made no effort that I ever heard of to keep open the communications with his base at Battle Creek or Chattanooga; nevertheless that was only one of his bases, but he did not choose to lose it for the reason that he had supplies in advance. On arriving again in Kentucky this again became his new base, and after a time he cut loose from that, and in neither case did he attempt to keep his communications open.

Question. Where did you learn the fact that Bragg carried twenty days' supplies from Chattanooga?

I learned it from the statements of his own men, as well as from our own officers.

Question. What number of wagons did he allow to a brigade for the purpose of carrying provisions from Chattanooga?

I do not know that I ever heard. I heard General McCook say something about the length of their train, but about what it was has escaped my memory. The impression made upon my mind was that it was a train of considerable length, but that they moved with less transportation than ourselves. General Wood or General Rousseau told me of the hard time they had in getting their train over Barren River.

Question. Did Generals McCook, Thomas, Wood, or indeed any officers of the Army of the Ohio tell you that Bragg left Chattanooga with more than ten days' provisions?

I do not know that I have heard so from any one of those you have mentioned, but certainly a number of them told me so. I think in a conversation in General Buell's headquarters at Louisville, when, as near as I remember, General Thomas, General

Nelson, General Wright (I believe), also, I think, General Rousseau, Mr. James Guthrie, and several other gentlemen, also General Finnell, were there, it was stated by one or by all that he did leave Battle Creek, in front of Chattanooga. That conversation made more impression on me than any that I recall. From some surgeons of Bragg's army who were prisoners I have had the same statement; also from officers who were left behind. I asked them if they had full rations, and they replied that they had no coffee, and I think they said they had but half rations of flour and salt meat. They had some beef that they drove along, and the cavalry picked up some beef and sheep in the country About their living better in Kentucky than they ever did before, that was their statement—that they had provisions in greater abundance and of better quality than they had found before or at any time during the war.

Question. General, I will ask you to tax your memory and state to the Commission precisely what General Thomas did say as to the amount of provisions taken from Chattanooga by Bragg.

It will be impossible. I cannot state that General Thomas said it. I am sure General Buell said it, and I judged it was the universal opinion, because there was no dissenting voice. It seemed a settled fact. It was one of those consultations or councils that occasionally took place, and where I took no notes as to what any individual said; it was one of those conversations, having only a momentary importance, where we were reviewing the history of the whole thing—the point started from, the length of time on the march, comparing the routes and about what distance the two armies had marched. It would be impossible to state whether General Thomas or General Rousseau said it, but this was the conversation in which the fact was stated. Gen Buell I am sure stated it on this occasion; how he obtained the knowledge I do not know. I suppose he obtained it as we all obtain such information. I had heard the same thing before.

Question. What time did Bragg take to march from Chattanooga to Sparta?

I do not recollect, sir.

Question. Did the officers of the Army of the Ohio inform you that he arrived at Sparta with his army very much distressed from fatiguing marches and lack of supplies?

Not that I recollect.

Question. Did they not inform you that from Sparta to Bardstown he lived upon the country he marched through?

Only so far as I have mentioned. They obtained only partial supplies—beef and mutton; and, further, I did not get that information from our own officers, but from Bragg's officers and men.

Question. Were your opportunities and means of obtaining information as to the force and position of Bragg's and Kirby Smith's army superior to those you had of obtaining information of the force and position of General Buell's army at that period of time?

At what period of time or between what periods of time?

Question. At the same time at which you are estimating the force and position of Bragg.

My facilities for ascertaining the number of Kirby Smith's force, I judge, must have been quite equal to if not better than those of General Buell up to his arrival at Louisville. I further judge that my means and facilities of information whereby to judge of the strength of Bragg's force after its arrival at Munfordville, or perhaps a little sooner, were about the same as his own. What information he had I believe he communicated to me freely; he had spies out, so had I, and sometimes I communicated with him two or three times a day and he with me. We had information from prisoners, spies, and deserters who were coming in; besides we had men in our employ who visited their camps, who would go and stay three or four days at a time. Previous to the arrival of Bragg's army of course General Buell's facilities must have been greater than those of any other officer, as he was in that immediate section of country. I will now add that I supposed I was the first officer that reported the movements of this army from the time it left Tupelo. I was then in position to know more, being at the time in command of the advance guard of the whole army of Corinth, from 25 to 40 miles in front of Corinth. Through spies and deserters, while at Booneville, Blackland, Rienzi, and Baldwyn, I was the first to learn that that army was moving in the direction of Chattanooga, and so reported it through General Rosecrans to the commander-in-chief. I took great pains to ascertain the number of troops, dates of departure, composition of the army, and its destination. The movements of the rebel army and the approximate numbers I reported from day to day in the months of July and August last. These facts gave me more early data, and perhaps quite as reliable, as to the strength of the expeditionary force which left Tupelo for Kentucky. This furthermore led me to watch with great care this movement to Chattanooga and all its subsequent movements till it reached Kentucky.

Question. You fix the strength of Bragg's army at 52,000 to 55,000 and Kirby Smith's at 18,000, making in all about 73,000. At what do you fix the force General Buell had before its arrival at Louisville and what was its strength when it left Louisville to meet Bragg?

I think I stated yesterday that my recollection of General Buell's force when concentrated at Bowling Green, after he left Nashville, was 42,000. I asked Colonel Fry, his chief of staff, not long since about what force they left Louisville with. He replied he could only tell me in round numbers, in consequence of the hurry of organizing the new troops which were coming in, and which was proceeded with day and night. He put it in round numbers at 65,000 to 70,000—70,000 was my impression. He added further, as a reason why he did not know exactly, that before they got accurate returns the battle of Perryville had been fought, and that on their way a great many had straggled and broken down from hard marching and want of water, and never would be accounted for, owing perhaps to the officers being new and ignorant of the mode of making out returns. Colonel Fry's statement I judge to be most reliable, though I have heard it stated by others, who were officers of the line and not of the staff, that it was 90,000, and by some 100,000.

Question. Did you understand him to say that those 70,000 included Sill's division?

Yes, sir; the entire force.

Question. Would not the returns, under the circumstances you have mentioned, be very interesting in giving the full force of the Army of the Ohio in its march from Louisville to Perryville?

I have so stated. I will qualify it by saying that about the returns of the old troops there would be no difficulty; it was with the new re-enforcements, which had but just arrived.

Question. Are not the officers more numerous in the rebel army in proportion to the number of men than in ours?

I will state that as to their organization I am not sufficiently familiar with it to give a positive answer. From their own officers, and from intercepted orders, letters, &c., I judge their regimental and company organizations to be the same as our own, but I am satisfied they have more staff officers than we have—major-generals, lieutenant-generals, and generals. I have been told that by themselves, and it has been corroborated by orders and military communications of theirs I have picked up.

Question. As a general rising of the people was anticipated in Kentucky, might not the excess of officers that accompanied Kirby Smith be accounted for by the fact that they were sent to organize the new levies?

I think it reasonable to suppose that this might account for any surplus of officers, if there were any. Having been stationed in the midst of the people where they attempted to raise troops, I had opportunities of knowing something of the organizations that were attempted there. Such troops as were organized were officered as far up as the grade of brigadier by gentlemen who were found in Kentucky on their arrival there. I heard it stated that Buckner came in expecting to raise a division or more of Kentuckians during his stay there, and that Mr. William Preston was to have a command that was to be raised. The only brigade I know of their raising, and that was a very feeble one, was officered by General Buford, who was in Kentucky on the arrival of the Confederate forces. One of the difficulties they found in Kentucky, I have ascertained, was this; that Bragg wished to fill up his decimated regiments with recruits obtained in Kentucky rather than form any new organizations until that was done. This statement was made by people there and by those who started off and returned. It was set forth as one reason why there were not more joining them; they were willing to make up organizations of their own, but they were not willing to fill up regiments in the Confederate Army just where they were required.

Question. Do you know that the Army of the Ohio left 18,000 [?] wagons at Bowling Green, and was therefore unencumbered by trains?

I cannot answer as to Bowling Green. I heard it stated that General Buell had left his transportation; I think it was between Munfordville and Louisville; I am not certain as to the point. I think it was after Bragg had changed his course and deviated in the direction of Bardstown that a brigade or division was ordered to fetch it up. They were making a forced march, and thought it better to lose the transportation than not to head Bragg off for Louisville or reach there the time he did. I only remember it being stated that the transportation was left somewhere on the road, and that it came in some two or three days after the arrival of the army.

Question. Was a junction formed by Kirby Smith and Bragg; and, if so, where and on what day?

The best information I have is that Kirby Smith marched from Harrodsburg on October 9, and became the rear guard of Bragg's army about the time of its arrival at Camp Dick Robinson. About this junction I never have been able to ascertain; I have not seen any one who seemed to know. There appeared to be some bewilderment or doubt about it. It was said that a portion struck off by Somerset and another portion followed in the rear of Bragg. I have made a great many inquiries and made a great deal of investigation, but no one seemed to know exactly what day, and I came to the conclusion that on or about the 9th or 10th of October he moved from Harrodsburg in the direction of Bryantsville and Camp Dick Robinson, and my belief is (though I have never been able to solve the thing by sufficiently reliable information to say what he did or what he did not do) that about that time he became the rear guard of Bragg's army. My reason for believing that he formed the rear guard is from the complaints of the citizens along the route. I have seen a great many of these people along toward Cumberland Gap, Barboursville, and London. They said that he murdered a great many; there were sixteen Union men hung at Rockcastle River, which Smith has the credit of doing. They spoke of this as being so very different from his conduct when he entered Kentucky. Then he met the people with smiles and affability and gave them more protection than they wanted; but after he failed in being able to obtain recruits he turned his troops upon them through his disappointment at finding that he was to be driven from the State.

Question. Supposing your calculation in your examination-in-chief to be correct, that Bragg's and Smith's army consisted of 73,000 men, with their guns, wagons, ambulances, &c.; these armies combined commenced their retreat from Camp Dick Robinson on the morning after the battle of Perryville; how long would it be before the rear guard of the army would leave the camp and where would the advance be at that time?

As to that it is hardly possible to suppose they were combined.

Question. In making that supposition that there were 73,000 men, upon the best of your caculation what would your answer be to that question?

Do you want a mathematical calculation as to how long it would take 73,000 men to get out of Camp Dick Robinson?

Question. Yes, sir.

I gave eighteen hours as a theoretical deduction, which is as far from practical as one could possible put it. I also stated that as you increase the force it becomes more unwieldy in a much larger proportion than the real increase of numbers. The head of such an army as that would reach Cumberland Gap before the rear would get out of Camp Dick Robinson. From Camp Dick Robinson to Cumberland Gap I believe is a distance of about 115 miles. In the forced marches they made it would take them forty-eight hours. They did not move, however, in that way. When Smith reached Camp Dick Robinson, Bragg's force was all out and on different roads.

Question. Did they separate on different roads before they reached Lancaster?

I am unable to answer that positively; the map does not show the country roads.

Their trail was 3 to 5 miles wide, through fields, country roads, and everything. The great object they had in view was to get into the mountains of Big Hill, where they would be safe from pursuit. The position they sought was very strong by nature. The appearance of the country and the statements of citizens who reside at Richmond and between there and Big Hill seem to show that they went off like a flock of sheep every one on his own hook, but that the rear kept in good order.

Question. What roads did they take after leaving Lancaster?

I learned that they took the great pike to London; thence to Barboursville; thence to Cumberland Gap. It was possible after reaching Barboursville, perhaps, from London that a portion of them went through Big Creek Gap and Rogers' Gap. Those gaps are very good for infantry and light-loaded wagons and very bad for anything else. The main body, however, passed through Cumberland Gap.

Question. Did not a portion of that army go through Lowell by Gum Spring and Valley and Big Hill?

I am unable to say. It is some time since this occurred, and I have had my head so full of other roads, streams, and other details that the particulars have escaped me. The supposition of yours that there were 73,000—my answer being on the record—it might be inferred that I considered there were 73,000; from this, however, we must deduct for loss from sickness, deserters, battle, and losses at Perryville, and from all I learn these could not be less than from 12,000 to 15,000 men. Kirby Smith left a good many sick in Frankfort and quite a number down on his march. This force, from the time of his entrance into Kentucky to his exit, instead of being augmented, was reduced several thousand. I sent off myself from sick alone some 3,000 or 4,000 that he left at different points.

Question. An army of, say, 60,000 men marching upon one road from Harrodsburg to Camp Dick Robinson, would Dick's River be no obstruction had that army been attacked by the Army of the Ohio while crossing?

If the army was attacked while crossing it certainly would be an obstruction, but had this army marching from Harrodsburg a few hours' start and its columns organized it would be a great advantage.

Question. General, please look at the copy of the letter marked A and state to the Commission if you know anything about it.

To the best of my recollection this is a copy of a letter shown me by General Nelson in Louisville some time about the 23d of September, the date of the letter.

(The letter is read to the Commission.)

Question. Was your advice to form a junction with the Army of the Ohio made previous to the reception of that letter or subsequently?

I am unable positively to state, but I think it was previous; what makes me think so was the little progress we had made in intrenching; we had done very little, and my advice was to drop it and call in the men. The intrenching was carried on very rapidly, but at the time I was advised to make this movement we had done very little. I urged as a further reason that by going on with the work we should only complete the trenches for the enemy's use against ourselves.

Question. Where was the Army of the Ohio, do you recollect, at the time you made your proposition?

I could not name the point. My calculation was this: leaving Louisville at dark, we would be enabled to reach Elizabethtown, by a forced march, some time late in the next day or night, and that General Buell on the advance of the Army of the Ohio would reach it at about the same time as we would. I do not remember, in fact I do not know, that I knew the names of the camping grounds; it was at such a distance that I deemed it possible and probable that both armies would come into Elizabethtown about the same time and form a junction there.

Question. Had your advice been acted upon, what would have prevented Bragg taking our army in detail, taking your raw recruits first?

The relative position of the three armies—the Army of the Ohio, the Army of Louisville, and Bragg's army—was such as to render it almost impossible, owing to the nature of the country. It would have been necessary for Bragg to have passed directly across General Buell's front in order to place his army upon our line of march, or to make so large a detour around by Bardstown pike as to give us more than ample time to form a junction. Had Bragg attempted this he would have been directly between the two armies and in the angle formed by Salt River and the Ohio, and from this position it would have been impossible to extricate himself. There are no roads suitable for movements of an army between the Salt River and the Bardstown pike, after leaving Louisville a few miles, till you approach the neighborhood of Elizabethtown.

Question. Had this junction been attempted what would have prevented Kirby Smith occupying Louisville and destroying the canal, &c.?

Nothing particular; that is just what I should have wanted him to have done had he come to Louisville; that means we would have forced him to a junction. We were afraid that Smith would try to keep open the route to Frankfort, in order to make his own escape. Had Smith moved on Louisville and had the junction of our forces been completed the entire rebel army, including Bragg's and Smith's, would certainly have been bagged in the angle formed by the Kentucky and the Ohio. By Smith's remaining in Central Kentucky he could have escaped at any time either by Pound Gap or Cumberland Gap, or as Bragg moved up he would have passed out of the State at New Haven.

Question. Bragg, you say, left Battle Creek direct for Glasgow; what object had he in view in making that march?

Well, sir, he had two objects. In the first place, there were two objective points, which he undoubtedly amply considered, and one of the great objects he was in hopes of accomplishing. The objective point was the city of Nashville and the second Kentucky. By this flank march of his he evidently intended, if possible, to force the evacuation of Nashville. Should he not succeed in this, however, he would move directly for Kentucky, thereby drawing the great bulk of our forces in that direction. Had General Buell been forced to evacuate Nashville for want of subsistence and supplies the first objective point was carried, the result being to relieve Tennessee of the possession of the Federal troops. Fortunately, however, we had both rations and force sufficient to hold Nashville and at the same time take care of Bragg. Had General Buell remained at Nashville with his entire force, supposing that he had subsistence, Bragg would have moved on his communications into Kentucky and taken Louisville and Cincinnati, the consequence of which you can all judge.

Question. Had Bragg made a successful stand at Munfordville would he not have accomplished both objects?

For him to have made a successful stand at Munfordville it would have been necessary for General Buell to have offered him battle. I believe I stated previously that it would not have been judicious for him to have done so, but to have passed Bragg and drawn him from his stronghold rather than to fight an unequal battle. Had Bragg overthrown General Buell or held him in check it certainly must have caused the destruction of his army. As to whether he had force sufficient to return and besiege Nashville and at the same time carry on operations in Kentucky is very doubtful. Under those circumstances General Buell would have been forced to have passed him, which had he done or attempted to do Bragg would have been forced to move. At the time General Buell got in his rear the order of things would have been reversed and Bragg's army would have been destroyed.

Question. You say it is contrary to the maxim and science of war to divide your force. Which was better, to leave 20,000 in Nashville or to throw 10,000 into Munfordville?

You must develop that question. I must say it is not clear.

Question. Which would be better, to divide the Army of the Ohio between Bowling Green and Nashville or between Bowling Green and Munfordville?

Well, with Nashville in General Buell's rear and Bragg on his flank and rather in advance, certainly it would be much safer to leave a force in Nashville than it would to send forward a force of 10,000 men to Munfordville, when Bragg's army was much nearer to it than he was himself with his main body. In my judgment 20,000 men are better anywhere than 10,000.

Question. Suppose General Buell had promptly massed his army at

Lebanon or Gallatin directly after Bragg passed out of the Sequatchie Valley at or near Sparta, would he not have covered Nashville and blocked Bragg's progress into Kentucky by way of Munfordville?

It occurs to me that this is supposing an impossibility. The supplies of the Army of the Ohio were in Nashville, it being its base. Bragg occupying the road spoken of, could it have been possible for him to have massed them there? I should say yes, though I do not see myself how it could have been done. To march on a road to a certain point it is very necessary to get possession of it before the enemy does. Whether that was possible, not being there at the time, I am unprepared to say. I have heard it stated, though, by officers of the Army of the Ohio that the Army of the Ohio was forced by the Nashville route for two reasons: first, for supplies, and, second, to place it in a defensive condition, as it was not their object to give it up if it could possibly be avoided. Furthermore, those routes are as follows: The direct route, the one that Bragg took, was a chord of a circle, while the route via Nashville was the circle itself, the latter much longer.

Question. Do you recollect the names of those officers of the Army of the Ohio who gave you that information?

Colonel Fry I know was one, and I think General Crittenden; but it is almost impossible for me to call names. I have talked with the general officers upon this campaign and subject a great deal, but I cannot say positively whether with this or that one. I talked a great deal with Colonel Fry, because he knew as much, perhaps more, than most of them.

Question. Allowing Generals Thomas, McCook, Negley, Wood, and other general officers who participated on the field and in all movements of the army to be equally proficient with yourself in the science of war, would not those officers be better able to explain the movements, plans, &c., of the campaign in Kentucky and Tennessee than yourself?

I must say that I do not see the advantages on either side particularly. They should be quite as much so, but I do not know particularly that they should be any more so. It does not follow, Mr. Judge-Advocate, neither is it important or necessary for an officer to tread over every acre of ground or to be there on the spot with an army to comprehend the plans of the campaign, the movements, or the reasons for those movements. Some of the worst descriptions of battles and campaigns I have received were from persons who were all through them. It depends a great deal upon the commander. Some commanders are always calling councils of war; others act upon their own judgment, give their orders, and hold themselves responsible for them. General McCook told me on one occasion that he never knew what General Buell was going to do. Again, the duties of a commander on the field with the troops are very arduous, or should be, if he takes good care of them.

Question. Are not the actual circumstances attending a campaign so varied and expanded and the maxims of war so numerous that a supposable case gives little or no light?

The rules and maxims of war, combined with experience such as a commander should have, may be fixed and infallible, and all the great disasters that have happened to armies have originated in nineteen cases out of twenty, I will venture to say, by deviating from them. When a general knows his front of operations, the configuration of the country, the strength of the enemy, and his capacity as a commander, the strength and quality of his troops, he is almost perfectly prepared to foresee and anticipate everything material that should take place. Those circumstances which appear to the casual observer or unprofessional soldier to be accidental are but the incidents and circumstances brought about by the different movements, such as feints, threats, marches, counter-marches, and many of the ways which are at the disposal of the contestants.

Question. Was not Bragg's extraordinary march in and out of Kentucky in violation of the more important maxims of war; and was not the attempt to meet him by the strict adherence to such maxims of war a hinderance to our success?

The march of Bragg was certainly a very extraordinary one. After he found he could not force the evacuation of Nashville he certainly did violate, to a certain extent, some of the fundamental rules of war; but he had in justification the fact of his newly established base in Kentucky. As to the adherence to the rules of war by the Army of the Ohio, it was certainly the only thing that saved it. If General Buell had pursued directly after Bragg he would have found himself in a short time many miles from any supplies, following in the wake of an army that had devastated and stripped the whole country in front of him. He would have lost Bowling Green for certain, perhaps Nashville, and perhaps his army. There is no doubt, although Bragg made a successful raid into Kentucky, that he certainly lost ten times more than he accomplished. He lost his reputation for one thing, and was removed from his command for a time; and I suppose the round trip cost him not less than 20,000 men, besides the wear and tear and destruction of his material of war. It is true, at the same time, it put us to a great deal of inconvenience and set us back in our operations, but I do not see how it advanced him. I think he would have done better to have remained in front of General Buell, kept in position there, and worried his communications, with a fair prospect of success in starving him out before the railroad could have been opened and kept open or before there was enough water in the Cumberland for transportation.

By General TYLER:

Question. When did Bragg's army leave Tupelo?

To the best of my knowledge and recollection it commenced the movement on July 8.

Question. By what route did it move and to what point?

The infantry, artillery, carriages, pieces, &c., moved down via Mobile by rail to Chattanooga; the cavalry, artillery, horses, and trains moved off across the country, passing through Tuscaloosa for one point; it then went direct to Rome, thence to Chattanooga.

Question. What time did the advance of Bragg's army arrive at Chattanooga?

His first advance met with a detention of some kind on the railroad. My best recollection is that it was about July 18. The two engineers on the road told me when they left and the number of cars; this was one of the most reliable sources of information.

Question. What was the amount of force that left Tupelo in July?

From information that I received from these men and the spy I had there, who was a railroad man, my estimate was 58,000 to 60,000. Everything was ordered to go away except the little force of Price and Van Dorn. I presume they did. Most of the cavalry force was left behind about that time. I think they sent over about 4,000 cavalry during the month of June. About this time they were very busy getting in conscripts to take the place of those troops, and for which they were holding meetings all over the country there. A small division of this force, under Breckinridge, was diverted subsequently; I think it went to Baton Rouge and Vicksburg; but that I understood was only some 7,000 or 8,000 men.

Question. Did I understand you to say that all the rebel forces that were at Corinth, with the exception of Van Dorn's and Price's divisions and this division of Breckinridge's, were sent to Chattanooga?

So I understood.

Question. Were the divisions of Van Dorn and Price in Mississippi the same they had at the siege of Corinth?

I understood all the Missourians remained behind, with a portion of the Texans and a portion of the Arkansians. The divisions were not the same; they took from them some Texas and Arkansas troops, but how many I am unable to say. The force at leaving (of which I had good opportunities of learning, for they were very careless about the camp) that Price and Van Dorn had was only from 16,000 to 18,000 men.

Question. I understand, general, from your testimony that all the troops that were at Corinth, the conscripts that were drawn in between the abandonment of Corinth and the time this army moved, with the exception of 23,000 men, were sent to Chattanooga?

Yes; that was my information.

Question. If Bragg had occupied Louisville would he not have destroyed the canal at that point; and, if so, what would have been the effect upon the transportation above the Falls and on the military operations then and since in progress?

I presume he would have destroyed the canal. I do not know enough about the nature of the Falls and the canal there to give an intelligent opinion. I only saw it once in passing through it; but I know nothing about the depth of water at low or high water. I know Beauregard recommended it to be destroyed as a compensation for the sinking of stone ships in Charleston Harbor.

Question. Would not the destruction of that canal cause the entire cessation of all transportation except at high water?

From the fact that there is a canal there I presume it would.

Question. Were you stationed at Louisville any length of time?

About two weeks, I think.

Question. At what time?

I think from about the 16th or 17th of September till the 1st or 3d of October.

Question. You never considered the value of that canal in reference to the military operations of the country or the defense of Louisville?

I did not consider it in reference to the defense of Louisville nor as to the effect it would have upon military operations. We had more than we could do to organize our troops and get our intrenchments in order.

Question. Between the 16th or 17th of September and the 1st to the 3d of October did you receive or see any dispatches from General Buell proposing or asking any co-operation on the part of the forces in and about Louisville with his military operations then in progress?

No, sir; except the paper marked A, presented to me this morning, respecting the sending of rations as far as Brandenburg.

Question. General, do you know of your own knowledge that Kirby Smith's army ever passed through Harrodsburg?

No, sir.

Question. You state in your testimony that they did pass through. Please give the sources of your information.

I obtained it from spies, residents of the country, prisoners, and from wounded and sick left behind.

Question. You stated in your examination this morning that Kirby Smith's army you understood formed the rear of Bragg's as it retreated from Camp Dick Robinson, although you did not know that it made a junction. What inducement would they have had to pass through Harrodsburg?

Because the direct and best pike leads through Harrodsburg. I call to mind, however, that a small portion of it for some reason did pass down on the north side of Kentucky, but it is a roundabout road, and came over in the direction of Hickman Bridge, crossed the country, and came into Camp Dick Robinson; but the great mass of it moved as I have described.

Question. Do I understand you to say that the direct road from Camp Dick Robinson is by Harrodsburg?

Yes, sir; the best route. The pike goes down by Lawrenceburg; thence to Harrodsburg; thence to Dicksville; thence to Bryantsville. It is the great traveled road and the only one suitable for the army.

Question. Is not the point Salvisa, on the Harrodsburg road, the point where they would naturally attempt to reach Camp Dick Robinson by the shortest road, and is not Harrodsburg some miles in advance of Salvisa?

Some little distance. I do not remember the number of miles just now. I never heard and can see no reason why they should go there except to come back again on the main road; they would get into a road that was almost impracticable, steep, and rugged.

Question. Did or did not the greater part of Bragg's army pass over Dick's River by a pass in the neighborhood of Salvisa?

Yes, sir; they passed over the only crossing there is. It is the only place to cross from Harrodsburg through Dicksville direct to Bryantsville.

Question. Do you mean us to understand that there is no practicable road passing from Salvisa to the crossing that Bragg's army made over Dick's River except by the way of Harrodsburg?

It is the only crossing of Dick's River, and the best road is to go through Harrodsburg. If you are at Salvisa on the left or Danville on the right you strike the same place and come into the common road.

Question. Just look on the map and fix your eye on McMinnville and Sparta. Suppose Bragg's army to be concentrated at Sparta and General Buell's at McMinnville and the destination of both had been Glasgow, which would reach Glasgow first, supposing transportation, &c., to have been equal?

Taking the roads as they are, Bragg seems to be several miles nearer Glasgow than the troops at McMinnville.

Question. Supposing General Buell's army had ten days' advantage, which should have reached there first?

Why, General Buell, of course.

Question. How did Bragg and Kirby Smith subsist their armies in Kentucky and Tennessee? Was it by voluntary contributions or by levies made on the citizens?

I understand Bragg's supplies and depots were at Columbus and Atlanta, just in his rear, on the line of railway; from these points he drew them, whatever the Confederate Government supplied. Whether they seized, impressed, or purchased them I am unable to say. Whenever I have been near them they took supplies and the people said did not pay for them. Kirby Smith's army, up to its departure for Kentucky, was supplied from the same depots. He carried enough to last him till he struck the blue-grass region of Kentucky; there he had his subsistence and paid for it in Confederate money. From Union people he took at his own price and in his own way.

Commission adjourned to meet February 20, 1863.

CINCINNATI, *February* 20, 1863.

Commission met pursuant to adjournment. All the members present; also the judge-advocate and General Buell.

JAMES B. BECK (a witness for the defendant), being duly sworn by the judge-advocate, testified as follows:

By General BUELL:

Question. State your name, if you please, and place of residence.

James B. Beck; Lexington, Ky.

Question. State, if you please, what information you have of the movements of the rebel force under the command of General Breckinridge in October last, and what reasons you have for believing that that force was expected in Kentucky about the time of the battle of Perryville or soon after.

I have no information from General Breckinridge personally; my information is all from his wife and friends, who purported to have information as to his arrival there. From their statements to me he was confidently expected with his force about the time of the battle of Perryville. I went to Richmond, Ky., with his wife, upon what she believed to be reliable information that he would meet her there on the Saturday or Sunday after the battle. He did not meet her, and I returned to Lexington. She went South with a friend.

Question. Were your former relations with General Breckinridge and his family such as to give you peculiar facilities for obtaining information upon a subject of that kind?

They were. I had been his law partner for a number of years. His wife visited my house frequently and seemed to rely upon me to advise her as to her husband's movements, and I supposed he would have communicated with me in relation to his family at least. Mr. Keene Richards, one of his aides, as I understood, called to see me. I did not see him, but he saw Mrs. Breckinridge and communicated his information to her, as she told me.

Question. State what your information was, if you please.

In substance that she must meet him in Richmond or Danville, and that he desired her to be with him; that he expected to be there in a very short time. This was a week or two before the battle of Perryville.

Question. State, if you please, whether this information to her was to the effect that he desired her to be with him or that he desired her to go South with him, and whether the information indicated that the object of this meeting was to go South at that time.

It did not; it was that he desired her to be with him.

Question. Did this information indicate that General Breckinridge was coming alone or that he was coming with his troops?

With his troops.

Question. State what information you had as to the strength of the column he was expected to bring at that time.

He was said to be a major-general, and his troops were variously estimated at from 10,000 to 20,000.

Question. Were you satisfied yourself that General Breckinridge, with his command, was expected in Kentucky at that time, and have you any reason now to doubt that he was expected and actually on his way?

I confidently believed that he was expected in Kentucky, and am satisfied from information that he was actually on his way.

Question. Did the people of Kentucky regard the invasion of the State by the armies of Bragg and Kirby Smith and the additional force that was expected under Breckinridge as a temporary raid, or did they regard it as a formidable effort to get possession of the State and secure it to the cause of the rebellion?

I think all regarded it as a formidable effort to hold permanent possession of Kentucky if possible.

Question. State, if you please, what steps were taken to inaugurate the provisional government under Confederate authority and what other steps were taken to enforce Confederate laws within the limits of the State during that invasion.

Richard Hawes was inaugurated as provisional governor by General Bragg at Frankfort. I am unable to give the exact date, further than that it was on a Saturday, and I think the Saturday before the battle of Perryville. Several members of his council were in Lexington claiming the authorities conferred upon them by the provisional governor. I saw three or four of them just before his inauguration. In answer to the other branch of the question I will state that they required Confederate money to be taken like any other currency, and claimed the right to punish by imprisonment or otherwise those who sought to depreciate it. They claimed also the right to punish persons who discouraged enlistments.

Question. Did they claim the right to enforce the conscription act and was that act enforced in any case?

I do not think it was in the neighborhood of Lexington. General Bragg issued an order, the purport of which I do not distinctly remember, threatening to enforce it at some early day in the future. That is my recollection of it, but I cannot now give the substance of the order.

Question. Were the people of Kentucky generally so provided with arms and munitions of war as to be able to increase very materially the efficiency of the invading army if they took part with it?

A great many men in my part of the State had rifles, shot-guns, and pistols; there were few farmers but had one or the other.

Question. What was your information in regard to the supply of these articles brought into the State by the rebel forces during their occupation of it?

I saw what appeared to me to be immense numbers of guns at their depot in Lexington; in fact at several depots they had large numbers. Where they obtained them I do not know, but they certainly had a large supply at Lexington during their occupation of it.

Question. Have you any means of making an accurate estimate?

I have not.

Question. Had they also supplies of provisions and other necessaries for an army at these depots?

They had at these or other depots. They kept their guns in one and their supplies in others.

Question. Were the guns you speak of in the depot in boxes or were they loose?

Mostly loose when I saw them. I saw some in boxes with the tops off, but not a great many.

Question. State, if you please, about the size of the rooms in which these arms were stored and in what manner they were stored; that is, as to the space that they occupied. I want to arrive at an approximate estimate of the numbers, if I can.

Their principal depot was what had been a livery stable, on Short street; the guns were laid in the stalls. One side of the stable was filled with guns lying flat and piled from 5 to 7 feet high; six or eight of these stalls being so filled when I saw them. Large numbers were standing about the door and the central portions of the stable, and were being divided out at times to different companies of volunteers who were being organized to take part. I saw also at the different depots where companies and regimental organizations were attempted to be perfected guns cleaned up and put in order, ready to be delivered to the men.

Question. About what time was it that you saw these arms stored in this way?

First shortly after their arrival, in the early part of September, 1862, and I saw them occasionally till within a week or two before their departure.

Question. Had the quantity seemed to increase or diminish when you saw them last?

I did not observe with sufficient accuracy to answer.

Cross-examination by the JUDGE-ADVOCATE:

Question. What time were you in partnership with Mr. Breckinridge and when did that partnership terminate?

It commenced the first part of 1855 and terminated about the time he was a candidate for the Presidency; I think in 1860.

Question. Was there any formal dissolution of that partnership?

General BUELL. I object to the question, Mr. President, as not being relevant to the matter under investigation.

The JUDGE-ADVOCATE. The witness has undertaken to state the movements and intentions and force of Breckinridge in reference to Kentucky at that time. For the purpose of showing how accurate and reliable his information could be he states himself in his examination-in-chief that he had been the law partner of Mr. Breckinridge. For the purpose of testing precisely what was introduced, as to how far his acquaintance with Mr. Breckinridge would justify his statements to this Commission and a knowledge of his movements or intentions, I ask this, because I think it is pertinent.

General BUELL. In calling upon the witness to state the relations which afforded him facilities for obtaining information in regard to the movements of General Breckinridge I did not base it upon business relations, but upon former social associations more particularly. I do not think that the business relations of General Breckinridge and Mr. Beck have any bearing upon this testimony; it was more particularly his relations with the family of General Breckinridge that I meant to inquire into.

(The court was cleared; after discussion it was decided the question be put.)

The WITNESS. We agreed to dissolve and did dissolve. There was no writing either in the formation or dissolution, and I soon after formed a partnership with F. K. Hunt, my present partner.

Question. Where was Mr. Breckinridge at the time you dissolved that partnership?

I saw him in Washington and spoke to him of my intention to form a partnership with Mr. Hunt, in which he fully concurred, we both agreeing that our partnership was at an end. I formed an actual partnership with Mr. Hunt after my return, and wrote to Mr. Breckinridge informing him of it, but I do not remember if he replied to me or not.

Question. Was Mr. Breckinridge in Lexington subsequent to that conversation in Washington?

Yes, sir.

Question. What was the cause of the dissolution at that time?

His political engagements were such that he was unable to attend to his law business, he being then Senator from Kentucky.

Question. How frequently was he in Lexington subsequent to that conversation in Washington?

He spent most of his time in and about Lexington from the time Congress adjourned in August, 1861, till September or October, 1861, when he went South.

Question. What became of the business after the dissolution?

I attended to the closing of it.

Question. Have you had any communication with him since of a business character or in reference to your former partnership?

I have had no communication with him since he went South directly. I have said to gentlemen going South that if they saw him to tell him how his family was; nothing more.

Question. Was not that dissolution of partnership really caused by his going South or by his intention of joining the rebel army?

No, sir; it was closed long before I had the least suspicion of any such thing and I think before the war broke out.

General BUELL. With the consent of the judge-advocate I should like to ask the witness one other question?

The JUDGE-ADVOCATE. I have no objection, with the consent of the Commission.

Question. (By General BUELL.) Do you know of any arms having been in the State Arsenal or stored elsewhere at the time of the invasion by Kirby Smith, and do you know whether the arms which you have stated to have seen in store may or may not have been part of the same?

I have no personal knowledge on that subject.

Question. (By General TYLER.) Are you in favor of the execution of all the laws passed by Congress and of all the orders issued by the President of the United States and his subordinate military officers, so far as they have come to your knowledge, for the suppression of the rebellion commenced at Fort Sumter and since carried on by the rebel Government at Richmond, of which Jefferson Davis is President?

General BUELL. I object to the question, Mr. President. It is totally irrelevant to the matters under investigation, and I shall not give my consent, whatever that may amount to, to continue to make this investigation of political opinions. The question has that tendency; it is in every sense irrelevant and improper. The witness may be a firm and devoted adherent of the supporters of the rebellion or he may not be; I do not know anything about it at all. I have no acquaintance with him. I saw him for the first time this morning, and have not conversed with him five minutes in all. He appears here only because I happened to hear that he had this information in regard to the movements of General Breckinridge.

The JUDGE-ADVOCATE. I do not propose to say anything as to the merits or demerits directly of this question; but certainly the question cannot be successfully objected to on the grounds General Buell placed it upon. It is no test of political opinion whatever as to the manner of conducting a government. Properly defined, the word politics cannot possibly enter into the queston whether the Government should exist or not. Whether his answer would affect his credibility as a witness or not I cannot say.

General BUELL. The term may not be well chosen. I do not pretend to say that it is. I use it in its popular sense, however, and not in any sense in which it can be interpreted as expressing support or opposition to the laws of the Government. I still contend that the question is irrelevant, because it has nothing to do with the validity of the witness' testimony, nothing to do with the matter under investigation, and nothing to do with the credibility of the witness.

General TYLER. I ask this question on my own responsibility, and I must confess that on the answer to it will depend the weight that I give to the gentleman's testimony.

The court was cleared for secret session.

On the court being opened the witness was informed that the question would be put.

The WITNESS. I will ask the court if I may be allowed to enter my protest on the record, that my answer to the question may not in any event be used against me.

General DANA. I think it would be right to advise the witness as to the power of the court to enforce an answer to any question put to him by the court.

The PRESIDENT. I will admonish the witness that if he believes his evidence will criminate him, and being a lawyer he will understand the meaning of this, he has a right to decline answering it upon that ground.

The WITNESS. I am not prepared to say that it would criminate me, in my opinion.

The PRESIDENT. As to the power of the Commission to compel an anwer to its questions from any witness, whether he be citizen or soldier, I have no doubt. The witness in this instance may understand, however, that this court has no criminal jurisdiction nor can a prosecution be begun or entertained in it; neither is it intended that answers given before it by witnesses shall be used as a foundation for any prosecution in any court of competent jurisdiction. It is proper to say in addition that it will be well for the witness to consider how his answer may affect his relations with his neighbors if his residence should be in a secession neighborhood.

The WITNESS. With that explanation I am prepared to answer.

General BUELL. Before the witness proceeds with his answer I wish to enter my formal protest against the question and all questions of that character, the tendency of which is to deter and intimidate my witnesses, both in appearing before the Commission and in giving their testimony. There is nothing more certain than that it has no earthly bearing upon the matter you are investigating, and there can be no charge made that it affects the reliability of a witness or the validity of his testimony. I repeat to you that it has the tendency to intimidate witnesses before the Commission. There will be a vague apprehension of something—nobody knows what—in the minds of many men when such questions are put to them before this Commission, the object and the authority and the legal sanction of which are not understood anywhere.

The preceding remarks of General Buell having been, according to rule, read aloud by the recorder, who read "intention" instead of "tendency," General Buell proceeded :

I will suggest from this particular case the importance and justice of an examination of the record that is made of the remarks of all persons. You see in this instance how important an error was made by the recorder. The day before yesterday I was refused the privilege of revising the remarks I made before the Commission.

The PRESIDENT. I beg your pardon, general ; it was no refusal of the privilege. It was intended, as has been the rule, to allow you to have a copy of the proceedings to examine afterward, and in this particular case to make any correction in your remarks if any were required. It was not intended to debar you from the privilege accorded you by the Commission, but only to expedite the proceedings of the court.

General BUELL. Will you allow me to remark on the inconvenience of correcting a particular word after it has passed two or three days ? There is a difficulty, too, in remembering what was actually said ; besides in the case referred to the Commission had already decided against the privilege of correction before I proposed to have the record read for emendations.

The PRESIDENT. The Commission required the record should stand as it was ; nevertheless you will remember, general, I said you could have the record to make any alteration it might require, and that privilege you have now.

General SCHOEPF. There are only two instances in which such questions were asked; consequently the statement of General Buell that it intimidates the witness is not a fact.

General BUELL. Does the Commission suppose that if questions of this kind are put it will not be known abroad and that witnesses will not be apprised of the fact?

The PRESIDENT. I will call your attention to the impropriety of speaking to a question decided by the Commission.

General BUELL. I am forced to reply when opposition is made to the protest I have made.

The PRESIDENT. All such questions would be in order before the question was decided by the Commission.

General TYLER. I do not see what right General Buell has to dictate to the Commission. Our proceedings are taking a very remarkable shape.

General BUELL. I think so myself. I may cite the question itself as evidence of it.

The PRESIDENT. That remark is a reflection upon the proceedings of the Commission, and I must be permitted to say I think uncalled for.

General BUELL. I do not mean to cast any reflection upon the proceedings of the Commission, only upon the question itself.

The PRESIDENT. The remarks of General Buell upon the proceedings of the Commission are, I think, uncalled for.

The remarks of the president having been again read to the witness, he proceeded:

The WITNESS. After what is recorded I desire to say many of the acts of Congress and acts of subordinate officers I have not read. I think I have read most of the orders of the President himself. Some of those I have read are not, in my opinion, calculated to promote the purposes for which they were intended, and I therefore do not agree with the policy of them. Others I deem unconstitutional, and therefore oppose them. I approve of all constitutional measures to restore the integrity of this Union, as I greatly desire the attainment of that object. I should like to be permitted to say that I have obeyed all laws, State and Federal, to the best of my ability and intend so to do, taking no part against the Government in any form in this rebellion.

By General DANA:

Question. At what time did Keene Richards, the emissary of Breckinridge, seek you in Lexington and have an interview with Mrs. Breckinridge?

I understood it was shortly before the battle of Perryville; how many days I am not prepared to say. He saw Mrs. Breckinridge, as I understood, in Scott County, where Keene Richards formerly resided.

Question. Was Lexington at that time within the lines of the United States forces or within those of the rebels?

I am not able to answer that question distinctly. It was not occupied in force by either side. That is my best recollection.

Question. At what time prior to the battle of Perryville did you know of the whereabouts of Breckinridge?

I did not know personally of his whereabouts at any time. Shortly before that, reports were reaching us of his approach frequently, but those reports were very conflicting.

Question. According to the best information that you have, where was the rebel force under him at the time that Keene Richards made his appearance at Lexington?

Between Chattanooga and Knoxville, was the best information I have.

Question. Were you informed about that time as to whether any other rebel emissaries were visiting Lexington or that vicinity?

There were a great many in that vicinity at that time, and reports of such were frequent, but I cannot specify them with any distinctness.

Question. Did you see any of these rebel emissaries yourself?

Do you mean emissaries from Breckinridge?

Question. Yes, or from other generals?

I frequently saw men during the occupation of the country by rebels about Lexington, who were coming from the South, from Bragg to Kirby Smith, from Marshall to Kirby Smith. A good many of them had been formerly citizens of Kentucky with whom I was personally acquainted.

Question. Prior to the time of the occupation of the vicinity of Lexington by the rebel forces and during the time that Lexington was supposed to be within the Union lines did you see any persons in that vicinity whom you knew to be from the rebel lines?

I do not think I did. I have no recollection of seeing any. I heard of them, but I had no conversation with any and I don't think I saw any.

Question. When Keene Richards visited Lexington was he an officer in the rebel service?

He was said to be on Breckinridge's staff; in what capacity I do not know.

Question. Did you derive any information from the dress he wore at the time he came?

I did not.

Question. Was it a military or citizen's dress he wore?

I had no information on the subject.

Question. Do you know whether any Union men at Lexington at the time these rebel emissaries made their visits to the vicinity of Lexington took measures to send information to the commanders of the Union forces of those visits?

I do not know.

Question. Is it your opinion that any Union man in Lexington would notify the commander of the Union forces if he knew of the visits of the rebel spies or rebel officers in disguise to his vicinity?

In my opinion there were some gentlemen in Lexington who stood so well in the opinion of the commanders of the Union forces that they could with propriety have done so and I suppose did; but I have no knowledge on the subject.

Question. Had you such information of the strength of the forces under Kirby Smith as would enable you to give a decided opinion of it?

I have not. I have heard it variously estimated, but cannot speak with any certainty myself as to its strength.

Question. Was the whole of his column supposed to be at Lexington at any time?

I think not. His advance passed through Lexington and beyond before other portions of his column reached the neighborhood.

Question. Do you think the whole of his column passed through Lexington or through that vicinity?

I suppose nearly all of it came into the vicinity of Lexington; but I do not know.

Question. What is the estimate of intelligent men of that part of the country as to the strength of Kirby Smith's column?

I should say not far from 15,000 is the estimate of the most intelligent men I have spoken to of it.

General BUELL. Although the rebel forces may not have been actually at Lexington——

The PRESIDENT. Allow me to interrupt you. I wish the judge-advocate to read the resolution adopted lately regarding the order of examination of witnesses.

General BUELL. It would be proper for me at this time to urge my right to re-examine the witness upon any new matter introduced either by the judge-advocate or any member of the Commission. I ask the decision of the Commission upon this question, and I do it without argument.

General SCHOEPF. I would like to know what is General Buell's idea as to what new matter has been introduced in this cross-examination.

The PRESIDENT. It is inquired of you, General Buell, by a member of the Commission, what is the point upon which you wish to examine the witness.

General BUELL. What I ask is a decision upon the principle and not upon the particular question I wish to put. They are different questions entirely.

(The court was cleared, when the decision of the Commission was reaffirmed, and on the opening of the court was announced to General Buell.)

General BUELL. Mr. President, as the right to cross-examine this witness upon the new matter introduced has been denied me, I will suggest to the member of the Commission who examined last an inquiry which may further the object of his investigation. I understand that object to be to ascertain under what circumstances emissaries of the rebel authorities were permitted to visit the vicinity of Lexington, as appears to have been done in the case of Keene Richards spoken of. I will therefore suggest to the Commission this question, and, if proper, I propose the question be put.

General TYLER. I would like to know what the question is before it is put.

The PRESIDENT. General Dana did, ask one or two questions touching upon new matter, and though I am of opinion that both questions and answers were very unimportant, I think in this case it would be nothing but fair for the question of General Buell to be put by General Dana.

General ORD. Before the question is put I propose that the judge-advocate read the ruling of the court.

The PRESIDENT. Will General Buell suggest the subject of the question?

General BUELL. Although the rebel troops may not have been actually in possession of Lexington at the time of the visit of Keene Richards to which you have referred in your testimony, nevertheless were not the rebel troops in possession of all that district of country and had they not virtually the entire control of it? That is the question.

The PRESIDENT. I understand General Buell wishes that question to be put by General Dana.

General BUELL. Yes, sir. But that is not the new matter upon which I proposed to examine the witness. That was in reference to the strength of Kirby Smith's force and which was entirely new matter.

General TYLER. I move that the court be cleared.

(The court was cleared. The question of General Buell is adopted by General Dana and put to the witness.)

The WITNESS. They had all that portion of country east and south of Lexington. That north and northwest of it was, I might say, debatable ground.

General BUELL. If now the Commission or any member of the Commission would accept the suggestion of another question, I have no doubt it would have a tendency to bring out information that has seemed to be desired.

The PRESIDENT. I would suggest, general, that you have the question written.

The question was as follows:

"Does your estimate of 15,000 as being the strength of the rebel force under Kirby Smith in Central Kentucky include the column under General Stevenson which came in somewhat later? State also what you understand to have been the strength of that column."

The WITNESS. The estimate I spoke of had no reference to General Stevenson's column. That column, as I understood, did not approach Lexington, but went from some point in Madison County toward Danville or Harrodsburg.

Commission adjourned to meet February 21.

CINCINNATI, *February* 21, 1863.

Commission met pursuant to adjournment. All the members present; also the judge-advocate and General Buell.

G. W. DOWNING (a witness for the defendant), being duly sworn by the judge-advocate, testified as follows:

By General BUELL:

Question. State your name, if you please.

George W. Downing.

Question. Are you a resident of Kentucky?

Yes, sir; I reside near Lexington.

Question. Did you see General Breckinridge, of the rebel army, in the month of October last? If so, please state where.

I did, sir; I saw him in Knoxville.

Question. State what information you received from General Breckinridge in regard to the movement of his division into Kentucky shortly previous to that time.

General Breckinridge stated to me that he was on his way to Kentucky, and within a days' march of the Kentucky line, when he received orders to return to Knoxville.

Question. What was the date of this interview with General Breckinridge; according to the information given you, about what time was this movement taking place and when was it countermanded?

I could not say exactly the date. I think it was in the latter part of October. I could not exactly state at what date the order was countermanded. He had received orders and his army had turned toward Knoxville before the other army had got to Cumberland Gap, but I do not exactly know the time.

Question. Where was his division at the time you received this information?

His army, or the most of it, had moved to Murfreesborough. A portion of it was gone on. While he was waiting to get upon the cars I had a conversation with him of twenty or thirty minutes.

Question. Was he moving his whole force by railroad, did you understand?

Yes, sir.

Question. Do you know where the army of General Bragg was at that time?

The most of it had arrived in the vicinity of Knoxville.

Question. Was this movement of General Breckinridge's division toward Kentucky going on while Bragg's army was in that State?

Yes, sir.

Question. Did General Breckinridge tell you what the strength of his division was? If so, please state what he told you about it.

General Breckinridge told me it was about 8,000 or 10,000.

Question. Have you reason to doubt the truth of the information given you by General Breckinridge both in regard to the destination of his division and the strength of it?

I have not.

Question. Do you know anything of the character of the country across from Somerset to East Tennessee in the direction of Knoxville?

Yes, sir; I know some little of it.

Question. Do you know the road that leaves the Cumberland River just above the mouth of the South Fork and goes through Jacksborough, thence on to Knoxville?

I do.

Question. Have you traveled that road?

Yes, sir.

Question. What is the character of it?

It is a pretty bad road.

Question. How does it compare with the Cumberland Gap road?

It is a worse road, I think.

Question. Is it a road that is much traveled?

No, sir; I think not.

Question. Is it used for wagons?

Not a great deal, I think.

Question. State as particularly as you can the general character of the country, its population, and agricultural resources, especially between the Cumberland River and Jacksborough.

I could not say exactly; there is not much of that country that is very productive.

Question. Is it a level country or is it a mountainous country, abounding in difficult passes and defiles?

It is a mountainous country.

Question. How do you get on to that road, starting from Somerset?

I could not state exactly. I never paid a great deal of attention to the country or the roads.

Question. From the information you received did you understand distinctly that General Breckinridge's division was not in Kentucky during the occupation or invasion of that State last summer by the rebel forces?

Yes, sir; I understood so from himself.

Cross-examination by the JUDGE-ADVOCATE:

Question. What were you doing in Knoxville at that time?

I left the State about the time Generals Smith's and Bragg's armies were leaving Kentucky, a little in advance of them sometimes.

Question. What reason had you for leaving the State at that time?

I was a good deal scared at that time, as a good many others were. We heard a great many tales about pressing men into the service, and as I did not care about going in I thought it better to leave.

Question. What service do you refer to?

To the Union service.

By General DANA:

Question. Do you know of any men pressed into the service of the United States; can you name any man?

No, sir; I have heard of a great many, but could not find out how it was. I heard a great many tales when the Confederates were in Kentucky where I live about what was being done at Louisville and Covington.

By General SCHOEPF:

Question. Was there a single Union officer or soldier near Lexington to press you into the service?

No, sir; not at that time.

By General TYLER:

Question. Are you in favor of all the laws passed by Congress and of all orders issued by the President of the United States and his subordinate military authorities, so far as they have come to your knowledge, for the suppression of the rebellion commenced at Fort Sumter and since carried on by the rebel Government at Richmond, of which Jefferson Davis is president?

The JUDGE-ADVOCATE. I am forced, Mr. President, to object to this question. I cannot see precisely the ground upon which the question can be pressed upon this witness or asked of him.

General BUELL. I desire to enter my objection to the question also for the reasons which I stated yesterday in an objection to precisely the same question to another witness.

The JUDGE-ADVOCATE. There is a difference between this witness and the former one. The former witness had, from the position he occupied, taken an oath to sustain the Constitution of the United States. That oath he may have violated, and violating that oath affects his credibility before this or any other court. But here is a witness occupying no such position, and I think on that ground the question is scarcely pertinent.

General TYLER. I propose to ask the question of every witness, whether presented by the judge-advocate or General Buell, as a means of obtaining information as to their credibility. On the answer given to that question will depend very much the force that I shall give to their testimony before the Commission. I would like to ask the judge-advocate if the witness examined yesterday had taken an oath? Nothing of the kind appears on the record.

The PRESIDENT. His being an attorney requires it. Every attorney is required to take the oath of allegiance to the United States.

General BUELL. It occurs to me to say a word in reference to the remarks of the judge-advocate in answer to mine, if it is not too late.

The PRESIDENT. Proceed, sir.

General BUELL. The question of General Tyler extends to matters which may not, perhaps, come within the constitutional obligations of citizens of the United States. This question does not speak of lawful orders; it not only specifies the orders of the President, which may be presumed to be constitutional always, but it specifies the orders of all officers under the President. He does not say whether they shall be constitutional or unconstitutional. The opposition to such orders or the violation of such unconstitutional orders by any person would not be a violation of the oath, and it would not therefore disqualify a witness before any tribunal.

General DANA. I move that the witness be informed that if he deems the answer to this question may commit him in any degree, either now or hereafter, he may not answer it.

The PRESIDENT. If you think the answer to that question will have the effect of criminating you in any manner, either now or hereafter, you are not required to answer it.

The WITNESS. I would rather not answer the question, sir. I do not think the answer would criminate me. I decline answering it.

By General TYLER:

Question. Have you ever been connected, directly or indirectly, with the rebel service?

No, sir.

Question. Under what circumstances were you brought in contact with General Breckinridge, and how did you become so intimate with him that he should give you the strength and position of his army?

I am an old acquaintance of General Breckinridge and his wife is a distant relative of mine.

Question. How long were you absent from Lexington at the time you visited Knoxville, and were you in contact with the Confederate army during the whole of that time?

I cannot be certain as to the time, but I think it was about two or three weeks from the time I left Lexington until I arrived at Knoxville.

Question. In whose company did you leave Lexington?

I had a few friends with me.

Question. How many? And please name them.

There were some 5 or 6. Mr. Reed, of Fayette County; Mr. John H. Cooper, of Fayette; Mr. Hern, of Fayette; two Mr. Armstrongs and Mr. Stuart, of Fayette County, composed the company.

Question. Did these gentlemen return with you?

Some returned and some have not.

Question. Did any of them join the rebel army?

No, sir.

Question. What route did you take from Lexington to Knoxville?

We went on to Richmond, then to London, and along that route.

Question. Did you fall in with the rebel army?

Sometimes we were with it; but every chance we had to get off the road we turned off to keep from being with it as much as possible.

Question. Did you return to Lexington because you had no sympathy with the rebel army?

No, sir; I did not have any sympathy with it. I am not a secessionist by any means.

Question. But you left Lexington to avoid the draft or being pressed into the Union service?

From reports that I heard I did; but I found out they were untrue and returned.

Question. Have you had any communication with General Breckinridge since you returned to Lexington?

No, sir.

By General SCHOEPF:

Question. Were you aware of an order of General Buell that persons who went with the army to Tennessee and came back into Kentucky should be arrested?

General BUELL. I gave no such order. I request that the orders referred to by General Schoepf be read.

(General Orders, No. 49, is read, as follows:

GENERAL ORDERS, }	HEADQUARTERS ARMY OF THE OHIO,
No. 49. }	*Louisville, October* 26, 1862.

I. All recruits for the rebel army captured or arrested by troops of this command will be regarded as prisoners of war and sent without delay to Vicksburg, and there paroled and left subject to exchange.

II. All persons who have actively aided or abetted in the invasion of Kentucky by rebel troops within the last three months will be immediately arrested and sent to Vicksburg, Miss., and forbidden to return to Kentucky. This order will not be understood as including persons indicted or held by the civil authorities for trial, nor will arrests be made on suspicion or insufficient evidence of guilt.

III. Brig. Gen. J. T. Boyle is charged with the execution of these orders, and will give such special instructions as may be found necessary.

By command of Major-General Buell:

JAMES B. FRY,
Colonel and Chief of Staff.

General BUELL. The order refers to particular classes of persons, not to persons in general; it refers to deserters from the rebel service and to persons who have actively aided and abetted in the invasion of Kentucky in the army of General Bragg.

The WITNESS. I was not aware of any such order.

General SCHOEPF. Were you not arrested when you returned?

Yes, sir. I was not—I want to correct that by explaining——

General BUELL. I beg the recorder ——

General SCHOEPF. I object to General Buell's interfering with the recorder all the time.

I reported myself to the commander of the post at Danville. I was not arrested I went and reported myself, and he gave me a letter to General Granger at Lexington, and I reported to him there.

By General SCHOEPF:

Question. Do you know that James Clay, of Lexington, raised a regiment in Kentucky before Kirby Smith left?

No, sir; he did not.

Question. Did he not issue a proclamation to the people to enlist?

He did.

Question. Did not a good many enlist or go with him to Tennessee for the purpose of enlisting?

I think not.

Mr. J. H. COOPER (a witness for the defendant), being duly sworn by the judge-advocate, testified as follows:

By General BUELL:

Question. State your name and place of residence, if you please?

J. H. Cooper; 8 miles north of Lexington, Fayette County, Kentucky.

Question. Were you in Lexington last summer during its occupation by the rebel troops under Kirby Smith?

Yes, sir.

Question. Did you see any arms belonging to the rebel force? If so, state where they were stored and about how many there were of them, as near as you know.

They were stored in a stable belonging to a Capt. O. B. Beard. I think there were from 8,000 to 10,000 muskets.

Question. Were they in boxes or in what manner were they stored?

They were piled up in the stable in the stalls and a good many were in boxes.

Question. Did the rebel troops bring these arms into Kentucky; if not, where did they come from?

I understood they were captured at Richmond, Ky. I heard of their being captured and curiosity led me to go and see them. I saw them brought in in wagons and I saw them unloaded.

Question. Were they those in boxes which you saw unloaded or were these loose in the wagons?

Most of those I saw unloaded were loose; yet there were several loads that were in boxes. My attention was more particularly called to those that were loose as I was passing along the street.

Question. When did you first see them? If you cannot remember the date, state with reference to the time of the arrival of the rebel troops.

It was within a very few days after the arrival of the troops—some three or four days; I don't remember the exact time they got there; it was three or four days after the Richmond fight that I saw them unload the guns.

Question. Were you at the time well apprised of the fact of a battle at Richmond and were you at Lexington when the rebel troops entered that place?

I was in the country the day of the fight. I heard the firing of cannon. I went up on Sunday, and on Monday morning I went back to Lexington, and the Confederate troops, I think, got there about 12 o'clock.

Question. Did you see General Breckinridge, of the rebel army, about the time that General Bragg retreated from Kentucky in October last? If so, state where, and give the date if you remember it.

I saw him in Knoxville, and to the best of my recollection I think it was about the 25th of October. He was then on his way to Murfreesborough; his force had gone ahead of him and he was there waiting. Hearing that I was in Knoxville he sent for me, and I went out to him and saw him a few minutes before he left.

Question. Did you have any conversation with him or hear any conversation between him and other persons with reference to the previous movements of his troops? If so, please state what that conversation was.

I think it occurred about in this way: At Lexington we understood that General Breckinridge had gone to Richmond with 20,000 troops, and at that time I stated this fact to him, and he told me he had started to Kentucky, and had got within one day's march with about half the number it was said he had taken to Richmond; that he was within one day's march of Cumberland Gap, or Kentucky, with about 10,000 men, and there he received countermanding orders and returned to Knoxville, understanding that General Bragg was retreating from Kentucky.

Question. Had you previously known General Breckinridge, and had you then or have you now any reason to doubt the truth of what he stated to you?

I have been acquainted with General Breckinridge for, I think, about fifteen years, and I have no reason in the world to doubt anything he stated to me.

Question. How were General Breckinridge's troops going to Murfreesborough, and how long had they started before you saw him on the occasion referred to?

I think they went on the railroad. My best recollection is that they left there a day or two before General Breckinridge left Knoxville himself.

Question. Do you know whether or not there was much dissatisfaction among the rebel troops on account of their withdrawal from Kentucky?

Yes, sir; there was a great deal of dissatisfaction among both the officers and troops, more particularly among the officers. I had more chance to talk with them than the men. There was a general dissatisfaction. They claimed that they came there to hold Kentucky and they saw no reason why they should leave it.

Question. Did you hear anything about a council of war among the officers of Camp Dick Robinson with reference to a retreat from Kentucky? If so, state what you heard and from whom you heard it and all that you know about it.

On Sunday morning I understood that they held a council of war among the officers at Camp Dick Robinson and that there was a majority of officers in favor of giving battle, but that General Bragg overruled them and ordered a retreat. I got this from Mr. Gilson Johnson, and I heard divers others speaking about it. My best recollection serves me now that it was Sunday or Monday the retreat was ordered, and I went on to Lancaster, and the next morning General Buckner's command came through there; his command came through Lancaster on Monday morning on the road to Crab Orchard.

Question. Who was this Mr. Johnson that you received this information from and what connection had he with the rebel army?

I think that he belonged to General Breckinridge's staff and he was out on furlough; but I met with him at Camp Dick Robinson, and he went back with the retreating army.

Question. How long was this council held after the battle of Perryville or was it before or after the battle?

It was after the battle of Perryville, the Sunday following the battle, which think took place on the Wednesday previous.

Question. What was the opinion of the people of Kentucky, as far as you know it, in regard to the object of the invasion; did they believe it was a temporary incursion or did they suppose that the rebel forces came there to hold the State permanently?

It was generally believed by the people of Kentucky that General Bragg's object in coming there was to hold Kentucky, and they held to that opinion up to the time of his retreat, when the people generally were taken by surprise, as they did not look for anything of the sort. General Bragg made a speech in Lexington to that effect and convinced the people that such was his object.

Question. Do you say you were at Camp Dick Robinson at the time the rebel army was there after the battle of Perryville?

Yes, sir. I got there on Friday, I think, and remained there till the retreat was ordered, which, as I stated before, I believe was on Sunday evening.

Question. Did you have an opportunity of having some knowledge of the intended movements of the rebel army; and, if so, was it supposed or understood when that army moved to Camp Dick Robinson that it was retreating out of Kentucky?

When it moved to Camp Dick Robinson I think it was generally understood that the intention was to give battle, from the fact of their concentrating their whole forces at that point, and it was believed so up to the time this council of war was held. After that I understood that the army would retreat to the south by way of Cumberland Gap.

Cross-examination by the JUDGE-ADVOCATE.

Question. Had you ever any facility for examining those arms you spoke of?

As I stated before, in passing, on coming down town, I saw the wagons unloading, and curiosity led me to go into the stable and see them. I saw them piled up there, and I saw there were a great many. I asked questions of those who were guarding the arms, the pickets—the number of guns and where they were captured. They were large stable doors, and any one passing could see them in the stalls, and the boxes that had not been opened.

Question. Did you go inside the stable?

Yes, sir; I think I was in there once or twice.

Question. How did you pass the guards who had charge of them?

I got permission to go in.

Question. Who gave you permission?

As well as I recollect now I think it was Captain Beard who went with me, and who was acquainted with the guard. It was a stable he rented out. The Government had it before the rebel army got there, and they took possession of it and were using it as a commissary store. There were a good many goods captured at Lexington, and some, I think, were stored in that building.

Question. What induced you, Mr. Cooper, to make that trip to Knoxville just at the time you did?

I suppose you want an honest answer?

Question. Certainly.

I was a Southern man in feeling.

The witness is cautioned by the judge-advocate to decline answering the question if he thinks his evidence will criminate him.

I don't believe it would be very criminal for a man to tell you the honest truth. I had no other object in leaving than that I believed I would be imprisoned if I remained, and I went South, and I staid there till I got pretty well satisfied that home was the best place. I made my intentions known there and came back to obey the laws existing. I left the Confederate Government and came back to the Federal, to obey the laws as a loyal citizen, and hope to remain. There was no compulsion used. I could have remained there, but I saw my error, and I went to General Bragg, told him my intentions, and he gave me a pass to go through his lines, and I returned home.

Question. You have a farm near Lexington, have you not?

Yes, sir.

Question. Are you one of the citizens of your country indicted for taking part and sympathizing with the rebellion?

I was indicted previous to the Confederates coming here, and General Smith got the notice and sent it to me, and they never renewed it. Our grand jury sat some ten days ago. I have not since been indicted. The other indictment was not served upon me. General Smith got it out of the clerk's office and sent it to me through the post-office.

Question. Was Mr. Downing also indicted?

I think he was indicted after leaving. I heard nothing of his being indicted previous.

Question. What passed between General Bragg and yourself when you announced your intention to return to your allegiance?

Nothing at all. It was done through young Mr. Johnson. I went to General Bragg's room, but Mr. Johnson, who was General Bragg's private secretary and an acquaintance of mine, applied for Mr. Downing, Mr. Reed, and myself. I was introduced to General Bragg, but I got the pass from Mr. Johnson, who made our intention known. He had refused to give passes to most persons, but he granted one to us. We intended to have gone by the way of Nashville. I was advised by Colonel Hunt and General Breckinridge that that would be the safest way, and give ourselves up to Rosecrans and make our intentions known, and they did not doubt he would give us a pass to return home; but we changed our notion and came by a different route.

By General SCHOEPF:

Question. What day did you arrive at Camp Dick Robinson?

I think it was the Friday before the Sunday that the army retreated from Camp Dick Robinson.

By General TYLER:

Question. Did you accompany any part of Kirby Smith's army to Camp Dick Robinson?

No, sir; I did not.

Question. Do you know the day on which the advance guard of Kirby Smith's army arrived at Camp Dick Robinson?

I do not.

Question. Was Kirby Smith's army at Camp Dick Robinson on your arrival there?

Yes, sir; it was.

Question. Do you know that Kirby Smith's army was at Camp Dick Robinson or in that vicinity on the day of the battle of Perryville?

I did not go to Camp Dick Robinson till after the battle of Perryville, and at that time—the battle of Perryville—Kirby Smith was stationed at Salvisa, between Harrodsburg and Frankfort.

Question. By what route did Bragg's army retreat from Camp Dick Robinson?

They went by two or three different routes; I think Buckner went by the way of Crab Orchard; Kirby Smith by way of Richmond. I went out with the rear of the army, but had nothing to do with it, considering I was a citizen.

Question. How long did you remain at Camp Dick Robinson?

As I stated before I got there on Friday, and I think I left there Sunday or Monday evening; according to my best recollection I left Sunday evening. From there I went to Lancaster with the retreating army.

Question. Were you in Kirby Smith's camp at Salvisa?

I was not.

Question. Did any of Kirby Smith's army occupy Harrodsburg or pass through Harrodsburg?

Not to my knowledge; but I understood they came through Harrodsburg up to Camp Dick Robinson. I do not think they could go there in any other way than by passing through Harrodsburg.

Question. You speak of your information as to the different movements of the rebel army from Knoxville to Murfreesborough and from Camp Dick Robinson; what were your means of information other than that of personal information?

None other than being acquainted with officers and hearing them talk about their movements after the retreat had become generally known. I was there as a citizen, and as such talked to by everybody, and being acquainted with officers of course heard their conversation.

Question. Name the officers who communicated to you the information as to the movements of the rebel army.

I do not know, sir, that I could mention them, as it was in the room of Mrs. Robinson's inn, where I heard the officers talking to each other, that I got my information. I do not want you to understand that they directed their conversation to me at all; it was my mixing with them at table after this retreat was ordered and became generally known that it was talked about.

Question. Had the rebels a line of communication between Knoxville and Murfreesborough by which they moved their troops?

Yes, sir; they had. I saw them move their troops from Knoxville to Murfreesborough.

Question. Are you in favor of the execution of all the laws passed by Congress and all the orders issued by the President of the United States and by his subordinate military officers, so far as they have come to your knowledge, for the suppression of the rebellion commenced at Fort Sumter and since carried on by the rebel Government at Richmond, of which Jefferson Davis is the president?

General BUELL. I object to this question, as I have done to the same question in all previous cases and for the same reason.

The court is cleared. In secret session it is decided that the question shall be put.

The PRESIDENT. It is proper to admonish you that you are not required to answer the question if in your judgment it would criminate you in any degree. Do you understand the meaning of my caution?

I do, sir. I would rather not answer that question. I can answer it. As I stated to you before, I have come back and taken the oath with the intention of becoming a loyal citizen. At the same time I do not approve of everything Mr. Lincoln has done.

The PRESIDENT. Do I understand that you decline to answer the question?

It is a very hard question for me to answer. I want you to understand that I am trying to be a loyal citizen and want to remain as such. I have taken the oath and intend to adhere to it, and I am in a loyal State and I intend to stay; but if you want my candid answer I will give it. I could answer it very quickly, but in doing so I might get myself into trouble.

Question. If you apprehend that you are not bound to answer it.

As I stated before, I have told you my object in going South and my object in coming back.

Question. Do you decline answering the question?

Please read the question again.

The question is reread.

I would rather not answer it at all; but if I am to answer it I will say it right out: I don't approve of Mr. Lincoln's January proclamation in regard to slavery.

Judge LANE (a witness for the defendant), being duly sworn by the judge-advocate, testified as follows:

By General BUELL:

Question. State your name and place of residence, if you please, judge.

G. W. Lane; Huntsville, Ala.

Question. Have you a good knowledge of the country of North Alabama and of its agricultural resources?

I have been a resident there for the last forty-five years; have traversed it in almost every manner, and profess to have a pretty correct knowledge of the physical geography and topography of the country, and I profess to have a knowledge of the agricultural resources of the country.

Question. State, if you please, what you know on these subjects.

Please describe the general features and character of the country, and state what its products are, and which are the productive regions and which the least so.

There is a spur of the Cumberland Mountains that passes through, dividing North Alabama rather from northeast to southwest. One-half of North Alabama is mountainous, with coves here and there; the other half is table-land, with the addition of what we call the river bottoms. The Tennessee passes through North Alabama. I should say that perhaps one-half was table-land and the balance was mountain coves and river bottom. The table-land is owned and cultivated by the wealthy class of the community that we term planters. On the table-land you find farmers owning from 3,000 acres of land down to 500. That part of the community denominated planters look to cotton as the source of their revenue. They have recently, for the last four or five years, been endeavoring more than formerly to raise their supplies of corn and meat on their own plantations. Up to ten years ago they would look to the Northwest for their meat. They usually raised corn enough for their needs, but for the last ten years they have tried to raise upon their plantations what they would consume, and as a general rule the best farmers have succeeded, but the rest look to the West for their supply of meat and flour. Owing to this fact there is but little surplus of corn and meat; but the planters are all satisfied if they raise corn, forage, fodder, and hay for their own consumption.

Question. I wish you first to describe the general features of the country; the limits of what you call the productive regions, particularly toward the east; to describe this feature of spurs running toward the Tennessee River and corresponding coves running up toward the mountains; to give some idea of that productive region, and what the amount of its production is, I should say, with reference to the amount that its population requires for its own consumption.

There are four counties lying on the north of the Tennessee River. Jackson County extends up to Nicojack; it is the most eastern county in the State, and extends up to the line. I should say four-fifths of Jackson County is very mountainous; the balance is what we call cove-land. But very little of that cove-land is adapted to the cultivation of cotton; it is a stiff, black limestone land, unfit for the cultivation of cotton. According to the size of this county and its population there are fewer negroes than in any county in the State; it is a poor white population. They raise principally corn, some wheat, and have been in the habit of bringing down to our country hogs for sale. The next county is Madison. I should say that four-fifths of that is good arable land, suitable for cultivation, and about two-thirds of that is cultivated in cotton. The next county is Limestone County. I should say two-thirds of that is arable and is cultivated in corn and cotton. The land in that county is mostly owned by the class I have described as the wealthier class of the community. The next county is Lauderdale, on this side of the river. There is very little mountain in that county, but a good deal of poor land. Large tracts of land are still owned by the United States Government. I should say one-half of that county is cultivated in corn and cotton, perhaps more than half of it, and owned and cultivated by planters, who look, as I have said, to their cotton as the source of their revenue. Jackson County is the only one in North Alabama that raises anything for exportation in the way of meat or breadstuffs, and that in but a small degree. The people are generally content, and eat what they raise. This embraces the counties on the north side of the river.

Question. You may give the same information with reference to the country on the south side within 10 or 15 miles of the river.

Commencing at the first county after crossing the river from Jackson County you strike De Kalb County; it is entirely mountainous for 20 miles and almost uninhabited. There is some bottom land on the south side of the river, lying in small tracts, that is perhaps the very best corn land we have in the country, but it is subject to inundation and the rises in the Tennessee River, which are frequently so late that planters are deprived of an opportunity of planting their corn, the floods extending into June, and it makes it a very uncertain business to raise corn on that side of the river. The next county is Marshall, and the same answer would be applicable to that. The next is Morgan County, and for a distance of 10 or 15 miles from the river the same answer would apply. The river seems to pass through the gorges in the mountains. There are mountains on both sides from the main gorge down to Morgan County. The main gorge is only about 15 miles west of Chattanooga by land, but I think it three times that by water, for the river is as serpentine as a corkscrew there. After getting out of Morgan County the next is Lawrence. There you strike a fine quality of land, what is called the Cortland Valley, extending down to Buzzard Roost, which is 95 miles from Huntsville. It is a fine valley, owned principally by rich cotton planters and cultivated in the way I have described before. When you get to Buzzard Roost you are near the Mississippi line, 8 to 15 miles to the Mississippi line west.

Question. Do the arable portions of the country south of the Tennessee afford any provisions beyond what is required for the support of the population?

It is inhabited by the rich planters I have already described, who are satisfied to make merely enough to carry on the operations of their plantations and look to cotton as the source of their revenue.

Question. Are there any practicable wagon roads leading into these coves that you speak of, judge, and where do these people find a market for the little surplus they have and how do they get it there?

There is no turnpike or roads that can be called highways running through those coves; there are roads that are used and the mountains are crossed by citizens, but the word "practicable" is scarcely to be applied. The mountains are crossed, but I should say there was no road running from Jackson County entering from the cove in Madison County to Huntsville that could be used or a load of anything brought. For instance, there is what is called the Big Cove; people live there, and bring to Huntsville their marketing with horse and buggy or carts, but they could not bring one-fourth of a load across the mountain; they could bring upon a mud road four times as much as they could bring across that mountain.

Question. What was the condition of all this region you have described, judge, in the month of July last, with reference to surplus supplies of provisions and forage?

I should say that 1861 was what was termed a bad year, for the grain crop was very short in North Alabama. Independent of that, in the month of February or March the Confederate army that fell back from Bowling Green and Fort Donelson passed through North Alabama and levied contributions upon the country as they passed through. These two facts, of a short crop and the Confederate army levying upon the people, made the supplies less than usual. The Confederate army passed right through the valley and levied contributions during the two weeks they were there.

Question. What was supposed to be the strength of this army that levied upon the country in that way?

It was said to be from 25,000 to 30,000 men. I saw a great many divisions pass. The secessionists of the country said there were from 25,000 to 30,000.

Question. Had the country also been drawn upon to a considerable extent by the United States troops previous to July, under the command of General Mitchel?

If my recollection serves me right I think General Mitchel reached Huntsville on the 11th of April. I do not know what time General Buell got there, but I suppose it must have been about the 1st of July. My impression is that General Mitchel left the 3d or 4th of July and General Buell got there three or four days before General Mitchel left. This would make two months and a half that General Mitchel had been there with an army of some 6,000 or 8,000 men; but I do not think General Mitchel had levied very heavy contributions, for I was frequently at his headquarters, and he evidently tried to avoid levying contributions, and got his supplies as well as he could from the army stores in Tennessee. There was some difficulty in getting provisions along the road; his trains were fired into and bridges were burned; but I think he brought a great many supplies from Nashville or Murfreesborough. He levied contributions for the forage entirely. I recollect on one occasion there was a considerable sensation, as it was said he was going to levy upon the smoke-houses, and it produced a great deal of consternation among the people. But I do not think he levied upon the people while I was there. He obtained his forage entirely from the country.

Question. What was the cause of this consternation produced by this anticipation that General Mitchel was about to take meat; was it because of the pecuniary loss, or because he would take that which was necessary for the sustenance of the population?

Upon consultation with General Mitchel I informed him that there was a great scarcity of the article of meat there, and the general appointed myself and two others as a committee to go around and assess the smoke-houses; the levying was to be made according to the quantity we each had in our smoke-houses; but in the mean time a wagon train arrived and the levy never was made. I had been a pork-buyer, and I think I had never given more than $5, but $3.50 was the ruling price there up to the year 1861, when, owing to the condition of the country and that we had failed to get our usual supplies from Kentucky and Tennessee, where we had been in the habit of getting our meat, it went up to $10 and $12, and consequently there was less put up than we were in the habit of doing.

The Commission adjourned to meet February 23.

CINCINNATI, *February* 23, 1863.

Commission met pursuant to adjournment. All the members present; also the judge-advocate and General Buell.

Judge LANE's examination continued.

By General BUELL :

Question. Can you state, if you please, judge, whether the inhabitants in and about Huntsville were very much in want of the necessaries of life—of provisions—at the time of my arrival there; that is, about the 1st of July last ?

Yes, sir; never to my recollection was there so great a scarcity and never were provisions so high; they were about 200 or 300, perhaps 500, per cent. higher than usual during the last summer. I paid as high as $2.50 for coffee. The usual price of bacon in Huntsville is from 10 to 12 cents per pound. It could not be bought there at that time (if it could be had at all) under 30, 40, or 50 cents per pound.

Question. How was it, sir, with reference to breadstuffs ?

Flour had advanced 200 or 300 per cent.; it was selling from $20 to $25 per barrel. Corn meal, which is usually bought for 37 to 50 cents per bushel, advanced to $1.50.

Question. Is the country you have described a cattle-raising region ?

No, sir; it is a cotton-raising country there, and cotton-planters have come to the conclusion that the raising of cattle won't pay; that the injury that is done to the crop, the ground in winter, is more than the stock is worth. To understand it, I should say that for the preparation of cotton it requires that the land should be well pulverized, and if the stock is allowed to run upon the land in the winter in the spring the ground breaks up in clods. They have avoided raising more stock than is sufficient for their own purpose, and have no more on their own plantations than is necessary for their own use as working oxen and milch cows.

Question. How is it with other stock that is used for provisions ?

We do not pretend to raise sheep there. Some poor planters raise a few. There are some planters that raise enough for their own purpose and that have cotton occasionally, but it is not a sheep-raising country; there is no attention paid to it. The farmers during the last ten years have got more in the habit of raising bacon than formerly. They used to raise cotton to buy bacon with, but now they raise other supplies upon their plantations.

Question. Am I to understand that as a general rule they raise no surplus of provisions ?

As a general rule that part of the planting interest known as planters are always satisfied if they can raise enough to supply their own plantations. There is another class—the poorer class—who raise some supplies; that class do not raise cotton; they raise some supplies for the home market. That part of the country lying on the north side of the river has never raised more than enough to supply the home consumption of this country. I doubt if they have ever raised enough for that.

Question. State, if you please, what you know of the products of that part of Tennessee bordering on Alabama, the agricultural products, and the quantity of provisions in proportion to what is required for the sustenance of the population.

The products there are more various than they are in Alabama. In all that tier of counties, commencing at Franklin, running east, coming down through Lincoln, Giles, and Lawrence, it is more or less a cotton-producing country. In that part bordered by Alabama, a greater proportion of meat and breadstuffs is raised than on the Alabama side. I cannot state what proportion of those counties send certain amounts of breadstuffs and meat into Alabama, but the amount of meat and breadstuffs sent by them would not be enough to supply the north of Alabama without sending into Middle Tennessee and Kentucky.

Question. Which of those counties is the most productive in supplies of provisions and forage ?

Lincoln, sir, produces more breadstuffs and meats than any of those counties. Lincoln is a mountainous county, containing a great deal of rich valley land not adapted to the cultivation of cotton; hence they raise other supplies—provisions.

Question. About what time were the supplies from the States north of Tennessee, from which you say Alabama and other Southern States have been in the habit of drawing supplies of provisions, cut off from that market by the rebellion ?

The rebellion was inaugurated in the winter of 1860 and the spring of 1861, and the supplies were cut off about that time. For instance, we put up our bacon in the winter; the bacon supply was cut off in the winter of 1861. Before the inauguration of the rebellion we had put up for 1861, but in the winter of 1861 our supplies were cut off by the rebellion.

Question. Did that circumstance throw a greater demand upon that region of Tennessee for its surplus of provisions ?

Yes, sir. That portion of Middle Tennessee and that portion that borders Alabama was overrun by the rebels, and there was a very large amount of Confederate stores put up all through that region of Tennessee.

Question. What route or routes did the rebel army pursue in its retreat from Nashville south in the spring of 1862 ?

I do not know. The larger proportion of the rebel army, and the whole of it as far as I know and believe, went from Nashville to Murfreesborough, from Murfreesborough to Shelbyville, from Shelbyville to Fayetteville, from Fayetteville to Huntsville, from Huntsville to Decatur. Some proportion of it may have gone by some other routes, but I am not certain.

Question. State, if you please, what you know of the agricultural resources of the country between Bridgeport and Chattanooga and within a circle of 10 or 15 miles around Chattanooga in all directions, explaining anything with reference to the topography of that country that may serve to illustrate the subject, if you please.

From Bridgeport to Chattanooga—the Memphis and Chattanooga Railroad crosses the Tennessee River at Bridgeport, and there on both sides of the river it is almost a perfectly mountainous country up to Chattanooga, and as to its productions they are extremely limited. It is only from 10 to 15 miles from Bridgeport to Chattanooga. From Bridgeport on the south and the north the country is entirely mountainous. When you get beyond, south of Chattanooga, there is some pretty good productive country within a distance of 15 miles; but I do not know much about that country beyond Chattanooga, except that there is some pretty good country, and I think the productions are entirely breadstuffs and meat.

Question. Do you know enough of it to be able to say whether there would probably have been much surplus provisions in that country last summer, considering the limits to which the Southern demand was confined by the circumstance of the rebellion ?

I could only give an opinion there; I should say that there was not. That opinion would be predicated on this: that Chattanooga had been in the possession of the rebels and the rebel army was there during the whole spring and summer.

Question. If not required for any force at Chattanooga, would it probably have been drawn off for other points to supply the demands of the cotton States ?

It is simply my opinion again and I must give my reasons. The Charleston Railroad passes right through that section of country, and the products of that country have been usually carried down to Macon, Augusta, and Savannah. None of the productions of that country have ever come down our way; they went from Chattanooga to Atlanta, Augusta, &c. The only channel for the products of that country was through the interior of Georgia, and it was from this country that the interior of Georgia got its supplies.

Question. Are there at any season fords across the Tennessee River within 10 miles of Chattanooga?

I have never heard of the Tennessee River being forded there at all. I have never known the Tennessee River forded anywhere except at the head of Muscle Shoals. I believe General Jackson forded there in 1814 with his army. It is called Colbert Shoals, and that is 150 to 200 miles from Chattanooga, and more by water.

Question. Do steamers ever cross the Muscle Shoals; and, if so, at what season of the year, and what is the greatest draught of a boat that can cross the shoals under the most favorable circumstances?

I have never known a steamer pass up the shoals—steamers built here in the West—but they were tugged up. There is no navigation, and never has been. No steamer has gone up unless it was carried up by force; that is, force independent of the steam itself.

Question. Was there formerly an attempt made to make the river navigable over the shoals by means of locks and dams?

Yes, sir; in 1828 there was an appropriation of land made by the General Government, of, I think, a million of acres. There was raised from that land about $3,000,000, and that money was expended in the attempt to cut a canal around the shoals, but it proved a signal and entire failure, and it is now in perfect ruin. I do not know that a boat has ever passed through it.

Question. Have you a general knowledge of the fact that depredations to a very considerable extent were committed by Government troops in various places in North Alabama in the spring and summer of 1862 and prior to my arrival at Huntsville? If so, please state what effect was produced upon the temper of the people and their sentiments toward the Union by those depredations.

The JUDGE-ADVOCATE. Mr. President, I object to that question. There is no earthly doubt but that depredations committed by soldiers will produce a bad effect upon the inhabitants of any country; the fact can be admitted without calling upon a witness to prove it; but if depredations were committed precisely at that time I cannot see what bearing it has upon the investigation we are engaged upon.

General BUELL. They have this bearing, Mr. President: that they go to explain to a considerable extent perhaps the cause of the dissatisfaction and demoralization which has been charged to have subsequently existed in the army under my command, and that has been one of the subjects of investigation before this Commission. It may serve as an answer, too, to the infamous denunciation that has been expressed in the public prints with reference to the measures which I adopted to suppress and punish those depredations and preserve discipline in my army. That is the object of the question.

The court was cleared; when, after discussion, it was decided that the question should be put.

General BUELL. I propose to modify the question by inserting after the words "Government troops" "more particularly those under the command of Colonel Turchin, Nineteenth Illinois Regiment."

The PRESIDENT. I suggest that you specify what troops you refer to in a separate question.

General BUELL. I request, sir, I may have permission to amend the question.

General SCHOEPF. I object to that amendment, because Colonel Turchin was tried by court-martial and has since been promoted.

The court was cleared; and, after discussion, it was decided that the proposed amendment to the question should not be put.

The WITNESS. Yes, sir. I have a general but not a personal knowledge of any depredations except in one particular instance. I do not know whether I am to speak from general knowledge or——

The JUDGE-ADVOCATE. The witness is to speak here as he would in any other court—from his personal knowledge, from what he knows.

General BUELL. I request that no greater restriction be placed upon this witness than has been practiced heretofore. I know no reason for a distinction at this particular time. I do not think the object of the investigation is to determine whether any particular person is to be hung for the crime of murder or whether he shall be adjudged to pay a certain forfeit. The object of the investigation is to get the best information we can in regard to the operations of the army and the exercise of my command. That has been the rule heretofore. The investigation has been pursued in a very general way, and I know no reason why it should be restricted now by a nice scrutiny.

The JUDGE-ADVOCATE. It certainly was not my intention, and if my memory serves me aright the rules governing the introduction of testimony have in no instance been departed from on the part of the Government, but I have permitted it on the part of the defense; but the departure from the established rules must not be carried too far.

General BUELL. I wish to say that I do not admit that any particular favors have been extended to the defense at all in this investigation or that any advantage has accrued from extraordinary liberality on the part of the prosecution. I do not admit that any greater liberties have been allowed to the defense in the introduction of evidence than can be found to have been used in the prosecution.

The JUDGE-ADVOCATE. The record will speak for itself.

General BUELL. That might have been a sufficient reason why the declaration of extraordinary liberality was unnecessary.

General SCHOEPF. The division referred to as having committed these depredations was subsequently under the command of General Rousseau, who testified that they were as good as any soldiers he wished to have. It is casting a reflection on the dead and can do no good at all.

General BUELL. That would have been a very good reason for approving of the proposed amendment. I do not wish to cast any reflection upon the troops at all. Many of the best officers in that command were outraged at these depredations, and, as I was told, threatened to resign their commission if these things were tolerated. I know that General Mitchel himself disapproved of them, except that he perhaps failed to enforce discipline which he would have himself approved. These violations were confined for the most part to a particular brigade. The question was put in the first place not very cautiously. It was for that reason I desired to amend it, so that it should apply to the troops to which the odium of this conduct properly belongs.

The court was cleared; when it was decided by the Commission that the witness may state any well-authenticated rumors or general information of depredations or misconduct, without involving any particular corps or regiment.

The WITNESS. I have a knowledge that there were general rumors that there had been various depredations committed; I might say that I got that information from General Mitchel himself and from various officers belonging to the different *corps* d'armée under his control. I will go further, and state that I was upon terms of the utmost intimacy with General Mitchel, and so far from having any disposition to do injustice to his memory I would say that I have known few men for whom I have had a higher regard. On one occasion, after there had been a very flagrant violation committed by the army, I accompanied General Mitchel from Huntsville to Athens, the adjoining town. The general had the different regiments assembled, and he made a speech to them, in which he deprecated very severely the course of conduct they had pursued, saying that he should certainly hold both officers and men to strict accountability for their conduct. As a matter of course those depredations that were charged to have been committed did produce some bad effect against the Federal army. I could go on further, and say that perhaps on the second day after General Mitchel arrived in Huntsville I sent for him, and we had a confidential interview, in which he asked my advice as a citizen as to what would be the proper policy to pursue there, and I have vanity enough to believe that the advice I gave him influenced his course of action. I could explain to the court what predicated the advice that was given. North Alabama had always been a Union State; the elections had taken place on the north side of the river, in which there had been an overwhelming demonstration, perhaps five Union votes to one secession, and I gave it to General Mitchel as my opinion that there was a Union sentiment, and that that sentiment should be fostered by a conciliatory course of conduct, and General Mitchel set out with the determination to pursue that policy. But I must say that my experience there convinced me that I was perhaps mistaken. No good came from the conciliatory policy; no good has since resulted from it, and I have seen fit to change my views on that subject.

The PRESIDENT. No good ?

No good, sir. I take more blame upon myself, for I advised General Mitchel to pursue this course: that there should be no discrimination made; that it should not be known who were and who were not secessionists; that contributions should be levied on all alike; but I think now that if the Union men knew that they were to be protected, while the burdens should fall alone upon the secessionists, it would have made the Union men more decided. Sharing the burdens with the secessionists I think had an unfavorable effect.

By General BUELL:

Question. Do I understand you to say that the depredations that were committed at Athens and other places ought to have been approved by General Mitchel; that the effect of such approval or the encouragement of such depredations would have strengthened the cause of the Union among the people?

By no means. I did not so intend to be understood; on the contrary, I intended it to be understood that these depredations did excite and inflame the people against the Federal cause. I intended to say that the conciliatory policy pursued by General Mitchel, being extended alike to secessionists and Union men, did not produce the good effect upon the Union men that I had hoped.

Question. Was it a matter of notoriety that depredations similar to those committed at Athens were committed at various other points in North Alabama, and perhaps also in Tennessee on the borders of North Alabama?

It was notorious that there had been depredations committed at various places, but none of so flagrant a character as those committed at Athens.

Question. By a conciliatory policy I understand you to mean a policy which discriminates in a marked manner between those persons who are loyal to the Government and those who are disloyal?

General SCHOEPF. I object to that question; that is more politics than a subject for a military investigation. The President of the United States will decide which policy to adopt; it is not for us to decide here.

General BUELL. My policy in the exercise of my command has been made the subject of investigation; the testimony goes to particularize that policy and to the wisdom or error of it. It was therefore pertinent.

The WITNESS. The question shows that I am not perfectly understood as to the policy I recommended to General Mitchel. I wish my ideas of what is a conciliatory policy to be understood by the court.

General BUELL. That is my object in asking the question.

The WITNESS. The question implies exactly what I did not mean.

On the expression of the wish by Judge Lane to correct his answer and make himself more fully understood General Schoepf withdraws his objection.

General BUELL. The policy which you now think wisest I understood to be one which discriminated in a marked degree between persons who are loyal and those who are disloyal in their sentiments, and this I understand you to put in contrast or opposition to the conciliatory policy. Please be precise and state exactly what you mean by a conciliatory policy.

This is the understanding that General Mitchel and myself came to: That it would be a sound and good policy to be as kind to the people generally, both secessionists and Union men, as was consistent with his duty as a United States officer, and that there should be no discrimination made between Unionists and disunionists. That was the policy which I wished General Mitchel to adopt. The conciliatory policy was that all should be treated alike. The policy that I would now recommend would be that he should discriminate in favor of the Union men, and that his contributions should have been levied entirely upon the disunionists. By this course the Union men would have felt themselves protected by the Government of the United States, while the secessionists would have felt the burden of the war falling entirely upon themselves.

Question. Was it a feature of this conciliatory policy that disloyal men should be allowed to talk and act disloyally?

No; I intended that the conciliation should be on the part of General Mitchel; that the kindness should proceed from him as a United States officer, not expecting or intending that he would submit either to rebellious or seditious language, acts, or conduct from the disunionists.

Question By a more rigorous policy do you mean that it would be wise for an army marching into a district of country to proceed at once to levy contributions, to take possession of their property, and treat them with severity and harshness personally merely on account of their opinions?

I should think that the commander of an army marching into a country should be governed by circumstances. If the country into which he marches was entirely rebellious, I should say that coercive means should be used to force that country into submission to the Constitution and the laws of the United States. If there was an element of Unionism, and one that I thought I could foster and encourage by pursuing a course of kindness and conciliation, I should certainly adopt that course. But wherever I marched an army into any portion of the rebellious States I should feel authorized to sustain that army, as far as I could, upon the sustenance that could be procured from the rebellious part of the community. I would go further, and say that no community in a state of rebellion to the Government of the United States has any right to claim the protection of that Government against which it was in rebellion. At the same time I would bring them into subjection in as civilized and Christianized a manner as I was capable of.

Question. Do I understand that you would take their property without compensation?

I should be governed entirely by what I considered military necessity required, and at the same time I should be opposed to any wanton destruction of property or any illegal or unconstitutional use of it. These are my present views, and not the views that I entertained at the time General Mitchel and yourself entered Tennessee with the Federal army. My views were then very different.

Question. In the whole district of North Alabama how many persons could General Mitchel have selected who, on account of their adhesion to the Government, would have been entitled to this favorable discrimination, as nearly as you can judge?

They would have been very scarce, although, as I have remarked, I had believed there was a strong Union sentiment there. When they came to take the responsibility of serving Jefferson Davis or the United States they were very cautious which side they took; and indeed I would say that there were not a dozen men in North Alabama who were willing to incur all the responsibility of coming out in favor of the Union and joining General Mitchel. But nevertheless there was a large number of what I term a sort of *quasi* Union men there who were anxious to receive the protection of the Government of the United States without incurring the responsibility of rendering themselves liable to be interrupted by the Confederate Army.

Question. Do you not believe that there is a very considerable portion of the population of the Southern States, at least of some of them, who would be very glad to place themselves again under the protection of the Constitution if the power of the rebel Government and its means of coercion did not render it impossible for them to do so?

I do, sir. I believe that four-fifths of the population of North Alabama would to-day be in favor of a reconstruction of this Government, and that they would be willing to unite with the Government of the United States if they could have a positive assurance that they could receive the protection of the Government without again being interrupted and interfered with by the Government of the Confederacy. I speak more especially of my own section, but from what I have heard from other sections of the country I believe the same would apply there.

Question. Is it true that those people who are at heart loyal to the Union are almost universally supporters of the rebellion?

Yes, sir; I believe there are a great many men (I speak more especially of my own section) who are loyal at heart, but who are professed secessionists; a state of things brought about by the fact that their personal safety, the safety of their families and property, depend upon their conforming to the requirements of the Confederate Government.

Question. Are or are not justice, the security of constitutional rights, and other results flowing from our institutions the considerations which have given rise to and have preserved this loyal sentiment in the people of the South toward the Constitution and the Government?

Yes, sir; I should say unhesitatingly that it was.

Question. What, then, would be likely to be the effect of the policy and conduct of an army upon these people which should violate all these principles? I do not speak now with reference to the people of the South more than to people everywhere.

The violation of justice and constitutional guaranties would in this case and everywhere be calculated to excite and enrage a loyal people, and I would go further, and say that it would be well calculated to estrange them from their Government.

Question. Suppose, then, these principles to be observed in any district of country, taking for example Middle Tennessee and North Alabama and the rebel power in that district of country to be destroyed and its armies kept out, which policy would leave those people in the best condition as regards their support to the Constitution and the Union, that which judges men according to their acts while they are at liberty to act according to their judgment and affection or that which punishes them harshly for acts which have been committed under the pressure of military force and a public sentiment which amounts almost to an insanity?

I should say that the preservation of justice, constitutional guaranties, and law to a loyal people would be well calculated to attach them to the Government, but that I know of no way of judging men's motives or their hearts but by their acts, and if their acts are rebellious I should say that they are rebellious at heart; but, at the same time, should the state of affairs take place as contemplated by the question, that the rebel army should be driven out of the country, a conciliatory policy would be best to pursue to bring them back again into the pale of the Constitution and under the protection of the Government of the United States.

Question. Suppose the rebel power not to be crushed and its armies not to be driven out, which line of conduct will leave these people in the best disposition in regard to the Union and the old Government, that policy which has respected personal rights or that which has violated them and treated the people with harshness and severity?

I should say that the mild policy, that which has treated them with the most consideration and in the mildest manner, would be the best calculated to attach them to the Government.

Question. Will you please state, judge, as far as you understand it, wherein my policy differed from that which General Mitchel entertained?

I do not know of any difference at all. Although I claimed to be very intimate with General Buell, perhaps I was not so conversant with his policy as I was with General Mitchel's; but, as far as I am aware, I know of no difference at all. I received as many favors asked for persons from General Mitchel as at the hands of General Buell, and perhaps as many at the hands of General Buell as from General Mitchel. Indeed I think their policy was the same; the only difference I know, I never held consultations with General Buell as to the policy that should be pursued, while I did with General Mitchel.

Question. If, then, General Mitchel's opinions and my own were not materially different upon the question of policy, was there any difference in our practice? If there was, please state what it was and what the effect of it was.

As far as I know there was no difference in their opinions as to the policy pursued. The only difference that now occurs to me was this: General Mitchel was a very impulsive man, and his practice did not in every instance conform to his opinions. For instance, some days, owing to circumstances, he would seem to act more harshly than at other times, while in the main he was kind and considerate. General Buell, on the contrary, seemed not to be under the same amount of impulse as generally actuated General Mitchel, and his practice was more uniform. I will state one fact. The general's trains on the railroad were very frequently fired into by guerrillas and nothing seemed to aggravate him and put him in a worse humor than for his trains to be fired into, and it not unfrequently happened when persons would come to me to ask favors or to have their wrongs redressed in some particular, knowing that his train had been fired into the previous day, I used to advise them to put off their application till I could find the general in a better humor, and I very rarely failed to obtain whatever I asked for the applicants. General Mitchel was also more communicative to me, while General Buell was disposed to be more reticent and to keep his own views to himself.

Question. Do I understand you to mean that this interference with his trains seemed to instigate General Mitchel to a harsher course of conduct toward the people?

By no means. It did not interfere with his practice, but with his professions. He would sometimes declare that he would do things that he did not do, and I would find him just as kind and as disposed to grant favors as before.

Cross-examination by the JUDGE-ADVOCATE:

Question. With a portion of the people in arms against the Government, what do you consider the personal rights of those who side with the rebels, at least so far as giving aid and comfort goes?

General BUELL. I object to the question, Mr. President. I have not examined the judge with reference to what are the personal rights of persons engaged in this rebellion.

The JUDGE-ADVOCATE. The question is based upon the proposition made by General Buell as to which were the better policy with the inhabitants of a country where our armies were, that which respected the personal rights of those inhabitants or that which treated them harshly. Now I want to know what are the personal rights of people who openly express their sympathy with the rebellion.

General BUELL. I do not think that in the whole course of my examination I have used the term "personal rights."

The JUDGE-ADVOCATE. General Buell is mistaken; he did use the very extraordinary expression, as it struck me at the time, "personal rights."

General BUELL. I wish to deny that a man under any circumstances loses personal rights, and that it is extraordinary that men under any circumstances should have personal rights. If I understand the effect of it, it is to bring them to the level of the beast and nothing less.

The record was examined and the words found to have been employed by General Buell.

General BUELL. I withdraw my objection; I am very well satisfied to have used the phrase; but what I meant was that I had not put that idea prominently forward. As I am not allowed to re-examine the witness I will make another objection to the question, and that is that the witness' explanation of what he understands to be personal rights shall not stand as expressing my views upon that subject, and that is an objection that I consider to be valid against the question.

The PRESIDENT. That is an objection to the answer rather than to the question. I don't imagine that anybody would suppose that Judge Lane's answer to the question would be fastened upon you as your opinion as to what were personal rights.

General BUELL. I have no objection to the answer.

The WITNESS. All who aid and assist in treason are principals; there are no accessaries. All aiders and abettors should be treated, in a legal point of view, precisely as the traitor himself, and all who give aid and comfort must be traitors and rebels, and should be treated precisely as the principal was treated. I should make this distinction between such and a sympathizer, if he merely sympathizes—if he had not reduced it to acts—that he had not given aid and comfort to the enemy.

General BUELL. If the judge will allow me I would ask him to answer as a lawyer.

The JUDGE-ADVOCATE. I have the witness, and I have asked a question which was to illustrate a question asked in the examination-in-chief.

The PRESIDENT. It was hardly fair, general, to interrupt a witness, unless it is to make an objection to his answer.

By the JUDGE-ADVOCATE:

Question. Do you know of any right which prohibits the army of the Government from living upon the country it invades if that country is in a state of rebellion?

General BUELL. I ask again that the witness may answer the question as a lawyer.

The JUDGE-ADVOCATE. I certainly must protest against this interference. I have the witness, and as to the manner of answering this question it is for me and the court to say.

General SCHOEPF. Mr. President, the judge-advocate is wrong. General Buell has complained that he has not been shown any favors. I propose that the court show him every favor and permit him to dictate to the witness.

General BUELL. I am very much affected by the judge-advocate's indignation that he should be interrupted in his investigation. I think, nevertheless, that my suggestion is a proper one and I urge it.

General TYLER. I move that the court be cleared.

The court was cleared; when it was decided by the Commission that when a witness is under examination the person having the right of questioning the witness shall not be interfered with except by objection made in the usual form.

The WITNESS. We have a clause in the Constitution of the United States which says that private or individual property shall not be appropriated without making fair and just compensation; but here comes up the question as to the law of military necessity, and without being a military man I do not know how far the military necessity or how far a commander-in-chief would have the right to claim individual and personal property; but I would suppose, and this would be my answer, that he would have the right to levy contributions upon the enemy to the amount of what was necessary for his present and pressing necessities.

Question. Abstaining, then, from levying contributions upon a country in a state of insurrection and granting safeguards and other protection to rebel property are to be regarded as favors and not as a recognition of rights?

Yes, sir; I so consider them.

Question. Has not the rebel Government been in the habit of prosecuting those they supposed to be the loyal men of the South to the furthest extent of their power?

Of that fact I have no personal knowledge, but from reliable information I believe they have.

Question. If we abstain from exercising our rights as a Government by levying contributions, &c., does it not in fact make it safer at the South to be a rebel than a loyal citizen?

Yes, sir; I should say that it did. But let me explain. The disloyal citizen would have two chances: he is protected by the Government of the United States, and let the rebels triumph he would be protected by the rebel Government, while the loyal citizen would only have one chance of protection.

Question. In a disputed territory where the two armies were contending, as in Tennessee or North Alabama, has not this conciliatory policy been taken on the part of the inhabitants as an evidence of weakness on our part and thereby worked our injury?

I should say not as an evidence of weakness, but as an extreme disposition to conciliate.

The Commission adjourned to meet February 24.

CINCINNATI, *February* 24, 1863.

Commission met pursuant to adjournment. All the members present; also the judge-advocate and General Buell.

Judge LANE's cross-examination continued.

By the JUDGE-ADVOCATE:

Question. Do you recollect, judge, how many counties you described in your evidence in chief lying along the line of the railway?

Yes, sir; I recollect there were only three. There are only four counties on the north side of the river—Limestone, Madison, Jackson, Lauderdale. The railroad passes through but three of them—Limestone, Madison, and Jackson.

Question. I refer to those counties of which you gave us a detailed description of their products.

There are five—De Kalb, Marshall, Morgan, Lawrence, and Franklin—on the south side.

Question. What is the population of those, if you can recollect?

I commence with Jackson County, the extreme eastern county, on the north side of the river: the voting population is about 2,000; Madison, about 800; Limestone, 1,200; Lauderdale, about 1,800; De Kalb (on the north side of the river), say, 1,400; Marshall, about 1,400; Morgan, 1,200; Lawrence, about 1,500; Franklin, about 1,800. The usual calculation there is ten inhabitants to a vote.

Question. Does that include the black as well as the white population?

Yes, sir.

Question. Was there subsistence—meat, corn, &c.—enough in those counties in July, 1861, to carry that population through to the next year?

I have no doubt they get through upon it, but I am satisfied it was a short allowance. I knew that on the south side of the river they were suffering for the substantials of life.

Question. In that term "substantials" what is included?

I mean meat and bread.

Question. Do you know, judge, whether the railroad from Huntsville to Stevenson is now in use by the rebels?

I so understand from the newspapers and rumors; but that they are running but one engine from Bridgeport to Decatur on that line of railroad.

General Buell desiring to ask further questions of the witness on the war policy, the court was cleared for a decision, when it was decided not to depart from the established rule.

JOHN B. YATES (a witness for the defendant), being duly sworn by the judge-advocate, testified as follows:

By General BUELL:

Question. State your name and position in the service of the United States, if you please.

John B. Yates; acting major of the First Michigan Engineers and Mechanics.

Question. Have you a commission in that regiment? State for what rank it is.

Captain Company A.

Question. Were you on duty in North Alabama last spring, under the command of General Mitchel?

Yes, sir; I was.

Question. Did you have anything to do in constructing what was called the gunboat Tennessee while you were there?

I had the charge of the construction of the gunboat Tennessee while I was there.

Question. State as particularly as you can what its construction was, its dimensions, and its subsequent operations.

It was made from a horse-ferry boat that ran from Whitesburg, 10 miles south of Huntsville, to the other side of the Tennessee River. Its dimensions were 52 feet long, if I remember correctly, and about 11 to 12 feet wide. It was built in the first place for the purpose of a gunboat, to run up and down the Tennessee River from Whitesburg to Bridgeport. The sides in the first place had barricades on them filled with cotton, to protect the men on the boat from the guns of the guerrillas; there was also one gun of Captain Loomis' First Michigan Battery. The machinery was a stationary engine, taken from a saw-mill and put on the boat. The intention was in the first place to case the boat with iron, to ward off more effectually the bullets of the guerrillas, but the tonnage of the boat was not sufficient to support it so as to make it bullet-proof. After it was discovered that it would not answer the purpose it was built for it was taken down the river to Decatur and there used as a ferry-boat by order of General Mitchel, who determined it could not be used with safety to patrol the river. As the machinery was continually getting out of order, he was afraid it would become unmanageable and be taken by the guerrillas, who would destroy the boat and take the gun.

Question. Did it ever make a trip up the river?

It made one trip up. How far I do not remember.

Question. Did it go as far as Bridgeport?

I do not know. As they were going up the river they were fired upon beyond Gunter's Landing by a party of guerrillas as the boat went near the bank, and some bullets went through the barricade. I heard they went nearly up to Bridgeport. That is my impression, though I do not know the exact distance they went.

Question. What was the defect or peculiarity in the engine which made it inefficient for that purpose?

It was, I think, a cast wheel, and the wheel was breaking. It was also a stationary engine, and had to be made so that we could reverse it, and the reversing gearing was constantly getting out of order. We had the castings made at Huntsville.

Question. How many men was it intended to carry as a guard or crew?

I do not know how many men it was intended to carry, but there was one company of the Tenth Ohio, Captain Steele, and one gun of Captain Loomis' Michigan Battery.

Question. What were its performances as a ferry-boat?

We built two boats, and placed one on each side of this ferry-boat, calculating to drive wagons on each side—two wagons to a boat—and distribute men on the ferry and on each of the two lighters, to ferry them across the river. We used it for some time—I do not know how long—with two boats. One of them became unserviceable, so that we were compelled to use but one.

Question. Could you carry animals with the wagons; and how many men could you carry in addition?

I never saw them carry any wagons or mules across or any men. I never was down there at the time the boat was running as a ferry-boat. When it was built it was put in charge of ferrymen that were sent there; but the calculation was to put two wagons and four mules to a boat; that was General Mitchel's idea.

Question. How many men was it estimated to carry in addition?

From 250 to 300 men was one calculation.

Question. Do you know whether in practice its capacity proved to come up to the estimate?

I think it did not, as I heard a great many complaints about it.

Question. What were the dimensions of those flats used in connection with the gunboat for ferrying?

The one we made was about 54 feet long and 14 feet wide; that was the good one. I do not remember the dimensions of the other, but it was smaller.

Question. What was the difficulty in replacing these boats when they became disabled?

It was impossible to get the sides or the lumber to cover the bottom. We had a great deal of trouble in getting those we had there; they were a little decayed, and we had to patch them up so as to make them serviceable.

Question. Do you know anything about the measures that were taken to get out the lumber for the construction of the pontoon bridge at Bridgeport after my arrival at Huntsville last summer?

I received an order from General Mitchel to set all the mills running between Huntsville and Stevenson to get out lumber for the pontoon bridges; and after a great deal of trouble I got two started; they were some 5 miles between Huntsville and Stevenson. But it was impossible to get the men to work at them; they were afraid of guerrillas running in upon them at night. It was considered dangerous to start them, and it being a dry season many of them were out of water; one of them had no water at all. At Jackson's Mill two of our men were taken prisoners after we had started it. Paint Rock Mill, one of the mills we had in operation, was idle a great deal of the time for the want of water.

Question. What was done from first to last to carry on and complete the work?

All the mills were started that we could start. Our regiment was sent to Stevenson to build the boats, and we thought when we moved there that when we got into camp the lumber would be ready, but we were delayed a number of days for the want of the lumber.

Question. Did you work the mills yourself or did you depend upon the owners to work them?

Paint Rock Mill was worked under the charge of the owner, a man named Douglas, and a detail from our regiment and a detail from the Tenth Wisconsin to assist. Jackson's Mill was under the charge of Jackson, the owner of the mill, with a detail from our regiment. Colonel Innes had the general supervision of both mills after they were fairly started.

Question. Notwithstanding these delays, were the boats for the bridges constructed before the completion of the railroads and the accumulation of supplies at Stevenson which would have enabled the army to use them?

The boats were not completed before the road was finished through to Bridgeport, but they were finished before there were sufficient supplies collected at Stevenson for the army.

Question. Do you know anything about the abundance or scarcity of supplies for the troops under the command of General Mitchel before my arrival there? State, if you please, whatever you know upon that subject.

We were on half rations at one time—I do not remember the exact date—and we had a great deal of trouble to get our trains through; they were attacked and captured by bands of guerrillas. At one time Captain Paul, a captain of the commissary department, informed me that he had no rations on hand for the next day, and wanted to know when our trains would be in; and then we were on half rations. We got an order that our men should have full rations, as they were hard at work on the bridges, but the rest were on half rations.

Question. Did you use all the supplies you could gather in the country?

I do not know that we used all we could gather, but we used a great deal that we gathered from the country.

Question. Was it the policy of General Mitchel to supply himself as far as possible from the country he occupied?

That I cannot answer directly, but he was always anxious about having supply trains come up, so as to be able to supply his army from his own department.

Question. Was your scarcity due to the difficulties in the transportation of supplies from the depots of Nashville?

Yes, sir.

Question. About what force had General Mitchel on that line that was supplied in that way?

We had the Third Division and about 600 to 700 negroes and men at work on the railroad.

Question. Estimate the number of men altogether, as nearly as you can.

I think 7,000 would cover them all.

Question. With the difficulties that you experienced in supplying 7,000 men, what would you think of the practicability of supplying 20,000 with the same means?

It would be worse in proportion.

Question. At what time did you get this order to prepare lumber for pontoon bridges and from whom did it emanate?

I got it about June 30, 1862. The order emanated from General O. M. Mitchel to me. General Mitchel said to me that he was ordered to get the lumber out.

Question. Did he state by whom?

We supposed it was by General Buell's order, although his name was not on the order.

Question. State whatever you know in regard to the service of your regiment during the summer of my arrival at Huntsville; and if you do not know particularly of the services performed by the whole regiment, state whether any portion of it, to your knowledge, was idle during that time.

No portion of it, to my knowledge, was idle during that time. Two companies with me, under General Mitchel, were hard at work from the time of our arrival at Huntsville, and also on the march from Nashville to Murfreesborough and from Murfreesborough to Huntsville.

Question. Does your answer include the time subsequent to my arrival at Huntsville? You will observe the question refers to that time.

It refers to the time we finished the pontoon boats.

Question. How were the companies under your command employed during that time?

In the building of bridges on the Nashville and Chattanooga Railroad, assisting in running the trains from Huntsville to Stevenson and from Huntsville to Elk River, also in building one of the bridges between Stevenson and the Tennessee River, and assisting in building the pontoon bridges.

Question. Have you traveled frequently on the railroad between Huntsville and Bridgeport?

I have.

Question. State what you know from observation of the character of that country and its agricultural resources.

About 16 miles east of Huntsville, on the railroad, the land is very good as far as you can see on each side of the road; from there on to Bridgeport it is through a broken, rocky country, and with only small clearings on each side of the road.

Question. Has this productive tract that you speak of any name by which you can designate it, and what is the extent of it along the road?

I cannot designate it by any name, and I do not know anything of its productions, save that once in a while we would pass what would look like a good farm from the car windows; and these points were between Huntsville and Brownsborough and Brownsborough and Paint Rock Station.

Question. Do you mean that the country for 16 miles is productive and cultivated or do you mean that isolated points for that distance are cultivated?

Occasional farms; not the entire stretch of country.

Question. What is the character of the country between these farms?

The road runs through rock cuts.

Question. Were you in the battle of Perryville?

I was.

Question. With what corps?

Three companies of the Michigan Engineers, under Major Hopkins, attached to General Rousseau's division.

Question. Did you see many officers and men the night and morning after the battle, and have an opportunity of becoming acquainted with their opinions in regard to the condition of affairs consequent upon that battle?

I saw quite a number; I do not know how many.

Question. As far as you know, what was the expectation of the officers and troops in regard to a battle the following morning; that is, the morning of the 9th?

I can speak for our command more than I can for any other. We expected to be called into action the next morning. Our men were very tired, and Major Hopkins told them they must get all the rest they could, for they would probably have to go into the fight in the morning. We were ordered by General Rousseau to take our position in the rear of Colonel Starkweather's brigade, and we were drawn up in line of battle when we got to our position.

Question. Was there, as far as you know or from any indications you could see, any other expectation than that the battle was to be renewed that morning?

All the officers with whom I talked thought we were going into battle again next morning.

Question. Do you mean by that that you expected to fight the enemy on that ground?

I did. I expected that we would fight the enemy, keeping the ground in the morning that we left after dark.

Cross-examination by the Judge-Advocate:

Question. At the time the troops were on half rations that you speak of in your examination-in-chief did they suffer any?

There were some complaints, but I was not around among the troops to see whether they suffered or not. I was posted at the depot, and attended there most of the time, assisting Captain Paul, by furnishing transportation. I only heard from him that the troops were on half rations and from the guards who were stationed around the building that they had not full rations.

Question. Except from the guards about the building you did not know anything of your own knowledge?

No, sir; not from my personal knowledge; only from hearsay and from our regimental quartermaster, who said that the rest of the troops were on half rations and that we were on full because we had hard work at daily labor.

Question. Do you not know, from what you observed of the guards about the building, that they lived about as well on half rations as when they were on full?

From their looks they seemed to. I did not see any signs of pinching hunger.

Question. Do you know anything about the ferry at Gunter's Landing and the ford there?

I never saw the ferry; but all the boats on this side were, I believe, destroyed by General Mitchel's orders. Of the ford I remember nothing, though I may have heard of it at the time.

Question. Was that the case with the boats at the other ferry besides the one you speak of?

I believe so. General Mitchel gave orders to have all the boats destroyed from

Decatur up the river to Bridgeport on this side of the river—all boats that guerrillas could get to cross over from the other side. Captain King, Fourth Ohio Cavalry, went over at one time and destroyed some boats that were over there by General Mitchel's orders.

Question. There was but one ferry in operation, and that was the steam-ferry you speak of?

Yes, sir.

By General SCHOEPF:

Question. What was the amount of transportation that each regiment had in that division?

About thirteen wagons to a regiment.

Question. How many wagons were in a brigade train to each of the brigades?

I do not remember.

Question. Do you know if there was a brigade train to each brigade?

I do not know for a certainty.

Question. Do you know the number of wagons in a division train?

One train that went out had two hundred wagons that I know of.

By General TYLER:

Question. What particular duties did you perform while this order for getting out timber was being executed?

I was acting as military superintendent of the railroad for General Mitchel at that time, and also started those men up the road to look up the mills and report their condition.

Question. Were these mills run under your orders or your supervision?

They were started under my orders. A short time after they were started I was relieved of the superintendence of the Memphis and Charleston Railroad, in order to report to Colonel Innes, who then took the supervision of the mills.

Question. What was the amount of lumber ordered to be cut up by General Mitchel for bridges, pontoon boats, &c., in feet, board measure?

I cannot estimate the correct amount. I have the bills of timber at my tent. It was somewhat less, though, than the bill of timber for the boats that we built.

Question. Was there as much as half a million of feet, board measure?

I think it was about 300,000 feet, as near as I remember, but I cannot answer correctly from memory.

Question. Was standing timber plenty for supplying your mills; and, if so, what kind?

Oak timber was plenty.

Question. How many mills did you put in operation?

Two mills; Paint Rock Mill and Jackson's mill.

Question. Were these the only mills that could have been put in operation at that time within your control?

General BUELL. Mr. President, I do not wish to object to the question at all, but suggest to the Commission that it is unnecessary. I do not pretend that the failure to complete the bridge in time was the cause of my not moving to Chattanooga. I only call evidence upon this point to show how the troops were occupied; that preparations were being made. With that explanation I have no objection to the question.

The WITNESS. Yes, sir; and I had an almost endless amount of trouble to get these two started and keep them running.

Question. What were the particular troubles you had to encounter?

Want of water, fear of guerrillas, and a want of machinery.

Question. Would not a single company or half a company guarantee these mills from incursions from the guerrillas?

It would have needed as much as one company, and that one company would have needed stockades for protection.

Question. Then I understand from your testimony that only two mills were available to cut your lumber out, and that these were where water is uncertain; that they were exposed to guerrilla incursions, and the machinery was inferior?

At one of these mills—Paint Rock—the water was all the while failing, though that mill was in the least danger. The mill at Stevenson was a pretty good one. The others were right in the infested region, near Woodville. I think that is the name of the station.

Question. I think in your direct testimony you say that the road was completed before there were sufficient supplies collected at Stevenson; what means had you of knowing what were sufficient supplies and when they were collected?

My means of knowing were from Captain Smith and from the trouble our quartermaster had occasionally in getting supplies and from the general talk of officers and men connected with the commissary department.

Question. Do you know that any particular amount of supplies was fixed upon as necessary; if so, what was that amount?

I do not know the amount or if there was any fixed upon.

Question. You were a captain in Colonel Innes' regiment, I understand; would Colonel Innes have had as good an opportunity of knowing or testifying as to the points upon which you have testified yourself?

With the exception of about the formation and building of the gunboat he could have spoken as to the efficiency or inefficiency of the gunboat while acting as ferry-boat at Decatur and about the trouble in starting those mills. He would not have known as much as I did of the complaints that the mills were not started sooner, but I have endeavored to explain to him many times why they were not started sooner.

Question. Then Colonel Innes was dissatisfied, was he, with the administration of that branch of the service?

He was dissatisfied with the delay in starting the mills, but he never complained of me as far as running the road was concerned.

Question. You stated in your direct testimony that General Mitchel's force was 7,000 men; did that include the whole force of General Mitchel, all told?

At Huntsville and supplied from that depot.

Question. What other divisions had he and where were they?

He had a brigade or part of a brigade a part of the time at Shelbyville, I think.

Question. Any other?

Not any that I know of that were supplied from Huntsville.

Question. That is included in the 7,000 men?

It is not included in the 7,000.

Question. Had General Mitchel any force under his command except the 7,000 men and this brigade or part of a brigade at Shelbyville?

There were some troops at Murfreesborough, but I do not know whether they reported to General Mitchel or not. I am not acquainted with part of General Mitchel's force. In this 7,000 men were included the employés and negroes on the Memphis and Charleston Railroad.

Question. To what amount?

I think 600 or 700, but I do not remember the exact number on the rolls.

By General SCHOEPF:

Question. Was that division train that you spoke of as containing two hundred wagons made up of regimental and brigade wagons or was it not a division train proper?

I think it was made up of details; so many wagons from each regiment and so many wagons from each brigade. At one time almost all the wagons in the division were called on to go for supplies.

After the examination was concluded, by permission of the Commission, Major Yates made the following addition to his testimony:

The WITNESS. At Jackson's Mill, near Stevenson, where we were getting out the lumber, we had to send to Nashville for a circular saw, the one being unfit for use; this was one cause of delay that I remember. I wish to make that statement to show that everything was done that could be done.

Capt. JOSEPH J. SLOCUM (a witness for the defendant), being duly sworn by the judge-advocate, testified as follows:

By General BUELL:

Question. State your name and position in the service of the United States.

Joseph J. Slocum; captain and commissary of subsistence.

Question. Were you on duty at Huntsville last summer, under command of Major-General Mitchel?

I was.

Question. Do you know anything of the measures that were adopted to procure supplies for the army in North Alabama during that time and what the difficulties were? If so, please state what you know about both.

The supplies were derived partly from the Government headquarters at Nashville, partly by foraging upon the country and pressing supplies. At times the army was on half rations. I have had great difficulty in getting supplies in that vicinity; that is, the neighborhood of Huntsville.

Question. Did you endeavor to get as much from the country as you could procure and was that General Mitchel's policy? Indeed, was it necessary, from the difficulty you had in transporting supplies from the depots at Nashville?

It was necessary. I was acting in the capacity of quartermaster to our army in North Alabama at that time and not as commissary.

Question. Did your position and duty nevertheless give you an opportunity of being acquainted with the facts you have stated?

They did.

Question. Did you know of complaints on the part of the inhabitants of the country in consequence of treatment which resulted from this method of procuring supplies?

They were constantly complaining, but it was necessary, and we paid no attention to them. The forage supplies in that portion of the country were all procured, up to the time of General Buell's arrival, from the inhabitants. Our supplies of forage were much more abundant after General Buell came to Huntsville, as they were all then directed to that place from Nashville; consequently we had more with which to supply the army, but not sufficient for the whole army. A portion of the time our troops were

in a suffering condi ion from he lack of supplies, principally in the vicinity of Bridgeport, toward Chattanooga and in that direction ; even after General Buell came there
it was impossible to get up supplies fast enough.

Question. How long did you remain on duty in Huntsville after my
arrival?

Not long; I think between two and three weeks.

Question. Did you still during that time continue to draw all the
forage you could from the country besides what you obtained from the
depots?

We continued to draw from the country, but I am not prepared to say that we drew
all we could; we had our forage trains out almost every day gathering in supplies.

Question. Do you mean by that that the country might have afforded
more supplies or that you did not avail yourself of the means of your
position to procure them—such as wagons, &c.

My impression is that the policy that had been pursued previous to that was such
that we did not want to draw supplies from the country if we could help it.

Question. That is during what time?

During the months of May and June, while General Mitchel was in command.

Question. How did the troops at Bridgeport and Battle Creek obtain
their forage?

I directed their quartermasters to forage upon the country, but they reported back
that forage could not be obtained ; consequently I was obliged to send supplies from
the neighborhood of Huntsville. They did procure some supplies, but not sufficient.

Question. Do you know that they were sometimes in very great want
of forage?

I do.

Question. What number of animals were kept at these points that
you remember ?

My memory fails me. I might answer that question with more reflection. General
Sill was at Battle Creek with one brigade, I think—two regiments, at least ; and the
animals belonging to the same I suppose he had with him and the cavalry that
were furnished him for scouting purposes.

Question. Was the number large or small in proportion to the number of troops; do you remember?

Small. Our means of transportation were strained to the utmost all the time to keep
up a sufficient supply. I mean by that that we had no sufficient transportation.
Our animals were worn-out. We had before that impressed a great many from the
country, particularly for cavalry purposes.

Question. Did you make use of your regimental train's baggage
wagons for hauling supplies as well as of your division train's?

I did.

Question. About what number of troops were in that part of the
country—say on the line from Huntsville to Battle Creek—prior to the
date of my arrival and before the arrival of troops from Corinth ? If
you cannot answer by numbers, give idea by brigades and regiments.

About 4,000.

Question. What troops did this include; what brigades or divisions?
It is not necessary to designate the regiments.

The troops of the Third Division, composed of the Seventeenth Brigade, the Eighth
Brigade, and I believe a portion of the Ninth Brigade, with the artillery of Loomis'
battery, Edgarton's and Simonson's battery, and the Fourth Ohio Volunteer Cavalry.

Question. Would not all of these have amounted to more than 4,000, or were some of these beyond the limits stated in the question.

I might say that my number perhaps was low, but they were beyond the limits. There was Colonel Turchin's brigade in the other direction. The troops were constantly moving up and down from east to west upon that road, sometimes more and sometimes less—moving from Decatur or Athens particularly, up and down the road, as they were required. At one time Turchin's brigade was at one end of the road and at other times at the other. I cannot now state about what time that was. I know one time that entire brigade was moved to a point north of Bridgeport; I think it was somewhere near La Vergne, in that direction, where they fought—I think at Winchester. General Negley had command of the expedition and drove the rebels back, but our troops were a good deal scattered.

Question. You mentioned to me the other day that you had by accident laid your hand upon a dispatch which exemplified the scarcity of supplies and the difficulty in procuring them. Have you it with you, captain?

I have. In looking over some of my old papers I found this dispatch a few days ago. I was searching for some other papers though:

"BATTLE CREEK, *July* 4, 1862.

"General BUELL:

"There is no forage here and no rations; everything is on short allowance. I have telegraphed and written, but could get nothing. Have no instructions in case of an attack. Enemy's pickets on the opposite side of the river. Sent General Mitchel official communication yesterday explaining everything. Refer you to it, as also to dispatches to-day.

" JOHN C. STARKWEATHER,
" *Colonel First Wisconsin Infantry.*"

This is indorsed on the back to General Smith:

"See to supplies at once. Have you received the communication of yesterday and the dispatch of to-day? Look into the matter.

"D. C. B."

Another indorsement:

Captain Slocum to Captain Paul.

"Attend with all diligence to the within matter, and report to me forthwith what you have done.

"WM. S. SMITH,
"*Brigadier-General, Third Division.*"

Question. Did this scarcity in this case occur under General Mitchel's administration?

It did. I suppose at the very time that dispatch was sent General Mitchel was relieved from the command, which accounts for its being indorsed by General Smith.

Question. On what day did General Mitchel leave his command?

I think on the 2d of July or thereabouts.

Question. Without reference to the inconvenience which the people of the country complained of on account of having their supplies taken from them for the use of the army, did they complain of abuses and wrongs practiced upon them by the parties engaged in collecting or pretending to be acting under authority for that object?

Not that I am aware of. I have suffered a great deal of abuse myself from these parties because they thought I was the responsible person, but I am not aware that the parties sent for the supplies inflicted any abuse upon them.

Question. "Abuse" is not perhaps the best word to use in the question. I do not refer to abusive language; injury might be a more ap propriate word; nor do I inquire whether they actually suffered these injuries, but whether they complained of them.

I do not recollect of any instance of that kind at Huntsville, though I am aware that complaints were made at other points. The rudeness of soldiers is about all I can remember now. In the matter of pressing horses particularly it was a very grievous one to them. Our men would sometimes, perhaps, use extreme language; the people would provoke it; but I remember nothing else.

Question. Is it a matter of notoriety that great outrages were committed by portions of the troops in that district of country?

If accounts are true of great outrages having been committed, it is. We had some regiments in that division who were extremely hard to control; but they were particularly good at the warfare that was carried on there, I suppose, of abusing the people. For instance, the Nineteenth Illinois has the credit of having a hard reputation. The Tenth Ohio was a pretty good regiment in that way, but it was under discipline. These regiments, particularly the Nineteenth Illinois, were kept out, I believe, as much as possible to the extreme for bushwhacking purposes, as we called it. They were very good at that and a very fine regiment when brought into action.

Question. With the difficulty you had in supplying the troops that you had on that line under the command of General Mitchel what would you think of the practicability of supplying 20,000 men at Bridgeport, with the same means of transportation and the railroads of the country as they were at that time?

I should say that it would be wholly impracticable. One thing I distinctly remember: It was the fact of our division train for this small army that General Mitchel had with him at Huntsville of about 5,000 men—that train of 85 to 100 or, say, 125 wagons—was kept so constantly at work that it did not give them time even to have their horses and mules shod in some instances.

Cross-examination by the JUDGE-ADVOCATE:

Question. Under whose command was General Mitchel at Huntsville?

General Buell's.

Question. Why, then, do you speak of General Mitchel's policy; was it not in fact the policy of the commanding general?

As I understood at that time General Mitchel's command was separate, at the same time being a portion of General Buell's army; but he was ordered to go to North Alabama to take possession of that country. I did not join him until after he arrived there.

Question. Were not the complaints of the inhabitants there really based upon your attempt to gather supplies from them and not from any depredation or abuse from the soldiers?

As I said, I am not aware of complaints having been made; they felt bitter, and would raise every possible objection they could at the most trifling thing. They were paid. I am not aware that anything was ever taken from them for which they were not paid. In some instances they preferred Confederate notes, but I could not supply them.

Question. What articles did our forces need; were we suffering there from a lack of subsistence?

Bacon was one thing in the way of subsistence. Hay and oats we never had for our animals. The cattle fed on corn and fodder altogether.

Question. Did not the men have a sufficiency of beef, mutton, and pork?

No, sir; we would send out into the country and get in beef cattle frequently and slaughter them. I do not know that we ever had any mutton. Pork we had occasionally, as we could get it from the North. I recollect in one instance we had a yoke of oxen sent to me, that were captured by one of our scouts, belonging to a Confederate officer. They were very poor and thin, but I was ordered to turn them over to the commissary to be killed. We had no fresh beef.

Question. I understand you to say that it was the lack of transportation that made it impossible to support 20,000 men where 5,000 or 6,000 suffered?

No, sir. I do not recollect saying transportation only. We had nearly exhausted the whole country in the way of supplies. I mean by that that our trains could not supply such an army. The distance they had to go was 25 to 30 miles. They had to be wagoned down to Alabama.

Question. Do you know anything more of this telegram than what appears upon the face of it?

I do not; except that I was two or three times called over to General Smith's headquarters—in fact I was at the headquarters all the time—to consult with him on the possibility of getting supplies from Battle Creek. General Sill and Colonel Starkweather both represented that the troops were in a suffering condition.

Question. Do you know whether this refers to forage and rations or as to what the country might supply or what they would have on hand from the stores of the army?

I think it refers to both, or, properly speaking, to what they had belonging to the army. Of course they looked to headquarters for their supplies as much as possible.

Question. The country about Battle Creek was about the worst region you had to live upon, was it not?

I believe it was.

Question. In the indorsement upon the back you are ordered to see to the supplies at once; do you recollect how you remedied the difficulty?

My impression is that the commissary sent supplies that he had received from Nashville directly down there. I sent wagons into the country that got in some corn and fodder, and that, together with some supplies that were received from Nashville, I believe were sent down. But it did not remedy the evil; it was only an alleviation of it.

Question. If the two regiments could not subsist there, how did Crittenden's and McCook's manage to subsist till late in August?

As I said before, supplies came in more abundantly after General Buell came to Huntsville; they were directed to that point. The steamboats were coming down to Nashville by the Cumberland River loaded for that army. These supplies were all sent direct to Huntsville as fast as they could be sent there, but our communication was very uncertain from Nashville. I was ordered away from Huntsville on the 11th of July, I believe.

Commission adjourned to meet February 25.

CINCINNATI, *February* 25, 1863.

Commission met pursuant to adjournment. All the members present; also the judge-advocate and General Buell.

RUSSELL HUSTON (a witness for the defendant), being duly sworn by the judge-advocate, testified as follows:

By General BUELL:

Question. State your name and place of residence, if you please.

Russell Huston; residence, Nashville, Tenn.

Question. What is your profession or calling?

I am a lawyer.

Question. I wish to submit to Mr. Huston and to the Commission an order which I published on entering Nashville in February last, and to ask him if he recognizes it as embodying the policy which I announced as that which I proposed to observe toward the people of Tennessee in the conduct of the war as far as my command was concerned. It is dated Nashville, February 26, 1862. General Orders, No. 13a.

I think I remember that order. My attention was called to the first order issued by General Buell, because I wished particularly to see what would be the policy of the Federal Army in our country. I recognize that order as embodying his policy in the conduct of the war in Tennessee.

Question. Will you please state what effect, upon general principles and from experience as far as you have had an opportunity of observing its practical operations, such a policy, if carried out, would have had upon the temper of the people of Tennessee with reference to the cause of the Union?

I take the object of the United States to be to restore the Union; not merely a physical conquering or reannexing of territory in which the people are in rebellion, but, as far as it may be in the power of the Government to effect it to restore the affections of the people to the Government. I take it to be of first importance to conquer the men in arms. After this is done I should say that such a course should be pursued as would effect the other purpose of restoring the love of the people for their country and Government. This may be accomplished to some extent, as I think, while the armies are passing through the country, but not by unnecessary harshness. I speak in reference to quiet and peaceable citizens. I think the order spoken of in the question is conciliatory, and if carried out was calculated to win back the affections of the people. I think that the course pursued by the army under that and like orders had a good effect upon the people of Tennessee as far as I had access to them. I think so from what I saw myself and I would say so from the knowledge I have of human nature. I think there was a better state of feeling toward the Government in Middle Tennessee as late as July, 1862, and has been since.

Question. Do you recognize in that order or in the practical effect of it anything which places loyal and disloyal people, those who are friendly or hostile in their conduct, on the same footing under all circumstances—anything that exempts from punishment conduct that is injurious to the interest of the Government?

I do not, sir. I recognize in that order a distinction in some cases between loyal and disloyal persons.

Question. From your knowledge of the people in Tennessee and the effect of the policy initiated there upon their disposition toward the Government, as far as it was faithfully executed, in what position do you believe the State of Tennessee would stand to-day if the rebel armies had been kept out of the State and the people left free to express their opinions and wishes?

By order of the president the Order No. 13a was here read to the Commission:

GENERAL ORDERS, }   HEADQUARTERS DEPARTMENT OF THE OHIO,
    No. 13a.   }   Nashville, Tenn., February 26, 1862.

The general commanding congratulates his troops that it has been their privilege to restore the national banner to the capital of Tennessee. We believe that thousands of hearts in every part of the State will melt with joy to see that honored flag reinstated in a position from which it was removed in the excitement and folly of an evil hour; that the voice of her people will soon proclaim its welcome, and that their manhood and patriotism will protect and perpetuate it. The general does not deem it necessary, though the occasion is a fit one, to remind his troops of the rule of conduct they have hitherto observed and are still to pursue. We are in arms not for the purpose of invading the rights of our fellow-countrymen anywhere, but to maintain the integrity of the Union and protect the Constitution, under which its people have been prosperous and happy. We cannot, therefore, look with indifference on any conduct which is designed to give aid and comfort to those who are endeavoring to defeat these objects; but the action to be taken in such cases rests with certain authorized persons, and is not to be assumed by individual officers or soldiers. Peaceable citizens are not to be molested in their persons and property. Any wrongs to either are to be promptly corrected and the offenders brought to punishment.

To this end all persons are desired to make complaint to the immediate commander of officers and soldiers so offending, and if justice be not done promptly, then the next commander, and so on till the wrong is redressed. If the necessities of the public service should require the use of private property for public purposes fair compensation is to be allowed. No such appropriation of private property is to be made except by the authority of the highest commander present, and any other officer or soldier who shall presume to exercise such privilege shall be brought to trial. Soldiers are forbidden to enter the residences or grounds of citizens on any plea without authority. No arrests are to be made without the authority of the commanding general, except in case of actual offense against the authority of the Government, and in all such cases the fact and circumstance will immediately be reported in writing to headquarters through the intermediate commanders. The general reminds his officers that the most frequent depredations are those which are committed by worthless characters, who straggle from the ranks on the plea of not being able to march, and where the inability really exists it will be found in most instances that the soldier has overloaded himself with useless and unauthorized articles. The orders already published on this subject must be enforced. The condition and behavior of a corps are sure indications of the efficacy and fitness of its officers. If any regiments shall be found to disregard that propriety of conduct which belongs to soldiers as well as citizens, they must not expect to occupy the post of honor, but may rest assured that they will be placed in positions where they cannot bring shame on their commands and the cause they are engaged in. The Government supplies with liberality all the wants of the soldier. The occasional depredations and hardships incident to rapid marches must be borne with patience and fortitude. Any officer who neglects to provide for his troops or separates himself to seek his own comfort will be held to a rigid accountability.

By order of General Buell:

JAMES B. FRY,
Assistant Adjutant-General, Chief of Staff.

The WITNESS. I can give only my own opinion. If the whole of Tennessee had been possessed by the Federal armies, and the people could have been assured that it would be held, I think the policy indicated in that order, as far as it was faithfully executed, would have had a good effect upon the people of the State in reclaiming their affections.

Question. And on the supposition which you have somewhat extended in your answer—that is, that they should be assured that the State would be held by the Federal armies—do you or do you not believe that the people of the State would by their own vote have returned to the Union and elected their officers under the Constitution of the United States?

Judging from what I saw and heard in the counties in Middle Tennessee and from what I know of East Tennessee I think it more than probable they would have elected their State officers and Congressmen. We had some large Union meetings in several counties of Middle Tennessee, and we regarded the prospects as very flattering for the return of the people to their allegiance.

Question. During this rebellion how has the disposition of the people in the counties you have referred to toward the cause of the Union compared with that of people of other portions of the State; have they been better disposed toward the Union or less so than the people of other portions of the State?

General TYLER. I object to the question. It is not definite. I can form no opinion of the force of the question, because I do not know what counties are included.

General BUELL. The question is not as to what is the disposition of the people of the particular counties. The object of the question is to draw a comparison between the disposition of the population which he has referred to—not the inhabitants of any particular district, but of the population he has referred to—with the disposition of the people of other portions of the State.

The PRESIDENT. I will suggest that if there is anything considered material by a member of the Commission it is his duty to draw out that information in his examination of the witness by himself.

The JUDGE-ADVOCATE. Neither the Government nor General Buell can be controlled in the examination of witnesses, and all information sought should be obtained by asking questions after the Government and General Buell get through. It is the rule we have established ourselves, and is a very good one if adhered to.

The PRESIDENT. That is my opinion—to make no interruptions except it is to make an objection to the question; and scarcely think an objection to the form of the question would constitute a serious objection. General Buell has undoubtedly the right to shape and form his own questions on any particular subject; so has the judge-advocate on the part of the Government. I think it would be safer and better for us to adhere strictly to the rule we have established.

General BUELL. I will ask the witness to specify the counties in which he observed this disposition of the people which seemed to be favorable and to encourage the hope of their voluntary return to the Union.

The counties of Robertson, Sumner, Wilson, Davidson, Williamson, Maury, Giles, Rutherford, and Bedford, and perhaps Lawrence, Hickman, Wayne, and Hardin, though my information in regard to them is not so certain.

In reply to the question that was objected to—

I am not able to answer the other part of the question with any degree of satisfaction to myself or others.

Question. Do you know about the time when by my withdrawal to the west bank of the Tennessee River I was removed from the immediate supervision and control of the military policy in Middle Tennessee and North Alabama, and did you subsequent to that time observe any marked departure from the policy which I had announced by the troops under my command in that part of Tennessee and North Alabama?

General Buell left Nashville with his army some time in March or April, I think—at all events before the battle of Shiloh; left Middle Tennessee, and was not again in Middle Tennessee until some time in the summer or fall of last year. I think after he left, for a time, in some parts of the country around Nashville, the policy indicated in that general order was followed. I think it was particularly in Murray and Giles Counties, where there were post commanders. In each of these counties there was a large Union meeting, and we regarded the proceedings as flattering. I am not advised as to whether the policy was changed in Giles County. It was, I think, in Giles County. I am not, however, fully advised.

Question. Do you know, by common report or in any other way, of the complaints of the people that that policy was not very fully carried out in North Alabama?

I heard from citizens of Athens, Limestone County, Ala., that the policy was not carried-out there. How it was elsewhere in North Alabama I cannot say.

Question. And from what you know was the departure from or neglect of that policy in this instance attended with good effects or bad with reference to the disposition of the people toward the Union?

With peaceable, quiet citizens I think a kind policy would have been best. My conversations with the citizens of Athens were had with Union men, or men who were disposed to return to the Union and to have North Alabama come back, as they assured me; and their statements to me were that the policy pursued there had a very injurious effect upon those people who were disposed to be friendly to the Government of the United States.

Question. From your knowledge of the people of the States that have ken part in the rebellion, is it to be expected that they will return to heir loyalty until the rebel armies are defeated and kept beyond their mits?

I do not think it is possible.

Question. As far as you know, what is the practice and policy of the rebel Government? I wish to distinguish between that and the practice of indiscreet officers and passionate citizens. What, I say, is the practice and policy of the rebel Government with reference to the inhabitants of those districts of country which are overrun alternately by the rebel armies and the Union armies?

I am not able to answer that question from positive knowledge; I only have information from others; that information leads me to believe in many instances, and particularly in East Tennessee, that their treatment has been very harsh. In other instances in Middle Tennessee my information has been that it has not been so. I make this latter statement from what I know of Murray County and Giles. There are many Union men in those counties remaining at home, I think, past the age of conscription. Since the Federal army left those counties, feeling an interest in those gentlemen, I have made frequent inquiries about them and their treatment. The information received was that they were at home unmolested, at least so far as their personal liberty was concerned. Whether any distinctions have been made in regard to seizing property of Union or secession men I am not advised. I know the fact that a great many young men have left some of the counties in Middle Tennessee (being, as I believe, Union men) to avoid the conscription. I know the fact that there are a great many refugees in Nashville and different parts of the State who left their homes to avoid punishment, as they feared, by the Confederate authorities. Whether they would have been punished I cannot say; doubtless some of them would have been had they remained at home.

Question. Is it understood that the harsh policy which the rebel Government has pursued toward the Union people of East Tennessee has impaired their affection and loyalty toward the Union; and is it supposed that this treatment, in the event of an occupation of that country by the Union armies, would prevent those people from giving expression to their loyalty and extending their support to the Government?

I do not think, from what I have heard from East Tennesseeans, that their treatment by the rebel armies or authorities has impaired their affection for the Union. I rather think there would be almost a universal rejoicing if the armies of the United States would enter East Tennessee. I think their bitterness for the rebel authorities is very intense, and has been increased by the manner in which they have been treated by those authorities.

Question. It has been supposed that while the policy and practice of the rebel authorities toward those who forget their allegiance to the rebel Government are severe and our policy and practice toward those who forget their allegiance toward the General Government are mild the effect is to offer an inducement to disloyalty. Do you consider that that is really true; that the practical operation of these systems is to weaken the influence of the General Government over such people as long as they are under the control and protection of the Union armies?

I think treason to the United States ought to be punished. If committed in the face of the Army, the military ought to punish it; if not, the civil authorities ought to. I think a course of consistent kindness on the part of the United States Army in the territory whose people are in rebellion would have a good effect upon those people. From what I have seen of the East Tennesseeans who have left Tennessee on account of their persecutions for their Union sentiments I am satisfied that the rebel cause has suffered by the treatment of these men. I think a milder course would have been better for it; and so I think of our own cause. Where it is necessary to be severe on account of offenses committed, then let severity come; but with peaceable, quiet citizens kindness, in my judgment, would be far preferable.

Question. Is it not true that the people of the States in rebellion against the Government have been compelled very generally to acquiesce in that rebellion, whatever might be their wishes and opinions?

On the first breaking out of the rebellion I think there was an apprehension on the minds of the people of Tennessee to some extent of physical force and injury, and in many instances there was a compulsion of public sentiment which the young men could not well resist, or at all events they did not. I presume that force is more recently used to swell their armies where force was necessary. I think on the 1st of April, 1861, that the people of Tennessee were for the Union. I know they were in February, 1861, from the vote they gave on the 9th of that month, in which the result was about 64,000 majority for the Union. I do not pretend to undertake to describe the state of things when this rebellion first broke out in Tennessee, but no man who was not there will ever comprehend it. Never.

Question. With, then, the existence of a latent or suppressed affection for the Union, has not the policy of severity the objection of punishing friends as well as enemies, the innocent as well as the guilty?

I think there is that latent feeling of regard and perhaps affection for the Union in the minds of a great many people of the South, and I think it can be cultivated much more effectually by kindness, where it can be extended, than by a contrary course. As to the effect of the policy referred to in the question, that can be judged of each man for himself.

Cross-examination by the JUDGE-ADVOCATE:

Question. How long have you been a resident of East Tennessee?

I am a native of Tennessee.

Question. Were you in the State subsequent to its withdrawal from the Union?

Yes, sir.

Question. How long did you remain under the rebel Government?

Until the advent of the Federal Army in February or March, 1862.

Question. As a Union man residing in the State at that time did you experience none of the harsh treatment we have heard of?

No, sir; I was not treated harshly personally.

Question. Were you understood by the rebel authorities to be a Union man?

I suppose so, sir.

Question. What was the number of troops furnished by Tennessee to the rebel Army up to the time of our occupation of Nashville?

I do not know, sir; I know that there was provision made in the Legislature to raise 55,000, but how many were raised I do not know, for I had nothing to say to or do with the authorities on that subject.

Question. Were those troops raised by volunteering or by conscripting or drafting.

A large portion of the first troops raised was by volunteering. In the fall of 1861 there was an attempt at a draft, and, judging from what I heard from others, in attempting to enforce the draft most of the called volunteered to avoid it. More recently in Tennessee my information is that they are conscripting them wherever they can find them, but I know nothing on that subject.

Question. Do you not know that that rebel army from Tennessee represents nearly the whole population of Tennessee?

Yes, sir; that is, they are from all parts of the State and a large majority of the families are represented.

Question. Did not that vote from which you drew your inference that there was a Union feeling in Tennessee stop short of an unconditional Union sentiment; that is, did it include coercion?

I think it did not stop short; that is my impression, from the fact that the majority voted against having a convention to consider the subject at all, lest that convention might take the State out. I do not know that that vote indicated a condition of coercion; at all events, it was a vote against holding a convention, but not by so large a majority as the 64,000.

Question. Was it not about the same thing as it was in Virginia;

that is, that the people were in favor of the Union, but not in favor of a Union that could be coerced?

I do not know how it would have been in the vote of February if that had been the leading question, nor do I know for certainty how it was in the State of Virginia; but I think there has always been a better state of feeling for the Union in Tennessee than in Virginia. I do not of course include Western Virginia.

Question. How is it possible to pursue a conciliatory policy, such as you speak of, toward a population who volunteered to the number of 50,000, say, in opposition to its Government, representing thereby the entire population of the State?

I would not pursue a conciliatory policy toward the 55,000 then in arms. I should subdue them if I could; but for the quiet people at home who have not volunteered or joined the army in any form, who are remaining peaceable and quiet in the face of the armies of the United States, I would extend to them kindness. That would be my judgment of the course to pursue toward all men and women under all circumstances where I wished to win their affections.

Question. Why do you make a distinction between the man who carries the arms and the man who furnishes the arms and the sustenance for him?

It is very rarely to be found in the history of any wars that I have read of that war has been made upon peaceable citizens, men and women, who have no arms in their hands, but the business is to fight the men that have arms; this, it seems to me, makes the distinction itself. In the presence of the armies of the United States in the rebel territory I see no chance for furnishing arms or anything else to the men in rebellion and in the field. I should certainly make a wide distinction between those two classes of persons. I would go even further, and say if I could I would induce these men to lay down their arms and come back to the Union. I would do it, but I see no hope for that course.

Question. Does this distinction that you speak of obtain in rebellion?

I think it ought to, when the object is to restore the greatest portion of the country to its loyalty. I know of no instance to the contrary where a distinction has not existed; at least I remember none such now.

Question. In what way do you think the Government of the United States lost the affection of this people now in rebellion?

I think, sir, it has been produced very largely by the discussion of partisan politicians and partisan newspapers in both sections of the country, in which falsehoods and misrepresentations have been stated as truth.

Question. Do you not know, Mr. Huston, that the deadly animosity of that entire population is almost without a parallel in the history of wars?

With a large majority of the people of the South there is that hostility; but I think if the armies of the United States were to be successful it could be overcome by judicious treatment.

Question. You rely, then, upon the strong arm of the Government really and not upon the conciliatory policy which has been spoken of?

I should rely mainly upon that; without that there is nothing to be done. Conciliation I should adopt with a view of overcoming the prejudices and winning the affections of the people after the other work is done and while it is being done.

Question. Until, then, our armies are successful, permanently so, is not all the effort of a conciliatory character taken as an evidence of weakness by the people of the South and laughed at accordingly?

General BUELL. I object to the question, inasmuch as it applies to the present time, when the disposition of the people toward the General Government may have changed and their opinion of its power changed from what it was when I inaugurated my policy. It may answer the judge-advocate's purpose to shape it a little differently and obviate the objection.

The JUDGE-ADVOCATE. I see no objection to the question as it stands. I do not propose to argue it.

General SCHOEPF. The witness stated that the people were very different until July last year, 1862, and that they have changed since then. There is a difference in the time and policy of the whole affair.

The court is cleared, and after discussion it is decided that the question should be put.

The WITNESS. I have spoken of a conciliatory policy toward peaceable and quiet citizens who remained at home. I do not myself regard that course as an evidence of weakness, nor have I any knowledge or information that the rebels so regard it. My information, though somewhat limited, is that they are delighted to hear of instances of hardship from people at home, because, as I suppose, they look upon it as a means of exasperating the public opinion of the country. From what I see and hear they are glad to be able to cite these things as a verification of what they pretended to predict at the onset of this contest.

Question. Did not the rebel States put forth their entire strength; and have they, in fact, needed any such incentive as that to embitter their feelings?

I think they needed that element of strength to some extent, for the reason that there were a good many people of Union feelings and a good number indifferent—at all events having a latent feeling for the Government of the United States; and I think they saw if they forced them into the army they would not make as good soldiers as if they were first exasperated and then induced to volunteer or come in by the conscription laws. I do not think a conscripted soldier makes as good a soldier as one who goes in willingly. I may be mistaken in that, but I do not think I am.

Question. As the concilatory policy you speak of that was inaugurated by the commander of the Army of the Ohio depends upon the application of the order referred to, please tell us from your experience who were designated as peaceable citizens, who were to be protected, not to be molested, in their persons and property.

I do not know of any specific designation outside of this order and others that I may have seen. I put a construction on it myself, and supposed it meant persons who staid at home and attended to their business and did or said nothing against the Government in any shape or form.

Question. I ask you from your experience, and not from your construction of that order, whether citizens openly avowing disunion sentiments, having sons in the rebel army and having until our army arrived there, furnished those sons with subsistence, and willingly supported the rebel Government, were included in that order as persons not to be molested in their persons and property?

I have no particular experience as to that matter; I remember no particular case now. But I would regard a man talking secession openly as not a peaceable citizen; and I do not include such when I speak of a conciliatory policy.

Question. If your recollection furnishes no instance in illustration of this sentence in the order, who were considered peaceable citizens and who were not, your observation has been somewhat limited, has it not?

I have been in Nashville most of the time since the Federal army arrived there. I do not know of any arrests under this order. I do not know whether there was anything to be observed or not; at all events I observed but little.

Question. Are you acquainted with or do you know of Judge G. W. Lane? If so, what weight would his opinion have as to the proper policy to be pursued in North Alabama?

I am acquainted with him, sir. He is a man of good sense, and I presume has an acquaintance with the people of North Alabama. I would rely upon his judgment about as I would upon any one man's. I should not regard it as unerring.

Question. Has not the treatment of Union men in East Tennessee by the rebel Government very effectually prevented any demonstration there in behalf of the Union?

The treatment and the presence of rebel armies there prevent any demonstration of Union sentiment among the people.

Question. Are you acquainted with or do you know of Parson Brownlow, of East Tennessee; and, if so, what weight would you give his opinion as to the proper policy to be pursued toward the rebels?

I am acquainted with him, sir. I should not give so much weight to his opinion as I should to that of many cooler men. I think he is too violent, and his judgment warped by his feelings honestly. He has been harshly dealt with, and feels it a great deal.

Question. I will ask you the same question with reference to Governor Andrew Johnson, of Tennessee.

I know of Governor Johnson. I would have a great deal more confidence in his judgment than in Mr. Brownlow's in regard to this whole matter.

Question. Would not his opinion very justly have great weight in settling a question of that sort?

It ought to have the same weight as that of any other sensible man of experience should have; but I do not know what it would have

Question. Is he not regarded as a man of more than ordinary intellect, and has not his experience on this very subject been very extended?

Yes, sir; he has more intellect than common, a great deal. He has had a great deal of experience in this matter.

By General SCHOEPF:

Question. You stated that you were at Nashville after the army commanded by General Buell occupied that place; where were you before that time?

I was at Nashville, sir.

Question. Did you practice law at Nashville previous to that time?

I practiced law in the State courts as long as there were any—in one of them, at least, the chancery court, as long as it was held. The Federal court was abolished and the Confederate took its place; I never was in that court, sir.

By General TYLER:

Question. Suppose both the Union and the rebel armies were out of Tennessee to-day and the people left to decide whether they would continue in the Union or join the Confederate Government, which do you think would be the decision of the population?

Under the present state of feeling I should say they would join the Confederate Government.

Question. What do you understand by latent and suppressed affection for the Union under this state of circumstances?

I mean a feeling that once existed in all its force and that has been to a great extent overcome. You may combine with this state of mind the fear of making a demonstration of it in a given case, lest the powers adverse to Government should become supreme. I mean, in other words, that feeling in the minds of a great many of the people of the South which, if cultivated and all fears resulting from its development and demonstration removed, will make good citizens of the United States.

Question. How is it that this latent feeling you speak of has been overcome?

It was not a latent feeling at the start. It is kept latent by all the appliances used

by the rebel authorities, and which are known to the whole country. I do not think
it is overcome; I think it now exists.

Question. Are you in favor of the execution of all the laws passed by
Congress and of all the orders issued by the President of the United
States and by his subordinate military officers, so far as they have come
to your knowledge, for the suppression of the rebellion commenced at
Fort Sumter and since carried on by the rebel Government at Rich-
mond, of which Jefferson Davis is President?

General BUELL. I object to the question, Mr. President, for the same
reasons I gave when the same question was put to a previous witness.

The court was cleared; when it was decided that the question should
be put.

The WITNESS. I am in favor of all the constitutional laws passed by Congress and
I am in favor of the suppression of the rebellion by all means known to civilized warfare.

Question. Do you believe that all laws passed by Congress should be
deemed to be constitutional until they are decided by the Supreme
Court to be unconstitutional.

I think the presumption is that all laws passed by the legislative department are
prima facie with authority until they are decided otherwise by the supreme judica-
ture of the land.

Commission adjourned to meet February 26.

CINCINNATI, *February* 26, 1863.

Commission met pursuant to adjournment. All the members present;
also the judge-advocate and General Buell.

Capt. JESSE MERRILL (a witness for the defendant), being duly sworn
by the judge-advocate, testified as follows:

By General BUELL:

Question. State your name and position in the service of the United
States.

Jesse Merrill; captain in the Seventh Pennsylvania Infantry, on detached duty as
an acting officer in charge of the signal corps.

Question. Were you on duty with the headquarters of the Army of
the Ohio last summer? If so, please state in what capacity.

I was with the headquarters of the Army of the Ohio; I joined them at Corinth,
and was with them as an officer in charge of the signal corps.

Question. Did you while at Huntsville prepare a code of signals to
direct the movements of the army under certain contingencies?

I did.

Question. If you have a copy of that code please present it to the
Commission.

(Code of signals presented by Captain Merrill, marked A.)

Question. I will submit this paper (the code of signals) as evidence,
and as showing the preparation that was made to direct the movements
of the army under my command, under certain contingencies, through
the assistance of the signal corps.

The communication and the direction that was given was by means of rockets.
There were officers under my command with four of the five divisions of the army at
that time, and the fifth division was to have been supplied with officers if this code
was carried into effect and it was found necessary to use them. The reason that the
two colors are represented here is that they are used to indicate different things when
differently combined. As a signal a white rocket was used to call attention, but when

combined with anything else meant "artillery;" in the same way a red rocket was used to acknowledge the receipt of a message, but when used in a combination it meant "infantry;" and the red and white combined meant "repeat the message," but when used in combination it meant "cavalry."

Question. Do you understand that the movements which are prescribed upon certain roads had particular reference to the information which was expressed in the preceding message, giving information in regard to movements of the enemy, or is the particular arrangement you have there accidental; is there any particular design in it?

The design was to direct the movements of the army, and was made for that special purpose. The code is so arranged that any brigade or division of the army could have been ordered to move on any particular points named in any of the messages which the different combinations represented, always provided that the communication by this system of signals could have been made; that is, that a rocket could be seen from the point where the order was given and the point where it was intended it should go.

Question. Take an example here. Here is a message: "The enemy is crossing in force at Chattanooga;" then follows a signal message to the troops: "Move on Therman road," "Move on Cane road," &c. What I want to know is whether this arrangement of messages with reference to each other was a matter of accident in preparing the code, or whether it indicated that because the enemy was crossing at Chattanooga then the movements expressed in the message following were to be made. Was there any necessary connection between the two? In other words, for example, might not a message to the troops which followed some other message containing information in regard to the movements of the enemy have been just as appropriate on the occasion referred to in the first message giving information of the movements as any other message?

There is no necessary connection between these messages. For instance, if the intelligence came to General Buell, commanding that army, that the enemy was crossing in force at Chattanooga, he could, by having any of these combinations used, order his force or any part of his force to move on any of these points named. The messages themselves are entirely distinct and separate from each other, and the first might as well be last or in any other part of the code; so that the arrangement of the messages in the order in which they are expressed in the code is purely accidental.

Question. Were the different parts of your corps provided with the necessary means of using this code?

They were.

Question. Was it found necessary to use it in the subsequent operations of the army?

It was not.

Question. Explain, if you please, the alterations which were made in that paper subsequently and the object of them.

The alterations were made to direct the movements of the army after arriving at Louisville in September (2d, I think it was). The combinations were altered as well as the messages, inasmuch as I have been supplied with rockets of a different color and not requiring to use so large a number.

(The code and copy of the order presented as evidence, marked B.)

Question. Was your corps in operation at Perryville on the 8th of October last? If so, please state what stations you established, what time they were established and in operation, and what officers were in charge of them respectively.

Communication was established on the hill near General Buell's headquarters to a point immediately in front of and in the direction of Perryville and near the pike on which this hill was. This was about 12 o'clock. There was one intermediate station between these two points, making three stations in all. The station at General Buell's headquarters was worked by Lieutenants Meeker, Taylor, and Thayer, I think. I know Meeker and Taylor were there during the afternoon. The intermediate station spoken of was worked by Lieutenants Hollopeter and Bachtell, and the one in front by Lieutenants Fitch and Sheridan. At one time during the day this station in front communicated with a station near General Rousseau's headquarters, at which Lieutenants Landrum, Quinton, and Connelly were operating, but the communication with that station was but for a very short time.

Question. At what hour of the day was that communication interrupted?

I cannot speak certainly as to the hour, but think it was between 2 and 3 o'clock, or a little after 2.

Question. Did you establish communication between headquarters and the right corps of the army also?

I did some time during the night of the 8th.

Question. Were you on the ground and in the immediate supervision of these various stations?

I was. I was in the front along the line until nearly dark, trying to establish communication with the left wing—from the left wing to this station in the center.

Question. Was any communication, official or otherwise, transmitted to headquarters that a battle was being fought on any part of the line?

I have no knowledge of any communication of that kind having been transmitted over the line, nor has it been reported to me, as it should have been if such communication had been sent. I speak entirely with reference to the line leading from General Buell's headquarters to the front; not the communication with the right wing. A number of messages passed over that line, but none of them in reference to the fight that was going on, because communication with the right wing was not established till the night of the 8th.

Question. Have you heard any talk of intelligence of that kind being at any of the stations? If so, please state at what stations, what officers were in charge of them, and all you know about it.

I have heard within the last two months, and not before that time, Lieutenant Fitch assert that while he was on the station in front he received a message from the officers on the station at General Rousseau's headquarters to the effect that the enemy were attacking them with infantry and artillery, and I think that he asserts that he sent it to the next station, but not in any official way, as it was merely a message from one officer of the corps to another, giving this information, not coming from any official source nor directed to any official person.

Question. Do you understand that he transmitted it as information that was important or was it merely an exchange of intelligence among themselves; how did he represent it?

I understood it as merely an exchange of ideas, giving what he received from the officer of General Rousseau's division and telling them what was going on, and that he sent it to the next station for the information of those officers. The line being open for communication, he would not need to give the information himself to General Buell when others who knew better the state of affairs had the same opportunity of communicating with General Buell that he had.

Question. Lieutenants Fitch and Sheridan were at the third station, I understand.

They were at the third station, counting the station at your headquarters as No. 1.

Question. Does Lieutenant Sheridan know anything about this message?

He says he does not.

Question. Were you near that station yourself, and about how far from it, when this message should have been received?

I was near that station until half past 3 or 4 o'clock. I think the message was received at the time or just before the communication was broken off with General Rousseau. I was within 200 rods of the station.

Question. Who were the officers to whom it should have been transmitted next by Lieutenant Fitch?

Lieutenants Bachtell and Hollopeter.

Question. Have you had conversation with those officers on the subject?

I have not. I never thought it of sufficient importance until I saw the assertion in what purported to be a letter written by Col. Dan. McCook to his brother, in which he repeated this message; and since that time it has never occurred to me to inquire in reference to it when I have seen them.

Question. Had you conversation with the officers who were at the first station, the headquarters station?

I have conversed with Lieutenant Meeker, who was the principal officer at that station, and he has no recollection of any such message having come to him.

Question. Is it a rule in that corps to keep a copy of messages that have been transmitted to different stations and is such a copy kept at each station?

It is a rule to keep copies of all official communications. Now we have books prepared for that special purpose; they have been introduced since the time of which we are now speaking.

Question. How far were you from this station at General Rousseau's headquarters during the time when the severe fighting was going on, as it is now understood?

I cannot speak positively as to the distance, though it was not a mile.

Question. Were you in sight of the ground upon which the battle was fought, and with what general officers were you?

I was at the third station, immediately in front of the headquarters, on the road leading to Perryville, with the troops of General Sheridan, until half past 4 or 5 o'clock, when I went over to the left to make another effort to establish communication with General McCook, and was on that side of the battle ground until nearly or quite dark, when I went back to General Buell's headquarters.

Question. Designate these stations by numbers, commencing with No. 1, at the headquarters, and name the officers who were at them respectively.

Station No. 1, at General Buell's headquarters, Lieutenants Meeker, Taylor, and Thayer; No. 2, in a corn field half way between No. 1 and No. 3, Lieutenants Hollopeter and Bachtell; Station No. 3, near the Perryville road and General Sheridan's command, Lieutenants Sheridan and Fitch; No. 4, to the left, near General Rousseau's and General McCook's headquarters (only until between 2 and 3 o'clock, when they were compelled to abandon that station), Lieutenants Landrum, Quinton, and Connelly.

Question. What impression was made upon your mind by what you saw and heard in regard to the severity of the engagement that day?

It was the first fight I had ever seen and the first fire under which I ever was, and necessarily I felt rather singular. At the time, and before I saw the battle of Stone River, I supposed it was rather a severe action; since then, comparing it with that, I have changed my mind as regards its being a very severe engagement, and do not think it was a very severe engagement from what I saw, though I was not in the same situation by any means and was not so close in the battle of Perryville as I was in the other case.

Question. Was it your expectation, from what you saw and heard, that the battle would be renewed the next morning?

It was, sir. It was a very general impression with all with whom I conversed.

Question. Did you expect to find the enemy on the same ground or to have to go in pursuit of them?

I expected to find them where they were the day before and had arranged our communications with that expectation.

Question. Was it considered by anybody that you saw and conversed with, or whose opinion you heard expressed, that the battle of that day had been of such severity and importance as to decide the contest which had been expected between the armies all the time?

Not that I know of. All the officers with whom I conversed—they were mostly, though, officers of my own corps, with two or three exceptions—thought the contest undecided.

Question. Was it supposed the enemy had suffered by comparison very severely in the engagement—more so or as much so as ourselves?

I have no recollection so far as regards that. I myself supposed that they had, but I do not remember that I had any conversation with any one on that subject.

Question. Did you know that General McCook's corps had been driven from its position and that it did not regain that position during the day?

Some time during the afternoon—I am unable to say at what hour—I saw General Rousseau's line of battle retire and saw Loomis' battery (at least it was represented as Loomis' and I have no doubt it was) taken from the front, where it was stationed, and run back through a corn field, and soon after a rebel cavalry regiment went past the line which had been occupied by General Rousseau, and this rebel cavalry regiment was opened upon and I think driven back—at least they retired by the battery on the hill, near General Sheridan's batteries, where our station was. That was the first intimation I had of our lines having been withdrawn from the position where they originally stood. I have no knowledge of what was going on farther to the left until later in the evening.

Question. Was the question considered by General Sheridan, in your hearing and your knowledge, whether it was considered to send intelligence to headquarters of what was going on in front at any time during the day? State anything you know on the subject.

Lieutenant Sheridan, one of the officers working that station, informed me officially, perhaps the same day, that General Sheridan had prepared a message to send, but of the contents of that message my memory does not serve me, but I think it had reference to the contest; but just as Lieutenant Sheridan was about to send it General Sheridan recalled it and told him it was not necessary to send it.

Question. Was this information from General Sheridan to you in the nature of an official report or conversation between you; was it information which it would have been proper to give to you as his superior officer?

It was not, sir. It was simply a conversation of our doings and workings during the day.

Question. Do you know at what time this message was supposed to have been prepared?

I do not, sir.

Question. Did you on the night of the 8th transmit orders to the right corps with reference to attacking the enemy next morning?

I did.

Question. Have you a copy of those orders, captain? Please present it if you have.

Here is the copy of the order given me by General Thomas:

"(Official.)

"GENERAL BUELL'S HEADQUARTERS.

"To General CRITTENDEN:
"Have your advance division ready to attack at daylight. Issue orders at once.
"THOMAS."

Question. At what time of the night was it given?

The order is not dated. It was given about half past 1 o'clock on the morning of the 9th of October.

Question. You have some messages which I understand were transmitted through your corps on the morning of the 9th. I will thank you to read them in the order in which they occurred.

The first message, I think, but I may be mistaken in reference to the order in which they were received, is:

"(Official.)

"To General BUELL:
"I am all ready. My post will be to the rear of the center of my line.
"CRITTENDEN."

The message just read was received, I think, soon after daylight on the morning of the 9th. There are two messages which I think were sent without any answer. As to the order in which they were sent I do not know positively, but I think they were sent in this order:

"OCTOBER 9—8 a. m.

"General CRITTENDEN:
"Have you commenced the advance? What delays your attack?
"JAMES B. FRY,
"Colonel."

The second message to General Crittenden is:

"Are you advancing, and what news? Answer.
"JAMES B. FRY,
"Colonel."

Here are two other messages giving information.

Question. Have you any answer to that?

I have no positive answer.

"To Colonel FRY:
"Colonel Murray, who is off to the right of the command, reports that this morning a regiment of cavalry and one of infantry had crossed the Danville road beyond Mitchell's, going south. I have ordered Colonel McCook to reconnoiter the woods and ascertain his whereabouts."

That message was from General Thomas or General Crittenden, I am unable to say which. There is no signature. It was received some time in the morning before 12 o'clock.

There are two other official communications, but I am unable to say whether these communications, giving information in reference to the movements of the enemy, were received before or after this order; but I think after. The order is dated—

"OCTOBER 9—12 o'clock.

"General CRITTENDEN or General THOMAS:
"In case the enemy has retired, as reported, put two of your divisions in position near Crawford Spring, on the Harrodsburg road, and a third near Walker's Spring, south of the town. Take the strongest positions you can find, and be ready at a moment's notice to march or fight.
"JAMES B. FRY."

The next is a communication official to General Buell:

"I have just conversed with a citizen of Parksville. He says there is no enemy at Danville nor on the Lebanon and Danville pike. He thinks they have turned toward Harrodsburg. I have sent McCook with his cavalry to observe and report. Crittenden's corps is advancing upon Walker's Spring. Have met no resistance for an hour."

This message was from General Thomas. I am unable to say whether it was before or after the order, which is dated 12 o'clock. All these messages were transmitted on the 9th of October.

There is another message to Colonel Fry:

"General Smith advancing. His skirmishers within three-quarters of a mile of Walker's Spring, on the Perryville pike. So far they have met no resistance."

I do not know the hour at which this was received.

Question. Do you know where Parksville is?

No, sir; I do not.

Cross-examination by the JUDGE-ADVOCATE:

Question. Would the transmission of such a message spoken of by Lieutenant Fitch be in accordance with the custom or rule governing your signal corps?

General BUELL. I have not the privilege of cross-examining the witness, and would suggest that the question is not as distinct as the judge-advocate himself would desire to make it. It might be in accordance with certain rules, but not in accordance with those rules which would make it an official message.

The JUDGE-ADVOCATE. (In continuation of his question.) In other words, is it the habit or would it be within the rule for any post of your signal corps to send information of an important character without its being sanctioned by an officer outside of the corps?

It would certainly; if he chose to take the responsibility of sending that message to General Buell it would be within the line of his duty. But it is usual, when there is a general officer with whom an officer is stationed, for any information of that kind to come from that general officer. There are times when our corps is sent out as reconnoitering or observing officers, and then they report on their own responsibility; but if they are with any general officer the communication comes usually from him.

Question. Would such a communication as that claimed to have been sent by Lieutenant Fitch have been recorded as the others were?

If he had sent it as an official communication from himself to General Buell, giving information, it would have been recorded and reported or should have been; but conversations between officers while on their stations are not reported, even though they contain information given from one to the other.

Question. Would it not have been the duty of officers at Station No. 1 to have communicated that intelligence to headquarters, whether it came officially or not?

I am hardly prepared to say whether it would or not, but I have no doubt they would have done so; knowing that the communication might have come from a general officer, they would perhaps not have done so. I do not think it would have been imperative for them to have done so at all.

Question. Do you know of any messages received or sent along the line that day from headquarters respecting the firing in front?

I do not, sir.

Question. Do you know of any information or any inquiries such as you considered of a conversational character passing from No. 1 to the front that day?

I do not.

Question. If there had been any such would you have known it?

Not necessarily. The conversations, if any, from the station at headquarters would have been carried on with the Station No. 2, while I was most of the afternoon at Station No. 3.

Question. Do you know that those stations were busily at work passing signals all that afternoon?

No, sir; I do not.

Question. Did Lieutenant Fitch accompany you to the court-room at Nashville at the time I sent for you or was it Lieutenant Sheridan?

Neither of them accompanied me as a witness. Lieutenant Sheridan was afterward subpœnaed as a witness, and went there, but the court had adjourned to Louisville.

Question. Do you know that Lieutenant Fitch was ordered to appear and did come to Nashville at that time?

I have no knowledge of it, sir.

Question. At what time did you leave Station No. 3 that afternoon to go to McCook's left and establish communications?

I think it was about half past 4 o'clock. I cannot speak positively, but I think it was about that hour.

Question. In fixing the date and attaching the signature to some of these dispatches you have introduced you rely exclusively upon your memory, do you not?

With reference to these that are not dated I do.

By General TYLER:

Question. From what source or sources did you get the impression that the battle would be renewed next morning? Please explain.

I cannot give the source of the impression. I suppose I got it from the fact that I thought the battle was as yet undecided, and that I knew of the order for this attack to General Crittenden, and that there were troops in reserve that had not been engaged.

Question. Was General Crittenden ordered to attack the enemy or to be ready to attack the enemy?

The order reads to be ready to attack the enemy.

Question. Do you know of any order having been given to General Crittenden to attack the enemy?

I do not.

Question. What reason had you for expecting to find the enemy "the next morning" where they were the night before, as stated in your testimony?

It was a result arrived at in my own mind by some course of reasoning which I cannot now explain.

Question. You did not find them there the next morning.

I did not. I was not out; I was at headquarters of the Army of the Ohio.

Question. What would be the effect if all the signal officers arrogated to themselves the right to judge of military movements and go and report them on their own authority to headquarters?

The effect would be merely an expression of their own opinion, to be judged of by the general commanding according to their merits.

Question. Under whose control was the signal corps in General Buell's army?

I was the general signal officer in General Buell's army.

Question. And to whom did you report direct?

I report to and am under the order of Maj. Albert J. Myer, Signal Officer of the Army.

Question. Are you under the immediate command of the commanding officer of the army under whom you are acting?

I am.

Question. Do you make daily reports to the commander-in-chief of the operations of your corps?

I make now a semi-weekly report. To General Buell I made a daily morning report of the efficiency and strength of the corps, and the operations of the corps are reported to the commanding officer of the army when they do any work.

Question. Was there any order communicated by the signal corps on the 8th or 9th of October not cited in your testimony as yet?

There is one, I think, from General Gilbert on the 9th.

Question. What is that order?

(Official.)

To General Buell:

Mitchell is close to the town and Sheridan closing up his right with Mitchell. His left retired, waiting for McCook to close up. McCook closing to his right slowly. When connection is complete and ready to advance Sheridan will move his left forward even with his right.

GILBERT.

Question. Then I understand you to say, captain, that we have on record the result of all the operations of the signal corps on the 8th and 9th of October?

You have, so far as I know them.

Question. You would from your official position know all, would you not?

All official business that went over the line I would.

Col. JOHN KENNETT (a witness for the defendant), being duly sworn by the judge-advocate, testified as follows:

By General BUELL:

Question. State your name and place of residence, if you please; whether you have been in the service of the United States, and in what capacity, and when you left the service.

My name is John Kennett; colonel Fourth Ohio Cavalry. On the 5th of September, 1862, I was detached in command of the First Cavalry Division. On the 25th of February, 1863, I resigned.

Question. Were you on duty in North Alabama from the time of the occupation of that country by our troops and did you continue so until they were withdrawn?

Yes, sir.

Question. State what the condition of your regiment was about the 1st of July last in regard to its horses and other necessaries affecting its efficiency.

Our regiment had been ordered about so much in North Alabama and Tennessee that the horses were all worn-out; that, however, was under General Mitchel, before General Buell came on from Shiloh. About that time, when we were waiting to get other horses, our clothing was defective, and so with respect to other quartermaster's stores.

Question. State, if you please, what was done to refit you again and with what result.

I sent 125 men, by orders from General Buell, to Pittsburg Landing after some horses, which were brought through to Huntsville; 155 horses, I think, was the number. Also, subsequent to that, I sent 200 to Nashville, by General Buell's orders, for horses there; upon their return most of the horses were unfit for service.

Question. State how your regiment was distributed during the summer and whether it was actively employed subsequent to the 1st of July.

Yes, sir. All the time "on the go" scouting. Part of the regiment was at Battle Creek, extending from Bridgeport and Stevenson to Battle Creek and through that section of the country. Four companies were there on active duty.

Question. How did you supply your regiment with forage?

We had to feed them on green corn.

Question. Was old forage to be found in any abundance?

No, sir; it was very scarce at that time.

Question. Do you know whether or not the army availed itself of the supplies of the country to as full an extent as it admitted?

I think they did, sir. We visited every farm-house in every direction to get forage, bacon, &c.

Question. Were you with the army in its movement in Kentucky in September? If so, please state what you know in regard to the movement of the train from Bowling Green to Louisville, the route it took, &c.

I was, sir. Colonel Zahm was detached in command of the Second Brigade, to take command of the train that went by way of Brownsville, Priceville, Millerstown, from there to Hayesville, Deep Spring, and from there to West Point. I did not go on that road; my duty was on the other road, to protect any approach to the train. I took the road to their right, with the First Brigade, to protect them on every cross-road from the rebel cavalry cutting it off, and went on to Elizabethtown. There I occupied the place, threatening every cross-road all the time during Colonel Zahm's march to West Point, and receiving daily reports three times a day as to the precise distance he had gone and whether he required any further assistance from the First Brigade. I did send him the Seventh Pennsylvania when there were reports of some rebel cavalry appearing on its flanks. Every road was also covered with scouting parties during the whole time the train was in transitu. In addition to that we captured a whole regiment of cavalry, the Third Georgia. In the performance of that duty we felt the daily pickets on our right, with scouting parties toward Hodgensville, Boston, New Haven, and Bardstown.

Question. You do not pretend to describe the road accurately, then?

No, sir. I do not know that I could describe it accurately without having my own map here; I did not charge my memory with the names of the little towns I passed through.

Question. Were you in command of the cavalry division at that time?

Yes, sir.

Question. What time did your division leave Bowling Green and on what roads; in other words, what disposition was made of your division on the march from Bowling Green?

I do not remember the date exactly. The First Brigade went right on to the bridge over Green River to the right of Munfordville, and we went to Bacon Creek, on the Louisville and Nashville road, thence to Elizabethtown. The Second Brigade, as I just described, was in charge of the train toward West Point.

Question. Were you in advance with any portion of your command during the retreat of the rebel army out of Kentucky? If so, please state in what condition you found the country in regard to supplies of forage for your animals and what road you were on.

We were in the advance from Harrodsburg, Danville, Stanford, and Crab Orchard, up to Mount Vernon. Up to Stanford we found forage; from Stanford to Mount Vernon we could not find any, and were ordered back from Mount Vernon to feed the horses at Crab Orchard.

Commission adjourned to meet February 27, 1863.

CINCINNATI, *February* 27, 1863.

Commission met pursuant to adjournment. All the members present; also the judge-advocate and General Buell.

General THOMAS L. CRITTENDEN (a witness for the defendant), being duly sworn by the judge-advocate, testified as follows:

By General BUELL:

Question. State your name and position in the service of the United States, if you please, general.

My name is Thomas L. Crittenden; age, forty-four years; major-general of volunteers.

Question. Were you on duty with the Army of the Ohio at Corinth; did you march with that Army into North Alabama and Middle Tennessee after the evacuation of Corinth by the rebel army, and what was your command at that time?

I was on duty with the Army of the Ohio at Corinth, and I did march with the Army of the Ohio from Corinth through North Alabama and through Middle Tennessee. I commanded the Fifth Division in the Army of the Ohio at that time.

Question. About what was the effective strength of your division at that time?

About 3,000, sir.

Question. Were you with your division when the movement toward North Alabama commenced in the month of June last?

I was near Baldwyn at the time the movement of the Tennessee commenced and through Middle Tennessee. I remember it because General Pope had called for some re-enforcements; he was near Baldwyn, and supposed the enemy in considerable force in front of him. General Buell sent up two divisions and went up himself with them. There we remained not more than two days, I think, possibly three; after which we commenced to march.

Question. Please state the route by which you marched from the vicinity of Booneville until you arrived at Athens and the more remarkable features of that route, as well as you can remember them, giving the dates as well as you can, the time of departure, and the arrival.

I marched from Booneville to Iuka. The only thing that dwells in my memory now is, that on the first day's march I encountered very considerable difficulties in crossing a bottom that was intersected by some streams and various little bridges that were destroyed. I managed, however, to get across, as I considered it important. I had but three days' rations, and was ordered to make the march within the time—three days. Supplies were sent to me at Iuka. As to the date on which we started I cannot be positive; I think it was about the middle of the month; from the 12th to the 15th I guess. I marched from Iuka to Tuscumbia. I remember nothing very particular on the march. The weather was intensely hot and the roads dusty. I marched at 3 o'clock in the morning and got into camp by 8 or 9. I was encumbered on that march somewhat with my reserve artillery—some six or eight batteries I had to carry along. I took them only from Iuka to Athens. At Tuscumbia we crossed the river; General McCook's division and my own ferried across the river there; and from Florence I marched to Athens, carrying along this reserve artillery. The roads were very dusty and the weather very hot. I remember no particular obstacle on the road. The river we had to ford. It is a considerable stream, and the ford was rather deep at the time, but we got across without any difficulty. I do not remember precisely when I arrived at Athens, but I marched from that place on the 5th of July to Huntsville. At Huntsville I was delayed a little while, perhaps a day, waiting for supplies. Supplies were scarce, and General Nelson, I understood, had taken all to Athens, so that none came on to Huntsville for me, and I had to start without sufficient quantity of supplies to take me to Stevenson. The general, however, determined to send my supplies to a point on the railroad between Huntsville and Stevenson, near which I passed on my march. I got to Stevenson on the 12th of July, and on the 13th I received an order from General Buell to go to Battle Creek and take command there. I reached Battle Creek on the 13th, and relieved General Hascall, who was there in command.

Question. In the march from Iuka to Athens what division did you follow and how far were you behind?

I followed General McCook's division; it was commanded by General Johnson. When I reached Stevenson I found General Johnson commanded the division. I think General McCook left his division at Athens, but I am not sure. The division left Huntsville on the day before I got there; they marched very shortly before I did from Athens; I do not remember the day; I marched on the 5th. General Johnson left, I think, the day before I got to Huntsville, for Stevenson, where I overtook him.

Question. What do you know about the condition of supplies at the time of your arrival at Athens and about the cause of the scarcity, if there was any?

I know that there was a scarcity of supplies, and I understood that there was a break in the railroad, which made it necessary to haul supplies a considerable distance. Of the exact distance I am not sure, but I heard it was about 22 miles. Our wagons had had to bring supplies along the road. Afterwards, on the very day I got to Stevenson, we received the news of the taking of Murfreesborough, and the interruption there made the supplies very scarce for a long time. We lived on half rations for, I should think, a month from the time I reached Battle Creek.

Question. Are you positive about the distance that supplies had to be hauled over that break in the railroad?

I am not, sir.

Question. Was your division train turned into the general train for the purpose of hauling supplies over this break?

I understood that it was. All our wagons were so used, I understood.

Question. Was exertion made to supply your command with forage while you were in the vicinity of Athens and did you find the supply in the country abundant or scarce?

I found the supply of forage quite scarce. I cannot say what exertions were made to supply the command with forage. I had expected some forage, had been notified that I might look for some, but none was ever supplied me. I supplied myself with a good deal of difficulty, taking the forage where I found it. I made every possible exertion. General Nelson was in command there, and I remember having some little quarrel because I thought his animals were living a little better than mine were. I thought he obtained it from the supply train; and I remember his telling me that I would have to work for myself—there was no other way of getting it; and I made every possible exertion to obtain forage. I moved my camp once during the few days I remained at Athens in order to get forage or to get nearer to it.

Question. Do you know about how long you remained in the vicinity of Athens and what was the cause of your halting there temporarily?

I was halted there because of the scarcity of supplies, I understood; but I do not remember when I arrived at Athens nor how long I remained there. I understood there was nothing for me at Huntsville, and we were living from hand to mouth at Stevenson, which I understood to be the cause of my detention there.

Question. How does the country about Athens and Huntsville compare with that about Stevenson and Battle Creek in supplies of forage?

I should say that the country about Athens and about Huntsville was a better one for supplies than either that around Stevenson or Battle Creek. We could not supply ourselves at Battle Creek, and supplies of forage were sent to us. I hauled forage from Bridgeport and from Stevenson to Battle Creek. We consumed everything around Battle Creek. We sent our wagons some distance up the railroad to haul forage for some distance in the country when it was hauled to the road and brought down by railroad to the camp.

Question. How did you find the country between Huntsville and Battle Creek in regard to supplies both of forage and provisions?

Scarcely anything; very poor.

Question. Do you remember anything about the orders that were given when the army was leaving Corinth for reducing the amount of baggage as much as possible and can you state about the substance of these orders?

My recollection is that when I left Corinth I did not know that we were going farther than Baldwyn. I do not think that I took all of my wagons; they were sent back. If my memory serves me, I was at Booneville when I received the order; I cannot remember the substance of it, except that it was to reduce the baggage as much as possible; but how many wagons were allowed and what the order was I do not now remember.

Question. Do you remember that orders were given reducing the allowance of tents and requiring the soldiers to turn over their overcoats and other surplus clothing? Do you know whether that order was executed; what disposition was made of this surplus?

I remember the order in reference to the overcoats and the order about the allowance of tents. My recollection is that the overcoats and tents were to be turned over at Iuka, but I cannot be positive.

Question. About what force was there at Battle Creek at the time of your arrival there till you left and how was that force composed—of what divisions or parts of divisions?

The force was composed of my own division, which numbered about 3,000 men, and a brigade under General Hascall which I found there. I do not certainly know what was the strength of that brigade; they had a battery; I think they had 1,500 men. Most of that brigade was ordered away when General McCook came up. General McCook's force, on its arrival, I understood to be about 6,000 men. Our entire force there was about 9,000 men, and this force continued there till we left.

Question. Had you instructions to inform yourself by all possible means of the strength and movements of the enemy while you were in command there and did you exert yourself in that way?

I was ordered to use every possible exertion to obtain information and to spare no expense in order to obtain it. I employed at once on my arrival there several men who were vouched for as trusty at considerable expense, and kept them going all the time. It was exceedingly difficult to get any reliable information there. The rebels occupied the bank of the river immediately opposite our camp; they were in sight every day and the men were very much afraid to go. We, however, got a man to go within a few miles of Chattanooga, who brought a message from a man who lived in that place.

Question. Do you remember that information now?

I cannot say that I remember it at all. I know that he mentioned that troops were at Chattanooga. I sent the information immediately to headquarters, as I did all information I received there; but I do not remember now what it was. It occurred about the middle of July and before we heard much about the movements of the rebel army; it was not fastened in my memory, as it would have been afterwards when events became more interesting.

Question. Was General McCook there at the time this information was reported?

I am not sure whether General McCook was there or not; he possibly reached there the very day my messenger returned. It is also possible I might have given the information to General McCook instead of sending it to General Buell, General McCook having taken command there.

Question. Do you know of General McCook's reporting to headquarters information which had been derived through your scouts or agents and which you probably reported yourself also?

I believe that that is the fact, sir. I have some recollection of General McCook's telling me that he had reported information to you which I also reported; but of course I cannot say that he did, though I think he told me so and showed me the dispatches.

Question. Do you remember what divisions of the army were embraced in the movement toward North Alabama from Corinth in the first place ?

General McCook's division, General Nelson's, General Wood's, and my own; that is, in the first movement toward North Alabama. General Thomas' division, I understood, was to remain at that time; it did not start with us, but came up afterward.

Question. Do you know positively the time of the arrival of General Thomas' division at Athens or Huntsville ?

I do not. General Thomas never reached me at any point on the march. I never saw him or any portion of his command until we reached Pelham, where I found General Schoepf in command.

Question. About what was the aggregate effective strength of the four divisions you have mentioned ?

My own division was very much the smallest. Of course my knowledge is not accurate about the others. I talked frequently with the commanders, and supposed their divisions were about 6,500, from that to 7,000, strong; my own, as stated, was about 3,000.

Question. Making an aggregate force of how much ?

Probably about 22,000.

Question. What did you learn with regard to the character of the country between Bridgeport and Chattanooga on the south side of the river and with regard to its resources of supplies; was there as much as would be required for the subsistence of an army ?

For information of that kind we had to rely upon Union men who lived or had lived in that country. It was a barren country, and we supposed was very much exhausted by the troops who had been there; but of that of course we could only conjecture; we could not go over there. It is a very hilly, broken country, narrow bottoms, and very barren.

Question. With your knowledge of the dependence of the army in that region of country upon its depots in consequence of the scarcity of supplies in the country, and of the difficulty of getting supplies forward in consequence of the destruction of the railroad and the great distance of the army from its base, and considering also the force that the enemy, from the best information, could concentrate at Chattanooga to make such an operation difficult, if not uncertain, what is your opinion in regard to the practicability of moving directly to Chattanooga when the army arrived in North Alabama ?

I do not think, sir, at any time the movement was practicable; I mean from the time of my arrival and the first arrival of the troops up to the time we left.

Question. What time was this ?

I arrived at Battle Creek on the 13th of July. At no time after the breaking of the roads was the movement practicable at all, in my opinion. With the roads broken by which they had to receive supplies, and the troops thus living on half rations, they could not have gone to Chattanooga even with a very small force to resist them. I should have considered it unsafe to go if there had been nobody there to resist us.

Question. Do you know at what date, from the best information, General Bragg crossed the Tennessee River in his advance through Middle Tennessee into Kentucky ?

About the 22d of August. Perhaps on the 22d General McCook with his division and I with my division were in the Sequatchie Valley, having left me some 6 or 8 miles up the valley beyond the town of Jasper, and General McCook being himself about 6 miles farther up the valley, on his way to a road called the Anderson road, I think.

General McCook received information that thirty-six regiments had crossed the river and marched so far that in his judgment they could meet him to the Anderson road. He also received at the same time and from the same source (one of his spies) information that a large force had crossed the river at some two or three points; and upon this information he came back, gave me his information, and told me that as I had been separated from his command by order of General Buell and posted in the position I then occupied, he gave me no orders, and I must act upon my own responsibility—remain there or go back with him, just as I pleased. The precise day when the enemy crossed the river I cannot state; this is the only information I had as to the time. I supposed General McCook sent the information to headquarters when the rebels crossed the river. We had heard of the crossing of the river by smaller commands several times before, and then heard afterward that they had recrossed and gone back; but between the 18th and the 22d I should say that the main force or the force of the army crossed the Tennessee River.

Question. Was the information ever current for some time previous that the rebel army was advancing or about to advance on Tennessee?

Yes, sir; we had many conversations as to what they were going to do. Some thought they were going up to Knoxville; some to cross the Tennessee at Nashville; some thought into Kentucky. These were the conjectures among the officers and men.

Question. From the best information that you were aware of at the time as to the movements of the enemy and his designs what was supposed to be his immediate destination and by what route or routes across the mountains was he expected to move?

I confess I thought it was exceedingly doubtful myself as to what his object was, whether he meant to go to Nashville or whether he intended to go into Kentucky or whether General Bragg was expecting any great re-enforcements and hoped to lead our army farther into East Tennessee. I confess it was doubtful all the time to myself. Most of the officers with whom I talked rather persuaded me that Nashville was the point. That was the general impression at first. I did not know much about the roads at the time, but supposed he would take the Anderson road, and go either through Altamont or keep off to the right and go through Sparta. There was another road, of which I do not remember the name, farther east than the Anderson road, by which he actually did go. If he was going to Murfreesborough, he would go from Sparta to McMinnville, or directly to Nashville if it was practicable to leave McMinnville to the left and go higher up into the State before he turned off for Nashville.

Question. Was the country across the mountains from Chattanooga into the plains of Tennessee understood to be very destitute of forage and water?

It was, sir.

Question. Do you know, in a general way, about how the troops in Tennessee were distributed at the time the rebel army commenced this advance?

I know in a general way only. I knew we had troops in Decherd, at Murfreesborough, if they had not been moved from there; we had troops at McMinnville, and I learned very soon after that we had troops at Pelham, that we had some troops at Stevenson, and we left a small force at Battle Creek. I understood too that we had some troops at Tullahoma and some over at Columbia.

Question. Had we troops in North Alabama and on the line of road from Decatur to Nashville, did you understand?

I did so understand.

Question. Was it probable, from the scarcity of water and supplies on the route, that the rebel army would make its march across from Chattanooga into the plains of Tennessee as rapidly as possible, should you say?

I should say so, certainly.

Question. Was there anything in the scattered condition of our forces that would have seemed to offer an inducement for the enemy to march into the midst of our forces as well as make his movement as rapid as possible?

Undoubtedly I should think that the enemy would avail himself of every opportunity of that kind; there was every inducement.

Question. From an examination of the map and the position of our troops at that time what route or routes would seem to answer his purpose best for such an object?

I thought it not at all unlikely, if General McCook's information was correct and General Bragg was as near to our command as he was reported to be, that he might rush upon our two divisions; but that would have led him out of the way for any grand achievement. I think he took about the only course that was open to him by making his march to Sparta and Gainesborough, or if into Kentucky by Carthage; if his purpose was to go on to Kentucky, there was no other way. The roads across the mountains, except the roads he took, were impracticable. General McCook tried to get over the mountains some 6 miles up the valley beyond Jasper, but found it altogether impracticable. It was with the greatest difficulty that he got across the mountains at Battle Creek. It took two days and a part of the night to get up the mountain with our two divisions.

Question. What was to prevent him from moving directly on the Therman road to McMinnville or on the road from Dunlap to McMinnville or on the road from Pikeville to McMinnville?

There is nothing, sir; I see no difficulty; there seems to be a good road. I know nothing of the road directly from Dunlap to McMinnville. There is one from Pikeville through Spencer, across the mountains from Chattanooga, toward Pelham and Hillsborough. I meant to say there was no road that General Bragg could have marched on in that direction except the road he took, which is a very difficult one. There is a road from Dunlap to McMinnville and a road from Sparta to McMinnville. From Chattanooga and Harrison's Landing both roads seem to converge to Dunlap.

Question. Suppose the object of the enemy to have been to strike into the midst of our scattered troops and then through to Nashville, would the road by Sparta have been the most direct or the most circuitous?

It would have been the most circuitous. The direct road would have been from Dunlap to McMinnville and through Altamont, if he could have reached that place but that seems to be an impracticable country and out of the way altogether. By the roads marked on the map, from Harrison's Landing to McMinnville and Murfreesborough is almost a direct line.

Question. You judge of the directness of this route by Altamont by the printed map that is before you?

Yes, sir; I was not on the road at all, and have no knowledge of the roads from Chattanooga to Dunlap and Altamont.

Question. Is your opinion as to the practicability of that road based upon the experience of General McCook in moving from Pelham to Altamont?

It is, sir. It was on that account that the road was considered by me impracticable. General McCook had told me of the difficulty he had in getting through from the broken nature of the country.

Question. Did General McCook ascend the mountain from Pelham to Altamont?

So he told me. I saw him start. I also knew he was ordered to go.

Question. What information did he give you in regard to the practicability of descending the mountain from Altamont?

I do not remember, sir, that he gave me any.

Question. Are you aware that a column of troops under General Negley actually crossed the mountains from Chattanooga on the Anderson and Therman road as far as Altamont and then diverged toward Winchester on another road?

I was not, sir.

Question. Do you consider that it was certainly to be foreseen that the enemy was destined for Kentucky when he commenced this march and that he was to pursue the road by Sparta?

I did not, sir; I was more afraid of that, I suppose, than of anything else. I am a Kentuckian; it is my home; and I felt a deep solicitude about it. I feared it sometimes, but did not feel convinced at all as to where General Bragg was going, as I said before. I do not believe now that he knew certainly where he was going.

Question. Do you know or can you acquaint yourself by reference to the maps as to how close General Bragg in crossing the mountains could come to McMinnville and Sparta before determining which of these points he would strike for?

Yes, sir; he might go to Spencer, I should say, without any difficulty. The points seem to be nearly equidistant between the two places.

Question. And how far would that point be from McMinnville and how far from Sparta?

I should suppose not more than 20 miles from McMinnville and 14 or 15 from Sparta.

Question. Could it ordinarily have been determined with any certainty which point he was aiming for until he actually developed his plans by his movements?

I should suppose he would have no difficulty in covering his movements for either point. Sometimes by demonstrations it would be difficult or impossible to tell until he had actually gone.

Question. Supposing the Army of the Ohio to have been concentrated at Sparta to oppose the advance of the rebel army, from your reading and your experience have you any doubt that the rebel army could substantially reach McMinnville before you could have a knowledge of his destination at Sparta?

I have none, sir; I think it would have been entirely practicable to have reached McMinnville or to have gone to Sparta. If the Army of the Ohio had been at McMinnville, the rebel army could have gone by Sparta, by a demonstration upon McMinnville, without anybody's knowing it almost. If the Army of the Ohio had been at Sparta, it would have been entirely practicable for the rebel army to have marched to McMinnville without its movements being known.

Question. Do you know anything of the character of the road between McMinnville and Sparta and of the creek which intersects that road; that is, Caney Fork of the Cumberland?

There is, I see (referring to the map), a creek crossing the road, but I know nothing of it.

Question. What advantage would the rebel army have had if it had reached McMinnville while the Army of the Ohio was at Sparta looking for it there, and what would have been the embarrassment of the Army of the Ohio from such a result?

With the rebel army at McMinnville, the Army of the Ohio at Sparta would have been deprived of all its source of supplies by reaching Murfreesborough and Nashville first, I should think. It would have been almost fatal to the Army of the Ohio to have been cut off from Murfreesborough and Nashville by the rebel army in our then condition of supplies.

Question. With these various routes by which the rebel army could cross the mountains and this uncertainty as to its destination what, in your opinion, was the best point at which to concentrate the Army of the Ohio to counteract the movements of the enemy, whatever they might be?

General McCook and myself frequently talked about it, and we thought the army ought to be concentrated at Murfreesborough.

Question. What was the advantage of the concentration at that point?

One great advantage that we looked to at that time, from our having been on half rations, was the advantage of getting supplies for the army, and the certainty that we could cover Nashville and be on the direct road to Kentucky in case we should be required there.

Question. Would it also have the advantage of opposing a greater force to the enemy than could have been brought against him at a more remote point?

Yes, sir; we had troops as far west as Columbia, and Murfreesborough was a nearer point at which those troops could be concentrated with the balance of the army than any point east of Murfreesborough. We had, besides, the advantage of railroad communication running into Murfreesborough.

Question. Is it true also that the main body of the army is diminished 'for the purpose of protecting its communications the farther it goes from its base?

Undoubtedly, sir; it must be so.

Question. Did the arrival of the rebel army at Sparta indicate with certainty that its destination was Kentucky, in your opinion?

No, sir.

Question. How far could it march upon the routes which it actually followed before that question would be determined with certainty?

I should say that it would be almost certain after passing Smithville that General Bragg would go to Nashville, unless Kirby Smith had met him at the Cumberland River. He might have gone through Lebanon, or he might have gone to Gallatin and taken Nashville from that side, or he might have gone to the Cumberland River and formed his junction there if Nashville had been the object which they intended to direct the rebel force upon. But if General Bragg was to operate alone against Nashville I do not know precisely what road he would take. He could go up to Lebanon and cross the river. It is a difficult road, and it would be a considerable obstacle; still it might have been done.

Question. Is there anything in the character of the country or the condition of the roads to have prevented Bragg from striking the river and marching down it on either side or on both sides?

There is on the south side of the Cumberland Stone River, that would have proved one obstacle; on the other side there is no obstacle. He would have had very good roads, I believe.

Question. Would such a route have had the effect of throwing him into a region of country in which supplies were more abundant than on any other route toward Nashville?

Supplies were very abundant about Lebanon. It is a good country. East of Stone River supplies were abundant—plenty of forage—and I suppose that that route would have furnished him better with supplies of every kind than any other. On the other side of the river is also a good country as far as Gallatin; but I know little of the country. I was up the Cumberland beyond Gallatin.

Question. From a careful consideration of all the information of which you have had any knowledge, from the time the rebel army crossed the Tennessee River until it arrived at Sparta, about what was your estimate and that of other officers who had the best opportunity of knowing as to the strength of that army?

My own opinion was that the enemy was about 40,000 strong. I had information that varied very much. It was placed as high as 60,000 and 100,000, but I never supposed he had more than about 40,000 to 45,000 men at Chattanooga.

Question. Was your estimate greater or less than that of other high officers in the army ?

I think my estimate was less than General McCook's. I am not prepared to say whether it was less or greater than that of other officers. I remember that after we got into Kentucky I had some conversation with officers as to the strength of Bragg's army, and the general estimate was that the enemy was about 60,000 strong.

Question. Did you find supplies of forage and provisions scarce or abundant in that part of Tennessee through which you marched in going from Battle Creek to Murfreesborough ?

Very scarce. Parts of the road very scarce, with the exception of perhaps one day's march, where we passed through a pretty good country, about 30 miles south of Murfreesborough.

Commission adjourned to meet February 28, 1863.

CINCINNATI, *February* 28, 1863.

Commission met pursuant to adjournment. All the members present; also the judge-advocate and General Buell.

Major-General CRITTENDEN's examination continued.

By General BUELL:

Question. Did you during the month of August last hear reports or rumors of an intended advance of the rebel troops from the vicinity of Knoxville; and, if so, what destination did those reports or rumors give to such an advance ? I mean prior to a knowledge in the Army of the Ohio of the invasion of Kirby Smith.

I did hear in August last rumors and reports of a large force of rebels gathering about Knoxville. I am not sure that I heard of the direction that they were going to take. It was a matter of frequent speculation and conjecture with us at camp as to which way they were going, whether they would come to Chattanooga; and after Bragg had crossed the Tennessee it was a matter of speculation as to the point at which they would concentrate.

Question. What do you mean by concentration; do you mean a concentration of Bragg's forces with the forces that were collecting about Knoxville ?

I do, sir. It would perhaps be proper to add that I think I now remember that at one time we heard of a very considerable force of Bragg's army moving from Chattanooga to Knoxville, but which I believe turned out to be a false rumor. Whether that occurred in August last or in the latter part of July I am not certain.

Question. In the statement previously given in your testimony in regard to the strength of your division are we to understand that it includes but two brigades; was the organization of your division subsequently changed, or rather was an additional brigade added to your division ?

In my statement with reference to the strength of my division it is to be understood, of course, to mean the strength at that time at Battle Creek. When I arrived there I had but two brigades. Subsequently, when I moved from Battle Creek, Colonel Harker's brigade reported to me, either as we returned down the Sequatchie Valley through Jasper or at Battle Creek, 5 miles up the creek, where I encamped, and continued to form part of my command until I reached Nashville, where I was directed to instruct General Harker to report to General Wood, to whose division he belonged and from which he had been detached for some time. Colonel Stanley Matthews was ordered to report to me, and his brigade formed a part of my command from that time till now, but the precise day he reported to me I cannot now remember.

Question. Did Colonel Harker's brigade form a part of General Wood's division while it was on this temporary service with you?

I believe so, sir; in fact I heard General Wood claim that Colonel Harker should be restored to his command at Nashville, on the ground that he had been detached from his division. He claimed that at headquarters and in my presence, and orders were accordingly given by Colonel Fry.

Question. How many regiments had you in your division after the permanent addition of a third brigade to it?

I had twelve regiments, sir.

Question. How many regiments were added to your division at Louisville after your arrival there in September?

One to each brigade, making three to that division.

Question. And what would have been the effective strength of your division at that time?

I should say about 8,500 men. This is my best impression from quite a decided recollection of my division before the three new regiments were added. As to the strength of the new regiments I am not positive in my recollection. They were new and numerically strong.

Question. I understand, then, that you make 8,500 by taking the effective strength with which you marched from Tennessee into Kentucky and adding to that the strength of the three regiments added to your division at Louisville?

Yes, sir. When I reached Louisville I was in command of two divisions. I speak with reference, of course, to the strength of the Fifth Division, which was my own, and which I am convinced was about 6,000 strong. I reported at the mouth of Salt River to General Nelson that I had reached the mouth of Salt River with 12,000 men— General Wood's division and my own.

Question. Do you know anything of a very great diminution in the strength of these two divisions, about the time of their arrival at Louisville until the battle of Perryville, by straggling and by men going to their homes in the various States to which their regiments belonged, and can you form any estimate of the diminution from this cause?

I know that there was a very decided diminution of strength in many regiments. Many men left. I know this by the complaints of my own officers to me on the subject. I also know that there was a great deal of straggling on the march, particularly in the new regiments, from Louisville to Perryville. It was reported to me several times that the road behind was filled with stragglers, but on that march until the battle of Perryville, until my return from Wild Cat, we had no regular returns, and it was impossible for me to know what the diminution had been.

Question. Can you mention an example of any particular regiment which will give some idea of the extent of this diminution?

My recollection now is indistinct, but there was a regiment which it seems to me now refused to march, so it was reported to me, because they did not have the transportation which they thought they were entitled to. I cannot name that regiment, nor am I positive that this occurred at Louisville; but that is my decided impression, because I had no other regiments that would have refused to march under any circumstances. It must have been one of the new regiments.

Question. Have you any doubt that it was one of the new regiments?

I have not.

Question. Did the regiment march?

I think it did, sir. I am sure it did.

Question. Was any report made to you of the extraordinary diminution in the strength of the regiment of which General Hascall was formerly the colonel on account of absentees who left the regiment and went to their homes in Indiana after the arrival of the regiment in Louisville?

I do not remember any report in reference to that particular regiment.

Question. In the whole of your connection with the Army of the Ohio can you point to an example of the refusal of any regiment in that army to march or perform any other service that was required of it?

I never heard of any such occurrence in the army before, sir. It certainly never occurred in my command.

Question. Do you know anything about the length of service and discipline of the new regiments formed at Louisville when the Army of the Ohio reached that point?

I know that the new regiments which were added to my command at Louisville, and which command was increased at that place to three divisions, were undisciplined and new troops. As to the time of their service, I infer from their want of discipline and instruction that it must have been very short.

Question. Do you know to what levy they belonged?

I understood that those troops were mostly raised after the invasion of Kentucky, when Louisville and Cincinnati were both supposed to be in danger, but I have no knowledge of the fact, and cannot say under what levy they were raised.

Question. What would be your judgment as to the ability of the force that was found in Louisville when the Army of the Ohio arrived there in September last to withstand a determined attack from Bragg's army at that place?

I do not think they could have withstood an attack from Bragg's army at all. They were all, as I understood, new troops. General Nelson, who was in command at Louisville when I reached Salt River, was of that opinion, I know, from a note which I received from him, in answer to a dispatch of mine from the mouth of Salt River, urging me in his note to come immediately to Louisville.

Question. With what command and when did you march from Louisville against the rebel army at Bardstown?

I marched with the Second Army Corps, which was composed of the Fourth, Fifth, and Sixth Divisions. It was on the 1st of October, I think.

Question. Was it known at that time at what point the rebel forces were to be met—at what point they could probably be brought to battle?

My understanding was, sir, that we would probably fight them at Bardstown.

Question. Did you find any rebel troops in Bardstown when you arrived there with your command?

We had rather a severe cavalry skirmish just on the edge of Bardstown, but found no infantry there. We drove the cavalry out, and in consequence of this cavalry skirmish, going up to support our cavalry there that met with a repulse there, my recollection is that we occupied Bardstown one day sooner than was expected.

Question. Was it known with any certainty at what point the rebel army would be found after its withdrawal at Bardstown?

I certainly did not know nor do I believe it was known. I remember, however, hearing you say at Bardstown, in a few minutes' conversation I had with you there while you were giving me instructions or orders for my march, that the enemy might make a stand at Perryville.

Question. By what road did you march after you left Springfield in advance upon Perryville, and at what point did you encamp on the night of the first day's march from Springfield?

I marched by the road which leads from Springfield to Haysville. General Thomas accompanied the command, and we went beyond Haysville to the fork of Salt River, some 3½ or 4 miles, I think, from the turnpike which leads from Haysville to Perryville. I remember the camp distinctly, because we had a very fatiguing march, and my last division did not get into camp until 3 o'clock in the morning, and we marched without water too.

Question. Did you encamp at the place at which you were expected to encamp when I parted with you at Springfield?

I did not, sir. I expected to encamp at Haysville, but when I reached that place General Thomas ordered the command to go on to this fork of Salt River. He was of opinion, I know, that it would take us only about 2½ miles out of our way, and he deemed it important that the men should have water; and this being the only water, or the nearest, he ordered us to go there.

Question. What position did General Thomas occupy at that time and did he move with your corps?

He was second in command of the Army of the Ohio, and he did move with my corps.

Question. Do you know how far it is from Haysville to Perryville and on what known turnpike road is the town of Haysville?

It is, I should think, about 10 miles from Haysville to Perryville. I am not sure about the distance, however. Haysville is on the main road from Danville to Lebanon or Harrodsburg; I do not know the name of the road however.

Question. Do you mean to say that it is on the road from Danville to Harrodsburg?

No, sir. There is no main turnpike road through Haysville either to Danville or Harrodsburg.

General BUELL. I will offer at this time the instructions issued to General Thomas on the night of the 7th of October in reference to the movements of General Crittenden's corps for the following day.

The JUDGE-ADVOCATE. I admit the instructions offered by General Buell to be those forwarded to me by General Thomas.

OCTOBER 7—7 p. m.

GENERAL: The Third Corps (Gilbert's) is within 3½ miles of Perryville, the cavalry being near, perhaps 2½. From all the information received to-day it is thought the enemy will resist our advance into Perryville. They are said to have a strong force in and near the place. We expect to attack and carry the place to-morrow.

March at 3 o'clock precisely to-morrow morning without fail, and if possible get all the canteens filled and have the men cautioned to use water in the most sparing manner. Every officer must caution his men on this point. Send back every team and animal that is not absolutely necessary with the troops, as they will suffer for water. All the wagons which come must move in rear of your troops. The right of Gilbert's corps rests opposite to Gordon's place, which is on the Lebanon pike, and from Gordon's to Gilbert's right is about 2 or 2½ miles. When the Second Corps gets up to that vicinity, that is to say, about 3 or 3½ miles from town, let the front be halted and put in order of battle and the whole column closed up, and the men allowed to rest in position and made as comfortable as possible, but not allowed to scatter. The commander of the corps must then immediately have the front reconnoitered and gain all the information he can of the position of the enemy and his strength, also of the nature of the country in his front. This must be done by inquiring of the inhabitants and personal examination of officers and by the reconnaissance. When the column has got into position you will please report in person at these headquarters, with all the information you may have been able to obtain, and instructions for the future movements will be given. Send orderlies back with bearer to learn where our headquarters are. All the usual precaution must be taken and preparation made for action. There is no water near us, and we can expect but little, if any, until we get it at Perryville. Nothing has been heard of you since we parted this morning.

Respectfully, &c.,

JAMES B. FRY,
Colonel and Chief of Staff.

General THOMAS, *Second in Command.*

A true copy.

GEO. E. FLYNT,
Major and Chief of Staff.

Question. Do you recognize those as the instructions which were received for the movement of your corps on the 8th?

Yes, sir; I think I received that order, or it was read to me by General Thomas, about 3 o'clock on the morning of the 8th. At this time the last of my rear division was still coming into camp when that order was received, at least when I first heard of it and saw it myself.

Question. State, if you please, in what manner it was executed.

We marched at 7 with the First Division; at 9 the Second Division was marched; and at 11 General Wood's division, which had been all night getting into camp, marched, being put in the rear again in order that the men might rest. We reached Perryville with the First Division about 10 or 11 o'clock. It was before 11 o'clock that General Smith had his division in line of battle within 2½ or 3 miles of Perryville. It was perhaps two hours afterward when the Second Division got into position. Between 3 and 4 o'clock it was reported to me by one of my aides that I had sent over to the left to bring me such information that my last division had formed on General Gilbert's right, completing my line of battle.

Question. Did you march through Haysville?

We did not, sir. I understand that to mean did we in marching from Salt River march through Haysville? The road by which we went to Salt River was not the road by which we returned to the pike. We came into the pike leading to Perryville some 2½ miles, as I understood, nearer to Perryville than Haysville is.

Question. Do you know the name of the creek near Haysville at which you were expected to find water on the night of the 7th?

I do not, sir.

Question. Suppose you had been where you expected to encamp that night and had marched at the time appointed in the order about what time would you have been in position in front of Perryville on the morning of the 8th?

My recollection of the distance from Haysville to Perryville does not enable me to state exactly what that distance is. I am sure it is not over 10 miles; it is possibly not more than 7. Of course the hour at which I could have reached Perryville, starting from Haysville at 3 o'clock, would depend somewhat on the distance. I should have marched on that road 2½ to 3 miles an hour. Starting at 3 o'clock, if it were 10 miles, I should have reached Perryville by a quarter past 6 o'clock with the head of my column; that would carry me actually to Perryville by that time. We were, however, ordered to halt some 2½ to 3 miles outside of Perryville, and that would put me there at that point an hour sooner—at a quarter past 5.

Question. What distance did you march on that day from the point at which you did actually encamp?

I should think about 8 or 9 miles.

Question. Do you know at what time your arrival in front of Perryville was reported at headquarters and in what manner it was reported?

I do not remember, sir.

Question. When were you first informed during that day that a severe action had been fought on the extreme left?

About 8 or 9 o'clock that night; I think it must have been about this time. I first got my information from Captain Fitzhugh, whom I found at General Thomas' headquarters.

Question. Please state what your impression was prior to the receipt of that information as to the character and extent of the operations of that day and of the position and condition of the army with reference to the rebel forces.

We had heard very considerable cannonading during the day, or for a long time in the early part of the day, which we all supposed was the rebels firing upon our cavalry in the advance. This opinion of mine that it was nothing more than this sort of skirmishing was based also upon two dispatches which I received from General Gilbert during the day. I received a note from General Gilbert at 12 or 12.30 in the day, in which he apprised me that a reconnaissance of some force was about to be made which might grow into a general engagement; that General Buell had directed him to apprise me of that change. I immediately handed the note to General Thomas, but I heard nothing of any general engagements or any increased firing after that. At 4 o'clock I received another note from General Gilbert, in which he apprised me of some little change made in the disposition of his troops since my aide-de-camp had been over there in the morning, and also said, " The noise you hear on the left is from McCook," and in a vein of pleasantry he added, " My children are all quiet, and by sunset we will have them in bed and nicely tucked up, as we used to do in Corinth." I have those dispatches somewhere.

The JUDGE-ADVOCATE. I should like to have them, general.

The WITNESS. In consequence of this I rode over with the note to General Thomas, and my impression was, and I so stated to him in the presence of a number of officers, that at last we had the rebels, and they could not possibly get away, so little did I know what was going on during the day.

O. P. BEARD (a witness for the defendant), being duly sworn by the judge-advocate, testified as follows:

By General BUELL:

Question. State your name and residence, if you please.

O. P. Beard; Lexington, Ky.

Question. Were you in or about Lexington when the rebel force under Kirby Smith entered that place last summer?

I was, sir.

Question. State what you know in regard to the strength of that force and how you obtained your information.

I counted General Smith's force as they came into town, with several other gentlemen. He had about 15,000 men. John Morgan had about 1,250 to 1,300. Humphrey Marshall came in with 3,500 to 4,000.

Question. I understand you to mean that these several numbers have to be added together to make up the whole force that came in?

Yes, sir; but not including General Stevenson's, that went through Danville?

Question. Did Stevenson's force go into Lexington?

No, sir; they did not.

Question. About how long did the rebel troops remain in Lexington?

I could not tell to a day. They commenced retreating from Lexington on the Thursday previous to the inauguration of Governor Hawes; that was in October, I think. They remained in Lexington until General Sill advanced upon Frankfort.

Question. Do you mean the Thursday previous to the inauguration or subsequent?

A good many of them left before and all of them a day or two afterward. A good many of the troops went toward Versailles as soon as they returned from Frankfort. They got back on Sunday to Lexington after the inauguration at Frankfort, and on Monday or Tuesday the whole force left, with the exception of a few mounted men that were on duty there.

Question. Which way did they go and where did they cross the Kentucky River?

They went both roads; they went both on the Harrodsburg and Versailles roads; and all the information of their crossing was from an aide of General Smith, Captain Allen, who told me that a good many of them crossed below Versailles. Humphrey Marshall went down the Harrodsburg road.

Question. To what point on the south side of the Kentucky River did they go? Can you place them?

Schryock's or Munday's Landing, or both. I would suppose they crossed at both ferries.

Question. Could they ford the river at these points without difficulty?

Yes, sir; the water was very low. I had crossed the river myself a few days before at Frankfort and the water was extremely low.

Question. Do you say that the force of Humphrey Marshall accompanied this movement toward Harrodsburg across the Kentucky River?

They did, from Lexington, sir; and went in the direction of the Kentucky River on the Harrodsburg road.

Question. Where did the force of Humphrey Marshall come from; by what road did they enter the State?

They came, as I suppose, from Mount Sterling (in an easterly direction) and Winchester into Lexington on the Winchester road.

Question. Mention the point on the border of the State at which they entered.

I talked with some of Humphrey Marshall's officers whom I knew personally, and they said they came through Piketon.

Question. From Virginia?

From Abingdon, Va., so they told me.

Question. Has this force or a similar force under Humphrey Marshall been operating from that quarter and on that route for the past year; in fact pretty much since the commencement of the rebellion?

It has been so reported at headquarters at Lexington and by officers connected with the army there to me.

Question. Is it a matter of notoriety that Humphey Marshall has been operating in that way during that time?

It is, sir.

Question. Was there anything to have prevented him from returning by that route instead of going with Kirby Smith's force in the direction of Harrodsburg if he had desired to retreat from the State.

None that I have any information of.

Question. State what you know, if you please, of any depots of arms that the rebel forces had in Lexington while they were there.

They had a very large depot of arms on my premises. I have two stables in Lexington; one of them has been occupied by the Federal troops since the commencement of the war, and upon the retreat of the Federal forces the rebels took possession of the same and used it as a depot for arms. They had a very large quantity there; all the stalls were filled and the middle of the stable piled up. The stable is now in possession of the Federal authorities and is used by General Gillmore, for which the Government is paying me. The rebels never paid me anything.

Question. Where did these stores come from?

They were captured, I suppose, at Richmond—a great many of them—and a great many were found in Lexington.

Question. Do you know that the rebel troops captured a large amount of arms and ammunition at Richmond? You may state at the same time what opportunity you had of knowing what you do in regard to the battle of Richmond and the circumstances following and connected with that battle.

Upon the night after the battle of Richmond I was ordered by Colonel Anderson and Colonel McCook to take a squad of men and go out in advance of their regiments and march to the Kentucky River and stop stragglers. I started ahead of the two regiments. I found the army completely demoralized—very much frightened. I could not stop them at all; they refused to be stopped by me. I did not use any force. I met the trains; they were full of soldiers and men holding on behind on the wagon-boxes. I went out about 9 miles on the road and returned to Lexington. The Federal forces came back and intended giving fight the next day, but from some cause of which I do not know they retreated that night, and the rebels came into Lexington on Tuesday morning, I think it was. It was the 1st of September. Having a depot opposite my premises within 40 yards, and being at the head of the street, I could see all their trains as they came in. We had great curiosity, us Union men, to see what was going on. I counted one train of 40 or 50 wagons loaded with guns and marked "U. S." I saw a great many cannon, and loaded wagons of all descriptions of stores with the Government mark on them. They were unloading ammunition there the entire day, blocking up the street so much that people had to go around the entire square. I had frequent talks with the ordnance officer in command, who told me that they had more than I believe they had. He told me they had 25,000 stand of arms, but I do not believe it at all, though I would judge from what I saw they had from 10,000 to 15,000. After the rebels had been there for several days the trains continued to arrive with boxes of ammunition. They had country wagons, in which they could not haul a very heavy load.

Question. Do you know anything about the capture of arms at Frankfort by the rebel troops at the time they came into the State?

I procured a pass from General Kirby Smith to go to Louisville to get my omnibuses and wagons that I had let Colonel McCook have for hospital purposes. It was about ten or twelve days after that they got into Lexington. On my return from Louisville I came through Frankfort, and Leadbetter's division was in possession of that place. My road home was directly by the arsenal. There was a train upon the road, and a good many wagons loaded, a great many empty, and there were two or three wagons loading with arms at the time I passed the arsenal, moving in the direction of Lexington after they were loaded. That is all I know about it.

Question. How soon after their arrival at Lexington did the rebel troops begin to send out trains of supplies?

The first I saw that led me to believe they were moving supplies out of Lexington was when I went with my family out on the road to see a relative the third day after my arrival. On my return I struck the turnpike about 3 miles from Lexington, and there was one continuous train of wagons nearly the whole distance from Lexington, loaded with flour, going down the Nicholasville road, in a southwesterly direction from Lexington. The Nicholasville road leads immediately to Camp Dick Robinson.

Question. About what date was that?

That was about the 4th day of September.

Question. In your estimate of the strength of the force which entered Lexington did you include stragglers and other soldiers that accompanied the trains or were the numbers you have mentioned those which you counted in the ranks?

The numbers I have mentioned were those which came in the ranks, not including stragglers nor the recruits obtained through the country.

Question. Do you know anything about the number of recruits obtained in the State?

I know nothing except the numbers I saw pass through Lexington, of which I formerly made an estimate. I think that the different rebel regiments that were raised through the country would amount to 4,000 or 5,000. The rebel army was very much disappointed with the number of recruits they obtained there. None of General Bragg's recruits or those raised south of the Kentucky River came to Lexington, to my knowledge. At one time it looked as if every rebel in the country was going to fall into the ranks, but from some cause they became lukewarm, and a great many of them slipped out of the ranks and returned home.

Question. What was the opinion of the people of the State, as far as you know, as to the object of this invasion, as to whether it was a temporary raid or with the design of holding permanent possession of the State?

They believed, sir, from General Smith's conversation and acts, that they had come to remain in Kentucky permanently, and so strong was the belief, that when I expressed the opinion that the Federal forces would drive them out in two weeks they arrested me and put me in jail for it and kept me there a day.

Question. What sort of treatment did you receive from the rebel authorities when they came in?

Well, I thought pretty bad. They took possession of my premises; sent out and issued an order and had my horses taken; fed from my grain for a week, and paid me nothing for it. They put me in jail twice and arrested me once besides; at least I was arrested the first morning they came in and twice afterward and put in jail once; the third time when I was arrested they kept me in the marshal's office.

Question. Did they require you to take any oath or give any parole?

They demanded it of me and I refused. Upon the interposition of a friend General Smith released me.

Question. Do you know anything about the number of Union troops that were at Louisville when the rebel troops came into Central Kentucky?

I do not, sir; I went to Louisville after my property, and was under special promise to General Smith not to divulge anything; consequently when I got to Louisville I asked no questions and derived no information whatever.

Cross-examination by the JUDGE-ADVOCATE:

Question. In this account of the forces under Kirby Smith do you mean to say that Marshall's and Morgan's are included in the 15,000 men?

I do not, sir.

Question. How many do you make the whole number?

From 20,000 to 22,000 it would add up.

Question. Do you not know that Kirby Smith entered Kentucky with from 8,000 to 10,000 men?

I do not, sir. The information I have on that subject is from a gentleman from our town, a Mr. Spencer, that he counted them in Barboursville, and his count was that 12,000 passed through that town.

Question. Upon what day did Kirby Smith enter Lexington and did his entire force come into town?

He first entered Lexington on the 1st of September. His army came in by divisions; some of them came in by different roads; one or two on the Tait's Creek road and the balance on the Richmond road.

Question. With his force entering the town by different roads how did you make up your estimate?

The two roads run into the main street, and the whole force of General Smith made a display down the main street.

Question. On the same day?

No, sir; on different days.

Question. Who assisted you in making that count?

Several gentlemen of our town, sir.

Question. Do you recollect their names?

J. M. Lawrence, David Hawkins. I do not recollect the others. I refused to do any business with the rebels while they were in Lexington, but made it my business to see all I could.

Question. How did you count; by regiments?

No, sir; I did not count by regiments. I counted them as they entered by divisions.

Question. Do you mean to say that you actually counted each man as he passed?

As near as I could. I do not think any person could make a really correct count.

It was as near as I could get it. I think it is impossible to, when a man's attention is attracted first to one thing and then to another; he may make mistakes. I do not mean to say that my count was perfectly accurate, but it was as near as I could make it.

Question. Counting under those circumstances might you not make a difference of 5,000 men, more or less?

I do not think I could make that much of a mistake, sir.

Question. Did you count the recruits in Kentucky in the same way?

I did not count the recruits at all; I only formed an estimate of them from seeing them in the different regiments. I was told there was a great many more than I made them, but I did not believe it.

Question. How were those recruits armed at the time you saw them?

They were all brought up in front of my stable and armed at the armory or the depot the rebels had there.

Question. Have you seen a statement by an ordnance officer connected with the rebel army in Kentucky, published in a Richmond paper, to the effect that he distributed 2,000 muskets and had lost the larger portion of them by recruits going home with them?

I did not, sir.

Question. If Kirby Smith recruited to the extent of 5,000 men would it not be reasonable to suppose that Bragg had gathered up to the same number?

From what I could learn from gentlemen who were with Bragg's army they scarcely got any. General Bragg, in his public speech at Lexington, said that he had been disappointed in getting troops.

Question. Are you so well satisfied with your estimate of the recruits that you could venture to contradict an official report stating the number to be about 2,000?

I should adhere to my opinion as to what I supposed to be the number. I may be mistaken; but I would adhere to what I saw and the conclusion I formed from it. I do not know how far the recruits went, but I know a great many of them returned. It was probable that not half the number went out of the State of Kentucky. I know of my own knowledge of a great many who volunteered out of Fayette County and went with the army, but when they got to the Big Hill deserted and came back and are now scattered all over the country, and others who went from other counties deserted and came back. I saw a great many of them.

Question. Was the abandonment of Kentucky on the part of the rebels really owing to their disappointment in obtaining recruits or from lack of co-operation of the people?

It was not so understood in Lexington; it was there understood to be in consequence of General Buell's marching into the southern part of the State.

Question. Was your imprisonment previous or subsequent to the visit to Louisville?

I was arrested once before I went to Louisville and twice afterward.

Question. Upon what ground were you released by General Smith?

When the fact of what I was arrested for was communicated to him he thought it was not sufficient and just ground for imprisoning a citizen and ordered me to be discharged, and cautioned me to keep my opinions to myself; that he intended to remain in Kentucky, and expected obedience to the laws from all the citizens. This, I believe, was about the substance of his remarks.

Question. After this knowledge of your opinions what reasons had he for permitting you to go to Louisville?

It was after I returned from Louisville.

Question. You say you were arrested and released previous to your going to Louisville and I ask you upon what grounds you were released?

There were no charges preferred against me. I was arrested by some soldiers and released.

Question. You were not then released upon the order of Kirby Smith?

No, sir; by the provost-marshal.

Question. Was Kirby Smith under the impression when you went to Louisville that you were a Union man?

Yes, sir; I was so represented to him by his aide, Captain Allen, who went with me and procured a pass for me. He also gave me a special permit for myself and Mr. Kenny, my partner, to protect seventy-five or eighty mules that we had bought for the Government and that were then on the road to Cincinnati; they had not been delivered to the Government, and he gave permission to Mr. Kenny to bring them to Cincinnati, which he did, and they were sold to the Government.

Question. Did Kirby Smith know at that time that you had been in the service of the United States at Richmond?

No, sir; I did not consider that I had any office when I went out temporarily. I had no commission; it was all volunteer on my part.

Question. Was this liberality on the part of Kirby Smith a common thing at that time?

Yes, sir; when he first arrived there. They were then on what I call their good behavior; but they afterward became pretty severe.

Question. This good behavior, I understand you to say, extended to the protection and delivery of seventy-five mules for the United States?

It extended to me and Mr. Kenny as individuals.

By General TYLER:

Question. You say you counted by divisions; how many divisions did you count; who commanded them?

I do not know whether I could tell all the divisions or not; I made no memorandum at the time. There were Cheatham's, Leadbetter's, Preston Smith's, Morgan's, and Marshall's. I do not recollect the names of the other commanders, sir.

Question. Did Marshall and Morgan command divisions?

They had separate commands. I do not know if they were entirely to themselves or not. I know the fact of their being called generals.

Question. Was there any great inequality as to the numbers of the divisions that you counted?

I do not recollect. My impression is that Cheatham had the largest division that moved down the Maysville road toward Cincinnati when they passed through Lexington, but I do not remember now the number that he had. I never expected to be called on to testify; it was merely a matter of curiosity with me.

Question. How large was Leadbetter's division, sir?

I do not recollect, sir. I cannot give you the number of any particular division now. I kept no memorandum of any division; we counted them as they came in.

Question. Then I understand you to say that Leadbetter's, Cheatham's, Preston Smith's, Marshall's, and Morgan's divisions made your whole amount of troops 20,000 men?

And the balance of them—I do not know who they were commanded by—make the number.

Question. How do you account for this balance? Where did they come from and where did they go to?

They came to Lexington; some of them marched toward Cincinnati and some of them marched down the Frankfort road. A gentleman by the name of Scott had command of the cavalry. I do not know whether he was a general or not; some called him General and some Colonel Scott. He had quite a smart force.

Question. How large a force had Scott?

I could not tell exactly, sir, because some of them went around Lexington and I did not get to see them.

Question. How could you count men you did not see?

I did not count them, sir.

Question. Were the Kentucky recruits organized into regiments; if so, how many regiments were organized?

I cannot answer how many regiments were organized. I know there were a great many advertised to be organized. Colonel Cluke had a pretty full regiment; the largest that was raised, I think. Colonel Thompson had a regiment. Colonel Chenault and Colonel Viele organized a regiment, but the number raised I could not state. There was also Colonel Blackman, but how many he got I could not tell, for I never saw his regiment.

Question. Did you see as many as 2,000 recruits first and last; I mean under arms in their regiments?

I think I saw as many as four or five thousand.

Question. Where did you see them?

At Lexington.

Question. Where were they encamped at Lexington?

They were encamped in two or three different places, some on the south side of Lexington and some on the east side. There were some out on the Cincinnati road, on the north side of the city, but I never went to their camp. I was not in a rebel encampment while they were there.

Question. How could you testify as to the exact number of their troops without having been in their camps?

I saw them all under arms in Lexington.

Question. Did you see them all at one time or at different times?

At one time. I suppose they were brought there for the purpose of being reviewed by General Smith.

Question. Who was in command of the recruits at the time you supposed this review was to take place?

General Abraham Buford.

Question. How many regiments were they divided into at this review.

I do not know exactly how many regiments there were. I formed my estimate from the number of recruits I saw under arms. There were a good many independent companies raised and in the act of being raised.

Question. How do you know that all these men under the command of General Buford were all recruits?

I supposed they were under the command of General Buford. I knew nothing of the movements of the rebels personally; it was only from observation.

General Buell wishing to ask a question of the witness, it was adopted by General Tyler, as follows:

Question. I wish to ask the witness whether he is confident that General Cheatham's division was at Lexington and whether he knows anything of the division of General Heth?

The WITNESS. General Heth's division passed through Lexington and went on toward Cincinnati. The name mentioned in my testimony as Cheatham I believe is Churchill. I am not certain whether it is Cheatham or Churchill, but it is one of the two. There were General Heth and General Reynolds commanding a division also with Kirby Smith.

The Commission adjourned to meet March 2, 1863, at 10 o'clock a. m.

CINCINNATI, *March* 2, 1863.

Commission met pursuant to adjournment. All the members present; also the judge-advocate and General Buell.

Major-General CRITTENDEN'S examination continued.

By General BUELL:

Question. Were you on duty in the lines in front of Corinth until the evacuation of that place by the rebel army in May last?

I was.

Question. Were there any general or partial engagements between the rebel army and the forces under the command of Major-General Halleck prior to that engagement?

I remember one very considerable engagement, and I heard the firing from numerous small engagements or skirmishes. I had some skirmishing there myself. It would perhaps be proper to add that I was not in line in front of Corinth when the considerable engagement to which I refer took place; I was some distance back. I refer to the fight at Farmington when I speak of the considerable engagement.

Question. What was the impression made upon your mind by any engagement in front of Corinth compared with that made upon you by the firing in front of Perryville on the 8th of October as to the severity of the action?

That question reminds me of a slight mistake which I made in the answer to the previous question. In answering it I wish to make a correction, which is that I now remember another very considerable engagement where I was in line and subsequent to the fight at Farmington, in which in addition to the cannonading there was considerable musketry firing. I heard no musketry at Perryville. I heard cannonading at Corinth several times as rapid, I should think, as any I heard at Perryville. At Murfreesborough I heard more rapid firing in skirmishing going on than I heard at either place on one day. My impression was, of course, when I heard nothing but artillery firing at Perryville, that there was no engagement of any considerable force. I had heard at Corinth on the extreme right of our line what it seems to me now was equal to any I heard at Perryville, but I never heard any explanation of it to this day and I do not know what they were firing about; I think it was skirmishing or an artillery duel. I supposed at Perryville, as I believe I have already stated, that the cannonading which I heard was principally from the enemy upon our cavalry, which I supposed was pressing them, and perhaps by the return firing of our cavalry also. Hearing no musketry, my impression was that there could not be any battle going on; merely an artillery duel. When General Pope's forces became engaged at Corinth and when the musketry firing began I supposed it might have been a battle, and that perhaps it was the beginning of a very serious battle.

Question. Do you think it very remarkable that, with an army occupying a front of 5 or 6 miles and in front of an enemy, such partial engagements should sometimes take place at various points without attracting unusual attention or giving cause for apprehension of a dangerous engagement, unless other circumstances indicated that such engagement was imminent?

I thought it remarkable that I could hear no musketry from such an engagement as did actually take place there when I was within 6 miles, and I thought I could hardly have credited the fact if I had not witnessed it myself. I do not think it remarkable that such artillery firing as I heard there should take place in a line of battle 6 miles long without exciting any extraordinary interest or anxiety, because I have known such things to happen, within my own short experience as a soldier, several times, and nothing serious to result from it.

Question. After hearing of the engagement that took place on the left on the 8th of October, were you or were you not in expectation that the enemy would be found in our front and that a battle would ensue the next morning?

I expected a battle the next morning, because I received an order, which I have in my pocket now, from General Thomas, dated at General Buell's headquarters, in which he orders me to have my command ready to attack at daylight. I have also a note from Colonel Fry, inquiring, on the morning of the 9th, what delayed my attack. I heard nothing of the enemy's leaving Perryville, and from these orders had no doubt they were there.

Question. Did you witness any of the movements of the enemy or did you have knowledge in any way of these movements such as to give you a different expectation if such orders had not been received from headquarters?

I certainly witnessed no movements of the enemy, nor was there any circumstance to produce the impression on my mind that the enemy intended to leave Perryville that morning or that they had left the night before. I knew nothing of Perryville. I had no judgment as to the eligibility of that place for the enemy to make a stand and fight a battle, but my impression was that as they had stopped there, had selected the place, and had actually fought there, they intended still to fight there. That was the only ground that I had for such an opinion.

Question. Have you with you the dispatches from headquarters of which you make mention?

I have, sir. These are the dispatches to which I refer as received from General Thomas and Colonel Fry. The one from General Thomas was received by me after night of the 8th. I cannot fix the hour:

"(Official.)

"GENERAL BUELL'S HEADQUARTERS.

"To General CRITTENDEN:
"Have your different divisions ready to attack at daylight. Issue orders at once.
"General THOMAS,
"By Captain CASE,
"Signal Officer."

The dispatch from Colonel Fry reads as follows:

"General CRITTENDEN:
"Have you commenced the advance? What delays your attack?
"JAMES B. FRY,
"Colonel."

It is difficult on the field to remember the hour, but my impression is this was not received till 9 or 10 o'clock in the morning. I had ordered my command to be ready for the attack at daylight. I had taken my position in rear of the center of my command, ready to execute General Thomas' orders, which you will notice is to be ready for the attack, but I never received any order to attack. After waiting a long time, till after 8 or 9 o'clock in the morning—I am not sure whether it was after receiving this dispatch from Colonel Fry or not—I rode to General Thomas, and about that time we commenced the advance.

General BUELL. I propose to introduce those dispatches.
The JUDGE-ADVOCATE. I have no objection to them.

OCTOBER 8—8.30 p. m.

GENERAL: The First Corps (McCook's) on our left has been very heavily engaged. The left and center of this corps gained ground, but the right of it yielded a little. Press your lines forward as far as possible to-night and get into position to make a vigorous attack in the morning at daylight. If you have got your troops into a position which you deem advantageous it will not be desirable to make a change for the purpose of complying with the general's instructions for you sent by Captain Mack. It may be as well to halt the division ordered to the center and let it wait where it is for further orders. The general desires to see you in person as soon to-night as your dut'es will permit you to come over.

Respectfully,

J. B. FRY,
Colonel and Chief of Staff.

General THOMAS.

A true copy.

GEO. E. FLYNT,
Major and Chief of Staff.

OCTOBER 9—10 a. m.

GENERAL: The general commanding in the center reports that the enemy appears to be moving toward our left, and a prisoner confirms this idea and says he thinks they are moving to Dicksville. This, if true, may be to pursue the advantage they gained yesterday over our left. You will move forward steadily, and when the action commences you must attack vigorously and get possession of Perryville, so as to be able to pursue your advantage by moving over the roads from that place to Dicksville, Cave Spring, or Harrodsburg. If the enemy attack our left, re-enforcements will be sent from the center, thus rendering the success of your attack the more necessary. Pursue with vigor any advantage you gain. Report more frequently.

Respectfully,

JAMES B. FRY,
Colonel and Chief of Staff.

General THOMAS or General CRITTENDEN.

A true copy.

GEO. E. FLYNT,
Major and Chief of Staff.

General BUELL. I will first ask the judge-advocate if he admits these copies to have been received from General Thomas and recognizes the transmission of them by General Thomas as an acknowledgment that the orders were received by General Thomas?

The JUDGE-ADVOCATE. Yes, sir; they come to me in response to a request from General Buell asking for all orders and instructions issued at the time indicated in this order, and being authenticated as they are I take them to be in response to that letter, and permit them to come in as such.

By General BUELL:

Question. Have you any knowledge of these instructions?

I cannot say that I ever saw the instructions. They sound familiar to me, and I infer that I either saw them or that General Thomas told me the substance of them.

Question. What position did your corps take on the night of the 9th and at what hour did it get into camp?

General SCHOEPF. I suggest that General Crittenden mark his position on the map, so that the position of the troops be marked by an officer who was present.

General BUELL. I suggest, Mr. President, that the map of Perryville and the neighborhood was prepared before we occupied Perryville and from such information as I could collect in advance. It has never been corrected or verified, and there can be no assurance of its accuracy for any important purpose now.

General CRITTENDEN. My recollection is that one of my divisions encamped at a spring, the name of which I forget. I was not with the division or at the spring; but it is on or near the Perryville or Danville road. The other two divisions I think encamped at Crawford Spring, some few miles from Perryville. I cannot be positive as to the time I reached my camp; I suppose at 1 or 2 o'clock. I am not positive that I did not go on that day to Harlan's, which would be to the east of the Perryville and Harrodsburg road some 3 or 4 miles; but my best impression is that I encamped at Crawford Spring and went to Harlan's the next day.

Question. Where would that position be in reference to Perryville and on what road?

The position at Crawford Spring would be on the Perryville and Harrodsburg road and about 3 miles I think toward Harrodsburg. The spring is not on the road, but near enough I presume to be called on the road.

Question. What position did your corps take on the 10th and at what hour was it entirely in camp?

On the 10th my recollection is that I was in camp at Harlan's; but whether I reached the camp that day or whether I went there on the evening of the 9th is a matter about which I cannot be positive in my statements. I cannot remember whether I went to Harlan's on the 9th or 10th, but I did not move from there on the 10th. I now remember that before I marched from Harlan's with my entire command I sent a brigade to make a reconnaissance toward Harrodsburg. I must leave the question unanswered as to when I got into camp, because I am not actually positive that I marched on the 10th. If I marched on the 10th it was from Crawford Spring, and as it was but a few miles I have no doubt I got into camp early in the day, but I do not recollect the hour.

Question. Who commanded the brigade that went into Harrodsburg, and are you positive that it returned to your camp at Harlan's or did it not join you after you moved from that position?

Colonel Harker commanded the brigade which I sent into Harrodsburg, and since the suggestion which the question makes I am inclined to think that Colonel Harker did join me afterward and that he did not return to Harlan's.

Question. Did you give Colonel Harker his instructions or did General Thomas?

My impression is that they were given by General Thomas. My impression is that I was present or that I gave the instructions myself to Colonel Harker. This is my impression, because Colonel Harker was not instructed to go into Harrodsburg and I was surprised to learn that he had been there. I did not expect him to go there when he started. He was making a reconnaissance to see where the enemy were. I supposed at the time they were at Harrodsburg.

Question. Was the whole of your corps at Harlan's? If not, describe the position of the different parts of it.

The whole of my corps was not at Harlan's. About two divisions were at Harlan's, which is 4 or 5 miles from Perryville, at a point, I should say, nearly equidistant between the Perryville and Danville road and Perryville and Harrodsburg road perhaps a little nearer to the Danville road than to the Harrodsburg road; and one division south of the other two divisions perhaps 2 miles, on or near the Danville road.

Question. Do you know of a brigade being sent from your right division, while occupying that position, to Danville and beyond Danville on a reconnaissance?

I do, sir. I sent Colonel Harker to Danville with his brigade.

Question. Was your corps in the advance in the pursuit of the rebel army in its retreat from Camp Dick Robinson?

It was, sir.

Question. At what time did it march from Danville to take up that pursuit?

I cannot remember the day at this time.

Question. At what hour did your march commence?

It is impossible for me to recollect and state at what hour I marched. A number of blunders delayed one of my divisions. I am inclined to think I was ordered to march very early that morning. I now remember that a sister I had living in Danville was very anxious to have me stay all night at her house, and that I could not do it in consequence of the early hour at which we were to start next morning. That would induce me to believe that it was at an earlier hour than 6.

Question. Can you remember whether you had orders to march at 12 o'clock at night and can you be positive that General Wood's division did not march at that hour?

I cannot remember positively that I was ordered to march at 12 o'clock that night. I do remember that one of my divisions could not march at the hour designated in the order, and I think it was because the commissary had failed to furnish us with supplies.

Question. Can you remember, with reference to the hour appointed to march, at what time it was known that the rebel army was retreating to Camp Dick Robinson?

I cannot, sir; my best recollection is that I did not know myself when I marched that the rebel army was retreating to Camp Dick Robinson.

Question. State, if you please, general, as briefly as possible, the more important particulars of the pursuit as far as it was continued.

Very soon after leaving Danville we skirmished with the rebel cavalry continually, but nothing like a serious engagement. We had no difficulty in driving them along on the march till we reached Crab Orchard. There they made more resistance than at any previous point, so much so as to make it prudent, in my judgment, to send a brigade in advance to drive them along. On the march I heard pretty considerable firing over toward Lancaster, which was on my left, and which made us rather cautious in our approach to Crab Orchard, as there was a road running into that place from Lancaster. I suppose we were delayed only an hour or two at Crab Orchard, and from there on as far as the enemy were pursued by my troops—and they were in advance—we had no serious engagement. The nature of the country was such as to enable very few men with light guns, such as the cavalry had, always to impede our progress. In addition to other difficulties placed before us with their guns, and taking advantage of extraordinary passes through this broken country, they also obstructed our way by cutting down trees and gave us a good deal of work by tearing up the road. I went as far as Wild Cat with my command. I sent one brigade within 2 or 3 miles of London. I also sent a brigade from Wild Cat to Manchester, or the vicinity of Manchester, to destroy some salt works there, and where we scattered a considerable force and took some provisions and pursued them and took 200 head of very fine cattle. The country is barren, and we had some difficulty in keeping the animals from perishing for want of something to eat. The brigade had been sent from Wild Cat by a cross-road which runs from the road leading from Wild Cat to London to the road running from Richmond to London.

Question. Were there any side roads, or was the character of the country off the main roads such that movements could be made to intercept the enemy, or were you obliged to pursue the main roads which the enemy followed?

There is no road by which the enemy could be pursued except the main road, nor is there any road by which they could have been intercepted.

Question. After discontinuing the pursuit was your corps ordered to Glasgow and did it proceed to that point under my orders?

I was ordered there and I proceeded there.

Question. Can you state the date of your arrival there?

I cannot.

Question. From your knowledge of all the circumstances under which Kentucky was invaded by the rebel forces last summer what was your judgment and what is your judgment now as to the probability that that invasion was intended for the purpose of holding the State permanently and as to the presumption that that object was not to be abandoned without a serious struggle?

From the time I knew the magnitude of the force with which the rebels had invaded Kentucky I never doubted at all that they intended to hold the State if it could possibly be done and that they would fight for it. Perhaps it would be wrong to say I never doubted it, for when they began to retreat I thought perhaps that their hearts had failed; but my impression, certainly up to Perryville, was that they intended to fight; but when they commenced their retreat there I may have possibly thought differently (I do not remember precisely what I did think then), and when they passed Crab Orchard I thought they meant to abandon the State.

Question. When it was first discovered that the enemy had retired from his position at Perryville what was your impression as to the force he had had there, and was it your impression that his force was concentrated there or that only a small portion of it had made a stand there?

My impression was that his entire force was there, but I cannot say that I derived that impression from any information. The fact that they fought there statisfied me that he had concentrated his force there. I do not know that I had any information beyond that which induced me to believe his entire force was there.

Question. Do you consider that the supposition that he had concentrated his whole force and had fought there, and on the other hand the supposition that he made a stand there with only a small portion of his force, might make a very decided difference as to the object of his withdrawal from that point; in other words, while in one case it might indicate that he was retreating, might it not in the other case indicate that he was moving to complete his junction or concentrate for the purpose of battle?

Undoubtedly it would make a great difference in the inference which I should draw myself as to the object of his withdrawal; in the one case I should think he would consider himself unable to encounter our army, and in the other case I should think his object was to unite his whole force, and that he intended to fight or run as he might think best.

Question. With Bragg's army proper at Bardstown and Kirby Smith's forces at Lexington and other points in Central Kentucky, with the direct roads open from these points to any points on which the enemy might desire to retreat—for example, the turnpike from Bardstown through New Haven and Glasgow and so on to Middle Tennessee, the turnpike from Bardstown to Lebanon and thence on either directly to Glasgow or by way of Columbia, the road from Bardstown to Danville, thence to Somerset, or on toward Cumberland Gap, and for the other forces the roads from Central Kentucky by the way of Richmond on to Cumberland Gap—what to your mind would such movements indicate as took these separate forces entirely off these various routes for the purpose of concentrating them at or in the vicinity of an out-of-the-way place like Harrodsburg?

To my mind it would indicate certainly a resolution to fight.

Question. State, if you please, what your judgment is in regard to the state of discipline in the Army of the Ohio from first to last, and as to the care with which its discipline was watched over and preserved by its commander and his subordinate officers under his direction.

I think the Army of the Ohio, from my knowledge of it, has always been in a high state of discipline, and that the very greatest care was taken by its commander to preserve that discipline. He was very efficiently aided by very many of his officers; and I think the army has demonstrated its discipline, from Shiloh and Perryville down to Stone River, by the very highest sort of testimony to its efficiency.

Question. Does anything occur to you in connection with the condition of that army last summer in Middle Tennessee which was calculated to impair its discipline in spite of the best efforts of its high officers? Please state what now occurs to you on that subject.

There were several things, I think, calculated to impair the discipline of an army situated as that army was in Middle Tennessee. It was scattered very much, and in some divisions composing the army there was some dissatisfaction because they thought they were so isolated. They did not know how they were supported or to be supported in case of difficulty, and when the movement began some of the commands supposed they were retreating, which always impairs the discipline of an army. In addition to that we were living on half rations very often. There was a great deal of ripe fruit in the country through which we marched and the men would break ranks. There was great difficulty in keeping the men in the ranks. I know of nothing else. I think the discipline of the army was very much restored again as soon as it was concentrated and began to feel its strength and began to think they were to fight again and not to run.

Question. Is it or is it not your opinion that the tone of a considerable portion of the public press encouraged in the minds of the men the idea that they were more or less at liberty to make use of private property wherever they could find it, if they wished?

I think there was much in the tone of a portion of the press that encouraged that idea in the men. Undoubtedly, from some reason or other, many men seemed to have adopted that idea, and it was with great difficulty and after a considerable time that marauding could be stopped.

Question. Have you ever known any army or do you suppose it is possible to have an army in which there will not be more or less complaining and fault-finding and animosity toward the commander?

I have certainly never known such an army, and I do not believe there ever was such an army or ever will be, that is composed of men.

Question. Have you observed any instance of such animosity in the Army of the Ohio toward its late commander, myself, and have you in your own mind been able to explain it? Do you know of any marked instances of that kind that you can explain now?

I have known of some instances in which officers of the army complained of their late commander, and the explanation to my mind was—and I am not sure whether I did those officers injustice or not, but my explanation was that they were dissatisfied with the general because of some orders that were personally disagreeable to them. I supposed the dissatisfaction was temporary, because it grew out of such a cause as that. By this I do not mean to say that I have not heard officers complain of the general commanding or that I have not complained myself of some things, but I mean to say that as far as I know his general course as a commander was satisfact ry to the army.

Question. I wish to submit to the witness General Orders, No. 13a, issued by me at Nashville a year ago, and ask him whether he recognizes that order as embodying the policy which I meant to pursue and did pursue, as far as my presence enabled me to enforce it, in the military operations of the army under my command.

I do not recognize the order, and I will state unhesitatingly that the whole time it was the commanding general's policy to carry out this order, and that he exerted himself, to my knoweledge, to have it carried out when we were on the march, and that he exerted himself to have it carried out by frequent instructions and orders to his command.

Question. Do you see anything in that order or was it the practice under it to treat persons who were active in their opposition to the Government or violent and offensive in their language in the same manner as persons who were loyal to the Government?

There is nothing in the order requiring loyal and disloyal persons to be treated in the same way, nor was it the practice, to my knowledge, to treat disloyal and loyal persons in the same way.

Question. Do you consider that there was a time in Kentucky when the policy to be pursued by the army would have had a very material effect upon the sentiments of the people toward the Union?

I think so, undoubtedly.

Question. What, in your judgment, was the effect of the policy announced in that order; was it good or bad?

I think it was good.

Question. What, in your opinion, has been the effect of that policy everywhere wherever it has been faithfully executed, and what the effect of a policy which denied that the people had any rights, which deprived them of their liberties without some positive and individual offense against the authority of the Government, and impoverished them?

In my opinion the policy announced in that order is the true policy of the Government, and of course I think its effects must be good everywhere wherever it is carried out. The policy of depriving people of their rights and impoverishing them, depriving them of their liberties, arresting them without having committed positive offenses, I consider tyrannical and a bad policy, and that its effect must be bad among such a people as ours.

Commission adjourned to meet March 3.

CINCINNATI, *Tuesday, March 3, 1863.*

The Commission met pursuant to adjournment. All the members present; also the judge-advocate and General Buell.

Examination of General CRITTENDEN continued.

By General BUELL:

Question. Have you any recollection of the visit which I paid to the camp of your division and other divisions near Pelham in the month of August last?

I remember your being at Pelham, and my division, General McCook's division, and General Schoepf's division were there ; in the latter part of August I think it was.

Question. Did you, subsequent to that visit or about that time, hear any comments upon any particular incident connected with that visit? If so, please state what you heard and all you know about it, and particularly an incident connected with my visit to the division of which Brigadier-General Schoepf was at that time in command.

I remember being at General Schoepf's headquarters the day after General Buell's arrival at Pelham, which I think took place at night, if I remember correctly, and to have heard as I rode to General Schoepf's headquarters that he had been arrested.

The JUDGE-ADVOCATE. Mr. President, before this question goes any further I think it would be proper for General Buell to state what he expects to prove by this line of examination that he is now entering upon.

General BUELL. I should like to inquire, Mr. President, by what right or upon what ground the judge-advocate requires me to explain the object of the evidence I introduce here any more than he should be required to explain the object of any question he may think proper to put. The explanation which he proposes I should be required to make might defeat the very object of the evidence itself. I can imagine no good reason for his objection.

The JUDGE-ADVOCATE. If I were to ask any question the answer to which traveled apparently outside of the issue or beyond the line of investigation called for by the Government and incumbent upon us to follow it would be proper for General Buell to ask me what I expected to prove by it. A great deal of time would be necessarily lost if we permitted the introduction of subjects, however interesting they might be, outside of what we are called upon to investigate. I cannot see myself the object of the question nor what the evidence has to do with the investigation under consideration.

General BUELL. I do not know that it is necessary that the judge-advocate should see what the tendency of this evidence may be. I think it is sufficient that the object is to defend myself before this Commission and before the country.

General SCHOEPF. Mr. President, here is a witness (General Crittenden) who was present, and if it is satisfactory to the Commission I will make a statement, which if correct——

The JUDGE-ADVOCATE. Mr. President, I would suggest respectfully to the members of the court that unless my objection is admitted to be in order a discussion upon it would be out of order. If my objection is in order then the court should be cleared for its consideration. If General Buell says that the answer, or what he anticipates will be the answer, would be defeated by stating the object for which he calls for it and that it is strictly within the line of investigation we are authorized to make, I have nothing more to say. The Commission will have to judge of that when they come to it on the record.

The PRESIDENT. I would like to call the general's attention to one point which I see involved in the question and on which I should like to hear the general's opinion. It appears that the question has reference to a member of the court. Now, if it is a question which involves misconduct of his, or involves him in anything the nature of which might hereafter be considered criminal, or which would affect his standing as a member of this court, charged like the rest of us with the investigation of the general's operations in the State of Tennessee and Kentucky, the general cannot but see that it would be but right that that member of the court should have an opportunity for a full explanation of the affair; and the making of that explanation might require the presence of witnesses, and it might require him in his own justification to go into a lengthened explanation by witnesses introduced before this Commission. As to the propriety of the question, therefore, I would like very much to hear the general's views.

General SCHOEPF. I would suggest that the explanation, which would only occupy two minutes, might be made to the court.

The PRESIDENT. Excuse me, general, the question which I propose for the general to speak to is whether a question involving the conduct of a member of this court, be it good or bad, could properly be considered as part of the issue pending before this Commission; and if in your opinion, general, it is properly a part of the issue, whether that would not require you to explain the purpose of your question and what is the particular fact which you seek from the witness.

General BUELL. It seems to me, sir, that the judge-advocate and the member of the Commission have both anticipated the answer. The question does not involve General Schoepf at all necessarily. General Schoepf is not mentioned in the question except as being the commander whose camp I visited near Pelham. I think, sir, that the objections are a little untimely. I will say further that I claim that it is my right to show to this Commission, though I am not coming to that point now, sir, that if any member of this Commission has disqualified himself by prejudice or by personal animosity to sit as an impartial judge upon this investigation, I claim the right to show that such a member would be incompetent to sit on this Commission. I do not say that I am coming to that point now, sir; but upon the other point I say that if any matter has been introduced in the course of this investigation which involves the conduct or opinions of any member of this Commission with reference to the exercise of my command, I have the right to introduce testimony to elucidate that matter fully.

The JUDGE-ADVOCATE. General Buell misapprehended me in the matter. Mr. President, I simply take the .broad ground, which is my duty, to keep this investigation as closely as possible to the matter called for by the Government, and it was because I thought we were traveling out of that line that I asked for an explanation. The ground taken by yourself is strictly correct and I agree with your opinion; but I must say in this connection that if there is anything which disqualifies a member of this court from sitting as an impartial judge or juror this is not the proper tribunal to bring it before; it belongs entirely to another place; we could not take up our time in trying members of this court; but if these facts are in possession of General Buell the proper time to have urged them was when this court was being organized and not after the court has been sitting three months: Your objection, Mr. President, is properly taken and is tenable, but I did not introduce the argument, because I did not dream for an instant that exception would be taken to members of this Commission.

General BUELL. The judge-advocate is very right as to the proper time to make objection to competency of any members of this Commission under certain circumstances. If I had knowledge of facts that would have disqualified them it was proper for me to make objection at the time. I have not asserted that I have such knowledge now. If I have, it is my privilege, and it is due to justice, and I have no doubt the right will be accorded me, to establish the facts before this Commission.

The JUDGE-ADVOCATE. I do not wish to prolong this discussion, Mr. President, but I would say that I still occupy the ground that I did. If the fact was not in possession of General Buell, but if the doubt was on his mind as to the propriety of any member sitting on this board, it should have been taken and discussed before this Commission at the time of its formation.

General TYLER. I move that the court be cleared.

The PRESIDENT. If this had been a court-martial or a court of inquiry I should have no right in the world to take exception to any individual members; but it is not a court-martial or court of inquiry, but a court of investigation. To show the distinction: General Buell is not charged with anything before this court; there is no charge, no specification. It is simply an investigation of general operations which certain officers of the Army are charged to make; and the point to which I would wish to call the general's attention is whether under the law or with propriety exception can be taken, either on the part of the Government or on the part of General Buell, to any member or members of this investigation.

General BUELL. This matter was not introduced by me, and I do not think it necessary to answer your inquiry negatively or affirmatively. When I come to that point then it will be time for you to give your decision upon it. I will make one remark in reference to any suspicion I might entertain. I will say that I should not object to any member sitting upon any court for the investigation of my conduct simply upon a prejudgment of his which might be rectified by the evidence. My presumption would be that all honorable men, in spite of slight prejudices or somewhat prejudiced conclusions, might in the end be able to do substantial justice, and therefore I should not object as a general thing to a member of this Commission, though I might know that he had expressed himself unfavorably. But I will say further that I was not apprised of that when this investigation commenced its sittings. I may have become apprised of it since, and I may say that I shall not fail to avail myself of that information.

On General SCHOEPF'S requesting permission to make a personal explanation.

The PRESIDENT. I think it would be improper. The answer to the question has not distinctly involved you, and until it is fairly defined that you are involved in an act which may be called out by the answer I think it hardly necessary to make an explanation, and I think an explanation at this point would be immature.

The JUDGE-ADVOCATE. I would remark, Mr. President, that this discussion is entirely out of order.

General TYLER. I move that the court be cleared.

The court was cleared; when it was decided that the question should be answered.

The WITNESS. I think I inquired upon my arrival, either of General Schoepf or General Fry, for both were there before I left their quarters, whether General Schoepf had been arrested or was under arrest. I think General Schoepf himself told me that he had been arrested, but that he was released from arrest, and then the conversation which followed was in reference to the cause of the arrest. Both General Schoepf and General Fry participated in the conversation. I think they told me that General Buell had ridden through the lines and into camp without being challenged, and that he came up to their quarters (whether he came to General Schoepf's or General Fry's quarters I am not sure) very angry indeed, and complained of it as a piece of great carelessness on the part of the commanders that any one should be enabled to ride into headquarters without being challenged by a sentinel. I remember but little more of that conversation. The generals were both excited and I thought a little indignant at General Buell's anger and censure, and laughingly said they would make the sentinels or outposts arrest General Buell if he did not mind how he rode around the lines; that is the impression made on my mind by what they said. I think the general had not come on the road, but through a fence, and had got into the lines without being challenged. I thought it was a sort of indignation that would wear off. I have been as mad as that often myself with my commanding generals and it made no great impression on me. This is the only incident that I remember connected with General Buell's visit to General Schoepf's headquarters.

Question. Are you positive that it was asserted by any officer whom you heard converse upon this subject that I had ridden into camp by any by-road or across any field out of the usual route? If so, what officer made that assertion?

I cannot say that any officer made that assertion, nor am I absolutely positive that the assertion was made. My impression is and my recollection is that some one at that time mentioned it as a fact that General Buell had approached the camp, not by the road, but had gone through a field. I have not conversed with any one since on the subject. My impression is strong that I must have heard it, because I had no idea what road General Buell did approach by. Such a fact I think could not have got into my head unless I had heard it from some one. I cannot name the officer who made this statement nor can I be more positive than I have been.

Question. Has the supposition which you say you entertained at that time been realized, that the irritation caused by that incident would speedily pass away from the minds of those officers or not? You may answer with reference to General Fry.

Since that time I do not remember to have had any conversation with General Schoepf in reference to his arrest or to have had any conversation with him which would have induced me to think otherwise than that the irritation was temporary. With reference to General Fry my impression has been that he was subsequent to that time, perhaps a month subsequent, still unfriendly to General Buell; but whether that impression was formed from a conversation with General Fry, or from incidental remarks that I may have heard him make, or from having heard others say that General Fry was hostile to General Buell, I cannot now distinctly remember; nor can I state that the unfriendly feelings of General Fry for General Buell was in consequence of what occurred when General Buell visited his camp at Pelham, and therefore General Fry's irritation at Pelham may have been, as I supposed originally, only temporary.

Question. At what time did this visit to General Schoepf's camp take place? Was it in the day or night?

I understood it was at night, but I have no positive knowledge.

Question. On the march from Bowling Green to Louisville do you know of any proposition among any of the officers of the army having for its object the removal of General Buell from command? State anything that you know upon that subject, if you please, and all you know.

I think it was on the march between Bowling Green and Louisville—I am sure it occurred somewhere between Nashville and Louisville—an officer came to me stating that there was great dissatisfaction in his command; the officers and men were unwilling to fight under General Buell. He came to talk with me on the subject because I was an officer of high rank and a Kentuckian, and he thought I ought to take some part in it; he thought something ought to be done. I replied to him that I had entire confidence in General Buell; that there was no dissatisfaction in my command that I knew anything about, and asked him what he proposed to do. I think he said that we ought to arrest General Buell. I told him that I did not want him to talk to me any more upon that subject. I have not named the officer, but can do so if necessary.

Question. I will thank you to name the officer, and state to whose brigade and whose division he belonged.

Col. John M. Harlan, of Kentucky, was the officer. I think he belonged to General Thomas' division, but I cannot state to what brigade he belonged.

Question. Did Colonel Harlan give you any explanation of the dissatisfaction which he said existed in the part of the army he was serving in, or could you from what he said, or from any other fact, trace the cause of that dissatisfaction and of his discontent in particular?

I think I have stated almost entirely the conversation which I had with Colonel Harlan. He did not give me any explanation of the causes for dissatisfaction nor did I believe that there was any dissatisfaction. I thought that I could trace Colonel Harlan's own dissatisfaction with General Buell to an order which General Buell had published censuring to some extent a portion of Colonel Harlan's regiment that had been on detached service somewhere in Alabama or the southern part of Tennessee, I am not sure where now, and I believed that Colonel Harlan had mistaken his own irritation at having any portion of his command censured for the general dissatisfaction in the command. I scarcely thought that Colonel Harlan could be serious in his proposition to me. I know that he felt very sore under the order to which I refer from a conversation he had with me on the subject not long after the occurrence.

Question. Have you any reason to believe that the proposition you allude to for my removal from command ever came to my knowledge while I was in command of the army?

None in the world, nor any reason to believe that the proposition ever came to any one else's ears than my own. I should have deemed it my duty to have apprised the commanding general at once if I had supposed that there was any conspiracy among officers, or if I had not supposed it was a proposition made by a single officer, who was irritated and not in the exercise of his own best judgment at the time, and if I had not believed the conversation with him would be the end of it.

Question. Can you remember whether Colonel Harlan belonged to the brigade which General Fry commanded at that time and do you know anything of the personal relations between those officers?

I am inclined to think that Colonel Harlan did belong to General Fry's brigade. I am quite sure that their personal relations were very friendly.

Cross-examination by the JUDGE-ADVOCATE:

Question. At what date did you move your division from Baldwyn, Miss., and when did you arrive at Athens?

I was not at Baldwyn. I think it was from the 12th to the 15th of June, as I now remember, that I marched from near Baldwyn to Iuka and thence to Athens. I cannot be positive as to the day I reached Athens, but it was in the latter part of June.

Question. How long had McCook's division been at Athens when you arrived and do you know when he left the vicinity of Corinth?

General McCook's division reached Iuka about the same time that I reached there and preceded me on the march to Athens. We crossed the Tennessee River at Florence together, he preceding me one day. Whether General McCook preceded me to Athens or not I am not positive. I know that he marched in advance of me to Huntsville and as far as Stevenson, but cannot now remember positively whether I left Florence in front of General McCook's command. General McCook I think must have left the vicinity of Corinth about the 15th to the 17th of June, and I believe that he could march from Corinth to Iuka in a day, and my recollection is that he did make that march.

Question. You say you arrived at Stevenson on the 12th of July. How far is Stevenson from Chattanooga?

I should say it is about 40 miles. I do not know the distance by any road.

Question. What is the distance from Baldwyn to Stevenson and how many days were you on the route and what did your march average per day?

I think it is about 180 to 200 miles from Baldwyn to Stevenson. I do not remember how many days I was marching. I do not now remember how many days I halted on the march. Whenever I did march my recollection is that my march would average from 12 to 15 miles. I was halted several times on the march; I had to stop at Iuka. I do not know how many days I was detained for supplies and turning over a number of things, such as overcoats and camp equipage; things we did not want on the march. I do not remember how many days we lost at Tuscumbia in crossing the Tennessee River; we had to make a road there; nor do I remember how long I was delayed at Athens waiting for supplies. It would be impossible for me to say how many days I was marching unless I had access to my papers.

Question. You can state, general, whether that march was pushed with vigor, no time lost, as if you had some object in view, or whether it was delayed and what was the cause of the delay.

So far as my own command is concerned I have no recollection of any delay. My halts were all made for specific purposes, and when they were accomplished, when I had got supplies and when we had made the road ready at the river and we crossed the river and marched, my recollection is that we marched direct to Athens, where I was delayed for want of supplies. I made no halt afterward except one day at Huntsville, waiting again for supplies, until I reached Battle Creek.

Question. On your arrival at Stevenson, on the 12th of July, where were the other divisions of the Army of the Ohio?

I found General McCook's division near Stevenson, and we left a division (I think General Mitchel's) at Huntsville, under the command of General Smith. I believe General Nelson's division was at Athens when I passed through. I do not remember where General Wood's division was; I think he was repairing a railroad, but I do not know exactly where, and there was a brigade at Battle Creek.

Question. Were not Athens and Battle Creek about the poorest places for supplies you encountered?

Battle Creek certainly was one of the poorest of places, and I remember having a great deal of difficulty at Athens about forage. On the march there were places which were worse for supplies. The road from Huntsville to Stevenson is a very bad one for supplies, and it was a very barren, mountainous country at the beginning of the march, shortly after we left Iuka, I think.

Question. When you were living on half rations at Battle Creek what exertions were made and how to obtain supplies from the country?

We sent out parties regularly for forage and driving cattle. We hired the Tennessee refugees that came into camp to go out and drive in cattle and haul in forage. I cannot remember precisely what extent of country, but we sent as far as we deemed it safe. At one time we sent back to Stevenson and out upon the Stevenson road and had forage hauled to the road; that would be some 25 to 30 miles in that direction. Up the Sequatchie Valley we could not send very far.

Question. How far on each side of your line of march from Huntsville to Battle Creek did you draw supplies of forage and provisions from?

We got no supplies on the road from Huntsville to Battle Creek except those that were sent to us by railroad. We were short of supplies when we started, and obtained them on the road at the point to which they had been sent from Huntsville. The supplies which we got on the march from Huntsville to Battle Creek we gathered in the immediate vicinity. We did not delay at all. We had no time to send any distance; we gathered what we could.

Question. What was the amount of your train on the march from Baldwyn to Huntsville?

I cannot say.

Question. General, what force had the enemy opposite you at Battle Creek and at Stevenson, as you estimate it?

We were never able to ascertain in any reliable way what force they had there. We could infer only from the names of officers who sent notes and dispatches that were sometimes brought into our camp across the river that there was some considerable force there, a brigade we supposed, as General Heth was there at one time; he signed himself as in command. I never saw 200 men there. Some distance back from the river they were encamped and entirely covered by woods. Their pickets were in view every day, and sometimes held conversations across the river when there was no one there to stop it.

Question. What force was there at Chattanooga at the time you arrived at Battle Creek?

My instructions were, and I considered it an important part of my business, to try to ascertain what force was really at Chattanooga. It was a considerable time before we got any sort of information that we deemed reliable. The men that I used as spies were not capable, at least many of them, of estimating a large force. My own idea as to the only way of ascertaining the number of men was to ascertain what officers were there. Upon my arrival at that place I really did not know anything at all about the force at Chattanooga, except the common rumor that there was a "considerable force" there.

Question. From your knowledge of the officers there and from reports of your scouts what did you make the number to have been?

I can only state now what my impression is. I cannot fix the date at which I received the information, but I suppose when I reached Battle Creek there were about 8,000 to 10,000 troops at Chattanooga.

Question. You state that General McCook's, General Nelson's, General Wood's, and your own division made the first movement toward North Alabama, and that General Thomas afterward came up. What do you estimate the strength of these divisions at?

My estimate of our force at that time was about 30,000 men.

Question. Was General Mitchel's division also in North Alabama and what was its strength and did this form a part of the Army of the Ohio?

General Mitchel's division was at Huntsville when I passed through, so I understood. I also understood that it did form part of the Army of the Ohio. I never was with General Mitchel's division, and had no opportunity of knowing anything personally as to its strength. I supposed it was about equal to the other divisions.

Question. You said the distance from Stevenson to Chattanooga was 40 miles. How many days' provisions would have been necessary to have made a dash at Chattanooga?

That would depend upon so many contingencies that I scarcely know how to answer. To have marched to Chattanooga with no opposition and with forced marches it might have been done in two days, but to have marched there and encountered such obstacles as an enemy could have interposed in that country I think it would not have been prudent to start with less than eight or ten days' provisions, and unless we were quite sure of succeeding when we got there it would be unsafe with that.

Question. Was not a movement on Chattanooga with ten days' subsistence as practicable as Bragg's movement across the Tennessee with ten days' and only three wagons to a brigade?

I think that Bragg's movement was a very extraordinary one certainly, and that the other movement would have been a very extraordinary one. As far as I understand the movement, I think that Bragg's was more feasible than the movement on Chattanooga with eight or ten days' supplies. Bragg had a railroad behind him. Bragg knew that he could avoid the enemy. Bragg had a people who sympathized with him very much through whose country he was to march, and I suppose he had an accurate knowledge, for I suppose that he obtained all such information possible of all our forces and our strength.

Question. State what reasons you have, general, for saying that Bragg knew he could avoid the enemy.

I suppose that Bragg knew the position of our forces and that he knew he could avoid us. Bragg having his troops concentrated and ready to move could by keeping his own counsel start just when he pleased. He knew that we could not or would not attempt to intercept him without concentrating our forces, and I think it was not possible for us to have concentrated our forces so as to intercept him.

Question. Was there not time between the knowledge of the fact of his crossing the Tennessee and his arrival at Sparta to have concentrated our forces?

I think it is possible that our forces might have been concentrated at Sparta before General Bragg reached there. I am not sure of that, but think it is possible; still I do not think that would necessarily have intercepted General Bragg.

Question. How could he have avoided our army concentrated at Sparta?

He might have kept still farther to the east and have avoided it, or he might have attempted to come west and avoid it.

Question. Had he turned to the east would it not have thrown him upon a line of country in which he would have found great difficulties to subsist his army, and had he turned west would it not have brought it to the front of Nashville instead of to its rear?

I do not know the nature of the country into which he would have been thrown by going farther east. He might have obtained supplies by the road from Chattanooga to Knoxville had he gone far enough, and if he had turned to the west I suppose he would have been tempted to go to Murfreesborough ahead of us. He might have got to Nashville by that route.

Question. Is it not now well known that all the rebel troops that could be spared were in demand at Richmond for the struggle with McClellan during that summer and that very few troops could be spared at the Southwest?

Question objected to by General Buell.

General BUELL. Mr. President, if it gives the witness the privilege of speaking from report it cannot be known as a matter of notoriety. If the witness is expected to speak from his own knowledge, very well. I will give a reason why the question cannot be answered. I can cite an example where the rebel troops were at a point where they were not absolutely necessary. For example, the expedition of Breckinridge's division against Baton Rouge. That was not an expedition of such vital importance that those troops could not have been spared for other points where the presence of an additional force was of vital consequence.

General SCHOEPF. As I understand, General Buell objects to the question so that he may answer it himself.

The JUDGE-ADVOCATE. I would remark that so far as any historical fact is concerned we are entitled to use it as we would any other fact. The struggle between McClellan and the rebel army at Richmond last summer is history, and we may introduce it in illustration of any fact that may come before this court. I apprehend that General Buell will not persist in his objection when he comes to think of it; it certainly is not tenable. So far as the illustration goes it is entirely out of the line of argument.

General BUELL. The question would require a distinct answer, yes, or no. It did not require that the witness should travel out of the path to explain his opinion—if he had that opinion—that all the forces at the service of the rebel Government were required and actually were in front of Richmond to stop the advance of McClellan's army. I had no idea of suggesting anything to the mind of the witness, and I do not think I did suggest anything that he could have been expected to state in answer to the question.

(The recorder is in doubt whether the foregoing remark of General Buell, marked in the margin, is fully reported.)

The JUDGE-ADVOCATE. Before General Buell goes I would remark that where a fact is notoriously a fact you can draw your conclusions from it, and it is proper for a witness to do so. For example, recollecting the terrible struggle we were engaged in in the front of Richmond, was it not reasonable to suppose and do you not believe that all the troops were drawn from the Southwest in order to support the rebel Government at Richmond?

General BUELL. For my own part I can answer that it is not a matter of notoriety that all the troops that could possibly be spared were sent to Richmond to support the rebel army. There was a sufficiency of rebel troops there to accomplish their object. Whether they had there all they could collect I do not know, or whether they could not have spared some of their troops for other purposes I do not know.

The court was cleared; when, after discussion, it was decided that the question should be put.

On the opening of the court General Crittenden replied as follows:

No, sir; I do not think it is well known.

The JUDGE-ADVOCATE. Do you understand that to be the fact?

I do not. I understand that a great struggle was going on there, and that the Confederate Government were using every means possible to maintain themselves there. I also understand at the same time they were struggling with equal pertinacity and assiduity to maintain themselves everywhere else where they had armies.

Question. With the army numbering over 30,000 men at the time there were but 10,000 at Chattanooga you say a movement on that place was not practicable?

I have not made that statement. A movement on Chattanooga with our army, which numbered 30,000 men at the time that there were as I supposed not more than 10,000 men at Chattanooga, would not be practicable at all with ten day's rations. At that time our army was scattered over a considerable extent of country. Portions of it could not have reached Chattanooga in less than six or seven days, I should think. That is my understanding of the position of the army at that time. Had the army of 30,000 men been within 40 miles of Chattanooga while there were but 10,000 men in Chattanooga I should think the enterprise could have been carried out, notwithstanding all the difficulties, and that Chattanooga could have been taken.

Question. Were there any other reasons than a lack of supplies which prevented the concentration of the army there in time to bring about that result?

I know of no reason which delayed the concentration of the army except the want of supplies, which was occasioned by the breaks in the railroads and some work that some portions of the army were required to do in repairing railroads; but had the army been concentrated at Stevenson I am very far from supposing that a much larger force would not have been thrown into Chattanooga by the rebels at an earlier day.

Question. You stated in your examination-in-chief that you considered it would have been unsafe to go to Chattanooga if there had been nobody there to resist. Please give your reasons, general.

I would have considered it unsafe to march with the command which we had at Battle Creek to Chattanooga if there had been no enemy there to oppose us, because we were cut off from our source of supplies and could not have expected to find supplies at Chattanooga. We should have been compelled to go back for supplies, and would have incurred some risk in passing through that country from even small parties of guerrillas We might have lost some transportation and could have accomplished nothing.

Question. You say the country across the mountains from Chattanooga was very destitute of provisions. Was the Sequatchie Valley, the route Bragg's army took, also destitute; and, if not, did it not make it almost sure that Bragg would come out at Pikeville or Sparta?

The Sequatchie Valley, I understand, was not destitute of provisions or supplies. I saw only a portion of it. I was not far up the Sequatchie Valley; as far as I did go it is a narrow valley and not very much cultivated nor very abundant in its supplies. I cannot say that I considered it certain at all that General Bragg would come out at Pikeville or Sparta. To tell the truth I was not sure that he would not come down the Sequatchie Valley in pursuit of McCook and myself.

Question. At McMinnville had not the Army of the Ohio its subsistence assured by railroad communication; and could it, with McMinnville as a base, supply itself at or near Sparta had it been concentrated there, the distance being only about 25 miles?

The Army of the Ohio concentrated at McMinnville had its supplies quite secure, but with its supplies at McMinnville and the Army of the Ohio at Sparta I should have considered its depot of supplies as very insecure.

Question. Will you give your reasons, general?

If General Bragg, on the road from Chattanooga to Sparta or McMinnville, were at liberty to take what road he pleased, and with such a force of cavalry as he had with him, it might have been possible for General Bragg to reach McMinnville before the army at Sparta could come back to defend its supplies.

Question. Do you not know that General Bragg's army arrived at Sparta very much demoralized from exhaustion from that march up the Sequatchie Valley?

I do not, sir; I understood that General Bragg's army suffered a great deal throughout that march; I do not remember to have heard that they were very much demoralized at that place.

Question. If his army suffered in that march up the Sequatchie Valley what would have been its condition if it had attempted to cross the mountains by any of those roads which you characterized as being destitute of provisions and I believe also of water?

If the Sequatchie Valley is a very rich valley he could not have suffered much coming up. If he had crossed the mountains he would have suffered the same hardships, I suppose, and encountered the same difficulties that we encountered.

Question. How long a time after the 20th of August, the date you gave Bragg to have crossed the Tennessee River at Chattanooga, would it have required to concentrate the Army of the Ohio at or near McMinnville?

I do not know precisely where the various portions of the army were at that time, but in seven or eight days, I suppose, if they had all supplies and had been ready to march, the entire army might have been concentrated there. This opinion is, of course, a mere guess as to the time it would have required. I do not know where the different portions of the army were precisely, nor the distance from McMinnville to these various points, nor the roads by which the different portions of the army would have been compelled to march; but in six or eight days, if everything had been ready, I suppose they might have been concentrated.

Question. Can you state what the Army of the Ohio was doing between the 12th day of July, when you arrived at Battle Creek, and the 20th of August, when Bragg crossed the Tennessee River at Chattanooga?

I do not think I arrived at Battle Creek till the 13th. My impression is I arrived at Stevenson on the 12th and at Battle Creek on the 13th. I can only state what that portion of the army I was with was actually doing, and that I have already stated. I know that a portion of the army was at Murfreesborough, where a battle had been fought. General Nelson was sent there. The roads were broken, and I know General Smith was sent—I think to Tullahoma; I do not know with what forces. Most of that time General Mitchel's division was at Huntsville, and I believe General Buell's headquarters were there until near that time, or from the 12th of July until about the 20th of August. It was somewhere about that time he changed his headquarters. A portion of the army was during that period of time at McMinnville. General Thomas and General Wood were there I think; that is my best recollection; but what they were all doing I cannot state, sir. They had to march some distance to get to these different points.

Question. Do you know that the Therman road was practicable for baggage wagons and artillery trains for a large army?

I have no personal knowledge of the Therman road. I only know from the fact that was brought out during my examination here that an army did pass over that road.

The Commission adjourned to meet March 4, 1863, at 10 o'clock a. m.

CINCINNATI, *Wednesday, March* 4, 1863.

The Commission met pursuant to adjournment. All the members present; also the judge-advocate and General Buell.

Cross-examination of General CRITTENDEN continued.

By the JUDGE-ADVOCATE:

Question. You say in your examination-in-chief that if the Army of the Ohio had been massed at Sparta it would have been practicable for Bragg's army to have marched on McMinnville without its movements being known; please explain how and by what routes this movement could have been made in the face of the Army of the Ohio.

My idea of the manner in which it would have been possible for Bragg's army to have reached McMinnville with the Army of the Ohio concentrated at Sparta, and before the army could have known certainly what direction Bragg's army was taking, would be in a movement somewhere about Spencer, where I understand there was a road running to Sparta and a road running to McMinnville. I do not see such a road upon that map, but my recollection is that there is a road from Spencer to McMinnville and a road from Spencer to Sparta; so that it would have been possible even for Bragg's army starting from Pikeville to have deceived the army at Sparta as to its destination until it substantially reached McMinnville. I think that armies of any considerable force, while lying near together, by feints and demonstrations may almost always deceive the opposing general as to their movements or at least leave him in a state of great uncertainty.

Question. Are you acquainted, general, with the stream Caney Fork? If so, please state to the Commission the character of that stream.

I have no personal knowledge of the stream at all. I have never seen it.

Question. Have you ever seen any reports in reference to it and the character of the country about it that would justify you in stating to the Commission what it amounts to?

I do not think I have, sir. I have heard only general opinions with reference to the stream itself; I have heard that it was a difficult stream to cross.

Question. You say supplies were plenty at Lebanon; suppose the Army of the Ohio had been massed at that point before or after Bragg passed Sparta, would it not have been in a position to oppose his advance into Kentucky or his farther advance into Tennessee?

If the Army of the Ohio had been massed at Lebanon I should have considered that it made it a more hazardous thing for General Bragg to attempt the passage of the Cumberland River where he did actually cross than if the Army of the Ohio had been massed at Nashville; but I am inclined to think, without any accurate knowledge of the distances, that General Bragg could still have crossed the river, and I should have considered the Army of the Ohio in a worse place at Lebanon than at Nashville for any future operations.

Question. Supposing General Bragg's army to have numbered 35,000 or 40,000 men and subsisting on the country through which they marched, was it possible for him to move upon one road; and if the Army of the Ohio had been massed at Lebanon would he have been forced to concentrate his forces so as to meet us?

I have not a sufficient knowledge of the country to know whether General Bragg could have marched his army and have subsisted on one road. I am inclined to think he would have been compelled to have arranged for such a march beforehand, if the country had sufficient supplies and with the large cavalry force he had. The people sympathized with him and would bring him over supplies. I suppose it would be possible, marching rapidly as he did, to subsist his army through that country. With such an arrangement as that I think he would not necessarily have been compelled to mass his forces for the purpose of fighting at Lebanon. I think it was practicable for him to have passed the Cumberland.

Question. Are you sufficiently acquainted with the details of the army and the exigencies of the service at the time as to be able to tell the Commission why out of an army of 62,481 men 50,000 could not have been massed at some point in Tennessee to have opposed the advance of an army of 35,000 or 40,000?

The knowledge I had of the Army of the Ohio at that time has been pretty well shown in my examination here by my estimate of the strength of the divisions. In my statement as to the divisions which compose the army I did not include General Morgan's force. My acquaintance with the details of the service would enable me to account for a very considerable difference between the effective force of an army in the field and the returns. General Rosecrans told me the other day that he had more men absent from his army than he had present on duty—some 40,000 men on duty and some 50,000 men absent. The only reason that I could assign, from my knowledge of the facts and my impression of the strength of the army, why 50,000 men could not have been concentrated was that there was no such force there in the Army of the Ohio.

Question. What was the force concentrated at Nashville at the time General Buell fell back toward Bowling Green?

I do not know what force General Negley had, who was I think in Nashville at the time of General Buell's arrival there, nor do I know what other forces had come into Nashville; some I think came in from Columbia. I cannot say to what extent the strength of the army was increased. My estimate of the force with which we marched to Nashville was about 30,000 men; but the strength that we acquired in Nashville I did not learn; I passed directly through Nashville.

Question. You state that General Negley crossed the mountains from Chattanooga to Altamont and Winchester. You are probably aware that General Negley commanded only a brigade and marched in a season when water was plenty. Is it your opinion that Bragg could have marched his army by that route in September?

I stated I think that I understood General Negley passed over that road. I have no knowledge of the fact. I ought to have so stated; whether I did or not I cannot say. I have no knowledge of the road, and only infer it is a practicable road for an army from the fact—assuming it to be a fact—that an army had actually passed over the road. It would make a great difference in going over a mountainous country whether water was scarce or abundant. I did not know the strength of General Negley's command, whether it was a brigade or a division. I supposed that General Bragg could have marched his army over that road, as a brigade had passed over it, because I crossed the mountains in the latter part of August with two divisions, when there was no water on the mountains, literally none for animals. I also had an additional reason for inferring that that was a practicable road from the fact that I knew General Buell had ordered General McCook up the Sequatchie Valley to that road, and my impression was that his object in sending General McCook there was that he might watch that road and hinder Bragg if possible from taking it.

Question. Do you recollect, general, what estimate General McCook placed upon the rebel force after the Army of the Ohio left Nashville and whether he did not fix the number at 25,000 or 30,000?

I do not remember, sir, hearing General McCook make any estimate.

Question. Did you not hear General McCook say in Bowling Green that there were but 25,000 or 30,000 ragged rascals there and that we ought to go and whip them?

I cannot remember hearing General McCook make such an assertion.

Question. Was not the Army of the Ohio exceedingly demoralized after it left Nashville, and was not that in a great measure in consequence of a general feeling of disappointment at not having been permitted to meet the enemy?

I think the *morale* of the army was very much improved after reaching Nashville—in truth, after reaching Murfreesborough. I think the army generally expected that they were going to battle on their march into Kentucky; therefore, of course, they were not demoralized, because they were going to fight.

Question. Were not the straggling and desertion almost without a parallel in the Army of the Ohio in that march from Nashville to Louisville?

There was considerable straggling and desertion; I suppose desertion is the proper term, though the men who left merely absented themselves without leave and as a general thing came back. There were a number of Kentucky regiments who passed near to their homes on that march, and I ascribe most of these desertions to that cause. I think the desertions were more than paralleled at Louisville after the junction of the two armies.

Question. Did not the Army of the Ohio lose from 8,000 to 10,000 men from desertion alone in that march and at Louisville?

I cannot say what the loss of the Army of the Ohio was from that cause.

Question. Is not that loss taken into account in the statement General Rosecrans made to you?

General Rosecrans gave me no particulars at all. I presume that every loss was included, from every cause, in his statement.

Question. What measures were ordered by the commander of the Army of the Ohio to put a stop to the men straggling or deserting from their regiments prior to the battle of Perryville and what did you do in your division to arrest desertion?

We had frequent orders. I cannot remember precisely what the orders were, but straggling or desertions of that kind seemed to provoke the general commanding more than anything else. Orders were again and again issued and rear guards were established and commanders were held responsible for their men. There was no particular measure that I adopted, that I remember now, except that I kept a rear guard to bring up stragglers and notified my subordinate officers that I would hold them accountable for their men—that they must keep them in their ranks. I am not positive, but I think we had to each regiment a rear guard to keep the men in their ranks. Many of the commanders adopted the rule to make the colonel commanding ride in the rear of his regiment to see that the men did not straggle. I am not sure that the general commanding did not issue an order to that effect, though I will not be positive about it.

Question. You say the army concentrated at Louisville could not have resisted Bragg with the Army of the Ohio for its support and on the heels of Bragg; was there ever any danger that Bragg would attack Louisville?

I think there was the greatest danger that Bragg would attack Louisville. All the information that I received on the march from Bowling Green to Louisville certainly indicated that the people at Louisville and the officers anticipated an attack upon the city by Bragg. General Nelson I know felt the greatest apprehension, and I have no doubt at all that General Bragg could have reached Louisville and have taken it before General Buell got there. The information which I also received was that Kirby Smith had united his forces with Bragg's at Bardstown, which made it of course still more practicable for Bragg to have taken Louisville.

Question. What time did you learn that Kirby Smith had not joined General Bragg at Bardstown?

I cannot remember when I first learned that Kirby Smith had not joined General Bragg at Bardstown.

Question. What was the strength of the Army of the Ohio when it moved from Louisville on Bardstown?

I do not know certainly the strength of the Army of the Ohio at that time. My own command I suppose was about 25,000 men; that was diminished considerably by desertion, but I do not know to what extent. I suppose the other corps of the army, and there were two of them, were about as strong as mine. I knew nothing about them, however.

Question. What reason did General Buell give you at Bardstown that Bragg must make a stand at Perryville?

I am not sure that General Buell gave me any answer at all. I am rather inclined to the opinion that I was present at a conversation between General Buell and General Thomas, in which General Buell suggested that Bragg must make a stand there and that Perryville was a point at which he *might* make a stand; and my impression is that he also suggested in that conversation that it was possible for Kirby Smith to unite his forces with Bragg at Perryville. My recollection of this conversation is somewhat vague. It was a hurried conversation. I was but a few moments in the room, and marched directly afterwards. I should never probably have remembered it but that a fight did actually take place at Perryville.

Question. Is it not your opinion that Bragg anticipated a junction at Perryville with Kirby Smith, and not finding him there was forced to check the Army of the Ohio until he could form such a junction?

I have no reason to suppose that Bragg expected a junction with Kirby Smith at Perryville any more than at any other point where they were likely to come together, and I really do not know why Bragg fought at Perryville, with Kirby Smith so near him, unless he thought it was the best way to check the pursuit of the Army of the Ohio by a violent attack and then retreat to Kirby Smith.

Question. Did General Buell when you left Springfield designate the place you were to encamp at that night?

It is my impression that he did, sir. I do not remember precisely whether General Buell gave me the order or whether I got it from General Thomas. I know I expected to encamp at Haysville, and was astonished when we turned from the road at Haysville and went to Salt River.

Question. Please look at the instructions of October 7, given to General Thomas, and tell the Commission whether those instructions were literally carried out; if not, please state the particulars in which they were not carried out.

Those instructions were not literally carried out. We were ordered by the instructions to march precisely at 3 o'clock on the morning of the 8th without fail. We did not march till 7 o'clock with the First Division, at 9 o'clock with the Second, and 11 o'clock with the Third Division, because, as I have stated I believe, the command was all night almost getting into camp, at least a portion of it, the rear division. This order was not received by me, and I knew nothing of its existence till very near the time named for marching, 3 o'clock in the morning. I believe these instructions in other respects were literally carried out, except that I do not think General Thomas reported in person on the morning of the 8th at General Buell's headquarters; of that I can't be positive, but my recollection is that he was with me or in my sight until late in the day or night.

Question. - These instructions were issued at 7 p. m. At what time ought they to have reached you ?

I cannot state, for I do not know where General Buell was when those instructions were written. I do not know the distance from his headquarters to our camp. I last saw General Buell on the road from Springfield to Perryville, at the fork in the road where we turn off to go to Louisville. At that point General Buell would perhaps be 8 or 10 miles from Haysville, which would make it 13 or 14 miles that the order would have to come, and if the order came from that point it would not probably take more than two or two and a half hours, and if from near Perryville not more than two hours.

Question. At what time in the morning of the 8th of October was your corps in line of battle near Perryville ?

My First Division I think was in line of battle between 10 and 11 o'clock, from 12 to 1 the Second Division got into line of battle, and somewhere between 3 and 4 o'clock I think the entire corps was in line of battle. I cannot be positive, but that is my best impression. Certainly between 9 and not later than 4 o'clock my divisions all got into line of battle.

Question. State, as near as you can recollect, at what hour General Gilbert's corps was in line of battle.

I cannot state when General Gilbert was in line of battle. I did not see his corps at all during the day.

Question. You will please inform the Commission the direction of your line of battle at that time with reference to General Gilbert and Perryville ?

My corps was in line of battle and at right angles with the road by which we marched, the road leading from Haysville to Perryville, with Perryville directly in front, perhaps 2½ to 3 miles distant. General Gilbert was on my left, and I understand General McCook was on the left of General Gilbert.

Question. By whose orders, general, was your line of battle formed, and did it make part of the general plan ?

I do not certainly remember whether I got my instructions from General Thomas on the field or from General Buell. I supposed of course it was a part of the general plan, though my instructions only required me to ascertain where General Gilbert's right was and to form my line so that my left should join Gilbert's right.

Question. Were not your forces suffering for want of water, then guarded by the enemy, and how long could you have stood in line of battle without making the attack for the purpose of relieving them ?

My own forces had an abundant supply of water the night before. They had been ordered to supply themselves and fill their canteens. I do not think my own forces suffered particularly for want of water that day. I do not know how long we could have staid there without water; not a great while certainly.

Question. At the time General Gilbert notified you by order of General Buell that a reconnaissance was about to be made that might bring on a general engagement, as General Thomas was present and in command, how do you account for this order being sent to you ?

Orders were frequently addressed either to General Thomas or to myself, frequently to both. I do not know why General Gilbert sent this to me. Possibly it was sent to me because an aide-de-camp of mine was there, and it might have come with an orderly of my own who accompanied this aide. However, I suppose General Gilbert would not have considered it material at all whether he directed the order to General Thomas or to me. General Thomas saw the order as soon as I read it.

Question. How do you account for General Gilbert's note dated 4 o'clock, when a severe action with McCook's corps was commenced and in progress, and Gilbert's the supporting corps, in which he stated that his "children were all quiet and by sunset he would have them all in bed, nicely tucked up, as we used to do at Corinth"?

General BUELL. Mr. President, I object to that question in its present form; it hardly does justice to General Gilbert. His corps was scarcely a supporting corps, unless it was specially so directed in an emergency. Like the other corps it had its proper position in line, but it was not in any proper sense a supporting corps.

The WITNESS. I accounted for it then as I account for it now, by supposing that General Gilbert did not know the serious battle that was going on any more than I did myself. I inferred from his note at the time that there was nothing more than a skirmish going on.

Question. Have you read General Gilbert's report of that battle and do you find the knowledge exhibited in that report in accordance with this note addressed to you?

I think I have read General Gilbert's report, but I do not remember it so as to be able to answer the question, nor am I positive that I have read his report; only I must have read it, because I always take a deep interest in such things and generally read all the reports.

Question. On what was your opinion predicated, as stated to General Thomas, that "at last we had the rebels, and that they could not possibly get away"?

It was predicated upon the idea that they were in Perryville and that our army was there too. I made that remark after I learned that our army was there and in line of battle, and I believed that we would destroy them if they undertook to fly and that we would whip them if they fought. I thought that we had got too near to them for them to run with any safety and that they must fight.

Question. You call the battle of Perryville a partial engagement; how many were killed and wounded there; do you recollect?

I do not remember that I called it a partial engagement. It might be called a partial engagement, as all the forces were not engaged. I do not remember the exact number killed and wounded. It was a very severe battle. My recollection is that General Rousseau in his report states that he lost from his own command some 1,800 killed and wounded. I will not be positive about that, but that is my recollection. I do not remember the entire number lost in killed and wounded.

Question. Were not 819 killed and between 3,000 and 4,000 wounded?

I cannot answer the question. My recollection is not certain as to that. I know it was a very severe battle and a bloody one, and I suppose it is about that number that were killed and wounded.

Question. You say that in a line of battle extending some 5 or 6 miles it is not strange that a partial engagement should take place without involving the whole army; is it not, however, remarkable that such an engagement, resulting in the death of over 900 men, in the wounding of more than 3,000, and the loss of very many valuable officers, occurring within 3½ miles of headquarters, connected by the signal corps, without the knowledge of the general commanding till it was all over?

General BUELL. I object to the question, Mr. President. The question does not state the facts. The facts are not such as the question assumes. I did have knowledge of the battle before it was all over, and if the evidence does not show it already it will show that I adopted measures with reference to it. How great the loss may have been up to that time I am not able to say and it is hardly possible to ascertain.

The JUDGE-ADVOCATE. I would simply remark that General Buell assumes, and this is not the first instance of the kind, that the question makes the evidence; in no case does it do so. It is for the witness in his answer to say whether it is so or not. I think the objection is not well taken.

The court was cleared; when, after discussion, it was decided that the question should be put.

On the opening of the court General Crittenden proceeded as follows:

Certainly, if these things were so, I should consider it very remarkable.

Question. You say you heard more furious cannonading than at Perryville before Corinth in an artillery duel; was such fighting without the knowledge of the general in command there?

I do not know whether the general commanding had knowledge of the fighting or not. At Corinth, however, I should infer that he did. We heard the cannonading there from one end of the line to the other. I do not know where the general's headquarters were, but I presume he could hear the cannonading, though I have no knowledge of the fact.

Question. Did you ever know of one corps being warmly engaged, severely punished, and eventually driven back, while another corps stood calmly by looking on and rendering no assistance?

General BUELL. Mr. President, I certainly must object to this manner of examination. It is not fair, sir. It is more fair to me than it is to others who are involved in this investigation. The question insinuates something which is not true. It is not true in any sense that there was a corps by General McCook's looking idly on while it was engaged. The reports show that the corps next to it was quite sharply engaged itself, and sustained a loss, if I remember rightly, of as many as 1,000 men. And the corps did render assistance; that assistance may not have come in as good time as might be desirable, but it did render assistance. The question misrepresents the whole matter. It is most unfair. There is no necessity for pursuing this investigation in this way. As far as the question applies to me I do not think it affects me at all, but it is not fair to others who are not here to defend themselves; it is not fair to the country; it does not represent the matter fairly and honestly.

The JUDGE-ADVOCATE. The question is based upon some evidence that I have great confidence in and believe.

The court was cleared; when, after discussion, it was decided that the objection should not be sustained.

I knew of this fight at Perryville, and I know my own corps was there and offered no assistance. They were calm enough, because they did not know that the other corps had been engaged in a battle and was severely punished and driven back. I certainly never knew any corps standing by, with a knowledge of such facts, looking on without rendering assistance.

Question. Do you know that there was an order issued by General Buell to attack the rebels on the morning of the 9th; if so, at what hour of the day and what day was that order issued?

I believe I have filed before the Commission the only orders I did receive that I had to attack the next morning. My recollection about them is that one was an order from General Thomas, dated from General Buell's headquarters, which I think was written on the night of the 8th, that I might have my command ready to attack at daylight the next morning, and a note from Colonel Fry on the morning of the 9th asking what delayed the attack. I had received no order to attack at that time. About the time of the receipt of that note we commenced to advance, and did go into Perryville. I cannot be positive as to the time that note was received. Whether the order to advance emanated from General Buell or from General Thomas I cannot remember now. General Thomas was present when the advance began. I do not know from whom I received the order to begin to advance.

Question. Did the enemy retreat from Perryville on the evening and night of the battle?

I have so understood since.

Question. What answer did you make to Colonel Fry's telegram or message to know why you had not commenced the attack?

I cannot remember; but I have no doubt, if I answered it at all, it was because I had received no order at that time. I took the note, however, as I did all orders and notes of that kind, immediately to General Thomas, and it is possible I may have left General Thomas to answer it, he being present on the field and my commanding officer.

Question. State the movements of your division [corps] and the parts of it day by day from the morning of the battle of Perryville till the next and the retrograde movement in pursuing Bragg, and by whose orders these various movements were made.

As I have before stated, I cannot remember positively where I encamped on the night of the 9th, whether at Crawford Spring or whether I moved farther out and went across to Harlan's with two of my divisions. One division encamped on or near the road from Perryville to Danville. I cannot state whether I got the orders from General Buell or from General Thomas to move from these camps. I cannot state precisely on what day I did move up to the Danville and Harrodsburg road, nor can I state with any certainty the day when I marched from Danville. My command moved from Danville to Stanford somewhere about the middle of October, from Stanford to Crab Orchard, and from there to Mount Vernon and Wild Cat, with the skirmishing that I have already mentioned. I think that we commenced the retrograde movement about the 22d or 23d from Wild Cat or about that time.

Question. How many miles per day were made in the pursuit of Bragg from Perryville?

We marched from Harlan's to Danville and the Harrodsburg road, which I suppose is not more than 6 or 7 miles. I marched from Danville to a little beyond Stanford, which is somewhere about 10 or 12 miles; I do not remember precisely. From Stanford we marched to beyond Crab Orchard, some 5 or 6 miles I think, and from there to Mount Vernon with a portion of the command, and a portion of it went beyond Mount Vernon. I cannot remember precisely whether we went from this point to Wild Cat in one day or not; I rather think we did, as the roads were more obstructed between Mount Vernon and Wild Cat by the felling of trees than at any other point; it was a more favorable country for the enemy to resist our advance. After leaving Danville we did not halt any day. These marches were made on consecutive days, and I think we moved as rapidly as we could have done.

Question. Please look at the map and state the points by and through which Bragg's army retreated from Perryville and out of Kentucky.

From Harrodsburg Bragg passed to Camp Dick Robinson, as I understood; marched through Lancaster, Crab Orchard, Mount Vernon, and London; after leaving London I do not remember what points he passed through. Bragg's entire force did not all go back by that road, so I understood; some of them I know got out by the road leading from Richmond to London.

Question. Your command led the advance in the pursuit of the rebel army toward London; please give your opinion whether the rebel army, as estimated by some officers from 55,000 to 65,000 men, was driven out of Kentucky, baffled and disappointed, or did it, in your judgment, march out at its ease, with all its transportation?

I think the army of the Confederates was driven from Kentucky, baffled and defeated in all its purposes, except perhaps that of carrying away some subsistence and some clothing.

Question. Are you personally acquainted with Brigadier-General Fry; if so, how far, in your estimation, would his statement of facts be affected by personal differences?

I am personally acquainted with General Fry, and consider him a man of the very strictest integrity and honor, a man of piety. I consider him a good man, and I do not believe that he would state anything that he did not believe was true.

Question. I wish to ask you, from your personal knowledge of General Fry, how far his temperament would affect and color his knowledge of truth or what he thought to be true?

I cannot say how far General Fry would be influenced by his prejudices. I think he is a man of very strong prejudices. I am quite sure, as I have stated before, that no prejudices would make him state what he did not believe, but as to how far the prejudices of any man would affect his opinions or his judgment is impossible for me to say. I can only say that I think he is a man of strong prejudices.

The following question is asked by the judge-advocate at the request of General Buell:

Question. With reference to the operations of an army and the conduct of a campaign, where there is always so much ignorance or at least so much lack of information with all officers who have not fully the confidence of the commander and where at any rate there may be so wide a diversity of opinion, do you or do you not believe that the prejudices of almost any man would warp his judgment against the commander toward whom these prejudices exist?

I think that to say a man is a man of prejudices is equivalent to saying that where his prejudices operate his judgment is warped already. I would say also that the case cited in question is a case in which I think the judgment of any one who was prejudiced would be more likely to warp his judgment than almost any other cause of which I can think.

By General TYLER:

Question. General, if the Army of the Ohio had been massed at Lebanon or Sparta would not Bragg by a movement on McMinnville or Nashville or into Kentucky have exposed his flank to an attack from the Army of the Ohio?

Undoubtedly an army attempting to move in the presence of another army as near as those two armies were might expose its flank to an attack, but it would altogether depend upon the nature of the country and the direction of the roads how great the danger of such an exposure would be.

Question. Suppose General Buell had massed his army at Sparta to meet Bragg there, and Bragg, advised of the fact, had turned toward McMinnville, as you supposed, would not General Buell with his army concentrated at Sparta have been in a better position to oppose Bragg's advance than he would have been had Bragg debouched at Sparta and General Buell's army been still near McMinnville?

I think not, sir. General Buell would have been nearer to his line of communications and to his supplies, nearer to Nashville I should think, and in a better and more feasible country to march over. I think, moreover, that at that time, with the Army of the Ohio at Sparta, it might have incurred another risk, for I thought there was a very considerable force at Knoxville, Tenn., and that that force might be coming into Tennessee at the same time that Bragg was moving up from Chattanooga. It was not known, at least I did not know, that Kirby Smith had gone into Kentucky. I did not know that he was not going down the Cumberland River from Knoxville to McMinnville to make his junction with Bragg there.

Question. Why, then, did it happen that Bragg, starting from Sparta at the same time General Buell started from McMinnville, should hold the advance clear to Munfordville?

I presume because General Buell had to divine the movements of Bragg, to watch his movements, and he could not tell to what point Bragg had actually moved or what direction he would take. This necessarily gave Bragg the start on the march.

Question. It is assumed in your direct testimony that the Army of the Ohio was scattered at the time Bragg crossed the Tennessee River at Chattanooga. What necessity existed for the army being scattered at that time and how far were they scattered?

I do not know precisely what the necessity was for the different portions of the army being in their various positions. I infer that it was necessary to keep the army somewhat scattered at that time in order to procure forage and subsistence; and this might not have been one of the reasons; there might have been other and better ones. I have stated already the points where I think the troops were located.

The Commission adjourned to meet March 5, 1863, at 10 o'clock a. m.

CINCINNATI, *Thursday, March* 5, 1863.

The Commission met pursuant to adjournment. All the members resent; also the judge-advocate and General Buell.

The examination of General CRITTENDEN continued.

By General TYLER:

Question. General, who was your immediate commander and to whom did you make your report? I have reference to the battle of Perryville and about that time.

I never made but one written report; that was addressed to General Buell. General Thomas was the second in command of that army and was with my command. All verbal reports I made to him. General Buell was the commander of the army and General Thomas the second in command. I received verbal orders from General Thomas alone to the best of my knowledge. I am not sure that my orders did not all come from General Thomas. I think there was an order from General Buell addressed both to General Thomas and to me. Whether I received it first or received it from General Thomas I cannot now testify.

Question. Did you stand in the same relation to General Thomas that a brigade commander stands to his division commander?

I consider myself in my relation to General Thomas as a subordinate officer. I was entirely under his command as much as I was under General Buell's, and I see no difference between the relation in which I stood to General Thomas and the relation a brigade commander stands to his own division commander.

By General DANA:

Question. With the rebel army under Bragg approaching Sparta from the direction of Pikeville and with the Army of the Ohio approaching Sparta from the direction of McMinnville would either of them expose his flank to the other?

I should think not. Perhaps when very near to Sparta, as the roads converge, the nature of the country and the roads, for aught I know, might expose the flank of either army.

Question. You stated that the rebel army in its march would necessarily have to approach McMinnville within the distance of a few miles before it could be decided whether it would approach McMinnville or approach Sparta from that point. Now, with the rebel army at this point, when it became decided that it would go to Sparta, and the Army of the Ohio at McMinnville in observation of the rebel army, would the flank of either army in approaching Sparta have been exposed to the other?

The rebel army having approached to within a few miles of McMinnville and the Army of the Ohio being in possession at McMinnville would expose its rear undoubtedly in an attempt to move on Sparta, because it would have to go back to Spencer in order to march to Sparta; but I cannot say that its flank would have been exposed at all. As I have said, when it approached very near to Sparta, where, if the country would admit of the passage of troops and the distance from the road by which our army would have necessarily had to go toward the enemy from the road by which the enemy would go, as the distance would be quite short, it might have exposed its flank there. But as I understand the road which approaches to McMinnville and the roads to Sparta, I do not see how the flank of Bragg's army would have been exposed except as I have stated.

Question. Is Spencer the nearest point to McMinnville and Sparta from which roads diverge to those two places, and what is the distance of Spencer from those two places?

I cannot say that it is the nearest point from which roads diverge to the two points. It is a point I had noticed frequently on the military maps we had, the only point, I believe, which I have noticed where roads were laid down. I have no other knowledge of the country than that. The distance, I suppose, would be from 14 to 20 miles, but it is a mere guess as to the relative distance from McMinnville and from Sparta. I presume there is no great difference in the distance, though I would not undertake to say positively.

Question. I understood you to say in your direct examination that there was some point within about 10 miles of McMinnville to which the rebel army might advance before it could be absolutely determined whether they were on the road to Sparta or on the road to McMinnville; what point is that?

I have no doubt I referred to Spencer. Spencer may not be more than 10 miles, though, as I have said, it might be 14 to 20.

Question. Is there no road that connects that road from Spencer to McMinnville with Sparta?

The only road I know connecting the McMinnville and Spencer road is the road that runs directly from Spencer a little east of north of Sparta. I know there is a direct road from McMinnville to Sparta.

Question. With the rebel army, then, arrived at Spencer and threatening an attack on the Army of the Ohio at McMinnville, was it practicable for it to move and take possession of Sparta before the Army of the Ohio could be advised of it?

That is my opinion.

Question. And in McMinnville was that movement threatened with a flank attack from the Army of the Ohio?

I think not, sir.

Question. The Army of the Ohio having discovered its movement in progress and attempting to make a rapid movement to Sparta would its right flank have been exposed to the rebel army or not?

When it approached near to Sparta, as I have already said, its right flank might have been exposed. If there were no natural obstacles through the country that would have made it impracticable for troops it would have exposed its flank, the other army being there in position.

Question. Now reverse the positions of the army. Suppose the Army of the Ohio to have taken position at Sparta, with a view to prevent Bragg from marching into Kentucky, having given up its line from McMinnville to Murfreesborough; suppose the rebel army to have elected an advance on Nashville and to have arrived at McMinnville; then the Army of the Ohio, in an effort to relieve Nashville, starts at the same time for that place with the rebel army from McMinnville—which, if either, would expose its flank to the other?

I do not know sufficient of the roads from Sparta by which the Army of the Ohio would have marched to relieve Nashville to say how much, or if at all, its flank would have been exposed or if it would have threatened the flank of the rebel army. I should think that with the rebel army, however, at McMinnville and the Army of the Ohio at Sparta the flank of neither army would be exposed. I should consider one army as considerably in rear of the other when marching for the same point, the army at McMinnville having the best roads and I should think the shortest distance to march.

Question. Had the Army of the Ohio taken its position at that time at Sparta with Bragg at McMinnville in how many days would it have been driven from there by want of supplies?

It would be impossible for me to state with what quantity of supplies the Army of the Ohio could have been placed at Sparta. I only know that supplies were very scarce, that we were required most of that time to live on half rations, and that the railroads were broken by which our supplies came. My impression is that the Army of the Ohio could not have been placed at Sparta with supplies that would have enabled them to remain there many days. It must necessarily have been a very short time they could have remained at Sparta with Bragg at McMinnville.

Question. With the Army of the Ohio at Sparta and its supplies exhausted was it possible for it to have reached its base of supplies at Nashville without fighting a battle with the rebel army?

I think not, sir. The rebel army at McMinnville, as I have stated, if I am correct in my judgment on the subject, had a better and shorter route to Nashville than the Army of the Ohio would have had in starting from Sparta; they would have had to fight on the way or at Nashville if General Bragg had so chosen. That is my belief.

Question. Then was it not at Bragg's option to make a flank attack on the Army of the Ohio during their retrograde movement?

I cannot state that it was at Bragg's option to make a flank attack. I can only say, as I stated before, that I considered him in the advance. He could have reached Nashville first, and it would depend entirely on the roads, with which I am not acquainted and the direction of the roads by which the two armies marched, whether he could have made a flank attack or not. I am not prepared to say. I think, being nearer to Nashville and having the best roads, we would have had to fight there or before if the nature of the country would have admitted of a flank attack.

Question. When both armies started north from the Cumberland River were they either of them exposed in their flanks to the other during that march?

I think not, sir.

Question. With the rebel army at Glasgow and the Army of the Ohio arriving by divisions at Bowling Green would it have been exposed in its flank from that point onward and just before reaching that point to an attack of the rebel army?

From Bowling Green onward perhaps to Munfordville, as well as I recollect the distance, the roads, and the country, with the rebel army at Glasgow and the Army of the Ohio moving on the road by which it marched, I think it was exposed to a flank attack from Glasgow. I thought of that when I answered that on the march neither army was exposed in its flank, but I did not refer to it, because when we moved from Bowling Green it was known that a considerable portion of Bragg's army had already left Glasgow about that time, which made me think that the flank of neither army was exposed.

Question. With the armies of about equal strength and enterprise, traveling over a considerable distance of country in the same direction on roads pretty nearly parallel and with cross-roads connecting those roads and a country practicable for infantry between the roads, at what distance do you consider it necessary those roads should be apart to make either army safe from a flank attack from the other?

It would depend entirely, in my judgment, upon the relative position of the two armies. If one was considerably in advance of the other it might cover its movements and have the time to march a very considerable distance. To attack an army in flank as it passed, with two armies marching with the heads of their columns nearly parallel, I should think that anything over a day's march (the distance of a day's march) would make either army secure in its flank.

Question. What is the distance from Carthage to Gallatin?

It seems to be about 28 miles in a direct line by the scale on the map; I do not know the distance by any roads; my impression was that it was considerably farther than that.

Question. Would the army which is in advance of the other on parallel roads—a day's march in advance of the other—always have it at its option to make a flank attack on the one which is in the rear?

I think not, sir, the distance separating not allowing such an attack.

Question. With two armies, with the conditions supposed, operating over a large extent of country and within a day's march of each other, may it not be very frequently necessary for both armies to expose their flanks to each other and use extra precautions to protect those flanks?

Undoubtedly. In such cases accidents will occur which will lose a march to one army and so gain one for another. This in such a case would expose the flank of the one and render extraordinary precautions necessary.

Question. On the day of the battle of Perryville whose fault was it that you did not know that McCook's corps was being beaten by the enemy?

I do not know, sir, that I ever ascribed it to the fault of any one. I have not a sufficient knowledge of the conduct of that battle, of its inception and progress, to know who should be blamed. I have sometimes found that I was blamed myself because I could not hear the guns and did not know that a fight was going on. It was an extraordinary affair. I had 20,000 men there, and no officer or man ever knew, or, if they did know, ever reported to General Thomas or myself, that a battle was going on. I should be altogether unwilling and I should consider myself unjust, with my knowledge of the facts, to undertake to lay the blame to any one.

Question. Is it your opinion that there was a criminal blame to be attached to somebody among the number of men who did know that the fight was going on because you were not called on for support with that large number of troops under your command?

I cannot say that there was blame to be attached to any one even on that account. I do not know at what hour the battle began. I do not know for what space of time it was fought. I do not know that I could have rendered more assistance than was actually rendered. I had one, perhaps two, brigades that participated in that fight late in the evening, but I believe, without any knowledge of the extent of the fight on the extreme left, they had but little to do with the fight. I remember that General Wood thought it necessary to make some report in reference to the conduct of a portion of his command which was on the extreme left of my line. I must say, however, that somebody was to blame, if there was time to notify General Thomas or myself of the very serious nature of the fight which was going on, that it was not done.

Question. Do you know that the commanding general of the army was equally unaware of the serious nature of the fight that was going on?

I remember that the commanding general of the army told me that he was never more astonished in his life than when he was informed of the character of the fight that had already taken place when he got his information. I cannot be positive about the time he stated to me that he had received this information. My best impression is that he told me it was after 4 o'clock. That conversation occurred between the commanding general and myself shortly after the battle, perhaps the next day.

Question. Do you know whose fault it was that General Buell did not know that General McCook was being beaten?

I do not, indeed, sir.

Question. Have you ever known that General Buell has cast censure upon anybody for this dereliction previously spoken of, or that he has made such criticisms upon the conduct of anybody as would imply that censure for that neglect?

I do not remember to have heard General Buell censure any one in this conversation to which I have just referred. I thought that by implication General Buell censured some one because he had not received earlier information of this fight. I did not know nor do I know now whether General Buell meant such an implication or not, whether he was cognizant of the fact that information had been started to him;

whether such information was ever started to him or not I do not know; and still I thought he did mean to censure somebody. It was a mere inference of mine from the fact that he told me he had not received this information until I suppose the most disastrous part of the battle was over.

Question. From the impression made upon your mind immediately after that conversation who, in your opinion, was censurable for that neglect?

I cannot say that in my opinion any one was censurable. I do not know the facts. Everything might have been done to give such information that a prudent man could do. I have no facts which would enable me to say that any one was censurable for neglect.

Question. Do you know of the existence in the army of the Ohio among colonels and general officers of such a feeling as would amount to a general belief as to who the person or persons are who were to be censured for the neglect?

I do not know, sir. As far as I know the opinions in the army have been as various almost as the officers on the subject. I scarcely know a man of any prominence in the army upon whom I have not heard censure cast for that fight. I know of no general opinion in the army attaching even the principal blame to any individual.

Question. How long after the battle did you become convinced that Bragg had retreated by way of Harrodsburg to Camp Dick Robinson?

I am somewhat in doubt as to the date when we moved from Perryville or when I knew that Bragg had moved to Camp Dick Robinson. I did not know it until one of my brigades had gone to Harrodsburg. After the battle, I think next day, my opinion was that Kirby Smith was in line of battle with his command near to Harrodsburg and on the Harrodsburg and Perryville road some mile or two outside of Harrodsburg.

Question. The question is intended to ascertain how long a time elapsed after the battle before you became convinced in your mind that Bragg's strategic operations had degenerated into a decided retreat by that particular route?

I saw the object of the question and stated my difficulty about the date as my reason for not being able to give a very satisfactory answer. The time when I first knew he was gone I can only fix by ascertaining the day on which I sent a brigade to Harrodsburg. It was then I first learned that the rebels had retreated from Harrodsburg in the direction of Camp Dick Robinson. I think it could not have occurred sooner than the 11th; it might have been the 12th. I am quite sure it was not later that my brigade went to Harrodsburg.

Question. Do you know why you did not know this before?

I do not know why I did not have the information earlier. I suppose it was because we had had a very severe battle. It was not considered at that time the victory that it has since been denominated. The general impression in my part of the command was that we had suffered a considerable disaster. The fact that Kirby Smith had reached Harrodsburg and the impression that Bragg had received re-enforcements was that we should have another battle. The general confusion, too, that ensues in any army after a battle made some delay necessary. I suppose that these were the reasons why we did not advance at once upon Harrodsburg and ascertain whether the rebels were flying or not; but this is my supposition only.

Question. Why did not the Army of the Ohio go right after General Bragg as soon as he left Perryville?

It was nearly night when Bragg left Perryville. I suppose night would have stopped us from any immediate pursuit, and suppose we did not follow up to Harrodsburg on the next day for the reasons that I have just stated. Kirby Smith was said to be in line of battle at Harrodsburg, and I suppose the commanding general thought it important to rest his army after the battle, and see what its condition really was before he advanced upon this army, which at that time was believed to have inflicted a disaster upon us and not to have been defeated. When it had been re-enforced by the army under General Kirby Smith he was only some 6 or 8 miles in front of us.

Question. Was it positively known on the 9th whether Bragg had gone to Harrodsburg or Danville or to any intermediate place between the two?

My best impression is that it was known; that was my information.

Question. With regard to the retreat of Bragg from Harrodsburg by way of Camp Dick Robinson and other places beyond there, is it to this day positively known what particular routes all the divisions of Bragg's army took?

I certainly do not know myself and I cannot say that it is positively known.

By General ORD:

Question. You were asked whether you are sufficiently acquainted with the details of the Army of the Ohio to know whether General Buell could not concentrate 50,000 men at some point to oppose the advance of General Bragg's army, and you stated in your answer that there was no such force there. Supposing such force had been there, does it or does it not necessarily follow that the best use of them would have been to concentrate them at some point in the mountains or elsewhere in front of or on such lines as General Bragg chose to pursue with his army?

I do not think it necessarily follows that if there had been such a force there it would have been the best use they could have been put to to place them or concentrate them in front of General Bragg. My opinion is that the best use to which the army could have been put at that time and under the circumstances was to cover and protect the line by which it received its supplies and to watch Bragg's army.

Question. Would or would not the movements for the concentration of such a force probably have been known beforehand and in time to have enabled the enemy to take another route?

I think so. The enemy always had information of our movements in that country.

Question. Is the nature of the country and the disposition of the people where General Buell and Bragg were operating at that time such that a movement might have been caused by feints or demonstrations or partly made before the concentration to meet it (where such concentration was desirable) could have been effected?

I think so.

Question. If General Buell could have concentrated 50,000 men in front of Bragg on the route he took to Tennessee or any route east of it, would or would he not have been compelled to draw in his detachments from guarding bridges, roads, depots, or strategic points.

Undoubtedly to have concentrated anything like such a force in front of General Bragg General Buell must have drawn in, in my opinion, not only all the troops he had on detached service in Tennessee, but he would have had to bring troops from Kentucky to make up 50,000 men. This is my opinion of the external position of the command.

Question. Were these troops guarding depots, bridges, roads, and important strategic points or not?

At the time that General Bragg crossed the Tennessee River to that time General Buell was guarding the road from Decatur to Nashville, the road from Decatur to Stevenson, the road from Stevenson to Nashville, some 300 miles of railroad. This shows that they were guarding bridges, roads, depots, that were of vital importance to the different portions of the army. General Buell was also, I suppose, guarding the road from Nashville to Louisville and from Cincinnati to Cumberland Gap, which would make some 300 or 400 miles more of roads that his entire army in Kentucky and Tennessee had to guard when keeping open their lines of communication, making in all some 600 or 700 miles.

Question. In case this detachment had been drawn in from these important points what do you think General Bragg would have done; gone and attacked the army of 50,000 men in its defensive position, or have sent cavalry and light troops to attack these depots, bridges, &c.?

I do not think General Bragg would have attacked 50,000 men. I think General Bragg might, if he had desired it, have got a fight out of 30,000 men at any time, and as he avoided that I am quite sure he would have avoided the 50,000. I think he unquestionably would have sent cavalry and light troops to break up these depots and railroads, seize these bridges, and that the effect of such a course would necessarily have been to force our army to retreat or to fight General Bragg where we could find him.

Question. Was the nature of the country such that you would probably have found him in a very strong and difficult position or not?

Certainly; he might have availed himself of strong positions almost anywhere in that country.

Question. Suppose either army to have received notice of the approach of the other, and to have occupied a defensive position, in such a country with which would the advantage be, the attacking party or the party on the defensive?

I hardly know whether I am competent to answer that question or not. There are supposed to be certain advantages always accompanying an attacking force, but I scarcely think there are many positions which would more than counterbalance any advantages growing out of the enthusiasm which an attack inspires in soldiers. It would depend upon the strength of the position and somewhat upon the strength of the two armies as to with which the advantage would be.

Question. Was there any similarity between the battle of Perryville and Murfreesborough in respect to the number and kinds of troops engaged on either side, in results, commanders of corps, manner of attack, or other important points? And, if so, please state the points of resemblance and in what the battles differed.

There were undoubtedly some points of resemblance in the two battles. Our troops in both battles approached the enemy to attack them; in both battles the enemy attacked our troops. There was also this other point of resemblance: that the enemy were successful in their attacks. At Perryville they drove back our left wing. At Stone River, or Murfreesborough (I think you call it), they drove back our right wing and our center. Very many of the same troops that composed both armies at Stone River composed the two armies that were at the battle of Perryville. As to the strength of the two armies, I cannot state the strength of the rebel army at Perryville nor the strength of either army at Stone River. At Stone River we fought with some 42,000 or 43,000 men. I believe at Perryville the troops engaged on our side were not so numerous, though we had a larger army there. We had different commanders. General Buell was in command at Perryville; General Rosecrans was in command at Stone River. I think there was another resemblance between the two battles: they were both very bloody and both very fruitless; no army was destroyed; nothing was accomplished at either place except to show the valor of our troops. There was also this similarity in the two battles: that we were suddenly and unexpectedly attacked. General McCook commanded the portions of the army which received the attack at both battles, at Perryville and at Stone River.

Question. Was the corps that received the attack in either instance routed; if so, in which?

I did not see any of the corps that received the attack at Perryville. I did not understand that they were routed. I saw a considerable portion of General McCook's corps at Stone River that received the attack. I did not consider them routed, although they were driven back with very considerable confusion and over a considerable distance. I remember that I was encouraged considerably at night on the 31st, after the battle, by the recollection which I had of the continual firing of our troops as they fell back. With some portions I suppose it might almost be called a rout, but most of them continued to fight as they retreated until the enemy were checked; at least so I inferred from the sounds of the musketry. They were covered from my view by the woods, and I had no other means of knowing in what condition they retreated except the one referred to—that they were fighting as they fell back.

Question. Have you seen the published report of that battle by General Rosecrans; if so, do you remember whether he states that that corps was routed?

General TYLER. I object to the question, Mr. President, simply on the ground that it relates entirely to the battle of Stone River, and has no connection with the campaign of General Buell in 1862. I have no objection except that it is encumbering our record with matters in no way submitted to the consideration of this Commission.

The court was cleared; when, after discussion, it was decided that the question should be put.

The WITNESS. I have seen and read the published report of General Rosecrans, but I did not remember nor do I now remember that the expression "rout" was used. General Rosecrans' report that that corps was routed would not alter my opinion. As I stated before, I do not consider a corps as routed that, when support is brought to it, can be stopped in retreat and reformed in a short space of time. They were in considerable confusion and had been very roughly handled by the enemy, but I do not consider that the corps was routed.

Question. What was the relative condition of the two armies after these two battles with regard to their fitness and ability to pursue the enemy?

At Perryville the enemy retreated immediately after the battle; at Stone River the question was whether we should retreat. The great question to be decided on the 31st (Stone River) was as to whether we could maintain our position or whether we would not have to fall back. The enemy remained for three days and attacked us frequently during that time at Murfreesborough. The condition of the army at Perryville was unquestionably far better for the pursuit of an enemy than was the condition of our army at Stone River.

Question. Upon the retreat of the enemy being known in these two instances after each battle were they first pursued when at Perryville or at Stone River by the whole of our army?

They have never been pursued at Stone River, to my knowledge, at all. They were pursued very shortly after the battle of Perryville, to a certain extent, the next day.

Question. In regard to the damage suffered by the whole army, at which of these two battles—at Perryville and Murfreesborough—do you consider that it was greatest in proportion to the injury inflicted upon the enemy?

It is a very difficult question for me to answer, because I lost a number of esteemed friends at the battle of Perryville and a considerable number of valuable officers were lost to the country. And perhaps an equal number of officers were lost at Perryville as at Stone River, but I do not happen to know them so well and could not appreciate them as I did my own friends. With reference to the damage done to our whole army in proportion to the damage inflicted upon the rebels at the two battles I cannot answer certainly, for I do not know the loss of the enemy at either of the battles. If the enemy were as numerous at Stone River as General Rosecrans supposes, my impression would be that the rebels had suffered, in proportion to their numbers, more at Perryville than at Stone River; but I do not think the rebels had so large a force at Stone River, and I am inclined to the opinion that they suffered more damage, in proportion to the numbers engaged, at Stone River than they did at Perryville. It was a much longer fight, and they were repulsed in several very fierce and bloody attacks which they made on portions of our lines. I think the damage inflicted upon our army, in proportion to the numbers engaged, was greater than the damage inflicted upon our army at Perryville.

Question. Was or was not the movement of the Army of the Ohio, when concentrated, upon learning that General Bragg had gone up the Sequatchie Valley and afterward followed it, a retreat?

No, sir; as soon as we found we were concentrating, the general opinion undoubtedly was that it was for the purpose of fighting General Bragg's army at some point.

Question. What was the extent of the straggling and desertion by the absenting of the soldiers visiting their homes previous to the arrival of the army at Louisville in proportion to what occurred after the army arrived at Louisville?

The straggling and desertion at Louisville and after the arrival of the army at Louisville was very much greater than at any time previous.

Question. Under the military laws of our service and the habits of the people were such absentings to be expected or not in any army of volunteers on arriving near home?

In any army of volunteers such absenteeism I think cannot be prevented by our laws of discipline. They always have occurred in similar cases since I have had any experience in the army.

Question. Were they milder or less in the army at that time than they would have been in any other army under similar circumstances?

I always considered that army one of the best disciplined armies of the country. It might perhaps be my partiality for that army which formed the opinion that they were less in that army than they would have been in any other.

Question. You refer in one part of your examination to the discipline instilled by General Buell having shown itself in that army from the battle of Shiloh to that of Stone River; what had General Buell's discipline to do with the battle of Stone River?

In my judgment a great deal. No one had had a part in disciplining that army before General Buell. General Rosecrans took command of it on the march; he never had it together except at Nashville. His time there was occupied necessarily in preparing an advance upon Murfreesborough. The entire discipline of that army I ascribe to General Buell. Up to that time perhaps it is reasonable to say that the entire discipline of the army is to be ascribed to General Buell. He had command of it for a year. General Sherman had preceded General Buell I believe in the command of that army. General Anderson had preceded him. A portion of the army had been somewhat disciplined by these two commanders; but I think it is only just to ascribe the discipline of that army to General Buell.

Question. In what manner were the effects of that discipline shown at Stone River?

It was shown, certainly in my command, by the steadiness with which the men met and repulsed the enemy under extraordinary circumstances. When their flank was turned, the right and center of our army driven away from them, when a fight was actually going on in their rear, the steadiness with which the troops still fought and maintained their ground was the very highest evidence of extraordinary discipline. I think that even with the troops who were driven back in considerable confusion the fact that the officers were enabled to stop them on the field to get them ready for another fight was a high evidence of their good discipline.

Question. Do you think that discipline had anything to do with saving the army at that fight?

I am sure it had everything to do with it.

Question. With Louisville as our base of supplies and the railroad north of Nashville interrupted and effectually broken up, as you stated in your testimony, could or could not the Army of the Ohio have been safe long at McMinnville as regards supplies even though communication was open to Nashville?

I should have considered it very unsafe.

The Commission adjourned to meet March 6, 1863, at 10 o'clock a. m.

CINCINNATI, *Friday, March* 6, 1863.

The Commission met pursuant to adjournment. All the members present; also the judge-advocate and General Buell.

Cross-examination of General CRITTENDEN continued.

General BUELL. Before the examination commences this morning, Mr. President, I want to call your attention to some inaccuracies in the map which I see has been prepared. They are calculated to mislead the Commission and witnesses that may refer to the map.

The first I see is a road represented directly from Chattanooga to Dunlap, and that is represented as the route pursued by the rebel army. There is no such road. The only road across the mountain at that point is called the Anderson road; it is a continuation of the Therman road, and that is the road on which the principal part of the rebel army marched.

The map does not represent correctly the roads across the mountain north of Dunlap. The road which is represented to pass from Pikeville ascends the mountain on the road 7 miles south of Pikeville; it forks on the top of the mountain, one fork going directly to McMinnville, another fork striking the road from McMinnville across the mountain by way of Spencer. That road also continues in the direction of Sparta, either passing through Spencer or leaving Spencer somewhat to the left in going toward Sparta.

The map does not represent correctly the routes pursued by the Army of the Ohio in its various movements. It does not represent the movement up the Sequatchie Valley at all, nor does it represent the march pursued by the divisions of General McCook and General Crittenden across the mountain from the Sequatchie Valley to Pelham.

It does not represent correctly the movements of troops from Altamont, Pelham, Decherd, and in that region toward Murfreesborough.

It does not represent the Glasgow and Bardstown turnpike, by which the rebel army when advancing into Central Kentucky moved a considerable portion of its wagon train.

It does not show the Lebanon and Danville turnpike, which is an important road in connection with the operations of the army in Kentucky.

It does not represent correctly the movements of the army at Perryville after the rebel army retired from that place.

It does not represent correctly the road from Harrodsburg to Camp Dick Robinson, which passes first to Bryantsville a mile north of Camp Dick Robinson.

It represents but one road from Camp Dick Robinson and Bryantsville to Lancaster, whereas there is one from each of these places.

It does not represent the movement of a portion of the Army of the Ohio from Danville to Lancaster and thence on to Crab Orchard.

It does not represent correctly the roads from Louisville to Salt River by which the army moved, though that perhaps is not very important; it is, however, as easy to be accurate as to be inaccurate in that matter. Those are the only material errors I observe now, though I have not examined the map very carefully.

By the PRESIDENT:

Question. After our troops took possession of Corinth how long was it before the Army of the Ohio moved in the direction of Chattanooga?

My impression is that it was from eight to ten days after the evacuation of Corinth until I moved up toward Baldwyn and from there marched on in the direction of Chattanooga; that I consider the commencement of our march toward Chattanooga, because two divisions that went up there went on from that point.

Question. What was the object of the movement on Chattanooga?

As I understood it the object was to free East Tennessee from the rebel troops.

Question. It embraced, I suppose, the capture of Chattanooga?

Yes, sir; of course.

Question. After the movement began, if General Buell had moved directly on Chattanooga what was there to prevent its capture?

I have this difficulty in answering the question: My own opinion is that General Buell advanced upon Chattanooga as rapidly as he could, and that the occupation of Chattanooga by the rebel army was the obstacle in addition to General Buell's want of supplies. The difficulty in getting supplies for the army in consequence of breaks made in the roads by the rebels delayed a portion of his command I know at several points on the march toward Chattanooga. If General Buell could have marched his entire army without any delay to Chattanooga, and if by a rapid march he could have reached there before any greater force of the enemy had been concentrated there, I should think he would have had no difficulty in taking Chattanooga, my impression being that at that time there was not a sufficient force of rebels there to resist General Buell's army.

Question. Why was Chattanooga considered a point of so much importance?

Chiefly, I suppose, because of the different railroads that center there and of the river that passes by it.

Question. With General Buell at Chattanooga and General Morgan at Cumberland Gap was not East Tennessee, including the railroad through it to Virginia, in General Buell's power?

I think so, sir.

Question. With Chattanooga in General Buell's possession, with his supplies collected from East Tennessee and all the region commanded by Chattanooga, could not the Army of the Ohio have been subsisted long enough at that point to have covered expeditions and detachments sent to destroy that railroad as far east as Jonesborough?

I know but little of the resources of the country commanded by Chattanooga, except in a limited portion along the Sequatchie Valley. My impression is that it is a barren country, and I suppose from the fact of the rebels having occupied Chattanooga for a considerable time that the country around was somewhat exhausted of its supplies. I suppose also that the force which General Buell would have driven from Chattanooga would have had it in their power to destroy any railroads that he could have used. But I do not believe that he could have subsisted his army upon the country around Chattanooga. General Buell must have reached Chattanooga with but a very limited quantity of supplies, and I think he must have relied for supplies upon the usual road, that is the Louisville and Nashville Railroad. A few days perhaps an army could have lived upon the country, but my impression is not longer than that. I do not think General Buell could have remained at Chattanooga un il an expedition could have been sent to Jonesborough. There would have had to be concert and understanding between the forces of General Buell and those at Cumberland Gap. He would have had to remain until the news of his occupation of that place was known at Cumberland Gap and to be apprised that an expedition had started to Knoxville, all of which would have occupied time, and I do not think it would have been practicable for him to have subsisted his army at Chattanooga until that could have been accomplished. General Bragg, we understood, derived his supplies while at Chattanooga from a depot at Atlanta, so far as he did not or could not supply himself from the country around Chattanooga.

Question. Was not the country or any portion of it along your line of march from Corinth to Chattanooga productive and capable of yielding supplies if energy had been used for that purpose?

From the time we got down into the valley perhaps until we reached Tuscumbia the country was a fertile one; the corn fields had been planted and the crops promised to be fine, but the corn was green and not fit for use for our animals. I do not think we passed through any country that would have subsisted such an army if the army had to rely upon the country for its supplies for any length of time. The cotton plantations do not raise much grain ordinarily, and our impression was that they had turned their cotton fields into corn fields, expecting to have great difficulty in getting subsistence for themselves. The old corn was not to be had in any great abundance anywhere on the march. It was a good enough country for meat. I suppose we could have gathered considerable quantities of beef.

Question. Was not the country at least capable of subsisting the army while on its march, without any reference to supplies ahead, supposing you had gleaned it thoroughly, making everything bend to the subsistence of your army?

It is possible that by moving slowly and gathering everything for a considerable distance along the route of the army it could have been subsisted through this valley in Alabama, which I have mentioned as a fertile valley, as far as Tuscumbia. My impression from what I saw of the country was that from there on its subsistence would have been meager if it had to be gathered in the country. The army might have gathered cattle enough, I am inclined to think; if they could have lived on meat alone it might have been done; but the army must necessarily have moved very slowly.

Question. What opposition did the enemy offer to your advance as far as Battle Creek going slowly as it did?

I encountered scarcely anything to be called opposition. I had a few men captured, perhaps a man or two killed, between Huntsville and Stevenson, which was done by small bodies of guerrillas. I saw no enemy.

Question. Was not East Tennessee at that time considered and represented as to a great extent loyal?

It certainly had been represented as loyal. My own experience in Tennessee prevented me from considering any portion of Tennessee as loyal. My impression was that the loyal men in East Tennessee had at that time generally left the State. This, however, is only my impression of what I saw of Tennesseeans generally. I have no doubt that in their hearts there are still great numbers of Tennesseeans all over the State who would prefer to be back in the Union, but they are overawed.

Question. Is there any question about the fertility and productiveness of East Tennessee, particularly the valleys?

I know nothing of East Tennessee; it is a portion of the State into which I have never been. I suppose my opinion on that subject is worth nothing.

Question. What is your general information on the subject?

My impression from general information is that it is a good country; not equal at all to the best portions of Tennessee, but a pretty good country.

Question. At what time and place on its march was it ascertained or did it come to be considered that the Army of the Ohio was not equal to the task of taking Chattanooga?

My own opinion is that the idea was never abandoned until Bragg crossed the Tennessee River. I supposed that we were endeavoring to repair the roads, to gather sufficient supplies, that we might go on to Chattanooga. This is my opinion, because we did not move back at once after the roads were broken, and because I understood that boats were being prepared to bridge the Tennessee at Bridgeport, and because I never received any orders that indicated anything else than a movement on Chattanooga. We were seeking information all the time from Chattanooga, and were directed by every possible means to obtain information as to the strength of the enemy there, their movements, and their resources.

Question. If General Buell believed his army unequal to that enterprise, what was his object in distributing it, as he did, over 400 or 500 miles of lines; mainly distributing it, however, with his right on Stevenson and his left at or about McMinnville?

I was never apprised of the object which General Buell had in view by this disposition of his forces. I infer that they were scattered somewhat with a view of having them supplied. Some were sent beyond the breaks. The roads were broken, and we were living on half rations for a great while. I suppose that the object with which he held on at Stevenson was with the hope that he could repair the roads and still take Chattanooga.

Question. Supposing Bragg's army at Chattanooga could have whipped the Army of the Ohio at any time it was so disposed, was not that a very unwise disposition of General Buell's forces, exposing them constantly to attack before they could have time to concentrate to repel it?

I do not see that by that disposition of General Buell's army it was in the power of Bragg to force General Buell into a fight before he could concentrate his army on the road or near his line of communication. Any disposition of his army that would have enabled Bragg to force him into a fight, supposing that Bragg could have whipped General Buell's army, would have been bad. But it seems to me in the case supposed, and as the troops were disposed, that those most advanced in General Buell's army might have retired, and that he could have concentrated his army as he actually did.

Question. If the Army of the Ohio had been fairly concentrated at any point convenient for action, and such as might have been selected by General Buell at his leisure, between Chattanooga and Nashville or between Chattanooga and the Cumberland River on the road to Kentucky, do you believe that Bragg could have whipped that army?

I do not, sir. I believe that that army could have whipped Bragg. I think that's a great army.

Question. If such was your belief, what necessity was there for General Buell's falling back on the defensive at any time?

I do not consider that General Buell did fall back on the defensive at any time, except in so far as he was defending his line of communication, already cut. I consider that General Buell was forced to protect that line of communication, because by that he derived all his supplies; and that he was moving back on his line of communication, ready at any time to fight Bragg if he came to that line; and that he could not go in pursuit of Bragg to force him into a fight, because of his want of supplies. That is my impression.

Question. With his line of communication reaching from Louisville to Nashville and from Nashville to Murfreesborough and from there to Stevenson, his army being distributed on a line from Stevenson to McMinnville, was not that line of communication constantly and continually exposed to precisely the kind of attack that Morgan, Kirby Smith, and Bragg afterward made upon him?

It is a very long line, and I think was always very much exposed, necessarily so. With that disposition of troops from Stevenson to McMinnville I do not think the line was exposed to an attack from Bragg; that is to say, it would be very difficult for General Bragg to get at the line without encountering General Buell. It was certainly exposed to Morgan before that disposition of the troops was made. The troops I believe were on the march, before they reached Stevenson, when Morgan had cut the road. I am not sure about the dates. At all events the upper part of the line was exposed to Kirby Smith and to light troops or cavalry that moved rapidly.

Question. Except such cover as was afforded by General Morgan at Cumberland Gap, was it not known to every intelligent man in the Army of the Ohio, and of course to General Buell, that Kentucky was left almost naked of troops?

I do not know myself what number of troops were in Kentucky, but supposed very few. I cannot say what the opinion of the intelligent officers in the army was with reference to that; but intelligent officers in the army generally acquaint themselves with the locality of any considerable bodies of troops, and I dare say many of them were better posted in regard to the forces in Kentucky than I was myself. I supposed there were but few there, though I did not know. I was very anxious about Kentucky, and feared that she was going to have a very hard time when I heard that Kirby Smith was there; but that was not until I reached Murfreesborough.

Question. If General Buell believed that the Army of the Ohio could not take Chattanooga, distributed as it was, did it not become a mere army of observation?

I cannot say that. General Buell might have undertaken some other enterprise that he considered feasible if he thought he could not take Chattanooga. If the army had remained in that position and undertaken no other enterprise, I should have considered it posted just to watch the movements of Bragg.

Question. Supposing it to have degenerated into an army of observation, to prevent, if possible, the foray into Kentucky or a march of the enemy against Nashville, where, in your judgment, was its true point of observation?

If General Buell had been simply undertaking to cover Kentucky and Nashville, I should think that a portion of his army, disposed as it was, would be somewhat out of place. I was not sufficiently acquainted with all the roads to say where perhaps would have been the true point of observation, but perhaps from McMinnville or from Sparta even to McMinnville and Murfreesborough. This is from a general recollection of the roads on the map. I suppose in those positions he would be enabled to throw himself between Bragg and either one of the points at his option. This is supposing Bragg to be at Chattanooga.

Question. Can you state with any certainty, general, how far Bragg's army had progressed *en route* for Kentucky before General Buell commenced his concentration of troops at Murfreesborough for the purpose of retiring to Nashville?

I cannot tell for a certainty. My impression is when I received orders to march to Pelham and on to Murfreesborough—which I now suppose was for the purpose of concentrating the army at Murfreesborough—General Bragg was either in the Sequatchie Valley or was coming down into the valley. I will not be positive about the date, but I think I got the order to move about the 24th or 25th of August.

Question. If the Army of the Ohio, instead of being posted from Stevenson to McMinnville, had been posted on the line between McMinnville and Sparta, with Collins Creek and Caney Fork for its front, would it not have effectually covered Nashville and at the same time been in position, if it could have whipped Bragg's army, to have pursued and overtaken Bragg's army before it crossed the Cumberland River; that is, supposing that army could have got by its flank?

I suppose, with the army posted at that point, that Bragg passing anywhere near to the army he could have been forced to fight before he crossed the Cumberland River; but I could not say, unless some point were designated showing the distance between the armies when it did pass the flank, whether they would have had to fight on the south side of the Cumberland or whether he would have had time to cross it. It would have been in a position I think to cover Nashville, and in a position to whip Bragg's army, supposing Bragg's army to have come near enough to that position to enable General Buell to force him into a fight.

Question. If the purpose was simply to hold Bragg with his army in Chattanooga what is the objection to taking up a position with the Army of the Ohio concentrated close to the Tennessee River on the north bank in front of Chattanooga; and in that event and with that disposition would not the Tennessee have been a very serious obstacle to Bragg's front and a very great advantage to our army?

The objection would be the want of supplies and the difficulty of getting them into that position. I think the Tennessee River would have been a very considerable obstacle.

Question. You see no objection to it, then, except the difficulty of getting supplies to the army at such a point?

I can think of no other objection.

Question. At any time after 4 o'clock on the day of the battle of Perryville what was there to have prevented you from cutting off the enemy's retreat while they were engaged driving McCook's corps and how long would such a movement on your part have required; that is, could you have accomplished it before night, supposing this driving of

McCook's corps of which you speak to have been between 2 and 4 o'clock?

My command was posted some 2½ or 3 miles on the side of Ferryville opposite to the side which was occupied by the enemy when they made that attack upon McCook. How far they were from the road by which they retreated to Harrodsburg after the fight I cannot say. If we had started simultaneously, my impression is I could have marched to the point where they probably came down into the road almost as soon as they overcame the natural obstacles. I would probably have encountered some resistance in Perryville. I have no doubt, in fact I know, they covered their flank by a considerable force in Perryville, and I suppose it would have been night by the time I could have reached the point near which they must have turned in the road, starting at 4 o'clock, and it would have been a pretty rapid movement then if resisted at all. I do not now remember at what time it was dark. I think I could have accomplished the distance in two hours.

Question. As I understand you, general, you make that answer upon the supposition that the enemy would have contested your advance into Perryville?

Yes, sir.

Question. But suppose that advance had not been contested; suppose a brigade from General Gilbert's corps had already marched through Perryville and reached a point in the enemy's rear on the other side of the town?

In that case I could have moved more rapidly, and supposing the distance would have been 5 miles, I could have done it in one and a half hours in an emergency.

Question. Would the movement of your corps that distance have been any way complicated?

Not at all, sir.

Question. What would have been your movement?

If I supposed I should have been resisted in Perryville I should have moved in line; but if I had known that there would have been no resistance and no enemy in Perryville, that they had retreated, I would have moved in column along the road; or if I could have moved more rapidly the different divisions through the woods where they were posted and through the fields I should have done so. I do not remember precisely the natural obstacles I might possibly have had to avoid; there were some perhaps on the extreme right; but I rather think I could have moved the three divisions in column right straight through the town of Perryville.

Question. If a council of officers composed of such men as Thomas, Wood, Negley, with all the facts that could be brought before them at the time, had determined that it was better to make a stand at Sparta or McMinnville against Bragg coming from Chattanooga, would you have concurred in that proposition?

I should be very loath to have taken a position antagonistic to officers of such attainments with my little experience and want of military knowledge; yet still I think it would depend entirely on my conviction and the strength of my conviction what course I would take if I were responsible for the movement. I think if the country had made me responsible that I should have relied upon my own convictions where they were firm and decided.

By General SCHOEPF:

Question. Was not Rockcastle River, Kentucky, a very serious obstacle in the pursuit of Bragg's army?

I cannot say that it was a serious obstacle; we soon crossed the river. We encountered very little resistance, and that was from a force of cavalry along there. The resistance was more by the felling of trees obstructing the road. It might have been made a very serious obstacle.

Question. Will you please give your opinion in regard to the means of crossing the river; also a description of the river itself, and the number of troops and the amount of transportation you had with you and the time it took you to cross?

The river is a narrow stream, running through a very mountainous, broken country, sometimes with very precipitous hills for its banks. It is a stream full of very deep pools, but at that season of the year there was little water in running over shoals. I cannot state what transportation I had; I do not remember. I am not sure what portion of my command crossed Rockcastle River. One division, I think, did not cross the river. I rather think two divisions did. As to means of crossing the river, I required none; I do not suppose there were 4 inches of water on the ford. We had no difficulty in crossing, and no more time was occupied in crossing, or very little more, than at any other portion of the march. It was up hill and down merely. The time we lost was not produced by any difficulty we encountered at the ford. I do not now remember certainly whether we were stopped at all by the rebel cavalry there. They planted their guns and resisted us a little at every advantageous place, but my recollection is that just at that ford we were not delayed, though I cannot be positive about that.

Question. Did not Major-General McCook, in failing to make the reconnaissance ordered by General Buell and reporting the same to headquarters, as he was directed to do, on the 8th of October, really bring on the disaster of that day and keep the general in command in ignorance of it until too late to remedy the disaster—supposing the fact is before you?

Even supposing the fact that he failed to make the reconnaissance which he was ordered to make, I cannot say what effect that neglect or failure of General McCook had upon the events of the day. I cannot say, therefore, that such failure brought on the disaster. I do not know precisely the object of the reconnaissance and I cannot say that General McCook kept the general in command in ignorance; but if he did keep the general in ignorance of so important a fact as the repulse of that day until it was too late for the general to remedy the disaster then undoubtedly he was greatly to blame in my judgment.

Question. As General Gilbert with two divisions was in close proximity to General McCook's army corps, was it not his duty to be in front instead of in the rear with the reserve division, and had he been so is it possible that he would have been ignorant of the battle?

My idea of the proper position for the general commanding an army corps is that it should be at some central point most accessible to all his command and that it should be in the rear. As to whether he should have been with the two front divisions or with the reserve division I cannot say. If the reserve division was near enough really to support his two divisions in front and occupied a central position, I should say that that was his proper position. I was not on the ground occupied by General Gilbert or any portion of his command, and I cannot say whether he would possibly have been ignorant of the battle had he been with his two front divisions. I was not very far from General Gilbert, I presume not over 2 miles, and I certainly was ignorant of it; but I do not know that the 2 miles which separated me from General Gilbert would have enabled me or him if up to the front to have heard the battle.

Question. Do you know that Captain Gilbert, quartermaster or assistant quartermaster, disguised himself in a major-general's uniform and reported himself as such to General Buell?

I do not, sir; nor do I believe that such is the fact.

Question. Have you not seen him wearing two stars on a major-general's uniform?

Frequently.

Question. Is he a major-general now?

I understand he is not.

Question. Do you think an officer educated at West Point would have known that no one but the President had the right to appoint a major-general?

Yes, sir; I suppose no officer educated at West Point is ignorant of the appointing power in this Government.

By General TYLER :

Question. You were a corps commander at the battles of Perryville and Stone River, were you not?

No, sir; I was a corps commander at the battle of Perryville, and at Stone River I commanded what was known as the left wing.

Question. What number of men did your command consist of respectively in these two battles?

At Perryville I suppose my command was somewhere near 23,000 men, and I believe, though my memory is bad about such things, that I commanded at the battle of Stone River somewhere about 13,000 men on the field.

Question. Did you, as corps or wing commander, receive in advance, from the commanders-in-chief respectively, plans of the battles of Perryville and Stone River, and was the part your command was to take in these battles pointed out to you by special instructions?

My testimony has shown that I had little to do with the battle of Perryville. The only instructions I received in advance of the battle are contained in an order which I believe has been submitted by General Buell to the Commission during my examination. I received no other instructions or orders in advance of the battle at Perryville. At Stone River I received no instructions except to advance upon Murfreesborough by the Murfreesborough and Nashville road. At one time the general supposed that the enemy were evacuating Murfreesborough, and I received a dispatch by the signal corps to occupy Murfreesborough with one division on the night of the 29th.

Question. Excuse me, general, you are getting away from the object of this question. The question is whether you received any specific orders as to what your corps was to perform in the battles of Perryville and Stone River?

I never did.

Question. In answer to a question yesterday you ran a parallel between the movements of the two armies of Perryville and Stone River respectively, and contrasted the conduct of the troops engaged in those battles. Please continue the parallel, and inform the Commission what you saw and heard as to the conduct of the two commanders of those armies on the battle field in directing the movements and leading the troops.

The JUDGE-ADVOCATE. I must object to the question, Mr. President. The subject was introduced yesterday, but it is going entirely out of the proper course of our investigation, and if it is allowed it is impossible to say where it will end. What has a parallel between those two battles to do with the operations of the army in the campaign of Tennessee and Kentucky? We might as well attempt to run a parallel between the battle of Bunker Hill and Bull Run defeat. It may be my ignorance, but I cannot see the pertinency of the question to the investigation we have on hand.

General BUELL. I request that the witness may be permitted to answer the question.

General TYLER. I foresaw the difficulty in introducing the course of testimony by General Ord and voted against it.

General DANA. I call the general to order. He has no right to expose the votes of this court.

General TYLER. The general is correct.

The court was cleared; when, after discussion, it was decided that the question should be put.

The WITNESS. I will state that in running the parallel between the two battles yesterday I was answering the questions which were propounded to me by the Commission. As to the conduct of General Buell at the battle of Perryville I can say nothing. During the day on which that battle was fought I do not think I saw General Buell. I remained with my command all day and I do not think he was there. At Stone River I saw General Rosecrans very frequently during the battle. I do not think that I contrasted the conduct of the troops in the two battles. As to my opinion about the two commanders it is a very decided one.

General TYLER: It is not a matter of opinion, general; it is as to what you saw and heard of the conduct of the two commanders on the battle-field.

As I said, I did not see General Buell at Perryville, nor do I now remember to have heard of him on the battle-field at any place except at headquarters. Since the battle undoubtedly I have heard General Buell's conduct criticised. I have heard it spoken of as a most extraordinary thing that he permitted a portion of his army to be engaged and repulsed by the enemy when he had a large force there that was not engaged at all. I have heard many other officers say that General Buell was not to blame at all for the matter. I stated that I saw General Rosecrans frequently on the battle-field at Stone River. I saw him galloping about the field in many directions. I have heard him censured by a great many officers for his impetuosity, for his great excitement during the battle. I have heard him censured by commanders because they said they could not turn their backs on their commands without his ordering portions of them away

General DANA. Would there be a manifest propriety or impropriety in the commanding general of an army of 40,000 men habitually exposing himself to a dangerous fire?

I do not think a commander who habitually exposes himself to a dangerous fire is qualified to command any large army.

By General DANA:

Question. In proportion as the size of this army and the importance of this command increases, say up to 65,000 or 70,000 men, would the disqualification be more or less apparent if he habitually exposed himself to danger?

In my judgment more dangerous. It would be a decided disqualification.

Question. Would there be propriety in the commanding general of an army, with less than half of his troops engaged, and with his reserves entirely fresh and out of action, to head an assault or to appear in the midst of a murderous fire?

There would be great impropriety in such conduct in my judgment.

Question. As a general rule is the sudden death or the sudden disabling of the commanding general of a large army among the worst disasters that can befall it?

As a general rule, yes.

Question. Do you or do you not consider it of doubtful propriety for the commanding general of a large army to lead a charge under any circumstances, except when his last reserves are being brought into action, his situation becoming desperate, and an absolute necessity exists for the moral courage of his troops to be restored by the impetuosity of daring and the encouragement which is inspired by the immediate presence of the commanding general?

I think that a commanding general of a large army ought never to expose himself by leading a charge so long as there is any place left for his judgment and coolness and discretion, and that he ought to remain out of the confusion of battle, where he could control and direct the movements of his entire army, and that only in the last resort, when everything depended upon the valor of his troops, only then could he be justified or excused by putting himself at the head of his men and leading a charge.

Question. Do you know of any other instance in the life of Napoleon than the desperate charges at Arcola and Lodi and the last desperate effort at Waterloo where he led charges, and did you ever hear of his conduct being impeached on the field of battle?

I remember no other charges led by Napoleon, and I think there are few military men bold enough to criticise the conduct of Napoleon as a commander.

Question. Do you remember whether General Scott, in throwing himself with 10,000 men in the heart of the enemy's country in the valley of Mexico, with an organized army in front of him of 30,000 men, a hostile country all around him, his line of communication gone entirely, ever headed a charge?

I do not remember any such instance and I think there was no such instance.

Question. Do you remember whether at the most desperate battle that General Zachary Taylor fought, at Buena Vista, where with 5,000 Union troops he successfully resisted after three days' fighting 25,000 Mexicans, in any of the assaults there he ever headed a charge?

I know that he never headed a charge at all at that battle.

Question. Did you ever know of General Grant heading a charge since he has been in the Army?

I never did, sir.

Question. Did you ever hear of General McClellan, when he was in command of an army of 120,000 men, heading a charge?

I never did, sir.

Question. Or did you ever hear that General Burnside at Fredericksburg headed the assault of his troops, or did he remain on his own side of the river?

The information I have had in reference to that is that he remained on his own side of the river.

Question. Did you ever hear of General Butler, in all his campaign in Louisiana, heading a charge?

I never did.

General DANA here offered the following resolution:

"Resolved, That in consideration of the unusual length at which the members of the Commission have examined the present witness an opportunity be now offered General Buell to question him again, making this case an exception to our rule."

Carried.

General SCHOEPF, in explanation of his vote in the negative, desired the following stand upon the record:

"The reason I vote no is because I think the resolution unnecessary, as whenever General Buell has desired to ask questions the members of the Commission have shown themselves willing to adopt them."

The Commission adjourned to meet March 7, 1863, at 10 o'clock a. m.

CINCINNATI, *Saturday, March 7, 1863.*

The Commission met pursuant to adjournment. All the members resent; also the judge-advocate and General Buell.

Examination of General CRITTENDEN concluded.

By General BUELL:

Question. State, if you please, when the enemy commenced his formidable cavalry operations in Kentucky against the line of communication of the army in Kentucky and Tennessee.

The JUDGE-ADVOCATE. I shall have to object to that question, Mr. President. I understand that the resolution passed last evening turned General Crittenden over to General Buell for examination simply upon such new matter as the Commission in its examination may have brought out. This certainly is not that new matter.

General DANA. It certainly is a great stretch of imagination on the part of the judge-advocate in supposing that any resolution was necessary to be introduced for the purpose of confining General Buell to an examination on the new matter introduced by the Commission. The resolution is to turn the witness over to General Buell in consideration of the witness having been put through such an extraordinary examination by the Commission.

General BUELL. I should like to know how the judge-advocate knows that the question I have asked has not reference to the matter introduced in the examination of yesterday. I do not know how he can be sure of it.

The JUDGE-ADVOCATE. I only judge, Mr. President, from the question itself. This matter of cutting the lines of communication had been gone into in the examination-in-chief, was cross-examined upon by myself and afterward by the Commission. It certainly forms no part of the new matter introduced by the Commission yesterday or the day before. If General Dana's explanation of the resolution is correct, then the witness has to be turned over to General Buell as if he had not been examined at all. The resolution itself does not express what was the intention.

The court was cleared; when, after the passage of a resolution introduced by the president, it was decided that the question should be put.

The JUDGE-ADVOCATE. I would ask General Buell to state to what matter this question has reference, because it evidently does not refer to the new matter introduced by the Commission.

General BUELL. The question refers to questions which were asked yesterday with reference to the force that was left in Kentucky to guard against inroads into the State and operations against communications of the Army in Tennessee. The object of the question is to explain that matter.

The JUDGE-ADVOCATE. I withdraw my objection.

The WITNESS. I cannot state precisely the date. I think the first formidable array of the enemy against our lines of communications in Kentucky was after we left Corinth and while we were on the Tennessee River, but I cannot remember the date. My impression is that it must have occurred in July. It might have been as early as the latter part of June.

By General BUELL:

Question. What force do you suppose would have been necessary in Kentucky to prevent such incursions?

I really would find great difficulty in stating what force would be necessary to prevent such incursions. I think it would have required a very large force. I would say that from 20,000 to 25,000 might possibly have guarded the State against such incursions.

Question. Would it have been possible, do you suppose, to spare a force for that purpose from the forces under my command and at the same time maintain the advanced positions which we occupied in Tennessee?

I think not, sir.

Question. Do you recognize any difference between the nature and objects of all military operations in this rebellion and the nature and objects of military operations against a foreign foe under ordinary circumstances?

The JUDGE-ADVOCATE. I object to that question, Mr. President, on the same ground that I objected to the other. It is not based upon any new matter introduced by the Commission.

General BUELL. The new matter which this question has reference to is the plan put forward in a portion of the examination of yesterday of a temporary advance into East Tennessee for the purpose of destroying the railroads, which it was supposed might be accomplished in a short time and with the supplies the army had last summer.

The court was cleared, and after discussion it was decided that the objection should be sustained.

General BUELL. The only object I had in the re-examination of General Crittenden was to throw light upon certain theories for a campaign which were started in the examination of yesterday. The question which has just been objected to and the objection to which has been sustained has reference to one of these theories, so that I suppose the same action would be had upon any further questions I would ask of General Crittenden, at all events the more material of them, and therefore I have no more questions to put.

The PRESIDENT. I think, general, you misapprehended the effect of this vote. If you have any questions with reference to new theories which were certainly introduced there would be no objection. The question of yours, general, as it stands upon the record, does not seem to come within the rule.

General BUELL. This question had reference to such theories, one in particular. I would rather not commence the examination at all than be restricted to any specific form of questions. In fact, sir, I am not particularly anxious to examine the witness at all. I do not see anything in the examination of yesterday that I think very important, and therefore, and for the reason already stated, I forego the re-examination of the witness.

General DANA. I have quite a number of questions to ask.

The question being raised whether it would be in accordance with the rule established, the court was cleared; and, on the question being put whether the witness should be recalled for further examination by the Commission, it was decided in the negative.

General DANA. I wish to state that there were certain questions put to this witness——

General TYLER. I moved that the court be cleared.

General DANA. I object to it.

On the order of the president the court was cleared.

On the opening of the court, by permission of the Commission, General Crittenden made the following explanation:

It was, I think, in answer to a question of yours, general (president), as to whether if I had received an order at 4 o'clock, how long it would have taken me to march to the enemy, or where I expected to encounter the enemy, on the road to Harrodsburg. Upon reflection, sir, I think I answered too hastily. The distance being about 5 miles, I could not have issued orders to my command and have moved that distance in the time stated. I do not remember precisely how the question was put, but I supposed myself at the time to be in motion with my command at 4 o'clock, and that in an emergency I could have accomplished it in the time stated. But to have issued the order at 4 o'clock, with a line 2 miles long and either to have marched in line or to have thrown that line into column and marched that distance, would have required much more time. It would have taken from half to three-quarters of an hour to have started. That is the correction I wish to make to the court.

Maj. C. S. COTTER (a witness for the defense), being duly sworn by the judge-advocate, testified as follows:

By General BUELL:

Question. State your name and position in the service of the United States.

C. S. Cotter; major of the First Regiment Ohio Artillery, and chief of artillery on Major-General McCook's staff.

Question. Were you on duty with the Army of the Ohio at the battle of Perryville?

I was.

Question. Were you taken prisoner by the enemy in that battle? If so, state where you were taken to afterward and when you were released?

I was taken prisoner on the 8th of October, on the Mackville road, about 50 yards on the left of the road, in rear of Russell's house. I was taken by Major-General Polk, and was taken to the rear as far as Harrodsburg. I was there released on parole on the 10th of October.

Question. Did you observe the movements of the enemy about Harrodsburg on the 10th of October?

I did, sir.

Question. What time did you return to the Army of the Ohio and did you report yourself at my headquarters?

I returned to the Army of the Ohio and was at your headquarters between 5 and 6 o'clock on the morning of the 11th of October.

Question. Did you visit my tent at that time for a particular object?

I did. Having observed the movements of the enemy, I thought it was necessary you should be prepared for them. I made for your headquarters the first thing I did on being released.

Question. Please state what report you made to me in regard to the movements of the enemy on that occasion.

I told you that on the morning of the 10th Kirby Smith had joined Generals Bragg, Buckner, Cheatham, and Hardee, and that he was moving with his whole force upon what I supposed was the Perryville road. General Smith was moving with his force of from 15,000 to 18,000, and while watching their movements I heard some little firing at the front, and couriers came back, riding very rapidly, and taking the direction to Camp Dick Robinson.

Question. Are you stating the report you made to me?

Yes, sir; and that I thought they were massing their troops on that road and that we should probably be attacked.

Question. What road do you refer to as the road on which the enemy was massing his troops?

The road running from Harrodsburg to Perryville.

Question. Did you state that the road on which they were moving was the Perryville road or one you supposed was the Perryville road?

The one I supposed to be the Perryville road.

Question. Was your report such as to leave any doubt upon that point or did you state distinctly that the enemy was moving and forming in our front?

I stated to you that they were forming on our front and that they had a heavy force of cavalry upon the Danville road and every indication that I could see or learn of was an indication of a movement to attack you.

Question. Had you at the time you made that report any doubt that that was the intention of the enemy or at least that he was forming in front of us to give battle?

I had no doubt in my own mind in regard to it. Of course I had no opportunity of knowing except from the information I could get or see or judge from, and I felt it my duty, although I had given my parole of honor, to inform you of the fact.

Question. Do you know what time the forces under Kirby Smith commenced passing through Harrodsburg to take their position?

On the morning of the 10th, about 7 or 8 o'clock; the advance guard of Kirby Smith came in about 6 o'clock.

Question. How long did they continue passing through the town or how long did you observe them?

They made a halt in the town for a few moments. General Kirby Smith rode up to General Bragg's headquarters. I saw him and watched the movements as close as I could, being under guard and having the liberty of the town at the time. They were passing from 8 to 12 o'clock.

Question. You say you were under guard when you obtained this information?

Yes, sir.

Cross-examination by the JUDGE-ADVOCATE:

Question. How did you come by the information you carried to General Buell?

I saw movement of troops and had conversation with some staff officers belonging to the different generals. I also had conversation with some Union men.

Question. Were the movements you saw in and about Harrodsburg?

They were.

Question. By what road did they come into Harrodsburg and by what route did they go out?

I could not tell you the name of the road by which they came into Harrodsburg. I do not recollect that point. They went out on the Perryville road. It must have been the Perryville road I came in on.

Question. Between what hours were they moving out on the Perryville road?

I judge from 8 to 12 o'clock in the morning; it might have been earlier and it might have been a little later; I did not notice the hour at the time.

Question. In what manner did they move out on that Perryville road—closed up, and was it a continuous column of men?

It was. It moved up with men in columns of fours, and with artillery. I paid more attention to the artillery, being in that branch of service, than to the infantry.

Question. Was that the morning of the 9th?

It was the morning of the 10th.

Question. What conversation had you with staff officers in reference to these movements that you reported to General Buell?

I had no conversation with them in regard to the movements.

Question. At what time were you paroled?

I was paroled at 9 o'clock. I refused to take the parole at first, because I thought I could be exchanged sooner by not taking the parole. I did take the parole on the evening of the 9th.

Question. How did it happen that you remained there till the afternoon of the 10th after being liberated?

They refused to let me go at first until they could send us out from their lines with an escort.

Question. Who do you mean by "we"?

The whole of the prisoners who were taken.

Question. There was no restraint placed upon your observation about that time, was there?

No, sir; they gave us the liberty of the town, but we had a guard following us all the time.

Question. Now state, if you please, what troops they were that were sent out on the Perryville road between 8 and 12 o'clock on the morning of the 10th.

The forces under Kirby Smith. I do not know the troops except by their battle-flags. There were troops moving in every direction. There were troops moving on the road leading from Camp Dick Robinson; also on the Perryville road. Cavalry was constantly going and couriers going and coming all the time. The troops of Kirby Smith did not go out by the road to Camp Dick Robinson (as laid down on the map), but on the road (as laid down on the map) leading from Harrodsburg to Perryville.

Question. Look at the map, if you please, and inform the Commission what road you mean by the Perryville and the road to Camp Dick Robinson?

(Referring to Perryville map.) It was upon this road from Harrodsburg to Perryville that I was taken in—the road from Camp Dick Robinson as laid down upon the map.

Question. Are you certain, major, that these troops you saw leaving Harrodsburg were moving down upon this road leading from Harrodsburg to Danville?

I am certain they did not come down on that road unless there were other roads across the country from which they could come on to this road, because they came up on the Perryville road.

Question. Where and how did you learn the fact that Hardee, Cheatham, and Kirby Smith united were moving down upon the Army of the Ohio?

When I was brought in from Harrodsburg on the morning of the 9th we then passed the troops retreating on the Perryville road to Harrodsburg. I was taken out upon the Danville pike on the cross-road; kept here till 3 in the morning; was then taken upon a cross-road, and passed the troops of Buckner, Hardee, and Polk retreating into Harrodsburg. That was on the morning of the 9th. They then took the road down to Camp Dick Robinson on that day. I could see them from the building in which I was placed and observed them going back. I saw their battle-flags and had explained to me which were Hardee's forces, which were Cheatham's, and which Buckner's. On the morning of the 10th Kirby Smith came in. I do not know what road it is that leads out of Harrodsburg; it was not the Camp Dick Robinson road or the Danville or the Perryville road on which Kirby Smith's forces came.

Question. If you saw Buckner's, Hardee's, and Cheatham's forces retreat down toward Camp Dick Robinson and Kirby Smith's forces march down toward Perryville how came you to report that there was a junction of those forces and that they were moving down to attack the Army of the Ohio?

This was upon the morning of the 9th that I saw these forces going down upon the road leading to Camp Dick Robinson. On the morning of the 10th Kirby Smith's forces came into Harrodsburg and the forces of Buckner and Cheatham came back upon the road leading from Camp Dick Robinson.

Question. What time on the morning of the 10th did you see these forces coming back from Camp Dick Robinson?

While Kirby Smith's forces were moving through Harrodsburg couriers came in riding very rapidly from Perryville and went out on the road leading from Harrodsburg to Camp Dick Robinson. I should judge it was between 10 and 11 o'clock that these forces commenced coming on the Camp Dick Robinson road. They came down the Perryville road and went up the Harrodsburg road.

Question. Did their forces form a part of the column you have described as marching out from Harrodsburg toward Perryville between the hours of 8 and 12?

I cannot state exactly whether they did form part or not. A part of them went out upon that road. I do not know exactly when Kirby Smith's whole force got to the end of it; they were moving when I left Harrodsburg, which was 3 o'clock in the afternoon.

Question. What force was it, then, you said moved out between 8 and 12 o'clock?

Kirby Smith's forces.

Question. What force, then, moved out between 12 and 3 o'clock?

I went to get some dinner at 12 o'clock at a hotel, and when I came out of it I saw the troops still moving on the Camp Dick Robinson road. How long it took Kirby Smith's force to get through there I do not know.

Question. In what direction were they moving on the Harrodsburg and Camp Dick Robinson road?

They were moving into Harrodsburg.

Question. Why cannot you then say, if you saw it, whether Buckner, Hardee, and Cheatham formed a junction with Kirby Smith?

I stated that I supposed they formed a junction; in fact I know that they formed a junction.

Question. By what road did you leave Harrodsburg to join the Army of the Ohio?

By the Danville road.

Question. At what point did you meet our forces?

We were taken out upon the Danville pike leading from Harrodsburg to Danville. We were then taken out upon the pike leading from Danville to Perryville for about 3, 4, or 5 miles perhaps. We were then taken upon a circuitous route; I do not know by what name the road is called; it was to the left of the Danville road going from Danville to Perryville. We met our pickets the other side of Perryville. We marched same 30 miles to get there.

Question. What time did you arrive at the point where you met our forces?

Probably about 3 or 4 o'clock on the morning of the 11th. I do not recollect the exact time.

Question. Where did you find General Buell's headquarters?

I went out upon the pike leading from Perryville to Harrodsburg and found General Buell's headquarters to the left of the pike.

Question. How far from Perryville?

I should judge it to be 2 or 2½ miles.

Question. Upon what day did you see General Buell?

On the morning of the 11th of October.

Question. Did you report to General Buell that you saw Buckner, Hardee, and Cheatham going down toward Camp Dick Robinson?

I do not recollect whether I did or not. It was but a short time after daylight that I got there, and I felt it necessary for him to know what information I had obtained, and do not know whether I told him I saw the forces retreating to Camp Dick Robinson or not on the morning of the 9th.

Question. Did you consider it right to violate your parole as you did in reporting to General Buell in regard to the movements of the enemy?

General BUELL. I object to the question, Mr. President. It is not necessary for any purpose of this investigation, and it is not the province of the judge-advocate to admonish this officer. I presume the Commission itself will not undertake to admonish him.

The JUDGE-ADVOCATE. The witness appears upon the stand precisely as any other witness would do and gives us a statement of facts. I have a right to inquire into his status as I would into that of any witness coming before this or any court. Now, I want to know whether this witness considers it right to violate his oath given under those circumstances; if he does, it may have a decided influence in the estimate of the facts he lays before us.

General BUELL. I desire to express my astonishment and my regret that this method should be adopted of instructing officers in regard to their duties. I do not think it is necessary nor do I think it is in good taste.

The court was cleared; when, after discussion, it was resolved that the objection should be sustained.

Question. State to the Commission whether you consider that you violated your parole in giving that information to General Buell.

No, sir; I did not.

Question. Did it turn out subsequently that the information you gave was correct?

I do not know, sir. I left the same day for the rear. I wished to remain, but was not allowed.

By General SCHOEPF:

Question. Were you with General McCook during the battle of the 8th. And, if so, please state where his position was from 12 till 4 in the afternoon of that day.

I was at the front when the battle commenced, and did not see Major-General McCook till 12 o'clock. I saw him several times on the field during the battle. At 4 o'clock he was with me at the point known as Russell's house. I did not see him afterward, as I was taken prisoner. I was in charge of the five batteries of artillery, that I was working to the best advantage that I could, according to my judgment, and consequently did not see the general only when he came by. I saw him several times riding by.

Question. What time in the afternoon did you first see General McCook?

I could not state positively what time; I should judge somewhere about 2 o'clock, when I rode up to him and told him I wanted some support for one battery, and he gave me the requisite order to move up the Thirty-eighth Indiana, Colonel Scribner's, to support Simonson's battery. I moved that regiment up and was engaged with my batteries and consequently did not see him. I saw him several times riding along the line of battle. I distinctly remember seeing him at 4 o'clock near Russell's house, where I placed two pieces of Hotchkiss' Minnesota battery. I showed him the rebel lines where they were planting a battery, and before we got away they fired upon us, and he immediately sent back to the end of the line. I was engaged upon the right entirely and did not go to the left at all. When I say the right of our line, I mean the center, to the right of McCook's corps.

Question. Was General McCook aware that the battle was in progress when you first met him?

He must have been aware of it, because they had been cannonading for some half or three-quarters of an hour before I saw him.

Question. You stated you met him on several occasions; did you see any of the members of his staff with him, particularly Captain Hoblitzell?

I could not be positive as to whether I saw Captain Hoblitzell with him or not. I saw one or two of his staff at the time referred to. I was very much occupied with my artillery, and did not particularly notice any one but the commanding officer, from whom I received instructions.

Question. Do you know at what time General McCook sent Captain Hoblitzell to General Buell with information about the battle?

I think it was a little before 4; I cannot say positively what time it was, whether before or after. I rode up to General McCook and said to him—he was at the front, at Russell's house—I said, "We must have more re-enforcements; they will drive in our right and I shall lose my batteries," and he immediately turned to one of his staff—I cannot recollect whether it was Captain Hoblitzell or not—and sent him to General Buell for re-enforcements. I think he sent some one to General Gilbert. He then rode down with me to Russell's house to show me the position of the rebel lines. They were then coming down four lines deep. It was at that time they fired upon us with their batteries.

By General ORD:

Question. Do you know whether General McCook had sent previous to this time for re-enforcements, to whom he sent, and about what time?

No, sir; I do not. We formed our line of battle upon the Chaplin Hills, and a section was moving from there as they attacked us. We were not expecting an attack. We had our line of battle formed there. I think they opened upon us about 2 or 3 o'clock. I was there when they fired the first shot. We were skirmishing then, as we had been all the morning, with the rear of the army.

Question. When do you consider that the battle was finally closed, and there was no further fight to front of fighting?

About 5 o'clock in the evening there was very heavy firing. We ceased firing at dark. When I was taken prisoner I was riding into the lines which I supposed was our army; it was after dark. I rode up to a point that half an hour before our forces were on, intending to put some artillery there to open out upon them by moonlight.

Question. Did the re-enforcements sent for come?

Just before dark—I do not recollect the exact time—there was one brigade of four regiments sent down to a point near Russell's house to the cross-road. I think the road runs from the Mackville road to the pike leading from Bardstown into Perryville. They came down upon that road. Probably we were there half an hour, and if we had had re-enforcements, probably at 4 o'clock—had they been there half an hour earlier we could have held our right.

Question. Do you know whether any other applications were made for re-enforcements than the one you have spoken of?

I do not, sir; because I was engaged entirely with the artillery on the right, and and did not know what the left was doing all the time.

Question. How far was the right driven back? Did the retreat begin before the re-enforcements came up?

From 400 to 500 yards.

Question. Was the retreat in good order or did it appear to be a panic?

The retreat was in good order. I fetched off all my artillery and did not lose a piece of the twenty-six I had.

The Commission adjourned to meet March 9, 1863, at 10 o'clock a. m.

CINCINNATI, *Monday, March* 9, 1863.

The Commission met pursuant to adjournment. All the members present; also the judge-advocate and General Buell.

General BUELL wishing to introduce a witness whose name was not included in the list furnished the judge-advocate by General Buell and who was therefore excluded by the resolution of General Tyler—

General ORD moved that the witness be considered as within the rule.

The PRESIDENT. I wish, general, you would state what you expect to prove by this witness.

General BUELL. I wish to show by this witness that the forces of Kirby Smith moved through Harrodsburg toward Perryville on the morning of the 10th. The evidence of this witness I expect will confirm the evidence given by Major Cotter on Saturday, and I may as well say that I shall have other witnesses to call upon the same matter until the Commission shall consider themselves satisfied on that point and that the rebel army occupied a position south of Perryville on the 10th, as is presumed, for the purpose of battle.

Mr. H. W. HIERONYMUS (a witness for the defense), being duly sworn by the judge-advocate, testified as follows:

By General BUELL:

Question. State your name and place of residence.

H. W. Hieronymus; Harrodsburg, Ky.

Question. Were you in Harrodsburg between the 8th and 12th of October last?

Yes, sir.

Question. State whether or not you witnessed the movements of the rebel troops about that place between those dates, and what you know of those movements from the 7th to the 12th inclusive.

On the 7th, in the afternoon, after dinner, all the forces that were at Harrodsburg went in the direction of Perryville. I made the inquiry where they were going, and they said they were going to re-enforce Bragg at Perryville. They returned that evening; they came in between 8 and 10 o'clock, and the next morning they all went in the direction of Perryville—that is, the 8th, the day of the battle. On the next morning some of them came into Harrodsburg, I suppose between 11 and 12 o'clock. I believe that was the first I saw, and I asked a young man I knew from Tennessee what was the matter, and he said, "I suppose we are retreating;" but what was the force that came into Harrodsburg I do not recollect. Bragg's army came up the Perryville and Harrodsburg turnpike road and they went on the Cave Run road in part; but there are three roads to Camp Dick Robinson from Harrodsburg; their names are the Danville, Bellus' Mill, and Cave Run roads; and then there is a ferry 8 miles from Harrodsburg called Baker's Ferry, but I never crossed it and do not know what facilities there are for crossing.

Question. Do you know whether the whole of Bragg's force passed through Harrodsburg the day after the battle?

No, sir; I do not.

Question. How far on the road to Camp Dick Robinson did these troops that you saw go?

I do not know. I do not know whether they encamped at the Big Spring or went farther. I cannot tell.

Question. On what road is the Big Spring and how far from Harrodsburg?

It is near the Lexington pike, where the Cave Run road leaves the Lexington road—just at the fork of the Lexington and Cave Run roads and some 150 to 300 yards from the forks of those roads.

Question. Is it on the left of the Lexington road or on the right and how far from the town?

On the left of the road. It is in the town limits, I think; it is three-quarters of a mile from the court-house.

Question. Where did the troops that started for Perryville on the evening of the 7th come from ?

From that spring; they were located around that spring.

Question. Do you know whether they belonged to Bragg's army proper or to Kirby Smith's ?

I do not know.

Question. How long had they been at the Big Spring ?

I do not know. They were moving all the time in and out, passing backward and forward.

Question. State now, if you please, what movements of the rebel army you witnessed on the 10th ?

Kirby Smith's army commenced coming into Harrodsburg and passing through it at 8 o'clock on the morning of the 10th; they passed on until 6.30 or 7 in the afternoon.

Question. Which road did they move on in passing through the town ?

A number moved on the Perryville road, but what number I do not know.

Question. Do you know of any of them going on any other road ?

No, sir.

Question. Did they all pass along the same street in going through the town ?

The soldiers did; the wagons did not.

Question. The soldiers, I understand you, passed on the Perryville road ?

Yes, sir; on the Perryville road—that is, the right-hand road; the wagons went on the left.

Question. On what road did these troops come into town and from what place, if you know ?

From the neighborhood of Lawrenceburg, on the Frankfort and Louisville pike, so I understood.

Question. Did the troops at the Big Spring remain there the day of the 10th ?

There were troops there, but how many I do not know.

Question. Do you know whether the troops you say stopped at the spring on the 9th moved from there on the 10th ? If so, where did they go to ?

I do not think they all left there on the 10th.

Question. Did they form part of the troops that passed through Harrodsburg toward Perryville on the 10th ?

That I am not exactly able to answer.

Question. Do you know when these troops that you say went through Harrodsburg toward Perryville on the 10th returned ?

Some of them were returning on the morning of the 11th, but how many passed through previous to that I cannot say.

Question. Where did the rebel army go after leaving Harrodsburg— the last you saw of it ?

From the best information I had it was to Camp Dick Robinson.

Question. When did the last of it leave Harrodsburg for Camp Dick Robinson ?

On Saturday morning, the 11th of October, the Federals came in, as I supposed, between 11 and 12; it may have been between 11 and 1 I saw them coming through.

Question. Did you on the 11th know positively that the rebel army had gone on the Camp Dick Robinson road?

I do not know that all went on that road, but a considerable number had gone that road, from the best information I could get.

Question. What kind of road is there from Dick's River to Camp Dick Robinson on what you call the Cave Run road?

It is a good road; that is, from Dick's River to Bryantsville and Camp Dick Robinson.

Question. Is it a graded road and perfectly practicable for wagons, or is it a difficult road?

It is a graded road and practicable for wagons, as I have been informed, and a good road, but I have not passed over it for some little time.

Question. Have you any idea of the quantity of water that is required for a large army?

No, sir; I have not.

Question. How is Harrodsburg and the vicinity supplied with water; are there many large springs or streams immediately about the town?

There is this one spring. That is a large spring and does not exhaust at all; all others do. That is the principal spring. At that time it was a dry season, and we had little water in the town except at this spring.

Cross-examination by the JUDGE-ADVOCATE:

Question. Which way did the troops go that came into Harrodsburg from toward Perryville on the 9th, when the young man told you they were retreating?

From the best information I could get they went on the Camp Dick Robinson or the Cave Run road.

Question. How far toward Perryville did Kirby Smith's army march on the 10th, when you saw them pass through Harrodsburg?

I do not know.

Question. When that army came back did it take the same road that Bragg's army had taken toward Camp Dick Robinson?

From the best information I could get it did.

Question. You say Kirby Smith's forces, coming from toward Lawrenceburg and passing through Harrodsburg down toward Perryville on the 10th, got through or ceased going through about half past six o'clock in the evening?

Yes, sir; that is correct.

Question. How long was Bragg's army going through Harrodsburg toward Camp Dick Robinson?

I do not know.

Question. They had got through, however, before Kirby Smith began moving down toward Perryville?

No, sir.

Question. Did the two forces pass each other at Harrodsburg?

There was Kirby Smith going down and some others coming up; they were mixed up. I cannot exactly explain how it was.

Question. When you say you saw the last of them leaving for Camp Dick Robinson what troops were they going through last?

It was a cavalry force that left last; what troops they were I do not know.

Question. How was Kirby Smith's force marching, rapidly or quietly, through Harrodsburg, when they moved off toward Perryville?

They were moving at what I should call medium pace; they were not in a particular hurry and not very slow. They were marching along all day.

Question. Where did you understand they were going to fight our forces?

After they had all passed through Harrodsburg I understood they were going to make a stand at Camp Dick Robinson.

Question. When did you first learn that they were going to make that stand at Camp Dick Robinson?

I do not know whether it was the 9th or 10th, but I think it must have been the 10th. There was a supposition that there might possibly be a battle at Harrodsburg or around there. The citizens were fearful of it.

Mr. TANCRED R. WILSON (a witness for the defense), being duly sworn by the judge-advocate, testified as follows:

By General BUELL:

Question. State your name and place of residence.

Tancred R. Wilson; Memphis, Tenn.

Question. Do you know Brigadier-General Schoepf, a member of this Commission?

Yes, sir; I know General Schoepf when I see him.

Question. Were you present at a conversation between General Schoepf and Colonel Mundy in Louisville in the month of October last?

The JUDGE-ADVOCATE. I object to that question. It has nothing whatever to do with the matters we are called upon to investigate, as far as I can see.

General BUELL. I should like to inquire of the Commission whether I am required to explain the object of the question I have put to the witness.

The PRESIDENT. As far as the rule referred to is concerned you are not. The objection of the judge-advocate, as I understand it, is that the question has nothing to do with the investigation. I should like to hear further from General Buell on that point. I do not think the nature of the conversation to which the general wishes the witness to testify has been sufficiently developed to enable us to judge whether it has anything to do with the investigation or not.

The JUDGE-ADVOCATE. It is impossible, Mr. President, to proceed with this investigation unless we confine our examination to evidence that properly comes within the line of investigation we have to pursue. The question in this instance is clearly outside the matter we are called upon to investigate, and the party asking the question should explain the object of the question before the case goes on.

The court was cleared; when, after discussion, it was decided that the objection should not be sustained.

Yes, sir; I was present at a conversation between General Schoepf and Colonel Mundy.

Question. Relate that conversation, as nearly as you can, and particularly state what remarks you heard General Schoepf make in reference to General Buell.

The JUDGE-ADVOCATE. I object to that question, Mr. President, on the same ground I did to the other.

The court was cleared; when, after discussion, it was decided that the objection should not be sustained.

I heard General Schoepf speak of the battle of Perryville. He said it was a very badly managed affair, and that he had sent several messages to General Buell asking him to allow him to re-enforce General McCook and General Rousseau. He spoke also of a difficulty between himself and General Buell in Tennessee, in which he defied General Buell, and I believe, if I remember aright, threatened him with personal violence. The whole tenor of his conversation at that time was in reference to General Buell, and in speaking of him he said he intended writing letters to Washington City to his friends there to let them know how matters were going on. He also stated that there were more brains in the Confederate Army than there were in the Federal Army. These are the only particulars of the conversation that I remember distinctly; these I do remember distinctly.

Question. What was the spirit manifested by the words and tone of this conversation of General Schoepf in reference to General Buell; was it friendly, or indifferent, or otherwise?

I thought he spoke very bitterly of General Buell. The whole tenor of his conversation was of that character.

Question. Do you remember whether he stated any other cause of difference between General Buell and himself?

No, sir; I do not think he did.

Question. Can you state about the date of this conversation?

It was either the first or second Sunday after the battle of Perryville.

Adjourned to meet March 10, at 11 o'clock a. m.

CINCINNATI, *March* 10, 1863.

(IN CLOSED SESSION.)

Commission met pursuant to adjournment. All the members present; also the judge-advocate.

General TYLER. Mr. President, before the record of yesterday's proceedings is approved I wish to submit, as follows:

That the act of the Commission yesterday in going into the trial of one of its members is so extraordinary that I feel myself obliged not only to object but to protest against this procedure, and I respectfully ask that this protest may be put upon your record to vindicate myself from any participation in such an uncalled-for course of investigation. It is immaterial to me whether the member whose conduct is attacked is willing or unwilling to have his conduct previous to the ordering of the Commission inquired into; but one thing is clear to my mind, that however willing he may be to meet personal accusations this is not the time nor is this the tribunal for such an investigation; and I enter my solemn protest against proceeding to investigate any matter not distinctly enumerated and ordered in the instructions of the Secretary of War dated November 4, 1862. And I now move, before the record of yesterday shall be approved, that the testimony of Tancred R. Wilson be struck from the record and that General Buell be notified of the fact, and that in future no witness shall be examined touching the conduct of any member of the Commission antecedent to the 27th day of November, the date on which this Commission convened.

General DANA. I would like to know if this resolution is in order before the minutes of yesterday's proceedings are read. I move that the usual order of business be proceeded with.

General TYLER. I move that we consider this resolution before the record of yesterday be read. The records of yesterday are not the records of the court till they are approved.

General DANA. I enter my objection to transacting this kind of business until the usual order of business is proceeded with. As to the difference between minutes and records, it is merely technical, to say the least. The record was as complete when we adjourned last night, as perfect as it can be made, with the exception of any clerical errors which may have been made by the clerk in taking the evidence of the witnesses. We have the right to correct the record in any clerical error, but there is no reason for departing from the regular order of business. The fact of interfering with the regular order of business cannot make the record any more complete than it is; neither would it be proper or right, nor can it be entertained, to expunge any portion of the record of this court for the purpose of its concealment from any one.

The PRESIDENT. The question is whether the resolution of General Tyler should be entertained in advance of reading the record.

The JUDGE-ADVOCATE. I do not see clearly the strength of the point urged by General Tyler in introducing his resolution before the minutes of yesterday's proceedings are read. After the reading of those minutes, before they are confirmed, any member may propose any correction or any alteration he may see fit to make, but until they are read we have no right to proceed with the consideration of any resolution. The proper way would be to read the minutes and the record, and before they are confirmed offer any protest or resolution that any member may see fit. As to our right to correct an error, on that I would like to be heard.

General DANA. I wish emphatically to deny the right of any one of this Commission to try any one of its members. I wish also to deny that any one of its members has been tried or that any attempt has been made to try him. I wish further to deny the right and the power of this Commission to alter its record or to expunge any portion of it. I wish also to state that in my belief no member of this Commission has been attacked in his character, nor has he been put upon his trial, nor has any attempt been made to introduce evidence militating against his character; and that the introduction of evidence before this court attempting to show that any member has expressed opinions prior to the organization of this court which he had an undoubted right to express, and which do not in any way militate against his character, is proper evidence to introduce. As to the evidence introduced yesterday, each member has his own opinion of it and as to its weight. I do not think it is important to go into that discussion; but the attempt to represent that a member of this court has been put upon his trial or his character impugned I consider a mistaken one.

The JUDGE-ADVOCATE. The question as to altering or obliterating or changing in any way any part of our record admits of no discussion. We clearly have the right. But the question that presents itself is, when any matter appears upon our record that is foreign to our inquiry, that has nothing whatever to do with our investigation, whether it got upon our record by error or by design and forms part of that record, have we the right to correct it? I hold that where any matter foreign to the issue, having no bearing whatever upon the points we are called to investigate, has been introduced upon the record, we have a right to wipe it off. This is a well-established rule. Now, so far as the fact is concerned, if the introduction of this witness yesterday, with the statements he made, in connection with the statements of like witnesses who may be brought forward—if that is not putting a member of this Commission on trial, if it is not thereby intended to impeach the impartiality of a member of this court, I should like to know what it is. It certainly has no other object that I can see. If it is not a trial, what is it worth? But I hold that no honorable man or officer would consent to sit upon the court were his mind so influenced that he could not judge impartially. And I have not the authority to send for witnesses to show that this man is a low gambler and cannot be believed under oath. I could not do it if the Commission so ordered. What is the effect of this? It places a member of this court under an imputation that an honorable and sensitive man would not submit to without the chance of a fair trial.

I would ask why was not this fact, occurring prior to the organization of the court and known to General Buell, presented to General Halleck or Secretary Stanton? Why was it preserved till we are nearly through with our labors and have collected a vast quantity of evidence, when it is too late to remedy the difficulty by a reorganization if it should prove to be true? It is improperly brought in here, it forms no part of our investigation and cannot make any part of our record, and the best thing we can do is to expunge it.

I came to this Commission this morning intending to object to the further introduction of testimony of this sort and to make my argument upon it in the presence of General Buell; then he might reply to it. In the shape it has now assumed, however, I am unwilling that my objections should go to General Buell. There are other reasons that might be urged against the introduction of testimony of this sort as not only improper but illegal.

General SCHOEPF. I vote against sustaining the resolution from a feeling of delicacy, as I do not wish to appear as shrinking from an investigation. I never saw this man Wilson that I know of nor do I believe that I ever saw him, as at the time he says he heard this conversation I was confined to my room by ill health.

General TYLER. It is an extraordinary proceeding on the part of General Buell to bring this gentleman in to back up the testimony of a witness who has not yet testified before the Commission, although Colonel Mundy has been here in attendance over a month. General Buell introduces this witness just before closing our proceedings, and by him undertakes to kill the Commission by an attack upon one of its members. I do think it is rather too late to bring up from Memphis this unknown gentleman to back up Colonel Mundy's testimony that is not yet before the court; and after getting from the witness the language said to have been used, General Buell then wanted, by another question, to get the *animus* of the language used by General Schoepf.

General SCHOEPF. In regard to the witness' statement that I expressed an intention to use violence against General Buell, it may be that he heard something of the affair in Tennessee, when on one occasion General Buell visited the camp, when General Fry rushed out of his tent, seized General Buell's bridle, and took out his pistol to shoot him, thinking he was a rebel, and the next day General Fry told General Buell that if he came in again in that way he would dismount him. He may have heard of that, and that perhaps may be the origin of Mr. Wilson's testimony.

General ORD. The judge-advocate has alluded to his desire to express his opposition to this testimony in the presence of General Buell, and one of the members of the Commission has expressed not only disapprobation but some reflections upon the propriety of the course pursued by the defense. As we are now discussing the evidence adduced by the defense as to the propriety of admitting that evidence, it seems to me we would be doing nothing but what was right if we were to ask General Buell to be present, that he might express his views and the reasons which influenced him to this course; that he might argue the case which has been argued at length by the judge-advocate in opposition to the defense. Would it not be right and proper to ask General Buell to be present, to have the judge-advocate's remarks read over to him, and ask him if he has any counter-arguments to make.

General SCHOEPF. There is time for the defense to make all the argument he desires.

General ORD. The defense is attacked; one of his witnesses is attempted to be thrown out. The Commission did not introduce this witness, but the defense, and the defense, I presume, considered this testimony proper or it would not have been introduced. Remarks have been made in opposition to the course pursued, and therefore I think the defense ought to be heard, and therefore move that General Buell be invited to have the proceedings of this morning read to him.

General SCHOEPF. The motion is to strike out the testimony of Mr. Wilson.

General ORD. As there has been a long argument made against the defense, I think it would be but justice to General Buell to ask him to be present, and I therefore repeat, I move that General Buell be invited to attend.

General DANA. I hope that General Buell will not be brought in to carry on a discussion of this sort. A great deal too much importance is attached and the minds of members of this court are influenced to feel that this is a more important matter than it really is. If it is necessary to advise General Buell of the proceedings of this morning for the purpose of having a reply from him, I think the best way would be to give him a copy of the proceedings and let him reply in writing— that is, if it is considered necessary. I do not see that it is necessary. If, however, such a course is deemed necessary I hope this method will be taken: that a copy of the proceedings will be given to him, that he make out a protest or argument in writing, and that the court adjourn for the purpose of considering it. I dislike to see an unimportant matter of this kind pressed in the way it is, and particularly have it rendered still more objectionable by asking General Buell to take part in the proceedings.

General Ord's motion, being put to vote, was lost.

General Dana's motion, being put to vote, was lost.

General SCHOEPF. The question is now on General Tyler's motion; and as I am personally interested in this matter, and am ready to answer before the Commission if it thinks itself competent to make an investigation, or to answer to any tribunal that may be ordered for the purpose, under the circumstances, and with perfect respect for the Commission, I request to be excused from voting upon that motion.

The PRESIDENT. Upon this question I shall vote against its being expunged from the record, and for the reason that if it is now expunged a correct and true history of our proceedings would show that such and such testimony was given and after having been given was stricken from our record, and I consider that it would have a worse effect to strike it from the record, leaving the world to form its own judgment and opinion and suspicion as to the nature of the testimony, its purport, and how far it went, than to have it remain upon the record.

The motion of General Tyler was then voted upon and lost.

General ORD. In voting as I have done in the matter that has just been before us, I take the view that as General Buell was not asked if he objected to any member of this Commission, the right of challenge not having been given him at the organization of the Commission and not at any time indeed, the only means he had of challenging a member of the Commission—a right given in all cases of trial by jury—was to challenge that member at some stage of the proceedings. I look upon the introduction of this evidence in the light of a challenge, and in referring to the authority upon the subject I find it stated that there is good ground for a court-martial to allow a challenge, though not supported by any proof, which does not exist in a like procedure in the courts of common law.

General TYLER. I do not know that it is necessary to have this upon the record. There is no business before the court.

General ORD. There is a motion to be offered.

The PRESIDENT. There being nothing before the court, those remarks are not, in my opinion, in order.

General ORD. I have been interrupted two or three times in this matter, but I must beg to be allowed to say that I consider it a matter of privilege, where a resolution has been offered by a member of the Commission, if a member ask to explain the reasons for his vote, and I therefore ask to be allowed to explain my reasons.

General TYLER. I object to it.

General Schoepf presented an application to be allowed to withdraw from the Commission, which was read.

General DANA. I suggest that, in that it charges a portion of the Commission with introducing evidence that impeaches his impartiality, it is hardly fairly drawn up. It certainly appears to me that no member of this Commission has attempted to introduce any testimony against any other member.

General ORD. I would suggest that General Schoepf make a change in the wording of his application. My vote was very much influenced by his own.

The PRESIDENT. I see two objections to this application of General Schoepf. The first is that it would necessarily have to be referred to the Secretary of War. General Schoepf is here by the order of General Halleck. It is therefore impossible for this Commission or for myself as president of this Commission to relieve General Schoepf from his present duty; that can only be done by General Halleck or the Secretary of War. The second objection is that it only proposes to suspend the proceedings of this Commission until the general can make his defense before the proper authorities; that would necessarily suspend the proceedings of this Commission for a considerable time, and thereby occasion delay, which I do not think would be advisable.

General SCHOEPF. I would ask, then, that my application to be relieved from this Commission be forwarded to General Halleck, while at the same time I deny most positively the truth of the testimony given by this man.

General DANA. As far as I am concerned, I would say that I voted in favor of introducing this testimony. At the same time I regret exceedingly that General Schoepf should take the view of it which he appears to take, and feel that a member, in voting, as in my opinion he is bound to do, according to his own best judgment, has entertained any other than the most cordial regard for him; and I furthermore wish to state that nothing has yet been introduced in testimony before this

Commission which makes it necessary for that member to withdraw or which places him on the defensive. He has been reported as engaging in a conversation which he had an undoubted right to engage in, and which does not incapacitate him as a member of this Commission.

General SCHOEPF. General Ord said that he voted for the admission of that evidence because I did so. Now, as I have said before, my vote was influenced by a feeling of delicacy in not wishing to appear to shrink from an investigation; but this affords no excuse for any other member of the Commission to vote as I did.

General ORD. General Dana's opinion is perfectly correct. An opinion previously formed or expressed does not disqualify a member from sitting on a court-martial or court of inquiry, though it might disqualify him as a juror. The law in reference to courts-martial specifies that we shall go into an inquiry of the ground where a party is challenged, but shall not admit or reject a member on account of slight reasons; and it was because members of military courts are frequently challenged and for such reasons that I looked upon this as a challenge offered on the part of the defense, an opportunity to challenge not having been offered earlier. I consider, too, that this is to some extent a trial of General Buell. The judge-advocate said he was sent here to examine into the offenses of General Buell, and adduced proofs which he thought would convict him of certain offenses; and the president said that he looked upon it as similar in its proceedings to a court of inquiry. It has about taken the form of a trial. Witnesses have been examined by the judge-advocate as for the prosecution; notice has been given that the prosecution was closed; witnesses have been called for the defense; and the rules by which we have been governed—when we have been governed by rules—were those of courts-martial. In all such tribunals the prisoner, the party before the tribunal, though he may not be on trial—it may only be an examination into the propriety of indicting him for offenses—has the right to challenge any member of the court in some form or other; and I presume this was the form taken by the defense in the present case, and I shall act in this case precisely as if I had been challenged. I have been on courts-martial where I have been challenged, and where the objection has been sustained I have left the court; but I did not think it was wrong or that it in any way affected my character as a gentleman. I may say that for some reasons I should have been very glad if I had been objected to in this case and had been allowed to retire. My vote in regard to this matter seems to have been entirely misunderstood. We have not refused an investigation to the member who states that his impartiality has been impeached; he has not asked for any.

The PRESIDENT. The general has misunderstood me. He has on previous occasions referred to my calling this investigation a court-martial or a court of inquiry, and I have as frequently called his attention to the fact that all through these proceedings I have held that it was not a court-martial nor a court of inquiry but of investigation—a board of officers appointed to investigate certain operations of the Army of the Ohio in the Kentucky and Tennessee campaigns.

General ORD. If there are no objections I suggest that we telegraph to General Halleck for instructions, and that we adjourn till the result of the dispatch be learned.

The JUDGE-ADVOCATE. In connection with the course pursued by General Schoepf, I will say that he advised with me in reference to his position before the Commission, and I told him what I firmly believe, that under the instructions given us by the Secretary of War General

Buell does not occupy the position of a defendant. There were no charges or specifications filed, and therefore he had no right to challenge any member of the court. If he had the right to challenge, and he was dissatisfied with any member of the court or all of them, he should have exercised the right then; this he failed to do, even supposing he had the right. The introduction of this testimony, therefore, was foreign to the issue, foreign to the subject-matter we are called upon to investigate, and I claim that General Buell had no power to introduce it for the purpose of challenging any member of this court; but having gone upon the record, the only power General Schoepf could appeal to to set him right was the President. What action the Commission will take upon his application to be relieved it is for the Commission to decide.

General ORD. I move that the application of General Schoepf to be permitted to withdraw be forwarded by the president of this Commission to General Halleck, and that in the mean time the Commission adjourn till an answer be received.

The motion was put and lost.

General TYLER. I move that General Schoepf's application asking permission to withdraw, together with such parts of the records of the Commission as the president and judge-advocate may see fit, for the past two days, be forwarded to General Halleck and instructions requested, and that this Commission adjourn from day to day until an answer be received.

General DANA. I offer the following in place of General Tyler's motion:

"That a full copy of the proceedings of the Commission, including General Schoepf's application, both in open and closed session, since the introduction of the last witness, be brought into court, and that after it has been read and approved it be turned over to the president to be forwarded to General Halleck, who ordered the Commission, in order that we may be instructed as to further proceedings in the case."

The motion was then put and lost.

General Tyler's motion was then put and carried.

The Commission then adjourned to meet at the call of the president.

CINCINNATI, *March* 20, 1863.

(IN CLOSED SESSION.)

The Commission met pursuant to a call of the president. Present, General Wallace, president; General Tyler, General Dana; also the judge-advocate.

The following communication from General Buell was received and read:

CINCINNATI, *March* 10, 1863.

To the Commission:

I desire the attendance of two witnesses not heretofore named, and in accordance with the rule established yesterday by the Commission I submit this statement of the object of their testimony:

The judge-advocate has attempted to show that my army was dissatisfied with its commander and had from that cause become demoralized. It is proper that I should trace the extent of that dissatisfaction and if possible explain its cause in each individual case.

Brigadier-General Schoepf was an officer under my command, and the witnesses for the prosecution have disclosed the fact that he was one of those who gave expression to his dissatisfaction, going to the extent of impugning my loyalty. I propose by the testimony of these witnesses and by other evidence that I shall introduce to trace the dissatisfaction in this instance to that discontent and personal animosity which are the inevitable consequence of command and are to be found in every army.

I shall show that in connection with these hostile manifestations this officer complained or asserted that I had not given him the command to which his rank entitled him, and had besides treated him with indignity; that while under my command he more than once avowed himself my enemy; that he more than once declared that I was a traitor, and expressed his determination to exert himself to effect my removal from the command of the army. I shall show that this inimical feeling evinced itself to a greater or less extent as early as a year ago this last winter, when he was in the habit of speaking disrespectfully of me in the presence of his subordinate officers and perhaps of soldiers.

The evidence in this light bears directly and materially on the question introduced by the judge-advocate as to the dissatisfaction and demoralization in my army; but it also has another bearing on which I should claim its admission, and that is as to the competency of this officer to sit in judgment on my official acts. In this connection I shall show also that his acquaintances have spoken to him on this point, and that he has excused himself by saying in effect that he had expressed his unwillingness to serve on the Commission, but could not avoid it. This is a fact which I deem it due to the War Department that it should be advised of.

It has already been claimed by the judge-advocate that the objection on account of prejudice should have been made before the Commission commenced its business. Undoubtedly that is true if I had known the prejudice to exist, but I hold the objection to be valid and admissible at any time when the fact becomes evident that the judgment of a member is so warped by prejudice that justice is not to be expected. That I think has been apparent in this case.

The facts with reference to Brigadier-General Schoepf are new to me. Had I been aware of them while in command I think I should have known what course my duty required me to pursue with reference to them. I do not propose, however, to insist that this officer shall vacate his seat or that the proceedings of the Commission shall be staid. I content myself with laying the facts before the Government.

The question as to the demoralization of my army is in my opinion an important one, and the investigation of it may be of the highest importance to the public good in explaining the influences which tend constantly to such a result in our armies.

D. C. BUELL,
Major-General.

The JUDGE-ADVOCATE. There is, I understand to be, a law authorizing courts-martial, military commissions, and bodies of this character to take the depositions of witnesses instead of calling them into the presence of the court, for the purpose of facilitating business, and not taking them away from the army, as has been done. I have not seen that law, but I gather from what Judge Holt told me in Washington that he has it in his power to order the deposition of a witness to be taken instead of forcing him to appear in court or before a commission.

All the testimony in the shape of rebutting evidence that I have to take I propose to take in that way, and I gather from what Judge Holt told me that the Commission, if it see fit, can call upon General Buell to do the same thing with his. The Commission will see the advantage arising from the adoption of such a course. By taking depositions or affidavits we can take the testimony of twenty or thirty witnesses while we would be examining perhaps one before the Commission, and instead of lengthening out this investigation we have it in our power to abbreviate our labors very much as far as time is concerned.

The PRESIDENT. I am not willing to act upon a law which I have not seen, although I am satisfied that so just a man as Judge Holt would never draught a law which proposed to do a willful and deliberate injury to a party accused by authorizing the taking of the deposition of a witness for rebutting purposes. Suppose the witness is in Kentucky or Nashville, how can General Buell go down there to examine a witness?

The JUDGE-ADVOCATE. Have the interrogatories sent to him.

The PRESIDENT. The deposition would of course have to be taken by some person legally authorized to take it; for instance, a judge-advocate there or some one appointed for that purpose.

The following communications from General Buell were read:

CINCINNATI, *March* 18, 1863.

To the Commission:

I desire that Mr. James Collier, of Nashville, Tenn., may be summoned before the Commission as a witness. I expect to prove by this witness that Brigadier-General Schoepf said in Louisville, soon after the battle of Perryville, that I was a traitor and had sold out my army; that he had begged me with tears to permit him to re-enforce Major-General McCook in the battle of the 8th, and that I had refused him, or words to that effect.

What I have already stated in a previous communication to the Commission in regard to the testimony of other witness whose presence I have requested will explain the object of the testimony of this witness also. It is first to throw light on the subject introduced by the judge-advocate of the alleged dissatisfaction in my army, and second to show the frame of mind which, so far as Brigadier-General Schoepf is concerned, was to shape this investigation and pronounce judgment on my official acts.

I desire also that J. M. Lawrence and David Hawkins, of Lexington, Ky., may be summoned to appear as witnesses. I expect by their testimony to multiply the evidence I have already introduced as to the strength of Kirby Smith's forces while they were in Central Kentucky. I desire also the attendance of Mr. Cosby, from the Fair Ground, Danville, Ky., by whom I expect to show that the retreat of the rebel army by way of Crab Orchard and Cumberland Gap was of sudden determination and contrary to the plans of its commander.

D. C. BUELL,
Major-General.

BURNET HOUSE, *March* 19, 1863.

Lieut. Col. DONN PIATT,
Judge-Advocate, &c. :

SIR: On the 10th instant, in accordance with a rule recently established by the Commission requiring a statement of the object of calling other witnesses whom I might desire, I gave in a communication to the Commission my reasons for calling two more witnesses. They are Brig. Gen. Speed S. Fry and Surgeon Strew. I request that they may be summoned. They are somewhere in Kentucky, and the general in command at Louisville will probably know where they are to be found.

You have the names of the following witnesses who have not yet appeared, besides those named to you yesterday; you will, of course, take steps to have them here whenever the Commission is ready to resume business: W. S. Downey, Lexington, Ky.; Richard S. Anderson (not Richard C. Anderson, who was summoned and is a different person), Lexington, Ky. ; —— Yates, Lexington, Ky.; W. G. Bruce, Lexington, Ky. Lieutenant-Colonel Darr is at Glendale, near this city. You are aware that Captain Bingham and other witnesses from Nashville have not appeared.

Out of regard for General Lytle's anxiety to return to the army I am disposed to take his evidence by affidavit.

Very respectfully, your obedient servant,

D. C. BUELL,
Major-General.

General TYLER. I move that the judge-advocate be directed not to call Mr. Collier, on the ground that we do not require more evidence as to the words said to have been spoken by General Schoepf.

The motion being put to vote, it was unanimously carried.

General DANA. I move that in reply to the communications of General Buell of the 18th and 19th instant the judge-advocate be directed to reply as follows:

That the Commission declines to call James Collier, for the reason that General Schoepf has been relieved from duty on this court; it also declines to call J. M. Lawrence and David Hawkins, for the reason that the Commission is satisfied by the evidence of witnesses already examined as to the strength of Kirby Smith's forces and does not intend to controvert it. The Commission also declines to call Mr. Cosby, for the reason that it will admit that he will testify to the fact as stated by General Buell and will consider it as sworn to by him. It also declines to call General Fry and Surgeon Strew, for the reason that the points on which their evidence is required are not stated.

Carried unanimously.

The judge-advocate introduced a deposition from General Lytle, which was read and received.*

The JUDGE-ADVOCATE. General Buell has propounded three questions to General Lytle, but I find nothing in the affidavit that requires a cross-examination.

Commission adjourned to meet March 21, at 10 o'clock a. m.

CINCINNATI, *March* 21, 1863.

(IN CLOSED SESSION.)

Commission met pursuant to adjournment. Present, General Wallace, president; General Dana, General Tyler; also the judge-advocate.

General TYLER. I object to receiving the deposition of General Lytle, read yesterday, on the ground that it has no place on our record. I move that the questions and answers be struck from our record, and that General Buell be notified that this Commission will not inquire into any matter outside of the investigation ordered by the Secretary of War.

The PRESIDENT. The Commission has the right to strike out matters that it considers out of place on its record, everything that is irrelevant to the business for which this Commission was organized.

The JUDGE-ADVOCATE. If when a deposition comes before the Commission I make an objection to any portion of it General Buell has a right to be heard. When a deposition is received by the Commission the court has the right to strike out any portion and retain just what it considers pertinent to the issue before the court. Nothing has been done with these questions that prevents that course being taken by the court.

General DANA. That testimony was received yesterday, and to strike it out now is not in the power of the court to do.

General Tyler's motion was submitted to vote and lost.

The judge-advocate then read the following communication from General Buell:

BURNET HOUSE, *March* 20, 1863.

To the Commission:

I did not have access to the Commission at its session to-day, but the judge-advocate informs me that it was determined not to call certain witnesses, because Brigadier-General Schoepf, to whose conduct they were expected to testify, had been relieved from the Commission, and that no testimony would be taken with reference to the conduct of that officer. In the communication which I submitted on the 10th instant I meant to explain the double bearing of such evidence; that is, it was to go first to the allegation of demoralization or dissatisfaction in my army, and second to the competency of Brigadier-General Schoepf to sit as an impartial judge of my acts. The removal of the latter question by relieving that officer from the Commission does not affect the former, which is one of the questions introduced by the judge-advocate.

I meant to be understood as not intending to notice the general statement of any witness that the army was dissatisfied with its commander, for that would virtually amount to putting the question to popular vote; I shall only answer specific statements of facts on that subject. To this end I propose to show that the demoralization was in the witnesses themselves who made the general assertion, and that it was in fact merely the dissatisfaction which results in every army from the exercise of command. Brigadier-General Schoepf was one of those who are shown to have expressed dissatisfaction. I desire to show that in this case personal irritation and disappointment were the real cause of dissatisfaction. I desire to show how that irritation manifested itself and how it must have affected the discipline of the portion of the army to which this officer belonged, and from which the evidence on this

* Not found.

subject has mainly been drawn. The judge-advocate informs me also that, contrary to my understanding, the rule of the court requiring a statement of what I propose to prove applies to witnesses that have been summoned as well as those whom I wish summoned, unless they are actually in attendance; and I am requested to give that explanation with reference to Messrs. Downey, Anderson, Yates, and Bruce. The evidence of the former will have reference to Brigadier-General Schoepf's expressions concerning me, and of the three latter to the strength of the rebel forces in Kentucky.

D. C. BUELL,
Major-General.

General DANA. I move to reconsider the vote of yesterday in reference to calling the witness mentioned by General Buell.

The motion, being put, was lost.

(IN OPEN SESSION.)

General Buell, having been notified that the Commission was ready to proceed with the taking of testimony, entered the court-room.

Lieut. Col. FRANCIS DARR (a witness for the defense), being duly sworn, testified as follows:

By General BUELL:

Question. Please to state your name and position in the United States service.

Francis Darr; lieutenant-colonel and commissary of subsistence of the United States Volunteers.

Question. State whether you were on duty with the Army of the Ohio during the past year; between what dates and in what capacity.

I was on duty in the Army of the Ohio, on General Buell's staff, as chief commissary in the field, from about the middle of January, 1862, until October 30, 1862, when General Buell was relieved. I was relieved at the same time.

Question. State, as circumstantially as you can, what measures were adopted for subsisting the army from the time it commenced its movement from the vicinity of Corinth to North Alabama until its arrival in North Alabama.

When the forces of General Buell commenced their movement from Corinth eastward I was stationed at Buell's Landing, on the Tennessee River, 2 miles above Pittsburg Landing, supplying his forces from that point. When the said movement was commenced I was ordered to move the supplies to Eastport, Miss., about 30 miles above Pittsburg Landing, from which point to a line of march from Corinth eastward to a place called Iuka it was only 8 miles, giving a first-rate road to supply General Buell's troops and saving about 20 miles of land transportation. As fast as the troops reached Iuka on their march eastward from Corinth they drew their supplies from Eastport sufficient to last them until they reached Tuscumbia, to which point from Eastport I was ordered to supply the forces by the river. For this purpose I secured the lightest draught boats, and had considerable difficulty in doing so, as the navigation between Eastport, Miss., and Tuscumbia, Ala., was dangerous and difficult on account of the low water on Colbert's Shoals, a few miles above Eastport.

It was at first considered impossible to so supply the troops on account of Colbert's Shoals. By General Buell's orders all the river pilots acquainted with those waters and living in the surrounding country were seized one night at midnight, and kept under close guard to run our steamers, because Union pilots then in the employ of the general were unwilling to undertake running boats to Tuscumbia. So difficult was the navigation that I went up on the first boat myself from Eastport to Tuscumbia. We stuck for half a day on the Shoals, and no boat went up the river without sticking there and having considerable trouble. Every boat had to be sent up by force, and threats were made against the captain and the crew. I mention this to show the difficulty of the navigation and the delay and the time consumed in supplying the troops. Boats drawing only 16 inches of water were only able to take about 30 or 40 tons to the trip. Besides commissary stores these boats were obliged to take forage and quartermaster's supplies, as the country through which the troops were marching was totally stripped of its resources by the enemy.

During my efforts to supply the troops at Tuscumbia we seriously damaged three of our steamers and were obliged for months to leave one of them above the Shoals. After the last of our troops had reached Tuscumbia and were provided with about ten days' rations of the essentials only—bread and meat, coffee and sugar—they were moved on without delay. I was then ordered to take all the available transportation of the army, fill the wagons with the essentials of subsistence—by that I mean bread and meat, coffee and sugar—to cross the river at Eastport with them, and proceed to Florence, on the north side of the Tennessee River, in Alabama. Taking about ten days' supplies of bread and meat, coffee and sugar, for the army, I left Eastport, Miss., crossing the Tennessee at that point on or about the 24th of June, 1862, and reached Florence, a distance of about 22 miles, the next day, where I found the columns in motion and crossing the river from Tuscumbia on its march to Huntsville, Northern Alabama.

My efforts to supply the troops from Eastport to Tuscumbia by river were unceasing, running the steamers day and night, and with all my efforts the column moved from Tuscumbia with altogether in the hands of regiments and in the supply trains about fifteen days' rations, and that only of the essentials of bread and meat, coffee and sugar. We expected, on our arrival at Athens, Ala., and Huntsville to find abundant supplies for our army, as orders had been issued to parties in Nashville to have supplies ready for us at least three or four weeks before we moved from Corinth. On arriving at Athens, Ala., to which place I rode ahead of the column, I discovered that no provisions whatever had been accumulated and that no forage either had been gathered. Upon inquiring the cause thereof, as it was a matter of great importance, I found that the railroad, sometimes called the Central Tennessee and Alabama Railroad, but generally called the Decatur and Nashville road, was so badly broken by the rebel raids and bridges burned that it was impossible to more than feed day by day the troops then under charge of General Mitchel, who was occupying Northern Alabama at Huntsville and the lines between that and Nashville. Inquiring as to the resources of the country from the inhabitants of the region through which we had passed and around Athens, I discovered that the country was entirely bare of resources along and near our lines of march, both of forage and subsistence, and that on account of the large bodies of guerrillas infesting the country it was dangerous to send out trains for foraging purposes without a larger guard than General Mitchel was able to afford. I came back to camp near Athens and reported the condition of supplies and asked for orders to remedy the evil. General Buell ordered me to make myself thoroughly acquainted as far as was in my power with the resources of the country and to make use of them wherever we could reach them. At the same time he told me to ascertain by what time the railroad would be completed from Nashville to Athens, in order to bring us supplies by rail. The break in the railroad was from Reynolds' Station to Elk River, the bridge over the latter stream being destroyed. The distance by railroad was only 24 miles, but on account of the impossibility of crossing by fording or ferrying Elk River, which was very high, and on account of an impassable mountain for loaded trains about midway between Elk River and Pulaski Station, I discovered it was necessary for our trains wagoning provisions around this break to make a detour of 40 miles, which going and coming made a trip of 80 miles. The train forded Elk River at the point called Elton, above the burnt bridge.

At the time that we reached Athens railroad repairing was going on, not only on the Decatur and Nashville road but on the Nashville and Chattanooga. I discovered also at Athens a great deal of irregularity in the use of army wagons and of railroad transportation, under the command of General Mitchel, which I have no doubt retarded the progress of getting supplies, by the uses made by quartermasters of this transportation for the purpose of hauling cotton. Immediately after the arrival of General Buell at Huntsville, which was next day after we reached the vicinity of Athens, an order was issued by General Buell restricting the use of army wagons for the uses of the army only in procuring forage and subsistence, and disallowing the use of railroad transportation when it interfered with the progress of supplies for the army. All the trains were immediately organized for the purpose of foraging, and the country in Northern Alabama as far south as the Tennessee River was scoured for forage and subsistence, and everything that could be gathered without absolutely starving the women and children was taken. Quartermasters were sent to different points along the railroad to receive and take care of the supplies so brought in. The country north of the Memphis and Charleston Railroad was also visited thoroughly by our forage trains. The result of these labors was but a small quantity of old corn, left by the rebels, and only gathered in a few bushels at the time from different plantations. Subsistence of no account was brought or could be found, except a few almost worthless cattle and sheep, and these not enough to justify the hunting for them.

In the mean time every effort was concentrated to complete the repairs on the Decatur and Nashville road first, all the force that could be put upon the different points in the break working day and night. Not only were the Michigan Mechanics and

Engineers employed on this work, but every negro that could be secured in the region through which the railroad passed was pressed into the service to expedite the work. When I first visited the burnt bridge on Elk River—this was about the last of June—I was told by the colonel commanding the Engineers that it would take one month of unremitting work to complete the repairs, on account of the impossibility to ferry and ford this river, and on account of the impassable mountains for loaded teams, which I have already alluded to. It was absolutely necessary for the trains around the break to make this detour by way of Elton until the very moment that the railroad was completed. To my certain knowledge every effort that mechanical skill and perseverance could do was used in making the repairs on this road, and it was a month, if not more, before the trains could be run over the road. During this time all the troops of General Buell had occupied their position from Tuscumbia on the left, where General Thomas was left in command, to Battle Creek on the east, near Stevenson. About July 14, discovering that the supplies wagoning around the railroad break did not come fast enough either to supply the army day by day or to accumulate a quantity for any forward movement, I asked of General Buell the propriety of placing the troops on half rations, which was done, not only to accumulate supplies if possible, but to increase their industry in making everything they could out of the resources, if they could be so called, of the country. This was about July 14. From my representations that the railroad would not be completed in time to accumulate any supplies, and that it was absolutely necessary to look to some other line of communication, General Buell sent me to Tuscumbia, Ala., on our extreme left, about the middle of July, I think, to urge General Thomas to bring with him all the provisions he could haul and all the cattle he could drive with his column when he should be ready to march from Tuscumbia eastward to join the rest of our forces. He also ordered me to place myself in communication with Colonel Hawkins, chief commissary of General Halleck at Corinth, and to see if supplies could not be brought by rail from Memphis and by river to Eastport, thence wagoning to Iuka, thence by rail eastward to Decatur, on the Tennessee River, where the railroad bridge was also destroyed, where we expected to boat the stores on flat-boats across the river.

On my arrival at Tuscumbia General Thomas informed me that instead of bringing any supplies he was scarcely able to receive supplies sufficient for his own troops. On telegraphing to Colonel Hawkins, at Corinth, and asking if anything better could be done, he told him that he could hardly supply the troops at Corinth, and that he must not look to him for any supplies. He also telegraphed that General McPherson informed him that he had but two locomotives to be used from Corinth to Tuscumbia, and that these were so heavy that it was pronounced impracticable by the railroad engineers to cross the railroad bridge at Bear River, about 8 or 9 miles east of Iuka, on account of the weakness of the bridge. This was, I think, about the middle of July. At the same time General Thomas informed me that the guerrillas were threatening the line of railroad between Decatur and Tuscumbia and between Tuscumbia and Iuka and Corinth, and the Tennessee River had become so low that the navigation above Pittsburg Landing was only practicable for the very lightest draught boats.

The next day after I had left Tuscumbia on my return to Huntsville the rebels made a successful attack upon a line of railroad at a place called Courtland, captured the forces there guarding it, destroyed the railroad bridges, and effectually closed that line against us. In the mean time the Cumberland River had fallen so low that we were entirely dependent on the Louisville and Nashville Railroad for the arrival of our supplies in Nashville. The raids of the rebels into Kentucky, and cutting the railroad and their successful raid against Murfreesborough on the very day that we had completed the Nashville and Chattanooga Railroad to Stevenson, made us entirely dependent for our supplies in Northern Alabama upon the Decatur and Nashville road.

With the opening of the Chattanooga and Nashville road, which, as I have said, was destroyed on the very day it was opened by the capture of Murfreesborough, the troops had been put again upon full rations a few days previously, but with the capture of Murfreesborough we were obliged to fall back again upon half rations. In procuring supplies from Nashville nothing but the essentials—bread and meat, coffee and sugar—were thought of. Every effort was made to obtain as large a supply as possible of these articles; and, as I have said before, the country was thoroughly scoured for supplies, but with very little success. I myself went out on one of these expeditions in order to satisfy myself that every effort had been made to obtain supplies for the troops. I saw with my own eyes and heard the additional testimony of the people that from the time the rebellion had broken out their country had been stripped of everything in the shape of army supplies. At no time was it a country which produced more than grain enough for their own simple wants. I found much suffering for the want of food. The country from Duck River in Tennessee to the Tennessee River in Northern Alabama, and between the Nashville and Decatur Railroad on the west and the Nashville and Chattanooga Railroad on the east, consisted mostly of cotton plantations, and had been up to the spring of 1862 planted with scarcely anything else, but in the spring of 1862 the farmers had planted corn. After exhausting all the old corn we could find in the country we had to use green corn, not only for the animals, but it comprised a large portion of the food of the troops. I mention this particularly to account for the scarcity of grain in that part of the country, and that was about the extreme range of the movements of our foraging trains. From Duck River to the Cumberland north the country had been thoroughly foraged by the forces at Nashville and occupying our line of communication.

When General Buell's headquarters were moved from Huntsville to Decherd Station, on the Nashville and Chattanooga Railroad, on or about August 20 or 21, the supply of rations in the hands of the troops and at the stations between Nashville and Stevenson, all points south of Nashville—for I include Murfreesborough, Franklin, Decherd Station, Stevenson, Huntsville, Athens, Columbia, and Franklin—was 628 [?] half rations. One week before that movement of General Buell to Decherd Station the following is the report of stores at Nashville: 300,000 rations of salt meat, 700,000 rations of hard bread and flour. Salt meat, as you will see by the figures, was largely inferior to the quantity of breadstuffs. This was owing to the difficulty of procuring fresh meat. The beef contractors of the army having met with heavy losses in the capture of herds of cattle by the guerrillas, I was ordered on our arrival at Huntsville to use every effort to absorb the resources of the country in fresh meat, and for that purpose all the cattle that could be gathered from Southern Kentucky and around Nashville and between Nashville and Huntsville were diligently sought after. In the movement of abandoning our line of communications in Northern Alabama and on the road between Columbia and Decatur all the other stores were carefully gathered up and sent northward, and in no case was anything lost except at Huntsville, where only a small quantity was lost. We succeeded in bringing everything safely forward. We arrived at Decherd Station, I think, on about the 21st or 22d of August, where we established our headquarters. While there I was ordered by General Buell to take four companies of cavalry and to thoroughly scour the north and south bank of Elk River as far as Fayetteville, and to bring in all the cattle that could be found, to ascertain what resources were still left in that region, as that was considered the best part of the country. I was absent five days and returned with 200 head of cattle, which was every hoof that could be gathered up on both banks of the river; but they were in very poor condition, so as hardly to justify the trip. I found in all the farms and plantations but a few bushels of old corn, and that not more than sufficient to feed the families and negroes living on the farms. On the McMinnville Railroad, leading from Tullahoma eastward, a branch of the Chattanooga Railroad, we gathered up a few hundred barrels of flour, a part of which proved afterward to be damaged. All this was brought forward and went toward Nashville with the movement of the army.

On our arrival at Nashville, about September 2, the following was the amount of stores on hand. I forgot to mention that already in July the commissary in Nashville was ordered to take all the supplies in the hands of dealers in Nashville, and all shipments of supplies out of Nashville on private account were stopped. I mention this to account for the enormous quantity of one item—salt—included in the following statement.

On the 1st of September the following was the condition of supplies in Nashville about the time our columns marched into the city: 345,000 rations of salt meats, 200 head of beef cattle, 1,000,000 rations of breadstuffs. The disproportion between breadstuffs and salt meats will account for our efforts to obtain all the fresh beef possible. Of salt Captain Macfeely had seized 5,000 barrels. That was the large item spoken of. I mention that because it might be thought we had taken up unnecessary transportation for the supply of this article, whereas that was taken from private parties. Constant complaint was made by our officers at Nashville of the inadequate means of transportation on the Louisville and Nashville Railroad. In order that no time should be lost and that no means should be left unused, Capt. W. Frank Harris, assistant quartermaster of volunteers in our command, and who at one time had been an agent on the Louisville and Nashville Railroad and was thoroughly posted in railroad matters, had been sent up to Louisville in the month of July with full powers to run the railroad to its utmost capacity. With all his efforts the railroad was unable to carry more than about 75 tons per day. This of course included not only subsistence but forage and quartermaster's supplies. In the mean time, discovering that subsistence was more requisite than that of forage, because our troops were making free use of the green corn in the fields, all the railroad transportation was applied to bringing subsistence. To provide for our march northward from Nashville in pursuit of Bragg, and at the same time to leave Nashville in as well supplied condition as possible, General Buell had ordered 1,000,000 of rations to Bowling Green, not only by railroad but by way of Green River.

The condition of our troops about September 1, when they reached Nashville on their march northward, was as follows (I have already stated the supplies at Nashville): General Crittenden's division had 20,000 rations of breadstuffs, but not so much of other articles; General McCook's train had forty days' rations complete; the Third Division, formerly commanded by General Mitchel, had 72,000 rations of breadstuffs only; the Fourth Division, formerly commanded by General Nelson, had 50,000 rations; General Wood's division had 36,000 rations of breadstuffs; and as General Thomas' division was over near McMinnville, I had sent him on about the last of August 35,000 rations. Besides these rations mentioned the troops had three days' rations on their persons, enough to allow them to reach Nashville. Besides these supplies mentioned as on hand at Nashville about September 1 and in the wagons of the division trains, I had sent to Nashville, and there were then in the depots there and *en route* in the cars waiting to be unloaded, 430,000 rations of breadstuffs, but nothing else. This, with the quantity on hand at Nashville, would give 1,100,000 rations of breadstuffs. General Buell ordered me to provide for the troops as far as Bowling Green on half rations, in order that we might leave every available and possible pound of supplies in Nashville, as we expected communication to be cut off in our rear with our forces left there. The troops were so supplied until we reached Bowling Green, and everything else turned over to the depots in Nashville. On our arrival at Bowling Green we were expecting to find the million rations ordered by General Buell beforehand for this emergency. The supplies which were taken with us from Nashville were exhausted.

On investigating the condition of supplies at Bowling Green I discovered that the essential parts of the rations ordered by General Buell were almost totally wanting, on account of the interruptions by the rebels at Munfordville and other places and of the inadequate power of the railroad to transport them in time. I found that no breadstuffs whatever were on hand, with the exception of a few barrels of flour and those not sufficient for the troops garrisoning Bowling Green for over four or five days. The meat rations amounted to only about one-third of the quantity ordered. It was necessary to halt the command and obtain sufficient supplies of meat and breadstuffs. Trains were immediately organized and sent out to gather all the wheat and flour in the surrounding country. Trains went as far as 20 and 25 miles westward in the direction of Russellville. Here we met the same difficulty in obtaining supplies, on account of the previous occupation of Bowling Green by the rebels and of the destitute condition in which they had left the people. I called upon the citizens of Bowling Green and induced them to send messengers throughout the country, promising immediate payment for all the wheat brought to the mills and for all the flour brought to Bowling Green. All the mills that could be put into operation within 18 miles around Bowling Green to the westward were put in operation, and by this means in about four or five days I had gathered about 400,000 rations of flour. Of salt meat I was unable to obtain more than about 10,000 rations. Upon the arrival of our troops at Munfordville the railroad trains from Bowling Green under my care were run to Munfordville day and night, supplying the troops as they passed Munfordville with provisions gathered in the manner I have stated. On the arrival of our troops at West Point, at the mouth of Salt River, on the Ohio River, provisions which had been ordered from Louisville down to West Point met us. One of the divisions, commanded by General Smith, formerly of the division of General Nelson, had been out of provisions for nearly a day where they arrived there. All the supplies that were left at Bowling Green of the quantity gathered in the manner I have stated were intended to be pushed into Nashville at the first favorable opportunity. When I left Bowling Green I so instructed the commissary there. During our march northward, according to my instructions, I used every effort to supply Nashville, even stinting the troops on the march, so that in case communication should be cut off with that city we had left everything possible with them.

We reached Louisville about the latter part of September. The troops on our arrival there were ordered to send in their trains and supply themselves with provisions immediately for ten days, so as to be able to march at an hour's notice. Arrangements were made also to supply the columns marching from Louisville in pursuit of Bragg at the rate of 100,000 rations per day.

The troops left Louisville about the 1st of October, marching in three different columns, by three different roads and routes, intending to concentrate in front of the enemy at or near Danville. The raids of the rebels under Kirby Smith by way of Frankfort, in the rear of the columns of General McCook, seriously impeded the movements of our trains following his columns to supply him, and they were consequently ordered from their route, barely in time to save them from the enemy, by way of Bardstown. It was a difficult matter to supply the troops on this march for these reasons: the Louisville and Nashville Railroad was destroyed; several important bridges burned on the main stem; the Bardstown branch was completely destroyed in every vulnerable point, as also the principal bridges on the Lebanon branch, which made it necessary to depend upon wagons alone from Louisville. Desiring to make use of the railroad as far as was in our power, the construction of the Frankfort Railroad and the Louisville and Nashville Railroad and its branches was pushed with the greatest energy. The raid of Kirby Smith in the rear of General McCook's column prevented us from making use of the Frankfort branch, and having taken supplies on the Louisville and Nashville as far as Shepherdsville, we had to abandon that route on account of the almost impracticable road between Shepherdsville and Bardstown, so that the column had to be supplied entirely by wagon trains starting from Louisville on the Bardstown pike.

The rebels having occupied the country in force as far as Bardstown and their pickets having come to within a few miles of Louisville they had stripped the country of forage, so that the trains hauling subsistence were obliged to haul the forage. Water was also very scarce upon the road, and we almost broke down our teams in pushing supplies up to the column at Crab Orchard and to the troops who had gone beyond that point a distance from Louisville of about 120 miles. I think that the total consumption of rations from Northern Alabama, while we were there, and on the march to Nashville was about 75,000 per day. Our effective force, I think, was about 45,000 men; the additional 30,000 rations is about the usual percentage of loss of rations in transportation, sick in hospitals, teamsters, and others. The difficulty in procuring forage, the bad roads beyond Crab Orchard, and the scarcity of water did not enable us to push our wagon trains over about 15 or 20 miles beyond Crab Orchard southward.

On motion, the Commission then adjourned to meet on Monday, March 23, 1863, at 10 o'clock a. m.

CINCINNATI, *Monday, March* 23, 1863.

The Commission met pursuant to adjournment. Members present, General Wallace, General Dana, General Tyler; also the judge-advocate and General Buell.

* Lieut. Col. FRANCIS DARR'S examination continued.

By General BUELL:

Submit to the Commission, if you please, colonel, any documents you have in confirmation of the particulars stated in your testimony on Saturday in regard to the amount of supplies on hand at the various periods mentioned. You may at the same time submit any of the instructions under which you acted in procuring supplies.

On June 3, a few days after the evacuation of Corinth by the rebels, I was ordered to make Eastport, Miss., the base of supplies for General Buell's command, the supplies to be wagoned thence to Iuka. Complying with this order, the supplies were moved from the neighborhood of Pittsburg Landing to Eastport. On June 9, at 11 p. m., I received orders to commence sending supplies to Tuscumbia and Florence. Up to the 20th instant I was engaged in so doing, and sent up about 300,000 rations, ten days' supply, at which time we were unable to run any more boats with any freight. From the 20th of June to the 25th instant I was engaged in loading wagons with five days' supply, which made fifteen days' supply from the 20th of June. From the 20th of June the forces were occupied at Jackson's Ford, ferrying across the river. On the 26th of June I fell into the column at Florence with my supply train.

In the neighborhood of Athens, Ala., the divisions of General Nelson and General Wood were obliged to wait for supplies. This was about July 5. About July the 4th or 5th the divisions of General McCook and General Crittenden, having exhausted their supplies with which they started from Tuscumbia and then being in the neighborhood of Huntsville and on the march toward Stevenson, had to be supplied day by day by railroad trains following their line of march. On July 15 the rebels destroyed at the capture of Murfreesborough 200,000 rations, breaking the railroad there on the day before on which we were to run trains from Nashville to Stevenson. This disaster, coupled with the difficulty already mentioned in my previous testimony by the breaks in the railroad between Athens and Nashville, induced me to apply to General Buell to put the troops on half rations. This was done on the 14th of July. At that time there were hardly any supplies in Nashville, on account of the Morgan raids in Kentucky.

Question. If you have any documents substantiating the statements you are making submit them to the Commission as you go along, that they may appear in the body of your testimony?

On the 14th July, in confirmation of the want of supplies at Nashville, I would submit the following dispatch from Capt. R. Macfeely, commissary of subsistence in the United States Army, and in charge of supplies at Nashville, addressed to Capt. F. Darr, commissary of subsistence, Huntsville:

"NASHVILLE, *July* 14, 1862.

"No stores sent to Elk River Bridge. I informed you on the 12th instant there were no provisions in this depot; if there had been they could not have been sent to Elk River Bridge (on the Decatur and Nashville road), as the trains have been unable to run through. No provisions received from Louisville in the past week, I presume on account of the troubles on the road.

"R. MACFEELY,
"*Commissary of Subsistence.*"

I submit another dispatch:

"NASHVILLE, *July* 12, 1862.

(This was the day before the rebels cut the railroad.)

"To Capt. F. DARR:

"I forwarded to Murfreesborough 100,000 rations. None to forward until received from Louisville. Nothing received since 6th instant. Will send stores required at Elk River as soon as received. Who is commissary of subsistence at Elk River? The transportation department at Louisville is responsible for delay in receipt of stores. They are sent forward from here as fast as received. Symonds [he means Capt. H. C. Symonds] has plenty, but cannot get cars.

"R. MACFEELY,
"*Commissary of Subsistence.*"

The indorsements on the back of this dispatch, made by me at the time, state that Captain Nigh, the chief quartermaster of General Buell at the time, reported to J. B. Anderson, military railroad superintendent, the lack of transportation at Louisville. It was to remedy any delay or neglect at Louisville that General Buell at once decided on sending Capt. W. F. Harris, assistant quartermaster, to Louisville.

On July 17 the guerrillas were so bad between Nashville and Huntsville that the sending of the mails was suspended. On July 21, eight days after the capture of Murfreesborough, the rebels destroyed an important railroad bridge at Antioch, 12 miles south of Nashville, on the Chattanooga road, also several small bridges on the Decatur and Nashville road between Reynolds' Station and Columbia, besides attacking and driving in our forage trains. About the same time, July 21 or 22, there were heavy rains; a flood on the Duck River washed away part of the bridge across Duck River at Columbia. These impediments to obtaining supplies from Nashville and the non-arrival of them at Nashville induced General Buell to send me to Tuscumbia to attempt to bring supplies for our army from that direction. On the 23d of July I left Huntsville and reached Tuscumbia the same evening. On the same night I telegraphed to Colonel Hawkins, the commissary of General Halleck at Corinth, the object of the mission I was on, and received from him the same night the following dispatch:

"CORINTH, *July* 23, 1862.

"To Capt. FRANCIS DARR, *Tuscumbia:*

"On account of the small means of transportation we are living from hand to mouth. It will be impossible for me to send you any supplies.

"JOHN P. HAWKINS,
"*Captain, Commissary of Subsistence.*"

In my testimony I have called him colonel; this is his present rank.

I left Tuscumbia on the 24th on my return to Huntsville. On the 25th the rebels destroyed the railroad communication between Tuscumbia and Decatur by a successful raid upon Courtland and neighboring stations. On the 24th of July the wants of the troops at and near Murfreesborough were so pressing, railroad communication to Nashville being destroyed, that we were obliged to wagon supplies from Nashville to them. In a letter dated July 26, at Louisville, Captain Symonds, commissary of subsistence, writes that he sends 75,000 rations per diem, and complains of the want of transportation; but he says that he will do his best to throw into Nashville 2,000,000 rations. Applying to him for a statement of the supplies shipped from Louisville to Nashville during the months of June and July I received the following statement: List of provisions shipped to Captain Macfeely at Nashville, Tenn., in the months of June and July, 1862, both by railroad and river, by Capt. H. C. Symonds, commissary of subsistence: 1,705,106 pounds, equal to 2,202,434 rations, salt meat; 2,711,243 pounds, equal to 2,202,434 rations, hard bread; and a proportionate quantity of the other parts of the rations.

On the 28th July the first train of the Chattanooga Railroad ran from Nashville to Stevenson, with 210,000 rations on board. On July 29 the troops were put upon full rations. By July 30 threw into Stevenson 160,000 rations additional. On August 6 a trial train of a few passenger cars was run over the Decatur and Nashville road for the first time from Nashville to Athens; the bridges were pronounced unsafe and the trains suspended. It was not until August 11 that loaded trains could pass safely over the road. On the 10th of August the line between Louisville and Nashville was again cut by the rebels by the capture of Gallatin, Tenn., and the garrison stationed there captured, and railroad communication between Louisville and Nashville again stopped. On August 19 the break of communication in Kentucky induced the order to put the troops again on half rations. In the mean time, by General Buell's orders, the lightest boats were seized at Louisville for the purpose of sending stores up the Cumberland River. This line of communication was also cut on the 20th of August by the rebels capturing Clarksville and seizing the first boat with supplies, which had just arrived there, and destroying the supplies on board. On the same day, I think August 20, General Buell's headquarters were moved to Decherd Station. I have before mentioned in my testimony the care taken to save all the supplies and carry them northward with the army and of the efforts made while at Decherd Station to gather all the supplies which could be found in the neighboring region.

In testimony on Saturday I also gave a statement of the means taken to supply the troops on their march from Nashville, by way of Bowling Green, to Louisville. In addition to that I will state that from the time of our arrival at Athens, about the last of June, until our march northward in pursuit of General Bragg, all the transportation of the army, except that which was absolutely necessary to carry the camp and garrison equipage of the troops, was put into requisition on the railway breaks for the purpose of wagoning supplies, and it was not until we reached Nashville, about the 1st of September, that the troops were able to get their proper transportation returned to them. I state that to show that we used every means in our power to bring forward supplies.

Question. Have you any memoranda which will enable you to give the dates at which the different divisions passed some given point on the march to Corinth? Can you state the date of their arrival at Tuscumbia, and, if you can, the date of their departure from the vicinity of Corinth?

On June 11 the advanced brigade of General Wood's division, commanded by General Hascall, was at Tuscumbia; I found them there. I think they got there the same day or the day before. On June 21, ten days afterward, General Nelson's division was at Iuka. From my being at Eastport I do not know the exact time of the arrival at Tuscumbia of the different divisions, but on the 25th, I think, General McCook's and General Crittenden's divisions had just succeeded in crossing the river at Jackson's Ferry or were in process of doing so. The wagons were taken across on large coal barges decked over, which we had hauled across the Shoals with great trouble.

I cannot exactly give the dates when those barges were taken up to Tuscumbia; I think they were taken up about the 20th. I know that General Thomas' headquarters were at Iuka on the 25th of June, because on that day I had sent him some prisoners. On July 23, while on my way to Tuscumbia, I met General Schoepf's brigade, of General Thomas' division, on the march for Decatur, where their wagons had to be ferried across the Tennessee River by a very small and fragile scow. They were several days in crossing. I think that the other two brigades of General Thomas' division crossed the river at Florence, commencing to do so on or about the 25th or 26th of July. The progress of this division marching eastward I have no other data to judge by except the murder of General Robert L. McCook, who was killed a few miles east of Athens, Ala., on August 5. I think that General Thomas himself was but a day or so in advance of him and had his headquarters at Decherd Station, from which place on August 6 he telegraphed to General Buell the report of the murder of General McCook on the day before. The brigade of General Robert L. McCook must have passed through Athens on or about the 4th of August.

Question. Do you know anything of the troops being employed in repairing the railroad from Corinth to Decatur during the movement in that direction? If so, state what you know about it.

I think that on about June the 10th or 11th the Michigan Mechanics and Engineers were put to work on the burnt railroad bridge across Bear River, a few miles east of Iuka. The fact is fresh in my mind on account of the murder of two of the Engineers by the guerrillas while at work there.

On my visit to Tuscumbia on June 11 I rode with General Hascall to examine the railroad bridge across Tuscumbia Creek a few miles west of Tuscumbia, and which was completely destroyed. Another bridge a few miles west of that was reported to me as also destroyed. With a view to putting the railway in order between Tuscumbia and Decatur, ahead of the construction of the bridges between Tuscumbia and Iuka, a locomotive and some freight cars had been ordered by way of the Tennessee River. I would state that at Tuscumbia all the rolling stock left by the rebels was useless. On the arrival of the locomotive at Pittsburg Landing, about June 15 or 16, I had it towed up to Eastport, transferred it, and towed it over the Shoals to Florence, where it was landed on the south side of the river and taken up the bank. On placing the locomotive on the rails and attempting to use it the engine was discovered to be useless, and after repeated trials to use it by some Michigan Engineers it was given up.

Question. Do you know who provided that locomotive or who is to blame that a locomotive in that condition was furnished?

I have no other reason than a military reason to know who provided it, and it is this: Col. Thomas Swords, assistant quartermaster-general, and in charge of furnishing quartermaster's supplies for General Buell's command, stationed then at Louisville, is, I presume, the party who procured it. I know it was a very old locomotive, having had some experience in railroad matters myself. I think the locomotive bore this mark: "W. and O. R. R." Had the locomotive been in good order and condition it would have assisted us very materially in bringing supplies forward to Decatur, a distance, I think, of 43 miles from Tuscumbia.

General Buell. I will state, in justice to Colonel Swords, that he is not responsible, as I believe, for the condition of that locomotive or that such a locomotive was forwarded.

Question. Do you know how far the work required to be done on the railroad and the preparation of the ferry was the cause of the delay of the troops along the road and in the vicinity of Tuscumbia until the 25th of June?

I think it was the only cause of the delay, because our troops repaired the railway bridges from Iuka eastward as they advanced.

Question. Can you give the date of the arrival of General Schoepf's brigade at Decatur and the date at which it had completed the passage of the river?

The head of General Schoepf's column reached Decatur on the evening of July 23. He himself with his staff arrived there about 1 or 2 p. m. He commenced crossing his wagons on the next day, and I think it took about three days to transfer his brigade from one side of the river to the other.

Question. Was the transfer of the troops across the river at Florence, with the means which we had prepared there, rapid or otherwise?

It was rather slow, because we had but one steamboat, the Lady Jackson, to carry and to tow the coal barges which were lashed alongside for the purpose of carrying the wagons. The road to the water's edge on the south side of the river came through a narrow defile. The landing on the opposite side (the north side) of the river, on account of the low and swampy nature of the ground, was very muddy. Temporary piers had to be constructed for the purpose of loading and unloading the wagons. The river at that point was very broad.

Question. What was the capacity of this ferry in comparison with the one at Decatur?

Having been only about an hour or two at Jackson's Ferry watching the ferry I could not state the exact number of wagons that could be crossed at the time, but I think it was in the neighborhood of ten, with their mules, whereas the ferry at Decatur, I think, could only take one or two wagons at the time. The Muscle Shoals, between Decatur and Florence, was an impassable barrier to navigation.

Question. Do you know what delayed General Thomas' division so long after the balance of the army in the movement from Corinth?

In a conversation held with General Thomas on the evening of July 23 he told me that he was obliged to wait; that he was occupying the country and line of railroad until troops from General Grant's army should come up to relieve him. I think General Morgan was the name of the general whom he expected to relieve him. He told me that he had been in readiness to move for some time, and had actually that evening ordered Brig. Gen. Speed S. Fry's brigade to be in readiness to march from Jackson's Ferry to cross in case the troops from Corinth came up. He remarked at the same time that he was fearful of withdrawing any portion of his troops from the line of railway until they had been actually relieved by General Grant's troops and not until the latter were in full possession, on account of bands of guerrillas who were hovering along the line of railroad.

Question. Do I understand you that the fifteen days' supplies of provisions which were forwarded to Tuscumbia for the use of the army dated from the 20th of July and that the previous supply was exhausted at that time?

Yes, sir.

Question. Do you know whether the supplies embraced in the statement of Captain Symonds which you have submitted to the Commission were actually received at Nashville?

I do not know, sir. I think that some supplies must have been detained along the line of the Louisville and Nashville road between the breaks, because a railroad line of that length could hardly be at any one time clear of railroad trains.

Question. Do you know anything about the shipment of supplies to Nashville by Captain Symonds during the month of August; whether such shipments were made and to what extent?

I have a dispatch dated Louisville, August 4, 1862, addressed to Capt. J. G. Chandler, quartermaster on General Buell's staff: "117 tons commissary stores (equal to 75,000 rations) forwarded and 100 tons of grain went forward this morning." Signed W. F. Harris, captain and assistant quartermaster. This is the officer whom General Buell had sent to Louisville to expedite shipments.

I have no consolidated returns of shipments in August. Seventy-five thousand rations per diem was about the capacity of the railroad when in running order; that was about equal to the total consumption of the army. There were interruptions on the Louisville and Nashville Railroad. On August 10 Gallatin was captured by Morgan, the railroad cut, and his subsequent defeat of General Johnson, commander of the Federal forces, and the constant interruptions, lead me to think that not over 600,000 or 700,000 rations were sent forward in August.

Question. Are you able to state whether the supplies for the army were generally well taken care of or whether they were wasted?

The utmost possible care was taken to preserve the supplies in transit and in depot; but large quantities must necessarily have been wasted in the frequent transshipment from Nashville toward Huntsville from rail to wagon and back again and in fording streams. There is always large wastage where supplies are wagoned over rough roads.

Question. As far as you know by comparison with other troops were the habits of the troops of the Army of the Ohio wasteful or economical and careful?

I have served in three departments since the commencement of the war, and I have known no troops managed better or make better use of their rations or use more care thereof than the Army of the Ohio.

Question. What was the amount of supplies left at Huntsville when that place was evacuated?

I do not think there could have been over ten days' supply left there for the forces under General Rousseau, and they took in their wagons all they could possibly haul away. I do not think over 10,000 rations were destroyed. I was present there at the time and this is my impression.

Question. Was there any loss of supplies at any other points when the troops commenced their concentration at Murfreesborough?

No, sir; most of the supplies at Stevenson, our main depot, had been forwarded north. Captain Bright, the commissary at that point, forwarded all the supplies before he left.

Question. Did you have an opportunity of observing the troops generally on the march from Nashville to Louisville? And, if so, please state in what manner that march was conducted. Was it orderly or otherwise?

My duties calling me frequently from the head of the column to the rear, I had often occasion to remark to my brother officers the excellent manner and close order in which the troops marched from Nashville to Bowling Green. I remember this distinctly, having had occasion to ride to the head of the column between Tyree Springs and Mitchellsville to learn the particulars of a skirmish between General Crittenden's advance and the rebels. I saw no straggling of any consequence, and for troops who had marched the distance they had passed over, in my experience I never saw troops march in better order or in better preparation for any attack or emergency which might occur. From Bowling Green to Munfordville, in the course of my duty, I passed up and down the column several times, both by rail and horseback, and still noticed the excellent marching order of the troops. At Munfordville, in the course of my duty, supplying each division as it passed Rowlett's Station, near Munfordville, I could not help but notice the excellent order of march, on account of the rapidity and regularity of each brigade drawing its supplies and the absence of stragglers in the rear of the line of march. After the troops had all passed Munfordville and were still on the march I rode along the column from its rear to General Buell at Elizabethtown, and had no reason to change my opinion already expressed. From Elizabethtown to West Point, at the mouth of Salt River, the troops marched with greater alacrity than ever and were going with the hope of soon meeting the enemy, and no depredations were committed along the road to my knowledge.

Question. Can you account for the large numbers of absentees from the army after its arrival at Louisville?

At West Point there was considerable conversation and discussion upon the subject of apprehended desertions, or rather an attempt on the part of the soldiers whose homes were in the neighboring counties of Indiana to visit them, and I have no doubt that on their arrival at West Point many crossed the river in skiffs and otherwise to gratify their desire to visit their homes, mostly by troops living in the southern counties of Indiana. I remember some instances of field officers doing so, and I have no doubt but that many company and regimental officers connived at this absenteeism of their troops.

Question. Have you observed the same thing in other cases when troops arrived near their homes after a long absence?

Yes, sir; in Western Virginia, where I served, the troops we had stationed along the Ohio River on the Virginia side caused us much annoyance by their visits to their homes; and even while at Pittsburg Landing I know there were great complaints among the officers of General Grant's army that the Illinois regiments gave him considerable trouble by soldiers escaping down the river in boats, so much so that the most stringent provost-marshal arrangements had to be made to suspend it. A more striking instance I remember when some of General Rosecrans' troops were transported from Western Virginia to General Buell's command in Kentucky in the fall of 1861, when two regiments from Cincinnati gave considerable trouble. The Ninth and Tenth Ohio being permitted to land at Cincinnati, their home, great annoyance and delay were occasioned in gathering them up, so much so that the Ninth Ohio had to be almost driven on board their boats at the point of the bayonet. This attachment for home was also exhibited by the Sixth Ohio Regiment, who, not being allowed to land at Cincinnati, their home, and being taken to Louisville, deserted almost in a body and visited Cincinnati.

Question. Did this absence of men from the Army of the Ohio on its arrival at Louisville to visit their homes indicate any demoralization in the army?

I do not think so, because many returned within a few days to join their regiments on the march toward Perryville, and in all cases that I heard of—and I spoke to many of them—they indignantly denied any intention of deserting; it was simply a desire to gratify an ardent wish to visit their homes before the impending battle.

Question. Would you consider that the same thing must be expected whenever troops return to the vicinity of their homes after a long absence from them with the mild discipline which is enforced in our armies?

I do; on account of the strength and natural desire of people absent a long time from their homes to see their families and on account of the non-punishment of previous examples of the same kind and on account of our people not having been used to the privations caused by war keeping them from their homes.

Question. State all that you know in regard to the amount of straggling from the army on the march from Louisville to Perryville.

On the march from Louisville to Perryville I rode with the center column, commanded by General Crittenden, on the line of the Louisville and Bardstown pike. On the arrival of the column at Springfield I was sent back to Bardstown, that being considered the most central point to superintend the movements of supplies for the army, and attend to any other business which might be forwarded to me there, that being the terminus and as far as we had erected the telegraph. General McCook's column having moved on a different road to the left and General Gilbert's command having joined our column at Springfield I can only speak of what I saw at that time of those two columns. I noticed that all the old troops, as we called the army that had come up from Tennessee, marched in their usual close order, and on account of this example kept the column composed of the new and old troops pretty well up; but returning from Springfield to Bardstown during the night I found many stragglers who had hidden during the day in the woods, but were mostly from the new troops absorbed by us at Louisville. On my arrival at Bardstown I asked of the officers in command of the post if there were many stragglers in town, and that it was General Buell's orders, if any such were there, that they should be sent forward immediately. From the march of the 7th or 8th stragglers who had hidden along the road during the days or who had loitered in Louisville came thronging through Bardstown, and up to about the 15th or 16th a great many passed through—in my judgment 5,000 or 6,000. I took particular notice of what part of the army the stragglers were composed, and with but rare exceptions I found them to be entirely of the new troops, who, either for purposes of plunder or not being accustomed to march, straggled behind the column. By General Buell's orders, twice a day stragglers were pushed through Bardstown at the point of the bayonet by the provost guard. By order of General Buell I directed Colonel Minty, of the Fourth Michigan Cavalry, who was coming up in charge of the ammunition train, to detail a portion of his cavalry to sweep the road and drive ahead of him every straggler.

Question. Do you know whether the orders were frequent and urgent for an accumulation of supplies in Middle Tennessee from Louisville during the last summer?

Yes, sir, they were; for it was our constant aim to hurry forward all the supplies possible. The frequent interruptions by the rebel raids kept us constantly on the alert to take every advantage of the river and railroad communication and wagoning to bring forward supplies.

Question. From your experience what do you think of the practice of supplying as large a force as was in Middle Tennessee last summer from the resources of that country, in the midst of active operations and in the midst of a population disposed as the people of Middle Tennessee were to the Government at that time?

I think it was impossible to subsist an army in that region of Middle Tennessee, strong enough to occupy the country, off the resources thereof, on account of the destitution of the people, they having been almost entirely stripped by the rebels. That the people were hostile to us there can be no doubt, because the rebel bands of guerrillas infesting that region were composed entirely of the inhabitants thereof.

Question. In an attempt to depend mainly upon the resources of the country which army would fare best, the Army of the Ohio or the rebel army? And give your reasons for whatever opinion you may have upon that subject.

In my opinion the rebel army, because the inhabitants of that region would have been volunteer foragers, and would have brought any supplies, pound by pound, te them; for no matter how poorly off they were, it was their boasted saying that the rebel troops should be the last to suffer for anything to eat wherever they and the people were concerned, when by connivance and preconcerted action supplies could be gathered for the rebels by the people themselves. Our army would have been compelled to visit every individual and to have taken supplies by force. My experience in foraging, even in a good country, induces me to believe that where an army subsists on a country's resources, without the aid of depots, it requires one day to forage for another.

Question. Did the organized bands of guerrillas give the enemy any advantage in this respect?

It did; because the guerrillas, at home in the neighborhood they infested, could be easily supplied by their families, on account of their knowledge of the country, whereas it would be impossible to have subsisted our troops; the rebel plan being generally to scatter and hide during the day and meet at night for the purpose of their raids, by this course making making them entirely independent of a commissariat requisite to handle our troops in the field, especially while we were in a hostile country.

Question. Can you form any estimate of the cavalry force that would be required to counteract this advantage which the rebels had, say in the district of country occupied by the Army of the Ohio last summer?

On account of the facilities enjoyed by the rebels in Tennessee and of their sympathizers in Kentucky, their knowledge of the country, and the rapidity of the movements of the rebel cavalry, it has always appeared to me to be necessary to have a cordon of cavalry or mounted men from Louisville to Huntsville strong enough at any available point on the railroad to meet any attack which the rebels in any force might hurl against them. This would have involved a large number of troops to effect a purpose, for which the small body of cavalry we had was totally inadequate. With my knowledge of military affairs I do not consider myself competent to estimate the number of cavalry required for this purpose. From the results of the rebel raids it was always my impression that no matter how much cavalry we had we never could have too much, for in a line of communication extending from Louisville to Nashville, and occupying two lines of railroad south from Nashville, as we did, embracing over 500 miles of communication, it appears to me almost impossible for such a line to be guarded thoroughly and safely, so as to make a constant communication certain, with less than 100,000 [?] troops of cavalry, doing nothing else but guarding the lines, because every vulnerable point in that line, if guarded at all, should be guarded so as to make certain defense against any attack whatsoever by the enemy; that is, such a certain defense as I consider was required by such a line of communication, liable to be broken at any hour.

Question. Taking the district of country which the Army of the Ohio occupied last summer, what amount of cavalry force do you think would be required, in an attempt to subsist on the country, to neutralize the inconvenience resulting from the unfriendly disposition of the people and the large guerrilla force scattered through the country, so as to enable the Army of the Ohio to derive all the benefit possible from the resources of the country?

I frequently heard cavalry officers occupied in guarding wagon trains say that 5,000 and 6,000 cavalry between Nashville and Huntsville was hardly sufficient to drive the guerrillas out. The line between Nashville and Louisville, it appears to me, would have taken a great many more, on account of the distance.

Question. Has your experience in commercial business given you an opportunity of knowing anything of the agricultural resources of Middle Tennessee?

It has. I am personally cognizant that Nashville has always been one of the largest markets for Cincinnati for the disposition of meat products, and the shipment of subsistence supplies. In my journeys through Middle Tennessee, in conversation with the planters, I have frequently asked the reason for purchasing their food in the North, when such a rich country as Middle Tennessee could produce it equally as well as our own lands. The reasons were these, that they scarcely would raise grain enough for their own negroes and animals, because they found it much more profitable to plant cotton, and for this reason they devoted their lands to the most profitable culture and obtained their food from the North.

Question. Up to how recent a period has this system of cultivation continued?

In the spring of 1861 they commenced planting corn. They were encouraged almost entirely to suspend the planting of cotton and substitute corn, because in the spring of 1861 shipments from Cincinnati, Pittsburgh, Louisville, and Saint Louis and other points to Nashville were either suspended or under such restrictions that it was impossible to get any amount of supplies through, and at the urgent solicitation of the press throughout the rebel States the system of corn planting was generally adopted. Large quantities of corn and meat were therefore raised and put into the market in Tennessee in the fall of 1861. Such home products were that year immensely in excess of any previous year. The grain so raised and the meats so packed in the fall of 1861 in that region of country composed the main supply of all the rebel force. Both in Virginia and other regions they were very active in the winter of 1861 in taking these supplies out of Tennessee. The Confederate authorities, in their eagerness to make use of the resources created in this year 1861 in Tennessee, packed the meats throughout Tennessee on their own account, either purchasing or taking by force the live stock from the owners or raisers. It was well known throughout the country, and I found it corroborated by my own inquiries, that from the supplies raised in Middle Tennessee in 1861 the main supplies for the rebel forces were drawn.

Cross-examination by the JUDGE-ADVOCATE:

Question. Colonel, what was the force leaving Corinth for North Alabama which you were called upon to subsist?

I think it was about 30,000.

Question. What was this force about the 14th of July, the middle of August, and the 7th of September?

About 45,000. They were about the same in the middle of August and the 7th of September.

Question. What was the force that you were called upon to subsist after the Army of the Ohio left Louisville to attack Bragg at Bardstown.

About 58,000.

Question. Have you any better means of making up the force of the Army than that of the consolidated reports submitted to the Commission by the assistant adjutant-general?

I have not had any experience in making up the number of troops in our army or as to the mode employed in doing so. I generally ascertained or gathered my idea of the number of troops I had to feed from headquarters.

Question. If the morning consolidated reports for the 20th of July exhibits 55,269 men present for duty and your recollection is that you fed 45,000 how do you account for the difference?

General BUELL. I object to the question, Mr. President. The force which the judge-advocate states is represented in the morning report is one thing and the force which the witness has stated that he subsisted is a different thing altogether. The witness will answer the question intelligibly I have no doubt, but it is a question that can have but one effect, and that is to mislead him.

The court was then cleared; when, after discussion, it was decided that the objection should not be sustained.

The WITNESS. The troops I mentioned as amounting to about 45,000 were those between Nashville and Huntsville. There were other forces under General Buell's command at other places, and whom I was not feeding and did not include in my estimate in Middle Tennessee. This may account for the difference in the morning report. There were troops at Cumberland Gap. Of course I did not include those; they were fed by way of Lexington, Ky.

Question. Were there any other forces besides those at Cumberland Gap which were not included?

There may have been on the line of the Louisville and Nashville Railroad and on the lines in communication with Cumberland Gap.

Question. If it should prove, however, that the consolidated morning report does not include the force at Cumberland Gap and those on the lines you have enumerated, are you still firm in your recollection that you fed only 45,000 men at that time?

It is my impression it was about that number.

The Commission then adjourned to meet on Tuesday, March 24, at 10 o'clock a. m.

CINCINNATI, *Tuesday, March 24*, 1863.

The Commission met pursuant to adjournment. Members present, General Wallace, General Dana, General Tyler; also the judge-advocate and General Buell.

Cross-examination of Col. FRANCIS DARR continued.

By the JUDGE-ADVOCATE:

Question. In stating that the available force was 45,000 men are we to understand it to include the two divisions that were added at Nashville after the army was massed there?

No, sir; in estimating the effective force 45,000 men I included our own command when we made the junction with General Mitchel's force at Huntsville and in that region. The two divisions from General Grant's army alluded to in the question joined us on or about September 1. The first division from General Grant's army joined the main column of General Buell's troops at Murfreesborough and the second division alluded to in the question reached Nashville a few days after the main body of General Buell's troops had left. I do not remember exactly the strength of the division of General Grant's army which joined us at Murfreesborough, but from my impression I think it amounted to about 5,000 men, which would have made our troops at that point after that junction about 50,000.

Question. Do you say that the two divisions only made about 5,000 men?

No, sir; the division that joined us at Murfreesborough. I did not see the other division, as they arrived at Nashville after I left.

Question. This 50,000, then, does not include the forces under Morgan at Cumberland Gap or the force stretched along the line to protect the communication?

This estimated force did not include Morgan's force at Cumberland Gap nor the troops north of the Cumberland River.

Question. At the time the various repairs were ordered on the railroads you enumerated was it not known that the lack of sufficient rolling stock would prevent this road being of use in supplying the army?

While our troops were repairing and on the march to Huntsville I inquired of Colonel Fry, chief of staff of General Buell, about the prospect of supplies when we reached Huntsville, and if I remember aright I think he told me that they had assurances from General Mitchel of the most encouraging kind; that with the wagons General Mitchel then had he (General Mitchel) thought he could supply a force of about 25,000 men. In order to make the supply more certain a large train of wagons had been sent from Tuscumbia, under the escort of cavalry, up to Reynolds' Station, on the Nashville and Decatur road, to assist in wagoning supplies around the break. This was done several times before the head of the column left Florence. As to the fact of the rolling stock not being sufficient to supply the troops after the railroad should be completed being known or not I am not aware, having been from about the 1st of April to the middle of June in and about Northern Mississippi.

Question. Were not the wagon and railroad trains used by General Mitchel's army to carry cotton confined to return trains, which would have been otherwise empty; and was not this explained in a satis factory manner to the Government?

The knowledge about the use of General Mitchel's wagons in carrying cotton which I gathered by inquiries was as follows:

Between Athens and Huntsville the wagons were used in bringing cotton to sundry railway stations. Cotton was hauled northward between Reynolds' Station and Athens on the return trip of the army wagons, which I consider a detriment to the service, because a bale of cotton weighing on an average 500 pounds, and generally putting about three or four bales in those wagons, made the return trip of the wagons as arduous and as wearing on the mules as the trip southward loaded with subsistence, and I urged that such transportation of cotton be suspended to enable the mules to get the rest by coming back empty. As for the explanation rendered by General Mitchel for so using the wagons I have no knowledge of it, and merely know that the condition of affairs in using these wagons induced the order which I have mentioned in my previous testimony about restricting the use of army wagons for army purposes only and restricting the transportation of cotton by railway where it interfered with Government supplies.

Question. Do you know what became of the slaves pressed into the service of the Government for the repairs of railways after such repairs were completed?

I cannot tell of their ultimate fate except of what I saw myself. A great many of them were sent to Nashville to assist in erecting the fortifications there, and on the line of march northward and along the Chattanooga Railroad, both by rail and by wagon road, they received every facility for being sent northward with the troops. Large crowds of them were on the railway trains, picked up from the stations as we relinquished them, and I saw a great many going north in wagons by the country roads about the same time that the troops were on the march. I know that there was a great sympathy felt for them by officers and soldiers and a general desire to help them along.

Question. Do you know of any orders issued in reference to that subject?

No, sir.

Question. In saying that the produce trade between Nashville and Cincinnati is very extensive, do you mean to say that this is confined to Middle Tennessee or Tennessee at all, or is it not rather that the Nashville trade extends throughout the whole South?

I have no doubt that other States besides Tennessee derived their supplies from Nashville, but I am satisfied that such shipments were made to Nashville for the benefit of Tennessee, because in time of peace they found it more profitable to raise cotton than grain as a general thing.

Question. Do you not know that the published statistics, such as those of 1850, made by the Government, show that the counties of Middle Tennessee and East Tennessee give a very large surplus in grain and produce of that sort?

I am not aware of that fact; but the fact of a region raising more produce than is requisite for the supply of the inhabitants thereof does not involve that it should be impossible for that region to import large supplies.

Question. Did the troops when put upon half rations suffer?

That I am unable to say. I was told, however, as a general thing, that they eked out as much as they wished to eat by living on the green corn.

Question. Did they not in fact live better than when they had full rations?

I do not know; but I would state that it was a by-word in the army that a soldier in full health cannot well eat the full rations allowed by the Government.

Question. State briefly the amount of subsistence in Nashville after the Army of the Ohio was massed there and all the supplies you enumerated had been brought in.

In my testimony the other day I gave the amount that was on hand September 1, and I stated the supplies were sent there by rail, and what each division had when they went into Nashville, which all summed up was the amount of supplies then in Nashville after the army had got there. I have my own report to Colonel Fry, dated September 4, and I have the report of the chief commissary in Nashville, dated two days before, so that would give a very accurate report.

Question. Does that include the number of rations of beans and mixed vegetables, said to be 1,217,888?

In Captain Macfeely's report of stores on hand in Nashville, dated September 2, he gives the number of rations of beans 100,000 and of mixed vegetables 200,000. McCook's train, having taken in 40,000 rations complete, must have had 40,000 rations of beans, but they had no mixed vegetables. General Thomas' train had 35,000 rations of beans. It does not amount to the quantity stated in the judge-advocate's question. The quantity of small rations was largely inferior to the essential rations—meat and bread.

Question. Does your statement made in your evidence in chief include 98,306 rations of tea and coffee?

Captain Macfeely's statement does not mention coffee; it mentions 300,000 rations of tea.

Question. If on August 31 there were on hand in Nashville 86,437 rations of meat, would not the days you speak of increase that largely beyond the amount you stated in your examination-in-chief?

Of all the salt meat taken into Nashville by the troops I do not think there was any left there, because I know there was a scarcity among the troops. It was not increased.

Question. Is the Commission to understand from that that there were no meat rations brought in by these various divisions to be added to the 86,437 rations?

None of any consequence of salt meat, but we left all the cattle on the hoof that we could spare.

Question. Does your statement of the subsistence on hand on the 2d September include the 106,039 rations of sugar?

It does not.

Question. Does it represent the 1,002,808 rations of mixed vegetables, not including the beans, pease, and rice enumerated in the number already stated?

It does not.

Question. Does it include the 223,144 rations of molasses.

It does not.

Question. If the number of bread rations was 527,786 on August 31 in Nashville, and represented to be 826,796 on September 30, how do you account for the difference?

On September 2, two or three days after August 31, Captain Macfeely reports 1,000,000 rations of breadstuffs on hand, which would account for part, and the troops on their arrival at Nashville had about 600,000 rations of breadstuffs.

Question. Do you consider a statement which leaves out such important items one of sufficient accuracy to make up an estimate as to what the subsistence of the army really was?

Yes, sir; because such articles as molasses and rice cannot be well used on a march, and Captain Macfeely in his statement mentioned only the leading articles.

Question. Are not beans, sugar, and coffee leading articles?

As to beans, yes, sir; but Captain Macfeely in his statement mentions beans and tea. From his not mentioning coffee I suppose the quantity must have been very small.

Question. Is the Commission to understand that the halt of four or five days at Bowling Green was owing solely to the lack of subsistence?

I have no doubt it partly was, because we consumed that time in getting in the wheat and flour. Besides this, the labor of loading the wagons with supplies consumed a great deal of time, and troops were necessary to guard the forage trains.

Question. Were the other halts, amounting in all to four or five days, between Nashville and Munfordville, owing to the same cause?

I do not know.

Question. Was not the Nashville and Louisville Railroad in operation from Louisville as far as Bowling Green at the time our advance guard reached Bowling Green?

The trains did not come through for several days, on account of the fear of guerrillas. I do not know the exact day when the last train left Louisville for Bowling Green.

Question. Did you not know that the railroad was in operation as far as Munfordville, and that soldiers were sent there to re-enforce that point after their arrival at Bowling Green by rail?

I heard so; but the rebel troops occupied positions on the railroad between Munfordville and Bowling Green.

Question. Had the four or five days, or the ten days in all, been used to secure Munfordville and the railroad, would you not have been in a better position in regard to supplies than in gathering them up all over the country near Bowling Green?

I am unable to say. Such an attempt may not have been successful or it may have been impossible.

Question. Was your information of such a character that you could say positively that the Army of the Ohio was not demoralized in its march from Bowling Green to Louisville?

I can only judge from my own impression and the feelings of my brother officers that at no time did they feel more buoyant with the hope and expectation of meeting the enemy.

Question. If out of twenty officers examined upon that subject of the Army of the Ohio not one could be found to dispute the fact that the army was demoralized, is your information of such a character that you could venture to dispute it?

I should say if there was demoralization I did not see it, nor do I think there was.

Question. Can you give any instance from your own observation in the service where the rebel inhabitants voluntarily furnished the rebel army with supplies other than those you have alluded to in Tennessee and Kentucky?

In Western Virginia the rebel sympathizers freely gave the guerrillas subsistence.

Question. Guerrillas were in a position to help themselves. Can you give an instance where the army was voluntarily supplied by the inhabitants in Western Virginia?

No, sir.

General BUELL. The judge-advocate in his cross-examination has touched upon some points which were not embraced in the examination-in-chief. Under the established rules governing the proceedings of military courts I should be allowed to examine the witness upon those points. The arbitrary rule which you have established precludes me from doing so unless by special permission. I have perhaps half a dozen questions I should like to ask the witness.

The JUDGE-ADVOCATE. If I have gone outside the examination-in-chief in this examination I shall make no objections to General Buell's additional questions, but I should like General Buell to state what those points were.

General BUELL. The departure from the limits embraced in the examination-in-chief is as to the time occupied by the army in the march from Nashville to Munfordville, and the witness may be able to give some information which you have not exactly upon your record in reference to that.

The JUDGE-ADVOCATE. I cannot admit that I went outside of my examination in that. The witness stated positively that the army stopped for lack of supplies between Munfordville and Nashville.

General BUELL. There was no attempt made in the examination-in-chief to explain a delay of four or five days at Bowling Green and a delay of four or five days between Bowling Green and Munfordville, a period of about ten days, which the judge-advocate has endeavored to explain by his cross-examination. I wish only to question the witness in reference to the dates of the arrival and departure of the army at several places.

The JUDGE-ADVOCATE. That we have already before us in the evidence of other witnesses. The only object in the cross-examination of Colonel Darr was to test the accuracy of his knowledge in reference to the facts he has given the Commission. As to the dates and the delays and the number of days on the march, that is already before the Commission, and I doubt if Colonel Darr could add anything new upon the subject.

General BUELL. If the Commission desire any further information upon this subject they may perhaps adopt my questions. I have no desire to put them myself.

The court was then cleared; when, upon motion whether the rule relating to the re-examination of witnesses should be suspended, it was decided in the negative.

By General DANA:

Question. How many days' halt of the Army of the Ohio was there between Nashville and Munfordville altogether?

I do not remember exactly. We arrived at Bowling Green the same day on which Munfordville was attacked by the rebels. As fast as the flour came in the troops were supplied and commenced moving. I think I was four or five days in Bowling Green while the troops were marching, but I think we halted two days at Prewitt's Knob; not exactly halted, but the headquarters halted. I can tell about the time that was consumed in marching from Nashville to Munfordville. We arrived at Bowling Green on the 14th, and I think that day week we arrived at Munfordville.

The witness was then dismissed.

General BUELL. I made application for all the signal officers. There seems to have been some difficulty about procuring their attendance. The judge-advocate expressed himself as satisfied that no message was received at headquarters during the day of the Perryville battle. I made this application upon the statement of Colonel McCook, who said in his testimony that he was under the impression that a message had been sent through the signal station giving information of the attack upon General McCook's corps, and also upon a statement in a published letter of Colonel McCook which I saw subsequently. The judge-advocate has said to me, and I suppose has said to the Commission also, that he was satisfied that no such message had been transmitted to headquarters, and that it does not desire further evidence upon that point. I understand that one of the members of the Commission is not satisfied.

One of the signal officers is now present, and in order to satisfy that member as far as possible I propose to examine him for further evidence on this point.

General TYLER. I have no particular desire for further evidence on this point. If the judge-advocate or General Buell so desire it may be obtained by deposition; that is, as to whether any messages were sent by the signal corps on that day.

The JUDGE-ADVOCATE. After examining that matter very carefully I satisfied myself that no message had been sent to General Buell by the signal corps on the day of the Perryville fight. General Buell has called witnesses since to that effect, and I will further state that no such message reached him, and upon that assurance being conveyed to General Tyler I understood him to say that he desired no further evidence upon that matter.

General TYLER. I yield my doubt on this point that no message was received by General Buell on the day of the battle of Perryville.

The attendance of Lieutenant Sheridan was not required, because it was acceded by the Commission that no such message was received by General Buell on the day of the battle of Perryville.

The JUDGE-ADVOCATE. Although there are yet Major-General Wright and Colonel Fry whom it is proposed to examine for the defense, I propose to examine, through questions reduced to writing, a certain number of witnesses as rebutting evidence. In accordance with the rule established I propose, although General Buell is not through, to state what witnesses I shall call and the points on which I wish to examine them and what I expect to prove by them. I propose to call Colonel De Courcy, to show that the testimony offered through Major-General Granger that East Tennessee could not be invaded successfully from Central Kentucky is erroneous.

General BUELL. Does the judge-advocate propose to examine that witness by deposition?

The JUDGE-ADVOCATE. Yes, sir; that is, by questions and cross-interrogatories by yourself at the same time.

General BUELL. I shall object to the introduction of testimony upon that question, upon the ground that it is not necessary and does not go to rebut anything that has been introduced in the defense. If it is claimed that my instructions restricted General Morgan from invading Eastern Tennessee farther than he did, those instructions will appear in the documentary evidence. The question of the invasion or the farther advance of General Morgan into Eastern Tennessee was introduced by the judge-advocate himself or by a member of the Commission, and I notified the Commission at the time of the wide field that was opened by this question. It is not possible that it could be fully explained by the testimony of one witness, and especially by the examination of that one witness in the manner proposed. I shall object to the introduction of this witness upon the broad ground that his testimony is not necessary to rebut any new matter that has been introduced in the defense. It was undoubtedly one of the subjects open to the investigation of the Commission at the beginning, and if it was to be introduced at all it should have been introduced in the inquiry on the part of the Government before the judge-advocate had ceased.

The JUDGE-ADVOCATE. General Buell hardly states the proposition that gives me the right to examine witnesses in rebutting evidence. I am not confined to new matter, as is well established in law governing rebutting evidence, but it is incumbent upon me to say that it has been introduced by General Buell in his defense; for I claim that in asking

General Gordon Granger as to the possibility or the practicability of invading Eastern Tennessee from Kentucky by the way of Cumberland Gap General Buell opened the way to this inquiry, and that I have an entire right to show that it was practicable and could have been done but for the instructions that retarded General Morgan.

General BUELL. The judge-advocate in stating the proposition with reference to introducing rebutting evidence may be accurate in so far as it has reference to civil courts, but the rule of proceeding is altogether different before military tribunals. My examination of General Granger upon the practicability of invading Eastern Tennessee by way of Cumberland Gap had reference to a different time and different circumstances altogether. The time to which the investigation which the judge-advocate proposes to enter upon applies is the time when General Morgan was in possession of Cumberland Gap with a small force. The time to which my inquiry applies was after the battle of Perryville, and had reference to the movement of a large army into East Tennessee. The time and the circumstances are all different.

The judge-advocate reads from General Gordon Granger's examination:

CINCINNATI, *February* 17, 1863.

By General BUELL:

Question. Have you had occasion in your official position to study the problem of throwing a force into East Tennessee from Central Kentucky?

Yes, sir; it is a matter to which I have given a good deal of study and reflection, and abandoned it as impracticable.

Question. In the course of your investigations what have you learned to be the character of the country and its agricultural resources between Somerset and East Tennessee directly across the mountains?

The character of the country is altogether mountainous.

General BUELL. The testimony which the judge-advocate proposes to introduce now has reference to the movements of the forces which were actually in East Tennessee. My examination of General Granger was in reference to the movement of a force across the mountains to Central Kentucky. There is not the slightest connection between them. In my question to General Granger there is nothing which refers to the force that was at Cumberland Gap under General Morgan. The examination had reference to the movements of the Army of the Ohio into East Tennessee after the battle of Perryville; a thing which I have heard has been supposed by some persons to have been possible.

The PRESIDENT. What is the question upon which the judge-advocate proposes to introduce the witness?

The JUDGE-ADVOCATE. I propose to examine Colonel De Courcy, who was with General Morgan, upon the possibility of having seized and held East Tennessee at the time General Morgan was in possession of Cumberland Gap and to ascertain the reasons why it was not done.

The PRESIDENT. You propose to show by this witness that it was practicable?

The JUDGE-ADVOCATE. Yes, sir. It was eminently practicable; it was a thing that could have been done, General Granger to the contrary notwithstanding.

General BUELL. General Granger did not answer at all with reference to what General Morgan might have done. General Granger's answer has no reference to that case at all.

General DANA. I should like to place on record my reasons for voting against the introduction of this witness: First, that it is in no form to be considered rebutting evidence, on account of the difference and distinction made by General Buell himself between the statements of the case at two different times; secondly, although it is a question which might properly have come before the Commission at the beginning of its labors, when General Buell could have introduced such testimony on that subject as he might have seen fit, it would at this stage of the proceedings be manifestly unjust to open a new investigation on new points, when the rule of the court not only prevents him from introducing testimony on that point, but if the court permitted it it would be impracticable for him to do so; and, thirdly, if the testimony were proper and the subject proper at the present time the proper witness would be General Morgan and not Colonel De Courcy.

The PRESIDENT. 1 would suggest that the judge-advocate alter the phraseology of his question so as to show if the invasion and occupation of East Tennessee from Central Kentucky was practicable.

The JUDGE-ADVOCATE. In showing that the thing might have been done of course I showed its practicability, and what I meant was to meet the question that was opened by General Buell in his questions to General Granger as to whether it was practicable to seize and hold Eastern Tennessee from that direction.

The court was opened; when the judge-advocate said that he had altered the proposition so as to bring it more within the rule and then read the proposition as altered.

General BUELL. I shall continue my objection to the question, and for the same reasons in general terms that I have previously stated. The examination of General Granger upon this point, it will be seen, evidently has reference to the practicability of the country between Central Kentucky and Eastern Tennessee—the mountainous region, that is, as to the practicability of throwing a large army into that country. The first question put to General Granger in reference to it is as to whether he has studied the problem of throwing a force into East Tennessee from Central Kentucky, and he answers that he has studied it and had abandoned it as impracticable. He studied it, of course, under the circumstances that existed at the time; it was a matter of consequence to him, and he answers as to its practicability with a view to those circumstances. It must be evident that he did not intend to say that it was impossible to march a force to East Tennessee, because the fact is before the country that a force had actually marched into East Tennessee and held possession of a point in that country for some weeks, perhaps some months. He answers as to the practicability with reference to the circumstances which he studied. The question which follows leads to the object of my inquiry; it was as to the character of the country and its agricultural resources between Somerset and East Tennessee, directly across the mountains, and the testimony goes on in reference to that. The judge-advocate has better evidence than any opinion that can be expressed by Colonel De Courcy, or any other witness, as to the practicability of doing what the judge-advocate says was practicable, and which the command of which Colonel De Courcy formed a part actually did. It is an established fact that that column marched to East Tennessee, and it is not necessary to produce evidence to show that it was practicable to do it; so that the proposition as the judge-advocate has shaped it is not less new matter than it was before; but, more than that, it is a mere shift to get at something which is not expressed in his new proposition.

The JUDGE-ADVOCATE. I hope General Buell will not indulge in reflections attributing it to any such motive.

General BUELL. I do not impute it to any motive which the judge-advocate has not himself expressed. For my own part I do not hesitate to say that General Morgan would have been captured bodily in less than ten days from the time he reached Knoxville, and I claim to know as much about the matter as Colonel De Courcy. I have seen so much disappointed valor in the course of my experience in this war that I am a little skeptical in regard to it.

The court being cleared; on motion whether Colonel De Courcy should be summoned to appear before the Commission the votes were—ayes: President, General Tyler; no: General Dana.

The PRESIDENT. I wish to explain my vote. I vote affirmatively for the reason that General Buell, in asking such a question of General Granger, brought out an opinion from that gentleman which is now upon the record, which opinion is that such an invasion of East Tennessee from Central Kentucky was altogether impracticable, and that this is a conclusion which General Granger has arrived at from long and profound study of that military problem. Such an opinion from so distinguished an officer being upon record, General Buell has the advantage of it, and for that reason it is nothing but fair that the judge-advocate should have the privilege of showing by a person who testifies from personal observation and personal experience that such an invasion would have been practicable.

Court opened.

The JUDGE-ADVOCATE. I propose to call Governor Johnson, of Tennessee, to examine him as to the policy exercised by General Buell toward Nashville, North Tennessee, and Northern Alabama, and what the effect of that policy was in furthering the purposes of the Government.

General DANA. I propose that Governor Johnson be summoned before the Commission at Baltimore and that his evidence may not be taken by deposition.

General BUELL. I shall not object to the presence of Governor Johnson before the Commission upon any question whatever. I do complain that he has not been brought before the Commission before; it was practicable to do so at Nashville and it has been practicable since. I have urged it upon the Commission, and I will venture to say that no good reason can be advanced why he has not been before the Commission before. I shall, however, object to any testimony by deposition.

The JUDGE-ADVOCATE. I could not tell, Mr. President, of what importance or of what significance Governor Johnson's testimony would be till I heard the defense. In that defense I find there is much in the knowledge of Governor Johnson, in the shape of rebutting evidence, that is important for us to have, and on that account I propose to bring him before the Commission.

The judge-advocate is directed by the President to summon Governor Johnson to appear before the Commission at Baltimore.

The questions to be submitted to Governor Johnson were then read to the Commission.

General TYLER. I move that Governor Johnson be subpœnaed to appear before this Commission if his personal attendance can be obtained; and, if not, that the judge-advocate be directed to obtain his deposition upon the subject-matter stated in the questions just read.

The questions to be submitted to Major Wright were then read to the Commission.

The JUDGE-ADVOCATE. I propose to call Major-General Wright to state what he knows of the capture of Munfordville by the forces under Bragg, and why that post, being in his department at the time, was not sufficiently re enforced by him, or why Colonel Wilder was not ordered to evacuate in time to prevent a capture.

General DANA. I move that the same instructions be given the judge-advocate as were given in the case of Governor Johnson.

General BUELL. I could object to the introduction of General Wright as a witness upon the ground that the matter should have been a subject of investigation in the original proceeding of the Commission. I complain that Major-General Wright was not called at the proper time. I shall object to so much of the questions of the judge-advocate as he may propound to him in regard to the strength of the rebel army after the battle of Perryville, for the reason that he should have exhausted the evidence he had upon that subject before he closed his case.

The JUDGE-ADVOCATE. I wish to recall Mr. J. H. Cooper, of Lexington.

The questions it was proposed to submit to Mr. Cooper were here read by the judge-advocate.

General BUELL. I do not object to General Wright being called, because there is matter that should have been explained by his testimony in the first instance. I complain that he was not examined at the proper time. I object to recalling this witness, Mr. Cooper, because in the first place it is not new matter upon which it is proposed to examine him. It is matter that should have been exhausted by the judge-advocate before he closed his case for the Government. I object to it also upon the ground that I have been precluded from calling witnesses that would have testified in reference to the matter that it is proposed to examine this witness upon.

The JUDGE-ADVOCATE. I wish to call attention to the last statement of General Buell and say that he has not been precluded from calling witnesses who would have testified to the matter on which it is proposed to examine Mr. Cooper. It is not upon this point. I was willing to admit that the fact was well substantiated as to Kirby Smith's forces; it is as to the strength of Bragg's army after the junction of Kirby Smith's forces that I want settled.

General BUELL. The evidence of Mr. Cosby, whom I requested should be summoned, would have testified as to the strength of the rebel army. Every witness I named would have testified to the strength of that army after the battle of Perryville.

The JUDGE-ADVOCATE. I admitted that they would swear to what was the strength of the whole force of the rebel army.

General BUELL. I made no distinct statement as to what I expected to prove by these witnesses. I only stated the subject on which I wished to examine them.

The court was then cleared; when, on motion whether Mr. Cooper should be recalled, it was decided in the affirmative.

On the opening of the court the questions were read by the judge-advocate which it was proposed to submit to Col. L. C. Houk.

General BUELL. I have no doubt that the evidence of Colonel Houk would be most invaluable. I understand that he is a most intelligent and refined man and I should be delighted to have him before the Commission, but I object to his testimony in the way proposed. I shall particularly object taking his evidence by deposition after he has been kept here, as I understand, for months, when he could have been examined during that time as well as at any other.

On the court being cleared, it was decided by vote of the Commission that the testimony of Col. L. C. Houk should be taken by deposition.

On the opening of the court the questions to be submitted to Captain Mussey were read by the judge-advocate.

General BUELL. I shall object to this witness for the reasons I have stated generally in reference to others.

The PRESIDENT. Who is this Captain Brent, referred to in the questions? Is his evidence of any importance; and, if so, is it not new matter?

The JUDGE-ADVOCATE. It is respecting a matter which has come to my notice since this investigation commenced. I do not attach much importance to it. The drift of it is that the condition of things at Munfordville was known to the commander-in-chief.

The court was then cleared; when, on motion that Captain Mussey's evidence should be taken by deposition, it was decided in the affirmative.

General BUELL. I understand that he is now actually in the city; do you propose to call him before the Commission?

The JUDGE-ADVOCATE. No, sir; I propose to receive his evidence by deposition.

General BUELL. Is it pretended that this witness has been here only since the prosecution was closed?

The JUDGE-ADVOCATE. Yes, sir; I have had no opportunity of examining him since he has been here.

General BUELL. Has he not been here all the time?

The JUDGE-ADVOCATE. All the time that the defense has been going on.

General BUELL. It appears to me that I saw an officer of that name when we first came to this city. If I remember rightly, he has been hovering about the Commission room from its first sitting here.

The JUDGE-ADVOCATE. You cannot mistake him when you once see him.

The PRESIDENT. Do I understand you that you have tried to introduce him.

The JUDGE-ADVOCATE. No, sir; I had no right to introduce him at the time I had him at my command here; that is, while the defense was going on.

General BUELL. I state to the Commission that I believe this officer has been in the city here from the very beginning of your session in this city.

The JUDGE-ADVOCATE. That, I believe, is a mistake, general; at least if he was it was without my knowledge. When he first came to me I told him the defense was going on and that I could not examine him.

The PRESIDENT. When did you send out the subpœna for him?

The JUDGE-ADVOCATE. I do not recollect the precise date.

General BUELL. I request, then, that this witness, as he is here to testify, be called before the Commission.

The JUDGE-ADVOCATE. I do not think his evidence is so important as to delay the Commission in its movements, and if General Buell insists upon it that the witness shall be brought into court, and if it is going to delay the Commission, I shall dispense with his examination altogether.

The PRESIDENT. If the witness is here in the city I see no reason why his deposition should be taken. The philosophy of taking depositions is to obtain evidence in the necessary absence of a witness, when it is impossible to obtain his personal attendance through sickness or any similar cause. I never heard of a deposition taken from a witness who was in attendance.

General BUELL. I think as good reasons could be given for Governor Johnson's presence before the Commission. Who is to decide in such a case?

The PRESIDENT. We must apply to the Secretary of War.

General BUELL. I take it for granted if it is left to Governor Johnson that he will not appear before the Commission.

The PRESIDENT. It is proposed to ask for an order for his appearance.

The JUDGE-ADVOCATE. There has been a good deal of the evidence that was expected from Captain Mussey, as to the time taken up in the marches from Corinth to Chattanooga, that has come out in evidence of witnesses examined since Captain Mussey has been here. It was deemed the most important part of his testimony, and I am not disposed to delay the Commission for his examination.

General BUELL. There is one point, with reference to the demoralization of the army, on which I should like him to be examined. I should like to find the man who can specify the grounds upon which he gives such evidence. If Captain Mussey can do it I shall be very glad to see him.

It was decided by the Commission to dispense with the examination of Captain Mussey.

The JUDGE-ADVOCATE. I propose to take the evidence of Mr. Brownlow (commonly known as Parson Brownlow) on the resources of East Tennessee and the character of the Sequatchie Valley and the roads leading out of it into Middle Tennessee.

General BUELL. If Parson Brownlow is brought before the Commission I shall not object to his appearance. I shall object to him otherwise. The information it is proposed to obtain I am very desirous the Commission should have, but I object to taking his testimony in the manner proposed.

The court was cleared; when, on motion, it was unanimously resolved to take the testimony of Mr. Brownlow by deposition.

The JUDGE-ADVOCATE. I propose, in addition to the witnesses already enumerated, to take the evidence of Colonel Loomis (of Loomis' battery), now at Murfreesborough, by deposition, as to the character of the Sequatchie Valley and the roads leading out of it into Middle Tennessee.

General BUELL. The only objection I shall make is as to giving his testimony by deposition.

The court was cleared; when, on motion, it was unanimously resolved to obtain the testimony of Colonel Loomis by deposition.

General DANA then moved—

In order to give the judge-advocate time to attend to his documentary matters and to prepare the necessary interrogatories for the witnesses, that we adjourn to meet on Wednesday next, April 10, [?] at Baltimore, at 12 o'clock.

On being put to the vote it was carried unanimously.

CINCINNATI, *Friday, March* 27, 1863.

The Commission met pursuant to adjournment. Members present, General Wallace, General Dana, General Tyler; also the judge-advocate and General Buell.

Col. J. D. BINGHAM (a witness for the defense), being duly sworn by the judge-advocate, testified as follows:

By General BUELL:

Question. Will you state your name and position in the service of the United States, if you please?

J. D. Bingham; lieutenant-colonel, and quartermaster of the Seventeenth Army Corps.

Question. State whether you have recently been on duty in Tennessee, at what place, and between what dates; state in what capacity also.

I have been on duty as depot quartermaster in Nashville, Tenn., from March 4, 1862, till March 19, 1863.

Question. Has it been your duty to acquaint yourself and have you acquainted yourself with the resources of the country about Nashville for those supplies which are required for the subsistence of an army?

It has been my duty to obtain that information, and I have obtained it as far as I could from inquiries throughout the country near Nashville.

Question. State what the condition of the country was during the last summer in that respect.

The supplies for an army in the vicinity of Nashville during the summer were very limited, as far I could ascertain. There were only two localities in which I could hear of supplies of any account.

Question. Go into the particulars, if you please, and state what you know in regard to that matter.

About the last of May I advertised for proposals for furnishing forage at the depot at Nashville. I received no bids in answer to the advertisement. I then applied to those who were represented to be acquainted with the country to know if they thought any supplies of forage could be obtained, and was informed that very little could be obtained near the city. Williamson County was represented as having a quantity of forage; the highest estimate that was placed upon it was 50,000 bushels of corn. I was informed that people were afraid to sell to agents of the Government, which probably was the reason I received no bids. I afterward ascertained there was forage and bacon and flour in Robertson County. I believe the estimated quantity in Robertson County was about the same as in Williamson County. Springfield, the county town of Robertson County, was about 40 miles distant from Nashville. Franklin, the county town of Williamson County, was about 18 miles from Nashville. I obtained from Williamson County about 28,000 bushels of corn and from the vicinity of Nashville about 8,000 bushels. I was informed by a quartermaster at Columbia, about 60 miles, I think, from Nashville, that hay could be obtained in that vicinity. I told him to purchase all that he could, but I never ascertained the amount purchased. Those were the only localities I heard of in which supplies could be obtained in that part of the State in any quantity.

Question. State whether proper means were used by your department to procure the supplies which could be obtained from the country; state what efforts you did use.

I sent agents throughout Williamson County and the country around Nashville to purchase all the forage that could be obtained. Where the people were afraid of known agents of the Government I sent agents who were not known to be such to purchase and forward to points on the railroad all the forage they could buy. I did not send agents into Robertson County until the guerrillas appeared in the counties south of the Cumberland River, when forage trains were sent into Robertson County to bring in what forage they could find on the north side of the river. I selected as agents people who were acquainted with the country and used every exertion to get forage in as rapidly as possible. The people were represented as afraid to sell to agents of the Government, for the reason that the guerrillas had threatened the destruction of their property if they were detected in furnishing any supplies to the troops of the United States.

Question. By what other means did you obtain supplies of forage for the army?

By requisitions on the depot at Louisville.

Question. And with what success?

The supplies could not be brought forward as rapidly as required. As an example, I remember one requisition that I sent in amounting to 5,000,000 pounds of grain. I received only 500,000 pounds.

Question. Do you know what means were used to forward supplies from Louisville and the cause of the failure to send them as rapidly as were required?

The supplies were forwarded over the Louisville and Nashville Railroad, and by boats of light draught to Clarksville, on the Cumberland River. I sent all the boats of light draught I could obtain at Nashville to Clarksville to bring forward supplies from that point. Boats that I could use to advantage over the Harpeth Shoals ranged in draught from 11 to 16 inches. The low stage of water in the Cumberland River was one cause of the delay in forwarding supplies from Louisville; and, as near as I could ascertain, the cause of the delay on the Louisville and Nashville Railroad was owing to the company not rendering available their total rolling stock on the road as far as possible for Government purposes.

Question. Do you know of any omission of the proper instructions from the commander of the Army of the Ohio or want of proper energy on the part of the staff officers in urging forward supplies into Nashville during the last summer or in collecting them from the country?

I received instructions frequently during the summer to bring forward and collect supplies for the quartermaster's department. I saw instructions to the same effect to the depot commissary at Nashville from the Headquarters of the Army of the Ohio. To my own personal knowledge, as far it extends, every exertion was made by the officers of the staff to accumulate supplies at the Nashville depot.

Question. Up to what time did you continue to use the Cumberland River for the transportation of supplies?

Up to about the 18th of August, the day Clarksville was captured by the enemy.

Question. What was the amount of freight you could receive in that way up to that time?

When I commenced using boats in June they could bring up eighty tons each from Clarksville. The river fell daily, and the quantity was reduced to such an extent that some boats could only bring eight or ten tons at a load. At the time Clarksville was captured I was sending horses down to the Shoals to tow the freight across in flat-boats.

Question. At what time do you consider the navigation of the river closed for all practical purposes in consequence of low water?

I think about the middle of July. The quantity of freight received by the river at that time scarcely justified the attempt to bring it up.

Question. Do you know at what date the railroad communication with Louisville was permanently broken?

I do not remember exactly the date, but I think between the 21st and the 31st of August.

Question. Do you know anything about the resources of the country about Nashville in regard to subsistence for the troops?

I heard of subsistence stores in Robertson County, consisting of bacon and flour, and I think I heard of some flour at Gallatin. Those were the only localities in which I heard subsistence stores could be obtained. Flour was also obtained from Gallatin during the summer; I think also from Robertson County. The bacon was principally obtained by the foraging parties that were sent out.

Question. How does the army in Tennessee obtain its supplies now?

Principally by the Cumberland River. Some Government supplies are received over the Louisville and Nashville Railroad.

Question. Is the forage for the army procured in that way?

At present I believe almost all the forage is procured by the way of the river. I believe during the month of January and part of February the forage for the army was obtained in the vicinity of Murfreesborough from the country; at least so I was informed, and we forwarded very little during that time from Nashville.

Question. How have the resources of the country during this spring and winter compared in abundance with what they were during the last summer?

I do not know, for the reason that no supplies have been obtained from the country about Nashville for the depot; some forage has been obtained from Kentucky in the counties bordering on Tennessee. It was impossible to send out to obtain forage around Nashville, in consequence of the country being infested by guerrillas, except by trains sent out with large escorts.

Question. To what extent was that the case last summer?

The guerrillas did not appear troublesome in the country about Nashville until about the time of the capture of Murfreesborough, which I think was between the 1st and 10th of July. After that no forage could be obtained beyond 5 or 6 miles from the city, except by sending trains under escort. The railroads were held after that time, a forage continued to be brought in from stations along those roads.

Cross-examination by the JUDGE-ADVOCATE:

Question. The country about Nashville that you have described is very productive, is it not?

Yes, sir.

Question. How did you pay for the supplies; cash down or give a certificate?

I paid cash down.

Question. The difficulty in obtaining supplies, I understand, did not originate from the lack of them in the country as much as from the fear the people had of guerrillas?

That was in the localities where I was informed forage could be obtained. In other localities that were not mentioned as having contained any quantity of forage none was procured until the new crop came in.

Question. In purchasing supplies from the country did you require the oath of allegiance before paying for them?

I did not up to the 22d of August; at that time I received instructions to give accounts bearing the conditions for payment, to be settled hereafter as the Government may direct.

Question. Did not our forces in Nashville at that time live unusually well while upon half rations and depending upon the country for supplies?

I do not know much about the way in which they lived. From information I obtained from reports I believe that they obtained large numbers of articles from the country, such as chickens, turkeys, geese, pigs, and sheep by the foraging parties during the blockade.

Question. How long have you been in the service, colonel?

Since 1854.

Question. What is your age now?

Thirty-one years.

General BUELL. I wish to ask the witness a few questions, Mr. President, on points which the judge-advocate has introduced in his cross-examination.

The PRESIDENT. What are the questions, general?

General BUELL. I wish to ask the witness first whether the orders requiring him to give accounts facilitated or embarrassed him in procuring supplies.

The JUDGE-ADVOCATE. I have no objection to that question if the Commission sees fit to suspend the rules.

The PRESIDENT. You have another question, general?

General BUELL. I wish to ask the witness whether these supplies that were procured by foraging parties, such as turkeys, geese, chickens, pigs, sheep, &c., were the results of plunder.

The PRESIDENT. What does the Commission say?

General TYLER. I move that the court be cleared.

General BUELL. I will withdraw the question.

The JUDGE-ADVOCATE. If the court will permit I will ask the first question General Buell suggested.

General BUELL. I object to the judge-advocate asking the question. I desire to ask it myself.

The court was cleared; when, on motion, it was decided that the rule should not be suspended.

The witness was then dismissed.

Col. MARC MUNDY (a witness for the defense), being duly sworn by the judge-advocate, testified as follows:

By General BUELL:

Question. Colonel, state your name and position in the service of the United States.

Marc Mundy; colonel Twenty-third Regiment Kentucky Infantry.

Question. Were you on duty with the Army of the Ohio in Middle Tennessee last summer? If so, state where, for how long a time, and the different localities.

I was on duty with the Army of the Ohio in Middle Tennessee. I was first ordered from Nashville with a squadron of cavalry and my regiment of infantry to occupy Lebanon, Tenn. That was in the spring. I remained at Lebanon some six weeks. I went from there to Murfreesborough, and during the month of May—I cannot give the exact date—I went with my regiment and a section of artillery and 500 cavalry to Pulaski, Tenn., where I remained till about the 4th of July. After being relieved from court-martial duty at Huntsville I rejoined my command at McMinnville some time in August. I remained with the Fourth Division of the army until it returned to Louisville, Ky., where it arrived about the last of September or the beginning of October.

Question. How long were you at McMinnville?

I was at McMinnville altogether about two weeks. I should state that I was at McMinnville three times. I went from McMinnville to Altamont and returned to McMinnville. I then went from McMinnville to Murfreesborough and returned to McMinnville, and then returned from that place to Murfreesborough.

Question. In what condition did you find the country around McMinnville in regard to supplies for subsistence and forage for the army?

Subsistence of every kind was very scarce; not enough to supply the army by any means. There was no forage except green corn and hay, and the corn was too green for the use of our stock at the time I speak of. Roasting-ears were about ripe enough for the use of the men, but too green for horses. There was some hay. We had to rely upon our subsistence department at Murfreesborough for our supplies entirely, except as to the green corn we got from the country. My command had only half rations while at McMinnville, owing to the difficulty of getting supplies down from Murfreesborough. I saw few, if any, cattle. Those I saw were not fit for use—what we Kentuckians call "scrubs," big-headed cattle, very poor and small. Hogs were also very scarce. I know it was with great difficulty we could keep our division supplied with the necessaries of life. I mean the Fourth Division, under the command of General Ammen. I saw no wheat there. The wheat crop had been gathered, I suppose, but I understood there was very little wheat in the country; in fact the country had the appearance of having been cleared out before I got there.

Question. Is it a productive country about McMinnville; how does it compare with the rich country of Central Kentucky?

It compares very poorly with the rich country of Central Kentucky. I should judge the soil is very thin. The corn crop was what I should call a very light crop. The land between McMinnville and Altamont, at the foot of the mountain, is pretty generally cultivated in what might be called the valleys, but produces comparatively little. Between McMinnville and Murfreesborough the country is not so good until you reach near Murfreesborough. To the north and east of McMinnville the country is hilly and broken, and you might almost call it a sterile country. I do not think they produce at the outside more than four or five barrels of corn to the acre from their land in their best seasons, whereas our best land in Kentucky produces from fifteen to twenty-five barrels to the acre.

Question. Describe the topography of the country about McMinnville, as far as you are acquainted with it.

To describe the part over which I went first, as you go from McMinnville toward Altamont, the country, till you reach the foot of the mountains, may be called a level country; there are very few, and those small, hills. To the northwest, toward Murfreesborough, the country is somewhat broken, but comparatively level. I have already said that on the northeast it is hilly and broken, and directly to the east it is a mountainous country and the knobs come to within two or three miles of McMinnville. There is a stream of water running by the town. I do not remember the name of it. When I was there it was a season of drought, but there was some running water in this stream, abundant for our men and stock. I think the mountain knob spoken of to the east of McMinnville is about two or three miles from the limits of the town. The roads about McMinnville are generally good; the one toward, I think, Manchester—at all events it is the one we went on toward Altamont—is a fine open road, and the one toward Murfreesborough is a good road. The road leading toward Smithfield is also a good road near the town. I have never been out far up that road.

Question. What is the character of this stream you speak of as passing near the town?

It is what might be called a large creek or small river. It is dammed at the town for mill purposes. It is clear, nice water. It is not deep; it may be forded except in the dam, and even across the dam I have forded it. In visiting the pickets and outposts I have ridden across the river at any point where I struck it; the water was not higher than to my horse's knees when I forded it.

Question. Is there anything in the topography of that country that would make it necessary for an army coming across the mountains from the south to pass through that particular point? Could it be avoided on either side at the option of the advancing army?

The country is open enough for an army to pass and avoid the town; it is not necessary that they should go through it. I do not know the state of the roads except those leading into the town.

Question. Do you know anything of the country about Sparta?

I have no personal knowledge of it.

Question. Please look at this order (General Orders, No. 13a) and state whether you recognize it as embodying the policy which was to be adopted by the troops under my command toward the people of the country in which we were operating.

Yes, sir; that is the order of which I received a copy, and I was governed by it.

Question. Was it the practice in that order to treat all persons alike, loyal and disloyal?

It was not my practice, sir. I made a great distinction between loyal and disloyal persons. The loyal persons I treated with every consideration and kindness. Disloyal ones, who were stirring up the people by denouncing our Government, in some instances I sent them through our lines to the Southern Confederacy, in other instances I put them under heavy bonds, and in some instances I compelled them to take the oath or go to prison. I did not make a distinction between citizens upon mere questions of sentiment. The distinction was made from their course of conduct and conversation.

Question. State what the effect of that policy was, colonel, upon the temper of the people, as far as your observation extended. State anything you know in illustration.

The policy was considered a just one, and he effect was beneficial as far as my experience goes. When I first went to Lebanon there were quite a number of what I call rabid rebels in the neighborhood who were exasperating the people very much, some of whom I imprisoned and some of them I sent through the lines. I warned them, however, by public notice that all who would behave themselves like good citizens should be protected. The policy I pursued at Lebanon had the effect of ridding the community of some very bad men and developed a very strong loyal sentiment. I had the approval of some of the best men in that part of Tennessee of the course I was pursuing; among others I would mention Ex-Governor Campbell, Mr. Jordan Stokes, and Col. William [B.] Stokes. The same policy I pursued at Pulaski when I first went there. I found the sum total of our Union men there amounted to two in the whole country. I pursued the same line of policy, having given the citizens notice that I was not there to war upon unarmed people, but to protect all who in their civil pursuits behaved themselves. After giving this warning to them I treated the people kindly, remedied some wrongs they were suffering, protected them from the marauding of the teamsters and trains that were passing through there, who were depredating very largely upon the people. I published an order forbidding any depredations upon the citizens, forbidding them from taking their property except by my authority, as I was instructed by General Buell's order No. 13.

In my intercourse with the people there I found the masses had been largely duped by their leaders in being led to believe that our purpose in coming into Tennessee was to take away all their civil rights and destroy their domestic relations. I permitted the country people to come into the town freely, in order that I might communicate with them more freely, and I discovered that while they were generally rebels they had been made so by falsehood. The policy I pursued made a practical contradiction to what had been taught them by their leaders, and the result in a short time was that they gained confidence in my course of procedure, and they themselves proposed that we should have what they called a county meeting, in order that all the people might hear my policy from my own lips.

I called a county meeting at their suggestion and invited the citizens to meet me at Pulaski. I was very agreeably surprised to find that we had a very large audience of citizens from every part of the country. I spoke to them in their court-house and assured them as I already had done by my order. The result of the meeting was that many of them declared themselves openly in favor of the restoration of the Union, and they themselves called another meeting of the people of Pulaski. At the second meeting Governor Neil S. Brown made them a speech, in which he publicly declared that his policy was changed and that he was then a Union man. He explained to them the impositions that had been practiced upon them, and at the end of the meeting they passed resolutions unanimously resolving to return to the Union and abandon the cause of the Southern Confederacy. A great many of the younger portion of the community in private conversation with me explained how they had been led away by the rebels assuring them that we were not only come there to take away their property, but to ravish their wives and daughters and do everything else that could be suggested that was bad. They expressed a great anxiety to return to their loyalty, feeling convinced that they had been deceived from the policy I was pursuing and the way I was treating them, but expressed fears that some leading men in the community who were bitter secessionists would mark them and have them punished by the Southern Confederacy.

To relieve these fears I summoned these gentlemen before me, frankly told them the apprehensions of the community, and insisted upon it that they should take the oath of allegiance and commit themselves in that way, so as to relieve the apprehensions of the community, or leave Pulaski and go to the Southern Confederacy. I think I summoned twenty of them, and perhaps all but six took the oath of allegiance and publicly proclaimed themselves for the Union. The six I sent through to General Beauregard. I think two of them were preachers. Having relieved the community of these men that they were afraid of, there was no longer any hesitation in declaring their Union sentiments, and I am satisfied that four-fifths of all the men in the country—fully four-fifths—returned to their loyalty and would have been glad to reconstruct the Union.

I advised Governor Johnson of the state of feeling and urged him to reorganize the State government by a popular election. We had considerable correspondence about the matter. He expressed great satisfaction at the result of my demonstrations at Pulaski, but declined to reconstruct the State government until all the rebels were out of Tennessee. He adopted another policy of mine and authorized me to proceed in it, which was to make the citizens of Pulaski reimburse the loyal men there whose goods had been seized in a rebel raid under Morgan, then Colonel Morgan. I had a commission organized, damages assessed, and made the citizens pay the money over. I believe that if the same policy had been pursued throughout Tennessee the loyalty of the people of Tennessee, which is overshadowed by the fears of the Southern leaders, would have been developed throughout the whole State. The people at

Pulaski had been much outraged by the depredations of these teamsters, and they seemed much gratified at the policy I pursued in relieving them from those wrongs. I think that of itself had great influence on the minds of the masses. I found the masses of the people of Tennessee were exceedingly ignorant, and depended entirely for their information upon their public speakers, the stump speakers, as they are called, which accounts for their gullibility by their leaders. Quite a large proportion of them I found could not read or write, and they necessarily relied upon their public speakers for all their information.

Question. Do you know any marked case of a departure from this policy by portions of our troops in the country they were occupying? If so, please mention the case and the effect.

Yes, sir; I know of one very aggravated case at Athens, Ala., in which a portion of troops under General Mitchel's command, the Third Division, plundered the people at Athens, robbed their store-houses and residences, making no distinction between those who were loyal and those who were disloyal, which exasperated the people of Athens very much. The people in North Alabama, particularly at Athens, had been considered a loyal people, insomuch that they kept the American flag flying at Athens until about the time General Mitchel's command went through to Huntsville.

The JUDGE-ADVOCATE. Colonel, you will confine yourself to the question.

The WITNESS. I am stating that they were loyal to show the effect upon them of such depredations.

The JUDGE-ADVOCATE. If it was the mere plunder of soldiers and not done by the authority of the officers it is not answering the question General Buell asked you.

The PRESIDENT. The rule is there should be no interference with the examination.

The JUDGE-ADVOCATE. The question is correct enough, but the witness is not answering the question.

The WITNESS. This plundering was done in the immediate presence of the officers who were commanding those troops, some commissioned officers taking part in it.

General TYLER. Did you see it, colonel?

No, sir; but it is testimony given me in court-martial under oath and from almost all the citizens of Athens who were present. I have it also from some of the officers who were themselves present and censured the commanding officer very much because he did not check them. The result of this was to estrange most of the citizens from our cause. They said to me themselves that they had lost confidence in our Government when they found they were subject to be plundered by our army. They complained bitterly that they had withstood the threats and supplications of the Southern rebels to join them and had been loyal to the Government, and yet their town was to be sacked and they were to be plundered because some rebels happened to make a raid into their town and drive out some Union soldiers. The people there also complained that these officers had taken away their horses without compensation or giving them any vouchers by which they might afterward obtain compensation. Other cases of departure from the rule I do not know of except those teamsters I spoke of, who plundered every man who lived on the road from Columbia, Tenn., to Athens, Ala. I know of one case which was reported to me which caused me to arrest the parties and send them to General Mitchel, in which they took all the bacon out of a man's smoke-house—some 6,000 pounds—drove his negroes off his place, and broke up all the furniture in his house. That was at the Elk River Crossing. When the men along the road who had been plundered found they would be protected by me they were pretty generally reconciled, expressed themselves in favor of the Union, and privately gave me advice of rebel bushwhackers and guerrillas who were prowling in the neighborhood. This Third Division had plundered the people.

The JUDGE-ADVOCATE. Mr. President, I object to this mode of examination, and I ask that this witness may be confined in his answer to the question that is asked him. The witness is asked what was the effect of certain departures from what is known as a conciliatory policy—a policy which recognizes the civil rights of the people who may openly sympathize with the rebellion and give aid and comfort to the enemy, but who are not found in arms; the opposite policy to which is that a people freely sympathizing with the enemy and giving aid and comfort to the rebels have no rights which the Government is bound to respect; but it does not follow that in pursuing either policy officers and soldiers guilty of such offenses as murder, rape, arson, and plunder may not be punished or can be said to have departed from either policy, and in giving instances of such offenses the witness is wide of the question asked him by General Buell.

General BUELL. In questioning this witness I have not spoken of a conciliatory or of a harsh policy. I have simply put before the witness an order which announced to my troops the rule of action by which they were to be governed. There are in fact two policies which may be pursued. One is that of justice and a reasonable respect for the rights of the people in whose country we are operating as far as is consistent with the success and efficiency of our military operations, and the other is one of plunder and pillage. If a country is laid under discretional and unrestricted contributions by authority, it will be plundered by individuals without authority. The testimony of the witness as to what was the result with respect to the condition of things at Pulaski is an exemplification of the policy I attempted to pursue and did enforce as far as I could. The proceedings of our troops at Athens were exactly the result of the other policy, and they are just such results as have followed wherever the policy of no rights to the people of the States in rebellion, " or living upon the enemy " as it is called, has been tolerated. I wish to exemplify the difference, and I request that the witness may be permitted to continue his evidence.

The JUDGE-ADVOCATE. If the witness is brought here to show the effect of unauthorized plunder and pillage on the part of the troops I answer that it is unnecessary, as the Government is prepared to admit it. I do not find in any orders issued from Washington permission to plunder, but it has been announced from headquarters at Washington that where a man is found in arms against the Government and giving aid and comfort to the enemy he has no rights which the Government is bound to respect, and his property may be taken, but in a legal and proper method, not by plunder and pillage. There are two courses which may be pursued, one only of which is authorized by the Government. Now if this witness merely shows that plundering, &c., is a bad policy, his testimony is unnecessary, for no one doubts it.

General BUELL. If it is necessary to show the propriety of the testimony which the witness is giving I think it would not be a difficult matter to establish before this Commission that the case which the witness has described is precisely the result of the reverse of that policy which I have insisted upon wherever I have commanded. It is undoubtedly true that the Government does not sanction such proceedings, and it must be assumed that they are the very reverse of what the Government desires to enforce, and that the men who have favored the free use of rebel property for public purposes would be as much outraged at the conduct which results from that course as anybody is; nevertheless that is the result, and it is a result which not only outrages humanity but trammels and impairs the efficiency of our armies.

The PRESIDENT. Is the point that you raise, colonel, whether the witness should be allowed to proceed further with this line of testimony?

The JUDGE-ADVOCATE. Yes, sir; I object to it for the reasons I have stated.

The court was cleared; when, after discussion, it was decided that the witness should be allowed to proceed with his testimony.

On the court being opened Colonel Mundy continued:

From Columbia to Athens they took their forage, for which they neither paid them nor gave them vouchers, and took their furniture out of their houses. I reported the matter to General Mitchel at Huntsville, and put the train-master under arrest, and sent him back to Huntsville to General Mitchel, and reported to him what I had done. That was as the train went down to Huntsville. In a few days afterward I found the same train-master with the train returning, which astonished me. I rearrested him at once upon their complaints of depredations he had committed upon that trip and reported the matter to General Mitchel again. He replied to me by telegraph to attend to my own business. I replied to him that it was my business, and that I intended to hang the man, under authority of the order of General Buell. The order did not give me authority to hang, only to check depredations and plunder. I reconsidered it, however, and sent the man back to Huntsville under arrest. I never knew what became of him afterward; he never came over my road any more. Under the aggravations of these depredations I found that our telegraph line was being cut continually, our railroad was being torn up, and bridges burned.

When I put a stop to the depredations the teamsters as well as the citizens found I was in earnest about it. I found that the citizens were freely disposed to give me notice of those who were interrupting our railroad and telegraphic communication; they freely supplied my hospitals with necessities gratuitously, and behaved generally as a loyal and Christian people. I now remember something more of that man: his name was Proctor; he afterward fell into the hands of General Buell, who ordered his trial by court-martial, but he escaped from the provost guard, and I do not know what became of him since. I might also say I had the sanction of Governor Johnson in pursuing this policy, who by proclamation advised the same as was recommended in General Buell's order. I reported the arrest of these citizens to Governor Johnson, with the reasons, and told him what I purposed to do; he approved of it, and directed me to proceed, but subsequently he relented so far as Colonel Jones was concerned, who was a member of the Southern Congress, and ordered me to permit him to remain in Pulaski.

By General BUELL:

Question. Was there any change in the disposition of this Colonel Jones that you speak of?

Well, sir, I cannot say as to that. If he talked any after that he did it so quietly that it did not come to my ears.

Question. Are any active demonstrations of loyalty to be expected from the people of the South so long as they have organized armies in their midst which control their actions and to a considerable extent their opinions also?

We cannot expect any demonstrations of loyalty from the people there unless we can assure them of protection against the rebel armies and guerrillas. I found that the great fear in the minds of the people in that portion of Tennessee where I held command. Those about Pulaski who were disposed to come out openly for the Union said to me that they feared they would be marked and destroyed by the rebels for it. If they were to incautiously develop the Union sentiment, and they had no protection from our forces and our Government it would be to seal their doom. I know of two cases near Pulaski where citizens who had declared themselves for the Union were hung by the guerrillas and left hanging in the woods. Their wives came to me to Pulaski and reported the facts. I afterward sent an officer with a party of men to have them decently taken care of and to search for the guerrillas till they could find them. I did not find them; if I had I should have retaliated by hanging them.

Question. In either event from which policy do you think the Government would derive most strength, the policy which is embodied in the order I have submitted to you or one which pays no regard to the private rights of the people among whom our armies operated?

In expressing an opinion based upon my experience with them I am satisfied that the policy of General Buell is the true one. I do believe that the whole of Tennessee could be restored to the Union by a strict pursuance of that policy. I might say the same thing for North Alabama. I had a great deal of intercourse with the people of both sections. I believe that the true policy of the Government to bring this war to a successful issue would be to pursue a course where the rights of the people would be respected and to disenthrall them from their leaders. Prisoners from the Army of Corinth who fell into my hands at Pulaski assured me that thousands of the soldiers from Tennessee, Kentucky, North Alabama, Arkansas, and North Carolina were disgusted with the war and would go back to their allegiance, but that they believed they would be shown no quarter and that their property as well as themselves would be destroyed. They seemed greatly surprised to find that I was not burning the houses, seizing the property, and ravishing the women in the neighborhood where I was in command. They said that representations of such procedures by all our officers were circulated in the Southern Army in order to keep alive the hatred and enmity.

Question. Do you know what measures were taken to punish the persons who committed those depredations about Athens which you have referred to?

They were arrested and tried by court-martial and punished according to the judgment of the court.

Question. What officers were punished in that way; how many were brought to trial, as near as you remember, and by whose orders were they brought to trial and punishment?

Colonel Turchin, who commanded the brigade, was dismissed by court-martial. Colonel Gazlay, who was commanding a regiment in the brigade, was also dismissed by court-martial. Captain Edgarton, who commanded a battery in the brigade, was tried, but acquitted, because it was shown that he acted by direct authority of his superior officer. Colonel Mihalotzy, who commanded a regiment in the brigade, was also tried by court-martial and punished. I do not remember what the punishment was; as he showed that he was acting by the authority of his superior officer, Colonel Turchin, the punishment, if any, was light. They were arrested and tried by the order of General Buell. Colonel Stanley was also tried, but I believe he was acquitted. I think the prosecution against him was abandoned. He showed that what he did was by authority of his superior officer, Colonel Turchin, and there was nothing to criminate him personally. These are all I remember now of the officers of that brigade who were tried.

Question. What effect did these disciplinary measures have upon the temper of the troops who were concerned in those depredations and others who sympathized with them toward the commander of the army?

I heard officers express great bitterness toward the commander of the army. I never heard private soldiers make any remarks about it, but I know the soldiers usually take their tone from their officers, and I have no doubt but what it embittered them against the commander of the army also.

Question. What comments were made upon those measures by the public press throughout the country generally?

The JUDGE-ADVOCATE. I object to that question. We are certainly traveling outside of our record. I do not see what the press has to do with the matter under investigation.

General BUELL. I think the judge-advocate is mistaken. Our record is a pretty comprehensive one; the subject is certainly a very comprehensive one. I wish to give some explanation of whatever ill temper may have existed in the army toward its commander. That is a matter which has been admitted already, and the question is pertinent to it. I will show how it is if the witness can be permitted to go on.

The court being cleared; on motion, it was decided that the objection should be sustained.

By General BUELL:

Question. Can you point to any circumstances in connection with these depredations and the measures that were adopted to punish them that were calculated to impair the authority of the commander of the army and to produce insubordination in its ranks?

The JUDGE-ADVOCATE. I object to that question, Mr. President. I have charged that after the army left Nashville, in falling back upon Louisville, it was demoralized, and witnesses have been before the

Commission who have said that they believed the army had lost confidence in its commander. Any evidence brought to bear upon that fact would be in order, but the witness should not be allowed to travel outside of the time specified by the Government in its charge. I am prepared to admit that up to the time to which the question refers the army had entire confidence in General Buell, believed in him, and sustained him as their commander, and that no general ever stood higher in the estimation of his troops than did General Buell.

General BUELL. And I wish to show that that confidence continued, if it ever existed, and that it was the tone of the public press and the censure passed upon the commander of the army for the measures now under consideration which encouraged that spirit of ill-will which can be found in any and every army, and is ready at any opportunity to express itself insubordinately with reference to its commander.

The court was cleared; when, after discussion, it was decided that the objection should not be sustained.

The WITNESS. Yes, sir; the dissatisfaction of the officers who were tried and their friends, as expressed both in the army and the criticisms of the public press, both upon General Buell and his court-martial, no doubt sowed the seeds of insubordination. I saw in some Northern papers, I think a Chicago paper——

The JUDGE-ADVOCATE. This is precisely the response that was ruled out here and I object to it now.

The PRESIDENT. If the witness states what any particular paper said it would bring his answer within the objection that was sustained to General Buell's former question.

General BUELL. I do not understand that the Commission meant to rule out anything I might introduce to establish the proposition I stated to you a few minutes ago.

The PRESIDENT. I would state, general, that the Commission had no objection to your showing any circumstances which were calculated to produce dissatisfaction and insubordination among your troops or alienate their confidence in yourself; but what this or that paper says the Commission would hardly think proper to admit as testimony. For instance, if the witness, in stating the circumstances that called forth the insubordination referred to in the question, should state that the tone and spirit of the public press commenting upon that affair were calculated to produce dissatisfaction and insubordination, such testimony would be perfectly proper.

General BUELL. I should think, sir, you were wrong in that. What would be objectionable in the evidence would be a general opinion. I should suppose it would be preferable that he should state the ground upon which he based his opinion, that the Commission might judge for itself whether the opinion was well founded or not.

The PRESIDENT. The decision of the Commission is as I have stated.

General BUELL. I wish, then, to put upon record that I desire not so much to call out the opinions of the witness as to establish the facts upon which those opinions might be based.

The PRESIDENT. The Commission has no objection to the witness proving facts; on the contrary, they expressly ruled that he should be allowed to state facts, and to show what those were on which he based his opinion. Among other facts may be enumerated the tone or spirit of the public press in its comments upon the affair you have alluded to.

General BUELL. I cannot understand, sir, the reason for the objection. The witness has given his opinion, and it seems to me to be very proper that he should give the reasons upon which he bases that opinion. So far from expecting that the Commission would stop him in his statement of the facts of the case, I should rather have expected that they would require him to give the explanation. It appears to me that it would be necessary to give his testimony substantial value; otherwise it is a mere expression of his own opinion.

The JUDGE-ADVOCATE. I object to the testimony offered for two reasons. In the first place, it is inadmissible unless General Buell can connect it with the time when it is charged by the Government that the army was demoralized; in other words, he is attempting to show that his army was demoralized when its *morale* was good; that is, at the time the press was commenting upon the trial of Colonel Turchin. In the second place, unless the witness connects the public press with the army and shows that these articles were read in the army and influenced it at the time that the Government charges the demoralization to have occurred it certainly is outside the case.

General BUELL. I have no doubt, sir, that the effects of these comments of the public press upon the army can be established very easily. I do not agree with the judge-advocate that it can be brought down to a particular point of time; he has not shown nor has he attempted to show that it commenced at any particular point of time or had reference to any particular act of mine.

The JUDGE-ADVOCATE. I would say that in this General Buell is mistaken. The question has been asked as to the *morale* of the army after it fell back from Nashville, and the testimony given has been confined to the condition of the army at that time, and the witnesses introduced by the Government have shown that the discipline and drill of the army previous to that period were excellent.

The court was cleared; when, after discussion, it was decided that the objection should be sustained.

On the opening of the court General Buell informed the Commission that Mr. Brownlow was at his home at Newport or Covington, and requested that his testimony should be given before the Commission instead of being received by deposition.

The court then adjourned to meet on Saturday, March 28, at 10 o'clock a. m.

CINCINNATI, *Saturday, March* 28, 1863.

The Commission met pursuant to adjournment. Members present, General Wallace, General Dana, and General Tyler; also the judge-advocate and General Buell.

Colonel MUNDY's examination continued.

By General BUELL :

Question. Were newspapers freely circulated in the camps of the army while we were in Tennessee last summer?

Yes, sir.

Question. Name the papers that were most frequently seen among the troops.

We had frequently the Cincinnati Times, Gazette, Commercial, Louisville Journal, and I frequently saw Pennsylvania papers. We also had Chicago papers, and many papers published in little inland towns, that came to soldiers from those localities. I remember the Cincinnati papers, because they came more directly to my camp than other papers. We also used to have the Nashville Union. There was quite an abundance of newspapers, though I cannot now give the names of all of them.

Question. Can you name all the Chicago papers that you saw frequently?

There was the Chicago Tribune and perhaps the Chicago Times. I cannot remember distinctly if that is the name of it.

Question. Were these papers unanimous in their condemnation of the commander of the Army of the Ohio?

Those that spoke of the conduct of the commander of the army particularly, with, I think the exception of the Louisville Journal, criticised his course severely. I do not mean to say that all these papers I have named spoke of the conduct of the commander of the army, but those that did, with the single exception of the Louisville Journal, spoke of it in condemnatory terms.

Question. What was generally the burden of this condemnation? And mention, if you please, those papers that indulged in it most freely.

I cannot give the exact language of any papers, nor can I specify which papers were most severe. The Chicago papers, I remember, condemned him very bitterly for his punishment of Colonel Turchin. The burden of complaint in the papers was this: that General Buell was protecting the people, rather than punishing them, generally; that he did not devastate the country and destroy all the rebel sympathizers, and that he treated the people generally too kindly; I mean the people of Tennessee and Alabama. In other words, they seemed to advocate what they called a "vigorous war policy," by which they seemed to mean general devastation.

Question. Did this sort of criticism have a good effect or a bad effect upon the temper of the troops and the discipline of the army?

I think it sowed the seeds of demoralization. I remember another thing which gave me a great deal of trouble in controlling my command. It was the general applause of the press for the orders and policy pursued by General Pope in Virginia, which the troops and papers construed into a right on the part of our soldiers to appropriate all the rebel goods they could find, to make themselves as comfortable as possible, and destroy the resources of the enemy. I know that many of our soldiers practiced the policy pretty freely, and I had great trouble and difficulty in restraining my own. I restrained mine not so much to protect the property of the people as to preserve the discipline of the troops, and in obedience to General Orders, No. 13, because that required me to do it.

Question. Have you any knowledge of the extent of the straggling that took place in the army after the march from Louisville in the pursuit of the rebel army? If you have, please state all you know about it.

Yes, sir; about the time we reached Louisville I suffered from a very violent hemorrhage, which incapacited me from field duty, and I was ordered to report to General Boyle for duty. I reported to him immediately. I think it was the same day or the day afterward I was enabled to get up to him, and not being able for specific duty he assigned me to the general superintendence of military affairs about Louisville under himself. Citizens from all the roads over which our army had gone out came in with constant complaints that the country was full of stragglers, who were committing all kinds of depredations upon them. I sent out cavalry patrols on all the roads, who gathered up a great many stragglers near the city of Louisville, some of whom they brought back to Louisville and some they sent forward to overtake their respective columns. These complaints were coming in continually until after the battle of Perryville. I have no idea now of the extent or the number of stragglers, except from the universal complaint from every part of the country between Louisville and Perryville. I know that during the month of November, when I had been assigned a command at the barracks at Louisville, I sent forward to Nashville over 5,000 and I sent forward during December about 4,000. This embraced not only stragglers, but a few convalescents sent from Louisville. The stragglers that I gathered up in the country were principally from new regiments, but a great many from our old regiments had gone home from Louisville. I remember in my own regiment, which was encamped in the island, surrounded by water and a strong guard, when ordered to march from Louisville toward Perryville left 125 guns in the stacks, and yet I had used every precaution, with a strong guard, to keep them in camp. I found afterward, by interrogating some of them that were captured, that they had waded and swum the Ohio River across the falls after night to get home. I sent out detachments as I had organized them in the city for recapturing them on the roads, under officers, with instructions to pick up all they could find and carry them to their commands.

Question. What was the cause of the large amount of absence with-out leave from the Army of the Ohio after its arrival at Louisville and while it remained there?

I think the principal cause was the desire of the soldiers to get home to see their families, from whom they had been absent a long while.

Question. Did they subsequently return to Louisville for the purpose of joining their regiments while the army was in front about Perryville and beyond there?

A great many of them did, sir. A great many of my own regiment returned within four or five days, took their guns, and went up to join their regiment. I made the detachment up and sent them forward under officers, with instructions to gather up stragglers on the road. I made them up largely from men who returned in that way, as being most reliable, adding to them the stragglers that I had gathered up by my cavalry patrol.

Question. What was the cause of the great amount of straggling from the army after it left Louisville to advance against the enemy?

I suppose there were two or three causes, one of which was they did not care much about fighting; another was they wanted to make use of the opportunity to plunder the people of the country. I suppose some straggling was the result of want of ability on the part of the new troops to keep up in the march, as they were raw, inexperienced, undrilled, and undisciplined; but if I should judge by the complaints that came in, I should say that the principal cause for the straggling was the great desire for plunder. I say this because I remember that when I took occasion to lecture some officers for the misdeeds of their commands they gave me to understand that they were in an enemy's country and had a right to plunder the people.

Question. Was this straggling to be ascribed to demoralization in the army or was it due to the want of discipline in the raw troops?

I may say it was done almost exclusively by the new troops, and therefore could not be from demoralization, but from want of discipline.

Question. In what manner was the march conducted from Nashville to Louisville; was it an orderly march or a disorderly one; were the troops obedient and under control; was there a great amount of straggling and were there desertions—any of those incidents which indicate demoralization in an army?

I consider the march to have been a very orderly one and generally well conducted. There was some straggling—comparatively little, however—and perhaps there may have been a few desertions, but, if so, they were very few. I have no doubt that some Kentucky troops as they reached the locality of their homes took occasion to go home to see their families; I know that a few did, because before we reached Louisville I saw some three or four who had stopped about Bowling Green and afterward came up and overtook the column. There was some complaint during the march of the fatigues incident thereto owing to the scarcity of water, the heat, and the great amount of dust. I think those three things combined made it the most terrible march that soldiers ever did make in this country. The troops were obedient and under control, and, I might add, under thorough discipline. There are always a few exceptions in every command, and there were in this army. I heard much more complaint from officers than from men. I do not mean to say complaint of the fatigues of the march and its hardships, but complaint against their commanding officer. I do not mean to specify the names of the officers; perhaps it would be improper to do so; but while our corps was lying at Horse Well, beyond Munfordville, I heard officers who outranked me publicly censure the conduct of General Buell, and one of the officers, major of a regiment, made a speech to his men, in which he questioned the loyal purposes of General Buell and censured his course of conduct. I was not near enough to catch the exact language used, but could hear the applause with which his men greeted his remarks. It was very near the headquarters of the commander of the brigade. I took occasion to say that if I commanded the brigade I would have put the officer in irons, which I would have done. I consider this demoralizing to a great extent, unbecoming in an officer, and injurious to the service.

Question. From what State did this regiment come in which this oc curred?

It was the Thirty-sixth Indiana Infantry.

Question. From what State did the officer come who commanded that brigade?

Indiana, sir; he was the colonel of the Thirty-sixth Indiana and commanded the brigade to which I was attached.

Question. Has that officer since been promoted?

The JUDGE-ADVOCATE. I object to that question. I do not see its purpose or what it has to do with this investigation.

After an explanation from the witness that he could not answer the question the judge-advocate withdrew the objection.

I do not know about the promotion of the commander of the brigade; the major that was is now the colonel of another regiment.

By General BUELL:

Question. Did you ever see an article published in the Indianapolis Journal which counseled the soldiers of the Army of the Ohio to take the life of their commander?

The JUDGE-ADVOCATE. I object to that question, Mr. President. It is hardly necessary to repeat what has already been said with respect to this outside matter.

The court was cleared; when, after discussion, it was decided that the objection be sustained.

By General BUELL:

Question. Do you know whether the Indianapolis Journal is recognized as expressing generally the sentiments of Governor Morton upon questions of public policy and the conduct of public officers, particu larly those concerned in the direction of the armies of the West?

The JUDGE-ADVOCATE. I object to that question also, Mr. Presi dent.

The court was cleared; when it was decided that the objection be sustained.

By General BUELL:

Question. Have you ever seen published in any newspaper a report of a public reception given to Colonel Turchin, at which in a speech he animadverted in terms of censure upon the conduct of the commander of the Army of the Ohio, and which was got up for the purpose of commending his conduct about Athens and at which the conduct of the commander of the Army of the Ohio in bringing him to punishment was denounced and received with hisses and groans?

The JUDGE-ADVOCATE. I object to that question, Mr. President.

The PRESIDENT. I should like to hear what the general has to say.

General BUELL. I have nothing to say, sir.

The PRESIDENT. Let the court be cleared.

As General BUELL was about retiring he remarked:

In order to show that I am not asking these questions simply at random and for the purpose of occupying time I will say that which I have expresed before, that I am bringing this matter forward to show what influences were brought to bear upon the army to produce demoralization if it could be produced by any means on earth.

The court was cleared. On being reopened it was announced that the objection was sustained.

Cross-examination by the JUDGE-ADVOCATE:

Question. What independent commands have you held since you have been in the service, colonel, and what were the specific duties attached to them?

First, the command of my own regiment. Then I was in command at Lexington, Ky., I think a month, with my own regiment. I was afterward at Rolling Fork, I think, for two or three weeks. I was next in command at Lebanon, Tenn., with my own regiment and a portion of the Seventh or Ninth (I forget which) Pennsylvania Cavalry. Subsequently I was in command at Pulaski, Tenn., with my own regiment, a large portion of the First Kentucky Cavalry, and a section of the First Kentucky Artillery. None of these commands can be said to be independent. I was always subject to the orders of my superior officers. This is, however, while I have been doing detached duty from my division. My regiment was not assigned to a division until, I think, about July last, when it was assigned to the Fourth and exchanged for the Seventeenth Kentucky.

Question. Is not McMinnville naturally a strong position, looking toward an enemy approaching from the Sequatchie Valley?

I should not call it a strong position; it has no natural defenses. It is overlooked by the knobs of the mountains, which lie on the east and within easy range of artillery. It is otherwise surrounded by an open country and acessible at almost any point, and I know that the commander of my division expressed great concern while there that the whole division would be gobbled up. The creek or river which runs near the town would be no defense, for the two reasons it is too near the town, and secondly you can cross it at almost any point. It would not retard the progress of troops at any point who wanted to make a dash over it.

Question. Do I understand from that answer that there is no position near and covering McMinnville from an approaching enemy coming from the Sequatchie Valley that is not naturally a strong position?

There are places where an army could be intrenched near McMinnville, but one of the great elements of strength—that is, sufficient supplies—would be wanting, and I therefore consider McMinnville to be a weak point in the general acceptation of the term.

Question. I understand you, then, that lacking supplies it is a weak point, but with supplies it is a strong position?

No, sir; I would not call it a strong position even with supplies, but an army might be intrenched near McMinnville so as to resist an assault of an equal force. I do not know how accessible the mountains are that look down upon McMinnville from a personal survey. I understand there is a road leading up the mountain from McMinnville, but a difficult road to pass. If an army were intrenched upon that mountain, with sufficient supplies to hold it, it would be in a very strong position. There are hills and a hilly country toward Woodbury, on the Murfreesborough road, where an army could intrench itself and make a stout resistance. There is, however, a scarcity of water, which would make that point objectionable. If intrenched on the knob of which I have spoken it might be supplied with water from the creek or river which runs at the base of it.

Question. How would you regard the opinion of such an officer as Major-General Thomas on that subject?

I would most certainly defer to his opinion.

Question. Do you not regard murder, rape, and plunder as the violation of a policy rather than a policy itself?

Most certainly I do. The practice of murder and rape could not be the furtherance of a policy, because the law expressly forbids them and affixes a penalty for them. To plunder an enemy may be considered as furthering a policy, but which I conceive to be a very bad policy; not so much on the enemy's account as because of its demoralizing effects upon the force that is permitted to plunder.

Question. Do you know of any policy inaugurated in this war which authorizes the plundering of the enemy?

Not under my construction of it, sir; but I know that plundering has been justified by officers as high or higher in command than myself, in pursuing a policy promulgated by General Pope in Virginia I thought to have been sanctioned by the administration.

Question. Please confine yourself to the question.

That is answering it fully. My view of it is that I do not think it authorized me to plunder anybody.

Question. What do you understand, then, to be the difference between what is known as a "conciliatory policy" and a "vigorous war policy"?

In answering that I must give the opinion of others.

Question. I ask you for your own, colonel.

In order fully to explain my construction of the two policies, a vigorous war policy, as generally understood in the army to which I have been attached, means the adoption of all means and measures not only to crush out the rebellion but to punish indiscriminately all persons who live in a rebellious territory. A conciliatory policy, as I understand it, means a vigorous prosecution of the war against the rebels in arms, an entire respect for the civil rights of those not in arms, and protection to the loyal and innocent.

Question. Is not that difference simply this: that in what is called a vigorous war policy the man in arms, or sympathizing or giving aid and comfort in any way to the rebellion organized against his Government, is considered to have no rights that that Government is bound to respect; while a conciliatory policy recognizes the civil rights of people who openly sympathize and give aid and comfort to the enemy but are not in arms?

No, sir; as I understand it a vigorous war policy not only wars upon those in arms and who sympathize and who give aid and comfort to the enemy, but would practice devastation and would destroy the very germ of rebellion. The conciliatory policy does not excuse those who openly sympathize with the rebellion and give it aid and comfort, but it silences the sympathizer or punishes him. Those who give aid and comfort they regard as rebels and treat them accordingly, but it defers to the law to punish by its established rules those who sympathize and who give aid and comfort to the enemy rather than resort to the strong arm of military authority. That is the difference, I understand, between them.

Question. Was or was not the Army of the Ohio demoralized?

Until the Army of the Ohio reached Louisville I should say that it was not demoralized; it certainly was inoculated with some demoralizing tendencies which I tried to explain in my direct examination, but having been detached from that army at Louisville I cannot speak of its subsequent character.

Question. Then the punishment of certain officers for plundering and the publication of certain newspaper articles had no effect upon the army until it reached Louisville?

It had not the effect of destroying the authority of the commander of the army, though that it had some effect there is no question, and that is what I mean by demoralizing tendencies.

Question. I understand you to say that they had an evil tendency, but not far enough to make the officers discontented or to demoralize the men?

I think until we reached Louisville the discontent was confined in a great measure to the officers; the discontent, however, of the officers did not reach to the point of insubordination, but expended itself in grumbling against the commanding general, and which in my opinion operated badly upon the men.

Question. Did you ever read an article in the Cincinnati Enquirer reflecting severely upon General Buell?

General Tyler having objected to the question it was withdrawn.

The witness was then dismissed.

The JUDGE-ADVOCATE. I would suggest that it is now a proper time for the introduction of such documentary evidence as General Buell wishes to bring before the Commission on the part of the defense. I have not had the privilege of seeing it, but I have been informed that General Buell has such documentary evidence.

General BUELL. I called the attention of the Commission yesterday to the fact that some of the witnesses whom the judge-advocate has been permitted to call for rebutting evidence are within reach of the Commission now. I mentioned Parson Brownlow and General Wright.

The PRESIDENT. An order has been issued to call Parson Brownlow before the Commission.

General BUELL. General Wright is in attendance.

The PRESIDENT. Do I understand that General Buell is through with his witnesses ?

General BUELL. No, sir.

General DANA. I suppose the same rule applies to calling witnesses for the Government as for the defense. If there are witnesses in the vicinity whose presence is not assured to us in future, I suppose we can introduce them in the same way that General Buell introduced witnesses for the defense before the prosecution closed. It certainly would not be right for us to allow witnesses to leave who are now within reach of the court and take their evidence by deposition.

The JUDGE-ADVOCATE. We have a law authorizing the taking of depositions which we had not at the time referred to. If a witness goes away his deposition can be taken as in a civil case. I can have General Wright and Mr. Brownlow after General Buell gets through with his evidence, and I propose that he should close.

General DANA. How about Colonel Fry ?

The JUDGE-ADVOCATE. I propose that we take his deposition. We cannot get him here; he is not allowed to leave the War Department and we are not permitted to go East. But the documentary evidence of the examination of General Wright I insist should be disposed of before we proceed with rebutting evidence.

General BUELL. The judge-advocate has already proceeded to take the deposition of witnesses who are within half an hour's walk of this room—witnesses that he calls rebutting witnesses. The judge-advocate claims that he did not intend to proceed with rebutting witnesses, when he had actually done so. He now insists upon my closing my case. One of the witnesses is now in Washington. When he comes to the question of bringing witnesses before the court, then he insists upon a certain order of procedure; then one of the Commission also insists upon a certain order of procedure, when he has before instituted a different order.

General TYLER. I am not aware that I have instituted a different order of procedure. There were five of us originally, and if there is any censure due I am willing to bear my part of it.

General BUELL. I speak of Brigadier-General Tyler as a member of the Commission. I do not speak of him personally. And perhaps I am wrong in assuming that he had anything to do with the order that was passed some days back directing that the depositions of certain witnesses should be taken. I may be wrong. I am willing to admit that I was wrong in assuming that he had anything to do with it.

The JUDGE ADVOCATE. I ask nothing that is unreasonable in insisting that General Buell close his case before I introduce rebutting evidence.

General BUELL. I would call the attention of the Commission to another fact. Notwithstanding the order of the Commission that Governor Johnson should be introduced, I have since been notified that the judge-advocate will proceed to take the evidence of Governor Johnson by deposition, before the Judge-Advocate-General at Washington, on Tuesday, March 31. It cannot be pretended that there is any necessity of the public service which keeps him away, and I demand his presence here. If it were not for the implied indorsement which my summons would give to his testimony I would demand him as my own witness.

The JUDGE-ADVOCATE. If the presence of Governor Johnson can be procured I for my part desire him to be summoned.

General BUELL. With reference to the documentary evidence I have to submit, I am not prepared to proceed with it at once. It has, I believe, been all copied, but I have to return it to the officer who had the supervision of that work for correction, and it may take him some little time to do it. It will, however, be completed as speedily as possible.

The PRESIDENT. Can you introduce it by Monday?

General BUELL. No, sir; there is a good deal of it; but it will be proceeded with industriously. The officer has been prevented from examining it by the use of the books by the judge-advocate; making copies, I believe, of what he requires. And I may as well call your attention to the fact that the judge-advocate has not actually submitted his documentary evidence to the Commission. He has designated it, but has not submitted it in due form.

The JUDGE-ADVOCATE. If it is not before the Commission it is the Government's loss. All the documentary evidence I have to offer is before the Commission.

The judge-advocate then proceeded to read the resolutions passed in reference to obtaining the evidence of Governor Johnson.

The JUDGE-ADVOCATE. That I have proceeded to do not only with reference to Governor Johnson, but General Halleck. As to what may be his engagements I know nothing, but I telegraphed to him and got his answer, which is on record; but I know of no process by which I can force Governor Johnson to appear before this Commission.

The PRESIDENT. There was a telegraphic message sent to Washington for the appearance of Governor Johnson; it was done by my own direction; but I do not recollect whether that was for his appearance at Baltimore or here.

The JUDGE-ADVOCATE. By the recent law authorizing depositions we can obtain Governor Johnson's, and I consider it quite as good to take his deposition as to have the officer present.

General BUELL. I should like to know whether the judge-advocate took any steps to procure the attendance of Governor Johnson. I am notified by the judge-advocate that on the 31st of this month he will proceed to take the deposition of Governor Johnson.

The JUDGE-ADVOCATE. I received a telegram from Judge Holt to the effect that Governor Johnson was in Washington. That was after I had asked for his appearance before the Commission at Baltimore. As we do not go to Baltimore, and as there is no prospect of getting Governor Johnson here that I can see, I proceeded to get his deposition.

General BUELL. The judge-advocate has certainly not complied with the resolution of the Commission. On the contrary, and in spite of it, he has proceeded to take the deposition of Governor Johnson at Washington.

General DANA. I do not see that there is any authority for taking Governor Johnson's deposition unless it is found impossible to get him before the Commission.

The PRESIDENT. I understood that if Governor Johnson could possibly be brought here his deposition was not to be taken.

General BUELL. The law for taking the depositions of officers is similar to that for taking the depositions of civilians. Heretofore there has been no compulsory process to enforce the attendance of civilians before the military courts; nevertheless it is a rule that the witness shall appear before the Commission if he can be produced at all. It never has been claimed that either party could insist that a deposition would be sufficient. It has been always considered that efforts should be made to bring the witness before the courts, but if that cannot be done, as military courts have no power to compel the attendance of such witnesses, then the law allows that the evidence shall be taken by deposition.

The PRESIDENT. It is in all cases preferable to have the personal attendance of a witness. I am not willing to concede that the gentlemen of Washington City can manage the business of this Commission better than we can ourselves, notwithstanding their claim. Has the judge-advocate written out the questions to be submitted to General Halleck?

The JUDGE-ADVOCATE. I have asked him a few questions covering the whole ground.

General BUELL. That is another matter to which I desire to call your attention. I am notified that the judge-advocate will take the deposition of Major-General Halleck on the 31st of this month at Washington City. The judge-advocate had no right to call for the testimony of General Halleck. The rule which the Commission established requires that he should state in writing what he expected to prove by the witness he wished to call.

General TYLER. That certainly is a matter between the Commission and the judge-advocate.

General BUELL. I think, sir, I have something to do with it. It is a rule of the court and it affects me.

General DANA. If a rule is adopted by the court which affects General Buell in any way I think he has a right to see that the rule is impartially applied.

The JUDGE-ADVOCATE. I did not, when calling for witnesses, give the name of General Halleck; he came since this rule was established. I have been notified by the Commission in the presence of General Buell that the presence of General Halleck would be required upon that point. I did not understand General Buell to object to General Halleck. If he does object to him he has only to say so.

The PRESIDENT. Do you not recollect some time ago, when a discussion arose as to whether the Government was through with its witnesses, I gave notice that I insisted upon the testimony of General Halleck and also of the testimony of General Wright? As a member of the Commission it is my judgment that the Government could not possibly be through until the testimony of those gentlemen was taken.

The JUDGE-ADVOCATE. Without recurring to the past at all, if General Buell objects to the evidence of General Halleck or objects to it in the form in which it is proposed to take it, he can do so and the Commission can decide.

General DANA. I consider the examination of General Halleck by a deposition will be very unsatisfactory to the Commission; but if it cannot be got in any other way I suppose it will have to be done, though it will be very unsatisfactory at the best.

The Commission then adjourned to meet on Monday, March 30, at 11 o'clock a. m.

CINCINNATI, *March* 30, 1863.

Commission met pursuant to adjournment. The members present, General Wallace, General Dana, General Tyler; also the judge-advocate and General D. C. Buell.

General DANA. I move that the Rev. W. G. Brownlow be called before the Commission.

The JUDGE-ADVOCATE. With the exception of Colonel Fry, I decline calling any more witnesses before the Commission on behalf of the Government. Besides, if Mr. Brownlow's testimony comes into the case at all, it would be as rebuttal testimony and after the defense had completed its case.

The court was cleared for deliberation. On being reopened the judge-advocate announced that the motion to call Mr. Brownlow was lost.

General DANA. Has anything more been heard of Governor Johnson?

The JUDGE-ADVOCATE. No, sir.

After informal talk as to the time General Buell would be ready with his documentary evidence—

General TYLER. As the Commission has determined not to call any more witnesses till General Buell is prepared with his documentary evidence, I move to adjourn till to-morrow, March 31, at 11 o'clock a. m.

Adjourned.

CINCINNATI, *March* 31, 1863.

Commission met pursuant to adjournment. The members present, General Wallace, General Dana, General Tyler; also the judge-advocate.

The JUDGE-ADVOCATE. Since the Commission adjourned I have learned that Mr. Brownlow is for the present residing in this city, and if he is called away he will give me such notice that he may be examined here or will give me his deposition.

There being no further business before the Commission, on motion it adjourned to meet on Wednesday, April 1, at 11 a. m.

CINCINNATI, *April* 1, 1863.

Commission met pursuant to adjournment. The members present, General Wallace, General Dana, General Tyler; also the judge-advocate and General Buell.

General BUELL. I propose to submit some documentary evidence. It is not all prepared. That which I have to present to the Commission I have arranged in different classes, according to its bearing upon the different questions that seemed to be before you. I propose that Major Wright shall read the copies that have been prepared and that Lieutenant Bush shall refer to the page where the dispatch is to be found and see that it has been correctly copied.

The Commission adjourned to meet April 2, at 11 o'clock a. m.

CINCINNATI, *April* 2, 1863.

Commission met pursuant to adjournment. Present, the President (General Wallace), General Dana, General Tyler; also the judge-advocate and General Buell.

The JUDGE-ADVOCATE. I propose to the Commission to agree to the documentary evidence that General Buell wishes to introduce in order to avoid the delay incidental to reading it before the court. That which was read yesterday, and which occupied the court till 2 o'clock, is, I am informed, about one-sixth of the whole. It therefore strikes me that the better and shorter way of disposing of it will be to agree to its admission.

The PRESIDENT. I have no objection. If the judge-advocate and General Buell can agree upon the matter I have no doubt such agreement will be coincided in by the Commission.

The JUDGE-ADVOCATE. I have made the same proposition to General Buell that I have submitted to the court, but General Buell does not assent to it. I must say that it occupies unnecessarily, as I consider, a great deal of the time of the Commission to read the evidence in this way, and if the Government is willing to admit it as General Buell submits it, I do not see how this refusal can be persisted in.

The PRESIDENT. The rule of the court can only be suspended by an agreement of parties. If General Buell and yourself were to agree I think it would make the reading unnecessary; but if there is no agreement possible, we must continue the reading.

The JUDGE-ADVOCATE. An agreement on my part makes an agreement for both parties. When General Buell offers evidence and the Government consents to its admission I cannot see why General Buell should object to it.

The PRESIDENT. General Buell has the advantage in this matter.

General TYLER. I wish to inquire if all the documentary evidence is ready, so that we may go on until it is completed.

General BUELL. It is not all ready, but it will be ready as fast as it can be read to the Commission, unless you should start now and read till the day after to-morrow. I suppose I have enough here to occupy you to-day. I should be glad, as the Commission listen, if each member would make notes of anything of importance as it is read, and 1 should be glad to have the attention of the Commission called to it. It is the only way in which I can present it, and it will facilitate your study of the matter hereafter.

The PRESIDENT. It has all to be read and studied, as a matter of course; but I do not know but that I, for my part, could use it better by having it before me to carefully read.

General BUELL. I have selected these documents with care, and have taken from the records everything that seemed to me important. I am willing to agree to withhold the reading to the Commission if it will be more agreeable to them. There is no advantage in reading the evidence here unless it will serve the purpose of information to the Commission.

The PRESIDENT. Notwithstanding the hearing of it here, every member of the Commission will feel it his duty to read very carefully each dispatch introduced.

General BUELL. I have no disposition to occupy the time of the Commission, and would submit that unless the reading here serves the purpose of informing them the reading is not necessary, and I am disposed to dispense with it to avoid the useless consumption of time.

The JUDGE-ADVOCATE. I propose to admit as evidence on the part of the defense all the documents General Buell may feel disposed to introduce, and the Commission will have to examine that may be placed before them at their leisure.

General BUELL. I understand it to be the desire of the Commission, then, that I prepare the documentary evidence and submit it to you without reading?

The JUDGE-ADVOCATE. There is only one way of introducing this evidence, namely, that when these documents are introduced I identify them and make a record of them.

The Commission adjourned to meet Saturday, April 4, 1863, at 11 o'clock a. m.

CINCINNATI, *Saturday, April 4, 1863.*

The Commission met pursuant to adjournment. Members present, General Wallace, General Dana, General Tyler; also the judge-advocate and General Buell.

Maj. J. M. WRIGHT (a witness for the defense), being duly sworn by the judge-advocate, testified as follows:

By General BUELL:

Question. State your name and position in the service of the United States, if you please, major.

J. M. Wright; major and assistant adjutant-general of volunteers.

Question. Were you on duty with the Army of the Ohio from the time of its departure from Corinth in June last until General Buell was relieved from the command of that army? If so, please state in what position?

I was not on duty the whole of that time. Previous to the evacuation of Corinth I was taken sick, and did not rejoin the army until the 5th of July, at Huntsville, Ala. I was then on duty as assistant adjutant-general at headquarters.

Question. How many divisions of that army marched into North Alabama at that time?

Four divisions marched from Corinth.

Question. Name the divisions, if you please.

Second Division, General McCook; Fourth Division, General Nelson; Fifth Division, General Crittenden; Sixth Division, General Wood.

Question. Refer to the first morning report of that force after the 1st of July, and state what the effective strength of that force was.

I have a memorandum, taken from a Sparta report, which is more correct than these returns (referring to returns before the Commission), which gives the effective strength as 24,638.

Question. What is the date of those reports?

They were taken from those in the early part of July. I have not the reports themselves. They were at Nashville.

The JUDGE-ADVOCATE. I object to the introduction of this testimony without the original reports; I want the reports themselves. The question of General Buell refers to the official returns on the table and the witness proceeds to reply from memoranda which he has obtained from other reports which we have not here.

General BUELL. If there is any discrepancy I shall call upon the witness to explain it.

The WITNESS. From the reports (before the Commission) of the 10th of July the effective strength is 25,215. I see that this includes some cavalry regiments which were not permanently attached to the division. There is one attached to the Fourth Division, the Third Kentucky Cavalry, which is included in the report.

Question. Does that explain the discrepancy between the report that is now before you and the one from which you have made up your memoranda?

The difference between the two statements is 577. The Third Kentucky Cavalry numbered 547. These general consolidated reports have a great many inaccuracies in them, some of which I detected myself and corrected. I found a very important mistake in the report of the 20th of August. Those reports were made up in Nashville, and frequently from reports two and three weeks old. They were made up from reports as they were received, and the commands being in the field, they were irregularly received.

Question. When did the last division which came from Corinth arrive at Athens and what was the strength of that division?

I do not know, sir; I was not in Alabama at the time.

Question. I speak of the last, the First Division, which composed the Army of the Ohio at Corinth—General Thomas' division.

I do not know the date of its arrival. It had about 6,000 men for duty. (Major Wright looking over the consolidated reports.) The First Division is not included in any of these consolidated reports of the general strength of the army. I got my information from a separate report which was received at my office.

Question. What was the date of that report, as well as you remember?

It was in the early part of August. I have forgotten the exact date.

Question. Refer to the last report for August that is before you and state the full effective strength of the force under my command in Tennessee and Kentucky at that date.

According to this report the total force was 45,454 men, and the aggregate strength of the entire force 68,749.

Question. Does that include the present and the absent?

It includes everything, present and absent.

Question. Does that report include the whole force in my command; is there any omission from it?

The First Division is not included.

Question. Is there any other omission from it?

None that I can discover, sir. The effective strength on August 20, as corrected, is 53,309.

Question. What is the error which you have corrected to make this strength as you now give it and how does the error occur?

It is an error in summing up the totals of the divisions.

Question. Add now the effective strength of the division which is omitted in that return and then state what was the whole effective strength of the force under my command.

It was 59,309.

Question. Examine the report carefully and state how that force was distributed; how much of it was on the south side of the Cumberland River, exclusive of the force at Cumberland Gap, and how the other part of the force was distributed; that is, that part not included in the item which I have given you.

South of the Cumberland River the effective strength was 47,537. I would like to call attention to another inaccuracy in this report in representing some of the regiments which were north of the Cumberland as being at Nashville. There are three regiments in the report which I have marked; one of them, the Seventy-first Ohio, Colonel Mason, was at Clarksville, and not in General Buell's command.

Question. The report, then, does not represent with accuracy the force that was on the south side of the Cumberland at that date?

No, sir; it does not. I discovered this inaccuracy when I was looking over the report at Nashville, when I was endeavoring to get more accurate information, which I prepared.

Question. What is that information?

It is relative to the effective strength of the army, which is made up from different reports, which I found to be more correct.

The JUDGE-ADVOCATE. That is what I objected to before. I want the reports from which these estimates of the witness are obtained, as being the better evidence.

Question. What, then, was the actual effective strength on the south side of the river?

As I gave it, 47,537. I deducted the regiments which were not south of the Cumberland, but which were so reported in this report of August 20.

Question. What other inaccuracies do you find in this report?

Those are the only ones I see and the one I referred to first in summing up the totals, which made a very material difference in the report.

Question. Do you mean to say that the information you derived from other reports gives a different strength from that which you have just stated?

The JUDGE-ADVOCATE. I object to that question; and now for the third time I ask to have it disposed of. If there are other reports, giving different estimates from those before us, I want them produced; they are the better evidence and I have a right to them.

General BUELL. I do not see that the question calls for any specific information in regard to what is shown in any other reports. The witness has undertaken to make an explanation which I do not understand myself and which I knew nothing of. I have not called for him to state the strength of the Army of the Ohio from any other source than from the reports which are now before the Commission; but I wish him to explain what is the discrepancy which he says exists. If it is found important I shall insist upon calling for the reports myself. I am just as anxious to do so as the judge-advocate himself.

The JUDGE-ADVOCATE. Any information which the witness may have derived from other documents is available to this Commission and is objectionable, because we have a right to the documents themselves. These reports were furnished to the Commission and were received as reliable; now we are told that there are other reports which show a different estimate.

General DANA. I do not see that the witness is precluded from testifying to the strength of the army, which many other witnesses have done. Other witnesses, I suppose, have got their information, both with respect to our own and Bragg's army, from all kinds of sources, and (as far as our own army is concerned) from these reports; and I do not see that any witness should be precluded from giving his testimony as to the effective strength of the army from any reliable source whatever.

The court was cleared; when it was decided that the objection should be sustained.

The PRESIDENT. This ruling of the court, general, does not preclude you from introducing the other reports that have been referred to.

General BUELL. I do not think it is a matter of any consequence. I simply desired to understand what the matter was that the witness had to explain.

By General BUELL:

Question. In this statement of the force on the south side of the Cumberland River have you included what is entered under the head of unattached cavalry in this report?

All except the Ninth Regiment Pennsylvania Cavalry.

Question. In that statement of the force on the south side of the Cumberland have you included all the regiments which are entered under the head of unattached infantry on this report?

No, sir.

Question. How many regiments have you omitted?

Three regiments were omitted. I see by glancing at it again another should be omitted, Colonel Warner's, the Eighteenth Kentucky, I think, which was also in Kentucky.

Question. What further change would that make in your statement as to the force on the south side of the river?

It would make a difference of 733, making the entire strength 46,504.

Question. What was the force at Cumberland Gap?

Seven thousand six hundred and two.

Question. How was the balance of the force employed that was not included in these two items?

It was in Kentucky, a portion of it, guarding the Louisville and Nashville Railroad. I do not know the exact disposition of the remainder, but it was posted throughout Kentucky.

Question. Does the form which is used for these official reports show the actual effective strength of the troops in the ranks?

No, sir.

Question. What does it include?

It shows the entire number for duty; it includes the extra and special duty men.

Question. When did the two divisions arrive which came from Corinth; I mean the two divisions that came from the Army of the Mississippi?

The first, General Mitchell's, arrived between the 1st and 3d of September, I believe, while we were at Murfreesborough. The other, General Paine's division, came into Nashville after we left there; it must have been after the 11th of September.

Question. What was the date of the arrival of the headquarters of the army at Bowling Green on its march to Kentucky?

We arrived at 6 o'clock on the morning of the 14th of September.

Question. How many divisions of the army were there at that time and whose divisions were they?

Two divisions were there; General Rousseau's and General Wood's.

Question. What divisions were yet in the rear?

General Ammen's, General Crittenden's, and General McCook's.

Question. Is that all?

General Mitchell's had marched from Nashville, I presume, as it overtook us at Bowling Green.

Question. Do you know when General Mitchell's division arrived at Bowling Green?

I do not know the exact date; it was either on the 15th or 16th of September.

Question. Do you know the date of the first attack on Munfordville?

It was on Sunday, the 14th of September, I think.

Question. When did the army march from Bowling Green north?

Most of it marched on the 16th of September.

Question. When did it reach Munfordville?

It was either on Sunday or Monday, the 21st or 22d of September; I do not recollect which.

Question. Had General Thomas' division arrived at Bowling Green when the army marched?

It had not arrived there when General Buell's headquarters moved on the morning of the 17th of September. I mean by that that I do not know whether they had arrived when the rear of the army left there.

Question. On what day of the march did the headquarters leave Nashville?

On the 11th of September.

Question. Did any division of the army leave at that time?

I think that General McCook's and General Ammen's left on the same day. General McCook's, I am certain, marched on that day. We overtook it at Edgefield Junction.

Question. How many days was it, then, from the time that division left until it arrived at Munfordville?

I am not certain, but I think it was ten days.

Question. What is the distance from Nashville to Munfordville?

I think it is 80 miles, according to the map.

Question. Is that the map prepared for the information of the Commission?

It is the one the judge-advocate called my attention to as such. It is probable I made a mistake in running over the distances on the map. From the position in which it hangs on the wall, I am unable to see the distances marked distinctly. By Lloyd's map the distance is 94 miles.

Question. What was the strength with which the army marched from Louisville after the accession of the new regiments that we had there?

The army which marched on Perryville was about 58,000. I cannot give the exact numbers, as I have no official reports. No official reports were ever sent to headquarters at that time. Previous to our leaving Louisville I called upon the corps commanders and they in the same manner called upon their division commanders for returns of their strength, but no official returns were made on the forms furnished for that purpose. So that we only arrived at a proximate estimate of the entire strength. The information asked for was sent afterward by the corps commanders in the form of letters.

Question. Can you produce those letters?

They are probably at Nashville, in the office there. They were filed with other papers that were left in General Rosecrans' office.

Question. Does that include the division of General Sill?

No, sir.

Question. Does it include the division of General Dumont?

No, sir; as they did not march from Louisville with the army toward Perryville.

Question. What would be the strength of General Sill's division?

It was between 8,000 and 9,000 strong.

Question. Would that be an average of the strength of all the divisions of the army?

No, sir; the Second Division was the largest, unless it was General Dumont's division, which may have been a little larger than that, which was composed entirely of the new regiments, which were full.

Question. How many regiments were there in General Dumont's division?

Fifteen regiments, if I remember correctly.

Question. Are you positive about that?

No, sir; I am not. My recollection fails me in regard to that division, as I never had any reports of it, and I merely remember from the order first organizing it.

Question. Were the new divisions organized with fifteen regiments?

The organization of the Tenth Division, General Jackson's, was not complete, but if I remember aright General Dumont's division was more complete in its organization. I know it was larger.

Question. How would this estimated strength of the army at the time it was at Louisville compare with its probable strength at Perryville, say about the 8th of October? If you know of any discrepancy explain the cause of it.

Fifty-eight thousand is the number which we had represented on paper on leaving Louisville. I am confident it was much larger than the number we had at Perryville, as there was a great deal of straggling from Louisville to Perryville. A great many of the regiments broke down and many men were left behind. The great number of stragglers from the new regiments, from their breaking down, was remarked upon throughout the army.

Question. Did you carry any instructions on the 8th of October for re-enforcing the left corps? If so, state when you received them, what they were, and how they were executed.

I did carry instructions to General McCook, commanding the left corps. About half past 4 in the afternoon we broke up our camp, when I received orders from Colonel Fry to prepare an orderly to carry orders to General McCook. He then told me that I had better go myself, and give the orders to General Gilbert, commanding the center corps, to send two brigades to re-enforce General McCook on the left. I rode forward and met General Gilbert about 2 miles in advance, and delivered him the order to send these re-enforcements to General McCook, when he told me that he had already sent one brigade and a battery. He told me to take any brigade I wished, and showed great willingness to send re-enforcements to General McCook. I told him I would only take one. I then went forward to General Schoepf, who was probably 300 yards in advance of General Gilbert. He had two brigades with him, the Third Brigade of his division being in reserve near General Buell's headquarters. When I met General Schoepf his troops were in motion, but moving very slowly through a corn field. He was riding along in the rear near his advance brigade. I think they were formed in two lines as they moved forward. I told him to move one of his brigades forward, and he designated General Steedman's, which was, I think, the larger of his two brigades. I then told him I would ride forward, and tell General McCook that they were coming and find the direction. There was an interval of some distance between General McCook's line and that of General Gilbert, and in this interval, though not entirely covering it, was Captain Gay's cavalry, and I tried to find from them the direction of General McCook's command; but no one knew where he was or could tell, or could tell me which direction I should take. I afterward found an ambulance train, which I followed for some distance, when we were met by an orderly, who turned them in another direction. He said he had just come from General McCook with orders to hurry them up. I told the surgeon in charge of the trains that I thought he was going in a wrong direction. At that time I heard no musketry firing. The road I was following led me to the rear of the right of General McCook's command. As I approached General McCook's line I met one of his staff officers half a mile in the rear, and I inquired where General McCook was; he said he had not seen him for two hours; he said he had been placed there to stop the stragglers. He spoke of the great numbers of stragglers there were; he also said that we had got the worst of it in the fight. As I rode up this line I met a battery about 300 yards in the rear of the line occupied by McCook's command. The captain of the battery rode forward to meet me and told me that the position of the battery marked the point to which the line had been driven back, but by the arrival of this new brigade they had been enabled to recover the intervening ground. This was, I presume, about 5 o'clock. I met General McCook immediately in rear of his line, which was about the center of the Third Division, which was on his right. I told him that re-enforcements were coming. I also told him that the general desired me to ask him how he was doing and whether the re-enforcements coming would be sufficient. He said that he had been driven back, but that he was now recovering his ground and was doing very well. I asked him how his new troops had done, and he said splendidly. I thought, however, he replied to the question without thinking what I had asked him. He may have misunderstood me, for his Tenth Division, composed of new troops, had been driven back.

I left him for about fifteen minutes to write a note to Colonel Fry, and had just returned to where General McCook was when Colonel Steedman rode up. As he came up General McCook turned to me and said, "Here come the Pea Ridge men; tell the general I am all right now." As I was about leaving him I asked him if he wanted any more re-enforcements; he first said no, but when I was on the point of leaving he recalled me and said he did not know but he might want more, as he did not know what might occur. I told him if he wished for more to send to General Gilbert, who would send him any re-enforcements he might ask for or that he could spare. I went back by the same road that I came by, and found Colonel Walker's brigade, of the First Division, near the end of it. I told him to form across this road, so that any one coming from General McCook would meet him. This was the remaining brigade of General Schoepf's division. I did not see him, though I searched for him to give him orders in regard to re-enforcements. I then rode back to General Gilbert, and told him where I had posted this brigade, and to send forward any re-enforcements he could spare, if General McCook wanted them. I left General McCook at sundown, about half past 5 o'clock (the sun set at 5.32 p. m. that day). I rode back at a gallop to where I had left General Buell, and in not more than ten or fifteen minutes after I arrived Colonel Fry wrote an order and sent it back to General McCook by an orderly I had taken up with me in the afternoon. I told the orderly to go by the exact road I had taken, and I found afterward that he had gone by that road to the exact place where I had left McCook's force probably not half an hour before. The orderly rode right into the midst of a rebel regiment and was captured. Colonel Walker's brigade was not called upon to go over to General McCook's assistance, so I presume he did not send for re-enforcements.

Question. Do you know what order that orderly took to General McCook?

No, sir; I did not see it. I thought it was to hold his ground that night and be ready to renew the fight in the morning.

Question. Do you know what time information was received at head-quarters that a battle was in progress on the left and that General Mc-Cook required re-enforcements, and how long was it before you started with the order for the re-enforcements?

I did not see the officer who came over to ask for re-enforcements, but Colonel Fry told me as he sent me off that an officer had just left them.

Question. What were the indications at headquarters that a battle was raging at that time?

No musketry firing could be heard, but toward noon and during the afternoon we heard artillery, but supposed it was in front; and I remember asking Colonel Fry if we were not going forward, and he replied that it was merely some artillery firing in front to hold the water that we had secured the previous night by sending forward a brigade. When I left General Buell to carry the order for re-enforcements to General Gilbert I had no idea that a battle was being fought, and did not know till I reached General McCook that one was in progress. During the time I was with General Mc-Cook his troops were advancing. I remember this distinctly, because as I was sitting on a log writing a note to Colonel Fry a battery came up and got into position immediately in front of us. I remember standing and looking at them for a few minutes as they were firing. They advanced their guns several paces by hand on the ridge from which they were firing and the troops on either side of the battery moved forward at the same time. General McCook afterward told me that this was the hottest part of the fight, and my impression was, as I told General Buell when I got back, that we were whipping the enemy.

Question. Do I understand you that subsequent to this the enemy actually occupied the ground you were on when you were with General McCook?

No, sir; I do not suppose that they did occupy that ground, as the point to which they had been driven back was fully 300 yards in rear of the line that our troops then occupied.

Question. Did you not state in your answer to a previous question that an orderly from headquarters was captured on this ground where you saw General McCook and where the advance was resumed?

Yes, sir; but that was after dark. The line had been driven back once before, but recovered their ground by the assistance of the brigade sent to them by General Gilbert. After dark they had been driven back again, and the orderly who went over to this place where General McCook was at sundown was captured.

Question. How, then, do you understand the previous question? Your answers, you observe, do not accord.

I supposed that the question had some connection with the fact that they were driven back some time in the afternoon previous to my arrival. The enemy did occupy that ground after dark and held it.

Question. Did you go to General McCook's corps on the morning of the 9th with any instructions? If so, please state what the object of your mission was and what you saw.

I did not carry any instructions to General McCook, though I was ordered to go forward by Colonel Fry to learn the positions occupied by McCook's command and see how they had progressed in issuing rations and in getting ready to advance. I left our headquarters about 8 o'clock and found General McCook near the Springfield and Perryville road. I told him what I had been sent forward for, and tried to get some information from him, but failed. He did not tell me anything about his troops. I then asked him where the Tenth Division was, but he did not tell me. I found them afterward on the left and to the rear of the other troops. His troops were formed in two lines. I think the intention was to have one regiment from each brigade in the second line, though it was not carried out through his entire line. The first brigade I found was Colonel Harris', Third Division. He told me he was on the extreme right and that there was nothing beyond him. Afterward I found Colonel Starkweather's brigade, of the same division, on his right. They gave me no information of the enemy, though I inquired of them. They were both formed on the skirt of some timber, looking out upon an open space several hundred yards across, toward the Mackville road. At this time General McCook's line was formed almost parallel to the Mackville road—the night before they had been almost perpendicular to it—so that in falling back the left had swept round and the right moved a very little to the rear. His entire force had moved to the right so as to connect with General Gilbert's corps. No one I saw knew anything about the enemy, though Colonel Starkweather told me that there had been large fires on the edge of the wood, probably not more than one-third of a mile from him, and that he supposed the enemy had bivouacked there. I asked him if he had seen any one moving about these fires during the night, but he had not observed any one there, and did not know whether the enemy had gone or not. The only one from whom I obtained any information was Captain Wickliffe. He told me that some guns of Parsons' battery which had been captured the day before were several hundred yards in advance, and if a brigade was advanced they could bring them in. I looked for General Rousseau and found him asleep. I awoke him and told him about these guns. He referred me to General McCook. I went in search of him, and told him that by advancing a brigade he could get these guns again; that a less force might attract the notice of small bodies of the enemy's cavalry who were moving about upon this open space in front of this line. General McCook called an aide, but I do not think he gave him any orders. I do not remember what he said to him. I told him it would be well to have another brigade to support this. He then said he would not send any. Afterward Lieutenant Parsons went out with, I think, Captain Wickliffe and drew in these guns without being molested. There were, I believe, three or four guns, though I did not see them. I tried to find out whether rations had been issued to the command or not, but no one could tell me. I went from regiment to regiment and found that some had received them and others had not, but no officer from any one's staff could tell me anything about it.

General Buell having finished his examination-in-chief, the Commission adjourned to meet on Monday, April 6, 1863, at 11 o'clock a. m.

CINCINNATI, *April 6, 1863.*

The Commission met pursuant to adjournment. Members present, General Wallace, General Dana, General Tyler; also the judge-advocate and General Buell.

Major WRIGHT'S examination continued.

By General BUELL:

Question. Take up the report for the 1st of September * and state, if

---

* Not found.

you please, what the whole effective force was, according to that report, including the First Division, which does not appear on that report.

This report is incorrect.

Question. Point out the error and explain it, if you can.

The report gives the total effective strength as 52,526. There is an error in summing up the totals of the divisions; it should be 47,711. (Major Wright, continuing the examination of the report.) I am mistaken; it is right as it stands in the report. I did not include the regiments which were in Kentucky. Including the First Division there are 58,526.

Question. Now see what effective force there was on the south of the Cumberland River at that date.

Forty-seven thousand six hundred and fifty-seven.

Question. Do those reports show the actual strength at the date of the report?

These consolidated reports were made up from the reports of the division commanders, which were forwarded as regularly as possible but were received in Nashville very irregularly. Sometimes the reports were two or three weeks old from which these reports were made up.

Question. In your statement of the effective force south of the Cumberland have you deducted the regiments which on that report are reported as belonging to Nashville when in reality they were not there?

I have deducted them.

Cross-examination by the JUDGE-ADVOCATE:

Question. Who was in command of the First Division; and can you explain why that was not included in these reports; and from what did you make up the number to be 6,000?

When General Thomas was put in command of the Army of the Mississippi, in front of Corinth, his division (the first which he commanded) went with him, and did not rejoin the Army of the Ohio until it entered North Alabama. This is the reason it does not appear in these reports. They either joined subsequent to the dates of most of these reports or his reports had not probably been received at Nashville. I said on Saturday that I had no report of General Thomas' division. I got its strength from reports at Nashville, and said its effective strength was about 6,000.

Question. Had Brigadier-General Schoepf the command of a division at that time?

No, sir; he was commanding a brigade of the First Division.

Question. Where were the two divisions that joined you subsequently from Grant's army on the 1st of September, 1862?

General Mitchell's division was near Murfreesborough, where they joined us. Paine's division was marched directly to Nashville. I do not know where it was on the 1st of September.

Question. What time did it reach Nashville?

I do not know the exact date; I think, however, it was after we left there.

Question. What was the number of these two divisions?

I never saw any official report of the strength of these divisions. General Mitchell told me on his arrival at Murfreesborough that he had about 5,000 men. The other division, I suppose, numbered about the same.

Question. At the date at which you give the effective force south of the Cumberland what force was there between Nashville and Bowling Green and at Bowling Green?

The reports of the troops at Nashville and north of the Cumberland were all sent to the office at Nashville and never came into my hands, and I never saw them. I remember, however, from dispatches I have read, that Colonel Bruce had, I think he said, 500 or 600 men at Bowling Green; probably not so many as that. I know that on the 20th of August he had not that number; probably not more than 450.

Question. Have you not included the troops at Nashville in your estimate of the forces north of the Cumberland?

Yes, sir.

Question. From what did you make it up?

I made it up from these reports before me, which include the whole command. These reports are tri-monthly reports of the whole command, which were forwarded to Washington. They were not sent down into the field at all. One was kept on file at the office in Nashville and the other was sent to Washington.

Question. Do these reports show upon their face where the troops were located?

These I believe do not. It is the intention, however, in the form in which they are furnished, that they should do so.

Question. Between what dates did the Army of the Ohio leave Nashville when it fell back to Bowling Green?

The troops moved forward from Nashville between the 5th and 11th of September.

Question. At what time did they arrive at Bowling Green?

The divisions arrived at Bowling Green successively. General Buell's headquarters arrived on the morning of the 14th; at that date two divisions had arrived, I think; two others had been there a day or two.

Question. What two divisions did you find there and what two divisions arrived there on the 14th?

Rousseau's and Wood's divisions were already there. General Ammen's and General Crittenden's divisions arrived that day.

Question. What time did General Wood's and General Rousseau's divisions arrive there?

I do not know the exact date; they preceded us by but a few days.

Question. At what time did McCook's division arrive there?

I think they came very near Bowling Green on the night of the 14th.

Question. Between what dates did the Army of the Ohio reach Munfordville?

I think it must have been between the 20th and 23d of September. The divisions arrived there nearly together, as they had taken up positions in front of Munfordville as they approached it, in anticipation, as I suppose, of a fight.

Question. What was the strength of the Army of the Ohio that marched into Louisville?

I have no means of giving the exact number, though in round numbers it was about 45,000 strong.

Question. Are not the returns made of new troops, when ordered into the field immediately, very unreliable, from the fact that many officers make no return at all, and those above them send in what they can get, if they give any report whatever?

I do not think they are reliable; as a general thing I think they overestimated the strength, from the fact that they took no report of the alterations occurring from day to day.

Question. Would they not rather underestimate them, or would they not in making up the force from the returns make an underestimate of that force, from the fact that many officers make no return at all?

I presume where officers do not make a return the strength is taken by the higher authorities from the average of the other regiments. The reason why they overestimate their strength is that they take no report of the alterations that occur, and in the new regiments more frequently than in the old ones. The officers of the new regiments do not fully appreciate the importance of having accurate reports, and frequently, to save time and trouble, would merely make a copy of their old report from day to day.

Question. Did not the difficulty with the new troops that you received at Louisville originate from the fact that many companies and some regiments made no report at all, neither old nor new?

I do not know what difficulty you refer to.

Question. In estimating the number of new troops you received at Louisville.

My understanding was that the authorities at Louisville had received reports from most of the new regiments. I was told by the general commanding that army very confidently what the strength of the troops was. I got no reports from them, because as soon as we removed into the field we were ordered to move light; that is, to leave all the unnecessary baggage; and many of the regiments left all their papers too. They did afterward join us at Lebanon. The troops had moved very rapidly in marching from Louisville, and could not carry all of their baggage, or even all of their office furniture and desks; indeed, after leaving Louisville no one had time to make up a report, as they were almost constantly on the march.

Question. What do you estimate the force under General Buell at subsequent to the battle of Perryville, including General Sill's and General Dumont's divisions?

General Dumont's division did not join at all. I think with the addition of General Sill's division it was not over 59,000 men. The army with which we marched from Louisville was estimated at 58,000. As I said, the new troops broke down very rapidly and fell out. There were a great many stragglers from the new regiments, and after the battle I do not think there were more than 50,000 of the army which appeared in front of Perryville. General Sill's division numbered between 8,000 and 9,000.

Question. You estimate the stragglers, then, at something like 16,000?

There were 58,000 men marched from Louisville, as I represented on paper; after the battle I supposed there were 50,000. There were several thousands killed, wounded, and missing at the battle of Perryville. I do not know how 16,000 stragglers are to be accounted for.

Question. I understand you to include Sill's division?

I spoke of the army that appeared before Perryville.

Question. I understood you to say that the explanation given you by Colonel Fry of the cannonading on the front on the morning of the 8th was that it was guarding the water that had been secured by our troops; is that correct?

On the night before the battle of Perryville Captain Gay, who had the advance with his cavalry, advanced to this water and held it until some time after dark. General Gilbert was ordered to throw forward a brigade at 2 o'clock in the morning to hold that water; it went, and the next morning the enemy made some demonstrations in front as if to recover the ground occupied by this brigade, and they commenced cannonading with a couple of batteries they had with them. Colonel Fry merely expressed his opinion on the subject when I referred to it. I asked if we were going to the front at that time—I presume it was not later than 12 o'clock then—and he said it was merely cannonading in front to hold the water we had secured in the morning. Captain Gay had been on this front, I think, but at the time this brigade was advanced his pickets were occupying it; his main body was farther back.

Question. Was it because of this explanation from Colonel Fry that you did not know that a battle was in progress until you saw General McCook?

No, sir; I heard no indications of the battle. I merely spoke to Colonel Fry in reference to the matter because I supposed he would have some information of what they were doing in front and why they were firing at intervals all the morning.

Question. Do I understand you that that firing of artillery was not unusual?

Do you mean the firing at different times during the morning?

Question. Yes, sir.

They very frequently had skirmishes in which a small number of pieces of artillery were engaged. We had been skirmishing all the afternoon before the battle.

Question. Was there no difference between the sound of the firing of these skirmishes and that of the 8th?

I remarked no difference between the sound. I only noticed it because it was continued longer. I do not think I paid any attention to it until toward the afternoon, when I remarked that it had been continued some time, and asked Colonel Fry what it was and what they were doing.

Question. Did you hear General Buell say that that was a waste of ammunition and should be stopped?

I do not think I heard him say so. I do not think I was near enough to General Buell that morning to hear him speak. I was busy attending to my own business. This was possibly the reason I did not inquire sooner what the noise was about.

Question. Did you not know that the enemy was in force at Perryville and that a fight at that place was anticipated?

I had no positive information of it. My understanding was that the enemy were not in force, and although I did not see the orders sent to the corps commanders I understood that they were ordered to approach to a convenient distance that day, and I supposed that we were to attack them on the following morning.

Question. And yet the cannonading in that direction caused no remark at headquarters?

It caused no remark, because the brigade was ordered to hold this water, which was very essential to us, as we had been without water, and it was absolutely necessary to our troops.

Question. At what hour in the afternoon was it that the officer arrived there demanding re-enforcements for General McCook?

I did not see the officer. As I was starting Colonel Fry told me that an officer had just been there; that was probably 4.30 in the afternoon that I started.

The JUDGE-ADVOCATE. Mr. President, I was instructed by the Commission to inquire into the facts relative to Captain Gay's being placed in command of a brigade. I was under the impression that I could get those facts from General Wright, but I find he knows nothing about it. I suppose Major Wright could give us some light upon the subject, and I would suggest that the Commission ask the necessary questions.

General BUELL. I have no objection to the judge-advocate asking the questions.

By the JUDGE-ADVOCATE:

Question. You will please state what you know of Captain Gay being put in command of a brigade.

General BUELL. I do not know that Major Wright knows anything about it, but I would like to ask him such questions, that his testimony may be clear upon this point.

The JUDGE-ADVOCATE. I have no objection.

The WITNESS. When we arrived in Louisville we found Captain Gay in command of a brigade. I was told that he had been recommended as brigadier-general and was expecting his appointment; that the colonels of the regiments which he commanded had yielded in expectation of his being made a brigadier-general. When we started from Louisville his appointment had not been made, but no objection was offered to his commanding the brigade. I heard one of his colonels say that he deemed him better qualified than himself. No difficulty arose in regard to this matter till the campaign was over and we were marching back to Louisville. As long as we were in the presence of the enemy the officers of the command never objected to his commanding the brigade, but after they got back to Lebanon I believe they did offer some objection to it, and he was removed for that reason.

By General DANA:

Question. Do you know whether Colonel Milliken, of the First Ohio Cavalry, gave his consent to being under the command of Captain Gay?

I do not know whether he objected to it or not. When we were at Lebanon he had been sent off to Munfordville with a separate command. If he had objected he was, I presume, relieved from duty under Captain Gay.

Question. Do you know by whose authority Captain Gay was first placed in command of the brigade at Louisville?

I always supposed it was by General Wright's authority; but I do not know.

Question. Do you know anything of the circumstances of Capt. C. C. Gilbert being placed upon duty as major-general in command of an army corps?

Previous to our arrival at Louisville I remember seeing one or two dispatches which were signed "C. C. Gilbert, major-general, commanding." When we arrived at Louisville, though he had then been superseded by General Nelson, he had been previously in command of the Army of Kentucky as major-general. He wore the uniform of a major-general, and in the reorganization he was made one of the corps commanders. Before the death of General Nelson he was left in charge of Louisville, and being next in rank he was placed in command at Louisville. When General Nelson was killed he was given the command of one of the corps. I always supposed he was a major-general until some circumstances arose and I was directed to call upon him for his commission and the date of his appointment, and it was found that he had been appointed a major-general by General Wright, subject to the confirmation of the President. He was then called upon for the date of his commission as brigadier-general, which was found to be September 25. We were then marched back to Lebanon, and a few days after he was relieved from the command of his corps—not more than three or four days afterward. I think in the order relieving him from the command of his corps and assigning him to a new command, which included the troops on the line of railroad, he was styled brigadier-general. I did not hear General Buell say anything about it, but I remember Colonel Fry expressing his astonishment that he was not a major-general. He told me he supposed he was, as he had worn the uniform and styled himself major-general.

Question. Do you remember the date of General Nelson's death?

I think it was the 30th September.

Question. During the time that General Gilbert was acting as a major-general in command of the Army of Kentucky was he then a captain in the regular service and not a general officer?

I am not positive as to the date of his appointment as a brigadier-general, but I know it was some time in September. I suppose at the time he was in command of the Army of Kentucky he was only a captain in the Regular Army.

By the PRESIDENT:

Question. Was he captain of an infantry regiment or in the quartermaster's department?

He was captain of an infantry regiment.

By General DANA:

Question. On the 8th of October did you receive from General Gilbert any message directed to General Buell? If so, what was it and did you deliver it?

As I came back from General McCook I met General Gilbert and stopped to speak to him for a moment. He spoke of a fight which was going on on the left of General McCook. There was a battery which we could see firing across in reply to one of General McCook's batteries, and he told me it was evident the enemy were massing their troops against McCook's, and he said "Thomas is the man that ought to be pushed forward." I told him that an officer had already been sent to push General Thomas' troops forward, and he said he doubted if they would get there in time or some remark to the same effect. This was just after sundown.

Question. To whose corps did Dumont's division belong and where was his division during the battle of Perryville?

It belonged to no corps; it was an unattached division and was in Frankfort.

Question. Where and at what date did General Sill join the Army of the Ohio after the battle of Perryville?

He joined us just beyond Perryville, on the 10th, I think.

Question. By how many regiments was the Army of the Ohio re-enforced at Louisville?

There were about thirty-eight regiments that entered into the organization of the army. There were two or three other regiments, which were unattached, under the command of General Buell, but were left in Kentucky, where they were when this army marched to Nashville.

Question. Does this number of regiments include infantry and cavalry?

There were thirty-eight infantry regiments.

Question. How many cavalry regiments?

I do not know. I did not get any reports and know little about them.

Question. Can you state whether there were many or few?

There were a few, I think.

Question. How many batteries of artillery were added to the army at Louisville?

There were not more than three or four. One of these batteries, Parsons', which belonged to the Tenth Division, was not regularly organized. It was manned by detachments from new infantry regiments.

Question. Would the number of cavalry regiments added to the army at Louisville exceed six?

No, sir.

Question. What in your idea was the maximum strength of the cavalry added to the army at Louisville?

I think there were not more than three regiments.

Question. Do the forty-one regiments of infantry added at Louisville embrace those that were placed in Dumont's and Sill's divisions also?

Yes, sir. Sill's division got no more than other divisions of the army. There was one new regiment attached to each old brigade. General Dumont's division was composed entirely of new regiments, as well as the Tenth, General Jackson's.

Question. What was the average strength of those forty-one regiments?

I suppose from the fact of the whole number of troops being 32,000 that they were about 800. General Nelson told me that his command was 32,000 strong.

Question. Would 32,000 men for the effective force of forty-one new regiments be a large or a small estimate?

I think that under the circumstances it was a large estimate. These troops were hurried into the field as soon as their organization was sufficiently complete to enable them to be on duty at all.

Question. Do you know whether any of these regiments were of the maximum standard?

I do not know, sir; I never saw a report of any of them.

Question. Do you know anything of any deserters and unwarranted absentees from the Army of the Ohio after its arrival on the Ohio at the mouth of Salt River?

I know that there were a great many absentees, particularly officers; but every precaution was taken at General Buell's headquarters to prevent it and very stringent measures were adopted, but I do not think these orders were fully carried out by brigade and division commanders. I heard that officers were absent with the permission of the brigade commanders. They got across the river by other means than those used by the public (ferry-boats), because there were guards to prevent them.

Question. Have you any means of arriving at an estimate of the number of officers and men absent without leave from the Army of the Ohio on its arrival at Louisville? If so, state the number.

In August there was an order issued from General Buell's headquarters calling attention to the number of absentees, officers and men, and putting it at 14,000.

Question. The question refers to the number of officers and men who absented themselves without leave from the time the army arrived at the mouth of Salt River until its arrival at Louisville—officers and men who were supposed to have gone to their homes without proper authority.

I have no means of ascertaining the number, but I suppose that in nearly every case the officers who went did so with the permission of their colonels, and they of course would not report it, and no reports were made up at that time which would show how many of these officers were absent.

Question. Is it or is it not a notorious fact that the Army of the Ohio during that interval suffered a great diminution of its numbers from this cause, and do you know anything about the facts?

It was not noticeable from the diminution of its numbers as much as from the fact that almost all those who went away without authority were officers and that these officers took advantage of their position to go off without permission and it was well known throughout the States where these officers went that they were absent without permission.

Question. In estimating the strength of the Army of the Ohio on its arrival at Louisville at 45,000 have you made any allowance for these absentees?

The estimate of 45,000 is taken from the report of the strength of the army before it left Nashville; it therefore does not include the absentees. I presume that in the Kentucky regiments there were more absentees when we left Louisville than from other regiments, as I know that one or two regiments raised near Louisville had a great many absentees, some of whom had to be brought in by force. Even after they had been searched for there were a great many still absent.

Question. Taking 45,000 as the number of the troops of the Army of the Ohio that left Nashville and deducting from them the losses from all causes on the march from Nashville to Louisville what would be the number of the old troops of the Army of the Ohio which left Louisville on its march toward Bardstown?

I presume there were about 43,000. On our march from Nashville we left quite a number at different points on the road, at Bowling Green and at other stations where there were hospitals. Many broke down from forced marches. The roads were very dusty, and we had a great many sick who had given out from exhaustion, and these were left behind on our march toward Louisville, and they did not rejoin us in time to march with the army towards Bardstown.

Question. Does this estimate include the old troops of Sill's and Dumont's divisions?

There were no old troops in Dumont's division; it was composed entirely of new regiments. It does include the old troops of Sill's division.

Question. What, then, was the aggregate effective strength of General Buell's army, including General Sill's and General Dumont's divisions, when he left Louisville?

I estimated it at 77,000. It is not more than 75,000. The estimated strength of the different corps averaged 22,000, as near as the corps commanders could make it; that would give the strength of the three corps at 66,000. Dumont's division had about 9,000 (and a few odd hundreds), making up a total of 75,000.

Question. Was the garrison at Munfordville ever embraced in any of the estimates of the strength of the Army of the Ohio at any time after it left Nashville?

No, sir.

By General TYLER:

Question. Were there any additions made to this 75,000 men that could be made available to the army before you reached Perryville by detachments left at Munfordville or at any other point?

No, sir; this estimate included everything.

Question. In your direct testimony you stated that you went to General McCook on the morning of the 9th to inquire whether he had rations, &c., issued to his men and that he would not give you any satisfaction on the point; did he understand that you were sent from headquarters to ascertain those facts?

When I met General McCook I told him that General Buell had sent me to learn the positions of the troops, how he progressed in issuing rations, and to learn what I could of the enemy. I first asked him some questions about his troops; he did not give a satisfactory reply. I asked if he knew anything of the enemy, and all he told me was that his brother, Colonel Dan. McCook, was skirmishing through the woods with them in his front. He said he was issuing rations to his troops. I asked one or two questions and he made some other remark about the skirmishing in his front, and I got on my horse and went to find out for myself what I could. I do not think it was General McCook's intention to avoid giving me information. He told me that he had been up nearly all the night; he was at the time lying on the ground, and he said he was almost worn-out. I think it arose more from that than any desire not to send information to General Buell.

Question. In your estimate of the effective force of the army in these reports submitted to you do you include all reported present, excluding the sick in hospitals, &c.?

The numbers which I gave were the effective strength for duty; the form gives "Present for duty."

Question. What did you do with the "extra-duty" men who were present?

The extra and special duty men are all included in the number reported as fit for duty. I suppose there were 25 or 30 men in each regiment who were on special and extra duty throughout the army.

Question. But those are included in "Present."

Yes, sir; but they are not available for duty as soldiers.

Question. Why are not these men available for duty?

They were detailed as teamsters, clerks, nurses in the hospital, and to perform all other little duties about the regimental camps.

By General DANA:

Question. In the march of the Army of the Ohio from Louisville to Perryville were not troops left at Bardstown, Springfield, or other places to occupy positions before the army reached Perryville? If so, how many?

There was a regiment left at Bardstown. The other points below that, I think, were not occupied.

Question. How many of these men reported as on extra and special duty were there in the whole of the Army of the Ohio at that time?

There were about 4,000.

Question. What would be the whole number to be deducted from the line of battle owing to this item and the detachment at Bardstown?

I should say about 4,400.

By General TYLER:

Question. Do I understand you to say that there were 4,000 men engaged as wagoners and hospital nurses, belonging to the army, that could not have been brought into line of battle?

There were nine divisions, with three brigades each, each brigade having five regiments—one hundred and twenty-two regiments. There was one unattached division which had twelve regiments. The one hundred and thirty-four regiments with 30 men in each regiment would be 4,020; I put it at 4,000. Those men were not available as soldiers; they could not leave their teams, and their service as hospital nurses could not, of course, be dispensed with, and those engaged as clerks never left the trains.

Question. Then one hundred and thirty-four regiments embraced the whole of General Buell's command, including those at Cumberland Gap and everywhere else?

No, sir; it included the three corps and General Dumont's division.

General BUELL. I should like the witness to verify his statement in regard to the arrival of General Sill's division with reference to the time the army marched.

The PRESIDENT. There is no objection, general, to your asking the question.

By General BUELL:

Question. In reference to taking up the march after the battle of Perryville, when did General Sill's division join?

The day after, I think.

Question. Explain what date you understand the question to refer to. The question refers to the time when the army continued its movements after the rebel army, subsequent to the 9th of October.

I answered in reference to our own movements and the movements of our own headquarters.

Question. How long was it before the headquarters went to Harrodsburg that General Sill's division joined?

We started on the morning after the evening of his arrival. I am speaking now from memory, and have nothing by which I can recall the exact time. I am quite certain, now that I reflect, about its not being on the 10th, as we remained in camp one day after the battle of Perryville, on the 9th, and on the 10th we moved forward to a camp beyond Perryville, where General Sill overtook us. I think it was on the 11th that he arrived.

General Buell here introduced the deposition of Captain Morton, which was read before the Commission.

The JUDGE-ADVOCATE. As this closes the evidence for the defense, with the exception of Colonel Fry, I propose to-morrow morning to commence with such rebutting evidence as I have on hand and proceed to a close.

The Commission adjourned to meet on Tuesday, April 7, at 11 o'clock a. m.

CINCINNATI, *Tuesday, April* 7, 1863.

The Commission met pursuant to adjournment. Members present, General Wallace, General Dana, General Tyler; also the judge-advocate and General Buell.

A communication from General Buell was read, desiring that the testimony of Lieutenant Fitzhugh might be taken as to the instructions that were sent to Major-General Thomas on the afternoon of the 8th of October.

After discussion it was decided in the affirmative.

Lieut. C. L. FITZHUGH (a witness for the defense), being duly sworn by the judge-advocate, testified as follows:

By General BUELL:

Question. State your name and your position in the service of the United States; whether you were on duty with the Army of the Ohio at the battle of Perryville and in what capacity, if you please.

My name is Charles L. Fitzhugh; first lieutenant Fourth Artillery; aide-de-camp to General Buell. I was on duty at the battle of Perryville as an aide-de-camp.

Question. At what time was it first known at headquarters that a battle was raging on the left at Perryville on the 8th of October?

At about a quarter after 4 in the afternoon.

Question. Did you on that occasion carry any instructions to Major-General Thomas. If so, state what they were, whether you delivered them, and any circumstances of interest connected with your visit to General Thomas' headquarters.

One of General McCook's aides-de-camp came to our headquarters and reported the state of affairs on the left about a quarter past 4 in the afternoon. I was immediately ordered to ride over, with a guide who was at headquarters and who belonged on the right, and order an advance on the right at once, and "press the attack on the right"—those were the words of the order—as General McCook had been driven back on the left; also to order a brigade to move at once over to the Springfield road, which was the road we were encamped on. I left our camp about half past 4 with this guide, and we reached the right and found General Thomas out in front at about half past 6, as well as I can judge. It was about an hour after sundown. I gave him the orders. He asked me then if it was intended to advance that night after dark, and I repeated the order and left him to draw his own inference from the order, which was to advance at once. I came back with him to his headquarters, which were half a mile to the rear of the place where we then were, and took tea with him. When I was about to ride home again he told me to tell General Buell that the enemy were in strong force right in his front, and that an advance of 100 yards on his part would bring on an engagement along the whole line; but that he would advance the next morning at the first sound of an action on the left; that he would advance with the first gun; and he told me to ride over and report that to General Buell, which I did. I suppose the ride took me an hour and a half. I reached our camp about half past 9, and reported to General Buell. As I rode out to the front on my way over in the first place I met Brig. Gen. William S. Smith, who I believe commanded the advance division on the right in that corps. He said that the enemy were only a few hundred yards from him, and had thirty pieces of artillery in position right on his front. I told him that they had had work on the left, and he said they would have harder on the right; that all the hard fighting was to be on the right. I reported that also to General Buell when I returned to camp.

General BUELL. I wish, Mr. President, to question the witness with reference to the circumstances of my visit to the camp of the First Division about the 23d of August last.

The JUDGE-ADVOCATE. I shall object, Mr. President, to going into an examination of that.

General BUELL. I will explain more fully the object of this testimony. I expect to show by this evidence the ground for the prejudice which certainly existed subsequently to that time in the minds of certain witnesses who have appeared before this Commission, quite enough prejudice to sway their judgment upon any matter of opinion where my official acts were concerned. The material part of the testimony of these witnesses—if a mere opinion can be considered material in such matters—is made up of opinion. I believe that this prejudice has rendered them incompetent to give a sound, impartial opinion. The evidence may or may not, depending upon the restriction which the Commission places upon it, extend to the motive and the disposition of Brigadier-General Schoepf, recently a member of this Commission. The Commission, however, have ruled out evidence upon that point heretofore. I do not know whether they will admit it now or not.

The JUDGE-ADVOCATE. I would like to remark in this connection that so far as any prejudice that might influence these witnesses goes General Buell is precluded from bringing forward anything to impeach them. General Buell in his cross-examination of these witnesses went outside of the examination-in-chief and made them his own. He now proposes to come in with other evidence to attack them before this Commission. He proposes to impeach his own witnesses. So far as General Schoepf is concerned I do not propose to occupy your time at all, but I will merely say that had that investigation gone on it would have shown a very different result from that which the record now implies.

General BUELL. I have no doubt of the propriety and admissibility of any evidence which shall affect the value of testimony that has been given before the Commission. I am satisfied of that without citing any authority. With reference to the motive that has been ascribed to Brigadier-General Schoepf, I challenge the judge-advocate or any other person to pursue that investigation.

The court was cleared; when it was decided that the objection should be sustained.

By General TYLER:

Question. Did you hear General McCook's aide make his report; and, if so, to whom?

I did not hear him make his report.

Question. Do you know to whom he reported?

I do not know of my own knowledge whom he reported to, but I suppose he reported to Major-General Buell in person.

Question. Whom did you receive the order from that you carried to General Thomas?

From General Buell.

Question. Was it written or verbal?

It was verbal.

Question. Was it usual to send an important order of that kind by verbal messages through an aide-de-camp?

It was done occasionally when there was great necessity or great hurry?

Question. What time, as near as you can make it, did you receive that verbal order?

About quarter after 4 in the afternoon.

Question. How long after General McCook's aide arrived in your camp?

I suppose while he was still there; immediately on his arrival.

Question. What is the distance from General Buell's camp to the point where you met General Thomas?

I suppose it was about 3½ miles, as near as I can judge.

Question. Did you consume all the time from a quarter past 4 to half past 6 in accomplishing that 3½ miles?

I stated that I left our camp at about half past 4.

Question. Did you require all the time from half past 4 to half past 6 to accomplish 3½ miles?

I was all that time hunting up the general, and discovered him accidentally. He was not at his own headquarters; he was out in front, and I lighted on him accidentally about the time I stated, which was about two hours after I left our own camp. He was off the road then in the field, and no one on the road knew anything of his whereabouts at all. .

Question. How was he engaged at the time you met him?

He had his aide-de-camp and was riding to his own headquarters; at least I suppose so, as he went straight there as I joined him.

Question. Did you receive this verbal order directly from General Buell or from his chief of staff?

I have answered that already, that I received it from General Buell.

Question. Repeat as near as possible the exact phraseology you used in communicating General Buell's order to General Thomas.

I repeat the words of the order exactly, which are: "To press the attack on the right, as General McCook had been driven back on the left, and to send a brigade on the Springfield road at once." I found at the time that I reached there that a brigade was on its way to the Springfield road.

Question. Had any attack been made on the right at that time?

They had had skirmishing on the right; that was all I knew of it.

Question. Did that skirmishing amount to an attack?

I heard it called heavy skirmishing, and that is the name I give it.

Question. How long did you remain at General Thomas' headquarters and what time did you leave there?

I must have staid there three-quarters of an hour, I think. I ate my supper, gave my horse a feed, and then started for home about 8 o'clock perhaps.

Question. Did you suppose the nature of the order you carried to General Thomas was to attack the enemy after dark?

I supposed when he received the order that he would advance at once; that was my own idea. There was a bright moon and it was almost as light as day.

Question. Would you infer from General Thomas' character as a soldier that if he received a positive order and understood the order to be positive to attack the enemy, he would not do it, night or day?

He received the order in the words I stated before. It could be judged whether the order was positive or not. The advance was not made.

Question. Did any conversation take place between you and General Thomas, after he received the order, by which you would infer that he understood the order to attack the enemy to be positive? Repeat any conversation as literally as possible.

I gave him the order at once when I reached him, and told him how long I had been gone from General Buell at his own headquarters; and he asked if the attack was to be made at night. I repeated the order to him at once, and left him to judge whether the advance was to be made at night. I carried him the words of the order right off in a great hurry.

Question. What observation did General Thomas make at the time as to the order?

I do not recollect that he made any observation at all.

Question. What time did you report to General Buell on your return to camp?

I have already stated, about half past 9, I should judge.

Question. Did you report that General Thomas had not obeyed the order?

I did not report in those words. I have already told how I reported.

Question. Have the goodness to repeat it.

He said that the enemy was in strong force on his front and that an advance of 100 yards would bring on an engagement all along the line, and that he would advance in the morning with the first sound of an action on the left; and I was given to understand that he would ride over to our headquarters himself in the course of the night; I so understood, though I do not know how I got the impression; and he did come to our headquarters.

Question. What comments were made by General Buell on the message you delivered to him from General Thomas; did he express any dissatisfaction?

I do not recollect whether he did or not.

General BUELL. I wish, Mr. President, in justice to General Thomas, to explain what interpretation I put upon this order myself. I never anticipated when I gave the order that it would be executed after night; and I think that under the circumstances General Thomas would have been justified in determining according to his own judgment whether it was necessary for him to undertake the execution of the order. If he thought it was impracticable he ought not to have undertaken it. I will add that I was apprehensive that very little could be done so late in the afternoon. I did not know how well General Thomas was prepared for such a movement. I will call your attention, furthermore, to the fact, which is shown upon your record, that owing to the cessation of the fight on the left and the change of the condition of affairs after the order which the witness has testified to was sent to General Thomas written instructions were sent to him at half past 6 o'clock. Those instructions required him to press his command forward as much as possible that night and be prepared to attack at daylight in the morning. I do not pretend to investigate whether he was to blame for not attempting it in some measure, nor do I charge anything upon him. I have not introduced this evidence for the purpose of attaching blame to General Thomas for the non-execution of that order.

The JUDGE-ADVOCATE. I propose to introduce as a witness this morning a Mr. McElwee, a gentleman from near Chattanooga, who is in possession of some intelligence in reference to the force there previous to and subsequent to the evacuation of Corinth. I wish to ask him a few questions in reference to that. He is in the employ of General Burnside, and is going away to-morrow morning. For that reason I wish to examine him to-day.

General TYLER. Is this the first rebutting evidence that is introduced?

The JUDGE-ADVOCATE. Yes, sir.

General TYLER. Then it is understood that General Buell is through?

The JUDGE-ADVOCATE. Yes, sir.

General BUELL. I think I must object to the introduction of this witness. I shall be very glad to have information on that subject, but the quality of information I expect you will derive from this witness can be multiplied to any extent. I doubt very much whether it will tend to enlighten the Commission. It is a subject that the judge-advocate ought to have exhausted before, I think.

The court was cleared; when, after discussion whether the witness should or should not be introduced, it was unanimously decided in the affirmative.

Mr. JAMES B. McELWEE (a witness for the Government), being duly sworn by the judge-advocate, testified as follows:

By the JUDGE-ADVOCATE:

Question. State your name and place of residence.

James B. McElwee, residing in Rhea County, East Tennessee.

Question. What distance is that from Chattanooga?

I think it is about 60 miles by land.

Question. State whether you were at Chattanooga or in its neighborhood in the spring or summer of 1862, when the Government forces first threatened it.

I was at Chattanooga when the Government forces were said to be near Bridgeport and they said there was to be a fight there.

Question. State as near as you can at what time that was and what occurred and all you know about it.

I am a bad hand to recollect dates; I cannot give them. It was at the time they had a fight at Bridgeport. I left Chattanooga and went down to Dalton, and part of the rebel force came there that night. My understanding was that they were taking the sick and wounded away. They stopped all the rolling stock on the road; they brought down all the rolling stock that was at Chattanooga and stopped any from going up. My understanding from rebel soldiers and others was that they were going to surrender Chattanooga.

Question. What was the number the rebels had at Chattanooga at that time?

I cannot tell what the number was, but it was not very large.

Question. What do you mean by saying that it was not very large; were there a thousand men?

There were not more than 1,000 or 1,500 men. That is my understanding; I am not positive. The force at Bridgeport retreated back to Chattanooga. I asked some soldiers how many Yankees they saw, and they said they only saw three or four on the other side of the river when they commenced retreating, and before the rebel infantry got across the bridge they turned a car loose and knocked several off into the river

Question. Had the victory at Bridgeport been followed up what would have been the consequence to Chattanooga?

Why Chattanooga, I think, would have surrendered.

General DANA. I take an objection to that question, that it is not rebutting evidence. If there is anything on the record to show that there has been a fight at Bridgeport I am mistaken.

The JUDGE-ADVOCATE. I do not recollect in what part of the testimony, though I think it can be found.

The PRESIDENT. It appears to me to be important to fix the date, so that it may be known whether the fight the witness speaks of was on the part of General Mitchel's or General Negley's forces or those of General Buell. I think it will be found by reference to General McCook's testimony that when his advance came to Bridgeport he saw the enemy's pickets, but it makes no mention of a battle; so if this fact occurred it must have had reference to General Negley's or General Mitchel's forces.

General BUELL. If it is admissible I request that he may be permitted to continue.

The JUDGE-ADVOCATE. I wish to fix the date if possible. State in what month this affair that you speak of occurred.

I cannot state the time. I do not think General Buell's forces were up there at that time. I think it was the force under General Mitchel. But I do not know much about the forces save what I heard reported throughout the country.

The JUDGE-ADVOCATE. It will be observed that the documentary evidence introduced on the part of the defense before the Commission takes us back to a period anterior to this affair of General Mitchel's at Chattanooga, for the purpose, I suppose, of giving us as clear a history of all the transactions connected with that campaign as possible, and that can only be effected by taking the events in connection with those that immediately preceded them. Now, it has been held that Chattanooga was a place of so much importance—the complaints from Washington that the Army of the Ohio did not advance with sufficient rapidity for the purpose of taking that place before the enemy could get there and fortify it or strengthen it by re-enforcements is responded to in this documentary evidence that it was a place of so much importance and the facilities for getting there were so great that it made no difference what time they got there; that Chattanooga would be defended to the best of their ability. In that light this evidence is important, because it shows that at that time the rebels made no efforts to defend the place, and that had our forces been pushed on Chattanooga would have been in our possession. I think it might be proper to go on and show what the condition of that place was and what was the character of its fortifications, for if there were any he certainly must have had some knowledge of them.

General DANA. In relation to rebutting evidence, if documentary evidence has been introduced here by the defense, and has not been examined by the Commission, which is irrelevant to the subject we have under consideration, it is only a reason why that much of it should be thrown out, because we do not wish to extend our investigations further than we are ordered, and it is not a reason for us to introduce irrelevant testimony, which is of no importance to us at all.

The PRESIDENT. Allow me to suggest that the court be cleared.

The court was cleared; when, after discussion, it was resolved that the examination of the witness should proceed.

By the JUDGE-ADVOCATE:

Question. Were you in Chattanooga subsequent to the arrival of Bragg and his forces?

Yes, sir; I was.

Question. State what the condition of that place was as a place of defense. Were there any fortifications? If so, state their extent, how many guns they had, and all you know about it.

I do not know whether they had any fortifications or not; I never heard any one say; nor do I know anything about their guns.

Question. If there had been any fortifications there would you not have known it?

I think I would.

Question. Do I understand you that at the time Bragg arrived there there were no fortifications?

I did not mean to say that. (Mr. McElwee here explained.) I did not understand the question as to whether I was in Chattanooga subsequent to the arrival of Bragg. I was not there.

Question. At what time were you there previous to the arrival of Bragg's forces?

I do not know, sir.

Question. I have no further questions to put to the witness, and under the ruling of the court, as I have elicited nothing, there is no ground on which a cross-examination can be had.

General BUELL. When did you leave your home in East Tennessee, Mr. McElwee?

The JUDGE-ADVOCATE. I shall have to object to this, Mr. President; there is really no evidence before the Commission on which to base a cross-examination. We occupy the position of having no witness at all before us, and General Buell, by going into new matter, will be making this witness his own.

General BUELL. I claim that under the rules of proceeding governing all courts it is my privilege to examine the witness on any subject connected with the pending examination. The position assumed by the judge-advocate that there is nothing to cross-examine upon I cannot admit at all. There is nothing in the question which I have asked to show that it may not be pertinent to a cross-examination.

The court was cleared; when, after discussion, it was unanimously decided that the objection should be sustained.

It was further decided that the witness' whole statement having been excluded with the consent of the judge-advocate there could be no cross-examination by General Buell.

Vote unanimous.

On the opening of the court—

The PRESIDENT. The Commission have decided, general, that as the testimony of the witness is so far immaterial it will be excluded from the evidence, and that therefore there is no ground for cross-examination.

General BUELL. Do I understand the Commission to decide that I have not the privilege of examining a witness except upon questions that are introduced by the judge-advocate?

The PRESIDENT. Yes, sir.

General BUELL. I should like to ask whether this ruling is based upon any authority or whether it is arbitrary?

The PRESIDENT. It is based upon a rule of law which applies in all cases of this kind. For instance, the judge-advocate introduces a witness in the way of rebutting testimony; after he has examined in chief you have by the rule of law the right to cross-examine, but you would not have the right to make him your witness originally. The same rule precisely applies to rebutting witnesses as to witnesses originally introduced, and the cross-examination of such witnesses is confined, as a matter of course, to evidence developed in the examination-in-chief.

Rev. W. G. BROWNLOW (a witness for the Government), being duly sworn by the judge-advocate, testified as follows:

By the JUDGE-ADVOCATE:

Question. Please state your name, occupation, and place of residence.

William G. Brownlow; Knoxville, Tenn.; editor and publisher of a newspaper for about a quarter of a century.

Question. State what you know of the resources of East Tennessee in reference to the wants of an army and what was the condition of the crops in the summer of 1862.

I could not say anything definite as to the crops of 1862. They put me in jail, and my information was therefore derived from hearsay and from newspapers. From these and from refugees I learn they were not so favorable as in former years. They started me out, before the crops were pitched or planted, on the 3d of March, and I cannot therefore say anything about the crops of 1862 of my own knowledge. The crops were not so good and the laborers not so abundant. The rebels had gone into the Southern army, and the Union men had absconded and broke over the mountains and joined the Federal army. There were not a great many slaves in East Tennessee—never were; the farming was chiefly done by white folks. I would not be surprised if not half the ground was occupied in 1862 that there was in 1861.

Question. State what you know of the resources of East Tennessee in the summer of 1862 as made up from the crops of 1861.

In 1861 I recorded as a journalist, on the authority of my correspondents from the various counties, unusually fine and abundant crops. We hardly ever had such a crop year. The corn was never so abundant; hay, timothy, and clover were abundant; so were oats; and wheat, the great staple of the country, was very fine, and reached an average crop. The rebels were engaged the latter part of the summer and fall and early winter of 1861 in gathering up the corn and wheat. The wheat they ran down to Atlanta, Ga., to the steam-mills. They boasted of salting down half a million of hogs. They said they had depots at Chattanooga, Athens, Sweetwater, Knoxville, and clear up to the Virginia line. Of hog-killing the largest was at Knoxville. We used to look out of our jail window upon the river, where they were killing hogs for weeks together, and as a matter of punishment they forced us to send our buckets and dip up our water below where they threw all their offal and refuse. We begged the officer of the jail to allow us to get our water from above, but he refused us the privilege. The rebels were alarmed at the result of the Fishing Creek fight, and, in expectation of the Federal army, threatened to burn the large stores of meat and grain in Knoxville; at least so they said. It was an abundant country for hogs and corn.

Question. If it had been possible for the army of the Government to seize and hold Chattanooga in the summer of 1862 what reliance could be placed upon East Tennessee for supplies?

That would depend entirely upon the extent of the crop, and I have no knowledge of that except from hearsay and from newspapers. The inhabitants, the owners of farms, were five to one on the side of the Union in the thirty-two counties of East Tennessee, and as long as they had anything they would have contributed it to the Government army. It could have had what there was, but to what extent they could have supplied the army I do not know. I was not there; I was in the North during the whole summer and fall. I was absent for thirteen months.

Question. State what opportunity you had of judging of the effects of the different policies exercised by our Government toward the disaffected districts and places. What, so far as you have observed, is the result of a kind and conciliatory policy?

In the winter and spring I was a good deal in Kentucky and Tennessee, at Murfreesborough and Nashville, and I saw and conversed with gentlemen from all parts of Tennessee—East, West, and Middle—and I consider—that is the impression made upon my mind—that a conciliatory forbearance would not work advantageously for the Union cause. It is proper to qualify that by stating that I am an ultra; that I would have ultra, stringent, measures used against them.

Question. So far as you have observed has not the effect of the policy that makes war upon the rebel in arms and gives the same protection to the man who sympathizes openly with the rebellion that it does to the good citizen been to convince the rebels that it arose rather from our weakness than from our sense of justice?

Yes, sir; this has been the result of my observation. They attribute our forbearance toward them to cowardice and think that we are afraid of them. It disheartens and discourages the Unionists. I heard them complain at Nashville even of Governor Johnson's forbearing and conciliatory course toward the rebels.

Question. Has this amiable policy been practiced by the rebels to any extent?

That is not my experience, sir; just the reverse.

Question. In disaffected districts, occupied first by one army and then another, has not the effect of the two policies, that is, the policy exercised by our Government heretofore and that of the rebels, been to make it much safer for a man to be a rebel sympathizer than to sympathize with the Union?

I have heard a leading and influential Union man assert that. I could not say of my own knowledge how it is. It is a very common remark, however, among the Unionists in Tennessee and Kentucky.

The court then adjourned to meet on Wednesday, April 8, at 11 o'clock a. m.

CINCINNATI, *Wednesday, April 8, 1863.*

The Commission met pursuant to adjournment. Members present, General Wallace, General Dana, General Tyler; also the judge-advocate and General Buell.

The JUDGE-ADVOCATE. I propose sending the following questions to General Thomas:

"Did Lieutenant Fitzhugh, aide-de-camp on the staff of Major-General Buell, bring you an order on the night of the 8th of October, at Perryville, commanding you to attack the enemy? If so, why was not that order obeyed? Give as nearly as you can the conversation between you and Lieutenant Fitzhugh in reference to that order and its meaning."

General BUELL. I shall make no objection to the question if it is put in the form in which the evidence has presented the matter to the Commission. General Thomas' position was not known to be such that he could instantly attack the enemy when that order was sent to him. The order, as testified to by Lieutenant Fitzhugh, required him to press forward and attack the enemy, or some such phraseology as that. The testimony of Lieutenant Fitzhugh explains that this order was given in the afternoon, and your record shows that General Thomas was not necessarily expected to execute that order after night. As the question now reads it will convey to the mind of General Thomas the impression that it has been asserted in evidence before this Commission that he was ordered to make an attack on the night of the 8th, whereas I have explained that that was not contemplated in the order when I gave it. If the question is amended so as to read " afternoon " instead of night I have no objection to it.

General DANA. I think it would be better for the question to read " afternoon or evening." As it stands at present it conveys the idea of a night attack.

The PRESIDENT. As that order is quoted by Lieutenant Fitzhugh it leaves a clear impression on my mind that General Thomas was ordered to make an attack as soon as he received that order. The words, I believe, were " to advance and press the attack." General Buell's explanation is that he was not expected to make a night attack, but the order, as conveyed by Lieutenant Fitzhugh, without General Buell's explanation, would leave only the impression that he was ordered to advance and press the attack, whether it was night or day. The nature of the order as given by Lieutenant Fitzhugh allowed no discretion to General Thomas that I can see.

General TYLER. It looks very much as if General Thomas was guilty of a disobedience of orders, and the only evidence showing he was not guilty of disobedience is the exculpation or explanation now offered by General Buell. There is no proof before the Commission that General Thomas is not guilty of disobedience of orders, and there is nothing to do away with the testimony of Lieutenant Fitzhugh except it is General Buell's admission.

General BUELL. I have not undertaken to exculpate General Thomas, but I have stated that it was not my expectation when that order was given that it would be executed after night. If General Thomas had seen that the execution of the order was feasible after night, that he could accomplish the object, and that the thing he was ordered to do was desirable and expedient at the time, I should say that he ought to have done it. But if he had considered it impracticable and injudicious I should have blamed him for executing it at that time. It was explained to him that a considerable time had elapsed since the order was given and the circumstances had very materially changed.

The question was then amended to read as follows:

" Did Lieutenant Fitzhugh, aide-de-camp on the staff of Major-General Buell, bring you an order at half past 6 o'clock on the 8th of October at Perryville commanding you to advance on the right at once and press the attack? If so, why was not that order obeyed. Give as nearly as you can the conversation between yourself and Lieutenant Fitzhugh in reference to that order and its meaning."

The court was cleared; when it was decided that the question as amended should be forwarded to Major-General Thomas.

On the opening of the court the following additional question to be forwarded to Major-General Thomas was read:

" How far are you responsible for General Crittenden's corps not being in line on the morning of the 8th of October, and what reason existed, if any, why that corps was not in line at the time ordered by General Buell, on the night of the 7th? "

General BUELL. There was no particular time ordered for General Crittenden's corps to be in line. He was ordered to march at a particular hour on the morning of the 8th, but there was no particular time appointed for him to be in line. I therefore object to the question in that shape. I would state also, Mr. President, that I might reasonably object to the whole of this matter. These are facts that were stated in my official report and in my telegraphic dispatch to the general-in-chief, and they should have been investigated by the judge-advocate at the time. However, I waive that. General Crittenden was not required, and there is nothing in the evidence before the Commision that states that he was required, to be in line at a particular time.

The JUDGE-ADVOCATE. I do not think, Mr. President, that this second question is a matter of much importance. General Thomas, I think, in his testimony states why they did not march at the time ordered and how they arrived there at the hour they did, and with the explanation now made by General Buell I see no object in asking the question. If, however, the Commission determines to ask either or both the questions of General Thomas they have the right to do so. These facts make a part of General Buell's defense, and I have a right to explain it away or contradict it if I have the evidence. Still I do not think the second question is of sufficient importance to press upon the Commission.

General BUELL. I have not introduced the testimony of Lieutenant Fitzhugh on that point in defense. As far as that matter is concerned I do not put myself in that attitude. I introduced it as a fact for the consideration of the Commission.

The question as amended read as follows:

"How far are you responsible for General Crittenden's corps not being in line on the morning of the 8th of October, and what reason existed, if any, why that corps was not on the march at the time ordered by General Buell, on the night of the 7th?"

General BUELL. I think it is all explained in General Thomas', testimony and in General Crittenden's too.

The court was cleared; when, after discussion, it was decided that the second question should be put to General Thomas.

The cross-examination of the Rev. W. G. Brownlow was then proceeded with.

By General BUELL:

Question. You have stated, I believe, Mr. Brownlow, in your direct testimony, that the rebel army drew freely upon the supplies of East Tennessee. What surplus above what would be required for the subsistence of the people until the new crops came in do you suppose there was on hand of the crop of 1861 at the time you left your home?

It was, as I remarked, a very abundant year, but the rebels had seized upon all they could find and had agents out purchasing. They ran it out of the country or stored it in various depots in great abundance in Knoxville, New Market, Greenfield, Bristol, Sweetwater, Cleveland, Chattanooga, &c. They had it in charge; it was out of the hands of the people; a great deal of wheat had been run off to the steam-mills at Atlanta. I should not consider that there was a great deal available outside of their hands. There was great complaint on the part of the people that they were oppressing them. Some men were put in jail for refusing to sell to the Confederate agents; that was the only offense they had committed. I could not say to what extent there were supplies. For three months of close confinement I could only learn from my fellow-prisoners, as they came in, what was going on out of doors. There was scarcely a day but there were accessions to our numbers in the jail, and they would give us the latest news.

Question. Considering the general scarcity of provisions in the South and the harsh policy which the rebel authorities practiced toward the loyal people of East Tennessee do you think it probable that there was any considerable surplus of provisions in the country as late as March of last year?

I should say not outside of what the rebel authorities had, for they bought it all up. There was a great deal, but they had it in their depots, and threatened to burn up and destroy it if the Federal army got in. There was also quite an abundance of beef cattle, hogs, and mutton which they seized upon; in addition to the abundance of grain hogs and cattle were abundant, but the rebel authorities had them all. I have been accustomed to lay in my pork, and never had to give $10 per hundred till then, which was the price I had to pay then.

Question. Have you frequently seen people from your country since you left there; and do they now give, as recently as you have seen any of them, any account with regard to the condition of the people and the abundance of their supplies?

I have seen them all the time; they come to see me here. I met with them at Nashville and Murfreesborough, and I went through the army and talked to them. They all agree, are harmonious in one tale, and that is that they are threatened with starvation all over East Tennessee; that destitution is very great, and they are very anxious that the Federal Army shall enter the country or they will starve. The labor, as I said, is chiefly performed by whites, and these have mostly gone into one army or the other or have absconded, and my information is that the present spring no crops of any consequence will be planted. This whole past summer was a season of great destitution and want. I think no people on this continent have suffered as severely as they have.

Question. Do you think that a temporary advance of our troops in East Tennessee would be wise or merciful to the people, as a general policy?

I think not, sir. I am perfectly satisfied in my own mind that if we are only to make a temporary advance upon them we had better stay away. Unless we go in and get possession of the country, leave it alone by all means. When we burned their bridges, a little over a year ago, they took our men and hung them in retaliation. I would deprecate our army going there, under the command of any one, only for a temporary hold of it. If it is not to be permanent I hope they will stay away. It would be better for the people to be left as they are.

Question. Have the Union people of East Tennessee generally remained loyal in spite of the cruel treatment they have received from the rebel authorities?

Yes, sir; I should say so. They have never shrunk from their devotion to the Government and to the Union.

Question. Suppose it had been evident that the Government which the rebels desired to establish would secure perfectly the equality and liberties of the people as well as under our Constitution, and that then the rebel authorities had pursued a mild course toward the people instead of a very severe one, whould they be in a better or worse disposition toward the rebel Government and the rebel authorities than they are now?

If they had adopted a more kindly course of conduct toward the people, instead of exasperating them, they would have felt more kindly toward them; but I have no idea that they would have indorsed secession or the rebel Government; that is, the Union portion of them. We held two large conventions for East Tennessee in May and July; we had Nelson, Johnson, and others speaking, and they were ultra men, and we had some conciliatory men, Colonel Baxter and others, who proposed that we should ground our arms, but the crowd would not listen to such a proposition, and called out, "They are damned secessionists; let them go and join them." The masses of the people were ahead of what we call the leaders. I witnessed those demonstrations. They sent Colonel Bell up there to set us right because we had voted largely, but we drove him back indignantly to Middle Tennessee. The people refused to hear him speak at all.

Question. Have you seen anything of the effects of the presence of large armies in a country, and is it or is it not your observation that under a system which requires that an army should live upon the country and its inhabitants, friends and foes suffer alike, as a general rule?

Yes, sir; the only fair view I have ever had of anything of that kind was in the vicinity of Murfreesborough, Nashville, and Gallatin, a country I was very familiar with. I have traveled over it in years gone by on horseback and by stage and rail, and I found, in returning from that country in the fall, in the winter, and again in the spring, all destroyed, and everybody's property suffered alike. There was a general using up of everything and everybody, a general deprecation of war, and a general wish with those I talked to that peace should be restored. All deprecate the war and devastation alike now, rebels and Unionists. This was the first manifestation of war I had ever witnessed. I have not been accustomed to war or to armies.

Question. Suppose our army should enter East Tennessee and should practice there a system which results in such universal devastation and ruin, do you think the affections of the people toward our cause would be strengthened by such a condition of things?

I think that in East Tennessee there would be a division. The Union party would submit to anything and indorse anything almost that the Federal Army did, and the other party would complain. I do not think the Federal Army could do anything there that would be offensive to the Unionists, provided they inflicted punishment upon the rebels in a spirit of retaliation.

Question. Suppose that in the execution of this system of retaliation the Union people should find that they suffered as much as their traitorous neighbors, do you or do you not suppose that they would soon learn to regard their friends with almost as much animosity as their enemies when they saw that they had no more protection under one than under the other; is that human nature or not?

Yes, sir; that is human nature. And if they were to suffer as much under the Federal Army as they have done under the other they would feel very greatly disappointed and it would have the tendency to cool them off. This is an opinion founded upon what I think human nature is.

Question. Do you believe that there are a great many people in the Southern States who are loyal at heart but compelled under the circumstances to acquiesce in the rebellion?

I do believe that the number is much greater than our friends and intelligent men here in the North suppose it to be, and that they are prevented from coming out for fear that when we take a place we shall not continue to hold it and that they will suffer for it afterward. It is fear that keeps them down. I would designate the State of Georgia as having a great many men loyal at heart, but who are crushed down. It may be that I am better acquainted with Georgia than with any other State out of Tennessee. I know they very reluctantly went into the rebellion.

Question. Do you think those people deserve punishment for a state of things which it was not in their power to prevent and which they still deprecate?

No, sir; I do not think they do. I should be sorry to have them punished if it could be avoided. I blame them, the whole of them, for not standing out and squarely avowing their sentiments. I censure them for knocking under rather than submit to punishment. I would rather be hanged myself.

Question. But is it not a very rare thing to find in human character firmness and constancy enough to endure such trials?

I could not say; it seems so to me, sir. In East Tennessee there were thousands of the most remarkable cases, that never came before the country, of men firm, unyielding, and spirited to the last, even under the lash and whip. They put them in jail, they starved them, and hung them under the gallows trying to extort confessions from them, but they said they would rather die first.

Question. Have you known of any policy practiced by any of our armies which regarded loyal people and traitors in the same light and treated them alike under all circumstances?

No, sir; I have not known anything of the kind personally. I have heard complaints, but they are matters of hearsay only. I have no knowledge of anything of the kind.

Question. What was the extent of these complaints, what did they amount to—those that have most attracted your attention?

Not very extensive, I think. I have heard our folks complain that a man to have his property and rights protected had better be a rebel. I heard it in reference to Cumberland Gap last year, but how well founded I do not know. I always thought it well to discourage grumbling both among citizens and soldiers, and when I heard anything of the kind among our East Tennessee troops I tried to reconcile them to their condition.

Question. Have you heard any of those complaints recently?

Yes, sir; on my last visit to Nashville. The complaint seemed to apply to the city authorities there—complaints of the military authorities in charge of the city and of Governor Johnson. But such complaints are always more or less going on; a great deal of such has come under my notice.

Question. Has Governor Johnson, as Governor of the State of Tennessee and in other prominent positions, been considered to have exhibited remarkable administrative and other qualities which fit a man to govern wisely, to shape a wise policy for the government of men?

The JUDGE-ADVOCATE. I object to that question, Mr. President. It certainly is traveling out of the examination-in-chief; and even if it were not, Governor Johnson is not on trial before this Commission.

General BUELL. A similar question was asked of a former witness by the judge-advocate himself. I do not know whether in putting that question the judge-advocate considered that it placed Governor Johnson on trial before this Commission. I do not think it did, nor do I think that this question places him on trial. I ask the question because it has been asked before by the judge-advocate in a somewhat different shape, because it is connected with the question of policy, and because I understand from the judge-advocate's question that Governor Johnson's opinion and practice may be supposed to have some importance in your deliberations on this question.

The PRESIDENT. When was the question asked, general?

General BUELL. It was asked of one of my witnesses.

The PRESIDENT. Was it asked in the examination-in-chief?

General BUELL. No, sir.

The court was cleared; when it was unanimously decided that the question should not be put.

By General TYLER:

Question. Was this devastation of which the people complained in the vicinity of Gallatin and other parts of Tennessee, that you speak of in your testimony, the result of regular foraging under the direction of proper officers of the army or was it occasioned by the plundering of our troops?

I could not say, sir; it was just a general complaint in a spirit of grumbling, but I heard nothing said of its being done either in a regular or an irregular manner. It was looked upon as the effects and consequences of the war, and I would infer that the people there were all very sick of it.

Question. Supposing that the Federal army should go to East Tennessee, and should, through the regular departments of the army, strip the country of all that is necessary to support that army, paying those men who could prove their loyalty and refusing compensation to those who were disloyal, do you or do you not suppose that such a course of policy would strengthen the hands of the army in East Tennessee?

It would meet with the hearty approbation of the whole Union population and would be doing just what they would expect.

Question. From what you know and from what you hear of the campaign of 1862 in Kentucky and Tennessee was that the policy pursued by the Federal army?

I know nothing personally, but from what I have heard they complained that it was not. It was merely a matter of complaint and rumor of those I heard talking about it.

General BUELL. I object to the question and to the answer. It is on record that an order was issued requiring certificates to be given to persons from whom supplies were received. The condition of payment upon those certificates is that the claimant shall prove his loyalty; so that no mere matter of opinion or hearsay evidence can be of any value or validity upon that point. I am willing it should pass.

By General DANA:

Question. Do you know whether, prior to the issue of an order by the Government making payment for produce or articles taken by the army for its use conditional on the loyalty or disloyalty of the parties from whom the articles were taken, there was any authority for any general commanding an army in the field to adopt that policy?

I am not able to answer the question satisfactorily.

Question. Do you know whether the policy of the Government of the United States in regard to the treatment of the population of States in rebellion to the United States has been changed since the first outbreak of the rebellion, so far as taking supplies from them and giving them vouchers with the conditions of payment predicated upon their loyalty or disloyalty is concerned?

I do not know, sir, of any change in the policy.

Question. Is it or is it not notorious that at the outbreak of the rebellion the policy of the Government toward the people residing in rebellious districts was what is termed a conciliatory and kind policy?

That was my understanding, sir, at the outbreak of the rebellion—that that was the policy of the Government and would continue to be. I have individually looked upon it as a mistaken policy.

Question. Are you informed whether the present policy of the Government is more or less severe than it was?

I cannot say that I am. I do not know whether the policy of the Government has been changed or not.

The court then adjourned to meet on Thursday, April 9, at 11 o'clock a. m.

CINCINNATI, *Thursday, April 9, 1863.*

The Commission met pursuant to adjournment. Members present, General Wallace, General Dana, General Tyler; also the judge-advocate and General Buell.

The JUDGE-ADVOCATE. There are three witnesses that the Commission and General Buell have expressed a desire to examine, whose evidence I have some difficulty in procuring—Major-General Halleck, Governor Johnson, and Colonel Fry. I would like to have some advice from the Commission as to what steps to take to procure their evidence. I presume I can get their depositions. I have about made up my mind that I cannot get them before the Commission.

The PRESIDENT. I thought you had forwarded questions to Major-General Halleck to be answered.

The JUDGE-ADVOCATE. I notified General Buell that I would take the depositions of Major-General Halleck and Governor Johnson, but by some irregularity of the mail the questions did not reach Washington until after the date of the notice. I certainly shall have him before the Commission or get his deposition on the same notice if General Buell does not object.

General BUELL. I have stated frequently and earnestly to the Commission my wish that Governor Johnson should appear before the Commission, and my conviction that for the sake of justice he ought to appear; and I must insist that he shall come or that the Government shall refuse to permit him. It is undoubtedly in the power of the Commission to bring him before them if they are not restrained by higher authorities.

The PRESIDENT. Has the judge-advocate heard from Governor Johnson?

The JUDGE-ADVOCATE. Yes, Mr. President; and I see I cannot get either of these witnesses before the Commission in any reasonable time. Governor Johnson is engaged in organizing some expedition in Tennessee; and I have received directions from Secretary Stanton that he will not permit me to take any officer out of active service to appear before this Commission when a deposition can be had.

General BUELL. Has the judge-advocate been informed by the Government that Governor Johnson is employed on such active service that he cannot appear before the Commission?

The JUDGE-ADVOCATE. No, sir.

General BUELL. Then the instructions of the Secretary of War to which the judge-advocate has referred do not apply to him. I take it that there must be some evidence of his being so employed before he can be considered within the prohibition of the Secretary of War.

The JUDGE-ADVOCATE. Governor Johnson, I believe, is brigadier-general of the volunteer service and Military Governor of Tennessee; he is not connected with Ohio in any possible form, and I have no process by which I can bring Governor Johnson before the Commission.

The PRESIDENT. Aside from these what other witnesses are there?

The JUDGE-ADVOCATE. Those are all.

General DANA. As soon as this documentary evidence is indorsed I propose to inform the Government that the Commission is through with this investigation, except receiving the testimony of Major-General Halleck, Governor Johnson, and Colonel Fry; and the Government must then let us know distinctly whether we can have those witnesses or not; if we cannot, we shall proceed to take their depositions.

The JUDGE-ADVOCATE. The Government will throw the responsibility of obtaining the evidence of these witnesses upon my shoulders; and why I do not take their depositions may be very pertinently asked by the Department, and unless I am prevented I shall proceed to take those depositions without delay. I understand you, general, that the wish for personal examination was more particularly confined to Governor Johnson?

General BUELL. Yes, sir. I do not know what deposition the judge-advocate proposes to take from Major-General Halleck.

The questions proposed to be submitted to General Halleck were here read by the judge-advocate, as follows:

"1st. What was the cause of the delay in the march of the Army of the Ohio from Corinth to North Alabama and who is responsible for that delay?

"2d. What were the circumstances attending the dispatch sent by General Buell from Nashville to the Department at Washington asking for instructions and what was the response and the circumstances connected with it?"

The PRESIDENT. Have you heard from General Halleck.

The JUDGE-ADVOCATE. Not directly. When I was in Washington he told me that he had too much business on hand to be taken before any court for examination.

The PRESIDENT. How about depositions?

The JUDGE-ADVOCATE. As I have stated, the questions arrived at Washington too late, and I have nothing definite to place before the Commission.

General BUELL. The first question of the judge-advocate is decidedly objectionable. It asks merely for the expression of an opinion on a question the Commission is to investigate. The business of the Commission is to inquire into the causes of the delay, and not to ascertain them by the expression of the opinion of any person. An expression of General Halleck on that question could be only one of opinion. He has not as good an opportunity of knowing the facts as the Commission, for they have all the records and the testimony of as many witnesses as they choose to call. The question calls for an opinion in regard to facts of which he has no knowledge. The second question refers to documentary evidence, and that evidence, I understand, has been furnished from Washington, and is to be presented this morning. So that of the two questions one is improper and the other is superfluous.

General DANA. It appears to me that we are now running against difficulties which I have seen all along we should encounter; and it appears to me that it is the most serious difficulty that can arise in our proceedings. I have remarked before this that there are no witnesses that have been introduced before the court whose testimony the court has a right to suppose will be more important than the testimony of Major-General Halleck and Colonel Fry. I do not believe there will be a dissenting opinion in the court as to the propriety of examining those two witnesses, but as to examining them by deposition I do not believe that any member of the court can consider that method will be satisfactory to either side in this case. I certainly would prefer not to have General Halleck examined at all than in the way proposed by those two questions, which do not reach the two important points that we have a right to investigate. Now, we all know that General Halleck cannot be brought here nor can Colonel Fry. The exigencies of the service will not permit it, and we find ourselves situated just as I feared we should be. I think, then, that in this case we ought to make such a representation to the Department of the actual necessity of having those two gentlemen before this Commission as has not heretofore been made to them. There has been no full representation made to the Department at Washington of the reasons which compel the Commission to feel the necessity of the presence of those two witnesses, and I think before we give up the expectation of having those witnesses present before the court that it is our duty to make a full representation of the necessity to the Government, and let them take the responsibility, where it properly belongs, of saying whether this Commission shall or shall not have this evidence that they consider so very important. Now I am unwilling to close this case without having the full evidence of these two witnesses. What their evidence will be I do not know, but I cannot believe that there is any evidence before the Commission that will be more important in this investigation than that of the general-in-chief, and who then commanded in front of Corinth, and who gave the orders to the Army of the Ohio which started it on its mission, and the testimony of the chief of staff of that army. As to the testimony of Governor Johnson, I have no very definite opinion about that, but if he is going to remain in Washington long enough for this Commission to get there I think his case may also be embraced in the represention that ought to be made of the absolute necessity that exists why this court should adjourn to where they can get the testimony of these witnesses; and if it cannot be obtained in that way I do not think it ought to be obtained at all.

The PRESIDENT. It is a matter of the most ordinary justice that, if these questions which have been read by the judge-advocate be submitted to General Halleck, General Buell should have the right to cross-examine. I am decidedly in favor of insisting that he should have that privilege; it is but a matter of justice to him, and if this evidence is taken by deposition he cannot have that permission.

General DANA. I imagine it would not be necessary to bring General Halleck into court. If the judge-advocate and General Buell were at Washington they could obtain his evidence from him at his own office. I think General Halleck's examination would be a very long one before the court.

General TYLER. I do not think we can judge whether General Halleck's testimony will be wanted till we have read this documentary evidence that is now before the Commission. It might fill up the gap for which his testimony is now required. And as to calling Colonel Fry before the Commission, I should be very glad to have him examined personally, but we have had Major Wright before the Commission. He was on General Buell's staff, was second in command, and is probably as conversant with the operations of the army at that time as Colonel Fry himself could be. As far as my recollection is concerned he has been examined on the main points on which it is proposed to examine Colonel Fry. As to making a proposition to adjourn to Baltimore, I think, the Government having rebuked that so positively, I am not myself willing to again place myself on the record as advising the Government as to the course of proceeding on the part of the Commission. We have our orders to remain here till our business is closed, and I for one am for obeying those orders.

General DANA. I suppose that that willingness would be made so by compulsion. We are here and ordered to remain here, but I wish to put myself on the record as representing the necessity of having the testimony of these two witnesses, and leaving the Government to take the responsibility of telling us to stop here and close up our case or ordering us to Washington, one of the two. When they are told of the necessity of the case they will know, but they cannot know till a full representation is made to them.

The PRESIDENT. I am opposed to taking the depositions of Major-General Halleck and Colonel Fry, and I am not in favor of asking the "powers that be" the privilege of going to Washington to take their testimony. The simple question now before us is whether we shall be allowed to take the depositions of these gentlemen, and I believe with General Dana as to the importance of the testimony of General Halleck. I have read the documentary evidence General Tyler alludes to with a great deal of care. It is very satisfactory in every respect save in one important particular, and that is, whose plan of operation that was; that can only be told by General Halleck himself, who was then commander of the Department of the West, as I think it was then called. We were ordered to remain in Cincinnati till our examination was completed. That is settled. The question now is whether we shall have the depositions of General Halleck and Colonel Fry, or shall the judge-advocate ask if we can have the testimony of these gentlemen. If there is no other way in which it can be done, the judge-advocate and General Buell can go to Washington and there conduct the examination. We may thus avoid disobedience of orders and accommodate the witnesses.

The documentary evidence received from Washington, and marked *—

Documentary evidence from Headquarters, Washington, for the Government, A ;

Documentary evidence from Headquarters, Washington, B ;
Documentary evidence from Headquarters, Washington, C ;
Documentary evidence from Headquarters, Washington, D ;
Documentary evidence from Headquarters, Washington, E ;

Letters marked No. 1 to 4, from Headquarters, Washington, F—was here presented to General Buell for his examination and his assent to its introduction as evidence before the Commission.

Glancing over the documentary evidence from Washington proposed to be submitted to the Commission General BUELL remarked:

---

* See note on page 690.

Of course I have no objection to these documents. They are more complete than my own files. I should desire them myself if they were not to be introduced by the Government. I find some verbal inaccuracies, which can perhaps be corrected as we go along. Before any decision is given as to the full effect of the recent act of Congress with reference to the testimony of absent witnesses I should like to have an opportunity to submit my views on that question. I am not prepared to do so at this moment with as much care as it requires. I will merely say now that if a literal interpretation is to be placed upon the wording of the law, it amounts to an abrogation of every principle of justice, as far as securing evidence is concerned. Justice could never be secured by any such practice as that. I do not suppose any intelligent man will pretend that that law would permit such a thing as this; that this Commission, sitting here, could compel me to submit to the introduction of evidence by deposition when the witness, living on the other side of the river, could be brought here in half an hour. If that is the case, an accused person could be prevented from ever confronting his accusers. The evidence of witnesses on the other side of the river having been admitted by deposition, the court could be transferred to that side, and the same process executed with reference to witnesses on this. The case of Governor Johnson presents almost such an example, though I do not wish to assert that it was so designed. I think I may say that it was the intention of the judge-advocate to call Governor Johnson at first. He failed to do so when the Commission was sitting in the same city and in the same building with him, and now, having gone beyond the State or district in which he lives, his deposition is insisted upon.

The JUDGE-ADVOCATE. So far, Mr. President, as any discussion upon that law would go, of course General Buell has an entire right to call your attention to it; but so far as my conduct is concerned I must beg leave to differ as to his right. There has been nothing before this Commission, that I can perceive, that would authorize such remarks. I inquired of Governor Johnson what he knew, and came to the conclusion that the testimony was not important. Since then, since our arrival in Louisville, documents and facts have come to my knowledge which I think make his examination important, and I proposed to call him. There is no wish on my part to take his deposition; I should infinitely prefer to have him before the Commission; but I shall take his deposition, as it seems I cannot get him.

General BUELL. The questions presented to the Commission by the judge-advocate to be submitted to Governor Johnson do not refer to any documents. If Governor Johnson's evidence is required with reference to any documents, I shall insist that the judge-advocate produce the documents or make his explanation more complete, and then we can judge whether Governor Johnson's evidence is necessary.

The JUDGE-ADVOCATE. The Commission can judge of the importance of that evidence when they get it and not before. I have already stated upon what points I wish to examine Governor Johnson. I submitted these questions in writing and had the action of the Commission upon them. As to how he will respond to them, it is of course impossible for me to say, but the Commission can judge of his reply after they get it.

General BUELL. The Commission will remember that in my presence the judge-advocate was asked by the President as to whether he was ready to call Governor Johnson in Nashville and he answered that he was not prepared to call him at that time. I inferred from that that he had given notice to the Commission that he intended to call him, and I have no doubt he did give that notice; and I shall be compelled to say that if Governor Johnson does not come before this Commission it will appear very badly in some respects at least. I wish to call the attention of the Commission again to the fact that I am notified now that the judge-advocate will on the 13th of April proceed to take depositions of Governor Johnson and Major-General Halleck. I call your attention to the fact that the Commission has not been informed that the presence of these witnesses cannot be obtained. If the Commission has not the power to bring them before it the Government certainly has the power, and the Commission has not been informed yet that the Government will not exercise that power. I therefore state my protest against the taking of the deposition of Governor Johnson; at all events as intimated in the notice of the judge-advocate. The judge-advocate has undertaken another responsibility in this matter, and that is to fix the notice that may be deemed sufficient under the law. I should like to know by what authority he limits that notice to three days after to-day.

The JUDGE-ADVOCATE. Under the law governing the taking of depositions in the State of Ohio that is the notice I have to give; that is the practice in civil courts.

The PRESIDENT. By the law governing the practice in civil courts that would be a sufficient notice; it is only required to give a reasonable time for the parties to attend at the place where the deposition is to be taken. There being no allusion to the length of notice made in this act of Congress, I presume that the customary practice would be followed.

General BUELL. Does the Commission understand that after this notice I am authorized to proceed to Washington to conduct this investigation as far as I am concerned?

The PRESIDENT. So far as I am concerned, the Commission would give you the privilege to go there at once in person or employ an attorney, or both.

General BUELL. I should like a decision on that question.

The JUDGE-ADVOCATE. Before any steps are taken in that matter I wish to say to the Commission and General Buell that he is laboring under a misapprehension in reference to Governor Johnson. I am expecting Governor Johnson here every day, and the moment he makes his appearance I will stop him. I am merely making every effort possible to get his evidence. If he remains in Washington I shall try to get it; if he come through Cincinnati I shall endeavor to examine him. There is no preference for taking his deposition instead of having him before the Commission, nor can I understand why General Buell is so anxious to have him before the Commission instead of taking his deposition. The Department at Washington does not recognize any difference between taking a deposition and having the witness in open court. The exigencies of the service forced that law. The first great difficulty was to get a court, and the next difficulty was to get witnesses from the Army. Many flagrant cases have occurred in which nothing could be done in consequence of the difficulty of getting a witness, and if I did not apply this law of the Government I do not know how I should proceed. I have no wish to take the deposition of Governor Johnson.

General BUELL. No doubt the law was adopted for the very reason that the judge-advocate has stated; but that does not authorize the judge-advocate or any tribunal to set aside without necessity the principle that a person accused has the right to confront his accusers. The law, I suppose, only applies to those cases where the public service or other circumstances render it impossible to procure the attendance of witnesses. That is not the case with Governor Johnson. Governor Johnson has been traveling through the States for a month; he could as well have been here as elsewhere, and I venture to say with as little detriment to the public service. It is a notorious fact that he could have been, and there is no excuse for his not having been, brought before the Commission. The Government has not undertaken to say he shall not appear.

The JUDGE-ADVOCATE. Nor has it.

General BUELL. Governor Johnson has no right to say he will not appear.

The JUDGE-ADVOCATE. Nor has he.

General BUELL. Nor has the judge-advocate the right to assume it.

After some conversation respecting the depositions of Governor Johnson and General Halleck General BUELL continued:

With reference to the notification of the judge-advocate that he would take the deposition of General Halleck I wish to call the attention of the Commission to the fact that he has not been authorized to take General Halleck's testimony at all. He has stated the proposition this morning, but it has not yet received the sanction of the Commission. I mention this in answer to the notification which has just been served upon me that his testimony will be taken by deposition, and I call your attention again to the objections which I made to the questions themselves and upon which no decision has been given by the Commission.

General TYLER. The order of the Commission with respect to Governor Johnson is that he shall, if possible, be brought before it. If he is not I do not see that we can take any action upon his deposition till it is brought before the Commission.

General DANA. I have no doubt it is General Buell's right to appear when the deposition is taken if he considers it necessary; and when the deposition is before the Commission I do not see that we can take any action upon it without some representation from General Buell himself, to which the court has to accede and by which it must shape its course.

The PRESIDENT. The language of the order authorizes General Buell to appear before this Commission. Now the word "appear" has a legal signification. Nothing is better defined than this word. To "appear" in a court of law is attended with certain consequences, certain rights, and when General Buell is ordered to "appear" before this Commission he is invested with all the rights and privileges of an accused party. Under these rights he can produce witnesses and examine them, both those introduced by himself and those of the Government. The result of this is that if General Buell thinks it necessary for him to go to Washington, where it is proposed to take these depositions, it would be our duty, under the order calling the Commission, to accede; we could do nothing else. I understand the notification was given to the judge-advocate when he was in Washington that officers would not be allowed to leave their commands to testify. Under the provisions of this act he is compelled, where their testimony is necessary, to take it by depositions; and when these depositions are taken General Buell has unquestionably the right to appear to cross-examine the witnesses, and it would be our duty in such cases to suspend the proceedings of the Commission while he was so engaged; so that, if the depositions of General Halleck and Colonel Fry be taken at Washington, General Buell has unquestionably the right to be there to cross-examine.

The JUDGE-ADVOCATE. The order "to appear" does not actually require that he should be present; he may appear by attorney.

The PRESIDENT. But if he thinks it necessary to be present he can do so.

The JUDGE-ADVOCATE. The wording of the order in the instructions given by the Government to the Commission is that General Buell would be ordered to Cincinnati, and have the privilege of appearing before the Commission and of examining witnesses, but it does not place General Buell in the position of a party accused or of having all the rights of an accused. To do so it would be necessary to make of the board a court, which it is not, and instead of permitting General Buell to appear he would be ordered to appear. In the investigation of these facts it may be found that blame should be attached to other officers of the Army or soldiers who have not the privilege of attending here. Under the correct reading of the order General Buell is permitted to attend, not to answer specific charges, but rather for the purpose of assisting in the investigation. General Buell has elected to appear in the light of a defendant, but it does not follow that all the belongings, attributes, and privileges pertaining to a person in that position are to be granted to General Buell. For instance, if General Buell was to go to Washington the proceedings of this Commission would have to be suspended till he returned.

The PRESIDENT. General Buell is authorized to "appear" before this Commission to examine witnesses, not only his own but those of the Government, and this clothes him with all the rights of a "party defendant." Were we to strictly follow the proceedings of courts of law notice would have to be given before the trial commenced of any deposition to be taken. Such a proceeding cannot be entertained in this case; it would be impracticable. Depositions not being possible to be taken before the trial, they must be taken during the trial, and the right of appearance follows as a matter of course. I suppose that no one would attempt to disguise the fact that this is an inquiry with special reference to General Buell's operations. When we speak of the operations of the Army of the Ohio they are the operations of the army as conducted by his command. The Government, therefore, gives special privileges to General Buell to appear and examine witnesses, &c., because he is more particularly interested in this investigation than any other officer in that army. Secretary Stanton is a lawyer; he knows the effect of the language employed in that order, which gives General Buell all the rights of a "party defendant" in this case.

The court was then cleared; when, on motion that the testimony of General Halleck and Governor Johnson should be taken by deposition, it was put to vote and decided in the affirmative.

After the decision was announced to General Buell the court adjourned to meet on Friday, April 10, at 11 o'clock a. m.

CINCINNATI, *Friday, April* 10, 1863.

The Commission met pursuant to adjournment. Members present, General Wallace, General Dana, General Tyler; also the judge-advocate and General Buell.

The following deposition was read to the Commission by the judge-advocate:

Deposition of Mr. John H. Cooper.

Mr. JOHN H. COOPER, of Lexington, Ky., being duly sworn by the judge-advocate of the Commission called to investigate the operations of the Army of the Ohio in Kentucky and Tennessee, responds to the questions submitted by the judge-advocate and the cross-interrogatories by Major-General Buell as follows:

Questions by the JUDGE-ADVOCATE:

1. State your name and place of residence, and whether you have once before been called and examined in this investigation.

I reside in Lexington, Ky., and was once before examined in this investigation, at Cincinnati, Ohio, and my statements reduced to writing. My name is John H. Cooper.

2. State what you know of Bragg's retreat after the fight at Perryville; at what time and by what route his forces reached Camp Dick Robinson, and whether after marching toward Camp Dick Robinson they returned through Harrodsburg and formed a line of battle between Harrodsburg and Perryville.

I was a mere spectator at Perryville and saw some of the fighting. On the day of battle I returned to Harrodsburg, and the next morning, after breakfast, went back in company with some others toward the battle-field, and met Bragg's army, or a portion of it, in full retreat, who turned us back toward Harrodsburg. The enemy, or this portion, retreated through Harrodsburg, and from the latter place to Camp Dick Robinson, by a new turnpike road crossing Dick's River at King's Mill, intersecting the turnpike from Lexington to Danville at Bryantsville, which is in Garrard County, a few miles from Camp Dick Robinson. Whether they, the rebel army or any portion of it, returned through Harrodsburg and formed a line of battle between Harrodsburg and Perryville I don't know.

3. State what you know of the number of Bragg's entire force after its junction with Kirby Smith's and others at Camp Dick Robinson and how you came by your information. What was, if you remember, the number of rations?

I was informed, either by Major Thomas or Captain Williams, both of whom were commissaries in the rebel army, that after the junction of Kirby Smith's forces with Bragg's they were issuing rations to 60,000 men. This is all I know, and I think is the substance of my former answer to this question when propounded to me at Cincinnati. Whether this number included all his forces I cannot say, but think it included all; and whether the officers knew or not I cannot say. And further saith not.

                                                            JOHN H. COOPER.

STATE OF KENTUCKY,
        Fayette County, sct.:

I, Charles D. Carr, presiding judge of the Fayette County court in and for the State and county aforesaid, do certify that John H. Cooper, the witness to whom the foregoing questions were propounded by me, was first duly sworn by me that the evidence he should give in answer to said questions should be the truth, the whole truth, and nothing but the truth, and that his answers were reduced to writing by me in his presence.

Given under my hand this 9th day of April, 1863.

                                                            C. D. CARR,
                                        Presiding Judge Fayette County Court.

The Commission adjourned to meet on Monday, April 13, 1863.

                                        CINCINNATI, *Monday, April 13, 1863.*

The Commission met pursuant to adjournment. Members present, General Wallace, General Dana, General Tyler; also the judge-advocate and General Buell.

General BUELL. The documents which I submit in evidence, including orders, letters, and telegraphic dispatches, are numbered from 1 to 716, inclusive, in addition to the fractional numbers $1\frac{1}{2}$, $3\frac{1}{2}$, $72\frac{1}{2}$, $80\frac{1}{4}$, $131\frac{1}{2}$, $138\frac{1}{2}$, $145\frac{1}{2}$, $218\frac{1}{2}$, $284\frac{1}{2}$, $327\frac{1}{2}$, $344\frac{1}{2}$, $469\frac{1}{2}$, $510\frac{1}{4}$, $510\frac{1}{2}$, $510\frac{3}{4}$, $511\frac{1}{4}$, $511\frac{1}{2}$, $511\frac{3}{4}$, $512\frac{1}{4}$, $512\frac{1}{2}$, $512\frac{3}{4}$, $549\frac{1}{2}$, $565\frac{1}{2}$, $673\frac{1}{2}$. Besides these I desire to include the dispatches received from Washington and submitted by the judge-advocate for the Government; they embrace many dispatches which I find have been lost from my files.* It will be seen that my file of dispatches to and from General Halleck embraces some that are not included in the file submitted for the Government. Some of the documents submitted do not come within the period to which the investigation has been confined. They might at first view not seem to have any immediate bearing upon the subject submitted to it; they, however, relate to circumstances which are general and permanent in their bearing upon my military operations, and to a greater or less extent entered into the plans which determined the operations of my army for the time to which the investigations of the Commission legitimately extend.

The Commission adjourned to meet Thursday, April 16, 1863, at 10 o'clock a. m.

CINCINNATI, *April* 16, 1863.

Commission met pursuant to adjournment. Present, the president (General Wallace), General Dana, General Tyler; also the judge-advocate.

The judge-advocate read the following letter to General Buell and the reply thereto:

COURT-ROOM OF COMMISSION,
Cincinnati, April 14, 1863.

Major-General BUELL, *U. S. Army, &c.*:

GENERAL: I have the honor to inform you that I have submitted to General Wright the questions authorized by the Commission, which asked him:

1st. As to the number of troops turned over to General Buell in Louisville.

2d. As to the number of enemy under Bragg after a junction with Kirby Smith and after the battle of Perryville.

3d. The circumstances attending the surrender of Munfordville and why that garrison was not relieved.

4th. The circumstances attending the illegal appointment of Captains Gay and Gilbert to the positions of brigadier-general and major-general.

If you will favor me with the cross-interrogatories I will have them asked and answered.

I have the honor to be, general, yours, respectfully,

DONN PIATT,
Lieutenant-Colonel and Judge-Advocate.

CINCINNATI, *April* 14, 1863.

Lieut. Col. DONN PIATT,
Judge-Advocate of Military Commission:

SIR: I have received your letter informing me that you have submitted certain questions to General Wright to be answered by deposition. It will be impossible for me to propound any cross-interrogatories until I know what is elicited from the examination-in-chief.

Very respectfully, your obedient servant,

D. C. BUELL.

---

* The copies substituted for the documentary evidence lost with the original record have been arranged either as "reports" in connection with the events to which they relate, or in chronological order in the "correspondence, orders, and returns." Such of these documents as relate to operations prior to March 4, 1862, are printed in Vol. VII of this series; those relating to operations between March 4 and June 10 appear in Vol. X, and the remainder appear in this chapter.

The following letter from General Buell was received and read:

BURNET HOUSE, *April* 16, 1863.

Lieut. Col. DONN PIATT, *Judge-Advocate:*

SIR: As soon as the Commission has finished with the proceedings which require my presence here I will proceed to Washington City to take the deposition of Colonel Fry, to be submitted in evidence to the Commission.

Very respectfully, your obedient servant,

D. C. BUELL,
Major-General.

There being no business before the Commission requiring the presence of General Buell, it adjourned to Friday, April 24, at 10 o'clock a. m.

CINCINNATI, *April* 24, 1863.

Commission met pursuant to adjournment. Present, the president (General Wallace), General Dana, General Tyler; also the judge-advocate and General Buell.

The JUDGE-ADVOCATE. After the close of our last session I received the following letter from General Buell:

BURNET HOUSE, *April* 16, 1863.

Lieut. Col. DONN PIATT, *Judge-Advocate:*

SIR: I will on Monday, the 20th instant, at 10 o'clock a. m., before some competent officer, commence, and continue from day to day until completed, to take the testimony of Col. J. B. Fry, Provost-Marshal-General, at Washington City, D. C., in the investigation now in progress concerning the operations of the Army of the Ohio in Tennessee and Kentucky, under my command.

Very respectfully, your obedient servant,

D. C. BUELL,
Major-General.

The JUDGE-ADVOCATE. To this letter I replied as follows:

LUDLOW, *April* 16, 1863.

Major-General BUELL, *U. S. Army, &c.:*

GENERAL: I have the honor to call your attention to the fact that the notice served upon me to-day to take the deposition of Colonel Fry is defective in two particulars: it does not state at what place the deposition will be taken nor does it give me time to reach Washington.

I have the honor to be, general, yours, respectfully,

DONN PIATT,
Lieutenant-Colonel and Judge-Advocate.

The JUDGE-ADVOCATE. General Buell then wrote as follows:

BURNET HOUSE, *April* 16, 1863.

Lieut. Col. DONN PIATT, *Judge-Advocate:*

SIR: I informed you this morning of my purpose to take Colonel Fry's deposition in Washington as soon as the business of the court would permit me to leave, and as soon as I was advised of the adjournment of the Commission until the 24th I notified you of the day. The deposition will be taken before the Judge-Advocate-General or other suitable officer.

Very respectfully, your obedient servant,

D. C. BUELL,
Major-General.

The JUDGE-ADVOCATE. I would state to the Commission that after the adjournment on Thursday, the 16th, I followed General Buell to Washington City, and on Wednesday, the 22d, we took two depositions, one of Colonel Fry and the other of Governor Johnson; but for the purpose of being back here by the 24th it was necessary for me to leave

Washington on Wednesday night, so that I had no opportunity to cross-examine Colonel Fry.   However, I have no objection to receive his deposition as it stands without cross-examining, if there is no objection on the part of General Buell to the deposition of Governor Johnson as it stands, General Buell having no time to cross-examine him.

The PRESIDENT. How was that?

The JUDGE-ADVOCATE. We had only one day, and some forty or fifty questions were put and answered.   The examination was held on Wednesday, and we had to leave that night in order to be here to-day.   As I left Cincinnati without any authority from the Commission to go to Washington, I would like, if it is not too late, to have some authority for my being in Washington at that time.

General TYLER. I move to amend the minutes of the 16th as follows: "That we adjourn to Friday, the 24th of April, to allow General Buell and the judge-advocate to proceed to Washington for the purpose of taking the depositions of General Fry and Governor Andrew Johnson." Carried.

The deposition of General H. G. Wright was then read by the judge-advocate:

Deposition of General H. G. Wright.

Questions by the JUDGE-ADVOCATE:

1. State what you know of the capture of Munfordville by the forces under Bragg, and why that post, being in your department at the time, was not sufficiently re-enforced by you or Colonel Wilder was not ordered to evacuate in time to prevent a capture.

The first attack on Munfordville was made on Sunday, the 14th of September, by a portion of Bragg's army, which was repulsed; and the garrison did not surrender, I believe, till the morning of the 17th, when, surrounded by Bragg's entire force, a retreat or further defense was impracticable.

The place was not further re-enforced because its garrison was as large as the importance of the place would justify.   It consisted of upward of 4,000 men, which, considering the strength of the position, was strong enough to hold the place against any force likely to be detached by Bragg to attempt its capture.   Any large force would not have accomplished more, as none which I could have furnished could have successfully resisted Bragg's army, which was finally brought against it and compelled its surrender.

Orders were not given for the evacuation of the place because it was intended to hold it until General Buell's army came up, as had been done in the case of Bowling Green; and from the information we had concerning the relative positions of his army and the rebel forces it was believed it could be held successfully.   It was not supposed that Bragg could bring his entire force against the place without coming in contact with Buell, though it was believed possible for him to attack with a strong detachment while watching General Buell with his main force.   This was exactly what he attempted in the first place; but on being repulsed he fell upon the place with his entire force.

I may have been in error in supposing it in the power of General Buell to relieve the place, but I fully expected it, or I should have withdrawn the garrison before the first attack.   As showing why Munfordville was held and General Buell depended on at all for its relief, I would state that after the defeat of our forces under Major-General Nelson at Richmond, Ky., it became necessary to concentrate all the forces of the department at points where a successful resistance could be made.   The points naturally selected, considering the strength of our forces and the character of the troops, all of which were new levies, were near Cincinnati (or more properly Covington and Newport) and Louisville.   Troops were accumulated at the two points as rapidly as possible till after the withdrawal of Kirby Smith's force from the front of Cincinnati, when all the available force was sent to Louisville, which in consequence of the advance of Bragg had become the important point.   During this time the line of the Louisville and Nashville Railroad as far as Bowling Green had been held as a part of the line of communication of the army under Major-General Buell in Tennessee.   At Bowling Green had been accumulated a large supply of rations (a million and a half, I believe) for General Buell's army, which could not be forwarded farther.

Satisfied of the impossibility of maintaining this long line with the force I then had, I applied to the general-in-chief for information regarding the whereabouts of General Buell and the importance of holding the line for him. On the receipt of his answer I ordered the withdrawal of the stores and the evacuation of Bowling Green, designing, if necessary, to evacuate Munfordville at a late day. On the same day I believe on which the order was given I received information regarding General Buell's position and movements which induced me to countermand the order and determine to hold both Bowling Green and Munfordville. The information in effect was that General Buell with his entire force was moving into Kentucky via Nashville, where, leaving a garrison, he was to proceed with the remainder of his troops into Kentucky to oppose Bragg, who was moving in the same direction that General Buell's army was without supplies, and I presumed would count on finding them at Bowling Green. In holding the line of road I therefore held it for him at some risk of the garrison being cut off, as I could not re-enforce them to such an extent as to secure them against an attack of an army. Their security against such an attack must depend upon General Buell's own movements, and, right or wrong, I relied upon it.

3. State as nearly you can the number of troops turned over to Major-General Buell at Louisville previous to his marching out to attack Bragg at Bardstown.

I cannot answer with any certainty, as I was never able to get a return of the troops at Louisville under the command of General Nelson. The regiments, with the exception of those sent from General Grant's army under General G. Granger, were all new, and General Nelson was not able to get returns. On the 15th of September there were at Louisville 18,250 infantry, 1,930 cavalry, and 550 artillery, according to General Gilbert's report. Subsequently there were sent from Cincinnati twenty-four regiments of infantry, two batteries of artillery, and one regiment of cavalry; from Illinois five regiments of infantry, and from Michigan one regiment of cavalry. I cannot say whether these were all or not, as the Governors of the States in the department were sending their troops as fast as they could be got ready, and may sometimes have neglected to notify the headquarters of the department.

4. State what you know, if anything, of the number of men of all arms combined under Bragg at or after the battle of Perryville?

I know nothing of the strength of Bragg's force except from reports which cannot be considered reliable. General Nelson furnished me the report of a friend of his who saw the troops at Munfordville, and gave their number as "about 30,000, a few more or less;" say they have "other troops coming on." He also reported that previous to the surrender of Munfordville certain officers demanded to see whether the enemy really encompassed the works with the force they pretended to have, and three officers went through their lines and reported as follows: "Total strength 45,000 men; eight batteries on the south side; on the north side they professed to have thirteen regiments and three batteries, about 10,000 men."

5. Inform the Commission what you know of C. C. Gilbert, U. S. Army, being placed and continued in command as a major-general without being legally appointed; also what you know of Capt. E. Gay, U. S. Army, being given the position of brigadier-general without legal authority.

I know nothing in regard to Captain Gay's being given the position of brigadier-general. Captain Gilbert was appointed by me a major-general subject to the approval of the President of the United States, and this was done upon the written request of Brigadier-Generals Jackson and Cruft, neither of whom desired to take the command of the forces after Major-General Nelson had been disabled in the battle of Richmond, Ky. A certified copy of the order appointing him is herewith, marked A, and a copy of the letter of Generals Jackson and Cruft, above referred to, marked B. This appointment was at once reported to Washington, and General Gilbert was subsequently appointed a brigadier-general of volunteers by the President, as was also General Terrill, who were appointed in the same order.

H. G. WRIGHT,
Brigadier-General Volunteers.

Subscribed and sworn to before me by H. G. Wright, brigadier-general, this day, 15th of April, 1863.

JOS. CLEMENT,
Justice of the Peace, Jefferson County, Kentucky.

Document marked A, September 1, 1862, and document marked B, were also introduced and read.*

The deposition of Col. JOHN F. DE COURCY was then introduced by the judge-advocate and read, as follows:

Col. J. F. DE COURCY, U. S. Volunteers, being duly sworn, responds to the questions submitted by the judge-advocate of the Commission called to investigate the operations of the Army of the Ohio, as follows:

By the JUDGE-ADVOCATE:

Question. State your name, present address, and your position in the United States service.

John F. De Courcy; colonel of the Sixteenth Ohio, commanding a brigade of five regiments near Vicksburg; present address, Lexington, Ky.

Question. State what occurred to the forces under General Morgan while on the march to and while in possession of Cumberland Gap, in the summer of 1862, and why that officer did not operate offensively with his forces in Eastern Tennessee.

The march undertaken by General Morgan to Rogers' Gap for the purpose of entering Powell's Valley, Tennessee, thereby turning the position of the Gap and cutting off the enemy from their communications with Knoxville, was suddenly arrested, when General Morgan's forces had nearly all concentrated at Rogers' Gap, by a telegraphic dispatch from General Buell, ordering a retrograde movement and stopping all further operations on the Tennessee side against the Gap. The countermarching began immediately, but owing to the narrowness of the road, proceeded very slowly. I was ordered by General Morgan to cover the movement, and to be the last to leave with my brigade. About thirty or forty hours after the main body of the force had retrograded I received the information that the enemy was evacuating the Gap. I immediately informed General Morgan of the same, and stated that I should not continue the retrograde movement with the troops under my command without further orders from him. General Morgan approved of this course, and sent me word that he would recommence the forward movement. The troops were once more reconcentrated at Rogers' Gap, and on the 18th of June the whole force moved and marched into the Gap, my advance guard entering the same a very few hours after the rear guard of the enemy had departed from it.

While in possession of Cumberland Gap General Morgan effected very little more than sending out some foraging parties on different occasions. I commanded two of those parties, and took the direction of Tazewell, about 13 miles south of Cumberland Gap. The first foraging expedition was perfectly successful; the second one, which began on the 3d of August and operated around Tazewell until the 6th, was also successful, the enemy always retiring and being evidently in very small force. On the 6th, however, my advance posts, composed of the Sixteenth Ohio, were very suddenly attacked by a very superior force, which I afterward discovered was under the command of General Stevenson, and which I have every reason to believe, from the reports of the enemy and from our own officers, prisoners in their hands, was composed of about 20,000 men, with a large amount of artillery. This force we held in check on the 6th of August from 11 o'clock a. m. till half past 3 p. m., when they retreated from my front, and merely continued an artillery fire until 6 in the evening, when I made my return to the Gap unmolested or without even an attempt being made by the enemy to follow me.

Two days afterward the Gap was invested on the southern side; and I believe about the 11th or 12th of August the investment of the Gap on both sides, on the Tennessee and Kentucky sides, was completed by the forces of Stevenson and Kirby Smith.

The success of the previous foraging expeditions will go far to show that Eastern Tennessee was not occupied in force by the enemy between the dates of the 18th of June and on or about the 15th of July. I remember distinctly asking General Morgan, shortly after our occupation of the Gap on the 18th of June, to allow me to proceed with my brigade toward a point near Morristown, Jefferson County, Tenn., to there tap the railroad, believing that said operation would have materially interfered with the commissary arrangements of the enemy. This permission was refused me by General Morgan, owing, I believe, to his instructions or orders from General Buell not allowing him to undertake any very decided initiative steps toward Knoxville.

---

* Not found.

I finally state that I believe General Morgan had every wish, inclination, and power to operate offensively in Eastern Tennessee, but was prevented by general instructions or orders, always premising, however, that this officer could not have undertaken any successful operation after the 15th of July.

Question. What was the force under General Bragg after the junction of all the rebel forces in Kentucky?

I can only answer this question on the basis of the opinions of others. I have now been two months in Kentucky, and from what I can gather of well-informed persons who saw a great deal of Kirby Smith's, Bragg's, and Stevenson's forces, and from what I can remember while we were at the Gap after the 6th of August and the information we gathered during our retreat toward the Ohio River, my opinion is that Bragg never could have concentrated at any one time a larger force than 60,000 men, and this is including the recruits he picked up in Kentucky during the rebel raid. I am more inclined to believe that Bragg had a force inferior to that number by several thousand, because I am of opinion that Stevenson never formed a complete junction with him, that officer being afraid to uncover the road to Cumberland Gap, and must therefore have kept a large fraction of his forces in that position in order to maintain it, to keep open their lines of retreat.

Question. Do you believe that Knoxville could have been taken by our forces after we had possession of Cumberland Gap?

I do. I believe, further, with most complete success could General Morgan have operated toward that town in co-operation with a real advance toward the east by the forces under Major-General Buell. For several weeks after our occupation of the Gap we received constant information that the enemy had never more than 6,000 or 7,000 men in and around Knoxville.

General BUELL. I must, Mr. President, object to this deposition. I could properly object to this testimony in any form. This officer, it appears, has the command of a brigade at Vicksburg, but at the time he gave this deposition he was at Lexington, I suppose on leave of absence. I understand moreover that he has been before the Commission.

The JUDGE-ADVOCATE. The deposition was taken in this room.

General BUELL. Then with what propriety is his deposition taken? Moreover the evidence is made up of opinion merely, without giving in any respect the ground upon which the opinion is based. Besides, it is not the best evidence upon some points it bears upon. He asserts that General Morgan received certain instructions. General Morgan's evidence is the best upon that point; at least better than Colonel De Courcy's. The statements, too, are untrue, many of them, and can be proved to be so. The documentary evidence shows that General Morgan had no such instructions upon that point; and there is a good deal of evidence before the Commission as to the movements of Stevenson's force which shows that this testimony is untrue, so that the whole matter is improper as evidence. But this cannot be fully shown without a close examination in court or the introduction of other evidence. It would afford an admirable text for a newspaper article, and that is the substance of its value. I could object to it also on the ground that whereas it is introduced as rebutting evidence it is not so at all in some essential particulars, but is purely original matter. That is particularly the case with refence to the possible movements of General Morgan's force from Cumberland Gap. If the deposition is admitted as evidence I shall desire the evidence of General Morgan upon points to which it relates, particularly as to the instructions he received. Whatever instructions he had were written and can be easily produced. They are in fact on your files, though there is perhaps nothing to show that they are all there. Upon that point General Morgan is the best witness. I do not suppose such testimony as this deposition contains would be received as evidence by any competent court.

The JUDGE-ADVOCATE. There is one portion of General Buell's remarks that I am compelled to notice, and that is as to the form in which this testimony appears before the Commission. As to the weight to be attached to Colonel De Courcy's affidavit, that is further along and for the Commission to determine. So far as the deposition itself is concerned I asked and obtained permission to introduce it. I forwarded certain queries to Colonel De Courcy at Lexington, where he was on sick leave, after having submitted them to General Buell. To my surprise Colonel De Courcy made his appearance here after we adjourned on the 16th, but it was too late to secure his evidence, and I proceeded to take his affidavit as it now appears before you. I do not care to go into an argument as to whether it is rebutting evidence or not or whether it is evidence worthy of belief; the first was argued before, and the last is out of my province and not pertinent to the objections raised by General Buell. I will say, however, that General Buell misapplies the term "better evidence." General Morgan's evidence might be more satisfactory, but could not be legally termed " better evidence," so as to bring it within the rule appealed to by General Buell.

General BUELL. The excuse for not taking Colonel De Courcy's evidence before the Commission when he appeared here is certainly not satisfactory. With reference to the evidence of General Morgan, it is only of value as verifying the documentary evidence that has been submitted and as showing whether he received any other instructions than those on record. I do not desire it for any other purpose, nor do I desire to have the opinion of General Morgan as to what operations could have been attempted by the force under his command in contradiction to the opinion of Colonel De Courcy. As far as my instructions are concerned they were determined by the dispatches I received from him. Most of these dispatches I have submitted to the Commission. I have more to submit this morning, and they give the Commission all the information I had from General Morgan so far as I know. I received information from another quarter which had some influence upon my instructions, but it is immaterial here. If the judge-advocate admits that the documentary evidence I have submitted includes all the instructions that were given to General Morgan it is sufficient; if he does not admit it, it is proper that General Morgan's evidence should be had before the Commission on that point. General Morgan's evidence is certainly better than Colonel De Courcy's in regard to it.

The court was then cleared; when, on vote, it was decided that the deposition of Colonel De Courcy should be received.

On the opening of the court—

General BUELL. I request the evidence of General Morgan. I wish General Morgan to produce any and all orders that he received while in command of the Seventh Division there, and that controlled his actions in any manner in moving on Cumberland Gap and while there. I request also that Colonel De Courcy may be called before the Commission for cross-examination. I understand he is still in the city. I request also that Col. John Coburn, who was an officer in General Morgan's command, and was with Colonel De Courcy in some of his operations, may be called before the Commission.

The JUDGE-ADVOCATE. I shall oppose going into any further evidence in this connection or disturb the resolution passed on the 16th It is a matter of regret to me that I did not have General Morgan before the Commission and go into the operations of the army in Tennessee; but it is too late now to do so. There is nothing whatever, as General Buell says, in this deposition of Colonel De Courcy that would require such an investigation as General Buell now calls for that I can discover.

General TYLER. I wish to inquire whether these interrogatories were submitted to General Buell before they were answered by Colonel De Courcy?

The JUDGE-ADVOCATE. The whole matter connected with Colonel De Courcy and his testimony is a matter of record. Half a dozen witnesses were proposed to be examined by deposition, and the questions which were read before the Commission were decided to be very proper. I asked General Buell at the time to add any cross-interrogatories he might wish to put to the witnesses, not only to Colonel De Courcy, but to all the witnesses I proposed to examine, and he returned me answer that he had none to ask.

General BUELL. I gave that answer because I did not admit the propriety of taking the evidence of these witnesses in this way. I asserted before that it was proper to have them before the Commission, and I will say now that it would be impossible to frame any system of questions that would meet such evidence as this. It would be impossible to cross-examine on evidence that never could have been anticipated.

The court was cleared; when, on vote, it was decided that the rule which prohibited the introduction of further testimony should be suspended, and that Colonel De Courcy be subpœnaed before the Commission.

On vote it was further decided that no other witnesses should be called.

On the opening of the court the judge-advocate introduced and read the deposition of Governor Johnson, as follows:

Deposition of Hon. Andrew Johnson, Military Governor of Tennessee, April 22, 1863.

Hon. ANDREW JOHNSON, Military Governor of Tennessee and brigadier-general U. S. Volunteers, being duly sworn, responds to the questions submitted by the judge-advocate of the Commission called to investigate the operations of the Army of the Ohio and the cross-interrogatories of Major-General Buell, as follows:

By the JUDGE-ADOCATE:

Question. State your name, present address, and position in the service of the United States.

Andrew Johnson; Nashville, Tenn. I was brigadier-general in the volunteer service and Military Governor of Tennessee.

Question. State what you know of Major-General Buell proposing to evacuate Nashville in the summer of 1862 on the approach of the rebel forces under Bragg.

In September, 1862, General Buell, on his retrograde move with his army from Huntsville, Ala., Decherd and Battle Creek, Tenn., reached Nashville. Upon General Buell's arrival in Nashville I sought and had an interview with him in regard to the army falling back and giving up the country we had once been in possession of. With the retreat of the army the rumor came, and it was repeated by the rebels, that Nashville would be evacuated and surrendered to the enemy in the same condition we had received it. It was also understood that a number of prominent persons who had formerly resided in Nashville, in Tennessee, were returning with Bragg and in the retreat of General Buell's army, with the understanding that Nashville was to be surrendered. These rumors caused me to be exceedingly solicitous as to what was to be done. In the first interview with General Buell, after some conversation in regard to the policy of a retreat, I asked him the question directly whether Nashville was to be given up to the enemy or evacuated without making resistance. I urged at some length and with much earnestness the great importance of holding

Nashville at all hazards, and in the end, rather than it should be retaken and held by the enemy, that it should be destroyed. This interview ended and another was had, in which the same arguments were repeated and urged as to the propriety of holding Nashville. General Buell replied with some little warmth that he was indifferent as to the criticism that might be made in regard to his policy or manner of conducting the campaign. He should rely upon his own judgment and convictions, without regard to consequences. The holding of Nashville in a military point of view was of no very great importance; that in fact upon military principles Nashville should have been abandoned or evacuated three months ago. In the third interview with General Buell, after repeating and urging again the importance of holding Nashville, he then stated that he had come to the conclusion to leave a force for the defense of Nashville, in answer to which I expressed my gratification and thanked him sincerely for doing so. He stated, though, in leaving a force for the defense of Nashville that he did not do it so much from military as from political considerations which had been pressed with so much earnestness upon him. We then separated. I think this was on Wednesday. On Thursday he left in pursuit of the army, which was then advancing toward Bowling Green, Ky.; on Friday a courier returned with a dispatch to General Thomas, who had been left in command of the forces for the defense of Nashville, notifying him to be in readiness to march with his division and General Palmer's on Sunday morning. Another dispatch was received from General Buell by General Thomas to march unless a certain portion of Bragg's army should be in striking distance of Nashville, and in that event he (General Thomas), in his discretion, to leave General Palmer with his command, which he did. It was understood, though, at this time that Bragg's army had passed into Kentucky. General Thomas, notwithstanding Bragg had passed with his forces, upon my earnest solicitation left General Palmer with his division and marched with his own in compliance with General Buell's dispatch. With the courier returning to General Buell on Sunday morning I forwarded a letter, in which I urged and pressed the importance of General Thomas remaining at Nashville or his being returned in the event he marched before the letter reached him; but General Thomas and his command did not return. There was much said *pro* and *con* by General Buell and myself in regard to the evacuation of Nashville which is deemed immaterial in this deposition. This deposition has been made in the absence of dispatches and letters which would be important to refer to as to dates and days, which are not remembered by me at this moment.

ANDREW JOHNSON,
Military Governor and Brigadier-General of Tennessee.

I hereby certify that the above-named Andrew Johnson, Military Governor of Tennessee and brigadier-general of volunteers in the United States service, was on the 22d day of April, A. D. 1863, at the city of Washington, duly sworn previous to responding as above.

DONN PIATT, U. S. V.,
Lieutenant-Colonel and Judge-Advocate.

General BUELL. I urge that the deposition of Governor Johnson shall be received. I also urge that he shall be called upon for the dispatches referred to in the deposition.

General DANA. I should like to ask if that last question is rebutting evidence?

The JUDGE-ADVOCATE. No, sir.

General DANA. Then, if the court is cleared, I will make a motion in regard to that deposition.

The court was cleared; when, on motion, it was decided that, the deposition of Governor Johnson not being in the nature of rebutting evidence, it be excluded from the record.

On the opening of the court—

The PRESIDENT. It is decided, general, that the deposition of Governor Johnson shall not be received.

General BUELL. I am very sorry for it, sir; I request that I may be allowed to take a copy of it.

General DANA. I move that the original be turned over to General Buell.

General TYLER. The Commission has no control over that document.

General DANA. I am of opinion that, an attempt having been made to introduce it, it is the property of the court.

The PRESIDENT. The practice of civil courts would make that the property of the judge-advocate.

General BUELL. Is it not a fact that that paper is before you as evidence, that it belongs to your records, and that you have decided not to recognize it as evidence? It has been read before the Commission, it was brought before the Commission in pursuance of its orders, and is it not properly a part of your record?

The PRESIDENT. It was read to the Commission, not as testimony, but for the purpose of gratifying your request, to see whether you would consent to receive it or object to it; but it was not received as evidence. It stands, then, in this shape: it is a deposition taken by order of the Commission; it was presented to it with a view to a decision whether it was to be received or not, and the Commission has decided not to receive it, and that at once makes it the property of the judge-advocate.

General BUELL. This appears to be a different case, sir. This paper stands precisely in the light of any evidence taken before the Commission. The Commission authorized and ordered it. The judge-advocate superintended it. I think, sir, that it belongs to your records.

General DANA. The record will show the fact that this deposition of Governor Johnson, like other documents prepared by the judge-advocate and presented to the court, belongs to the Commission; that upon the question being raised as to whether it should be received or not it was rejected. It presents the fact that it was offered as evidence and was rejected; not that it was received as testimony or that it becomes part and parcel of our record.

General BUELL. The judge-advocate has offered it to you as evidence; if it is not valuable to you it may be to me. The paper forms part of your record; you may determine not to receive it as evidence for any reason you may think proper; but I am of opinion that it forms part of your record.

The court was cleared; when it was moved to reconsider the vote taken in regard to the deposition of Governor Johnson and carried.

It was then moved that the deposition of Governor Johnson be admitted.

Carried.

On the question whether the dispatches referred to by Governor Johnson in his deposition and asked for by General Buell shall be called for it was put to the vote and negatived.

On the court being opened—

The JUDGE-ADVOCATE. This deposition of Colonel Fry, Mr. President, was taken at Washington in an informal manner, and I had no time to read it over or prepare a cross-examination. I desire to read it over, Mr. President, before I submit it to the Commission.

General BUELL. I am astonished at the proposition, sir. This evidence is as valid as though it had been delivered by the witness before the Commission. As for the judge-advocate not cross-examining him because he had not time, I do not know any reason why he had not. If he had started twenty-four hours after I did he could have been at Washington on Sunday at 1 o'clock. We delayed two days in Washington for him.

The JUDGE-ADVOCATE. I will ask why there was a delay of two days in Washington for me?

General BUELL. Because the judge-advocate gave the excuse that sufficient time was not allowed him when I served the notice upon him. I therefore did not know but there might have been something to interfere with his journey, and I therefore delayed till the last moment when the evidence could be prepared.

The JUDGE-ADVOCATE. I see nothing unreasonable in my request. I have had no opportunity to read it.

General BUELL. I notified the judge-advocate that the examination would continue from day to day.

The JUDGE-ADVOCATE. Did the examination commence on Monday, the 20th of April?

General BUELL. No, sir; it did not. I am astonished at this objection.

The JUDGE-ADVOCATE. I make no objection. I simply desire to have an opportunity of reading the deposition. All that I have yet seen was the rough draught I read over at Colonel Fry's office.

General BUELL. The judge-advocate fails to be present at the taking of the deposition and then takes advantage of the informality.

The JUDGE-ADVOCATE. The informality was not on my part. The informality was in General Buell's not beginning the examination when he should have done so. The examination was not commenced when I got there, and then it occupied all the time we had to spare before leaving.

General BUELL. Did you not read this evidence?

The JUDGE-ADVOCATE. Certainly; but I had no time to form a cross-examination upon it.

General BUELL. How could you have done it, then, had the examination been commenced in advance?

The JUDGE-ADVOCATE. It would then have been completed, and I would have had the whole of Wednesday to myself. I was surprised to find on reaching Washington that no steps had been taken to get Colonel Fry's deposition. But I say now I make no objection to it.

The PRESIDENT. Why do you wish to read it before reading it to the Commission?

The JUDGE-ADVOCATE. To see if there is anything requiring cross-examination.

General BUELL. I have several other papers to present, as this is the last day on which you have decided to receive them. Some of these papers may appear in the files already presented; others do not.

The PRESIDENT. Are they copies or originals?

General BUELL. Some of them are copies and others are originals. Some of them are copies made at Washington, and of whose existence I was not aware till my late visit there.

The JUDGE-ADVOCATE. I shall object to the introduction of any evidence except such as is included in the resolution of the Commission, and that is Colonel Fry's deposition only. It was understood that General Buell had introduced all his documentary evidence. To come in now with additional evidence is to open up the whole case.

General BUELL. These are papers that came into my possession at Washington; they were not within my reach before.

The PRESIDENT. What is the subject of these papers, general, that you propose to introduce?

General BUELL. They are upon different subjects connected with the operations of the army under my command. Some of them are dispatches from General Morgan at Cumberland Gap.

The PRESIDENT. Is not your file complete without them?

General BUELL. No, sir. These (a portion of the papers held by General Buell) are dispatches I found in Colonel Fry's possession at Washington; another is a dispatch to me from the Secretary of War, dated the 12th of May, representing the necessity of increasing the Government forces in East Tennessee and Kentucky; another is a dispatch from General Thomas to General Halleck, requesting that the order assigning him to the command of the army at Louisville shall be revoked. I desire this dispatch to be received particularly, as it has been represented that that request was made from motives of generosity. The dispatch gives a different reason for it. I have another paper which I have been advised by my friends to submit. I should not otherwise have done it. It is a copy of some resolutions which were passed at the recent session of the Legislature of Kentucky, expressive of thanks for the services which were rendered to Kentucky by the army under my command.

The JUDGE-ADVOCATE. I have no objection to that last-named paper being introduced, but I shall object to the others. I see no reason for violating the practice of civil courts and certainly none for violating the decision of the Commission. That dispatch of General Thomas makes it incumbent upon me not to admit it. It is really opening up the whole case again, and I do not think it would be proper at this late day. The resolutions passed by the Legislature of Kentucky I have no objection to. I would introduce them myself as to that matter.

The court was cleared; when it was decided that, the judge-advocate having objected to the introduction of the papers offered by General Buell, with the exception of the resolution of thanks by the Legislature of Kentucky, the objection be sustained.

On the opening of the court—

General BUELL. As you have refused to receive the other documentary evidence I offered, I decline to present the copy of the resolution of thanks offered by the Legislature of Kentucky for the services performed by my troops in Kentucky last fall.

Col. JOHN F. DE COURCY was then introduced, and his cross-examination proceeded as follows:

Cross-examination by General BUELL:

Question. You have stated in your deposition presented to this Commission that the march of General Morgan to turn the enemy's position at Cumberland Gap last summer was suddenly arrested, when General Morgan's forces had nearly all concentrated at Rogers' Gap, by a telegraphic dispatch from General Buell ordering a retrograde movement and stopping all further operations on the Tennessee side of the Gap. State what knowledge you have of such instructions.

I was in the same house at Rogers' Gap with General Morgan the day when his troops were nearly all concentrated there. I may as well state that we marched by two routes, some by Rogers' Gap and some by Big Creek Gap, and we were expecting to move next day on toward the Gap, when General Morgan sent for me some time in the afternoon and showed me a telegraphic dispatch which he had just received from General Buell. The dispatch was to the effect that he should not proceed with the enterprise, and compelled him to give us orders to countermarch all the troops. I read the dispatch myself, but do not remember the exact wording of it.

Question. Do you mean to say that that was the necessary effect of the dispatch or that that was the result?

I do. I remember distinctly discussing with General Morgan whether the order could be read in such a manner as to allow him to carry on the operations after having carried them to that point. I remember, further, even discussing whether it was necessary to return to the Cumberland Ford, or whether he might not change his base of operations and take a base more toward the west, somewhere near Barboursville, so as to threaten more continually the enemy's communications with the Gap and Knoxville.

Question. Did you concur with General Morgan in the interpretation of that dispatch that it required him not only to cease further operations in advance but to fall back?

I did interpret it as General Morgan did, but deemed that General Morgan's not strictly obeying the orders was almost imperative on him at the time, owing to the demoralization that had come over his troops on receiving this order. I deemed, further, that had General Morgan disobeyed the order he would not have been blamed by General Buell, because our information of the enemy's weakness in the Gap was so certain (I may say) that we felt equally certain of taking possession of it as soon as we had cut off that communication, which we did the very day we appeared on the south side of the Gap. This discussion was a very long one, and General Buell's interests in the matter as a soldier were as much looked to as General Morgan's. I felt convinced at the time, and I believe so expressed it to General Morgan, that General Buell would have approved of the course of conduct under the circumstances, as General Buell could not have known when he sent his dispatch that General Morgan had advanced so far on so long and so difficult a march. One part of the march, I being in advance with my brigade, we had to construct 2 miles of road, besides cutting out about 6 miles of blockade, extending with interruptions about 6 miles. If my memory serves me, I believe no communication had taken place between General Buell and General Morgan for several days previous to the receipt of the dispatch now in question.

Question. Were those instructions executed according to the interpretation you placed upon them?

They were to a degree.

Question. Was the enemy supposed to be in possession of Cumberland Gap at that time?

He was.

Question. Did General Morgan subsequently depart from those instructions, according to your interpretation of them, by going to Cumberland Gap?

Strictly speaking he did, and I was the principal cause of it. Immediately after the receipt of the dispatch General Morgan ordered a counter-march of all the troops then assembled at Rogers' Gap, and directed me to cover the movement with my brigade, the enemy then being in the valley skirmishing with my advance post. The movement began and was completed, so far as the other brigades were concerned, and I had ordered one regiment of my brigade to follow. This regiment had proceeded about half a mile on its way back when a well-known Union man, a Tennesseean, arrived at the mill at Rogers' Gap, where I was staying, with information that the enemy was leaving the Gap. I made inquiries of this man, and his answers were of such a nature as to convince me that he was telling the truth. I immediately stopped the movement of my brigade and of two batteries which were to move through Rogers' Gap, and forwarded a dispatch of my action to General Morgan, who had been then gone about twenty-four or thirty hours, I believe. He answered, approving of what I had done, and informed me that he would return and concentrate there once more all our troops.

Question. If those instructions were of so vague and indefinite a character that General Morgan could depart from them when there was no enemy to oppose him, do you not think that he could with greater propriety have departed from them when there was some danger but great advantage to be gained by such departure?

I do not think the instructions were vague. The discussion which took place as to obeying was not so much a question of interpreting the order, but respected more the necessities of the case as it then stood, keeping in view that General Buell probably could not have been at that time well informed as to the position of General Morgan's troops. The disobedience of the order, if disobedience there be in the act, after we had heard that the Gap was evacuated, was, in my opinion, imperative on General Morgan, because the enemy would certainly hear of our retrograde movement that evening and might have returned to the Gap and we should have had all our trouble over again, whilst by marching directly upon him from Rogers' Gap—a much shorter route than the other one would have been and a much easier one—we made certain of taking and holding the position. There were also some political considerations connected with this: the appearance of Union troops in that valley was necessary to give encouragement to the loyal Tennesseeans, who had been suffering for a long time from the enemy's occupation of Cumberland Gap.

Question. Was there any reasonable doubt of the success of your movement against Cumberland Gap when General Morgan received those instructions ?

I for one had none ; not that I supposed we should take the Gap by assault from the south side, but I deemed that our appearance there would so embarrass the enemy, by cutting off his line of communication, that before many days he would have to capitulate or retreat by one of his flanks along by the train of one of the Cumberland Mountains.

Question. Which would have been the greater advantage, that which resulted from the occupation of Cumberland Gap by the capitulation or the forced withdrawal of the rebel garrison—which you have supposed probable—or the marching into that position and occupying it when there was no enemy there to oppose you ?

Taking possession of the Gap after the capitulation of the enemy would have been the most advantageous.

Question. Do you not think, then, that the circumstances which justified the departure from those instructions for a lesser advantage would have justified a similar departure for a greater ?

I can only answer this question by stating that when discussing General Buell's dispatch at Rogers' Gap with General Morgan I was in favor of considering that General Buell did not know the difficult marching we had pursued for so many days on our way to attack the Gap, believing and trusting that General Buell would have approved of the conduct after our success.

Question. Can you give the date of these instructions, colonel, and state by whom they were signed ?

I cannot, sir.

Question. Can you give the date approximately ?

Approximately about the 10th of June; but there may be a difference of two or three days in the date.

Question. How soon after the receipt of those instructions did General Morgan assume the offensive against Cumberland Gap ?

He had reconcentrated all his troops by the evening of the 17th of June, when we marched on the morning of the 18th, my brigade being the advance guard, and the cavalry of my advance entered the Gap about 2 o'clock p. m. the same day, the infantry about 6 o'clock.

Question. Do I understand you that the 17th was the date when the retrograde movement was suspended and the advance resumed ?

Several days took place betwixt the suspension of the movement and the resumption of the advance.

Question. Can you state about how many days ?

It was a very confused backward and forward movement. I could not state positively.

Question. Can you state the date of your recommendation of the resumption of the march ?

I did not recommend the resumption of the march, and informed General Morgan that I had not obeyed his order, but had halted with my brigade and some artillery. I believe this took place about the 12th of June. It took place about forty-eight hours after the receipt of General Buell's order.

Question. Were you ever informed that General Morgan was authorized to act on the offensive or not, at his own discretion, after the receipt of the instructions you have referred to ?

I do not remember his receiving such distinct instructions before our occupation of the Gap.

Question. Read this dispatch, if you please, colonel, and see if this is the one you have in your mind.

The dispatch presented to the witness was as follows:

> "HEADQUARTERS, *June* 10, 1862.
>
> "General MORGAN, *Cumberland Ford:*
>
> "Considering your force and that opposed to you, it will probably not be safe for you to undertake any extended offensive operations. Other operations will soon have an influence upon your designs, and it is therefore better for you to run no risk at present.
>
> "JAMES B. FRY,
> "*Colonel and Chief of Staff.*"

This does not appear strongly enough worded to have allowed General Morgan to doubt for one moment the advisability of his advancing on the Gap, considering the difficulties he had to overcome, unless the word "other," which appears in this dispatch, may have had an influence at the time in inducing General Morgan to obey strictly the slightest wish, for fear of embarrassing the movements of General Buell; and yet I must believe that this is the identical dispatch which caused the retrograde movement, because I cannot now remember any other dispatch similar to this, and I do remember the latter part of the dispatch, namely, "other operations will soon have an influence upon your designs, and it is therefore better for you to run no risk at present," having been read by me in some dispatch shown to me by General Morgan.

Question. I wish to submit this dispatch to you also, colonel, and ask whether in view of this dispatch the other ought not to have been considered suggestive rather than imperative:

> "CUMBERLAND FORD, *June* 8, 1862.
>
> "Major-General BUELL:
>
> "Baird's brigade marches this morning and Carter will close up the rear to-morrow. It has become necessary to station the Forty-ninth Indiana, with two pieces of artillery, at Barboursville. On yesterday a spy, pretending to be a deserter, was brought into camp. He left Cumberland Gap on the day before yesterday at 2 o'clock a. m. He reports the enemy's force at Cumberland Gap at over 5,000; at Big Creek Gap at 18,000, with troops at Clinton and Knoxville. Should their forces concentrate they outnumber us nearly three to one. What is General Negley doing? Answer at once, as I start at noon to go to the head of the column. I send copy of this to Governor Johnson and to the Secretary of War.
>
> "GEORGE W. MORGAN."

After reading this communication from General Morgan I consider the dispatch from General Buell as suggestive rather than a direct order.

Question. Colonel, look at this dispatch also, if you please, and state whether you ever saw it or were informed of its contents:

> "HEADQUARTERS, *June* 10, 1862.
>
> "General MORGAN, *Cumberland Ford:*
>
> "Your information with regard to the evacuation of Cumberland Gap may be true; and, if so, it probably resulted from General Mitchel's force appearing before Chattanooga. If the Gap is evacuated you should seize and hold it and take any other advantage that may present itself, but not advance to points from which you would have to fall back.
>
> "JAMES B. FRY,
> "*Colonel and Chief of Staff.*"

I think I have seen this dispatch before.

Question. Do you consider that this dispatch restrained General Morgan from pursuing any advantage that might present itself to him?

I cannot answer the question in relation to the dispatch, but I can remember distinctly General Morgan telling me, shortly after the occupation of the Gap, that he was restrained from acting offensively by the orders or instructions contained in a dispatch that he had received from General Buell. Whether General Morgan referred to the dispatch just read or some other received previous to our conversation I cannot say. But he gave me this information in consequence of my asking him to allow me to proceed and tap the railroad at Morristown.

Commission adjourned to meet on Saturday, April 25, 1863, at 11 o'clock a. m.

[APRIL 25, 1863.]

Testimony of Col. J. B. FRY, Provost-Marshal-General.

By General BUELL:

Question. State your name and position in the service of the United States; whether you were on duty with the Army of the Ohio, under the command of Major-General Buell; in what capacity and for what period.

My name is James B. Fry; I am lieutenant-colonel in the Adjutant-General's Department of the Army, and additional aide-de-camp with rank of colonel, and at this time I am Provost-Marshal-General of the United States. I was on duty with the Army of the Ohio, commanded by General Buell, from the time he assumed command of that army, on 15th of November, 1861, until he relinquished the command of it, on 30th October, 1862, and during this period I was assistant adjutant-general and chief of staff of that army.

Question. State what you know of the movement of the Army of the Ohio from Corinth to North Alabama in June, 1862, the orders under which it marched, the points from which it marched, the dates of arrival and departure, the causes of any delay that may have occurred on the march, the strength of the army, the measures taken by its commander to supply it on the march and after its arrival, and whether the march and the measures on which it was dependent were prosecuted with industry.

Corinth fell into our hands on the 29th of May; within two or three days from this time Wood's division of the Army of the Ohio was by order of General Halleck pushed to the east and along the Memphis and Charleston Railroad, with orders to repair the railroad as it proceeded, the intention being, as it was understood, to establish railroad communication with Mitchel's division, then in North Alabama; and General Halleck intimated his intention of sending the Army of the Ohio to operate against Tennessee. On this intimation orders were at once, about June 1 or 2, sent to the staff officers at Louisville and Nashville, warning them to be ready with supplies to meet such a movement, and orders were given to send supplies at once to Eastport, the highest point at which the Tennessee is navigable for ordinary boats, to meet Wood's division, and be in readiness for the rest of the army when ordered to the eastward. On the 4th of June, General Buell, with Nelson's and Crittenden's divisions, started, in pursuance of orders from General Halleck, to join General Pope, who was pursuing the enemy down the Mobile and Ohio Railroad and who asked for re-enforcements. The pursuit of the enemy ceased near Booneville, Miss.; and on or about June 10 orders were received for the Army of the Ohio to proceed to North Alabama. Orders were immediately sent to officers of the supply department in Louisville and Nashville directing them to throw forward supplies to meet the   now actually ordered, and General Mitchel was again directed to push repairs on Nashville and Tennessee River Railroad and to accumulate supplies as rapidly as possible. The two divisions above mentioned marched from Booneville on the 10th of June; McCook's division marched from Corinth on the 11th of June. McCook and Crittenden, according to orders, proceeded to and reached South Florence on the 15th of June. Nelson was halted at Iuka to guard the railroad and aid in repairing it and wait until the ferry should be ready at Florence. The preparation of a suitable ferry was at once commenced under Lieutenant Morton, the engineer, and by the 22d was completed, and was capable of crossing a division a day, with its transportation, and perhaps more. No other delay occurred on the march but that required to arrange this ferry; the labor was pushed with industry and energy, and no time was lost. The Memphis and Charleston road and our forces working upon it were at this time threatened by the enemy, who lay within striking distance to the south of us, and considerable apprehension was felt for the safety of Wood's division if it should be left scattered along the railroad at the work required of it after the rest of the army had crossed the river. It was therefore doubted whether if the ferry could have been completed in less time than it was it would have been judicious to cross until Wood's division had pushed so far along toward Decatur as to be out of danger. A demonstration actually made upon the line by the enemy was checked or watched by the movement of a division from Corinth under the orders of General Halleck. The divisions of the Army of the Ohio at the time of crossing the Tennessee at Florence averaged a little less than 6,000 effectives. The crossing was commenced on the 23d and continued as rapidly as the troops could take up the line of march with proper intervals on the opposite side, Nelson's division being brought forward from Iuka to the ferry. Baggage was reduced at Florence before crossing, the surplus being sent off by water. All the wagons that could be spared from the troops were sent from Florence to Reynolds' Station to haul supplies over the break in the Nashville and Decatur road, a break of about 40 miles by the route which had to be taken. The leading division (McCook's) camped near Huntsville on the 28th of June; the other two (Crittenden's and Nelson's) were at prescribed distances in rear. The distance marched in the twenty-four days between the 4th and 28th of June was about 150 miles. During this time the ferry was constructed on the Tennessee River, and the troops, animals, and wagons crossed by means of it. I am therefore of opinion that the march was prosecuted with industry and energy. Among the causes of the delay, if there is deemed to have been any delay in the march herein referred to, may be mentioned the suffering of the troops and animals from extreme heat and from dust and a scarcity of water. During all this march forage was obtained from the country.

Question. After the arrival of the four divisions of the Army of the Ohio in North Alabama, about the last of June, what further obstacles were to be overcome in a farther advance upon Chattanooga; what supplies could be procured in the country through which the army had to march; what difficulties interfered with the ready procuring of supplies from Louisville or other points where they could be obtained; what were the natural obstacles to be overcome between North Alabama and Chattanooga; what measures were taken to overcome the difficulties above alluded to; were those measures prosecuted with zeal and energy; and, under the circumstances, was it possible for the army to pursue its march uninterruptedly to Chattanooga, its point of destination?

The third brigade of Wood's division did not complete its labor on the railroad and cross the Tennessee River until about the 6th of July. The further obstacles to be overcome in a farther advance on Chattanooga were a want of supplies and a want of means to procure them. The country between Huntsville and Chattanooga is poor; in fact is almost destitute of supplies. No provisions of consequence could be obtained, and forage enough to subsist the animals in the move could not have been procured along the line. It was expected that the railroad to Nashville would have been completed by 1st of July. General Mitchel reported that such would be the case, but it was not so, and the ready procurement of supplies from Nashville was prevented by the condition of the railroads; supplies did not go from Louisville to Nashville as rapidly as they should have done for some reason not known. The commissary at Louisville reported that he could send but 75,000 rations per day over the Louisville and Nashville road. That was not more than the daily consumption. I know the accumulation at Nashville was not as rapid as it should have been. No proper effort seemed to have been made in North Alabama before the arrival of General Buell to hasten and husband the supplies from Louisville or gather the few which were in the country, and I am satisfied that army transportation, which should have been hauling corn from the country and provisions over the break in the railroad, was hauling cotton, and that this cotton passing over railroads under military control interfered with the accumulation of supplies in anticipation of the arrival in North Alabama of the forces under General Buell. The natural obstacles to be overcome between North Alabama and Chattanooga were the Tennessee River (which had to be bridged, as there was no means of constructing an adequate ferry) and the broken nature of the country. All the material for a bridge had to be got out of the standing timber, and the work done by men not schooled in that species of labor. This required some time, and the labor was prosecuted with zeal and energy. All the spare wagons in the army were necessary in hauling supplies over the break in the railroad heretofore mentioned. No advance from the Tennessee River could therefore be made until the break was repaired, so as to release the wagons and leave them free for hauling from the depot at Stevenson or the river to supply the army as it moved forward. South of the river, on the line to Chattanooga, the country is very barren and broken; the roads are difficult; the march of an army over them would necessarily be slow and its progress could readily be impeded by a very inferior force. Supplies and transportation and means of crossing the river were [not] there, being absolutely necessary in an advance on Chattanooga, and it was impossible for the army to have pursued its march uninterruptedly to Chattanooga. It may be proper to state that there was not much subsistence in North Alabama, and what there was was so scattered as to render it impracticable for a concentrated army to gather enough for its daily use. There was no salt meat, but few cattle, and the corn was standing in fields often at a considerable distance from each other.

Question. When did the division of General Thomas join the army in North Alabama and what delayed its arrival? Pending the preparation to advance on Chattanooga, and before the rebel army crossed the Tennessee River in force, what were the operations of the enemy's cavalry on the lines of communication of the army and with what effect, and what dispositions were made of the troops comprising the army; for what reasons and with what object?

The division of General Thomas joined the army in North Alabama on the 2d or 3d of August. I understand its arrival to have been delayed because it was deemed necessary to keep it west of the river. On the 30th of June General Halleck telegraphed General Buell that General Thomas' division could not join him, and that he (General Halleck) might have to take another division from General Buell. I understood this to be in consequence of some orders or contemplated orders for the movement of a large part of General Halleck's force to some other field of operations. Pending the preparation to advance on Chattanooga the enemy's cavalry and guerrillas operated boldly and effectively on the lines of communication of the army. The first bridge was destroyed on or about the 9th of July, and from this time to the end of the campaign the road was destroyed almost as fast as it was repaired. On the 13th of July the enemy's cavalry captured our forces at Murfreesborough, and destroyed the road the next day after it was in running order for the first time. Other less important breaks were made and important bridges were twice injured by floods. The success of the enemy's cavalry at Murfreesborough not only destroyed the Chattanooga Railroad just completed and disorganized our forces at that place, but endangered Nashville. The dispositions made on this account were to send one division and all the available cavalry from the main army to Murfreesborough via Nashville. The reasons for this were that the state of affairs required it, and in addition to this General Halleck telegraphed that these raids should be stopped even if the Chattanooga expedition had to be delayed. The object was to re-establish the line of communication and establish a force at McMinnville to cover this line and Nashville. The brigade captured or broken up at Murfreesborough was to have taken post at McMinnville for this purpose. The cavalry was to operate directly against that of the enemy. It was found impracticable to hold the road against large columns of cavalry, with field batteries, by small infantry posts, however well intrenched. After capturing Murfreesborough and disposing of the prisoners and stores the enemy's cavalry proceeded to the Louisville and Nashville road, captured a regiment of infantry at Gallatin on the 10th of August, and soon after met and defeated our cavalry column, and were thus at liberty to complete the destruction of our lines and ride over Kentucky. In answer to that part of this question which calls for a statement as to the effect of these operations I will state that in my opinion they constrained, in fact controlled, all the subsequent operations of the Army of the Ohio, for they cut it off from its depots, and it was not possible for the army to maneuver in the face of an enemy equal or superior in numbers and gather its supplies daily from the fields in a sparsely settled country, even if the country afforded enough.

Question. When were the railroads from Nashville to the Tennessee River completed; what further preparations were made to advance, and why did not the Army of the Ohio then at once advance on Chattanooga?

The first freight train passed from Nashville to Stevenson on 28th July. Supplies were immediately sent by rail to Stevenson, which was selected as the depot for the advance on Chattanooga, and further detailed preparations made for the advance. On the 10th of August, however, as previously stated, the post of Gallatin was captured and our cavalry soon after defeated and the Louisville and Nashville road completely destroyed, and a large cavalry force of the enemy was in Kentucky and not an adequate amount of supplies in Nashville. It was also known at this time that the enemy was strong at Chattanooga. Not more than four divisions (Thomas', Wood's,

McCook's, and Crittenden's) could have been carried against him at this time. If the condition of affairs in our rear had permitted the advance I do not think this force was sufficient at this time.

Question. From what points did the rebel forces come which were collected to oppose the advance of the Army of the Ohio into East Tennessee; by what means were they moved, and, considering the railroad facilities which the enemy possessed, what was the probability of his being able to concentrate at Chattanooga all his available force not required for defense at other points before the Army of the Ohio could march to that point from Corinth, a distance of — miles, crossing the Tennessee River twice by means which had to be created?

The rebel forces collected at Chattanooga to resist the advance of the Army of the Ohio came mainly from Northern Mississippi (from Beauregard's Corinth army). The infantry moved by railroad; the cavalry and part of the artillery marched. I have no doubt of the enemy's ability to have concentrated at Chattanooga or any other point in East Tennessee all the forces he could spare from other operations before the Army of the Ohio could march from Corinth to the point in question, it having to march 200 miles and cross the Tennessee River twice by means which it had to create, the second crossing being probably opposed by the enemy.

Question. Under such circumstances what probability was there of the successful advance of 25,000 or even 30,000 men into East Tennessee unless the enemy was occupied by offensive operations at other vital points, and to what extent, as far as you know, was the large force of the enemy which retired from Corinth so occupied while the advance toward East Tennessee was being made?

Under the foregoing circumstances I think there was no probability of a successful advance of 25,000 or even 30,000 men into East Tennessee unless the enemy should be so occupied at other points as to be unable to spare troops to oppose this advance. To the best of my knowledge and belief the force of the enemy which withdrew from Corinth was not so occupied as to prevent its concentration for the purpose named, and I am satisfied that not as much as four regiments of that army was sent to Virginia.

Question. When did the rebel forces in East Tennessee commence their advance; at what points were they understood to have crossed the Tennessee River; what, according to the best information, was their immediate object; what route or routes did they intend to pursue, and what steps were taken by the commander of the Army of the Ohio to oppose the designs of the enemy?

From my recollection of the best information received at the time I should say the rebel forces in East Tennessee commenced their advance early in August. They were understood to have crossed the Tennessee River at Harrison, Blythe's Ferry, and Kingston. Their immediate object was understood to be the reoccupation of Middle Tennessee and capture of Nashville. The evidence on this point was as strong as could well be obtained on such a subject. There was reason to believe that they would pass into the Sequatchie Valley by the Poe and Anderson roads, and move thence down the valley by Jasper and Battle Creek, or continue on the Poe and Anderson roads and pass by Altamont or McMinnville, and thence by Winchester. Steps as follows were taken by the commander of the Army of the Ohio to oppose the design of the enemy. The Decatur road was abandoned; two divisions (Nelson's and Wood's) were sent to McMinnville; two (McCook's and Crittenden's) were already at Battle Creek; one (Schoepf's) was near Decherd, and the other (Rousseau's) was in part at Decherd and in part guarding the Chattanooga Railroad. After the movements to take these positions were completed and before the enemy had commenced to cross to the Sequatchie Valley the two divisions at Battle Creek were ordered to dispense with baggage, take only enough wagons to gather supplies, and move up the Sequatchie Valley, which is productive, subsist themselves on the valley as far as possible, and take a strong position near them, so as to control the valley and render the enemy's retreat to it unsafe. If forced back, these divisions were to retire on the Therman road via Altamont and join the main army. This movement was commenced, but the senior general received information which led him to fear that it could not be completed in time, and he abandoned it and returned to Battle Creek and moved thence to Altamont. When it was known that the enemy was not going to pass down the valley via Battle Creek the Chattanooga road was abandoned as far north as Decherd, and soon after as far as Murfreesborough, the army being concentrated at that point.

Question. While the rebel army was advancing in front were the communications of the Army of the Ohio unmolested. If not, how were they interfered with and what cavalry force had the commander of the Army of the Ohio to guard against the danger from that cause?

As heretofore stated, the communications of the Army of the Ohio were molested by the rebel cavalry while the main army advanced. The cavalry force of the Army of the Ohio was insufficient to guard against the dangers to which the army was exposed by the operations of the rebel cavalry. The commander of the Army of the Ohio was able to concentrate only eight regiments of cavalry, and this was done by stripping the divisions; the regiments were much reduced in numbers, were run down by having been overworked, and in some cases not well managed and cared for, and in most cases having been insufficiently well armed, equipped, or instructed.

Question. What, according to the best information, was the strength of the rebel force which advanced into Middle Tennessee under General Bragg; when did the two divisions of the army under General Grant join the Army of the Ohio, and prior to that time what force of the Army of the Ohio could have been concentrated at a point as far in advance as McMinnville to oppose the enemy?

The accounts in regard to the strength of the rebel forces were various, eye-witnesses of their columns having given their numbers as high as 150,000 men. I think, however, their strength was quite accurately determined. The various items of reliable information were collected and reasonable calculations made, and from these and the accurate knowledge of the organization, chief officers, &c., it may be safely stated that their strength was between 45,000 and 60,000 men; probably something over 45,000. One division from General Grant's army joined the Army of the Ohio at Murfreesborough on September 1. Previous to this time the divisions of McCook, Nelson, Wood, Crittenden, and Schoepf, between 25,000 and 30,000 men, could have been concentrated at McMinnville if the question of forage and provisions were disregarded. The other division from General Grant's army entered Nashville about the 12th or 13th of September, after the main army had gone into Kentucky.

Question. Read the dispatch now shown you, dated the 22d of August, from Major-General Thomas; repeat the dispatch in your answer, and state what its meaning was according to your knowledge of the circumstances which gave rise to it.

I have read the dispatch, which is as follows:

"McMinnville, *August 22.*

" Major-General BUELL, *Decherd:*

" By all means concentrate here. The enemy cannot reach Nashville by any other route across the mountain unless by Sparta or Altamont. I am positively informed that the enemy would have an equal advantage with ourselves here. We will have a most decided advantage, and by being here, should he march by Sparta, we can meet him either there or at Allen's Ford, across Caney Fork. He is obliged to pass Sparta to reach Nashville. I have six days' rations and plenty of ammunition. Did you get my dispatch of to-day? I cannot think that Bragg is coming here either by the Hill or by Therman road. My reconnoitering party went into Dunlap yesterday.

"THOMAS."

I was aware of the circumstances which gave rise to it, and its meaning was that concentration at McMinnville was preferable to concentration at Altamont, and it was written in connection with a consideration of those two points with regard to each other.

Question. Was it supposed or was there any ground to suppose that the rebel force which was in the Sequatchie Valley under the immediate command of General Bragg would cross the mountain to Sparta, and when was it known that that was his route?

It was not to my knowledge supposed, nor was there any ground to suppose, that the rebel army immediately under Bragg in the Sequatchie Valley would cross the mountains to Sparta; nor do I believe that that army intended to do so until it entertained the belief that its enemy were in force at Altamont and McMinnville. It was supposed that a force heard of as crossing at Kingston, and having a temporary depot at Crossville, might pass by Sparta. To the best of my knowledge and belief it was not known that Bragg was moving by Sparta until his advance actually reached that place early in September.

Question. Do you know any reasons for the belief that General Bragg changed his plan of campaign after leaving the Tennessee River, making Kentucky instead of Nashville his immediate object? If so, state what they are and when the change probably took place.

I have expressed the belief that General Bragg's object was to retake Middle Tennessee. Among other reasons for this opinion I give the following letters from Isham G. Harris and General Beauregard and telegram from Jefferson Davis, captured by our forces. I think the change took place after General Bragg crossed the Tennessee River and ascertained the disposition of troops made to meet his advance in Middle Tennessee. The communications referred to are as follows:

"Confidential.]

"CHATTANOOGA, *July* 28, 1862.

"Hon. ANDREW EWING:

"MY DEAR SIR: I have just returned from Tupelo, where I had a full and satisfactory conference with General Bragg, the result of which has made me very hopeful, if not entirely confident, as to the early consummation of our hopes.

"I succeeded in getting the general to send two brigades of Cheatham's division of Tennessee troops (General Maury's and General Donelson's) to this place, the two amounting to about 5,000 effectives; with this force added to General Kirby Smith's command we can successfully prevent Buell from crossing the river, and indeed defend our line of railroad from this to the Virginia line.

"I shall return to Tupelo in a few days, to accompany General Bragg in his forward movement. He assures me that he will carry me to Nashville before the last of August, and I have every confidence in his assurance. The army is greatly improved in health, discipline, and spirit, and is in better fighting trim than it has ever been before, while the Federal Army is evidently greatly demoralized and discouraged, in addition to which they have divided the army they had at Corinth, until there is no doubt about our ability to whip them at any point we may attack them before they can concentrate.

"The only difficulty between Tupelo and Nashville is the crossing of Tennessee River, but the general is confident he can cross his army over without serious loss or difficulty, and is at present delayed in his movement north for want of transportation, which he is collecting rapidly and will doubtless be in motion in a few days. He was not determined when I left as to the point at which he would cross—I suppose at Tuscumbia or Florence, but this must of course depend somewhat upon the position of the enemy, &c.

"I should be much pleased to have you go with me to Tupelo and from thence forward to Nashville, but I am satisfied that you can perform more important service by remaining in Middle Tennessee and rallying all the men that can possibly be raised to re-enforce Forrest. It is of the highest importance that Forrest should remain in that country at some point from which he can strike their lines of communication and keep them constantly cut, so as to prevent the concentration of troops upon us as we advance. His success thus far has been brilliant. He has proved himself a scourge to the vandal cut-throats. God grant he may continue so. He should be very active now for the next few weeks, burning bridges and attacking all small parties of the enemy, which will divert their attention from our movements at Tupelo and perhaps make the impression on their minds that they are to be attacked from this quarter. Our forces from Tupelo will destroy the Memphis and Charleston road, while Forrest is expected to keep the Tennessee and Alabama and the Nashville and Chattanooga roads useless to the enemy. If General Bragg succeeds in crossing the Tennessee River and marching rapidly through Middle Tennessee it places him in rear of Buell's force, now threatening Chattanooga, and compels Buell to fall back, if indeed we do not cut him off. When he falls back General Smith will probably concentrate and pursue him vigorously.

"You will see the propriety of not saying a word to any one as to the concentrated movement of the army, as much depends upon perfect secrecy in these matters. I have written to Forrest fully and inclosed to him full instructions from General Bragg. Col. John H. Morgan will be with him soon.

"I am pleased to learn that a firm spirit pervades the whole country, and that our people have not been seduced into error or won from their allegiance to the Government of their choice by the short-lived tyranny of that infamous wretch Andy Johnson or the treachery of Brown and Campbell. I have sent General Bright :o you with funds for the support of such men as may organize for State service, while Forrest will provide for those going into Confederate service, though those in State service must be ordered for the present to report to Forrest for duty. Send couriers there as often as you have anything to communicate, and if I have left here let dispatch be telegraphed to me at Tupelo. I will make arrangements there to have them forwarded to me promptly.

"Hoping that we may soon, very soon, meet under our own flag within the walls of our own capital, and rejoice together at the redemption of our beloved State from the thraldom of the invader, I subscribe myself, very truly, your friend,
                                                             "ISHAM G. HARRIS.

"P. S.—How did the Herald learn that we were at Altamont and Beersheba, planning the Forrest raid on Murfreesborough? Some traitor in that country must have given the correspondent information. I care nothing for the fact disclosed, yet would like to know the traitor.
                                                                       "I. G. H."

"Confidential.]   CULLUM'S SPRINGS, BLADEN, ALA.,
                                                   "28th of July, 1862.

"General BRAXTON BRAGG,
    "Commanding Department No. 2, Mobile, Ala. :

"MY DEAR GENERAL: Your letter of the 22d instant was only received last night. I give you with pleasure the following views on your proposed operations from Tupelo, for I wish you the amplest success, both on your and the country's account.
    "You had evidently but one of four things to do :
    "1st. To attack Halleck at Corinth.
    "2d. To attack Buell at or about Chattanooga.
    "3d. To attack Grant at or about Memphis.
    "4th. To remain idle at Tupelo.
    "From what you state the first is evidently inadmissible and the last cannot be entertained for one moment, for action, action, and action is what we require. Now, with regard to the other two propositions, it is evident that unless you re-enforce General E. K. Smith at Chattanooga he will be overpowered by Buell, and then our communications with the east and our supplies at Atlanta, Augusta, &c., will be cut off; also that a partial re-enforcement would so weaken you at Tupelo as to paralyze you for any other movements from there; hence you have adopted the wisest course in sending to Smith all your available forces, except just enough to guard your depots, &c., to the rear of your present position at Tupelo.
    "The third proposition would have afforded you some success, but not as brilliant or important in results as the second one, if the newspapers will permit you to carry it successfully into effect, for Halleck and Buell, occupying the base of a long isosceles triangle, of which Mobile is the apex, could get to Chattanooga before you, if they should become aware of your movement, and you would then have to contend again with superior forces, as usual to us. The moment you get to Chattanooga you ought to take the offensive, keeping in mind the following grand principles of the art of war: 1st. Always bring the masses of your army in contact with the fractions of the enemy. 2d. Operate as much as possible on his communications without exposing your own. 3d. Operate always on interior or shortest lines. I have no doubt that with anything like equal numbers you will always meet with success.
    "I am happy to see that my two lieutenants, Morgan and Forrest, are doing such good service in Kentucky and Tennessee. When I appointed them I thought they would leave their mark wherever they passed. By-the-bye, I think we ought hereafter in our official papers to call the Yankees "Abolitionists" instead of "Federals," for they now proclaim not only the abolition of slavery, but of all our constitutional rights, and that name will have a stinging effect on our Western enemies. I intend to issue a general order on the subject whenever I assume a command again.
    "Sincerely, your friend,
                                                       "G. T. BEAUREGARD."

"For Brig. Gen. Thomas Jordan's files. (Private.) Chattanooga, Tenn., from General G. T. B.

"Received at Knoxville, September 4, 1862, at 10 o'clock p. m., by telegram from Richmond 4th.

"To General BRAXTON BRAGG,
    "Care General J. P. McCown :

"I approve of your alternative in relation to General Smith, and hope you will be able to execute the movement in time. We heard last night of the glorious result at Richmond, Ky., and anticipate the accomplishment of much in that direction. You have the field before you, and I rely upon your judgment.
                                                        "JEFFERSON DAVIS."

Question. Supposing it had been known that General Bragg designed to cross from the Sequatchie Valley to Sparta, what would have been the effect of concentrating the Army of the Ohio at that point?

The effect would have been to divert him from the difficult road from the valley to Sparta and leave open to him the better and parallel roads to Altamont and McMinnville, thus throwing him between Sparta and Nashville and other points in Middle Tennessee and on the best roads in that country. That is to say, it would have opened the route the enemy most desired, and probably been fatal to the army at Sparta.

Question. What would have been the effect of dividing the Army of the Ohio between Sparta and McMinnville, with the view of opposing him at either of those points?

The effect of this division would have been but little different to that of concentrating at Sparta. By moving to Spencer the enemy would be at liberty to overwhelm the force at McMinnville and would probably subsequently destroy that at Sparta. A rapid advance to Spencer on the part of the enemy, with suitable demonstration on Sparta, would have prevented that force from getting back to McMinnville before the force there should be overcome.

Question. What circumstances or considerations induced the concentration of the Army of the Ohio at Murfreesborough?

The operations of the enemy's cavalry, affecting the means of supply of the Army of the Ohio, rendered any extended offensive operations of that army impracticable; a want of forage about McMinnville and Altamont rendered it impossible to keep a large force there for any length of time, and if the enemy did not choose to give battle the army would have been compelled to go to Murfreesborough, and perhaps Nashville, to restore the line to Louisville. It was hence best to put it at Murfreesborough at once and watch the further movements of the enemy.

Question. What do you know of the determination of General Buell to hold Nashville when the bulk of the Army of the Ohio moved north into Kentucky after Bragg, and have you any reason to believe, or do you believe, that he was influenced in that determination by any expostulations or persuasions of Governor Andrew Johnson?

As the army was concentrating at Murfreesborough about 1st September it was learned that Kirby Smith, with a strong rebel force, was in Kentucky and had defeated Nelson at Richmond, and that the State was pretty much in his hands. This, added to the fact that the Army of the Ohio was already cut off from Louisville, imposed the necessity of turning attention immediately in that direction. It was therefore with great pleasure and satisfaction that the Army of the Ohio learned about this time that Bragg was moving toward Kentucky. This enabled the army to cover and restore its line from Louisville to Nashville and hold the opportunity of fighting Bragg. In determining the disposition of the army to meet this new state of affairs I know that the first question the commander of the Army of the Ohio entertained was, what arrangements should be made to hold Nashville. I know he was determined to hold it; he told me he considered this necessary. As soon as he got to Nashville he rode over the line of defense to designate the points to be held; some of them were already in process of being fortified in pursuance of previous orders. The troops to garrison the place were designated and organized, and after considerable deliberation the commander was named and received his instructions. I have no reason to believe, and I do not believe, that he was influenced in his determination in this matter by Governor Andrew Johnson. I know that after these arrangements were all completed he informed me that he was going to tell Governor Johnson what he had determined to do, and that he went out and returned and told me that he had informed Governor Johnson of his determination, and gave me an account of the interview. I know of no other interview than the one just mentioned between the commander of the Army of the Ohio and Governor Andrew Johnson on this subject.

Question. Do you identify the letter now submitted to you as one received at Bowling Green by General Buell from Governor Johnson? If so, state what action was taken on that letter, and whether it in any manner changed the dispositions previously made for holding Nashville. Repeat the letter in your answer to this question.

I identify the letter as one received at Bowling Green by General Buell from Governor Johnson. It is as follows:

> "STATE OF TENNESSEE, EXECUTIVE DEPARTMENT,
> "*Nashville, September* 14, 1862.
>
> "Major-General BUELL,
> "*Commanding, &c., District of the Ohio:*
>
> "GENERAL: It is all-important that Major-General Thomas and his forces, as now assigned, should remain at Nashville. There is the utmost confidence in his bravery and capacity to defend Nashville against any odds. I am advised that, including your division of the army, there are not less than 75,000 men in Kentucky and the number increasing, so that you will be enabled to meet Smith and Bragg successfully.
>
> "I was reliably informed on yesterday that a portion of Bragg's forces were lingering about Carthage and the Cumberland River, Bragg no doubt with them, daily informed as to the number of our forces passing into Kentucky and the forces left here. If our strength is much reduced at this point he will be induced to attack Nashville as a matter of course.
>
> "In conclusion I express the strong and earnest hope that the present assignment of forces under General Thomas for the defense of Nashville may not be disturbed.
>
> "Very respectfully, your obedient servant,
>
> "ANDREW JOHNSON,
> "*Military Governor.*"

It in no manner changed the dispositions made previous to its date for holding Nashville.

Question. What was supposed to be the position of General Bragg's army when the Army of the Ohio marched from Bowling Green on the afternoon of the 16th of September; with what object did the Army of the Ohio start on that march, and what dispositions were made with a view to that object? When was it first known that the rebel army had left Glasgow? When was it first known that the garrison at Munfordville had surrendered to the rebel army, and where was the Army of the Ohio at that time? How far from Munfordville?

When the Army of the Ohio marched from Bowling Green, on the 16th of September, Bragg's army was supposed to be at Glasgow, and the object was to attack it at that point. I have no notes in reference to this part of the campaign and do not recall distinctly the dispositions made. The orders for the first day's march, however, I remember, placed the troops the first night at Dripping Springs, on the main Louisville pike, and Wright's store, on the direct road from Bowling Green to Glasgow. A brigade of cavalry was in advance on each of these roads, and the brigade on the Glasgow road had orders to push forward to Merry Oaks, the enemy's outpost from Glasgow, and ascertain the state of affairs and act accordingly. This brigade drove in the rebel cavalry at Merry Oaks and pushed on to Glasgow, learning that the main body had left. An important rebel mail was captured by it. This cavalry reconnaissance developed the fact that the rebel army had gone toward Munfordville. According to my recollection we heard of the surrender of Munfordville on the second day after leaving Bowling Green and while we were at Dripping Springs, about 26 miles from Munfordville.

Question. Do you know anything of the opinions of the higher officers of the army as to the desirability or expediency of attacking the rebel army in its position at Munfordville? If so, state what that opinion was and whether you heard of any difference of opinion on that point among the higher officers.

I heard the opinions of the highest generals in the army as to the expediency of attacking the rebel army in its position at Munfordville. The opinion was unfavorable to such attack, as the position was known to many of our officers to be one of unusual strength. I heard no difference of opinion on this point.

Question. Was the post of Munfordville under the command of General Buell at the time it was threatened? Had he any knowledge of its defenses or control over the strength of its garrison or over its action?

I answer no to all the branches of this question.

Question. What route did the extra wagon train of the Army of the Ohio pursue on the march from Bowling Green to Louisville?

According to my recollection it marched from Bowling Green to Brownsville, Litchfield, and West Point, to Louisville.

Question. What were the evidences of disorganization in the Army of the Ohio on its march from Nashville to Louisville; was the march conducted in good order and in proper preparation for battle; were the troops obedient and prompt in the execution of orders; were there many deserters and stragglers during the march?

I saw no evidence of demoralization in the Army of the Ohio during the march from Nashville and Louisville; the march was conducted in good order and in proper preparation for battle; the troops were obedient and prompt in the execution of orders. I heard of no desertions, and there was but little, if any, straggling. This was commented upon at the time.

Question. How can the absence of so large a number of men from the army after its arrival at Louisville be accounted for?

I account for the absence of men who left the army after its arrival at Louisville by the fact that they had come near their homes; that they had been a long time absent and passed through many dangers and hardships, and they knew that they were going in a few days to encounter new dangers and hardships in another campaign, and they could not resist the temptation to absent themselves.

Question. How is the large amount of straggling from the consolidated army on the march from Louisville against the rebel army under Bragg to be accounted for and were any efforts used by General Buell to prevent that evil?

I account for the large amount of straggling on the march of the consolidated army from Louisville against Bragg by the fact that many of the troops were entirely raw and undisciplined and that they had been raised under a state of feeling in the country which was unfavorable to regularity and discipline in armies in the rebel States, and which, in favoring a rigorous policy toward the rebels, led the men to think they were justified by their friends at home in indiscriminate plunder when operating in the seat of war. Straggling was a natural and necessary consequence of this state of feeling. General Buell was very active in trying to prevent this evil.

Question. At what hour on the 8th of October was it known that a severe conflict was going on between the rebel forces and the left corps under Major-General McCook; how was the information received; what action was taken by Major-General Buell in consequence of it, and what was the result of his orders with reference to it?

It was about half past 4 in the afternoon of the 8th of October, 1862, when it became known to General Buell that a severe conflict was going on between the rebel forces and the left corps under Major-General McCook. The information was received by an aide-de-camp from General McCook. Major-General Buell immediately on receipt of this information gave orders for two of General Schoepf's brigades to be sent to re-enforce General McCook. An aide-de-camp was mounted immediately and sent to General Thomas, commanding on the right, with information as to the state of affairs on the left, and with orders to push forward an attack as rapidly as possible and to send a division to the center column to replace the strength it would lose by re-enforcing McCook on the left. The result was that the re-enforcements sent to McCook, part of them however by General Gilbert before he received General Buell's order to send them, checked the enemy on the left, and night came on before the order to attack on the right could be executed.

Question. What were the reasons in the mind of the commander of the Army of the Ohio, as far as you know, which caused the delay of the army in advance of Perryville after the battle; when did the division of General Sill join the army; how soon after its arrival did the army march, and how, pending that delay, was the time employed in bringing forward necessary supplies and ascertaining the movements of the enemy?

To the best of my knowledge and belief the reasons in the mind of the commander of the Army of the Ohio which caused the delay of the army in advance of Perryville after the battle were that the left corps was badly crippled, and that the division of General Sill, which belonged to that corps, had not yet joined it. General Sill's joined in the afternoon of the 11th and the army marched next morning. The time between the 9th and 11th was occupied in bringing forward necessary supplies and in reconnaissance.

Question. When was it first ascertained that the rebel army was retreating from Camp Dick Robinson; what movement was the Army of the Ohio executing when that information was received, and what steps were taken in consequence of it to pursue them?

It was known on the evening of the 13th that the enemy was retreating from Camp Dick Robinson; the Army of the Ohio was then moving to attack at that place; the main features of the plan of attack having been determined on, orders were given for the pursuit to be commenced at 12 o'clock that night.

Question. When did Major-General Buell first see Major-General Thomas after the battle of Perryville? Did General Thomas at any time recommend the movement of the corps which he was with to Danville; and, if so, when and in what manner.

I do not think General Buell saw General Thomas after the battle of Perryville until they met at Danville on the evening of the 13th. I was hardly out of General Buell's presence during this time, and hence give an opinion on this point. The only recollection I have of a recommendation from General Thomas to move the corps he was with to Danville was one made on the 13th after orders had been given by General Buell for that move.

Question. What instructions were given to General Morgan at Cumberland Gap relative to his operations in that region; upon what grounds were those instructions based, and did they restrain him from operations against the enemy's forces on his railroad communication through East Tennessee which might have been undertaken with a reasonable prospect of success?

I have no means of reference to the instructions given to General Morgan at Cumberland Gap, but they were made matter of record, and I should prefer that they be referred to in answer to the thing in question. I, however, distinctly recall their general tenor. They left it discretionary with him whether to act on the offensive or defensive; he was told he could not be re-enforced from the main army; on reports from General Morgan that the enemy in his front was vastly superior to him in numbers cautionary orders were given; he was told that he was not required to attempt any desperate operations, &c., but on his reporting that he had abundance for a cavalry raid on the railroad, which he had planned, he was told expeditions of that kind were thought to be within his power and were deemed sufficiently safe and promised good results.

Question. Were your relations with General Buell such as enable you to say that you had full and unrestricted access to the information which influenced his actions and a full knowledge of his views and plans?

My relations with General Buell were such as to make me say that I had full and unrestricted access to the information which influenced his actions and full knowledge of his views and plans.

I hereby certify that the above-named J. B. Fry, colonel and Provost-Marshal General, and in the service of the Government of the United States, was duly sworn previous to the responses given by him to the questions asked by Major-General Buell on the 22d of April, 1863, at the War Department, in the city of Washington, D. C.

DONN PIATT,
Lieutenant-Colonel and Judge-Advocate.

CINCINNATI, *Saturday, April 25, 1863.*

The Commission met pursuant to adjournment. Members present, General Wallace, General Dana, General Tyler; also the judge-advocate and General Buell.

Col. JOHN F. DE COURCY'S examination continued.

By General BUELL:

Question. How long was it after the receipt of the first telegraphic dispatch from General Buell's headquarters to General Morgan, of the 10th of June, before the orders were given for the retrograde movement?

Almost immediately.

Question. Can you state with reference to the date of this telegraphic dispatch of the 10th when it was received by General Morgan—about how long after its date, as accurately as you can?

I cannot state accurately, but I think it must have been some time in the afternoon of the 11th or 12th.

Question. On the 13th of June General Morgan telegraphed to General Buell's chief of staff as follows: "On yesterday I received your telegram, giving me authority to operate offensively or not, according to my judgment." How happened it that it required till the 18th of June to recover the ground which had been lost in those few hours between the telegraphic dispatch upon which General Morgan commenced his retrograde movement and the telegraphic dispatches of the same date which authorized him to act at his discretion?

Because General Morgan had been concentrating his troops at Rogers' Gap by two roads. General Baird's and my brigade started from Cumberland Ford toward Rogers' Gap; General Carter's and General Spears' brigades marched through Big Creek Gap by Barboursville, with the view of threatening the enemy which was supposed to be guarding that Gap. After the receipt of the order countermanding the forward movement General Carter's and General Spears' brigades were ordered back by telegraph, the wires having been conducted the greater part of the way on their line of march. The roads were narrow and much encumbered; at Big Creek Gap General Spears' brigade had had a large amount of work to do in clearing a blockade. The delays therefore had been great, and when everything was ready for the concentration all the labor and time were lost. The men were fatigued and demoralized by the counter order, and the subsequent forward movement was not made with the same alacrity as had been evinced by all ranks in the first instance. Countermarching on narrow roads always takes a great deal of time, and the roads we had to countermarch on were of that kind—difficult and narrow. All expedition was used, as far as my memory serves me, in reconcentrating at Rogers' Gap; but notwithstanding every exertion said reconcentration was not effected until the evening of the 17th of June; by this I mean the complete reconcentration of all trains, batteries, infantry, and cavalry. It must be remembered that Generals Carter's and Spears' brigades had at the very least 25 miles longer march to make than the brigades of General Baird and myself. A glance at the map will at once show that I am probably understating the excess of march which Generals Carter's and Spears' brigades had to make.

Question. That does not quite answer the question. It appears that these two telegraphic dispatches were received within a very few hours of each other. I would like you to explain, if you please, how it happened that the order for the retrograde movement was obeyed with so much greater alacrity than the order for the reconcentration.

I was not present when the second order was received by General Morgan, that officer being then more than 20 miles distant from Rogers' Gap, and I almost imagine that he did not receive the order, from the fact, probably, that he had no telegraphic operator to take the dispatch off the wires. I suppose the dispatch was taken first of all off the wires and then had to be sent after and in search of General Morgan. The courier that I sent myself to General Morgan, telling him that I should not move, had to search for the general and had some difficulty in finding him.

Question. Where was General Morgan when he received the first dispatch?

At Rogers' Gap.

Question. How long after receiving that dispatch did he leave there?

Not till several hours afterward.

Question. Was it the same day?

I cannot state, because I had to proceed to the front, the enemy having engaged some of my outposts.

Question. Can you state about how many of those foraging expeditions were sent out while you were at Cumberland Gap? What was the greatest distance reached by them?

I can remember distinctly seven foraging expeditions of some importance, though I cannot give their dates; two conducted by General Carter, one by General Baird, two by General Spears, and two by myself. Of these expeditions, one by General Spears and two by myself proceeded farther than any other. General Spears' expedition proceeded to a point in Campbell County, Tennessee near Clinch River; he marched by a direct road from Cumberland Gap toward Clinch River about 30 miles, but in reality his troops covered a greater distance, inasmuch as they marched due west from Cumberland Gap, and only took a southern direction when they reached Big Creek Gap. On this expedition General Spears met the enemy in small force and captured some 50 or 60 prisoners, I believe. The expeditions under my command proceeded in a due southerly direction as far as Tazewell and operated around that town. On the second expedition to Tazewell I operated in a zone of about 8 miles east and west of Tazewell, and on two occasions approached to within 1 mile of the Clinch River. On the last expedition I encountered the enemy every day and forced him from my front until I was attacked by Stevenson, as already stated in my deposition. I went south about 15 miles from Cumberland Gap.

Question. Were these expeditions always for the purpose of procuring supplies?

I believe all except General Spears' expeditions, one of which, I think, was intended to harass the enemy.

Question. To what extent did that expedition accomplish its object?

All I know of its success is that I was informed in conversation that General Morgan was much pleased with what General Spears had done.

Question. How far would you have had to go any time within the first month after your arrival in Cumberland Gap to find an enemy that it was worth while to chastise?

I do not think we should have found any force of the enemy of importance north of Clinch River until after the 20th of July.

Question. Was that as far as General Spears marched for the purpose of harassing the enemy?

Yes.

Question. What is the distance from Cumberland Gap to Knoxville?

About 40 miles, by the direct road through Tazewell.

Question. Do I understand you to say that Clinch River is more than 30 miles from Cumberland Gap?

I have not so stated, but it must be remembered that when I approached the Clinch River I had marched only 15 miles from Cumberland Gap; General Spears approached it where the river tends in a southwesterly direction. Clinch River at some points of its course is not more than 20 miles from Cumberland Gap, at some 15, and at other points 60 or 70.

Question. I understood you to say that the enemy was to be found on the south side of Clinch River at any time of the first month after your arrival at Cumberland Gap; if that is not what you mean please explain.

I have not stated, that I am aware, anything that would bear that inference. What I have stated will show that our expeditions from Cumberland Gap on different occasions found the enemy in small force near the mouth of Clinch River. Of course I intend by this to refer only to the zone of General Morgan's operations, which never at any one time extended in a westerly direction farther than Jacksborough.

Question. Then, if you please, I will repeat the question put in the first instance. Within how short a distance of the Gap could you at any time within the first month after your arrival there have found the enemy in sufficient force to be worth the trouble of chastising?

I think that any time within one month after our occupation of the Gap, after the 18th of June, we should have found something like a force of 6,000 or 7,000 of the enemy between Clinch River and Knoxville; and if my memory serves me right, and I think it does, I can remember that all the information brought us by our own spies, of loyal Tennesseeans, refugees from the districts between Clinch River and Knoxville, tended to show that General Morgan might have operated toward Knoxville by two or three roads without much danger to his forces.

Question. Have you meant to be understood in your evidence that from the 18th of June until the 15th of July there were not more than 6,000 or 7,000 troops in all Eastern Tennessee?

I did not mean to convey that that was the number the enemy had in Eastern Tennessee, except as far as General Morgan's zone of operations was concerned. I consider that zone of operations to have extended south as far as Knoxville, west toward Jamestown, not farther than Jacksborough, and east to some point near Bean's Station, Granger County.

Question. Have you any knowledge of the enemy's force in East Tennessee beyond the limits of this zone you have described?

I have a pretty good knowledge of the forces east of the zone under Humphrey Marshall, and I do not believe that he ever had at any one time after our occupation of Cumberland Gap a force exceeding 1,800 or 2,000, and this force in a very poor state of organization. I have no positive knowledge of the forces south and west of the zone above described further than what was derived from loyal East Tennesseeans, who seemed to think that the enemy had not a very large force beyond the zone, and that force fully occupied in defending or preparing for the defense of Chattanooga.

Question. Did you and General Morgan exchange views on this subject freely and were your opinions about the same?

We exchanged opinions on this subject often and very freely, and we coincided in the opinion that shortly after our occupation of the Gap he could have operated toward and against Knoxville.

Question. You mean by that of course that he could have defeated the enemy and occupied Knoxville?

I do; and I here repeat what I have already placed in my deposition, that shortly after the occupation of the Gap I asked General Morgan to allow me to proceed with my brigade of three regiments and one battery toward a point near Morristown, to there tap the railroad; and a letter which I found in the post-office in one of my foraging expeditions to Tazewell convinced me that said expedition would have been successful, the letter being written by an officer then in charge of that post and addressed to some rebel general, asking that he might be re-enforced, inasmuch as he had not men enough to carry on the daily fatigue duty and guards.

Question. What was the date of that proposition of yours to General Morgan?

It must have been three or four days after our taking the Gap.

Question. Might you have done the same thing in a month after taking the Gap?

I think I could have done it with two brigades, but not with one, by rapid marching at night on first starting from the Gap, so as to prevent the enemy concentrating on their right by drawing troops which were beginning to assemble in position on Clinch River, in Anderson County.

Question. You have testified to the ability and willingness of General Morgan to operate successfully against the rebel force in East Tennessee? Have you equal confidence in his reports to the headquarters of the army on that subject?

I have testified to my opinion as to his ability to operate successfully in Eastern Tennessee immediately after the occupation of the Gap, and I further stated my opinion as to the possibility of thus operating; but as to General Morgan's willingness to thus operate at any period not immediately after taking the Gap is an answer which I do not think I have made and certainly am not willing to make; because, though shortly after our taking the Gap the encampment of my brigade enabled me to see General Morgan frequently and this enables me now to state with some kind of accuracy what General Morgan's views were then, I could not so testify at a later period, because some ten days after we had taken the Gap I moved my brigade encampment to the Kentucky side of the Gap, and from that period until the retreat to the Ohio I only saw General Morgan when compelled by important business to go to his headquarters.

Question. How large a force would you have required to advance successfully against the 6,000 or 7,000 men that you say were within General Morgan's zone of operations?

I shall consider this question as asking my opinion as a soldier, and I shall naturally answer, then, I would have advanced with all the troops I could, and I believe that I should have found more than sufficient in General Morgan's force, keeping in view his strength in artillery, to encounter and defeat the enemy.

Question. I want to know, colonel, what you would think sufficient.

An equal force to the enemy.

Question. What force would you have thought necessary to leave at Cumberland Gap when you advanced?

Two weak regiments.

General BUELL. (To the court.) I do not think it necessary to question Colonel De Courcy any further with reference to the operations of General Morgan about Cumberland Gap. The telegraphic dispatches which passed between General Morgan and myself, if they are studied carefully, will make this matter perfectly plain, and I do not desire to add anything to it.

Question. (To Colonel De Courcy.) You have expressed the opinion that when Stevenson came into Kentucky he took a position to cover the road to Cumberland Gap. Do you know what position he took for that purpose?

I do not think I have stated that he took a position for that purpose, if that means that he took a position north of Cumberland Gap. I have stated that probably Stevenson did not form a complete junction—with the entire of his forces—with Bragg, fearing that if he did so he would uncover the road to Cumberland Gap by leaving the Gap undefended. I think that will be found in my deposition. He, however, very likely had a force between Flat Lick and Barboursville, on the Cumberland River, with detachments toward Manchester and London.

Question. It is your opinion, then, that he did not come farther into Kentucky than Flat Lick with any part of his force?

My opinion is that he did come into Kentucky farther than that point with a certain part of his force, but I do not deem my opinion on this point of any great value.

By General TYLER:

Question. Considering all the circumstances and the telegram now submitted to your inspection, marked No. 20, in "Telegrams Received Book, No. 1," are you positive that the telegram quoted yesterday from General Buell to Morgan, dated June 10, 1862, was the telegram upon which the retrograde movement of General Morgan was made?

I did not state positively that that was the telegram upon which the movement was made. I stated that I remembered the latter part of that telegram, and do remember to this very minute. My impression is that the telegram which ordered the retrograde movement was couched in more direct and positive terms.

Question. Do you recollect any of the circumstances under which that telegram was submitted to you?

I do not.

General BUELL. The deposition of this witness has brought out new and distinct matter. It is the allegation that General Morgan had peremptory orders, which required him to retrace his steps after he had commenced his advance into East Tennessee and forbidding his operating offensively in that direction at all. I therefore think it is necessary that the question should be investigated more carefully, unless the Commission should be satisfied that the telegraphic dispatches submitted in evidence explain the whole matter. I do not know any better way of getting the desired information than by calling on General Morgan himself. I therefore request that General Morgan be called upon to furnish copies of any telegraphic dispatches which he received controlling his movements while he was in command of the division of my army which operated against Cumberland Gap and about there.

The court was cleared, when, on the question being put "Shall the dispatches sent and received by General Morgan and asked for by General Buell be ordered?" it was negatived.

On the opening of the court—

The JUDGE-ADVOCATE. After examining the somewhat remarkable deposition of Colonel Fry I withdraw my request to make a cross-examination upon it and admit it. It is indeed already admitted as evidence before the Commission. That closes the case, Mr. President. We are through now.

The deposition of Capt. J. St. C. Morton was read.

The PRESIDENT. (To General Buell.) With reference to the paper you have to submit to the Commission, can you give us an idea of the time you will need, general, to complete it.

General BUELL. I may say ten days.

The PRESIDENT. Does the judge-advocate propose to submit any paper?

The JUDGE-ADVOCATE. From the nature of this Commission, or board of officers, as I understand it, called to investigate the operations of the Army of the Ohio, I am not required to sum up the evidence. Indeed, so voluminous is the evidence that it would not be possible to do so within any reasonable time. Most of the questions under consideration are matters of opinion, and as military men the board is better able to treat of these than I am. There is very little conflict of testimony coming within my particular province, and I therefore ask to be excused. I think, Mr. President, that ten days is a somewhat unreasonable length of time to ask, considering the time the case has already been in progress.

General TYLER. For myself I am unwilling to give that length of time, considering we have now been five months in session.

General BUELL. I have nothing more to say, if the Commission will name the time they think proper to allow.

General Buell then retired.

General TYLER. It is very evident we have done all we can till we get the paper General Buell proposes to submit to us. Considering we have been in session since the 27th of last November, I do not think that General Buell should be permitted to detain this Commission so long after the testimony is closed. If General Buell has been doing what the court has he has been preparing his papers in advance, and now merely requires time for closing it up.

General Tyler moved—

"That General Buell be allowed till April 28 at 12 o'clock to prepare and present his defense to the Commission, and that the Commission adjourn till that time."

An amendment was offered by the president substituting Thursday (for Tuesday), April 30, and that the Commission adjourn to that day at 12 o'clock.

Carried unanimously.

The Commission thereupon adjourned to Thursday, April 30, 1863.

COURT-ROOM OF COMMISSION,
Louisville, Ky., January 12, 1863.

Maj. R. SKINNER,
Judge-Advocate, Army of the Cumberland, &c.:

MAJOR: Inclosed I have the honor of forwarding you certain questions which I wish asked Captain Morton under oath in behalf of Major-General Buell.

You will attach the oath and answers to the inclosed paper and mail them to this place. You will also ask the inclosed questions on behalf of the Government.

By attending to this as soon as practicable you will oblige, yours, respectfully,

DONN PIATT,
Major and Assistant Adjutant-General, Judge-Advocate.

Copy of questions to Captain Morton.

1. State your name and position in the service of the United States and whether you were on duty with the Army of the Ohio last summer.

2. Give a detailed statement of the service on which you were engaged and the work you executed in preparing pontoon bridges, ferries, and defenses for railroad bridges and other points, from the time you joined the Army of the Ohio until the departure of the main part of the army from Nashville to Kentucky in September last.

3. State by whose orders the works were executed; whether they were necessary and why; what means you were authorized to employ for them, and whether they were prosecuted with industry and energy. Give the dates of the commencement and completion of the several works, and if there was any delay in either state the cause of it.

4. What is the length of the capitol at Nashville?

5. What length of line will a regiment 475 strong occupy in line of battle or on parade?

Cross-examination:

What became of the improvements upon railroad lines and defenses constructed by our forces in Tennessee at the time the Army of the Ohio fell back to Nashville?

HEADQUARTERS PIONEER BRIGADE,
ARMY OF THE CUMBERLAND,
Camp near Murfreesborough, —— —, 1863.

Maj. R. SKINNER, *Judge-Advocate:*

MAJOR: In reply to the questions propounded in yours of the 5th instant I have the honor to state:

1. My name is James St. Clair Morton; a captain of engineers. Was on duty with Army of the Ohio last summer as chief engineer from date of June 9.

2. On June 11, being ordered by General Buell to provide for the crossing of his army over the Tennessee River, I went to Pittsburg Landing and Eastport, where I procured two suitable barges and a steamboat, of which, together with the floors,

rafters, and joists of store-houses in Florence, I made a steam-ferry bridge at the last-named place. I got the tools, spikes, nails, cordage, &c., from Pittsburg Landing. The bridge was capable of carrying across at a time about fifty loaded wagons; each trip took two hours. The army began to cross about the 25th. This was the best that could have been done, as the pontoons were, when inspected by me June 13, found unfit for use

About July 6 I drew up plans and specifications for pontoon bridge across Tennessee River near Bridgeport. (I believe one was made accordingly.)

On July 9 General Buell ordered me to build stockades at the bridges on the Nashville and Chattanooga Railroad between Elk River and Stevenson. By July 25 I had laid out and put in course of construction by the labor of troops fourteen such works, as per following table:

Designation of works.	Size inside of square or length of development in yards.	Number of garrison.	Station on Nashville and Chattanooga Railroad.
Stockade A..	16 yards square	One company	1 mile below Anderson.
Stockade B..	...do	...do	Bass.
Stockade C..	...do	...do	1½ miles below Bass.
Stockade D..	...do	...do	2 miles below Bass.
Stockade E..	...do	...do	2¼ miles below Bass.
Stockade 1..	...do	...do	Anderson.
Stockade 2..	...do	...do	4⅞ miles above Anderson.
Stockade 3..	8 yards square	Half company	5 miles above Anderson.
Stockade 4..	16 yards square	One company	8½ miles above Anderson.
Stockade 5..	24 yards square	Two to three companies ..	Tantalon.
Stockade 6..	16 yards square	One company	Cowan.
Stockade 7..	...do	...do	Do .
Redoubt 1. ..	95 yards developed	Two to three companies ..	Elk River.
Redoubt 2..	97 yards developed	...do	Do.
Stockade 8.*	16 yards developed	One company	Duck River, South Fork.
Stockade 9.*	...do	...do	Duck River, North Fork.

On July 28 General Buell ordered me to fortify the bridges between Huntsville and Stevenson, authorizing me to impress negro labor to help along the work. At this time some citizen mechanics joined me, and were subsequently used by me to direct the labor at the different points. August 1 I sent to Nashville and procured implements and hardware, blocks, falls, &c., for use on said works. August 7, being at Duck River, on Nashville and Chattanooga Railroad, I got a telegram from General Buell to fortify Nashville. At Nashville I organized a camp, impressed negroes, &c., and began work with them and fatigue parties of soldiers. When General Buell came there on the retreat the capitol was defensible, also Saint Cloud Hill and the bridge. I gave as my opinion that Nashville could be held during his absence with the main army.

3. This interrogatory is replied to above.

4. I am not prepared to answer this of my own knowledge.

5. A battalion will occupy, in line of battle, as many paces as it has files, less one-fifth; 475 men in two ranks will occupy 188 paces or 140 yards.

Cross-interrogatories:

The improvements on the railroad as far as Murfreesborough I found in great part demolished on our recent advance here and all the timber stockades. The earth-works were left in tolerable order. Of the rest I know nothing of my own knowledge.

I am, major, very respectfully, your obedient servant,

J. ST. C. MORTON,
Chief Engineer, Army of the Cumberland.

* The two last were laid out subsequently, but are added in the above list for convenience; so are the following:

Designation of works.	Size inside of square or length of development in yards.	Memphis and Chattanooga Railroad.
Bridge Defense 1	One company	Flint River.
Bridge Defense 2	...do	Viaduct.
Bridge Defense 3	...do	Hurricane River.
Bridge Defense 4	...do	Paint Rock.
Depot Defense 5	...do	Larkinsville.
Stockade 10	...do	Near Bellefont.
Stevenson Redoubt No. 3	50 yards square, seven companies, four guns.	Stevenson.
Stockade 11	16 yards square, one company	Do.
Depot Defense 6	Two companies	Do.

HEADQUARTERS DEPARTMENT OF THE CUMBERLAND,
Murfreesborough, Tenn., February 15, 1863.

Sworn to and subscribed before me this day by said J. St. Clair Morton, chief engineer Army of the Cumberland, who states upon oath that the foregoing are true answers to the interrogatories and cross-interrogatories hereto appended.

RALSTON SKINNER,
Major and Judge-Advocate this Department.

CINCINNATI, *April* 30, 1863.

Commission met pursuant to adjournment. Present, the president, General Wallace, General Dana, General Tyler; also the judge-advocate.

The statement from General Buell not being completed the Commission adjourned to Monday, May 4, 1863, at 12 m.

CINCINNATI, *May* 4, 1863—12 m.

The Commission met pursuant to adjournment. Present, the president, General Wallace, General Dana, and General Tyler; also the judge-advocate.

The following communication from General Buell was read:

To the Commission:

On examination I have found the record of the Commission to be deficient and inaccurate in several particulars of greater or less importance.

It will be remembered that at an early stage of the proceedings I proposed an examination of the record for the purpose of correcting such errors, but the Commission deemed it best to defer the examination until the investigation should be closed. I desire now to call attention to the more important of them. While the first witness, Colonel Lytle, I think, was giving his evidence the Commission was cleared at the motion of one of the members for some purpose not stated at the time. After the Commission had been in secret session some time I was invited in and the president directed or intimated to the judge-advocate to swear me to secrecy in regard to the proceedings of the Commission. I declined to be sworn, and the Commission was again cleared. The judge-advocate subsequently came out and informed me that it had been determined that the investigation should be continued without my presence. I objected to this decision, and the judge-advocate returned to the Commission and I presume stated my objection. He subsequently returned to me again and informed me that it had been concluded to admit me to the sessions of the Commission, but that it had been decided that I should not cross-examine witnesses, though I could introduce witnesses in the defense. I objected to this also. I returned to the Commission and stated in person my objections to its decisions. I was asked by the president whether I based my claim to be present and cross-examine witnesses on the privilege belonging to a party accused. I answered that undoubtedly the pending investigation implied some sort of accusation or imputation against me, but that I did not think it necessary to say whether I considered myself in the light of a party accused or not; that for the present I based my claim upon the instructions of the Secretary of War, under which they were acting, which stated that I would "be permitted to appear and produce and examines witnesses before the Commission." Without coming to any final decision on the questions the Commission adjourned.

The following morning I submitted a written statement of what I considered to be my right with reference to these several points, and that statement was sustained by the Commission. It is proper that these facts should appear on record, and I request that they may be placed there. They are stated here very briefly. It will be remembered that some discussion took place at the time with reference to the rights which I claimed. It is impossible for me now to repeat the precise words in which I presented them.

If there should be any question in regard to these several points then I desire to establish them by evidence, in order that the record may be corrected.

The other errors, so far as I have observed them, I have noted in my copy, and they can be pointed out more conveniently by referring to the record.[*]

BURNET HOUSE, *Cincinnati, May* 2, 1863.

D. C. BUELL,
Major-General.

[*] The literal errors referred to were, by order of the Commission, corrected in the official record.—REPORTER.

General Buell not having yet completed his statement—

General Dana moved that the Commission adjourn till May 6, at 12 o'clock, to receive General Buell's defense, and that the judge-advocate notify General Buell that the Commission will then proceed to make up their opinion.

The Commission adjourned to Wednesday, May 6, at 12 o'clock.

CINCINNATI, *May* 6, 1863.

The Commission met pursuant to adjournment. Present, the president, General Wallace, General Dana, and General Tyler; also the judge-advocate.

The following was received from General Buell and read to the Commission:

BURNET HOUSE, *Cincinnati, May* 6, 1863.

To the Commission:

As it was impossible for me to prepare the statement which I desired to submit to the Commission in the time allowed by their resolutions, I supposed I should not have an opportunity to lay it before the Commission at all, and therefore occupied more time with it than I had intended. In that way it has happened that I have consumed more time even than I asked—ten days. It is now in the hands of the printer in the rough original manuscript. I am the more anxious to lay it before the Commission because they have since extended the time first allowed.

I will hasten its preparation as much as possible, and if it should not be too late will then lay it before the Commission.

D. C. BUELL,
Major-General.

After the reading of the above communication it was ordered—

That the judge-advocate, in reply to the communication of General Buell, addressed to the Commission, just read, be directed to notify General Buell that they notice with some concern the announcement therein contained that the statement that has occupied his time during the last eleven days has been placed in the hands of the printer without any previous notice to them that such action would be taken by him. They perhaps have no right to assume that any portion of their record will be embraced in such publication, and therefore do not express themselves as their duty would require them to do if so unwarrantable a use were made of the journals of the Commission.

There being no further business before the Commission it adjourned to May 10, at 12 o'clock m.

WASHINGTON, D. C., *January* 25, 1873.

I hereby certify that the papers to which this certificate is appended, consisting of the proceedings of the Court of Inquiry, or Military Commission, in the case of Maj. Gen. Don Carlos Buell, United States Volunteers, and of the testimony taken before said Court or Commission (including the exhibits and papers connected with such testimony) are a true and complete transcript of the phonographic notes taken by me as reporter of said Court or Commission, during the investigation thereby of said case; and that the said transcript was made by me in pursuance of an act of Congress of June 5, 1872, directing the Secretary of War to employ me for such purpose.

BENN PITMAN,
Reporter of the Buell Court of Inquiry.

AIRDRIE, *December* 20, 1872.

BENN PITMAN, Esq., *Cincinnati, Ohio :*

SIR: I have looked over the record which you have prepared from the original notes and manuscripts to replace the lost record of the "Buell Commission," as it is called.

My examination of the oral evidence has been extremely cursory; indeed I have only endeavored to ascertain the general completeness of the work without pretending to verify its verbal accuracy. For that your professional standing is the best security.

In examining your abstract of documentary evidence I find that it contains a number of official dispatches which were not actually filed for the defense, and which give the subject the appearance of being burdened with details ; they have no other effect, however, than perhaps to detract somewhat from the dignity of the defense, and I deem it unnecessary on that account to suggest an alteration that could not be made with much exactness, and which would involve a good deal of time and trouble and mar the work you have executed with so much care.

The discrepancy grew out of the circumstance of your copying from records which, when the investigation was in progress, I marked as bearing more or less on the questions put forward by the Commission, but which I sifted very much when they came to be presented.

I find also that some of the documents which I presented do not appear in the new record. This has arisen from the fact that copies of the originals were not retained or cannot now be found. I send you a list of these, as far as I have been able to discover, and I suggest that you specify them separately at the end of the new index. They are not of great importance to the subject, though of course I regarded them at the time as having some significance in an inquiry which was so general and the object of which was so indefinite.

Your abstract of documents handed in for the side of the prosecution appears to be complete. There is missing, however, a map which may be regarded as belonging to both sides, and of which there is no copy extant. I suggest that you file instead an official historical map which was compiled with great care under the supervision of General George H. Thomas and published by the Engineer Bureau at Washington, to show the operations of the Army of the Cumberland (originally the Army of the Ohio), under its several commanders, from the beginning to the end of the war. I send you a copy of that map, which I have amended only so far as to add in a general way the lines of operation of the rebel army in the invasion of Kentucky in the fall of 1862, and also to show distinctly, by merely a change in the coloring, the operations of the army under my command.*

In the original arrangement of the documentary evidence the documents were placed in their appropriate relation to each other and to the questions upon which they had a bearing. The records from which you have had to copy are not arranged in that way, and I observe that you have copied in the order in which you found them. Indeed, you could not well do otherwise. The inconvenience of this defect will in a measure be modified by your arrangement of the index, which affords the ready means at least of following up questions involved in any particular chain of correspondence. That result will be facilitated by numbering all of the documents in one continuous series in the order in which they appear in the new record.†

---

* Map to appear in Atlas.

† This plan was not adopted by the reporter and the compiler I as disregarded the arbitrary numbering of the documents substituted for those lost. See note on p. 690.

With these explanations the new record will, I have no doubt, be substantially complete, as much so as it is possible to make it; and I suggest that you file some such statement with it, as a preface to it, perhaps, in order that it may contain the explanation of any discrepancy that may possibly exist between it and the original. If you think proper, I have no objection to your using this letter in that way.

Very respectfully, your obedient servant,

D. C. BUELL.

[Inclosure.]

Abstract of documentary evidence submitted to the Commission by General Buell for the defense, but of which copies cannot now be found.

Date.	From—	To—	Remarks.	Remarks of compiler.*
1861. Dec. 29	Buell	Thomas	Instructions for attacking Zollicoffer.	Vol. VII, p. 78.
1862. Jan. 20	Greene	Garfield	Instructions concerning operations against Humphrey Marshall.	Vol. VII, p. 23.
Jan. 24	Fry	Garfield	Same as above	Vol. VII, p. 23.
Jan. 26	Buell	Carter	Instructions for operations against Cumberland Gap.	Vol. VII, p. 566.
Jan. 27	Buell	Adjutant-General		Vol. VII, p. 568.
Feb. 19	Buell	Garrett Davis		Not found.
Mar. 12	Headquarters Army of the Ohio.		Special Orders, No. 12	Vol. XVI, Part II.
July 1	...do		Special Orders, No. 89	Do.
July 2	...do		Special Orders, No. 90	Do.
July 5	...do		Special Orders, No. 93	Do.
July 10	Wood	Fry		Not found.
July 11	Headquarters Army of the Ohio.		Special Orders, No. 99	Vol. XVI, Part II.
July 16	...do		Special Orders, No. 104	Do.
July 18	...do		Special Orders, No. 106	Do.
July 21	...do		Special Orders, No. 109	Do.
July 22	...do		Special Orders, No. 110	Do.
July 23	...do		Special Orders, No. 111	Do.
July 24	...do		Special Orders, No. 112	Do.
July 25	...do		Special Orders, No. 113	Do.
Aug. 2	...do		Special Orders, No. 121	Do.
Aug. 7	...do		Special Orders, No. 126	Not found.
Aug. 8	...do		Operations against guerrillas.	Do.
Sept. 1	Buell	Thomas		Do.
Sept. 3	Buell	Thomas		Do.
Sept. 25	Bragg	Buell		Vol. XVI, Part II.
Oct. 18	Schoepf	Buell	Letter of resignation	

* References are to the volumes of this series.

JUNE 20–23, 1862.—Affairs in Owen County, Ky., and skirmish (20th) near Lusby's Mill.

Report of Lieut. Col. John J. Landram, Eighteenth Kentucky Infantry.

CAMP FRAZIER, *near Cynthiana, Ky., June 28, 1862.*

DEAR SIR: The following is a list of prisoners captured by the officers and men under my command in the expedition to Owen County, and who are detained as prisoners, to wit.* Brombach and Foster appear to be the ringleaders. I have them closely confined in jail. I herewith inclose a memorandum of evidence against Brombach. One Bullett,

---

* Nominal list omitted shows 18 prisoners to have been taken.

from Louisville, appears to have been a leader of the party also; he escaped. Brombach says he was commissioned a colonel in the Confederate Army and was here recruiting. Many of those persons who were engaged in the guerrilla warfare had been mustered into the service by him.

I detached Lieutenant Chrisman with 12 men from Owenton to go into Grant and capture some of the parties engaged in the fight near the mills. I understand that he has captured several of them. Captain Wileman, of the Eighteenth Kentucky, who was in the neighborhood on private business and who had come previous to that time with 100 men to Lusby's Mill and did nothing, went to Lieutenant Chrisman, assumed command, as he said by order of Warner, and took the prisoners to the stamping ground (Warner's headquarters), very much to the mortification of Lieutenant Chrisman and not altogether agreeable to my feelings. I think such conduct in Warner and Wileman reprehensible. It is truly a small matter, but indicative of the spirit. I would be much pleased if you would order Warner to send them here, Chrisman in charge. I could then make out the charges and transport them wherever you may order or try them here with the others should a trial be ordered. I am unable to report to you the facts connected with the prisoners taken by Lieutenant Chrisman for the above reasons.

Lieut. James Dunlap, who is under my command, and who I sent to take command of Captain Baker's, Captain Bradley's, and Captain Humes' Home Guards, in the capacity of major, captured some 12 or 13 prisoners before the attack made upon them and before I arrived in the county, and took command. Those prisoners are at Lexington, I presume, in charge of the provost-marshal. I am unable to make out the charges against them.

Lieutenant Dunlap and the Home Guards did good service before I arrived. The Home Guards of this place, under Capt. W. C. Smith, and those above mentioned, acted in concert with the troops sent to me by Warner. All were placed under my command, and I think we cleared out Owen effectually. It appeared to be intensely Union when I left. I ordered the capture of all the arms, horses, and bridles of the men who were engaged in guerrilla warfare, and also all the arms I could find in that neighborhood in the hands of boisterous and noisy rebels.

Inclosed you will find an inventory of horses, saddles, arms, &c.

Warner ordered the mills burned. I would not allow it done, because they are owned by one Kindman, and from all the evidence I could get Kindman was a quiet, peaceable man, and had used his influence in favor of peace and submission to the laws. He rendered good service in ferreting out those persons engaged in the attack on the Home Guards, and he promises to arrest all the parties he can find in that community that were guilty and deliver them to me. He with many other persons in that vicinity have resolved to put down guerrilla warfare by force of arms and not allow any of these men to remain in their community. I acted in the premises as my own judgment dictated. I received no instructions from you. I did understand that Warner had; if so, he never communicated them to me.

I think we captured some 300 or 400 live Owen County secessionists first and last. Those who were not guilty of crime I ordered to report to the marshal, take the oath, and execute bond, &c.

The attack made upon the Home Guards was on the 20th instant, about 1 mile east of Lusby's Mill. Two men and one horse were killed on the spot. One of the rebels was shot through the thigh; we captured him in the woods; his name is William Osborne. A rebel by the name of Nash was also killed. Osborne is left at Williamstown; he was unable to travel to this place in consequence of his wounds. From the best information I can get the rebel force was between 30 and 40. The Home Guards numbered 22 men and officers. The rebels had chosen an excellent place, and had prepared themselves by cutting the bushes out of their way from the trees along the road, behind which they stood to protect themselves from the fire of the Home Guards. I was much discouraged when I arrived on the ground at the prospect of capturing or finding any of the parties. The country is remarkably bushy and hilly. I threw the men out as skirmishers in every direction and scoured the country. I found their camp about 2 miles northwest of Lusby's Mill. The wounded man Osborne was in the camp.

All of which is respectfully submitted.

J. J. LANDRAM,
Lieutenant-Colonel, Commanding.

General J. T. BOYLE.

JULY 3, 1862.—Skirmish near Russellville, Ala.

REPORTS.

No. 1.—Maj. Gen. George H. Thomas, U. S. Army.
No. 2.—Col. Minor Milliken, First Ohio Cavalry.
No. 3.—Lieut. Leonard Erwin, First Ohio Cavalry.

Reports of Maj. Gen. George H. Thomas, U. S. Army.

HDQRS. FIRST DIVISION, DISTRICT OF THE OHIO,
Tuscumbia, Ala., July 3, 1862.

Lieutenant Erwin, First Ohio Cavalry, just arrived from Russellville, reports two companies of his regiment, scouting toward Russellville, were attacked this morning by a force of the enemy's cavalry (four companies) and driven back. Captain Emery and 4 men were killed. Four of the enemy were known to be killed and one sergeant captured. I can get no information from the prisoner which is reliable. From the report of the lieutenant I think Captain Emery must have acted imprudently in not withdrawing in time. The force of cavalry I have is too small for so extended a line as that from Iuka to Decatur. A regiment of cavalry stationed at Iuka could, by patroling in the direction of Fulton as far south as the Frankfort and Russellville roads, drive the enemy's scouts from that section, and would leave only the country from Frankfort to Decatur to be watched by my cavalry, which work could be accomplished more effectually than with the present disposition of the troops.

GEO. H. THOMAS,
Major-General, U. S. Volunteers.

Major-General HALLECK, *Corinth, Miss.*

TUSCUMBIA, *July* 4, 1862.

The party sent out yesterday went as far as Russellville. The commanding officer reports that Captain Emery was not killed, but dangerously wounded. The citizens report that the enemy retreated in great haste and have not been seen near Russellville since. The sergeant taken prisoner says that the enemy were about 250 strong; that their special business was to burn cotton and arrest certain Union men and take them South.

I am informed by deserters that Hardee is in command of the forces remaining at Tupelo; that the larger part of the army has left. One part under Van Dorn gone to Vicksburg; another part has gone South, they suppose to Columbus, and that a few days ago orders were given for those remaining to prepare for a move. Great dissatisfaction exists among the troops, especially the Tennessee and Kentucky regiments. Several arrests of officers high in rank have been made and regiments put under guard.

GEO. H. THOMAS,
Major-General.

Major-General HALLECK.

No. 2.

Report of Col. Minor Milliken, First Ohio Cavalry.

HDQRS. FIRST OHIO CAV., *Tuscumbia, Ala., July 9, 1862.*

MAJOR: I have the honor herewith to inclose to you the report of Lieutenant Erwin, of Company G, detailing the incidents of the skirmish had by my men near Russellville.

Captain Emery, then reported dead, has been recovered and is now lying at my hospital very low, but in an improved state. The other wounded are doing well.

I have since learned that the forces were three companies of cavalry, two of the Second Alabama and one of the First Mississippi, the whole commanded by Captain Roddey, and aggregating 193 men. The enemy certainly lost four horses dead and two wounded. They left one private and one lieutenant dead on the field, retreating immediately after our forces retired without securing any of the subsistence left by us or taking anything but a few articles of clothing. Their exact loss I cannot learn, but suppose from the testimony of citizens that they had others killed and took off 6 wounded. Below is a statement of my own loss:

Killed.—Corporal Bell and Private McMullen, Company B.

Wounded.—Captain Emery, Company G; 3 privates in Company B and 1 in Company G.

The loss of property appears on Lieutenant Erwin's report.

Very respectfully, your obedient servant,

MINOR MILLIKEN,
Colonel First Ohio Cavalry.

Maj. GEORGE E. FLYNT, *Assistant Adjutant-General.*

No. 3.

Report of Lieut. Leonard Erwin, First Ohio Cavalry.

HDQRS. FIRST OHIO VOLUNTEER CAVALRY, COMPANY G,
Camp near Tuscumbia, Ala., July 3, 1862.

SIR: At about half past 3 o'clock this morning we were attacked by an armed force of between 200 and 250 rebel cavalry, commanded by one Captain Roddey. My own company and Company B (which agreeably to your instructions had joined us on the evening of the 30th from Frankfort) were encamped in an open piece of woods on the left of the road, about 3 miles from Russellville. Capt. A. B. Emery had posted pickets on the main road toward Tuscumbia and Russellville and on a road coming into the rear of our camp or fronting the main road. The attack began by a furious dash of cavalry, of about 25 in number, on our pickets nearest Tuscumbia, who, after firing their carbines and pistols, started immediately to camp to give the alarm. By the time they reached the camp Captain Emery had the men in line and gave the enemy a volley as they passed by on the road, bringing down several horses and doing other execution not known by reason of the darkness. The enemy immediately returned the fire, wounding 1 man in Company G. Almost at the same time, and before our own men were yet mounted, firing began from the right, rear, and left; also from points in the woods. Captain Emery, thinking his retreat cut off and knowing himself to be entirely surrounded, at once made a determined stand. He sent one platoon (arranged the night previous) under my command to the right, with orders to dismount and deploy as skirmishers. Another platoon he placed under command of Orderly Sergeant [William H.] Woodlief to be sent to the front. The third platoon were dismounted and sent to the left. Company B was divided so as to leave a few skirmishers on the left, but placing the main part of said company facing the rear, commanded by Sergeant-Major [Hugh H.] Siverd. In this position we sustained a fight of about one hour and a half, being dark when the contest commenced and not entirely light when it ended.

Most of the fighting done with my platoon was a hand-to-hand combat. The firing on all sides was sharp and rapid. The enemy were partly armed with Maynard carbines, which, however, did not prevent our men from loading and firing their Sharps carbines with great effect. The fighting had continued for over an hour when Sergeant-Major Siverd came to me with the news that Captain Emery was killed and the enemy pressing hard upon our rear. In about twenty minutes from this time, knowing the wagons were ready to move and feeling the force opposed to us were far superior in numbers and being, by the unfortunate illness of Lieutenant Fordyce, Company B, who was unable to do duty, left as sole commander, I thought best to draw off my force and try and cut my way back on the Tuscumbia road. Getting the wagons in the road, I drew my men off in columns of fours, finding no enemy in this move, neither did they pursue me.

The efficient men of Companies B and G in this engagement numbered 70.*

*   *   *   *   *   *   *

LEONARD ERWIN,
Second Lieut., Co. G, First Batt'n First Ohio Vol. Cav.

Col. MINOR MILLIKEN, *First Ohio Volunteer Cavalry.*

-----

* Nominal list of casualties shows 2 men killed and 1 officer and 4 men wounded.

JULY 4–28, 1862.—Morgan's first Kentucky raid.

SUMMARY OF THE PRINCIPAL EVENTS.

July   4.—Morgan's command sets out from Knoxville, Tenn.
     5.—Affair at Walden's Ridge, Tenn.
     9.—Capture of Tompkinsville, Ky.
   12.—Skirmish near and capture of Lebanon, Ky.
  14(?).—Skirmish near Mackville, Ky.
   17.—Capture of Cynthiana, Ky.
   19.—Skirmish near Paris, Ky.
   28.—Morgan's command arrives at Livingston, Tenn.

REPORTS, ETC.

No. 1.—Brig. Gen. Jeremiah T. Boyle, U. S. Army, commanding at Louisville, Ky.,
     with resulting orders and correspondence.
No. 2.—Col. John F. Miller, Twenty-ninth Indiana Infantry, commanding at Nash-
     ville, Tenn.
No. 3.—Col. Sanders D. Bruce, Twentieth Kentucky Infantry, of the capture of
     Tompkinsville.
No. 4.—Maj. Thomas J. Jordan, Ninth Pennsylvania Cavalry, of the capture of
     Tompkinsville.
No. 5.—Lieut. Col. John J. Landram, Eighteenth Kentucky Infantry, of the capture
     of Cynthiana.
No. 6.—Brig. Gen. G. Clay Smith, U. S. Army, of operations July 13–25, including
     skirmish near Paris.
No. 7.—Col. Cicero Maxwell, Twenty-sixth Kentucky Infantry, of operations July
     18–24.
No. 8.—J. V. Guthrie, of operations July 16–21.
No. 9.—Lieut. Col. Sidney Burbank, Thirteenth United States Infantry, commanding
     at Cincinnati, Ohio.
No. 10.—Maj. Gen. E. Kirby Smith, C. S. Army, commanding Department of East
     Tennessee.
No. 11.—Col. John H. Morgan, Second Kentucky Cavalry (Confederate), commanding
     expedition.
No. 12.—Maj. R. M. Gano, Cavalry Battalion.
No. 13.—George A. Ellsworth, telegraph operator Morgan's command.
No. 14.—Lieut. Col. F. M. Nix, First Georgia Partisan Rangers, of the capture of
     Cynthiana.
No. 15.—Lieut. Col. Basil W. Duke, Second Kentucky Cavalry, of the capture of
     Cynthiana.
No. 16.—Lieut. Joseph E. Harris, commanding Morgan's artillery.

No. 1.

*Reports of Brig. Gen. Jeremiah T. Boyle, U. S. Army, commanding at
Louisville, Ky., with resulting orders and correspondence.*

LOUISVILLE, KY., *July* 10, 1862.

The rebels under Starnes, over 2,000, with three pieces of artillery,
crossed from Sparta, Tenn., into Kentucky; cut to pieces Major Jordan
with three companies of the Ninth Pennsylvania Cavalry at Tompkinsville, and are moving on Glasgow. I have concentrated all my available forces at Munfordville and Bowling Green, but I have not sufficient force to drive back the enemy. Kentucky will be overrun and

the railroad seized and destroyed without more force. I have asked for aid at Nashville, but they stand on some etiquette, which I pay no attention to. I beg you to send re-enforcements sufficient to drive the enemy and to prevent his coming upon us from Tennessee.

J. T. BOYLE,
Brigadier-General, Commanding.

Major-General BUELL,
  Commanding Army of the Ohio.

—

HEADQUARTERS, Huntsville, July 10, 1862.

Captain GREENE, *Nashville:*
  Instead of bringing back part of the Eleventh Michigan send five companies of it to Bowling Green and five to Munfordville.

JAMES B. FRY,
Chief of Staff.

—

HEADQUARTERS, Louisville, July 10, 1862.

The rebels under Starnes, 2,000 strong, with three pieces of artillery, passed from Sparta, Tenn., crossing the Cumberland River into Kentucky, cutting up Major Jordan's command of three companies of Ninth Pennsylvania. They are moving from Tompkinsville to Glasgow. I have all my available force at Munfordville and Bowling Green. I have not sufficient force to drive them out. I have called for re-enforcements from Nashville. I have advised General Buell by telegraph. We are much in need of more troops in Kentucky. I can extemporize a good force if I could pay them soldiers' wages.

J. T. BOYLE,
Brigadier-General, Commanding.

Hon. E. M. STANTON, *Secretary of War.*

—

LOUISVILLE, July 11, 1862.

I have 1,800 men at Munfordville and one company of artillery. Bowling Green is not threatened now. Morgan issued proclamation yesterday (10th) at Glasgow. He has moved forces toward Lebanon. Firing going on at Lebanon to-night. Train with 500 soldiers left Lebanon Junction at 8 o'clock; has not arrived at Lebanon at this time. Will send other re-enforcements to-night and in the morning. General McCook was expected here to-night. If he comes I will avail myself of his aid. With assistance from Nashville by Gallatin and Scottsville, Ky., we could cut off Morgan.

I have used all the convalescent soldiers here. Governor Morton will send to-morrow 600 men. I am fearful of matters at Lebanon, as my re-enforcements did not reach there by rail. I will telegraph you fully to-morrow.

J. T. BOYLE.

Maj. Gen. D. C. BUELL.

HEADQUARTERS, *Huntsville, July* 11, 1862.

General BOYLE, *Louisville:*

I have just received your dispatch of yesterday. Report at once what troops you have and what dispositions you have made. The bridges at Bowling Green and Munfordville will be secure against any attack likely to be made by any force of cavalry if protected by two companies in a field work so placed as to command the bridge perfectly. The works can be thrown up in a very few hours, and it should be done at once. This will leave your main force available for active operations. A stockade with loop-holes sufficient to hold from 10 to 15 or 20 men must be made at every bridge on the road, and while the road is in danger each train must carry a guard of about 40 men. The force of the enemy is doubtless greatly exaggerated. A regiment of infantry and your cavalry, if properly managed, will force him to recross the Cumberland or destroy him. The dispositions I am making on this side will indirectly assist that object. Troops can illy be spared from here, and it is necessary not to transfer them for a protracted service north of the Cumberland if it can be avoided. No person at Nashville was authorized to divert troops from the destination I had given them. Your report should have been made to me.

D. C. BUELL.

—

LOUISVILLE, *July* 12, 1862.

Morgan has over 1,500 men; his force is increasing; all the rebels of the State will join him if there is not a demonstration of force and power sent in cavalry. The State will be desolated unless this matter is attended to. This city is so endangered that I am bound to keep force here. Send me cavalry and other re-enforcements. I know more of Kentucky than you can possibly know, and unless it is intended to abandon Kentucky I must have the force.

J. T. BOYLE.

Col. J. B. FRY.

—

LOUISVILLE, *July* 12, 1862.

Morgan passed around and escaped and burned Lebanon; is moving on Danville and toward Lexington.

I have no cavalry and but little force. The whole State will be in arms if General Buell does not send a force to put it down. Can we not have two of the regiments? Morgan is devastating with fire and sword. I have protected the railroad but cannot protect the whole State with my force.

J. T. BOYLE.

Capt. OLIVER D. GREENE, *Assistant Adjutant-General.*

—

LOUISVILLE, KY., *July* 12, 1862.

I ordered 1,600 of my men to attack Morgan this morning. They have moved. Colonel Moore, of the Thirty-third Ohio, ordered by me into service, attacked 450 of Morgan's men near Lebanon last night at 11 o'clock, killing 1, wounding several, and routing them. They retreated toward Greensburg. I ordered pursuit of them.

J. T. BOYLE,
Brigadier-General.

Capt. OLIVER D. GREENE.

LOUISVILLE, *July* 12, 1862.

It is certain Morgan cannot be caught without cavalry. He will lay waste large parts of the State. He is aiming at Lexington. I have no force to take him. If Buell would save Kentucky it must be done instantly. I know of what I speak. If I had the necessary troops I could hold everything straight. Morgan has some accessions—several hundreds; these can be stopped by proper force. What will you do?

J. T. BOYLE.

Capt. OLIVER D. GREENE.

—

LOUISVILLE, KY., *July* 12, 1862.

Morgan is reported at Danville and Harrodsburg. His force is too large to be driven back with my force of infantry. Colonel Bruce telegraphs me that a rebel Captain Meriwether has several hundred, and threatening Bowling Green. He raised these men in counties south of Green River. It will be necessary to move a force into Kentucky. What will you do for us?

J. T. BOYLE,
Brigadier-General.

Major-General HALLECK.

—

LOUISVILLE, *July* 12, 1862.

Rebel Morgan issued proclamation at Glasgow on the 10th. Part of his force was attacked last night near Lebanon by my men and number of his men wounded and force routed. They retreated toward Greensburg. I have ordered attack of Morgan's main force to-day. I am in great want of the 1,800 cavalry arms and equipments. I trust they will be hastened forward. Send agent with the arms, otherwise they will be stopped in some depot on the route.

J. T. BOYLE,
Brigadier-General.

Hon. E. M. STANTON, *Secretary of War.*

—

HUNTSVILLE, *July* 12, 1862.

After the favorable reports just sent you General Boyle now says

Morgan passed around and escaped and burned Lebanon; is moving on Danville and toward Lexington.
I have no cavalry and but little force. The whole State will be in arms if General Buell does not send a force to put it down. Morgan is devastating with fire and sword.

This is excited language, but the facts make it evident that Kentucky cannot be left without troops to guard against such incursions and their consequences. I shall have to use some of my force for that purpose. There should be at least five more regiments of cavalry in those two States.

D. C. BUELL,
Major-General.

General HALLECK.

HEADQUARTERS, *Huntsville, July 12,* 1862.

General BOYLE, *Louisville:*

Morgan ought not to escape without a severe blow, but he will effect no doubt a good deal of harm, and the mischief will be done before troops could arrive from here to prevent it. You must use the force you have and can collect to the best advantage to protect important points. Small guards in stockades will protect bridges. Much of your infantry and all of your cavalry can be used as an active force. Five hundred infantry can cope with the enemy at any one point, if I am not mistaken in his force. Warner's regiment, excepting small bridge guards, should be moved instantly to Lexington. Glasgow, Columbia, and Somerset are important points to intercept the enemy in his retreat. Order one of the regiments and the squadron of cavalry from Prestonburg to Mount Sterling and the other regiment to Lexington. These are proper general dispositions, but the movement of the enemy may make it necessary to vary them.

Morgan's principal object besides rapine will be to strike at the line of supplies for Cumberland Gap. I have warned General Morgan, and hope he can send a regiment or two to defeat it. I shall at once send more troops toward Kentucky, but it is not possible for them to be in time to do more than to endeavor to intercept the enemy in his retreat. I have in fact not a man to spare from the work to be done here.

D. C. BUELL.

—

CINCINNATI, *July 12,* 1862—12 p. m.

I received the following:

LOUISVILLE, *July 12.*

Mayor HATCH:

Send artillery to Lexington and as many men as possible by special train without delay.

J. T. BOYLE,
Brigadier-General, Commanding.

I have been in communication with General Boyle. He wants assistance. Five hundred men go to-night from here and Camp Dennison. Governor Tod says he sends force and 1,000 stand of arms from Camp Chase. General Boyle says Governor of Indiana sends a regiment; to be in Louisville to-morrow morning. Great excitement here. Meeting called for to-morrow morning.

Have you about fifteen 12-pounders, new?

GEORGE HATCH,
Mayor.

Hon. E. M. STANTON, *Secretary of War.*

—

WAR DEPARTMENT,
July 12, 1862.

Hon. GEORGE HATCH, *Mayor of Cincinnati, Ohio:*

No information has been received here from General Boyle of any such pressing need of men or artillery as his request to you and his call for a public meeting indicate. The Department must have more definite knowledge before it can act intelligently. Send here immediately copy of General Boyle's telegram to you and any other information you may have on this subject.

EDWIN M. STANTON,
Secretary of War.

WAR DEPARTMENT,
July 12, 1862.

General J. T. BOYLE, *Lexington, Ky.:*

The mayor of Cincinnati has just sent the following telegram to the Department:

CINCINNATI, *July* 12.

Brigadier-General Boyle, Lexington, Ky., asks me to send artillery and men without delay. What shall I do? Have called public meeting.
GEORGE HATCH,
Mayor.

To-day you telegraphed me from Louisville announcing the rout yesterday of part of Morgan's force and that you had ordered attack to be made on his main force to-day. The Department has received no further information from you. What means this sudden call on the mayor of Cincinnati to send men and artillery immediately and why have you not advised this Department of the real or supposed necessity for such a step?

EDWIN M. STANTON,
Secretary of War.

—

NASHVILLE, *July* 13, 1862.

I have the honor to forward the following dispatch just received:

LOUISVILLE, 13*th.*

Morgan's force is increasing. The rebels are rising in the counties on the Ohio. The State will be under the domination of Morgan in a few days. He will take Frankfort and Lexington if forces are not sent immediately.
J. T. BOYLE,
Brigadier-General.

Capt. OLIVER D. GREENE, *Assistant Adjutant-General.*

OLIVER D. GREENE,
Assistant Adjutant-General.

Col. J. B. FRY.

—

LOUISVILLE, *July* 13, 1862.

Morgan has invaded Kentucky with 3,000 men, robbed the bank, and is murdering and stealing everywhere. My force is inadequate to drive him out. Can you not send us assistance? If you can throw a heavy force in his rear he can be cut off.

J. T. BOYLE,
Brigadier-General.

Major-General HALLECK.

—

LOUISVILLE, *July* 13, 1862.

Morgan's force increases. There is evident disposition of rebels to rise in the State. Can Governor Yates send a force to Paducah at once? I have over and again asked for re-enforcements of General Buell's headquarters at Nashville. All forces in Ohio and Indiana should be sent to Kentucky.

J. T. BOYLE,
Brigadier-General, Commanding.

Hon. E. M. STANTON.

LOUISVILLE, *July* 13, 1862.

It is quite certain that Morgan's force has grown since he entered the State and that it is about 2,800 to 3,000 now. It will require more force than is in the State to drive him out. If we had two of the six Kentucky regiments of cavalry, with more infantry, we could maintain ourselves. Could we get the Third Kentucky cavalry and one other? They are somewhere south.

J. T. BOYLE,
Brigadier-General.

Hon. E. M. STANTON, *Secretary of War.*

—

WAR DEPARTMENT, *July* 13, 1862.

General J. T. BOYLE, *Louisville, Ky.*:

We cannot venture to order troops from General Buell. We know not what condition he is in. He may be attacked himself. You must call on General Halleck, who commands, and whose business it is to understand and care for the whole field. If you cannot telegraph to him send a messenger to him. A dispatch has this moment come from Halleck at Tuscumbia, Ala.

A. LINCOLN.

—

LOUISVILLE, *July* 13, 1862.

I have just received the following dispatch, dated July 13:

I cannot send you any aid. About 3,000 rebels surprised our force at Murfreesborough this morning, and a courier has arrived and says our troops were cut to pieces. Have sent your dispatches to General Buell fast as received, but get no reply.
OLIVER D. GREENE.

Morgan's force is represented as increasing. I do not believe that he has any material increase. I believe his force from 1,000 to 1,500. It is reported just double this estimate. There are other guerrilla bands in other parts of the State. Morgan may contemplate attacking this city, to destroy public stores and rob banks. I have about 1,500 men here, besides several hundred Home Guards, and may be able to raise the citizen soldiers to 1,000. We are in great need of troops. Can you order reenforcements from General Buell?

J. T. BOYLE,
Brigadier-General, Commanding.

Hon. E. M. STANTON.

—

LOUISVILLE, *July* 13, 1862.

Telegraph from Nashville says our forces cut to pieces at Murfreesborough, Tenn., and calling for re-enforcements. The rebels undoubtedly have control of telegraph all around us. There is great danger in Kentucky. We have not sufficient force.

J. T. BOYLE,
Brigadier-General.

Hon. E. M. STANTON, *Secretary of War.*

LOUISVILLE, *July* 13, 1862.

Have telegraphed General Buell in person at Huntsville and his adjutant-general at Nashville of Morgan's raid and the extent of it. I advised the Governors of Indiana and Ohio. Morgan was not attacked by our men as expected, because they were all mounted and well mounted and ours were infantry. He eluded them and passed on to Lebanon, and has passed from there to Danville and Harrodsburg, in the direction of Lexington and Frankfort. His force is variously estimated from 1,500 to 3,000 men. He is reported as having three pieces of artillery. A considerable portion of the force I have been using I have taken from the convalescents at hospitals. The forces that I have at my command are stationed along the Nashville road to prevent destruction of bridges and track, over which road all the supplies go for the army in Southern Tennessee. There is a small force at Paducah and Henderson. I called on the Governors of Ohio and Indiana in pursuance of your orders heretofore given. Did not advise the War Department except in the general dispatch, believing that the report to the headquarters of the Army of the Ohio at Nashville and to the call upon the Governors of Ohio and Indiana would secure the necessary re-enforcements. I have received no reply from the headquarters at Nashville, but have had one regiment sent up the road from Nashville, enabling me to move a portion of the troops already there to other points threatened by Morgan. I do not believe that Morgan's force exceeds from 800 to 1,200 men, with one to three pieces of artillery.

J. T. BOYLE,
Brigadier-General, Commanding.

Hon. E. M. STANTON, *Secretary of War.*

—

WAR DEPARTMENT,
July 13, 1862.

Major-General HALLECK, *Corinth, Miss.*:
They are having a stampede in Kentucky. Please look to it.

A. LINCOLN.

—

CORINTH, MISS., *July* 13, 1862.

General Buell thinks that the measures he has taken will destroy Morgan's expedition into Tennessee and Kentucky. He reports that he finds the forces of General Mitchel in an utter state of disorganization.

H. W. HALLECK.

Hon. E. M. STANTON, *Secretary of War.*

—

WASHINGTON, *July* 13, 1862.

General J. T. BOYLE, *Louisville, Ky.*:
Your several dispatches received. You should call on General Halleck. Telegraph him at once. I have telegraphed him that you are in trouble.

A. LINCOLN.

WAR DEPARTMENT,
July 13, 1862.

MILES GREENWOOD, Esq., *Cincinnati:*

You will deliver on the order of Mayor Hatch any cannon made for the Government you may have on hand, in order that they may be used for the defense of Cincinnati or sent to General Boyle in Kentucky.

EDWIN M. STANTON,
Secretary of War.

—

WASHINGTON, *July* 13, 1862.

GEORGE HATCH, Esq., *Mayor, Cincinnati:*

General Halleck, in command of the department embracing the State of Kentucky, telegraphs that General Buell thinks that the measures he has taken will destroy Morgan's expedition into Tennessee and Kentucky. The forces for the defense of Kentucky are under command of General Buell, the commanding officer of General Boyle, who no doubt has reported the state of affairs. Mr. Greenwood has been authorized to deliver on your application any Government cannon he may have for the defense of your city or to be used in Kentucky.

EDWIN M. STANTON,
Secretary of War.

—

HEADQUARTERS, *Huntsville, July* 14, 1862.

General BOYLE, *Louisville:*

I am moving troops toward Kentucky as rapidly as possible, but they are too remote from railroad communication to get there instantly. The movement of the enemy against Nashville may also, I fear, delay them a few days. I am not afraid of Kentucky rising nor of any fatal public consequences, but I deplore the mischief that will be done to individuals.

D. C. BUELL.

—

LOUISVILLE, *July* 14, 1862.

President of Military Board telegraphs me Morgan has withdrawn his force from vicinity of Frankfort. His whereabouts not certainly known to me. He was reported at Danville and Harrodsburg on yesterday. It is believed he is falling back. He may pass out by way of Somerset if he is retreating or in rear of General Morgan at Cumberland Gap. I sent a messenger to General Morgan, informing him that the rebels were in Kentucky; might fall in his rear. I concentrated at Lexington and at Frankfort. Forced to hold those places. I will endeavor to mount a thousand men, and send infantry to engage him if possible. I have organized all the convalescent and convalescing soldiers here into battalions, and ordered officers here, on their way to regiments, to take command. This was absolutely necessary. I have ordered Captain Jenkins, in command of the artillery here, and ordered Major Sidell and Major Sitgreaves to duty in the emergency. I mounted all privates of cavalry here and some of the infantry for duty, and placed them under command of Lieutenant-Colonel Stewart, of Second Indiana Cavalry. I have so far protected the Nashville Railroad, over which supplies pass to General Buell's army. I have called citizen soldiers to aid in this. Henderson and Owensborough, on the Ohio River, have been troubled by rebel bands in their vicinity. I have, from necessity here, withdrawn part of force there. If I can succeed in getting the Home Guard soldiers to organize and arm I hope to suppress them. I have not force sufficient to protect any point. So far I have done the best that could have been done, considering my force and condition of officers. I have sent by special train to Nashville Colonel Moody's regiment, at the earnest request of Governor Johnson, who says Nashville is threatened and Murfreesborough taken by the rebels from various parts of the State. Officers of cavalry companies are made to do duty in Kentucky. Will you authorize my raising some companies of cavalry to do duty in this State and have them paid as regularly enlisted cavalry?

J. T. BOYLE,
Brigadier-General, Commanding.

Hon. E. M. STANTON.

—

WAR DEPARTMENT,
July 14, 1862.

GEORGE HATCH, Esq., <i>Mayor, Cincinnati, Ohio:</i>

Since my dispatch to you a telegram from General Boyle has reached here stating that Morgan has retreated. As there will be no occasion for the cannon to be sent to Kentucky at present the order to Miles Greenwood has been countermanded.

EDWIN M. STANTON,
Secretary of War.

—

LOUISVILLE, July 15, 1862.

I have organized all convalescents into regiments to defend this place and some of the bridges. I have ordered Major Sidell, Captain Gay, Colonel Maxwell, and other officers to duty. It was absolutely necessary. I advised the Secretary of War. I will report at another time names of all equally. Morgan's band is divided up and recruiting. He is gathering accessions. We need cavalry. I am mounting an infantry regiment. Governor Morton has sent me one regiment and sends 400 more men to-day. Governor Tod sent one. I use them to defend Frankfort and Lexington. General Ward is commanding at Lexington.

J. T. BOYLE.

Major-General BUELL.

—

LOUISVILLE, July 15, 1862.

Morgan has moved on Lebanon, burned the depot, robbed the bank and burned a considerable portion of the town. He is now at Danville and Harrodsburg, on the roads to Lexington and Frankfort. He is variously reported at 1,500 to 3,000 strong, with three pieces of artillery. After calling into service all the convalescents I have hardly sufficient force to protect the railroads of the State.

Mounted and equipped as Morgan is he cannot be overtaken by infantry. We must have infantry and cavalry. I have advised your headquarters at Nashville from time to time and looked for force

Cannot a brigade of infantry and two regiments of cavalry be sent to Kentucky immediately?

J. T. BOYLE.

General D. C. BUELL.

—

LOUISVILLE, *July* 15, 1862.

I am persuaded Morgan has not over 1,000 men and two brass howitzers. Jack Allen probably has over 100 and there are several squads raised by domestic rebels. The secessionists have lied for Morgan and magnified his forces. He has divided them up and is burning bridges on Central Railroad between Paris and Lexington. Are well mounted and armed and move fleetly. I have no cavalry properly armed to pursue them. I am mounting some.

You are right in your judgment as to no evil effects except loss of individuals and destruction of property. Only the low and evil will join him. His recruits are few. He will escape, though, between Somerset and Lebanon. I know that Morgan's force is about as stated by me. I have sent reliable men, who learned the facts; one of them joining him to get the facts.

As Mr. Temple informs me, with Metcalfe's regiment of cavalry completed, with one other cavalry regiment, with force in Kentucky, such raids can be stopped if I am allowed to pursue a more rigid policy. Can we not make it to interest of domestic rebels to aid in stopping it?

J. T. BOYLE,
Brigadier-General, Commanding.

Major-General BUELL.

—

LOUISVILLE, KY., *July* 15, 1862.

When will the carbines and cavalry equipments arrive here? Morgan's band are recruiting and gaining more accessions. They are divided up for that purpose. General Buell telegraphs that he is sending force to Tennessee and Kentucky, and sent Colonel Moody's regiment to Nashville yesterday afternoon.

J. T. BOYLE,
Brigadier-General, Commanding.

The PRESIDENT OF THE UNITED STATES.

—

LOUISVILLE, *July* 15, 1862.

Morgan continues his raid. He has several bands marauding and burning bridges. One band north of Lexington burned bridge on Covington Railroad. Morgan's main force supposed to be between Frankfort and Lexington. His operator has his instrument and attempted to deceive us by dispatches, but was detected. Morgan will not retreat until driven by cavalry, which I have not. Can the Governor of Ohio send regiment to Covington and along that road to quiet Covington?

J. T. BOYLE,
Brigadier-General, Commanding.

Hon. E. M. STANTON, *Secretary of War.*

NASHVILLE, *July* 15, 1862.

The following dispatch has just been received by telegraph :

LOUISVILLE, *July* 15, 1862.

Colonel MILLER:

News just received. Shelbyville occupied by rebels at dark last night; 1,200 strong reported. Eleventh Michigan cannot be spared yet.

J. T. BOYLE.

JNO. F. MILLER,
Colonel, Commanding Post.

Col. J. B. FRY, *Chief of Staff.*

—

CINCINNATI, *July* 15, 1862.

Landram, lieutenant-colonel, commanding Cynthiana, says bridge at Kiser's Station was attacked by 100 guerrillas and burned last night. It is the most important bridge on railroad. We have no military head here. Can't you send an officer ?

GEORGE HATCH,
Mayor.

Hon. E. M. STANTON, *Secretary of War.*

—

CINCINNATI, *July* 15, 1862—10.31 a. m.

General W. T. Ward telegraphed me at midnight that he had positive information from reliable eye-witnesses that at 9 o'clock Morgan was in Versailles, 2 miles distant, with the greater part, if not the whole, of his force. He wishes to have as many men sent as possible. Will you give an order for the cannon ?

GEORGE HATCH,
Mayor.

Hon. E. M. STANTON, *Secretary of War.*

—

CINCINNATI, *July* 15, 1862.

Hon. JOHN A. GURLEY:

Danger of serious trouble here, external if not internal. Men enough for emergency, but no arms; no head. Military commander should be appointed immediately for this post. Press this upon Stanton at once. Immediate action important.

RICHARD SMITH.

—

LOUISVILLE, *July* 16, 1862.

It is difficult to ascertain Morgan's force. They have united. Captain Lupton, quartermaster of Fifty-fourth Indiana, informs me that he counted over 1,500 passing toward Georgetown. They are perfectly mounted and armed. They are stealing horses and bridge-burning. They do no other violence. It appears to be an effort at recruiting and to ascertain whether the rebels in the State will join them. They are not meeting with much success. The home rebels are deterred by the forces sent into the State. I have no cavalry to pursue, and can only hold the important points with the raw recruits I have. I am endeavoring to mount men, but find it very difficult. Nothing but cavalry will answer. I will proceed to raise the regiment authorized if it will not be forbidden. I will take steps to prevent persons hostile to the Government and desiring its overthrow from standing for office. I believe this should be done. I have done so in some localities. It is a delicate subject and great responsibility, but I will do it (as it is for the preservation of the Government) if not forbid.

J. T. BOYLE,
Brigadier-General, Commanding.

Hon. E. M. STANTON, *Secretary of War.*

—

WAR DEPARTMENT,
July 16, 1862.

General BOYLE, *Louisville, Ky.:*

You are authorized to raise a regiment of cavalry for the service if it can be done in your State.

I will immediately telegraph the Governor of Ohio to ascertain whether any men can be had there.

EDWIN M. STANTON,
Secretary of War.

—

NASHVILLE, *July* 17, 1862.

The following dispatch just received from General Boyle at Louisville:

JULY 17.

Morgan is at Paris, and fighting reported at Cynthiana, on Covington Railroad. Morgan is gathering recruits. Must have force. Said to be two or three regiments of infantry and one of cavalry. Morgan's force increasing. You will communicate to General Buell instantly in forwarding troops to me at this place.

J. T. BOYLE,
Brigadier-General, Commanding.

General D. C. BUELL, *Huntsville.*

General Nelson is here with his force. Please dispatch me here to reply to General Boyle.

W. H. SIDELL.

Col. J. B. FRY.

—

LOUISVILLE, *July* 17, 1862.

If force is sent on the Tennessee border and up the Cumberland River I wish to be advised of it. I shall expect the forces at Nashville to protect and keep open the railroad. Morgan is in Scott and Bourbon Counties. I ordered General Ward to attack the enemy. He did not obey. I ordered Generals Smith and Ward to pursue and attack. I have no officers fit for an emergency.

J. T. BOYLE.

Capt. OLIVER D. GREENE.

—

LOUISVILLE, *July* 17, 1862.

Best information is Morgan at Georgetown and Paris. Report from Covington of an attack at Cynthiana to-day. Morgan will probably escape through Montgomery County by way of Pound Gap. He is stealing horses and tearing up railroads. Has about 1,200 or 1,600 men, having gathered some recruits. He has done most damage he can. I ordered an attack by General Ward, an officer at Frankfort, but could not have the order executed. Nothing but cavalry would avail anything. I have ordered pursuit of him, with part of Ninth Pennsylvania Cavalry and infantry I have mounted. I have but little hope of overtaking him. I have few officers and raw recruits. With fair officers I could have taken him or cut him up. No man ever had such times.

If you will prevent the villains from coming through Cumberland from Sparta, &c., I will put the scoundrels through. It would hardly justify you bringing your command over. Orders if necessary I will telegraph. I am not satisfactorily advised of the position of the enemy.

J. T. BOYLE,
Brigadier-General.

General NELSON.

—

LOUISVILLE, KY., July 17, 1862.

Governor Campbell, Jordan Stokes, and Trimble, of Tennessee, and the prominent men of Kentucky desire that I ask leave to raise cavalry regiment for term of twelve months or for three years, to serve in Kentucky and Tennessee. Twelve-months' men would only need a jacket to distinguish them, and arms and horses, many of which should be taken from secessionists. Twelve-months' men can be had in very short time. Since the rebels have mounted so many of their men we must have cavalry to protect the railroads or General Buell will have to fall back with his whole army for subsistence. We can clear the two States of these villains from the South and at home in less than twelve months. I trust I may have this authority at once. I feel it all-important. Rebels are becoming impudent and propose to celebrate Manassas at Hopkinsville. They have driven off the best Union men at Henderson, on the Ohio River.

J. T. BOYLE,
Brigadier-General, Commanding.

E. M. STANTON.

—

CINCINNATI, July 17, 1862.
(Received Washington July 17, 1862, 9 p. m.)

Have received no reply to my several dispatches last few days. Rebels reported to have attacked Cynthiana. Have sent all the force I can raise, some arms and ammunition. Appeals constantly made for assistance, which we cannot render.

GEORGE HATCH,
Mayor of Cincinnati.

SECRETARY OF WAR.

—

LOUISVILLE, KY., July 17, 1862.

Recent events in Kentucky prove that infantry cannot protect the State against the inroads of hostile cavalry, and we cannot have cavalry force to meet cavalry invaders. Kentucky is in imminent danger of being overrun. The internal strength of sympathizers in this rebellion is underrated.   Let General Boyle raise cavalry for twelve months if he cannot get them longer.

J. R. UNDERWOOD.

The PRESIDENT OF THE UNITED STATES.

—

HEADQUARTERS, *Huntsville, July* 18, 1862.

General BOYLE, *Louisville:*

I observe a marked difference in the tone of your dispatches of yesterday to me and to General Nelson.   As there is nothing in them to determine priority of date, I request you to inform me as exactly as possible what the state of the case is according to your latest information.   The condition of things here requires the services of every soldier that can be mustered and perhaps more.   No detachments should be sent from here except in case of the greatest necessity.   I have not yet received the information called for in regard to the number and disposition of your troops.

D. C. BUELL,
Major-General.

—

LOUISVILLE, *July* 18, 1862.

I shall look for re-enforcements from you.   It is reported that Breck inridge, with 8,000 men, is 25 miles from Lebanon.   I do not believe it, but have ordered out scouts to see.

J. T. BOYLE,
Brigadier-General.

Major SIDELL, *Assistant Adjutant-General.*

—

LOUISVILLE, KY., *July* 18, 1862.

Cynthiana surrounded by Morgan.   At last accounts he was 8 miles north of that place.   His forces are divided.   He has gathered re-enforcements.   His force is reported to me as about 2,500; it is estimated by some as over 3,000.   I do not believe these reports, though his army increases daily.   They spread every possible lie.   They have it now that Breckinridge is coming into Kentucky with 8,000 men.   He is coming this way by Snell Springs and Somerset or Lebanon.   There may be some truth in these reports.   I have sent spies and scouts on the border to report facts.   Colonel Maxwell moved from Frankfort last night with 1,800 men, cavalry and infantry, and two pieces of artillery, in pursuit of Morgan.   I ordered General Smith to march from Lexington in pursuit, directing force to be left at each place to protect them. It is of first moment that I have re-enforcements.   You will send this telegram to General Buell.

J. T. BOYLE,
Brigadier-General, Commanding.

Major SIDELL, *Assistant Adjutant-General.*

—

LOUISVILLE, *July* 18, 1862.

Morgan continues his raid.   Has gathered some recruits.   I have in pursuit of him 1,800 men, part of Ninth Pennsylvania Cavalry and some infantry mounted and on foot, under Colonel Maxwell. I have some force at Lexington which I had ordered to engage one division of the enemy's force, but orders not obeyed. With such officers as General Ward and General Smith I cannot hope to accomplish much. I shall report their conduct in writing. I have telegraphed General Nelson at Nashville for aid and asked him to come in person. Deficiency in cavalry will prevent the cutting off of Morgan's retreat. I have force at Frankfort and raw recruits from Ohio, and send to-day to that place battalion of three-months' men from Indiana. I have gathered all the force it is possible to get except from Nashville.

J. T. BOYLE,
Brigadier-General.

Hon. E. M. STANTON.

—

CINCINNATI, OHIO, *July* 18, 1862.

I have reliable information that Morgan was at Cynthiana last night. My informant shook hands with him and was disarmed by him. Cynthiana surrendered at 5.30 p. m. Boyd's Station, this side of Cynthiana, expects to be attacked every moment. Morgan reported to have 2,500 men. We have no organized forces here. A few arms and some ammunition.

GEO. HATCH.

Hon. E. M. STANTON.

—

LOUISVILLE, *July* 19, 1862.

The boldness of Morgan's raid gives reason to believe that he is to be re-enforced and that they will fall upon Kentucky in her helpless condition. Major Sidell telegraphs that Baxter is threatening at Murfreesborough and that I can have no re-enforcements from there.

J. T. BOYLE,
Brigadier-General.

Major-General BUELL.

—

LOUISVILLE, *July* 19, 1862.

I moved from Frankfort a force of 1,800 men, consisting of cavalry, infantry mounted and on foot, and two pieces of Thirteenth Indiana Battery, under Colonel Maxwell, in pursuit of Morgan in direction of Georgetown. I ordered General Smith with smaller force from Lexington on Paris. He attacked part of Morgan's force at Paris this morning about 10 o'clock, driving them out, killing 12, and putting others to flight. Morgan was moving rapidly in direction of Winchester, General Smith in pursuit. I ordered Colonel Warner with 500 men to move on him and engage him at Winchester, and after these positive orders, accompanied with a threat, he is just moving now, at 6 o'clock. I ordered Colonel Wolford on yesterday with volunteer cavalry to move toward Richmond and Winchester to intercept Morgan and protect the trains to Cumberland Gap. I ordered Lieutenant-Colonel Cochran, of Second Kentucky Cavalry, in command of men mounted by me and part of Ninth Pennsylvania Cavalry, to march this morning from Danville for Winchester in pursuit and to cut off retreat. If General Ward and others had obeyed my orders I would have prevented the great extent of Morgan's raid. I relieved Ward and put Smith in command as soon as he could reach Lexington. Morgan has done great damage and stclen a great number of horses and other property. I shall levy heavy contribution on his uncles and other secessionists; it is the only way to prevent a repetition of his raids. I shall publish orders forbidding any secessionists standing for office, and see that those who desire the overthrow of the Government do not acquire influence from official positions to render effective their efforts to overthrow the Government.

I have advised the President and Secretary of War of every purpose. I believe Morgan will pass out by Pound Gap; he may fall down below Cumberland Gap into East Tennessee. The domestic rebels will subside for a season, though there are bands over the State.

J. T. BOYLE.

Major-General BUELL.

—

LOUISVILLE, *July* 19, 1862.

General G. Clay Smith telegraphs me that he drove Morgan from Paris at 10 o'clock to-day, killed 10 or 12, and took as many prisoners. He is in pursuit of Morgan. I have ordered Colonel Warner to advance from Lexington on Winchester and sent cavalry from Danville toward Winchester. I ordered Colonel Wolford, with volunteer cavalry, on yesterday to proceed to Richmond and cut off retreat and protect General Morgan's trains going to Cumberland Gap. No loss on our side.

J. T. BOYLE,
Brigadier-General, Commanding.

Hon. E. M. STANTON, *Secretary of War.*

—

HEADQUARTERS, *Louisville, July* 19, 1862.

The State is in imminent danger of being overrun by Morgan and those joining him. If he should succeed in a fight with our forces there is danger of an uprising of the traitors in our midst. I telegraphed General Buell, also General Nelson, who is at Murfreesborough, and he replied to me that 30,000 rebels threaten him at that place and that he expects an engagement. There must be some mistake as to their number. There is a concerted plan between the traitors at home and the rebels in arms. The pretended deserters who have taken the oath and received paroles and prisoners turned loose are agencies in the plans and spies in our midst. Morgan's force has increased—is estimated at from 2,500 to 3,500. I do not believe it so large. Every species of falsehood is circulated by the traitors at home, producing consternation among the people, to get the people to rise. Morgan proclaims that Breckinridge is coming with 30,000 men. Traitors through the State circulate it.

J. T. BOYLE,
Brigadier-General, Commanding.

Hon. E. M. STANTON.

—

LOUISVILLE, *July* 20, 1862.

Last heard of Morgan he had been attacked and defeated near Paris, losing 30 men. Returned toward Winchester. I have ordered Colonel Warner to march with 600 men from Lexington and attack him at all hazards; have sent Colonel Wolford to intercept his retreat at Richmond. I do not believe now he had over 1,000 or 1,200 men; he has received only 150 or 200 recruits in the State. Will keep you fully advised of progress of events.

J. T. BOYLE.

Major-General BUELL.

—

LOUISVILLE, KY., *July* 20, 1862.

Morgan was at Winchester; General Smith was moving after him. I ordered Colonel [Warner] from Lexington with one piece of artillery and 500 infantry to move toward Winchester and co-operate with Smith. I ordered Lieutenant-Colonel Cochran with 500 cavalry to march this morning from Nicholasville. He did not leave until this morning, when I ordered him to move to Winchester or Richmond, as his information determined position of Morgan. Wolford I had ordered two days ago to go to Richmond. If he obeyed he should be there this morning. Green Clay, formerly of Jackson, gives information that 200 or 300 rebels entered Richmond before day or last night. Rebels send back word that Hon. John Williams is furnishing re-enforcements to Morgan. I believe it is a lie. Every conceivable lie is told. Morgan has not received more than 100 to 200 re-enforcements, if so many. His whole force does not exceed 1,200, if that, though our men aver they counted over 1,500. The rebel lies alarmed some of my commanding officers and produced consternation among the people. There are bands of guerrillas in Henderson, Davis, Webster, and Union Counties. A rebel captain (A. R. Johnson) issued a proclamation at Henderson that the Yankee Government had surrendered Kentucky to Jeff. Davis, and C. Merywether celebrated the anniversary of Manassas at Hopkinsville. As soon as I am rid of Morgan I will clear out that region. I think Morgan will pass out through Whitley County or by Somerset and Mill Springs. If a cavalry regiment with infantry force and artillery were at Sparta, Tenn., it would protect our border and relieve greatly East Tennessee.

J. T. BOYLE,
Brigadier-General.

Major-General BUELL.

—

LOUISVILLE, KY., *July* 20, 1862.

At last accounts Morgan was at Richmond; part of his men reported as being at Lancaster. General Smith was between Lexington and Richmond with 600 cavalry. I have heard nothing of Colonel Wolford. Colonel Maxwell has not kept me advised of his routes. Sent couriers to order him to move to Lexington. Morgan may attempt to return the route he went. I have so small a force that I have to ship them from point to point.

J. T. BOYLE,
Brigadier-General.

Major-General BUELL.

—

LOUISVILLE, *July* 21, 1862.

Morgan at Crab Orchard, going toward Somerset; my force pursuing him. He is too far ahead to overtake. Wolford may overhaul him at Somerset and harass him so that forces can overtake him. He will go out by Mill Springs. Will rest and recruit at Sparta, Tenn.

J. T. BOYLE.

Major-General BUELL.

LOUISVILLE, *July* 21, 1862.

No information of Morgan since last dispatch. I have ordered General Smith to continue pursuit and not allow Morgan to take position at Mill Springs. General Morgan telegraphs from the Gap that 1,100 Louisiana cavalry, to be re-enforced with artillery and infantry, are at Kingston. General Morgan says scouts from Morristown state Kentucky is to be invaded through Pound Gap. General Morgan has sent a regiment to Barboursville. I will send to London. There are rumors of bands in every part of the State.

J. T. BOYLE,
General.

Major-General BUELL.

—

LOUISVILLE, *July* 21, 1862—11 a. m.

Morgan at Somerset. He is moving from Somerset. My force pursuing. Colonel Wolford is on way for Somerset with 600 mounted men. May overhaul Morgan there, and detain him until pursuing force comes up. Morgan will go out by Mill Springs. He has been in retreat for three days before my forces. He has the best mounted men in the world.

J. T. BOYLE,
Brigadier-General.

Hon. E. M. STANTON, *Secretary of War.*

—

LOUISVILLE, *July* 21, 1862—10 p. m.

No information since my last as to Morgan. He is probably at Somerset. I have ordered my force to continue pursuit, and not allow him to remain at Mill Springs. General Morgan telegraphs from Cumberland Gap that 1,100 Louisiana cavalry, to be re-enforced with artillery and infantry at Kingston, Tenn., are to invade Kentucky. He says scouts state that Kentucky is to be invaded by Pound Gap. This may all be rebel lies. They have bands in many parts of this State. Many of the best men in the State believe there is preparation for a general uprising. I believe there is such purpose and plans.

J. T. BOYLE,
Brigadier-General, Commanding.

Hon. E. M. STANTON.

—

WAR DEPARTMENT,
Washington City, D. C., July 22, 1862.

Brig. Gen. J. T. BOYLE, *Louisville, Ky.:*

SIR: You are hereby authorized to raise in Kentucky three regiments of cavalry, to be organized in accordance with the plan of organization hereunto attached, and to be mustered into the service of the United States for one year unless sooner discharged.

Horses will be supplied as far as possible by taking them from disloyal persons within the boundaries of your command. The muster rolls will be promptly and carefully made out and copies forwarded to the Adjutant-General as soon as practicable.

By order of the Secretary of War:

C. P. BUCKINGHAM,
Brigadier-General and Assistant Adjutant-General.

HEADQUARTERS,
Louisville, July 22, 1862—4.45 p. m.

Only 820 carbines have been received. Can I not have 1,200 more immediately, with pistols? We want more muskets for Kentucky. I can and will put the rebels down in the State if General Buell will hold them south of the Cumberland.

J. T. BOYLE,
Brigadier-General, Commanding.

Mr. WATSON, *Assistant Secretary of War.*

—

LOUISVILLE, *July 23, 1862.*

Our forces are at Somerset. Morgan passed through there yesterday. I ordered General Smith to drive him from the State. Colonel Bruce informs me to-night that 3,000 rebel cavalry are at or near Scottsville, invading the State. I do not believe there is such a force. Morgan may join with another force they have and return. I shall issue orders directing guerrillas and armed squads to be shot and not taken prisoners. I shall seize horses of secessionists to mount my men, and at proper time require them to pay for Union men's property stolen and destroyed. A more vigorous policy must be pursued in Kentucky or all is lost.

J. T. BOYLE.

Major-General BUELL.

—

LOUISVILLE, *July 23, 1862.*

Have about 1,000 to 1,200 cavalry ready for equipments. I have no new infantry. Kentucky has distributed her guns to Home Guards. I have armed convalescent infantry. Another invasion threatened upon Kentucky from Tennessee. Gallagher guns worthless. Officers do not want them—prefer muskets to them. We need pistols for cavalry.

J. T. BOYLE,
Brigadier-General.

P. H. WATSON, *Assistant Secretary of War.*

—

LOUISVILLE, *July 23, 1862—1.30 p. m.*

General Ripley asks for objections to Gallagher carbines. They snap often; the cartridge hangs in after firing; difficult to get the exploded cartridges out often with screw-driver; men throw them away and take musket or any other arm. They are unquestionably worthless. Can we get Sharps, or Wesson's, or Ballard's, or some other kind? Sharps best. We are much in need of carbines and pistols. I beg we be supplied. Wesson's carbines can be had at Cincinnati at $25, probably for less.

J. T. BOYLE,
Brigadier-General, Commanding.

Hon. E. M. STANTON, *Secretary of War.*

—

LOUISVILLE, *July 23, 1862—1.30 p. m.*

Can I furnish arms to the Home Guards in this city? Military Board have distributed all their arms. I have given out some arms to

Home Guards. Morgan passed through Somerset, General Smith still pursuing. Ordered him to drive Morgan out of the State.

> J. T. BOYLE,
> *Brigadier-General.*

Hon. E. M. STANTON, *Secretary of War.*

HEADQUARTERS, *Huntsville, July* 24, 1862.

General BOYLE, *Louisville:*

I approve of punishing the guilty, but it will not answer to announce the rule of no quarter even to guerrillas. Neither will it be judicious to levy contributions upon secessionists for opinions alone. But with those who have given aid and comfort to Morgan's raid it will be proper to deal in the strictest manner. I approve of your preventing any avowed secessionist from being run for an office.

> D. C. BUELL.

HEADQUARTERS,
Huntsville, July 24, 1862.

General BOYLE, *Louisville:*

Is it true that your troops surrendered to Morgan at Cynthiana? What number were there?

> D. C. BUELL.

LOUISVILLE, KY., *July* 24, 1862.

No official report of affair at Cynthiana received. About 100 men were engaged; nearly 30 taken prisoners, and few of them mustered into service. Enemy's loss greater than our own. Morgan left Monticello yesterday for Sparta, Tenn.

> J. T. BOYLE,
> *Brigadier-General.*

Major-General BUELL.

LOUISVILLE, KY., *July* 25, 1862.

Morgan has left the State. General Smith ought to have taken him. Will report fully as I have time. Morgan gone to Sparta. There is rebel cavalry at Huntsville, Salina, and near Sparta. I trust they may be taken. There are bands over the State; nearly all the pretended deserters from the rebels and paroled soldiers and those who have passed our lines form their bands or the nucleus. If they could be cut off at Sparta we could give protection to other parts. I have the Fifteenth Kentucky at Lexington and on the Covington Railroad; the Fifty-fourth Indiana at Frankfort. Pickets fired on at Frankfort last night by band of 25 secessionists. I have Sixteenth Kentucky from Big Sandy here. The Eleventh Michigan is here on way to Russellville to drive the rebel bands from Logan, Christian, Trigg, and Todd Counties. Parts of the Twenty-eighth Kentucky and Fiftieth Indiana are on Nashville Railroad. The Sixtieth Indiana and Ninth Pennsylvania Cavalry, who were after Morgan, I have ordered to Lebanon. I have some 500 convalescents here; sending them forward gradually. Shall I arm them from the arsenal here?

> J. T. BOYLE,
> *Brigadier-General, Commanding.*

Major-General BUELL.

LOUISVILLE, *July* 29, 1862.

Morgan is at Livingston or Sparta, resting their party for another raid. The rebels are recruiting a larger force in Tennessee. I have over 2,000 cavalry ready for arms, &c., under orders issued to me last week by War Department. I will soon have between 3,000 and 4,000 cavalry, if I can get equipments and arms. I seize my horses from secessionists by written authority from the Government. Could not get horses otherwise. Can we not catch Morgan? Shall I move into East Tennessee; leave the guerrillas to be destroyed by other forces? We ought not to give up that part of Kentucky to them. If I had any officers to aid me could get on. Can I have General Johnson? Don't you want General G. Clay Smith?

J. T. BOYLE.

Col. J. B. FRY, *Chief of Staff.*

HEADQUARTERS, *Huntsville, July* 30, 1862.

General BOYLE, *Louisville:*

I am gratified to hear that you are getting so considerable a cavalry force. In the phase the war is assuming it is daily becoming more important. If you have four or even three regiments the best disposition of them to protect Kentucky against any more Morgan raids would be to place two in the vicinity of Cookville, Tenn., and the rest at Columbia, Ky. The former would be in a position to act in conjunction with the latter and with the movements I am making in Tennessee. After all, the security of Kentucky depends on depriving the enemy of any resting place in Tennessee. You cannot operate advantageously toward East Tennessee except in conjunction with the troops moving from Nashville or those at Cumberland Gap, and the former would be best at this time.

If your cavalry is not sufficient to divide in the way I mention, Columbia or Glasgow is the best position for it. With the bridges fortified with stockades as I have directed nearly your whole force can be used in a body wherever required. I cannot spare General Johnson, as he is in command of the cavalry and other troops about Murfreesborough. Let me know what effective cavalry force you now have and where posted.

D. C. BUELL,
Major-General.

LOUISVILLE, *July* 30, 1862.

Morgan went from Livingston, taking road to Sequatchie Valley, saying his intention was to go to Knoxville. He left 400 or 500 10 miles southward of Livingston. He declared his purpose to return to Kentucky. Two hundred and fifteen of Morgan's recruits, from Owen and other counties, were overtaken by Major Bracht, Eighteenth Kentucky, and Home Guards, at Flemingsburg, and routed, 13 killed, 78 captured, pursuing the others. We had 3 wounded. I shall send Ninth Pennsylvania Cavalry into Clinton and Wayne Counties to protect people at election. The regiment turns out to be a poor concern. Metcalfe's regiment cavalry (three years) nearly completed. Almost 2,000 recruits for new cavalry regiments. I can't get horses.

J. T. BOYLE.

Major-General BUELL.

HEADQUARTERS,
Huntsville, July 30, 1862.

Have stockades been built at the bridges as ordered? With such an arrangement 30 or 40 men can protect the road at any point except perhaps Bowling Green and Green River, where there ought to be from two to four companies.

D. C. BUELL,
Major-General.

General BOYLE, *Louisville.*

No. 2.

Reports of Col. John F. Miller, Twenty-ninth Indiana Infantry, commanding at Nashville, Tenn.

NASHVILLE, *July* 9, 1862.

The following dispatch was received this evening from General Boyle:

LOUISVILLE, *July* 9, 1862.

Four companies Ninth Pennsylvania Cavalry defeated with great loss this morning at Tompkinsville by Starnes' rebel cavalry, 1,000 strong. Are marching rapidly to Bowling Green. They took no prisoners, but killed without mercy. Can you assist us, and how? Send up a regiment to Bowling Green and send cavalry to cut off retreat of rebels.

Later he says:

The rebels are making a raid in force of 1,500 or 5,000 into Kentucky. Are near Glasgow. Send us one or two regiments to Munfordville to-night by railroad; it is of moment.

I sent the Eleventh Michigan Regiment about midnight up the railroad to his assistance. A courier from Major Ballard at Lebanon has just arrived with dispatches from Lieutenant Vale, commanding detachment of Seventh Pennsylvania Cavalry, at Alexandria, Tenn., dated this day, reporting upon what he calls reliable information that John Morgan is now at Sparta, with a force of 4,000 men, pressing horses, forage, &c., rapidly preparing for an expedition, either toward Nashville or into Kentucky, the latter being his avowed destination.

Major Ballard has sent out scouts toward Sparta.

JNO. F. MILLER,
Commanding Post.

Col. J. B. FRY.

HEADQUARTERS U. S. FORCES,
Nashville, July 12, 1862.

COLONEL: Since my dispatch to you I sent five companies Seventy-fourth Ohio and one section Bush's battery to Bowling Green, having sent the Eleventh Michigan before Morgan menaced Bowling Green and Munfordville.

The following dispatch just received from Bowling Green shows result thus far:

Colonel Moore routed them at Lebanon, Ky., yesterday. They are reported retreating toward Greensburg. Colonel Owen cut party of 500 to pieces above Burkesville. Colonel Stoughton and other forces are marching to intercept them at Bear Wallow. Six hundred men under Colonel Moody, with one piece of artillery, have marched to Scottsville to cut them off there. Rivers rising, which is favorable to us.

S. D. BRUCE,
Colonel, Commanding.

I will send First Tennessee, Colonel Gillem, one section Bush's battery and two companies cavalry to Lebanon, Tenn., to-day. Have there now four companies infantry and two companies cavalry. Some forces may go over from Murfreesborough also.

We will move northeast from Lebanon above Sparta to take or scatter Starnes, who is in that region with from 500 to 1,000 men, and to intercept retreating rebels from Kentucky.

JNO. F. MILLER,
Colonel, Commanding Post.

Col. J. B. Fry.

No. 3.

Report of Col. Sanders D. Bruce, Twentieth Kentucky Infantry, of capture of Tompkinsville.

BOWLING GREEN, KY., *July* 10, 1862.

Send more force and some artillery, if they can be spared. One thousand five hundred rebel cavalry and two pieces of artillery attacked Major Jordan at Tompkinsville and killed or captured his three companies. Confirmed by Judge Graham, from Tompkinsville. We are after them. Show this to Governor Johnson.

S. D. BRUCE,
Colonel, Commanding.

OLIVER D. GREENE, *Assistant Adjutant-General.*

No. 4.

Report of Maj. Thomas J. Jordan, Ninth Pennsylvania Cavalry, of the capture of Tomkinsville.

LOUISVILLE, KY., *December* 29, 1862.

SIR: On July 6 I was in command of the post at Tompkinsville, Ky., having with me Companies C, I, and M, of the Ninth Pennsylvania Cavalry. During that day I was informed that a large body of the enemy were collecting at Salina, a little village on the south side of the Cumberland River, some 20 miles from me. About the same time I learned that Company E, of my regiment, was at Glasgow, Ky., 27 miles north of me. I at once ordered that company to join me, which it did about noon on the 7th, thus making my command about 230 effective men. With this force I determined to attack Salina, and, if possible, capture or disperse the forces of the enemy at that point before they could be fully concentrated.

At 8 o'clock on that night I moved from my camp with my whole command, leaving only a detachment of Company M to guard my tents and stores. I succeeded in crossing the Cumberland at a point 12 miles north of Salina, and at daylight on the morning of the 8th entered the place, but I was disappointed in not finding the enemy. I made every inquiry probable from the inhabitants, but all denied any knowledge of forces being either there or in the neighborhood. Thinking that I had been misled, but far from being satisfied, I marched back to my camp, at which I arrived about 8 o'clock in the evening. I at once ordered the usual pickets to be posted on all the roads leading to my position, and also an extra one far out on the Salina road, so as to secure my camp against surprise during the night.

As day broke on the morning of the 9th reveille was sounded, and in a few moments my men were busily engaged in feeding and cleaning their horses. My officers were all at their posts, when a faint discharge of fire-arms was heard far out on the Salina road. I at once ordered the horses to be saddled, and in a few moments my pickets reported the enemy approaching in large force, and within a minute the head of Colonel Morgan's command began to deploy from the woods into an open field some 300 yards from me. I soon found that his force outnumbered mine by six to one, but as he showed no disposition to charge me I deemed it prudent not to retreat. His command soon opened to the right and left in front of me, displaying two pieces of cannon in position, which at once opened upon me with shell. I replied with my carbines, and could distinctly see that we were doing good execution.

Finding at the tenth round of the enemy that they were getting my range and seeing a movement from their right flank intended to gain my rear I gave the order to wheel and retreat. This movement was done with the precision of a parade, my men remaining perfectly cool and obedient to my orders. To gain the Burkesville road it was necessary that my retreat should be through a deep woods in my rear. I had not entered it but a few yards when I was opened upon by a line of the enemy, consisting of two squadrons of Texas Rangers, who had been thrown in my rear. I at once ordered my men to charge the line, which they did in the most gallant style, literally overturning the Rangers and driving them from the field. The Burkesville road being gained, my retreat was conducted in a most orderly manner, the enemy not pursuing us until we had gained some 2 miles, when, hearing firing in my rear, I deemed it proper for me to personally look to my rear guard, that I had placed under charge of Lieutenant Sullivan, of Company E. For this purpose I rode to the rear of my column and found that the firing proceeded from beyond a turn in the road some 200 yards behind my rear guard. Fearing that some of my men might have been separated from my command and were being attacked I rode back to the turn, so as to be able to see, when I discovered Lieutenant Sullivan in the act of being murdered by some 20 of the enemy, who had surrounded him. I at once turned my horse for the purpose of rejoining my command, when I found two of the enemy already in the road before me and in a moment after they were increased to 6, thus entirely cutting me off from my men. I determined to try and force my way through them, with my pistol answering their shot-guns, but I soon found that resistance would be madness and surrendered myself a prisoner of war. After I had surrendered I was fired upon at the distance of but a few feet, the charge, happily for me, missing its mark, but blackening the side of my face with the powder.

The forces of Colonel Morgan on that occasion consisted of his own brigade, Colonel Hunt's (Fifth Georgia) regiment of cavalry, a regiment of Alabama cavalry, two squadrons of Texas Rangers, and the independent companies of Captains Bledsoe, Hamilton, McMillin, and Ferguson, numbering in all some 2,000 men, with two pieces of artillery.

My loss was 4 killed (including Lieutenant Sullivan), 7 wounded, and 19 prisoners. I also lost my tents, wagons, mules, and personal baggage of my command. On the part of the enemy I have been informed that 19 were killed or mortally wounded and 28 slightly. Colonel Hunt was mortally wounded and died at Tompkinsville.

I cannot speak too highly of the coolness and bravery displayed by my officers and men. My orders were promptly obeyed and every one did his whole duty.

Respectfully submitted.

THOS. J. JORDAN,
Major, Ninth Pennsylvania Cavalry.

Brigadier-General BOYLE.

No. 5

Report of Lieut. Col. John J. Landram, Eighteenth Kentucky Infantry, of the capture of Cynthiana.

HEADQUARTERS,
Cynthiana, Ky., July 24, 1862.

On Thursday, the 17th instant, about 3 p. m., I was attacked at this place by the forces under command of Col. John H. Morgán, comprising three regiments, composed of Kentuckians, Tennesseeans, Georgians, Mississippians, Texans, and South Carolinians, estimated variously at from 1,500 to 3,000 men, reported by Captain Alston, his adjutant-general, at 2,200 strong, and two pieces of artillery. The forces under my command were composed of about 15 men of the Eighteenth Kentucky Volunteers and the following Home Guards: About 60 men under Capt. J. B. McClintock and from 50 to 60 men under Capt. Lafe Wilson, from Cynthiana and vicinity; Capt. John S. Arthur, of Newport, 50 men; Capt. J. J. Wright, of Cincinnati, 40 men; Captain Pepper, of Bracken County, 35 men; 75 men of the Seventh Kentucky Cavalry (raw recruits), under Maj. William O. Smith, and one brass 12-pounder and a small artillery squad, under Capt. W. H. Glass, of Cincinnati, amounting in the aggregate to about 340 men, the majority of them poorly armed and nearly all totally undisciplined.

After my pickets were driven in and before I had time to dispose my little force the enemy commenced shelling the town without notice to me to remove the women and children. I immediately ordered Captain Glass to occupy the public square with his artillery, from which point he could command most of the roads entering the town, Captain Arthur's company to support it. I also at the same time ordered a portion of my force to take position on the Magee Hill road, south of town, and soon hearing considerable firing in that quarter presumed they were approaching in that direction in heavy force. I then posted a portion of my force on the river bank, on the west side of the town, near the Licking Bridge, from which direction Morgan's main force seemed to be approaching, with instructions to hold the bridge at all hazards. At this time I ordered Captain Glass to put his piece in position, so as to command Morgan's battery and, if possible, to silence it, which was done at the second discharge. I then discovered that the town was circumvented, and we were completely surrounded by a superior force, the enemy approaching by every road, street, and by-path, and deployed as skirmishers through every field, completely encircling us. I ordered Captain Glass to put his gun in position to command the Millersburg road and give the enemy grape and canister, which was done with good effect By this time my little band was engaged at every point. The fighting on both sides was terrific. The enemy, having possession of the streets, were pouring a galling fire upon us from the shelter of houses, fences, &c., and the artillery squad, being subjected to a cross-fire, was compelled to abandon their piece. My men at the bridge were, after a most desperate conflict, driven back by very superior numbers and a cavalry charge made through the streets by Morgan's forces. At this time I rallied a part of my forces at the railroad depot, at which point our boys gave them a warm reception, emptying several saddles. I then went again for the purpose of rallying the artillery squad, so as to place it on the hill near the residence of M. L. Broadwell, from which position we could have commanded the town and several roads leading to it, but was unable to find either men or gun, the streets in every direction being in possession of the rebels.

My men were exhausted and out of ammunition, but I rallied them, and at the depot distributed cartridges to them. The firing at this time having nearly ceased I rode along the railroad to Rankin's Hotel, to ascertain what position the enemy was taking and from what direction they were coming in heaviest force. Here I met an officer of the rebel band, aide to Colonel Morgan, a son of the late Beverly L. Clark, who demanded my surrender. I replied, "I never surrender," and instantly discharged three shots at him, two of which took effect in his breast. He fell from his horse and I thought him dead, but he is still living and will probably recover, notwithstanding two balls passed through his body. Captain Rogers also discharged a shot at him, which took effect. I then rallied a part of my force, about 40 in number, determined to make a charge on the enemy at the Licking Bridge and take their battery, which had been brought to that point and was being used with effect upon my little band of patriot heroes. The force sustaining their artillery outnumbered ours more than ten to one, and were all the while under cover of houses, &c. Besides this a force of the rebels at least 300 strong were pouring an incessant and deadly fire upon my little band from the rear about 125 yards distant.

It was here that Jacob Carver, of Company E, Eighteenth Kentucky, fell severely wounded—as brave a man as ever pulled trigger—and I received a slight wound in the ankle. It was here too that the lamented Thomas Ware, United States commissioner for this county, one of the oldest citizens of Cynthiana, was instantly killed, nobly and bravely doing his duty as a patriot. Here, too, were killed Jesse Current, young Thomas Rankin, Capt. Lafe Wilson, young Hartburn of Cincinnati, and others, besides many—including F. L. St. Thomas, John Scott, Captain McClintock, John McClintock, Thomas Barry of Cincinnati, and Thomas J. Vimont—who fell severely wounded.

In consequence of the terrific storm of balls, and as but few of my men were left, among whom was William W. Trimble and J. S. Frizell, of this place, who was also wounded (others not remembered), I ordered a retreat.

In the mean time Maj. William O. Smith had command of the Seventh Kentucky Cavalry and was posted north of town to hold the Claysville road and prevent the enemy from gaining the streets from that direction, where he made a gallant resistance near the Episcopal Church, until overpowered by superior numbers and forced to fall back toward the Reform Church and thence to the court-house, where he and his command were compelled to surrender.

At this time more than three-fourths of my men were killed, wounded, and prisoners, and I determined to cut my way through the enemy and escape with the remainder if possible. I rallied together from 20 to 25 of my men at the depot and started in a southeasterly direction through Redmon's pasture, where we met a body of the enemy, who had crossed from the Millersburg road. They were secreted behind fences, trees, and hay-cocks. We at once engaged them and soon routed them. Upon turning around I discovered that the enemy had pursued us from town, and were on our rear not more than 40 paces distant. I ordered my handful of men to cross the hill-side and fight them from behind the fences, which they did, and held them in check until nearly surrounded by a body of cavalry at least ten times their number. I then ordered my men to retreat beyond a fence in a southeasterly direction to avoid a cavalry charge. Here a part of my men became exhausted, some falling by the wayside to await their fate, their ammunition all expended, when I informed the little Spartan band we could do no more; to save themselves and I would do likewise, if possible, and bade them good-by.

Each and every man of this noble little squad fought with desperation and the coolness of veterans. Among them were James F. Ware, John R. Smith, William Kimbrough, Lieut. William M. Dayton, Company I, Eighteenth Kentucky Volunteers; Lieut. W. C. Sleet, Company E, Eighteenth Kentucky; Silas Howe, sergeant, Company E, Eighteenth Kentucky; Albert Roper, sergeant, Company I, Eighteenth Kentucky; Capt. J. J. Wright, of Cincinnati, and others not now remembered, to any one of whom too much praise cannot be awarded.

Capt. Lafe Wilson fell near the depot, and continued to discharge his revolver as long as life lasted. His last words were, "Never surrender, boys."

Capt. J. B. McClintock fell severely wounded while urging his men to the charge.

Capt. S. G. Rogers, Company I, Eighteenth Kentucky, was wounded while gallantly resisting the foe.

I cannot particularize further; it is enough to say that all my men fought like heroes and veterans in the face of a greatly superior force, as is evidenced by the slaughter that ensued, having held them in check for nearly three hours against a most galling fire, which was poured in upon us from every side. I think it beyond doubt one of the most sanguinary conflicts of the war, considering the numbers engaged.

Rev. George Morrison, of this place, rendered me very important service before and during the engagement in conveying orders to the different commands under me.

It is quite difficult to ascertain the number in killed and wounded on their side, as the enemy had possession of the field, and our men, all being prisoners, had no opportunity to make examination until paroled, at which time the enemy had buried their dead and sent off most of their wounded.

I herewith append a list* of Federals killed and wounded, furnished me by Dr. W. T. McNees, assistant surgeon of Seventh Kentucky Cavalry.

I can give no accurate account of the rebel dead, Morgan having taken off eight burial-cases from this place and his men having been seen hauling off their dead toward Georgetown, the Magee road, and Millersburg road after the fight. Two of their wounded died at Winchester and two beyond that place. Since Morgan left 13 of his dead have been taken from the river near Cynthiana, where they were thrown for concealment. Morgan himself admitted at Paris a loss here of 24

---

* Nominal list omitted shows 17 killed and 34 wounded.

killed and 78 wounded, and that of seventeen engagements participated in by him since the beginning of the war the affair at Cynthiana was much the fiercest and most desperate.

I append also a list* of rebel wounded left in Cynthiana. Nine of their wounded are also at Paris, besides a number left along the road between this place and Richmond, Ky., to which point we pursued him, by command of General G. C. Smith.

We are under great obligations to the companies from Cincinnati, Newport, and Bracken County, Kentucky, under Captains Wright, Arthur, and Pepper, for their invaluable aid, who distinguished themselves on that occasion and fought like heroes.

The friends and relatives of the wounded of both sides are greatly indebted to Surg. W. T. McNees, Seventh Kentucky Cavalry; Drs. J. C. Frazier, A. Adams, W. O. Smith, J. A. Kirkpatrick, John A. Lair, and —— McLeod, for their unremitting attention to the wounded, and to the ladies of Cynthiana unbounded praise is due for their untiring ministrations upon the wounded, &c.

I have the honor to be, with much respect, your obedient servant,

J. J. LANDRAM,
Lieutenant-Colonel, Commanding.

Capt. JOHN BOYLE,
   Asst. Adjt. Gen. for the District of Kentucky, Louisville, Ky.

No. 6.

Report of Brig. Gen. G. Clay Smith, U. S. Army, of operations July 13–25, including skirmish near Paris.

LEBANON, KY., *July* 26, 1862.

SIR : By order of General Boyle I left the southern part of the State on the 13th, and assumed command of some forces in Frankfort, Ky., on the 16th day of this month. As soon as I reached that point I immediately set to work to organize a sufficient force to move against General John Morgan, said to be in camp near Georgetown.

At 9 p. m. of the day I reached Frankfort I was ready to march with 1,320 men, 430 of which were of Colonel Williams' (Ninth Pennsylvania) cavalry, which I had brought with me from the lower part of the State; two pieces of Captain Nicklin's (Thirteenth Indiana) battery, and two pieces gotten up by Home Guards, under Captain Goins ; Colonel Mahan's Indiana regiment of infantry, and one company of regulars under Captain Biddle.

On the cars at 9 p. m. Colonel Maxwell reached Frankfort with Colonel Stoughton's Michigan regiment and orders to assume command of that point and the forces, and directions for me to proceed to Lexington and take control of matters there. I left as early as possible with 230 of Colonel Williams' cavalry and reached Lexington at 7 o'clock in the morning. General Ward, by orders from General Boyle, turned over his command to me. I learned that General Morgan was in the neighborhood of Paris and would probably take possession of that town during the day or that night. I organized a force of 595 men—230 Ninth Pennsylvania Cavalry, under Maj. John Marshall; 165 Eighteenth Ken-

---

* Nominal list omitted shows 14.

tucky Infantry, under Colonel Landram; 100 Cincinnati police, under Captain Dudley, and 100 Home Guards, under Captain Faulkner, of Garrard, leaving balance of force to protect Lexington.

At 12 o'clock at night I moved from Lexington toward Paris and overtook Colonel Metcalfe within 6 miles of Paris with a portion of his regiment and some Home Guards, numbering about 500, and three pieces of large artillery, of little use on a chase. With this column I moved on toward Paris, determining to govern the disposition of my command by the position of the enemy.

At 9 o'clock the evening before I sent an order to Colonel Maxwell, who had reached Georgetown, to move on toward Paris without delay, and when within 4 or 5 miles of the town halt and notify me; that he should be in that distance of Paris by daylight. When I reached Metcalfe's camp I dispatched a messenger to Colonel Maxwell to move on rapidly and occupy the Lexington road, that I might cross over to the Winchester pike, which could have been done in a short time. I did not deem it prudent to leave the Lexington road without a force. I heard nothing from Colonel Maxwell. In a few minutes afterward my advance began to fight. I dispatched another messenger to Colonel Maxwell to let me know his position, and also to move in haste and hold the position I had before designated. I heard nothing from him. In half an hour more I sent the third messenger, but with same result; therefore I did not know whether Colonel Maxwell was in reach or not. My advance by this time was skirmishing heavily and I had thrown out Colonel Landram's command to clear the woods, my column moving on with them a quarter of a mile in rear. From all indications and the advantages of the ground, with a creek and bridge in front to cross, I believed the enemy had taken position on the Lexington pike and intended to give fight on that side of Paris. I could not divide my force, for half were raw Home Guards, badly armed, without sabers, and many without pistols. I pressed on, however, determining to give him battle wherever found.

At or near the bridge 1 mile from Paris, on Lexington pike, I received a dispatch from a very reliable gentleman living in Paris that General Morgan, 1,500 strong, was in line of battle and somewhat fortified in Garrett Davis' woods, south of the town, and would make a stand. With fighting in front and the information that the enemy was ready to receive me I could do nothing else than advance. As I did, my advance pushed back the enemy and made a dash into town, when I found that Morgan had retreated rapidly toward Winchester. I occupied his encampment, and in a short time Colonel Maxwell came up, when I learned that 4 miles from town he had formed line of battle and remained so for near two hours.

When Colonel Maxwell reached me I found his troops, as well as my own, jaded, tired, and hungry, but intended to move forward without delay. My orders had been issued, when Captain Brunt [?], of Paris Home Guard, came to me in great speed with the intelligence that Morgan had been re-enforced 7 miles from town by 2,000 men, under Colonel Williams, and were returning to Paris. He told me his informant was a reliable man and had seen the forces. I could not doubt the report, and therefore prepared to receive him in the position I occupied. I sent, however, Colonel Metcalfe, with 250 of his men, to examine the country and ascertain the facts. He returned in the evening with report of no one in front of him.

In the mean time the men got something to eat, horses fed, and orders were given to march, when a very heavy, drenching thunderstorm came up, which lasted the greater portion of the night. Many of the Home Guards left for their homes, and thereby reduced my cavalry force.

Early in the morning I moved for Winchester, leaving Colonel Metcalfe and his command in Paris. Captain Wadsworth, with his Home Guards, accompanied me. When I reached Winchester I ordered Colonel Mahan to remain with his regiment, and Colonel Guthrie and Captain Dudley and the three large pieces of artillery to return to Lexington as soon as possible. At Richmond I was joined by Colonel Cochran with five companies of Colonel Williams' (Ninth Pennsylvania) cavalry, some of Colonel Metcalfe's, under Colonel Halisy, and a company of Home Guards, under Colonel Worthington. I left Colonel Maxwell with the remainder of infantry at this point and pushed on in pursuit.

From the time I left Paris until I drew near to Somerset I halted only long enough to feed, as best we could, once a day; traveled day and night, yet was unable to overhaul the running enemy. When crossing Paint Lick, between Garrard and Madison, I learned Morgan had burned the bridge over Dick's River, on the Crab Orchard road, hence I took the Lancaster and Stanford route, with the hope of overtaking him somewhere in Pulaski, but when within 12 or 13 miles of Somerset I learned reliably that he had passed out of Kentucky into Tennessee and was moving on from the line. I halted and turned my course to Stanford.

On the entire trip I am forced to say that I never received a word of intelligence as to the movement or whereabouts of the enemy save through the scouts I sent out from my command and from intelligence received at and near Paris. It was my conviction that Morgan intended to attack Lexington, believing the troops had all been withdrawn and in pursuit of him. I was therefore anxious and particular to protect the city and the Government stores deposited there; hence I kept the woods watched until I ascertained the line of Morgan's retreat was through Richmond. I could receive no communication from a force anywhere in front of me until after I left Richmond and almost reached Lancaster, then I ascertained that Colonel Wolford, with 300 or 400 Home Guards, was somewhere in Pulaski. I immediately dispatched him to fall in front of Morgan and impede him as much as possible. I do not know that the messenger reached him; but after I got into Pulaski I sent another messenger to him and learned for the first time his troops had been disbanded, with no prospect of using them under three or four days; hence I abandoned the pursuit and returned under orders to this point, which I reached Friday evening.

The endurance with which the men under my command submitted to the deprivation and hardship of that expedition deserves the gratitude of the country and entitles them to my thanks and confidence. Officers and all obeyed my orders promptly.

From the best information received by me the result of the fighting at Paris and on expedition was, rebels:

Killed	29
Wounded	30
Prisoners	18
Total	77

Loss on Federal side none.

I will remark that it was the general impression of all with whom I advised that Morgan would make his escape through Mount Sterling, his escape being much more probable that way than any other.

Respectfully, &c.,

G. CLAY SMITH,
Brigadier-General, Commanding.

Capt. JOHN BOYLE, *Assistant Adjutant-General.*

No. 7.

Report of Col. Cicero Maxwell, Twenty-sixth Kentucky Infantry, of operations July 18–24.

LOUISVILLE, KY., *July* 24, 1862.

CAPTAIN : In obedience to an order from General Boyle, commanding United States forces in Kentucky, I proceeded from this place to Frankfort, Ky., Thursday afternoon, July 17, and assumed command of the United States forces there.

At 2 a. m. Friday, 18th, the forces under my command—consisting of the Eleventh Michigan Volunteers, Colonel Stoughton ; the Fifty-fifth Indiana Volunteers, Colonel Mahan ; Company B, Second Battalion, Sixteenth U. S. Infantry, Capt. James Biddle ; a small portion of the Ninth Pennsylvania Cavalry, Colonel Williams, and two sections of artillery, under command of Captain Nicklin, about 1,200 in all, after leaving a small force for the defense of Frankfort—moved toward Georgetown, Scott County, distant 17 miles from Frankfort, where we arrived about 11 a. m. same day, and found that the marauder (Morgan) and his band had left early on the day before. A messenger was sent immediately to General G. Clay Smith at Lexington, with whom I was ordered to co-operate, to inform him of our arrival at Georgetown.

About 12 o'clock Friday night I received an order from General Smith to move the force under my command toward Paris, Bourbon County, distant 18 miles from Georgetown, and when within 4 or 5 miles of that place communicate with him at Lexington.

Between 2 and 3 a. m. Saturday, the 19th instant, just as soon as our pickets could be called in, we moved toward Paris, though slowly at first, owing to the fact that the men had made a long march the day before and had slept but little, the officers urging them forward as fast as possible.

When about half way from Georgetown to Paris an order was received from General Smith, dated 5 a. m., 6 miles from Paris, directing me to press on rapidly, stating that Morgan had moved toward Winchester, and that, though the general's force was small, he would hold Morgan in check until we could get up. I urged the men forward as rapidly as possible and pressed all the wagons and horses we could find along the road for the use of the sick and worn-out men.

Between 8 and 9 a. m., when about 4 miles from Paris, we were met by a young man, who said Morgan was still in Paris with his force, posted on the Hon. Garrett Davis' farm, and prepared for battle. I immediately sent a messenger to General Smith to communicate this fact, moved the command a short distance forward, halted it, sent out some scouts, and being informed that some horsemen were seen in front, the command was quickly formed in line of battle, the officers and men acting very promptly. In a short time a messenger came from General

Smith, who stated that the general was with his force about 2 miles from Paris, on the Lexington turnpike, and that he directed that the force under my command move as quickly as possible to the Fair Grounds, on the same road, the messenger saying he had thought it proper to destroy the general's written order. The command was moved forward as rapidly as possible, but before we had gone half a mile a gentleman rode up and informed us that Morgan had been driven from Paris by General Smith's forces and was retreating toward Winchester. We still pressed on as fast as we could, arrived at Paris about 10.30 a. m., and found that the marauders had left about 8 a. m.

The force under my command was joined to General Smith's, and we remained at Paris until Sunday morning, the 20th instant, about 7 or 8 o'clock, when General Smith, taking all the cavalry and Captain Nicklin's artillery, moved toward Winchester. By his order I was placed in command of all the infantry, consisting of the forces before named, some of the Cincinnati police, and a portion of the Eighteenth Kentucky Volunteers, under the command of Lieutenant-Colonel Landram, and the artillery from Lexington, and directed to move on after him toward Winchester, distant from Paris 18 miles, where we arrived about 5 p. m., having obtained all the wagons we could along the road to haul our weary soldiers, but found that Morgan had gone through the town Saturday evening.

Shortly after we arrived at Winchester General Smith directed me to detail about 150 infantry and place them in wagons, to be ready to move that night with the cavalry toward Richmond, Madison County. At my suggestion the general modified his order so far as to allow me to put in wagons all of the Eleventh Michigan (Colonel Stoughton) that were fit for duty, the company of regulars, and as many of the Eighteenth Kentucky (Colonel Landram) as we could get wagons for, leaving the remaining forces under the command of Colonel Mahan, Fifty-fifth Indiana, and before 11 o'clock that night we had upward of 500 infantry in wagons and moving toward Richmond, and though we had to ferry the Kentucky River, we arrived at Richmond, 22 miles from Winchester, about 10 a. m. Monday, the 21st instant, but found that the marauders had left the evening before about 3 o'clock.

Late Monday evening I received orders from Generals Boyle and Smith to move to Lexington, 26 miles from Richmond, with the infantry, which I did on Tuesday, 22d instant. By order from General Boyle turned over my command to Colonel Warner, commanding post, and returned here on Wednesday. At Lexington I sent home all the wagons and horses that I could find that we had taken in our march.

While it is cause of bitter mortification to us all that we were unable to overtake the marauding chief and his lawless band, we feel that we did all that we could under the circumstances.

I cannot close this report without returning my sincere thanks to Colonels Williams, Stoughton, and Mahan for their energetic co-operation during our rapid and fatiguing marches, all acting the part of prompt and efficient officers. Colonel Stoughton was with me all the time with his gallant regiment, and I feel indebted to this brave officer for his hearty and efficient aid.

The gallant Lieutenant-Colonel Landram also was prompt and attentive to his command.

Lieutenant Chadwick, of the Eleventh Michigan, who acted as assistant adjutant-general until we arrived at Paris, where he was taken ill, rendered me great service.

Col. James M. Shackelford, formerly commanding officer of the

Twenty-fifth Kentucky, always brave, manly, and true, went with me as aide, and I am much indebted to him for his efficient services.

Several others acted as aides. Lieutenants Richardson, Towns, and Colonel Shackelford, and all deserve my thanks.

Captain Biddle showed himself to be a skillful, attentive officer.

While Captain Nicklin was not called on to use his artillery, it could not escape my attention that he is an officer of rare merit, skillful and prompt.

Very respectfully,

CICERO MAXWELL,
Colonel Twenty-sixth Kentucky Volunteers.

Capt. JOHN BOYLE,
Assistant Adjutant-General, U. S. Forces in Kentucky.

No. 8.

Report of J. V. Guthrie of operations July 16–21.

CINCINNATI, *July* 25, 1862.

In compliance with your order of the 16th the undersigned took the cars on the Central Kentucky Railroad from the depot in Covington, with about 100 men, for Cynthiana, Ky., at which place Lieutenant-Colonel Landram, of the Eighteenth Kentucky, was in command.

Receiving orders to move toward Paris and distribute my forces at the different stations to guard bridges, I proceeded to Paris, which place was reached at 2 o'clock in the night. There were at this post detachments of companies—35 from Captain Whittlesey's camp, under command of his lieutenant; 30 men under command of Captain Pugsley, of the Eighteenth Kentucky Regiment, and the Home Guards of Paris, numbering 67 men, infantry. There were also 60 men on horseback, under command of the Hon. Mr. Wadsworth, member of Congress from the Maysville district, making a total of forces in Paris, as reported to me, of 233 men, rank and file. During the day re-enforcements to the number of 60 men from Mount Sterling, under Captain Evans, came in. These were Home Guard cavalry. Brigadier-General Ward ordered me to take command of this post. Upon assuming the command I immediately proceeded to organize the forces for service, and appointed the Hon. Mr. Wadsworth, with the rank of major, to the command of all the Home Guard cavalry. Pursuant to orders, he took command of 40 men and proceeded toward Lexington on a scouting expedition. At 11 o'clock p. m. Major Wadsworth returned, and reported that John Morgan, with a force of from 1,000 to 1,200 men, was moving down the road to Cynthiana. I immediately telegraphed Lieutenant-Colonel Landram, at Cynthiana, of Morgan's movements and his advance on that place. I also sent a message to Captain Ayres, commanding the bridge guards between Paris and Cynthiana, to join me with his forces at Paris. I also telegraphed to General Ward at Lexington the position of affairs, and asked for re-enforcements to hold Paris. He answered that I should send to him at Lexington all the men I could spare. Satisfied that I could not weaken my force I did not send any men to Lexington. About 7 o'clock in the evening Lieutenant-Colonel Landram reported the fall of Cynthiana. Upon consultation it was deemed advisable to fall back on Lexington. We moved at 11 o'clock that night, and proceeded 14 miles on the Lexington road. About daylight we had reached Colonel Metcalfe's advance post from Lexington, where he had encamped.

Colonel Metcalfe was ordered to move forward with all his force on Paris, and started about 4 o'clock. I was again detailed to take command of all the infantry and support the batteries. Thirty-five of my men were reported as unable to travel, and by my order were sent by the surgeon to the Lexington hospital. We moved on toward Paris, and at dark encamped 5 miles from the town. During the night our pickets were driven in three different times, and, as the infantry with the artillery held the advance, I formed them all in line of battle at the road.

On the morning of the 19th we again took up our line of march, Brigadier-General Smith in command. Our advance continually drove in the rebel scouts, killing 7 and taking 8 prisoners. Arriving at the entrance to Paris, our column was halted. The center, composed of the Ohio troops and the artillery, was 1 mile from the town. We were informed that an attack was expected and the men stood by their guns one hour and a half, when we learned to our chagrin that Morgan had retreated toward Winchester.

It is but justice to the Ohio troops to inform you that they were eager and ready for the fight. Two companies of the Cincinnati police took off their coats, and under their chief, Colonel Dudley, were anxious to meet the enemy. The detachment of Captain Whittlesey's Cincinnati company deserve commendation for their gallantry, while the troops from Camp Dennison, under Captain Ayres, were prompt and efficient, and had opportunity offered would have earned for themselves a creditable reputation.

After the retreat of the enemy we encamped for twenty-four hours. On the morning of the 20th we were ordered to move, the rear guard being assigned to my command. I found it impossible for the troops sent out with me to follow on to Winchester. I therefore left them at Paris, under command of Captain Ayres, with instructions to remain until further orders from me after I had arrived at Winchester.

Receiving orders from General Smith to proceed to Lexington, I moved my command the next day (the 21st) and reached Lexington at night. I rode over with Dr. Bush to Paris that night and found that the men left in charge of Captain Ayres had gone to Cincinnati the morning previous. I returned to Lexington the same night and found Colonel McCook with your orders. After instructing the lieutenant in charge of the sick at Lexington to report to Colonel McCook the condition of the men I obtained leave to return home and arrived here this morning.

I have been thus particular in explaining to you how I became detached from my particular command, which was intrusted to me by your orders, and to do justice as near as I can to the Ohio troops under my charge.

I am, general, your obedient servant,

J. V. GUTHRIE,
Commanding.

General GEORGE B. WRIGHT, *Quartermaster-General, Ohio.*

No. 9.

Report of Lieut. Col. Sidney Burbank, Thirteenth U. S. Infantry, commanding at Cincinnati, Ohio.

CITY OF CINCINNATI, OHIO, *July* 19, 1862.

SIR: The movements in Kentucky of Morgan's forces have assumed so important an attitude that I deem it essential that you should be placed in immediate possession of the views entertained by parties best informed on the subject for the information of the War Department.

The first impression, that it was merely a raid for the purpose of capturing provisions and beating up a few recruits and then retreating, has now given way to the conviction that it is a preconcerted movement made by previous concert with the secessionists in various districts of the State for the purpose of securing and maintaining within the State a formidable force under arms to threaten constantly the position of the Union forces and hoping to regain control of the entire State.

It becomes therefore in my judgment absolutely necessary that prompt measures be adopted to place in Kentucky the necessary force to expel the invaders ere they succeed in drawing together sufficient forces to enable them to maintain their positions, to visit with punishment those who have openly aided and encouraged them, and to encourage the Union men in their struggle.

I have the honor to be, your obedient servant,

S. BURBANK,
Lieutenant-Colonel Thirteenth Infantry, Commanding.

Brig. Gen. LORENZO THOMAS, *Adjutant-General.*

No. 10.

Report of Maj. Gen. E. Kirby Smith, C. S. Army, commanding Department of East Tennessee.

KNOXVILLE, TENN., *July* 24, 1862.

Colonel Morgan sends a dispatch, dated Georgetown, Ky., 16th instant, stating that he has taken eleven cities and towns with very heavy army stores and has a force sufficient to hold all the country outside of Lexington and Frankfort, which places are chiefly garrisoned by Home Guards. The bridges between Lexington and Cincinnati have been destroyed.

E. KIRBY SMITH,
Major-General, Commanding.

General S. COOPER.

No. 11.

Reports of Col. John H. Morgan, Second Kentucky Cavalry (Confederate), commanding expedition.

BRIGADE HEADQUARTERS,
Tompkinsville, Ky., July 9, 1862.

SIR: I have the honor to report that I arrived with my command at the Cumberland River and passed the ford at about 2 p. m. yesterday, 8th instant. My forces consisted of Colonel Hunt's Georgia regiment cavalry, my own regiment, and a squadron of Texas Rangers; we were joined at the river by two companies under Captains Hamilton and McMillin. I received information that the enemy had passed the Cumberland River at Salina the day of my arrival with about 180 men, but did not deem it right to attack that force, as I was aware that a considerable body of cavalry, about 380 or 400 strong, were stationed at this town, and I thought by a rapid night march I might succeed in surprising them. I left the river at 10 p. m. on the 8th instant, and at 5 a. m. this day I surprised the enemy, and having surrounded them, threw four shells into their camp, and then carried it by a dashing charge. The enemy fled, leaving about 22 dead and 30 to 40 wounded in our hands. We have 30 prisoners and my Texas squadron are still in pursuit of the fugitives. Among the prisoners is Major Jordan, their commander, and two lieutenants. The tents, stores, and camp equipage I have destroyed, but a valuable baggage train, consisting of some 20 wagons and 50 mules, is in my possession; also some 40 cavalry horses, and supplies of sugar, coffee, &c. I did not lose a single man in killed, but have to regret that Colonel Hunt, while leading a brilliant charge, received a severe wound in the leg, which prevents his going on with the command. I also had three members of the Texas squadron wounded, but not seriously.

Very respectfully,

JOHN H. MORGAN,
Colonel, Commanding.

Maj. Gen. E. KIRBY SMITH,
Commanding, Knoxville, Tenn.

—

HEADQUARTERS MORGAN'S COMMAND,
Knoxville, Tenn., July 30, 1862.

GENERAL: I have the honor to report that upon the day of the engagements at Tompkinsville, a full report of which I have already sent you, I moved my command (consisting of my own regiment, the Georgia regiment of Partisan Rangers, commanded by Col. A. A. Hunt, and Major Gano's Texas squadron, to which were attached two companies of Tennessee cavalry) in the direction of Glasgow, which place I reached at 12 o'clock that night.

There were but few troops in the town, who fled at our approach. The commissary stores, clothing, &c., together with a large supply of medical stores found in Glasgow, were burned, and the guns were distributed among my command, about 200 of which were unarmed when I left Knoxville. From Glasgow I proceeded along the main Lexington road to Barren River, halting for a short time at a point near Cave City, my object being to induce the belief that I intended destroying the railroad bridge between Bowling Green and Woodsonville. I caused wires connecting with the portable battery that I carried with me to be attached to the telegraph line near Horse Cave and intercepted a number of dispatches.

At Barren River I detached three companies, under Capt. Jack Allen, to move forward rapidly and destroy the Salt River Bridge, that the troops along the line of railroad might be prevented from returning to Louisville.

On the following morning I moved on toward Lebanon, distant 35 miles from Barren River. At 11 o'clock at night I reached the bridge over Rolling Fork, 6 miles from Lebanon. The enemy had received information of my approach from their spies and my advance guard was fired upon at the bridge. After a short fight the force at the bridge was dispersed and the planks which had been torn up having been replaced the command moved forward to Lebanon. About 2 miles from the town a skirmish commenced between two companies I caused to dismount and deploy and a force of the enemy posted upon the road, which was soon ended by its dispersion and capture. Lieut. Col. A. Y. Johnson, commanding the troops in the town, surrendered and I entered the place. The prisoners taken, in number about 65, were paroled. I took immediate possession of the telegraph and intercepted a dispatch to Colonel Johnson, informing him that Colonel Owen, with the Sixtieth Indiana Regiment, had been ordered to his assistance, so I at once dispatched a company of Texas Rangers, under Major Gano, to destroy the railroad bridge on the Lebanon Branch, which he successfully accomplished in time to prevent the arrival of the troops. I burned two long buildings full of commissary stores, consisting of upward of 500 sacks of coffee and a large amount of all other supplies in bulk, marked for the army at Cumberland Gap. I also destroyed a very large amount of clothing, boots, &c. I burned the hospital buildings, which appeared to have been recently erected and fitted up, together with about 35 wagons and 53 new ambulances. I found in the place a large store of medicines, 5,000 stand of arms, with accouterments, about 2,000 sabers, and an immense quantity of ammunition, shell, &c. I distributed the best arms among my command and loaded one wagon with them to be given to recruits that I expected to join me; I also loaded a wagon with ammunition; the remainder of the arms, ammunition, and the hospital and medical stores I destroyed.

While in Lebanon I ascertained from telegraph dispatches that I intercepted that the force which had been started from Lebanon Junction to re-enforce Lieutenant-Colonel Johnson had met and driven back the force under Capt. Jack Allen, killing one of the men, and preventing him from accomplishing the purpose for which he had been detached.

I proceeded from Lebanon on the following day through Springfield to Mackville, at which point I was attacked by Home Guards. Two of my men were taken prisoners and one severely wounded. I remained at Mackville that night to recover the prisoners, which I did the next morning. I then left for Harrodsburg, capturing a Federal captain and lieutenant on the road; reached Harrodsburg at 12.30 o'clock. Found that the Home Guards of all that portion of country had fled to Lexington; a force was also stationed on the bridge where the Lexington road crossed the Kentucky River.

My reception at this place was very encouraging. The whole population appeared to turn out and vie with each other as to who should show us most attention. I left Harrodsburg at 6 o'clock the same evening and moved to Lawrenceburg, 20 miles distant, threatening Frankfort, in order to draw off the troops from Georgetown. Remained there until the return of my courier from Frankfort, who brought the information that there was a force in Frankfort of 2,000 or 3,000 men, consisting of Home Guards collected from the adjacent counties and a few regular troops. From Lawrenceburg I proceeded to Shryock Ferry, on the Kentucky River, raised the boat which had been sunken, and crossed that evening, reaching Versailles at 7 o'clock. I found this place abandoned by its defenders, who had fled to Lexington; remained there that night, and on the next morning marched toward Georgetown.

While at Versailles I took about 300 Government horses and mules. I passed through Midway on the way to Georgetown, and was informed just before reaching the place that a train from Frankfort was nearly due with two regiments of Federals. I tore up the track and posted the howitzers to command it and formed my command along the line of the road, but the train was warned of our presence and returned to Frankfort. Having taken possession of the telegraph office, I intercepted a dispatch asking if the road was clear and if it would be safe to start the train from Lexington. I replied to send the train and made preparations to receive it, but it was also turned back and escaped. I reached Georgetown, 12 miles from Lexington, that evening. Just before entering the town I was informed that a small force of Home Guards had mustered to oppose us. I sent them word to surrender their arms and they should not be molested, but they fled.

The people of Georgetown also welcomed us with gladness and provided my troops with everything that they needed. I remained at Georgetown two days, during which time I sent out a company under Captain McMillin to destroy the track between Midway and Lexington and Midway and Frankfort and to blow up the stone bridge on that road, which he successfully accomplished. Hearing that a company of Home Guards were encamped at Stamping Grounds, 13 miles distant, I dispatched a company under Captain Hamilton to break up their encampment, burn the tents and stores, and destroy the guns. This was also accomplished, Captain Hamilton taking 15 prisoners and all their guns and destroying a large amount of medical and commissary stores. I also while at Georgetown sent Captain Castleman with his company to destroy the railroad bridges between Paris and Lexington and report to me at Winchester. This was done.

Determining to move on Paris with a view of returning, and hearing that the place was being rapidly re-enforced from Cincinnati, I deemed it of great importance to cut off the communication from that place while I drew off the troops that were already there by a feint on Lexington. I therefore dispatched a portion of two companies toward Lexington, with instructions to drive the pickets to the very entrance of the city, while I moved the command toward Cynthiana. When I arrived within 3 miles of this place I learned that it was defended by a considerable force of infantry, cavalry, and artillery. I dispatched the Texas Squadron, under Major Gano, to enter the town on the right, and the Georgia regiment to cross the river and get in the rear, while I moved my own regiment, with the artillery, under the command of Lieut. J. E. Harris, down the Georgetown pike. A severe engagement took place, which lasted about an hour and a half before the enemy were driven into the town and compelled to surrender. I took 420 prisoners, including about 70 Home Guards.

I regret to have to mention the loss of 8 of my men in killed and 29 wounded. The enemy's loss was 194 in killed and wounded, according to their own account. Their excess in killed and wounded is remarkable, as they fought us from behind stone fences and fired at us from buildings as we charged through the town. We captured a very fine 12-pounder brass piece of artillery, together with a large number of small-arms and about 300 Government horses. I found a very large supply of commissary and medical stores, tents, guns, and ammunition at this place, which I destroyed. The paroled prisoners were sent under an escort to Falmouth, where they took the train for Cincinnati.

I proceeded the next morning toward Paris, and was met on the road by the bearer of a flag of truce, offering the unconditional surrender of the place. I reached Paris at 4 o'clock. Remained there that night, and started toward Winchester the next morning. As my command was filing out of Paris on the Winchester pike I discovered a large force of Federals coming toward the town from the direction of Lexington. They immediately countermarched, supposing no doubt that my intention was to get in their rear. This enabled me to bring off my entire command without molestation, with the exception of two of my pickets, who probably were surprised; reached Winchester that day at 12 o'clock; remained until 4 o'clock, when I proceeded toward Richmond. At Winchester I found a number of arms, which were destroyed.

I arrived at Richmond at 12 o'clock that night and remained until the next afternoon, when I proceeded to Crab Orchard. I had determined to make a stand at Richmond and await re-enforcements, as the whole people appeared ready to rise and join me, but I received information that large bodies of cavalry, under General Clay Smith and Colonels Wolford, Metcalfe, Munday, and Wynkoop, were endeavoring to surround me at this place, so I moved on to Crab Orchard. There I attached my portable battery to the telegraph leading from Stanford to Louisville, and learned the exact position of the enemy's forces and directed my movements accordingly.

Leaving Crab Orchard at 11 o'clock, I arrived at Somerset, distant 28 miles, at sundown. I took possession of the telegraph and countermanded all the previous orders that had been given by General Boyle to pursue me, and remained here in perfect security all night. I found a very large supply of commissary stores, clothing, blankets, shoes, hats, &c., at this place, which were destroyed. I also found the arms that had been taken from General Zollicoffer, together with large quantities of shell and ammunition, all of which were destroyed. I also burned at this place and Crab Orchard about 120 Government wagons. From Somerset I proceeded to Monticello, and from thence to a point between Livingston and Sparta, where my command is now encamped.

I left Knoxville on the 4th day of this month with about 900 men, and returned to Livingston on 28th instant with nearly 1,200, having been absent just twenty-four days, during which time I traveled over 1,000 miles, captured seventeen towns, destroyed all the Government supplies and arms in them, dispersed about 1,500 Home Guards, and paroled nearly 1,200 regular troops. I lost, in killed, wounded, and missing, of the number that I carried into Kentucky about 90.

I take great pleasure in testifying to the gallant bravery and efficiency of my whole command. There were individual instances of daring so conspicuous that I must beg the privilege of referring to them. Private Moore, of Louisiana, a member of Company A, of my regiment, particularly distinguished himself by leading a charge which had an important effect in winning the battle. The reports of the regimental commanders, which are inclosed, are respectfully referred to for further instances of individual bravery and efficiency. I feel indebted to all my aides for the promptness with which my orders were executed, and particularly to Col. St. Leger Grenfell for the assistance which his experience afforded me.

All of which is respectfully submitted.

JOHN H. MORGAN,
Acting Brigadier-General, C. S. Army.

R. A. ALSTON, Assistant Adjutant-General.

No. 12.

Report of Maj. R. M. Gano, C. S. Army, commanding Cavalry Battalion.

HONORED SIR : I have the pleasure of reporting to you the action of the battalion under my command in the recent expedition to Kentucky. This report is intended to embrace only the action of the battalion while separated from the other troops under your command. The battalion was composed of four companies—the two Texas companies under my command, known as the Texas Squadron, Company A (commanded by Lieutenant Speer), and Company B (commanded by Captain Huffman), and two Tennessee companies, viz: Company C (commanded by Captain McMillin) and Company D (by Captain Hamilton). Having left Knoxville on the morning of July 4, we reached Walden's Ridge on the evening of the 5th, where the bushwhackers fired upon our foraging party, mortally wounding Mr. J. N. O'Brien, of Company A, of the Texas Squadron. He lived twenty-four hours, suffered much, was a model soldier, a fond husband, affectionate father, and a worthy man in all the relations of life. Cut down in the prime of life, he died in a noble cause—the defense of his country from the invader.

We reached Tompkinsville on the morning of the 9th about sunrise. I was then ordered to the right of the town, on the Old Mill road, to attack from that point and cut off all retreat from that quarter. I proceeded as directed and drove in the pickets, giving the alarm in the enemy's camp. When we came in sight of the enemy they were forming on horseback, apparently with the intention of attacking us, not dreaming of the reception prepared before breakfast for them. I arranged my command to receive them, but only had the opportunity of firing a few long-range guns at them, as the well-aimed shell from your howitzers drove them back from their position, and I then thought from their movements that they would retreat on the Burkesville road, and I immediately ordered Captain Huffman through the woods upon our right with two companies to intercept them there, but the rapid and well-aimed fire from the Georgians, under Colonel Hunt, from one point and of your regiment from another, drove the enemy into such a hasty retreat that they passed out through a wood-land trail some half mile or more, and then, falling into the Burkesville road, put their horses to their utmost speed. The Texans, so famous for horsemanship, started in pursuit, and a portion of the squadron on faster horses soon came up with some 75 of the enemy, under Major Jordan and two lieutenants, trying to cover their hasty retreat. They did not surrender to our demand, but fired back at us, wounding Thomas Huffhines. Then commenced a running fight, 75 Yankees against about a dozen Texans, and many an invader bit the dust; among the number 1 lieutenant, 1 sergeant, and 2 corporals. We captured Major Jordan, 1 lieutenant, 1 sergeant, and 4 privates.

Our casualties were in this running fight 2 wounded, viz : T. Huffhines, a flesh wound in the thigh, and J. Loose, a saber cut on the head, severing the outer table of the skull; neither dangerous. The enemy lost 9 killed, 7 captured. Number of wounded unknown.

At Bear Wallow, on the 9th, Captain Huffman's company was detailed from my command upon an expedition under Capt. Jack Allen. For their movements I refer you to his report.*

After the bushwacking from New Market to Lebanon on the night of

---

* Not found.

the 10th and after the surrender of Colonel Johnson and his forces, he having stated that the Home Guards would fire upon us from the houses if we entered the town, you will recollect how nobly the three companies of my battalion, at the still hour of the night, marched through to receive their fire, Lieutenant Speer in front, Captain McMillin next, and Captain Hamilton third; but the fire came not, the women waved their handkerchiefs, and the place was ours, as witnessed by the shout that rent the air; and then, without rest, having been in the saddle twenty-four hours, how cheerfully we posted off 5 miles in the country, in compliance with the order to burn the bridge, which we did, capturing the guard. Captain Huffman and his company rejoined us at Mackville on the night of the 11th, and next morning I was ordered forward to take possession of Harrodsburg.

The Home Guards had assembled at this place to drive us back, but before we came in sight they fled precipitately to the Kentucky Cliffs to re-enforce Joshua Bell, who was collecting all the Home Guards at the bridge on the Danville and Lexington road, and the aforesaid militia general (Bell) was exhorting his assemblage to deeds of heroism and valor when a party of 65 Home Guards came from Lancaster to re-enforce them. They came shouting and waving their hats. Bell's pickets fled, and reported Morgan coming with his forces at full gallop. Their heroic leader then announced that they could not possibly make a stand there and every man must take care of himself, and they all fled in the direction of Lexington, some on horseback, some on foot. The author of this, Mike Chrisman, made several miles on foot and fainted by the wayside. "The wicked flee when no man pursueth." The excitement and dread at Harrodsburg on the part of the Unionists was intense. Strange that any person in Kentucky could be deluded by the lies of George D. Prentice to believe that the Southern people, noted for their chivalry, liberality, and sympathy, could be guilty of the baseness ascribed to us by those base hirelings of the North. But now have they been shown better by actions which speak louder than words. A few words, guaranteeing respect to person and property, quieted their fears, and all united in preparing us a repast. But the ladies, God bless them, true and loyal to their native South, are bright examples of patriotism and fidelity to our country, our institutions, and the liberties vouchsafed to us by the struggles of our forefathers.

From Harrodsburg, per order, I proceeded toward Paris, intending to avoid the pickets at Lexington (having only 92 men with me), but accidentally coming upon them I feigned an attack, and crossing several roads and frightening in the pickets, they reported a large rebel force coming in from different roads. The greatest excitement prevailed, and with cannon and huge proclamations they prepared for defense, compelling every man of whatever sentiment to take up arms. I did not attack the city with my small force, but leaving Lexington on my right, and passing in by Payne's Depot, on the Frankfort road, I halted my company at the residence of John Payne, near Georgetown, for dinner. Mrs. Payne, not knowing any better, sent word to her husband in town that a body of Union cavalry were there. He immediately called upon the provost-marshal to accompany him home. He could not go, but sends his deputy, Alexander Long. Soon another messenger arrived in the person of Oliver Gaines, with an order to me to take my forces over to the Frankfort road and cut off Morgan's forces, for the rebels were certainly coming that way. I answered all right, and administered the oath of secrecy and non-interference to the two messengers, with three others that had assembled there by accident. I then passed up the Iron Works road, followed, as I afterward learned, at long distance by a party of Home Guards, mounted upon such horses as they had been able to pick up on the streets of Georgetown—some riding with bridles and some with halters; but when they came in sight of the rear of our little column they concluded discretion was the better part of valor and turned off on another road.

We passed through the farm of Victor Flournoy, stopping to refresh ourselves at the spring of the Rev. R. J. Breckinridge, where the ladies came out, and one, whose bright eyes bespoke a southern heart, was very curious to know what party we belonged to. This accidental call was construed into an attempt to arrest the doctor, and his son, Capt. Will. Breckinridge, whom we had not seen, was accused of being accessory. It is not surprising they should judge thus, meting by their own measure. The enemy may feel the effect of Captain Will.'s steel upon the field of battle, but they will never find a man of his noble Southern soul trying to secure his father's arrest. Taking tea at my father's, I proceeded on to Kiser's Station, on the Paris and Covington road, and fired the bridge. The burning bridge fired an old shed beneath, which I afterward learned was Mr. Kiser's distillery. I regretted the loss of private property, but, as it did happen, better be a distillery than anything else. I here lost 7 pickets through their mistaking the road, and we hunted them until day, and consequently did not destroy the Townsend Bridge, as I had contemplated. We then proceeded toward Georgetown, and while encamped in a wood-land near that place R. P. Tannehill, of Company A, Texas Squadron, was by the accidental discharge of a gun launched into eternity. Robert was a brave soldier boy, always ready, devoted to the Southern cause, and the main prop of his widowed mother; but we laid our bold soldier boy to rest more than 1,000 miles from his fond mother, who little dreams of the removal of her boy.

On this the evening of the 18th we rejoined you in Georgetown, and by order arrested Mr. Samuel Thompson, the provost-marshal of that place.

On the 17th instant, near Cynthiana, in accordance with your order, I proceeded with my command across to the Millersburg pike, arresting the guard at the bridge, driving in the picket, and commencing the fight on that side of town. We drove the enemy back from that portion of the town. They soon returned in pretty large force, waving their hands. I ordered to cease firing, thinking they wished to surrender, but they had mistaken us for Home Guards, and commenced cursing us for firing on our own men. I ordered them to lay down their arms, when they fired and ran. We opened a brisk fire and they dropped their guns for two squares down the street. We killed some 10 or 12, wounding many, and capturing as many more in town, and when they retreated from the town we pursued on horseback, capturing many. The loss from my battalion was 1 killed (in Captain Hamilton's company) and 3 badly wounded, viz, Lieut. R. Speer, of Company A, of the Texas Squadron; Clark Aldridge, of Captain Huffman's company, and 1 from Captain McMillan's company; there were two others slightly wounded. Captain Huffman is of a brave stock and is an honor to the name. On all other occasions the forces were together and your report will embrace the whole.

My command conducted themselves with the bravery that has always characterized them, securing lasting honors to themselves, while rendering such efficient service to their country; and to their honor be it said they never failed to show kindness to the captured and wounded of the enemy and respect to the rights of others. I think the kindness of your entire command to the enemy when in their power will be a good example to those of our enemies who have, throughout the State of Kentucky, busied themselves with tyrannizing over and oppressing those who honestly differ with them in political opinion. Let all those who wish to serve their country join the army and show to the world they are not cowards, and not employ their time in trying in a cowardly manner to secure the arrest of those neighbors who differ with them in political sentiment.

We are now, on the 29th instant, again at Knoxville, Tenn., having returned from one of the most daring and adventurous expeditions on record with a very small loss in numbers, but having struck a blow from which the enemy will not soon recover.

Yours,

R. M. GANO,
Major, Comdg. Batt. Cav. in Morgan's Brigade, C. S. Army.

Brig. Gen. JOHN H. MORGAN,
Comdg. Brigade in the Kentucky Expedition of July, 1862.

No. 13.

Report of George A. Elsworth, Telegraph Operator, Morgan's command.

KNOXVILLE, TENN., *July* 30, 1862.

SIR: On July 10 General Morgan, with a body guard of 15 men and myself, arrived at a point half a mile below Horse Cave, on the Louisville and Nashville Railroad, where I took down the telegraph line and connected my pocket instrument for the purpose of taking off all dispatches as they passed through. Owing to a heavy storm prevailing south the atmospheric electricity prevented me from communicating with Bowling Green or Nashville. The first I heard was Louisville calling Bowling Green. I immediately put on my ground wire south, and noticing particularly at the same time what change it would make in the circuit. It did make it stronger, but owing to the storm mentioned above affecting telegraphs more or less, Louisville did not suspicion anything wrong, and I answered for Bowling Green, when I received the following message:

LOUISVILLE, KY., *July* 10, 1862.

S. D. BRUCE, *Commanding, Bowling Green:*

You and Colonel Stoughton move together. I fear the force of Colonel Stoughton too small to venture to Glasgow. The whole force should move together, as the enemy are mounted. We cannot venture to leave the road too far, as they may pass around and ruin it.

J. T. BOYLE,
Brigadier-General, Commanding.

I returned the usual signal, after receiving the message, of O. K.

Louisville immediately called Nashville, and I answered for Nashville. Receiving business for two hours. This business was mostly of a private nature and I took no copies. It could be plainly seen by the tenor of the messages that Morgan was in the country, and all orders to send money and valuables by railroad were countermanded (as they supposed); but little did the operator at Louisville think that all of his work would have to be repeated the next day. Louisville also sent the news of the day, and thus we were furnished with New York and Washington dates of that day.   During the whole of the time it was raining heavy; my situation was anything but an agreeable one, sitting in the mud, with my feet in the water up to my knees.

At 11 p. m. the general, being satisfied that I had drained Louisville of all the news, concluded to close for the night, and he verbally gave me the following message to send, dating and signing it as below :

NASHVILLE, TENN., *July* 10, 1862.

HENRY DENT, *Provost-Marshal, Louisville, Ky.* :

General Forrest, commanding brigade, attacked Murfreesborough, routing our forces, and is now moving on Nashville.   Morgan is reported to be between Scottsville and Gallatin, and will act in concert with Forrest, it is believed.   Inform general commanding.

STANLEY MATTHEWS,
Provost-Marshal.

I am not aware that General Morgan claims to be a prophet or a son of a prophet, but Forrest did attack Murfreesborough and rout the enemy.

On arriving at Lebanon, July 12, I accompanied the advance guard into town and took charge of the telegraph office immediately.   This was, as you know, at 3.30 a. m.   I adjusted the instrument and examined the circuit.   No other operator on the line appeared to be on hand this early.   I then examined all the dispatches of the day previous; among them I found the following:

LEBANON, KY., *July* 11, 1862.

General BOYLE, *Louisville, Ky.* :

I have positive information that there is 400 marauders in 20 miles of this place, on the old Lexington road, approaching Lebanon.   Send re-enforcements immediately.

A. Y. JOHNSON,
Lieutenant-Colonel, Commanding.

At 7.30 a. m. an operator, signing Z, commenced calling B, which I had ascertained by the books in the office was the signal for Lebanon office. I answered the call, when the following conversation between Z and myself ensued :

To B: What news?   Any more skirmishing after your last message?—Z.
To Z: No; we drove what little cavalry there was away.—B.
To B: Has the train arrived yet?—Z.
To Z: No.   About how many troops on train?—B.
To B: About 500.—Z.

My curiosity being excited as to what station Z was, and to ascertain without creating any suspicion, I adopted the following plan :

To Z: A gentleman here in the office bets me the cigars you cannot spell the name of your station correctly.—B.
To B: Take the bet.   L-e-b-a-n-o-n Junction.   Is this not right?   How did he think I would spell it?—Z.
To Z: He gives it up.   He thought you would put two b's in Lebanon.—B.
To B: Ha! ha!   He is a green one.—Z.
To Z: Yes; that's so.—B.
To Z: What time did train with soldiers pass, Z?—B.
To B: At 8.30 last night.—Z.
To Z: Very singular where the train is.—B.
To B: Yes, it is.   Let me know when it arrives.—Z.

At 8.20 Z called me up and says :

To B: The train has returned.   They had a fight with the rebels at New Hope. The commanding officer awaits orders here.—Z.

To Z: Give us the particulars of the fight.   Colonel Johnson is anxious to know all about it.—B.

To B: I will soon as possible.—Z.

To B: Here is Moore's message to General Boyle:

"LEBANON JUNCTION, KY., *July* 12, 1862.

"General BOYLE, *Louisville, Ky.* :

"At 11 o'clock last night, at New Hope Station, 5 miles beyond New Haven, part of my command encountered a force of rebel cavalry posted on the county road one-half a mile south of the railroad.   After a brisk fire of musketry for twenty minutes the enemy was routed and fled.   Skirmishers were sent out in different directions, but were unable to find the enemy.

"At 3 o'clock this morning, apprehending that an effort might be made to destroy the bridges in our rear, we moved down to New Haven and remained until after daylight, when the train went back to the scene of the skirmish.   A Mr. Forman, of Owen County, was found mortally wounded.   He reported the rebel force at 450, under command of Capt. Jack Allen, and that they had fallen back toward Greensburg.   One horse was killed and three captured.   The books of the company were found.   In the field blood was found at different places, showing that the enemy was severely punished.   No casualties on our side.   Here with train waiting orders.

"O. F. MOORE,
"*Commanding.*"

Lebanon Junction being the repeating station for Louisville business, he forwarded the following telegrams just from Louisville 9 a. m.

LOUISVILLE, KY., *July* 12, 1862.

Colonel JOHNSON, *Lebanon, Ky.* :

Leave good guard and join Colonel Owen.   Pursue the enemy and drive him out. Be cautious and vigorous.   Make no delay.

J. T. BOYLE,
Brigadier-General, Commanding.

LOUISVILLE, KY., *July* 12, 1862.

Colonel OWEN, *Lebanon, Ky.* :

You will move after the enemy and pursue him.

J. T. BOYLE,
Brigadier-General, Commanding.

You will see by the above message that Colonel Owen must have been *en route* for Lebanon.

Up to the time of our leaving Lebanon, which was about noon, Colonel Moore, in command of those 500 troops at Lebanon Junction, had not received his orders or I could furnish you with them.   This I greatly regretted, but General Morgan, having no fears of "Lincoln's web-foot soldiery," told me I could close my office, and to allay all suspicion at not being able to communicate with Lebanon during the afternoon I told the operator at Lebanon Junction as follows:

To Z: I have been up all night and am very sleepy.   If you have no objections I will take a nap until 2 or 3 o'clock.—B.

To B: All right; don't oversleep yourself.—Z.

Wonder if I did!

Arrived at Midway, on the Lexington and Louisville Railroad, about 10 a. m.   At this place I surprised the operator, who was quietly sitting on the platform of the depot enjoying himself hugely.   Little did he suspicion that Morgan was in his vicinity.   I asked him to call Lexington and to ask Lexington the time of day.   He did so.   I demanded this for the purpose of getting his style of handling the key, which corroborated my first impression, from the fact that I noticed paper in the instrument; to use a telegraphic phrase, he was a "plug operator."   I adopted his style of writing and commenced operations.

In this office I found a signal-book, which, by the way, came very useful. It contained the calls for all the offices. Dispatch after dispatch was going to and fro from Lexington, Georgetown, Paris, and Frankfort; all contained something in reference to Morgan. I tested the line and found by applying my ground wire it made no difference with the circuit, and as Lexington was headquarters I cut Frankfort off.

I omitted to state that on commencing operations at this place I discovered that there were two wires on this railroad. One was what we term a through wire, running direct from Lexington to Frankfort and not entering any of the way offices. I found that all military business was sent over that wire, and as it did not enter Midway office I ordered it cut, thus forcing Lexington on the wire that did run into this office. Midway was called and I answered, when I received the following:

LEXINGTON, KY., *July* 15, 1862.

J. W. WOOLUMS, *Operator, Midway, Ky.*:

Will there be any danger in coming to Midway? Is everything right?
TAYLOR,
Conductor.

I inquired of my prisoner if he knew a man by name of Taylor. He said Taylor was conductor. I immediately gave Taylor the following reply:

MIDWAY, KY., *July* 15, 1862.

TAYLOR, *Lexington, Ky.*:

All right. Come on. No signs of any rebels here.
WOOLUMS.

The operator in Cincinnati then called Frankfort. I answered and received about a dozen of unimportant dispatches. He had no sooner finished when Lexington called Frankfort and again I answered, receiving the following message:

LEXINGTON, KY., *July* 15, 1862.

General FINNELL, *Frankfort, Ky.*:

I wish you to move the forces at Frankfort on the line of the Lexington Railroad immediately, and have the cars follow and take them up as soon as possible. Further orders will await them at Midway. I will in three or four hours move forward on the Georgetown road. Will have most of my men mounted. Morgan left Versailles this morning at 8 o'clock with 800 men on the Midway road, moving in the direction of Georgetown.
WARD.

This being our position and intention exactly, it was thought proper to throw General Ward on some other track. So in the course of half an hour I manufactured the following dispatch, which was approved by General Morgan, and I sent it:

MIDWAY, KY., *July* 15, 1862.

Brigadier-General WARD, *Lexington, Ky.*:

Morgan, with upward of 1,000 men, came within a mile of here and took the Old Frankfort road, bound, as we suppose, for Frankfort. This is reliable.
WOOLUMS,
Operator.

In about ten minutes Lexington again called Frankfort, and as I was doing the work of two or three offices, I answered the call and received the following:

LEXINGTON, KY., *July* 15, 1862.

General FINNELL, *Frankfort, Ky.*:

Morgan, with more than 1,000 men, came within a mile of here and took the Old Frankfort road. This dispatch received from Midway and is reliable. The regiment from Frankfort had better be recalled.

WARD.

I receipted for this message, and again manufactured a message to confirm the information General Ward had received from Midway, and not knowing the tariff from Frankfort to Lexington I could not send a formal message. I waited until the circuit was occupied and then broke in, appearing greatly excited, and told those using the wire I must have the circuit, and commenced calling Lexington. He answered with as much gusto as I called. I telegraphed as follows to Lexington:

Tell General Ward our pickets just driven in. Great excitement. Pickets say force of enemy must be 2,000.

FRANKFORT.

It was now 2 p. m. and General Morgan wished to be off for Georgetown. I run a secret ground connection and opened the circuit on the Lexington end. This was done to leave the impression that the Frankfort operator was skedaddling or that Morgan's men had destroyed the telegraph.

We arrived at Georgetown at sundown. I went to the telegraph office, found it locked; inquired for the operator. He was pointed out to me. I hailed him and demanded admission into his office. He very courteously showed me into his office. I discovered the instruments had been moved. I asked where they were. He replied that he had sent them to Lexington. I asked him what time he had Lexington last. He said 9 o'clock, and since that time the line had been down. I remarked that it must be an extraordinary line to be in working condition when it was down, as I heard him sending messages to Lexington when I was at Midway at 1 o'clock. This was a stunner; he had nothing to say. I immediately tested the line by applying the ends of the wires to my tongue and found the line O. K. I said nothing to him, but called for a guard of two men to take care of Mr. Smith until I got ready to leave town.

I did not interrupt the line until after tea, when I put in my own instrument, and after listening for an hour or two at the Yankees talking I opened the conversation as follows, signing myself "Federal Operator," as I had done before successfully at other places:

To LEXINGTON: Keep mum. I am in the office reading by the sound of my magnet in the dark. I crawled in when no one seen me. Morgan's men are here, encamped on Dr. Gano's place.

GEORGETOWN.

To GEORGETOWN: Keep cool; don't be discovered. About how many rebels are there?

LEXINGTON.

To LEXINGTON: I don't know. I did not notice, as Morgan's operator was asking me about my instruments. I told him I sent them to Lexington. He said, "Damn the luck," and went out.

GEORGETOWN.

To GEORGETOWN: Be on hand and keep us posted.

LEXINGTON.

To LEXINGTON I will do so. Tell General Ward I will stay up all night if he wishes.

GEORGETOWN.

To GEORGETOWN : Mr. Fulton wishes to know if the rebels are there.
                                                                    CINCINNATI.

To CINCINNATI : Yes; Morgan's men are here.
                                                                    GEORGETOWN.

To GEORGETOWN : How can you be in office and not be arrested ?
                                                                    CINCINNATI.

To CINCINNATI : Oh, I am in the dark and reading by sound of the magnet.
                                                                    GEORGETOWN.

This settled Cincinnati. Question after question was asked me about the rebels and I answered to suit myself. Things had been going on this way about two hours, when Lexington asked me where my assistant was. I replied, "Don't know." He then asked me, "Have you seen him to-day ?" I replied, "No." Well, from this time out no telegraphing could I do in the beautiful city of Georgetown.

Wishing to keep myself busy and make myself useful, I concluded to call on Mr. Smith, the operator, who was under guard in my room. I did so. I informed Mr. Smith that I would furnish him with a mule in the morning and I should be pleased to have him accompany me to Dixie, as I understood he was in the employ of the United States Government. This was anything but agreeable to the said Smith. It seemed to me I had hit the young man in the right place, and I remarked that had he not sent his instruments to Lexington I would have taken them in preference to his person. His face brightened and an idea struck him very forcibly that he would make a proposition. He did so, and it was to furnish me the instruments if I would release him. This I agreed to, as telegraph instruments are of much more value to the Southern Confederacy than Yankee telegraphers. I accompanied Mr. Smith to the servants' room, and there under a bed in a chest were the instruments. After Mr. Smith's giving me his word of honor not to leave town for twenty-four hours he was at liberty to visit his wife and young Smiths.

On arriving at Cynthiana I found that the operator had skedaddled. I tested the wires, and found no fluid from either Cincinnati or Lexington, nor were the wires in working condition when I left the next day.

At Paris the operator had made a clean sweep. He left the night before, taking all his instruments.

At Crab Orchard there was no office, and I put in my pocket magnet. This was at 11 a. m., and the first message I heard was the following:

                                                    LOUISVILLE, KY., *July* 21, 1862.
Colonel WOLFORD, *Danville, Ky.* :
Pursue Morgan ; he is at Crab Orchard, going to Somerset.
                                                                    BOYLE.

No sooner had the Danville operator receipted for this than the operator at Lebanon suggested the following :

To LEBANON JUNCTION : Would it not be well for Danville and offices below here to put on their ground wires when they send or receive important messages, as George Elsworth, the rebel operator, may be on the line between here and Cumberland Gap ?
                                                                    LEBANON.

The operator at the Junction agreed with him and said it would be a good idea, but it was not carried into effect.

Arrived at Somerset that evening. I took charge of the office. I ascertained from citizens that the office had been closed for three weeks up to the very hour our advance guard arrived in town and then it was opened by the operator from London, who came to work the instrument for the purpose of catching Morgan, but unfortunately for Uncle Sam the operator had no time to either send or receive a message, but I am glad to say he had it in fine working condition for me. I had been in the office some time when Stanford called Somerset and said:

> I have just returned from Crab Orchard, where I have been to fix the line. The rebels tore it down. I left there at 8 o'clock. The Ninth Pennsylvania Cavalry had not then arrived. What time did you get in from London?
>
> STANFORD.

> To STANFORD: Just arrived and got my office working finely.
>
> SOMERSET.

> To SOMERSET: Any signs of Morgan yet? He left Crab Orchard at 11.30 a. m. to-day.
>
> STANFORD.

> To STANFORD: No; no signs of him as yet.
>
> SOMERSET.

> To SOMERSET: For fear they may take you by surprise I would suggest we have a private signal. What say you?
>
> STANFORD.

> To STANFORD: Good; before signing we will make the figure 7.
>
> SOMERSET.

This was mutually agreed upon. I asked when would Wolford be at Somerset, and he said Wolford had telegraphed Boyle that his force was green and insufficient to attack Morgan.

Seeing there was no use of my losing a night's rest I told Stanford I would retire, and that I had made arrangements with the pickets to wake me up in case Morgan came in. The operator at Lebanon Junction urged me to sit up, but I declined on the ground of being unwell. This did not satisfy him, but after arguing with him some time I retired.

JULY 22.

Opened office at 7 o'clock. Informed Stanford operator Morgan not yet arrived; made inquiries about different things, and after everything in town belonging to the United States Government was destroyed the general gave me the following messages to send:

SOMERSET, Ky., *July* 22, 1862.

GEORGE D. PRENTICE, *Louisville, Ky.:*

Good morning, George D.! I am quietly watching the complete destruction of all of Uncle Sam's property in this little burg. I regret exceedingly that this is the last that comes under my supervision on this route. I expect in a short time to pay you a visit and wish to know if you will be at home. All well in Dixie.

JOHN H. MORGAN,
Commanding Brigade.

SOMERSET, Ky., *July* 22, 1862.

General J. T. BOYLE, *Louisville, Ky.:*

Good morning, Jerry! This telegraph is a great institution. You should destroy it, as it keeps me too well posted. My friend Elsworth has all of your dispatches since July 10 on file. Do you wish copies?

JOHN H. MORGAN,
Commanding Brigade.

SOMERSET, Ky., *July* 22, 1862.

Hon. GEORGE DUNLAP, *Washington, D. C.:*

Just completed my tour through Kentucky. Captured sixteen cities, destroyed millions of dollars' worth of United States property. Passed through your county, but regret not seeing you. We paroled 1,500 Federal prisoners.

Your old friend,

JOHN H. MORGAN,
Commanding Brigade

The following is an order I issued to all operators while at George-town:

GENERAL ORDERS, } HDQRS. TELEGRAPH, DEPARTMENT OF KENTUCKY, C. S. A.,
No. 1.   }   *Georgetown, Ky., July* 16, 1862.

When an operator is positively informed that the enemy is marching on his station he will immediately proceed to destroy the telegraph instruments and all material in his charge. Such instances of carelessness as exhibited on the part of the operators at Lebanon, Midway, and Georgetown will be severely dealt with.

By order of

G. A. ELSWORTH,
General Military Superintendent C. S. Telegraph Department.

The above report contains but a few of the dispatches I received and sent during General Morgan's late expedition through Kentucky. Those of the greatest interest and importance are respectfully submitted.

I remain, your obedient servant,

GEO. A. ELSWORTH,
Morgan's Telegrapher.

Capt. R. A. ALSTON, *Assistant Adjutant-General.*

No. 14.

Report of Lieut. Col. F. M. Nix, First Georgia Partisan Rangers, of the capture of Cynthiana.

HEADQUARTERS, CAMP SMITH,
Near Knoxville, Tenn., July 30, 1862.

SIR: I have the honor to submit the following report of the action of the First Regiment Georgia Partisan Rangers in the battle of Cynthiana on Thursday, 17th instant:

On Thursday, the 17th instant, when the brigade had arrived within a few miles of Cynthiana, I was ordered by General Morgan to detach my regiment and attack the town on the west side at the report of the cannon. Having made a circuit of 5 or more miles through plantations and over many obstructions not anticipated, with all possible dispatch I arrived in the suburbs, and formed a line a few minutes after the signal of attack was heard, when I observed a body of the enemy's cavalry advancing toward my line, which were promptly repulsed by a volley from my command. Having advanced a short distance, I ordered Captain Jones to deploy his company (A) to the right of the pike, in order to cover the whole of the rear of the town and prevent the escape of the enemy in case of their defeat. Before the whole of Company A, however, could be deployed it encountered a body of cavalry advancing on the pike, which were repulsed after a sharp contest. Advancing farther, Captain Jones encountered a force of artillery, with one brass field piece, which he charged and repulsed, the enemy leaving the piece behind

them. Still advancing, and completing the deployment to the right of
the pike, Company A captured 68 prisoners, marched then to a corner
of the main street, and left them in charge of a squad under command
of Lieut. R. H. Chapman. At this juncture, intelligence having reached
Captain Jones, through a prisoner, that a re-enforcement of 700 men
was coming in by railroad, he ordered Quartermaster Sergt. John C.
Allen to take a file of men and burn a long railroad bridge in his rear,
which was promptly executed, the remainder of the company advancing until the firing ceased.

Company B, advancing along Main street, driving before it a body of
the enemy, killed some and captured many—Lieutenant Meadows and a
private of said company, and Private S. T. Moore, of Company A, being
the first to approach the brass field piece, which was captured. Advancing along Main street this company was ordered to dislodge a party
of the enemy from a garden, which was promptly executed. Companies
B and C and a portion of Company A were then ordered to charge the
depot and a neighboring brick building from which the enemy was pouring an incessant fire. After a severe conflict they drove the enemy from
both these strongholds, killing and capturing several of them, and afterward pursuing the enemy to the corn field, in which they made their
last stand.

The only casualty in Company B was 1 man wounded; in Company
C, 2 killed and 6 wounded (3 slightly and 3 severely); among the latter
was Second Lieut. Thomas N. Pitts.

The left wing, viz, Companies D, E, and F, under command of Maj.
Samuel J. Winn, advanced steadily on the left of the pike, engaging
the enemy at several points and driving them into the center of the
town, having killed and captured a number of them and not halting
until the enemy was routed. The left wing sustained no loss either in
killed or wounded.

I feel that many thanks and much praise are due to the officers and
soldiers of my command for their highly creditable and heroic conduct
on the occasion of this battle.

All of which is respectfully submitted.

F. M. NIX,
Lieut. Col., Comdg. First Regiment Georgia Partisan Rangers.

Capt. R. A. ALSTON,
Assistant Adjutant-General, Morgan's Brigade.

No. 15.

Report of Lieut. Col. Basil W. Duke, Second Kentucky Cavalry, of the
capture of Cynthiana.

CYNTHIANA, KY., July 17, 1862.

SIR : During the engagement to-day the regiment engaged the enemy
on the Georgetown pike, and after a desperate fight of about an hour
and a half succeeded in driving them into the town, where a hot street
fight occurred, lasting until near dark. We took the 12-pounder brass
piece that had so annoyed us during the early part of the action.
Where all engaged acted so nobly, it is difficult to particularize; but

It is generally conceded that Company A covered itself with glory, which is acknowledged by the regiment.

P. H. THORPE,
Adjutant.

Capt. R. A. ALSTON, *Assistant Adjutant-General.*

[Inclosure.]

—————, 1862.

In the action referred to above my regiment was deployed upon the Georgetown pike, Companies A and B upon the right, Companies E and F upon the left. After a stubborn fight the enemy were driven from all the positions in the edge of the town. Company B was then sent to the extreme right to engage a force which threatened our right flank and succeeded in dispersing it. Companies E and F charged up to the bank of the river under a severe fire of musketry and grape, and were prevented from entering the town only by the depth of the water at that point. Company A crossed the river at a ford near the bridge, charged across the bridge, and after a very severe contest drove the enemy from the houses near the bridge. Company C, previously held in reserve, charged through the town on horseback, and forced the enemy to abandon their artillery and cleared that street. The two last-named companies, then uniting with the Georgians (who had dashed in upon the left), forced the enemy to abandon the depot and subsequently the town.

It is almost impossible to speak in terms too high of the different officers under my command; good conduct and individual gallantry were so common that it almost ceased to be a matter of remark. Captain Hutcheson and Webber led their companies in perfect order through a fire that was unusually severe. Lieut. J. A. Smith and Bowyer, of Company A, were both severely wounded in front of that company and in the midst of the enemy. Captain Bowles and Lieutenant Myers, of Company C, behaved with great gallantry; the latter was struck from his horse, but fortunately the wound was but slight. Lieutenant White, commanding Company B, performed the duty assigned him, and kept his company in front of a superior force for nearly an hour, finally dispersing it. I have the pleasure to report the gallant and efficient conduct of Captain Thorpe, adjutant of my regiment, and my thanks are due him for the manner in which he superintended the execution of every order. I cannot too highly compliment Col. St. Leger Grenfell, who acted with my regiment, for the execution of an order which did perhaps more than anything else to gain the battle. His example gave new courage to every one who witnessed it.

I have the honor to report that every one in my regiment gave satisfaction to myself and their respective company commanders.

B. W. DUKE,
Lieutenant-Colonel, Commanding Regiment.

Capt. R. A. ALSTON, *Assistant Adjutant-General.*

No. 16.

Report of Lieut. Joseph E. Harris, commanding Morgan's Artillery.

MORGAN'S BRIGADE,
Cynthiana, Ky., July 18, 1862.

SIR: In obedience to special instructions I have to report that my battery entered the engagement of 17th instant on the turnpike road leading to this place, about 300 yards from the bridge, at — o'clock, and commenced shelling the enemy, who were occupying the latter position, which was kept up, under showers of musketry-balls and grape from the enemy's artillery for an hour, at which time they retired before a charge of cavalry. By order of the general the pieces were then moved by hand to the front across the bridge, again coming under galling fire of the enemy's sharpshooters, who occupied the depot and surrounding buildings, about 80 yards distant.

I regret here to have to report the inefficiency of my command for a short time, resulting mainly from a want of discipline and drill, which you know I have scarcely had time to produce. Under these difficulties, however, the firing continued slowly until the enemy evacuated his final position.

The casualties in this command are as follows, viz: Wounded— Cannoneer W. B. Shelton, slightly in the head; Cannoneer Thomas Shanks, flesh wound in leg, and three horses killed.

In conclusion I cannot but mention the gallant conduct of Cannoneer W. B. Shelton as setting an emulous example to others, who, when having been wounded in the head and lain senseless for ten minutes, on recovering himself resumed his post, where he continued throughout the engagement.

I am, captain, your obedient servant,

> JOS. E. HARRIS,
> *First Lieutenant, Commanding Artillery, Morgan's Legion.*

Captain ALSTON, *Assistant Adjutant-General, Morgan's Legion.*

JULY 7–11, 1862.—Operations about Cumberland Gap, Tenn.

Report of Brig. Gen. John S. Williams, C. S. Army, commanding Army of Eastern Kentucky.

> HDQRS. DEPARTMENT SOUTHWESTERN VIRGINIA,
> *Camp near Narrows, Ky., July 13, 1862.*

SIR: I have the honor to inclose a letter from General John S. Williams, furnishing information of the enemy at Cumberland Gap. He mentions an engagement between our cavalry and that of the enemy. This communication will show the active services of this energetic and valuable officer. We had a skirmish on the 11th instant in the direction of Greenbrier River, driving the enemy back to his lines.

I have the honor to be, very respectfully, your obedient servant,

> W. W. LORING,
> *Major-General, Commanding.*

Hon. G. W. RANDOLPH, *Secretary of War.*

[Inclosure.]

> HEADQUARTERS ARMY OF EASTERN KENTUCKY,
> *Camp near Liberty Hill, Ky., July 12, 1862.*

GENERAL: I am this morning in receipt of yours of the 10th, informing me of the movements of the enemy across Greenbrier and directing reconnaissances in the direction of Flat Top Mountain. I have kept all the time a company scouting in the vicinity of Flat Top with com petent guides. My information is that the enemy has moved his camp down to the foot of the mountain in consequence of the scarcity of water. One of my scouts returned from Logan last night reports one regiment of 400 at Chapmanville, 5 miles below the Court-House. I have sent two spies into Raleigh, neither of whom has returned.

Some days ago I sent three companies of mounted men down the Clinch and Holston into Tennessee, under command of Captain Witcher. I have a dispatch from him of the 9th. He had a fight with a company of Yankee cavalry on the 7th instant within 8 miles of Cumberland Gap. Killed 16 of them and captured their colors, which he sent to me by the courier. Our loss none.

The enemy has three brigades in the neighborhood of Cumberland Gap, to wit: Garfield's brigade of Ohioans on Copper Creek between the Gap and Cumberland Ford; Garrard's Kentucky in the Gap, and Spears' Tennesseeans between the Gap and the ford of Clinch. With this force there is 500 cavalry. The entire force is about 8,000.

My effective force is very much reduced by measles and mumps among the new troops and by the large scouting parties sent agreeably to your instructions toward Tennessee and Kentucky. I will keep a sharp lookout and let no opportunity escape of hitting the enemy a blow.

Yours, respectfully,

JOHN S. WILLIAMS,
Brigadier-General, &c.

Maj. Gen. W. W. LORING, *Commanding, &c.*

P. S.—Since writing the above a courier has arrived from Buchanan, who reports 150 Yankees from Logan to be in that county plundering the people.

JULY 12–16, 1862.—Expedition from Decatur, Ala., and skirmish (12th) near Davis' Gap.

REPORTS.

No. 1.—Col. Abel D. Streight, Fifty-first Indiana Infantry.
No. 2.—Capt. Stephen C. Writer, First Ohio Cavalry.

No. 1.

Report of Col. Abel D. Streight, Fifty-first Indiana Infantry.

HEADQUARTERS FIFTY-FIRST INDIANA VOLUNTEERS,
Camp near Mooresville, Ala., July 16, 1862.

SIR: While in command at Decatur there were several small parties of loyal Alabamians who came into our lines begging me to give them protection and a chance to defend the flag of our country. The tale of suffering and misery as told by each as they arrived was in itself a lamentable history of the deplorable condition of the Union people of the South. Notwithstanding the oft-repeated assertion that there was a strong Union sentiment in portions of the cotton States, I had long since given up all hopes of finding the people entertaining it; hence I was at first incredulous as to what they said and even suspicious that they were spies belonging to the enemy, but as their numbers increased, each corroborating the story of the other, I at last became convinced that the matter was worthy of notice.

About this time (10th instant) I was informed by a courier that there was a party of about 40 men some 5 or 6 miles toward the mountain trying to come to us and about the same number of the enemy's cavalry were between them and Decatur trying to intercept and capture them. As my orders were to defend the town only I did not feel at liberty to send out assistance to the Union men without further orders, and there being no telegraphic communication with you I at once informed General Buell by telegraph of the circumstances, whereupon I received the following reply:

HUNTSVILLE, ALA., ——— —, 1862.

Col. A. D. STREIGHT, *Fifty-first Indiana Volunteers:*

Send out what force you deem sufficient to assist the Union men in and drive off the rebel cavalry, and see that they are not playing a trick to draw you out by these reports.

JAMES B. FRY,
Colonel and Chief of Staff.

Owing to a storm that was passing over the telegraph lines at the time the above was not received until near three hours after I sent General Buell the first dispatch. As soon as I received the foregoing instructions from Colonel Fry I at once ordered three companies of my regiment, under Major Colescott, to cross the river with their arms and full 40 rounds of cartridges. This was done in the least possible time, but just as the three companies were in line ready to march another courier arrived, stating that the Alabama boys had succeeded in avoiding the rebels and had got within our lines; but a short time elapsed before they arrived. Such were the manifestations of joy and gladness exhibited by them that all doubts were fully expelled from my mind, whereupon I resolved to go to the assistance of those who were left behind, providing I could get permission to do so. Consequently I telegraphed the following:

DECATUR, ALA., *July* 10, 1862—7 p. m.

Col. JAMES B. FRY, *Assistant Adjutant-General, Chief of Staff:*

SIR: I have the honor to report to you that the party of Alabama volunteers has just arrived and 40 of them have been mustered into the service of the United States. Their accounts of the hardships endured are sufficient to enlist the sympathies of the hardest heart. They report that there are several hundred who would come but for the danger of passing from the foot of the mountains here, some 25 miles distant. If you will give me one company of cavalry to take with my regiment I am fully satisfied that I could, by going, say, 15 miles toward the foot of the mountains and then sending out a few of these new recruits to notify their neighbors, within four days' time bring back with me at least 500 volunteers. If you will allow me to make the experiment, my word for it I will return safely with my command.

I am, sir, your most obedient servant,

A. D. STREIGHT,
Colonel Fifty-first Indiana Volunteers.

Nothing was heard from the foregoing dispatch till about 2 p. m., the next day (July 11), when Captain Lennard handed me the following communication from Colonel Fry to General Wood, with verbal instructions to carry out its provisions:

HEADQUARTERS,
Huntsville, Ala., July 11, 1862.

General WOOD:

Colonel Streight reports that there are several hundred men about 25 miles south of Decatur who are trying to come on to join our army and Colonel Streight is anxious to go with his regiment to bring them in. You can order an expedition of this kind. In doing so it will be necessary to send another regiment to take Colonel Streight's place near Decatur. It will not be practicable for you to cross cavalry over to send, but the colonel can take any cavalry that may be at Decatur. Instruct Colonel Streight to be cautious, and not expose his command to ambuscade or surprise or to attack from superior force. He should not be gone more than three or four days, and must take no baggage. He must be careful and not let the people suppose that his presence indicates a permanent occupation, and thus lead them into demonstrations for which the rebels would make them suffer after our withdrawal. Give such orders for the details and precautionary instructions as the case may seem to you to require.

JAMES B. FRY,
Colonel and Chief of Staff.

Upon the receipt of the above I proceeded to get my command in readiness for the expedition as quickly as possible. Four days' rations were ordered and one camp kettle to each company. The haversacks holding only three days' rations, we filled the kettles and buckets out of the remainder, and decided to get along as best we could under the circumstances. The guides were selected to conduct us to the Union settlement, who were also to act as couriers to inform their friends of the nature of our mission. There were but 16 men and the captain of Company D, First Ohio Cavalry, at Decatur, who were also put in readiness to march.

In accordance with these arrangements, we moved off at daylight on the 12th instant in the direction of a place called Davis' Gap, some 9 miles southeast of Danville and 25 south of Decatur. The cavalry were thrown out in the advance a suitable distance to give notice of the approach of an enemy, and a strong advance and rear guard was at all times kept in readiness for immediate action. When we had proceeded some 12 miles on our way, being unable to hear anything of the enemy, I ordered the captain commanding the cavalry to proceed with his command in advance with three of the guides and escort them as far toward Davis' Gap as he should deem safe, so as to allow the guides to give the information to the Union people that we were coming. I gave him the most positive instructions to make diligent inquiry relative to the enemy, and to go no farther than he could with perfect safety, and as soon as he arrived near enough to the mountains to enable the guides to get through he should fall back at once and rejoin me, I at this time having ascertained that it would in all probability be necessary for me to go about 23 miles, instead of 15, the distance I at first expected, but did not expect to be able to get through the first day.

Under these instructions he proceeded somewhat faster than the infantry could march, consequently when he arrived some 22 miles from Decatur (10 miles from where he left us) he was probably not more than 5 or 6 miles ahead of my regiment; but it being very hot in the middle of the day, we halted to rest, expecting the cavalry to rejoin us, as ordered. In direct disobedience to my orders, the cavalry spent about an hour's time in scouting about the country after they had escorted the guides to within 3 miles of the mountains, after which they stopped at a Mr. Menter's house and ordered dinner; there they spent about three hours more. The captain was warned when he first arrived in the neighborhood that 40 of the enemy's cavalry were within 6 miles of him; yet with these facts before him, as I have above shown, he spent nearly four hours in the neighborhood and at Mr. Menter's house—a sufficient time to have returned to Decatur, if necessary, much less to rejoin me.

At about 5.30 o'clock he was attacked by upward of 40 of the enemy's cavalry and guerrillas. Here again his conduct seems to have been very injudicious, for although there were several log buildings that he could have held against any force the enemy could bring to bear against him, yet, instead of occupying them, after exchanging a few shots, in which 1 of his men was wounded and 2 of the enemy killed and 2 wounded, he ordered a retreat across the field, which seems to have been accomplished very precipitately, especially when taking into consideration the fact that the enemy did not pursue him but a few rods, and that too on foot. Four of his men got lost from the balance. He proceeded in a westerly, circuitous route to Decatur, where he arrived the evening of the same day with 12 of his men.

In the mean time I had arrived to within 2 miles of the place where he was attacked before the enemy had left, and think I would have been in time to have done them justice had I not halted to chastise some guerrillas who had the impudence to fire into my rear guard; but as it was we arrived just in time to see the chivalry put spurs to their horses and leave hurriedly to the eastward, thus showing conclusively that the enemy did not follow our cavalry. We bivouacked that night 23 miles from Decatur and within 1 mile of where the skirmish took place.

The next day was spent in ascertaining what we could relative to the extent of the damage done to the cavalry and in notifying the people in the mountains that they could now have a chance to join the Union Army. I ascertained the loss of our cavalry in the engagement to be 1 man missing, who, when last seen, some 2 miles from where the skirmish took place, was wounded in the thigh (not seriously), and 1 taken prisoner; 1 horse killed and 1 disabled. Three cavalrymen came in early in the morning without horses, but our boys succeeded in finding the horses and equipments near where they were left. The captain's sword was also found about 100 rods from where the fight occurred.

I soon became convinced that the time set for me to return was insufficient to fully accomplish the object of my mission. The news of the defeat of our cavalry spread over the country like a fire on a prairie, causing great consternation among the Union people and boldness on the part of the guerrillas. The guides became frightened, and it was very difficult to induce them to leave my command. However, after laboring under all these difficulties we succeeded in bringing back with us 150 volunteers. Several small parties that started to join us failed to get there in time. One party, numbering 34 men, were within 20 miles of us at daylight the morning we left, and although a messenger arrived giving me that information when we had marched but a short distance on our return, yet I was ordered to return within four days' time and could wait no longer.

At 11 a. m. yesterday we took up our line of march for Decatur, and when we had proceeded about 4 miles from our encampment we were informed that the enemy's cavalry, about 500 strong, were posted at the crossing of the road, about 1 mile ahead. The country being thickly wooded, I had nothing to fear from mounted men, but supposing that they might dismount and act as infantry, I deployed Companies A and F on each side of the road in advance as skirmishers, at the same time ordering Company D forward in the road to form a reserve, and also to deploy 6 men in advance to act as signal-men, one company having been previously detailed to act as rear guard. They too were ordered to throw out skirmishers on the flanks, to avoid an undiscovered approach from either of these directions. The Alabamians had previously been placed next to the rear guard. Having advanced the skirmishers and advance reserves some 400 yards I ordered the whole battalion to move forward, each individual and company to keep their relative positions. In this order we proceeded, but as we approached the position occupied by the enemy they fled before us without firing a gun.

It now became apparent to me that the intention of the enemy was to harass our march, and as the country was mostly wooded, I concluded to continue the march in the order above referred to, thus avoiding the possibility of running into an ambuscade or of being surprised. The enemy fell back as we approached for about 2 miles, when they turned eastward. For some time afterward I was expecting a demonstration upon our rear and made preparations accordingly. We proceeded to march in this manner for 12 miles, frequently relieving the skirmishers by sending out others, without further molestation. It was now getting dark and we were within 7 miles of Decatur, when we concluded to bivouac for the night. Strong pickets were thrown out in every approachable direction. The boys were allowed to sleep till 3 o'clock the next morning, when they were awakened, and as soon as it was daylight we were on our way, and arrived at Decatur at 6.30 a. m., bringing back every member of my regiment who went with us.

I wish to say a word relative to the condition of these people. They are mostly poor, though many of them are, or rather were, in comfortable circumstances. They outnumber nearly three to one the secessionists in portions of Morgan, Blount, Winston, Marion, Walker, Fayette, and Jefferson Counties; but situated as they are, surrounded by a most relentless foe, mostly unarmed and destitute of ammunition, they are persecuted in every conceivable way, yet up to this time most of them have kept out of the way sufficiently to avoid being dragged off by the gangs that infest the country for the purpose of plunder and enforcing the provisions of the rebel conscription act. Their horses and cattle are driven off in vast numbers. Every public road is patrolled by guerrilla bands, and the Union men have been compelled to seek protection in the fastnesses of the mountainous wilderness. They cannot hold out much longer. This state of things has so disturbed them that but very little attention has been paid to farming, consequently many of them are now destitute of food of their own and are living off their more fortunate neighbors. Such examples of patriotism as these people have set are worthy of being followed. One old lady, Mrs. Anna Campbell, volunteered to ride 35 miles and return, making 70 miles, with about 30 recruits, within thirty-six hours. When it is taken into consideration that these people were all hid away to avoid being taken by the rebels and that the country is but sparsely settled this case is without a parallel in American history. There are many cases of a similar nature that came under my observation, but I do not desire to weary your patience with them. Suffice it to say that I have never witnessed such an outpouring of devoted and determined patriotism among any other people. I am now of the opinion that if there could be a sufficient force in that portion of the country to protect these people there could be at least two full regiments raised of as good and true men as ever defended the American flag. So confident am I that my views are correct that if the commanding general will grant me permission to do so I will take my regiment (the boys all want to go) and two weeks' rations of bread, salt, sugar, and coffee (meat we can get there), and 500 extra stand of arms, with a sufficient supply of ammunition, and locate at least 30 miles south of Decatur, where I will rally around me a sufficient number of the brave mountaineers to protect the country effectually against anything except the regular rebel army, which, by the way, would find it a difficult country to operate in.   Never did people stand in greater need of protection.   They have battled manfully against the most unscrupulous foe that civilized warfare has ever witnessed.   They have been shut out from all communication with anybody but their enemies for a year and a half, and yet they stand firm and true.   If such merit is not to be rewarded, if such citizens are not to receive protection, then is their case a deplorable one indeed.

I am, sir, your most obedient servant,

A. D. STREIGHT,
Colonel Fifty-first Regiment Indiana Volunteers.

Capt. W. H. SCHLATER, *Assistant Adjutant-General.*

No. 2.

Report of Capt. Stephen C. Writer, First Ohio Cavalry.

DECATUR, ALA., *July* 16, 1862.

SIR : I should have sent you the following official information with regard to my late expedition sooner, but I did not until this morning learn the full details from some of my men who were detained with the infantry regiment which accompanied us at the time of starting.

Late on Friday evening of the 11th, Colonel Streight, of the Fifty-first Indiana Regiment, informed me that he had received permission from General Buell to march his regiment 24 miles into the hills and remain four days for the purpose of recruiting its numbers, as many had already come in and many more would come in were they protected from the bushwhackers in their immediate neighborhood, and also received permission from the general to take any cavalry he might find upon this side of the river.

We left Decatur the following morning at sunrise and went out 6 miles.   Colonel Streight then ordered that I should take five of the new recruits which had accompanied us and escort them through to Colonel Davis', 17 miles farther on, with my cavalry, which consisted of 1 sergeant, 2 corporals, and 11 privates, carrying in all 12 guns.   I was instructed when I arrived at Colonel Davis' to impress any number of horses that they might require to ride all through the country to inform Union men wishing to join our army that he was there ready to receive them, they to go on that night and require a change of horses, it being considered too hard a day's work to use the horses they had that day ridden through.

At the time of parting with Colonel Streight he told me that his regiment would undoubtedly come up with me that night ; but if it did not, and I considered it dangerous to remain there alone, to fall back upon his regiment.

I arrived near Colonel Davis' all safe, put out pickets, fed horses, and sent forward three men and procured horses for three others.   I supposed at the time I reached Colonel Davis' the infantry was 8 or 10 miles back. The place we selected to feed was a farm-yard, well fortified by corn-cribs, stables, hen-houses, and pig-pens, and might easily have been held had I had any respectable number of men.   I suppose I had been there altogether two and a half hours when I heard an alarm firing from our rear pickets.   We immediately mounted our horses, rode out to the pickets, and found the enemy were approaching us with some force mounted and a very considerably larger force dismounted, and deploying right and left of the road under cover of the woods and a rail fence, evidently intending to flank us on all sides and capture us. I then ordered the men to return to the barn-yard, tie up the horses, and take position behind our defenses and defend ourselves as best we could. The men fired steady and with precision, and staid their advance for the time being; but as their force was being constantly augmented from the woods I finally gave the order to mount and make our retreat, that being the only way I could then see to save our horses. We retreated toward the woods parallel with their line, they keeping up a constant firing, it being now the only route left open to us. While running the gauntlet 3 men were wounded, 1 in the thigh and 2 about the head; the latter 2 not seriously. Two horses were shot and disabled and left behind.

When we reached the woods I gave directions that we should turn the enemy's flank, go back by their rear, and join the infantry on the Decatur road, which I then supposed to be about 4 miles back of where we had the skirmish. I then for the first time discovered that five of my men were missing, and supposed that they had got scattered from the main body and would join the infantry that night or in the morning. The country through which we retreated was a secession, guerrilla neighborhood, and when within $2\frac{1}{2}$ miles of the main road four more shots were fired upon us, and one of my men had his saber and scabbord shot entirely off the belt. One mile farther on I was shot, the ball entering the body near the upper point of the hip bone, traversing down and around the hip, lodging on the inside of the thigh nearly one-third of the way down to the knee, giving me a gunshot wound in my body of considerably over one foot in length. I then determined to change my course and come into camp by a by-road, which I did that night by 12 o'clock, having ridden 18 miles after being shot.

Three of my missing men returned this morning and state that they made their way to the infantry the next forenoon. They report two men still missing, one having been taken prisoner and the other either a prisoner or killed, they were not able to say positively which.

I have lost 3 horses (2 shot and disabled and the third taken with the prisoner), 2 full horse equipments, 2 carbines, 3 sabers, and 4 pistols.

The enemy had between 75 and 100 men, and report 2 killed and 2 severely wounded upon their side.

S. C. WRITER,
Captain, Comdg. Company I, First Ohio Volunteer Cavalry.

Col. MINOR MILLIKEN,
Commanding First Ohio Volunteer Cavalry.

JULY 13, 1862.—Action at and surrender of Murfreesborough, Tenn.

REPORTS, ETC.

No. 1.—Maj. Gen. D. C. Buell, U. S. Army, commanding Army of the Ohio, including General Orders, No. 32.
No. 2.—Brig. Gen. T. T. Crittenden, U. S. Army, commanding at Murfreesborough.
No. 3.—Findings of a Court of Inquiry.
No. 4.—Maj. James J. Seibert, Seventh Pennsylvania Cavalry.
No. 5.—Capt. John M. Hewett, Battery B, Kentucky Light Artillery.
No. 6.—Col. John C. Walker, Thirty-fifth Indiana Infantry.
No. 7.—Col. William W. Duffield, Ninth Michigan Infantry.
No. 8.—Lieut. Col. John G. Parkhurst, Ninth Michigan Infantry.
No. 9.—Col. Henry C. Lester, Third Minnesota Infantry.
No. 10.—Col. John F. Miller, Twenty-ninth Indiana Infantry, commanding at Nashville.
No. 11.—Maj. Gen. J. P. McCown, C. S. Army.
No. 12.—Brig. Gen. N. B. Forrest, C. S. Army, commanding Cavalry Brigade.

No. 1.

Reports of Maj. Gen. D. C. Buell, U. S. Army, commanding Army of the Ohio, including General Orders, No. 32.

HUNTSVILLE, ALA., *July* 15, 1862.

My information, up to the night of the 13th, from Murfreesborough was that the Ninth Michigan had been captured, but that Colonel Lester's regiment and Hewett's battery were doing well, and felt confident of being able to hold out. Re-enforcements were being started from Nashville. It appears that before they arrived Colonel Lester surrendered, at 4 p. m. the same day. I have no particulars, and at present no remarks to make upon what appears to be a most disgraceful affair. Of course it may embarrass me considerably. I have been busy to counteract it. The worst is the interception of the Chattanooga road, which was just completed. I had taken the precaution to place some twelve regiments on that route until it should be securely established. We will go to work again.

D. C. BUELL,
Major-General.

General HALLECK.

—

HUNTSVILLE, ALA., *July* 19, 1862.

As nearly as I can ascertain the force captured at Murfreesborough on the 13th consisted of nine companies of the Third Minnesota, under Colonel Lester; six companies of the Ninth Michigan, four companies of the Fourth Kentucky Cavalry, three companies of the Seventh Pennsylvania Cavalry, and two sections of Hewett's Kentucky battery. All except Colonel Lester's regiment and the artillery, including Colonel Duffield and General T. T. Crittenden, seem to have been completely surprised in the town and captured without time or opportunity for resistance. The case of the rest of the command was but little better. They maintained their position until 4 o'clock and then surrendered. I had concentrated a larger force at that point to occupy McMinnville, but a considerable portion of it had been sent away a day or two before to Kentucky to meet the difficulties there.   I regard the whole affair as most disgraceful and demanding prompt and vigorous treatment.   It has also caused serious delay in the means of supplying the army so that it can move on the Decatur route.   The difficulty has been increased by damages to bridges by swollen streams.   Every effort is being made to remove these difficulties and I hope to have the Murfreesborough road repaired and in working order in a very few days.   It is not my habit to plead difficulties or represent them even; but it is important that they should be somewhat understood, lest impossible expectations should be formed, and the opinion taken up that this army is idle and has nothing to do but march rapidly along the road.   Our lines of supply are very long and difficult to protect; for, without ascribing hostility to the mass of the people, there is still enough of hostile and bad element to involve us in all the difficulties of operating in an enemy's country.

D. C. BUELL,
Major-General, Commanding.

Major-General HALLECK, or
ADJUTANT-GENERAL U. S. ARMY.

GENERAL ORDERS, }   HEADQUARTERS ARMY OF THE OHIO,
     No. 32.   }   *In Camp, Huntsville, Ala., July 21, 1862.*

On the 13th instant the force at Murfreesborough, under command of Brig. Gen. T. T. Crittenden, late colonel of the Sixth Indiana Regiment, and consisting of six companies of the Ninth Michigan, nine companies of the Third Minnesota, two sections of Hewett's (Kentucky) battery, four companies of the Fourth Kentucky Cavalry, and three companies of the Seventh Pennsylvania Cavalry, was captured at that place by a force of the enemy's cavalry variously estimated at from 1,800 to 3,500. It appears from the best information that can be obtained that Brigadier-General Crittenden, and Colonel Duffield, of the Ninth Michigan, with the six companies of that regiment and all of the cavalry, were surprised and captured early in the morning in the houses and streets of the town or in their camp near by, with but slight resistance and without any timely warning of the presence of an enemy.   The rest of the force, consisting of the Third Minnesota and the artillery, under Colonel Lester, left its camp and took another position, which it maintained with but few casualties against the feeble attacks of the enemy until about 3 o'clock, when it was surrendered and marched into captivity.

Take it in all its features, few more disgraceful examples of neglect of duty and lack of good conduct can be found in the history of wars. It fully merits the extreme penalty which the law provides for such misconduct.   The force was more than sufficient to repel the attack effectually.   The mortification which the army will feel at the result is poorly compensated by the exertion made by some—perhaps many—of the officers to retrieve the disgrace of the surprise.   The action fit to be adopted with reference to those who are blamable, especially the officers highest in command, cannot be determined without further investigation.

In contrast to this shameful affair the general commanding takes pleasure in making honorable mention of the conduct of a detachment of 22 men of Companies I and H, Tenth Wisconsin Regiment, under the command of Sergts. W. Nelson and A. H. Makinson.   The detachment was on duty guarding a bridge east of Huntsville, when it was attacked on April 28 by a force of some 200 or 300 cavalry, which it fought for two hours and repulsed in the most signal manner. Such is the conduct that duty and honor demand of every soldier; and this example is worthy of imitation by higher officers and larger commands.

By command of Major-General Buell:

JAMES B. FRY,
Colonel and Chief of Staff.

No. 2.

Report of Brig. Gen. T. T. Crittenden, U. S. Army, commanding at Murfreesborough.

I submit the following report of the affair of July 13, 1862, at Murfreesborough, Tenn.:

While at Athens, Ala., I received the special order of Major-General Buell assigning me to the command of the post of Murfreesborough, and went there as speedily as possible. I arrived there on the same train with Colonel Duffield, of the Ninth Michigan, on July 11. The next day I assumed command of the post and Colonel Duffield of the Twenty-third Brigade. Having no instructions, and knowing nothing of the affairs at the post, I had several interviews with Col. [Henry C.] Lester [Third Minnesota], then in command, and from his statements, made both to myself and Colonel Duffield, it was evident that he apprehended no danger. He stated that the only points from which the enemy could approach were McMinnville and Lebanon, that there was no force between Chattanooga and Murfreesborough, and that Morgan's force was far beyond Lebanon, *en route* for Kentucky.

Colonel Lester had separated his forces on or about June 23, 1862, leaving five companies of the Ninth Michigan and about 80 men of the Seventh Pennsylvania Cavalry at the old camp, and removing the Third Minnesota Regiment and Hewett's First Kentucky Battery (four guns) about 1¼ miles northwest of the former camp. This was the whole force there on July 13, except one company Ninth Michigan posted in the court-house as provost-guard, altogether numbering about 950 effective men.

I appointed Lieut. [Henry M.] Duffield, Ninth Michigan, acting assistant adjutant-general, Lieut. C. H. Blakey, who had been previously acting, having left for Minnesota on recruiting service on July 12.

Lieutenant Duffield, under my orders, proceeded at once to prepare a morning report, but did not complete it that day.

I then went with Colonel Duffield to look for a proper camp for the whole force, as I would not permit it to remain separated. I found the water, the scarcity of which Colonel Lester assigned as the reason for such division, abundant to supply 5,000 men and a good camp ground within a quarter of a mile of the former camp. I examined other camp sites, but preferred the first, and ordered Colonel Duffield to concentrate his force there.

The same day I rode out with the officer of the day and made an examination of the pickets. Being dissatisfied with its strength and locations, I directed Major Seibert, commanding the cavalry, to double his cavalry force on all the roads to Lebanon and McMinnville, which he did, but withdrew them at night, in accordance with the custom and orders of Colonel Lester under which he had previously acted, of which custom and order I was entirely ignorant. There was no such order on the order-book, it being merely verbal. I had doubled the cavalry on the points of danger, as a temporary strengthening of the pickets, until next day, when I had ordered a much larger detail for picket duty from the infantry. My temporary headquarters were opposite to and about 75 yards from the court-house.

I have been informed that Colonel Lester had some intelligence of a cavalry force of the enemy assembling near McMinnville, but he did not inform me nor did I have any information of impending danger. I found things negligently and loosely done at the post and attempted to remedy all the negligence I saw there.

At daylight of July 13 General Forrest, with 2,500 cavalry, consisting of four regiments and one battalion—among them the First and Second Georgia and Seventh Texas, having marched 48 miles between noon of the 12th and that time—surrounded and captured the pickets on one of the roads to McMinnville without the firing of a gun, rushed at full speed into the camp of the Seventh Pennsylvania Cavalry and into the court-house square and streets of the town. Passing through the cavalry camp they attacked the Ninth Michigan, which was ready to receive them. Severe fighting at this point resulted in driving the enemy back some 300 yards after repeated assaults, both sides losing heavily.

Colonel Duffield, commanding Twenty-third Brigade, was severely wounded early in the action and carried from the field. He was paroled at once, and I have had no report from him.

Lieutenant-Colonel Parkhurst, commanding the Ninth Michigan, after holding his camp nearly eight hours against superior numbers, finding the enemy were surrounding him with their whole force and having no hope of re-enforcement (not receiving any reply to several messages for assistance sent by him to Colonel Lester), surrendered his force, then reduced to 134 men. This fragment of a regiment, under its gallant lieutenant-colonel (Parkhurst), fought splendidly, and deserves honorable mention. Their loss was 11 killed, 86 wounded, and 36 missing.

Company B, Ninth Michigan, the provost guard, made a resolute defense of the court-house for three hours during repeated assaults, killing 12 and wounding 18 of the enemy. They did not surrender until the court-house was set on fire. During these hours of suspense only an occasional shot was heard from the Third Minnesota and Hewett's battery. Of course their comparative quiet showed that they were not attacked in force. From the reports of Colonel Lester and Captain Hewett and from other sources I learned that their commands turned out promptly, marched unattacked nearly half a mile, and were there halted by Colonel Lester. Except slight changes of position, they remained there from 4.30 a. m. until 2.30 p. m., twice or three times menaced by small squads and once attacked by about 300 cavalry. The latter were repulsed by the fire of the skirmishers and one volley from two companies on the left flank of the regiment. Within three-quarters of a mile of their position they heard the fighting at the court-house for three hours and during seven hours and a half the fight at the Michigan camp.

The Third Minnesota was a splendidly drilled regiment. The officers and men were anxious to fight, but Colonel Lester held them there without seeing any enemy in force. Colonel Lester received two dispatches from Lieutenant-Colonel Parkhurst, begging for aid, but would afford none. When all was lost except his own command Colonel Lester went under a flag of truce to see Colonel Duffield, and there saw the enemy, who had not dared to come within range of his artillery, and was so impressed with what he saw that he returned, determined to surrender. This is proved by his calling a council of his company commanders and his lieutenant-colonel [Chauncey W. Griggs]. They, by a *viva-voce* vote, decided to fight. Part of them went from the council. Colonel Lester reopened and reargued the matter. A ballot vote was taken and the force was surrendered. This was done by the statements and influence of Colonel Lester. Lieutenant-Colonel Griggs bitterly opposed the surrender and voted against it to the last. Not a man was killed in the line of the Third Minnesota during the day. I state the facts without comment.

With a few men I held my headquarters until after the court-house was taken. I early sent a messenger, in citizen's clothes, with orders to Colonel Duffield, but he could not pass through the enemy's lines. They had my quarters surrounded from the time they entered the square. I submit copies of reports made to me and refer to them. I respectfully demand a court of inquiry into the disaster at Murfreesborough.

T. T. CRITTENDEN,
Brigadier-General, late Commanding Post.

Lieut. Col. J. P. GARESCHÉ,
 Assistant Adjutant-General and Chief of Staff.

[Indorsement.]

HEADQUARTERS DEPARTMENT OF THE CUMBERLAND,
Nashville, Tenn., November 26, 1862.

Respectfully forwarded to the Adjutant-General of the Army, with the request that this case may receive prompt attention and that Colonel Lester be ignominiously dismissed the service.*

As Capt. [John A.] Tanner is under my command, I propose to avail myself of the authority delegated to me by the Secretary of War and shall dismiss him.† General Crittenden I will order to duty.

W. S. ROSECRANS,
Major-General, U. S. Volunteers, Comdg. Department.

No. 3.

Findings of a Court of Inquiry.

GENERAL ORDERS, }   HDQRS. DEPT. OF THE CUMBERLAND,
 No. 4.   }   *Murfreesborough, Tenn., January 24, 1863.*

I. At a court of inquiry, convened at the city of Nashville, December 17, 1862, by Special Field Orders, No. 19, Headquarters Fourteenth Army Corps, Department of the Cumberland, on the request of Brig. Gen. T. T. Crittenden, to investigate and give an opinion on the facts connected with the surrender of the troops at Murfreesborough, under his command, of which court Brig. Gen. James G. Spears was president, and Col. Joseph R. Scott, Nineteenth Regiment Illinois Volunteers, was recorder, the following facts were found upon the testimony:

1st. That he (General Crittenden) assumed command of the post at

---

*Dismissed December 1, 1862.   †Dismissed, to date September 22, 1862.

Murfreesborough on the 12th day of July, 1862, between the hours of 9 and 10 o'clock a. m.

2d. That he found the camp had been divided for three weeks previous and the forces separated.

3d. That he rode out on the morning of the 12th July, with Colonel Duffield, commanding the Twenty-third Brigade, and selected a camp, and told Colonel Duffield to concentrate the whole force there at once.

4th. That he rode out and inspected the pickets with the field officer of the day, and not being satisfied with their strength and location, ordered Major Seibert, commanding the cavalry, to double his cavalry patrol on the roads leading to Lebanon and McMinnville.

5th. That the pickets on these roads were re-enforced, but were withdrawn at night without the knowledge of General Crittenden, as was the custom of the post by order.

6th. That he ordered morning reports to be made out and one-fifth of the entire effective force to be detailed as grand guards.

7th. That he examined the brigade order books, and ordered a plot of the town and its approaches to be made.

8th. That he consulted fully and freely with Colonels Lester and Duffield, did a large amount of executive business, and was constantly employed until 9 p. m. July 12.

9th. That he was informed, on what should have been good authority, that there was no force of the enemy nearer than Chattanooga, with the exception of small parties of guerrillas, and that there was no danger of an immediate attack.

10th. That the attack was made upon the Ninth Michigan Infantry and Seventh Pennsylvania Cavalry and the town at daylight on the morning of the 13th July.

11th. That the Seventh Pennsylvania Cavalry was immediately overpowered. That the Ninth Michigan Infantry was promptly formed and repeatedly repulsed the enemy. That about 8 o'clock a. m. they took a more sheltered position, which they held until 12 o'clock, when they surrendered; their commanding officer being wounded and having lost nearly one-half their number in killed and wounded.

12th. That one company of the Ninth Michigan Infantry, acting as provost guards, held the court-house in the town until 8 o'clock, when they surrendered after it was set on fire.

13th. That General Crittenden surrendered himself and staff at 8 o'clock, having endeavored to communicate with the troops, but failed, owing to the stopping of his message by rebel guards.

14th. That the Third Minnesota Infantry and Hewett's battery of four guns, under command of Colonel Lester, being 1¼ miles from town and about the same distance from the Ninth Michigan Infantry and cavalry, immediately on hearing the attack on these places marched up the turnpike and took position in an open field, with woods in front, about 600 yards distant, where they remained until about 12 o'clock, cavalry occasionally appearing in their front in small parties, which were driven off with shot and shell from the battery, after which they fell back about one-half mile, near their camp, and remained there until they surrendered.

15th. That the estimated number of troops at the post was about 1,040; that of the enemy 2,600.

Upon which statement of facts the court give the following opinion:

"We therefore are of the opinion from the evidence that Brig. Gen. T. T. Crittenden did all that should be expected of a vigilant commander from the time he took command until the surrender. We find no evidence that impugns his skill or courage; on the contrary, he was very active on the day before the attack up to 9 p. m. in obtaining information and placing the post in a proper state of defense. Although it may be said that he should have immediately concentrated his forces and that any delay in so doing was dangerous, yet we find an ample apology for the delay in the facts that he was an entire stranger to the place and country, and that he was assured by Colonel Lester, who had preceded him in the command for two months, that there was no danger of an attack and that no enemy of importance was nearer than Chattanooga."

All which is published for the information of the army.

II. The general commanding, after a careful examination of the testimony adduced before the court of inquiry, is of opinion that the defeat of our forces under Brig. Gen. T. T. Crittenden at Murfreesborough was chiefly owing to the withdrawal of picket guards from the roads leading to the town during the night and to the separation of the forces at the post; that the post was taken by surprise and the forces overpowered by being attacked in detail, all which would have been provided against had the timely orders of General Crittenden been obeyed.

By command of Major-General Rosecrans:

C. GODDARD,
Assistant Adjutant-General and Chief of Staff.

No. 4.

Report of Maj. James J. Seibert, Seventh Pennsylvania Cavalry.

GENERAL: I respectfully submit the following as my report of the battle at Murfreesborough, Tenn., on Sunday, July 13, 1862:

I first assumed command of the cavalry attached to that command, consisting of the Third Battalion Seventh Pennsylvania Cavalry, and one squadron of the Fourth Kentucky Cavalry, on May 29, but was called to Nashville on duty on June 19, returning again on July 6.

When I first assumed command it was the custom, as well as the order, of Colonel Lester, then in command, to send out daily from the cavalry a patrol of 5 men on each of the seven pikes leading to and from the town, starting out in the morning and returning in the evening. This order was not changed while I was in command until the day before the occurrence. When you assumed command you ordered me to double the number of the patrols on the roads to Lebanon and McMinnville, which was done. When the patrols returned in the evening I received the report daily from each of the non-commissioned officers in charge, which, after committing to writing, I handed to Colonel Lester.

The attack was made at daybreak in the morning, and I first saw the enemy when charging on my camp, which was a short distance to the right of the Woodbury pike. I had not over 80 duty-men in camp at the time of the attack, most of whom were captured there. We then left my camp and joined the Ninth Michigan and surrendered with them at noon. I lost 5 killed and 20 wounded.

Before closing this report I would state that a report reached me about midnight that several men were seen in the night between our pickets and the town on the Bradyville pike. I immediately mounted

12 men and went to the points named, but after examining the fields
and several houses and barns on the Bradyville and Woodbury pikes
and discovering no signs of the enemy I returned with the men to camp,
having reached it only a little more than an hour before the attack.

I am, general, very respectfully, your obedient servant,

JAMES J. SEIBERT,
Major, Seventh Pa. Cav., Comdg. Cav., Twenty-third Brigade.

General T. T. CRITTENDEN,
Commanding Forces at Murfreesborough, Tenn. :

No. 5.

Report of Capt. John M. Hewett, Battery B, Kentucky Light Artillery.

GENERAL: I have the honor of making the following report of the
part taken by my command in the fight at Murfreesborough, Tenn., on
July 13, 1862:

Before it was fairly daylight my camp was alarmed by rapid discharges of musketry in the direction of the Ninth Michigan camp and
in town, distant 1½ miles. I immediately ordered my horses harnessed
and hitched in, supposing that an immediate advance would be made
on the town. I left my park with the guns of one section advanced and
the other passed to the rear, my caissons in the center.

I rode to the color-line of the Third Minnesota Regiment, which was
forming, and informed Colonel Lester that I was in motion. He
ordered me to wait till he came up. On his joining us I asked in what
order we would advance on the town. He said he would halt in the
old field on our left and wait for orders. The firing was still brisk in
town. Twenty minutes or half an hour later the enemy was seen on
our left flank, 1,000 or 1,500 yards distant. I opened fire on them; they
instantly dispersed. I then placed the other section on the turnpike
(the extreme right), in charge of Lieut. [Alban A.] Ellsworth, who
was in position but a few moments when the enemy were discovered
advancing from the town in considerable force. A few rounds drove
them for protection into the woods immediately in our front and half
a mile distant from our line. We then briskly shelled the woods for a
few minutes, driving them out. Nothing further was seen of the enemy
for nearly an hour, when they were discovered in our rear and about
the same time saw the smoke from our camp, which they had gained.
I ordered the guns from one section to shell them out, which was done.
In a few minutes after a charge was made on us by 200 or 300, which
was repulsed, the enemy retiring into the woods in front of the line.
We again shelled the woods briskly for several moments. An hour
later they were discovered tearing up the railroad track, half or three-
fourths of a mile below. They were shelled from this. The train from
Nashville had before this passed up and stopped under our guns. We
saw them but occasionally for the next five or six hours. They made
no further demonstrations of attack. We remained during this time,
say from 4.30 a. m. till 2 p. m., in an open field, front, rear, and both
flanks open to cavalry. About 2 o'clock we were ordered to fall back
500 yards toward our camp and take position in front of a frame house.
We remained here about an hour, when Colonel Lester, in answer to a
flag of truce, went into town. Returning, he surrendered the entire

command. Up to the moment of surrender the utmost confidence was evinced by the officers and men. My command bore themselves like men. I turned over, by order of Colonel Lester, three 6-pounder smoothbore and one 10-pounder Parrott gun, with the general property of the company. Officers and men lost all their clothing, blankets, &c., in the burning of the tents.

Lost 1 killed, 3 wounded and 9 missing. Seventy men were surrendered, though but 51 were fit for duty.

I have the honor to be, very respectfully, your obedient servant,

J. M. HEWETT,
Captain, Comdg. Hewett's Battery, Kentucky Vol. Artillery.

No. 6.

Report of Col. John C. Walker, Thirty-fifth Indiana Infantry.

SHELBYVILLE, TENN., *July 13, 1862.*

SIR: An engagement has been going on at Murfreesborough nearly all day between our troops at that place and the enemy under Colonel Starnes. I give you the reports as they come to me through messengers of Colonel Hambright, who is stationed at Wartrace. It seems from these reports that Colonel Starnes, with about 5,000 cavalry and two pieces of artillery, attacked Murfreesborough this morning. After two or three hours' fighting he succeeded in taking prisoners seven companies of the Ninth Michigan Regiment and the entire provost guard. It is said that General Crittenden, of Indiana, is also taken prisoner. Since this the First Kentucky Battery was engaged for several hours in shelling the rebels. The battery, I believe, is sustained by the Third Minnesota Regiment. Toward evening the enemy withdrew to the woods.

I cannot vouch for the details of this statement, but will add that the cannonading has been heard distinctly at this place during nearly the entire day. Colonel Matthews, Fifty-first Ohio, arrived at this place this evening and will await further orders. Under existing circumstances I have taken the responsibility of ordering my regiment to this place, for the purpose of co-operating, if necessary, with the other troops in this vicinity. In the course of a day or two I will have the regiment proceed to Elk River Bridge, unless orders are received directing me to do otherwise.

Trusting that my action in the premises will meet with your approbation, I have the honor to be, sir, very respectfully, your obedient servant,

J. C. WALKER,
Colonel Thirty-fifth Indiana.

Col. J. B. FRY, *Chief of Staff, Huntsville, Ala.*

No. 7.

Report of Col. William W. Duffield, Ninth Michigan Infantry.

MURFREESBOROUGH, TENN., *July 23, 1862.*

COLONEL: Although I had not yet formally assumed command of the Twenty-third Brigade, yet, as Brig. Gen. Thomas T. Crittenden and the other officers of the command have been captured and forwarded to Chattanooga, permit me to submit the following report of such portion of the attack made on the 13th instant as came under my own personal observation :

I arrived here, after an absence of two months, on the afternoon of the 11th instant, coming down on the same train with Brig. Gen. Thomas T. Crittenden, the newly appointed commander of the post, and found that several material changes had been made in the location and encampment of the Twenty-third Brigade since my departure. Instead of the whole command encamping together, as it had done, it was separated into two portions and several miles apart. The brigade had never been drilled as such nor a brigade guard mounted. Each regiment furnished its quota of officers and men and watched certain roads; and, worse than all, the commanding officers of the respective regiments were on ill terms with each other, and this feeling, upon one occasion, had broken out into an open personal quarrel. The result was a great lack of discipline and a bitter feeling of jealousy between the different regiments, manifesting itself in the personal encounters of the men when they met upon the street. There was no order, no harmony. The parts of the machine did not fit well, and the commanding officers seem either not to have possessed the will or the ability to adjust them. General Crittenden and myself, immediately after our arrival, visited the several camps, discussed the impropriety of a divided command, and decided upon a concentration ; but as neither of us had assumed command we deferred it until the morrow. But on the morrow the blow fell, and the danger we anticipated became a reality. General Crittenden made his headquarters in town, while I preferred camping with my own men, and therefore pitched my tent with the five companies of the Ninth Michigan Volunteers.

The force then at Murfreesborough was as follows : Five companies (A, C, G, H, and K), Ninth Michigan Volunteers, Lieutenant-Colonel Parkhurst commanding, 200 strong, together with the First Squadron Fourth Kentucky Cavalry, Capt. Levi Chilson, 81 strong, were encamped three-fourths of a mile east of the town, upon the Liberty turnpike; one company (B) Ninth Michigan Volunteers, Captain Rounds, 42 strong, occupied the court-house, the other companies of the Ninth Michigan Volunteers having been ordered to Tullahoma a month since, while nine companies of the Third Minnesota Volunteers, Colonel Lester (one company being on detached duty as train guard), 450 strong, and Hewett's First Kentucky battery, two sections, 72 strong, occupied the east bank of Stone River, at a distance of more than 3 miles from the encampment of the detachment of the Ninth Michigan Volunteers.

Orders were received from Nashville the evening of the 12th instant directing the First Squadron Fourth Kentucky Cavalry to proceed immediately to Lebanon. The total effective strength of the command at Murfreesborough on the morning of the 13th instant did not therefore exceed 814 men, including pickets.

The attack was made at daybreak on the morning of the 13th instant by the Second Cavalry Brigade, C. S. Army, Brig. Gen. N. B. Forrest, over 3,000 strong, consisting of one Texas regiment, Lieutenant-Colonel Walker; the First and Second Georgia Regiments, Colonels Lawton and Hood ; one Alabama regiment, Colonel Saunders, and one Tennessee regiment, Colonel Lawton[?]. The noise of so many hoofs at full speed upon the macadamized roads was so great that the alarm was given before the head of the column reached our pickets, about 1 mile distant, so that our men were formed and ready to receive them, although they came in at full speed. The Texas and a battalion of one of the Georgia regiments, in all over 800 strong, attacked the detachment of the Ninth Michigan Volunteers. So fierce and impetuous was their attack that our men were forced nearly to the center of the camp; but they fell back steadily and in order, with their faces to the foe. But upon reaching the center of the camp their line was brought to a halt, and after twenty minutes of nearly hand-to-hand fighting the enemy broke and fled in the wildest confusion, followed in close pursuit by one company as skirmishers. A squadron of cavalry at this time launched at their heels would have utterly routed and annihilated them. Indeed so great was their panic that their officers were unable to check the fugitives for a distance of 7 miles, and Colonel Wharton,[?] commanding the Georgia regiment, was subsequently arrested by General Forrest for misconduct under the fire of the enemy.

During this attack both officers and men, with one single exception, behaved very handsomely. There was no excitement, no hurry, and no confusion. Everything was done calmly, quietly, and in obedience to orders. But it is with the deepest shame and mortification that I am compelled to report that one officer of Michigan has been guilty of gross cowardice in the face of the enemy. Capt. John A. Tanner, of Company K, Ninth Michigan Volunteers, at the first alarm left his quarters, abandoned his company, and fled from his command under the enemy's fire, and I therefore inclose you herewith charges preferred against him for violation of the Fifty-second Article of War. Capt. Charles V. De Land, Company C, Ninth Michigan Volunteers, deserves special mention for cool and gallant conduct throughout the action and the fearless mode in which he led his company as skirmishers in pursuit of the enemy when repulsed. Also First Lieut. Hiram Barrows, of Company A, same regiment, for the tenacity with which he held his ground, although sorely pressed by the enemy. The loss of the detachment of the Ninth Michigan Volunteers has been very severe for the number engaged, amounting to 1 officer and 12 men killed and 3 officers and 75 men wounded. The enemy's loss has been much more severe than our own. More than double the number of their dead were buried with ours and their wounded are found in almost every house. Among their wounded are a colonel, a major, two adjutants, and one surgeon. I inclose you herewith the surgeon's report of the killed and wounded of the Ninth Michigan Volunteers.

Not having been present at the subsequent surrender of the detachment of the Ninth Michigan Volunteers, under Lieutenant-Colonel Parkhurst, I can only state the facts as reported to me, which show that this force, isolated and reduced by killed and wounded to less than 75 men, after having held their ground from 4 a. m. to 1 p. m., were compelled to surrender or be cut to pieces by the entire force of the enemy. I am reliably informed that Company B, Ninth Michigan Volunteers, under command of First Lieut. L. J. Wright, held the court-house against an incessant attack by a greatly superior force from 4 a. m. till 7.30 a. m., and did not surrender till the enemy had possession of the lower story of the building and had started a fire, with the evident intention of burning them out.

Of the surrender of the Third Minnesota Volunteers and Hewett's First Kentucky Artillery, under command of Colonel Lester, I cannot speak from personal knowledge nor have I received any information from sources sufficiently reliable to warrant my communicating to you any details. Indeed I would much prefer not to do so. The circumstances of the case, as reported, bear painfully on the honor of a brother officer now a prisoner of war, and who is therefore unable to defend himself.

I inclose a list of killed and wounded of the Third Minnesota Volunteers, furnished me by the assistant surgeon of that regiment, amounting to 2 killed and 8 wounded,* one of whom was killed and 2 wounded in line, the remainder in camp.

In the early part of this attack I received two gunshot wounds, one passing through the right testicle, the other through the left thigh. These, although very painful and bleeding profusely, did not prevent me from remaining with my own regiment until the attack was repulsed, when, fainting from pain and loss of blood, I was carried from the field, and was therefore not a witness of what subsequently occurred. At noon the same day I was made prisoner by General Forrest, but, in my then helpless condition, was released upon my parole not to bear arms against the Confederate States until regularly exchanged.

I remain, colonel, your obedient servant,

WM. W. DUFFIELD,
Colonel Ninth Michigan Infantry, Comdg. Twenty-third Brigade.

Col. J. B. FRY,
Asst. Adjt. Gen., Chief of Staff, Huntsville, Ala.

[Indorsements.]

SEPTEMBER 20, 1862.

Respectfully forwarded to the Adjutant-General. It is gratifying to discover anything to mitigate the mortification of the affair at Murfreesborough. This report seems to do so as far as Colonel Duffield is concerned, but does not alter the general features of the affair.

D. C. BUELL,
Major-General.

I respectfully recommend that Capt. John A. Tanner, Company K, Ninth Michigan Volunteers, be dismissed from the service for cowardly abandoning his company at the battle of Murfreesborough.

H. W. HALLECK,
General-in-Chief.

Approved.

EDWIN M. STANTON,
Secretary of War.

No. 8.

Report of Lieut. Col. John G. Parkhurst, Ninth Michigan Infantry.

LIEUTENANT: I have the honor to make the following report of the battle of Murfreesborough, Tenn., on July 13, 1862. Before giving the particulars of the battle I beg leave to report the strength and condition of the Ninth Regiment Michigan Infantry at the time of the attack:

This regiment, with the Third Regiment of Minnesota Infantry, Hewett's Kentucky battery, and a portion of the Seventh Pennsylvania

---

*Nominal list omitted.

Cavalry, had been encamped in one encampment, in the city of Mur-freesborough, for some months, under the command of Colonel Duffield, when, on May 9, he was assigned to command of the troops of Kentucky, and Colonel Lester, of the Third Minnesota, assumed command of the forces at Murfreesborough.

On June 26 the force at Murfreesborough was divided and its strength greatly reduced by the Third Minnesota Regiment and Hewett's battery being sent 1½ miles north of the city of Murfreesborough, on the Nashville pike, leaving the Ninth Michigan and a squadron of the Seventh Pennsylvania Cavalry occupying the old camping ground, and the only troops in the city.

On June 30, agreeably to an order received from Colonel Lester, this force was further reduced, and Companies D, E, F, and I, of the Ninth Michigan, were sent to Tullahoma. Company B, Capt. [Oliver C.] Rounds, of the Ninth Michigan, was occupying the court-house, situated three-fourths of a mile from camp, and acting as provost guard for the city, leaving only five companies of my regiment in camp. From these companies heavy details for picket and other duties were constantly made, so that the force in camp was about 250 strong.

The weakness of my camp and the divided condition of the forces at Murfreesborough were observed by General Crittenden upon his arrival and viewing of the camp on the 12th, and the danger to be apprehended in consequence of such division was remarked upon by both General Crittenden and Colonel Duffield, who returned to Murfreesborough in company with General Crittenden, and it was by them determined to reunite the forces at once.

At 4 o'clock on the morning of the 13th I was aroused by the sentinel at my tent and informed that the enemy was advancing upon the camp. I at once turned out an gave the alarm in camp. The companies in camp turned out with alacrity, but before they had time to form square the enemy, mounted and some 1,200 strong, with terrific yells, dashed upon us from three directions, armed with double-barreled shot-guns and Colt's navy revolvers. Some of my men gave way under this charge, but the majority of them stood firm and returned the first fire with great precision and fatal effect. After discharging their pieces the enemy retired and dismounted a part of his force and advanced upon us mounted and on foot. I rallied my force, and, although the effect of the fire of the enemy was terribly severe, my officers and men stood their ground with heroic courage and poured a destructive fire into the enemy's ranks until he began to yield. Seeing this, I took advantage of it and ordered my force to advance and charge upon him. In obedience to this order my men, with a yell equal to that of the Texans, made a charge, driving the enemy before them until he was completely routed from my camp and driven out of and beyond reach of the camp of the Pennsylvania cavalry and brigade headquarters. I immediately ordered Company C, Capt. [Charles V.] De Land, to advance in pursuit, as skirmishers, as far as the second street in our front, which he did in good style, doing good execution and holding the line I had indicated to him and driving the enemy still farther in retreat.

Finding an opportunity I immediately occupied my time in preparing for another attack, and marched my force into a garden in front of camp, which was inclosed by a cedar-post fence, and made use of such forage as I had in camp to barricade Maney avenue, which led to our right, and made use of the transportation wagons for a protection on our left, thus securing quite a formidable position. After having se-

surrender my horse, which General Forrest instantly appropriated. Other officers were deprived of their horses.

I remain, lieutenant, most respectfully, your obedient servant,

J. G. PARKHURST,
Lieut. Col., Ninth Regiment Michigan Infantry, Comdg.

Lieut. H. M. DUFFIELD,
Acting Assistant Adjutant-General, Murfreesborough, Tenn.

No. 9.

Report of Col. Henry C. Lester, Third Minnesota Infantry.

LIEUTENANT: I have the honor to report the share taken by my regiment in the action at Murfreesborough, Tenn., on Sunday, July 13, 1862.

The attack was made about daylight upon the camp of the Ninth Michigan, the pickets having been captured without firing a shot. With the first alarm my regiment was formed in line and marched from camp toward town, for the purpose of effecting a junction with the other troops, the camping ground of the two regiments having been necessarily separated about 1½ miles in consequence of scarcity of water. We had proceeded nearly half a mile when the enemy appeared in force in the woods in our front, and also upon our left flank. Line of battle was at once formed upon the crest of a hill and we opened upon the enemy with shell. The firing was principally directed to the woods in front, where they were evidently forming for a charge. In the mean time a small force had made its way through a corn field on our left and attacked our camp, which, after a sharp skirmish with the camp guard they took, killing or capturing the guard and firing the tents. Some time was passed in shelling the woods, when a train arrived from Nashville, and was only stopped when it had reached a point opposite our position and distant from it about 100 yards. As soon as the enemy had seen the train pass they commenced to tear up the track between it and Nashville, and were repeatedly driven off by the artillery. A charge was made upon our left from the woods, but was easily repulsed, with some loss to the enemy. At this time a scout returned from the camp of the Ninth Michigan, reporting the enemy in strong force on the Lebanon road between the Michigan regiment and our position; and as the force in front seemed to be still too strong to attempt to push through with any prospect of success I determined to maintain my own position for the present. The firing in town having ceased for some time I sent a scout through the corn field to try and get news from our friends, but the effort was unsuccessful, the enemy being still in strong force on the Lebanon road. Shortly after a soldier of the Ninth Michigan came through and reported his regiment as having surrendered. Thereupon we fell back to a farm-house a short distance in our rear, which being surrounded by a fence I expected to make as strong as possible and to hold until the end.

While taking up our new position a flag of truce appeared, borne by yourself, and sent at the request of Colonel Duffield, commanding Twenty-third Brigade, for the purpose of procuring an interview with me. I returned to town with the flag and had an interview with the colonel commanding, in which I learned that we were attacked by the rebel General Forrest with a brigade of cavalry. Learning from the colonel that the enemy were in overwhelming force, and that even should the road be uninjured the forces at Nashville were absent upon an expedition and that there was no hope of re-enforcements, at his suggestion I agreed to refer the matter of surrender to my officers. Accordingly the matter was represented to them as derived from Colonel Duffield, and the great majority, looking upon further resistance as involving the certainty of an ultimate defeat with great loss, and with no possibility of an escape or assistance, it was decided to surrender, which was done at 3.30 p. m.

The force surrendered by me consisted of about 450 infantry. The enemy's force consisted of about 2,600 troops, together with some hundreds of citizens of the country between McMinnville and Murfreesborough, being in all about 3,000 men.

I have the honor to be, very respectfully, your obedient servant.

H. C. LESTER,
Colonel, Commanding Third Minnesota.

Lieut. H. M. DUFFIELD,
Acting Assistant Adjutant-General, Twenty-third Brigade.

No. 10.

Report of Col. John F. Miller, Twenty-ninth Indiana Infantry, commanding at Nashville.

NASHVILLE, *July* 19, 1862—12 p. m.

GENERAL: Statements of prisoners and others establish these facts: Complete surprise of the Ninth Michigan and cavalry at about 4 a. m. Enemy attacked Michigan camp and provost guard in town simultaneously, approaching in two directions between roads; no grand guard; pickets only in roads; Michigan troops in discord; men killed in tents attempting to form square; Colonel Duffield wounded; failed to form, and surrendered. Provost guards in court-house did most fighting, holding enemy at bay perhaps an hour, killing 10 rebels; surrendered; part cavalry attempted to join Michigan regiment; did little fighting; surrendered.

Third Minnesota, 1½ miles in rear, formed on alarm; had Hewett's battery; left their camp and reserve ammunition; marched short distance, halted, took position, waited for attack; enemy, some in front and flank. At 7 a. m. burned camp, charged on battery; were repulsed with slight loss; made several weak attempts to charge. Infantry hovered about in woods; but little firing by infantry. Enemy showed signs of intention to retreat; burned depot supplies; surrender demanded; men anxious to continue fight; colonel and six captains anxious to surrender. Infantry had plenty ammunition; battery short, but had 64 rounds left; surrendered at about 3 p. m.; loss, 2 killed, 5 wounded in Michigan. Colonel Lester reported as having been stupid with fear, some complain, cowardly; strength of enemy, five regiments; average estimate, 1,800. Marched the prisoners 7 miles beyond McMinnville. Whole force left for Chattanooga, moving rapidly.

Jealousy of officers, causing separation of troops beyond supporting distance in sudden emergency. Bad picketing, lack of skill, vigilance.

and personal courage on part of officers caused the disaster according to testimony.

Loss of Ninth Michigan, 14 killed and 63 wounded.

Respectfully,

JNO. F. MILLER,
Colonel, Commanding Post.

Maj. Gen. D. C. BUELL.

No. 11.

Report of Maj. Gen. J. P. McCown, C. S. Army.

CHATTANOOGA, TENN., *July* 17, 1862.

Colonel Forrest dispatches me as follows:

Attacked Murfreesborough 5 a. m. last Sunday morning; captured two brigadier-generals, staff and field officers, and 1,200 men; burnt $200,000 worth of stores; captured sufficient stores with those burned to amount to $500,000, and brigade of 60 wagons, 300 mules, 150 or 200 horses, and field battery of four pieces; destroyed the railroad and depot at Murfreesborough. Had to retreat to McMinnville, owing to large number of prisoners to be guarded. Our loss 16 or 18 killed; 25 or 30 wounded. Enemy's loss 200 or 300.

Leaves to-day for re-enforcements coming from Kingston.

J. P. McCOWN.

General BRAXTON BRAGG.

[Indorsement.]

HEADQUARTERS ARMY OF MISSISSIPPI,
Tupelo, Miss., July 18, 1862.

Brigadier-General CHALMERS,
Commanding Cavalry, Army of Mississippi:

GENERAL: The general commanding directs that the above dispatch be read to the troops.

Respectfully, general, your obedient servant,

D. H. POOLE,
Acting Assistant Adjutant-General.

No. 12.

Report of Brig. Gen. N. B. Forrest, C. S. Army, commanding Cavalry Brigade.

HEADQUARTERS DEPARTMENT OF EAST TENNESSEE,
Knoxville, Tenn., July 22, 1862.

GENERAL: I have the honor to forward the report of an engagement of our forces under the command of Col. N. B. Forrest and the enemy at Murfreesborough, Tenn., the 13th instant. A portion of the captured property has been brought in and turned over to the department. Colonel Forrest is now on his way to Columbia, Tenn., purposing the destruction of the railroad and bridges between Nashville and that place.

Very respectfully, your obedient servant,

E. KIRBY SMITH,
Major-General, Commanding.

General S. COOPER, *Adjt. and Insp. Gen., Richmond, Va.*

——— —, 1862.

SIR: We left Chattanooga on July 9 with the Texan Rangers, under Colonel Wharton, and the Second Georgia Cavalry, under Colonel Lawton. We made a forced march of nearly 50 miles, reaching Altamont on the night of the 10th instant. After resting one night we passed on to McMinnville, where I was joined on the night of the 11th by Colonel Morrison with a portion of the First Georgia Cavalry, two companies of Colonel Spiller's battalion, under Major Smith, and two companies of Kentuckians, under Captains Taylor and Waltham. After this junction my whole force was about 1,400 men, and both men and horses were much jaded and worn by their long travel. After feeding and refreshing for a single day and being joined by some few volunteers I left on the 12th at 1 o'clock for Murfreesborough. It was over 50 miles to our destination, but there was no halt except for a short time to feed the men and horses.

We approached Murfreesborough about 4.30 a. m. and fortunately captured the pickets of the enemy without firing a gun. I then learned that there were two regiments in and near Murfreesborough, one the Ninth Michigan and the other the Third Minnesota, 200 Pennsylvania cavalry, 100 of the Eighth Kentucky, and Captain Hewett's battery of four guns, numbering in all 1,400 or 1,500 men, under the command of General Thomas Crittenden, of Indiana. There were said to be two camps, one in Murfreesborough of one infantry regiment and the cavalry, the other with the artillery about a mile distant, and a small force with the officers in the court-house and private houses around the public square. I decided immediately to attack the camp in town and the buildings, while the camp with the artillery should be held in check until the first was stormed and surrendered. Colonel Wharton with his Texan Rangers was ordered to charge the camp in town. He moved forward in gallant style at the head of his men, but owing to the urgent necessity of using a portion of the Rangers for the attack on the buildings he did not carry with him but two of his companies. This fact, however, did not abate his courage or that of his men. They charged over the tent ropes right into the camp. Colonel Wharton was soon severely wounded and the command of his Rangers devolved on Colonel Walker.

Colonel Morrison with a portion of the Second Georgia was ordered to storm the court-house while the balance of the Texan Rangers were attacking the private buildings. After two or three hours' hard struggle the court-house was fired and surrendered to Colonel Morrison. The private buildings were also cleared by the Rangers and General Crittenden and his staff surrendered.

Lieut. Col. [Arthur] Hood, of the Second Georgia, with a portion of his force was ordered to storm the jail, which he did, releasing many prisoners confined for political offenses; he also took the telegraph office, capturing the operator.

Colonel Lawton, with the First Georgia, the Tennesseeans and Kentuckians, was ordered to attack the second camp with the artillery, which he did with great efficiency for several hours. The Tennesseeans, under Major Smith, and Kentuckians, under Captains Taylor and Waltham, stood the fire of shot and shell like veterans. The Georgians, under Captain Dunlop and Major Harper, made a gallant charge almost to the mouths of the cannon. After fighting them in front two or three hours I took immediate command of this force and charged the rear of the enemy into their camps and burned their camps and stores, demoralizing their force and weakening their strength.

The force of Texan Rangers sent to attack the first camp was so small that, although they fought with desperate courage and great skill, they were gradually driven back.

After the court-house and private buildings were surrendered and the fight had lasted five or six hours I prepared my whole force to storm both camps and summoned them to surrender. After some parley Colonel Duffield surrendered the infantry and artillery.

My aide, Colonel Saunders, rendered me efficient aid until he was severely wounded by a ball from the court-house. Major Strange, my adjutant, also performed his whole duty. Lieutenant-Colonel Walker and Major Harrison, of the Rangers, acted with their usual daring and bravery. All the officers and men who acted bravely cannot be particularly mentioned, but they acted their part nobly.

After the action was over I detached Major Smith to burn a railroad bridge below Murfreesborough, which he executed well. I intended to burn a railroad bridge above Murfreesborough and gave orders for the purpose, but by mistake they were not executed. I had the telegraph wire cut and a large portion of the railroad track torn up. I found four car-loads of provisions on the railroad track and the depot house full of stores, all of which I burned.

There were between 1,100 and 1,200 privates and non-commissioned officers captured and brought to McMinnville and paroled on condition not to serve until exchanged. The officers have been already sent to Knoxville, in charge of Colonel Wharton (and I trust have safely reached their destination), except one or two who were wounded and left at Murfreesborough, on condition to surrender when restored to health.

I captured four pieces of artillery—three brass pieces and one Parrott gun—which are still in my possession, with harness and ammunition. There were some 50 or 60 large road wagons with the mule teams, harness, &c., captured. I burnt some of the wagons, which could not be got away, and sent you the balance. There were a large number of cavalry horses, saddles, and small-arms, with the ammunition, captured, and such as I have not been compelled to use are also forwarded to you.

In consequence of our being compelled to leave Murfreesborough, and not having received reports of the killed from some of my command, it is impossible to report accurately my loss. My best information is that we had about 25 killed and from 40 to 60 wounded. Among those killed is Lieutenant Green, of the Tennessee Battalion. The reports of the officers under my command when furnished will show more definitely the loss.

The enemy lost about 75 killed and 125 wounded. The pecuniary loss to the enemy must be near half a million of dollars.

Yours, respectfully,

N. B. FORREST,
Brigadier-General, Commanding Brigade of Cavalry.

Maj. H. L. CLAY,
Adjutant-General, Army of East Tennessee.

JULY 15, 1862.—Skirmish at Wallace's Cross-Roads, Tenn.

REPORTS.

No. 1.—Brig. Gen. George W. Morgan, U. S. Army.
No. 2.—Maj. H. L. Clay, Assistant Adjutant-General, C. S. Army.

No. 1.

CUMBERLAND GAP, *July* 18, 1862.

General Spears has returned. The enemy was routed at Wallace's Cross-Roads. The attack was a complete success. The enemy's loss was 10 killed, 18 prisoners, 30 horses, 30 sabers, and 100 fire-arms.

As I hope to be immediately relieved from command at post I deem it fair to ask instructions as to which brigade I shall send to guard the line between this place and Lexington.

GEORGE W. MORGAN,
Brigadier-General Volunteers, Commanding.

Col. J. B. FRY.

No. 2.

Reports of Maj. H. L. Clay, Assistant Adjutant-General, C. S. Army.

HEADQUARTERS DEPARTMENT OF EAST TENNESSEE,
Knoxville, Tenn., July 15, 1862.

GENERAL: It is proper that I communicate to you the fact that our cavalry at Wallace's Cross-Roads (four companies), under the command of Captain Mims (Colonel McLin's Second Tennessee Cavalry), was surprised by the enemy at 11 o'clock this morning. Captain Mims reports from Mynatt's Cross-Roads that no scouts had been ordered out to-day, and when his pickets were driven in he advanced to meet, as he supposed, a small force, when he discovered two full regiments advancing upon his flank. He retreated with the loss of about 20 men (captured, killed, and wounded), all his baggage, &c. It is not stated in the report whether the enemy's force consisted of cavalry or infantry, but four fugitives of the command affirm that they saw infantry only. Captain Mims sent information of the surprise to Colonel McLin at Maynardville. I have no information from what quarter the enemy came.

Very respectfully, your obedient servant,

H. L. CLAY,
Assistant Adjutant-General.

Brig. Gen. C. L. STEVENSON,
Commanding First Division, Bean's Station, Tenn.

HEADQUARTERS DEPARTMENT OF EAST TENNESSEE,
Knoxville, Tenn., July 16, 1862.

GENERAL: Captain Owen, First Tennessee Cavalry, was sent last evening from this place to ascertain the result of the engagement at Wallace's Cross-Roads yesterday, the number of the enemy, and their movements. He reports that our loss was 1 man wounded, with 4 or 5 taken prisoners. The force of the enemy consisted of three regiments (Houk's, Cooper's, and Shelley's), under command of General [James G.] Spears. It left yesterday evening, going to Big Creek Gap.

Very respectfully, your obedient servant,

H. L. CLAY,
Assistant Adjutant-General.

Brig. Gen. C. L. STEVENSON,
Commanding First Division, Bean's Station, Tenn.

JULY 18, 1862.—Raid on Henderson, Ky., and Newburg, Ind.

REPORTS.

No. 1.—Gov. O. P. Morton, of Indiana.
No. 2.—Brig. Gen. William K. Strong, U. S. Army, commanding District of Cairo.

No. 1.

Reports of Gov. O. P. Morton, of Indiana.

INDIANAPOLIS, IND., *July* 18, 1862.

The rebels have taken possession of Henderson, Ky., on the Ohio, below Evansville. They have also crossed the river and taken Newburg, Ind.; killed one of our men and taken 250 of our sick in hospital prisoners. They took 250 arms and destroyed the hospital stores. A boat has left Evansville with arms. I will send an extra train with artillery, arms, and infantry immediately.

O. P. MORTON.

To the SECRETARY OF WAR.

--

INDIANAPOLIS, IND., *July* 19, 1862.

Yesterday the rebels passed the Ohio River and seized Newburg, in Indiana, capturing a hospital with 80 sick and wounded soldiers. Indiana has a river border of 300 miles exposed to raids from Kentucky. A regiment of cavalry stationed in detachments and a gunboat would furnish great security. Arms for the State Legion are greatly needed.

O. P. MORTON,
Governor.

Hon. E. M. STANTON, *Secretary of War.*

--

INDIANAPOLIS, IND., *July* 21, 1862.

The rebels under Johnson remained at Newburg, in our State, long enough to steal and destroy all the hospital stores, parole the sick and wounded soldiers, steal a few horses and wagons, then recross to Kentucky. The boys in hospital were armed and wanted to fight, but the surgeon ordered them to lay down their arms. Governor Morton has ordered the arrest of the surgeon. Two citizens of our State, who brought the rebels over and remained after they left, were killed by our citizens. We have sent a sufficient force to Henderson, under General Love, of our State Militia, to clean out Henderson, Webster, Davis, and

Union Counties, at the request of General Boyle. Governor Morton has gone with him.

W. R. HOLLOWAY,
Governor's Private Secretary.

Hon. E. M. STANTON, *Secretary of War.*

No. 2.

Report of Brig. Gen. William K. Strong, U. S. Army, commanding District of Cairo.

HEADQUARTERS DISTRICT OF CAIRO,
Cairo, Ill., July 19, 1862.

SIR: I have received telegraph this morning from General Boyle, dated Louisville, 18th, saying:

Henderson is taken by rebels. Governor Morton telegraphs Newburg, Ind., taken and 200 stand of arms. Can you send force to Henderson? Order gunboat up the river.

Also telegraph this morning from commander of post Evansville confirming above, and adds—

Also rebels have taken possession of the hospitals and have fired into passing steamer.

There is no gunboat here to send nor any force to spare. I have seen Captain Wise, of the Navy, and he has ordered the receiving boat Clara Dolson fired up. There are some 150 sailors on board that he can arm and he will put on some half dozen navy howitzers and ammunition, with arms for the men, and I shall put on board 200 infantry, well armed, with six days' rations. There will also go a small tug in company, with a howitzer or two. This is all we can do here.

I dispatch my aide, Lieutenant-Colonel Holt, with this, to suggest to you the importance of your doing all you can in the emergency to drive back or capture these marauding rebels. You have plenty of transportation. Now, if you can, spare for a few days two or three companies of cavalry, a battery of artillery, and three or four companies of infantry, well armed and rationed for five or six days and proceed at once to the points captured. If you could not spare all indicated above spare all you can, and if you cannot go yourself send Colonel Duff or some other brave officer and have those marauders wiped out in quick-time. I hope you will agree with me as to the propriety of prompt action. There is no communication to-day by telegraph to Saint Louis, therefore all we can do in the emergency is to act upon our own judgment. I have contributed all I could to the expedition and hope you will do the same on your part promptly.

I inclose you copies of telegrams received by me.

Very respectfully, your obedient servant,

WM. K. STRONG,
Brigadier-General, Commanding.

Brigadier-General QUINBY, *Columbus, Ky.*

[Inclosures.]

LOUISVILLE, 18*th*, 1862.

UNITED STATES COMMANDER, *Cairo:*

Henderson is taken by the rebels. Governor Morton telegraphs Newburg taken and 200 stand of arms. Can you send force to Henderson? Order gunboat up the river. Cannot the Governor of Illinois send force to Paducah?

> J. T. BOYLE,
> *Brigadier-General, Commanding.*

EVANSVILLE, 18th, 1862.

General STRONG, *Cairo*:

Send a gunboat to this point, as Henderson, Ky., and Newburg, Ind., are occupied by the rebels. Also have taken possession of the hospitals and have fired into passing steamers conveying troops to the latter place. I have detained the Hornet for the present.

> F. H. EBRMAN,
> *Lieutenant, Assistant Quartermaster and Commanding Post.*

JULY 21, 1862.—Skirmishes around Nashville, Tenn.

REPORTS.

No. 1.—Brig. Gen. William Nelson, U. S. Army, commanding at Murfreesborough.
No. 2.—Col. John F. Miller, Twenty-ninth Indiana, commanding at Nashville.
No. 3.—Brig. Gen. Nathan B. Forrest, C. S. Army, including operations July 18-24.

No. 1.

Report of Brig. Gen. William Nelson, U. S. Army, commanding at Murfreesborough.

HEADQUARTERS,
Murfreesborough, Tenn., July 24, 1862.

GENERAL : You will have heard that on the 21st instant Forrest went down the Lebanon road to within 5 miles of Nashville and burned a bridge and some trestle work. When this occurred I had only the cavalry companies I picked up at Nashville, Haggard having joined after the damage was done. I determined at once to cut off Forrest's retreat, and gave orders for the cavalry to march to Readyville (see inclosed paper*), and thence to Statesville, and close up to Milton, and I would march with infantry to the point where the Jefferson pike crosses the road from here to Lebanon, 2 miles beyond Stone River, it being my impression that Forrest, having gone by way of Lebanon, would return this way. Twenty minutes before marching a courier came to me from Franklin, bringing a dispatch that Forrest, with 2,500 or 3,000 men, was at Nashville. All sorts of reports came by the courier. I immediately, to save the stores at Nashville, changed the order and sent Haggard with all the cavalry to move rapidly to Nashville and attack the enemy wherever he could find them, telling Colonel Haggard that he would find the enemy scattered, marauding, and having his own men in hand all he had to do was to attack and destroy them as fast as he came to them. I immediately followed with the infantry, and at 10 p. m. was in 10 miles of Nashville. Colonel Haggard sent me several messages with various accounts of the supposed strength of the enemy in front. I answered him in writing to attack—to attack all the time.

---

* Not found.

When I arrived at the junction of the Old Franklin road, at 10 p. m., I found him and all the cavalry there awaiting my arrival. He had been there five or six hours. The enemy were so strongly posted, &c., that he had determined to wait for me and report, having held a council of war and all that sort of nonsense. In an hour's examination I was satisfied that there was not only no enemy, but that they had retreated over the identical road that I had expected they would. Being so sure that he would go that way in any event, I sent messengers back to Colonel Barnes at Murfreesborough for him to take the regiment remaining there and abandon everything there and move up that road; but, alas! he got there just after Forrest had gone by.

By the telegram sent me by Colonel Miller, indicating that Nashville was in danger, Forrest escaped; the 80 men that were guarding the bridge that was burned are lost, 3 of them killed, the rest taken. They were of the Second Kentucky. That regiment is much reduced since leaving Athens; 3 were killed and 48 wounded on the railroad; now 3 are killed and 81 taken, making a loss of 6 killed and 129 lost by death and prisoners.

Forrest was last heard of near Liberty. I have ordered a battalion of Wolford's cavalry to come here by way Shelbyville; a battalion of Board's by way of Versailles. When they do come I will have about 1,200 cavalry, and Mr. Forrest shall have no rest. I will hunt him myself. Where, O tell me, where is General Jackson? It's a chance for him.

I have called in 500 negro laborers from the country to build the field work indicated. When it is finished it will relieve the men here, and I can take the field with the whole force, and I will clear out the country if it can be done. I have stationed three regiments at the crossing of the Jefferson and Lebanon pikes, and will move on McMinnville from that point instead of from here.

Your order has been received to forward 100,000 rations to Stevenson, and I am using all energy to carry it into execution. I will be able to-morrow to send a train to within 5 miles of Nashville, when I will load it and send it along.

If you will send me the rest of my division I will settle the rest of this country in no time. The troops I find here are without discipline, and your orders in relation to marauding, stealing, and rascality generally are dead letters as far as many of them are concerned.

By the burning of the bridges provisions are scarce, and a train I have not, but will go ahead. I inclose some papers. Reports are constant that a large force is coming in at this point. Every man in this country yesterday, so soon as the troops changed direction, started, and I heard of several parties hurrying to Forrest to carry him the news.

I must tell you something that has transpired since you left here. The hostility to the United States Government and the troops has increased 1,000 per cent. It seems settled into a fierce hatred to Governor Johnson, to him personally more than officially, for in questioning many people they cannot point to an act that he has not been warranted in doing by their own showing; but still, either in manner of doing it, or that it should be done by him, or from some undefinable course touching him their resentment is fierce and vindictive, and this country, from being neutral at least, as you left it, is now hostile and in arms, and what makes it bad for us it is in our rear. The continual rumor of a large body of infantry coming into this country tends to make the discontented bold and active. Wherever Forrest stopped he found prepared (notice no doubt having been given) food and forage in ample quantities. Every man is an active spy, and guerrillas are now aiding him.

I send this letter by Messrs. William Spence and William Elliott, two good and true Union men, whom I beg to recommend to your favorable consideration.

Very respectfully,

W. NELSON,
Brigadier-General.

Major-General BUELL,
   Commanding Army of the Ohio, &c.

[Inclosures.]

PROCLAMATION.

HEADQUARTERS FOURTH DIVISION,
Murfreesborough, Tenn., July 18, 1862.

Information has been received at these headquarters that arms and other property belonging to the United States, captured with the troops last Sunday, were distributed yesterday to the disloyal citizens of this town. All persons having such arms or property in their possession will bring them immediately to the court-house and turn them over to the provost-marshal there. Those failing to do so will be arrested and sent to a military prison on the charge of treason.

By order of Brigadier-General Nelson, commanding.

J. MILLS KENDRICK,
Assistant Adjutant-General.

SPECIAL ORDERS, }   HDQRS. FOURTH DIV. ARMY OF THE OHIO,
   No. ——.   }   *Murfreesborough, Tenn., July 21, 1862.*

The inhabitants of the county will furnish negro laborers to the amount of 200 for the use of troops at this point. These laborers will report here to-morrow morning.

By command of Major-General Nelson:

J. MILLS KENDRICK,
Assistant Adjutant-General.

No. 2.

Report of Col. John F. Miller, Twenty-ninth Indiana Infantry, commanding at Nashville.

HEADQUARTERS, *Nashville, July 22, 1862.*

General Forrest, with forces variously reported from 1,200 to 4,000 strong, advanced yesterday on Lebanon pike within 8 miles of city, then marched across to Mill Creek Bridge, 7 miles out on Chattanooga Railroad; destroyed three bridges, taking 80 prisoners Second Kentucky Volunteers, killing 2; 1 wounded. Rebel loss reported, 20 killed and wounded. Took prisoners on Murfreesborough road 12 miles from this place, camped, paroled the prisoners this morning, and marched at daylight toward Murfreesborough to capture wagon train with 360 of Thirty-sixth Indiana, who left here yesterday morning for Murfreesborough, and supposed to have been 12 miles this side of Murfreesborough this morning.

The enemy menaced this place yesterday evening; drove in our pickets; captured 3 of our scouts. They are divided into parties and endeavored to draw out my forces after them. I held and will hold my forces under arms in city. I have no cavalry to pursue, but will hold the city. I telegraphed to Franklin last night and this morning to send couriers to Murfreesborough with all information. The paroled men have just arrived.

JNO. F. MILLER,
Colonel, Commanding Post.

Major-General BUELL.

No. 3.

Report of Brig. Gen. Nathan B. Forrest, C. S. Army, including operations July 18-24.

HEADQUARTERS SECOND CAVALRY BRIGADE,
McMinnville, Tenn., July 24, 1862.

SIR: I have the honor to report to you that on Friday, the 18th, at noon I left my camp on Mountain Creek, 10 miles from this place, with about 700 effective men of this brigade, in the direction of Nashville, for the purpose of making a reconnaissance. On my arrival at Alexandria with a portion of my command (the Texas Rangers) I was advised that during the day some 700 Federal cavalry had been sent from Nashville to Lebanon. I immediately ordered forward the balance of my command, being portions of the First and Second Georgia Cavalry and the Tennessee and Kentucky squadrons, and by a forced march reached Lebanon soon after sunrise. We dashed into the city in fine style, but found that the enemy, having notice of my approach, had retired about 12 o'clock, leaving me in the undisturbed possession of that place. I found the entire population true and loyal, with perhaps a single exception.

I remained at Lebanon until Monday morning, and moved then with my command toward Nashville. On reaching the vicinity of Nashville, say 5 or 6 miles, I captured 3 of the enemy's pickets. I moved then around the city, semicircling it and the Nashville and Chattanooga Railroad, passing within 3 miles of the city, and capturing on the way 2 additional pickets. I moved on the road for the purpose of destroying the bridges on the railroad near the city, and to my entire satisfaction accomplished the purpose, destroying three important railroad bridges over Mill Creek and cutting the telegraph wires. At each bridge I found heavy pickets, and had some considerable skirmishing at each, and also at Antioch Depot.

In the several skirmishes there were 10 killed and some 15 or 20 wounded, 97 prisoners (94 privates and 3 lieutenants), besides destroying a considerable amount of stores at Antioch Depot. Our forces were reported to be four times their number, so I afterward learned.

The necessity of rapid marching to secure the end desired having exhausted to a very considerable extent both men and horses, I found it necessary to fall back to this point, with a view of recruiting, which I did in good order, having the satisfaction to report that I did not lose a single man on the expedition, either in killed or wounded. I regret the limited time allowed me in which to make this report will not permit me to enter minutely into the details of this exploit. I hope it will fully meet the approbation and expectation of the general.

Permit me to add that the entire force, officers and men, under my command acquitted themselves with great credit, and bore the fatigue and risk of the expedition in a manner only to be borne by Confederate troops. My demonstration on Nashville, I am advised, created great excitement in that city, by which the greater portion of the force at Murfreesborough was ordered to that point. I regretted then, and now sincerely regret, that the limited force I had with me, which was all that I had which was available, did not permit me to make a more solid demonstration against that city. They were evidently frightened. A few thousand would then have placed that city in our possession.

On my return I sent a flag of truce to Murfreesborough and found the troops at that point in great confusion and evident fright. They are attempting to fortify the place and have partially blockaded the road between that city and this. I am credibly informed that the same state of confusion and terror pervaded their entire army at Wartrace and all other points within my reach. I regret that my force will not permit me to avail myself of this terror.

The officers and men of my entire command, flushed with victory and our past success, are anxious and ready to meet the enemy. I feel secure in my present position. Should events render this an insecure place I will fall back to a less exposed point.

I am, very respectfully, your obedient servant,

N. B. FORREST,
Brigadier-General, Second Cavalry Brigade.

Maj. H. L. CLAY,
Assistant Adjutant-General, Knoxville, Tenn.

JULY 25, 1862.—Operations at and in the vicinity of Courtland and Trinity, Ala.

REPORTS, ETC.

No. 1.—Maj. Gen. D. C. Buell, U. S. Army, including General Orders, No. 37.
No. 2.—Capt. James H. Boyl, Tenth Indiana Infantry.
No. 3.—Col. John M. Harlan, Tenth Kentucky Infantry.
No. 4.—Col. Moses B. Walker, Thirty-first Ohio Infantry.
No. 5.—General Braxton Bragg, C. S. Army, including congratulatory order.
No. 6.—Brig. Gen. Frank C. Armstrong, C. S. Army.

No. 1.

Report of Maj. Gen. D. C. Buell, U. S. Army, including General Orders, No. 37.

HUNTSVILLE, ALA., *July* 26, 1862.
(Received July 27, 10.10 p. m.)

On yesterday the enemy's cavalry attacked the guards at several points on the road between Decatur and Tuscumbia; captured the one at Courtland; drove others into Decatur, and probably destroyed the bridge. These disgraceful and serious results are due to the neglect and disobedience of my repeated orders in regard to construction of stockades, and I shall bring every offender to trial. I am trying to make our lives secure against such occurrences, for they are fraught with the most serious consequences to an army operating on such long lines. I have requested General Grant to open the road again, for it is important to both of us.

D. C. BUELL.

Major-General HALLECK.

GENERAL ORDERS, }   HEADQUARTERS ARMY OF THE OHIO,
No. 37. }   *In Camp, Huntsville, Ala., August 1, 1862.*

The major-general commanding has to announce other instances of disgraceful neglect and contrast them with another of gallantry:

The guard at Courtland Bridge—consisting of Companies A and H, Tenth Kentucky, under the command of Captain Davidson, and a part of Captain Eggleston's company, First Ohio Cavalry—was completely surprised and captured with but trifling loss on the morning of the 25th ultimo by a force of irregular cavalry. On the same day the companies of Captains Boyl and Goben, Tenth Indiana, which were ordered to protect two bridges on the same road, respectively 6 and 12 miles east of Courtland, deemed it wiser to bring in an empty train which came up than to defend their posts, threatened with an attack from the same irregular cavalry, and so put themselves on the train and arrived safely at Decatur, a few miles distant, without the loss or injury of a man. On the same day and on the same road, 8 miles from Decatur, a guard, consisting of 24 men, of Company E, Thirty-first Ohio, under the command of Lieutenant Harman, were suddenly attacked by a greatly superior force of the same cavalry. They defended themselves gallantly, however, and repulsed the enemy, killing several of the number. Lieutenant Harman and 11 of his men were wounded, himself in two places, and 2 of his men were killed.

The general submits these examples to the reflection of the troops. He reminds them that neglect and bad conduct on the part of guards bring dishonor upon them and may even jeopardize the safety of an army. If these appeals to their personal and professional pride should fail of their object, he warns them that the extreme penalty of the law must intervene to punish the guilty and save the army from the jeopardy in which they place it. The duty of guarding the communications of the army is among the most important with which an officer and his troops can be intrusted. Vigilance, determination, and the preparation of suitable defenses in the way of intrenchments or stockades will prevent such attacks or enable a small force to repel a greatly superior one. Had the orders for bridge guards to fortify their posts been promptly executed and proper vigilance been observed the attacks referred to, if made at all, would have had very different results.

This order and General Orders, No. 32, will be read at the head of every company and detachment.

By command of Major-General Buell:

JAMES B. FRY,
Colonel and Chief of Staff.

No. 2.

Report of Capt. James H. Boyl, Tenth Indiana Infantry.

CAMP, NEAR DECHERD, TENN.,
August 9, 1862.

SIR: I have the honor to report that on the 25th ultimo I learned by the conductor of the train running from Decatur to Tuscumbia, Ala., and which had left the former place that morning, that the Federal forces at Courtland, commanded by Capt. [Henry G.] Davidson, Tenth Kentucky Volunteers, had been attacked by a superior force of the enemy and his entire command captured, the two companies of infantry and a large portion of the First Ohio Cavalry, Captain Eggleston, being prisoners. The road-master was on the train which brought the information, and requested me to put my command on board the cars, thereby protecting the interests of the Government in conducting the same to a place of safety, he representing that the train there was all the rolling stock that was available on the road, it having been transported across the river with great labor and expense, and that it would be impossible to procure another locomotive should the one then attached to the train be destroyed. After mature deliberation I determined to hold my position, and instructed the road-master to proceed to the camp of Captain Goben, some 6 miles distant, in the direction of Decatur, where he might learn more of the movements of the enemy. Arriving there, the road-master informed Capt. [Frank] Goben of the destruction of the Courtland Bridge and the capture of the companies of Captain Davidson's command, asking him, in the name of the Government, for his company, numbering about 40 effective men, to conduct the train through to Decatur. The captain, not thinking it advisable to abandon his position, gave the road-master orders to proceed in the direction of Decatur at a cautious rate of speed, keeping a good lookout for any troops that might attempt the capture of the train, and if attacked in front to fall back to his camp. The train had proceeded but about a half mile when it was attacked by a cavalry force, numbering about 300 men. The engine was reversed and the train run back to Captain Goben's camp, closely followed by the rebel cavalry, who advanced until within about 300 yards of the camp, where, finding Captain Goben's company drawn up in line of battle, they slowly retreated, placing obstructions upon the road of cross-ties, which they set on fire to destroy those laid down, intending to render the road unfit for the passage of trains. After consultation with the road-master in regard to the value and importance of the bridge at which his company was stationed both agreed that it was of but little importance, being merely constructed of square sills thrown across a small creek, which I will here state was exactly the case of the one I was guarding, and Captain Goben placed his company on board the cars and joined my command.

Both the positions, that of Captain Goben and the one occupied by myself, were rendered valueless by the destruction of the long bridge at Courtland and the burning of a wooden culvert on the road. After the arrival of Captain Goben I placed my entire command, camp equipage, &c., on board, preparatory to leaving. This was not done because I deemed the position untenable, but I was satisfied it was valueless, having been informed by a citizen captured by my pickets that Courtland was in possession of the rebels and that an attack upon Decatur was threatened by a large force of rebels. Other circumstances convinced me that his information was correct, and I decided to endeavor to get the train through to Decatur, knowing that if the attack was made upon that place my command could render efficient service there and my force being sufficient in my judgment to protect the train. After proceeding about 1 mile I formed my command in line of battle and proceeded in advance of the train a short distance, when the enemy, numbering some 300 infantry and cavalry, emerged from the woods, and I immediately advanced to meet them, firing a few shots to ascertain their distance, when the entire force, infantry and cavalry, fell back. I pursued them on double-quick for nearly half a mile, but finding it impossible to overtake them, I returned to the train and ordered the engineer to move forward.

A short distance in advance of the encampment of Captain Goben we found the cross-ties of the railroad for about 100 yards on fire and the wooden culvert over a small ravine burned. I put my men to work immediately, and in a short time had so far repaired the road as to allow the passage of the train. This work was considerably retarded from the fact that the iron rails had been much drawn and warped by the burning of the ties upon which they had been placed. While engaged in these repairs Lieutenant Harman, of the Thirty-first Ohio, with his command, was surprised, and, after a gallant fight, repulsed, falling back upon me. The lieutenant received two wounds while contesting the field with the rebels, and had 1 man killed and 12 wounded. He represented the attacking force as numbering from 300 to 400, and as his dead and wounded had been left upon the field, I proceeded with him to the place where the battle occurred with all possible dispatch. Arriving there, we discovered some 40 or 50 cavalry near, all of whom fled when they discovered we were advancing upon them. Placing his dead, wounded, camp equipage, and command aboard the train, we proceeded to Decatur, where we arrived without further accident.

Hoping that this plain statement of facts and my conduct in regard to the affair will meet your approval, I am, respectfully,

JAMES H. BOYL,
Captain Company C, Tenth Indiana Volunteers.

Colonel KISE.

[Indorsement.]

I herewith forward the report of Captain Boyl for your consideration and disposal. It contains a full report of the action of Companies C and B, of the Tenth Regiment Indiana Volunteers, in the late affair near Courtland, Ala.

W. C. KISE,
Colonel, Commanding Tenth Indiana Volunteers.

Brigadier-General FRY.

No. 3.

Report of Col. John M. Harlan, Tenth Kentucky Infantry.

HEADQUARTERS TENTH KENTUCKY REGIMENT,
Winchester, Tenn., August 8, 1862

SIR: I seize the earliest moment since my regiment joined the brigade from detached service at Eastport, Miss., to advise you officially of the capture by the Confederate forces, on July 25, of Companies A and H, of this regiment, stationed at Courtland, Ala., together with such facts connected with their capture as I have been able to gather.

In the outset allow me to state that within a few days after the arrival of our division at Tuscumbia I was ordered to send one company to Courtland, Ala., 23 miles east of Tuscumbia. Company A, Capt. Henry G. Davidson, was detailed for that service. Shortly thereafter, in compliance with orders from division headquarters, I sent Company H, Capt. B. R. Pendleton, to re-enforce Captain Davidson, the two companies being placed by me under the command of the latter, who was the senior captain. A small force of cavalry from the First Ohio was stationed at the same point.

On the same day that Captain Pendleton left for Courtland the remainder of my regiment left for Eastport, Miss., where it continued on detached service until the 24th ultimo, when it left Eastport to rejoin the brigade.

The first reliable information received by me in regard to the affair at Courtland was when *en route* from Florence, Ala., to Pulaski, Tenn., when most of the men from Companies A and H joined the regiment. Being separated from my brigade and division commanders, I deemed it my duty to telegraph to Major-General Buell the substance of that information. At that time I also received a brief communication from Captain Davidson, which was written from Moulton, Ala., while a prisoner in the hands of the rebels. It was written, as I learn from my men, hurriedly, a few moments before they separated from him.

He writes that on the morning of July 25, about 8 o'clock, he was attacked by a large force of Confederate cavalry, under Brigadier-General Armstrong, believed to number 800. Seeing the enemy coming, he formed Companies A and H in line behind the railroad embankment and near the bridge, intending to give the enemy battle, and determined to guard that which he was sent there to do as long as he could possibly do so.

The position which he selected was so advantageous for defense against a force coming from an opposite direction that the presence of his men behind the embankment was not observed by the enemy until they came quite close to him. He fired two volleys into their ranks as they charged, which killed and wounded a number of the rebels, and also killed the horse of the rebel general. Seeing the enemy, with their greatly superior force, was flanking him and getting into his rear, Captain Davidson passed with his command by the left flank across the creek, running under the bridge, and took position in some gullies. About this time he observed a considerable force of cavalry coming from the direction of Courtland, and what appeared to be infantry (but which proved to be cavalry dismounted) in a corn field supporting the cavalry. Captain Davidson ordered bayonets to be fixed, intending to charge through them, get into the corn field, and from there into the woods near by, but finding himself surrounded, with no possible chance of escape, he surrendered his command.

He writes that his men behaved splendidly, obeying every command with promptitude and alacrity and fighting gallantly until the last moment. He says further that Captain Pendleton, Company H, Lieutenant Reynolds, Company A, and Lieutenants Barry and Shively, Company H, are worthy of all praise for the brave and gallant manner in which they managed their troops.

The loss on our side was as follows: William Farmer, Company H, killed; James Rogers, Company A, wounded severely in thigh; Mattis

Cortes, Company A, wounded slightly in arm and cheek, and James Cable, Company A, in left arm.

Captain Davidson writes that the loss of the enemy greatly exceeded his. From my men I learn that the rebel loss was 11 killed and more than 20 wounded. The enemy took both officers and enlisted men to Moulton, Ala., at which place the latter were paroled and the former retained and sent to Tupelo, Miss.

I herewith inclose a complete list of the enlisted men who were taken prisoners and paroled (with the exception of James Rogers, who was too badly wounded to travel and was left with the rebels at Moulton). The paroled men were forwarded to Nashville, Tenn., with orders to report to Maj. W. H. Sidell, assistant adjutant-general, and from that place, I learn, were forwarded to Camp Chase, Ohio.

Justice to Captain Davidson requires that I should say that the unvarying testimony of all the men of Companies A and H is that he acted as became a brave and dauntless soldier under the trying circumstances surrounding him. The admirable manner in which he disciplined his company and his high character afford every assurance that he performed his whole duty. I feel sure that he did all that he could do with the small force at his command. The infantry numbered about 97 effective men. The cavalry force stationed there did not exceed, as I learn, 35 or 40 men, composing parts of two companies, under command distinct from Captain Davidson. They performed the picket duty for the station. Their operations upon the occasion alluded to will doubtless be detailed by others.

The enemy captured the entire camp equipage of Companies A and H, including 2 company wagons, 12 mules, and a small quantity of forage and provisions.

In conclusion, I beg that you will take such steps as will effect a speedy exchange of such of the officers and men of Companies A and H as were taken prisoners. They deserve to be returned to the service of the United States.

I should have stated that the rebel commander and his men were so enraged at Captain Davidson and his command because of the resistance made by them, attended by the killing and wounding of some of their number, that he (General Armstrong) and they threatened to kill them all. General Armstrong denounced Captain Davidson because he did not surrender, without fighting, to such a superior force. This is stated because it was rumored that my companies surrendered without fighting or firing a gun.

Respectfully,

JNO. M. HARLAN,
Colonel Tenth Kentucky Regiment.

G. D. HUNT, JR., Acting Assistant Adjutant-General.

No. 4.

Reports of Col. Moses B. Walker, Thirty-first Ohio Infantry.

DECATUR, July 26, 1862—1 a. m.

General Scheopf is on the north side of the river with three regiments of his brigade. He directs me to say that all guards between this point and Tuscumbia have been attacked on yesterday and driven from their posts. Eighty men of the Tenth Kentucky have been captured at Court-land. The town is now in possession of the rebels. Captain Boyl, of the Tenth Indiana, stationed at trestle work near Courtland with one company Tenth Indiana, fell back on Company B, same regiment, at trestle work 12 miles this side of Courtland, defended the train, and brought it in safely to this place.

Company E, Thirty-first Ohio, stationed at Trinity, 6 miles from this place, was attacked at 4 p. m. Lieutenant Harman stood his ground, and with the small force he had of effective men repulsed the rebels, num-bering 350 men, with a loss to his command of 2 killed and 12 wounded. Lieutenant Harman is himself wounded in two places, but not mortally.

The general wishes your order as to whether he should move from here at this time.

The Thirty-first Regiment is now all under my command in and about this place, having re-crossed the river to-night.

The wires are cut, bridges and trestle work burned, between here and Tuscumbia.

M. B. WALKER,
Colonel Thirty-first Ohio.

General D. C. BUELL.

—

HDQRS. THIRTY-FIRST OHIO VOLUNTEER INFANTRY,
Winchester, Tenn., August 3, 1862.

GENERAL: I beg leave to report that about 4 o'clock in the afternoon of the 24th [25th?] ultimo Lieut. M. B. W. Harman, in command of Com-pany E, Thirty-first Ohio Volunteer Infantry—having one platoon of his company, numbering 25 men, including non-commissioned officers, stationed at a place called Trinity, near Decatur, Ala., for the purpose of guarding the Memphis and Charleston Railroad—was attacked by a force of rebel cavalry, numbering about 350 men. The attack was made at a time when Lieutenant Harman and his little force were engaged in erecting a stockade fort and had not their guns in their hands. They were fired upon and several of the men wounded by the first fire. They sprang to their arms, which were stacked near by, and then commenced the most Spartan-like resistance which the history of this war so far will probably furnish, killing 12 of the enemy certain and wounding not less than 38 or 40. The precise number killed and wounded of the enemy cannot be ascertained, as they were able to carry off all but 5 of their dead and all of their wounded. Lieutenant Harman held his position, fighting himself like a lion at bay, though badly wounded in the face and painfully, though not seriously, in the left arm. His example inspired his men to emulate his conduct, and all but 2 of the 26 fought with a most desperate valor.

You will see by this report that one-half of this little band was killed or wounded in the fight. Their work of fortification had not advanced far enough to afford them any protection. They remained masters of the field, remaining upon it until a late hour at night, when they were brought to Decatur, Ala., upon the train.

The same force, as is believed, which attacked Lieutenant Harman did much mischief on the railroad the same day and took about 80 pris-oners from the Tenth Kentucky Volunteers, who were stationed near Courtland to guard the railroad, driving away two companies of the Tenth Indiana Volunteers and burning bridges and trestle work along the line between Courtland and Decatur, Ala.

This report would have been furnished at an earlier date but for the reason that we have been upon the march ever since the fight occurred.
Respectfully submitted.

M. B. WALKER,
Colonel, Commanding Thirty-first Ohio Volunteer Infantry.

Brig. Gen. A. SCHOEPF.

No. 5.

Report of General Braxton Bragg, C. S. Army, including congratulatory order.

CHATTANOOGA, TENN., *July* 31, 1862.

A cavalry expedition sent from Tupelo on 18th, under Col. Frank C. Armstrong—three Louisiana regiments—attacked the enemy at Courtland, Ala., on the 25th instant; took 133 prisoners (8 commissioned officers), 10 wagons and teams, quantity of forage, many horses and equipments, large number of arms, and the camp equipage of four companies; destroyed railroad depot, bridges, and telegraph. We lost 3 killed and 5 wounded; the enemy, 3 killed and 6 wounded. The men were paroled; officers sent to Columbus, Miss. Another small expedition to Town Creek, near by, captured 16 prisoners.

BRAXTON BRAGG,
General, Commanding.

General S. COOPER.

GENERAL ORDERS, } HEADQUARTERS DEPARTMENT No. 2,
No. 111. } *Chattanooga, Tenn., August* 12, 1862.

The commander of the forces is gratified to call the attention of the army to another well-planned and vigorously executed cavalry movement on Courtland, Ala., led by General Armstrong, which resulted in a serious loss to the enemy in the capture of a number of prisoners, their baggage and camp equipage, arms, ammunition, and other military supplies, and in the destruction of the telegraph lines and railroad bridges on the enemy's line of communication. This expedition reflects credit upon the skill of the commander and bravery of all engaged, and gives another proof of what a few resolute men intelligently handled can accomplish. The commander of the forces is especially pleased to notice the gallant conduct of Capt. P. D. Roddey and the officers and men of his command, who on this occasion exhibited the same coolness and circumspection, and when necessary daring, which have enabled them in previous operations in the same quarter to accomplish results so highly creditable and satisfactory. These late successes of our cavalry should be regarded as presages of the coming campaign. Other arms of the service will emulate the example set them until by bold, rapid, and repeated blows our foe is driven from our soil.

By command of General Bragg:

THOMAS JORDAN,
Chief of Staff.

No. 6.

Reports of Brig. Gen. Frank C. Armstrong, C. S. Army.

HEADQUARTERS ARMY OF THE WEST,
Tupelo, Miss., August 2, 1862.

Brigadier-General JORDAN,
  Chief of Staff, Department No. 2.:

GENERAL: I have the honor to forward to you the inclosed reports made by acting Brigadier-General Armstrong of two very successful engagements which he has had with the enemy in the vicinity of Courtland, Ala. I regret that the smallness of my cavalry force and the consequent necessity of concentrating it all here have compelled me to order Armstrong to return with his command to this point. I beg leave to commend him to the favorable notice of the general commanding the department and of the President.

I am, with the greatest respect, your obedient servant,
STERLING PRICE,
Major-General.

—

HDQRS. CAVALRY BRIGADE, ARMY OF THE WEST,
Moulton, Ala., July 26, 1862.

MAJOR: I have the honor to report that I reached here on the evening of the 24th instant. After conferring with Captain Roddey, from whom I gained all the valuable information I could desire, I determined to move early on the morning of the 25th to Courtland, 16 miles north of this, on the line of the Memphis and Charleston Railroad, and take the place, it being the center of guards and patrols for the portion of the road between Tuscumbia and Decatur. Sending Lieut. Col. D. C. Kelley with 140 of Forrest's cavalry to a point 7 miles west and two Partisan companies that are in the neighborhood 12 miles east of Courtland, to destroy and ambush the road from both directions, I moved from here with about 550 men, including the independent companies under Captain Roddey, at 1 a. m. on the morning of the 25th instant. Having arrived near Courtland, avoiding all roads as much as possible, I sent two companies under Captain Roddey and a detachment of 60 men, with long-range guns, selected from the several battalions, under Captain Champion, to advance upon the flank. I succeeded, through corn fields and by-paths, in getting within 500 yards of the enemy's camp, when I charged them with the main body of cavalry, the two commands of Captains Roddey and Champion moving promptly to the positions previously assigned them. The enemy's infantry fell back under cover of the railroad and fired a volley, but I soon crossed the railroad and charged down it on the north side, which drove them from the trestle work and forced them to take shelter under the bank of a creek, where it was impossible to get at them on horseback. I immediately pushed around some dismounted men to charge them on foot. Seeing this they ceased firing, threw down their arms, and surrendered. In getting to this infantry command I had to charge through the cavalry encampment, dispersed their cavalry, taking the commander and many others prisoners, captured 2 wagons and teams, 500 bushels sacked corn, many horses and equipments, a large number of arms, all the camp and garrison equipage of four companies, and six days' supplies; destroyed the telegraph line, three pieces of trestle work and a bridge, burned a depot, and took 133 prisoners (8 commissioned officers).

My loss was 3 killed and 5 wounded; the enemy same number killed and 6 wounded. From the statements of the officers I am satisfied that not more than 12 of the command made their escape.

My command was composed of portions of Webb's Louisiana Squadron, Barteau's Independent Battalion, McCulloch's Missouri Battalion, Captains Hill's, Sanders', Roddey's, and Newsom's companies. The officers and men behaved with coolness and gallantry, and I can proudly say gave entire satisfaction to myself, and gave evidence of what our cavalry can do if they are used with energy and boldness.

My thanks are due to Captain Hyams, assistant adjutant-general; Lieut. D. J. Armstrong, aide-de-camp, and to Col. T. J. Foster, volunteer aide-de-camp for the prompt manner in which my orders were delivered and for their gallant example in leading troops to the charge. Captain Roddey and Dr. Jones have my thanks for rendering me invaluable assistance, as it was from their information I based my plan that succeeded so well.

I would respectfully request that the balance of my brigade be sent to me, as I am satisfied that with it I can hold the valley of the Tennessee from Decatur to Tuscumbia, and prevent any communication by railroad or telegraph. This country is peculiarly adapted for cavalry service of this kind. Forage in abundance can be procured; subsistence, except sugar, coffee, and salt, can be purchased.

I am, sir, with respect, your obedient servant,

FRANK C. ARMSTRONG,
Brigadier-General.

Major SNEAD.

—

HDQRS. CAVALRY BRIGADE, ARMY OF THE WEST,
Moulton, Ala., July 26, 1862.

MAJOR: I send, under Major Smith (McCulloch's battalion), 8 Federal officers taken at Courtland on the 25th instant. The non-commissioned officers and privates I have paroled, numbering 125. I could not feed them and had not the men to spare to guard them to headquarters of department. I brought them to this place last night and will send them into Tuscumbia to-morrow. General Thomas' division has crossed at Florence and ordered to Huntsville. General Buell was at the latter place a few days ago. General Rosecrans' division is now or will be to-night at Tuscumbia. The railroad has been destroyed by my command, and I am fully under the impression that there are to-day no troops between Tuscumbia and Decatur. With the remainder of my brigade I can stop all communication on this side of the river between the two points. I can easily forage my command, and can also procure subsistence, excepting sugar, coffee, and salt. Corn meal and beef I can get in abundance. I hope the general will send every available man of my brigade immediately forward via Russellville and Mount Hope. After leaving Fulton forage sufficient can be obtained along the whole route. Major Smith would be a suitable officer to bring them up. I would request that you order my brigade commissary and quartermaster to procure funds and join me. The horses sent to Aberdeen might remain a few weeks longer. Instruct the officer who may bring the command to me to push up to Russellville rapidly and then to report his arrival to me, as I will have need of a force in that direction.

I have the honor to be, with respect, your obedient servant,

FRANK C. ARMSTRONG,
Brigadier-General.

Maj. THOMAS L. SNEAD,
Acting Assistant Adjutant-General.

P. S.—Since writing the above I learn that a very large force moved up the railroad to-day toward Courtland from Tuscumbia.

JULY 25, 1862.—Skirmish at Clinton Ferry, Tenn.

Report of Assistant Adjutant-General H. L. Clay, C. S. Army.

HEADQUARTERS DEPARTMENT OF EAST TENNESSEE,
Knoxville, Tenn., July 25, 1862.

COLONEL: Captain Blalock, commanding company of cavalry at Clinton, reports that at sunrise this morning his pickets at the ferry were fired upon by the enemy. He sent re-enforcements, when a skirmish occurred, resulting in the wounding of one man. Believing he was about being surrounded he retreated.

The major-general commanding directs me to give you the report of Captain Blalock, and suggests that the enemy may be a foraging party. If they cross the river you will move your brigade promptly forward and drive them back. You will be supported in the movement by Colonel Taylor's brigade.

Very respectfully, your obedient servant,

H. L. CLAY,
Assistant Adjutant-General.

Col. A. W. REYNOLDS, *Commanding Fourth Brigade.*

(NOTE.—Similar letter to Col. T. H. Taylor, commanding Fifth Brigade.)

—

HEADQUARTERS DEPARTMENT OF EAST TENNESSEE,
Knoxville, Tenn., July 26, 1862.

GENERAL: The enemy attacked our cavalry at Clinton yesterday morning. It was reported by our secret police last night that it was also intended to attack Knoxville with cavalry and infantry this morning at daylight. It seems that some of their scouts were within a very short distance from this place some time during the night. Information of these facts was sent to Colonels Reynolds and Taylor, with instructions to forward it to you without delay.

The major-general commanding directs that a regiment be ordered to this place from Colonel Reynolds' command, and dispatches to that end have been already forwarded to Colonel Reynolds. He further directs me to say that you will send some infantry to Clinton.

Very respectfully, your obedient servant,

H. L. CLAY,
Assistant Adjutant-General.

Brig. Gen. C. L. STEVENSON,
Commanding Division, Bean's Station, Tenn.

JULY 26, 1862.—Action near Spangler's Mill, near Jonesborough, Ala.

REPORTS.

No. 1.—Maj. Gen. Ulysses S. Grant, U. S. Army, commanding District of West Tennessee.

No. 2.—Maj. Gilbert Moyers, Third Michigan Cavalry.

No. 3.—General Braxton Bragg, C. S. Army.

No. 1.

Report of Maj. Gen. Ulysses S. Grant, U. S. Army, commanding District of West Tennessee.

HEADQUARTERS DISTRICT OF WEST TENNESSEE,
Corinth, July 28, 1862.

GENERAL: A report received late last night from General Morgan states that three companies of cavalry, under Major Moyers, went out southeast from Tuscumbia to attack a party of rebel cavalry which had surprised and captured two companies of General Thomas' command and burned the bridge near Courtland. They found the enemy about 200 strong and made the attack, losing 23 killed, wounded, and missing. Does not state whether the enemy were repulsed with loss or not and gives no dates.

General Ross, at Bolivar, is threatened by a strong force, possibly Price's. I have had him re-enforced as much as possible from Jackson and have sent six regiments of infantry and one battery from here. There was some skirmishing yesterday at the crossing of the Hatchie, northwest of Bolivar, about 8 miles distant. This change of troops is only intended to be temporary, but the necessity may arise to keep a larger force on the line of the Hatchie than we have had.

There is an evident disposition on the part of many of the citizens to join the guerrillas on their approach. I am decidedly in favor of turning all discontented citizens within our lines out south.

Colonel Sheridan has gone, with all the available cavalry belonging here, to attack and drive out a body of rebel cavalry that are pressing or conscripting men in that neighborhood. I will probably hear from them to-morrow.

I am, general, very respectfully, your obedient servant,
U. S. GRANT,
Major-General.

Maj. Gen. H. W. HALLECK, *Washington City, D. C.*

No. 2.

Report of Maj. Gilbert Moyers, Third Michigan Cavalry.

HDQRS. THIRD BATTALION THIRD MICHIGAN CAVALRY,
In Camp, near Tuscumbia, Ala., July 27, 1862.

SIR: Having been ordered at 1.30 o'clock on the morning of the 26th instant to take Companies L, H, and M, of the Third Regiment Michigan Cavalry, and move out to the south of Leighton and scour the country, for the purpose of intercepting whatever of the enemy's forces there might be in that direction, I respectfully submit the following report:

At daybreak I had gained the Tuscumbia and Chattanooga road, and moved southward on the road leading to La Grange until I came to the county-line road, which I followed until I came to a point about 8 miles south of the Tuscumbia and Chattanooga road, where I took a by-road, leading southeastward to the Russellville road; thence to Spangler's Mill, near which the Moulton and Courtland roads intersect. After I had gained the Russellville road, and when within about one-half mile of the mill, I halted near a school-house, standing in the edge of the woods on the left of the road, sent forward Company M, in command of Lieutenant McEntee, for the purpose of making a dash upon the mill, to secure, if possible, a small force of rebel pickets which I had learned were stationed at that point, and after having extended the advance and rear guards a little I ordered my men to dismount. While in this situation I was suddenly apprised of the approach of a column of rebel cavalry, since variously estimated at from 150 to 300 strong. I immediately formed my force, consisting of Companies L and H, in column of squadrons in the margin of the woods fronting the enemy's point of ingress. Scarcely had this movement been effected when the enemy dashed down, formed a line under our fire nearly parallel and not to exceed 6 rods in distance. For about ten minutes the fire from both sides was sharp and withering, both ranks being sensibly thinned. But the enemy still continued to rush down the road in overwhelming numbers, increased their front, and concentrated a fire upon my force, compelling them to give way, which movement was effected in tolerable order at a point about 10 rods in rear of my first position. I partially succeeded in forming a second line on the bank of a ravine, for the purpose of holding the enemy in check until I could rally upon the opposite bank. This I effected under a galling fire, and with a loss, by accident, of several horses and perhaps one or two men. While my men, thus formed, were pouring an irregular fire upon the enemy, Company M, having returned from the mill, formed in the road and poured in volley after volley with terrible effect. This timely and well-executed movement of Lieutenant McEntee diverted the attention of the enemy and gave me time to change my position to the enemy's left, upon which I advanced with dismounted skirmishers. Meanwhile Lieutenant McEntee, perceiving himself flanked, drew his men off in good order, but was hotly pursued for about 4 miles. He returned by way of the Courtland road.

Finding it impossible to push my men forward to a new engagement I deemed it proper to withdraw, which was done in good order. After proceeding a short distance I came to a by-road leading back to the same point, and induced my men to return again, to look after the wounded, and, if possible, to form a junction with Lieutenant McEntee; but, on coming within sight of the enemy, we were repulsed and forced to retreat for some distance through the woods.

The strength of my command was as follows: Company L, 33; Company H, 24; Company M, 32.

Our loss was 11 men missing and about 20 horses. The loss on the part of the enemy must have been far greater.

G. MOYERS,
Major, Third Michigan Cavalry, Comdg. Third Battalion.

CHARLES WILLS,
Actg. Asst. Adjt. Gen., First Brig., Cav. Div., Army of the Miss.

No. 3.

Report of General Braxton Bragg, C. S. Army.

CHATTANOOGA, TENN., *August* 3, 1862.

General Price reports another successful attack on the enemy by Armstrong's cavalry on 26th instant [ultimo], near Jonesborough, Ala., routing four companies. Their loss, 9 killed, 5 wounded, and 16 prisoners. Ours, 1 wounded.

BRAXTON BRAGG.

General S. COOPER:

JULY 27–30, 1862.—**Expedition from Woodville to Guntersville, Ala., and skirmishes (28th) at Guntersville and Law's Landing, and (29th) at Old Deposit Ferry.**

Report of Maj. James W. Paramore, Third Ohio Cavalry.

WOODVILLE, ALA., *July* 31, 1862.

SIR: I have the honor to report the entire success of the expedition sent out under my command on the 27th instant for the purpose of destroying the ferries on the Tennessee River from Law's Landing down to Whitesburg.

In accordance with instructions, the expedition—consisting of the Fifteenth Kentucky Infantry, commanded by Major Campbell, and a section of Loomis' battery, commanded by Lieutenant Chandler—left Huntsville on the morning of the 27th and proceeded by rail to Woodville, where we were joined by the Third Battalion of the Third Ohio Cavalry, in command of Maj. [Charles B.] Seidel, from which place I proceeded with the whole command, as above stated, for the Tennessee River, which we reached about 8 o'clock the same day, and encamped opposite Matthews' Landing, a distance of about 20 miles from Woodville, and over a rough, mountainous road. This was the first point on the route where we could get forage and water for our animals, and although it was a fatiguing march, it was accomplished without a murmur, so eager were the officers and men for the accomplishment of the purpose for which they were sent. I sent out the same evening of our arrival a strong picket, consisting of infantry and cavalry, to each of the ferries at Law's and Matthews' Landings, and also a squadron of cavalry, in command of Major Seidel, down to Guntersville, to watch the movements of the enemy, guard the boats, and prevent any one from crossing to give information of our approach. A courier from Major Seidel informed me that he was apprehensive that they would move their boats from Guntersville unless prevented by our artillery.

Accordingly I left the guards at Matthews' and Law's Ferries and proceeded with the command by daylight the next morning to Guntersville. I found the town strongly garrisoned by Forrest's cavalry and some independent companies of guerrillas and bushwhackers raised in the vicinity, with a heavy picket guard down at the landing guarding their boats and a warehouse filled with forage and commissary stores. I concealed most of my forces and artillery in a wood a short distance back from the landing, and deployed two companies of infantry as skirmishers to reconnoiter the position and ascertain the whereabouts of the enemy at the landing. True to their bushwhacking mode of warfare the enemy soon fired on them from their concealed positions behind trees and the old buildings on the opposite side of the river. The fire was returned by our skirmishers and cavalry pickets and continued for a short time sharply on both sides, when I ordered one piece of artillery to be placed on the high bluff above the landing in a position to command their camp and the town and the other so as to command the landing and buildings opposite.

At about 7 a. m. we commenced a simultaneous shelling of their camp and the woods on the island above the landing with an occasional round of canister, which soon scattered the astonished rebels in every direction and set them to riding and running in the utmost confusion, and with the assistance of our carbines and long-range rifles soon cleared the opposite shore. The enemy having taken all their boats and skiffs to the opposite shore and concealed them in the creek between the town and the island (as shown in the accompanying diagram*), it was necessary that we should cross the river to destroy them.

Accordingly I set some men to work constructing a raft with such material as we had at our command for the purpose of crossing the river to destroy their boats. The enemy, perceiving our object, gathered in the old buildings opposite and commenced firing on the workmen. I then directed Lieutenant Chandler to shell those buildings, which he did, and they were soon discovered to be on fire, and the flames spread rapidly and consumed that part of the town.

As soon as the raft was completed Captain Allen, of the Fifteenth Kentucky, and 10 men volunteered for the daring feat of crossing the river in search of the boats, and the raft not being large enough to carry more, one brave fellow swam the river to assist them. The party crossed safely to the island, and proceeded under cover of our guns up along the bank of the creek, and found that their boats had just been destroyed and sunk in the creek, all except one large one, which laid near the mouth of the creek partially sunk, but not destroyed. This they tried to raise and bring across, but the fire of the enemy's sharpshooters rendered it too hazardous, and Captain Allen abandoned it, and returned safely with his men to the command. I then ordered one of the guns down to a position below the landing, where the boat could be seen, and a few well-directed shells totally destroyed it. A vigorous fire was kept up on both sides from about 7 a. m. till 12 m., when the well-directed fire of our artillery had driven them from their camp and town to the mountains for safety, and the firing gradually subsided into an irregular skirmish of sharpshooters with long-range guns from concealed positions. This was continued until about 6 o'clock in the evening, when, having completed the destruction of their boats, and having no sufficient means of crossing my command to pursue the enemy further, I withdrew all the command except one company of cavalry and one of infantry (which I left on picket at that place to hold and watch the movements of the enemy) back to our old camp near Matthews' Landing.

All this was accomplished without any loss on our side except one man of the artillery slightly wounded in the foot. The loss of the enemy we could not ascertain definitely, but learned from a citizen who crossed the river the next day that their loss was about 30 killed and wounded, besides their camp and town badly damaged by our shells and about

---

*Omitted as unimportant

ten buildings, including the warehouse, filled with forage and commissary stores, burned.

Their force at that point and Law's and Matthews' Landings was variously estimated at from 600 to 1,200, all mounted, with no artillery, and is said to consist of a battalion of Forrest's cavalry or battalion of Adams' cavalry and two or three companies of guerrillas and bushwhackers raised in that vicinity.

During that night (Monday, 28th) the boat from Matthews' Ferry was moved up to Law's Landing and an attempt was made to cross under cover of night and get in our rear, but by the vigilance of Captain Spaulding, of the Fifteenth Kentucky, and his company, who were on picket guard at that place, they were prevented from crossing, and compelled to leave their boat, with a loss of 2 killed and several wounded.

The next morning I took a part of my forces, consisting of one company of cavalry and one of infantry and one gun, and went to that point and destroyed their boat, also giving them a farewell salute of a few shell in their camp, about a mile distant, but with what effect we could not ascertain. Having previously sent out scouting parties and thoroughly canvassed the shore for boats and ascertained that there were none, at least that could be found between that point and Guntersville, we returned to camp and collected our forces and proceeded down the river toward Whitesburg and encamped at Cottonville, near the Old Deposit Ferry. Then I sent a small force, consisting of one company of cavalry and one gun, under command of Major Seidel, down to the ferry to destroy the boat at that point. On their approach the rebel pickets cut the boat loose and it floated down the stream over a mile before it was discovered, when the first shot from the artillery struck and sunk it. Having accomplished their object they returned to camp.

The next morning I sent Major Seidel with a detachment of cavalry on a scout to Ferrin's Landing, about 4 miles below Deposit, to ascertain if there were any boats at that place, and report if necessary to destroy them. I then left one piece of artillery and one company of cavalry and one of infantry at the road leading to this point to assist in destroying the boats, if necessary, and proceeded with the balance of the command to Vienna, and there awaited their arrival. When they came up Major Seidel reported that he found one large boat on this side of the river at that point and another on the opposite side. He dismounted a part of his cavalry and crossed in the boat lying on this side, and procured the other and brought them both to this shore, and totally destroyed and sunk them without the aid of the other forces. They then pushed on and joined us at Vienna, where our command separated, Major Campbell, with the infantry and artillery, proceeding toward Whitesburg, and I returned with the cavalry the same evening (Wednesday, 30th) to our camp at Woodville.

I regret to record that while proceeding with the command near Vienna one of my men—James Weldon, of Company K, Third Ohio Volunteer Cavalry—was shot and instantly killed by a villain concealed in the thick woods near the road. I immediately sent out scouting parties in all directions, with instructions to shoot down all persons found in arms and arrest all male citizens found in the vicinity. Only one was found and arrested—McDonald, living in sight of where the man was shot. He denies all connection with or knowledge of the murder, but I think it almost impossible that he could not know something about it, if he was not actually engaged in it. I therefore send him to your headquarters for such punishment as you may think proper, fully satisfied that to put down bushwhacking vigorous and severe measures must be used, and all the citizens in the vicinity where these outrages are committed must be held responsible for them.

It would be injustice to close this report without speaking more particularly of the bravery and gallant conduct of all the officers and men composing the expedition. Without mentioning their names, I would say that all are entitled to great credit for the promptness with which they obeyed and executed all orders given and the energy they evinced in accomplishing the object for which they were sent; and I would particularly mention the names of Major Campbell, commanding the infantry; Lieutenant Chandler, commanding the artillery, and Major Seidel, commanding cavalry; also Captains Spaulding and Allen, of the Fifteenth Kentucky, and Lieutenant Heflebower, of Company G, Third Ohio Volunteer Cavalry, for their co-operation and valuable services rendered in the expedition.

During the route we destroyed seven boats, viz: one at Law's Landing, three at Guntersville, one at Deposit, and two at Ferrin's Landing; but I was hardly satisfied with our operations at Guntersville. I think that nest of treason and rendezvous of guerrillas and bushwhackers should be entirely destroyed and purified by fire, for as long as it is permitted to remain their facilities for reconstructing their boats and its proximity to the railroad will make it a dangerous place for the safety of our trains and railroad bridges and require it to be closely watched.

All of which is respectfully submitted.

J. W. PARAMORE,
Major, Third Ohio Volunteer Cavalry, Comdg. Expedition.

Lieutenant-Colonel MURRAY,
    Commanding Third Ohio Cavalry.

JULY 29, 1862.—Skirmish at Russellville, Ky.

Report of Brig. Gen. Jeremiah T. Boyle, U. S. Army.

LOUISVILLE, *July* 29, 1862.

COLONEL: Guerrillas infest the Green River counties. Fight in Russellville to-day. Lieutenant Burgher, of Twenty-sixth Kentucky, killed; Captain Morrow badly wounded, and others wounded in the fight. Fifty-fourth Indiana will reach them to-night.*

J. T. BOYLE,
General.

Col. J. B. FRY.

AUGUST 2–6, 1862.—Operations at Cumberland Gap and skirmish (6th) near Tazewell, Tenn.

Report of Brig. Gen. George W. Morgan, U. S. Army.

CUMBERLAND GAP, *August* 7, 1862.

COLONEL: To obtain forage and feel and learn the strength of the enemy, De Courcy was ordered to Tazewell on the 2d instant. He

----

* Some matters of detail omitted from above dispatch.

secured 200 wagon loads of forage, all of which safely arrived on the 5th. Some slight picket skirmishing took place, in which we had 2 men wounded, while the enemy had 1 killed and several wounded.

Early in the morning of the 6th instant, not wishing to bring on a general action, I ordered Colonel De Courcy to return to this post, but he was attacked at daybreak on that day. Considering enemy's forces the attack was feeble. Two of his regiments surrounded two companies of the Sixteenth Ohio, detached to protect a section of artillery. The enemy's movement was well executed, and had it not been for the coolness and gallantry of Lieutenant Anderson we would have lost two pieces of artillery. Although surrounded by a vastly superior force, the two infantry companies, under command of Captains Edgar and Taneyhill, fought heroically, and three-fourths of them succeeded in cutting their way through to their regiments. But we fear that Captain Edgar, an officer of great merit, was killed, and Captain Taneyhill taken prisoner. There were several instances of distinguished conduct both on the part of officers and soldiers. A soldier of the Twenty-second Kentucky was shot through the neck and fell. His gun dropped from his hands; his foe contrived to advance upon him, when the wounded hero grasped his gun, rose to his feet and shot the rebel soldier dead when within five paces of him, when he again fell weltering in his blood. Two soldiers of the Sixteenth Ohio had lost their way and were going toward the enemy, when Lieutenant-Colonel Gordon, of the Eleventh Tennessee, hailed them, demanding their regiment. With coolness and courage they required him to declare his rank and regiment and took him prisoner. Resuming their march by a circuitous route they rejoined their commands. Gordon speaks highly of their courage and courteous treatment. At 3.30 p. m. a courier arrived from Colonel De Courcy and asked for aid. Leaving three regiments to guard the Gap I marched with my remaining force to his assistance, but when within 2 miles of Tazewell I met him on his return. The enemy left the field at 5 o'clock and maintained his position until 7 o'clock p. m. The enemy's loss is believed to be considerable. I did not pursue, lest with a superior force, he should gain my rear.

GEORGE W. MORGAN,
Brigadier-General.

Col. J. B. FRY.

AUGUST 4–7, 1862.—Attack on Union pickets near Woodville, Ala. (4th), and reconnaissance from Woodville to Guntersville, Ala. (5th–7th).

Reports of Lieut. Col. Douglas A. Murray, Third Ohio Cavalry.

HEADQUARTERS THIRD OHIO CAVALRY,
Woodville, Ala., August 4, 1862.

COLONEL: I have the honor to inform you that between the hours of 3 and 4 our outward pickets on the Guntersville road were fired at from the bushes by a party of 10 guerrillas or bushwackers. One of the men was shot dead—the sergeant, a most worthy, good man, mortally wounded through the head, who died shortly afterward; the two other men were both dangerously wounded, only one of five escaping uninjured, who, being driven by the murderers, was forced to fall back. He describes the scene above as follows:

"The party, consisting of a sergeant and 4 privates, belonging to Company G, Third Ohio Cavalry, who were in the advance of the rest of the company at the outpost of the line of pickets on the road, about a mile and one-fourth distant from the camp, between the hours of 3 and 4 o'clock p. m., were fired on by a party of 10 or 12 armed men. The first intimation they had of their approach was a volley of ball and buckshot. He, being the only one of the party who escaped its fatal effects, fired his carbine and revolver upon the party, but being so hardly pressed by the entire number had to retire. All this was so quickly done that the other pickets had not time to come to the assistance of the unfortunate man. The murderers turned into the bushes, which just at that place were thick, the mountain steep and rocky. Lieutenant Heflebower, the officer in charge of the picket, dismounted some of the men and searched all over for them without success."

Hearing the firing in camp from the line of pickets I immediately sent out a squadron to scour the country in the neighborhood of the scene. After much trouble, found the tracks of the murderers up and across the mountain; taking a circuitous route to some houses about 1½ miles from where the firing took place, finding 4 men who could not account for themselves and from their contradictory statements were arrested. Finding any further efforts to make discoveries fruitless the command returned to camp. I brought each of the prisoners separately before the wounded men, then in the regimental hospital, one of whom, N. J. Fletcher, was identified immediately by Private [Lewis H.] Palmer, who is positive that he is the man that fired on him. Private Steckel, the only one of the party uninjured, also identified him, Fletcher, and one other, John Peters, jr., as being two of the men of the party of ten. The other two state that they were in company with Fletcher and Peters all day, and further their statements are both contradictory and changeable, and I have no doubt that each and all of them are guilty of the murders committed.

I had to use, assisted by the other officers of the regiment, the most strenuous efforts to prevent the men from lynching them, their guilt being so palpable. I hear from good authority that three of the ten men that are now in this vicinity bushwhacking are of those I have sent down to headquarters and who have been recently released, and are now boasting of being Union men.

Very respectfully, I have the honor to be, your obedient servant,

D. A. MURRAY,
Lieutenant-Colonel Third Ohio Cavalry, Commanding.

P. S.—Since writing the above Private Steckel has recognized Lewis Turner, another of the prisoners, also John Peters, as being two that were of the party. Private William Smith, Company C, recognizes one of the prisoners, Fletcher, as being one that fired upon him a few days since; Private Smith is now lying in hospital from wounds received, he states, by his hands.

Respectfully, yours,

D. A. MURRAY,
Lieutenant-Colonel Third Ohio Cavalry, Commanding.

Col. J. B. FRY, *Chief of Staff, Army of the Ohio.*

———

HEADQUARTERS THIRD OHIO CAVALRY,
In Camp, Woodville, Ala., August 7, 1862.

COLONEL: I have the honor to report for your information that the squadron of the Third Ohio Cavalry that left these headquarters on the morning of the 5th instant on a reconnaissance to the river opposite to Guntersville returned this day at noon.

The officer in command of the squadron reports that the encampment of the enemy has been moved back from the river about 2 miles, and there appears to be a larger force there now than when our troops, accompanied by artillery and infantry, were there. The enemy have dug rifle pits, and have also mounted two pieces of artillery to command the old ferries at that point. The ferry-boats destroyed by our troops are being repaired, and I have heard from good authority will be ready for use this day or to-morrow. It is rumored that they, the enemy, will cross with the intention of destroying the bridges on the railroad as soon as they possibly can. If not too great a liberty, might I suggest that two pieces of artillery may be sent to this point or the bridge near by. I have no doubt if artillery were here and could be spared they would render good service. The country being so miserably adapted for cavalry being as effectual as they otherwise would be on more suitable ground might be obviated by having the assistance of artillery. If artillery cannot be spared, two companies of infantry would, I have no doubt, prevent any damage being done to railroad in our vicinity.

The squadron arrested Mr. Hornbuckle, a noted bushwhacker, who attempted after his arrest to escape, and did succeed in getting off some distance; would have made good his escape but for the steps taken to prevent it.

Very respectfully, I have the honor to be, your obedient servant,

D. A. MURRAY,
Lieutenant-Colonel Third Ohio Cavalry, Commanding.

Col. J. B. FRY, *Chief of Staff.*

AUGUST 5, 1862.—Skirmish near New Market, Ala.

REPORTS, ETC.

No. 1.—Maj. Gen. D. C. Buell, U. S. Army, commanding Army of the Ohio.

No. 2.—Maj. Gen. George H. Thomas, U. S. Army, commanding First Division, with order announcing death of Brigadier-General Robert L. McCook.

No. 3.—Col. Ferdinand Van Derveer, Thirty-fifth Ohio Infantry, commanding Third Brigade.

No. 1.

Report of Maj. Gen. D. C. Buell, U. S. Army, commanding Army of the Ohio.

HUNTSVILLE, ALA., *August 9, 1862.*

It is with pain I inform you that Brig. Gen. Robert L. McCook died at 12 m. on the 6th of a gunshot wound or wounds inflicted by guerrillas on the previous day near New Market, Ala. He was indisposed, and was riding in an ambulance some distance ahead of brigade, with a member of his staff and a small escort. He had stopped to see about a camping ground for his command, when the party was attacked by a band of guerrillas, one of whom rode up to the ambulance and shot him in the side.

D. C. BUELL,
Major-General, Commanding.

Brig. Gen. LORENZO THOMAS.

No. 2.

Reports of Maj. Gen. George H. Thomas, U. S. Army, commanding First Division, with order announcing death of Brigadier-General McCook.

HDQRS. FIRST DIVISION, DISTRICT OF THE OHIO,
Decherd, Tenn., August 7, 1862.

GENERAL: General R. L. McCook died of his wounds yesterday at 12 o'clock. It seems that he was riding some distance ahead of his command in an ambulance (being sick), with his escort, and stopped at a house belonging to a man named Petit to inquire about water and a camping ground; sent his escort a short distance ahead to the edge of a woods, where they were fired upon, and before he could turn his ambulance around and return to his command the escort retreated, and a man riding alongside of the ambulance shot him through the side.

His regiment were very much enraged, and before they could be stopped burned and destroyed some four or five farm-houses; but Colonel Van Derveer, by great exertions, succeeded in subjugating them to discipline before night, and they are now quiet.

GEO. H. THOMAS,
Major-General, U. S. Volunteers.

Major-General BUELL.

—

DECHERD, *August 7, 1862.*

The attack on General McCook occurred not far from New Market, on the road between Hazel Green and Winchester. Colonel Van Derveer thinks they were guerrillas, but Captain Brooke, who was captured, wrote a note to Colonel Van Derveer, stating that the attack was made by regular Confederate States cavalry, and that he was a prisoner of a Captain Hambrick, who offers to exchange him for his (Hambrick's) brother, a prisoner in Huntsville. I am inclined to the belief that citizens were giving assistance, but do not know who.

GEO. H. THOMAS,
Major-General.

Col. J. B. FRY, *Chief of Staff.*

—

GENERAL ORDERS, }   HDQRS. FIRST DIV., DIST. OF THE OHIO,
    No. 8.   }   *Camp near Decherd, August 7, 1862.*

The major-general commanding announces with deep regret to the troops of this division the death of Brig. Gen. Robert L. McCook, who departed this life at 12 o'clock m. on the 6th instant from wounds received from a party of guerrillas, who attacked him while proceeding in an ambulance *en route* from Athens, Ala., to this place.

General McCook entered the volunteer service at the commencement of the rebellion; won a name for himself and command by his daring exploits in Western Virginia, and added greatly to his fame at the battle of Mill Springs, where he was severely wounded whilst conducting a charge with his gallant regiment. He was affable in his manners and a courteous gentleman. A brave officer and a congenial friend is lost to this division, and the country has been deprived of a general who was firm and devoted to its interests.

Whilst we deplore his loss let us be steady in our efforts to maintain such discipline as will insure to our arms a just retribution upon the dastardly foe who could take advantage of his defenseless condition.

In respect for his memory the usual badge of mourning will be worn for thirty days.

By command of Maj. Gen. George H. Thomas:

GEO. E. FLYNT,
Assistant Adjutant-General and Chief of Staff.

No. 3.

Report of Col. Ferdinand Van Derveer, Thirty-fifth Ohio Infantry, commanding Third Brigade.

HEADQUARTERS THIRD BRIGADE, ARMY OF THE OHIO,
Camp near Winchester, Tenn., August 9, 1862.

SIR: It becomes my melancholy duty to report that while a portion of the Third Brigade, composed of the Ninth Ohio Volunteers, the Second Minnesota Volunteers, and the Thirty-fifth Ohio Volunteers, under the command of Brig. Gen. Robert L. McCook, were on their march from Athens, Ala., to this point, at a point near the southern line of Tennessee General McCook, who was sick and riding in an open carriage upon his bed, about 3 miles in advance of the troops, accompanied by Capt. Hunter Brooke, of his staff, and Major Boynton, of the Thirty-fifth Ohio, together with nine members of his escort, was suddenly attacked by a band of mounted guerrillas, numbering between 100 and 200 men, about noon on the 5 h instant.

Major Boynton, with one of the escort and a citizen mounted on the horse of another, had been sent a half a mile to the rear, and three members of the escort, including the sergeant, a like distance to the front, in search of suitable camping ground for the brigade, thus leaving but four of the escort with General McCook, one of whom was dismounted, and Captain Brooke, who was unarmed and in the carriage attending upon the general, when the attack began.

The general succeeded in turning his carriage, but not before the guerrillas were within range and firing. He was soon overtaken and surrounded, although his horses were running at the top of their speed. In reply to the oft-repeated cry of "Stop!" "Stop!" the general rose in his bed and exclaimed, "Don't shoot; the horses are running; we will stop as soon as possible." Notwithstanding this surrender those riding within a few feet by the side of the carriage fired, one ball passing through his hat and one inflicting a mortal wound in the abdomen, which produced death twenty-four hours after, at noon of August 6.

The alarm having reached the column, it was hurried up at double-quick and almost immediately encountered the advance of the band, but a few shots from the head of the Thirty-fifth scattered them instantly. General McCook was found in a house near where he was shot, whither Captain Brooke and the driver of the carriage had carried him. Of those in advance, Captain Brooke, two members of the escort, and two teamsters of the Ninth Ohio, who were driving General McCook's own wagons, were captured, and one member of the Ninth Ohio band wounded by a saber cut on the head. General McCook's wagons were fired but not greatly damaged. The three horses attached to this team and the mules of one other brigade team were taken.

The condition of General McCook could not but have been known to the attacking party, as he was on his bed, divested of all outer clothing, except a hat used as a shade, and the curtains of the carriage being raised on all sides. There are good reasons for supposing that the attack was planned solely for General McCook's capture or murder.

Infuriated by this cowardly assassination, many of the soldiers of the brigade spread themselves over the country before any measures could be taken to check them, and burned all the property of rebels in the vicinity and shot a rebel lieutenant who was on furlough and supposed to be connected with the gang.

I have the honor to be, very respectfully, your obedient servant,

FERDINAND VAN DERVEER,
Colonel Thirty-fifth Ohio Volunteers, Comdg. Third Brigade.

Maj. GEORGE E. FLYNT, *Assistant Adjutant-General.*

AUGUST 7, 1862.—Attack on convalescent train near Decatur, Ala.

REPORTS.

No. 1.—Lieut. Col. Luther P. Bradley, Fifty-first Illinois Infantry.
No. 2.—General Braxton Bragg, C. S. Army.
No. 3.—Maj. Gen. Sterling Price, C. S. Army.

No. 1.

Report of Lieut. Col. Luther P. Bradley, Fifty-first Illinois Infantry.

HEADQUARTERS FIFTY-FIRST ILLINOIS VOLUNTEERS,
Decatur, Ala., August 7, 1862.

Wires cut, so I cannot telegraph you. The convalescent train from Tuscumbia was attacked this a. m., about 5.30, near Moseley's plantation, about 2½ miles from here. There were over 200 men in the column, and of these one-half are missing. One hundred came in, and we have 2 killed and 2 wounded.

The attack was made by some 250 rebel cavalry. They came from their camp, some 9 miles south of here, last night, and crossed over to the Courtland road before morning. Their designs were to attack and cut off our patrol, and if they had not fallen in with the convalescents would have done it without doubt. Major Koehler turned out promptly as soon as we heard of it and took the road after them. He followed them to Silses' plantation, near Minty, across the railroad and nearly to the foot of the mountains, but could not overtake them. I do not think they have taken a large number of prisoners. Most of the missing men are probably scattered through the woods and will come in to-day or to-morrow. You will see from this that the rebels are showing some little enterprise. It is already unsafe to send foraging parties over 2 or 3 miles out, and when Colonel Starkweather leaves (he is already under marching orders) you may expect to see a part of your command in trouble. Unless we are re-enforced we cannot protect this part of the line. They can run us into our defenses any day and keep us there if they choose.

Captain Rose sent out a corporal and 4 men yesterday to repair telegraph. Returning they were fired upon by a band of 50 rebels. One man mortally wounded, 1 slightly, and 1 missing.

L. P. BRADLEY,
Lieutenant-Colonel, Commanding.

Colonel HARRINGTON, *Comdg. First Brig., First Div.*

No. 2.

Report of General Braxton Bragg, C. S. Army.

CHATTANOOGA, TENN., *August* 15, 1862.

Captain Roddey reports his attack, with three companies cavalry, upon the enemy near Decatur, Ala. Captured 123 prisoners. One officer killed and wounded many, and brought off 56 small-arms.

BRAXTON BRAGG.

General S. COOPER, *Adjutant and Inspector General.*

No. 3.

Report of Maj. Gen. Sterling Price.

TUPELO, MISS., *August* 14, 1862.

Captain Roddey, commanding scouts, reports a charge made by him with three companies upon a force of the enemy near Decatur. Captured 123 men, 1 officer, brought off 56 guns, killed and wounded many of the enemy; lost 1 man killed and 3 wounded. Reports enemy fortified at Town Creek, Courtland, Mallett's Creek, Fox's Creek, and Trinity. All their movements continue to be eastward.

STERLING PRICE.

Brig. Gen. THOMAS JORDAN,
      Chief of Staff, Chattanooga, Tenn.

AUGUST 11, 1862.—Affair near Kinderhook, Tenn.

Reports of Brig. Gen. James S. Negley, U. S. Army.

COLUMBIA, TENN., *August* 11, 1862—3 p. m.

My movement against the guerrillas who have committed the great outrage has been completely successful. Megowan's command of Third Kentucky Cavalry and First Tennessee Cavalry, 108 men, engaged 175 of the enemy near Kinderhook at 5 a. m., continuing the contest fiercely for four hours. Seven were found killed, numbers wounded, 27 prisoners, among whom are a number of officers. Our loss was 3 killed. The woody and broken character of the country and the combatants scattered prevents an accurate estimate of the enemy's loss. I have received news from Maj. F. H. Kennedy, of my staff, commanding another portion of the expedition. He is driving the enemy in every direction.

JAS. S. NEGLEY,
      Brigadier-General, Commanding.

Hon. E. M. STANTON.

COLUMBIA, *August* 16, 1862.

Maj. Rogers, Kennett's cavalry, has just returned from Centreville, having driven the guerrillas from that place.

The Third Kentucky are just in from a scout. Part of the battalion is in Nashville getting horses.

The two companies First Kentucky are in readiness to surprise a small party of guerrillas at Cedar Springs.

The defeat of the guerrillas at Kinderhook was of greater importance than first reported, both in killed, wounded, and dispersion of the band.

> JAS. S. NEGLEY,
> *Brigadier-General.*

Col. J. B. FRY.

—

COLUMBIA, *August* 17, 1862.

You will be pleased to hear that the defeat of Napier's and Anderson's guerrillas near Kinderhook was more complete than reported. Upwards of 20 are reported killed, the band stricken with terror, and scattered in every direction. A prisoner captured yesterday gives the following, I believe, reliable information : Headquarters Cooper's band removed to Persimmon Branch, 6 miles west of Ashland; Col. Jake Biffle's headquarters 5 miles south of Ashland; Tom Williams' Buffalo Creek, 8 miles southwest of Henryville.

When the Third Kentucky get their horses if they could be used against these nests it would be good policy. These sudden surprises frighten many of the scoundrels back to their homes. Six hundred citizens of this county have taken the oath this week. I hope to have every prominent citizen in this county under oath or out of the lines by the end of next week.

> JAS. S. NEGLEY,
> *Brigadier-General.*

Col. J. B. FRY, *Chief of Staff.*

AUGUST 12–13, 1862.—Capture of Gallatin, Tenn., and destruction of bridges in that vicinity (12th), and skirmish (13th).

REPORTS.

No. 1.—Col. John F. Miller, Twenty-ninth Indiana Infantry, of skirmish August 13.

No. 2.—Maj. William H. Sidell, Fifteenth U. S. Infantry, and Acting Assistant Adjutant-General.

No. 3 —Capt. Walworth Jenkins, Assistant Quartermaster, U. S. Army, of the surrender of Gallatin.

No. 4.—General Braxton Bragg, C. S. Army, of the surrender of Gallatin.

No. 5.—Asst. Adjt. Gen. J. F. Belton, C. S. Army, of the surrender of Gallatin and the destruction of bridges in that vicinity.

No. 1.

Reports of Col. John F. Miller, Twenty-ninth Indiana Infantry, of skirmish August 13.

GALLATIN, *August* 13, 1862.

MAJOR: It is ascertained that the rebel loss this morning was 4 killed and 10 wounded; 1 captain and 1 lieutenant killed. We had nobody hurt. The rebels were completely surprised. I am arresting nearly all the citizens, they being implicated in the destruction of property, &c.

JNO. F. MILLER.

Major SIDELL.

—

GALLATIN, August 13, 1862.

MAJOR: We have found 6 of the enemy killed, among whom is Captain Breckinridge, making 2 captains killed, 1 lieutenant, and 3 privates, and 2 wounded.

Please obtain answer as to what troops shall be left here as soon as possible. I desire to start back.

JNO. F. MILLER,
Colonel, Commanding.

Major SIDELL.

———

No. 2.

Report of Maj. William H. Sidell, Fifteenth U. S. Infantry, and Acting Assistant Adjutant-General.

NASHVILLE, August 13, 1862.

COLONEL: Colonel Miller has returned with his force, as by your dispatch ordered. Miller did not see Boone; he left in a wagon for Bowling Green, on parole, soon after Miller came. Cassilly saw Boone and also many paroled men, who accused Boone of complicity. These paroled men disappeared before they could be collected; supposed following Boone to Bowling Green. Only about 125 were captured; the rest guarding bridges and two companies absent on an expedition supposed escaped to Bowling Green. Boone and his staff were captured; no other field officers present. Morgan attacked at daylight; no gun was fired on either side. The pickets were asleep; were brought in by the enemy. Boone was in bed; all the others conveniently at hand for capture except 6 or 8, who were accidentally absent. When Miller saw the rebel force at Gallatin he found it difficult to distinguish between citizens and rebel soldiers either by appearance or conduct. One small bridge was destroyed 2 miles this side of Gallatin. Miller left his train there and marched into town. He drove such rebels as were there, killing a few. He sent out parties during the day to seek the enemy and examined damages. Fair Ground buildings destroyed; also 30 cars, of which 20 had Government forage and horses; depot was saved; wood work of tunnel and one bridge beyond Gallatin destroyed. A note-book found on a dead rebel captain revealed intentions some of which Miller prevented. The citizens helped burn the cars, and Morgan was highly applauded by the population; who came out from all the country around. On the other branch road bridge at Red River destroyed, thus interrupting both routes; supposed done by citizens.

This evening when Miller's men and guns were on cars to return rebel force closed in from all directions, firing. He got his men and guns down and the latter in battery; drove off the rebels, killing not less than 30. His loss, 1 killed, 3 wounded. Supposed enemy's intention to divert and detain him while their main force should come this way destroying bridges. Miller's success and return over the road to town prevented this.

W. H. SIDELL,
Major, Fifteenth Infantry and Acting Assistant Adjutant-General.
Col. J. B. FRY, *Assistant Adjutant-General.*

No. 3.

Report of Capt. Walworth Jenkins, Assistant Quartermaster, U. S. Army, of the surrender of Gallatin and destruction of bridges in that vicinity.

LOUISVILLE, KY., *August 25, 1862.*

SIR: I have the honor to transmit herewith my report in reference to the surrender of Gallatin, Tenn., by Colonel Boone, Twenty-eighth Kentucky Volunteers, and a statement of the officers and men on that subject, which are marked respectively A and B, and inclosed herein.

I am, captain, very respectfully, your obedient servant,

W. JENKINS,
Captain, Assistant Quartermaster, U. S. Army.

Capt. H. C. McDOWELL,
Assistant Adjutant-General, Louisville, Ky.

LOUISVILLE, KY., *August 23, 1862.*

SIR: In compliance with Special Orders, No. 31, dated Headquarters United States forces in Kentucky, Louisville, August 17, 1862, directing an investigation of the circumstances attending the surrender of Gallatin, Tenn., I have to report as follows:

I have examined several of the officers and men belonging to Colonel Boone's command at Gallatin, Tenn. The results of this examination are embodied in a series of statements herewith inclosed, together with a copy of a rough pencil sketch* of the town of Gallatin and its approaches, made by Lieut. J. R. Boone, adjutant of the regiment. This sketch also shows the position of the various night pickets.

The statements of the various officers and men differ in many points, so that the true state of affairs can, in my judgment, only be reached by a properly constituted court of inquiry, which I would recommend be instituted.

With the slight information derived from these statements I cannot in justice to myself or the officers of Colonel Boone's command frame and prefer definite charges against them. I can only express the following general opinion and state a few facts which have been elicited by the examination:

It appears that Colonel Boone had been expecting an attack for some three weeks prior to the surprise and surrender of his command on the 12th instant, and that he had at various times applied to Colonel Miller at Nashville and to General Nelson at Murfreesborough for re-enforcements, which however, for reasons not within my knowledge, but doubtless known to those officers, were withheld.

Arrangements had been made to fortify the town and guard the

---

* Omitted.

bridges by stockades, but beyond cutting the timber for this purpose nothing had been done.

Colonel Boone's command consisted of five companies of his regiment (Twenty-eighth Kentucky), averaging, according to his statement, about 75 men each, making a force of about 375 men. Of this force one company (Captain O'Neill's) was detached from the main camp, guarding the tunnel and railroad bridges on the line of the Louisville and Nashville Railroad.

On the night of the 11th instant Colonel Boone, at the request of Colonel Bruce, commanding at Bowling Green, detached two of the remaining four companies after a drove of beef cattle, intended for the rebel forces. This was done, notwithstanding the rebels were known to be in the vicinity, threatening his command. Although this was doubtless done with the best intentions, it appears to have been a very serious error. These two companies did not and could not return, and, as from all reports they threw away their arms when no enemy was in sight, it is perhaps as well that they did not return to their main body. As to their reasons for thus relinquishing their only means of defense I know not, as none of them were present to be examined. Future examination must decide upon their conduct. The absence of these two companies reduced the strength of the command to about 124 muskets.

It appears that the pickets were posted by Lieutenant Boone, the adjutant of the regiment, and cautioned to extra vigilance. The pickets were in the habit of relieving themselves at reveille and returning to camp. No pickets, mounted or foot, were posted during the day-time, and the excuse given for this great neglect is that the command was too weak.

It appears that Colonel Boone visited the pickets in and near the town between 1 and 2 a. m. on the 12th and then went to his hotel, where his wife was lying sick, and remained there until about 4 o'clock. As he was about returning to his camp, and just as he was leaving the room, some dozen or more rebels confronted him and made him prisoner. No alarm whatever had been given either by the mounted pickets stationed on the Scottsville and Hartsville pikes respectively, at a distance of some 4 miles from town, or by the pickets between the town and the mounted pickets, or by the guards stationed in the city. Not a gun was fired by any of those to whom the safety of the command was intrusted, and everything goes to show that they were either asleep or shamefully neglecting their duty. The result was a shameful and complete surprise within two hours after Colonel Boone had left his guards "on the alert and doing their duty," and the surrender of the whole command in camp, on guard, and at the tunnel and bridges without a shot being fired for the defense of their position, the reputation of their State, or the honor of their country.

The sleeping of sentinels on their posts appears to have been of no uncommon occurrence, and yet no punishment proportionate to this offense appears to have been inflicted; and from the statement of one of the officers it seems that there was an almost total want of discipline in the command.

Colonel Boone appears to have been vigilant and endeavoring to perform his duty as well as possible with the means at his disposal. Whether or not the command could have made any defense with a hope of success after they were surprised and surrounded I will not attempt to decide; but the fault of the surprise must rest on the pickets and guards in a great measure.

The absence of all guards and pickets during the day, and especially when an attack was expected, indicates great carelessness or wanton neglect on the part of the officers in command. I would recommend that a list of all the men forming the guards or pickets be furnished and a court of inquiry instituted to report on the conduct of each and every man on this duty.

Respectfully submitted.

W. JENKINS,
Captain and Assistant Quartermaster, U. S. Army.
Capt. H. C. McDOWELL, *Assistant Adjutant-General.*

[Inclosure A.]

Statement of Colonel Boone, Twenty-eighth Kentucky Volunteers.

I took command at Gallatin, Tenn., about 1st May, 1862, with five companies of Twenty-eighth Kentucky Volunteers, averaging about 75 men each. After being detached for some time at Lebanon and other points, guarding bridges, returned to Gallatin.

I have been apprehensive for about three weeks that an attack would be made on my position. This I made known to General Nelson, and applied for re-enforcements, and especially for some cavalry, for the purpose of scouting. Expected the enemy was at Sparta or above Carthage in that direction. Carthage is 32 miles above Gallatin, on the Cumberland River, and same side. Communicated my information to Colonel Miller at Nashville by telegraph, and also by adjutant, asking for re-enforcements. Morgan was supposed to have about 1,200 men and Starnes from 800 to 1,500, and were expected to combine forces.

My troops were disposed as follows: Captain O'Neill was sent with his company to the south tunnel, 7 miles north of Gallatin, on the railroad, with orders to have at least 20 men there, and the balance distributed between five bridges and the tank on the line of the road between the tunnel and the Kentucky line, the most distant being 7 miles north of the tunnel and 14 miles from Gallatin. The remaining four companies were distributed as follows: One sergeant and 10 men at tunnel 4 miles north of Gallatin; 1 sergeant and 10 men at bridge 2 miles south of Gallatin; 1 sergeant and 10 men at bridge at Pilot Knob, 7 miles south, and a regular daily detail of 1 sergeant and 10 men to guard the depot and tank at Gallatin.

The evening before the attack Colonel Bruce, at Bowling Green, sent to me to re-enforce a party of his command who were after a drove of beef cattle, moving in the direction of Carthage, for the Confederate forces. After some hesitation and on receiving a second dispatch from Colonel Bruce I finally concluded to scout in that direction, and sent out two companies, under Captains Noble and White, of about 50 men each, to scout toward La Fayette and Carthage (that being the direction from which I feared an attack), ordering them to press horses and mount the men as soon as they were about 5 miles from town, and to get all their men mounted. This was the only disposition possible to form a junction with the detachment of Colonel Bruce. But fearing they might be intercepted by Morgan's forces ordered them to retreat to our camp in case they discovered anything of them. I did not make known this movement or send the force out until late at night, when the people had retired, so as not to have my weakened position known. They were instructed to keep an advanced guard not less than 2 miles in advance (about 10 men), and a similar guard on each flank as scouts, so as to embrace a considerable tract for observation. Being more apprehensive of an attack on account of my weakened condition, I gave orders for greater diligence on the part of the pickets. The main camp was at the Fair Grounds, three-fourths of a mile westwardly from Gallatin, consisting of parts of two companies. The camp was encircled by the usual camp guard, and an infantry picket guard, more extended, in the fields and woods, encircling the camp at a distance of about 300 yards. The adjutant placed the pickets. Infantry pickets were posted also at the bridge near town, at the court-house, and at the upper end of the street running in front of the court-house. Cavalry pickets were stationed on the various roads leading from Gallatin at distances from 3½ to 7 miles. The mounted pickets were ordered in case of an alarm or advance of the enemy to fall back to the vicinity of the infantry pickets and fire so as to give the alarm, and the infantry pickets were then to fall back firing so as to alarm the camp guard.

I occupied the time, after sending out the two companies above mentioned, in visiting the infantry pickets, to see that all were on the alert until 2 o'clock at night, and found them all at their posts doing their duty, and I cautioned them to extra vigilance. I then went to my hotel, where my wife was dangerously ill, and spent about an hour and a half there. I then adjusted my pistol, and just as I was starting out to make my final tour of the pickets I heard a knock at my door and supposed it was some of my pickets, as I had told those nearest where to find me if anything occurred. On opening the door some 20 men were seen, about a dozen of them presenting their revolvers at me and demanded my immediate surrender. Their pistols were cocked and the men much excited, apparently being afraid of shots from my pickets. I endeavored to gain time in parley, hoping my pickets would take the alarm and come up. On my asking by what authority their demand was made one of them stated that he was Captain Desha, of Brig. Gen. John Morgan's cavalry; that I was completely in their power, as my camp was surrounded by 1,200 cavalry, and demanded the surrender of myself and camp. I told them that I didn't believe it, and that I would never surrender my camp. They then demanded the immediate surrender of my person. I told them I would surrender my person if they would state the terms and I liked them. They replied, "As a prisoner of war, with the privilege of an immediate parole." I replied, "On these terms I will surrender." They then took my pistol and hurried me away in the direction of the court-house, where they said 2 of my pickets were found asleep. Morgan's whole force then filled the town and were eager to go to the camp. Morgan's adjutant-general came to me as soon as the greater portion had passed toward the camp (the men were going as fast as they could) and called on me to surrender my camp. I replied I had no command, as I had surrendered personally to Captain Desha. They threatened to shoot me if I did not surrender the command. I told them I could not and would not; that no one could do it but Captain Hughes, the senior officer at the camp. Captain Desha commanded them to desist; that I had surrendered as a prisoner of war to him, and that I should not be shot. They then said they would take me to General Morgan and let him decide whether I should surrender the camp or not. When we came up to General Morgan he received me very kindly, and first concurred with the adjutant-general that I should surrender the camp, but afterward concurred with me that my position was correct, and would not force me to do so. By this time we were within 300 or 400 yards of the camp. A flag of truce was sent in to Captain Hughes, who came out and spoke with General Morgan. I informed him that I had surrendered, and it was now for him to say whether the men in camp should fight. He asked for time to consult with his officers, which was granted. We then returned to General Morgan and surrendered the camp. General Morgan ordered the arms to be stacked, which was done, amounting to about 120 guns. The troops in camp were in line, ready to fight.

Subsequently Captain O'Neill's guard at the tunnel were captured. They were in position for action in a sort of block-house, and were ready to fight until they saw the large force opposed to them.

Morgan insisted on my surrendering the forces out, as they were not under Captain Hughes' command. I declined to do so, as I was confident they could escape. I gave a line to Captain O'Neill, saying that Morgan's forces had possession of our camp, so that he might understand the position of affairs and not rely for re-enforcements upon the camp.

My command was all paroled, except Captains Noble's and White's commands, who were not taken. Captain Benson, commanding the other company in camp, had gone to Nashville in charge of a prisoner.

Statement of Capt. F. M. Hughes.

There were 120 guns stacked at the time of the surrender. I considered Colonel Boone's words to me as an order to surrender.

Colonel Boone wrote a letter to Captain O'Neill, as I understood, to surrender his command. Our pickets were surrounded. We never had pickets out during the day and no scouts. The men in camp were anxious to fight. Lieutenants Davis and Conaway usually slept about half a square out of camp, having their wives with them, in a house.

Colonel Boone was in town when the attack was first made. He was generally in the habit of visiting the pickets and camp guards.

I called several times for my officers to give me their attention, as I wished to consult with them, but could not get their attention.

Two companies had been detached the evening before. I think some of the pickets were asleep. It was usual for the pickets on the same post to take turns sleeping.

I told my first sergeant I thought we would have to fight. We had about 30 men on guard and picket duty. I think Morgan had 1,200 or 1,500 men. When I saw the two detached companies, after the surrender, they had their arms, but threw them away. I do not know who ordered them to do so.

Statement of Capt. H. J. O'Neill.

I had 36 men with me at the time of the attack. Some were washing and cooking and the balance of my company were distributed about at bridges. I usually had pickets out in the immediate vicinity of my camp. We never had pickets out during the day. I often found pickets sleeping on their posts while I was in camp. We had no guard-house or systems of punishment, and what we lacked most was discipline. There was no discipline among the men. I would not have surrendered could we have made any reasonable resistance.

[Inclosure B.]

Statement of Corpl. James E. Mullin, Company B, Twenty-eighth Kentucky Volunteers.

I was on picket duty and posted about a half a mile from camp in the direction of the city, on a path running through the woods and a corn field, with orders to arrest any one, not a commissioned officer, going to or from the camp with or without the countersign after tattoo. The first I heard of the attack was after I was relieved from picket duty. Private Selvage, of Company B, who was on picket, came running back and said the rebels or some one were in the city and that it was filling up with cavalry. At that time I was cooking breakfast in camp. There were no day pickets out. None of the officers, so far as I could see, noticed his statement. I heard nothing until I saw the flag of truce coming in about 5.30 a. m. Soon as it arrived the officers ordered the men to fall in. The flag was in camp two minutes after we first saw it and the rebels were closing in all the time. My company being absent I fell in with Company A. Captain Hughes went to meet the flag, and the next I knew the camp was surrendered. There were about 83 men in camp for duty at the time the flag came up. As I was told, there were from 1,100 to 1,500 rebels opposed to us. I don't think there would have been any use in resistance at that time. There were no scouting parties sent out, only a heavy camp guard and pickets. There were a few mounted pickets sent out on the roads at night about a mile from camp on impressed horses. I was not visited during the night by any one. I always found Colonel Boone with his clothes on at night, and think he was as watchful as possible, and as far as he was able did his whole duty. I never knew Colonel Boone to be out of camp except the night of the attack, when his wife was very sick. Have often seen him late at night visiting the guards and pickets. The enemy kept closing in and surrounding us while the flag was being received.

Statement of Corpl. T. T. Baldwin, Company E, Twenty-eighth Kentucky Volunteers.

I was on camp guard and had 8 men on guard; but after 10 o'clock, on account of the absence of two companies, only had 4 men. The pickets relieve themselves about reveille, and most of them were in camp at the time of the surrender. The first I saw or heard of an attack was a soldier of our camp running in and saying the town was full of cavalry. The next was I heard the men saying the rebels were coming and had our colonel prisoner. They then fell in of their own accord and appeared anxious to fight. We formed around the amphitheater, and some one asked if they were going to fight, and the reply was made that there was no use, as there were too many of them. The adjutant, Lieutenant Boone, said, "For God's sake let us fight and show them that the Twenty-eighth was not afraid of them!"

Captain Hughes went out to see the flag of truce. I met him coming in and asked him what was the prospect. He said, "I expect we will have to fight them." He said they claimed 1,500. The rebels, as far as I could see, were on both sides of the road and in the corn fields all around us.

Statement of Private John Shirley, Company E, Twenty-eighth Kentucky Volunteers.

I was a mounted picket, posted about 3 miles from camp, on the Hartsville road. Was ordered not to interfere with citizens coming into camp and to pay no attention to what was going on off the road. These orders were given by the adjutant. Was not visited during the night. Was on post until about daybreak with Private Hardy; he was watching while I laid down to sleep. The first I knew we were surrounded by the rebels and captured.

Statement of Private James Coomes, Company E, Twenty-eighth Kentucky Volunteers.

I was an infantry picket, posted at the depot in Gallatin, in sight of the court-house. Colonel Boone visited my post between 12 and 1 o'clock that night. I left my post as usual about sunrise and went into camp. The pickets had not all got into camp when the camp was surrendered. The adjutant gave orders for us to fall into line. The men were anxious and willing to fight. I think Colonel Boone was very watchful and did all he could, but don't think him capable of commanding the post.

Private George Hand, Company B, Twenty-eighth Kentucky Volunteers, states substantially the same as Private Coomes, being on the same duty with him. States that there were 83 muskets stacked at the time of the surrender.

Statement of Private John C. Hardin, Company A, Twenty-eighth Kentucky Volunteers.

I was posted at the court-house, with orders to keep soldiers out of town who had not the countersign. I was visited twice by Colonel Boone during the night of the attack; the first time when he was sending out the two companies and the last time between 1 and 2 o'clock a. m. Near 4 a. m. some 8 or 10 men in citizens' dress, armed, came upon me from the rear of the court-house, apparently through the fields and corn, as they were very wet and covered with grass-seed, &c. I was in front at the time they came up. They demanded my surrender, pointing their guns at me, and I was obliged to do it. Osborne and the sergeant were with me at the time and were arrested also. The main force came up about ten minutes after. We had returned from Lebanon about two months before the attack.

Statement of Private Layton Jones, Company E, Twenty-eighth Kentucky Volunteers.

I was on picket duty about 500 yards from camp. Was not visited during the night. Was in camp when the cavalry came up. No pickets were posted during the day-time. We could have done nothing in the way of defense. No defensive arrangements had been made in the way of stockades, though we were expecting an attack.

Statement of Private Benjamin Fuell, Company A, Twenty-eighth Kentucky Volunteers.

I was posted 4 miles from camp, on the Scottsville road, mounted, with one other man. Was sent out as an advanced guard to the two companies which were sent to intercept cattle. I returned about 8 o'clock to Gallatin, not knowing the rebels were there, and was arrested at the court-house. Most of the enemy were in town at the time. I don't think the camp had been captured at that time.

Statement of Lieut. J. R. Boone, adjutant of the regiment.

On the 1st day of May five companies of Twenty-eighth Kentucky Volunteers (Companies A, B, D, E, and F) arrived at Gallatin, Tenn.; the remainder of the regiment was scattered along the railroad line back to Lebanon, Ky. These five companies were together at Gallatin doing duty until after the fight at Lebanon, Tenn., when Companies A and E were sent as a garrison for Lebanon, Tenn., and Company F sent to Hartsville, Tenn., and Companies B and D were left at Gallatin, together with one company of the Fiftieth Indiana. In about three weeks Company F was recalled to Gallatin and Company D ordered to Lebanon. There were then three companies of the Twenty-eighth Kentucky and three companies of Ninth Pennsylvania Cavalry at Lebanon and two companies, B and F, of Twenty-eighth Kentucky at Gallatin. These two companies were called to Nashville to go with General Dumont to Murfreesborough; they were again sent back to Nashville, and from there to Franklin, Tenn., where they guarded the whole line of the railroad down to Columbia. They were finally relieved and returned to Gallatin. Upon their return the three camps which were at Lebanon were ordered to report to Colonel Boone at Gallatin, and it was promised that the regiment which had for so long a time been doing guard duty should be brought together and put forward. But in a few days we were ordered to guard the two tunnels and eight bridges on the railroad from the Kentucky line to within about 15 miles of Nashville. Accordingly Company D was stationed at the tunnel 7 miles above Gallatin. The captain was ordered to keep at least 20 men there, and with the rest of his company keep guard at the other tunnel, water-tank, and bridges north of him. This left Companies A, B, E, and F at Gallatin, generally averaging about 65 men each fit for duty. To the bridge north of Gallatin and south of tunnel and to each of the three bridges south of Gallatin were sent a sergeant and 10 men, until we were relieved by a lieutenant and a squad of men, who took charge of the bridge nearest Nashville. This duty, besides guarding the depot and water-tank at Gallatin and the necessary picket and camp duty, we performed until Murfreesborough was attacked and Nashville threatened, when we were ordered to leave one company at Gallatin and with the other three companies repair by rail to Nashville. We were on the cars and off in twenty minutes.

At Nashville we did a heavy duty; slept on the bare ground under the canopy of heaven, and could get nothing to eat from Sunday at 11 o'clock, when we started, till Monday at 12. When General Nelson was near Nashville with his re-enforcements we were ordered back to Gallatin, and found evidence that had the place not have been re-enforced Company F stationed there would have been cut off. We had reports of a force concentrating at Sparta and Hartsville and apprised the authorities at Nashville of the fact, and asked for some cavalry to scout in that direction, but got none.

About this time Forrest, who had taken Murfreesborough, where two regiments were posted, was advancing on Lebanon, where the Fifty-fourth Ohio was stationed. They burned their camp equipage and baggage and retreated to Nashville. Thus we were left at Gallatin with four companies, reduced to mere squads by heavy details, and Forrest, with a force supposed to be about 3,000, at Lebanon, 17 miles distant. Time and again we apprised Colonel Miller, commanding at Nashville, of our critical situation and asked to be re-enforced. They told us they could not even send us a company of cavalry to watch the river, and we were ordered to press horses, saddles, and bridles. This we did, but between the two armies the country about Gallatin was about stripped of horses; but we pressed some fifteen horses, and with blind bridles, and in some cases no saddles, began picketing the roads with mounted men along the river and between Gallatin and Hartsville. We burned all the ferry-boats from Hartsville down between Gallatin, and waited for Forrest in the court-house, where we had determined to give him an obstinate fight. An accident, which appeared like an interposition of Providence, saved us. The river, which was fordable in many places, raised to an impassable height in one night. For a day or two we felt comparatively easy, when we were notified that a mounted infantry force, supposed to number 1,500, had possession of the railroad at Richland. Colonel Boone called in the company at the tunnel and bridge guards, and with the five companies determined to force a passage for the cars through to Louisville. We went as far as Mitchellsville, a few miles above Richland, and found no enemy, the small force which had been there having left in the direction of Hartsville. We returned to Gallatin, distributed the force as before stated, and called for re-enforcements. Some paroled prisoners, who had been taken about Murfreesborough and carried by Forrest to Lebanon and up to Sparta and then let go and who came down to Gallatin, were surprised to find so small a force at that post, and said we were in the greatest danger and had no force to fight the numbers that were preparing to come against us; that Forrest and Starnes were up there and would undoubtedly attack us in a short time. We again called for re-enforcements, and Colonel Boone tried until 1 o'clock at night to get a telegraphic dispatch to General Nelson at Murfreesborough, but could get no response.

Our scouts reported the country full of the rebels' scouts and pickets above Gallatin about 6 miles. Other information received led us to believe we would certainly be attacked by an overwhelming force; and that night a messenger was dispatched on horseback at the dead hour of night (for we could get no word from there by telegraph), and went to Nashville in two hours.

Mr. Fowler, comptroller of the State of Tennessee, was at that time in Gallatin and saw our critical situation, and promised Colonel Boone to do all in his power to have him re-enforced. The next day Colonel Boone sent me with these paroled prisoners to Nashville, and directed me to take them to Colonel Miller, and let him hear from them the danger of keeping so small a force at Gallatin. Mr. Fowler went with me. We first saw General Campbell, late Ex-Governor Campbell, and told him of these things, and he expressed surprise at the small force at Gallatin, and said he had been assigned to no command at that time, and if he had the authority he would send a strong force there.

We then went to Colonel Miller's headquarters, but he was absent, and we went around to Governor Johnson's. He was also surprised at our little squads being left with no re-enforcements, and after having heard the statement of the prisoners he jumped up out of his chair and walked across the floor and said emphatically, "I have said all along that a strong force should be kept at Gallatin;" that he could see how exposed the post was, and had urged the military authorities to put a force there, but they had paid little attention to what he had said. He said he would do anything in his power for us, and would telegraph or write to General Nelson and urge him to send a force to Gallatin. We then took the paroled men to Colonel Miller's headquarters again and explained to him our situation; and Mr. Fowler, who knew the country about Gallatin, having resided there, pointed out our exposed position and impressed upon him the importance of sending re-enforcements immediately. He said he had telegraphed General Nelson about it and had received no answer. We asked if he could not let us have a few cavalrymen for scouts and pickets, and if he could not do that could we not get a few saddles? That it was bad enough to have to send the men out on old broken-down horses and brood mares without having to send them out barebacked and with blind-bridles; but we could get neither. Mr. Fowler and myself asked if we could get no cannon. Colonel Miller said that there was a howitzer there that was not in use and he would send it up to us. I then left, but called again after supper to see if an answer had been received from General Nelson. Colonel Miller was out, but I found a gentleman who had been run off from his home at Lebanon at 2 o'clock the night before because he was a Unionist and feared Starnes' men, who were then in Lebanon. With him was a brother-in-law of Colonel Stokes or General Campbell—I do not exactly remember which—but they waited with me until Colonel Miller came and told him what they knew. Col. Jordan Stokes came in to warn the authorities of danger. He had received a letter from his wife at Lebanon, in which she reported Starnes at that place. They all thought we should be re-enforced at Gallatin. Colonel Miller had received word from General Nelson to re-enforce us if he thought best; said he had telegraphed to Colonel Boone about it. I then reminded Colonel Miller of his promise to send the cannon and left. The next morning I returned to Gallatin, and the next morning succeeding my return the Thirty-first Indiana arrived and encamped near us. Brigadier-General Cruft was commanding the regiment. He thought there should be at least one regiment of infantry and two or three companies of cavalry there. The second day after their arrival they were ordered to go back to Murfreesborough, leaving us as exposed as before. Colonel Boone then was notified by Colonel Miller that he would send 150 men with axes and tools to put up stockades at each of the bridges and a fortification at Gallatin. The day following a lieutenant and 26 men from an Ohio regiment arrived and reported for duty. They brought no axes or tools and none had arrived. The next day they were ordered back to Nashville, and authority came to Colonel Boone to press negroes and build the fortifications; and that night Lieutenants Keegan and Platt, of Eleventh Michigan, arrived with some 60 men and some wagons, but no tools of any kind. The same day a lieutenant of Sixty-ninth Ohio arrived from Nashville with 37 negroes, and we were getting a pretty good force on hand, but no tools to work with. Colonel Boone telegraphed to Nashville after axes and picks, and was ordered to press axes. In a country where everybody is an enemy it soon became known that we were pressing axes, and although we started out two wagons, one under charge of Lieutenant Platt and a squad of men and the other under charge of a sergeant and a squad instantly, they found it difficult to get the axes, and it took several days to collect enough to go to work with. Lieutenant Keegan was ordered by Colonel Boone to take charge of the business, and to employ all the available force in the construction of the stockades and to shove the work forward as rapidly as possible. Nearly every ax that was pressed needed a new handle and grinding; they were put in order and employed immediately in cutting timber for the stockades. Still we had no plans nor pickaxes, and not near enough axes; but all that we had were employed.

About this time, say four or five days after the arrival of Lieutenant Keegan with the Eleventh Michigan men, Lieutenant Howland, aide-de-camp and acting assistant adjutant-general to Colonel Miller, came up, and brought with him plans and specifications for building stockades at the bridges, but no plan was sent for the fortifications at Gallatin.

Lieutenant Howland inquired about how we were progressing with the stockades, and seemed satisfied that we were pushing their erection forward as rapidly as possible. Lieutenant Keegan went to Nashville that same evening to get some to work with. A box of some fifteen axes came up, but Lieutenant Keegan never returned, and Lieutenant Platt and men were ordered next day to Nashville.

At this time we had about 68 negroes on hand, and knew that this, together with the fact that it had become known that we were putting up fortifications, would only greatly increase our danger at Gallatin, and our vigilance was increased as much as possible.

The negroes were sent about 7 miles above Gallatin, to where the timber was most plentiful and better suited to the purpose, and Lieutenant Weatherford was appointed to oversee the work, and a guard was furnished him to protect the negroes and keep them at work. He is a pushing, industrious man, and worked the negroes hard. They were getting along well. The stockades were about cut, and Colonel Boone had telegraphed to Nashville to have a construction train sent up to distribute the stockades at each of the bridges, and a part of the negroes were brought to camp to begin the erection of the fortifications at Gallatin the next day, and had we been undisturbed for two days longer the fortifications would have been about completed.

Monday evening, August 11, Colonel Boone received a telegraphic dispatch from Colonel Bruce, commanding Bowling Green, to send about 100 men out the Scottsville pike toward La Fayette, to intercept some fine beef cattle that the rebels were driving south. This dispatch came about 3 o'clock p. m. We had no way to mount the men, and if they marched out there they could not drive the cattle back very well, they being on foot; so Colonel Boone did not send them.

Late in the evening, however, Colonel Bruce sent another dispatch, saying he had sent a force of cavalry in that direction, and wanted Colonel Boone to send those men to operate with the cavalry. They were going directly in the direction from which we apprehended an attack; and as we had previously been ordered to co-operate with Colonel Bruce Colonel Boone thought that sending out this force spoken of would serve three purposes: to reconnoiter the country in the direction of the enemy, to press horses, which were much needed, and to get the cattle if possible. Accordingly Companies B and F were detailed for that purpose, and Captain White, commanding, was ordered by Colonel Boone to press horses for all the men after they had got some 6 miles from Gallatin; to keep out a good advanced and rear guard, and if they came across the rebels in force to fall back upon the camp at Gallatin. The precaution was taken to slip them out quietly at night after the people had retired, and they got off without being observed, and no one but Captains White and Noble knew whither they were going. Captain Noble, commanding Company F, was officer of the day. As he was going with his company I took his place. The rest of the officers were pretty well worked down, and Colonel Boone ordered the very strictest vigilance; so I took the place of officer of the day myself. I had posted the new picket at sunset and given them good instructions. I put out 34 pickets (foot), 1 sergeant and 1 corporal, a patrol for the town, and guards for the water-tank and depot, and 2 mounted pickets of 2 men each. I sent one out the Hartsville pike and the other out the Scottsville pike with instructions to keep the strictest watch, and keep moving about between a distance of about 4 miles out and the picket stationed at the forks of the roads above town, and in case they should see an enemy to fall back, and as soon as within hearing of the other pickets to fire, so as to alarm them, and they to alarm the camp.

The guards at camp were directed to give the alarm in case they heard the report of a gun and the sergeant of the guard to have the long-roll beat instantly. The companies were then to be quietly formed on the color front.

The sergeant of the guard and myself visited the sentinels frequently during the night, and cautioned them to be watchful and attentive. I had every light in camp extinguished and all noise silenced, and staid with the sergeant of the guard and corporal of relief at post No. 1 all night. We went the grand-rounds before and after 12 o'clock.

About 2 o'clock the hospital steward came in from the hospital in town, and with him I visited the pickets below town and renewed the instructions and charged them to keep on the alert; that any negligence on their part would not only jeopardize their own but the lives of those who were sleeping quietly, thinking their comrades would warn them of any danger. Colonel Boone had just visited the pickets and in town.

I then went back to camp, and the first intimation I had of an enemy was about 4.30 o'clock. One of the pickets which I had placed at the intersection of a dirt road with the pike leading to Cumberland River, about a mile from town (a place where I had not placed pickets before), made their escape and got into camp and reported a force of cavalry in Gallatin. Immediately I ordered the long roll to be beat. I also ordered my horse and some men to go with me to reconnoiter, but saw what was up and helped form the men. We got formed and counted the men and am certain we had not more than 96 men to fight with. They had captured our pickets, and by the time we got formed closed in around us so that the Texas Rangers, on our left, were no farther than 40 yards from us. At this juncture a flag of truce came in. Captain Hughes, the senior officer present, went out to receive the flag. They told him they had captured Colonel Boone, just as he came out the door on his way to visit the picket, and that the camp was surrounded, as he could see himself, by 2,500 men. Captain Hughes said he saw that our little squad would soon be cut down, situated as they were, but told the bearers of the flag, Colonel St. Leger Grenfell and Lieutenant-Colonel Duke, that he did not like to take upon himself the responsibility of surrendering the men, and requested a short time to confer with the other officers, which was granted. Captain Hughes called the officers together, and after a short consultation they concluded that it would be sinful to have the little batch of brave men cut down by a force that was supposed to be about 1,800, and accordingly agreed that Captain Hughes should surrender us upon condition that officers and men should be well treated and paroled. We then surrendered 124 guns, including the guns of the pickets. After we surrendered they sent out and picked up the little squads along the railroad.

Officers and men were well treated. The officers were allowed to retain all personal property. I saw no officer or soldier who appeared frightened in the least, and believe if it would have conduced any to the good of the country every man in the little band would have fought while a spark of life glowed in his bosom.

Additional statement of Lieutenant Boone.

There were no pickets posted during the day on account of the weak condition of the camp. Colonel Boone did not direct the surrender of the camp. Was informed that the rebels came down between the Scottsville and Hartsville roads till they got in rear of our mounted pickets and then sent parties back and captured them. Was informed by the rebels that one of the pickets at the court-house was asleep. There was no drunkenness among the officers or men. Occasionally found men asleep on post, but had no way to punish them except by a regimental court-martial, which the men did not mind. We asked for a general court-martial several times, but were ordered to try them by a regimental court.

I think the rebels were piloted by citizens living around, who knew the whereabouts of the pickets. The pickets relieved themselves about 8.30 o'clock. It was about 5 o'clock when the flag of truce came up. Only one of our pickets had reached camp that I knew of, and that was the man stationed on the pike to Cumberland River near the dirt road leading through the woods and a corn field.

No. 4.

Report of General Braxton Bragg, C. S. Army, of the surrender of Gallatin.

CHATTANOOGA, TENN., *August* 18, 1862.

Colonel Morgan has captured Gallatin, Tenn., taking 300 prisoners and destroying three railroad tracks and the tunnel, so as to obstruct the road for a month. The first blow in General Smith's expedition.

BRAXTON BRAGG.

General S. COOPER.

No. 5.

Report of Asst. Adjt. Gen. J. F. Belton, C. S. Army, of the surrender of Gallatin and destruction of bridges in that vicinity.

KNOXVILLE, TENN., *August* 17, 1862.

Col. John H. Morgan reports that on the 11th [12th] instant he captured Gallatin; about 200 Federal soldiers, including Colonel Boone, commanding, and other officers of the Twenty-eighth Kentucky, were taken and paroled. The tunnel and trestle work between Bowling Green and Gallatin were set fire to; totally destroyed. The bridge between Nashville and Gallatin blown up and 40 cars burned. A large quantity of Government stores were destroyed. Over 100 horses taken.

J. F. BELTON,
Assistant Adjutant-General.

General S. COOPER.

AUGUST 13, 1862.—Skirmish at Huntsville, Scott County, Tenn.

Report of Col. William Clift, Seventh Tennessee Infantry, including operations of his command in East Tennessee, July 1–October 31.

HEADQUARTERS,
Somerset, Ky., October 28 [31?], 1862.

DEAR SIR : I avail myself of the present opportunity of reporting to you my movements for the last three months. The way has been so blockaded by the enemy as to entirely prevent my reporting to you sooner.

I was ordered by Major-General Morgan about June 1 to go to Scott County, Tennessee, and commence recruiting and making up the Seventh Regiment Tennessee Volunteers, and was also ordered that so soon as I had a sufficient number of men to attack the small bodies of rebel troops stationed in different parts of East Tennessee to do so. Accordingly about July 1 I made a scouting expedition to Montgomery, Morgan County, Tenn., to engage a party of rebels that were in the habit of coming up to that place from Kingston, Tenn., but the enemy had left on the day before we got to Montgomery, and we had to return without any engagement.

About July 20 I made another expedition to Anderson County, Tennessee. Our friends in that county had promised to provide means for us to cross Clinch River to engage same cavalry from Alabama that was stationed near Clinton, Anderson County, Tenn.; but no preparation was made as promised. I then turned my course, after taking several guerrillas prisoners near Clinton, Tenn., and returned by way of Wartburg and Montgomery, Morgan County, Tenn., to Huntsville, Scott County, Tenn.

About August 8 I made another expedition into Anderson County, Tennessee, at the request of our Union friends of that county, who had again promised to provide means for us to cross Clinch River, but again failed and we were disappointed.

At intervals when I was not scouting I was busily employed fortifying an eminence near Huntsville, Scott County, Tenn.

On the morning of August 13, about 8 o'clock, our pickets were driven in by the enemy. My command, numbering about 250 men, were soon in order for battle. I was attacked about 9 o'clock by the enemy, numbering from 1,500 to 2,000 men. On the appearance of them in such disproportionate numbers my men (who were mostly new recruits) left my breastworks in wild confusion. But while I speak in dishonorable terms of a part of my command I am proud to speak in the most honorable terms of a part of the officers and men that remained under my command. About 50 men held our breastworks for one hour and forty minutes against the enemy, at least 1,500 men. Maj. James S. Dunan, Captains Robins, Wilson, and Shelton fought with great coolness and deliberation. When our numbers in the breastworks were reduced to about 20 men I ordered a retreat, which was conducted in good order, carrying with them our guns without any loss.

My position in Scott County, Tennessee, has been very perilous until within the last few days; but I kept my men in the most obscure parts of the county, and posted my pickets from 20 to 25 miles from my camps and within a short distance of the enemy's lines, and in this way I evaded collision with the enemy until General Bragg's army retreated out of Kentucky.

I again sent out a scouting party October 1 and we passed over the counties of Scott and Morgan and a part of Fentress County, Tennessee, capturing some prisoners and a little of the rebels' property.

I sent out another scouting party about October 15, which returned on the 29th instant, and report that they passed over Scott, Morgan, and Fentress Counties, Tennessee, and had a skirmish with Ferguson's guerrillas, killing 4 of them, and among the number was the cruel murderer Captain Milliken. They also captured some property.

On October 31 I sent out another scouting party from Somerset, Ky, to traverse the country toward Monticello and Jamestown, Tenn.; thence from the line of Kentucky and Tennessee to Post Oak Springs, in Roane County, Tenn., with a view of breaking up several guerrilla companies that are roaming in the mountains between the line of Kentucky and Tennessee and the Tennessee River and sometimes in the counties of Clinton and Wayne, Kentucky. I have been subsisting my troops on corn bread and beef since the fight at Huntsville, Tenn., at a cost to the Government from about 10 to 15 cents for each soldier per day and about the same for about 50 horses for mounted infantry.

I deem it highly indispensable to break up these guerrilla companies as speedily as possible, as there can be no safety to the peace of the country while they are permitted to exist.

About August 1 I had a correspondence with General Boyle, of Kentucky, in which he proposed to co-operate with me along the line of the States of Tennessee and Kentucky, and authorized me to mount a part of my men for that service. I find but little trouble in procuring horses, but find a great deal of trouble in getting saddles and bridles suitable for such a service. If the War Department will furnish me with cavalry saddles, bridles, &c., suitable for such service, I can place myself in a condition for active operations in a few days.

I hope for the future to be able to keep up a regular correspondence with you by way of Louisville, Ky.

Your obedient servant,

WM. CLIFT,
Colonel, Comdg. Seventh Regiment of Tennessee Vols.

The ADJUTANT-GENERAL U. S. ARMY.

AUGUST 14, 1862.—Skirmish near Mount Pleasant, Tenn.

Report of Brig. Gen. James S. Negley, U. S. Army.

COLUMBIA, *August* 14, 1862.

Major Kennedy attacked Williams' guerrillas 8 miles south of Mount Pleasant this morning at 7 o'clock, killing 2 and taking several prisoners. The enemy fled to woods after the first fire. Our horses were too much exhausted to follow them.

JAS. S. NEGLEY.

Col. J. B. FRY.

AUGUST 16–22, 1862.—Operations about Cumberland Gap, Tenn., including action at London, Ky., and skirmishes at Flat Lick, Ky., and Pine Mountain, Tenn. (17th).

Reports of Brig. Gen. George W. Morgan, U. S. Army, commanding Seventh Division, Army of the Ohio.*

> CUMBERLAND GAP, TENN., *August* 19,
> *Via Lexington, Ky., August* 22, 1862.

GENERAL : On the night of the 16th the enemy, said to be 20,000 strong ,arrived in our front and drove in our pickets. The morning following there was a brisk skirmish, in which there were trifling losses on either side. During the morning the enemy commenced to emerge from Patterson's woods, and with his artillery opened upon our cavalry. We returned the fire from the pinnacle forts on the right and left and compelled the enemy to withdraw his guns. We also drove him from the adjacent woods. He now envelops our entire front.

On the 16th instant 6,000 infantry and cavalry, with one battery of mountain howitzers, passed through Rogers' Gap. Deserters say that that column is 15,000 strong, but an intelligent scout estimates it at only 6,000. It cannot be the strength of the column which passed Big Creek Gap, for it is said to be 20,000 strong. I had stationed five companies of infantry at Cumberland Ford, five at Barboursville, and a similar force at London and Richmond. I requested General Boyle to re-enforce Richmond and London, and on the 11th instant he informed me that he would do so, but as Boyle's troops were elsewhere ordered London was not re-enforced, and I ordered Colonel Houk to concentrate his regiment and fall back upon Cumberland Gap. It is rumored that Houk was attacked on the 16th instant and his command captured.

On the morning of the 16th I sent Captain Martin via Cumberland Ford to observe Big Creek and Rogers' Gap. On the 17th instant he was attacked by Ashby's cavalry, 600 strong, and 60 of his men are missing.

I have called in my force from Barboursville and Cumberland Ford and they have safely arrived with 150 wagons of forage and subsistence.

Two men who left Knoxville three days ago report that 30,000 men are *en route* from that place to attack and surround us. My troops are in good condition and spirits and the position shall not be yielded while we have a pound of meat and an ounce of powder; but I trust that the road to Lexington may soon be cleared by a column from Lexington.

A letter received from Kingston states that John Morgan, with 6,000 cavalry and artillery, will be in Nashville in less than twenty days, and confirms the reports of our scouts that the rebel forces in East Tennessee are from 80,000 to 100,000 strong. Kirby Smith commands the column invading Kentucky, and Bragg is at Loudon, 30 miles southwest of Knoxville.

This telegram is sent to Generals Halleck and Buell by courier to Lexington.

> GEORGE W. MORGAN,
> *Brigadier-General.*

Brigadier-General CULLUM, *Chief of Staff.*

---

*See also reports of J. S. Scott, pp. 937, 938 ; G. W. Morgan, p. 992.

CUMBERLAND GAP, TENN., *August 23,*
Via Lexington, Ky., August 27, 1862—8.30 p. m.

On the 17th instant Colonel Houk, Third Tennessee, with part of five companies, amounting to 180 men, was attacked at London [Ky.], by a large force of cavalry. After a gallant resistance of an hour's duration, in which the enemy lost one lieutenant-colonel and a number of soldiers, Colonel Houk retreated to the mountain ridges, and after five days of privations and dangers reached this stronghold. Among the prisoners sent in by the rebels on the 20th instant are two soldiers, not paroled, who estimate the enemy's force at Barboursville and Flat Lick at 15,000 men. Rebel soldiers said that when their heavy guns arrived they would attack us, and others claimed that we were already prisoners. On yesterday I sent a flag of truce, with 11 prisoners, to Pogue's, near Flat Lick, but the officers in charge have not yet returned. A forage train of 100 wagons, protected by the guns of the fort, and a convoy of three regiments of infantry and a section of artillery, went up the Virginia road 3 miles to get fodder for the mules. The forage was obtained and there was a slight skirmish, during which 6 or 8 of the enemy were killed and a number wounded. We captured 8 horses, 12 swords, 15 rifles, and 8 barrels of salt, which had been smuggled through the mountains. The enemy's force, as far as seen, consisted of one regiment of infantry and a body of cavalry. On last evening he concentrated his forces 5 miles in front. I believe that he has now but two brigades in our front and that the other three have gone into Kentucky. Our troops have been on half rations for six days, but they are in high spirits and feel confident of victory. Should the enemy attack, Nashville is certain to be attacked. Bragg and Hardee are at Chattanooga.

GEORGE W. MORGAN,
Brigadier-General.

Major-General HALLECK,* *General-in-Chief.*

AUGUST 17, 1862.—Skirmish near Mammoth Cave, Ky.

Report of Capt. W. E. Wortham, Rock Creek (Kentucky) Home Guards.

LITCHFIELD, KY., *August 26,* 1862.

DEAR SIR: On the 17th instant a party, composed of small squads from five different Home Guards, after pursuing a company of guerrillas about 40 miles, came upon them near Mammoth Cave, in this State, killed and captured the entire gang, numbering 66, together with their horses, there being 43 horses. After restoring to the owners the horses which had been stolen, upon proof of the fact, under the order of General Boyle, the 43 horses have been divided among the men who captured them, 9 of said horses falling to the company under my command.

My company has been in service eleven months, and has done good service in guarding roads, capturing contrabands of war, &c., all of which has heretofore been turned over to the Government, we paying our own expenses up to the time of the last capture and have never received any compensation whatever. My men are poor men, some of them having no horse to ride upon a scout and not able to buy. We have no arms but the common musket.

---

*Same report to Generals Buell and Wright.

We now hold these captured horses subject to the order of the United States Government; some of said horses are unfit for any kind of military service. I wish an order from my Government to dispose of the 9 horses in my care to reimburse my men for the expense they have been at during the past eleven months and purchasing such side-arms as we can after mounting men who have no horses.

If this meets with the favor of my Government address me at Litchfield, Ky.

Yours, with due respect,

W. E. WORTHAM,
Captain, Rock Creek Home Guards.

P. S.—Not being acquainted with the military law it may be that I am not addressing the proper authority. If so, you will please lay this before the proper authority.

Your obedient servant,

W. E. WORTHAM.

Hon. E. M. STANTON, *Secretary of War.*

AUGUST 18, 1862.—Surrender of Clarksville, Tenn.

REPORTS, ETC.

No. 1.—Maj. Gen. U. S. Grant, U. S. Army.
No. 2.—Col. Rodney Mason, Seventy-first Ohio Infantry, with War Department General Orders, No. 115, of 1862.
No. 3.—Lieut. Col. George W. Andrews, Seventy-first Ohio Infantry.
No. 4.—Statement of Company Officers of the Seventy-first Ohio Infantry, with War Department General Orders, Nos. 120, 133, of 1862.
No. 5.—Maj. William H. Sidell, Fifteenth U. S. Infantry, Acting Assistant Adjutant-General.

No. 1.

Report of Maj. Gen. U. S. Grant, U. S. Army.

CORINTH, MISS., *August* 22, 1862.

Colonel Mason, with a portion of the Seventy-first Ohio, surrendered Clarksville to guerrillas. Prisoners were paroled and sent down the river. I ordered them to Benton Barracks. I have put Forts Donelson and Henry under command of Colonel Lowe, and have ordered six companies of infantry up to re-enforce him.

U. S. GRANT,
Major-General.

General H. W. HALLECK, *Washington, D. C.*

No. 2.

Reports of Col. Rodney Mason, Seventy-first Ohio Infantry, with War Department General Orders, No. 115, of 1862.

PADUCAH, *August* 20, 1862.
(Received August 21, 1862.)

GENERAL: I report my detachment, being the garrison at Clarksville as paroled prisoners. I applied to Buell for re-enforcements in vain. With the support of artillery we were attacked on Monday by a force of cavalry and infantry, 800 strong, with a battery of 6 and 12 pounders, under command of Cols. (A. R.) Johnson and Woodward. They were immediately joined by large numbers of armed citizens. My little force was reduced by details on telegraph and river to 150 effective men in camp. It was thought best to surrender. I refused to give my parole, but otherwise would do it. I then gave it for thirty days, when I am to surrender myself at Hopkinsville, Ky. Where shall I take my men? Other forces are organizing to attack Donelson and Henry. Donelson is very weak, and will, I think, be overwhelmed unless immediate relief is given. The enemy will be able to overrun this country again. They can any day bring over 2,000 armed men to Donelson.

R. MASON,
Colonel Seventy-first Ohio.

Major-General GRANT.

—

CAMP CHASE, Columbus, Ohio, August 27, 1862.

GENERAL: Pursuant to your orders I reported with paroled prisoners at Benton Barracks, and then, by order of Major-General Halleck, proceeded with them to this camp.

Before receiving your command, through Colonel Lowe, to leave Clarksville I had repeatedly asked re-enforcements from General Buell, whose stores were accumulating at that point to a considerable amount. After receiving that order I went to Nashville, and explained fully to Major Sidell, Fifteenth U. S. Infantry, acting assistant adjutant-general to General Buell, the situation of affairs. I told him that forces had been collected; that Lieutenant-Colonel Bristow, of the Kentucky cavalry, had sent me notice they were going to attack me; that I should be attacked in overwhelming numbers, and would not hold myself responsible for the stores, but would hold my camp against infantry. He still insisted on my remaining until you were heard from, and I consented. I received your orders to remain on the day I had fixed for departure.

On Monday, August 18, I had, according to the morning reports, for duty: Commissioned officers, 18; enlisted men, 225; on extra duty, 36; sick, 34; in arrest, 7; total, 320. The extra-duty men were at the stables and post commissary and quartermaster's offices in the city.

A little before 9 a. m. I was informed that the enemy were in force near town. I immediately started for camp (I was at my headquarters in the city), and arrived there just as the enemy came into the city, a party of about 150 dashing at a gallop for my headquarters, where they had hoped to capture me. The men in camp had been formed (according to instructions previously given by me) by their officers, the immediate command of the camp having been devolved upon Lieutenant-Colonel Andrews.

The enemy halted, deployed a considerable portion of their forces, and held the remainder in mass out of range and under cover of houses, placing a battery in position in a corn field southeast of the college, about which we were encamped. They then sent in a flag of truce, demanding a surrender. I laid the matter before the commissioned officers. While they were considering the matter I returned to the flag and asked whether I would be permitted to verify the statement of their forces. He went away and returned, saying that Colonel Woodward, who commanded the force attacking us, requested a personal interview, to which I saw no objections, and we met midway. I made the same inquiry of him and he assented. I sent Lieutenant-Colonel Andrews to examine and count their force, which he did, and on his return stated that they were over 800 strong one company armed with volcanic rifles (16-shooters); one with Sharps carbines; the remander of the cavalry with double-barreled shot-guns, and part of the infantry with muskets. They had a battery of three guns, with caissons, in the corn field, but he did not go to them. They were afterward found to be 6 and 12 pounder field pieces. This report was made to the officers, and their vote was reported to me as about three-fourths for surrender and the remainder against it. I told them to rejoin their companies; that notwithstanding the disparity of force I would fight them.

Before or about the time I reached the flag I was called by Lieutenant-Colonel Andrews, who informed me that owing to the overpowering force opposed, their display of artillery, to which we had nothing to reply, and only brick walls to oppose, the men were found, in some companies at least, to be discouraged, and that the officers unanimously recommended a surrender.

Of the 225 men reported for duty 22 were on river guard, 7 on telegraph guard, and 6 out on telegraph line, repairing it—in all 35; leaving of those who ought to have been in camp 190; but of those only 152 were reported to me as in camp, including the camp guard of 42 men. Where the other 38 were I do not know.

I was then to determine whether I would, with this force of 152 men, or may be 175, by arming prisoners and bringing in men who might not be in line, fight over 800 men, armed as well as we were for the sort of a fight that was impending, most of their men being soldiers of the regular army, who had been sent home to recruit under Johnson, Woodward, and Garth, the 800 being increased by several hundred citizens who had appeared already in arms, and who were being constantly increased by men coming in from every direction. Had it been simply a fight of small-arms there would have been a general willingness to attempt to hold the college against any odds; but their artillery gave them complete control of this, and then we had nothing left. We had, as you are aware, no artillery. A little gun (found at the rolling-mill), that would not chamber a grape-shot, had been sent from Fort Donelson, and mounted on a gun carriage for a 24-pounder, was of no earthly value, and if it had been we had no ammunition for it. All the men in the city, nearly one-third of my aggregate, were already in the hands of the enemy. We had no hope of re-enforcements and no possibility, with the Cumberland and Red Rivers on three sides of us and an enemy indefinite in numbers in front, to retreat. To me then was submitted the question whether, against the judgments of all my commissioned officers, and my own most deliberately formed judgment (for I was dealing with a state of facts that for weeks I had contemplated and attempted to provide against), I should sacrifice the lives of my soldiers to the hope of retrieving a reputation for myself and survivors. However strongly personal considerations required my making a desperate resistance my conscience required me to surrender, and now, reviewing all the facts, I think I did my duty.

Anxious to save every possible chance, I stipulated that the surrender should not be made until sundown, at which time I yielded my camp, the entire mass of public property outside having been inevitably in the hands of the enemy from the beginning. I advised against giving parole, and refused to give my own, as did also Lieutenant-Colonel Andrews, Captain Houck, of Company I, and Lieutenant Hetzler, of Company H, acting commissary of subsistence at the post.   Lieutenant-Colonel Andrews afterward made an arrangement for a parole for thirty days, at the end of which time we agreed to report to the officer commanding the Confederate forces at Hopkinsville, Ky.   The other officers and the enlisted men gave their parole not to take up arms against the Confederate States until exchanged.   These paroles I suppose to be binding, as Lieutenant-Colonel Woodward held the commission as lieutenant-colonel of the C. S. Army, and his men were all regularly mustered into service.

I am, general, respectfully, your obedient servant,

R. MASON,
Colonel Seventy-first Ohio Volunteers.

Maj. Gen. U. S. Grant, *Headquarters, Corinth, Miss.*

—

GENERAL ORDERS, ⎱ WAR DEPARTMENT, ADJT. GEN.'S OFFICE,
No. 115.   ⎰   *Washington, August 22, 1862.*

Col. Rodney Mason, Seventy-first Regiment Ohio Volunteers, is, by order of the President of the United States, cashiered for repeated acts of cowardice in the face of the enemy.

By order of Secretary of War:

E. D. TOWNSEND,
Assistant Adjutant-General.

—

SPECIAL ORDERS, ⎱   WAR DEPT., ADJT. GENERAL'S OFFICE.
No. 130.   ⎰   *Washington, March 22, 1866.*

*   *   *   *   *   *   *

III. By direction of the President, General Orders, No. 115, August 22, 1862, from this office, relating to Col. Rodney Mason, Seventy-first Ohio Volunteers, is hereby revoked, and he is mustered out of the service of the United States to date August 22, 1862.

*   *   *   *   *   *   *

By order of the Secretary of War:

E. D. TOWNSEND,
Assistant Adjutant-General.

———

No. 3.

Report of Lieut. Col. George W. Andrews, Seventy-first Ohio Infantry.

COLUMBUS, OHIO,
Camp Chase, September 30, 1862.

SIR : Understanding some censures have been cast upon me by officers dismissed I submit the following :

After the surrender of Clarksville, while the detachment was on its way up the Mississippi River to Benton Barracks. to which General

Grant had sent us by telegraphic dispatch, several of the company officers asked me to sit down and write a short statement of the facts as to the surrender. Just as we were going into Saint Louis I sat down and hastily drew for the company officers such a statement as a favor to them, acting, as I supposed, as a mere secretary. I read it over to them, and some of them took it and read it for themselves. One or two read it before it was finished. There had been a difference of opinion as to the surrender between most of them and myself. I was opposed to it, as every one of them well knew, and I supposed they wished to justify their votes by the circumstances, which I was willing they should undertake to do. I had no earthly object to represent them improperly, as we well understood our relative positions on the subject of the surrender.

Previous to that unfortunate affair not a word within my recollection of unpleasantness ever passed between myself and any one of the company officers concerned. For nearly four months I had been separated from them and had a separate command at Fort Donelson of the balance of our regiment. I had never visited Clarksville but once, and then to stay but a very short time, which visit was made nearly three months before the surrender. I was at this time, as I supposed, upon a mere visit, expecting to very shortly return to my own command at Fort Donelson. I had thrown up a small fort at Donelson, the old fort of the enemy being greatly too large for my small force to occupy. I had got up a couple of pieces of artillery that were attempted to be disabled by the enemy at the old fort, repaired them, and so arranged the little fort, as I believed, and as I expressed to Colonel Mason, I could defend and hold it against any force that could, in the then condition of the country, be brought against it.

I was at Clarksville but a short time when the attack was made, and knew little or nothing about the approaches to the town or the arrangements made by our force to resist attacks, and though believing the force menacing us much superior to us in numbers, I thought we ought to fight with the hope of driving the enemy back. For the first time I had unpleasant words with some of the company officers.

I think Colonel Mason committed a great error in calling the company officers together, and so expressed my opinion at the time. I had the men drawn in line ready to fight when he came and when the flag of truce came, and I thought then, as I think now, a good fight could have been made. But the vote stood greatly against it; that is to say, when first taken four company officers with myself voted to fight and balance to surrender, and part of the latter were exceedingly eager so to do. Now that the Government has condemned the act of surrender I am informed that the officers who voted to surrender desire to excuse their conduct by saying, among other things, that they did not understand a statement they asked me to write for them. It was right their position should be known.

They voted to surrender and of course advised it. If they had done otherwise no responsibility but to fight would have rested on them. In this I only desire to set myself right, and having done so I subscribe myself, very respectfully,

GEO. W. ANDREWS,
Lieutenant-Colonel Seventy-first Ohio Volunteer Infantry.

Hon. SECRETARY OF WAR.

No. 4.

Statement of Company Officers of the Seventy-first Ohio Infantry, with War Department General Orders, Nos. 120, 133, of 1862, &c.

The undersigned, commissioned officers of the line, who were at Clarksville, Tenn., on duty at the time of the surrender, have read with deep regret a telegraphic dispatch purporting to come from Russellville and comments thereon, giving a basely false report of the action. To the end of obtaining simple justice we submit a faithful statement of the facts :

About ten days after the battle of Shiloh our regiment was sent from thence to garrison and hold Fort Donelson and Clarksville. Four companies were stationed at the former place, under Lieutenant-Colonel Andrews; the other six at Clarksville, under Colonel Mason. We had lost 137 men in the battle of Shiloh out of 510, balance of regiment being sick in hospital at the time.

We were divided to garrison the above places. After sending back to Ohio the sick we did not all told number 300 men fit for duty; still both places have been held for more than three months. Our number for duty has never at Clarksville numbered 200. Colonel Mason constantly called on superior officers for re-enforcements and for artillery, but because of supposed greater necessity at other places neither were sent. Rumors of designed attacks upon us were received for seven days, and by Colonel Mason's order several temporary rifle pits were constructed. A few days before the attack Lieutenant-Colonel Andrews came up from Donelson, 45 miles distant, and Major Hart was sent to take his place at the fort.

On the morning of the attack Colonel Mason was near the river attending to the duties of the post, and upon hearing of the enemy's approach made his way to the camp. Upon the approach of the enemy Lieutenant-Colonel Andrews immediately placed all men in camp in line of battle. Detachments had been sent to guard steamers with Government stores on the way to Nashville, others on telegraph line, and still others to guard Government stores on the landing, so that at the time not more than 125 were in line.

As Colonel Andrews was preparing to open fire upon the enemy Colonel Mason had by a circuitous route and rapid movements reached the camp. At that moment a flag of truce approached from the enemy. Of course all movements were halted, and the messenger was sent to Colonel Mason. He immediately summoned us to his quarters in council. The messenger stated he was sent to demand a surrender, with the condition that private property should be respected and the force allowed to retain its colors.

The true condition of affairs was for a moment canvassed. It was certain that a force of from 800 to 1,000 was drawn up before us, supported by two batteries of artillery; the messenger said a greater number. Colonel Woodward, commanding, conjointly with Col. A. R. Johnson, the enemy, was called, and Lieutenant-Colonel Andrews asked to be permitted to pass along the enemy's lines to ascertain the true number. After some parleying the request was granted. He returned and reported that as near as he could ascertain about 400 cavalrymen were drawn up in line some 400 yards distant, one company armed with new 16-shooter rifles, one company with carbines and sabers, balance with double-barreled shot-guns; at the left and rear were drawn up about 100 infantry; at other points of street crossings were stationed probably

200 men; besides these about 150 cavalry had dashed through the city to the landing. This was Colonel Andrews' report. But several others had reconnoitered and discovered two batteries of artillery planted within 500 yards of us. The people, 6,000 or 7,000 in number and containing at least 1,000 fighting men, were rising and turning out armed. There were but five or six Union families in the city. We had not the sign of artillery but a little bell-muzzled piece Colonel Andrews had patched up at Donelson and brought along; a grape-shot could not be put in its chamber; we had no ammunition for that. Under these circumstances we thought it madness to hold out, and we unanimously advised Colonel Mason to surrender.

N. J. HARTER,
  First Lieutenant Co. I.
ISAAC MANN,
  Second Lieutenant Co. C.
IRA L. MORRIS,
  First Lieutenant Co. C.
SMITH H. CLARK,
  Captain Co. D.
J. R. WOODWARD,
  Captain Co. C.
T. W. BOWN,
  Captain Co. K.

C. H. KRAMER,
  Captain Co. F.
SOL. J. HOUCK,
  Captain Co. I.
THOS. T. MORE,
  Adjutant.
WM. H. CALLENDER,
  Captain Co. E.
H. M. DRURY,
  Lieutenant Co. D.
S. W. BEAMAN,
  Lieutenant Co. F.

GENERAL ORDERS, } WAR DEPARTMENT, ADJT. GEN.'S OFFICE,
  No. 120.   }   *Washington, August* 29, 1862.

The following officers of the Seventy-first Regiment Ohio Volunteers are, by order of the President of the United States, cashiered, they having published a card stating that they advised Col. Rodney Mason to surrender Clarksville, Tenn., to the rebel forces, for which and other like acts the said Colonel Mason has been cashiered:

First Lieut. N. J. Harter.
Second Lieut. Isaac Mann.
First Lieut. Ira L. Morris.
Capt. Smith H. Clark.
Capt. J. R. Woodward.
Capt. T. W. Bown.

Capt. Sol. J. Houck.
Capt. C. H. Kramer.
Adjt. Thomas T. More.
Capt. William H. Callender.
Lieut. H. M. Drury.
Lieut. S. W. Beaman.

By order of the Secretary of War:

E. D. TOWNSEND,
  Assistant Adjutant-General.

GENERAL ORDERS, } WAR DEPARTMENT, ADJT. GEN.'S OFFICE,
  No. 133.   }   *Washington, September* 18, 1862.

*   *   *   *   *   *   *   *

II. Satisfactory evidence having been submitted that Capt. Sol. J. Houck, Seventy-first Ohio Volunteers, did not advise the surrender of Clarksville, Tenn., and that he signed the card justifying the surrender under a misapprehension of its contents, the President directs that so much of General Orders, No. 120, as cashiers him be revoked.

*   *   *   *   *   *   *   *

By order of the Secretary of War:

L. THOMAS,
  Adjutant-General.

SPECIAL ORDERS, }   WAR DEPT., ADJT. GENERAL'S OFFICE,
No. 242.   }   Washington, July 19, 1864.

*   *   *   *   *

II. So much of General Orders, No. 120, August 29, 1862, from this office, as dismissed First Lieut. Ira L. Morris, Seventy-first Ohio Volunteers, is hereby revoked, he being now in service as a private soldier of the Union Light Guards, Ohio Volunteer Cavalry. Lieutenant Morris will be considered as honorably discharged as an officer from the date the General Orders, No. 120, took effect, but held to service under his present enlistment.

*   *   *   *   *   *   *

By order of the Secretary of War:

E. D. TOWNSEND,
Assistant Adjutant-General.

—

SPECIAL ORDERS, }   WAR DEPT., ADJT. GENERAL'S OFFICE,
No. 206.   }   Washington, May 3, 1866.

*   *   *   *   *   *

XIII. By direction of the President, General Orders, No. 120, August 29, 1862, from this office, is hereby revoked, and the following-named officers of the Seventy-first Ohio Volunteers (names corrected), are hereby mustered out of the service of the United States, to date August 29, 1862:

Capt. W. H. Callender, Capt. Smith H. Clark, Capt. J. R. Woodward, Capt. T. W. Bown, Capt. C. H. Kramer, First Lieut. Thomas T. More, First Lieut. N. J. Harter, Second Lieut. Isaac Mann, Second Lieut. H. M. Drury, Second Lieut. Stephen W. Beaman.

*   *   *   *   *   *   *

By order of the Secretary of War:

E. D. TOWNSEND,
Assistant Adjutant-General.

———

No. 5.

Report of Maj. William H. Sidell, Fifteenth U. S. Infantry, and Acting Assistant Adjutant-General.

NASHVILLE, *August* 20, 1862.

GENERAL: Five companies Seventy-first Ohio, 350 men; one small gun, with intrenchments and rifle pits, captured without resistance on Monday noon. Enemy entered suburbs at 10; sent flag of truce and received capitulation at 12.

Steamboat Fisher just coming up with corn and oats and other stores taken and grain thrown in river. Mason and his men sent down (destination Camp Chase) with Confederate guard as far as latter could safely go. Enemy only 300 strong, all cavalry, under Johnson, Woodward, and Garth. Nothing but shot-guns, and their vicinity known to Mason at the time. Postmaster, collector, and railroad engineer kept prisoners on demand of citizens, who want to hang them, but Johnson opposes. Half the Confederates left yesterday, supposed for Fort Donelson, and remainder probably went last night. Enemy had no artillery or wagons or respectable arms; came from Hopkinsville and State Line.

Public goods were sold at auction; private respected. The wires were cut both ways prior to attack.

Respectfully,

W. H. SIDELL,
Major, Fifteenth U. S. Infantry, Actg. Asst. Adjt. Gen.

Maj. Gen. D. C. BUELL.

AUGUST 19–20, 1862.—Scout from Woodville to Guntersville, Ala., and vicinity.

Report of Maj. James W. Paramore, Third Ohio Cavalry.

CAMP THIRD OHIO CAVALRY,
Woodville, Ala., August 21, 1862.

SIR: I have the honor to report the safe arrival on last evening of squadron A and D, sent out on the 19th instant, under my command, on a scout to Guntersville and vicinity. I proceeded via Vienna and around the bend of the river, and returned by Law's Landing, camping at Henryville. On the first [day] of the scout I captured as prisoners Capt. J. B. Turney, Company K, First Tennessee, and Private John T. Wilson, same company and regiment, with a large number of letters, which they were attempting to smuggle through our lines into Tennessee; took as prisoners, with their horses, Thomas B. Yates and A. C. Shaffner, with Southern papers, letters, and about $960 in Confederate bonds and money, which they were also smuggling through our lines from rebel officers and soldiers. I think they are also connected with the rebel army as soldiers or spies.

On Wednesday, the second day of the scout, I seized 12 good working mules from the estate of Alexander Erskine, and receipted for the same for the use of the United States; also 6 negroes, belonging to the same estate, who have recently been employed in the rebel service at Guntersville, Ala., in constructing earthworks, digging rifle pits, &c. I also seized 1 mule of John Rayburn, 3 from John Ryan, and 1 from William Read; also 14 head of cattle and 3 mules from B. Mathews, for which no receipts were given. These last-mentioned persons were all over the river, having deserted their homes, and are engaged either as members of companies or aiders or abettors of the guerrillas and bushwhackers in the vicinity. No responsible person could be found to whom to receipt for said property, but I left word that if the owners would call at our headquarters proper vouchers would be given. I sent a small detachment of my command, under command of Lieutenant Williams, to Law's Landing, who captured as prisoners G. W. Morgan, of Colonel Howard's Alabama cavalry, and Ira T. Cobb, an active aider and abettor of the rebels, and also thought to be a bushwhacker. He was armed at the time of his arrest. Also a colored boy, private servant of Major Weeden. He also destroyed two skiffs in which they had crossed the river. The forces across the river continue about the same as contained in my last report.

The letters captured contained valuable information of the movements of the rebel army.

The highest praise is due the officers and soldiers of the command for their energy in procuring the property taken and prisoners captured and the good behavior and gallant conduct during the scout. All of which property is hereby turned over to you, together with the prisoners taken, for your disposal.

Respectfully submitted.

Your obedient servant,

J. W. PARAMORE,
Major, Third Ohio Volunteer Cavalry.

Col. L. ZAHM.

AUGUST 19-21, 1862.—Raid on Louisville and Nashville Railroad; skirmishes at Pilot Knob, Drake's Creek, and Manscoe Creek, near Edgefield Junction (20th), and action (21st) on the Hartsville Road, near Gallatin, Tenn.

REPORTS, ETC.

No. 1.—Brig. Gen. Richard W. Johnson, U. S. Army, of action August 21.

No. 2.—Col. Edward M. McCook, Second Indiana Cavalry, of action August 21.

No. 3.—Lieut. Col. Robert R. Stewart, Second Indiana Cavalry, of action August 21.

No. 4.—Capt. Levi Chilson, Fourth Kentucky Cavalry, of action August 21.

No. 5.—Col. George C. Wynkoop, Seventh Pennsylvania Cavalry, of action August 21.

No. 6.—Col. John H. Morgan, Second Kentucky Cavalry (Confederate), commanding Cavalry Brigade, including proclamation.

No. 1.

Report of Brig. Gen. Richard W. Johnson, U. S. Army, of action August 21.

HARTSVILLE, TENN., *August 22, 1862.*

I have the honor to report that on the 11th instant I left McMinnville, Tenn., in command of three regiments of infantry, one battery of artillery, and 640 cavalry, taken from the Second Indiana, Lieutenant-Colonel Stewart; Fourth Kentucky, Captain Chilson; Fifth Kentucky, Major Winfrey, and Seventh Pennsylvania, Colonel Wynkoop. With this force I marched to Smithville, where I was joined by two additional regiments of infantry. With this command I proceeded to Liberty. Here I received an order recalling my infantry and artillery, and I sent them back to McMinnville.

Hearing that the enemy, under Colonel Morgan, was encamped in an old field, in the angle formed by the Cumberland and Caney Fork, with my cavalry I marched to the point designated, and found that I had been incorrectly informed, but was here told that the force had left for Kentucky. I determined to return to Liberty, thence to Cookville, and await their return.

On my arrival at Cookville I received reliable information to the effect that the enemy was encamped in or near Hartsville, and I took up the march for that place; but on reaching it found that he had left the evening before, going in the direction of Gallatin. I took possession of his old camp, captured several prisoners, a number of wagons, mules, horses, &c., which had been taken from Colonel Boone's command.

At this place I heard of the approach of Forrest in my rear, and decided upon uniting my force to the one in Gallatin, for the purpose of resisting an attack from the combined forces of Forrest and Morgan; but on my approach to Gallatin I found that it was in the possession of Morgan's forces, which I was satisfied did not exceed 800 men. I immediately ordered an attack. Lieutenant-Colonel Stewart and Major Winfrey, gallantly leading the charge of their respective regiments, threw their whole strength against the enemy with terrible effect. Colonel Wynkoop and Captain Chilson also brought their commands handsomely into action, and for some time the conflict seemed to progress finely for us. Soon some horses were wounded, riders killed, and confusion began to appear. Regimental and company organizations were lost, and without any apparent cause at least half of my command precipitately fled, throwing away their arms, &c. Many of the men, after getting a thousand yards from the enemy, wildly discharged their revolvers in the air. I sent back a staff officer to rally them, but they could not be induced to reappear on the field. Seeing my advance wavering, I ordered a retreat and tried to rally them behind a hedge and fence, but as soon as the firing became general the whole line gave way. I tried to get them to stand at several different points with the same result. Finally, seeing that I could get them to fight no longer, I ordered a retreat, and marched to the rear about 3 miles, and undertook to reform them.

While reforming, seeing that I was not pursued, I sent in a flag of truce and asked that I might be allowed to bury the dead, but was informed that the dead were being buried, and I was requested to surrender, men and officers being promised their paroles. This request I declined.

Being well satisfied that my men would stand no longer I took up the line of march for Cairo, on the Cumberland, hoping to be able to take a strong position on the river and hold it; but my rear being hotly pressed I formed line of battle with the Second Indiana and Fifth Kentucky and made my arrangements to fight on foot. Soon the firing became brisk, and my line of battle broke and the men fled in every direction, leaving only about 75 on the ground.

Seeing Lieutenant-Colonel Stewart and Major Winfrey I asked them if they thought it possible for them to rally their men, and they replied that they could not, and that a surrender of the few left was all that could be done. Lieutenant-Colonel Stewart made his escape.

With the few left I remained and held the enemy in check long enough to enable the greater portion of my command to ford the river, but finally, being completely surrounded by overwhelming numbers, I was compelled to surrender.

I regret to report that the conduct of the officers and men as a general thing was shameful in the lowest degree, and the greater portion of those who escaped will remember that they did so shamefully abandoning their general on the battle-field, while if they had remained like true and brave men the result of this conflict would have been quite different.

I turn from the mortifying recollection of their action to mention the names of those whose conduct was meritorious in the highest degree. My assistant adjutant-general, Capt. W. C. Turner, exhibited the same cool courage which characterized his conduct on the field of Shiloh. Lieutenant Hill, Second Indiana Cavalry, and acting aide-de-camp, was of great service to me, and proved himself a man of courage. Adjutant Wynkoop, when his regiment became disorganized, joined me, and his gallantry and courage were conspicuous. He was killed at my side assisting me to rally the troops. Lieutenant-Colonel Stewart, commanding the Second Indiana, was foremost in the charge, and exhibited great coolness and courage. Captain Leabo, Second Indiana, had command of four companies of his regiment and handled them well, but was taken prisoner early in the action. Captain Starr, with his company (C), did good execution. Major Winfrey, Captain Duncan and his company, Lieutenants Campbell and Cheek, and Captain Carter and his company, all of the Fifth Kentucky, behaved well, and managed their troops with skill and proved themselves gallant men.

My loss was 30 killed, 50 wounded, and 75 taken prisoners. About 200 horses were killed or disabled in this action.

Very respectfully, your obedient servant,

R. W. JOHNSON,
Brigadier-General.

Col. J. B. FRY, *A. A. G., Chief of Staff, Huntsville, Ala.*

No. 2.

Report of Col. Edward M. McCook, Second Indiana Cavalry, of action August 21.

MURFREESBOROUGH, *August 31, 1862.*

SIR: I have the honor to inclose the report of Lieut. Col. R. R. Stewart, commanding that portion of my regiment engaged in the fight with Morgan's rebel forces at Gallatin on the 21st instant. It is a plain and concise statement of facts, to which I would most respectfully call your attention.

At the time the last expedition in pursuit of Morgan started I was absent on special duty, but from the past good conduct of my regiment, as well as reports, official and unofficial, which I have carefully compared, I feel satisfied that none, either officers or men, in Lieutenant-Colonel Stewart's command were responsible for this disaster or should share its disgrace.

I have carefully preserved and examined the reports of company officers, and of course drew my conclusions concerning this fight from them. These conclusions differ so widely from the statements contained in a printed paper published in the Louisville Journal, purporting to be the official report of Brigadier-General Johnson, that I feel it to be my duty to respectfully request a court of inquiry, to convene at the earliest day practicable.

If my command or any of them have conducted themselves in a manner unworthy brave soldiers and true men I desire to know it, that their shame may be exposed; if otherwise, then simple justice demands that they shall be fully exculpated from any disgrace which may attach to this affair. If there has been cowardice or incompetency, or both combined, on the part of either officers or men, is it not due the gallant Army of the Ohio, upon which no stain has ever yet rested, that the responsibility should be fixed where it belongs?

I have the honor to inclose herewith a list of killed, wounded, and missing of my regiment in the engagement,* and should the general commanding deem copies of reports of company officers necessary to

---

* Nominal list omitted shows 14 enlisted men killed; 2 officers and 40 enlisted men wounded, and 1 officer and 29 enlisted men missing.

sustain my request for a court of inquiry I will forward them so soon as required.

Very respectfully, your obedient servant,

EDWARD M. McCOOK,
Colonel, Commanding Regiment.

Col. J. B. FRY, *Chief of Staff, Army of the Ohio.*

No. 3.

Report of Lieut. Col. Robert R. Stewart, Second Indiana Cavalry, of action August 21.

NASHVILLE, TENN., *August* 22, 1862.

SIR: I have the honor to report herewith the part taken by my command in the engagement which occurred between General Johnson and General Morgan on the 21st instant near Gallatin.

Leaving McMinnville on the 11th instant, our efforts to find or obtain intelligence of the whereabouts of the enemy were fruitless until the 19th instant, when at Cookville we obtained reliable information that General Morgan, with a command 800 strong, was at Hartsville. This intelligence we got by intercepting the enemy's mail.

General Johnson here asked my advice as to whether we should follow in pursuit. I replied that we had been in search of the information just received, and urged that we should follow in the morning, with a force of cavalry about 700 strong, consisting of detachments of the Second Indiana, Seventh Pennsylvania, Fourth Kentucky, and Fifth Kentucky Regiments. We took up the line of march and moved 2½ miles beyond Hartsville, where we recaptured some prisoners, horses, mules, and wagons which had been taken from Colonel Boone a few days previous. At this place we learned that Morgan had gone to retake Gallatin. Early next morning we pushed forward in the direction of Gallatin. My command—the Second Indiana—composed the advance of the column. I threw forward Companies C and D as an advance guard. After moving some 9 or 10 miles, Captain Johnson, of Company D, sent back word that they were in sight of the enemy's pickets. I returned the order to the advance guard to press them. This being done, and 1½ miles farther advanced, word was returned from the front to the column that the enemy in force were moving to the right and left. We also received reliable intelligence that Morgan had been re-enforced, and that his command was at least 3,000, consisting of cavalry and infantry, all of which I communicated to General Johnson, who in reply ordered me to engage them.

I here halted the advance guard, and the enemy appearing in heavy columns on my right, I had my men to throw down the fence of an open field, marched my regiment in, formed it into line, gave the command forward, and opened fire upon the enemy's column, which after two volleys was broken, and we drove them about 500 yards, when a terrific fire was opened upon the right and left flanks of my command. Seeing that no support came to my aid, I ordered Captain Leabo to take command of the right squadron, face it to the right, and protect the right flank. Discovering that this force was insufficient for the purpose I ordered Companies A and B to charge in aid of Captain Leabo, which they did, but the fire being so destructive, they were compelled to retire after severe loss. At the same time I made an effort to change front to the left, but here I received orders from General Johnson to fall back, which command my men executed in perfect order, marching off the field in a walk.

I gained my second position and formed my command front to the rear on the left of an old log stable, and held the ground until the Fifth Kentucky, panic-stricken, fled from the field in disorder. Here I again received orders from General Johnson to fall back. In the execution of this order the enemy pressed us hard, yet I am proud to report that my men moved in order and gained their third position unconfused at a place called the Cross Lanes, a distance of 1½ miles.

General Johnson at this time remarked to me, "Your men have acted most nobly in this fight, but the Kentuckians have disgraced me and my State." Said he, "I believe I will send in a white flag, asking permission to bury my dead." I replied that the idea was a good one, as it would give us an opportunity to restore order and fortify. He called for a white flag, and Captain Turner, with one of my orderlies, proceeded with it to the enemy's lines. While this was transpiring, with my command I gained the advantage of 100 yards of picket and rail fence, which by means of some labor I formed into fortifications, protecting the right and left flanks of my command. This was by far the best position we had occupied, and here we determined to make our best effort. I dismounted my men and ascertained the number of cartridges left, which I found to be an average of 7 rounds to the man.

When Captain Turner returned he reported that the wounded would be properly cared for and the dead decently interred and that General Morgan desired an interview with General Johnson. Whereupon General Johnson, with the white flag, rode to General Morgan, and in about twenty minutes returned and informed me of the result of the interview, namely, that Morgan had demanded an immediate surrender and would parole without delay both officers and men—allowing the former to retain their side-arms—which he had refused, and, said he, "We must get out of here," and ordered a retreat.

I commanded my men to mount, and taking my place in the advance marched off in column of fours and in a walk. We had gone about 1½ miles in the direction of Cairo when the report came forward that the enemy were charging our rear. General Johnson here ordered me to face my men front to the rear and resist the enemy's charge, which I executed, and had formed line, when the Fifth Kentucky came dashing through in a style of confusion more complete than the flight of a drove of stampeded buffaloes, if possible disgracing their former inglorious conduct. There appeared to be a question of rivalry between officers and men for which should outvie in the disgrace of their cowardly scamper. After they had got through my ranks order was restored, and we waited some ten minutes for the reported enemy, giving my men orders to reserve their fire; they faithfully did so until the rebels advanced to within 25 yards, then, upon order given, opened a volley which broke the rebel line and threw them back in confusion some 500 yards. In the mean time General Johnson's whole command, save the Second Indiana, had left and taken up a hurried retreat.

Here General Johnson rode up to me and asked what he should do. I replied that no officer could command those damned cowards, pointing toward the Fifth Kentucky retreating. He then said to me, "I shall surrender," and asked me for a white hankerchief, which I refused to give. He then asked my chief bugler to sound a parley; the bugler replied that he "did not know the call." General Johnson then obtained a white handkerchief from some one and started it through the lines of my regiment. It was here that I rode in front of my regiment and told my men that they were about to be surrendered; and, said I, "Indianians, never surrender; follow me!" and moved off with all of my men who had heard the order. We found the enemy on our right and left. On our retreat luckily we found a negro, whom I pressed, and who guided me to a ford, and we were enabled to cross the Cumberland River. Having crossed in safety, I posted Captain Ross and 5 men as pickets, to watch and report the movement of the enemy. I had proceeded about 5 miles when Captain Ross reported a portion of the rebels had crossed and were in pursuit. I ordered the "Trot—March," but soon learned that it was a portion of my own men, with Captains Johnson, Kessler, Adjutant Woolley, and Lieutenants Beck, Barnett, and Barnes, who, occupying a position at the left of my line, did not hear my order to follow. I ordered a halt and waited until they came up; then moved to Stone River and encamped for the night.

Along the whole line of retreat evidences of the disgraceful conduct of the Fifth Kentucky appeared. Enfield rifles, pistols, sabers, saddlebags, canteens, curry-combs, brushes, and hats had been thrown away and abandoned in helter-skelter style. Perfect disorder must have prevailed during this cattle-like scamper.

With my command I arrived at Nashville on the morning following at 8 o'clock a. m., when I learned that the Fifth Kentucky and other portions of General Johnson's command had been swift enough to reach Nashville on the evening before.

Although the result of the engagement was an unfortunate one, yet I am happy to report the uniform good conduct of the Second Indiana Cavalry.

Further evidence of the gallantry of my command appears by reference to the printed report of Adjutant Woolley, to which your attention is most respectfully called.*

I have not space to enumerate individual acts. Suffice to say that the highest compliments which I could pay to any one is due to all.

Very respectfully, your obedient servant,

R. R. STEWART,
Lieutenant-Colonel Second Indiana Cavalry.

Col. E. M. McCook.

No. 4.

Report of Capt. Levi Chilson, Fourth Kentucky Cavalry, of action August 21.

NASHVILLE, TENN., *August* 26, 1862.

SIR: I herewith send you a report of the casualties in the First Squadron of Fourth Kentucky Cavalry in the battle at Gallatin, Tenn., on the 21st instant.

Company A, commanded by Capt. Levi Chilson, went in the fight with Lieut. William D. Hooker and 28 men: Wounded, officers, 1; killed, enlisted men, 2; wounded, enlisted men, 2; missing, 3; total, 7.

Company C went into the fight with First Lieut. Sylvester W. Raplee

---

* Not found.

and 26 men: Killed, enlisted men, 2; wounded, enlisted men, 1; missing, enlisted men, 7; total, 10.

L. CHILSON,

Captain, Comdg. First Squadron Fourth Kentucky Cavalry.

Major SIDELL.

No. 5.

Report of Col. George C. Wynkoop, Seventh Pennsylvania Cavalry, of action August 21.

NASHVILLE, *August* 26, 1862.

SIR: I have the honor to submit the following report of the forces engaged near Gallatin, Tenn., on the 21st instant, under command of Brigadier-General Johnson, now a prisoner of war.

We left Hartsville early on the morning of the 21st instant and marched in the direction of Gallatin, which is 14 miles west of Hartsville, with the Second Indiana Cavalry, under command of Lieutenant-Colonel Stewart, numbering 287 men, in the advance; then my command, consisting of detachments of three companies of my regiment and two of the Fourth Kentucky Cavalry, numbering in all 187 men, and a detachment of the Fifth Kentucky Cavalry, under command of Major Winfrey, numbering 293 men, in the rear; our force, including officers and men, numbering some 767 men.

We marched on slowly until about 8 o'clock, when General Johnson was informed that the rebel pickets were driven in 3 miles from Gallatin. We were then ordered to march in close column by fours. Soon after the general received word by a courier from the advance guard that the enemy were flanking us right and left. We then moved on rapidly about 1 mile, when we were ordered to halt and take down the fence on our right, and soon our line of battle was formed in the field.

The enemy then made a stand to our right, and the Second Indiana was ordered to charge upon them; the charge was a complete success, and threw the rebel line into great confusion. Too great praise cannot be awarded Lieutenant-Colonel Stewart for the manner in which he conducted this charge.

My command was ordered to engage the enemy on the left, where they were firing from behind trees and bushes, but owing to the superiority of their arms I could not do effective service. I ordered my men to take down a fence and was about to charge upon them, when I was ordered by General Johnson to fall back.

About this time the Fifth Kentucky seemed to have been panic-stricken and retreated in great disorder. I fell back to the brow of a hill and formed a line, men dismounted; the rebels pushed forward and a fiercely contested battle ensued.

The general, seeing the superior numbers of enemy, ordered us to retreat to a cross-road, where we halted, and the general sent in a flag of truce by his adjutant, asking permission to bury his dead. Col. John H. Morgan, who seemed to be in command of the rebel forces, sent word that he would attend to our wounded and bury our dead, and solicited an interview with General Johnson. The general rode over and had an interview with Colonel Morgan, who demanded an immediate and unconditional surrender, saying he was prepared to march three heavy columns of cavalry on us.

General Johnson returned, saying that further resistance would be useless, owing to the superior number of the enemy. He immediately ordered a retreat, and after retreating about 1 mile found that the enemy were charging on our rear guard. We then halted and again formed a line of battle, with the men dismounted. We held our fire until the enemy advanced within about 50 yards, when we poured in a volley which scattered them in all directions.

We now fell back to a ravine and awaited their coming; they soon advanced, and met with the same result as before. We were about to charge upon them when to our right a heavy column of rebel cavalry dashed forward and was about to cut us off from the river. General Johnson, seeing them, hoisted a white flag and proposed to surrender his whole force. Seeing that to stand now would be useless, I, with part of my command and parts of the Second Indiana and Fifth Kentucky, numbering in all about 200 men, dashed forward through their lines and made good our escape; the balance of our force, consisting of parts of the three commands, broke to the left and crossed the Cumberland River about 4 miles to the east of the town of Lebanon. We arrived in Nashville about 2 o'clock next morning.

The force of the enemy I estimate at about from 1,400 to 1,500 of Morgan's cavalry and about 1,000 armed citizens.

The following is a list of the killed, wounded, and missing of the three different commands, as near as can be ascertained:

Of my command—

Commissioned officers killed, 1 (Adjt. N. Wynkoop); commissioned officers wounded 2 (Capt. Levi Chilson and Lieut. Joseph Vale). Non-commissioned officers and privates killed, 8; missing, 43.

Of the Second Indiana Cavalry—

Commissioned officers wounded, 2; missing, 1. Non-commissioned officers and privates killed, 12; wounded, 40; missing, 31.

Of the Fifth Kentucky Cavalry—

Commissioned officers wounded, 3. Non-commissioned officers and privates missing, 101.

Total killed, wounded, and missing, 244.

The report of killed may not be correct, as many of the missing may have been killed. All the officers and men of my command fought with great courage and coolness during the engagement, promptly obeying all commands.

Great credit is due Captain Chilson and Lieutenant Raplee, of the Fourth Kentucky, as well as their men, for courage shown throughout the engagement.

My report would have been handed in much sooner had it not been for my illness since my arrival here.

I am, sir, with high respect, your most obedient servant,

GEO. C. WYNKOOP,
Colonel Seventh Pennsylvania Cavalry.

Col. J. B. FRY, *Assistant Adjutant-General.*

No. 6.

Reports of Col. John H. Morgan, Second Kentucky Cavalry (Confederate),
including proclamation.

HEADQUARTERS MORGAN'S BRIGADE,
Gallatin, Tenn., August 22, 1862.

GENERAL: I have the honor to report that having received information while at Hartsville that a force of 300 Federal infantry had arrived in this place on the morning of the 19th and were committing depredations on the inhabitants, robbing houses and arresting all those citizens who had shown kindness to the officers and men of my command while stationed here, I left my camp near Hartsville at 12 m. on the same day and encamped about 5 miles from Gallatin.

Fearing that the Federals would return by rail to Nashville, I dispatched Capt. [J. B.] Hutcheson with Company F and a portion of my advanced guard to burn up the trestle work at Saundersville, and thus cut off their retreat, while I attacked Gallatin. Some delay was experienced owing to the difficulties of the ground during a dark night, but the plan met with entire success. The trestle work was burned, and the guard of about 60 men driven into a stockade were followed so closely by my men that they ran them out on the other side, killing some and taking 16 prisoners; the remainder got into the woods and escaped.

The 300 Federals having, I suppose, advice of my arrival, attempted to leave by train with some 60 citizens they had arrested in Gallatin, with no other charge against them than that of being favorable to our cause, but cut off by Company E, of my command, they were obliged to leave the cars and march their prisoners along the Nashville railway track. I pushed on with four companies and came up with a detachment of about 80 men, under command of Captain [Abraham H.] Miller; 35 prisoners were taken by my men and the remainder either fell or escaped into the woods. A second detachment were reached who had charge of the prisoners. I recovered 40 of these poor fellows, who had been treated with great cruelty; the remainder were hurried on by the Federals and lodged in a block-house, or stockade, which I attacked, but met with such determined resistance that I retreated toward Gallatin. Before this fort I lost 2 of my best officers and 3 men.

I took in this expedition some 120 prisoners, killed and wounded some 60 of the enemy, and carried off at least 200 muskets, which I have distributed among my new recruits.* Had I not been obliged to leave my howitzers at Knoxville to repair the carriages worn-out in my last expedition to Kentucky I could have captured every detachment of guards on bridges between Gallatin and Nashville; but these stockades are not to be taken by troops unaccompanied by artillery.

When evening came I was with my command within 8 miles of Nashville, having destroyed every bridge between Gallatin and the Edgefield Junction. I have learned also from an engineer of high standing that the tunnel burned on the last expedition is so completely destroyed that it never can be repaired, the rocks having fallen in in every direction.

I have the honor to be, with the highest respect, general, your most obedient servant,

JOHN H. MORGAN,
Colonel, Commanding Cavalry.

General RANDOLPH.

—

HDQRS. MORGAN'S REGT., *Hartsville, Tenn., Aug. 22, 1862.*

GENERAL: I beg to confirm my dispatch of the 22d instant announcing the result of yesterday's expedition. My command, consisting of my own regiment, 700 strong, and a squadron of Texas Rangers, numbering about 100 men, returned that day, worn-out, to Gallatin.

---

* As reported by the regimental records the Union loss in the skirmishes at Pilot Knob, Drake's Creek, and Manscoe Creek, near Edgefield Junction, August 20, was 2 men killed, 3 men wounded, and 5 officers and 158 men captured.

At 11 p. m. I received information from one of my friendly scouts that the enemy's cavalry were encamped on the road-side between Castalian Springs and Hartsville, a distance of only 12 miles from my camp. Judging from the fact that they had halted by the road-side, I concluded that they intended to march at night and attack early in the morning, and I made my preparations accordingly, dispatching scouts upon whom I could depend to bring me positive information as to the enemy's movements. At daybreak my column was on the move, and as the advanced guard reached the head of the town my pickets came galloping in, followed by my principal scout, who reported that he was closely pursued by a large body of cavalry. Not wishing, on account of the inhabitants, to make Gallatin the scene of our contest, I advanced my column, and was greeted on reaching the Hartsville pike by a heavy fire from that direction. I dismounted the two leading companies to fight and threw them into the woods on the left of the road. The enemy increased his fire and I gradually had my whole command engaged.

The fight began at 6.30 o'clock and was maintained without much advantage on either side, the enemy having perhaps rather the best of it at first, until about 8.30 o'clock, when they began to fall back and my men to redouble their efforts. At 9.30 o'clock I had driven them 4 miles and was preparing for a final charge, when a flag of truce was brought proposing an armistice in order to bury their dead, My reply was that I could entertain no proposition except unconditional surrender. I learned then that the troops were commanded by Brigadier-General Johnson. During the parley the enemy had formed into line of battle, and were evidently ready to defend themselves from any fresh attack. I divided my force into three divisions, leading one myself in the direction which I thought General Johnson had taken. Maj. [G. W.] Morgan had five companies under his orders on my left. Lieut. Col. [B. W.] Duke, on my right, had three companies and his advanced guard. Some delay was occasioned by the non-arrival of my gallant Texas Rangers, who formed part of the body under my own immediate orders. They had been separated from their horses during the preceding fight and had not been able to recover them in time to come to the front. On their arrival we marched on in the direction of the enemy, and Colonel Duke's division, coming within sight, advanced at a canter and opened fire. General Johnson's forces, being on a good pike, retreated for some time faster than my men, who were on difficult ground, could follow, but after a pursuit of some 2 miles they were overtaken and compelled to fight.

They were dismounted and formed behind their horses. The position they had selected was a very good one, especially as they considerably outnumbered Colonel Duke's force, which was the only one opposed to them; Major Morgan and my own detachment, in the eagerness of pursuit, having taken too far to the left.

Colonel Duke reports that on perceiving that the enemy had halted he formed his three companies and the advanced guard into columns of squadrons, preserving the regular distances between each, so as to be able to form into line at command and attack. This was done with admirable precision and coolness by his men, and nothing could exceed their gallantry. The enemy were formed under the brow of a hill, and my men were drawn up above them, so that their fire told with effect on my line, while that of the attacking party went over their heads. After a very sharp engagement of about fifteen minutes they broke and ran. General Johnson, his adjutant-general (Captain Turner), Major Winfrey, and a number of privates were captured, but the main body escaped to the hills through the woods and high corn, making for the Cumberland River.

Thus ended an action in which my command, not exceeding 700 men (one whole company being in the rear with prisoners), succeeded in defeating a brigade of 1,200 chosen cavalry, sent by General Buell expressly to take me or drive me out of Tennessee, killing and wounding some 180 and taking 200 prisoners, including the brigadier-general commanding and the greater part of the regimental officers.

My loss in both actions amounted to 5 killed, 18 wounded, and 2 missing. Among the wounded was Captain Huffman, who had his arm shattered by a ball while leading gallantly on his brave Texan Rangers, a small body of men commanded by Maj. [R. M.] Gano, of whom I cannot speak too highly, as they have distinguished themselves ever since they joined my command not only by their bravery, but their good, soldier-like conduct.

To all my officers and men my best acknowledgments are due. Nothing but hard fighting carried them through.

To my personal staff I am deeply indebted. Col. St. Leger Grenfell, acting adjutant-general, ably supported me; Captain Lewellen, my quartermaster, and Capt. Green Roberts, who acted as my aides-de-camp, were most active and fearless in carrying my orders, and the captains of companies cool and collected in the performance of them.

Lieutenant-Colonel Duke led on his regiment, if possible, with more than his usual gallantry, and contributed, by the confidence with which he has inspired his men, to insure the success of the day. Lieutenant-Colonel Duke makes particular mention of the cool and determined manner in which Lieut. [W. S.] Rogers, commanding advanced guard, Capts. Hutcheson, [J. T.] Cassell, and Lieut. [George] White, respectively, commanding the three companies composing his division, behaved. In fact the conduct of both officers and men deserves the highest praise.

I received every assistance from the patriotism and zeal of the neighboring citizens, among whom Major Duffey and Capt. R. A. Bennet were pre-eminent.

I have also to report that I have received a dispatch from General Forrest, stating that he has encamped within 8 miles of me with a re-enforcement of 800 men, but no artillery. The want of this arm cripples my movements and prevents my advance with that certainty of effect which a battery would afford.

Recruits are daily and hourly arriving. The population seems at last to be thoroughly aroused and to be determined on resistance.

I hope shortly, general, to be able to report further successes, and rest assured that no exertions on my part shall be wanting, no sacrifices on that of my officers and men will prevent our giving as good an account of the enemy as our small numbers will admit of.

I have the honor to be, with the greatest respect, general, your most obedient servant,

JOHN H. MORGAN,
Colonel, Commanding Cavalry, C. S. Army.

The ADJUTANT-GENERAL.

P. S.—This morning I received positive information as to General Nelson's intentions and movements. He is retreating from Nashville to re-enforce Bowling Green at the head of 1,500 infantry, 200 cavalry, and 12 cannon.   It is evidently the intention of the Federals to attempt the defense of the line at Bowling Green and Lebanon.

—

Proclamation.

HEADQUARTERS MORGAN'S BRIGADE,
Hartsville, Tenn., August 22, 1862.

SOLDIERS: Your gallant bearing during the last two days will not only be inscribed in the history of the country and the annals of this war, but is engraven deeply in my heart.

Your zeal and devotion on the 20th at the attack of the trestle work at Saundersville and of the Edgefield Junction stockade, your heroism during the two hard fights of yesterday, have placed you high on the list of those patriots who are now in arms for our Southern rights.

All communication cut off betwixt Gallatin and Nashville, a body of 300 infantry totally cut up or taken prisoners, the liberation of those kind friends arrested by our revengeful foes for no other reason than their compassionate care of our sick and wounded, would have been laurels sufficient for your brows; but, soldiers, the utter annihilation of General Johnson's brigade, composed of twenty-four picked companies of regulars and sent on purpose to take us, raises your reputation as soldiers and strikes fear into the craven hearts of your enemies.   General Johnson and his staff with 200 men taken prisoners, 64 killed, and 100 wounded, attest the resistance made, and bear testimony to your valor.   But our victories have not been achieved without loss.   We have to mourn some brave and dear comrades.   Their names will remain in our breasts; their fame outlives them.   They died in defense of a good cause; they died like gallant soldiers, with their front to the foe.

Officers and men, your conduct makes me proud to command you. Fight always as you fought yesterday and you are invincible.

JOHN H. MORGAN,
Colonel, Commanding Cavalry.

———

AUGUST 22, 1862.—Skirmish at Trinity, Ala.

REPORTS.

No. 1.—Col. John K. Mizner, Third Michigan Cavalry.
No. 2.—Maj. Gen. Sterling Price, C. S. Army.

No. 1.

Report of Col. John K. Mizner, Third Michigan Cavalry.

HEADQUARTERS FIRST BRIGADE CAVALRY DIVISION,
Tuscumbia, Ala., August 24, 1862.

Having been directed to furnish a special report touching the conduct of the cavalry in the affair at Trinity, in which our force was driven off by the enemy and a train destroyed, I have the honor to submit the following, which has been furnished me by Major Nelson, Seventh Illinois Cavalry, stationed at Courtland:

Lieut. S. F. Lee, commanding 26 men of Company F, Seventh Illinois Cavalry, reports that when within about 2 miles of Trinity he became aware that three companies of the enemy were moving to intercept the train. On advancing farther he learned that there were six companies one-quarter of a mile from him taking dinner. Here he took 2 prisoners (surgeons) and 3 horses and then turned toward Trinity. Half a mile above Trinity he found the train off the track. He dispatched a messenger to Fox Creek, requesting re-enforcements, the whole force at the train being 20 infantry and 26 cavalry. They formed a line to defend the train, and remained in line about an hour before the enemy advanced. Lieutenant Lee then dismounted his men, leaving one man to hold four horses, and placed his men behind the embankment of the road, when the enemy, advancing to within gun-shot, commenced firing. He says:

We returned the fire, which caused our horses to break loose, and the enemy closed rapidly upon both flanks, and I saw, if we remained, we would be cut off. I therefore ordered my men to fall back, but too late for all to escape. There are 1 commissioned officer and 18 men missing. I learn that 4 were wounded.

Lieutenant Voris, in command of 27 men, Seventh Illinois Cavalry, reports that he had patrolled the road to Fort Rose, and started back for Decatur at 10.30 a. m. Had got as far as Bolding's farm when he met the messenger from Company F, informing him of the condition of the train and threatened attack. He says:

I proceeded through the woods and fields until within about one-half mile of the railroad, where I met Lieutenant Lee, in full retreat. The timber and brush was so thick I could not form my men in line, so I fell back one-half mile, where I endeavored to form a line in a small open space. Before one-half the men were in line the enemy were upon us, breaking my ranks and scattering the men in every direction. I succeeded in getting them together at the Decatur road.

His loss is stated at 1 man dangerously wounded and 2 missing.

Major Nelson says that although Lieutenant Voris is quite a young man there is no braver officer. He is reported to have killed 2 of the enemy with his own hand.

It is possible that more might have been done, but our force being so small, the train off the track, and the enemy appearing in such greatly superior numbers, compelled our men, for their own safety, to abandon the train to its fate.

Major Koehler's report, since received, is the same in substance. Reports from other sources reflect great discredit upon the cavalry, but the faults of others are more easily seen than our own, hence the probable cause of discrepancy. I understand that many reported missing have since returned.

I am, colonel, very respectfully, your obedient servant,

J. K. MIZNER,
Colonel, Commanding Brigade.

Lieut. Col. H. G. KENNETT,
Chief of Staff, Army of the Mississippi.

No. 2.

Report of Maj. Gen. Sterling Price, C. S. Army.

HEADQUARTERS DISTRICT OF THE TENNESSEE,
Tupelo, Miss., August 31, 1862.

GENERAL: I have just received from Captain [P. D.] Roddey a

report of an engagement which he had with the enemy on the 22d instant at Trinity, near Decatur. He states that the enemy's loss in killed and wounded cannot be less than 30; that he captured 37 prisoners, 4 of whom, being wounded, were released on their verbal parole; that he took 5 horses and their equipments, 37 stand of small-arms, and $407 in specie, together with some clothing and sutler's stores. He also destroyed a locomotive and train of cars.

Captain Roddey asks permission to increase his command to a regiment, which he says he can easily raise for the war. I submit the matter to the decision of the general commanding, and respectfully suggest that the four companies of Forrest's cavalry, commanded by Capt. [W. C.] Bacot, which were lately near Guntersville, might be placed under Captain Roddey. These companies were detached by the general commanding some six or eight weeks ago under orders which were not communicated to me, and I do not know therefore whether they are still under my command or not. The headquarters of their regiment are here. It might be well to disband this regiment and to attach the four Alabama companies to an Alabama regiment under Captain Roddey and to consolidate the Tennessee companies here into another regiment.

Yours, very respectfully,

STERLING PRICE,
Major-General, Commanding.

Brig. Gen. THOMAS JORDAN,
Chief of Staff, Chattanooga, Tenn.

AUGUST 23, 1862.—Action at Big Hill, Ky.

REPORTS, ETC.

No. 1.—Maj. Gen. Lewis Wallace, U. S. Army.
No. 2.—General Orders, No. 2, Headquarters Army of Kentucky.
No. 3.—Col. John S. Scott, First Louisiana Cavalry, commanding Brigade, C. S. Army.

No. 1.

Report of Maj. Gen. Lewis Wallace, U. S. Army.

LEXINGTON, KY., *August 24, 1862.*

GENERAL: I regret to report that the enemy moved against Colonel Metcalfe yesterday afternoon. The colonel led his men to attack them on the Big Hill, but they broke and fled, leaving him and his lieutenant-colonel alone on the field. A small body of the Third Tennessee stood and fought, but were driven back to Richmond, after rescuing Metcalfe and Oden. Then enemy advanced and demanded surrender of Richmond. Metcalfe refused to surrender. Link's brigade reached the place in time and is now ready to defend it. Link has three regiments and three field pieces. The conduct of Metcalfe's men was most disgraceful. He refuses to command them any longer. He thinks his loss about 50. I am arresting his runaways as they come to town. Link will whip the rebels if they attack him.

LEW. WALLACE,
Major-General.

Major-General WRIGHT.

No. 2.

General Orders, No. 2, Headquarters Army of Kentucky.

GENERAL ORDERS, }   HDQRS. OF THE ARMY OF KENTUCKY,
No. 2.   }   *Richmond, Ky., August 26, 1862.*

On Saturday, the 23d instant, the Seventh Kentucky Cavalry, under Colonel Metcalfe, together with a battalion of Houk's Third Tennessee Regiment, under Lieutenant-Colonel Chiles, attacked the enemy on Big Hill, in Rockcastle County. Colonel Metcalfe led the attack with much gallantry, but had the mortification to find that not more than 100 of his regiment followed him; the remainder, at the first cannon-shot, turned tail and fled like a pack of cowards, and are now dispersed over a half dozen counties, some fleeing as far as Paris.

All provost-marshals are hereby ordered to arrest and commit to jail any of this regiment, officers or men, who may be found, under any pretense, to be in their neighborhoods, and report their names and rank to the adjutant-general at these headquarters, and to hold them subject to orders.

The conduct of the Tennessee battalion, under Lieutenant-Colonel Chiles, presents a refreshing contrast to the foregoing. They met the enemy bravely, checked his advance, rescued Colonel Metcalfe, abandoned by his own regiment, and, though too few to retrieve the action, at least saved the honor of our arms. Lieutenant-Colonel Chiles will accept the thanks of the major-general, and convey to his officers and soldiers his high appreciation of their gallantry and good conduct.

By order of Major-General Nelson, commanding:

J. MILLS KENDRICK,
Assistant Adjutant-General and Chief of Staff.

No. 3.

Reports of Col. John S. Scott, First Louisiana Cavalry, commanding Brigade, C. S. Army.

HEADQUARTERS KIRBY SMITH'S BRIGADE,
Big Hill, Madison County, Ky., August 24, 1862.

GENERAL: After leaving you I moved the evening of the 21st with the remaining portion of my command toward Mount Vernon to sustain Colonel Morrison, who had been sent two days previous with instructions to occupy Mount Vernon and Crab Orchard. The latter place he failed to occupy, General Smith, with his brigade, having taken possession several hours previous to his arrival. Finding the forces of General Smith too strong to be dispersed, I concluded to drive in his pickets and engage his attention until I could remove all the wagons along my route, hoping by that time to be re-enforced by Colonel Starnes. Having accomplished my objects, and the re-enforcements failing to arrive, I determined to cross over to the Richmond road and move against that place.

On the morning of the 23d instant I left Mount Vernon and took a mountain path that led me into the London and Richmond road. About 3 o'clock in the evening I came within the vicinity of their pickets and learned that Colonel Metcalfe was posted in a strong position on Big Hill with 800 or 900 cavalry and 300 or 400 infantry. My force now numbered about 650, but notwithstanding his advantage in numbers and position I determined to give him battle, and immediately ordered my men forward and the fight commenced. After an engagement of one hour and twenty minutes I succeeded in driving them from the strongest natural position I have ever seen in complete rout toward Richmond, when night put an end to the pursuit. The jaded condition of my horses alone prevented my capturing the whole command. Learning this morning that Richmond was re-enforced during the night with a brigade of infantry and four pieces of artillery from Lexington I fell back to this place.

My loss in the engagement is 4 killed, 12 wounded, and 21 horses. The enemy left upon the field in killed and wounded 120 men. I have captured and paroled near 150 prisoners and my men are still bringing them in from the mountains.

I captured and brought away from the vicinity of Richmond a wagon train (27 in number), with 40 to 50 extra mules. I have taken up to the present time about 175 wagons and 650 mules and horses. I am unable to give you a report of the contents of the wagons, as I have not received the statement from my brigade quartermaster and commissary, who are stationed at London to forward the trains to you.

I refer you to the inclosed letter* for the numbers and positions of the enemy, so far as I have been able to ascertain.

I cannot close my report without making mention of the gallant conduct of the troops comprising the Kirby Smith brigade—First Georgia Cavalry, Colonel Morrison; First Louisiana Cavalry, Lieutenant-Colonel Nixon commanding, and the Buckner Guards, a Kentucky company, commanded by Captain Garnett. They all bore the privation and fatigue of the trip without murmur and conducted themselves most gallantly in the presence of the enemy.

Very respectfully,

J. S. SCOTT,
Colonel, Commanding Brigade.

Maj. Gen. E. KIRBY SMITH.

HEADQUARTERS KIRBY SMITH'S BRIGADE,
Big Hill, Madison County, Ky., August 24, 1862.

SIR: I have forwarded to General Smith through you a report of my engagement near this place. During the chase I captured the horses of Colonel Metcalfe and his coat containing his private papers, among which was a letter from General L. Wallace, commanding at Lexington, stating that he would move a brigade of infantry and four pieces of artillery to Richmond on the 23d. A portion of this force reached Richmond on the 23d and the remainder on the morning of the 24th. I would have taken Richmond on the night of the 23d, but had ridden 25 miles over a very broken country before the fight commenced and chased the enemy 10 miles, which so completely crippled up my horses I could go no farther. General G. Clay Smith has a brigade of cavalry at Crab Orchard.

Enlisting is going on rapidly under the various appliances of the Federals and the State is in great excitement. The camp of instruction has been changed from Dick Robinson to Cynthiana, in Harrison County. The Legislature is in session. George McDuffie has resigned and James F. Robinson elected in his stead. Forty or fifty Kentuckians came into my camp this evening to join me, and report large numbers in the adjacent counties anxious to enlist in the Confederate service,

---

*Not found.

but have no means of escape. They are hemmed in by the Home Guards and Federal troops. I have now captured all the trains on both roads to the Gap, and do not see how I can subsist many days longer without going down into the blue-grass region, and this I cannot do without being sustained by infantry. The troops in this State are all raw recruits, and could be scattered to the winds by one-third their number if the move is made at once. My men are very much fatigued and my horses broken down. I would like to have a few days' rest, unless the necessities of the service demand my immediate assistance. I will be on the road (the London and Richmond) between this point and Rockcastle River until I receive orders.

Very respectfully,

J. S. SCOTT,
Colonel, Commanding.

Col. J. PEGRAM, *Chief of Staff.*

AUGUST 27, 1862.—Skirmish at Round Mountain, near Woodbury, Tenn.

Report of Col. William Grose, Thirty-sixth Indiana Infantry.

MURFREESBOROUGH, TENN., *August 30, 1862.*

GENERAL: I arrived here this morning at 6 o'clock. The forces under my command had an engagement with General Forrest between 3 and 4 o'clock p. m. on the 27th instant at Round Mountain, 2½ miles from Woodbury. He made the attack upon our rear, and as he supposed upon our train. But instead of my train his heavy force came in contact with the Twenty-third Kentucky, under Colonel Mundy. The enemy was handsomely repulsed, and with a portion of Captain Mendenhall's battery, the right wing of the Thirty-sixth Indiana, and Colonel Mundy's regiment we pursued and drove them over 2 miles, scattering them in every direction.

Our loss is 4 of Twenty-third Kentucky and 1 of Lieutenant-Colonel Cochran's cavalry wounded. The loss of the enemy is much larger.

Your obedient servant,

WM. GROSE,
Colonel, Commanding Tenth Brigade.

Brig. Gen. JACOB AMMEN, *McMinnville, Tenn.*

AUGUST 27, 1862.—Skirmish at Bridgeport, Ala., and attack on Fort McCook, Battle Creek, Tenn.

REPORTS.

No. 1.—Col. Leonard A. Harris, Second Ohio Infantry.
No. 2.—Brig. Gen. Samuel B. Maxey, C. S. Army, with congratulatory orders.

No. 1.

Report of Col. Leonard A. Harris, Second Ohio Infantry.

SIR: I have the honor to report that on the 21st of August I was directed by Major-General McCook to occupy the fort at the mouth of Battle Creek. On that night I marched into the fort with two regiments of infantry (the Second and Thirty-third Ohio), Edgarton's Ohio battery, and 110 of the Fourth Ohio Cavalry.

On the 22d Major-General Buell directed me to send four companies to Bridgeport to take the place of a regiment of infantry withdrawn from that point.

On the same day I received an order to send one regiment and the battery to General McCook. This left me six companies of the Thirty-third and the cavalry to hold this fort.

On the evening of the 26th, all of the stores having been removed from Bridgeport, in pursuance of orders I withdrew the command of Major Lock to the fort.

On the morning of the 27th I received information that the enemy were crossing at Bridgeport. I ordered the cavalry to Bridgeport, with instructions that if the enemy had crossed to attack him at once, and if possible to drive him into the Tennessee River. I also directed the cavalry on picket on the Jasper road to push forward as far as Jasper and report promptly the advance of the enemy in that direction.

Major Pugh, with the cavalry, had no sooner engaged the force at Bridgeport than the enemy put a battery of four guns, one a siege gun, in position on the opposite bank of the Tennessee River, about 800 yards from the fort. They opened on the fort and camp and shelled it without intermission, except to allow their guns to cool, for twelve hours. I soon received information that the enemy had crossed in force at Bridgeport; that the cavalry had attacked them without success, and were then falling back to the fort. I was satisfied that my scouts would report the Decherd road in possession of the enemy. I therefore made preparation as a last resort to hold a small mountain path which I understood tapped the Decherd road about 8 miles from the fort. I placed three companies of infantry and the cavalry, which had just arrived, at that point, with instructions to hold it to the last extremity.

In the evening my scouts from Jasper reported that the enemy were not advancing in that direction. I immediately directed two companies to proceed to the Battle Creek Ford, where the Jasper road joins the Decherd road, and to hold it against any force that might be brought against them. I also threw a company of riflemen in the pits to annoy the enemy and cover the withdrawal of our forces and stores from the fort. The wagons were loaded with the most valuable stores; the balance were piled up ready to be burned. The tents were cut up and the wagon wheels were wrapped with them. As soon as it was dark I commenced the withdrawal of the forces and the stores for which I had transportation. This I succeeded in doing without loss.

The casualties in the fort were 1 killed and 9 slightly wounded, including my acting assistant adjutant-general, Vandegrift, and orderly, Henry Norris, who is a brave and cool little fellow.

An hour after the last of the forces had been withdrawn Captain Mathews, of the Fourth Ohio Cavalry, applied the torch to the stores which were left behind, completely destroying them.

I arrived with the command at Decherd on the 29th and reported to Major-General Buell at that point.

The enemy had on the day before the attack four regiments of infantry and a battalion of cavalry, under command of General Maxey, and were also in direct communication with Chattanooga, 27 miles by rail, from which place they could receive re-enforcements to any extent.

My force, all told, for duty were 450 of the Thirty-third Ohio Regiment and 110 of the Fourth Ohio Volunteer Cavalry. Lieutenant-Colonel Moore, who commanded the Thirty-third Ohio, his officers and men, with few exceptions, acted gallantly and to my entire satisfaction. I cannot speak too highly of Captain Mathews, of the cavalry, who executed with promptness and fidelity the arduous duties assigned him. I am also under many obligations to my acting assistant adjutant-general, who acted coolly and gallantly in communicating my orders to the command. Brigade Quartermaster Bird, Commissary Hills, and Quartermaster Colburn, of the Thirty-third Ohio, conducted themselves so as to meet with my entire approbation. They coolly and effectually, under a heavy fire, directed the loading and removal of the stores. Under the circumstances, the necessity of longer holding the fort having passed, I acted according to instructions in withdrawing my command. I believe that the enemy, relying on their command of the Decherd road by their artillery and infantry fire, neglected until it was too late to throw a force in my front as they had done in my rear, which would have necessitated a retreat through the mountains by uncertain and difficult paths.

Very respectfully,

L. A. HARRIS,
Colonel, Commanding Ninth Brigade.

Captain JONES, *Assistant Adjutant-General.*

No. 2.

Report of Brig. Gen. Samuel B. Maxey, C. S. Army, with congratulatory orders.

CHATTANOOGA, TENN., *August 31, 1862.*

COLONEL: I send with this a copy of Brigadier-General Maxey's report of the affairs at Bridgeport and Battle Creek, in which a part of his command was engaged on the 27th instant. The affairs were conducted with judgment and spirit, deserving high commendation, and I shall be gratified if the general commanding sees proper to notice it in general orders. Such notice of the good conduct of new troops in their first engagement with the enemy would be gratifying and encouraging

Respectfully, your obedient servant,

SAM. JONES,
Major-General.

Lieut. Col. GEORGE G. GARNER,
Assistant Adjutant-General.

[Inclosure.]

HEADQUARTERS CONFEDERATE STATES FORCES,
Near Graham's, opposite Mouth of Battle Creek, Tenn.,
August 30, 1862.

CAPTAIN: I have the honor to submit the following report of the affairs in which a portion of the troops under my command were engaged on the 27th instant:

Early in the morning I ordered Capt. P. H. Rice, commanding Company A, [J. R.] Howard's battalion Georgia and Alabama cavalry, to ford the Tennessee River about 2½ miles below Bridgeport, and cautiously approach that place and attack the enemy. Captain Rice found, however, that the enemy had precipitately evacuated the night before. This being communicated to me, I ordered the Thirty-second Alabama Regiment of Infantry, Col. [A.] McKinstry, which was concealed on the bank of the river, to cross. Captain Rice was in the mean time ordered to throw his cavalry well out on the Battle Creek and Stevenson roads. Scarcely had the Thirty-second crossed when the cavalry reported enemy's infantry and cavalry approaching in force, the truth of which was made apparent from the clouds of dust in the roads. I immediately ordered the Thirty-second to be formed in line of battle near the crest of the hill in the town, and in a few moments the enemy's cavalry (Fourth Ohio and one other, name not known) dashed up in full speed, and were permitted to come within less than 50 yards of the infantry before a gun was fired, when a galling fire was poured into them and they retreated in great confusion. In a short time clouds of dust warned me of the enemy's approach on our left, and to meet it I had the front of the left wing changed forward in time to receive another dash of cavalry, which was again thrown in confusion by another volley more effective than the first, and he again retreated but reformed, and by the dust I soon saw he was approaching the center. A company of the Thirty-second Alabama, armed with the Enfield rifle, commanded by Lieut. [A.] Sellers, was placed in the center in ambush, and as the enemy came up the hill in very close range this company arose and delivered its deadly fire simultaneously with the wings (separated for cover), and this time they broke and fled in perfect confusion. While this portion of the fight was going on my batteries, consisting of Capt. [S. L.] Freeman's [Tennessee] and Capt. [G. A.] Dure's [Georgia] artillery and one 24-pounder rifle gun, opened out (by previous agreement) on the enemy's works at the mouth of Battle Creek, about 5 miles distant up the river, and continued incessantly during the entire day. The heavy columns of dust bearing toward Stevenson from the enemy's camps around there showed a general commotion. At night I ordered the battery commanders to keep the fire up, believing the enemy, if properly managed, would evacuate before day.

At about 2 o'clock in the morning the work was abandoned in great confusion, the enemy burning most of his commissary stores, but leaving in our possession some $30,000 worth of valuable property, embracing some commissary stores, ordnance stores, quartermaster's stores, clothing, all his tents, 32 horses and 4 mules, a few wagons and ambulances, and some few medicines, and a splendid case of surgical instruments, besides some sutlers' stores, a number of officers' trunks, many of the post commander's papers, and some very valuable maps.

It is proper to observe that after the fight commenced at Bridgeport the Third Georgia Cavalry and Twenty-fifth Tennessee Infantry were ordered across, but did not reach the place in time to participate; indeed it was only after the fight had opened that I received notice that the Third Georgia was placed at my disposal temporarily.

I was informed by the major-general commanding several days ago that some cavalry under Colonel Lay would move down the Sequatchie Valley, and I had hoped to have its assistance. At 10 p. m. on the 27th I received a note from Colonel Lay, dated Jasper, 5.30 p. m., informing me that he was there with 550 cavalry, and desired me to inform him of my movements, stating that he heard the cannonading, &c. This I did, with an expression of belief that the enemy would be shelled out before morning, and saying to him in substance that if he would take his position about the mouth of Sweeden's Cove about daylight he would probably get them. It is unfortunate that these suggestions were not acted on, for if they had been the enemy, being panic-stricken by throwing cavalry in his front, the hills on either side, and my forces in rear, would have been easy prey.

I am indebted to Capt. T. M. Scott, assistant adjutant-general; Capt.

C. G. Schultz, assistant inspector-general; Capt. W. H. Lewis, ordnance officer of my staff, and my aide, Lieut. R. C. Andrews, for valuable and efficient aid. The work between the two points kept the first three constantly busy, Captain Scott personally superintending the throwing forward re-enforcements. My aide, Lieutenant Andrews, was with me at Bridgeport, and did his duty coolly and well.

The Thirty-second Alabama did nobly, fighting like veterans, under their able colonel (McKinstry), seconded by Lieutenant-Colonel Maury, distinguished for gallantry and coolness on the field.

Captains Freeman and Dure and the officers under them did their whole duty. Lieutenant Holtzclaw, of Captain Dure's battery, worked the siege gun most of the time and splendidly. It was handled part of the time by Captain McCreery.

Captain Rice and his command acted in a manner worthy of all praise. In short I never saw troops behave better than did the Thirty-second Alabama, Rice's cavalry, Freeman's and Dure's batteries, and the detachment with siege guns. I particularly call your attention to the boldness of this regiment of infantry in wading a broad sheet of water, such as the Tennessee, up to their arm-pits, with retreat cut off and the enemy known to be strong in front.

Should I be furnished with sufficient cavalry to reap the fruits of this movement our cause will be greatly benefited. The work out of which the enemy was shelled is a splendidly constructed field work, admirably executed; is the key to the Sequatchie Valley, and its possession completely breaks the enemy's chain up the Tennessee River. With cavalry to operate from that point toward Stevenson and Huntsville the enemy could be kept in constant alarm.

I neglected in its appropriate place to say, which I do with gratitude, that our loss was trifling—only 6 wounded and 1 missing; thus small owing to the fact that the grounds on which the fight took place at Bridgeport were perfectly well known to me, and the men most of the time had the advantage of cover. The enemy's loss for such an affair was heavy, variously estimated from 50 to 75 killed and wounded in the two engagements—certainly not less than 50, and the indications are it was greater.

Very respectfully, your obedient servant,

S. B. MAXEY,
Brigadier-General, Commanding.

Capt. C. S. STRINGFELLOW, *Assistant Adjutant-General.*

—

GENERAL ORDERS, }   HDQRS. ARMY OF THE MISSISSIPPI,
No. 2.   }   *Pikeville, Tenn., September 2, 1862.*

In the attack on the 27th ultimo on the enemy's works at Bridgeport and Battle Creek by the troops under Brigadier-General Maxey the general commanding finds a display of gallantry and boldness, rewarded by complete success, which has rarely been surpassed. He congratulates the brigadier and his gallant officers and men upon one of the most dashing achievements of the day.

By command of General Bragg:

JNO. M. OTEY,
Assistant Adjutant-General.

AUGUST 27, 1862.—Skirmish near Cumberland Gap, Tenn.

Report of Brig. Gen. George W. Morgan, U. S. Army.

CUMBERLAND GAP, *August 29, 1862.*

GENERAL : Nothing of interest on the 28th instant. On the 27th, a small detachment from the First and Second Tennessee, commanded by Captains Meyers and Robbins, attacked and surprised a party of the enemy's cavalry, commanded by Acting Brigadier-General Allston, of South Carolina. Allston, his colors, and 3 privates were captured. The enemy left 4 dead men upon the field and had a considerable number wounded.

The affair was a complete surprise, and we did not sustain any loss.

GEORGE W. MORGAN,
Brigadier-General, Commanding.

Brig. Gen. G. W. CULLUM, *Chief of Staff, Washington.*

AUGUST 27–OCTOBER 22, 1862.—Operations of Wheeler's Cavalry in Tennessee and Kentucky.*

SUMMARY OF THE PRINCIPAL EVENTS.

Aug.   27, 1862.—Command crosses the Tennessee at Chattanooga.

      30, 1862.—Skirmish at Altamont, Tenn.

Sept. 6, 1862.—Affair on the Gallatin Road, Tenn.

      8, 1862.—Affair at Kentucky Line.

      9, 1862.—Skirmishes on the Franklin and Scottsville Roads, Ky.

     10, 1862.—Skirmish at Log Church, Ky.

     11, 1862.—Skirmish at Smith's, Ky.

     12, 1862.—Skirmish near Woodburn, Ky.

     16, 1862.—Skirmish near Oakland Station, Ky.

     17, 1862.—Skirmishes on Bowling Green Road and at Merry Oaks, Ky.

     18, 1862.—Skirmish near Cave City, Ky.

     19, 1862.—Skirmishes at Horse Cave and Bear Wallow, Ky.

  20–21, 1862.—Actions near Munfordville, Ky.

     22, 1862.—Skirmish at Vinegar Hill, Ky.

     28, 1862.—Skirmish near Lebanon Junction, Ky.

     29, 1862.—Skirmish on the Elizabethtown Road, Ky.

Oct.   1, 1862.—Skirmish on the Louisville Pike, Ky.

     2, 1862.—Skirmish on the Shepherdsville Road, Ky.

     4, 1862.—Action on the Bardstown Pike, Ky.

     6, 1862.—Skirmishes at Fair Grounds, Springfield, Burnt Cross-Roads, Beach Fork, and Grassy Mound, Ky.

     7, 1862.—Skirmishes at Brown Hill and at Perryville, Ky.

     8, 1862.—Battle of Perryville, Ky.

     9, 1862.—Skirmishes on Mackville Pike and Bardstown Road, Ky.

    10, 1862.—Skirmish at Danville Cross-Roads, Ky.

    11, 1862.—Skirmish at Danville, Ky.

    12, 1862.—Skirmish at Dick's Ford, Ky.

---

* See also October 10–22. Pursuit of the Confederate forces from Perryville to London, Ky.

Oct.   13, 1862.—Wheeler placed in command of all the cavalry of Bragg's army.
               Skirmish on the Lancaster Road, Ky.
        14, 1862.—Skirmishes at Lancaster and on Crab Orchard Road, Ky.
        15, 1862.—Skirmishes at Crab Orchard and Barren Mound, Ky.
        16, 1862.—Skirmishes at Mountain Gap and Mount Vernon, Ky.
        17, 1862.—Skirmishes at Valley Woods and Rocky Hill, Ky.
        18, 1862.—Skirmishes at Cross-Roads, Big Hill, Little Rockcastle River, and
               Mountain Side, Ky.
        19, 1862.—Skirmish at Wild Cat, Ky.
        20, 1862.—Skirmish near Wild Cat, Ky.
        21, 1862.—Skirmish at Pitman's Cross-Roads, Ky.
        22, 1862.—Command arrives at London.

Report of Brig. Gen. Joseph Wheeler, C. S. Army.

HEADQUARTERS CAVALRY,
Knoxville, Tenn., October 30, 1862.

COLONEL: I have the honor to report that on August 27 I moved
across the Tennessee River at Chattanooga with a brigade of cavalry,
consisting of parts of the First Alabama and First Kentucky Regiments.

On the 28th we moved in front of General Hardee's wing. The next
day I received an order to march toward Altamont and drive in the
enemy's scouts on the mountain. We arrived near Altamont at daylight on the morning of the 30th and drove in their pickets on three
sides, firing into their camp and killing, as we afterwards learned, 1
colonel, 1 captain, and 2 privates. The enemy were so alarmed and
deceived that General Buell reported in his official statement, subsequently made to a council of war at Nashville, that General Hardee
attempted to cross the mountain with his corps, but by his placing a
large force at Altamont he had compelled General Hardee to fall back
into the valley. A few hours before we reached Altamont the enemy
had an infantry brigade in ambush on the road, but on our approach
they marched in and joined their main body. After having menaced
their flanks until 12 m. we returned to Sequatchie Valley. We then
moved northward, covering the rear and left flank of the army, having
a slight skirmish near Fleming's.

We arrived at Carthage on September 7, where we were joined by the
Third Georgia Regiment, and the First Alabama was detached. That
night I received orders to proceed toward Nashville and harass the
enemy, &c. At Hartsville I was joined by Col. [J. D.] Bennett
[Ninth Tennessee Cavalry], with about 200 men. The enemy being on
the march from Nashville to Bowling Green, we hovered along their
flank, occasionally skirmishing and making captures and destroying
the railroad and telegraph at every opportunity. A scout succeeded
in capturing a stage, containing a Federal colonel and lieutenant bearing important dispatches. The two Federal officers and the dispatches
were sent to the main army.

On the night of the 11th General Crittenden's entire division encamped
at Woodburn, Ky. My entire command, consisting of nearly 700 men,
were placed in ambush on the road he would have to pass in moving on
his way to Bowling Green. Soon after daylight he commenced to move,
but when near our position the head of the column, discovering us, turned
back. After waiting for some time, having captured a captain and several privates, we withdrew about 2 miles from the pike to rest and feed
the command.

About 2 p. m. the enemy followed us with infantry and cavalry. After warmly engaging them for some time we endeavored to draw them down to a position where the bulk of our force was stationed and where we could develop their strength, and, if possible, separate their infantry from their cavalry. In this we failed. The enemy soon retired, leaving 1 man dead on the field and carrying off 1 major and 10 privates wounded, some of them seriously. We followed them a short distance with about 200 men, but as night was coming on and we were near their strong force we soon rejoined our reserves. General Forrest came up in the rear while the fight was going on, but finding he could not engage the enemy to advantage he retired toward Glasgow.

The next day we proceeded to Merry Oaks, a place midway between Bowling Green and Glasgow, to cover our army and watch the movements of the enemy. We remained at this point, watching the several approaches to Bowling Green, until the 16th, when we moved down to Oakland Station, 7 miles east of Bowling Green, leaving a small force at Merry Oaks to watch the movements of the enemy on the two lower roads.

That night the enemy moved Rousseau's division and a large cavalry force over the river on the Glasgow or Cave City pike, while at the same time more extensive arrangements were being made for a movement across the river in a northerly direction, which led me to believe that the bulk of General Buell's army was to move in that direction. This was also the opinion of all my agents who had been sent into the town. In this we were deceived. The wagon train of General Buell's army, consisting of over 2,000 wagons, crossed in the northerly direction with a comparatively small guard, while the rest of the army moved toward Cave City. Col. [John F.] Lay had been sent to Dripping Springs, with orders to report to me, and Colonel Bennett's command was detached. The enemy pressed upon my pickets during the night, which, together with other movements on their part, convinced me that an early advance was intended. About daylight the enemy's cavalry in large force moved up rapidly in good order toward Cave City, followed by infantry. Finding that they had passed our position we moved rapidly by a circuitous route to gain their front, having previously directed Colonel Lay to remain at his post until our arrival, in order that our combined forces might more effectually retard the enemy. Orders were also sent to the battalion at Merry Oaks to join me at the same place. On arriving there, however, I found Colonel Lay had been gone some time, and also heard that the detachment at Merry Oaks had been driven in by a large force of cavalry. After resisting the enemy's advance until late in the day we finally moved toward Glasgow to collect all detachments on the lower roads and protect some trains at that point. These trains we escorted to Munfordville, arriving at that point about 8 o'clock the next morning.

Our total loss in killed and wounded was 2 officers and 3 privates.

At night we moved down to Horse Cave, near Cave City, to picket the front and watch the enemy, who was concentrating his troops at that place. We were here joined by the First and Third Alabama Regiments, Colonel Lay having been detached. We continued picketing the front, frequently skirmishing heavily with the enemy, with some loss on both sides.

On the morning of the 20th the enemy advanced and deployed their lines in front of their advanced pickets. Our army being now moving from Munfordville, our front was kept unchanged and every effort made to prevent the enemy from learning our movements. Toward evening

Col. [John A.] Wharton arrived with his brigade, which was, however, kept in reserve. The enemy continued deploying their lines all day and in the morning commenced their advance. Our pickets held their ground so well that it was noon before my main body became engaged, which had fallen back to a point about 4 miles from Green River. Here the enemy's infantry advanced in line of battle upon the First and Third Alabama Regiments. After a heavy engagement the enemy, finding that they were simply opposed by cavalry, sent a brigade to turn our right flank. After a gallant resistance and a handsome charge by the First Alabama, in which Lieut. Col. [T. B.] Brown was killed, both regiments were compelled to retire slowly, but in good order, to prevent being entirely cut off, the enemy's dense lines of infantry being in full view and within range both in front and on the right flank. Our artillery, consisting of two guns, attached to Colonel Wharton's and my own brigade, had been placed upon the north side of the river and commenced good work as soon as the enemy came within its range. The First and Third Alabama Regiments retired slowly and finally were compelled to cross the river, which was done in good order. The lines were again formed on the north side of the river, and as the enemy came up we received them warmly with artillery and small-arms. The enemy, discovering that our army had left Munfordville, sent an infantry brigade to turn our right flank. We contested the crossing under a heavy fire of infantry and artillery until this brigade of the enemy had crossed the river about half a mile below the town and was advancing in line perpendicular to our lines. We then fell back about 300 yards and again formed our lines, which allowed the enemy to cross several brigades of infantry and a large force of cavalry, all of which promptly formed line of battle, engaging us as they came up. Their cavalry sounded the charge, but could not be moved toward us. After a short but severe fight, the sun having gone down, we slowly withdrew. The fighting on the north side of the river was done by the First Alabama, Third Georgia, and First Kentucky Regiments, all of which acted as well as could be expected with such disparity of numbers, the Third Georgia suffering most severely. Colonel Wharton's Texas regiment was at all times ready and maneuvered well, but circumstances did not call it into action.

About noon I sent orders to the various pickets beyond the scene of action directing them how to come in; they all joined us safely during the night. We were obliged to move on some 8 miles that night to procure forage and water. Early in the morning Colonel Wharton moved with his brigade some miles farther on to Red Mills to procure rations. The enemy's advance reaching me about noon, my brigade was moved rapidly to a favorable position to receive him. The artillery and most of my cavalry were secreted until the head of a column of not less than 1,500 cavalry had arrived within about 350 yards of our position, when we opened upon them with canister and shell, killing and wounding many men and horses. The enemy deployed as skirmishers and brought up their artillery, engaging us warmly until dark, when they went into camp. Colonel Wharton was notified of the advance when the action first commenced and moved promptly to my assistance. Finding, however, that he was not needed at that point he moved his command toward Hodgensville to watch the other roads leading north from Munfordville, and on which we learned the enemy were also advancing.

Having received written orders from General Hardee to be at Hodgensville by daylight Tuesday morning [23d] at furthest, we moved late that night in that direction, leaving a small picket to watch the enemy during the night. Picked men were also sent to watch General Buell's army as it passed up the pike toward Louisville. They easily counted the regiments, batteries, and wagons which passed, a report of which was sent to headquarters. I will here state that during the entire campaign reports in writing were made several times each day to the major-general commanding the left wing or to the general commanding the army of everything relating to the movements of the enemy which could be ascertained.

On Wednesday morning Colonel Wharton's brigade was ordered to Bardstown, while I remained at Hodgensville and New Haven watching the enemy on the roads from below and toward Elizabethtown.

On September 27 I received orders to move with 250 men toward Glasgow, but after marching 8 miles was ordered to return and proceed with my command to Boston. Orders were also sent to leave Col. [M. J.] Crawford's (Third Georgia) regiment [cavalry] at New Haven. I regret to state that a few days after a superior force of the enemy surprised and captured Colonel Crawford and 250 of his command at Boston.* We picketed and scouted well down toward Elizabethtown, frequently skirmishing with the enemy, until we were ordered to Bards-town, at which place we arrived about daylight on the morning of the 4th instant,† when I was ordered to follow and cover the rear of the left wing of the army, which was moving toward Glenville. All roads leading to the town were immediately picketed, and about noon we moved the remainder of the brigade on the road on which we were to march. Hearing firing in advance we moved rapidly in that direction, when I discovered that it emanated from a wood to our left and that a large force of the enemy had moved up between my position and the point where the firing took place. At this moment I received a message from General Johnson that his brigade—the infantry rear guard of the left wing—was but a short distance in front. A large portion of my command was left to protect his rear, and I moved back with the remainder to reach the scene of the firing and relieve my pickets which had been left around Bardstown. On arriving at the town I found that Colonel Wharton had engaged the enemy but had passed on toward Spring-field. We drew in our picket and remained near Bardstown until nearly dark, when I moved back to my command. The enemy in the mean time having placed a large force in and about the road, I was obliged to make a circuit with my little force to avoid capture. Having reached my brigade we moved on, in accordance with orders, to Glenville, and the next morning continued the march toward Mackville, before reaching which place I was ordered to Springfield, where we remained until the morning of October 6, at which time the enemy came up in strong force, reaching the town about 8 a. m. Our pickets having been driven in, we engaged them with artillery and small-arms, compelling them to advance very slowly, frequently deploying their infantry. We were obliged to fall back slowly when their infantry fired too heavily, but succeeded in so checking their progress that they only advanced about 4 miles from 8 a. m. until dark. They attempted several times to turn our flank, but were easily checked by our flankers. In this series of engagements the enemy suffered quite severely.

The next morning we ambushed the command at a position about 6

---

* See September 29, 1862. Capture of Third Georgia Cavalry, near New Haven, Ky., post.

† See October 4, 1862. Action near Bardstown, Ky. Report of Maj. Gen. George H. Thomas, U. S. Army.

miles west of Perryville. The enemy came up in fine style to within about 200 yards, when they discovered our position. We then fired upon them with excellent effect, thoroughly stampeding their entire front. So effectual and unexpected was this stampede of so large a force of cavalry, artillery, and a portion of their infantry that our cavalry could not be placed in a position to charge them in time to accomplish all that could be desired. As it was we succeeded in capturing 1 officer and 8 men, together with about 50 stand of superior arms, and great numbers of blankets, saddle-bags, &c., which they had thrown away in their flight. In a few hours they returned in a force which finally compelled us to retire slowly before them, skirmishing with their advance during the entire day. Toward evening we succeeded in making a successful charge with a few men, driving in their advance and capturing several prisoners. In this charge we lost about 7 officers and men killed and wounded, including Captain Cathey and Lieutenant Clanton. Unfortunately, before we withdrew, our flank was so warmly attacked that most of the prisoners made their escape during the fight which ensued.

By keeping our lines continuously skirmishing until night we prevented the enemy from making any demonstration that day upon our infantry, which had deployed in line of battle to meet the enemy on the field of Perryville.

During the night I received orders to place my brigade on the left of our general line of battle for the engagement which was to take place the following day.

At daylight the skirmishing again commenced, and at about 8 o'clock my brigade was deployed as directed. Pickets and scouts were immediately thrown out on all the approaches to Perryville from the south and southwest as far as the Lebanon and Danville road and all precaution taken to prevent a flank movement of the enemy.

Seeing myself confronted by a large body of troops of all arms deployed in line of battle and gradually increasing their front my line was advanced to hold them in check sufficiently to prevent their farther advance.

About 10 a. m. my pickets on the Perryville and Lebanon road were pressed in by a large body of cavalry, which proved to be the First Kentucky and Seventh Pennsylvania Regiments, which were moving down the Lebanon and Perryville road with a large force, partly dismounted, deployed on each side. At this moment, receiving orders from General Polk to clear that road of the enemy, we charged the enemy, throwing their entire force of cavalry into confusion and putting it to flight.

We pursued them at full charge for 2 miles, capturing many prisoners and horses in single combat and driving the remaining under cover of their masses of infantry. The enemy also fled terror-stricken from a battery placed in advance of their general line and left it at our disposal. The charge, one of the most brilliant of the campaign, was made in column; detachments of the First and Third Alabama Cavalry with the gallant Cols. [W. W.] Allen and [James] Hagan being in advance. Colonel Hart, who had just come up with a body of about 400 cavalry, followed for a short distance, but owing to some mistake turned off the road, carrying all his own command, together with all in his rear, thus leaving the combat to the few brave men of the First and Third Alabama Regiments. With these few, who, after sending our prisoners to the rear, numbered only about 80 men, we were confronted by such forces that we were prevented making any farther advance. I therefore withdrew a short distance and again deployed our line, engaging the enemy with both cavalry and artillery until night, and prevented this large force from taking any other part in the contest of that day. Early in the day I sent a battalion under Major Adrian to re-enforce the picket on the Perryville and Mitchellsburg road, the enemy having pressed upon us at that point with apparent indication of an attempt to gain our rear. Major Adrian skirmished with them and held them at bay until we retired the following morning.

On the morning of the 9th I received orders to hold the enemy in check until our army had withdrawn from the field and then to follow on toward Danville, retarding the enemy as much as possible. In complying with this order we frequently engaged the enemy that day and the day following, besides keeping a force in observation of the road from Perryville to Harrodsburg.

On the evening of the 10th I learned from this force that the enemy were moving from the Perryville and Harrodsburg pike toward Danville, which information was promptly communicated to the general commanding.

On the morning of the 11th,* after a severe engagement, in which Colonel Wade's regiment participated, he having just arrived from Tennessee and reported to me, we were obliged to fall back behind Danville, where we remained until the evening of the 12th, when I received orders to move across Dick's River and guard the fords below Camp Dick Robinson.

On the morning of the 13th I received orders directing me to assume control of all our mounted forces as chief of cavalry and make the necessary dispositions to cover the movement our army was about to commence. I therefore recrossed Dick's River, and finding that the general advance of the enemy was toward Lancaster and Stanford, I left small forces, with all necessary orders to guard the several fords and the Bryantsville road, and with the bulk of my own and Wharton's brigades moved over to the roads leading from Danville to Lancaster and Stanford. My own brigade was placed on the former road and Colonel Wharton's on the latter. The enemy were pushing forward, but, by continually fighting them, they repeatedly deployed their lines for battle, and consequently progressed very slowly.

We arrived at Lancaster on the afternoon of the 15th [14?], and after a fight, in which we disabled a battery, prevented the enemy from approaching nearer than to within 2 or 3 miles of the town. Col. John H. Morgan and Colonel Ashby reported to me with their brigades, but they were not called into action.

Having received information from Colonel Wharton, then near Stanford, that he was warmly pressed, after ascertaining from a personal reconnaissance that the enemy in my front were not in large force, and that they had fallen back and gone into camp for the night, I started at about 10 p. m. to assist Colonel Wharton, leaving Colonels Morgan and Ashby to cover the road from Lancaster to Big Hill.

We arrived at Colonel Wharton's position early on the morning of the 16th [15?], and allowed him to move in toward the main army with his brigade, while with my own we engaged a large force of the enemy,

---

* See October 10-22 1862. Pursuit of Confederate forces from Perryville to London, Ky.

falling back slowly through Crab Orchard. We engaged the enemy all day and reached Mount Vernon late that night.

The next morning, together with Colonel Wharton, we commenced obstructing the road, continuously skirmishing with the enemy until the evening of October 22, we having then arrived at London, where the enemy ceased to pursue us.

At Wild Cat we were directed to hold our position for two days, which we had but little difficulty in accomplishing.

On the evening of the 19th I took a small portion of Colonel Frazer's infantry regiment, which was sent back to assist me, to feel the enemy, during which my brave young aide, Lieutenant Pointer, was severely wounded.

This was the only occasion where any infantry engaged the enemy after the battle of Perryville, although the enemy used infantry almost continually to engage our cavalry.

After guarding the roads at London and Barboursville until our infantry had reached Cumberland Gap I moved on to Tennessee with my brigade, Colonel Wharton having preceded me the previous day.

When our army first left Camp Dick Robinson I issued the most stringent orders to the several cavalry commanders that all stragglers from the infantry should be forced on to the main body. As far as I could observe this duty was most thoroughly performed. In my own brigade a company was kept at work gathering up the foot-sore and weary, whom the troopers placed on their horses and walked themselves by their side.

In this manner all stragglers on the roads we traveled were conveyed to their commands, no one being left behind to be taken by the enemy except those who willfully left the road for a great distance to avoid our guards.

In closing this report I cannot speak in too great praise of the gallantry of the officers and men of the First and Third Alabama Regiments, who were always ready to meet the enemy at any moment, performed all duties assigned them, and endured all hardships and privations without a murmur or complaint. The confidence I naturally placed in such noble officers and men caused me to call upon them perhaps too frequently for posts of danger and hardship, yet never did they intimate that their details were more frequent than other commands, but with the greatest cheerfulness right bravely performed their double task thus imposed simply because their commander placed in them unshaken and implicit trust and confidence. To the brave officers and men of these regiments and their gallant leaders, Colonels Hagan and Allen, I tender my warmest thanks.

Col. [J. W.] Grigsby's excellent Kentucky regiment was with me during several engagements and did most excellent and efficient service. Though just organized, the gallantry, skill, and intelligence of their commander, which seemed to characterize the officers and men of his regiment, made up in some measure for deficiency in instruction.

The First Kentucky Battalion, commanded by Major Caldwell; Eighth Confederate Regiment, under Col. [W. B.] Wade, and the First Confederate Regiment, under Lieut. Col. [C. S.] Robertson, were with me at times and did good service.

The gallant Colonel (now General) Wharton did good work with his brigade; but as his operations were for the most part of a separate character I leave it for him to do justice to the noble officers and men of his command.

I must also mention the gallantry and uniformly good conduct through the many fights of Capts. Oliver, [J. D.] Farish, and [W. W.] Lang, of the Third Alabama; Maj. [John S.] Prather and Capts. [T. W.] Golding and [B. B.] McCaa, of the Eighth Confederate, and Lieuts. [G. P.] Fuhrman and Burford and Adjutant Ledyard, of the First Alabama Cavalry.

I also tender my thanks to my adjutant, Capt. D. G. Reed, and my volunteer aides, Lieutenant-Colonel McGuirk and Lieutenant Pointer, all of whom conducted themselves with marked bravery.

Lieutenant Hanley, who commanded a section of artillery, was always gallant and skillful and efficient in performing all duties assigned him.

For the deeds of many other officers and men who deserve mention for gallantry and endurance I must refer to reports of subordinate commanders.

The gallant dead, who fell nearly every day of the campaign, including field and company officers of every grade except that of colonel, indelibly mark the road of the cavalry rear guard of our army.

I have the honor to be, with great respect, your obedient servant,

JOS. WHEELER,
Brigadier-General.

Col. GEORGE WILLIAM BRENT, *Assistant Adjutant-General.*

AUGUST 29-30, 1862.—Skirmishes at Short Mountain Cross-Roads (29th) and Little Pond (30th), near McMinnville, Tenn.

REPORTS.

No. 1.—Brig. Gen. Thomas J. Wood, U. S. Army, of skirmish at Little Pond.
No. 2.—Capt. Henry R. Miller, Eighteenth Ohio Infantry, of skirmish at Short Mountain Cross-Roads.
No. 3.—Col. Edward P. Fyffe, Twenty-sixth Ohio Infantry, of skirmish at Little Pond.
No. 4.—Col. George P. Buell, Fifty-eighth Indiana Infantry, of skirmish at Little Pond.

No. 1.

Reports of Brig. Gen. Thomas J. Wood, U. S. Army, of skirmish at Little Pond.

HEADQUARTERS SIXTH DIVISION,
In Camp, near McMinnville, Tenn., August 31, 1862.

MAJOR: Immediately after my return to camp yesterday from the mountain expedition, on which I had been absent two days, I heard that Forrest's command was crossing the railroad 3 miles west of my camp, going northward. I at once sent out three regiments of infantry and four pieces of artillery, under Colonel Fyffe, Twenty-sixth Ohio, to cross to the north side of Barren Fork, near to my camp, move out to the Murfreesborough road, take the road to that place, and try to cut Forrest off. By a very rapid forced march (part of it at the double-quick) of 9 miles Colonel Fyffe reached the junction of the cross-road by which Forrest was moving and the Murfreesborough road just as about one-half of the enemy had got onto the latter road. Colonel Fyffe deployed a part of his command, immediately ordered up the artillery, and opened a fire of shell and musketry. He divided the enemy, forced a portion back on the cross-road, and utterly routed and scattered him in all directions. The pursuit was continued for 1½ miles, till it was too dark to see.

Colonel Fyffe captured a number of horses, mules, shot-guns, sabers, revolvers, carbines, saddles, bridles, cartridge-boxes, &c. He captured General Forrest's light spring wagon, riding-horse, and the riding-horse and body servant of Captain Forrest, brother to the general.

The rebels fled in the utmost consternation and confusion. Forrest's forces numbered between 1,400 and 1,500.

I am, sir, very respectfully, your obedient servant,

TH. J. WOOD,
Brigadier-General of Volunteers, Commanding.

Maj. GEORGE E. FLYNT,
Assistant Adjutant-General.

P. S.—A cavalry scout, sent out by me early this morning, reports, from information received of citizens, that several of Forrest's command were killed and wounded.

TH. J. WOOD,
Brigadier-General of Volunteers, Commanding.

—

HEADQUARTERS SIXTH DIVISION,
August 31, 1862.

MAJOR: My people captured last evening a very intelligent negro who belonged to a Texan Ranger who was killed in the attack on the stockade on the 29th. This negro gives a very intelligent account of General Forrest's movements for the last two weeks. He says Forrest left his train at Decatur, in Meigs County, on the Tennessee River, two weeks ago, since which time he has been roaming around, hunting for small parties and trains to capture, and subsisting on the country; that when he came down on the 29th he was on his way back to Decatur to his train, intending to cross the mountains by the way of Altamont; that after the repulse at the stockade he moved on toward the foot of the mountains and halted for the night. There he learned that our forces were at Altamont. He probably learned also that troops were moving to Hillsborough (Crittenden's), though the negro does not say so. But he says Forrest made a speech to his men yesterday, telling them they were surrounded and would be caught if they did not get out of the trap at once. Hence the rapid movement northward, across the railroad, yesterday afternoon. Doubtless Forrest will try to make his way around by Sparta or Rock Island, crossing, to get into the valley, and make his way down to Pikeville, Washington, &c., or from Pikeville directly to Decatur. Cannot you send a force promptly into the valley, beyond Spencer, to cut him off? I think it might be done. The negro says Forrest was repulsed in an attack on a train at Woodbury a few days since.

Respectfully, &c.,

TH. J. WOOD,
Brigadier-General Volunteers, Commanding.

Maj. GEORGE E. FLYNT,
Assistant Adjutant-General.

HEADQUARTERS SIXTH DIVISION, *August* 31, 1862.

MAJOR: The more information I obtain the more certain I am that an attempt ought to be made to cut up, capture, or at all events prevent Forrest from joining Bragg. I am still more certain that the object of Forrest's movement down this way was to cross the mountains and effect a junction with Bragg, and having been disappointed in this movement, he will attempt to effect the same purpose by the way of Sparta and down the Sequatchie Valley. The junction should by all means be prevented, as Forrest's command would be of the greatest advantage to Bragg in his advance. That the advance will be made sooner or later I am quite certain. The attempt will be made to sweep everything to Nashville, retake it, and then invade Kentucky. I have got hold of some information to-day on this point. I think General Thomas is mistaken in not believing Bragg to be on this side of the Tennessee River. I am satisfied the advance will be made by one of two roads—by the road by which I went out the other day, the Hills' Truce road to Dunlap, or up the valley and around by Sparta, or perhaps by both roads at once. The general, I think, ought to have both roads watched clear to the other side of the mountains.

I sent out a party of cavalry this morning beyond where my people encountered Forrest yesterday evening, which has just returned, with information that as late as 11 o'clock to-day Forrest, with the bulk of his command, was near to Short Mountain. I understand Short Mountain is near and a little to the right of the McMinnville and Lebanon road. Cannot the general send out a force there to rout him out? He probably halted there to collect his scattered forces.

Respectfully,

TH. J. WOOD,
Commanding.

Major FLYNT, *Assistant-Adjutant-General.*

No. 2.

Reports of Capt. Henry R. Miller, Eighteenth Ohio Infantry, of skirmish at Short Mountain Cross-Roads.

HDQRS. DETACHMENTS 18TH OHIO AND 9TH MICH. REGTS.,
August 30, 1862.

Yesterday at 1 p. m. we were attacked in our position, 8 miles west, on the Manchester and McMinnville Railroad, by General Forrest's rebel cavalry, consisting of one regiment Texas Rangers, Colonel Wharton; one battalion Alabama Cavalry, Captain Bacot; one battalion Tennessee Cavalry, Major Smith, and one battalion Kentucky Cavalry. We repulsed the enemy, with a loss of 9 killed and 40 wounded, several mortally. Among the killed, Captain Houston; among the mortally wounded, Lieutenant Butler, who died this morning. Our loss, 9 wounded, 5 severely. The rout complete, the rebels throwing away arms and fleeing, leaving on the field their dead and several of their wounded. They set on fire a small trestle between us and Manchester, half a mile distant from us, which we put out, and have now repaired the damage. The enemy have gone in the direction of Sparta.

H. R. MILLER,
Captain, Commanding

General HASCALL,
Commanding Fifteenth Brigade, McMinnville, Tenn.

SHORT MOUNTAIN CROSS-ROADS, TENN.,
August 30, 1862.

COLONEL: On Friday, August 29, the troops under my command, numbering 100 effective men, of Company A, Eighteenth Ohio Volunteers; Company I, Eighteenth Ohio Volunteers, Capt. Charles C. Ross, and Company D, Ninth Michigan Volunteers, Lieutenant Wallace, had just completed the inclosure of a stockade at this place 30 by 40 feet square, of round timber, 12 feet high. The men were eating dinner at about 1 o'clock p. m. in a grove, distant from the stockade about 100 yards, and in which also we had the ammunition belonging to the command, except such as was in boxes, when the enemy, 1,500 strong, made his appearance, formed in line of battle along the skirt of woods extending from the railroad along the south side of the stockade at the distance of about 200 yards, and rapidly extended his line on east and west sides. My men ran rapidly to the stockade, and at the same time the enemy, with a terrific yell, fired a volley and rushed to cut us off from the stockade. The attacking force consisted of 900 dismounted cavalry, commanded by General Forrest, and led to the charge by him. My men kept up a sharp running fire on the way to the stockade, checking the impetuosity of the enemy, and all but some 10 of Company I and the men on picket got inside the fort before the enemy. The men cut off kept up a constant fire from the railroad and woods during the engagement and got in in safety. The race to the stockade was a desperate one. On getting within the stockade I at once sent three parties of 6 men each, one from each company, to bring in the ammunition. These squads were commanded by Sergeant [Edward] McLaren, Company A; Sergeant [James K.] Williams, Company I, and I regret that I do not know who from Ninth Michigan company. They ran to the thicket under a terrible fire from the enemy's skirmishers and succeeded in bringing in the ammunition.

The enemy now made an attack from three directions with great desperation, approaching within 50 feet of the stockade. I kept up a constant and well-directed fire upon him for ten minutes, when, finding it impossible to dislodge us or seriously injure our men and his own falling rapidly around, he made a rapid retreat to the woods in great confusion. His men ran in every direction before our fire, throwing down their arms, and immediately fell back out of range. Soon after an attempt was made to destroy the railroad above us. I went out with a party and drove them away.

I at once sent messengers to Manchester and McMinnville on foot through the enemy's lines with information. To do this dangerous duty I called for volunteers, and from those offering to go I sent Clinton L. Lee, private Company A, to McMinnville, and Henry F. Thayer, private Company D, Ninth Michigan, to Manchester. They both got safely through and gave information of our situation.

The enemy's forces consisted of Colonel Wharton's Texas Rangers; one battalion Alabama Cavalry, Captain Bacot's; one battalion Tennessee Cavalry, Major Smith, and one battalion Kentucky Cavalry, numbering, as I learn from Dr. Houston, surgeon Texas Cavalry, 1,500 strong. I have also the same information from Lieutenant Butler and other prisoners.

We buried 12 of the enemy left dead and dying on the field, and have 41 of his wounded in our hands and scattered among the houses of citizens in the vicinity. Among the dead are Capt. W. Y. Houston and Lieutenant Butler, Texas Rangers. Our loss is 9 wounded, to wit: **Seven of Company I**, Eighteenth Ohio Volunteers; **1 of Company A,**

Eighteenth Ohio Volunteers, and 1 of Company D, Ninth Michigan Volunteers. Two are wounded dangerously and the others slightly. I send list of wounded.

Drs. Johnson and Mills, surgeons Eighteenth Ohio Volunteers, arrived at midnight and at once proceeded to give all possible attention to the wounded. At daylight Drs. Stimmel and Sabine, Twenty-sixth Ohio Volunteers, arrived from McMinnville, and assisted in attentions to the wounded and suffering. To all the gentlemen my thanks are due for their promptness, industry, and skill in ministering to the wounded.

We captured 8 horses, 3 saddles, and 30 guns.

The conduct of all the officers and men of the command was such as to compel my admiration. They fought from the first with great coolness, bravery, and determination. The enemy outnumbered us as nine to one.

I have the honor to be, your obedient servant,

H. R. MILLER,
Captain Eighteenth Ohio Volunteers, Commanding.

Col. T. R. STANLEY, *Eighteenth Ohio Volunteers.*

No. 3.

Report of Col. Edward P. Fyffe, Twenty-sixth Ohio Infantry, of skirmish at Little Pond.

HEADQUARTERS FIFTEENTH BRIGADE,
Near McMinnville, Tenn., August 31, 1862.

SIR: In pursuance to orders from Brigadier-General Wood to cut off General Forrest and his command, who was passing to the westward and within 2 miles of this camp, making his way northward, and upon five minutes' notice, after procuring a guide, I marched in a circuitous route through the woods to the Murfreesborough and McMinnville road, a distance of 6 miles from camp. I pushed forward in the direction of Murfreesborough in quick-time until I came to an open country, where at some distance across the fields I discovered the column of General Forrest, consisting entirely of cavalry.

The enemy having become aware of my presence at this time there commenced an exciting race between his command of cavalry and my column of infantry for the intersection of the two roads. I ordered my command forward at a double-quick, which they obeyed cheerfully, although they had marched several miles at quick-time without water. I discovered when about 400 or 500 yards distant from the junction of the roads that General Forrest had formed his command in line of battle to receive my attack. I immediately ordered Lieutenant Estep, commanding Eighth Indiana Battery, to take up a position on an elevated piece of ground in the field to the left of the road, with instructions to commence firing, and the advance guard (Companies A and F, Captains James and Peatman, of the Twenty-sixth Ohio), under Major Degenfeld, to deploy in front of the artillery on the low ground, advance, and commence firing. In the mean time Lieutenant-Colonel Young, commanding the Twenty-sixth Ohio Regiment, agreeably to instructions, formed his regiment in rear of the advance guard and followed it closely in line of battle. After firing a few rounds the enemy's lines gave way in the center. His right wing (the Texan Rangers and some Alabama troops) were forced to take the back track to our left, while General Forrest, with his left wing, scampered off in the direction of Murfreesborough. I ordered Lieutenant Jervis forward on the main road with one section of artillery to fire on General Forrest's detachment, and gave instructions to Lieutenant-Colonel Gorman, commanding Seventeenth Indiana, to support him with his regiment. I then ordered Lieutenant Voris, with the other section, supported by the Fifty-eighth Indiana, Colonel Buell commanding, to follow up and to fire on the Texan Rangers, leaving the Twenty-sixth Ohio to occupy the center.

In a very short time the enemy were entirely dispersed in every direction; so much so that it was with great difficulty I could determine on which road it would be must profitable to pursue him. I immediately concluded to follow him on the Murfreesborough road, but it had grown so dark that I was enabled to pursue him but about 2 miles, when I was forced to abandon the chase in consequence of the men and animals suffering for water. I returned to camp the same night, arriving about 11 o'clock.

The ground over which we fought presented every indication of the utmost confusion and consternation on the part of the enemy, the woods and roads being strewn with arms, wearing apparel, &c. Accompanying this I have the honor to present a list of the property that fell into our hands.

The actual loss of the enemy I had no means of ascertaining, but from the statements of citizens subsequently received and from his own admissions his loss must have been from 18 to 20 in killed and wounded.

It is with pleasure that I inform you that these fine regiments of your division never came into line in better order at their battalion drills than they did upon this occasion. The artillery, commanded by Lieutenant Estep, was well handled, quickly got into position, fired rapidly and with precision.

The command of that portion of the brigade that accompanied the expedition devolved upon me in consequence of the severe illness of Brigadier-General Hascall, who was at the time confined to his room.

It is proper to state that the Third Kentucky Regiment did not participate, in consequence of just having returned from a severe march of two days' duration, thus entirely incapacitating them for further immediate service.

I cannot speak too highly in praise of the members of the general staff. Capt. Ed. R. Kerstetter, assistant adjutant-general, and Lieuts. James R. Hume, Jules J. Montagnier, and Charles H. Bruce, aides-de-camp, were active in conveying my commands to every part of the field. I would respectfully commend them to your favorable notice.

I have the honor to be, very respectfully, your obedient servant,

E. P. FYFFE,
Colonel Twenty-sixth Ohio Volunteers, Commanding.

Capt. W. H. SCHLATER, *A. A. G, Sixth Division, Army of the Ohio.*

No. 4.

Report of Col. George P. Buell, Fifty-eighth Indiana Infantry, of skirmish at Little Pond.

ON THE ROAD, *August* 31, 1862—11 a. m.

This armed body was commanded in person by General Forrest. He has passed north, via Sparta, to avoid our troops, and thus join Bragg on the other side of the mountains. He also expects to join Morgan soon, who will also join Bragg. Can they not be cut off somewhere northeast of McMinnville? He went toward Short Mountain from here, thence via Sparta. If we had deployed along this road last night it would have been better. We entirely cut off 500 Texas Rangers, who fell back into the woods, and after we left they went on north.

GEO. P. BUELL,
Colonel, Commanding.

General WOOD.

P. S.—I start immediately. The wagons captured at Murfreesborough are at Pikeville, and very little force there—two pieces of artillery and a little cavalry.

AUGUST 30, 1862.—Battle of Richmond, Ky., or engagements at Mount Zion Church, White's Farm, and Richmond.

REPORTS, ETC.

No. 1.—Maj. Gen. Horatio G. Wright, U. S. Army, commanding Department of the Ohio, with instructions to Maj. Gen. William Nelson.

No. 2.—Maj. Gen. William Nelson, U. S. Army, commanding Army of Kentucky.

No. 3.—Return of Casualties in the Union forces.

No. 4.—Brig. Gen. James S. Jackson, U. S. Army, Chief of Cavalry, including operations August 28–30.

No. 5.—Brig. Gen. Mahlon D. Manson, U. S. Army, commanding First Brigade.

No. 6.—Lieut. Col. John R. Mahan, Fifty-fifth Indiana Infantry.

No. 7.—Brig. Gen. Charles Cruft, U. S. Army, commanding Second Brigade.

No. 8.—Lieut. Luther F. Hale, Battery F, First Michigan Light Artillery.

No. 9.—Capt. John F. Baird, Sixty-sixth Indiana Infantry.

No. 10.—Capt. Jasper N. Rodman, Sixty-sixth Indiana Infantry.

No. 11.—Maj. Frederick G. Bracht, Eighteenth Kentucky Infantry.

No. 12.—Col. William L. McMillen, Ninety-fifth Ohio Infantry.

No. 13.—Lieut. Thomas P. Jones, Ninety-fifth Ohio Infantry.

No. 14.—Maj. Bill Cross, Third Tennessee Infantry (Union).

No. 15.—Maj. Gen. John P. McCown, C. S. Army, commanding Department of East Tennessee.

No. 16.—Maj. Gen. E. Kirby Smith, C. S. Army, commanding Army of Kentucky, including operations August 30–September 16, and congratulatory orders.

No. 17.—Col. John S. Scott, First Louisiana Cavalry, commanding Cavalry Brigade, including operations from August 13–September 11.

No. 18.—Brig. Gen. Thomas J. Churchill, C. S. Army, commanding Third Division.

No. 19.—Col. T. H. McCray, Thirty-first Arkansas Infantry, commanding First Brigade.

No. 20.—Col. Evander McNair, Fourth Arkansas Infantry, commanding Second Brigade.

No. 21.—Brig. Gen. P. R. Cleburne, C. S. Army, commanding Fourth Division.

No. 22.—Col. Preston Smith, Provisional Army of the Confederate States and Acting Brigadier-General, commanding First Brigade, Fourth Division.

No. 23.—Col. Benjamin J. Hill, Thirty-fifth Tennessee Infantry, commanding Second Brigade.

No. 1.

Reports of Maj. Gen. Horatio G. Wright, U. S. Army, commanding Department of the Ohio, with instructions to Maj. Gen. William Nelson.

HEADQUARTERS DEPARTMENT OF THE OHIO,
Cincinnati, Ohio, August 31, 1862.

Nelson has been badly beaten, I fear, in an encounter with the enemy near Richmond, Ky., his force being, as he says, hopelessly broken and scattered.   He is in Lexington, wounded, and I leave for that place in a couple of hours, to see what can be done.   He gives no particulars. My orders were to make the Kentucky River the line of defense, and his orders in pursuance seem to have been disregarded.   At any rate his force has been routed.

H. G. WRIGHT,
Major-General, Commanding.

Maj. Gen. H. W. HALLECK, *Washington, D. C.*

LEXINGTON, KY., *August* 31, 1862.

I find matters here in a very bad condition.   The force engaged in the late battle is scattered, there being only about 800 of them here, with what was not engaged in the fight.   I am not strong enough to resist the rebel forces, and shall be forced to fall back if they approach. The battle was fought in direct disobedience to my orders and those of General Nelson.   General Manson, who was in immediate command until General Nelson came up, and who brought on the battle, has not been heard of.   He is probably a prisoner.   Have directed troops still coming in to rendezvous at Covington and Louisville until further orders and those in advance to fall back on these points on approach of a superior force.   This until I can better understand matters.

H. G. WRIGHT,
Major-General, Commanding.

Maj. Gen. H. W. HALLECK.

HEADQUARTERS DEPARTMENT OF THE OHIO,
Louisville, Ky., September 2, 1862.

GENERAL: I have the honor to report that I left Lexington last evening about 5 o'clock, arriving here about 4.30 a. m. to-day.   On reaching Lexington I found that the force engaged in the battle in front of Richmond was utterly broken up, and that after all the exertions that could be made to collect the stragglers only some 800 or 900 could be found. The remainder of the force were killed, captured, or scattered over the country.   The only force then at Lexington and its vicinity not engaged in the fight were six regiments of infantry, two of cavalry, all new except the Ninth Tennessee [Pennsylvania] Cavalry, and much demoralized by the reverse that had been sustained.   Under these circumstances it would have been madness to attempt the defense of Lexington or the Kentucky River with the forces there or with any re-enforcements that could have been brought up in time, and I therefore reluctantly gave orders for the evacuation of the place on the advance of the enemy in force, falling back on Covington or Louisville, as might be proper.

There were two general officers left with the command, neither of which desired the position of commander of the forces, and I therefore at their request appointed Capt. C. C. Gilbert, First Infantry, U. S. Army, a major-general, subject to the approval of the President, and Capt. W. R. Terrill, Fifth Artillery, U. S. Army, a brigadier-general, subject to a like approval, assigning the former to the command of the Army of Kentucky during the absence of Major-General Nelson, wounded in the battle. A copy of the order is herewith inclosed.*

I believe in making these appointments I have acted for the best interest of the service.

General Gilbert is favorably known throughout the regular service, and in this section of the country commands the confidence of officers and citizens, and I trust for the good of the service the appointment may meet the approval of the authorities. General Terrill is also favorably known to the service, has served gallantly through the war, and is, I am sure, entitled to some such mark of recognition of his services, zeal, and intelligence.

If the force at Lexington is brought off safely it will be due mainly to the good management of those officers.

I am, general, very respectfully, your obedient servant,

H. G. WRIGHT,
Major-General, Commanding

Maj. Gen. H. W. HALLECK, *General-in-Chief.*

INSTRUCTIONS TO MAJ. GEN. WILLIAM NELSON, U. S. ARMY.

LOUISVILLE, KY., *August* 24, 1862.

If enemy is in force get your troops together, and do not risk a general battle at Richmond unless you are sure of success. Better fall back to a more defensible position, say the Kentucky River, than to risk much. If the enemy's force is cavalry he may have designs against [Green Clay] Smith, who should be ready to fall back and join you. Do not let him be overwhelmed. It is the enemy's game to fall upon our detachments. Your lowest estimate of enemy's strength probably nearest the truth; keep me advised.

H. G. WRIGHT,
Major-General, Commanding

Major-General NELSON, *Commanding at Lexington, Ky.*

P. S.—To be sent forward by telegraph if General N. has left.

No. 2.

Report of Maj. Gen. William Nelson, U. S. Army, commanding Army of Kentucky.

HEADQUARTERS, *Lexington, Ky., August* 31, 1862.

GENERAL: I have to report that on yesterday morning at 2.30 o'clock I, much to my surprise, received a dispatch from General Manson, stating that the enemy was in force in his front and that he anticipated an engagement. I immediately sent couriers, with orders for him not to fight the enemy, but to retreat by way of the Lancaster road. I had ordeerd General Dumont to proceed from Lebanon to Danville, where he would

---

* Not found.

find further orders. Also Col. Charles Anderson, with a brigade of three infantry regiments, to proceed in the same direction, it being my intention to mass the troops, knowing that the enemy would not cross the Kentucky River while 16,000 men were on their flank. My anxiety was such that I started myself to see that the troops at Richmond moved in the proper direction and in order. Upon my arrival at Lancaster, at 9.30 a. m., I heard the artillery. I procured fresh horses and took the Richmond road, but was compelled to take by-paths because of the enemy's cavalry on it and being accompanied only by a single member of my staff. I arrived on the field, 3 miles south of Richmond, at 2 p. m., and found the command in a disorganized retreat or rather a rout. With great exertion I rallied about 2,200 men, moved them to a strong position, where I was confident I could hold them in check until night, and then resume the retreat. The enemy attacked in front and on both flanks simultaneously with vigor. Our troops stood about three rounds, when, struck by a panic, they fled in utter disorder. I was left with my staff almost alone. The enemy's cavalry was now in our rear, and the panic at such height that it was a sheer impossibility to do anything. What the motive of General Manson was in bringing on an action under the circumstances, and marching 5 miles to do so, I will leave him to explain to you.

W. NELSON,
Major-General.

No. 3.

Return of Casualties in the Union forces.

[Compiled from nominal list of casualties, returns, &c.]

Command.	Killed.		Wounded.		Captured or missing.		Aggregate.
	Officers.	Enlisted men.	Officers.	Enlisted men.	Officers.	Enlisted men.	
General and staff officers			2		3		5
12th Indiana Infantry		25	6	142	22	586	781
16th Indiana Infantry	1	24	4	116	21	374	540
55th Indiana Infantry	1	10	4	43	4	425	487
66th Indiana Infantry	2	21	5	63	10	506	607
69th Indiana Infantry	1	16	3	108	22	476	626
71st Indiana Infantry	3	26	3	88	23	570	713
6th Kentucky Cavalry (battalion)				1	1	61	63
7th Kentucky Cavalry	1	4		25	5	233	268
3d Kentucky Infantry		1	1	13	7	66	88
18th Kentucky Infantry	3	36	7	104	7	230	387
Lanphere's Battery (improvised)		1		3	1	10	15
1st Michigan Light Artillery, Battery F		6		9		54	69
95th Ohio Infantry		24	6	88	22	526	666
3d Tennessee Infantry (battalion)					11	27	38
Total	12	194	41	803	159	4,144	5,353

Officers killed.—Lieut. Col. Joel Wolfe, Sixteenth Indiana; Lieut. William L. Thompson, Fifty-fifth Indiana; Lieuts. Charles H. Cornwell and Samuel P. Reid, Sixty-sixth Indiana; Lieut. Alvin M. Cowing, Sixty-ninth Indiana; Lieut. Col. Melville D. Topping, Maj. William Conklin, and Lieut. William O. Norris, Seventy-first Indiana; Maj. Charles T. Milward, Seventh Kentucky Cavalry; Capt. Orin M. Lewis, Lieuts. James Dunlap and John W. Washburn, Eighteenth Kentucky.

Officers mortally wounded.—Col. William H. Link, Lieuts. Henry S. Westcott and Caleb Day, Twelfth Indiana; Capt. W. W. Culbertson, Eighteenth Kentucky.

NOTE.—To avoid counting them twice the wounded who fell into the enemy's hands are omitted from the column of "captured or missing." The whole number of prisoners was about 178 officers and 4,650 men.

No. 4.

Report of Brig. Gen. James S. Jackson, U. S. Army, Chief of Cavalry, including operations August 28–30.

HDQRS. FIRST DIVISION, ARMY OF KENTUCKY.

GENERAL : On Monday, August 25, you gave me the following verbal order :

You will proceed to Nicholasville and take command of the two battalions of Jacob's Ninth Kentucky Cavalry, and go thence to Hickman's Bridge, and take command of the Ninth Pennsylvania Cavalry, commanded by Colonel Williams. You will then take position on the flank of the enemy and observe his movements. You will be very cautious. Colonel Jacob's regiment is just recruited, and you must not risk an engagement unless the chances are in your favor. You will from time to time send me such information as may be obtained.

In obedience to these instructions I proceeded to Crab Orchard, throwing out my advance to the Big Hill and Mount Vernon, also keeping a close watch on the road from Somerset to London and Barboursville. I ascertained distinctly at 9 p. m. on Thursday, August 28, the actual force of the enemy, and dispatched the same to you at Richmond by a reliable courier. Knowing the force of the enemy, as I did, you may be satisfied that I was astounded at receiving from you the following dispatch, dated Saturday, August 30, at 1.30 p. m.:

They are fighting at Richmond. Proceed there at once.

With my entire command of two regiments of cavalry, Colonel Williams' Ninth Pennsylvania, and Colonel Jacob's Ninth Kentucky, I proceeded at once in the direction of Richmond. Reports of disaster to our forces reached me when within 14 miles. When I arrived within 6 miles of Richmond I became satisfied that you were falling back, if not routed. I determined at once to pass around the town and fall in with your command on the road to Lexington. At 4.30 a. m. the next day I halted near the Lexington and Richmond road, on the farm of Maj. Gen. C. M. Clay, and undertook at once to ascertain the whereabouts of your command. At 7.30 a. m. I observed from an elevation a force of the enemy's cavalry, artillery, and infantry passing to Clay's Ferry, in the direction of Lexington. It was also reported that a column was advancing toward Lexington on the Tait's Creek road. My command lying at this time between the two roads, I crossed the Kentucky River at the mouth of Jack's Creek, with the view of passing around to the front of the enemy on the Clay's Ferry road, leading from Lexington to Richmond. I there fell in with a force of infantry, under the command of Col. Dan. McCook, of the Fifty-second Ohio, and fell back slowly and in order with him to Lexington, and there reported to Major-General Wright.

I am, sir, very respectfully, your obedient servant,

J. S. JACKSON,
Brigadier-General Volunteers, Chief of Cavalry.
Major-General NELSON, *Commanding Army of Kentucky.*

No. 5.

Report of Brig. Gen. Mahlon D. Manson, U. S. Army, commanding First Brigade.

INDIANAPOLIS, IND., *September* 10, 1862.

SIR : I have the honor to transmit the following report of the part taken by the troops under my command in the battles fought near Richmond, Ky., on the 29th and 30th days of August, 1862.

On Friday, the 29th of August, a courier arrived at my headquarters, some 2 miles south of Richmond, at 11 o'clock a. m., bearing a communication from Lieutenant-Colonel Munday, commanding a small detachment of cavalry in the neighborhood of Kingston, 5 or 6 miles south of me. Colonel Munday informed me in this communication that he believed the enemy were advancing in considerable force. I caused two copies of Colonel Munday's letter to me to be made out, one of which I sent to Lancaster and the other to Lexington directed to you, not having been informed at which place you might be found. I also sent a written message to Colonel Munday, directing him to hold the enemy in check and ascertain if possible his strength and position; also to learn if the enemy had left the main road and taken either to the right or left from the turnpike road near the foot of Big Hill with any of his forces. I ordered the men to stand to arms in the First Brigade and be ready to move at a moment's warning. I also sent forward four additional companies to strengthen the picket which I already had in that direction, under the command of Lieutenant-Colonel Wolfe, of the Sixteenth Indiana.

At 2 o'clock p. m. of the same day a messenger arrived and informed me that the cavalry, under command of Colonel Metcalfe and Lieutenant-Colonel Munday, and the infantry picket, under command of Lieutenant-Colonel Wolfe, were retreating as fast as possible to the camp, and that the enemy, to the number of 4,000 or 5,000, was pressing hard upon them. The only question for me now to determine was whether I should allow the enemy to attack me in my camp or whether I should advance and meet him. It did not take me a moment to decide which course to pursue, as all the hills 1½ miles south of me completely commanded my camp, and I did not think it my duty to allow the enemy to obtain possession of them without a struggle. I therefore ordered forward the First Brigade, consisting of the Sixteenth, Fifty-fifth, Sixty-ninth, and Seventy-first Indiana Regiments, and the artillery under command of Lieutenant Lanphere. When I had advanced three-quarters of a mile I discovered a heavy column of the enemy's cavalry half a mile east of the road. I immediately ordered Lieutenant Lanphere to get a section of his artillery in position and open upon the enemy, which he did with admirable effect, scattering them in every direction.

I then moved forward a mile and took possession of a high ridge, formed line of battle upon the right and left of the road, with artillery protecting each flank and commanding the open country and turnpike road as far south as Rogersville. The enemy in a few minutes made his appearance in considerable numbers, of cavalry, infantry, and artillery. I opened fire upon him with my artillery, and after a sharp skirmish of an hour's duration succeeded in driving him in some confusion from the field, capturing some prisoners, horses, and one cannon.

I advanced again to Rogersville, distant about 1 mile, where I had the men bivouac, with orders to sleep on their arms, and sent forward Colonel Metcalfe with his cavalry to pursue the enemy and ascertain if possible what his strength was. Colonel Metcalfe returned about 11 o'clock p. m. and stated that he had passed down the road in the direction of Big Hill 6 miles, and had there encountered some of the enemy's cavalry pickets, who, after a slight skirmish retired and fell back some distance. Colonel Metcalfe here had 2 men killed and 2 wounded. At the same time I sent out the cavalry to scout the road I also sent an order to General Cruft to place a strong picket on the

Lancaster pike and on the road that comes into Richmond on the east side, and to hold his brigade in readiness to move at a moment's notice.

On the morning of the 30th, at 4 o'clock, I caused the men to stand to arms, directing that there be details from each company to make coffee and fill the canteens with fresh water.   At 6 o'clock I ascertained that the enemy was advancing upon me, and sent an order to General Cruft to join me with all the forces under his command as quickly as possible; whereupon I gave orders for a forward movement, taking the advance myself with the Fifty-fifth Indiana.   I met the enemy's advance half a mile beyond Rogersville and drove them back, took possession of some woods and high ground upon the left of the road, and formed line of battle, the Fifty-fifth on the left of the road behind a fence, the Sixty-ninth Indiana on the right of the road, artillery on the left of the Fifty-fifth on high ground, the Seventy-first Indiana 300 yards in rear as a support for the battery and as a reserve. I ordered skirmishers to be thrown in front, which was done, those of the Fifty-fifth Indiana opening the battle in the most gallant style.   In a few minutes, the Sixteenth Indiana coming up, I ordered it to take position upon the left of the Fifty-fifth in the woods, which they did, gallantly maintaining their ground against a very heavy force of the enemy for more than an hour, when an attempt was made to turn their flank.   I ordered the Seventy-first Regiment to go forward to their support, which in moving to the point indicated was exposed to a heavy fire from the enemy.   I regret to state that Major Conklin, of the Seventy-first Indiana, was killed while thus moving to the support of the Sixteenth and bravely cheering on his men, and that very shortly afterward Lieutenant-Colonel Topping fell from his horse, mortally wounded, while encouraging the men of his command.   The rebels seemed determined to turn my left flank, and I was compelled to transfer seven companies of the Sixty-ninth Regiment from the right to the left, where, together with the Seventy-first, they faced the enemy and fought bravely.

In the mean time General Cruft arrived on the field with two sections of artillery and the Ninety-fifth Ohio Regiment in advance.   I directed him to place this regiment on the ground that had been occupied by the Sixty-ninth to support the three companies of skirmishers now warmly engaged, and to charge upon a battery that the enemy was then endeavoring to plant upon an eminence only a short distance to the front and right.   In attempting to take this position they were exposed to a severe and raking fire, which threw them into some confusion, and the enemy pressed forward with a heavy force and drove all the troops upon the right before them.   At the same time we were entirely outflanked upon the left, and the enemy, having gained the cover of a large corn field and the woods, made a descent upon the left wing, which gave way and retreated in great disorder.   Up to this time I had maintained my first position for three hours and forty minutes, during all of which time the artillery, under command of Lieutenant Lanphere, had kept up a constant fire, except for a very short time, when the ammunition had become exhausted and before they had received a supply.   The Fifty-fifth Indiana, Colonel Mahan, the Sixteenth Indiana, Colonel Lucas, the Sixty-ninth Indiana, Lieutenant-Colonel Korff, and the Seventy-first Indiana, Lieutenant-Colonel Topping, occupied prominent and exposed positions from the commencement of the engagement, and contended against the enemy with a determination and bravery worthy of older soldiers.   The three remaining regiments of General Cruft's brigade arrived just at the time when our troops were on full retreat and the rout had become general, the Eighteenth Kentucky being in advance, under command of Colonel Warner. This regiment was immediately deployed into line and made a desperate effort to check the advancing enemy, and contended with him single-handed and alone for twenty minutes, when, after a severe loss, they were compelled to give way before overwhelming numbers. The Twelfth and Sixty-sixth Indiana Regiments not having arrived in time to take part in the first battle retired in good order, and were formed in line of battle on a high position near Rogersville, about a mile in the rear of the first battle-field. Taking these two regiments as a nucleus I rallied the remainder of the division, but saw at once that it would not do to fight upon that ground. I deployed the cavalry of Colonels Metcalfe and Munday upon the high ground in front of the infantry, placed one piece of artillery in the road, directing the fire toward the enemy, who were forming line of battle near Rogers' house. I then gave orders to the infantry to face by the rear rank and move to the rear in line of battle. They moved in this manner about three-quarters of a mile, halted, and about-faced. I had now arrived on the ground which I had occupied in the skirmish with the enemy the evening before, and I here ordered General Cruft to move off with his brigade to the right and take position on elevated ground, putting two regiments in the woods on the extreme right and two behind the fence fronting a field of corn and to throw skirmishers forward into the corn field and woods. The first brigade I formed behind fences on the left of the road. The artillery was placed on the right and left, on the same ground occupied the previous afternoon.

I now signaled the cavalry and artillery, which had been left on the ridge in front and which until now had held the enemy in check, and they retired rapidly and took their proper positions in the new line. The enemy now began advancing in great force through the open fields in line of battle, and while they were thus advancing a courier rode upon the field and delivered to me your written order, dated at Lexington, August 30, directing me to retire by the Lancaster road if the enemy should advance in force. It was then 12.30 o'clock p. m., and in less than five minutes from the time I received your order the battle raged with great fierceness along my whole line. The enemy's right soon gave way under the fire from the artillery upon our left, and his whole attention was then turned to our right, upon which a vigorous assault was made by infantry advancing through the woods and open fields. They were met in the most gallant manner by General Cruft's brigade. The Twelfth Indiana and Eighteenth Kentucky Regiments, being placed in the woods, contended against fearful odds and repulsed the rebels several different times. At this point the gallant Colonel Warner, of the Eighteenth Kentucky, was dangerously wounded. The Sixty-sixth Indiana and Ninety-fifth Ohio Regiments held their positions and drove the enemy back a short distance. The enemy soon rallied and again attacked our right wing, which, after a terrific engagement, which lasted from its commencement over one hour, was compelled to fall back and retreated in confusion. I was then forced to order the left wing to fall back, which they did in tolerably good order, the enemy crowding close upon them.

On arriving at my camp I made another effort to rally and reform the troops, and had only partially succeeded when I heard that you were upon the field. I at once reported to you for orders. You informed me that we would make a stand near the town and cemetery. I directed the troops already formed in my camp to move to the place specified. On arriving upon the ground, under your direction the men were formed in line of battle about 2,500 strong, and after contending with an unequal and overpowering force of the enemy for about thirty minutes our whole line was broken and repulsed and the men retreated in the greatest confusion. I regret to say that in this battle Colonel Link, of the Twelfth Indiana, was dangerously wounded, and Colonel McMillen, of the Ninety-fifth Ohio, was shot in the hand.

After passing through Richmond, by your permission I organized a rear guard of the scattered men of most all regiments that had been in the several battles, and took command myself, for the purpose of covering our rear on the retreat. The rear guard behaved well, keeping back the enemy's advance until we had retreated 2 miles on the turnpike road to Lexington, when the scattered troops in advance came to a halt. I left the rear guard in charge of Major Morrison, of the Sixty-sixth Indiana, and pressed forward myself to ascertain the cause of the halt. On arriving in front I found a small squad of the rebel cavalry formed in the road. I attempted to form an advance guard, but owing to the fact that the troops had been defeated in three engagements they were so perfectly demoralized that I found it impossible to rally more than 100 men. This small guard cleared the road in a few moments and continued steadily to advance, driving the rebels from three different stand-points. After passing a little over 4 miles from Richmond we discovered the enemy in heavy force concealed in a corn field on the left side of the road. In attempting to drive them my little band was completely cut to pieces, having 17 killed and 25 wounded. Lieutenant-Colonel Wolfe fell at this point while cheering forward the men. Lieutenant Osborn, my aide-de-camp, was severely wounded. Lieutenant Kercheval, quartermaster Seventy-first Indiana Volunteers, received a severe wound in the left arm, which rendered amputation necessary. The enemy killed and crippled a large number of horses here, which entirely blocked up the road.

It being now about 7 o'clock in the evening, and having no men to make any further resistance with, I attempted to make my escape, accompanied by Colonel Lucas, Captain Baird, and several other officers. We rode through the enemy's lines and proceeded in a westerly direction for half a mile, when we came upon a squadron of the enemy's cavalry, who commanded us to halt, and at the same time fired upon us. My horse was killed and fell upon me, injuring me severely in the breast, and a short time afterward I was arrested by the enemy's cavalry and made a prisoner.

I cannot say with certainty the extent of our loss in killed, wounded, and prisoners, not having received any reports from the officers who commanded on the field, except Colonel Mahan, of the Fifty-fifth Indiana. I do not think, after an examination of the field, that our loss will exceed 200 in killed, 700 wounded, and 2,000 prisoners.* I understand the enemy took quite a number of the men of my command prisoners after they had escaped as far as Lexington. The enemy informed me that they had only captured 24 of our wagons and teams, nine pieces of artillery, and a small amount of camp equipage.

I deem it proper here to state that the troops which I found at Richmond when I arrived there three days before the battle had only been in the service from ten to twenty-five days. Some of the regiments never had had a battalion drill and knew not what a line of battle was.

---

* See revised statement, p. 909.

They were undisciplined, inexperienced, and had never been taught in the manual of arms. The artillery which I had was composed of men of different regiments, some of infantry, and a few artillerymen who had been separated from their commands at the Cumberland Gap. They had been sent from Lexington without caissons or a proper supply of ammunition, being quite deficient in fuses and friction primers. The ammunition of some of the pieces was entirely spent in the first engagement of the morning and the ammunition of all had been quite exhausted at the close of the last battle in the evening.

Taking into consideration the rawness of our troops, there has been no battle during the war where more bravery was displayed by officers and men, with a few exceptions, than there was in the four battles near Richmond. I have neglected to state in the proper place that I was joined in the second engagement by a portion of the Third Kentucky Infantry, who had passed from General Morgan's command at the Cumberland Gap with some Government horses. These men dismounted, hitched their horses, and did excellent service. I do not know the names of any of the accomplished officers who commanded this detachment, or I should gladly give them a place in this report.

I cannot close my report without referring specially to the gallant acts of some of the officers which came directly under my own observation. Capt. R. C. Kise, my assistant adjutant-general; Captain Biddle, U. S. Army; Lieutenant Osborne, Fifty-fifth Indiana; Colonel Metcalfe; Mr. William Goodloe, of Lexington, Ky.; Mr. Bennett, of Madison County, and one or two other citizens, whose names I do not remember, who composed my staff on the day of the battles, are entitled to great credit for the services which they rendered me, and for the prompt manner in which they discharged their duty, regardless of personal danger. I am under particular obligations to Captain Biddle for valuable suggestions in relation to the posting and ranging of the artillery.

I am greatly indebted to the gallant Lieut. Wickliffe Cooper, Dr. Irwin, Captains Baldwin, Stacy, and Kendrick, of your staff—some of whom had traveled 25 miles after hearing the cannonading in the morning—for valuable aid given me during the second and third engagements.

Colonels Lucas, Link, Mahan, Korff, Landram, Munday, Oden, McMillen; Majors Kempton, Orr, and Morris; Captain Baird; Lieutenant Lanphere, and Sergeant Brown, of the battery, greatly distinguished themselves during the action, together with other officers whose names I have not got.

The enemy say they had about 12,000 infantry, 4,000 cavalry, and fifteen pieces of artillery, who were all veteran troops, most of them having been in the army since the commencement of the war. Their loss in killed was about 250 and in wounded probably not over 500. The Union troops did not exceed 6,500, and of these there was not engaged at any one time over 3,500. It is to be regretted that we had not some drilled and disciplined soldiers to meet the enemy in the battles near Richmond. I am satisfied the result might and would have been different.

In conclusion allow me to express a wish that the wound which you received in the last action near Richmond may speedily heal and that you may soon be able to take the field again.

I herewith transmit the report of Colonel Mahan, of the Fifty-fifth

Indiana, and as soon as reports are received from the other regiments of my command I will forward them to you.

I am, sir, very respectfully, yours,

MAHLON D. MANSON,
Brigadier-General, Commanding at Richmond.

Maj. Gen. WILLIAM NELSON, *Commanding Army of Kentucky.*

No. 6.

Report of Lieut. Col. John R. Mahan, Fifty-fifth Indiana Infantry.

CAMP MORTON, *Indianapolis, September* 10, 1862.

I have the honor to submit to you a report of the part taken by the Fifty-fifth Regiment Indiana Volunteers in the late engagement at Rogersville and Richmond, Ky. On the 29th instant, at about 1 o'clock p. m., in pursuance of your order, a part of the regiment, consisting of Companies B, C, D, E, and G, were formed in line of battle on our camp ground about 2 miles south of Richmond, and was moved down the road in the direction of Rogersville at a point about 1½ miles from our camp, being followed immediately by four pieces of artillery, under command of Lieutenant Lanphere. At this point, the enemy having been discovered in considerable force on the left in the valley, two pieces of artillery were placed on the left of the road and opened an effective fire on the enemy, who had ingeniously concealed himself in the woods. The Fifty-fifth Regiment, in pursuance of your order, here remained in position in the rear of the battery until the woods had been thoroughly shelled in that direction, when they moved forward to a point one-half mile farther toward Rogersville, and formed again upon the right of the road at a point designated and wisely selected by you. Here the artillery was placed again in front of the Fifty-fifth Regiment, the Seventy-first Indiana Regiment, under command of Lieutenant-Colonel Topping, being now upon the left of the Fifty-fifth, and the Sixty-ninth being upon the left of the Seventy-first and across the road in line of battle, with two pieces of artillery.

The enemy appearing in our front and upon our left at this point in large numbers, the artillery upon the right and left again opened upon them, bearing upon the road in the direction of Rogersville and the valley and woods upon our left. The enemy here opened a lively fire upon us, directed toward our battery and the Fifty-fifth Regiment upon the right, and for a short time we had the promise of a lively engagement, but the enemy was soon discovered to be falling back. At your suggestion I here deployed one company of my command, Company E, Capt. [Charles] Emery, and sent them down the road toward Rogersville as skirmishers. They found the enemy in front retreating through Rogersville, and pursued so closely that they captured and brought back to us one piece of the enemy's artillery, which had been used, with but little effect, upon us but a short time previous. The enemy was now found to be retreating in dismay, and the column, the Fifty-fifth being in front, upon your order moved 1 mile farther south to Rogersville, where they slept upon their arms.

At about 6 o'clock in the morning of the 30th I formed the Fifty-fifth Regiment again, and, as you directed, moved in front of the column, being followed by the artillery to a point about one-half mile south of

Rogersville, when the enemy were discovered upon the right of the road and in front, having previously killed a part of our pickets and driven the remainder in. I here, in accordance with your direction, formed my front company—Company C, Capt. [Abner E.] Purcell—into sections and moved them a short distance down the road as an advance guard, when the first section fired upon a squad of cavalry upon our right. I then formed my command upon the left of the road and caused them to lay down under cover of a hill, and deployed Company B, Capt. [Carter L.] Vigus, upon the extreme left as skirmishers. This company had been out but a few minutes until they found the enemy in heavy force upon the left and threatening a flank movement, which you discovered, and placed the Sixteenth Indiana, under Colonel Lucas, upon our left. I caused the Fifty-fifth Regiment to fall back to the fence a few paces in our rear and to form a line there and to support the battery which you had caused to be placed there. At this point the Fifty-fifth Regiment became engaged, as did also the Sixteenth, upon our left. The enemy opened their artillery upon us with a fierce and constant firing, their second ball killing two corporals in Company G, Capt. [David H.] Hamilton's company. My command remained here for about two hours and a half under a heavy fire and returned it like old soldiers until the enemy had turned our left flank and the Sixteenth Indiana was compelled to give way. The Fifty-fifth Regiment became somewhat confused in the retreat, having been divided previously for skirmishers, but they rallied again in good order and formed at the place designated by you, about 1 mile north of Rogersville. Having fired their 40 rounds, some little time was spent in procuring a new supply of ammunition; but in due time I placed the five companies upon the extreme left and held our position until almost entirely surrounded by the enemy's cavalry, when I again moved them back to a point on the left of our camp 2 miles south of Richmond, where we again formed and were ready for the contest, when I was ordered to fall back to a point just south of Richmond, in the suburbs of the town. In this movement I experienced some embarrassment from the confusion which had reached my own command to some extent. The field officers and many of the company officers of the Seventy-first Regiment having been killed or disabled left that regiment without a commander and unavoidably confused. But I found the men all willing to fight, and with pleasure saw many of them fall in with other regiments and do good service. At this last stand the Fifty-fifth Regiment stood and held their position until they had been entirely surrounded by the enemy's cavalry and the force upon our right gave way, when I moved the Fifty-fifth Regiment on the east of the town of Richmond and forced our way through the line of the enemy, killing many of them, and passed over the Kentucky River that night, skirmishing with the enemy at intervals, who were to be found in every field in the country. Having learned that no stand would be made at the river I moved the regiment on to Lexington, where, in accordance with the order of General Nelson, we turned our arms over to another regiment, our term of service having expired.

I am under obligations to my company officers for the valuable aid they rendered me in commanding our little command. Adjt. [Frank A.] Rose also rendered me efficient aid until the artillery firing commenced on the 30th, when his horse fell with him and disabled him so much that he had to be carried from the field, and is now among the wounded at the hospital. It pains me to record the death of Lieut. [William L.] Thompson, of Company E. He fell about 11 o'clock on the 30th. In the midst of danger he acted nobly and fell with his face toward the foe, having fired upon them after he had received his mortal wound. No better blood ever stained a battle-field. It would afford me pleasure to allude to the many acts of gallantry and courage of my officers and men. They did their duty and did it well. I congratulate you upon your success in disposing of the various regiments upon the field and your final success in the narrow escape through the heavy fire of the enemy, and trust that you may soon recover from the wounds received on that memorable day. I append a list of killed and wounded of my regiment as near as can now be ascertained.*

I have the honor to be, your obedient servant,

JOHN R. MAHAN,
Lieutenant-Colonel, Commanding Fifty-fifth Regiment.

Brigadier-General MANSON.

No. 7.

Report of Brig. Gen. Charles Cruft, U. S. Army, commanding Second Brigade.

HDQRS. SECOND BRIGADE GENERAL NELSON'S COMMAND,
In the Field, near Louisville, Ky., September 5, 1862.

CAPTAIN: The following report of the operations of the Second Brigade of General Nelson's command in the battles near Richmond, Ky., on the 29th and 30th ultimo, is herewith submitted:

The brigade consisted of four regiments and a battalion of volunteer infantry and a volunteer battery, as follows, to wit: The Eighteenth Kentucky Volunteers, Col. W. A. Warner; Ninety-fifth Ohio Volunteers, Colonel McMillen; Twelfth Indiana Volunteers, Colonel Link; Sixty-sixth Indiana Volunteers, Major Morrison; battalion of Third Tennessee Volunteers, Lieutenant-Colonel Chiles; Andrews' Michigan battery, Lieutenant Hale. The effective strength of the brigade on the morning of the 30th ultimo was 3,085.

On the afternoon of Tuesday, the 26th ultimo, 1 was assigned to the command of the brigade. It was bivouacked a short distance from the town of Richmond, in a line of battle, which extended from the Irving turnpike, across the State road leading to Cumberland Gap, to the edge of the woods west of the cemetery. The men were all fresh recruits, except the Eighteenth Kentucky, which had seen no field service, very little drill, and was now, for the first time since its formation, collected as a regiment. The men knew nothing of the duties or habits of soldiers. Most of them had been less than a fortnight away from their homes. They could but indifferently execute some of the simplest movements in the manual of arms, but knew nothing whatever of company or battalion drill. Both officers and men were earnest and brave, but wholly inexperienced and untrained. There were no regular camps ; neither had the men any of the ordinary camp equipage or conveniencies. They were lying exposed to the hot sun by day and heavy dews by night, without the means of instruction or improvement in any way. One regiment had no field officers yet appointed, and, save the exception above noticed, all were but a mere collection of citizens, hastily assembled, armed, and thrown together without the least knowl-

---

* Nominal list omitted shows 12 killed, 46 wounded, and 2 missing ; but see revised statement, p. 909.

edge of military rules or discipline. The battery, though some time recruited, had never received its guns, horses, or appointments until within the week preceding the battle. It was a sad spectacle to a soldier to look at these raw levies and contemplate their fate in a trial at arms with experienced troops.

Such was the material of the command at the time the brigade was constituted. The same is true of the First Brigade, commanded by Brigadier-General Manson. All that experience could suggest, everything that incessant labor could accomplish, was done by me during the three days preceding the battle to put the regiments and battery into working shape. Not a moment was unnecessarily lost from drills and instruction. Manifest improvement was becoming daily visible. Yet, owing to the almost entire ignorance of the officers, this was necessarily slow. There was but a single staff officer of any experience with me. No subalterns were found in the whole command of sufficient military knowledge to assist upon the general staff.

Upon assuming command the town and bivouacks were at once thoroughly picketed. Cavalry patrols and scouting parties were kept constantly on the roads leading south and southeasterly for a distance of 12 miles out. Every exertion was used to guard against surprise and to procure intelligence from the front. Colonel Metcalfe had met with a repulse at Big Hill a few days previously. It was known that the enemy held this position some 15 miles to the front, but it seemed to be impossible to ascertain his force. Numerous plans were resorted to in order to ascertain this, but all were unavailing.

On Friday, the 29th, it was reported that the enemy had descended from the hill, but nothing could be learned accurately in regard to his approach toward our lines or whether such was his purpose. Duties elsewhere had called Major-General Nelson from Richmond, and the command fell to Brigadier-General Manson.

General Manson's line was 2 miles to the front and parallel to that of the Second Brigade. He had a half battery of artillery belonging to my command on one of his flanks and another half battery upon the opposite one, and was earnestly and laboriously endeavoring to instruct his officers and men and watching matters to the front.

About 4 o'clock on Friday afternoon the discharge of cannon was heard to the front in the direction of General Manson's lines. This continued for some minutes; no intelligence reached me, however, as to the cause. A messenger was sent forward forthwith. The brigade was put under arms, in readiness to march on command. A Rodman gun, from the artillery under command of Lieutenant Andrews, was sent forward on the Irving road, with five companies of the Eighteenth Kentucky Regiment, under Major Bracht, to support it, and every disposition made to move forward rapidly when ordered. The piece upon the Irving road was heard to fire four times, when everything became quiet. The messenger returned from the front with the intelligence that General Manson had advanced some 3 miles to a ridge near the village of Rogersville, had encountered the enemy, driven him off, captured one piece of artillery, and was able to hold his position. The officers in charge of my detachment on the Irving road reported having seen a small force of rebel cavalry attempting to flank General Manson's left, which he had dispersed by his fire. Nothing further was heard from General Manson, but the command was kept under arms till 10 p. m. The men then retired and were aroused again and placed in line of battle at 3 o'clock on Saturday morning. Still nothing was heard from General Manson directly. My command breakfasted half regiment at a time and were placed in line again.

About 7.15 a. m. on Saturday a heavy cannonade was heard to the front. It continued for some minutes, and was evidently being actively replied to. Occasional musketry was also heard. After waiting a sufficient time for a dispatch to reach me I sent forward for orders. The cannonading now increased, and it became evident that a general engagement was imminent. I waited no longer, but wheeled the artillery and infantry into the road and took up march for the front. After proceeding 4 miles I encountered my messenger, who informed me that he had been unable to communicate with General Manson, though the fight was progressing rapidly on both sides with artillery and would doubtless soon become general. The column, already wearied with heat and thirst, was pressed rapidly up. Near Rogersville, a mile to the rear of the scene of the first action, a messenger from General Manson reached me, urging immediate re-enforcements. The artillery was sent forward on a trot and the infantry hurried up.

The locality of the first battle was a piece of broken woodland on the left of the State road, near a small church, about 1 mile beyond Rogersville and 5 miles from my encampment. As our re-enforcements approached the place we met the artillery wagons driving back to Richmond for ammunition, the supply in the boxes having been already exhausted. My artillery was immediately placed and the fire renewed. The re-enforcing regiments were soon in position, the Ninety-fifth Ohio on the right, Eighteenth Kentucky on the left, while the Sixty-sixth and Twelfth Indiana were held in the rear in reserve. In a few moments after these dispositions were made the enemy's cannonading ceased, and an advance of his infantry was made, showing not only a superior front to ours but very large numbers at each flank. His approach was manfully resisted. Our raw troops went to work in earnest, and for some forty minutes the rattle of musketry was terrible. It was apparent, however, to any experienced eye, that the conflict was too unequal to be of long duration. The enemy's skirmishers were at first driven off and the advance of his main body for a time checked. It was, however, impossible, with the troops composing our lines, to stand against the impetuosity of his charge. The center gave way, then the right flank. The left made still a show of resistance, and the Eighteenth Kentucky, Colonel Warner, was brought up to its aid. This regiment made here a gallant fight, and by its brave stand broke the force of the enemy's attack and prevented the retreat at this time from becoming a rout. The men and officers of most of the regiments, however, fled in confusion to the rear through the fields. A few companies were brought off in tolerable order, but the panic was well-nigh universal. This was 10.30 a. m. At this juncture the whole thing was fast becoming shameful. No appeals availed at first to stop officers or men. The men, however, began to rally. I had the Twelfth and Sixty-sixth Indiana formed on the left of the road across the fields about 1 mile in the rear of the battle-field and in front of the retreating mass, and placed a line of cavalry still to their front. Here the greater portion of the retreating regiments were eventually rallied. A line of battle was established extending across the State road, and all the regiments marched in tolerable order back for a distance of 2 miles through the fields.

Upon conferring with General Manson it was determined to make another fight. It had now reached 1 p. m. My brigade was ordered to take position on the right of the road and occupy a ridge there. It was soon formed in line, the Ninety-fifth Ohio on the left next the road, the Sixty-sixth Indiana to their right, and the Eighteenth Kentucky in cover of the wood, with the Twelfth Indiana on the extreme right. The artillery was placed upon the high ground near the road. Skirmishers were thrown out well to the front. I endeavored in vain to urge some of the cavalry standing to my rear to explore the woodland to my right. The reply, however, returned by my aide-de-camp from their commanding officer was that they were a pack of cowards and would not go.

The First Brigade was formed to my rear several hundred yards, inside a corn field on the left of the road, with its artillery in front. The enemy approached first through a corn field in front of my left wing and opened a severe fire. My line was advanced up the fence and a sharp conflict ensued, in which the Ninety-fifth Ohio and Sixty-sixth Indiana took part. The behavior of these regiments here was excellent, and they succeeded in driving the enemy out of the field and holding their position. The attack now commenced on the right in the woodland. The Eighteenth Kentucky and Twelfth Indiana held their ground for some time in a sturdy manner, but, yielding to overpowering numbers, broke and fell back in confusion. At this time I attempted to change the front of my left wing to oppose the enemy that was crossing the meadow-land on the left of the road. The attempt to maneuver, however, was a failure, and the men broke and fled down the road. The entire First Brigade had gone previously, without having opened fire during the engagement. The flying masses drifted up the road and through the fields in the direction of Richmond. General Manson and myself rode forward, endeavoring to stay the flight and panic in every possible way. Our respective staff officers and some of the field officers of the various commands nobly assisted in the hopeless task.

The general ordered a third rally to be made at the ground formerly occupied by his camp. Here we were striving to collect the scattered soldiers when Major-General Nelson reached the field. He ordered another halt and reformation of line, and chose for the place that formerly occupied by the Second Brigade. Here such of the men as could be rallied were collected and formed in line of battle, the left resting on the State road near the toll-gate, occupying the cemetery and stretching off through the woods on the right. The entire number of men in the last fight in both brigades did not exceed 2,500. My brigade was formed on the left, occupying the cemetery and adjoining corn field and skirt of the woods. The enemy came upon us as soon as the line was formed. His skirmishers were held back for a short while by ours. The attack soon became general and was stoutly resisted for a few moments, when the whole line broke in wild confusion and a general stampede ensued. Both officers and men became reckless of all restraint or command, and rushed pell-mell to the rear, amidst a mingled mass of horses, wagons, artillery, &c., in an utter rout. Every effort possible was made to rally the men behind the artillery, trusting, with the few shots left in the ammunition-chests of the howitzers, to make our way to the rear. Officers, or men wearing shoulder-straps, deliberately refused to render any assistance or respond to any order.

Before the last battle the enemy had flanked our line and passed large bodies of cavalry to our rear. These fell upon the helpless and demoralized mass of fugitives, and either slew or captured them, without much show of resistance. It now became a matter of individual safety, and the mass scattered, each one taking such course as he was able. At times during the battles of the day every regiment in my command exhibited great courage and endurance. Heavy and continued volleys were given, and the enemy was often severely handled. His loss seemed to have exceeded ours, but the perfect discipline of his troops enabled him to break our front, while his superior numbers made it easy to fank our lines in masses that were irresistible. His force at all times engaged must have exceeded ours three times in numbers. He seemed to have in each attack a superior number to our front, with as many on each flank. The account of the whole battle may be summed up in a few words. It was an attack by at least 15,000 well disciplined troops, under experienced officers, upon 6,250 citizens, ignorant of war, without officers of experience. The wonder really is that the latter fought so well for a whole day, could be twice rallied after being panic-stricken, and that any escaped slaughter or capture.

Before closing the report of this disastrous fight it is just to say that there were many instances of great personal valor exhibited by individual officers and men which came under my observation. Colonel Warner, Lieutenant-Colonel Landram, and Major Bracht, of the Eighteenth Kentucky, exhibited proper courage and daring. The former, I regret to say, is reported mortally wounded, and the latter two had their horses shot under them. Colonel Link, of the Twelfth Indiana, was badly wounded in the fearless discharge of his duties. Colonel McMillen, of the Ninety-fifth Ohio, was cool and brave during the whole day, and was wounded in the last fight. Major Morrison and Capt. John F. Baird managed the Sixty-sixth Indiana in a creditable manner and exhibited soldierly qualities upon the field. They were both captured during the retreat. Lieutenants Hale and Andrews, of the Michigan battery, acted gallantly throughout the day, using their pieces effectively, and, with their gunners, standing by them in every extremity. They brought them safely away from all the engagements, but lost them in the retreat. Lieutenant-Colonel Chiles, of the Third Tennessee, was left in rear of the town during the engagements, and his command took no part in them. It was, however, engaged with the enemy's cavalry during the retreat and is reported to have behaved well. Lieutenant-Colonel Chiles was captured by the enemy. Copies of the reports of the regimental commanders and commanding officer of Andrews' battery are herewith appended, marked respectively A, B, C, D, E, and F. In these reports many instances of individual bravery are noted and commended to the consideration of the major-general commanding.

The detailed report of Surg. Joseph Fithian, acting brigade surgeon, is herewith submitted. The report exhibits the following summary of the casualties of the brigade, to wit:

Regiment.	Killed.			Wounded.			Aggregate.
	Officers.	Men.	Total.	Officers.	Men.	Total.	
12th Indiana Volunteers		7	7	3	31	34	41
95th Ohio Volunteers		10	10	5	33	38	48
66th Indiana Volunteers	3	21	24	5	63	68	92
18th Kentucky Volunteers	4	28	32	6	101	107	139
Andrews' battery		2	2		9	9	11
Total	7	68	75	19	237	256	*331

* But see revised statement, p. 909.

It is due to Surgeon Fithian to say that he was unremitting in the discharge of his duties on the field during the engagements, and that he shrank from no personal danger or exposure in ministering to the wounded and dying. He further reports good conduct on the part of all the regimental surgeons of the brigade.

It is impossible to state the number of prisoners captured by the enemy with accuracy. It is presumed, however, from concurrent reports that have been received at my headquarters that nearly half the command were taken prisoners and subsequently paroled. The remaining troops of both brigades were reorganized by me, under orders from Major-General Wright, at Lexington, and marched to this encampment.

In concluding this report it affords me pleasure to make honorable mention of the officers who acted upon my brigade staff, and to express my obligations to the gentlemen from civil life who volunteered their services and exposed their lives in the thickest of the battles. Capt. Wickliffe Cooper, of General Nelson's staff, my acting assistant adjutant-general, bore himself gallantly throughout the engagements and rendered efficient service at all parts of the field. Lieutenant Reeder, of the Eighteenth Kentucky Volunteers, detailed as aide-de-camp, evinced a high degree of courage and coolness. Acting brigade quartermaster, Lieut. J. T. Clark, of the Eighteenth Kentucky, obeyed orders—staid with his teams and stores, got his trains safely away, and thereby saved a large amount of Government property from the enemy. Messrs. Green Clay, of Madison County; Hartwell Boswell, L. P. Shaw, and Wharton M. Moore, of Lexington, and William Holloway and John Miller, of Richmond, volunteered their services as aides-de-camp, and acted throughout the day in that capacity upon my staff. Their bearing on the field was gallant in the extreme and coolness under fire admirable. They were constantly exposed to the enemy's bullets, but escaped unhurt, except Mr. Miller, who was mortally wounded in the second engagement and has since died—a martyr to his high-toned patriotism. Captains Kendrick, Stacy, Baldwin, and Horton, of Major-General Nelson's staff, joined my staff before the second engagement and conducted themselves handsomely on the field, rendering marked service in rallying and assuring the men.

With assurances of regard to Major-General Nelson, and the hope that he will soon recover from his wounds and be again able to take the field, I am, captain, yours, respectfully, &c.,

CHARLES CRUFT,
Brigadier-General, Commanding Second Brigade.

Capt. J. Edward Stacy, *A. A. G., Army of Kentucky.*

No. 8.

Report of Lieut. Luther F. Hale, Battery F, First Michigan Light Artillery.

Camp Gilbert, *Louisville, Ky., September 9, 1862.*

Sir: I have the honor to submit to you the following report of the casualties which occurred in and the part taken by Andrews' Michigan battery in the action at Richmond, Ky., August 30, 1862:

Enlisted men, killed, 2; wounded, 9; missing, 4.*

---

* But see revised statement, p. 909.

Of the conduct of the officers and men under my command I cannot speak too highly. They were prompt in obedience to my orders regardless of personal safety, and in no instance leaving their post until all support was withdrawn. Lieutenant Andrews displayed great energy and precision in all his movements. Lieutenant Paddock also displayed great coolness and presence of mind at all times. Each piece, with the exception of one commanded by Lieutenant Andrews, was successfully withdrawn from the field. Three of the horses upon the one left on the field were shot down, when it was found necessary to abandon it. The battery commenced the retreat in good order. After proceeding to a point about 2 miles this side of Richmond, being unsupported and without ammunition, was attacked and captured, together with all camp equipage, company books, officers' baggage, &c., by the enemy, with the exception of about 25 horses and some harness, the amount of which I am unable to state definitely, which by your order was turned over to General Terrill.

All of which is respectfully submitted.

I remain, sir, your obedient servant,

L. F. HALE,
Senior First Lieutenant, Commanding Battery.

Brig. Gen. CHARLES CRUFT,
Comdg. Second Brig., Second Div., U. S. Forces in Kentucky.

No. 9.

Report of Capt. John F. Baird, Sixty-sixth Indiana Infantry.

The Second Brigade, commanded by Brigadier-General Cruft, was ordered to the support of Brigadier-General Manson's brigade that was engaging the enemy in the morning. General Cruft's brigade commenced moving Saturday morning at 11 o'clock; advanced about 3 miles, the Sixty-sixth forming in line of battle to the left of the pike. While General Manson's brigade was falling back in some disorder a large number from different regiments under General Manson was rallied by our gallant general and his aides. About 100 of this number was formed on the left wing of the Sixty-sixth. The Sixty-sixth remained in line of battle on a commanding ridge, with cavalry in front, till ordered by General Cruft to march in line of battle to a position about 1 mile to the rear. The Sixty-sixth then halted and formed in line of battle on the left, supporting one brass piece of the Michigan battery in an open field, with a corn field in front and timber on the right. The Sixty-sixth opened fire on the enemy in the corn field till they exhausted their ammunition, driving the enemy from the field with great slaughter to the timber on the right. The Sixty-sixth then made a charge for a short distance in the field. General Cruft in the mean time ordered the field piece to be fired promptly with canister and grape, which thinned their ranks, causing the enemy to halt, which gave the Sixty-sixth time to fall back by a left-flank movement to the left in direction of the pike and toward Richmond. We followed the pike some 3 miles. The Sixty-sixth then formed in line of battle in the grave-yard near Richmond. Captain Rodman and Captain Jordan were thrown to the front as skirmishers, lying down. They remained in that position till the enemy came on the Sixty-sixth parade ground, within 60 yards. They then opened fire, the regiment firing immedi-

ately after, killing about 100. The Sixty-sixth then fell back to Richmond. I was then ordered by General Cruft to rally the men in the
streets, which was done. The Sixty-sixth retired in order through the
streets, firing as they went. The Sixty-sixth then followed the pike
toward Lexington for 3 miles, the enemy shelling us in the rear. We
soon discovered the enemy's cavalry directly in our front and on our
right and left, supported by a heavy body of infantry. They commenced firing on us from every direction, men and horses falling. We
soon discovered that we were bagged and completely surrounded and
our retreat cut off. We were ordered to lay down our arms and that
we would not be hurt. Then our brave Sixty-sixth surrendered, and
not till then. During the engagement in the grave-yard General
Cruft's horse received a ball in the jaw. The general dismounted
when the enemy's bullets were falling thick around him and examined
the wound with that coolness that belongs to none but the brave. The
general then mounted his gallant steed and called on the Sixty-sixth
to remember Indiana. All praise is due to General Cruft and his aides,
who distinguished themselves nobly. They were galloping in every
direction on the field, delivering orders from the general. Major Morrison conducted himself nobly and was not excited. He is a brave
officer. He was at all times a mark for the enemy. His horse was
shot in the last engagement. After his horse fell he was taken prisoner
and paroled.

The officers and men of the Sixty-sixth are brave men; they never
flinched or shrank from duty. You could hear their voices above the
roar of artillery and the volley of musketry shouting, "Remember
Indiana." But, alas, the gallant Sixth-sixth was forced to surrender
to an overwhelming force.

JOHN F. BAIRD,
Captain, Commanding at Richmond.

No. 10.

Report of Capt. Jasper N. Rodman, Sixty-sixth Indiana Infantry.

CAMP NEAR LOUISVILLE, KY., *September* 7, 1862.

CAPTAIN: I beg leave to submit the following report of the part
taken by the Sixty-sixth Regiment Indiana Volunteers in the recent
engagements before Richmond, Ky., on the 30th and 31st [29th and
30th] ultimo:

On the morning of the 30th ultimo (Saturday) the regiment commanded by Major Morrison was ordered under arms at 3 o'clock to be
ready to march to the scene of action and at 8 o'clock took up their
line of march. Arriving at Rogersville we met our forces on the retreat. After forming the line of battle they rallied, the Twelfth Indiana being upon our right. After remaining there a short time we
were ordered to fall back about a mile, which was done in order. A
new line of battle was formed on the right of the road, and we remained there until the enemy made their appearance on the right and
front. The Sixty-sixth then advanced to the fence of a corn field
through which the enemy were advancing and opened fire, and after
firing about 20 rounds forced the enemy to retire, which they did, and
concentrated their forces upon the right. The fighting there was very
severe, and the Twelfth Indiana being forced back left our right ex-

posed, and the enemy, seizing the opportunity, outflanked us in that direction. The Ninety-fifth Ohio had given way on our left some time before, and in the attempt to change front to the left we were exposed to a galling cross-fire from both wings of the enemy. Being thus almost entirely surrounded, the command was given to fall back to the main road, which was done in as good order as possible, and the retreat was continued for 2 miles, when a new line of battle was formed, and after awaiting the approach of the enemy for some time we were ordered to fall back to Richmond.

The Sixty-sixth was then formed in the cemetery and the woods on the right and waited for the attack of the enemy, which was made on the whole line and both flanks. We held our position until the whole right had given way, and we were again outflanked and obliged to retreat, the Sixty-sixth being detailed to bring up the rear. After passing about half-way through the town of Richmond we halted, and three companies formed in line across the street and opened fire on the enemy. The entire column was then in full retreat toward Lexington, the Sixty-sixth still bringing up the rear and covering the retreat. After marching about a mile the enemy made their appearance on our front between our advance and Lexington. The wildest confusion then prevailed, and each one tried to save himself. It is thought that there Major Morrison was taken prisoner. It is impossible to make any further report at this time, the whole force being scattered in all directions. During the night many escaped to Lexington, some 316 of the Sixty-sixth being among the number.

I have the honor to be, very respectfully, yours,

J. N. RODMAN,
Captain Company B.

Capt. W. H. FAIRBANKS, *Assistant Adjutant-General.*

No. 11.

Report of Maj. Frederick G. Bracht, Eighteenth Kentucky Infantry.

The following statement of the action of the Eighteenth Regiment Kentucky Volunteers, U. S. Army, in the engagement of Friday and Saturday, near Richmond, Ky., is respectfully submitted:

On Friday evening, when the roar of artillery in the direction of Rogersville announced that the contest had commenced, the Eighteenth was promptly drawn up in line, and two companies detached and sent out, with a couple of field pieces, on the Irving road, from which excursion only one of the companies returned, the other remaining on picket duty till after the battle.

At 3 o'clock in the morning of Saturday our camp was quietly awakened, and fell into line more promptly and in better spirits than I have ever before observed, manifesting as laudable a desire to meet the invading foe in deadly conflict as ever inspired a veteran regiment, and when the roar of artillery announced that the conflict had again commenced the countenances of all were lit up with an enthusiasm which promised well for their action on the field. When the order to march was received they stepped off with as light a tread as ever inspired the true soldier, and when we approached the field and the rattle of musketry told of the close proximity of the combatants, a new zeal and an increased enthusiasm were constantly growing on every countenance.

When we came in sight of the struggling combatants we were informed that the left wing of our army was retiring under a terrible fire from the right of the enemy, and we were ordered into an open field at double-quick to sustain them. We crossed a ravine, and then came forward by companies into line, the right of our regiment resting in the head of a hollow, yet in plain view of the foe, and the left extending off into a high ridge in front of a wood and near a field of corn on our left. During the time of forming our line a terrible fire was poured into us from the foe in front, screened and concealed by a fence and thick brush. Before we were yet formed considerable numbers of each company had bit the dust and many more were groaning with ghastly wounds; and yet, notwithstanding all the discouragement which such a state of affairs was destined to produce, our men stood boldly up and poured a steady fire into the fence and wood from which the deadly missiles were falling around us, while scarce one single visible foe was seen before us; and to make our position more terrible and untenable a severe cross-fire was opened upon us from the corn field on our left and from a still hidden foe. Seeing it was suicide to stand the men were ordered to fall upon the ground, which they promptly did, and continued (*a la Zouave*) from that position to pour into the fields from which the balls were raining so thick upon us a prompt and steady fire. Numbers had already fallen in every company in the regiment. Several company officers had become victims. Captain Mullins, Company A, was wounded in the leg and taken back; Captain Lewis, Company H, killed; Captain Culbertson, Company K, mortally wounded; Lieutenant Washburn, Company F, killed. The horses of Colonel Warner, Lieutenant-Colonel Landram, and my own had been shot under us. The line of our troops which we were ordered up to support had fallen far back in our rear. Destruction seemed to await us, and yet every officer and man of the regiment stood up to his post, but it could not be supposed that men under their first fire could long be held to their position under such an array of terrible discouragements.

The right wing commenced falling back, the center and the left soon followed, nor could any effort of officers prevent a confused and precipitate retreat from a position which under all the circumstances we could not long have maintained without utter annihilation. In this retreat Lieutenant-Colonel Landram, while engaged in an effort to rally the men, received a painful wound in the face, and was sent by the surgeon to Richmond in an ambulance, where he was subsequently taken prisoner. Colonel Warner and myself mounted fresh horses and succeeded, with the assistance of Lieutenant Robbins, acting adjutant, and company officers, in collecting together about 300 of our men for the second conflict, in which we took position on the right, between the Twelfth Indiana on our right and the Ninety-fifth Ohio on our left, Company B, under command of Captain Johnson, having been sent out as skirmishers. During the first part of this engagement we stood silent spectators of a hard-contested combat on our left. Finally, however, by a flank movement, the enemy in overwhelming numbers passed around a corn field and made a precipitate rush upon our line in front, while they outflanked us in the woods and subjected the right of our line to another severe cross-fire, by which means they quickly turned our right, threw it in confusion, and produced another unavoidable retreat, in which Colonel Warner received a mortal wound through his chest, and Lieutenant Dunlap, commanding Company I, was shot in the head, producing instant death.

About this time Major-General Nelson appeared on the field and made an effort to force another stand. Lieutenant Robbins and Captain Fisk had taken Colonel Warner off the field, whence he was sent in an ambulance to Richmond. Lieutenant Robbins, of whose meritorious conduct on the battle-field I cannot speak in too high praise, being disabled by a fall from his horse, was also conveyed to Richmond.

Our forces were by this time badly scattered and confused. The different officers, however, who were yet fit for service, were unceasing in their efforts to collect and bring into the final contest at Richmond as many of our forces as possible, but it very soon became manifest to myself, as well as to many others, that no good result could be expected from a force three times beaten, fatigued, and prostrated from want of water The whole force was soon stampeded, and I took what I could collect of our own regiment, with many stragglers from others, and struck off for Boonesborough, where we crossed the Kentucky River at 2 o'clock at night, and I finally succeeded, after a most fatiguing march, in bring ing into Lexington about 300 men. The Eighteenth Regiment Kentucky Volunteers report now 236 enlisted men, under two captains— A. G. Wileman, Company D, and W. H. Littlejoin, Company F ; six first lieutenants—J. W. Robbins, Company A, acting adjutant ; J. D. Chrisman, Company B ; W. C. Reeder, Company C ; D. Boys, Company G ; J. J. Hall, Company H ; J. B. Heltemes, Company K ; and two second lieutenants—A. B. Clark, Company C, and J. H. Johns, Company D.

F. G. BRACHT,
Major Eighteenth Kentucky Volunteers, U. S. Army.

Brig. Gen. CHARLES CRUFT, *Commanding Second Brigade.*

No. 12.

Report of Col. William L. McMillen, Ninety-fifth Ohio Infantry.

HDQRS. NINETY-FIFTH REGIMENT OHIO VOLUNTEERS,
Camp Chase, Ohio, September 20, 1862.

GENERAL: I have the honor to submit the following report of the part taken by the Ninety-fifth Regiment Ohio Volunteers in the battles before Richmond, Ky., on Saturday, August 30, 1862 :

About 3 p. m. on Friday, August 29, I received an order from Brigadier-General Cruft, commanding the Second Brigade of the Army of Kentucky, directing me to form my regiment quietly in line of battle and to wait further orders. The regiment remained in line until about dark, at which time, the skirmishing in front having ceased, supper was prepared and the men dismissed, one-half at a time, to eat it. During the night the regiment lay on their arms, and at 3 o'clock on Saturday morning again formed in line of battle. At daylight arms were stacked and breakfast prepared. As soon as possible thereafter the line was again formed, and at 7 o'clock we received marching orders. Taking the advance of the brigade, we were marched rapidly (a portion of the distance on the double-quick) 7 miles to the front to a point between Rogersville and Kingston, where General Manson's brigade had already engaged the enemy. Without being permitted to halt for rest or the men to close up we were marched at once upon the field, and required to form our line of battle under a heavy artillery fire from the enemy and in advance of our own guns. This movement was being executed with alacrity by the men, but before it could be completed we were ordered by General Manson to move across the road and charge a battery which the enemy was planting some 400 yards to our front. I moved at once with that portion of the regiment which had come up, forming on the right of the road, and advancing rapidly at a charge-bayonet on the battery indicated. While we were thus engaged the enemy advanced his right and left wings, outflanking and driving our forces before him. Seeing that it would be reckless and useless to continue our assault upon the battery I ordered the regiment to halt and fall back, which they did for a time in good order, losing, however, in addition to our killed and wounded, 160 men and a large number of officers captured at this point. In forming for this charge Captains Allis and Tate, Lieutenants Bull, Chittenden, Tate, and Potts, as well as other company officers, deserve great credit for the coolness and courage they displayed.

We continued falling back for about 1½ miles, where we found our cavalry drawn up in line, and where a halt was ordered and the regiment reformed. Notwithstanding my men were very much exhausted and suffering for want of water, which was difficult to obtain, they again formed with spirit and promptness. Taking our place in line, the whole army was ordered to fall back and take up a position on two commanding hills some 2 miles this side of Rogersville, where the second engagement, lasting about one hour, occurred. Here the Ninety-fifth and the other regiments forming General Cruft's brigade fought with a gallantry and determination unsurpassed by raw troops, holding the enemy in check and at one time driving him some distance, but were finally overpowered, outflanked, and compelled to fall back. The retreat from this point very soon degenerated into a complete rout, and no effort was made to rally the men until in sight of the town of Richmond. There we succeeded in collecting about 300 of the Ninety-fifth, including Captain Taylor's company, which had been on picket duty during the former engagements and was relieved by order of General Nelson, who had recently arrived upon the field. We were posted at the edge of a corn field to the right and in sight of our old camping ground, with the Sixty-sixth Indiana on our left and the Twelfth Indiana on our right. We there awaited some time the advance of the enemy, who came up each time with fresh brigades and increased confidence and engaged us in front at short range until we were again outflanked and compelled to abandon the field. The last engagement was the bloodiest of the day, our men fighting with a desperation worthy of a better result. Our loss here was sad and severe—14 killed and 52 wounded. Here Major Brumback and Captain Thomas received severe wounds, which still detain them at Richmond. Captain Darety and Lieutenant Peters were painfully wounded also during this engagement.

Too much cannot be said in praise of the endurance, spirit, and gallantry exhibited by the officers and men composing my regiment upon that unfortunate day. Only one week in the field, and during all that time bivouacked in line of battle in the face of the enemy, with heavy picket and other duties, consequent upon our advanced position, to perform, but little time or opportunity had been given to organize or drill the regiment. Laboring under difficulties and disadvantages which few if any regiments from Ohio have ever experienced, the men went into the engagements with an eagerness which only novices in war ever exhibit, and maintained themselves with a gallantry which would have done honor to veterans.

Where all did so well it may seem unnecessary and unjust to designate any by name, but I cannot close without calling your attention to the gallant conduct and valuable assistance rendered me that day by Maj. Jefferson Brumback and Capt. J. M. Stuart, Company A, who after the first engagement acted as one of my field officers. Among the officers who were in the several engagements and who displayed great personal courage I desire to mention Captains Thomas, Darety, and Wylie, Lieutenants Peters and Yeomans. Lieut. A. G. Tuther, adjutant, although captured early in the day, displayed great gallantry and rendered valuable assistance during the time he was engaged. Captain Taylor's company at the commencement of the last engagement was deployed as skirmishers, and he deserves great credit for the gallant and skillful manner in which he handled his men.

I am, general, most respectfully, your obedient servant,

W. L. McMILLEN,
Colonel Ninety-fifth Regiment Ohio Volunteer Infantry.

Brig. Gen. L. THOMAS.

No. 13.

Report of Lieut. Thomas P. Jones, Ninety-fifth Ohio Infantry.

SEPTEMBER 12, 1862.

DEAR SIR: I submit to you a report of the Ninety-fifth Regiment Ohio Volunteer Infantry in the engagement near Richmond, Ky., on August 30, 1862:

The total strength of the regiment on the morning of the battle was 975. Colonel McMillen, commanding, with lieutenant-colonel, major, and 26 company officers, and 835 privates and non-commissioned officers, moved to the battle-field at 7 a. m., and went into the battle. Sixty were left on guard duty, 65 were left at Lexington, and 15 were in the hospital. I gathered on the road and around Lexington 168 of the privates and 3 commissioned officers that were in the battle. With these and the 65 privates left at Lexington to guard camp I moved in the column to the camp near Louisville. The total number now in camp is 4 commissioned officers and 233 privates and non-commissioned officers. Of those of the regiment who have not reported at camp near Louisville, 100 escaped to Ohio, 550 were taken prisoners and paroled, and the remainder killed, wounded, and missing.

Respectfully, your obedient servant,

T. P. JONES,
First Lieut., Comdg. Ninety-fifth Ohio Volunteer Infantry.

General CHARLES CRUFT, *Commanding Second Brigade.*

No. 14.

Report of Maj. Bill Cross, Third Tennessee Infantry (Union).

IN CAMP NEAR LOUISVILLE, KY.

GENERAL: I have the honor to submit the following report of officers and men of my command:

Its original strength, when I first came to Richmond, Ky., was 250 men, with the proper company officers. One hundred of these men were taken to escort a battery to London. They were ordered to remain at London, which they did, until Colonel Houk, with his command, was ordered from Barboursville to London, and they ordered to join me at Richmond, which they did the day before the fight at Big Hill, when the whole command were scattered, some captured, and others went to Cumberland Gap, and about 100 men came back to Richmond. Again in the battle of Richmond were my men scattered, and I now have but 75 men, 3 captains, and 2 lieutenants.

I am, general, your most obedient servant,

BILL CROSS,
Major, Comdg. Detachment Third Regt. East Tenn. Vols.

Brig. Gen. CHARLES CRUFT, *at Quarters.*

No. 15.

Report of Maj. Gen. John P. McCown, C. S. Army, commanding Department of East Tennessee.

KNOXVILLE, TENN., *September* 3, 1862.

The following just received from General Smith, dated Richmond, Ky.:

We had three fights on the 30th near this place; enemy completely routed; General Nelson wounded in the thigh; General Miller killed; 3,000 prisoners captured, including General Manson and staff, together with all their artillery, small-arms, wagons, &c.; our loss small.

J. P. McCOWN,
Major-General, Commanding.

General S. COOPER.

No. 16.

Reports of Maj. Gen. E. Kirby Smith, C. S. Army, commanding Army of Kentucky, including operations August 30–September 16, and congratulatory orders.

HEADQUARTERS ARMY OF KENTUCKY,
Richmond, Ky., August 30, 1862.

SIR: It is my great pleasure to announce to you that God has thrice blessed our arms to-day. After a forced march, almost day and night, for three days, over a mountainous wilderness, destitute alike of food and water, I found the enemy drawn up in force to oppose us at a point 8 miles from this place. With less than half my force I attacked and carried a very strong position at Mount Zion Church after a hard fight of two hours; again a still better position at White's farm in a half hour, and finally in this town, just before sunset, our indomitable troops deliberately walked (they were too tired to run) up to a magnificent position, manned by 10,000 of the enemy (many of them perfectly fresh), and carried it in fifteen minutes. It is for me now to give you the exact results of these glorious battles:

Our loss is comparatively small; that of the enemy many hundred killed and wounded and several thousand prisoners. We have captured artillery, small-arms, and wagons. Indeed, everything indicates the almost entire annihilation of this force of the enemy. In the first two battles they were commanded by General Manson; in the last by General Nelson. Re-enforcements must be sent up to me at once. We have large numbers of adherents here, who, if we can show an ability to maintain ourselves, will flock to our standard.

I am, sir, respectfully, your obedient servant,

E. KIRBY SMITH,
Major-General, Commanding.

General S. COOPER, *A. and I. G., C. S. Army, Richmond, Va.*

—

P. S.—   AUGUST 31.

GENERAL: I have only time to add that the commander of the enemy (General Nelson) was wounded in the thigh; its second in command (General Manson, and staff) a prisoner in this place, and General Miller killed; all their artillery taken; some 3,500 prisoners and their whole force dispersed in every direction. The cavalry continues to bring in prisoners.

Respectfully, and in haste,

E. KIRBY SMITH,
Major-General.

—

HEADQUARTERS ARMY OF KENTUCKY,
Lexington, Ky., September 3, 1862.

GENERAL: On the 30th ultimo our forces met and repulsed the enemy in three separate engagements. General Cleburne's division, which was in advance, came upon the enemy's advance about 6 miles from Richmond early in the day and drove it from the field before the remainder of my column was brought into action. Falling back about $3\frac{1}{2}$ miles and receiving re-enforcements the enemy again made a stand and were again driven from the field in confusion. My cavalry having been sent to the enemy's rear I could not pursue rapidly, and he formed his line of battle in the outskirts of Richmond, his force having swelled to the number of 10,000 men, General Nelson commanding. Within an hour after our column was deployed for the attack the enemy were utterly routed and retreated in terrible confusion. The cavalry came in upon their flank and scattered them in all directions, capturing all their artillery and train. Not a regiment escaped in order.

The enemy's loss during the day is about 1,400 killed and wounded and 4,000 prisoners. Our loss is about 500 killed and wounded. General Miller was killed, General Nelson wounded, and General Manson taken prisoner. The remnant of the Federal force in Kentucky is making its way, utterly demoralized and scattered, to the Ohio.

General Marshall is in communication with me. Our column is moving upon Cincinnati. The country is rising in arms, and all that is needed to accomplish the objects of the campaign is to have our left in communication with your right. If I am supported and can be supplied with arms 25,000 Kentucky troops in a few days would be added to my command. Breckinridge and Buckner should be here.

I am, general, very respectfully, your obedient servant,

E. KIRBY SMITH,
Major-General.

General BRAXTON BRAGG, *Commanding Army of the West.*

HEADQUARTERS ARMY OF KENTUCKY,
Lexington, Ky., September 6, 1862.

GENERAL : I have the honor to report that after giving my men one day's rest at Richmond, a rest which I deemed absolutely essential, I pushed on toward this place on the 1st instant, and entered it with a portion of my infantry on the 2d. The cavalry I sent forward in pursuit of the enemy, who had retreated by the Frankfort road. It would be impossible for me to exaggerate the enthusiasm of the people here on the entry of our troops. They evidently regarded us as their deliverers from oppression and have continued in every way to prove to us that the heart of Kentucky is with the South in this struggle. They are rapidly rallying to our flag, and my especial object in writing this letter is to urge upon the Confederate Government to support the people of this State in the present movement by rapidly throwing to our aid men and arms. If Bragg occupies Buell we can have nothing to oppose us but raw levies, and by the blessing of God will always dispose of them as we did on the memorable August 30.

I am still unable to give you a detailed report of the combats of that day. The killed and wounded of the enemy exceed 1,000 ; the prisoners amount to between 5,000 and 6,000; the loss—besides some twenty pieces of artillery, including that taken here and at Frankfort—9,000 small-arms and large quantities of supplies. Their scattered forces are represented by every one as being totally demoralized. They escaped by mounting their infantry behind their cavalry and upon the wagons.

Our cavalry, under Colonel Scott, pursued the enemy to within 12 miles of Louisville, when the jaded condition of their horses forced them to abandon the pursuit. The remnants of the enemy's force are in Louisville and Covington. I have sent a small force to Frankfort to take possession of the arsenal and public property there. I am pushing some forces in the direction of Cincinnati in order to give the people of Kentucky time to organize. General Heth, with the advance, is at Cynthiana, with orders to threaten Covington. At both Louisville and Cincinnati the troops are said to be collecting in large numbers. At the former place there are said to be fully 30,000. Although the people about here are rapidly enrolling their names, yet without some immediate aid from the Government we can hardly hope to resist successfully the hosts that are preparing to meet us.

Hoping that this matter will receive the prompt attention its importance demands, I am, very respectfully, your obedient servant,

E. KIRBY SMITH,
Major-General, Commanding.

General S. COOPER, *A. and I. G. C. S. Army, Richmond, Va.*

—

HEADQUARTERS ARMY OF KENTUCKY,
Lexington, Ky., September 16, 1862.

GENERAL : In my short letter of the 30th ultimo I gave you the results of my actions of that day, of which I have the honor now to make a more detailed report.

Before leaving Barboursville for this part of Kentucky I wrote to you, fully explaining the reasons that prompted me to take that step. Until my advance descended the Big Hill it met with no opposition from the enemy. Here, on the morning of the 29th, the enemy was discovered to be in force in our front, and a bold reconnaissance by the cavalry, under

Colonel Scott, in the afternoon, indicated a determination to give us battle. Although Churchill's division did not get up until late in the afternoon, and then in apparently an exhausted state, I determined to march to Richmond the next day, even at the cost of a battle with the whole force of the enemy. The leading division, under General Cleburne, was moved early the next morning, and after advancing 2 or 3 miles they found the enemy drawn up in line of battle in a fine position near Mount Zion Church, about 6 miles from Richmond. Without waiting for Churchill's division Cleburne at once commenced the action, and when I arrived on the field at 7.30 o'clock the fire of artillery was brisk on both sides. As my force was almost too small to storm the position in front without a disastrous loss I sent General Churchill with one of his brigades to turn the enemy's right. While this move was being executed a bold and well-conducted attempt on the part of the enemy to turn Cleburne's right was admirably foiled by the firmness of Col. Preston Smith's brigade, who repulsed the enemy with great slaughter. It was about this time, and while he was riding from his left to his right, that General Cleburne was badly wounded in the face, and thus at a critical moment I was deprived of the services of one of the most gallant, zealous, and intelligent officers of my whole army. The command of this division then devolved upon Col. Preston Smith.

In the mean time General Churchill had been completely successful in his movement upon the enemy's right flank, where by a bold charge his men completed a victory already partially gained by the gallantry of our troops on the right. In this action our loss was quite heavy on the right, but in comparison with that of the enemy was small.

It being reported that the enemy had taken up a new position on White's farm, 2 miles in front, I ordered Churchill with one brigade to again turn his right, intending to bring up Preston Smith on the other flank; but a desperate attempt on the part of the enemy to crush Churchill caused the action to commence before the arrival of Smith's division, and so this gallant brigade (Colonel McCray's) of Texans and Arkansians had to fight the battle alone. Although the odds opposed to them were fearful, yet by reserving their own fire under the deafening roar of the enemy's guns, and by a well-timed and dashing charge upon the advancing line they completely routed and put to flight the hosts of the enemy just as the cheers of Smith's division announced their arrival in the field. The loss of the enemy here was very great, including one piece of artillery; ours almost nothing.

Scott's cavalry having been sent around to our left by another road to get in the rear of Richmond, I felt during the whole day much need of cavalry to follow up our different successes. It was then that in this second repulse of the enemy I ordered Captain Nelson, commanding a company of Partisan Rangers, to charge the retreating masses of the enemy. This was promptly and admirably obeyed, the result being the capture of numerous prisoners. In passing a deserted camp of the enemy I found from some of the wounded that General Nelson with reenforcements had arrived after the second battle. A march of 2 miles brought us within sight of the town, in front of which and on a commanding ridge, with both flanks resting upon woods, Nelson had determined to make a final stand. For the third time Churchill with a brigade (McNair's) was sent off to the left, when a deafening roar of musketry soon announced the raging of a furious combat. In the meanwhile Preston Smith, bringing up his division at a double-quick, formed with wonderful precision and rapidity in front of the enemy's center and left. Almost without waiting for the commands of the officers this division coolly advanced under the murderous fire of a force twice their number and drove them from the field in the greatest confusion and with immense slaughter.

Owing to the open character of the country our loss in the last fight was quite heavy, including some valuable regimental officers. The exhausted condition of my men, together with the closing in of night, prevented the pursuit of the enemy more than a mile beyond Richmond, but the timely arrival of Colonel Scott with his cavalry upon their two lines of retreat enabled him to greatly increase the fruits of the hard labors of the day by capturing large numbers of prisoners, including General Manson and staff, as also eight pieces of artillery and a number of wagons, &c. While my whole force was not more than 5,000 that of the enemy was more than 10,000. In the last engagement we took prisoners from thirteen regiments.

Our loss, killed and wounded, is about 400; that of the enemy over 1,000, and his prisoners about 5,000. The immediate fruits of the victory were nine pieces of artillery, some 10,000 small-arms, and large quantities of supplies. These latter were greatly increased by our capture of this place and Frankfort, the whole number of cannon taken being about twenty.

I regret that I am unable to forward with this the reports of all the different commands of the forces engaged. Those inclosed (General Churchill's and Colonel Scott's) will show you how much cause the Confederacy has to be proud of her sons. I almost fear to particularize lest I do not full justice to all; but I cannot close without expressing my admiration at the promptness and intelligence with which Generals Churchill and Cleburne and Col. Preston Smith executed the orders given them.

My thanks are due to the following members of my staff, who were with me on the field, for their active assistance to me during the day, viz: Cols. [John] Pegram and [W. R.] Boggs, Lieut. Col. [G. W.] Brent; Majs. J. A. Brown, [H. McD.] McElrath, and Thomas; Capt. [John G.] Meem, [jr.]; Lieuts. [E.] Cunningham and Pratt; and Capts. Walworth and Hammond, and Mr. Freret, volunteer aides. Too much praise cannot be given to the medical director, Surg. S. A. Smith, and to his assistants, for their untiring devotion in the arduous labors that devolved upon them.

As regards the intrepid behavior of the true patriots (the men in ranks) I can only say that as long as the destinies of the South remain in such hands we need never fear Northern subjugation. But even more than their noble courage before the enemy are we called upon to admire that higher courage which enabled them to undergo without murmur the fatigues and privations of one of the most difficult marches of this war. For several days and parts of the nights, through a country almost entirely without water, over stony roads, with their almost bare feet, and with green corn and beef without salt as their only food, did these gallant men trudge along, inspired only with the desire of being led against the invaders of their homes and the oppressors of their liberties.

I refer you to the reports of the division and brigade commanders, only a part of which I am now able to forward, for notices of special cases of good behavior.

I remain, general, very respectfully, your obedient servant,

E. KIRBY SMITH,
Major-General.

General S. COOPER, *A. and I. G., Richmond, Va.*

Table of Casualties, battle of Richmond, Ky., August 30.

	Killed.	Wounded.	Missing.	Total.
ARMY OF KENTUCKY.				
Second Brigade, Third Division:	8	18	......	26
1st Arkansas Mounted Riflemen	1	10	.....	11
2d Arkansas Mounted Riflemen	6	17	.....	23
4th Arkansas Regiment	1	9	......	10
30th Arkansas Regiment	......	6	......	6
4th Arkansas Battalion				
First Brigade, Fourth Division:	4	16	......	20
154th Tennessee Regiment	5	27	......	32
12th Tennessee Regiment	12	35	1	48
13th Tennessee Regiment	8	24	......	32
47th Tennessee Regiment				
Second Brigade, Fourth Division:	......	1	......	1
Staff	6	23	......	29
13th Arkansas Regiment	2	19	......	21
15th Arkansas Regiment	17	95	......	112
2d Tennessee Regiment	2	23	......	25
5th Tennessee Regiment	4	42	......	46
48th Tennessee Regiment	2	4	......	6
Texas Battery	......	3	......	3
Company of Sharpshooters				
RECAPITULATION.				
Second Brigade, Third Division	16	60	......	76
First Brigade, Fourth Division	29	102	1	132
Second Brigade, Fourth Division	33	210	......	243
Aggregate	78	372	1	451

CONGRATULATORY ORDERS.

GENERAL ORDERS, }   HEADQUARTERS ARMY OF KENTUCKY,
                                Richmond, Ky., August 30, 1862.
   No. 10.   }   (Received at Richmond, Va., Sept. 6, 1862.)

The major-general commanding returns his heartfelt thanks to the troops of this command (officers and men) for their exceeding gallantry in the several actions of this day, their patient and unmurmuring endurance of fatigue during two days' and nights' forced marches, and fighting three battles in twelve hours. The country shall know of your sufferings on the march, as well as the bold, pressing charges of this day.

To-morrow being Sunday, the general desires that the troops shall assemble and, under their several chaplains, shall return thanks to Almighty God, to whose mercy and goodness these victories are due.

By command of Maj. Gen. E. Kirby Smith:

                                    JNO. PEGRAM,
                                     Chief of Staff.

—

GENERAL ORDERS, }   HEADQUARTERS DEPARTMENT No. 2,
   No. 128.   }   *Sparta, Tenn., September 5, 1862.*

I. The signal triumph of our arms in Virginia over the combined forces of McClellan and Pope had hardly been announced to the whole of this command before we are again called upon to rejoice and give thanks to God for a victory as brilliant and complete achieved in our own campaign by the troops under Maj. Gen. E. Kirby Smith at Richmond, Ky., on the 30th ultimo. The enemy, under Major-General Nelson, was completely routed, with the commander wounded, one general killed, and one captured, with 3,000 other prisoners. Not the least important of the fruits secured was the whole of the enemy's artillery, small-arms, and transportation.

II. Comrades, our campaign opens most auspiciously and promises complete success. Your general is happy and proud to witness the tone and conduct of his army. Contented and cheerful under privations and strictly regardful of the rights of citizens, you have achieved a victory over yourselves which insures success against every foe. The enemy is in full retreat, with consternation and demoralization devastating his ranks. To secure the full fruits of this condition we must press on vigorously and unceasingly. You will be called on to make greater sacrifices still, to suffer other, perhaps greater, privations, but your generals will share them and a grateful people will reward you. Alabamians, your State is redeemed. An arrogant foe no longer treads her soil. Tennesseeans, the restoration of your capital and State government is almost accomplished without firing a gun. You return to your invaded homes conquerors and heroes. Kentuckians, the first great blow has been struck for your freedom. The manacles will soon fall from your limbs, when we know you will arise and strike for your freedom, your women, and your altars. Soldiers from the Gulf, South Carolina, Georgia, and Arkansas, we share the happiness of our more fortunate brothers, and will press on with them, rejoicing in the hope that a brighter future is in store for the fruitful fields, happy homes, and fair daughters of our own sunny South.

BRAXTON BRAGG,
General, Commanding.

No. 17.

Reports of Col. John S. Scott, First Louisiana Cavalry, commanding Cavalry Brigade, including operations from August 13–September 11.*

HDQRS. KIRBY SMITH'S BRIG., *August* 17, 1862.

COLONEL: I reached London at 8 o'clock this morning, after a ride of 160 miles in seventy hours. I failed to surprise the telegraph office at Somerset and found the force at this place in position to fight me when I arrived. We soon cleared the town, took 75 prisoners, killed and wounded about 50. Lost 1 lieutenant and a private killed; 3 or 4 wounded. Captured 40 or 50 wagons, 175 mules, camp and garrison equipage, some ammunition, about 50 guns, very small commissary stores. My men have been skirmishing to-day between this and Barboursville.

Bearer is instructed to tell you my whereabouts to-night. Kentuckians will not fight us much this trip. There is quite a large camp at Dick Robinson. Do have Starnes sent to me, for I must go to the bluegrass region for forage.

Yours, respectfully, &c.,

J. S. SCOTT,
Commanding.

Colonel PEGRAM, *Chief of Staff, Dept. of E. Tenn.*

---

*See August 17–22, 1862. Operations near Cumberland Gap, Tenn. Report of Brig. Gen. George W. Morgan, U. S. Army.

HEADQUARTERS KIRBY SMITH'S BRIGADE,
Lebanon, Ky., September 11, 1862.

The evening of August 13 I left Kingston, Tenn., with the First Louisiana Cavalry, Lieut. Col. [James O.] Nixon commanding; First Georgia Cavalry, Col. [J. J.] Morrison, and the Buckner Guards, Captain Garnett, numbering in the aggregate 896, and passing through Montgomery and Jamestown, Tenn., Monticello and Somerset, Ky., reached London on the 17th. During the night of the 16th, when 25 miles from London, I learned that five companies of the Third[*] Tennessee Volunteers, U. S. Army, were stationed there. I selected 500 men from the command and made a forced march, reaching the town about 7 o'clock the next morning, when I attacked the place, and after a brief resistance by the enemy I captured it, killing 13, wounding 17, and taking 111 prisoners. My loss was 1 officer and 1 private killed; none wounded. I took a large number of wagons laden with quartermaster's and commissary stores, and a number of horses and mules, and several hundred stand of arms, all of which I have forwarded to you.

After leaving London I employed my command gathering mules, horses, and wagons that had been left along the road by the affrighted Federals from London to Mount Vernon and Richmond.

The evening of the 22d, learning that a train was coming (intended for the Gap), guarded by infantry and cavalry, I moved my command to meet them. My advance came upon them at Big Hill, 17 miles from Richmond, when the fight commenced, and resulted as stated in my former report.[†]

After driving in their pickets within 2 miles of Richmond the morning of the 24th and gathering up all the trains, horses, and mules, I fell back slowly to the junction of the Wild Cat and Richmond roads, which I reached the evening of the 25th.

On the 27th the Third Tennessee Cavalry, Col. [J. W.] Starnes, was added to my command, and I moved on in the direction of Richmond.

On the 29th I made a reconnaissance of the enemy with my whole command, and finding them in position about 3 miles from Richmond I fell back 4 miles to the infantry and reported to General Cleburne, who was in command of the advance division.

On the morning of the 30th, in obedience to your orders, I passed around to the west of Richmond and took possession of the roads leading to Lexington. The majority of my forces were posted on the Lexington road and one company on the Lancaster road; the remainder between the two roads. About 4 o'clock stragglers from the battlefield commenced passing into my lines and gradually increased in numbers until 6 o'clock, when the main body of the enemy, apparently about 5,000 strong, with nine pieces of artillery, came upon us. My forces, being well ambuscaded, poured a destructive fire into their ranks, killing about 60 and wounding a large number—the firing commenced in obedience to my orders on the extreme left, extending to the right, which was nearest Richmond—after which almost the entire force immediately surrendered. Owing to the smallness of my force (about 850) I was unable to still guard the roads and remove all the prisoners to the rear, and consequently a large number escaped, wandering through

---

[*] See September 17–October 3, 1862. Evacuation of Cumberland Gap, Tenn., and march of its garrison to Greenupsburg, Ky. Report of Brig. Gen. George W. Morgan, U. S. Army, p. 922.

[†] See August 23, 1862. Action at Big Hill, Ky.

the corn fields and woodlands, it being now too dark to distinguish them when a few paces distant. I am unable to state positively the number of prisoners taken by my command, owing to the fact that they were captured principally after dark, and during the same night were turned over to General Preston Smith, in obedience to your orders, but am confident they could not fall short of 3,500. I captured also nine pieces of artillery, a large number of small-arms, and wagons loaded with army supplies. Among the prisoners captured was Brigadier-General Manson and a number of field and staff officers.

On the morning of the 31st I moved to the Kentucky River and drove the rear guard of the enemy from the opposite bank.

September 1 I moved on and encamped near Lexington, and on the 2d moved around Lexington and encamped near Georgetown; on the 3d we moved on to Frankfort and hoisted the battle flag of the First Louisiana Cavalry (in default of a Confederate flag) on the capitol of the State, while the rear guard of the enemy (now about 8,000 strong) were quiet spectators from the opposite hills. The same evening I detailed all my command with horses in condition to travel (450 in number) to pursue the enemy and harass his rear.

The next morning, September 4, about sunrise they came upon the enemy near Shelbyville, and drove them into and through the town and then crossed over the railroad and destroyed the bridges in obedience to your orders, and returned to camp near Frankfort. The 6th and 7th remained in camp near Frankfort.

The evening of the 8th left Frankfort and reached this place at 9 o'clock this morning.

My loss since leaving Kingston is 1 officer and 6 privates killed, 21 wounded, and 9 taken prisoners.

Since reaching London I have captured near 4,000 prisoners (including those turned over to General Smith and those paroled by me), about 375 wagons, mostly laden with provisions and army stores, near 1,500 mules, and a large number of horses. It has been impossible to keep an account of the wagons, &c., captured by my command, owing to the rapidity of my movement.

I cannot close this report without bearing testimony to the soldierly conduct of my command; they have endured unusual privations and fatigues without murmur.

I cannot compliment the commanders of the regiments composing this brigade too highly for the assistance rendered me.

I would mention that the first 106 miles of our march, over a rough and barren country, was made in forty-two hours, having been delayed one day on account of getting my horses shod.

The statement of the property captured at Frankfort was handed in at your headquarters by me in person on Saturday last.

My forces have been materially reduced by the numerous details which I found it necessary to make in order to remove wagons and stock to the rear, and I shall use my utmost endeavors to concentrate my command at as early a day as possible.

Hoping that the results achieved by the Kirby Smith Brigade may prove satisfactory to you, general, I remain, very respectfully, your obedient servant,

J. S. SCOTT,
Colonel, Commanding Brigade.

Maj. Gen. E. KIRBY SMITH,
Commanding Army of Kentucky, Lexington, Ky.

No. 18.

Report of Brig. Gen. Thomas J. Churchill, C. S. Army, commanding Third Division.

HDQRS. THIRD DIVISION, ARMY OF KENTUCKY,
Cynthiana, Ky., September 8, 1862.

I have the honor to report that on the morning of the 30th ultimo, according to instructions, I moved my division, composed of the First and Second Brigades, commanded by Colonels McCray and McNair respectively up the road in the direction of Richmond. When I arrived in the neighborhood of Kingston I heard the artillery open on our right, showing that General Cleburne had met the enemy. It was now about 8 a. m. It was at this time that you arrived on the field and ordered me to hold one of my brigades in reserve while with the other I was to make a flank movement on the enemy's right. In accordance with these instructions I left Colonel McNair with his brigade as a reserve force, and proceeded with Colonel McCray's brigade (composed of Arkansas and Texas troops) to execute the movement on the enemy's flank, and by proceeding cautiously through a corn field and a ravine had almost perfected the move when the enemy, pressed by our forces on our right, commenced to give way, but after falling back some distance they formed in a skirt of timber, when my forces fired and charged upon them. Then for the first time discovering my position they commenced a precipitate retreat, but not before we had killed a great many and taken a large number of prisoners. I was again ordered to move up on the left with the same brigade, while General Cleburne was to move on the right. After proceeding some 2 miles in the direction of Richmond I found the entire force of the enemy, numbering 8,000 or 10,000, in a strong position on the left of the road, concealed by a corn field and a skirt of timber. I then sent word to General Cleburne to move up, that I was ready to engage the enemy. I then placed one section of Capt. [John T.] Humphreys' battery [Arkansas], under command of Lieutenant ———, on my right, within 200 yards of the enemy, to more effectually rake his lines. Before General Cleburne's division came up the fight had commenced in earnest. The fire of the enemy's artillery and musketry was most terrific, while we replied only with artillery. I then ordered my command to lie down, protected by a fence and ditch, and for full five minutes we did not fire a gun in response to their terrible fire. The enemy were at this time advancing in heavy force, and when they had arrived within less than 50 yards of my lines the order was given to rise, fire, and charge, which order was promptly and gallantly obeyed. The enemy could not withstand the desperate courage of my men, but still for a while they contested every inch of ground as they were driven from it, until finally, finding it impossible to check this gallant charge, they gave way in every direction. The victory was complete. The field was covered with the dead and wounded of the enemy, and some (though comparatively few) of the gallant sons of Arkansas and Texas fell martyrs to the cause of liberty. Here we captured a large number of prisoners, guns, and equipments of all kinds. In this charge one splendid rifle cannon was taken. This was perhaps the most severely-contested fight of the day.

Finding this brigade now worn down by incessant fighting, I ordered up Colonel McNair to follow in pursuit of the fleeing enemy. After pursuing them some 2 miles we found them again drawn up in line near the outskirts of Richmond, having collected their whole force for a last and final struggle. Here I took position on the right of the enemy's line. Soon my skirmishers engaged those of the enemy, which was soon followed by a general engagement of my forces. I was driving back the enemy's right wing when I heard firing on my right, showing that General Cleburne had engaged the enemy on their left. The engagement then became general along the entire line. For a time the contest was sharp and the rattle of musketry almost deafening, but again and for the third and last time the enemy fled in great confusion through the streets of Richmond as night closed upon our victorious arms.

I captured in this engagement a large amount of ordnance and ordnance stores, together with 400 or 500 prisoners.

I cannot speak too highly of the gallantry and coolness displayed by Colonels McNair and McCray throughout the entire day, and I have to thank them for the promptness and skill with which they executed all orders.

Of the two batteries in my division the one commanded by Capt. [James P.] Douglas [Texas] was ordered the evening previous to report to General Cleburne for orders. The other, commanded by Captain Humphreys, was with my division the whole day, and it gives me great pleasure to say that his pieces were handled with surprising skill and ability and did great execution in the ranks of the enemy.

My loss during the entire day in killed, wounded, and missing was 225.

Before closing I must particularly mention for their daring, bravery, and gallant bearing on the battle-field the following members of my staff: Capt. B. S. Johnson, adjutant-general; Capt. B. F. Blackburn, inspector-general; Capt. John Rennick, volunteer aide; Captain [Elcon] Jones, Signal Corps, and Lieut. J. M. Rose, ordnance officer. These officers were ever seen bearing orders through the thickest of the fight and at times in the front of battle, cheering on my men to victory.

My division surgeon, Dr. C. H. Smith, in addition to his professional services upon the field to the wounded, rendered me many valuable services.

The officers and men of my entire division always met the enemy with unflinching gallantry and were the proud victors of every battle-field; and for the privations, hardships, and almost unequaled marches, all of which they have borne without a murmur, they deserve the thanks of their country.

I have the honor to be, general, very respectfully, your most obedient servant,

T. J. CHURCHILL,
Brigadier-General, Comdg. Third Div., Army of Kentucky.

Maj. Gen. E. KIRBY SMITH.

No. 19.

Report of Col. T. H. McCray, Thirty-first Arkansas Infantry, commanding First Brigade.

CAMP NEAR CYNTHIANA, KY., *Sept. 6, 1862.*

GENERAL: I have the honor to report that the troops of this brigade, consisting of the Tenth Texas Regiment, dismounted cavalry, commanded by Col. C. R. Earp; the Eleventh Texas Regiment, dismounted cavalry, commanded by Col. J. C. Burks; the Fourteenth Texas Regiment, dismounted cavalry, commanded by Col. M. D. Ector; the Fifteenth [Thirty-second?] Texas Regiment, dismounted cavalry, commanded by Lieut. Col. James Weaver, and McCray's Arkansas regiment of sharp-shooters, commanded by Maj. J. W. Clark, were twice engaged with the enemy on the 30th ultimo before Richmond, Ky., after a forced march of 13 miles.

At about 9 a. m. I was ordered to march my brigade, left in front, to a skirt of woods about 1 mile to the left of the turnpike road leading to Richmond, for the purpose of flanking the enemy, who was already briskly engaged with Brigadier-General Cleburne's division. At the place designated the brigade was moved in line of battle directly on the right wing of the enemy's line, which was immediately turned, and they fled in confusion, leaving on the field a large number of killed, wounded, and prisoners. The enemy retreated about 2 miles and again formed line of battle, covered by a skirt of woods and a field of very heavy corn. I was ordered to attack him with my brigade, numbering at that time not exceeding 1,500 effective men. The line of battle was immediately formed and marched directly in front of the enemy's lines, who numbered not less than 6,000 infantry, supported by a full battery of six pieces and one regiment of cavalry. When within about 400 yards of the enemy he opened his battery upon us, which was rapidly followed with volleys of musketry; but my gallant troops pressed steadily forward under a galling fire of bombs, rifle-shot, and Minie balls to a fence not exceeding 200 yards of his lines, where, finding the air literally filled with bomb-shells and Minie balls, I ordered the troops to lie down under cover of the fence to prevent the little command from being crushed out by overwhelming numbers. I remained in this position for fully twenty minutes, during all of which time the most incessant firing of cannon and musketry I have ever heard was kept up by the enemy, without being replied to except by one section of Captain Humphreys' Arkansas battery, commanded by Lieutenant ———, who did very efficient service. The two pieces of artillery were posted on my extreme right. The enemy, misconstruing my silence and thinking he could crush me before re-enforcements could arrive, ordered a charge, and on came his solid columns. I immediately ordered my command to lie still and not fire a gun until ordered to do so, and when his lines had advanced to within less than 50 yards the order fire was given and promptly responded to by the entire command. The effect was terrific. The advancing columns of the enemy faltered and staggered from one end of his lines to the other. My command was ordered to load rapidly, mount the fence, and charge, which were admirably and gallantly executed. The enemy soon commenced falling back, but obstinately contested every inch of ground, taking shelter and firing at us from behind trees, some hay-stacks, corn-pens, and a fence that happened to be on the line of his retreat, for about half a mile, where, being so closely pursued and pressed, they fled in all directions, leaving on the field 500 in killed, wounded, and prisoners, 1 piece of rifled cannon, 600 Minie rifles, 300,000 Enfield rifled cartridges, wagons, teams, ambulances, &c.

It is impossible for me to speak in terms of too high praise of the gallantry and intrepid valor of the officers and privates of this command. Each one, it seemed, tried to excel his comrade in deeds of daring. I will mention a few names of the officers who were under my immediate observation : Cols. M. D. Ector and J. C. Burks, Lieut. Col. James Weaver, and Majs. R. Redwine and J. W. Clark particularly distinguished themselves, being in the front of battle and cheering on their men during the entire engagement, and my staff officers, Captain Kilgore, assistant adjutant-general; Captain Ford, brigade quartermaster: Dr. Graham, brigade surgeon; Captain Spencer, brigade commissary; Captain Fitzpatrick, inspector-general, and Lieutenant Lane, aide-de-camp, were each at their proper post and rendered me very efficient service. Captains Kilgore, Spencer, and Fitzpatrick, and Lieutenant Lane were on the field, and I will add on every part of the field, and unflinchingly did their duty in all respects. Captain Ford was in command of the train, and Dr. Graham was at the hospital rendering his surgical aid to the dying and the wounded soldiers. Lieutenant Nichols, assistant provost-marshal, acted with great gallantry and justly merits praise.

In this connection it would be an act of injustice in me not to mention the names of Captains Johnson and Rennick, of your staff. I have never seen cooler and more determined bravery displayed by any one. They were a great part of the time in front of my skirmishers inspiring my men to press forward.

I must also return my most grateful thanks to Dr. Smith, division surgeon, for his efficient surgical aid to the wounded on the field.

The loss in killed, wounded, and missing is 149, as follows: Killed, 20; wounded, 120, and missing, 9.

The battery belonging to this brigade, commanded by Captain Douglas, was with General Cleburne's division. Inclosed herewith I send you the captain's report* of the engagement, as also the reports of the different regimental commanders of this brigade..

All of which is respectfully referred.

I am, general, respectfully, &c.

T. H. McCRAY,
Col., Comdg. First Brig., Third Div., Army of Kentucky.

Brig. Gen. T. J. CHURCHILL,
Commanding Third Division, Army of Kentucky.

No. 20.

Report of Col. Evander McNair, Fourth Arkansas Infantry, commanding Second Brigade.

HEADQUARTERS SECOND BRIGADE,
September 6, 1862.

GENERAL: I have the honor to report the following loss and casualties† in the Second Brigade, Third Division, Army of Kentucky, in the action near Richmond on August 30.

In regard to the part my brigade took in the late battle near Richmond, Ky., I will only say that both officers and men did their whole duty. I will not particularize, lest I do some one injustice, but will leave you and the country to judge of us.

I am, general, your obedient servant,

E. McNAIR,
Col., Comdg. Second Brig., Third Div., Army of Kentucky.

Brigadier-General CHURCHILL.

---

* Not found

† See p. 936.

No. 21.

Reports of Brig. Gen. P. R. Cleburne, C. S. Army, commanding Fourth Division.

HDQES. 2D BRIG., 4TH DIV., ARMY OF KENTUCKY,
Richmond, Ky., September 1, 1862.

GENERAL: On the morning of the 29th ultimo I was ordered by you to advance on the Richmond road to a point where the road emerged from a gap in the hills about 5 miles from the foot of Big Hill, and to act as advance guard of the army.

About 5 p. m. I heard cannonading in my front, and learned that Colonel Scott's cavalry were being driven in and they had already lost one of the mountain howitzers. Subsequently the cannonading ceased, and Colonel Scott, coming into camp, informed me he was encamped in the road in my front; that our whole front was well picketed; that the enemy were not advancing. Still feeling uneasy about our situation, with an unknown force of the enemy in our front, I determined, as a matter of precaution, to form line of battle facing the supposed direction of the enemy. This was not accomplished until some time after dark. I then warned commanders of regiments at the first alarm to bring their regiments to their prescribed positions on this line, and then dismissed them, retaining, however, my battery and company of sharpshooters on the line. I had scarcely dismissed them, however, before firing and yelling was heard in our front, and almost simultaneously a multitude of stragglers, consisting of part of Colonel Scott's cavalry brigade, sick men, baggage wagons, servants leading horses, came flying in in the utmost consternation, closely pursued by the whole of Colonel Metcalfe's command of United States cavalry, who were firing on them and yelling as though they were all excited with liquor. I reformed my line rapidly, leaving the road clear. When within 25 steps two companies of the Forty-eighth Tennessee fired on the enemy's advance and checked it. The enemy then dismounted one regiment of cavalry and again advanced. It was very dark and they could not see my line of battle, but they kept up a continuous fire on our camp-fires, which were blazing brightly 300 yards in our rear. A few sharpshooters were now pushed forward, the enemy showing great reluctance to advance, and in spite of curses and threats, which we could plainly hear, the whole force of the enemy precipitately retreated.

In this affair we had but one man wounded. The enemy had several dangerously wounded. We captured 30 prisoners, 100 stand of arms, and several horses. The enemy retreated in such haste they cut the reins of their horses, which, as before stated, they had hitched for the purpose of advancing on foot, fearing it would take too much time to unhitch them. My men slept in line of battle without any supper, and at daylight again advanced in search of the enemy.

I have the honor to be, sir, your obedient servant,

P. R. CLEBURNE,
Brigadier-General, Commanding Second Brigade.

Maj. Gen. E. KIRBY SMITH, *Commanding Army of Kentucky.*

[Indorsement.]

HDQES. DEPT. OF E. TENN., *Knoxville, Tenn., Nov. 16, 1862.*

Respectfully forwarded. Owing to movement from Kentucky this communication, being mislaid, could not be sooner forwarded.

E. KIRBY SMITH,
Lieutenant-General.

RICHMOND, KY., *September* 1, 1862.

GENERAL : On the night of the 29th ultimo I was informed by Colonel Boggs, of your staff, that you desired me to move forward with my division and the two batteries attached at daylight and attack the enemy, supposed to be immediately in my front. At daylight I commenced the movement. The Second Brigade and the battery of Captain Douglas (commanded by Col. B. J. Hill) was in front. The First Brigade, under Acting Brig. Gen. Preston Smith, with the battery of Captain Martin, followed at the distance of a quarter of a mile. I sent the Buckner Guards (a company of Scott's cavalry) in front to find the enemy. Half a mile north of the village of Kingston the cavalry encountered the advance guard of the enemy and soon after discovered their line of battle about 500 or 600 yards in rear of their advance guard. Going forward to reconnoiter I could distinctly see their first line facing us at right angles to the Richmond road, with one regiment to the right of the road, the others in the timber to the left. They had a battery masked near the Richmond road. I immediately placed Colonel Hill's brigade in line behind the crest of a low hill which ran parallel to and about 500 yards from the enemy's line. I placed Douglas' battery on the crest near my center. I ordered Smith's brigade to be formed in line within supporting distance ; he accordingly formed his brigade in line behind the crest of a second hill in my rear. While making these dispositions the enemy, showing only one regiment, kept up a ridiculous fire on us from a little mountain howitzer which they had captured the day before from Colonel Scott.

I now ordered the battery of Captain Douglas to open on what appeared to be a squad of cavalry on the Richmond road. In a moment this squad disappeared, unmasking a battery, which opened a rapid fire. I sent out skirmishers along our front and toward our right flank, and extended my line to the left across the Richmond turnpike with a strong company of skirmishers. This company held the regiment of the enemy's infantry on the same side of the road in check during the whole of the first fight and effectually protected my left flank. Finding a good position for a second battery I sent orders to acting Brig. Gen. Preston Smith to send Martin's battery to the front. I placed it on the hill near the right of my brigade and opened on the enemy. At this juncture I received an order from you, directing me to avoid a general battle until General Churchill's division could get up. I now directed the artillery to fire very slowly and not waste a round. The battle continued a mere fight of artillery and skirmishers for over two hours, when the enemy commenced moving toward my right flank, driving back my skirmishers on that flank. I ordered a regiment of Smith's brigade (the One hundred and fifty-fourth Tennessee) to be sent forward, and placed it in line on the right of my brigade. A close fire soon commenced on the right, and became so heavy I found it necessary to sustain the right with a further re-enforcement. I detached Col. [L. E.] Polk, commanding the Thirteenth and Fifteenth Arkansas Regiments, to the support of the One hundred and fifty-fourth Tennessee. A very heavy musketry fight ensued, and learning that the enemy were still concentrating against my right, and believing that General Churchill must now be within supporting distance, I ordered Acting Brig. Gen. Preston Smith to immediately move forward the remaining three regiments of his brigade, to place them on the right of the line already engaged, and if his line overlapped that of the enemy to lap around their left flank. At this time it was evident that the enemy had staked everything on driving back or turning our right flank and that they had weakened their center to effect this object. I therefore determined the moment I could hear Smith's musketry on the enemy's left flank to move Hill's brigade rapidly on the center. With this view I galloped to the right to satisfy myself that Smith's brigade was getting into position. I found them moving into the position rapidly and in admirable order. I then moved back to give my personal attention to the advance of Hill's brigade, including the two batteries. Before I got far, however, I was addressed by Colonel Polk, who was being carried wounded to the rear. I stopped an instant to reply and while doing so received a very painful wound in the mouth, which in a few minutes deprived me of the powers of speech and rendered my further presence on the field worse than useless. I sent aides to inform General Preston Smith of my mishap and to direct him to take command of the division; also to inform Colonel Hill and yourself of the situation of affairs.

Including the batteries, I had less than 3,000 men in my division.

I have the honor to be, sir, your obedient servant,

P. R. CLEBURNE,
Brig. Gen., Comdg. Fourth Division, Army of Kentucky.

Maj. Gen. E. KIRBY SMITH, *Commanding Army of Kentucky.*

No. 22.

Report of Col. Preston Smith, Provisional Army of the Confederate States, and Acting Brigadier-General, commanding First Brigade, Fourth Division.

HDQRS. FOURTH DIVISION, ARMY OF KENTUCKY,
September 16, 1862.

COLONEL: I have the honor to submit the following report of the part taken by my command in the series of battles before the town of Richmond, Ky., on the 30th ultimo:

Early on that morning (4 a. m.) this division, Brigadier-General Cleburne commanding, was moved forward in line of battle from the place of bivouac, 5 miles south of Rogersville, and in the direction of that place, the Second Brigade, Colonel Hill commanding, being in advance, the First Brigade about 500 yards in the rear thereof.

At 7.30 a. m., the Second Brigade having passed the town of Rogersville and the First emerging therefrom, the enemy, some half a mile north of the town, opened fire upon us with his field battery. The division was speedily thrown in position for action, having been changed from line of battle to moving by the flank a short distance south of the town. The battery of the Second Brigade was soon in position and replied to the fire of the enemy, which was continued for more than an hour, skirmishing being kept up the while between the advanced forces of the two armies. About this time I received an order from Brigadier-General Cleburne to send my battery forward and to the right of the position occupied by the battery of the Second Brigade, which was done, and the guns were soon heard from this position. I also received an order from Brigadier-General Cleburne to send a regiment forward and to the right of the line of the Second Brigade, to be posted in woods and near a corn field on the right of this line. The front line being thus so extended by an additional regiment and the battery, I found it necessary to change the position of my brigade in order that I might be in more easy supporting distance. My line was therefore advanced to the front and to the right of my old position, the increasing fire from the right indicating that the regiment sent forward by me was already engaging the enemy. This regiment (the One hundred and fifty-fourth Senior Tennessee Regiment) was in fact already engaged when this new position was taken.

Very soon after this it was reported to me that the enemy was moving forward with the apparent design of flanking the front line on its right. I therefore moved forward my command and to the right until the front line was unmasked, at which time I was advised that the enemy with three regiments had certainly succeeded in entering the woods and corn fields on the right of the One hundred and fifty-fourth Senior Tennessee Regiment and would soon be in the rear of this regiment, now considerably advanced. Having assured myself of this, I caused a change of front forward on the left regiment to be executed, thus throwing the two right regiments entirely in the rear of the enemy, from which position my brigade advanced on him, taking him by surprise, and after a few well-directed volleys compelling him to abandon his cover and flee in great confusion toward his reserve. At this time the One hundred and fifty-fourth Senior Tennessee Regiment advanced and formed on the left of the line, and, the enemy having rallied, the whole brigade was again soon engaged, but under their steady advance and galling fire from Minie and Enfield rifles the enemy soon broke and fled for his rear, leaving the ground strewn thickly with his killed and wounded.

Some 500 prisoners were taken at and near this place by my command and turned over to Lieutenant Seay, detailed for the purpose of taking charge of the prisoners by the major-general commanding. The troops, being almost exhausted from previous hard marching, loss of sleep, and scanty fare, were compelled to desist from the pursuit and rest, during which their cartridge-boxes were replenished with ammunition preparatory to again advancing on the enemy.

At this time I was advised that Brigadier-General Cleburne had been wounded and had retired from the field. I therefore assumed command of the division, and the major-general commanding having arrived, by his direction I moved the division forward on the right-hand side of the road toward Richmond, Brigadier-General Churchill's division having been previously advanced on the left of the road and engaging the enemy soon after my division was put in motion.

This engagement was spirited, the enemy contesting the ground stubbornly with their force on the left of the road and shelling my command as we advanced toward him through the open fields; but being very hotly pressed by Brigadier-General Churchill's command he again fled, and by his superior speed secured to himself another ground on which to rally. The troops under my command were by this time almost famished for water, having only had about one canteen of muddy water to the man during the entire day. A scant supply of water having been obtained by the troops, we again pressed on and soon came in sight of him, posted in the south edge of the town of Richmond and in the country near that place. In this position he attacked the Third Division on the left of the road and the Second Brigade of the Fourth Division on the right of the road—the Twelfth and Forty-seventh Tennessee Regiments held as a reserve and the One hundred and fifty-fourth Senior and Thirteenth Tennessee Regiments on the right of the Second Brigade—whence after a stubborn resistance for half an hour he was driven, his ranks so thinned, broken, and scattered that it was again impossible for him to rally, and seeking safety in flight, the town with his stores, &c., were abandoned to us, and after an ineffectual pursuit 3 miles beyond the town we went into camp after twelve hours' hard fighting and marching.

A list of the prisoners taken by this command is already in your office.

It is with deep sorrow that I mention the fall of Col. Ed. Fitzgerald, of the One hundred and fifty-fourth Senior Tennessee Regiment, who fell early in the morning at the head of his regiment. As a man he was kind and gentle in his bearing, as a soldier he was equal to the discharge of his duty, as an officer diligent in executing the orders of his superiors, and as a leader in battle was ever to be found in the foremost ranks.

I would also mention Lieut. Col. [J. A.] Butler, of the Second Tennessee Regiment, who fell while leading his regiment in the last charge before Richmond. His life was given to the country while driving the vandal hordes from Southern soil and from the sacred precincts of the last resting place of the dead, which their commander had not scrupled to profane with his iniquitous clan. He sleeps there with the gallant dead of his command around him.

The gallant conduct of Col. B. J. Hill is worthy of conspicuous mention. Two horses were shot under him and three bullets struck his person. In spite of this he led his brigade without an apparent intermission, each casualty to him being so speedily succeeded by a quick remedy as to cause his appearance in the lead of his command to appear without interruption in the various contests through which he so valiantly passed.

Col. A. J. Vaughan, jr., who commanded the Second Brigade after I assumed command of the division, repeated the exhibition of judgment and coolness which he had displayed in leading his regiment in the first engagement of the day.

I cannot close this report without bearing testimony to the gallant conduct of the officers and privates of the command generally, and to say that I refrain from particularizing because of the great length to which this report would be extended.

I feel it due to a gallant foreigner to call your attention to his bearing throughout these several bloody conflicts—Lieut. Col. [C. J.] Polignac. Though not born on our soil, a stranger to nearly the entire command, not prompted by the many incentives which impel us to battle for our rights, but led on to see the right prevail and the sordid meanness of our foe punished, he has freely exposed himself to all the dangers of warfare, leading the gallant little band of which he was temporarily in command through the thickest of the fight and cheering them on to victory. He deserves the thanks of this country.

I here take great pleasure in speaking of the material service rendered me during the several engagements by Capt. M. W. Cluskey, assistant adjutant-general; Capt. J. H. Edmondson, brigade inspector; Maj. A. M. Looney, volunteer aide-de-camp, and Mr. F. B. Rodgers, my aide-de-camp, who in his personal encouragement of the troops when in the most desperate moments of the first engagement attracted my attention as well as that of his brother members of my staff and won the admiration of the entire command; to Lieutenants Hanly, Mayo, and Jetton, of Brigadier-General Cleburne's staff, who reported to me for duty after their general was wounded.

Herewith inclosed I submit the reports of Colonels Hill and Vaughan,* commanding the brigades of this division, to which reference is made

---

* Not found.

as to the bearing of the officers and men of the several commands; also, marked A and B, the lists* of the killed and wounded of the brigades.

I have the honor, colonel, to be, your obedient servant,

PRESTON SMITH,
Acting Brigadier-General, Commanding.

Col. J. PEGRAM, *Chief of Staff.*

No. 23.

Report of Col. Benjamin J. Hill, Thirty-fifth Tennessee Infantry, commanding Second Brigade.

CAMP NEAR FLORENCE, KY., *September* 15, 1862.

The Second Brigade, of which I am in command, having been placed in the advance on August 29 for the attack on the enemy's forces before Richmond, Ky., I beg leave to submit the following report of its action:

Halting in line of battle on either side of the Richmond and Big Hill turnpike, in the afternoon of Friday, August 29, some 10 miles south of the former place, we awaited the result of the movement of the cavalry, under Colonel Scott, of Louisiana, which had been sent forward to ascertain the force and position of the enemy.

About 5 o'clock quick and heavy artillery discovered to us a skirmish some 5 miles in our front going on between the cavalry and Federals, and a few minutes after dark Colonel Scott's forces came into our lines on a brisk trot, reporting an advance of both infantry and cavalry troops from the Lincolnites. The brigade was then moved up some 50 yards in line of battle upon a range of small hills which commanded the pike and fields on both sides for more than half a mile. The battery under Captain Douglas was thrown into position on an eminence to the left of the road, supported by the sharpshooters, the Second and Forty-eighth Tennessee Regiments. The regimental skirmishers were placed 200 yards in front of their respective commands. Almost instantly with the completion of these preparations a regiment of Federal cavalry, commanded by the notorious Metcalfe, came thundering down the road, crying "Charge, and shoot down the rebels." They were allowed to approach sufficiently near to ascertain by the sound on the road something of their exact whereabouts, when the skirmishers of the Forty-eighth Tennessee, whose right rested near the pike and who were commanded by Capt. [O. T.] Plummer, of Company A, were ordered to fire, throwing the cavalry into utter confusion, causing a pell-mell retreat. One of the enemy was here killed, several wounded, and three captured. Thirty breech-loading Sharps cavalry carbines were picked up by my men and the place strewn with blankets and accouterments.

The brigade here lay upon its arms until early light Saturday morning, the 30th, when the order was given to advance in line of battle, which was done for a distance of 1½ miles. The cavalry scouts here reported the position of the enemy in large force three-quarters of a mile north of the little village of Kingston. The brigade was marched in column along the road a half mile beyond the latter place and formed into line of battle on the right of the pike at 7 o'clock. The enemy then commenced a heavy artillery fire upon our line and also on the

---

*Not found.

village, from which direction the other brigade of this division, then under command of yourself, and the division of General Churchill were approaching. Our artillery was here ordered to advance to a nearer position, and our line of battle followed immediately on under a rapid fire from the field pieces of the enemy. The guns of our battery were thrown into position upon an uncovered field about 600 yards from the enemy's line of battle, which was formed some 50 yards in rear of their batteries. Our line of battle rested its center immediately in the rear of our battery in the following order: The Second Tennessee, under Lieutenant-Colonel Butler, on the left and toward the pike; the Fifteenth and Thirteenth Arkansas (temporarily consolidated), under command of Colonel Polk and Lieut. Col. [A. R.] Brown, on the right; the Forty-eighth Tennessee, under Colonel Nixon, and the Fifth Tennessee, under Lieutenant-Colonel Smith, in the center. An artillery duel, continuing an hour and a quarter, now commenced, which resulted in a loss to our side of 7 wounded of the Forty-eighth Tennessee, 2 killed and 1 wounded of the Second Tennessee. The dead and wounded of the enemy by grape, canister, and shell, which their ground afterwards exhibited, showed that our artillery had been worked with great skill.

In pursuance of an order from General Cleburne I here detailed a company from the Second Tennessee, under command of Capt. J. J. Newsom, as sharpshooters, to occupy a position near the barn, situated upon a hill to the left of the pike, for the purpose of picking off the horses and gunners from the enemy's battery. A similar detail was also made from the Fifteenth Arkansas, under Capts. [O. S.] Palmer and [G.] Dixon, to occupy a position upon the right of our line in a skirt of woods and ascertain the extreme left of the enemy's line. This company was under the eye of General Cleburne, who was preparing for a flank movement upon the enemy with Colonel Vaughan's brigade, then under your personal command and which you had formed in line of battle upon the right of my brigade. Sharp work soon took place between the enemy and the companies of Captain Newsom on the left and Captains Palmer and Dixon on the right. The position of my brigade remained unchanged until the forward movement was commanded to the entire division. The enemy commenced a confused retreat; their scattered forces extended from the right of the road through the corn fields on the left for half a mile. In this charge the Forty-eighth Tennessee, under Col. [G. H.] Nixon, captured 165 prisoners, including several commissioned officers of high rank. Our success, I am sorry here to say, in the capture of a greater number of prisoners was interfered with in the detachment of two of my regiments by a staff officer of another division, who, it seems, was ordered to have a section of battery supported, and mistaking his own line of battle, thus unfortunately detached two regiments of my own people. The error was remedied as soon as possible, but unfortunately not early enough to carry out what my brigade would otherwise have accomplished.

The loss of the brigade in this engagement was small in the number ber of killed. Captain Douglas and Lieut. [Benjamin] Hardin, of the battery, were slightly wounded; Colonel Polk, Fifteenth Arkansas, badly wounded in the head, and Capt. J. J. Newsom, company of sharpshooters, Second Tennessee, seriously, if not mortally.

The brigade was ordered to rest for one hour about 1½ miles in advance of the scene of the first action in a woodland to the right of the road near a building called Zion's Church, after which it was again formed in line of battle. This was near the hour of 1 o'clock—the sun beating down with oppressive heat and the canteens of my men scarce of water. T1e enemy had rallied and again thrown their batteries into position, when we advanced through the open fields under a hot fire of shell, which, however, proved fruitless upon our unbroken line. In this stand the enemy had thrown his heavy line of infantry in the skirt of woods on the left of the road, which were soon engaged by a brigade of General Churchill's troops and after a short engagement began to waver. The order then reached us to move across to that portion of the field in double-quick, which we did for over half a mile, but their hordes gave way before our gallant companions in arms ere we had time to give them a volley.

Another halt was given along the line about 3 o'clock at a point some 2 miles south of Richmond and the scattered men gathered to their proper commands. When rested for the space of an hour the line was again formed, and Captain Yancey, of the Second Tennessee Regiment, was placed in command of all the skirmishers of the brigade, which again resumed its position to the right of the road, marching steadily forward toward the town without an indication of a stand from the Federals until we came in half a mile of its spires. Our skirmishers were then thrown some 400 yards in advance to feel the enemy's strongest positions, and the repeated shots along our entire front soon told of their whereabouts and showed them to number a large force. The men under Captain Yancey maintained their advanced ground firmly and were driving back the enemy's sharpshooters when our line advanced at a quick-pace, opening a warm fire, and discovering the enemy densely massed along the fences, in the corn fields, and behind the hay-stacks bordering a turn of the pike into the environs of Richmond. Here the loss was slight to several regiments of the brigade, but the men moved on most gallantly, although grape and canister were plowing the earth all around them in every direction. When we reached the pike the order was given to charge across an uninclosed field lying between the road and the cemetery, the enemy being posted behind the fence and tombstones and in the corn fields and woods stretching off to the left. As we cleared a rise in the ground the deadliest fire was poured into us that occurred during the entire day, and although the bullets hailed our brave troops did not falter, but with volley after volley and shout after shout routed them from their stronghold and pursued them through the streets of Richmond, and when night closed in we were, as we started in the morning, still in the advance line.

In this last engagement our loss in killed and wounded was severe:

	Killed.	Wounded.
15th Arkansas		
13th Arkansas	2	15
5th Tennessee	3	19
48th Tennessee	2	12
2d Tennessee	5	54
	15	94
Total	27	194

The gallant Lieutenant-Colonel Butler, of the Second Tennessee, was here killed, and Colonel Nixon, of the Forty-eighth Tennessee, received a severe contusion from a canister-shot while bravely leading his regiment.

The killed and wounded of the enemy at this point outnumbered our loss very seriously. We captured squad after squad of prisoners continuously through and past the town.

The Second Brigade, when formed into line on the morning of the 30th, showed the following strength: Fifteenth and Thirteenth Arkansas, 390; Fifth Tennessee, 295; Forty-eighth Tennessee, 312; Second Tennessee, 300.

In concluding this report I must speak in the highest terms of the gallant conduct of the officers and men of my command. They stood unflinchingly before the galling fire of a superior force, and no troops battling for the defense of our noblest cause could have acquitted themselves more nobly. While I make no invidious distinction between the actions of officers and men under my command, I feel it obligatory to mention the gallantry of Lieutenant-Colonel Polignac, who, in the last fight before Richmond, seized the colors of the Fifth Tennessee, bearing them triumphantly through the thickest of the fight and encouraged the men to withstand a terrible fire.

My thanks are due Capt. James F. Lanford, assistant adjutant-general, for the assistance rendered me on the field by his unwavering coolness and courage.

Respectfully,

BENJ. J. HILL,
Col., Comdg. Second Brig., Fourth Div., Army of Kentucky.

Brig. Gen. PRESTON SMITH,
Commanding Fourth Division, Army of Kentucky.

P. S.—The conduct of Lieutenant-Colonel Murray, who commanded the sharpshooters on Friday night and assisted at the guns of the battery on Saturday, was highly creditable to him as a brave and gallant officer.

I herewith append a list of the killed and wounded of the brigade during the series of fights on Saturday.*

AUGUST 31, 1862.—Skirmish at Stevenson, Ala.

Report of Maj. Gen. Samuel Jones, C. S. Army.

HEADQUARTERS CONFEDERATE STATES FORCES,
Chattanooga, Tenn., September 1, 1862.

COLONEL: When I ordered the Twenty-fifth Tennessee Regiment, which was stationed near Shell Mound, to come to this place to proceed to Sparta, agreeably to instructions conveyed to me in your letter of the 30th instant [ultimo], I was not aware that it formed a part of the force sent to attack the enemy at Stevenson. I received last night a telegram from Lieutenant-Colonel Maury, dated at Stevenson, informing me that after a few hours' fighting the enemy was driven from Stevenson and the place occupied by our troops, the Twenty-fifth Tennessee being a part of them. I have directed Brigadier-General Maxey to keep that regiment only so long as it may be necessary to enable him to secure all property that may have been captured, and then to comply with the order sending it to Sparta.

---

* See p. 936.

It is estimated that the enemy's force at Stevens on was 1,000 infantry (probably one regiment), a squadron of cavalry, and five pieces of artillery; our force was about 900; and the enemy was strongly intrenched. No detailed report of the affair has yet been received.

I regret the delay in sending forward the Twenty-fifth Tennessee as directed by the general. It will only be a delay of a day, or perhaps two, however, as I expect the regiment up to-night or to-morrow.

Very respectfully, your obedient servant,

SAM. JONES,
Major-General.

Lieut. Col. GEORGE G. GARNER, *A. A. G., &c.*

AUGUST 31, 1862.—Skirmish at Rogers' Gap, Tenn.

REPORTS.

No. 1.—Brig. Gen. George W. Morgan, U. S. Army.
No. 2.—Maj. Gen. J. P. McCown, C. S. Army.

No. 1.

Report of Brig. Gen. George W. Morgan, U. S. Army.

CUMBERLAND GAP, TENN., *August* 31,
Via Louisville, Ky., September 14, 1862.

At noon on the 29th I sent 60 picked infantry, under Captain Myers and Lieutenant Rogers, First Tennessee, by a circuitous route through the mountains to Rogers' Gap, with instructions to harass the enemy, and, if possible, intercept dispatches. This morning at daylight Captain Meyers surprised Captain Rhodes' company of rebel cavalry on the southern side of Rogers' Gap. He killed 6, wounded 6 or 8, and captured 19, among whom is Captain Rhodes, a renegade Ohioan; also 30 horses and equipments, including carbines, &c. Captain Myers and party reached Cumberland Gap at 6 o'clock p. m. to-day. This brave little band performed a march of 60 miles, over a route almost impracticable, in fifty hours, and surprised and captured one of the enemy's outposts, and returned to this place without the loss of a single man. A portion of the enemy were absent on a scout; of those present one lieutenant escaped, and he only clothed in his shirt. This morning I sent Lieut. Col. [Joel W.] Ridgell, with 275 men, to join Garrard, Third Kentucky, *en route* to General Wallace. The forces of the enemy under General Smith, about 25,000 strong, have gone forward from Cumberland Ford and Barboursville toward Lexington. The condition of his army is desperate; his whole force is doomed. Sixty of his men will be in to-morrow morning to surrender. Those who have arrived represent that a considerable portion of the conscripts are for the Union. Were it not for the immense importance of this stronghold I would advance with two brigades by rapid marches to gain Smith's rear; but were we to lose the Gap it would cost a sea of blood to retake it. Colonel Garrard has fought and whipped the enemy near McKee to-day. I established a battery on Poor Valley Ridge, 1 mile south of the Gap, and shelled the enemy's camp, indicated by their fires, at several points. We could see the rebels scatter. The Knoxville Register of the 27th instant declares that we have but three days' rations. The telegram of the general-in-chief has been received. He need not feel anxious in regard to this post. Officers and soldiers are in fine spirits and prepared for any sacrifice which duty may require.

GEORGE W. MORGAN,
Commanding.

Brigadier-General CULLUM, *Chief of Staff.*

No. 2.

Report of Maj. Gen. J. P. McCown, C. S. Army.

KNOXVILLE, TENN., *September* 2, 1862.

A Federal force through Rogers' Gap captured and dispersed the company there; they also threaten our trains through Big Creek Gap. All the force at my command will be required to protect these points. Where is Breckinridge's division?

J. P. McCOWN,
Major-General, Commanding.

Maj. Gen. SAMUEL JONES, *Chattanooga, Tenn.*

SEPTEMBER 2, 1862.—Skirmish near Nashville, Tenn.

Report of Col. William B. Stokes, First Middle Tennessee Cavalry.

HDQRS. FIRST MIDDLE TENNESSEE CAVALRY,
Camp Campbell, September 2, 1862.

SIR: I have the honor to report that after leaving Colonel Miller, on the Dickinson pike, in obedience to verbal orders I proceeded with two companies of my regiment, accompanied by a regiment of infantry, to Center Meeting-House, where I left the pike, taking a pathway to the left. This I followed to Mr. Driver's, where I met with Colonel Miller. I was then instructed to move on a pathway to the rear of Mr. Driver's, which was supposed would lead to the camp of the enemy. After following this road for 2 miles I met with a farmer, who said he knew and would lead me to where the enemy was, which he did, after traveling 2 miles farther.

I immediately attacked him with my advance guard, capturing 8 prisoners, among them Capt. Robert Bennett, and wounding his brother, Col. James Bennett, putting the remainder to flight. Here I left the infantry and pursued the enemy 4 miles farther, taking 18 more prisoners, killing 4, wounding 6. I captured 26 horses and a great many shot-guns and rifles, which I ordered to be destroyed, as I could not carry them. The way was strewn with clothing, arms, &c., showing it was a complete rout. I then gave over the pursuit and returned to where I left the infantry, and not finding them I moved to the White's Creek pike. Here I learned that Colonel Stoughton, with the train, was 2 miles above. We here rested an hour, when I decided to return to the city, arriving at 3 p. m.

Of the officers and men of my command I cannot speak in terms strong enough to show my satisfaction for the good conduct and the alacrity with which they obeyed orders.

I am, sir, very respectfully, your obedient servant,

WM. B. STOKES,
Colonel, Commanding First Tennessee Cavalry.

ASSISTANT-ADJUTANT GENERAL, *Seventh Brigade.*

SEPTEMBER 5–10, 1862.—Expedition from Fort Donelson to Clarksville, Tenn., and skirmishes (6th) at New Providence and (7th) at Riggin's Hill.

Report of Col. William W. Lowe, Fifth Iowa Cavalry.

HEADQUARTERS, *Fort Donelson, September 10, 1862.*

SIR: I have the honor to state that I have just returned from an expedition to Clarksville, and have to report as follows:

On the morning of the 5th instant I started from this post with parts of the Eleventh Illinois, Thirteenth Wisconsin, Seventy-first Ohio Infantry, part of the Fifth Iowa Cavalry, one section of Flood's battery, and one section of Stenbeck's battery, numbering in all about 1,030 men. During the day and night I marched to a point called Blue Springs, about 16 miles from Clarksville. About midnight I received a dispatch from the general telling me I need not attempt to take Clarksville at present. I immediately replied that I was now already on the way, and within 16 miles of Clarksville. "Shall I return?" stating also, "Awaiting your reply, I shall menace them."

Acting in accordance with this assertion, and because the point where I had stopped was not well supplied with water, I moved on slowly during the morning of the 6th to a good position, within 10 miles of the town, receiving from time to time during the day positive information that the enemy, about 1,100 strong, were in good position 3 miles from the town, and had determined to give us battle.

During the afternoon a small reconnoitering party, under Lieutenant Moreing, Fifth Iowa Cavalry, came in sight of their pickets, and immediately gave chase, running them more than a mile, when they were fired upon by some 50 or more rebels in ambush. Though within 15 yards of the road, with their guns at a rest, not a man was injured by the volley, and but 1 horse was killed and 3 wounded. I immediately ordered Lieutenant-Colonel Patrick, of the Fifth Iowa Cavalry, to move forward with four companies of cavalry, three companies of infantry, and one piece of artillery, with a view to driving in their pickets and creating the belief that we were advancing upon them. Early in the morning of the 7th (having received the necessary permission) I moved on in the direction of the town, driving their pickets before us for more than two hours. About 10.30 a. m. we came in view of the enemy's position and immediately opened upon them a fire of shell and canister, and in thirty-five minutes they were completely routed, both sections of artillery being well served and doing fine execution. Finding that the enemy were rapidly retreating, I immediately formed line (the right commanded by Colonel Ransom and Major Hart, the left by Lieutenant-Colonel Chapman, followed immediately by the sections of artillery and the detachment of cavalry), and pushed on rapidly in pursuit. They fled so rapidly, however, that they could not be overhauled by infantry, and I immediately pushed forward some companies, under Lieutenant-Colonel Patrick, to prevent them from tearing up the Red River Bridge, the only practicable approach to the town. He caught them in the very act, charged them, drove them from the bridge, and held his position until I succeeded in planting two pieces of artillery on a bluff commanding the town. The enemy fled precipitately through the place and scattered in all directions.

Their loss, according to the report of their commander, Colonel Woodward, was 17 killed and from 40 to 50 wounded. Some of their dead were buried on the field and others taken to Providence and Clarksville.

We captured about 40 horses and a considerable quantity of arms and accouterments. I occupied the town during the night and the greater part of the next day, requiring the citizens to furnish rations for my command. While there I burned about 1,000 bales of hay, destroyed some 250 boxes of commissary stores, captured 3 Government wagons and several prisoners. By pressing teams into the service I was enabled to bring away nearly 200 boxes of commissary stores. I also brought with me several Union families, who were afraid to remain in the place.

I am, sir, your obedient servant,

                        W. W. LOWE,
            Colonel Fifth Iowa Cavalry, Commanding.

ASSISTANT ADJUTANT-GENERAL, U. S. ARMY,
      Headquarters District of West Tennessee, Corinth, Miss.

SEPTEMBER 7, 1862.—Surrender of outpost at Shepherdsville, **Ky.**

Report of Capt. Stephen R. Tinker, Fifty-fourth Indiana Infantry.

                   LOUISVILLE, *September* 8, 1862.

DEAR SIR: I would respectfully make the following report, viz:

On yesterday, 7th instant, my command, stationed at Shepherdsville, Ky., to guard the bridge at Salt River, had to surrender to a superior force, under the command of Colonel Hutcheson, of the so-called Confederate Army. Said forces consisted of cavalry and at least three pieces of artillery. The first that we saw of them one of the captains came through our guards with a flag of truce, demanding an immediate and unconditional surrender, saying at the same time that we would all be paroled, which conditions I at once rejected. He (the captain) then told us that they had plenty of artillery, and unless we surrendered that he should commence firing, and that soon. I did not believe they had any cannon, but kept up a parley until my first lieutenant sent his son—a youth, who was visiting his father in camp, and dressed in citizen's clothes—to spy out whether or not they had any cannon. On his return he reported three field pieces and a number of my men made the same assertion, and that there must have been not less than 500 of the enemy. At this moment, the flag of truce being delayed so long, which was near three-quarters of an hour, the rebels opened fire by throwing a shell, which exploded near our stockade and wounded 1 of my men. They fired a number of rounds, when I thought, after consultation, it best to surrender on the following terms: That the commissioned officers and non-commissioned officers should retain all their private property and side-arms, the privates all their clothing, blankets, &c. All the balance they either destroyed or carried away, and accomplished their design in partially destroying the bridge over Salt River.

I am satisfied had the enemy no artillery we could have held the position until we could have been re-enforced, although they outnumbered us more than three to one, we having the advantage of our stockade.

All of which is respectfully submitted.

S. R. TINKER,
Captain Company C, Fifty-fourth Regiment Indiana Vols.

Captain McDOWELL.

SEPTEMBER 10, 1862.—Operations at Rogers' and Big Creek Gaps, Tenn.

Report of Brig. Gen. George W. Morgan, U. S. Army.*

HEADQUARTERS UNITED STATES FORCES,
Maysville, Ky., September 18, 1862.

MAJOR: The inclosed dispatches were received this evening from General Morgan, inclosed in a horse-collar. I forward them forthwith.

I am, sir, very respectfully, your obedient servant,

H. B. WILSON,
Lieutenant-Colonel, Commanding.

Major McLEAN, Assistant Adjutant-General.

[Inclosure No. 1.]

HEADQUARTERS UNITED STATES FORCES,
Cumberland Gap, September 11, 1862.

GENERAL: I have already had the honor of reporting to you the success of expeditions against Baptist and Rogers' Gaps since our investment by the enemy, and I now report that on yesterday Rogers' Gap was blockaded by Lieut. Col. [M. L.] Phillips at the head of 200 picked men from the First and Second Tennessee Volunteers, and that Big Creek Gap was blockaded by Colonel Cooper at the head of 400 picked men taken from Spears' brigade. Colonel Cooper likewise attacked a body of McAfee's Kentucky cavalry on their march through Big Creek Gap to join General Smith, and Colonel McAfee and 95 officers and soldiers were made prisoners, while 10 or 12 of the enemy were left dead upon the field; among them was one of the aides-de-camp of Major-General Smith and 2 captains. Colonel Cooper also brings in 98 horses and equipments.

I ordered the expeditions so that both Gaps should be blockaded at the same time and that each party should cover the other's flank.

It is a remarkable fact that in these affairs we did not lose a single man, while the enemy had upward of 30 killed, a considerable number wounded, and lost 230 prisoners. These were complete surprises.

Inclosed I send you the general order of Major-General Bragg to his army. You will observe that he crossed the Tennessee River on the 24th ultimo.

---

* See also Morgan's report of evacuation of Cumberland Gap, etc., September 17–October 3, 1862; and McCown to Cooper, Part II, p. 814.

My aide de-camp, Lieutenant Medary, will give you much information which I do not desire to commit to paper, and I will be happy to receive your instructions through him. Whatever may be your orders, if within the power of men they shall be executed.

Since we have been surrounded I have had at the same time 4,000 men detached on various expeditions, all of which have been successful.

Stevenson is still in my immediate front and I daily send him paroled prisoners, and our pickets have frequent skirmishes.

A few days since I sent Lieut. R. Montgomery, of my staff, with an escort of 5 cavalry to Barboursville to take possession of that place. He captured and paroled 100 prisoners, among whom was a captain; they were generally convalescents. He also captured a supply of hospital stores.

I am, general, with high respect, your obedient servant,
GEORGE W. MORGAN,
Brigadier-General Volunteers, Commanding.

Major-General WRIGHT, U. S. A., *Cincinnati, Ohio.*

P. S.—I will thank you, general, to send me a list of the officers and soldiers of the Third Kentucky (Garrard's), Third East Tennessee (Houk's), and First Battalion Kentucky Cavalry (Munday's), captured and paroled by the enemy. I have no other means of ascertaining their names, and have now an opportunity of effecting the exchange of many of them.

[Inclosure No. 2.]

GENERAL ORDERS, }   HEADQUARTERS DEPARTMENT No. 2,
    No. 124.   }   *Chattanooga, Tenn., August 25, 1862.*

The troops of this command will be in readiness to move at an hour's notice. Ample time for the preparation having been allowed and everything necessary having been promptly supplied, the general trusts the movement will be made with that alacrity and regularity which can alone inspire confidence.

The enemy is before us, devastating our fair country, imprisoning our old and venerated men, even the ministers of God, insulting our women, and desecrating our altars. It is our proud lot to be assigned the duty of punishing and driving these deluded men, led by desperate adventurers and goaded on by Abolition demagogues and demons. Let us but deserve success and an offended Deity will certainly secure it. Should we be opposed, we must fight at any odds and conquer at any sacrifice. Should the foe retire, we must follow him rapidly to his own territory and make him taste the bitters of invasion.

Soldiers! The enemy are before you and your banners are free. It is for you to decide whether our brothers and sisters of Tennessee and Kentucky shall remain bondmen and bondwomen of the Abolition tyrant or be restored to the freedom inherited from our fathers.

By command of General Bragg:
GEO. G. GARNER,
Assistant Adjutant-General.

P. S.—General Bragg crossed the Tennessee with his army on the 24th of August.

[Addenda.]

Humphrey Marshall marching from Pound Gap by way of Mount Sterling to join Kirby Smith. His force estimated at from 8,000 to

15,000. About 300 rebel troops at Mount Sterling and 100 at Winchester. Kirby Smith's forces, which were at Lexington and Frankfort, have moved on toward Cynthiana and Covington. Rumored that a portion of his forces are moving toward Louisville. Colonel De Courcy, of General Morgan's command, is at Manchester with his brigade, and is collecting supplies for the army at Cumberland Gap. General Morgan's entire force numbers about 7,000 effective men. He has thirty pieces of cannon, with a moderate supply of ammunition for them; has plenty of ammunition for small-arms. Provisions will hold out eighty days yet.

General Bragg crossed the Tennessee River on the 25th of August. General Stevenson has from 10,000 to 15,000 men immediately in front of Cumberland Gap. Kirby Smith's forces altogether in Kentucky number from 30,000 to 40,000. Recruits for the rebel army are being raised very rapidly in Kentucky.

SEPTEMBER 14–17, 1862.—Siege of Munfordville and Woodsonville, Ky.

REPORTS, ETC

No. 1.—Col. John T. Wilder, Seventeenth Indiana Infantry.
No. 2.—Col. Cyrus L. Dunham, Fiftieth Indiana Infantry.
No. 3.—Return of Casualties in the Union forces.
No. 4.—General Braxton Bragg, C. S. Army, commanding Department No. 2.
No. 5.—Brig. Gen. James R. Chalmers, C. S. Army, commanding Second Brigade, right wing Army of the Mississippi, including operations September 12–17.
No. 6.—Lieut. James Garrity, commanding W. H. Ketchum's Battery.
No. 7.—Col. John W. Frazer, Twenty-eighth Alabama Infantry, of operations September 16.
No. 8.—Col. W. H. Bishop, Seventh Mississippi Infantry, of operations September 14.
No. 9.—Col. Thomas W. White, Ninth Mississippi Infantry, of operations September 14.
No. 10.—Capt. James L. Finley, Tenth Mississippi Infantry, of operations September 14.
No. 11.—Col. Edward C. Walthall, Twenty-ninth Mississippi Infantry, of operations September 14.
No. 12.—Maj. John C. Thompson, Blythe's Forty-fourth Mississippi Infantry, of operations September 14.
No. 13.—Col. A. J. Lythgoe, Nineteenth South Carolina Infantry, of operations September 16–17.
No. 14.—Capt. O. F. West, commanding Richards' Battalion, of operations September 14.

No. 1.

Report of Col. John T. Wilder, Seventeenth Indiana Infantry.

CAVE CITY, KY., *September* 18, 1862.

SIR : I have the honor to report that on September 8, 1862, according to a special order from General Boyle, I assumed command of the forces at Munfordville, Ky. I immediately set to work building fortifications for defense of the railroad bridge over Green River.

On Sunday, September 9, I was informed that the railroad bridge at Salt River was burned by the rebels. Our supplies being sufficient for one day only I immediately began collecting flour and bacon in the country about us and got some bread from Bowling Green, and managed to get rations for fifteen days. At the same time I ordered all the Home Guard companies and recruits for the Thirty-third Kentucky, who had no arms, to scatter out over the country and act in the capacity of scouts. They served me admirably in this respect, giving notice of Bragg's approach when over 50 miles distant, and notifying me of his numbers, pieces of artillery, direction taken, &c., in every movement made by him on his advance from Cumberland River.

On Saturday, September 13, Colonel Scott, with a brigade of cavalry and a battery of five mountain howitzers, came down the north side of the river from Greensburg, and at 8 p. m. demanded an unconditional surrender of the place. I peremptorily refused, and at 3 o'clock the next morning he commenced an attack by firing on our pickets. They contested the ground so stubbornly that he was compelled to bring up his artillery to drive them in, which he accomplished at daybreak, after losing his guide and a lieutenant-colonel killed.

At daylight a furious attack was made on the pickets on the south side of the river by a large force of infantry. I immediately sent Company K, Seventy-fourth Indiana, out to a belt of woods about a quarter of a mile in advance, to act as a reserve, for the pickets to rally on. They held their ground until nearly surrounded, and only fell back when peremptorily ordered to do so by Major Cubberly, of the Eighty-ninth Indiana, who had charge of the pickets and skirmishers on the south side of the river. Our advanced line fought them stubbornly for an hour, and only came in when ordered to do so by me, as I did not wish to lose the advantage of our works. At 5.30 the fighting became general along the whole line, the enemy having advanced to within 200 yards of our works in large numbers.

At 6.30 a. m. the enemy advanced in line of battle upon our west, or main work, and seeing their intention to storm our position I ordered the men to fix bayonets, when the rebels came forward with a cheer, supposing our cessation of fire was a sign of retreat. When they came within about 30 yards I directed the men to fire, which was repeated by Col. [Charles D.] Murray and the officers along the line, and a very avalanche of death swept through the ranks, causing them to first stagger and then run in disorder to the wood in the rear, having left all of their field officers on the ground either killed or badly wounded. The regiments that made this charge were the Seventh and Tenth Mississippi and Seventh Alabama. Immediately after this repulse a similar one was made on the redoubt by the Ninth and Twenty-ninth Mississippi and a battalion of sharpshooters. They were literally murdered by a terrible fire from the gallant defenders of the work.

Maj. [Augustus H.] Abbott sprang upon the parapet, with his hat in one hand and a drawn saber in the other, urging his men to stand to the work, until he was shot dead under the flag he so nobly defended. A braver man never fell. The flag had 146 bullet-holes through it and the staff was struck eleven times.

Lieutenant Mason, of the Thirteenth Indiana Battery, commanding the artillery, in the mean time was riddling them with grape and canister, when they broke in all directions, fleeing as from a belching volcano, many dropping as they fled. At this juncture I sent Colonel Emerson, of the Sixty-seventh Indiana, with one more company, to reenforce the redoubt and to take command. The enemy soon rallied, however, and seemed to be more cautious in their movements, keeping up a constant fire from the best cover they could obtain until 9.30 a. m., making several weak efforts to charge us again, but they had learned a dear lesson and profited by it.

At 9.30 they sent in a flag of truce, demanding again that I should surrender. I again refused, when they asked the privilege of removing their dead and wounded. I gave them leave to do so. The following is the correspondence that passed between the two parties:

Col. J. T. WILDER, *Commanding U. S. Forces at Green River:*

You have made a gallant defense of your position, and to avoid further bloodshed I demand an unconditional surrender of your forces. I have six regiments of infantry, one battalion of infantry sharpshooters, and have just been re-enforced by a brigade of cavalry, under Colonel Scott, with two battalions of artillery. I have two regiments on the north side of the river, and you can't escape. The railroad track is torn up in your rear and you can't receive re-enforcements. General Bragg's army is but a short distance in the rear.*

JAMES R. CHALMERS,
Brig. Gen., Comdg. First Brig., Right Wing Army of the Mississippi.

To this demand and these arguments Colonel Wilder returned the following answer:

Brig. Gen. JAMES R. CHALMERS,
Commanding First Brigade, Right Wing, Army of the Mississippi:

Your note demanding the unconditional surrender of my forces has been received. Thank you for your compliments. If you wish to avoid further bloodshed keep out of the range of my guns. As to re-enforcements, they are now entering my works. I think I can defend my position against your entire force; at least I shall try to do so.*

J. T. WILDER,
Colonel Seventeenth Indiana Volunteers, Comdg. U. S. Forces at Green River.

At 9 a. m. I was re-enforced by six companies of the Fiftieth Indiana, under Colonel Dunham, who had come up on the railroad from Louisville and were thrown off the track 6 miles back. At daylight they pushed through by a circuitous route, missing Scott's cavalry on the north side of the river, and getting into the works without any loss except 1 man slightly wounded.

After the night closed, Colonel Dunham, being the ranking officer, assumed command, and will no doubt make a report of the events occurring on Monday and Tuesday following Sunday's fight. My whole force consisted of the Sixty-seventh and Eighty-ninth Indiana Regiments, one company of the Eighteenth Regulars, 204 recruits of the Seventeenth Indiana, two companies Seventy-fourth Indiana, one company of cavalry, Louisville Provost Guard, Lieutenant Watson commanding; one 12-pounder heavy gun, one 12-pounder Napoleon, one 12-pounder howitzer, and one 3-inch rifled gun, under Lieutenant Mason, Thirteenth Indiana Battery; 60 men Thirty-third Kentucky, Captain Wilson. The whole force amounting to 2,122 men for duty.

If I were to give a list of those who did their whole duty it would simply be a muster roll of all who were there. No man flinched or held back a particle. I must, however, mention W. A. Bullitt, adjutant Third Kentucky, who conveyed orders for me through the hottest of the fire with as much coolness as if on review, and Capt. Frank White, Fifteenth Indiana, who superintended the earthworks, and whenever a point was exposed to a raking fire from the enemy's batteries immediately threw up traverses to protect the men.

Our entire loss was 37 killed and wounded.† The enemy admit a loss

---

* Compare with Inclosures Nos. 2 and 3, Chalmers' report, p. 981.
† But see p. 967.

of 714 killed and wounded on Sunday alone. I cannot give as complete a report as I could wish, not having yet received a report from the different commands engaged.

On Tuesday evening at 7 p. m. I was again placed in command. By this time General Polk had crossed the river 10 miles above with the right wing of Bragg's army, and coming down on the north side took up a position on the river hills commanding our works, the left wing, under Hardee, having taken position on the hills on the south side. Bragg had sent a summons to surrender, and a consultation had been held late Tuesday evening with commanders of regiments, in which it was the unanimous expression that unless enabled by re-enforcements to hold the north side of the river we could make no successful resistance. All, however, decided to resist unless full evidence should be given of the overwhelming force of the enemy, and having been informed that General Buell's army had not left Bowling Green at 2 p. m. the day before, and having been notified by you that we could get no help from Louisville, our ammunition for small-arms being very limited, and our men worn out by constant work and fighting for four days and nights, and being satisfied that further resistance was no less than willful murder of the brave men who had so long contested with overwhelming numbers, I determined, after counting forty-five cannon in positions commanding our open field works, and surrounded by over 25,000 men, with no possible chance of assistance from any quarter, although promised such by you from Bowling Green, to surrender the entire force, which I did on Wednesday morning at 2 a. m., marching out of the works at 6 a. m. with all the honors of war, drums beating and colors flying, we being allowed by the terms of surrender our side-arms and all private property and four days' rations. Officers and men were immediately paroled and are about to start for the Ohio River.

I have the honor to be, your obedient servant,

J. T. WILDER,
Col., Seventeenth Ind. Vols., Comdg. U. S. Forces at Green River.

J. E. STACY, *Assistant Adjutant-General, Chief of Staff.*

—

HEADQUARTERS UNITED STATES FORCES,
Munfordville, Ky., September 14, 1862.

Brig. Gen. JAMES R. CHALMERS,
Commanding Confederate States Forces:

GENERAL: Your note is to hand. If you will agree, in case hostilities are resumed, not to fire from or on any building in either Munfordville or Woodsonville, as it is probable a number of them may be needed for our wounded as well as yours [sic]. Our sick are at a house near the river bank in Woodsonville. Thank you for your kind wishes and allow me to reciprocate.

I am, sir, very respectfully, yours, &c.,

J. T. WILDER,
Colonel, Commanding.

—

HDQRS. SECOND BRIG., RIGHT WING ARMY OF THE MISS.,
September 14, 1862.

Col. J. T. WILDER, *Commanding:*

COLONEL: Your proposition to permit any wounded that I may have at the depot near here to remain undisturbed has been received through Major Morgan. Permit me to thank you cordially for the proposal, and I will avail myself of it, as the roads are very rough. Hoping that when we cross swords again I may be able to render you a similar service, I remain, very respectfully,

JAMES R. CHALMERS,
Brigadier-General.

—

FORT CRAIG, KY., *September* 14, 1862.
Brig. Gen. JAMES R. CHALMERS,
Commanding Confederate States Forces:

GENERAL: Your acceptance of my propositions is received. One of my sergeants went outside of my works to relieve a wounded comrade after your flag of truce came in; some of your men engaged in removing your wounded took him prisoner. I expect you to return him.
Respectfully, yours,

J. T. WILDER,
Colonel, Commanding.

———

No. 2.

Report of Col. Cyrus L. Dunham, Fiftieth Indiana Infantry.

LOUISVILLE, KY., *September* 30, 1862.
SIR: I have the honor to report that, in obedience to an order from Major-General Gilbert, I, on the 13th instant, at 11 p. m., left the depot of the Louisville and Nashville Railroad with six companies of the Fiftieth Regiment Indiana Volunteers and one company (K) of the Seventy-eighth Indiana (attached to the Fiftieth, for duty), in all 446 strong, rank and file, for Green River, near Munfordville, to re-enforce Colonel Wilder in the defense of that point. The train ran very slowly until some distance below Elizabethtown, when I went forward and earnestly urged the engineer to greater speed, assuring him that it was all-important for us to reach Green River before daylight. He did increase the speed as far as safety would permit. Just below Bacon Creek, about 7 miles from Green River, the train stopped for wood. I immediately passed along the cars, aroused the men, and bade them stand by their arms in readiness for any emergency, as we were approaching dangerous ground. I took position on the engine, and the train moved cautiously forward. We had proceeded about a mile when we ran upon a portion of the track which had been undermined by the enemy, and slid to one side in such a manner as not to make the injury apparent to the engineer or myself. The train was thrown off, and several of the cars completely wrecked; yet, strange to say, not a man or a horse was seriously injured. The men seemed inspired with even greater confidence, as if feeling themselves under the especial protection of an overruling Providence. They were immediately formed in line of battle, an instantaneous attack being expected. The woods, which skirted the sides of the road were promptly reconnoitered. No enemy appearing, the regiment was put in rapid march for Munfordville, presuming that the road had been destroyed to prevent re-enforcements from reaching that place. We had not proceeded far before cannonading was heard in that direction. It had now become day-

light, and the men deposited their knapsacks and blankets in a thicket by the road-side and moved on rapidly. We soon met crowds of frightened and fleeing citizens, from whom no satisfactory information could be got of the situation of affairs at or of the forces investing our works. When within 3 or 4 miles of the place we were met by an intelligent citizen of my acquaintance, who informed me that a cavalry force of the enemy, at least 2,000 strong, and a battery of artillery were posted some distance this side of the river and covering the road approaching our works, which were upon the south bank; that guns were also so planted upon both banks of the river as to cover the bridges, and that he deemed it impossible for us to pass them and get in. But, nothing daunted, our little force made a detour to the right, and, by keeping under the cover of the woods and corn fields and down ravines, eluded the enemy, and reached the river just below the bridges and opposite our works. Here a momentary halt was made, under the cover of the woods, to close up the column and give the men a little rest. They then plunged into and forded the river at the double-quick between the two bridges, the first notice the enemy having of our approach being the hearty cheers of our beleaguered troops in the works. Fortunately for us the guns of the enemy upon the northern bank bearing upon the crossing had just before, by a well-directed fire from our own, under Lieutenant Mason, been silenced, and from those upon the southern side he had only time to throw a shell or two at our rear as it disappeared under cover of the bank, resulting only in slightly wounding one man. His cavalry came dashing down upon us in an attempt to cut us off, but only in time to be as hastily driven back by our little band, who promptly turned and fired upon them.

We found the engagement still progressing. By General Gilbert's written order the command was to go according to seniority, and I being the senior officer, Colonel Wilder promptly tendered me the command, but I as promptly refused to assume it, feeling that to do so during the progress of the engagement would be ungenerous in me and unjust to him, but I placed myself and my forces under his command. He has reported the proceedings of that day.

On Monday, the 15th, I assumed command. The enemy had under cover of the night withdrawn from before us, the infantry and artillery to Cave City and the cavalry up the river. Work upon the intrenchments was at once resumed and pushed forward with vigor that day, the night following, and in fact throughout all the affair of Tuesday. Wagons were sent to the wrecked train for the provisions upon it, and steps successfully taken, by the aid of Mr. William Gibson, a patriotic Union citizen of Munfordville, of whom I cannot speak in too high praise, to bring in the ammunition which had been upon it, but which the loyal men of the neighborhood had carried to the wood and concealed. Efforts were also made to repair the telegraph line. Messengers were sent to different points northward to communicate to the headquarters in this city our situation, inform them that we expected a renewal of the attack by a largely increased force, and ask reenforcements. Messengers, with a like object, I was informed, had been sent by Colonel Wilder to Bowling Green. I regarded the place as of great importance to the Government and made every effort to save it. Monday night re-enforcements, under command of Colonel Owen, Sixtieth Indiana, were received from Lebanon Junction, consisting of a part of the Sixtieth Indiana, 420 men, including one company (I) of the Twenty-eighth Kentucky, Lieutenant Conaway, which had been attached to it for duty; a part of the Sixty-eighth Indiana, Colonel King,

570 men, and six pieces of the First Ohio Artillery, 150 men, Captain Konkle in command.

On Tuesday, the 16th instant, at about 9.30 a. m., the advance of the enemy attacked our pickets on the south side of our works and from the direction of Cave City. His advance was sternly resisted by Companies A, B, and H, Fiftieth Indiana, and part of Company K, Seventy-eighth Indiana, under Maj. [Samuel T.] Wells, who, as well as the officers and men under him, in this little skirmish displayed great coolness and courage. They held the enemy's advancing columns at bay for over an hour and were only pressed back by overwhelming numbers. The object evidently was to avoid the field work on our left, known as Fort Craig, from which he had been so fatally repulsed on Sunday, and, under cover of the woods to approach and carry by storm the breast-works on our right; but the promptness and energy with which he was met seemed to deter him from the attempt. Before 11 a. m. the engagement had become general along our south line, the heavy pressure being upon the west or right. The men were cool and eager for the expected assault. The fire was rapid and continuous on the part of the enemy, who kept himself closely under cover of the woods. Between 2 and 3 o'clock it slackened, and by 3 o'clock it had almost ceased, and, supposing the enemy had withdrawn from the wood which fronted our entire south line, and being anxious to occupy the farther edge of it, that I might be advised of and check a renewed attack, Company A, Fiftieth Indiana, Captain Burrell, was thrown out as skirmishers, to feel through it. They soon became hotly engaged with the enemy, who attempted to turn their left flank. I immediately ordered Captain Carothers' company (G, same regiment) to his support. The order was promptly obeyed, and the company gallantly deployed, under a galling fire. This was a brilliant little affair. In it Lieutenant Burton, of Company G, fell, severely wounded, nobly doing his duty. Finding that the enemy still occupied the woods in force, our men were withdrawn, under a fire from the works. I should also mention that Company A, Sixtieth Indiana, was thrown out as skirmishers upon the left early in the engagement, and there remained for some time, doing excellent service, with the loss of 1 man wounded. By 4.30 p. m. the firing on both sides had nearly ceased, there being only an occasional shot from our guns, as opportunity offered, to prevent the planting of batteries by the enemy.

Between 5 and 6 o'clock a flag of truce from the enemy was seen approaching. I sent Colonel Wilder to receive it. It covered a note from General Bragg, commanding the enemy's forces, asserting that we were surrounded by an overwhelming force, all hopes of re-enforcements cut off, and demanding a surrender to save the loss of human life, which must result from carrying the works by storm.* I promptly and peremptorily declined; but when Colonel Wilder returned, after the delivery of my reply, and informed me that so far as he had been able to observe the force against us was truly overwhelming, and especially in artillery, and our situation critical, and being only a senior officer of equal rank with several others in the works, some of whom had had greater experience, I, at his suggestion, deemed it my duty to call a council of war of those officers. I desired also to gain time, in hopes of relief from this place or from Bowling Green. I therefore sent a note to General Bragg, asking a further suspension of hostilities, to give me time for such consultation. He consented to such suspension un-

---

*See inclosures to reports of Bragg.

til 9 p. m. This was a point gained, as by that time it would be too late for further attack, except by assault, which I felt able to repel. By this time I had got telegraphic communication with Louisville, and immediately telegraphed General Gilbert, in substance that we had held the enemy (said to be Bragg's and Polk's whole army) at bay all day; that evidently fresh columns were being moved against us, and whether we should be able to continue to hold our position without assistance remained to be seen ; that we should do the best we could. I received an answer, ordering me to turn the command over to Colonel Wilder. I replied that, under the circumstances, I regarded the order as unjust, but should obey it. In the mean time the council had been convened, consisting of Colonels Owen, Wilder, King, Emerson, and Murray, and Captain Konkle and myself. The unanimous conclusion was, if that they had the force claimed, viz, over 25,000 men and sixty pieces of artillery, besides cavalry, it would be a useless sacrifice of human life to resist, and especially as by their artillery they could in spite of us occupy the heights north of the river, which completely covered our works. But it was also unanimously resolved that we should be permitted by some competent officer or officers to have actual observation of their strength or that we should demonstrate it by actual trial of arms.

At the conclusion of the council I formally relinquished the command to Colonel Wilder, who has reported the further proceedings. I at once telegraphed General Gilbert, in substance, that I had so relinquished the command, and that I should take my musket and go into the trenches; that, as a senior officer, under the circumstances, I would not, as an officer, fight under a junior. I was immediately ordered by him to report to Colonel Wilder under arrest, which I did. It is but just to observe that I did not object to serving under Colonel Wilder. Between him and myself had existed and yet exists the most friendly and cordial relations. We had in all things agreed, and no praise from me would add to his reputation as an officer. The proper authorities must judge from subsequent events whether my telegram to General Gilbert was such evidence of weakness as justified my removal from command, or whether it was simply evidence that I saw our peril and was not afraid to look it in the face. To that authority I shall also appeal for the justness of my arrest.

Of the coolness and determined courage of the men I cannot speak too highly. Of officers, where all did their duty well, especial praise seems almost out of place; yet some of course had better opportunities than others to display tact, coolness, and courage. Justice requires me to acknowledge my obligations to Lieut. Col. Edward A. King, of the Nineteenth Regulars, but now colonel of the Sixty-eighth Indiana Volunteers. He had position about midway of the south line of the works west of the railroad. Six companies of his regiment were held in a hollow near by as a support, the assault being anticipated in that direction. His experience, coolness, and close observation, even when shells and musket-balls flew thick and fast, were invaluable and cannot be too highly praised. Colonel Owen was in command of the field works on the left (Fort Craig), with discretionary authority. I need scarcely say that it was trustworthily confided. I should also mention the excellent conduct of Adjt. John R. Simpson, of the Fiftieth Indiana, and Lieutenant Pumpelly, of the Sixteenth Kentucky, who acted as my aides. On Sunday they boldly reconnoitered the woods along our march to guard us against surprise. On Tuesday they did their duty with a quiet fearlessness that deserves favorable notice.

Our loss, 1 officer (Lieutenant Burton) and 6 privates wounded (one private mortally and Lieutenant Burton dangerously, a musket-ball passing through both legs and shattering a bone of one). The enemy's loss was over 100, said to be 105.

The forces under my command during this affair were those mentioned by Colonel Wilder in his report and the re-enforcements thereto hereinbefore noticed.

I am, respectfully,

C. L. DUNHAM,
Colonel, Commanding U. S. Forces at Green River.

ASSISTANT ADJUTANT-GENERAL AND CHIEF OF STAFF,
Army of Kentucky.

N. B.—It is probably but just to Major-General Gilbert and myself to add that since my arrival in this city he has informed me that within a few moments after issuing the order directing me to report to Colonel Wilder under arrest he sent me a dispatch, not only releasing me from arrest, but restoring me to the command; but, telegraphic communication being in the mean time cut off, it did not reach me.

Respectfully,

C. L. DUNHAM,
Colonel, Commanding, &c.

No. 3.

Return of Casualties in the Union forces.

[Compiled from nominal list of casualties, returns, &c.]

Command	Killed.		Wounded.		Captured or missing.		Aggregate.
	Officers.	Enlisted men.	Officers.	Enlisted men.	Officers.	Enlisted men.	
Indiana Light Artillery, 13th Battery (detachment)....					1	40	41
17th Indiana (detachment)					2	62	64
50th Indiana, Companies A, B, D, F, G, and H			1	4	12	383	400
60th Indiana				2	17	389	408
67th Indiana	1	10		32	32	856	931
68th Indiana				2	25	533	560
74th Indiana, Companies C and K		1		2	6	161	170
78th Indiana, Company K					3	49	52
89th Indiana		3		14	35	892	944
28th Kentucky, Company I					2	50	52
33d Kentucky (detachment)					5	60	65
34th Kentucky, Company G					2	78	80
1st Ohio Light Artillery, Battery D					2	120	122
18th U. S. Infantry, Company H, 2d Battalion					2	116	118
Miscellaneous detachments, &c					9	132	141
Total	1	14	1	56	155	3,921	4,148

Officer killed.—Maj. Augustus H. Abbott, Sixty-seventh Indiana.
Mortally wounded.—Lieut. Caswell R. Burton, Fiftieth Indiana.

NOTE.—All the wounded fell into the hands of the Confederates, and to avoid counting them twice they are excluded from the column of "captured or missing."

No. 4.

Reports of General Braxton Bragg, C. S. Army, commanding Department No. 2.

MUNFORDVILLE, KY., September 17, 1862.
(Received September 26.)

The garrison at this place surrendered last night without our firing a gun. We get 4,000 prisoners, 4,000 small-arms, pieces of artillery, and munitions of war in large quantities. My junction with Kirby Smith is complete. Buell still at Bowling Green.

BRAXTON BRAGG.

General S. COOPER, *Adjutant and Inspector General.*

—

HEADQUARTERS DEPARTMENT No. 2,
Munfordville, Ky., September 17, 1862.

SIR: Since my last dispatch this army has moved on steadily in the accomplishment of its secondary object, a junction with Maj. Gen. E. K. Smith. Waiting two days in Glasgow to collect a supply of bread-stuffs, an advance brigade thrown in this direction to cut the railroad and observe the enemy was indiscreetly advanced by its commander to the attack of a superior force here strongly fortified. After a most desperate fight they were repulsed with a loss of about 300 in killed and wounded. As soon as I heard of this misfortune my whole command was put in motion, and in less than twenty-four hours we had the place (some 25 and 35 miles distant by the routes taken) completely surrounded, and in a few hours an unconditional surrender of the whole garrison was made without our firing a gun. We received some 4,000 prisoners, an equal number of small-arms, 10 pieces of artillery, and munitions. The prisoners will be paroled and sent to General Buell at Bowling Green, the nearest point of the enemy's lines. My position must be exceedingly embarrassing to Buell and his army. They dare not attack me, and yet no other escape seems to be open to them.

My admiration of and love for my army cannot be expressed. To its patient toil and admirable discipline am I indebted for all the success which has attended this perilous undertaking. The men are much jaded and somewhat destitute, but cheerful and confident without a murmur.

We move soon on a combined expedition with General Smith.

Very respectfully, your obedient servant,

BRAXTON BRAGG,
General Commanding.

The ADJUTANT-GENERAL C. S. ARMY.

—

EXHIBITS RELATING TO SURRENDER OF MUNFORDVILLE, KY.

HEADQUARTERS CONFEDERATE STATES TROOPS,
Near Munfordville, Ky., September 16, 1862.

To the OFFICER COMMANDING U. S. FORCES
Near Munfordville, Ky.:

SIR: Surrounded by an overwhelming force, your successful resistance or escape is impossible. You are therefore offere l an opportunity by capitulation of avoiding the terrible consequences of an assault. The bearer, Lieut. Col. [H. W.] Walter, of my staff, will receive your reply.

I am, sir, very respectfully, your obedient servant,

BRAXTON BRAGG,
General, Commanding.

—

HEADQUARTERS UNITED STATES FORCES,
Camp Dunham, near Munfordville, Ky., September 16, 1862.

General BRAXTON BRAGG,
Commanding Confederate States Forces:

SIR : Your note of this date is received. As much as I shall regret the terrible consequences of an assault upon the works under my command I shall defend them to the utmost, and God help the right.

I am, respectfully, your obedient servant,

C. L. DUNHAM,
Colonel, Commanding U. S. Forces near Munfordville, Ky.

P. S.—I regret to say since your note has been received two Confederate officers have been observed near our works with glasses making observations thereof. I regard this as a violation of the true spirit of a flag of truce.

Respectfully,

C. L. D.

—

HEADQUARTERS UNITED STATES FORCES,
Munfordville, Ky.

General BRAXTON BRAGG,
Commanding Confederate Forces near Munfordville, Ky.:

SIR : On further reflection I ask a further suspension of hostilities until I can hold a council of war with officers of equal rank now with these forces.

Respectfully, your obedient servant,

C. L. DUNHAM,
Colonel, Commanding U. S. Forces.

—

HEADQUARTERS ARMY OF THE MISSISSIPPI,
Near Munfordville, Ky., September 16, 1862.

Col. C. L. DUNHAM, *Commanding U. S. Forces :*

SIR: Your request is granted, and no firing will take place, if your troops keep within their lines, before 9 p. m. I sincerely trust an honorable arrangement may be made which will prevent an unnecessary effusion of blood. And I must say, in all candor, no chance exists for your escape, successful resistance, or re-enforcement.

Please forward the inclosed note to my forces in your rear, so as to prevent any accident. My route being circuitous is the reason of this request.

BRAXTON BRAGG,
General, Commanding.

HEADQUARTERS UNITED STATES FORCES,
Near Munfordville, Ky., September 16, 1862.

General BRAXTON BRAGG, *Commanding Confederate Forces :*

SIR: The command of the forces at this place is turned over to Colonel Wilder, who will conduct the corrrespondence hereafter.

Respectfully, your obedient servant,

C. L. DUNHAM,
Colonel Fiftieth Indiana.

—

HEADQUARTERS UNITED STATES FORCES,
Munfordville, Ky., September 16, 1862.

General BRAXTON BRAGG, *Commanding C. S. Army of Kentucky :*

SIR: Your forces are planting batteries under cover of cessation of hostilities in near proximity to my works. This is contrary to all rules of honorable warfare. Will you have this stopped? I presume you are not aware of this or it would not be.

I am, sir, very respectfully, yours, truly,

J. T. WILDER,
Colonel, Commanding.

—

HEADQUARTERS CONFEDERATE STATES FORCES,
Near Munfordville, Ky., September 16, 1862—10 p. m.

Col. J. T. WILDER, *Comdg. U. S. Forces, Munfordville, Ky. :*

SIR: By reference to my note you will see it was only stipulated that "no firing will take place, if your troops keep within their lines, before 9 p. m." This condition has been complied with.

Very respectfully, your obedient servant,

BRAXTON BRAGG,
General, Commanding.

—

HEADQUARTERS UNITED STATES FORCES,
Munfordville, Ky., September 16, 1862.

General BRAXTON BRAGG,
Commanding C. S. Forces near Munfordville, Ky. :

SIR: At a consultation of officers of this command, held since dark this evening, it is agreed upon that if satisfactory evidence is given them of your ability to make good your assertions of largely superior numbers, so as to make the defense of this position a useless waste of human life, we will treat as to terms of an honorable surrender.

I am, sir, very respectfully, yours, &c.,

J. T. WILDER,
Colonel, Commanding.

—

HEADQUARTERS CONFEDERATE STATES FORCES,
Munfordville, Ky., September 16, 1862—9 p. m.

Col. J. T. WILDER, *Comdg. U. S. Forces, Munfordville, Ky. :*

Your dispatch is just received. The only evidence I can give you of my ability to make good my assertion of the presence of a sufficient force to compel your surrender, beyond the statement that it now exceeds 20,000, will be the use of it. An unconditional surrender of your whole force, &c., is demanded and will be enforced.   You are allowed one hour in which to make known your decision.

I am, sir, very, respectfully, your obedient servant,

BRAXTON BRAGG,
General, Commanding.

—

Lieut. W. A. Bullitt will receipt for and deliver any message sent me.

J. T. WILDER,
Colonel, Commanding.

—

ROWLETT'S, HART COUNTY, KY.,
September 16, 1862.

Col. J. T. WILDER, *U. S. A.:*

SIR: I am directed by General Bragg to say that no other conditions than those prescribed in his late note can be given.   He requires an unconditional surrender of your forces and stores, &c., and authorizes me to accept the surrender.

I am, colonel, respectfully, your obedient servant,

S. B. BUCKNER,
Major-General, C. S. Army.

—

ROWLETT'S, HART COUNTY, KY.,
September 17, 1862.

General BRAXTON BRAGG,
Commanding C. S. Forces in Kentucky:

SIR: Your demand for an unconditional surrender of the forces under my command at Green River is received.   I am unwillingly forced to comply with your demand.   Allow me to ask the usual courtesies for my command.

I am, sir, very respectfully, your obedient servant,

J. T. WILDER,
Colonel, Commanding U. S. Forces at Green River.

———

No. 5.

Reports of Brig. Gen. James R. Chalmers, C. S. Army, commanding Second Brigade, right wing Army of the Mississippi, including operations September 12–17.

HDQRS. SECOND BRIGADE, RESERVE DIVISION,
RIGHT WING ARMY OF THE MISSISSIPPI,
Cave City, Ky., September 15, 1862.

MAJOR: At 5 p. m. on yesterday, having buried my dead and sent all of my wounded who could bear transportation to this place, I notified the enemy that the truce was ended.   They replied that they had not finished burying their dead and asked that it might be continued for an hour longer, to which I consented.   In accordance with my previous determination I then withdrew my forces and returned without molestation to this place, where we arrived at a late hour in the night. The movement was made in good order.

The position of the enemy at Munfordville is too strong to be taken by infantry or such light artillery as I had; they can, however, be easily shelled out with heavier guns, either from this side of the river or the other. When hostilities ceased on yesterday my guns were within 200 yards of the works and my infantry had driven all the enemy inside of them and [they were] compelled to keep themselves closely concealed behind them. There are points more distant from which the works could be easily shelled with 12-pounder guns, if none heavier could be got. The best approach to the place from Glasgow on this side the river is by the Burkesville road. Points from which the works can be shelled can be reached with but little danger of injury from their heavy guns.

The information upon which I made the attack deceived me completely as to the number of the enemy, the strength of their works, and the possibility of their being re-enforced. I was told that they had from 1,200 to 1,800 men, that no re-enforcements could possibly reach them, and was led to believe that their works were nothing more than rifle pits, and they perhaps unfinished, which could be easily taken by a bold dash with an infantry force, when in truth they had not less than 2,500 men; their works were extensive and complete and mounted with heavier guns than I had, and I am credibly informed that on Saturday they received a re-enforcement of 200 men, and during that night or early on yesterday morning a regiment of 500 old troops, under Colonel Dunham, arrived. In the last interview had with them at the termination of the truce Colonel Dunham had assumed the command. He had been in the fort for some time, but had declined to supersede Colonel Wilson [Wilder] until the termination of the truce. It is due to Colonel Scott, Louisiana cavalry, from whom I received my information, to say that he was himself misled as to the strength and disposition of the enemy by the fact that on Saturday night, when he demanded the surrender of the fort, the commander answered that he could not surrender to a cavalry brigade, leaving the inference to be drawn that if he had been supported by an infantry force they would have surrendered to it. I do not understand how he was deceived as to the possibility of re-enforcements coming to them.

I fear that I may have incurred censure at headquarters by my action in this matter, but with the information in my possession I felt that it was my duty to make the attempt and I could only believe that the result would be successful. This impression was strengthened at the beginning of the attack by the following incidents: A large force of the enemy, estimated at from two to three regiments, which we found drawn up in line of battle, retreated with but little resistance before the advance of my battalion of sharpshooters, who drove them into their rifle pits, and at the same time the enemy set fire to what I supposed to be the railroad bridge, but what, as I afterwards found, was a church near their principal work. In addition to this their artillery refused to reply to ours except by an occasional shot until ours had been moved up within a few hundred yards of them. These facts, connected with the information which I had previously received, forced me to the belief that the enemy were preparing to retreat or that they could be easily forced to surrender.

My heaviest loss was on the left, which was under the immediate command of Colonel Smith, of the Tenth Mississippi Regiment. I had originally instructed him to advance upon the left and observe the enemy, and, if he thought he could do so successfully, to charge the intrenchments; but afterwards, when I had gained a position upon the enemy's left and in rear of the intrenchments upon which Colonel Smith was moving, I sent an order to him to join me with his command; but unfortunately before the order reached him he had made the fatal charge in which he and Lieut. Col. [James G.] Bullard and many of his officers and men fell. Colonel Smith was found in advance of his own regiment almost at the very foot of the intrenchments. A number of Federal officers who witnessed his conduct testify in glowing terms to his dauntless intrepidity.

Lieutenant-Colonel Moore, of Blythe's Mississippi regiment, who was ordered with his regiment to support Colonel Smith, fell mortally wounded while leading his men on. I shall not attempt to express my admiration of the conduct of my troops. There was not an officer nor a man who did not discharge his whole duty with a cheerfulness and courage worthy of all honor. After marching for the greater part of two nights in succession and fighting unceasingly for four hours without food or water the only murmurs that I heard were when the flag of truce demanding the surrender of the fort was sent in, and some of the troops who did not understand its object feared that it was designed to make terms in our own behalf; and as we fell back last night their only wish seemed to be that the enemy might leave the cover of his walls and follow us.

We took one prisoner, who had been sent out as a skirmisher, and a Missourian who was in the enemy's service and who was on picket deserted to us; both of these are now here. I captured and brought off from the depot at Woodsonville 1 hand car and 3 barrels salt. I captured here 3 boarding cars, 4 box cars, 2 hand cars, 9 hogsheads tobacco, 1 barrel salt, 2 boxes new clothing, 6 boxes worn clothing, and 1 box boots. The salt has been turned over to the commissary, and the clothing and boots to the quartermaster, who has distributed them to the troops. The tobacco belongs to citizens. I shall send all my wounded who can bear it to Glasgow to-day.

I am, major, very respectfully, your obedient servant,

JAMES R. CHALMERS,
Brigadier-General.

Major HUGER, *A. A. G., Res. Div., Right Wing Army of the Miss.*

—

HDQRS. SECOND BRIGADE, RESERVE DIVISION,
RIGHT WING ARMY OF THE MISSISSIPPI,
Fort Craig, near Munfordville, Ky., September 19, 1862.

MAJOR: I have the honor to submit the following report of the action of this brigade from the 12th to the 17th instant inclusive:

In obedience to orders from Major-General Withers, received on the afternoon of the 12th while passing through Glasgow, Ky., I halted my brigade at Beaver Creek, about 3 miles from that place, on the Louisville turnpike, to cook rations, and then moved forward at 8 p. m., leaving all my wagons except the ordnance train in camp at Cave City. I sent forward a small detachment of cavalry which had been furnished to me by General Withers, under the command of my aide-de-camp, Lieut. G. T. Banks, with orders to enter the town without giving any alarm, if possible, to take possession of the telegraph and post-offices and to place guards on all the avenues of approach so as to prevent all passing, and I followed them as rapidly as possible with the infantry and artillery. After a march of 11 miles, which was made in excellent order, we reached Cave City at 11.30 p. m. The town was completely taken by surprise, and possession was immediately and quietly taken of the telegraph and post-offices and of the railroad depot. It being expected that one or more trains of the enemy's troops would pass up the road from Bowling Green toward Louisville the track was torn up and other preparations were made to capture it, but the train did not make its appearance.

The brigade was encamped near the town and strong pickets were thrown out on all the roads leading to it. By the aid of Sergeant Bradford, First Regiment Louisiana Infantry, who had been detailed to accompany me for that purpose, I established telegraphic communication with Louisville and intercepted a few messages passing to and from the enemy at that place, the most of which, together with those found on file in the office, I forwarded to you. Unfortunately the wires had been cut by our troops south of Cave City, and the operator at Louisville soon began to suspect that something was wrong; otherwise I might have obtained more valuable information.

On the morning of the 13th I made a reconnaissance of the country in the direction of Munfordville, and finding a mill near Horse Cave containing a considerable quantity of wheat I ordered the Tenth Mississippi Regiment (Col. R. A. Smith) and Blythe's Mississippi regiment (commanded by Lieut. Col. James Moore) up to take possession of it, with the view of having the wheat ground for the use of the troops. During the day I learned from intercepted dispatches that the advance of our army to Glasgow had thrown the enemy into consternation along the whole line from Louisville to Bowling Green, and that they were under the impression that the force occupying Cave City was 7,000 strong and was advancing on Munfordville, where they had a camp of instruction, from which place they were asking for re-enforcements and provisions.

Late in the afternoon I intercepted a dispatch from General Gilbert, commanding at Louisville, ordering transportation to be ready at 7 p. m. to convey Colonel Dunham's regiment, 500 strong, and five days' rations for 3,000 men to Munfordville. About 9 p. m. I received a message from Colonel Scott, commanding brigade of cavalry, through one of his officers, to the effect that the force of the enemy at Munfordville was not more than 1,800 men, entirely raw troops, and that they were fortifying their position, but that the railroad and telegraph had been destroyed in their rear, cutting them off completely from all communication and re-enforcements. He also informed me that he intended to attack them at daylight on the following morning, and desired that I would co-operate with him with a part of my force.

Relying upon the information thus received and that gleaned from the intercepted dispatches I determined to support him with my whole brigade, leaving only a sufficient force behind to protect Cave City and its approaches, and accordingly moved out of the town at 10 p. m., and, after a march of 12 miles, I reached the enemy's lines in front of Munfordville at daylight on the 14th instant. The enemy's works, as I afterward found, consisted of three distinct parts. On their right was a range of rifle pits sufficient to contain 3,000 men, semicircular in form, and terminating on the extreme right in a strong stockade, which stood upon the brink of the lofty bluff overlooking Green River. About 100 yards to the left of this was another rifle pit capable of sheltering at least one regiment, and still farther to the left and upon higher ground stood their principal work, a regular bastion earthwork, in and about which were stationed about 300 men. The passages between these works were almost entirely protected from our fire by the nature of the ground. The whole work protected the railroad bridge over Green River, and was connected with the opposite bank by a pontoon bridge. While on the march I had learned from citizens who had been in the works that they were much stronger than I had at first been led to believe; but I was unable to obtain any definite or clear description of them, and the foggy nature of the morning prevented me from making any satisfactory reconnaissance. I learned, however, that the right of their works could be shelled from an eminence known as Mrs. Lewis' Hill, and my original intention was to open a fire upon them from that point for some time before making an assault. With this view the battalion of sharpshooters was ordered forward to drive in the enemy's pickets, who were stationed in the woods on the left of the turnpike.

The firing commenced at 5 a. m. by the sharpshooters driving the enemy's pickets from the hill across an open field to their supporting line, which was supposed to be two regiments of infantry. Maj. W. C. Richards, commanding battalion of sharpshooters, was severely wounded at the first fire, and Captain West, who succeeded to the command, having sent back information of the force by which he was opposed, the Ninth and Twenty-ninth Mississippi Regiments were ordered up to his support, but the enemy were driven into their intrenchments by the sharpshooters before they could be brought into action. At the same time the battery (Ketchum's, under the command of Lieut. James Garrity) was ordered to take position on Mrs. Lewis' Hill and to open fire on the intrenchments, and the Tenth Mississippi Regiment was ordered to support it.

A heavy volume of flame and smoke which arose at this time near the enemy's work was supposed to proceed from the railroad bridge, and this, coupled with the fact that they had retired so rapidly before our advance and had refused almost altogether to reply to the fire of our artillery, led me to the belief that they were preparing to evacuate their position. I therefore determined to press forward at once against the works, and moved one section of the artillery, under the immediate command of Lieutenant Garrity, with the Seventh Mississippi (Col. W. H. Bishop), the Ninth Mississippi (Col. T. W. White), and the Twenty-ninth Mississippi Regiments (Col. E. C. Walthall), to the knob, an eminence in front of the bastion fort, from which I opened a fire on it. Blythe's regiment was left to guard the ordnance train, and the sharpshooters were pressed forward to keep the enemy within their works. The section of the battery left on Lewis' Hill, under the command of Lieutenant Bond, was ordered to move farther down the hill and nearer to the rifle pits on our left, and Colonel Smith was instructed to move with the Tenth Mississippi Regiment to the banks of the river and to advance up it toward the fort as near as possible, and, if he saw a favorable opportunity, to storm them. The artillery on the knob opened a rapid fire on the bastion fort, but owing to the light caliber of the guns and the very defective character of the ammunition with but little effect. From this point I discovered a house surrounded with woods on the right of the fort and within range of it, and I at once ordered the Ninth and Twenty-ninth Regiments to move forward and occupy the woods opposite the fort, with instructions to keep the men under cover, to approach the works as closely as possible, and to storm them if they could do so successfully. The Seventh Regiment was ordered to follow them within supporting distance. This was accomplished with small loss, the enemy stationed in the woods falling back at once before our advance. Our regiments attained a position under cover within range of the fort, and the sharpshooters, who were deployed in front as skirmishers, kept the enemy closely within their walls. I immediately ordered up the artillery from the knob and planted it near the house, not more than 200 yards from the fort, and in a position where it was protected in some measure from the fire of the enemy by a depression in the ground and by the timber. This position completely flanked the enemy's rifle pits and stockade on the center and left of their works, and if my guns had been of longer range I could have rendered them untenable. The distance was, however, too great for my guns, which could only reach the bastion and the rifle pits in the center, from the latter of which their fire drew every man. The fire of my artillery was maintained from this point during the continuance of hostilities.

When making this movement I notified Colonel Smith of it, and repeated my previous instructions to him.

In attempting to carry out these instructions, being entirely ignorant of the ground to be passed over, he came within range of the enemy's guns from the right of their work and in front of the abatis of fallen trees, in a position where it was equally dangerous to advance or retreat, and immediately advanced against the works. Hearing the firing, I ordered Blythe's regiment to support the Tenth, and that regiment was soon engaged with the enemy in endeavoring, under a very heavy fire, to force its way through the abatis. In this attack Colonel Smith, of the Tenth Mississippi Regiment, was dangerously wounded; Lieutenant-Colonel Bullard, of the same regiment, was killed; Lieutenant-Colonel Moore, commanding Blythe's Mississippi regiment, was mortally wounded, with a large number of their officers and men. By the fall of these officers the command of Blythe's regiment devolved upon Maj. [J. C.] Thompson, and that of the Tenth upon Capt. [J. M.] Walker, both of whom discharged that duty during the remainder of the engagement in a highly satisfactory manner. As soon as I was informed of the loss of these officers I instructed Maj. [James] Barr [jr.], of the Tenth Mississippi Regiment, who was acting on my staff as inspector-general of the brigade, to assume command of his regiment, but before he could reach it the firing had ceased. Before I knew the disastrous nature of this attack, believing that the bastion fort could be carried by a combined attack by my whole force, I sent orders to Colonel Smith to move to the right and join me with the two regiments under his command; but he was wounded before the order reached him, and his regiment was so engaged that it would have been impossible to withdraw it without great loss. Perceiving, however, after the order was sent that a furious struggle was going on upon the enemy's right, I thought it a favorable opportunity to move against them upon the left, and I at once ordered the three regiments under my immediate command to advance from their cover, the Seventh on the right, the Ninth on the left, and the Twenty-ninth in the center, and to storm the fort. This movement was made in fine style. The regiments moved in a perfect line across the road and up the hill upon which the fort stood to a point where they were in some measure protected by a depression in the ground and by the ruins of a church which the enemy had burned early in the morning and which we had supposed to be the railroad bridge. Here they halted and poured in so deadly a fire that the enemy were compelled to seek shelter behind their walls, and only ventured to return the fire from their artillery or by holding their guns at arm's length over the walls without exposing their persons. Seeing that the Ninth Mississippi Regiment was more exposed than the others I ordered it to move by the right flank in rear of the others, intending to form it on the right of the Seventh and to advance it against the fort from the direction of the river. The order to advance was repeated and the foremost files were within 25 yards of the ditch and pressing rapidly forward toward it when a fire from artillery was unexpectedly opened from a hill in our rear, the shells falling among our ranks. Supposing that the enemy must have established a battery in our rear I ordered the Seventh and Ninth Regiments to about-face and charge it. This order was promptly obeyed and these regiments were already within a short distance of the battery, which fell back before them, when I was informed that it was attached to Colonel Scott's cavalry brigade and had come up to our relief. I immediately halted the two regiments, intending to lead them again upon the fort, but unfortunately the other regiment, not understanding in the confusion the object of the movement which had been made and supposing that a retreat had been ordered, had fallen back. It being impossible to renew the attack at once under the circumstances, the whole force was withdrawn in good order to a position in the woods near that from which they had made the attack. It was then 9.30 a. m.

A careful examination of the ground since the engagement has satisfied me that had we not been surprised and disconcerted by the unexpected fire from Colonel Scott's artillery in our rear this attack would have been successful. The enemy had in that work, as I have since learned, only about 300 men, who had been driven by our fire to hide themselves, while I had before it not less than 700 men, who were pressing forward toward it in the most gallant and determined manner. A few steps farther would have carried them into the ditch, and once in close contest the issue could not be doubted. That work once taken and the rest lay at our mercy. Its guns could have been turned to rake the other works, and the remainder of the enemy's force would have had no choice but to surrender or be slaughtered.

Soon after regaining our position I had an interview with Colonel Scott, who said he had made repeated efforts to inform me of his presence and of his intention to plant his battery upon the hill from which it fired. Unfortunately none of them had reached me. He also stated that he was inclined to believe that the enemy would surrender if a demand was made upon them, from the fact that when he had approached the place on the afternoon of the day before from the opposite side of the river and demanded its surrender Colonel Wilder, the officer in command, had replied that he could not surrender to a cavalry force, leaving it to be inferred that he would surrender if attacked by infantry and artillery; and he repeated what his messenger had told me on the night before in reference to the destruction of the railroad and telegraph in their rear and the impossibility of their receiving any re-enforcements. At his suggestion I addressed a note to Colonel Wilder by Maj. [J. B.] Morgan, of the Twenty-ninth Mississippi Regiment, under a flag of truce, stating my strength and renewing the demand for a surrender, to which Colonel Wilder replied, saying that he had also been re-enforced since the engagement began and refusing to surrender, but proposing a truce to enable both parties to remove their dead and wounded. I acceded to this proposition, stating in my reply that I would take as much time as might be necessary and would notify him of its conclusion. Copies of the notes which passed between us are herewith inclosed and numbered from 1 to 3.

Fatigue parties were immediately sent out to remove the dead and wounded, but as tools for burying the former had to be obtained from the enemy, from whom I could get only a few, and as the latter had to be removed more than a mile in order to put them in comfortable quarters, this work was not accomplished until 5 p. m. In accordance with the terms of the truce I then notified Colonel Wilder that it was at an end, when, much to my surprise, Colonel Dunham, who had assumed command of the fort in the mean time, requested that it might be prolonged in order to enable them to complete burying their dead. Major Morgan, who bore my message, promised that I would make no offensive movement, and afterward Colonels White and Walthall, whom I sent to communicate with Colonel Dunham as soon as I heard of his request, agreed that this might continue for one hour.

After my interview with Colonel Scott in the morning I determined that I would not renew my attack upon the works. My previous attempt had satisfied me that I had been deceived as to the strength of the enemy's works, as well as their numbers and disposition and the possibility of their being re-enforced. They had at the commencement of the engagement, as I have since learned from their officers, about 2,300 men, and were re-enforced by Colonel Dunham with 500 men from the north side of the river during its continuance. Their works were mounted with ten guns, of which there were two 12-pounder Napoleon guns, one 3¼-inch Parrott gun, and the others 6-pounders, mostly rifled. My own force, owing to the heavy details left as pickets at Cave City, numbered only 1,613 officers and men, including Ketchum's battery of two 6-pounders and two 12-pounder howitzers. The force with which Colonel Scott joined me was 300 cavalry, with two small mountain howitzers, and he reported that there were two regiments of cavalry belonging to his brigade on the opposite side of the river. I felt assured that with this force, disproportioned as it was to that of the enemy, I might, by a determined assault, have taken the fort, but the heavy loss which I had already sustained, especially on my left, and the certainty that it would be greatly increased by a renewal of the attack, coupled with the conviction that the place could be easily and speedily taken by a larger force without loss of life, determined me not to make another attempt upon it. As soon therefore as notice had been given to the enemy of the termination of the truce I withdrew my troops under cover of the woods to the turnpike. While on the march I was informed of the request of Colonel Dunham that the truce might be prolonged, and immediately sent Colonels White and Walthall to communicate with him, as I have before stated. I halted the brigade on the turnpike just beyond the bridge crossing the railroad and remained there until the expiration of the hour agreed on, when I resumed the march and proceeded without molestation to Cave City, which I reached about midnight.

My loss in this affair was 3 officers and 32 men killed, and 28 officers and 225 men wounded, of whom some have since died. Of these the greater part in proportion to the numbers engaged fell in the attack on the right of the enemy's works. The wounded were first removed from the field to the depot and other buildings at Rowlett's Station, where their wounds were dressed, and afterward those who could bear transportation were conveyed in ambulances and wagons to Cave City, where they were placed in the hotel and depot and every possible arrangement made for their comfort. Those whom it was not thought proper to remove were left at Rowlett's Station under the charge of surgeons and with the assurance from Colonel Wilder that they should not be molested, which assurance, I am glad to say, was fully carried out.

On the following day (15th instant), having taken the pledge of the telegraphic operator captured at Cave City not to give any information to the enemy, I sent him into their lines under the charge of Capt.

[R. A.] Bell, of the Tenth Mississippi Regiment, with a flag of truce. I at the same time sent by Captain Bell a note to Colonel Dunham, requesting permission to remove such of my wounded from the hospital as might be able to bear it, and also the bodies of such as had died, which he granted at once, and in his reply stated that I could have access to my wounded at Rowlett's Station at any time. Copies of this correspondence are herewith inclosed, numbered 4 and 5.

At 5 o'clock on the morning of the 16th instant, in obedience to orders from Headquarters Right Wing Army of the Mississippi, this brigade moved from its camp at Cave City in advance of the main body toward Munfordville. About 8 a. m., when within 2½ miles of the fort, my cavalry scouts encountered those of the enemy and fired upon them, killing one horse. A detachment from the battalion of sharpshooters was immediately ordered forward as skirmishers, and soon after the whole battalion, under the command of Captain West, was ordered to advance and drive back the enemy's skirmishers, who began to show themselves in considerable numbers in the woods on the crest of Mrs. Lewis' Hill.

At this time Brigadier-General Duncan came up with his brigade and I at once resigned the command to him. A section of my battery (Ketchum's) was ordered forward to shell the woods in which the enemy's skirmishers were concealed, but after a few shots they were compelled to cease firing, as their shells were endangering our own men who were driving the enemy before them. The Seventh Mississippi Regiment was then ordered forward to support the sharpshooters, but before it could be brought into action the enemy had fallen back, and did not make another stand until they had reached their works. The sharpshooters continued to annoy the enemy until 6 p. m., when they rejoined the main body of the brigade. The remainder of the brigade was ordered to move to the left of the turnpike and was halted behind a spur of Mrs. Lewis' Hill, and afterwards, by order from General Bragg, it moved farther to the left and took position with its left resting on the river and right extending toward the turnpike, where it was entirely protected from the fire of the fort by a hill. Here we remained until the next morning, the 17th, when we were ordered up to witness the surrender of the garrison of the fort, and afterwards, by order of General Bragg, in compliment, as he stated, to our gallant attack upon the place, we took possession of the works.

The only loss sustained in this movement was by the battalion of sharpshooters, who had 3 men severely wounded while engaged with the enemy's skirmishers.

In the attack on the 14th instant I took 2 prisoners, who have since been turned over to the proper officers to be paroled with the others At Cave City we captured 3 boarding cars, 1 box car, 2 hand cars, 1 telegraphic machine and battery, 2 boxes new clothing (uniforms), 6 boxes worn clothing (uniforms), 1 box boots, and 1 barrel salt; and at Woodsonville I captured and brought off to Cave City 1 hand car and 3 barrels salt. The cars were left on the track at Cave City when our forces moved out of that place. The telegraphic machine and battery were sent to Major-General Polk. The salt was turned over to the commissary department, and the clothing and boots were turned over to the quartermaster of this brigade and issued to the men, who were greatly in need of them.

I cannot close this report without expressing my admiration of the conduct of the officers and men under my command. The cheerfulness with which they endured the hardships of the march from Chattanooga;

the alacrity with which, after a march of ordinary length during the day, they made the night march from Glasgow to Cave City and then on the succeeding night from that place to Woodsonville; the courage with which they first drove the enemy into his works and then attacked him in them, and which drew encomiums even from their foes; the endurance with which they fought for four hours against heavy odds without an opportunity for rest and with but little food or water, and the orderly manner in which, after a day of such toils, they retraced their steps to Cave City, entitle them to the highest praise that I can give; nor can I omit the opportunity to express my regret at the loss of the many brave officers and men who were killed or wounded. Most prominent among these—not more by their rank than by their high soldierly qualities—were Colonel Smith, of the Tenth Mississippi Regiment, who fell severely wounded in advance of his regiment and within a few yards of the enemy's works while leading a charge against them; Lieutenant-Colonel Bullard, of the same regiment, who was killed, and Lieutenant-Colonel Moore, commanding Blythe's Mississippi regiment, who was mortally wounded in the same attack, and Maj. W. C. Richards, commanding battalion of sharpshooters, who was severely wounded early in the action. They fell where they would have but liked to have fallen, in the very face of the enemy and while leading their men against them, but their loss will be severely felt in this brigade and their places cannot easily be supplied.

My thanks are due to the members of my staff for their gallant and efficient conduct in the separate departments. During both engagements Capt. W. A. Goodman, assistant adjutant-general; Lieut. G. T. Banks, aide-de-camp; Walter L. Strickland, volunteer aide-de-camp, whose horse was twice wounded; Maj. James Barr, jr., of the Tenth Mississippi Regiment, and acting brigade inspector, and Maj. H. H. Chalmers, acting commissary of subsistence, were constantly and actively engaged in bearing orders often under a heavy fire. Lieut. T. B. Mattison, ordnance officer, was active and efficient in the management of his train. Dr. J. H. P. Westbrook, senior surgeon of the brigade, proved himself eminently fitted for his position by his skill and energy displayed in the care and treatment of the wounded, and Maj. [J. M.] Thompson, brigade quartermaster, was exceedingly prompt in bringing up wagons and other vehicles from Cave City for their removal to that place.

I am, major, very respectfully, your obedient servant,

JAMES R. CHALMERS,
Brigadier-General.

Maj. D. E. HUGER,
  A. A. G., Res. Div., Right Wing Army of the Miss.

[Indorsement.]

HEADQUARTERS DEPARTMENT No. 2,
Knoxville, Tenn., November 3, 1862.

This attack was unauthorized and injudicious; but the conduct of the troops and commander in action reflects credit on both, and adds but another proof to the many of their distinguished gallantry. The loss of the gallant and admired Colonel Smith, with the other valuable officers and men of this distinguished brigade, will be mourned by their comrades and the country.

BRAXTON BRAGG,
General, Commanding.

[Inclosure No. 1.]

———— —, 1862.

Col. J. T. WILDER, *Comdg. U. S. Forces near Munfordville, Ky.:*

SIR: You have made a gallant defense of your position, and in order to prevent further bloodshed I demand an unconditional surrender. I have five regiments of infantry and one battalion of infantry sharp-shooters. I have just been re-enforced by a brigade of cavalry under Colonel Scott, and also one battery of artillery. A short distance in my rear is General Bragg's army, and you cannot escape; the track has been torn up behind you on the other side of the river.*

Very truly, yours, &c.,

JAMES R. CHALMERS,
Brig. Gen., Comdg. Second Brig., Right Wing Army of the Miss.

[Inclosure No. 2.]

FORT CRAIG, *September* 14, 1862.

Brig. Gen. JAMES R. CHALMERS,
Comdg. Second Brig., Right Wing Army of the Mississippi:

SIR: Allow me to thank you for your compliments. Re-enforcements have arrived for me. I shall defend myself until overpowered. Your men fight gallantly. If you wish you can remove your wounded and dead. Notify me if you wish to do so. I think I can hold my position against any force you can bring; at least I will try to do so.*

I am, sir, respectfully, yours, &c.,

J. T. WILDER,
Colonel, Commanding U. S. Forces at Munfordville, Ky.

[Inclosure No. 3.]

HDQRS. SECOND BRIGADE, RESERVE DIVISION,
RIGHT WING ARMY OF THE MISSISSIPPI,
September 14, 1862.

Col. J. T. WILDER, *Comdg. U. S. Forces, Munfordville, Ky.:*

COLONEL: Your note has just been received. I will accept your proposition to remove my wounded and dead, and for that purpose will take sufficient time to remove them to my hospital, which is some 2 miles in my rear, and will notify you when I have removed them. I will set about the work at once.

I have the honor to be, very truly, yours,

JAMES R. CHALMERS,
Brigadier-General, Commanding.

[Inclosure No. 4.]

HDQRS. SECOND BRIGADE, RESERVE DIVISION,
ARMY OF THE MISSISSIPPI,
Cave City, Ky., September 15, 1862.

Colonel DUNHAM, *Comdg. U. S. Forces, Munfordville, Ky.:*

COLONEL: I send Capt. R. A. Bell, Company E, Tenth Mississippi Regiment, with flag of truce in charge of Mr. Scott, telegraphic operator at this place, who has been allowed to pass from our lines to yours. I respectfully ask that permission be given to Captain Bell to remove

---

* See these as quoted in Wilder's report, p. 961.

some of our wounded and the bodies of those of our dead which remain unburied.

I am, colonel, with great respect, your obedient servant,

JAMES R. CHALMERS,
Brigadier-General.

[Inclosure No. 5.]

ROWLETT'S STATION, KY., *September* 15, 1862.

Brig. Gen. JAMES R. CHALMERS,
Comdg. Second Brigade, Army of the Mississippi:

GENERAL: Your note by Capt. R. A. Bell, with flag of truce, is received. Your request is granted. You can have access to your hospital at Rowlett's Station until notice to the contrary is given. Your communication must be by way of pike or railroad, accompanied by flag of truce.

I am, sir, yours, respectfully,

C. L. DUNHAM,
Colonel, Commanding,
By J. T. WILDER,
Colonel Seventeenth Indiana.

—

[Addenda.]

Casualties at battle of Munfordville (or Woodsonville), Ky., September 14–17, 1862.

	Killed.	Wounded.	Missing.	Total.
ARMY OF THE MISSISSIPPI.				
Second Brigade, Reserve Division, Right Wing:	4	16	......	20
7th Mississippi Regiment	9	44	......	53
9th Mississippi Regiment	13	95	......	108
10th Mississippi Regiment	5	36	......	41
29th Mississippi Regiment	4	40	......	44
Blythe's (44th) Mississippi Regiment	......	12	......	12
Battalion of sharpshooters	......	7	......	7
Ketchum's battery				
Total	35	250	......	285

No. 6.

Report of Lieut. James Garrity, commanding W. H. Ketchum's Battery.

CAMP AT CAVE CITY, KY., —— —, 1862.

SIR: I have the honor to report the part taken by Ketchum's battery in the engagement of yesterday:

We took possession on an elevation in front of the enemy's works about 1,000 yards distant about 5 a. m. and immediately opened fire, which we kept up until the two howitzers under my immediate command were ordered to a position on the right and in front of the fort; but finding it was out of range I was ordered forward and took position within point-blank range of the enemy's principal work, and kept up a steady and continuous fire on the fort and breastworks until about 9 o'clock, at which time the firing ceased on both sides.

The casualties in this section were 7 men wounded, 1 horse killed, and 6 wounded.

The left section, commanded by Lieutenant Bond, remained in the position the battery first occupied until 6 a. m. It was then ordered to move to a hill half a mile distant to the left, and kept up a steady fire on the enemy's breastworks until he ceased firing. Casualties none.

I take pleasure in being able to represent the conduct of the officers and men under my command as being highly commendable.

Number of men engaged, 100.

Very respectfully,

JAMES GARRITY,
First Lieutenant, Commanding Ketchum's Battery.

Brig. Gen. JAMES R. CHALMERS,
Comdg. Second Brig., Withers' Div., R. W. Army of the Miss.

No. 7.

Report of Col. John W. Frazer, Twenty-eighth Alabama Infantry, of operations September 16.

MUNFORDVILLE, KY., *September* 18, 1862.

CAPTAIN: In obedience to circular just received I have the honer to report:

On reaching the range of the guns on the fortifications on the 16th instant this command was moved in line of battle to the left of the position previously occupied by the battery of Captain Waters and halted, supporting the battery. Before the battery opened fire the regiment was ordered to move by the right flank and take position on the side of the mountain on the right of the Munfordville road. Here it rested in line for an hour or more, when, in accordance with orders, we marched to the brow of the mountain to support our skirmishers. While here we received an occasional shell from the works and were fired on by the enemy's skirmishers. Two companies from our left were then detailed to drive in the enemy's skirmishers occupying a wood in front and on the opposite side of the valley from us. This detachment, commanded by Capt. John H. Turpin, Company B, moved quickly forward, and after exchanging a few shots drove in the enemy's [skirmishers], as it is reported, with some slight loss or damage to them. These woods were held by this detachment until the command was relieved from its position on the mountain by a portion of the command of Major-General Buckner. After being relieved, as above stated, I reported with my command at the foot of the mountain, and marched with the brigade to a point a half mile northeast of the works, when the brigade bivouacked for the night.

One private of Company L, wounded by a spent ball in the finger, constituted all the damage sustained by this command.

It gratifies the commanding officer to be able to say that the men and officers were calm, cool, and cheerful during the entire day and obeyed every command with great alacrity and promptness.

I have the honor, captain, to be, very respectfully,

JNO. W. FRAZER,
Commanding Twenty-eighth Alabama Regiment.

Capt. P. H. THOMSON,
A. A. G., Fourth Brig., Res. Div., R. W. Army of the Miss.

No. 8.

Report of Col. W. H. Bishop, Seventh Mississippi Infantry, of operations September 14.

CAVE CITY, *September 15, 1862.*

CAPTAIN: I have the honor to submit to you the following report of the part taken in yesterday's engagement by this regiment:

About sunrise I received orders to follow after the right section of the battery which took position on a hill on the right of the Munfordville road. Here I received orders to take my position on the left of the Ninth Mississippi Regiment. This regiment had already passed the battery and entered a corn field beyond to the northeast, and before I could reach the position to which I was ordered I received another order to hold my regiment in reserve behind the Ninth and Twenty-ninth Regiments. This order was in a few minutes followed by another order to move forward and make the attack between the Ninth and Twenty-ninth. I ordered my regiment forward on the right of the Twenty-ninth, supposing the Ninth to be already on my right in advance, where I heard pretty brisk firing. I moved into a small corn field about 150 or 200 yards from the breastworks and on the left of their fort or stonghold. From this position I intended making a charge, but immediately after entering this field the firing in advance on my right almost entirely ceased, and no attack having been made by the Twenty-ninth on my left, I ordered my men to lie down, intending to confer with Colonel Walthall for an immediate and simultaneous charge, my own regiment being too small to charge alone. Almost instantly after this order the center of my regiment, which was imperfectly screened from observation, received a severe fire of grape, which killed 3 men and wounded 5 others. I immediately ordered the regiment back about 20 yards to the fence, behind which they could be effectually screened and protected. Here a lieutenant, commanding a company of sharpshooters (whom I had previously mistaken for a portion of the Ninth), asked me for assistance to drive the enemy back on the right. I ordered three companies forward deployed as skirmishers. Shortly afterward, on being informed that these companies were exposed to a severe cross-fire from the right, I moved the regiment in that direction, and soon after with the Ninth and Twenty-ninth made an attack near the enemy's fort. This attack had progressed only a few minutes when I was ordered to fall back and attack a battery on the right and to our rear. While moving in that direction I received word that the battery was a Confederate battery. A flag of truce ended further aggressive movements.

I would remark that the heavy details for picket duty, the number left sick and unable to march from this place, besides infirmary details, &c., left me only about 123 effective men and 141 aggregate in the action Of this number 4 were killed, 15 wounded, and 1 missing The men generally were cool and acted with courage.

I am, captain, very respectfully, your obedient servant,

W. H. BISHOP,
Colonel, Commanding.

Capt. W. A. GOODMAN,
Assistant Adjutant-General.

No. 9.

Report of Col. Thomas W. White, Ninth Mississippi Infantry, of operations September 14.

SEPTEMBER 19, 1862.

SIR : I have the honor to report the part taken by my regiment in the attack made by the Second Brigade of Withers' division on the enemy at Woodsonville, Sunday, the 14th instant:

We left Cave City with the brigade at 10 p. m. Saturday, and marching all night reached the hills near the railroad while the sharpshooters were driving in the pickets and skirmishers of the enemy. We followed them in and were formed in line in the field north and east of the railroad depot at Rowlett's Station. We then marched by the flank through the woods on the hill to our right, and on reaching the orchard, on its northern base, were ordered to form in line in the woods near the house of Woodson and charge the fort on the northeastern end of the enemy's lines. The regiment formed as desired, but on examining the fort and rifle pits supporting it I concluded to wait a few moments until Colonel Walthall arrived, who was directed to form near and support me. In the mean time two guns of Ketchum's battery were brought and put in position in the grove in front of the house and commenced to fire on the fort and lines of the enemy. General Chalmers arriving now on the ground, and my regiment being formed in line with the Twenty-ninth, we moved up amid a very heavy fire toward the fort through a corn patch and over several fences, and crossing the turnpike road, took shelter under a bank on the road-side about 100 yards from the fort and commenced a very heavy and well-directed fire on the men who were firing from the walls of the fort. In passing through the field and while firing behind the bank we lost several men. The Twenty-ninth being on my right and the ground being sheltered for them near the fort, part of my right wing moved up nearer the fort on the left of that regiment. We had now been over the road some fifteen or twenty minutes when I heard the order to charge given and passed along the line from the right. The regiment advanced at a run through a very heavy fire of grape-shot and small-arms toward the fort. Our men got within some 40 steps, but recoiled and returned in confusion to the bank near the road, when they formed and prepared to charge again, all of them stopping as soon as the road was reached. At this time I received an order to move the regiment by the right flank to charge a light battery which was reported to be firing at us from the hill on our right. As the noise was great and the order given on our right flank the regiment did not get off in good order, some leaving in advance of others as the word was passed along the line. We formed, however, in a corn field back of a house and prepared to charge on the battery above mentioned, when we were informed by an aide of General Chalmers that the battery was one of Colonel Scott's command, and ordered [us] to retire under cover of the woods, where the sinks in the ground gave shelter from the enemy's fire.

In the charge on the fort I lost several most gallant officers wounded and many brave men killed. Where all behaved so well I will not particularize, but the regiment, officers and men, did all that could have been expected or required of them.

I inclose a list * herewith showing the casualties, from which it will

---

* Embodied in Report No. 5, p. 982.

be seen that out of an aggregate of 282 men engaged we lost 9 killed and 44 wounded.

I am, captain, your most obedient servant,

T. W. WHITE,
Colonel Ninth Mississippi Regiment.

Capt. W. A. GOODMAN, *Assistant Adjutant-General.*

No. 10.

Report of Capt. James L. Finley, Tenth Mississippi Infantry, of operations September 14.

SEPTEMBER 27, 1862.

CAPTAIN: I have the honor to make the following report of the part taken in the action of September 14 by the Tenth Mississippi Regiment, 340 men, Col. R. A. Smith commanding:

After marching from Cave City on the night of the 13th instant and arriving near the crossing of the Cave City road and the Louisville and Nashville Railroad filed to the left with and in support of Ketchum's battery. After standing in line of battle some fifteen or twenty minutes was ordered to charge the enemy's works, which order was obeyed. After being under fire some three hours a flag of truce made its appearance. Demanding the object of the flag of truce, was informed by the officer bearing said flag that it was for the purpose of clearing the field of the killed and wounded. We immediately removed our killed and wounded, arms and accouterments, buried our dead, then retired at the proper time to the Cave City road, where we were joined by the balance of the brigade and marched back to Cave City.

I beg leave to state that the conduct of George Fugel, of Company D, color-sergeant, and B. F. Bonds, of Company E, and R. B. Tatom, of Company C, color-guards, was highly commendable and worthy of notice in this report.

I am, sir, very respectfully, your obedient servant,

JAMES L. FINLEY,
Captain, Commanding.

Capt. W. A. GOODMAN,
Asst. Adjt. Gen., Second Brigade, Withers' Division.

No. 11.

Report of Col. Edward C. Walthall, Twenty-ninth Mississippi Infantry, of operations September 14.

SEPTEMBER 15, 1862.

CAPTAIN: I respectfully submit the following as a report of the engagement on yesterday near Munfordville in what concerns this command:

About 6 o'clock in the morning, near the forks of the road near the bridge, I was ordered by Brigadier-General Chalmers to move forward my command within supporting distance of the battalion of sharpshooters, which I did, and drew up the regiment in line of battle about 200 yards in their rear, they having been previously deployed as skirmishers in the woods in front. Soon after this I received an order from General Chalmers, through Capt. [M.] Conly, to move my command across the road to the left. This done I received an order through Mr. Strickland to move to the right of the road and form on the left of the Ninth Mississippi Regiment, and just as the command was in the act of moving Captain Conly brought me an order to advance through the open field to the right of the position I then occupied as soon as I saw the Ninth Mississippi Regiment pass out of the woods into a field still farther to the right. In passing through this field I was fired on from the earthworks on the left and 2 privates were killed. After crossing the field I received an order through Major Barr to move to the right and support the sharpshooters and carry the works. On reaching the place indicated I discovered the Seventh Regiment in front of me, and they immediately moved off to the right. While they were moving General Chalmers came up and ordered me to move up under shelter of some houses on the hill in front of one of the forts of the enemy and fire on them. The command was moved up, the companies on the right partially sheltered behind the houses, and then advanced partly under the protection of a small hill in front to within 20 yards of the fort. After firing and receiving a heavy fire for a few moments a bayonet charge was ordered by General Chalmers. I gave the command and the charge was attempted but without success, the earthworks being about 10 feet high and surrounded by a deep ditch about 8 feet wide. After this the firing on either side was kept up for ten or fifteen minutes, when, it being manifest that my command could effect nothing in the position it then occupied, I retired to the woods in rear of the houses above named and halted under cover of a hill. I came off in good order. As soon as I reached this position I was ordered by General Chalmers to move my command to a depression in the hill-side near the battery to support it if necessary. Soon after I reached that point the firing ceased and was renewed no more.

I carried to the field 25 officers, 50 non-commissioned officers, and 232 privates. The number of killed and wounded is furnished below.*

I am, sir, very respectfully, your obedient servant,

E. C. WALTHALL,
Colonel, Commanding.

Capt. W. A. GOODMAN, *Assistant Adjutant-General.*

No. 12.

Report of Maj. John C. Thompson, Blythe's (Forty-fourth) Mississippi Infantry, of operations September 14.

CAMP NEAR CAVE CITY, KY., *September 15, 1862.*

SIR: In obedience to your order of to-day I have the honor to report that at about 7 o'clock on the morning of Sunday, the 14th instant, the Blythe Mississippi Regiment, consisting of 281 rank and file aggregate, commanded by Lieut. Col. James Moore, was ordered to leave the railroad depot at Woodsonville, to proceed to the battle ground, distant about three-fourths of a mile, and report to Col. [R. A.] Smith, com-

_____
* Nominal list omitted shows 5 officers wounded, 5 enlisted men killed, and 34 wounded.

manding the Tenth Mississippi Regiment. Having no guide, and being unacquainted with the position of the regiment, we had to be guided by the sound of the guns. When arrived near the breastworks of the enemy we were saluted with heavy and successive volleys of musketry. Colonel Moore was at the center, Capt. [W. P.] Malone on the left, and I on the right of our regiment. Their fire was immediately returned and was kept up with animation on both sides for about two hours, when I was informed that Colonel Moore was shot down. Proceeding at once to the center, I found him lying on the ground apparently mortally wounded. I immediately ordered the firing to cease and the men to lie close to the ground. This order was given to induce the enemy to believe that we had withdrawn under cover of the smoke. The firing by the enemy having partially ceased, the men were ordered to fall back quietly and with as little noise as possible. The retreat was made in fine order, and we halted at a distance of 80 or 100 yards to ground where we were partially protected by a slight elevation. The line was formed, but seeing that we were still exposed I again ordered them to fall back to a distance of about 100 yards, where they were again halted and formed. The falling back was done in fine order and without the loss or injury of a man. About this time the flag of truce was sent in.

The Blythe regiment was animated with the most heroic spirit, and throughout the conflict displayed a coolness and courage that defied all obstacles. The retreat was made without loss, and when the line was reformed the same eagerness was displayed which had been exhibited at the onset. The regiment is entitled to high commendation for its conduct on the occasion.

Appended I send the report* of killed and wounded, with the nature of their wounds, made by the regimental surgeon, Dr. D. A. Kinchloe, from which it will be seen that the number of killed was 4, wounded 38.

Respectfully submitted.

JNO. C. THOMPSON,
Major, Commanding.

Brigadier-General CHALMERS.

No. 13.

Report of Col. A. J. Lythgoe, Nineteenth South Carolina Infantry, of operations September 16–17.

SEPTEMBER 18, 1862.

The Nineteenth Regiment South Carolina Volunteers left the camp near Cave City at 4 a. m. on the morning of the 16th instant, moved with the Fourth Brigade, to which it is attached, to a short distance of the fort at Woodsonville, where the general commanding the brigade assigned it to a position on an eminence on the right of the road. In passing to it the regiment was for a short time exposed to the fire of grape and shell. One man, a private in Company I, had his haversack strap cut by a grape-shot. The regiment was placed in the position to which it was assigned, when one company was thrown out as skirmishers. This company soon became engaged with the pickets of the enemy at long range. Two companies of the Twenty-eighth Alabama Regiment were sent out by Colonel Frazer to join the company of this regiment. The three companies then drove the pickets of the enemy into

---

* Embodied in Report No. 5, p. 982.

their trenches, when the firing ceased and the regiment was ordered to move still farther to the right into a body of woods, where it remained until the morning of the 17th instant, when it was moved with the brigade to the camp in the vicinity of Munfordville.

Very respectfully,

A. J. LYTHGOE,
Colonel, Comdg. Nineteenth South Carolina Volunteers.

Capt. D. E. HUGER, *Assistant Adjutant-General.*

No. 14.

Report of O. F. West, commanding Richards' Battalion, of operations September 14.

CAMP AT CAVE CITY, *Monday, September 15, 1862.*

SIR: I have the honor to report that the battalion under the command of Maj. W. C. Richards encountered the enemy's pickets in strong force on the Munfordville road, about 1 mile south of Green River, on Sunday, September 14, at early dawn. They fired on us, and Company A was instantly deployed, and Company C was soon ordered to follow. They executed the maneuver promptly and in fine order under a heavy fire. Major Richards was at this time severely wounded, and ordered a sudden and quick forward movement. We advanced, driving the enemy before us without check, until we found ourselves within range and in full view of their intrenchments. Here I ordered a halt and firing ceased; our advanced position was held until the main body of our forces came up and the engagement became general. As soon as a line was formed for action Capt. T. W. Richards, with his company, charged on the enemy, who were concealed behind houses, and drove them before him; here he fell wounded. Lieut. J. D. Nesbitt, then taking command of his company, led it in the charge on the fort and fell dangerously wounded. The company then being without officers, Lieut. [J. T.] Fant, of the Ninth Mississippi Regiment, was ordered to take command; he was soon after severely wounded, and I ordered this company to be attached to Company A, under command of Lieutenants Day and Jones. Capt. T. Brownrigg's company was held as reserve and moved close behind the line of skirmishers in fine order.

The officers and men of this battalion conducted themselves with commendable coolness and gallantry during the entire battle.

The battalion went into the engagement with 130 men effective strength and came off with 116, having 6 men wounded and 8 missing; the missing have since reported.

Very respectfully, your obedient servant,

O. F. WEST,
Captain, Commanding Battalion.

Capt. W. A. GOODMAN.

SEPTEMBER 17, 1862.—Skirmish near Falmouth, Ky.

Report of Capt. G. W. Berry, commanding Home Guard.

CAMP 5 MILES FROM FALMOUTH, KY., *Sept.* 18, 1862.

GENERAL: On yesterday 28 cavalry attacked us at 3.30 o'clock; my men all being on scout except 11. We fought them for about forty minutes under cover of a house, when 23 of them retired, leaving 5 men and 5 horses on the ground; how many wounded were carried off I cannot tell. I counted cartridges, and saw I could not stand another forty minutes' attack, and at night fell back here.

We had only 1 wounded and he very badly. I send you the prisoner we took in hopes you can get some information from him. He tells me they have eighty pieces of artillery; also tells me that he can't understand why they are retreating.

Respectfully,

G. W. BERRY,
Commanding Home Guard.

General LEW. WALLACE.

SEPTEMBER 17–OCTOBER 3, 1862.—Evacuation of Cumberland Gap, Tenn., and march of its garrison to Greenupsburg, Ky.

REPORTS, ETC.

No. 1.—Maj. Gen. Horatio G. Wright, U. S. Army, commanding Department of the Ohio.

No. 2.—Brig. Gen. George W. Morgan, U. S. Army, including operations August 16–October 3.

No. 3.—Maj. Gen. John P. McCown, C. S. Army, commanding Department of East Tennessee, of the evacuation of Cumberland Gap.

No. 1.

Report of Maj. Gen. Horatio G. Wright, U. S. Army, commanding Department of the Ohio.

HEADQUARTERS DEPARTMENT OF THE OHIO,
Cincinnati, Ohio, October 15, 1862.

GENERAL: I have the honor to transmit herewith a copy of the report of Brig. Gen. George W. Morgan, dated the 12th instant, detailing the circumstances occasioning the withdrawal of his command from Cumberland Gap:

It appears from this report that the evacuation, which was in pursuance of the unanimous opinion of a council of the general officers of the command, was a matter of necessity, arising from their provisions being exhausted, their communications cut off, and no information of any prospect of relief being received. While the evacuation of the Gap is to be regretted, I do not see how, with starvation staring him in the face and with no certainty of relief being afforded, he could have come to any other conclusion than the one arrived at. The several communications which I had addressed to him appear not to have reached him. After the unfortunate battle near Richmond the entire country between the Ohio River and Cumberland Gap was in possession of the rebels, and communications could be sent only through the agency of individuals familiar with the country, and who of course ran great risk of capture. Several persons were found to undertake the mission, but none seem to have succeeded in getting through. The march of General Morgan from Cumberland Gap to the Ohio River was most successfully accomplished and reflects much credit on him and his officers for the skill with which it was conducted, and upon the men for the cheerfulness with which they bore the hardships of a toilsome march of over 200 miles, on scanty fare, over a country affording little subsistence, and often, for long marches, on an inadequate supply of water. The holding of Cumberland Gap has generally been considered as of the greatest moment, it being viewed as the only practicable avenue for the passage of an army into Kentucky from the Southeast. Its importance has, however, I apprehend, been much overestimated, there being several passes through the mountains which, though less easy, are nevertheless practicable, as is shown by the fact that Kirby Smith, with a rebel force of over 20,000 men, passed into Kentucky through one of them. This knowledge diminishes, in my judgment, the importance hitherto attached to the possession of the Gap, unless the neighboring avenues through the mountains into Kentucky are also held.

Very respectfully, your obedient servant,

H. G. WRIGHT,
Major-General, Commanding.

Brig. Gen. G. W. CULLUM,
    Chief of Staff, Hdqrs. of the Army, Washington, D. C.

No. 2.

Reports of Brig. Gen. George W. Morgan, U. S. Army, including operations August 16–October 3.

HEADQUARTERS UNITED STATES FORCES,
Greenupsburg, Ky., October 3, 1862.

GENERAL: On the night of the 17th of September, with the army of Stevenson 3 miles in my front, with Bragg and Marshall on my flanks, and Kirby Smith in my rear, my command marched from Cumberland Gap mid the explosion of mines and magazines and lighted by the blaze of the store-houses of the commissary and quartermaster. The sight was grand. Stevenson was taken completely by surprise. At 5 o'clock p. m. on the 17th instant I sent him three official letters. The officers of our respective flags remained together in friendly chat for an hour. I have brought away all the guns but four 30-pounders, which were destroyed by knocking off the trunnions. During our march we were constantly enveloped by the enemy's cavalry, first by the Stevenson and since by the Morgan brigade. Throughout I maintained the offensive, and on one day marched twenty hours and on three successive nights drove Morgan's men from their supper. Morgan first assailed us in the rear and then passed to our front, blockading the road and destroying subsistence. For three successive days we were limited to the water of stagnant pools and that in small quantities. We expected to meet Humphrey Marshall at this place, but have been disappointed. Unless otherwise ordered I will proceed with my column to Camp Dennison to rest and refit.

With high respect,

GEORGE W. MORGAN,
Brigadier-General, Commanding.

Maj. Gen. HORATIO G. WRIGHT,
    Cincinnati, Ohio.

HDQRS. LATE ARMY OF THE CUMBERLAND,
Portland, Ohio, October 12, 1862.

MAJOR: On the night of the 16th of August last the army of Stevenson, claimed by the enemy to be 20,000 strong, arrived in front of Cumberland Gap, and I immediately ordered Captain Martin, of Munday's cavalry, to proceed, by forced marches, to observe Rogers' and Big Creek Gaps. When within 18 miles of Rogers' Gap he encountered the advance guard of Maj. Gen. E. Kirby Smith's army, then invading Kentucky. Martin's company was attacked and routed by a greatly superior force of the enemy. General Smith, with 25,000 men, afterward increased to 30,000, established his headquarters at Barboursville, and sent two divisions, under Major-General McCown, to occupy Cumberland Ford. We were now closely enveloped by two armies, numbering 45,000 men, and our supplies were entirely cut off. In consequence of bad roads and want of proper transportation our subsistence stores were short, and I immediately placed my command on half rations, with the determination of holding out to the last extremity. In order to save the artillery, cavalry, and wagon horses from starvation, and for the further purpose of sending tried troops to re-enforce the column organizing at Lexington for our aid, I ordered 400 men of the Third Kentucky, under the gallant Colonel Garrard, to be mounted, and directed him to proceed, with Munday's cavalry, to join the United States forces then en route for our relief. A battalion of the Third Tennessee, under Colonel Houk, had been attacked by a greatly superior force at London, and after a brave resistance was compelled to retreat; but, after a fatiguing march through the mountains, succeeded in gaining Cumberland Gap. The other battalion, under Lieutenant-Colonel Chiles, did gallant service at the Big Hill and at Richmond, for which the hearty thanks of Major-General Nelson were tendered. At Richmond three battalions of my command participated in the battle against immense odds; and, though defeated, by their good conduct they preserved untarnished the honor of our flag.

The enemy's forces having been withdrawn from Cumberland Ford on September 1, I sent De Courcy's brigade to Manchester to secure supplies, though the entire country within 50 miles had been already exhausted. In the mean time I seized every available opportunity to assail the enemy, and sent two expeditions against Baptist and Rogers' Gaps, one against Big Creek Gap, and small expeditions to capture the enemy's stragglers left at Barboursville and London. In all we captured about 500 prisoners and killed and wounded 170 of the enemy, with trifling loss to ourselves. We resorted to every means to draw the enemy into a fight in front of Cumberland Gap. At one time I caused the brigade of De Courcy to be placed in ambush beyond the Poor Valley Ridge, and sent Baird's brigade 4 miles up the Virginia Valley with 50 wagons for corn, which was obtained and brought in; but the enemy adhered to his adopted policy and refused to fight, though Baird formed in line of battle in his immediate front and awaited his coming till 5 p. m. The bands struck up "Dixie," but to no effect. At that time the pickets of the two armies were within hailing distance of each other. In the hope that the enemy would be defeated in front I caused Rogers' and Big Creek Gaps to be heavily blockaded and determined to attack the enemy as he attempted to escape; but the action at Richmond was lost and the country around the Gap was stripped of every stalk of corn.

On the 9th of September I addressed a letter to Major-General Wright, by Lieut. Charles S. Medary, one of my aides-de-camp, with a verbal message that by eating the mules we could hold out sixty days. But on the 12th of September Capt. M. C. Garber, the able and energetic division quartermaster, informed me that it was impossible longer to feed the mules, and suggested that they should be sent toward the Ohio River by way of Manchester. For two reasons I decided not to do so—the hope that the mules could be converted into food, or it might become necessary to harness them to the cannon to prevent them from falling into the hands of the enemy. But without forage the mules must soon perish from hunger and the air become pestilent from their carcasses.

At this time we had been six days without bread, and the mill at Manchester supplied but little more than sufficient flour for De Courcy's brigade, and no more wheat was to be obtained. The other supplies were rapidly being exhausted, and not one syllable of intelligence had been received since the action at Richmond as to the position of Buell's army or as to what force was being organized in Kentucky under the national flag.

It was now certain that the enemy would not attack our position, and it was equally certain that two weeks from that day we would not have the means of transportation for our cannon should the enemy continue to occupy our front. While in the Gap our position was one of comparative ease and entire safety. To evacuate was to brave the worst horrors of war and the chance of being taken at disadvantage by an overwhelming force of the enemy. To hold the Gap until compelled by hunger to yield would have transferred to the enemy thirty-two guns, 14,000 stand of small-arms, vast magazines of ammunition, and palsied the arms of more than 10,000 brave men, who had been seasoned to all the hardships of war. I determined to convene a military council, and without expressing an opinion learn the views of my colleagues. Up to this time I had impressed upon the minds of my command the belief that under no circumstances would I evacuate, nor would I have ever done so had I not been convinced that it was the only wise course left open for me.

On the 10th of August I telegraphed General Buell that I had "about three weeks' supplies for my entire command." On the 8th of August I telegraphed to Captain Brown, assistant quartermaster at Lexington—

Twenty-five thousand men are between this place and Knoxville, and they are constantly arriving by way of Dalton. The safety of this place depends upon the supplies which you can rush forward. Not a second is to be lost. Give us supplies and we will be regardless of the enemy's force.

The enemy gained our rear and cut off our supplies.

A council of war, composed of Brigadier-Generals Spears, Baird, and Carter, with Lieutenant Craighill as recorder, assembled on the 14th of September, and it was unanimously decided that we had only the alternatives of evacuation or surrender. Such was my own opinion; but I waited one day longer, in the hope of receiving intelligence which would justify our remaining in our position. No intelligence came, and I devoted every energy to secure a rapid and successful evacuation of the Gap. In this, as in all else, I was nobly sustained by every officer and soldier of my command. Evacuation was peculiarly trying to the soldiers from East Tennessee, but both Generals Spears and Carter, from that State, strongly advised that policy.

Capt. W. F. Patterson, an officer of great merit, and of whose valuable services I have before spoken, under the general direction of Lieut. W. P. Craighill, chief engineer, was directed to mine the road and mountain cliffs, so as to prevent my column from being annoyed on its march by the army of Stevenson. This was well done. We had mounted thirty-two guns, and I determined to withdraw all but four 30-pounders, for which there was no possible means of transportation. Captain Tidd, a skillful and ingenious mechanic of the telegraph corps, was instructed to spike the 30-pounders, cut off their trunnions, wedge the bores with shot and spikes, and then hurl them over the cliffs. This was all effectually done.

On the night of the 16th of September a large train was sent toward Manchester, under the convoy of the Thirty-third Indiana and two companies of the Third Kentucky and the Ninth Ohio Battery, under the command of Colonel Coburn, an able and intelligent officer. The entire night of the 16th and the day of the 17th were occupied in busy preparation. At dark on the latter day the regular picket guards were withdrawn, and Lieutenant-Colonel Gallup, provost-marshal of the post, aided by Captain McNeish, with 200 chosen men, assumed the delicate and dangerous duty of holding the enemy in check during the night. Late in the day Lieutenant-Colonel Gallup bore three letters, under a flag of truce, to the enemy's lines, and, while well employed in an hour's chat with the officer accompanying the enemy's flag, some indiscreet person set fire to a portion of the quartermaster's establishments. The red flame and smoke soon curled over the mountains, and seemed like a proclamation to the enemy of what was then going forward. But, thanks to the tact of Gallup, for whose many valuable services I here make acknowledgment, the fire and smoke were ascribed to the burning of brush upon the mountain-sides. About 10 p. m. a breathless courier came in to announce the desertion of a sentinel, as was supposed, to the enemy. It was a moment of intense suspense. All of the guns but of one battery had been withdrawn from the fortifications and sent northward through the Gap, which was masked from the enemy's view by a mountain ridge $1\frac{1}{4}$ miles to the south of the Gap. The fire had spread from building to building, and the little valley, encircled by the mountains at the foot of the Gap, was one sea of flame. Captain Patterson now commenced to explode his mines, and the enemy seemed to be startled into a knowledge of what was going on. His pickets advanced by the Cottrell and Tazewell roads, but were driven back by a well-directed fire from Gallup's pickets. Spears had been ordered to form his brigade in line of battle at the foot of the mountain on the north side of the Gap, with a section of Foster's battery in the intervals between the regiments. Thus the approaches from Baptist Gap were commanded. At midnight Carter descended the mountain, followed by Baird. The descent was slow, difficult, and dangerous. Had the enemy boldly attacked he could have done much harm. But he was taken by surprise and evidently feared our mines. Gallup kept out his pickets till nearly dawn, when he caused the remaining buildings containing Government property to be destroyed, and with his own hands fired the train which blew up the principal magazine. The night was dark and the difficult march was continued until the advance brigade reached Flat Lick, a distance of 20 miles from the Gap. From this point we advanced by two parallel roads along Goose and Stinking Creeks, and reached the vicinity of Manchester on the night of September 19. At this place I halted one day to perfect the organization for the march, which was resumed on the 21st ultimo. The enemy's cavalry now appeared on our rear and endeavored to cut off one of our trains, but was gallantly repulsed by the Sixth Tennessee, under Colonel Cooper, who had before rendered good service in attacking the enemy's force near Big Creek Gap, which place he afterward blockaded. Captain Adams, the faithful and energetic commissary, had sent forward to Booneville and Proctor to obtain supplies, and, as the road diverged at Morris' farm, I sent the brigades of Baird and Carter via Booneville and those of Spears and De Courcy directly to Proctor. A brigade of cavalry, under General John H. Morgan, now commenced to annoy us, and, the night before our arrival, burned the steam-mill at Proctor; but upon our approach Morgan discovered that I was about to surround him and made a precipitate retreat. Already the troops had suffered greatly for want of water, but the route to Hazel Green was still more difficult. The ridge was almost entirely destitute of water, and where it did exist it was found in small quantities in holes down 80 or 100 feet among cliffs. The North Fork road had been destroyed by the spring and winter rains, but water was plentiful. I determined to advance in parallel columns, and directed Spears and De Courcy to march by the ridge and Baird and Carter by the North Fork road. Thanks to the skill and devotion of Captain Patterson, and to the officer-like bearing of the brigade commanders, regimental officers, and the heroic endurance of the soldiers, all of these terrible difficulties were nobly met and overcome, and the advance brigade halted one day at Hazel Green. At this place we captured two rebel officers. Morgan had already attacked us on the flank and rear, and now passed to our front and commenced a more serious system of annoyance, by blockading the narrow ridges and deep defiles which abound on that almost impracticable route.

After a day's rest the column was again put in motion toward West Liberty, where we expected to meet Humphrey Marshall, as we had been informed that he had left Mount Sterling with his command on the Saturday night previous and that on the day following Kirby Smith arrived with a column at that place. On this march the enemy's cavalry attacked the rear of De Courcy's brigade and scattered eighty or a hundred of our cattle. The cavalry soldiers dismounted and skirmished as infantry, but not until six horses and their riders were stretched upon the ground.

At West Liberty I halted for two days to concentrate my command and await Humphrey Marshall; but our scouts and spies penetrated in every direction without learning anything of his position. We had now cut his line, and occupied a central position between his divided forces. A portion of his command from Virginia arrived within 15 miles of West Liberty, but on learning of our approach rapidly retreated. The column now moved toward Grayson. In several places the roads were heavily obstructed by timber, and in one instance we were compelled to make a detour and construct a new road. Whenever opportunity offered we assumed the offensive and attacked the enemy while engaged in blockading the road. On three successive evenings so closely did we push him that we drove him from his hot supper. Morgan left Grayson late on the afternoon of October 1st and our advance reached there at 11 o'clock the same night. Here he ceased to annoy us.

Our loss, in killed, wounded, and prisoners, is about 80 men. His exact loss I do not know, but from the bloody evidences which were found in the positions occupied by his troops his loss must have been double our own.

On October 3 my column reached Greenupsburg, on the Ohio River. I had sent forward Captains Garber and Patterson to procure transportation for the passage of the river, which was effected in good order.

Colonel Byrd, of the First Tennessee, forded the river with the trains of Baird and Carter. To avoid too lengthy a report many incidents of interest have been omitted.

It affords me great pleasure to speak of the admirable bearing of my entire command, officers and soldiers, during that most difficult and trying march of 219 miles. It was worthy of all praise and receives my sincere gratitude. Especial credit is due to Brigadier-Generals Spears, Baird, and Carter, and to Colonel De Courcy; to Lieutenant-Colonel Gallup and Capts. W. F. Patterson, M. C. Garber, and G. M. Adams; to Lieut. W. P. Craighill and Lieutenant Burroughs, engineers; to Captain Foster, chief of artillery, and Lieutenant Burdick, acting ordnance officer, and to Lieutenant-Colonel Ridgell and Lieutenant Reeder, Third Kentucky Volunteers. And my cordial thanks and acknowledgments are due to my personal staff, Capt. C. O. Joline, assistant adjutant-general; Lieutenants Saunders and Medary, aides-de-camp; Lieutenant Montgomery, acting aide-de-camp, and Lieut. H. G. Fisher, chief of signal corps. In mentioning the names of these officers there is no distinction intended to the prejudice of any one, for all have behaved nobly.

It is proper that I should make particular mention of the services of Brigadier-General Baird during our occupancy of the Gap for the zeal displayed by him in aiding Lieutenant Craighill in executing his plans for the defense of that important post; nor can I close the report without respectfully calling the attention of the commanding general to the important services rendered me by Lieut. W. P. Craighill, of the Engineer Corps. He is an officer of distinguished merit, and is thoroughly informed on all the subjects connected with the art of war. He would make an able chief of any staff or fill with high credit any other position to which he may be assigned, and deserves a much higher grade than he now holds.

The evacuation of Cumberland Gap was dictated by a solemn sense of public duty. My command captured it without the loss of a single life, and, though a place of great strength, it can again be taken, should such be the policy of the Government; but the first step toward that end should be the construction of a good military road from Lexington to Cumberland Ford.

I respectfully call your attention to the reports of brigade and corps commanders.

I have the honor to be, major, very respectfully, your obedient servant,

GEORGE W. MORGAN,
Brigadier-General, Commanding.

Maj. N. H. McLEAN,
Asst. Adjt. Gen. and Chief of Staff, Cincinnati, Ohio.

—

HEADQUARTERS U. S. FORCES AT PORTLAND, OHIO,
October 16, 1862.

MAJOR: In the hurry of preparing my report of the march of my command from Cumberland Gap I inadvertently neglected to refer to the meritorious services of Lieutenant-Colonel Ridgell, Third Kentucky, and Capt. Sydney S. Lyon, acting topographical engineer, which I now take pleasure in doing. Also the valuable and highly creditable services of Dr. B. Cloak, acting medical director, and the corps of surgeons under him. Their conduct was admirable and is worthy of the highest praise.

I am, major, very respectfully, your obedient servant,

GEORGE W. MORGAN,
Brigadier-General.

Maj. N. H. McLean, *Chief of Staff, Cincinnati, Ohio.*

—

MOUNT VERNON, OHIO, *June* 6, 1863.

GENERAL : On the 6th of December, 1862, I wrote to you from Memphis (see Exhibit A) that the journals of that date announced that General Halleck, in his report of December 2, 1862, stated that "the alleged cause of the retreat from Cumberland Gap was the want of supplies;" but that the commanding officer had just before reported that he had "several weeks' provisions," and that "under no circumstances" would he abandon "that important post," and that an "investigation" had "been ordered."

As two months had elapsed since General Halleck had been informed of the evacuation, and as I had not been notified that an investigation had been ordered, so that I might have an opportunity of producing evidence of the facts upon which I acted, and as no intimation had been given of any dissatisfaction at Washington as to my conduct, save an anonymous telegram, which was discredited by the country, by the army, and by myself, in the exercise of the right guaranteed to every officer I demanded a prompt hearing before a court of inquiry or court-martial. To that demand, on the 20th of December, 1862, General Halleck, through Assistant Adjutant-General Kelton, replied (Exhibit B) that "Major-General Wright was directed some time since to investigate and report the facts concerning that affair," and that "if that report should be satisfactory no further proceedings" would be required, and that I would be held free from all blame.

You will observe, sir, that this assurance of General Halleck was made on the 20th of December, 1862, and that his report of general censure was made on the 2d of that month. My astonishment therefore was great when, in reply to my letter of January 6, 1863, General Wright, on the 27th of that month (Exhibit C), informed me that on the 15th of October, 1862—six weeks before General Halleck wrote his report—he, General Wright, had made his investigation and had written to General Halleck commending my policy in evacuating Cumberland Gap, and had stated that he "did not see how, with starvation staring him (Morgan) in the face and with no certainty of relief being afforded, he could have come to any other conclusion than the one arrived at." General Wright further informed General Halleck that "the evacuation was in pursuance of the unanimous opinion of the general officers of the command" (Exhibit D, record of council of war) "was a matter of necessity, arising from their provisions being exhausted, their communications cut off, and no information of any prospect of relief being received." And yet with this report of the investigation, made in accordance with his directions, and by the officer selected by himself, with this report lying before him, General Halleck published to the world that he had ordered an investigation, but suppressed the fact that the investigation had been made six weeks before the publication of his report and that my action had been fully sustained.

Although I have suffered public wrong I feel too deep an interest in the great issue for national existence now being tried on the battle-field to add a new disturbing element by making a public vindication. But I would be unworthy of the cause in the defense of which I drew my sword were I to allow any personal consideration to prevent me from placing on the record a statement of facts as set forth in this paper.

Having waited in vain for a further reply from General Halleck, on the 18th of January, 1863 (Exhibit E), I wrote to you that I had "patiently remained under the public censure of General Halleck for the period of four months, believing that time and investigation were only necessary to secure the approval of my course," and I requested to be informed "whether my conduct in the evacuation of Cumberland Gap met with the approval or disapproval of the General-in-Chief." To that communication General Halleck has not found it convenient to reply; but in his letter of February 8, 1863 (Exhibit F), in response to General Wright's letter of February 4 (Exhibit G), General Halleck says, "The facts as now presented justified General Morgan's retreat."

What facts? General Halleck possessed no facts on the 8th of February, 1863, which he did not know on the 2d of December, 1862, when he published his report. In his letter of February 4, 1863, General Wright simply reaffirmed the facts and opinions already stated by him in his official report of the investigation made October 15, 1862. And in reply to General Wright's letter of February 4, 1863, General Halleck says in his letter of February 8:

In this letter [of February 4] and your former letter [Wright's report of October 15] you fully exonerated General Morgan from all blame in abandoning Cumberland Gap. No further investigation will therefore be made.

In substance General Wright's letter of February 4, 1863, and his report of October 15, 1862, are identical, as General Halleck admits. Upon what principle then did he censure me upon the one and justify me on the other?

He expresses "regret that General Wright did not make a full and formal investigation at the time it was ordered." And yet when General Halleck penned the expression of that regret he knew that the investigation was as full and formal as it could have been made except by court of inquiry or court-martial. He says that such an investigation "was due to General Morgan as well as to General Wright and to the Government." If due to me, why did General Halleck refuse to grant me a court-martial or court of inquiry? If due to the Government, why did not General Halleck procure an order for a court of inquiry or himself order a court-martial? General Halleck ought to know that General Wright had not the power to order a court of inquiry. He (General Halleck) refused me a court and did not order one himself, but, on the contrary, he directed the investigation to be made by a single officer, selected that officer himself, and at this late day he grudgingly justifies my conduct on the report of that officer.

General Halleck further says:

General Morgan represented his force as able to hold Cumberland Gap against any number of troops which the enemy could bring against him. He was almost boastful in his confidence that he could do this. On these assurances the Government believed that the post would be held by us and serve as a serious obstacle to the retreat of General Bragg's army.

General Halleck strangely confounds "force" with "subsistence." I did hold my position against a force more than four times greater than my own; the enemy completely surrounded but dared not attack me; and had not General Halleck failed to open communication between Lexington and Cumberland Gap, as he promised to do (Exhibit H), that stronghold would be ours to-day.

I had sufficient force to beat the enemy if he attacked me, but had not subsistence sufficient to keep my troops two weeks longer from starvation.

In his report of December 2 General Halleck says that just before the evacuation I reported that I had "several weeks' supplies;" but in his letter of February 8 he asserts that in a dispatch of September 11, 1862, alleged to have been written by me six days before the evacuation, I said that I had "supplies for seventy or eighty days." But in that same letter General Halleck says, "it is true that he (Morgan) stated in his dispatches that his supplies were limited."

How then does General Halleck reconcile the assertion of seventy or eighty days' supplies with his admission that I reported that my supplies were limited? He says that I so stated in my dispatch of September 11, 1862. But I deny having at any time written such a dispatch to General Halleck, General Wright, or any other officer. No such dispatch was ever written by or for me, and if any purporting to be such is in existence I denounce it as a forgery.

In my official report of October 10, 1862, to General Wright (Exhibit I) I said:

On the 9th of September (Exhibit J) I addressed a letter to Major-General Wright by one of my aides-de-camp, with a verbal message, that by eating mules we could hold out sixty days (Exhibit K, statement of aide). But on the 12th of September the able and energetic division quartermaster informed me that it was impossible longer to feed the mules, and suggested that they should be sent to the Ohio River.

I further stated that my troops had been six days without bread, and that De Courcy had failed to obtain the hoped-for supplies at Manchester.

These facts were all before General Halleck while he was writing his report of December 2, for which he so ungracefully apologizes in his letter to General Wright of February 8, 1863.

General Halleck further says:

Had his (Morgan's) true condition been known measures might have been taken to relieve him.

Does General Halleck mean to say that he did not do all he was able to do at Big Hill, Richmond, and Lexington? Does he admit that he did not cause Bragg and Smith to be driven from Kentucky at the earliest possible moment? If so, then it is certain that General Halleck is responsible for the loss of Cumberland Gap, for the enemy maintained his position 100 miles north of Cumberland Ford until more than two months after my troops had been starved out of Cumberland Gap.

However ill-informed General Halleck may have been as to the general theater of operations, I propose to prove that he had no excuse for being ignorant of the condition of my command. He had been duly notified that my division was surrounded on the barren summit of the Cumberland Mountains; that Stevenson was in my immediate front with a force much larger than my own; that Bragg was on my right flank with a vast army; that Kirby Smith had gained my rear with a force three times greater than mine, and that Marshall occupied the sterile region to the north between the Gap and the Ohio River. He had been further informed by my official report of the capture of that stronghold, dated June 22, 1862, that—

While at Cumberland Ford I was compelled to haul forage for my animals (Exhibit L) a distance of 90 miles; and that during the months of April and May the roads were so bad that a train of ten wagons could only advance 3 or 4 miles per day.

That on the 30th of June, 1862, I telegraphed to Lieutenant-Colonel

Swords, assistant quartermaster-general, "We are in want of everything; we are destitute of forage."

That on the 21st of July, 1862, Chief Engineer Craighill, detailed for service at the Gap from the Regular Army, telegraphed to Brigadier-General Totten at Washington City, "The country in our rear is exhausted; that in our front soon will be."

That on the 23d of July I telegraphed to the Secretary of War and to General Buell, "My supplies are very short."

That on the 29th of July, in my letter of instructions to Chief Engineer Craighill, about to proceed to General Halleck's headquarters, I stated that "East Tennessee and Kentucky to the blue-grass region are exhausted." (The former had been ravaged by the enemy.)

That on the 10th of August I telegraphed to the Secretary of War and to General Buell, "I have about three weeks' supplies."

That on the 16th of August I telegraphed to the Secretary of War and to General Buell, "Smith cannot possibly remain three weeks in my rear, while I can hold this place five weeks with my present command." (I did hold the Gap four weeks and five days from the date of that dispatch.)

That on the 19th of August I telegraphed General Halleck that "150 wagons laden with forage and subsistence have arrived." Those supplies were principally of forage, which had been hauled over 100 miles, and as the teams had to be fed while on the road from the wagons the amount was greatly reduced.

Here then is the proof that General Halleck was informed of my true condition, and that if he had the means to have given me relief, as he says he "might have done," he is beyond all doubt responsible for the loss of Cumberland Gap.

General Halleck says that "the Government believed that Cumberland Gap would form a serious obstacle to the retreat of the enemy." If the administration so believed it was the duty of General Halleck to have corrected so erroneous an impression. He was aware that I had invaded East Tennessee in June, 1862, through two other gaps, and that Kirby Smith had invaded Kentucky by the same routes during the August following. Hence, even had General Halleck furnished me with supplies, as he says he might have done, the forces of Bragg and Smith would have retreated by two or three roads instead of by one.

It was not by my order that Kentucky was denuded of troops nor through my neglect that Rogers' and Big Creek Gaps were left invitingly open to invasion. In obedience to instructions from the Secretary of War I kept him advised of my movements, and on the 11th of May, 1862, and twice afterward, I suggested the importance of protecting the lines of communication between Louisville and Nashville and between Lexington and Cumberland Ford; and afterward I strongly recommended the occupation of the last-named gaps. But neither gap was occupied and both lines were left unprotected; the cavalry I had repeatedly asked for was not furnished me, and the natural results of the weakened and exposed condition of Kentucky were the raids of John Morgan and the invasions by Smith and Bragg.

Regarding the occupation of East Tennessee as of vital importance, in vain I made every effort to have a rail or other good military road constructed to Cumberland Gap, from thence to be extended to intersect the great road from Richmond which connects East Tennessee with Virginia, the Carolinas, Georgia, Alabama, and Mississippi.

East Tennessee is overwhelmingly devoted to the Union, and with proper cultivation is capable of feeding its own population and an army of 150,000 men. Once in our possession the rebels would be compelled to evacuate Virginia, for they would be cut off from their only practicable route to the Gulf States, and have lost the vast supplies, upon which they so much depend, from Tennessee, Arkansas, Louisiana, and Texas.

Three times I earnestly requested to be allowed to advance upon Knoxville, and pledged myself to sweep East Tennessee from Bristol to Chattanooga. I had surplus arms for six additional regiments of patriotic Tennesseeans. I could have destroyed all communication with Virginia until Buell could have advanced from the Southwest, but I was ordered not to act on the offensive, and Buell was not allowed to attack Bragg near Chattanooga while I advanced against Kirby Smith upon Knoxville. Had not these plans been interfered with the invasion of Kentucky would not have taken place and East Tennessee and Cumberland Gap would be in our possession to-day.

General Halleck complains that I was "almost boastful" in my confidence "that I could hold my position against any number of troops which the enemy could bring against me." There was a stern necessity for a tone of confidence upon my part, for I had reason to know that there was panic from Washington to Louisville. And although cut off from supplies and threatened by a force vastly greater than my own my command maintained a "boastful confidence" and sought to inspire at least a moderate degree elsewhere. In answer to an official telegram I said:

I am surprised to hear that there is consternation at Louisville or elsewhere. Here (Cumberland Gap) all is quiet and orderly. We are prepared for the enemy whenever he may show himself.

The enemy did show himself and the result proved that we were ready to receive him. During the thirty-two days that we were invested we captured over 500 officers and soldiers, making an equivalent of 542 privates, and killed or wounded 170, making an aggregate loss of over 700 on his part against a loss of less than 40 on our side. These facts were duly reported.

On the 19th of August I telegraphed to General Halleck:

This position shall not be yielded while we have a pound of meat or an ounce of powder. But I trust that the road may soon be opened by a column from Lexington.

General Halleck replied:

I will see that you are very soon re-enforced.

His promises only resulted in defeat and disaster to our arms. On the 19th of August his re-enforcements were driven from Big Hill; on the 30th of the same month they were routed at Richmond, and on the 2d of September in hot haste he abandoned Lexington and Frankfort, and retreated to Covington and Louisville; and Bragg maintained his position in the blue-grass region, more than 100 miles this side of Cumberland Gap, for more than two months after General Halleck promised his speedy re-enforcements.

Inasmuch as my advance against Cumberland Gap has been made a subject of investigation before the Buell Commission, and as I have not been summoned as a witness, it is proper that I should here state a few facts, some of which were unknown to me when my official report was written.

My camp at Cumberland Ford was 14 miles north of the Gap, and to reach the Gap in front was a six hours' march. But to turn it by a flank movement by way of Big Creek Gap required from my position an almost impracticable march of ten or twelve days over a distance of

95 miles. To deceive the enemy as to my intention I advanced in two columns, one passing the mountains at Rogers' and the other by Big Creek Gap, thus threatening at the same time Cumberland Gap, 19 miles east of Rogers', Knoxville, 45 miles south of Rogers', and Clinton, about 20 miles south of Big Creek Gap. Clinton was a base of supplies for the enemy.

Before advancing from the ford I informed General Buell that Smith's force was three times greater than my own, and requested that a diversion should be made in my favor against Chattanooga. My request was complied with, and Smith believed the feint to be an attack, and recalled Barton from Big Creek Gap, and with 12,000 men started to the relief of Chattanooga. But when Smith reached London he received a telegram stating that East Tennessee was being invaded by two columns. This recalled to him a ruse rumor which I had several weeks previously caused to be circulated of my intention to attack the Gap in front with 12,000 men, while at the same time I would advance by a flank movement with two columns into East Tennessee.

On the 16th of June I learned that Smith and Barton were advancing to attack me (Exhibit N), but it was not until a week or ten days after our occupation of the Gap that I learned fully of the disposition of Smith's forces. He left Stevenson with 6,000 men to defend Cumberland Gap, sent Barton with 4,000 men to the Big Valley to observe the approach to Knoxville by the Rogers' Gap road, while with 8,000 men he took position at Clinton.

Smith's disposition of his troops indicates his belief that I intended to advance upon Knoxville, and he hoped to meet me with his forces concentrated. My order of march (Exhibit O), shows that I anticipated his plan and was prepared for him, and my rapid advance upon Stevenson foiled the execution of his design, and Cumberland Gap was thus captured without the loss of a man.

General Buell knew that I was maneuvering against a force three times greater than my own, and this explains his anxiety for the safety of my command.

Upon assuming command at Cumberland Gap I adopted a conciliatory policy (Exhibits P and Q), and the citizens of the adjoining counties of Virginia and Tennessee flocked in to resume their allegiance to the United States.

. I am, sir, very respectfully, your obedient servant,

GEORGE W. MORGAN,
Brigadier-General Volunteers, U. S. Army.

LORENZO THOMAS, *Adjutant-General U. S. Army.*

EXHIBIT A.

DIVISION HEADQUARTERS,
Memphis, Tenn., December 6, 1862.

LORENZO THOMAS,
Adjutant-General, U. S. Army, Washington, D. C.:

SIR: To-day's journals announce that the general-in-chief has submitted to the honorable Secretary of War a report, in which it is stated "that an investigation has been ordered of Morgan's strange abandonment of Cumberland Gap."

I have therefore the honor respectfully to request that I may be relieved from my command, and that the investigation may take place at the earliest moment practicable; that the trial may be by court of inquiry or court-martial, and that the judge-advocate be instructed to furnish me at his earliest convenience a copy of the charges and specifications preferred against me.

Annexed please find a list of witnesses whom I desire to have summoned,* and after being furnished with the specifications I will forward to the judge-advocate the names of such other witnesses as circumstances may require.

As I am extremely anxious for prompt action in the premises, I trust that you will pardon any irregularity which may appear in my request.

I have the honor to be, sir, very respectfully, your obedient servant,
                                    GEORGE W. MORGAN,
                                        Brigadier-General Volunteers.

ExHIBIT B.

HEADQUARTERS OF THE ARMY,
                        Washington, D. C., December 20, 1862.
Brig. Gen. GEORGE W. MORGAN, *Memphis, Tenn.:*

GENERAL: Your communication to the Adjutant-General of the Army, asking that an investigation of your abandonment of Cumberland Gap may take place at the earliest practicable moment having been submitted to the general-in-chief, I am directed to say that Major-General Wright was directed some time since to investigate and report the facts concerning that affair. If that report should be satisfactory to the War Department no further proceedings will be required, and you will be relieved from all blame.

Very respectfully, your obedient servant,
                                    J. C. KELTON,
                                        Assistant Adjutant-General.

ExHIBIT C.

HEADQUARTERS DEPARTMENT OF THE OHIO,
                        Cincinnati, January 27, 1863.
Brig. Gen. GEORGE W. MORGAN, U. S. Vols.,
            Gaines' Landing, via Memphis, Tenn.:

GENERAL: I am instructed by Major-General Wright to acknowledge the receipt of your communication of the 6th instant, and to inclose to you a copy of his letter to the general-in-chief, transmitting your report of the evacuation of Cumberland Gap.†

It is presumed that these reports were satisfactory, as nothing has been heard of the matter.

Very respectfully, your obedient servant,
                                    C. W. FOSTER,
                                        Assistant Adjutant-General.

ExHIBIT D.

HEADQUARTERS CUMBERLAND GAP,
                                September 14, 1862.
A council of war, convened by Brigadier-General Morgan, commanding the United States forces at Cumberland Gap, assembled at these headquarters at 11 a. m. to-day. Present, Brig. Gen. G. W. Morgan,

---

* Omitted.   † See Report No. 1, p. 990.

commanding general; Brigadier-General Spears, commanding First Brigade; Brig. Gen. A. Baird, commanding Second Brigade; Brigadier-General Carter, commanding Third Brigade. The brigade of De Courcy (Fourth) absent on detached service.

The proceedings were opened by General Morgan, stating in detail the information in his possession relative to the positions and numbers of the Union and rebel forces in Virginia, Kentucky, and Tennessee, and as to the probabilities of succor both in force and supplies reaching this post, and of the condition of the force as to supplies of food, clothing, and ammunition.

General Morgan stated that the council was convened to consider the question of remaining here or evacuating the position, and that he should be governed, as far as that question was concerned, by the decision of the council. After a free interchange of opinion it was agreed unanimously that in view of all the circumstances of the case the position should be evacuated.

GEORGE W. MORGAN,
Brigadier-General, Commanding.
JAMES G. SPEARS,
Brigadier-General, Commanding First Brigade.
A. BAIRD,
Brigadier-General, Commanding Second Brigade.
S. P. CARTER,
Brigadier-General, Commanding Third Brigade.

WILLIAM P. CRAIGHILL,
  First Lieut. of Engineers, Recorder of the Council.

EXHIBIT E.

HDQRS. THIRTEENTH ARMY CORPS, U. S. FORCES,
Napoleon, Ark., January 18, 1863.

LORENZO THOMAS, *Adjutant-General U. S. Army:*

SIR: I trust that I shall be pardoned for again requesting the attention of the general-in-chief to the subject of the evacuation of Cumberland Gap. Four months have elapsed since that event, and I have respectfully and patiently remained under the implied censure of the general-in-chief, believing that time and investigation were only necessary to secure the approval of my course. In the communication I had the honor to receive from your department in December, 1862, I was informed that the investigation of the subject had been committed to Major-General Wright, whose report would be final.

My reputation is my only fortune; it belongs to my children, and a sense of duty to them, to the service, and myself induces me to respectfully request to be informed whether General Wright has yet made his report, and whether my conduct in the evacuation of Cumberland Gap meets with the approval or disapproval of the general-in-chief.

I am, sir, very respectfully, your obedient servant,

GEORGE W. MORGAN,
Brigadier-General.

Respectfully forwarded through the headquarters of Major-General McClernand.

EXHIBIT F.

HDQRS. OF THE ARMY, *Washington, D. C., Feb.* 8, 1863.

Major-General WRIGHT, *Cincinnati, Ohio:*

GENERAL: Your letter of the 4th instant [following] is just received. In this and your former letter you fully exonerate Brig. Gen. G. W. Morgan from all blame in abandoning Cumberland Gap. No further investigation will therefore be made. It however is to be regretted that you did not make a full and formal investigation at the time it was ordered. This was due to General Morgan as well as to yourself and to the Government.

All of your reports, as well as those received from General Morgan, almost to the day of his abandoning his post, represented his force as able to hold it against any number of troops which the enemy could bring against him. He was almost boastful in his confidence of his being able to do this. On these assurances the Government believed that the post would be held by us, and serve as a serious obstacle to the retreat of General Bragg's army. Great disappointment was therefore felt at learning that so important a point had been abandoned at a most critical moment in the campaign.

It appears now from your letters and from General Morgan's report that he was forced to abandon Cumberland Gap for want of supplies. It is true that he had stated in his dispatches that his supplies were limited and that he was collecting all he could from the surrounding country, but he did not intimate that they were so short as to compel him to abandon his post. On the contrary, in your dispatch to me of September the 18th you report that in his dispatch of September 11 he says he has supplies for from seventy to eighty days and feels secure. It now appears from his report that he had actually abandoned his post for want of supplies before the above dispatch was received here.

There is but one way of accounting for this discrepancy between the dispatches and the report—that the former were purposely made incorrect in order to deceive the enemy, if intercepted, in regard to General Morgan's real condition. They certainly deceived our Government. Had his true condition been known it is possible that measures could have been taken in time to relieve him. Seventy or eighty days' supplies on hand on the 11th day of September would have served him till near the end of December, before which time he was very certain to be relieved by you or by the army of General Buell.

The facts as now presented justified General Morgan's retreat, but the facts as understood by the War Department at the time, derived from his dispatches, furnished no possible justification for his abandoning Cumberland Gap in the middle of September. If the opinion of the Department was unjust toward General Morgan it was due entirely to incorrect information derived from his dispatches.

Very respectfully, your obedient servant,

H. W. HALLECK,
General-in-Chief.

EXHIBIT G.

HEADQUARTERS DEPARTMENT OF THE OHIO,
Cincinnati, Ohio, February 4, 1863.

Brig. Gen. G. W. CULLUM, &c.:

GENERAL: I have the honor to acknowledge the receipt of the dispatch of the general-in-chief of this date, saying that I had been "directed some time ago to investigate and report upon the conduct of Brig. Gen. Morgan in evacuating Cumberland Gap" and that "no report has yet been received."

Soon after the command of General Morgan reached the Ohio River I saw and conversed with many of the higher officers of the command in regard to the circumstances attending the evacuation, and was satisfied, even before General Morgan's official report came to hand, that the course adopted by him was one of unavoidable necessity. This I stated in my letter of the 15th October last, transmitting the report of General Morgan, and I considered this report as being all that I was called upon to furnish, being satisfied myself of the propriety and actual necessity of the evacuation of the Gap. I conceived that report to be conclusive, unless the commanding general desired some further investigation.

I would further remark that subsequent statements of officers of General Morgan's command have confirmed the correctness of the opinion expressed in my letter of October 15, above referred to, and have satisfied me that he could not have held out more than twenty days longer at the utmost, and then only on much reduced rations, with no provisions with which to subsist his troops on the march, and with a loss of animals meanwhile for want of forage, which would have compelled him to abandon his artillery and wagons.

No formal investigation was instituted, because I did not conceive it to be called for by the general-in-chief or to be necessary.

Referring to my letter of October 15 and General Morgan's report, transmitted therewith for further information, I am, very respectfully, your obedient servant,

H. G. WRIGHT,
Major-General, Commanding.

EXHIBIT H.

WASHINGTON, D. C., *August 22*, 1862.

General MORGAN, *Cumberland Gap, Tenn.:*

Hold on firmly; you will very soon be re-enforced. Do not yield an inch. Fight the enemy wherever he appears, and I will see that you are very soon supported by other troops. Try to open communications with General Buell. If you cannot do this, telegraph General Wright at Cincinnati.

H. W. HALLECK,
General-in-Chief.

EXHIBIT I.

[See Report No. 2, of date October 12, 1862, p. 992.]

EXHIBIT J.

[See September 10, 1862. Operations at Rogers' Gap and Big Creek Gap, Tenn., and Barboursville, Ky. Report of Brig. Gen. George W. Morgan, U. S. Army, p. 957.]

EXHIBIT K.

Statement of Lieut. Charles S. Medary, Third U. S. Artillery, Aide-de-Camp, relative to his interview with Maj. Gen. H. G. Wright, at Cincinnati, Ohio, September 18, 1862.

On the 10th of September, 1862, I left Cumberland Gap as bearer of a dispatch dated September 9, 1862, from General Morgan to Major-General Wright, commanding the Department of the Ohio.

Colonel De Courcy, with his brigade of four regiments, had been sent by General Morgan with a large wagon train to collect supplies of bacon and flour at Manchester. On the night of the 11th I reached that place, and was informed by Colonel De Courcy that General Morgan had been misinformed as to the provisions which could be there obtained; that very little bacon could be had, and that his brigade consumed three-quarters of all the flour that could be ground at the mill, and that he had collected all that could be obtained.

To guard against the loss of the dispatch in the event of my being captured I made an abstract of General Morgan's dispatch, and then delivered the dispatch to a Union citizen, who promised to send it to General Wright, which was done, and the dispatch safely reached him two or three days after my arrival.

I reached Cincinnati on the evening of the 17th of September, and on the day following I had an interview with General Wright. I delivered to him a copy of my abstract of General Morgan's report, and informed him that I had been instructed to communicate certain facts to him not contained in the dispatch, which were substantially as follows:

That there was an effective force of between 7,000 and 8,000 men at the Gap; that Garrard had been sent with a force to join General Nelson at Lexington; that there were in all thirty guns, among which were four 30 and six 20 pounders (Parrotts), and that there was a large supply of ammunition; that the troops at the Gap had been on half rations for three weeks and had been without flour or bread for a week prior to the date of the dispatch; that General Morgan had sent De Courcy's brigade to Manchester, where he hoped to obtain considerable supplies of flour and bacon, upon which he depended; that if he succeeded in obtaining those supplies General Morgan thought he might hold out sixty days.

I then remarked to General Wright that, in my own opinion, after learning that Colonel De Courcy had failed to obtain the anticipated supplies, I did not think that General Morgan could hold out over twenty or thirty days from the time I left the Gap even if the soldiers used the mules as food. And I should here state that when General Morgan spoke of holding out sixty days he said that he would kill the mules for food if necessary; but I do not recollect whether I mentioned that fact to General Wright or not.

Having finished the foregoing verbal statement, General Wright requested me to make a memorandum of the facts I had stated. I made a brief memorandum, in which I also gave the position and strength of Kirby Smith, Stevenson, and Humphrey Marshall, but it was not so full as the verbal statement.

CHARLES S. MEDARY,
Lieutenant, Third U. S. Artillery, Aide-de-Camp.

EXHIBIT L.

[See Series I, Vol. X, Part I, pp. 57–64.]

Telegram from the Secretary of War.

WASHINGTON, *June* 22, 1862.

Brigadier-General MORGAN:

This Department has been highly gratified with your successful occupation of Cumberland Gap, and commends the gallant conduct and labors of your officers and troops, to whom you will express the thanks of the President and this Department. Cumberland Gap is regarded as a strategic point of great importance, which, unless you have orders from your commanding officer, this Department will consider you well employed in holding and strengthening that position so that the enemy can by no chance recover his position. I have been striving ever since receiving the intelligence of your success to aid and send you a skillful officer of the Engineer Department to place and construct the necessary works. That has delayed my communication to you. The great demand in this quarter has absorbed the whole engineer force, but to-morrow I hope to send you an officer highly recommended by General Totten for his professional skill. It is out of the power of this Department to supply you at present with any cavalry for offensive operations, and as your force for some time can be advantageously employed defensively in its present position, I trust you will not need it.

With thanks for your diligence and activity, I remain, yours, truly,

EDWIN M. STANTON,
Secretary of War.

EXHIBIT M.

GENERAL ORDERS, }   HEADQUARTERS ARMY OF THE OHIO,
No. 29.   }   *In Camp, Huntsville, Ala., July 11, 1862.*

The general commanding the Army of the Ohio takes pleasure in announcing the success of an arduous and hazardous campaign by the Seventh Division, Brig. Gen. G. W. Morgan commanding, by which the enemy's fortified position at Cumberland Gap was turned and his force compelled to retreat as our troops advanced to attack.

The general thanks Brigadier-General Morgan and the troops of the Seventh Division for the ability displayed in the operations against this important stronghold, and for the energy, fortitude, and cheerfulness which they exhibited in their struggles with difficulties of the most formidable magnitude for an army.

By command of Major-General Buell:

JAMES B. FRY,
Colonel and Chief of Staff.

EXHIBIT N.

HDQRS. SEVENTH DIVISION, ARMY OF THE OHIO,
Rogers' Gap, Tenn., June 16, 1862.

Maj. Gen. D. C. BUELL, *Booneville:*

My division is concentrated. I have reliable information that Barton and Kirby Smith, with all their available forces, are marching to attack me.

If possible have a serious feint made on Chattanooga.

GEORGE W. MORGAN,
Brigadier-General Volunteers, Commanding.

EXHIBIT O.

[See Series I, Vol. X, Part I, pp. 62-64.]

EXHIBIT P.

GENERAL ORDERS,) HDQRS. SEVENTH DIV., ARMY OF THE OHIO,
No. 44. } *Cumberland Gap, June 20, 1862.*

It has been with mortification and regret that the general command-ing has learned that outrages have been committed upon private prop-erty of citizens, some of whom are loyal to the Union, by a few bad men, who have disgraced their uniforms by their unsoldier-like conduct.

Private citizens and private property must be respected, and the honor of our flag and of the brave men who are ready to die beneath its folds shall not be sullied by a handful of desperadoes who have crept into the ranks of the army, and if any such act is committed after this order has become promulgated and known the perpetrator of the outrage shall suffer the penalty of death, as prescribed by the Rules and Articles of War.

It is directed that this order be at once published at the head of every company in the command and that commanding officers will look to its enforcement.

By command of General Morgan :

CHAS. O. JOLINE,
Assistant Adjutant-General.

EXHIBIT Q.

HDQRS. SEVENTH DIVISION, ARMY OF THE OHIO,
Cumberland Gap, June 24, 1862.

Hon. E. M. STANTON, *Washington, D. C.:*

Citizens of Virginia, Kentucky, and Tennessee come in by the dozen to take the oath of allegiance to the United States. A moment ago 13 Virginians came in, and when I welcomed them back to the old flag every eye was dimmed with tears.

GEORGE W. MORGAN,
Brigadier-General Volunteers, Commanding.

CUMBERLAND GAP, *June 27, 1862.*

Hon. E. M. STANTON,
Secretary of War, Washington, D. C.:

Citizens from Lee County, Virginia, and East Tennessee continue to come in to take the oath of allegiance. I have adopted a conciliatory policy, and it has inspired confidence among the people generally, [but to a great extent it gives dissatisfaction to the Tennessee troops. Gen-eral Spears called upon me this a. m. to ask permission to dispose of certain prisoners whom he has caused to be arrested. It appears they were concerned in the arrest of Nelson. Spears desired to hang them. I have requested that they should be turned over to the provost-guard, to be sent as prisoners of war to Indianapolis or Columbus. I am now satisfied if additional regiments of Tennessee troops are to be organ-ized that they should be employed elsewhere and other troops be sent here].* This morning [Dr. Ewing], of Virginia, son of [Dr. Joshua D.

---

*The words bracketed in dispatch were omitted in the extract appended by Brig-adier-General Morgan. They are in the original as received.

Ewing], came in and gave his parole, and avowed his allegiance to the United States. His father [Dr. Joshua D. Ewing] and [Robert M. Bales] are members of the rebel Legislature. They desire to come in and take the oath if we will grant them protection. I am disposed to do so, and I am unfit by nature to carry out a policy of vengeance. [I can see trouble ahead after we have driven the enemy from East Tennessee. A decided majority of the troops taken from other States], formerly officers and soldiers of the Home Guard and rebel army, desire to take the oath of allegiance. Shall I permit them to do so? How shall I act as to [Bales and Ewing]?

GEORGE W. MORGAN,
Brigadier-General.

No. 3.

Report of Maj. Gen. John P. McCown, C. S. Army, commanding Department of East Tennessee, of the evacuation of Cumberland Gap.

HEADQUARTERS DEPARTMENT OF EAST TENNESSEE,
Knoxville, Tenn., September 22, 1862.

GENERAL: I have the honor to report that the enemy evacuated Cumberland Gap in the night of the 17th instant, blowing up his magazines and destroying small-arms and stores in large quantities. He left six pieces of artillery, including two 4½-inch Parrotts, which were rendered unfit for service.

General Stevenson's advance started in pursuit on the morning of the 18th. Owing to the absence of his supply train the rear guard did not move until the morning of 20th. Colonel [H. W.] Hilliard's legion and a regiment of infantry are now garrisoning the Gap. Enemy reported yesterday at Manchester. Stevenson close by.

Respectfully, your obedient servant,

J. P. McCOWN,
Major-General, Commanding.

S. COOPER, *Adjutant and Inspector General, Richmond, Va.*

SEPTEMBER 18, 1862.—Affair at Glasgow, Ky.

Report of Col. Lewis Zahm, Third Ohio Cavalry, commanding Second Cavalry Brigade.

HEADQUARTERS SECOND CAVALRY BRIGADE,
Glasgow, September 18, 1862—4 p. m.

COLONEL: I have the honor to report my arrival here between 1 and 2 o'clock this p. m. I took about 200 prisoners, sick and well; have the well ones in my column, nearly 100. Took some 10 or 12 officers; had them paroled. Captured 5 wagons loaded with flour; a number of arms, &c. I learn from citizens, especially the editor here, that six divisions of the rebel army have passed northward to Green River and, as they suppose, to Louisville. The divisions are as follows: Generals Withers', Cheatham's, Hardee's, Buckner's, Anderson's, and Brown's, altogether estimated at 45,000 men, with about eighty pieces light artillery, mostly 10 and 12 pounders.

General Bragg left here on Tuesday morning. They expect Breckinridge in to-morrow with a division numbering about 6,000. I sent out detachments on the pikes leading to Cumberland and Tompkinsville and other points. They returned without having made any discoveries. It is rumored that General Price is at Hopkinsville with his forces. I am getting my column in motion for Prewitt's Knob.

I am, very respectfully, your obedient servant,

LEWIS ZAHM,
Second Cavalry Brigade.

Col. J. B. FRY.

I also captured a mail, which I send with this.

SEPTEMBER 25, 1862.—Skirmish near Snow's Pond, Ky.

Report of Brig. Gen. Quincy A. Gillmore, U. S. Army.

HEADQUARTERS UNITED STATES FORCES,
Snow's Pond, Lexington Pike, Ky., September 25, 1862.

SIR: Your two letters of to-day are received.

I have to report an attack on my lines this morning at 11 o'clock by over 500 rebel cavalry, with one field piece. They made a sudden dash on the pickets from the direction of California, capturing several small posts. Fifty men are missing, but I am in hopes that some of them will make their appearance. They disappeared (as suddenly as they came up) toward Crittenden. I learned their number from parties who met them on the Crittenden road. It is doubtless the identical party that I have heard of before, numbering 508.

I am gratified that more cavalry are coming, and I wish they were here now. It is next to impossible to resist these sudden dashes with infantry, and my pickets will be in constant danger of being driven in unless I have enough mounted force to scour the country for miles around.

Very respectfully, your obedient servant,

Q. A. GILLMORE,
Brigadier-General, Commanding.

Brig. Gen. A. J. SMITH,
Commanding U. S. Forces near Covington, Ky.

SEPTEMBER 27–28, 1862.—Skirmishes at Augusta (27th) and Brookville (28th), Ky.

REPORTS.

No. 1.—Lieut. Col. H. Blair Wilson, Forty-fourth Ohio Infantry.
No. 2.—Capt. A. D. Wilson, master of gunboat Allen Collyer, of skirmish at Augusta.
No. 3.—Joseph Doniphan, of skirmish at Augusta.

No. 1.

Report of Lieut. Col. H. Blair Wilson, Forty-fourth Ohio Infantry.

HDQRS. U. S. FORCES, *Maysville, Ky., Sept.* 29, 1862.

SIR: About dusk on the evening of the 27th instant a special messenger brought me the intelligence from Ripley that Col. Basil W.

Duke, with about 750 of John Morgan's gang of rebels and two small pieces of artillery, had attacked Colonel Bradford's command at Augusta, 18 miles below this place, and, after a most desperate resistance on the part of Colonel Bradford and his men, had succeeded in capturing Colonel Bradford and his entire force. I immediately assembled all the available force at my command, being 325 infantry and one 6-pounder piece of artillery, and sent them, under command of the Hon. William H. Wadsworth, to Germantown, 12 miles distant from Maysville. I also dispatched a courier after 100 cavalry (the only mounted force I had) that I had sent to Flemingsburg, about 2 o'clock that afternoon, to capture or drive off a rebel recruiting party and some of Humphrey Marshall's cavalry, which were there. I instructed Colonel Wadsworth to reach Germantown before daylight and remain there until I could arrive with re-enforcements. In the mean time a boat had been sent up the river about 8 miles to bring down a body of Home Guards to take possession of Maysville and repel any attempt that I feared might be made to make a raid on that place in my absence. I then took a boat and went to Ripley, where I found 175 of the armed and organized militia and one smooth-bore 6-pounder field piece. I appointed Lieutenant-Colonel Edwards, of the Militia, commander of this force, and immediately crossed the Ohio to Dover, and started with them to Germantown, 11 miles distant, where we arrived a little after daylight. I ordered Col. E. Grand-Girard, of Ripley, to procure provisions for my men, and after collecting all the force he could to press on after me.

Colonel Wadsworth had reached Germantown before daylight. He had posted pickets on all the roads and had taken every necessary precaution to aid my design of surprising the enemy. My original design was to march down from Germantown to Augusta, having ascertained that a march of only 3 miles from Germantown in that direction would bring me completely in the rear of the enemy and render a successful retreat on his part quite improbable, my design being, however, to surprise him at Augusta; but some scouts that Colonel Wadsworth sent out brought in the intelligence that Colonel Duke, after burning the best part of the town of Augusta, had retired in the direction of Brookville, and had probably reached that place before midnight. I at once set out for Brookville, 7 miles distant from Germantown, and was overtaken on the way by the cavalry from Flemingsburg, which had then marched since 2 o'clock the preceding evening more than 60 miles. I arrived within three-quarters of a mile from Brookville about 8 a. m., when I halted and ordered Captain Youart, commanding detachment of the Forty-fourth Ohio Volunteers, to proceed by a circuitous route and take possession of the Falmouth road, concealing himself from the view of the enemy. I did this, being well assured that the enemy would retreat on that road. Captain Youart had just started when Judge Bush, who had been sent with his cavalry to the heights to reconnoiter, informed me that the enemy was forming in line of battle. I was then satisfied that the enemy had notice of our approach, and my principal force being militia and undrilled recruits, and knowing that the enemy outnumbered me, I thought it imprudent to divide my force, and countermanded my order to Captain Youart. It was very unfortunate that I did so. The truth was that the enemy had no notice of my presence, and had formed his line with the view of marching out on the Falmouth road. This was detected upon my arrival at the heights overlooking the town. It was then too late to take possession of the Falmouth road, and I could not, from any position on that side of the town, play on the rebels with artillery. I therefore ordered my detachment of the Forty-fourth Ohio Volunteers to charge at double-quick time down into the town, and I ordered the artillery and the remainder of my force to follow them promptly at quick-time. This was the first notice that Colonel Duke had of our presence. He, with a guard of 25 men, was in the court-house at that moment, and he was paroling prisoners. Some of my cavalry, seeing the Forty-fourth running into town, became excited, and imprudently and without orders rushed in advance of the Forty-fourth down a road leading to the rear of the court-house. Colonel Duke rushed out, mounted his men, and dashed off on the Falmouth road, passing within 25 yards of my detachment of the Forty-fourth Ohio, which mistook them for our own men, who had charged around the court-house. They were dressed very much as our own cavalry. I felt greatly annoyed, but under the circumstances I could not censure the men for not firing on them. We pressed to the other side of the town, and perceiving that the main body had halted about half a mile distant on hearing the alarm, I ordered the artillery into position and commenced shelling them. The third shot exploded in their midst, killing 6 and wounding 1, when they retreated precipitately toward Falmouth and were soon out of the range of our cannon. Between 30 and 40 prisoners were released that Duke did not have time to parole. Some of them rushed out and fled, and I do not know the precise number thus released.

Our loss was 1 killed. He belonged to the Fourteenth Kentucky Cavalry. He was shot from an alley, I think, by a citizen of Brookville about the same time Colonel Duke escaped from the court-house.

At noon we started for Augusta, 9 miles distant, and were overtaken by two wagon loads of provisions and 100 more men, under Colonel Grand-Girard. We reached Augusta before sundown, where boats were procured, and we arrived at this post the same night before 9 o'clock.

I do not think men could be found who will bear up with more fortitude under privation, hunger, and a most fatiguing march than did all the men on this occasion. Col. Charles A. Marshall, Hon. William H. Wadsworth, and Judge Bush, of Maysville; Colonel Edwards and Colonel Grand-Girard, of Ripley, volunteered to accompany me, and I feel under great obligations to them for the part taken by each. More than half of my command were citizens, but all marched and behaved like veteran troops, excepting on the occasion when the cavalry charged without orders, and their zeal and eagerness deprived us of Colonel Duke and 25 of his men. They made, however, a most handsome dash.

I am, sir, your obedient servant,

H. B. WILSON,
Lieutenant-Colonel, Commanding Post.

Maj. N. H. McLean,
  Asst. Adjt. Gen. and Chief of Staff, Dept. of the Ohio.

No. 2.

Report of Capt. A. D. Wilson, master of gunboat Allen Collyer, of skirmish at Augusta.

GUNBOAT ALLEN COLLYER,
Off Foster, September 27, 1862—p. m.

DEAR SIR: I went up to Augusta to get some ammunition from the

Belfast. Was there at 12 m. While there the Florence Miller passed down. Colonel Bradford sent a note requesting me to stay, as he expected an attack before night. About an hour after the Florence Miller came back, blowing her whistle. I then started down the river, and when I met her I understood them to say that the rebels were crossing the river at Chilo. I hurried down and found that it was a party of scouts that went out from Augusta yesterday and were returning. I hurried back as soon as possible, and found that the rebels had attacked Augusta with artillery, compelling Colonel Bradford to surrender, burning the town, the Belfast and Florence Miller going up the river.

Had it not have been for the blowing of the Miller's whistle and the misunderstanding of information I would have been there and assisted the Belfast. I have returned to watch the part of the river assigned to me.

Yours, truly,

A. D. WILSON,
Master.

Capt. JOHN A. DUBLE.

I understand that the rebels are 1,000 strong, with three pieces of artillery.

The Belfast and Miller are above Augusta, and I do not think can run by the guns planted on the hill back of town. I went within one mile of town, and did not think I could do any good attacking them, as Colonel Bradford and men were prisoners.

A. D. WILSON.

No. 3.

Report of Joseph Doniphan, of skirmish at Augusta.

AUGUSTA, KY., [*September* 28, 1862].

SIR: On Saturday, about 12 o'clock m., Colonel Bradford received intelligence of the approach of between 400 and 500 rebels, under command of Basil Duke. The colonel immediately prepared to defend the town, his force consisting of about 100 Home Guards and militia, and the gunboat Belfast, Captain Sedam commanding.

About 1 o'clock the gunboat Allen Collyer moored alongside the Belfast, and Colonel Bradford dispatched a messenger to the Collyer, requesting her to remain, as we would certainly be attacked by 2 o'clock.

A few moments later the Florence Miller, carrying a gun, came along and anchored in front of our town.

Colonel Bradford then posted his men in the houses along Front street and up Pine street to Second. The enemy in the mean time had reached the hill back of the town and were rapidly surrounding us. Hardly had our forces gotten their positions when the rebels with two small pieces of artillery appeared on the hill. The Belfast threw a shell, and so well was it aimed that it struck within 30 feet of the enemy's gun, killing 2 or 3 of the rebels, and causing them to change the position of their gun. The enemy then opened fire, throwing shell with little or no accuracy, and the Belfast fired two more shots with good effect.

Up to this time the forces in the houses were not engaged; but, to the surprise and sorrow of our people, the Belfast weighed anchor and abandoned us to our fate. The Florence Miller, without firing a gun, did the same thing. The Allen Collyer, although importuned to stay with us, steamed off before the fight and never returned.

Then came a shout from the rebels and they were upon us. From every window our true and trusty boys were firing, and for one-half hour the leaden hail was doing its work of death. Rebel after rebel was made to bite the dust, while our boys thus sheltered were fighting for their homes and firesides.

But what a scene now followed! The houses in which our forces were in were set on fire; the cannon of the enemy was planted in our streets, and, disregarding women or children, they were firing shell into the houses. Yet true to their work, the little band of Union men fought on until it was useless to try to hold out longer.

Colonel Bradford ordered a surrender. So soon as this was done then commenced the pillage and plunder, every rebel acting for himself. Stores were broken open and rifled of what was wanted by the rebels. This, however, was soon over. The rebel bugle was sounded, and the enemy retired from our town in good order, though in haste.

The fighting was desperate, and although our loss is small, yet gallant and brave men have gone from us forever. Our killed and wounded amount to 12 or 15, while that of the enemy number between 75 and 100; among them some 8 or 10 officers. We had no means of ascertaining the names of all the rebels killed and wounded, but among the number wounded mortally is a son of George D. Prentice, of Louisville. Capt. W. Rogers, of Harrison County, was killed, and a Lieutenant Wilson. The rebels left some of their dead and wounded in our hands, all of whom have been properly cared for. They took our horses, buggies, wagons, and all means of transportation to carry off their dead and wounded.

Among the killed on the Union side was Dr. W. Taylor, N. B. Worthington, John B. Story, George Byers, Oliver Stairs, John Gephart, John Perkins, and W. Gregg.

The prisoners were all taken from town as rapidly as they could march. Some have been paroled and returned home.

The conduct of the gunboats seems to us as cowardly in the extreme. Just above our town is a large sand bar, and so soon as the rebels could cross the bottom they ran out on this bar 100 or 150 strong, drew up in line of battle, and fired volley after volley at the Belfast and Florence Miller, and not one shot was fired in return. With one fire of grape the whole horde of rebels could have been mowed down; but the gallant commanders fled, fled! Ay, and when they got to Higginsport actually hauled their cannon ashore and moved off up the river with their boats.

Much of our town is destroyed; the loss will reach $100,000. The principal sufferers are Thomas Myers, J. B. Ryan, W. D. Diltz, W. P. Taylor, Mrs. Hooke, T. F. Marshall, V. Meldin, J. T. McKibben, and Mrs. Barr.

The Confederate forces are a battalion of Morgan's. Colonel Bradford, Colonel Harris, and F. L. Cleaveland, esq., are still in the hands of the enemy.

On yesterday Colonel Wilson and Colonel Wadsworth, commanding the forces from Maysville, Ripley, &c., passed on to Brookville in the effort to overtake the rebels, but were there only in time to fall upon their rear guard, they having retreated in great haste in the direction of Falmouth.

All of which is respectfully submitted.

JOSEPH DONIPHAN.

SEPTEMBER 29, 1862.—Capture of the Third Georgia Cavalry, near New Haven, Ky.

REPORTS.

No. 1.—Col. John Kennett, Fourth Ohio Cavalry, commanding Cavalry Division.
No. 2.—Col. Edward M. McCook, Second Indiana Cavalry, commanding First Cavalry Brigade.
No. 3.—Findings of General Court-Martial in case of Col. Martin J. Crawford, Third Georgia Cavalry.

No. 1.

Report of Col. John Kennett, Fourth Ohio Cavalry, commanding Cavalry Division.

ELIZABETHTOWN, KY.,
September 29, 1862.

COLONEL: A courier from Colonel Zahm having arrived this evening I have the honor of inclosing it. By this morning's dispatch I acquainted you with the victory part of my command achieved over the Third Georgia Cavalry, having surprised them at break of day, surrounded them, and captured the entire regiment, without the loss of a man or firing a single shot. We have their horses—poor stock—and arms. I sent them in to you as prisoners. I could not take time to parole them, and I hurried them away to secure so signal a victory, anticipating an attack to rescue them and being absorbed with field preparations for our enemies. We are surrounded by heavy bodies of cavalry, and we should have a section of artillery, with a portion of infantry.

Colonel Zahm being detained we will await his safe arrival and then leave, unless otherwise ordered. Telegraph line cut yesterday at noon. Our horses are saddled nightly; we sleep on our arms, and will be drawn up in the order of battle to-morrow morning by 4 o'clock. Such are our precautions to prevent surprise.

Not a word from you since we have been here. All quiet to-night.

Your obedient servant,

JNO. KENNETT,
Colonel, Commanding Cavalry Division.

Col. J. B. FRY.

No. 2.

Report of Col. Edward M. McCook, Second Indiana Cavalry, commanding First Cavalry Brigade.

HEADQUARTERS FIRST CAVALRY BRIGADE,
Elizabethtown, Ky., September 30, 1862.

SIR: I have the honor to report that a detachment of my brigade, under command of Lieutenant-Colonel Stewart, Second Indiana Cavalry, surprised and captured the Third Georgia Regiment of Cavalry, with their arms, equipments, and horses. All of their field officers and staff officers were taken with the regiment.

From the information gained I learn that the enemy's infantry and artillery are within 3 miles of where this force was taken. They have some 25,000 or 30,000 bushels of wheat at mills in that vicinity, being ground for the use of the army, and I suppose the enemy's force is left there for the purpose of protecting this.

Citizens of the neighborhood say there is one brigade of infantry and one of cavalry and three pieces of artillery between New Haven and Bardstown. Their object in concentrating this force seems to be to protect these mills.

Very respectfully, your obedient servant,

EDWARD M. McCOOK,
Colonel, Commanding Brigade.

Colonel KENNETT.

No. 3.

Findings of General Court-Martial in case of Col. Martin J. Crawford, Third Georgia Cavalry.

GENERAL ORDERS, }   HEADQUARTERS DEPARTMENT No. 2,
No. 160.   }   *Murfreesborough, Tenn., December 26, 1862.*

I. At a general court-martial, convened at Murfreesborough, Tenn., December 15, 1862, in pursuance of Special Orders, No. 60, from these headquarters, and of which Maj. Gen. J. M. Withers, Provisional Army of the Confederate States, is president, was arraigned and tried Col. M. J. Crawford, Third Georgia Cavalry, on the following charge and specifications:

CHARGE—Conduct prejudicial to good order and military discipline.

Specification 1.—In this, that he, Martin J. Crawford, colonel Third Georgia Cavalry, being in command of a portion of his regiment at New Haven, Ky., did allow the enemy to surprise and capture his command. This at New Haven, Ky., on or about September 29.

Specification 2.—In this, that he, the said Martin J. Crawford, colonel Third Georgia Cavalry, being in command of a portion of his regiment at New Haven, Ky., did surrender his command to the enemy without offering them any resistance whatever. This at New Haven, Ky., on or about September 29.

To which charge and specifications the accused pleaded as follows:

To 1st specification, not guilty.

To 2d specification, the accused admitted that he surrendered his command to the enemy without offering them any resistance, but denied that there was any criminal or improper conduct on his part in so acting.

To the charge, not guilty.

FINDING AND SENTENCE.

The court, after mature deliberation on the evidence adduced, finds the accused as follows:

Of the 1st specification to charge, guilty.

Of the 2d specification to charge, not guilty.

Of the charge, guilty.

The court do therefore sentence the said Col. Martin J. Crawford, Third Georgia Cavalry, to three months' suspension from rank and pay and to be reprimanded in orders by the general commanding.

II. The proceedings, finding, and sentence in the foregoing case are approved. To an intelligent, conscientious, and patriotic officer like Colonel Crawford no reprimand can add to the sting of a conviction and sentence on such a charge. The neglect of duty by which an outpost is surprised and captured not only involves the officer and his immediate command, but the very safety of the army, which is reposing on confidence misplaced and undeserved. Tending to the same result it is second only in criminality to a willful betrayal of a sacred trust, involving the safety of the country. Colonel Crawford will report his address monthly during his suspension to these headquarters.

III. The general court-martial of which Maj. Gen. J. M. Withers, Provisional Army of the Confederate States, is president, is dissolved.

By command of General Bragg:

GEO. G. GARNER,
Assistant Adjutant-General.

SEPTEMBER 30, 1862.—Skirmishes at Russellville and Glasgow, Ky.

Report of Col. Sanders D. Bruce, Twentieth Kentucky Infantry.

BOWLING GREEN, KY., [*October* 1], 1862.

GENERAL: Rebels burnt bridge at Black Lick, near Auburn, Monday night. I sent Seventieth Indiana and part of Eighth Kentucky down, rebuilt the bridge, surprised the enemy at Russellville, and routed them completely, killing and wounding 50, taking 15 prisoners and 40 horses and saddles. Also routed party at Glasgow yesterday, taking 10 prisoners; among them Lieutenant-Colonel Crews, Capt. J. M. Brown, and Lieutenant Thomas. One of prisoners has pass from General Bragg directed to General Breckinridge at Chattanooga, showing that he was expected in that direction.

No enemy in force near here; small parties stealing horses through the country. I intend to whip them all out.

S. D. BRUCE,
Colonel, Commanding.

General J. T. BOYLE.

OCTOBER 3, 1862.—Skirmish at Cedar Church, near Shepherdsville, Ky.

Report of Col. Minor Milliken, First Ohio Cavalry.

HEADQUARTERS FIRST OHIO CAVALRY,
Camp at Shepherdsville, Ky., October 3, 1862.

CAPTAIN: Agreeably to instructions received from the general commanding the division I crossed the river this morning, and proceeded on the road to Bardstown until I came to Cedar Church, 5 miles from this point. A body of the enemy had encamped there last evening. I here turned to the right, proceeded a mile and returned, and took the road to Woodbridge, proceeding on it 2½ miles, and returned. When I had proceeded a mile a lad met me, who lived on the Bardstown road, who told me a squad of cavalry had followed us back toward the church. I immediately sent a company across the country to intercept their return and pushed on to the church. I had been there but a moment and was endeavoring to find which road they had gone on when my intercepting party opened fire. I hurried to them and found them driving the enemy toward us. I formed one company in the road and, letting down the fence, placed a company on their left flank. When they came up resistance was impossible. They threw down their arms and surrendered.

We took 2 captains (Gray and Conner), 1 second lieutenant (Young), 19 privates and non-commissioned officers, 22 horses, some of them good; 23 stand of arms, shot-guns, sabers, and carbines, and 22 sets of horse equipments, good. We lost nothing and fired but a few shots. The troops were of Colonel Lay's (Tennessee) regiment.

The prisoners have already given you the only information my reconnaissance revealed.

The officers' horses I have returned to them. The horses and horse equipments I have taken up on my return as captured property. The arms are at your disposal.

I am, very truly, your obedient servant,

MINOR MILLIKEN,
Colonel First Ohio Cavalry.

Capt. WILLIAM KESLEY,
Asst. Adjt. Gen., First Div., Third Corps, Army of the Ohio.

P. S.—My force was Companies B, D, and G, First Battalion, numbering about 100 men.

OCTOBER 4, 1862.—Skirmish near Bardstown, Ky.

Report of Maj. Gen. George H. Thomas, U. S. Army.

HEADQUARTERS, *Bardstown, October 4, 1862.*

GENERAL: Bardstown is in our possession, after a pretty sharp skirmish of our advance cavalry with Wharton's brigade.

I intended to have camped on Cox's Creek, 4 miles from here, but the cavalry were drawn into a fight by the rebels, which made it necessary to send assistance, when the enemy retired and yielded the town. We have several hundred prisoners sick in hospital, all of whom I will have paroled to-morrow.

It is supposed by the citizens that the infantry of Wharton's brigade has been cut off by the advance of our troops. I have disposed the troops so as to intercept them if possible, but I believe they have all escaped. The last of their infantry left this morning on the Springfield pike, and on another road, which the citizens call the Little Beech Fork road. A Dr. Cowan informed me that the adjutant of a Florida regiment told him that Bragg's force consisted of sixty-five regiments, averaging 400 each, and that there was a great deal of sickness among them. The doctor is convinced that they are concentrating at Danville.

Bragg left here last Sunday morning for Danville and has not been back since. Polk left here this morning.

Very respectfully,

GEO. H. THOMAS,
Major-General.

General BUELL.

P. S.—We have some sick officers prisoners. The loss sustained by our cavalry was about 20 killed and wounded and a great many missing.

OCTOBER 4, 1862.—Skirmish near Clay Village, Ky.

Report of Brig. Gen. Joshua W. Sill, U. S. Army.

HEADQUARTERS SECOND DIVISION, *October 5, 1862.*

GENERAL: Yesterday, at 11 a. m., the advanced guard of the Fifth Brigade (Colonel Kirk) engaged Scott's cavalry, estimated at 600, 3 miles beyond Clay Village, and took 13 prisoners and killing and wounding 7 or 8. The brigade bivouacked at Clay Village. Information reached me from several sources during this day that the enemy had evacuated Frankfort, but full credit was not attached to these reports, as they came from second-hand sources. I have just conversed, however, with two reliable men direct from Frankfort. On Friday evening and Saturday morning the rebels had massed at Frankfort an army estimated at from 12,000 to 20,000. They inaugurated Richard Hawes as Governor at 12 m. yesterday; at 3 p. m. they began to evacuate, and during the evening burnt the railroad bridge over the Kentucky River, and also tore up the flooring and timbers of the turnpike bridge. The river can be forded.

I have ordered the march at 4 a. m. to-morrow. Bragg, Smith, Marshall, Heth, and Stevenson were there. The retreating troops took the road to Versailles. Stevenson's troops took the road to Lawrenceburg. General Dumont has arrived here with three brigades and two batteries and 500 cavalry.

Respectfully, your obedient servant,

J. W. SILL,
Brigadier-General, Commanding.

Maj. Gen. D. C. BUELL.

OCTOBER 7, 1862.—Skirmish near La Vergne, Tenn.

Report of Brig. Gen. James S. Negley, U. S. Army.

HEADQUARTERS UNITED STATES FORCES,
Nashville, October 9, 1862.

SIR: Maj. Gen. S. R. Anderson, Brigadier-General Forrest, and Governor Harris have been rapidly concentrating a large rebel force at La Vergne, 15 miles east, with the avowed intention of assaulting Nashville. Deeming it a favorable opportunity to check this project by a sudden blow, a concerted movement was made on the night of the 6th instant by a force of 400 infantry and 400 cavalry and four pieces of artillery, under command of General Palmer, sent via Murfreesborough road. At the same time 1,800 infantry, under Colonel [John F.] Miller, marched by a circuitous route to the south of La Vergne. The enemy's pickets and vedettes were in considerable force on the roads and skirmished with our advance 10 miles, enabling the main force, consisting of one regiment (the Thirty-second Alabama Infantry), with one steel rifled cannon and 3,000 cavalry, to assume a position, forming their lines in anticipation of our entire force advancing on the Murfreesborough road, which was part of our object.

The enemy commenced the action by opening fire with three pieces of artillery at a distance of 300 yards. This was soon silenced by a shell from one of our guns exploding their ammunition-chest. At the moment the enemy were directing their movements against the right flank of General Palmer's force Colonel Miller's infantry arrived, advancing in splendid line of battle, delivering a well-directed fire into the enemy's ranks, which was followed by a skillful deployment of the right and left to cut off their retreat. The Confederates held their ground for thirty minutes and then fled in the wildest disorder, leaving 175 prisoners in our hands, among whom were 2 lieutenants, 2 lieutenant-colonels, and a number of line officers, three pieces of artillery, ordnance and quartermaster stores, a large amount of provisions, camp equipage, personal effects, stand of regimental colors, and three railroad cars, which we destroyed. Their defeat was complete. Their loss in killed and wounded was about 80.

The conduct of our officers and men was highly meritorious, with numerous instances of individual bravery and efficiency.

A report in detail will be forwarded by the first opportunity.

Our loss is 5 killed, 9 wounded, 4 missing.

I have the honor to remain, yours, very truly,

JAS. S. NEGLEY,
Brigadier-General, Commanding.

Col. J. B. FRY, *A. A. G. and Chief of Staff.*

OCTOBER 8, 1862.—Battle of Perryville, or Chaplin Hills, Ky.

REPORTS, ETC.*

No. 1.—Maj. Gen. Don Carlos Buell, U. S. Army, commanding Army of the Ohio, including operations October 1–30, with congratulatory orders.

No. 2.—Return of Casualties in the Union forces.

No. 3.—Capt. Ebenezer Gay, Sixteenth United States Infantry, Inspector and Chief of Cavalry, including operations October 7.

No. 4.—Maj. Gen. Alexander McD McCook, U. S. Army, commanding First Army Corps.

No. 5.—Brig. Gen. Lovell H. Rousseau, U. S. Army, commanding Third Division.

No. 6.—Col. Leonard A. Harris, Second Ohio Infantry, commanding Ninth Brigade.

No. 7.—Col. Benjamin F. Scribner, Thirty-eighth Indiana Infantry.

No. 8.—Maj. Frederick J. Lock, Thirty-third Ohio Infantry.

No. 9.—Col. Joseph W. Frizell, Ninety-fourth Ohio Infantry.

No. 10.—Col. Alfred R. Chapin, Tenth Wisconsin Infantry.

No. 11.—Capt. Peter Simonson, Fifth Indiana Battery.

No. 12.—Col. George Humphrey, Eighty-eighth Indiana Infantry, Seventeenth Brigade.

No. 13.—Col. John Beatty, Third Ohio Infantry.

No. 14.—Capt. Percival P. Oldershaw, U. S. Army, Assistant Adjutant-General, Tenth Division.

No. 15.—Capt. William P. Anderson, U. S. Army, Assistant Adjutant-General, Thirty-third Brigade.

No. 16.—Col. Albert S. Hall, One hundred and fifth Ohio Infantry.

No. 17.—Lieut. Ellis E. Kennon, Ninety-eighth Ohio Infantry, Acting Assistant Adjutant-General, Thirty-fourth Brigade.

No. 18.—Lieut. Col. Silas A. Strickland, Fiftieth Ohio Infantry.

No. 19.—Col. William B. Hazen, Forty-first Ohio Infantry, commanding Nineteenth Brigade, Fourth Division, Second Army Corps.

---

* For report of Brigadier-General Wheeler, C. S. A., see August 27–October 22, 1862, p. 893.

No. 20.—Col. George D. Wagner, Fifteenth Indiana Infantry, commanding Twenty-first Brigade, Sixth Division.

No. 21.—Maj. Gen. Charles C. Gilbert, U. S. Army, commanding Third Army Corps.

No. 22.—Col. William C. Kise, Tenth Indiana Infantry, Second Brigade, First Division.

No. 23.—Brig. Gen. James B. Steedman, U. S. Army, commanding Third Brigade.

No. 24.—Brig. Gen. Robert B. Mitchell, U. S. Army, commanding Ninth Division, including skirmish October 7.

No. 25.—Col. Michael Gooding, Twenty-second Indiana Infantry, commanding Thirtieth Brigade.

No. 26.—Brig. Gen. Philip H. Sheridan, U. S. Army, commanding Eleventh Division.

No. 27.—Col. Daniel McCook, Fifty-second Ohio Infantry, commanding Thirty-sixth Brigade.

No. 28.—Lieut. Col. Daniel D. T. Cowen, Fifty-second Ohio Infantry.

No. 29.—General Braxton Bragg, C. S. Army, commanding Department No. 2, with orders and correspondence, and including operations August 28–October 24.

No. 30.—Casualties in the Confederate forces. (Incomplete.)

No. 31.—Maj. Gen. Leonidas Polk, C. S. Army, commanding Army of the Mississippi.

No. 32.—Maj. John Knight, Forty-first Georgia Infantry, Maney's Brigade, Cheatham's Division, Right Wing.

No. 33.—Col. H. R. Feild, First Tennessee Infantry.

No. 34.—Col. George C. Porter, Sixth Tennessee Infantry.

No. 35.—Maj. George W. Kelsoe, Ninth Tennessee Infantry.

No. 36.—Lieut. Col. W. Frierson, Twenty-seventh Tennessee Infantry.

No. 37.—Maj. Gen. William J. Hardee, C. S. Army, commanding Left Wing.

No. 38.—Brig. Gen. Daniel W. Adams, C. S. Army, commanding Second Brigade, Second Division.

No. 39.—Brig. Gen. Bushrod R. Johnson, C. S. Army, commanding Third Brigade, Third Division.

No. 40.—Col. A. S. Marks, Seventeenth Tennessee Infantry.

No. 41.—Lieut. Col. R. H. Keeble, Twenty-third Tennessee Infantry.

No. 42.—Col. John M. Hughs, Twenty-fifth Tennessee Infantry.

No. 43.—Col. Moses White, Thirty-seventh Tennessee Infantry.

No. 44.—Col. John S. Fulton, Forty-fourth Tennessee Infantry.

No. 1.

Reports of Maj. Gen. Don Carlos Buell, U. S. Army, commanding Army of the Ohio, including operations October 1–30, with congratulatory orders.

HEADQUARTERS ARMY OF THE OHIO,
Perryville, October 9, 1862.

I have already advised you of the movement of the army under my command from Louisville. More or less skirmishing has occurred daily with the enemy's cavalry since then. It was supposed the enemy would give battle at Bardstown. The troops reached that point on the 4th, driving out the enemy's rear guard of cavalry and artillery. The main body retired toward Springfield, whither the pursuit has continued. The center corps, under General Gilbert, moved on the direct road from Springfield to Perryville, and arrived on the 7th within 2 miles of the town, where the enemy was found to be in force. The left column, under General McCook, came up on the Mackville road about 10 o'clock yesterday, the 8th. It was ordered into position to attack and a strong reconnaissance directed.

At 4 o'clock I received a request from General McCook for re-enforcements, and heard with astonishment that the left had been seriously engaged for several hours and that the right and left of that corps were being turned and severally pressed. Re-enforcements were immediately sent forward from the center ; orders were also sent to the right column, under General Crittenden, which was advancing by the Lebanon road, to push forward and attack the enemy's left, but it was impossible for it to get into position in time to produce any decided results. The action continued until dark; some sharp fighting also occurred in the center. The enemy was everywhere repulsed, but not without some momentary advantage on the left.

The several corps were put in position during the night and moved to attack ; at 6 o'clock this morning some skirmishing occurred with the enemy's rear guard. The main body has fallen back in the direction of Harrodsburg. I have no accurate report of our loss yet. It is probably pretty heavy, including valuable officers. Generals Jackson and Terrill, I regret to say, are among the number of killed. I will report more in detail as soon as possible.

D. C. BUELL,
Major-General, Commanding.

Major-General HALLECK.

—

LOUISVILLE, KY., *November* 4, 1862.

SIR : It is due to the army which I have commanded for the last twelve months, and perhaps due to myself, that I should make a circumstantial report of its operations during the past summer. Such a report requires data not now at hand, and would occupy more time than can be spared at present from the subject of more immediate interest, namely, the operations from Louisville against the rebel forces in Kentucky under the command of General Bragg. I therefore commence this report from that period, premising only, in a general way, that my attention to the condition of affairs in Kentucky was demanded, first, by the minor operations of the enemy, which by the destruction of the railroad had completely severed the communications of my army and left it at a distance of 300 miles from its base with very limited supplies ; and, second, by the formidable invasion, which not only threatened the permanent occupation of the State, but exposed the States north of the Ohio River to invasion.

Leaving a sufficient force to hold Nashville, the remainder of the army under my command was put in march for Kentucky. The rear division left Nashville on the 15th and arrived at Louisville, a distance of 170 miles, on September 29. The advance arrived on the 25th. The particulars of the march will, as I have said, be given in a subsequent report, in connection with other matters.

I found in and about the city a considerable force of raw troops, hurriedly thrown in from Illinois, Indiana, and Ohio, for the defense of the city against the formidable force that had invaded the State under Generals Bragg and Kirby Smith. Under the command of Major-General Nelson, whose untimely death cannot be too much deplored, these troops had been organized into brigades and divisions, and they had some able and experienced officers in Generals Boyle, Jackson, Cruft, Gilbert, Terrill, and others. But the troops were as yet undisciplined, unprovided with suitable artillery, and in every way unfit for active operations against a disciplined foe. It was necessary to reorganize the whole force. This was done as far as possible by intermixing the new troops with the old without changing the old organization. The troops were supplied with shoes and other essentials, of which they were greatly in need; among them certain light cooking utensils, which the men could carry, and dispense with wagons, the allowance of which was reduced to one for each regiment, to carry a few necessary articles for officers and one for hospital supplies, besides the ambulances.

The army was to have marched on September 30, but an order, which was subsequently suspended, relieving me from the command delayed the movement until the following day.

The army marched on the 1st ultimo in five columns. The left moved toward Frankfort, to hold in check the force of the enemy which still remained at or near that place; the other columns, marching by different routes, finally fell respectively into the roads leading from Shepherdsville, Mount Washington, Fairfield, and Bloomfield to Bardstown, where the main force of the enemy under General Bragg was known to be. These roads converge upon Bardstown at an angle of about 15° from each other.

Skirmishing with the enemy's cavalry and artillery marked the movement of each column from within a few miles of Louisville. It was more stubborn and formidable near Bardstown; but the rear of the enemy's infantry retired from that place eight hours before our arrival, when his rear guard of cavalry and artillery retreated after a sharp engagement with my cavalry. The pursuit and skirmishing with the enemy's rear guard continued toward Springfield.

The information which I received indicated that the enemy would concentrate his forces at Danville. The First Corps, under Major-General McCook, was therefore ordered to march from Bloomfield on Harrodsburg, while the Second Corps, under Major-General Crittenden, moved on the Lebanon and Danville road, which passes 4 miles to the south of Perryville, with a branch to the latter place, and the Third Corps on the direct road to Perryville. My headquarters moved with the Third (or center) Corps. Major-General Thomas, second in command, accompanied the Second (or right) Corps. After leaving Bardstown I learned that the force of Kirby Smith had crossed to the west side of the Kentucky River near Salvisa, and that the enemy was moving to concentrate either at Harrodsburg or Perryville. General McCook's route was therefore changed from Harrodsburg to Perryville.

The center corps arrived on the afternoon of the 7th, and was drawn up in order of battle about 3 miles from Perryville, where the enemy appeared to be in force. The advance guard, under Captain Gay, consisting of cavalry and artillery, supported toward evening by two regiments of infantry, pressed successfully upon the enemy's rear guard to within 2 miles of the town against a somewhat stubborn opposition.

The whole army had for three days or more suffered from a scarcity of water. The last day particularly the troops and animals suffered exceedingly for the want of it and from hot weather and dusty roads. In the bed of Doctor's Creek, a tributary of Chaplin River, about 2½ miles from Perryville, some pools of water were discovered, which the enemy showed a determination to prevent us from gaining possession of. The Thirty-sixth brigade, under the command of Col. Daniel McCook, from General Sheridan's division was ordered forward to seize and hold a commanding position which covered these pools. It executed the orders that night, and a supply of bad water was secured for the troops.

On discovering that the enemy was concentrating for battle at Perryville I sent orders on the night of the 7th to General McCook and General Crittenden to march at 3 o'clock the following morning, so as to take position respectively as early as possible on the right and left of the center corps, the commanders themselves to report in person for orders on their arrival, my intention being to make the attack that day if possible. The orders did not reach General McCook until 2.30 o'clock, and he marched at 5.

The Second Corps, failing to find water at the place where it was expected to encamp the night of the 7th, had to move off the road for that purpose, and consequently was some 6 miles or more farther off than it would otherwise have been. The orders did not reach it in time, and these two causes delayed its arrival several hours. Still it was far enough advanced to have been pressed into the action on the 8th if the necessity for it had been known early enough.

The engagement which terminated at night the previous day was renewed early on the morning of the 8th by an attempt of the enemy to drive the brigade of Colonel McCook from the position taken to cover the water in Doctor's Creek. The design had been discovered, and the divisions of Generals Mitchell and Sheridan were moved into position to defeat it and hold the ground until the army was prepared to attack in force. A spirited attack was made on Colonel McCook's position and was handsomely repulsed.

Between 10 and 11 o'clock the left corps arrived on the Mackville road. General McCook was instructed to get it promptly into position on the left of the center corps and to make a reconnaissance to his front and left. The reconnaissance had been continued by Captain Gay toward his front and right, and sharp firing with artillery was then going on. I had somewhat expected an attack early in the morning on Gilbert's corps while it was isolated; but, as it did not take place, no formidable attack was apprehended after the arrival of the left corps.

The disposition of the troops was made mainly with a view to a combined attack on the enemy's position at daylight the following morning, as the time required to get all the troops into position after the unexpected delay would probably make it too late to attack that day.

The cannonading, which commenced with the partial engagement in the center, followed by the reconnaissance of the cavalry, under Captain Gay, extended toward the left, and became brisker as the day advanced, but was not supposed to proceed from any serious engagement, as no report to that effect was received.

At 4 o'clock, however, Major-General McCook's aide-de-camp arrived and reported to me that the general was sustaining a severe attack, which he would not be able to withstand unless re-enforced; that his flanks were already giving way. He added, to my astonishment, that the left corps had actually been engaged in a severe battle for several hours, perhaps since 12 o'clock. It was so difficult to credit the latter that I thought there must even be some misapprehension in regard to the former. I sent word to him that I should rely on his being able to hold his ground, though I should probably send him re-enforcements. I at once sent orders for two brigades from the center corps (Schoepf's division) to move promptly to re-enforce the left. Orders were also sent to General Crittenden to move a division in to strengthen the center and to move with the rest of his corps energetically against the enemy's left flank. The distance from one flank of the army to the other was not perhaps less than 6 miles, and before the orders could be delivered and the right corps make the attack night came on and terminated the engagement.

The roads going from Mackville and Springfield enter Perryville at an angle of about 15° with each other. The road from Lebanon runs nearly parallel to the Springfield road to within 5 miles of Perryville and then forks, the left-hand fork going to Perryville and the right continuing straight on to Danville, leaving Perryville 4 miles to the north. There is also a direct road from Perryville to Danville. Perryville, Danville, and Harrodsburg occupy the vertices of an equilateral triangle, and are 10 miles apart. Salt River rises midway between Perryville and Danville, and runs northward 2 miles west of Harrodsburg. Chaplin Fork rises near and passes through Perryville, bending in its course so as to run obliquely away from the Mackville and Perryville road, on which the left corps advanced. Doctor's Creek, running north, crosses the Perryville and Springfield road at right angles about 2½ miles west of Perryville, and empties into Chaplin Fork about 3 miles from town. The ground bordering the Chaplin is hilly, with alternate patches of timber and cleared land. The hills, though in some places steep, are generally practicable for infantry and cavalry and in many places for artillery. The ground afforded the enemy great advantages for attacking a force on the Mackville road, taken in the act of forming, as was the case in the battle of the 8th. General McCook's line ran nearly parallel with Chaplin Fork, the right resting on the road and the left to the north of it. Two of General Rousseau's brigades (the Seventeenth, under Colonel Lytle, and the Ninth, under Colonel Harris) were on the right; then the Thirty-third Brigade, under General Terrill, of Jackson's division; then on the extreme left and to the rear of Terrill the Twenty-eighth Brigade, under Colonel Starkweather, of Rousseau's division. The other brigade of Jackson's division, under Colonel Webster, was at first in the rear of Rousseau's two right brigades, and in the course of the battle was brought into action on the right. General Gilbert's corps was on the right of Rousseau, but the space between them was somewhat too great—first, Sheridan's division, then Mitchell's, and Schoepf's in reserve opposite the left of the corps.

The fight commenced early in the day, as has been described, with a feeble attack on the center corps; then, later, the attack fell with severity and pertinacity on Rousseau's right brigades; then, somewhat later, on Terrill's brigade, and on Rousseau's third brigade on the extreme left. It was successful against Terrill's brigade, composed of new regiments.

The gallant commander of the division, General J. S. Jackson, was killed almost instantly. The heroic young brigadier, Terrill, lost his life in endeavoring to rally his troops and ten pieces of his artillery were left on the ground. Two of them were carried off by the enemy the next morning; the rest were recovered.

The main weight of the battle thus fell upon the Third Division, under General Rousseau. No troops could have met it with more heroism. The left brigade, compelled at first to fall back somewhat, at length maintained its ground and repulsed the attack at that point.

Taking advantage of the opening between Gilbert's left and Rousseau's right, the enemy pressed his attack at that point with an overwhelming force. Rousseau's right was being turned and was forced to fall back, which it did in excellent order, until re-enforced by Gooding's and Steedman's brigades from Gilbert's corps, when the enemy was repulsed. That result was also promoted by the fire which the artillery of Sheridan's division poured into the enemy's left flank. Simultaneously with the heaviest attack on Rousseau's division the enemy made a strong attack on Sheridan's right. Sheridan was re-enforced from Mitchell's division by Colonel Carlin's brigade, which charged the enemy with intrepidity and drove him through the town to his position beyond, capturing in the town 2 caissons and 15 wagons, loaded with ammunition, and the guard that was with them, consisting of 3 officers and 138 men. This occurred about night-fall, which terminated the battle.

The corps of General Crittenden closed in, and Wagner's brigade, of Wood's division, became engaged and did good service on the right of Mitchell's division, but knowing nothing of the severity of the fight on the extreme left the rest of the corps did not get into action.

No doubt was entertained that the enemy would endeavor to hold his position. Accordingly orders were sent to the commanders of corps to be prepared to attack at daylight in the morning. They received instructions in person at my headquarters that night, except General Crittenden, for whom instructions were given to Major-General Thomas, second in command. General McCook supposed, from indications in his front, that the enemy would throw a formidable force against his corps, in pursuance of the original attempt to turn our left. He represented also that his corps was very much crippled, the new division of General Jackson having in fact almost entirely disappeared as a body. He was instructed to move in during the night and close the opening between his right and General Gilbert's left. His orders for the following day were to hold his position, taking advantage of any opportunity that the events of the day might present. The corps of Generals Crittenden and Gilbert were to move forward at 6 o'clock and attack the enemy's front and left flank.

The advance the following morning, in pursuance of these orders, discovered that the enemy's main body had retired during the night, but without any indications of haste or disorder, except that his dead and many of his wounded were left upon the field. The reconnaissance during the day showed that his whole force had fallen back on Harrodsburg, where the indications seemed to be that he would make a stand.

It will be impossible to form any correct judgment of the operations from this time, particularly without considering the condition of the two armies and the probable intentions of the enemy. The rebel army has been driven from the borders of Kentucky without a decisive battle. It is spoken of as if it were a comparatively insignificant force and pursued by an overwhelming one, which had nothing to do but to send out patrols and gather in the fragments of a routed and disorganized army. The very reverse was the case. The rebel force which invaded Kentucky, at the lowest estimates, has been rated at from 55,000 to 65,000 men. It was composed of veteran troops, well armed, and thoroughly inured to hardships. Every circumstance of its march and the concurrent testimony of all who came within reach of its lines attest that it was under perfect discipline. It had entered Kentucky with the avowed purpose of holding the State; its commanders declared that to be their intention to the last. Intercepted communications, disclosing their plans and the disappointment expressed by the Southern press at the result, show that to have been their purpose. The enterprise certainly seemed desperate, but it was entered upon deliberately, was conducted by the best talent in the rebel service, and there was nothing to indicate that it would be abandoned lightly. Some maneuvering for advantage and one decisive battle were to be expected before Kentucky could be rid of her invader. Everything goes to show that the final retreat of the enemy was suddenly determined on, and that it was not at the time to be calculated upon as a matter of course. Any movement on my part, solely in anticipation of it. would only have turned the enemy in a different direction, and any presumptuous attempt to capture a superior force by detachments would, according to all probabilities, have been more likely to result in defeat than in success.

The effective force which advanced on Perryville on the 7th and 8th under my command was about 58,000 infantry, artillery, and cavalry. Of these about 22,000 were raw troops, with very little instruction, or none at all. The reports show an actual loss of upward of 4,000 killed, wounded, and missing in the battle, which would leave the effective force about 54,000 after it. I did not hesitate therefore, after crossing Chaplin River and finding the enemy had fallen back, to await the arrival of General Sill's division, which had marched to Frankfort, and had been ordered to join, via Lawrenceburg and Chaplintown, when it was ascertained that Kirby Smith's force had marched to form a junction with Bragg. That division on the march from Louisville encountered a strong outpost of the enemy on the Frankfort road about 12 miles out, and skirmishing was kept up until its arrival at Frankfort.* It was followed closely by the division of General Dumont which remained at Frankfort.

In marching from Frankfort to join the main body Sill's division was attacked near Lawrenceburg by a portion of Kirby Smith's force, which it drove off, and then continued its march, arriving at Perryville on the evening of the 11th. Pending its arrival the army took position, with its right 4 miles from Danville, its center on the Perryville and Harrodsburg pike, and the left near Dicksville, on roads converging on Harrodsburg.

On the 11th three brigades from Crittenden's and Gilbert's corps, with Gay's and Colonel McCook's cavalry brigades, were sent out to reconnoiter the enemy's position. He was found in some force 2 miles south of Harrodsburg in the morning, but retired during the day, and his rear guard was driven out in the evening, with the loss of some stores and about 1,200 prisoners, mostly sick and wounded. It was probable that he would retire his whole force to Camp Dick Robinson, though it was not certainly ascertained what portion of it had crossed Dick's River. To compel him to take at once one side or the other, and either give battle on this side or be prevented from recrossing to attack our communications when a move was made to turn his position, the left corps moved on the 12th to Harrodsburg (General Sill's division having arrived the night before), the right corps moving forward and resting near and to the left of Danville, and the center midway on the Danville and Harrodsburg road, while a strong reconnaissance was sent forward to the crossing of Dick's River. The enemy was found to have crossed with his whole force.

The ground between the Kentucky River and Dick's River, as a military position, is rendered almost impregnable on the north and west by the rocky cliffs which border those streams, and which are only passable at a few points easily defended. Such is the character of Dick's River from its mouth to where the Danville and Lexington road crosses it, a

---

* See skirmish near Clay Vil'age, p. 1020.

distance of about 12 miles. It could only be reached by turning it to the south, while the passes to the west, by which our lines of communication would be exposed, were suitably guarded. The army was moving with that view, when I learned, on the evening of the 13th, at Danville, that the enemy was retiring from his position toward the south. Pursuit was immediately ordered for the purpose of overtaking or intercepting him if he should attempt to pass toward Somerset.

General Wood's division marched at 12 o'clock that night, and engaged the enemy's cavalry and artillery at Stanford at daylight the next morning. The remainder of General Crittenden's corps and General McCook's corps followed on that road and General Gilbert's marched on the Lancaster road. The enemy kept the road toward Cumberland Gap, opposing with cavalry and artillery the advance of both of the pursuing columns, which, however, progressed steadily.

At Crab Orchard the character of the country suddenly changes. It becomes rough and barren, affording scarcely more than enough corn for its sparse population, and the road passes through defiles, where a small force can resist with great effect a large one; where in fact the use of a large force is impracticable. The little forage the country afforded was consumed by the enemy in his retreat, rendering it impossible to subsist any considerable number of animals. The corps of General McCook and General Gilbert were therefore halted at Crab Orchard, while that of General Crittenden, with General W. S. Smith's division in advance, continued the pursuit as far as London on the direct road and on the branch road to Manchester.

I have not received the formal report of the operations of this corps, but the pursuit was conducted by its commander, according to my orders, with judgment and energy. The road was cleared of the trees felled across it by the enemy and his rear guard attacked successfully at several points. Some prisoners were taken, and about 300 head of cattle and other property, to no very great amount, captured.

It was not expedient to continue the pursuit beyond London, partly because it was impracticable in a manner to afford any material advantage; partly because, without advantage, it took the troops out of the way when they were likely to be required elsewhere. They were therefore promptly turned upon other routes toward Tennessee. A portion were to be at Bowling Green and the rest at Glasgow on the 31st ultimo, and thence continue their march by certain routes.

In that position I relinquished the command of the army on the 30th to Major-General Rosecrans, in obedience to instructions from the general-in-chief. In the mean time the railroads, which had been broken up by the enemy and suspended for two months, had been repaired as far as Bowling Green to carry forward supplies.

I have no means at this time of reporting the casualties that occurred in the minor engagements or skirmishes that took place during the campaign, nor is it possible for me to do justice to the services of the officers and soldiers engaged in them, as the subsequent movements of the troops and my separation from them have prevented me from obtaining detailed reports, except concerning the battle of the 8th. The particulars referred to outside of the battle are based on the brief and sometimes oral reports made at the time, and are unavoidably less complete and definite than I could wish. For the same reason many such I am unable to mention at all. In regard to the battle of the 8th, the reports of the several commanders go much more into detail than is necessary in this report, and I beg leave to commend them to your consideration, especially in relation to the services of many officers whose names are not herein mentioned. Where I have mentioned troops by the name of their commander, unless otherwise expressed, I wish to be understood as commending him for their good conduct.

The daily services of officers in an active campaign, though less brilliant, are often more arduous and important than those of the battlefield, and in this respect also the commanders of corps, Major-General McCook, Major-General Crittenden, and Brigadier-General Gilbert, are entitled to my thanks and the approbation of the Government. This commendation should extend also to many other officers in proportion to their responsibilities, particularly to the commanders of divisions.

I am indebted in the highest degree to the members of my staff for their assistance, especially to my chief of staff, Col. James B. Fry, whose efficient aid I have had during the whole period of my command in Kentucky and Tennessee.

The difficult and responsible duty of supplying a large force by wagon transportation over a line of about 140 miles was ably performed by Capt. J. G. Chandler, chief quartermaster, and Capt. Francis Darr, chief commissary.

Capt. H. C. Bankhead, acting inspector-general; Capt. J. H. Gilman, chief of artillery and acting ordnance officer, and Capt. N. Michler, Topographical Engineers, discharged their duties in the most satisfactory manner. At Perryville they were active and useful in reconnoitering the ground with a view to posting troops for battle.

Maj. J. M. Wright, assistant adjutant-general; Lieut. C. L. Fitzhugh, aide-de-camp, and Lieut. T. J. Bush, aide-de-camp, conveyed my orders to different commanders during the 8th, and at all times performed their duties with intelligence and zeal. The duties of his office have been ably and faithfully performed by Surg. Robert Murray, medical director.

The intelligent officers of the Signal Corps, Capt. Jesse Merrill and Lieutenants Meeker, Sheridan, and Fitch, attached to my headquarters, rendered good service at Perryville and other points.

Private Oakford, of the Anderson Troop, in carrying orders late on the evening of the 8th, fell into the enemy's lines and was captured, but had the presence of mind to destroy his dispatches.

I cannot omit to make honorable mention of the Michigan regiment of Mechanics and Engineers. It has not only rendered invaluable service in its appropriate duties during the past year, but at Chaplin Hills and on other occasions it has, in whole or in part, gallantly engaged the enemy. I especially commend Colonel Innes, Lieutenant-Colonel Hunton, and Major Hopkins for the efficient services of this fine regiment.

The cavalry, under Col. John Kennett, Fourth Ohio, commanding a division; Col. Lewis Zahm, Third Ohio, commanding a brigade; Col. E. M. McCook, Second Indiana, commanding a brigade, and Capt. E. Gay, commanding a brigade, rendered excellent service.

The brigade of Captain Gay was conducted with gallantry and effect by that officer at Perryville on the 7th and 8th.

The other brigades were not in the battle, but came in contact with the enemy on other occasions during the campaign. When the army marched on Louisville they were left on the south side of Salt River, under the command of Colonel Kennett, to escort the train of the army from Bowling Green and watch the enemy in the direction of Bardstown. The train was conducted in the most successful manner by Colonel Zahm.

The brigade of Colonel McCook also acquitted itself in the most satisfactory manner. A portion of it, under Lieut. Col. R. R. Stewart, captured Colonel Crawford and the principal part of his regiment of Georgia cavalry near New Haven on September 29.

Colonel Kennett, with Colonel McCook's brigade, rejoined the army at Bardstown on the 5th. Colonel Zahm's marched across from the mouth of the Salt River to join the column at Frankfort and thence to the main body at Danville.

The campaign, the history of which I have sketched, occupied a period of about twenty days. The result can be stated in a few words: An army, prepared for the conquest and occupation of Kentucky, with full knowledge of our means of resistance and with a confident expectation of prevailing over them, has been driven back, baffled and dispirited, from the borders of the State. It is true that only one serious battle has been fought, and that was incomplete and less decisive than it ought to have been. That it was so is due partly to unavoidable difficulties, which prevented the troops, marching on different roads, from getting upon the ground simultaneously; but more to the fact that I was not apprised early enough of the condition of affairs on my left. I can find no fault with the former, nor am I disposed at this time to censure the latter, though it must be admitted to have been a grave error. I ascribe it to the too great confidence of the general commanding the left corps (Major-General McCook), which made him believe that he could manage the difficulty without the aid or control of his commander. As before stated, there was skirmishing along the whole front, but after a certain hour, for the reasons stated, no general engagement was anticipated that day, and no sound of musketry reached my headquarters by which the sharpness of the action on the left could be known or even suspected, and when the fact was ascertained it was too late to do more than throw in succor before night set in. But although this lack of information was attended with disappointment and unfortunate consequences, yet the unequal struggle was marked by no disaster and conspicuously displayed the courage and discipline of the troops.

From first to last I suppose 4,000 or 5,000 prisoners, sick, wounded, and well, were taken; and at various points some stores and property fell into our hands, among them 2,500 barrels of pork and two pieces of cannon, abandoned by the enemy at Camp Dick Robinson. I do not believe that he carried off in his retreat any large amount of stores. He may have sent off a good deal, from first to last, while he was in quiet occupation of so much of the State.

The reports show a loss of 916 killed, 2,943 wounded, and 489 missing. Total, 4,348 in the battle of the 8th.* It includes many valuable lives. The loss of such men as James S. Jackson, William R. Terrill, George P. Jouett, George Webster, W. P. Campbell, Alexander S. Berryhill, and John Herrell would be mourned in any army and any cause where true manliness and earnest devotion are appreciated.

I inclose herewith the reports of subordinate commanders as far as received and a map showing the lines of operation of the army.†

Major-General Thomas acted as second in command during the campaign, and I am indebted to him for the most valuable assistance.

Very respectfully, your obedient servant,

D. C. BUELL,
Major-General.

General Lorenzo Thomas,
Adjutant-General U. S. Army, Washington, D. C.

---

* But see revised statement (Report No. 2), following.
† Map to appear in Atlas. See note on page 725.

GENERAL ORDERS, ⎱   HEADQUARTERS ARMY OF THE OHIO,
    No. 47b.   ⎰   *October* 12, 1862.

The battle of Chaplin Hills, fought near Perryville on the 8th instant, will stand conspicuous for its severity in the history of the rebellion. It deserves to be commemorated for the determined valor displayed by the portion of the army that was engaged.

The principal force of the enemy, on chosen ground, under General Bragg, attacked our left wing as it was moving into position after a fatiguing march. The suddenness and strength of the attack, and the fall of two of their gallant leaders, Jackson and Terrill, caused some of the new troops of the Tenth Division to fall into disorder, and threw the weight of the battle mainly on the Third Division. This was subsequently re-enforced by two brigades from the center corps, which itself had met with considerable opposition in moving into position. The enemy was repulsed with heavy loss, and when the army advanced to the attack at 6 o'clock the following morning was found to have retreated during the night.

The good conduct exhibited by the troops on this field only realized that which the general has always confidently expected from them. Fortuitous circumstances, which so often affect the incidents of war, screened the enemy from a combined effort of the different corps until night intervened to prevent his defeat from terminating in the destruction of his army, but the thanks of the general are not less due to the gallant officers and men under his command. In the battle and on the march the old troops have given the highest proofs of discipline and courage. The new troops already vie with them. Let them preserve order, remembering that lawlessness in an army is both disgraceful and fatal. The sacredness and dignity of the cause for which they are battling demand nothing less. The nation will mourn the loss of the heroes who fell at Chaplin Hills; it will honor those who prove worthy to fill their places.

By command of Major-General Buell:

                                    JAMES B. FRY,
                             Colonel and Chief of Staff.

No. 2.

Return of Casualties in the Union forces, commanded by Maj. Gen. Don Carlos Buell, at the battle of Perryville, or Chaplin Hills, Ky., October 8, 1862.

[Compiled from nominal lists of casualties, returns, &c.]

Command.	Killed.		Wounded.		Captured or missing.		Aggregate.
	Officers.	Enlisted men.	Officers.	Enlisted men.	Officers.	Enlisted men.	
ARMY OF THE OHIO.							
Maj. Gen. Don Carlos Buell.							
Maj. Gen. George H. Thomas.*							
ESCORT.							
Anderson Troop, Pennsylvania Cavalry							
4th U. S. Cavalry, Companies B, C, D, G, I, and K†						1	1
UNATTACHED.							
7th Pennsylvania Cavalry, Companies A, D, F, and I.				4		3	7
FIRST ARMY CORPS.							
Maj. Gen. A. McD. McCook.							
THIRD DIVISION.							
Brig. Gen. Lovell H. Rousseau.							
Staff					1		1
Ninth Brigade.							
Col. Leonard A. Harris.							
38th Indiana		27	4	121			152
2d Ohio	2	25	3	74		6	110
33d Ohio		21	4	74		10	109
94th Ohio	1	6		17		25	49
10th Wisconsin	1	36	1	108	1	3	150
Indiana Light Artillery, 5th Battery		2		13		6	21
Total Ninth Brigade	4	117	12	407	1	50	591
Seventeenth Brigade.							
(1.) Col. William H. Lytle.‡							
(2.) Col. Curran Pope.							
Staff	1		1		2		4
42d Indiana		20	7	126		21	174
88th Indiana		2		20			22
15th Kentucky	3	63	7	123			196
3d Ohio	3	40	1	146			190
10th Ohio	2	58	7	162			229
Michigan Light Artillery, 1st Battery		1		6			7
Total Seventeenth Brigade	9	184	23	583	2	21	822
Twenty-eighth Brigade.							
Col. John C. Starkweather.							
24th Illinois		28	4	75		8	115
79th Pennsylvania	2	38	3	143		30	216
1st Wisconsin		58	5	127	1	13	204
21st Wisconsin	3	35	5	98	2	54	197
Indiana Light Artillery, 4th Battery		3		8			11
Kentucky Light Artillery, Battery A		3		9		1	13
Total Twenty-eighth Brigade	5	165	17	460	3	106	756

*Second in command.   †No loss reported.   ‡Wounded.

Return of Casualties in the Union forces, commanded by Maj. Gen. Don Carlos Buell, at the battle of Perryville, or Chaplin Hills, Ky., October 8, 1862—Continued.

Command.	Killed.		Wounded.		Captured or missing.		Aggregate.
	Officers.	Enlisted men.	Officers.	Enlisted men.	Officers.	Enlisted men.	
FIRST ARMY CORPS—Continued.							
UNATTACHED.							
2d Kentucky Cavalry (six companies)				4		1	5
1st Michigan Engineers and Mechanics, Companies A, C, and H				14		3	17
Total unattached				18		4	22
Total Third Division	18	466	52	1,468	7	181	2,192
TENTH DIVISION.							
Brig. Gen. JAMES S. JACKSON.*							
Staff	1						1
Thirty-third Brigade.							
(1.) Brig. Gen. WILLIAM R. TERRILL.*							
(2.) Col. ALBERT S. HALL.							
Staff	1						1
80th Illinois	1	10		45			56
123d Illinois		35	2	117		35	189
101st Indiana †							
Garrard's detachment ‡				6		33	39
105th Ohio	2	41	3	144		13	203
Parsons' battery §		10	1	18		10	39
Total Thirty-third Brigade	4	96	6	330		91	527
Thirty-fourth Brigade.							
Col. GEORGE WEBSTER.*							
80th Indiana		25	3	113		16	157
50th Ohio	2	20		32		79	133
98th Ohio	2	33	3	159	1	31	229
121st Ohio	2	1	2	21	3	13	42
Indiana Light Artillery, 19th Battery		2		13		3	18
Total Thirty-fourth Brigade	6	81	-8	338	4	142	579
Total Tenth Division	11	177	14	668	4	233	1,107
Total First Corps	29	643	66	2,136	11	414	3,299
SECOND ARMY CORPS.							
40th Indiana ¶					2		2
Indiana Light Artillery, 10th Battery ¶							
Total Second Corps					2		2
THIRD ARMY CORPS.							
Maj. Gen. CHARLES C. GILBERT.							
FIRST DIVISION.							
Brig. Gen. ALBIN SCHOEPF.							
First Brigade.							
Col. MOSES B. WALKER.							
82d Indiana							
12th Kentucky							

† Detached.

* Killed.
‡ Composed of detachments of Seventh and Thirty-second Kentucky and Third Tennessee.
§ Manned by details from various volunteer infantry regiments.
¶ The only organizations belonging to the Second Army Corps which appear to have been actually engaged in the battle.

Return of Casualties in the Union forces, commanded by Maj. Gen. Don Carlos Buell, at the battle of Perryville, or Chaplin Hills, Ky., October 8, 1862—Continued.

Command.	Killed.		Wounded.		Captured or missing.		Aggregate.
	Officers.	Enlisted men.	Officers.	Enlisted men.	Officers.	Enlisted men.	
THIRD ARMY CORPS—Continued.							
17th Ohio	......	......	......	......	......	......	......
31st Ohio	......	......	......	......	......	......	......
38th Ohio	......	......	......	......	......	......	......
Total First Brigade*	......	......	......	......	......	......	......
Second Brigade.							
Brig. Gen. SPEED S. FRY.							
10th Indiana	......	4	......	7	......	......	11
74th Indiana	......		......		......	......	
4th Kentucky	......		......		......	......	
10th Kentucky	......		......		......	......	
14th Ohio	......		......		......	......	
Total Second Brigade	......	4	......	7	......	......	11
Third Brigade.							
Brig. Gen. JAMES B. STEEDMAN.							
Staff					1		1
87th Indiana				2			2
2d Minnesota				1			1
9th Ohio				1		2	3
35th Ohio					1	3	4
18th U. S				3			3
Total Third Brigade				6	2	6	14
Cavalry.							
1st Ohio (detachment)*							
Artillery.							
1st Michigan Light Artillery, Battery D*							
1st Ohio Light Artillery, Battery C*							
4th U. S. Artillery, Battery I				1			1
Total Artillery				1			1
Total First Division		4		14	2	6	26
NINTH DIVISION.							
Brig. Gen. ROBERT B. MITCHELL.							
Thirtieth Brigade.							
Col. MICHAEL GOODING.							
59th Illinois	2	23	3	56		29	113
74th Illinois *							
75th Illinois	2	44	8	159		12	225
22d Indiana	5	44	1	86		23	159
Wisconsin Light Artillery, 5th Battery		1		1			2
Total Thirtieth Brigade	9	112	12	302		64	499
Thirty-first Brigade.							
Col. WILLIAM P. CARLIN.							
21st Illinois				6			6
38th Illinois*							
101st Ohio*							
15th Wisconsin*							
Minnesota Light Artillery, 2d Battery				4			4
Total Thirty-first Brigade				10			10

*No loss reported.

Return of Casualties in the Union forces, commanded by Maj. Gen. Don Carlos Buell, at the battle of Perryville, or Chaplin Hills, Ky., October 8, 1862—Continued.

Command.	Killed.		Wounded.		Captured or missing.		Aggregate.
	Officers.	Enlisted men.	Officers.	Enlisted men.	Officers.	Enlisted men.	
THIRD ARMY CORPS—Continued.							
Thirty-second Brigade.							
Col. WILLIAM W. CALDWELL.							
25th Illinois							
35th Illinois							
81st Indiana							
8th Kansas							
Wisconsin Light Artillery, 8th Battery							
Total Thirty-second Brigade*							
Cavalry.							
36th Illinois, Company B							
Total Ninth Division	9	112	12	312		64	509
ELEVENTH DIVISION							
Brig. Gen. PHILIP H. SHERIDAN.							
Thirty-fifth Brigade.							
Lieut. Col. BERNARD LAIBOLDT.							
44th Illinois		1	1	11			12
73d Illinois		2	1	32			35
2d Missouri	1	17	2	49		1	70
15th Missouri		1		7			8
Total Thirty-fifth Brigade	1	21	3	99		1	125
Thirty-sixth Brigade.							
Col. DANIEL McCOOK.							
85th Illinois		5		38		9	52
86th Illinois		1		14			15
125th Illinois		1	1	7			9
52d Ohio				3			3
Total Thirty-sixth Brigade		7	1	62		9	79
Thirty-seventh Brigade.							
Col. NICHOLAS GREUSEL.							
36th Illinois		9	7	57		4	77
88th Illinois		5		38			43
21st Michigan			3	19			22
24th Wisconsin		1					1
Total Thirty-seventh Brigade		15	10	114		4	143
Artillery.							
2d Illinois Light Artillery, Battery I				3			3
1st Missouri Light Artillery, Battery G*							
Total Eleventh Division	1	43	14	278		14	350
Total Third Army Corps	10	159	26	604	2	84	885
THIRD CAVALRY BRIGADE.							
Capt. EBENEZER GAY.							
9th Kentucky*							
2d Michigan		4	2	11			17
9th Pennsylvania*							
Total Third Cavalry Brigade		4	2	11			17
Total Army of the Ohio	39	806	94	2,757	13	502	4,241

* No loss reported.

No. 3.

Report of Capt. Ebenezer Gay, Sixteenth United States Infantry, Inspector and Chief of Cavalry, including operations October 7.

LEBANON, KY., *October 21, 1862.*

SIR: Being in the advance on October 7, with 500 of the Ninth Pennsylvania Cavalry, under Lieutenant-Colonel James; 500 of the Ninth Kentucky Cavalry, under Lieutenant-Colonel Boyle, and 350 of the Second Michigan Cavalry, under Lieutenant-Colonel Campbell, I drove the enemy a distance of 9 miles, skirmishing from daylight until dark, to a point on the northwest of the Chaplin Hills, within 3 miles of Perryville, on the road from Springfield. In this action the rebel General Cleburne was mortally wounded. I occupied the point held by the enemy's battery this day with a portion of my command during the night, and removed the main body to a place of rest in the rear.

At 3 a. m. on the 8th instant my advance was joined by a brigade under Colonel McCook. At daylight, hearing firing in front, I moved my command to that position, still held by Colonel McCook, where I found slight skirmishing going on between him and the enemy. I moved on to take the advance, and had hardly passed our skirmishers when I was received by a volley of musketry from a wooded hill on the left side of the road. I formed the Ninth Pennsylvania to the left and perpendicular to the road (its right resting near it) and fronting the woods, supporting the Second Michigan, which was dismounted and sent forward as skirmishers. The Ninth Kentucky was held in reserve. My skirmishers had not advanced far when a heavy musketry fire from the enemy showed that he held the position in force. Four men of the Second Michigan were killed here and 2 commissioned officers and 11 privates wounded.

The Ninth Pennsylvania was now ordered to take position to the left and front, in open ground, in order to ascertain the situation of the enemy's batteries. They had proceeded about a quarter of a mile when the enemy opened upon them from two batteries and his position became known. I placed two pieces of artillery, under Captain Hotchkiss, in position opposite these batteries, and opened fire upon them. In twenty minutes they were silenced and the enemy was driven from the wooded hill. Observing that the enemy were showing themselves farther to my left and front, I moved forward to a more advanced position, near a fork of Chaplin Creek, placing my battery in position on a knoll near it, and throwing out portions of the Ninth Pennsylvania and Second Michigan as skirmishers in advance. The enemy's batteries were again silenced here, and his cavalry, broken and disordered, were driven toward Harrodsburg.

The advance of General McCook's army was now seen on the Mackville road, to the rear and left. At my request, General Rousseau sent forward two Parrott guns, from which a few shells were thrown into the woods far in advance without meeting with any response. My command was then dismounted and rested for about an hour and a half. At the end of this time clouds of dust were seen rising in the direction of Harrodsburg, and it became evident that the enemy was being strongly re-enforced. In a few minutes fire opened from a heavy battery in front, to which my howitzers replied without effect, the distance being too great. The two Parrott guns before mentioned, belonging to Loomis' battery, opened with apparent effect, and were soon joined by the rest of the battery. Another battery of the enemy now opened farther to the left and soon another to the right and his infantry was seen advancing in line, and it became evident that the engagement would become general. An infantry regiment coming to the support of the battery, I withdrew my command to a position to the left of the one first occupied, holding the interval between the Springfield and Perryville and the Mackville and Perryville roads. In an hour the engagement had become general, the enemy attacking the extreme left of General McCook and General Gilbert's left (on my right). I sent a regiment to operate on the extreme left of General McCook and opened fire with my howitzer on the advancing line of the enemy. These howitzers were in position on the right of General McCook and remained there until nearly dark, effectively checking the enemy. Observing that our lines to the left were gradually giving way, I moved my command to the left. Arriving on the ground, I found that a portion of General Schoepf's division, of General Gilbert's army, had come up and checked the enemy's advance. Night came on and the battle ended.

The Second Michigan in this action well sustained the good reputation it had previously earned. The Ninth Pennsylvania sustained a fire from three batteries for forty-five minutes without any disorder in its ranks. The Ninth Kentucky, although a new regiment, which had not been in action before, behaved admirably.

Too much praise cannot be awarded Captain Hotchkiss and his men for their brave and effective services. To Mr. E. McKinney, chaplain of the Ninth Pennsylvania, volunteer aide, and to the members of my staff, Captain Newlin, Seventh Pennsylvania, Lieutenant Farrell, Ninth Pennsylvania, and Lieut. J. M. Bacon, Fourth Kentucky, I am much indebted for their gallant action and valuable services.

I am, colonel, very respectfully, your obedient servant,

E. GAY,
Inspector and Chief of Cavalry.

Col. J. B. FRY,
Chief of Staff, Army of the Ohio.

No. 4.

Report of Maj. Gen. Alexander McD. McCook, U. S. Army, commanding First Army Corps.

HEADQUARTERS FIRST CORPS, ARMY OF THE OHIO,
Camp, near Crab Orchard, Ky., October 18, 1862.

COLONEL: I have the honor to report that, in compliance with written instructions from you, dated October 7, 8 p. m., and reaching me at my camp at Mackville, Ky., at 2.30 a. m. on the morning of the 8th instant, I marched at 5 a. m. on the Perryville road. I had but a portion of my corps with me—Rousseau's and Jackson's divisions—the Second Division, under General Sill, having been detached to march upon Frankfort, Ky. The Tenth Division (General Jackson's) was entitled to the advance, but it being composed entirely of new troops, I ordered General Rousseau's division to take the lead. General Rousseau was ordered to march with great caution, I having heard previously that the enemy were in force at Harrodsburg; also your letter informing me that the enemy would resist your advance into Perryville; also that you intended to attack them that day. Hearing artillery in the morning, our march was hastened. Mackville is equidistant from Perryville and Harrodsburg—distance, 10 miles. My instructions required me to advance on the Perryville road until I reached a point 3 or 3½ miles of Perryville or until I came up abreast with Gilbert's corps. The head of my column reached the point designated at 10.30 a. m. General Rousseau advanced his cavalry and a portion of his infantry to the front in order to see if the ground was clear, the artillery (Loomis' battery) being halted on the hill in rear. General Rousseau soon sent me word that the enemy was reported advancing in force on the position assigned my corps. I then rode forward and examined the ground, and saw a few of the enemy skirmishing with the left of Gilbert's corps. My attention was then directed to General Gilbert's left. I saw his infantry in line about 400 or 500 yards to our right. I called General Rousseau's attention to this fact, marked out my line of battle, and ordered him to form on it, having directed Loomis' battery to be brought up and put in position on a commanding piece of ground to the left and near Russell's house (called Clarke's on your map). I had previously ordered General Rousseau to throw forward a line of skirmishers to examine the woods on our left and front; also sending Captain Wickliffe, with his company of the Second Kentucky Volunteer Cavalry, to reconnoiter the ground on the left of the skirmishers. General Gay's cavalry was making a reconnaissance in front and toward Perryville. I was then well satisfied that the enemy that had engaged Gilbert's left had retired from the field.

I then informed General Rousseau that my instructions required me to report in person to General Buell; that I was about to leave the field, but would return in a short time. I had given particular instructions to Capt. J. A. Campbell, my assistant adjutant-general, to post General Jackson's two brigades on a commanding piece of ground immediately to the right of the Mackville and Perryville road, and to hold them there in column, so that they could be moved in any direction that occasion required. I then galloped off to report to General Buell, whose headquarters were about 2½ miles in rear and right of my line. Having reported, I then received verbal instructions from General Buell to make a reconnaissance down to Chaplin River. I immediately returned to my troops, finding that General Rousseau had advanced the line on the right, occupying a commanding ridge about 800 yards in front and to the left of Russell's house. The enemy had placed three batteries in position and were firing upon his line; Loomis' and Simonson's batteries were replying. There being then no infantry of the enemy in sight, I sent an order for these batteries to cease firing and economize their ammunition. The command suffering greatly for water, I then prepared to make the reconnaissance toward Chaplin River, as ordered. Having been informed by my guide, Capt. Beverly D. Williams, acting assistant quartermaster on General Jackson's staff, and also by Col. L. A. Harris, commanding the Ninth Brigade, that by moving a short distance to the left of the Perryville road I could get high commanding ground for a portion of my line, I went forward in person to the high ground overlooking a portion of Chaplin River, advanced to within 600 yards of the river, and saw the water. Having previously ordered a portion of the Thirty-third Ohio Volunteers into the woods on the right as skirmishers to ascertain if any enemy was present in that vicinity, I then sent for Generals Jackson and Terrill, showed them the water, marked their line of battle, and ordered a battery to be posted on this line, with strong support. General Terrill was ordered to advance a body of skirmishers cautiously down the slope of the hill to the water as soon as the line was formed.

During my presence on this ground no enemy was seen, save some rebel cavalry on the opposite hills, across the river, who I suppose were threatening my train in the rear. A few well-directed shots from Stone's First Kentucky Battery, posted to the left and rear of this position, put them to flight. Not being apprehensive of an attack, I left this position and moved toward the right of the line. This was about 1.30 p. m. in the day.

At 2 p. m. an attack was made by the enemy on the skirmishers of the Thirty-third Ohio Volunteers. I then ordered the remainder of the regiment, under Lieutenant-Colonel Moore, to support the line; also the Second Ohio Volunteers to support the Thirty-third.

My line of battle at this moment was formed as follows: The right of Rousseau's division rested near a barn on the right of the Perryville and Mackville road, extending to the left, on a commanding ridge, through a corn field (the corn being cut and shucked), to the skirt of woods occupied by the Second and Thirty-third Ohio Volunteers. The right of Terrill's brigade, of Jackson's division, resting on some woods running along to the left, on the commanding ground overlooking a portion of Chaplin River to the north, his left forming a crotchet to the rear, in order to occupy the high ground on his left and rear. Starkweather's brigade and Stone's and Bush's batteries, of Rousseau's division, were posted to the left and rear of Jackson's left, on high, commanding ground. Webster's brigade, of Jackson's division, was posted to the left of Russell's house, and in the rear of the center of Rousseau's line, on the right.

The attack on my line now became general. My attention was directed principally to the left, where the attack was most fiercely made. I had no apprehension about my right, as it rested near Gilbert's left. A fierce attack being made on Terrill's brigade, General Jackson being killed at the first fire, this brigade in a few moments gave way in confusion, General Terrill doing everything in the power of a man to steady them.

At this juncture, at 2.30 p. m., seeing that I was assailed by at least three times my numbers, I dispatched my aide-de-camp, First Lieut. L. M. Hosea, Sixteenth U. S. Infantry, to General Sheridan, commanding Gilbert's left division, to request him to look to my right and see that it was not turned.

At 3 p. m. I dispatched Capt. Horace N. Fisher, of my staff, to the nearest commander of troops for assistance. He first met General Schoepf, marching at the head of his division, and reported my condition to him. General Schoepf expressed a desire to come up, replying that he was moving to the front for some purpose, and requested Captain Fisher to see General Gilbert, who was riding with the column. Captain Fisher then reported to General Gilbert that my entire command was engaged and the reserves were all in line and the safety of my corps was compromised. General Gilbert referred this officer to General Buell, to whom this officer reported at 3.30 p. m.

I also dispatched another aide, Capt. W. T. Hoblitzell, to General Schoepf, commanding the First Division and reserve of Gilbert's corps or to the commander of the nearest troops in the rear to inform him of my condition and ask for troops.

I remained in rear of my left center until I saw the enemy's right completely routed and driven back by the gallant brigade of Starkweather, so admirably posted for the work they performed so well. I then galloped to the right of the line, but only in time to see it turned by a large force of the enemy. I then ordered Colonel Webster, of the

Ninety-eighth Ohio, to move his troops to the right and repel this attack, if possible. It was in obeying this order that this gallant officer received a mortal wound. Retiring to Russell's house, I ordered my chief of artillery, Maj. C. S. Cotter, to bring up a section of artillery to stop their advance. This was done promptly. The guns were well handled, but could not stop this determined attack.

At this time the right of Rousseau's line was compelled to fall back to prevent it from being enveloped by the enemy. The enemy then placed a battery in the open field, about 800 yards from Russell's house, near Bolton's barn. The fire from this battery was so heavy that the point near Russell's house could not be held. Loomis' battery, having exhausted all its long-range ammunition, had been retired from its position in the afternoon to a commanding ridge about 150 yards in rear of Russell's house and on the right of the Perryville road, supported by three companies of the Michigan Mechanics and Engineers, commanded by Major Hopkins. I ordered Captain Loomis to reserve his canister for close work. This battery opened fire and repulsed this wicked attack for the first time. I then went to the point where the Dicksville and Springfield road crosses the Mackville and Perryville road. Near this point I met Captain Hoblitzell, with a brigade of General Robert B. Mitchell's division. This brigade was commanded by Colonel Gooding, of the Twenty-second Indiana, and consisted of his own regiment, the Fifty-ninth and Seventy-fifth Illinois Volunteers, and Capt. O. F. Pinney's Fifth Wisconsin Battery. I ordered the posting of his infantry, and then placed Captain Pinney's battery in position near the cross-roads and in a small skirt of timber to the right.

Gooding's attack, assisted by Pinney's battery, drove back the enemy and reoccupied the position at Russell's house. At this moment Brig. Gen. James B. Steedman reported to me with his brigade, of Schoepf's division. It was now nearly dark. He posted his battery on the right of Pinney's and opened fire. I then conducted his brigade to a position on the right and front of these batteries. The two battalions of the Eighteenth Regulars, under Maj. Frederick Townsend, were posted on a commanding ridge in an open field, the right resting on a wood; the Ninth Ohio on the right of Townsend, the right resting on a field. The other regiments of this brigade were in the second line and supporting the batteries. The line of Steedman's brigade was about 200 yards to the rear and right of Russell's house. By this time it was dark and the firing had ceased on both sides.

I remained in front of Steedman's line until 9 p. m., when I rode to the left and found the line there had been retired by General Rousseau. Believing that the enemy would renew the attack at daylight I ordered him to throw his line back, his left resting upon the Mackville and Perryville road, and his line extending to the right, on commanding ground, to the left of Steedman's brigade. This movement was executed about 12 o'clock at night. When General Terrill's brigade gave way, a portion of his troops fell back with him to the position occupied by Stone's and Bush's batteries, and at this point, when in the act of rallying his broken troops, at 4 p. m. he was struck in the side by the fragment of a shell, carrying away a portion of his left lung. He died at 11 p. m. When Terrill's brigade gave way seven guns of Parsons' eight-gun battery fell into the hands of the enemy. At 6 p. m. four of the guns of Harris' Nineteenth Indiana Battery also fell into the hands of the enemy.

The posting of Starkweather's brigade and Stone's and Bush's batteries saved my left and secured to us the Mackville road, upon which stood our entire ammunition train and ambulances. The ground to the right of the road being rough and rugged prevented the train from being taken off the road and parked.

I have previously stated that the firing on both sides ceased at dark. The enemy posted their pickets about 50 yards from ours, but the main body escaped during the night, and with such precipitation that they left their dead and wounded and could not carry the guns captured from the new batteries from the field. The guns were all recovered next morning, except two Napoleon guns of Parsons' battery, that were kindly exchanged by the enemy for two 6-pounder field guns. The enemy retreated across Chaplin River to the Harrodsburg turnpike, about 1½ miles distant from the battle-field; thence to Harrodsburg.

The battle-field was a chosen one for the enemy. They marched from Harrodsburg to give our army battle at or near Perryville. The ground upon which the battle was fought was very much broken by hills and deep ravines, which afforded every facility to them for concealing their troops. I was assailed by at least three divisions of the enemy. The bluffs and dry channels of Chaplin River and Doctor's Fork afforded them every advantage for concealing and massing large bodies of troops.

I have since been reliably informed that General Bragg commanded the enemy in person and that Polk's and Hardee's corps were present upon the field.

Thus ends my account of the part taken in the battle of Chaplin Hills by my corps, the bloodiest battle of modern times for the number of troops engaged on our side. Rousseau had present on the field 7,000; Jackson, 5,500; the brigade of Gooding amounted to about 1,500. The battle was principally fought by Rousseau's division, and if there are or ever were better soldiers than the old troops engaged I have neither seen nor read of them.

Great discrimination must be exercised in making a perfectly fair statement respecting the conduct of the new regiments; exposed as some of them were to a terrific fire at the onset of the enemy, it would be extraordinary to expect in them the steadiness and composure of veterans. It was also clearly perceptible that the resolution and obstinate resistance displayed by the old troops in the same brigade or in close proximity had a salutary effect in animating and encouraging the new troops; for instance, the Ninth Brigade. When the Second and Thirty-third Ohio, Thirty-eighth Indiana, and Tenth Wisconsin fought so well, I was proud to see the Ninety-fourth and Ninety-eighth Ohio vie with their brethern in deeds of heroism. Commanders have found occasion for severe reflection on individuals, whose conduct did not entirely justify the confidence reposed in them by their State and country. These cases, happily but few, compel me the more strongly to awaken the attention of our authorities to a more rigid and careful selection of officers who may join to their other qualifications the essential ones of courage and honor. The material of the new levies is evidently as good as in the old regiments. My apology for the misbehavior of some on this day is want of discipline and confidence in their field and line officers.

If it were not a great pleasure my duty compels me to call the attention of my superiors and my Government to the conspicuous gallantry and good conduct of Brig. Gen. L. H. Rousseau on this hotly contested field. The manner of posting his left and the way it was maintained render him one of the most conspicuous lights of the war. The attention of my superiors is called to the good conduct and gallantry of Col. L. A. Harris, Second Ohio, commanding Ninth Brigade; Col. J. C. Starkweather, of the First Wisconsin, commanding Twenty-eighth Brigade; also Col. W. H. Lytle, of the Tenth Ohio, commanding Seventeenth Brigade. These officers deserve promotion.

Captain Loomis, of the First Michigan Battery, handled his battery with great success and ability. Capt. O. F. Pinney, of the Fifth Wisconsin Battery, greatly distinguished himself during the close of the action, as did the entire brigade of Colonel Gooding, sent me from General Robert B. Mitchell's division.

For favorable mention of other officers and men I refer you to the reports of General Rousseau; also to the adjutants-general of Generals Jackson and Terrill and Colonel Webster, herewith inclosed.

To my personal staff, Lieut. Col. J. V. Bomford, Sixteenth U. S. Infantry; Lieut. Col. E. Bassett Langdon, First Ohio Volunteers; Capt. J. A. Campbell, assistant adjutant-general; Capt. W. T. Hoblitzell, aide-de-camp; Second Lieut. S. W. Davies, First Ohio Volunteers, aide-de-camp; First Lieut. L. M. Hosea, Sixteenth U. S. Infantry, aide-de-camp; Maj. Caleb Bates, volunteer aide-de-camp; Capt. H. N. Fisher, volunteer aide-de-camp, and Capt. James P. Collier, volunteer aide-de-camp, I return my sincere thanks for their conspicuous gallantry and intelligence displayed on the field of battle. Lieutenant-Colonel Bomford was twice wounded while posting a regiment in line.

My orderlies, Privates Isaac Bailey, Second Indiana Cavalry; George L. Richardson, Thirty-fourth Illinois Volunteers; Henry Kline, First Ohio Volunteers; Avery Lapham, Thirty-fourth Illinois Volunteers, and Privates G. Benning Jenness, William Edwards, and Harvey Knowles, escort, behaved with coolness and bravery on the field, and I recommend them to their superiors for promotion.

To Surg. G. B. Beebe, medical director of my corps, my thanks are due for his good conduct on the field and the kind care he has taken of the wounded. Favorable mention is also made of Surgeons Marks, Tenth Wisconsin; L. J. Dixon, First Wisconsin; Williams, One hundred and twenty-first Ohio Volunteers; Wright, Seventy-ninth Pennsylvania; Beckwith, Thirty-eighth Indiana; Sinnet, Ninety-fourth Ohio, and Fowler. Also Assistant Surgeons Taft, One hundred and fifth Ohio; Devendorf, First Wisconsin; Albright, Seventy-ninth Pennsylvania; Mitchell, Tenth Wisconsin; Reeve and Fuller, Twenty-first Wisconsin, and Shannon, of the Second Ohio.

Maj. C. S. Cotter, First Ohio Artillery, my chief of that arm (artillery), behaved with conspicuous gallantry and good judgment during the entire action. He was unfortunately taken prisoner after dark.

Capt. Beverly D. Williams, assistant quartermaster, was my guide during the entire day. The battle was fought near his birthplace. He was of inestimable service to me.

Lieut. M. B. Gratz and Volunteer Aide Henry Duncan, of Kentucky, of Jackson's staff, reported to me for duty after the fall of their gallant general.

Lieut. C. C. Parsons, Fourth U. S. Artillery, also reported to me for duty after his battery had fallen into the hands of the enemy. He behaved with great bravery the entire day and the loss of his battery was no fault of his; he remained with it until deserted by every man around him.

Capt. W. P. Anderson, assistant adjutant-general to General Terrill, also reported to me after the fall of his chief, and behaved with coolness and bravery during the day.

My casualties during the day were very large. The nation is called upon to mourn the loss of such spirits as Jackson, Terrill, Webster, Jouett, Campbell, Berryhill, Herrell, and others, who fell upon this bloody field.

A list of killed and wounded of the Third and Tenth Divisions is herewith inclosed.*

All of which is respectfully submitted.

A. McD. McCOOK,
Major-General, Commanding First Corps.

Col. J. B. FRY, *Chief of Staff.*

No. 5.

Report of Brig. Gen. Lovell H. Rousseau, U. S. Army, commanding Third Division.

HDQRS. THIRD DIVISION, ARMY OF THE OHIO,
In the Field, October 17, 1862.

SIR: I have the honor to submit the following report of the part taken by the Third Division, Army of the Ohio, in the battle of Chaplin Hills, fought on the 8th instant:

On the morning of the 8th, on the march, General McCook showed me an order of General Buell, in which it was said he should move cautiously on approaching Perryville, as the enemy would probably make resistance in that vicinity.

When near Chaplin Hills battle ground, and perhaps 3 miles from Perryville, the report of artillery to our right and front was heard, and General McCook ordered me to advance my cavalry and infantry in reconnaissance, leaving the artillery on an eminence in the road. I moved on with the infantry, preceded by six companies of the Second Kentucky Cavalry (Col. Buckner Board), and when near the field of battle Colonel Board reported the enemy in sight. I halted the column and sent back for General McCook, and he and I rode forward to the front, examined the ground, and chose a line of battle, to be adopted if the enemy advanced upon us, and soon after moved up to Russell's house, on the hill overlooking the field, and there halted the head of the column. While there the artillery (two pieces) of Captain Harris' [Hotchkiss'] battery, with Gay's cavalry, continued to fire, and small-arms were also heard.

Gay addressed a note to me, saying he had been pursuing the enemy all the morning, was pressing him then, and much needed a regiment of infantry to support his pieces. I ordered the Forty-second Indiana Regiment to do so, and rode forward to his pieces and found him and Captain Harris [Hotchkiss] there. The enemy was just disappearing in the woods far to the front, and out of the range of Harris' [Hotchkiss'] ordinary brass pieces. I then ordered up Loomis, with two of his Parrott guns, and he shelled the woods, the enemy now and then appearing, until finally he was no longer to be seen, and the firing was ordered to be stopped. Everything indicated that the enemy had retired and it was so believed. General McCook rode off to see General Buell, understood to be 2 or 3 miles to our right.

Waiting perhaps an hour, I concluded to resume the march to Chaplin Creek, then probably a mile to our front, to get water for my men,

---

* Embodied in revised statement, p. 1033.

who were suffering intensely for the want of it. There was a small pool in the bed of a little stream to the right of Loomis' two pieces, to which the Forty-second Indiana was directed in order to obtain a supply, and the main column was then ordered forward; but when the head of the column was within a hundred or two yards of Loomis' pieces I halted it and went forward to see what was reported to be the enemy reappearing in the woods beyond, and in a few minutes I could see him plainly, and the discharge of shell from three batteries massed gave unmistakable evidence of his presence in force. I ordered Loomis to reply and bring up the remainder of his guns, and sent an order to Captain Simonson, Fifth Indiana Artillery, to join Loomis; all of which was promptly done. I then sent an order to Colonel Lytle to form his brigade on the right in good position, and galloped back to place Harris' brigade in position to resist the advance of the enemy, which I was just informed by a messenger from Captain Wickliffe, of Colonel Board's cavalry, was being made in that direction in great force, of cavalry, infantry, and artillery. I aided Colonel Harris, commanding Ninth Brigade, to form his brigade in two lines, the Second Ohio, Lieutenant-Colonel Kell; the Tenth Wisconsin, Colonel Chapin, and the Thirty-third Ohio, Lieutenant-Colonel Moore, being in the front line. Soon after this, by a messenger, Colonel Starkweather, commanding Twenty-eighth Brigade, announced his arrival on the left, his brigade having been unfortunately cut off and separated from my division by General Jackson's column that morning at Mackville; but he had the good sense when he heard firing in front to abandon the road, move around Jackson's column, and, by going through the field, to fall in on our left, and I found his brigade on the very spot where it was most needed.

A large body of the enemy's cavalry, appearing that moment 1½ miles to the front, was admirably shelled and dispersed in great disorder by Captain Stone, First Kentucky Artillery.

I then directed Colonel Starkweather to place Stone's battery and that of Captain Bush, Fourth Indiana Artillery, on a high ridge, on the extreme left, and extending diagonally to the front, and to support those batteries with the First Wisconsin (Lieutenant-Colonel Bingham), placed on that ridge, and by the Seventy-ninth Pennsylvania (Colonel Hambright), placed on another ridge, running at almost right angles to the one on which the batteries were planted. This formation gave a cross-fire, and proved of infinite value in maintaining that all-important position during the day. These formations were made in great haste and in a few moments, but without the least confusion or disorder, the men moving into line as if on parade.

I then returned to Harris' brigade, hearing that the enemy was close upon him, and found that the Thirty-third Ohio had been ordered farther to the front by General McCook and was then engaged with the enemy, and needed support. General McCook in person ordered the Second Ohio to its support, and sent direct to me to order up the Twenty-fourth Illinois also, Captain Mauff, commanding. I led the Twenty-fourth Illinois, in line of battle, immediately forward, and it was promptly deployed as skirmishers by its commander, and went gallantly into action on the left of the Thirty-third Ohio. The Second Ohio, moving up to the support of the Thirty-third Ohio, was engaged before it arrived on the ground where the Thirty-third was fighting. The Thirty-eighth Indiana, Col. B. F. Scribner commanding, then went gallantly into action on the right of the Second Ohio. Then followed in support the Ninety-fourth Ohio (Colonel Frizell). I wish here to say of this regiment that, although new and but a few weeks in the service, it behaved most gallantly, under the steady lead of its brave Colonel Frizell.

Colonel Harris' whole brigade, Simonson's battery on its right, was repeatedly assailed by overwhelming numbers, but gallantly held its position. The Thirty-eighth Indiana and Second Ohio, after exhausting their ammunition and that taken from the boxes of the dead and wounded on the field, still held their positions, as did also, I believe, the Tenth Wisconsin and Thirty-third Ohio. For this gallant conduct these brave men are entitled to the gratitude of the country, and I thank them here, as I did on the field of battle.

After the Twenty-fourth Illinois went into action I saw the undisciplined troops of General Jackson in front, in support of Parsons' battery, of Jackson's division, yielding the field in great confusion under a most terrific fire of the enemy, who was moving in the direction of my extreme left. General Jackson was killed. The support to Parsons' battery giving way, the guns were captured, but the gallant captain brought off his horses and company.

Seeing the enemy moving toward our left in great force with the apparent view of turning it, driving some broken and disordered regiments before them, I galloped around to Colonel Starkweather, on the left, and directed him to open his batteries (Stone's and Bush's) on the enemy. The order was promptly and effectually executed. The firing was admirable, and the heavy musketry of the advancing enemy was received by the gallant First Wisconsin with shouts of defiance, placing their caps on their bayonets. I ordered the regiment to lie down under cover and await the nearer approach of the enemy, but the artillery repulsed the enemy again and again, and held him in check for several hours, until finally a fresh and overwhelming force moved straight forward toward the guns.

I should have stated that the Twenty-first Wisconsin, Colonel Sweet, was to the front of these batteries, in a corn field, lying down, awaiting the approach of the enemy, and when he approached with his overwhelming force this new regiment poured into his ranks a most withering fire. The steady advance and heavy fire of the enemy caused a portion of this regiment to break in confusion, but the most of it, under its gallant officers, stood manfully to its work till forced to retire, which it did in pretty good order. The enemy were then in reach of the First Wisconsin and Seventy-ninth Pennsylvania. I had great confidence in the gallantry of these two regiments, and was not disappointed when this time of trial came. They drove back the enemy several times with great loss, and when their ammunition was exhausted bravely maintained their position, and then quietly (not under fire) retired under orders to the line of battle originally selected by General McCook and myself, where they got a supply of ammunition and were again ready for action. Their loss is very heavy.

The fire of musketry on them and the batteries was terrific, Captain Bush at that place losing 35 horses; but he and Stone, taking all their pieces, fell back with their supports, and at once renewed the conflict and continued it until after dark. At the time this retrograde movement was ordered I sent an order to Colonel Harris to fall back also. The right, Colonel Lytle's brigade, had an hour before been drawn in, thus contracting and rendering more compact the line so thin and depleted by our loss in killed and wounded.

Before this final struggle on the left I had heard that Lytle's brigade had been outflanked on the right by an overwhelming force of the enemy and was falling back. During the day I was so hard pressed on the left and center by the continuous and persistent assaults of the enemy, and knowing if our left was turned our position was lost and a total rout of the army corps would follow, I felt the importance of my presence there, and could not look after the interests of the Seventeenth Brigade; but the whole division fought under the eye of Major-General McCook, commanding First Army Corps, Army of the Ohio, and I felt no fear that anything necessary for its safety would be neglected; and, besides, Lieut. F. J. Jones, my assistant adjutant-general, was often sent to learn its condition, and reported to me, although severely assailed, it had triumphantly repulsed the enemy in several attacks, and that Colonel Lytle felt that he could easily maintain his position; but late in the afternoon an immense force of fresh troops of the enemy, moving around to his right, concealed by the undulation of the ground, turned his right flank and fell upon the right and rear of his brigade, and drove it and forced it to retire, which it did under the orders of Colonel Lytle, who was at the same moment wounded, as he thought, fatally, and, refusing to be taken from the field, was taken prisoner by the enemy.

Hearing of this condition of things I galloped over toward the right, and found the brigade formed in line of battle, the right (the Fifteenth Kentucky Volunteers, Colonel Pope) resting on the hill at Clark's house, with Loomis' battery immediately in the rear on an eminence, the Tenth Ohio, Lieutenant-Colonel Burke, and the Third Ohio, Colonel Beatty, on the left of the road. These regiments had, without support, struggled hard to hold their line of battle for several hours, and were only forced to retire after immense loss and the movements of the enemy above referred to.

While near the Fifteenth Kentucky I saw a heavy force of the enemy advancing upon our right, the same that had turned Lytle's right flank. It was moving steadily up, in full view of where General Gilbert's army corps had been during the day, the left flank of which was not more than 400 yards from it. On approaching the Fifteenth Kentucky (though broken and shattered) it rose to its feet and cheered, and as one man moved to the top of the hill, where it could see the enemy, and I ordered it to lie down.

I then rode up to Loomis' battery and directed him to open upon the enemy. He replied that he was ordered by General McCook to reserve what ammunition he had for close work. Pointing to the enemy advancing, I said it was close enough, and would be closer in a moment. He at once opened fire with alacrity and with fearful effect upon the ranks of the enemy. It was admirably done; but the enemy moved straight ahead, his ranks now raked by the battery and terribly thinned by the musketry of the Seventeenth Brigade, but he scarcely faltered; and finally hearing that re-enforcements were approaching, the brigade was ordered to retire and give place to them, which it did in good order, as did also Captain Loomis.

The re-enforcements were from Mitchell's division, as I understood, and were Pea Ridge men. I wish I knew who commanded the brigade, that I might do him justice. I can only say the brigade moved directly into the fight like true soldiers, opened a terrific fire, and drove back the enemy. It was a gallant body of men.

After repulsing the enemy they retired a few hundred yards to a piece of woods, to encamp, and during the night the enemy advanced his pickets in the woods on our left front and captured a good many of our men, who went there believing we still held the woods.

It was in this way that my assistant adjutant-general, Lieut. F. J.

Jones, and Lieut. J. A. Grover, assistant adjutant-general of the Seventeenth Brigade, were captured by the enemy. I regretted the capture of these young gentlemen deeply. They had behaved most gallantly during the day, and I can truly say deserve well of their country.

Major Hopkins, with three companies of the First Michigan Mechanics and Engineers, remained on the field during the day, and late in the evening formed a line of battle on a line with a portion of the Seventeenth Brigade on the left of the road. Their force was too small to oppose the advancing column of the enemy. They took shelter behind Clark's house, but were forced to retire with the Seventeenth Brigade, which was done in good order. They lost quite a number in wounded and missing.

The conduct of the officers and men under the fire of the rebels was admirable. The Eighty-eighth Indiana, Colonel Humphrey, was with the Seventeenth Brigade on the right. It was not under my eye, but I was informed that it (though a new regiment) behaved well.

I have thus given a general statement of the battle and such incidents as occur to me. It was a hard and gallantly fought field, and the country is called upon to mourn the loss of many brave men who fought in it. My division fought it under many disadvantages. It was attacked on ground well known to the enemy and fixed upon by him as the battle-field, and while it was on the march and it was impossible for us to know much of the nature of the ground on which we fought. My men too were suffering intensely for want of water, having been scantily supplied for a day or two; but they fought it bravely and against three or four times their number of the best soldiers of the rebel army and under the directions and eyes of Bragg, Buckner, Polk, Cheatham, and other prominent generals of the rebel army. If of the old troops any man flinched I do not know it and have not heard of it. Very few men of the undisciplined new regiments behaved badly.

I had an opportunity of seeing and knowing the conduct of Colonel Starkweather, of the Twenty-eighth Brigade; Colonel Harris, of the Ninth Brigade, and the officers and men under their commands, and I cannot speak too highly of their bravery and gallantry on that occasion. They did cheerfully and with alacrity all that brave men could do.

Colonel Lytle, of the Seventeenth Brigade, fell severely wounded while gallantly maintaining his position on the right, and doubtless the country is as much indebted to him and the brave men of his brigade as to those whose conduct I witnessed.

To the whole division I tender my sincere thanks for their gallantry on that bloody day.

I also acknowledge my indebtedness to Lieut. F. J. Jones, my assistant adjutant-general, and to Lieuts. William P. McDowell, L. S. Hartman, D. L. Rousseau, and Harrison Millard, my regular aides, and to W. F. G. Shanks, my volunteer aide, for gallant bearing and efficient services rendered on the battle-field.

I also acknowledge my indebtedness to Lieuts. George W. Landrum, of the Second Ohio; William Quinton, of the Nineteenth Illinois; James H. Connelly, of the Thirty-seventh Indiana, and the Signal Corps of the Third Division for gallantry and valuable services on the field. They attended me voluntarily, though not their place to do so, through the thickest of the fight.

My orderlies, Sergt. Damos Emory and the rest, behaved gallantly through the battle.

Col. Buckner Board, of the Second Kentucky Cavalry, and his command rendered efficient service in making reconnaissances to the front and skirmishing with the enemy.

I herewith transmit the reports of Colonels Starkweather, Harris, and Pope,* and also a list of casualties in my division, amounting in all to 1,950 in killed and wounded.† My division was about 7,000 strong when it went into action. We fought the divisions of Anderson, Cheatham, and Buckner.

I am, very respectfully, your obedient servant,

LOVELL H. ROUSSEAU,
Brigadier-General, Commanding Third Division.

Capt. JOHN A. CAMPBELL,
Actg. Asst. Adjt. Gen., First Corps d'Armée, Army of the Ohio.

No. 6.

Report of Col. Leonard A. Harris, Second Ohio Infantry, commanding Ninth Brigade.

SIR: I have the honor to report the part taken by the Ninth Brigade in the action of the 8th of October at Chaplin Hills.

At the commencement of the action the brigade was on the right center and on the left of the Seventeenth Brigade. By direction of the general Captain Simonson's Fifth Indiana Battery was placed on my right, where Loomis' battery was engaged, and the Tenth Wisconsin Regiment directed to support it. The Thirty-third Ohio was on the left, with skirmishers well advanced to the front in the woods; the Second Ohio and Thirty-sixth Indiana in the center, with the Ninety-fourth as a reserve.

The firing becoming very warm on the right, by direction of Major-General McCook the Thirty-eighth Indiana was sent to their support. I placed them in the rear of Simonson's battery, Loomis having withdrawn. The action had now become general along the whole line. Captain Simonson, with two batteries playing on him and a heavy infantry force advancing on him and firing, nobly fought his battery, until, having lost 16 horses and 14 men in killed and wounded, by direction of Major Cotter, chief of artillery, he retired his battery. I immediately directed the Thirty-eighth Indiana to take position where the battery had been. This was not done a moment too soon, as the enemy were advancing on us. By a well-directed volley from the Thirty-eighth Indiana, Col. B. F. Scribner commanding, and the Tenth Wisconsin, Col. A. R. Chapin commanding, they were driven behind the crest of the hill. They again advanced, but were driven back. This was done for the third time, when they took position behind the crest of the hill.

At this time the firing was very heavy. I now sent back for the Ninety-fourth Ohio, Colonel Frizell commanding, but was informed that they had been directed by Major-General McCook to support a section of artillery which General Terrill was working. The positions of the other regiments had all been changed. The Second Ohio, Lieut. Col. John Kell commanding, and the Thirty-third Ohio, Lieut. Col. O. F. Moore commanding, were fiercely engaged with the enemy, who were making desperate efforts to pierce the center. It was at this point that Lieutenant-Colonel Moore was wounded and taken prisoner.

---

* The reports of Starkweather and Pope not found.
† Embodied in revised statement, p. 1033.

I saw the necessity of holding my position, with or without support, until the right was successful or compelled to retire, and I determined to do so. If I had been driven back the Seventeenth Brigade would have been cut off from the main body and in my judgment irretrievably lost. During this part of the engagement Colonel Scribner informed me that the regiment on the right was not firing. I sent Lieutenant Spencer, my aide, to inquire the cause and to ascertain what regiment it was. On his return he informed me that it was the Tenth Ohio, and that Colonel Lytle said that they were reserving their fire. Half an hour afterward I sent to Colonel Lytle, informing him that I had been compelled to withdraw the Tenth Wisconsin for want of ammunition. The withdrawal of this regiment left an interval of 200 yards on the left of the Thirty-eighth Indiana. In the mean time the Fifteenth Kentucky and Third Ohio, which were on the extreme right, were compelled to retire. Colonel Scribner now informed me that they had exhausted their ammunition and were using the ammunition of the dead and wounded. My aide that I sent after support and ammunition informed me that no support could be had and that ammunition was some distance to the rear. The only aide I now had with me having had his horse shot under him, I rode over to Colonel Lytle and informed him of the condition of things. Upon my return to the Thirty-eighth Indiana I found they had exhausted the cartridges of the dead and wounded. Colonel Scribner then directed his men to fix bayonets and hold the position, which was promptly done. Without a round of ammunition, under a heavy fire in front and an enfilading fire from the artillery, they held their position for twenty-five minutes. Seeing the hopelessness of longer attempting to hold the position I gave the order to retire, which was done in perfect order. I had not fallen back more than 100 yards when a tremendous fire from a column of infantry, which had turned the right flank of the Tenth Ohio, was poured in upon their left and my retiring column.

I retired to the woods in the rear of the corn field, where I met the Thirty-third Ohio, who had just replenished their cartridges. I directed Major Lock, who was commanding, to place them in position parallel to the fence separating the woods from the corn field, and at right angles to the road and immediately opposite the white house, directing them to hold the enemy in check until the Thirty-eighth Indiana and Third Ohio were supplied with cartridges. The Tenth Ohio came up at this moment, under the command of the gallant Colonel Burke, and took position on the left of the Thirty-third Ohio. At this time the Second Ohio were warmly engaged with the enemy on our then left, stubbornly falling back, and husbanding their ammunition, which was nearly exhausted. I also met the gallant and lamented Colonel Webster rallying a regiment of his brigade which was in confusion. I assisted him, and as soon as order was restored requested him to form in the rear of the Thirty-third and Tenth Ohio Regiments, so that the balance of my command might supply themselves with ammunition. This he promptly did. At this moment I again met General Rousseau riding among and encouraging the soldiers.

As soon as the Second and Third Ohio, the Thirty-eighth Indiana, and the Tenth Wisconsin were supplied with ammunition I formed them into line to cover the retiring of the Thirty-third and Tenth Ohio and that portion of Webster's command engaged, directing the Tenth Wisconsin to move obliquely to the right, to support a battery engaged to the right of the road. From this point by your orders I retired the line about 100 yards, when I met and attached to my command the

Fiftieth Ohio, under command of the lieutenant-colonel, and bivouacked for the night.

When all have done so well it is sufficient to say, from reports of commanding officers of the regiments and my own observations during the day, that the field and line officers, without an exception, conducted themselves nobly and to my entire satisfaction. Too much praise cannot be awarded the soldiers, every one acting like a hero. My acting assistant adjutant-general, Lieut. George A. Vandegrift, and aides, and Lieuts. F. J. Fitzwilliam and H. E. Spencer were of great service to me during the day, coolly and bravely carrying my orders to all parts of the field. Major Johnson, Tenth Wisconsin, Captain Berryhill, acting major Second Ohio; Capt. John Herrell, Second Ohio, and Captain Drury, Ninety-fourth Ohio, fell gallantly fighting at their posts.

I thought proper to mention other regiments as they became attached to my command during the progress of the action through the loss of their brigade commanders. I also send you reports of regiments which were not under my immediate eye during part of the day. The following is the loss of the brigade :*

Command.	Commissioned officers.		Non-commissioned officers and privates.		
	Killed.	Wounded.	Killed.	Wounded.	Missing.
2d Ohio	2	3	25	77	10
33d Ohio		4	21	70	18
38th Indiana		1	29	121	1
10th Wisconsin	1	2	40	103	4
94th Ohio	1		7	25	7
5th Indiana Battery			2	16	3
Total	4	10	124	412	43

This list is furnished from the men actually buried and the wounded in the hospitals. Some of the missing have since returned, having been taken prisoner while going for water and paroled. The brigade went into action 2,250 strong, including Simonson's battery.

Very respectfully,

L. A. HARRIS,
Colonel, Commanding Ninth Brigade.

Captain McDOWELL, *Assistant Adjutant-General.*

No. 7.

Report of Col. Benjamin F. Scribner, Thirty-eighth Indiana Infantry.

HDQRS. THIRTY-EIGHTH INDIANA VOLUNTEERS,
Near Harrodsburg, Ky., October 13, 1862.

SIR: I have the honor to report the following facts concerning the part taken by my command in the battle of Chaplin Hills, October 8:

After having occupied several positions during the preliminary arrangements for the contest I was ordered to the front to support a

---

* But see revised statement, p. 1033.

battery, but upon arrival at the position indicated the battery was retired. I was ordered to form on the brow of the hill, on the right of
the Tenth Wisconsin, which was there warmly engaged, which we did,
under a heavy fire from the enemy's infantry in front of the right of my
line. We occupied this position about two and a half hours, my men
taking deliberate aim at every shot. They here spent the 40 rounds in
their boxes and then used those in the boxes of the killed and wounded.
After this they fixed bayonets and awaited orders.

About this time the right and center of the brigade on our right was
seen to give way, when you ordered us to retire, which we did in good
order, under a terrific fire from the enemy, who had turned our right
and opened upon us with a battery on our right. We halted at your
order on the hill on the edge of the woods, and while awaiting the
arrival of ammunition were trampled over by a regiment of our troops
in full retreat, and my men, to their credit be it spoken, remained firmly
in their places. Not a man was observed to share the panic, but, with
bayonets fixed, were prepared to repel whatever should come.

The retiring regiments having again formed we were ordered to pass
our column to the rear, which was promptly done. We there found
our ammunition wagon and supplied our wants immediately. From
this position we were ordered to move down the hill to support a battery which was threatened from the left, and where we maintained our
position until the close of the engagement.

I have been thus brief in the description, from the fact that during
the day we were under your personal observation.

I cannot close without specially noticing the gallant conduct of Lieut.
Col. D. F. Griffin, from whose judgment and self-possession I received
much assistance.

The conduct of my adjutant, George Devol, was most praiseworthy.

With regard to the officers of the line, it would be invidious to specify
by name when all did their whole duty so nobly. They, without exception, remained in their places and gave their whole attention to the
work before them, cautioning their men to be sure of their aim and
preventing them from uselessly exposing themselves.

Of the men I can only say that they were never more obedient and
manageable on drill than upon this occasion, and I believe would have
died on the spot rather than to have moved without orders.

The severity of the engagement may be correctly inferred from the
following facts: That of the color rank and guard but 3 remain; 5 were
killed, and the color-bearer severely wounded in two places. Two
others had their clothes penetrated by balls, and but one remained un-
scathed. The colors were riddled almost to shreds, the top of the staff
shot away, and the center cut in two.

Our loss on the field was: Killed, 27; officers wounded, 4; enlisted
men wounded, 119. Total, 150.*

We lost in prisoners (taken after they had passed through the engagement with us) 7, 2 of them while assisting the wounded from the
field; the others, while in search of water, wandering within the enemy's
lines.

B. F. SCRIBNER,
Colonel Thirty-eighth Indiana Volunteer Infantry.

Lieutenant VANDEGRIFT,
  Acting Assistant Adjutant-General.

---

* But see revised statement, p. 1033.

No. 8.

Report of Maj. Frederick J. Lock, Thirty-third Ohio Infantry.

HDQRS. THIRTY-THIRD REGT. OHIO VOL. INFANTRY,
Camp near Harrodsburg, Ky., October 13, 1862.

SIR: I have the honor to submit herewith my official report of the loss sustained by this regiment in the action at Chaplin Hills on the 8th instant:

It is deemed unnecessary to enter into a minute detail of the action of my command on that day. The brigade commander, by his presence at the different parts of the field, is no doubt familiar with the conduct of this regiment.

At an early period of the action Lieut. Col. O. F. Moore, commanding, was wounded while gallantly encouraging his men, and, refusing assistance to leave the field, fell into the hands of the enemy. His wound, I am happy to state, was not dangerous, and he has since been paroled.

With the conduct of my officers and men I am perfectly content. My orders were at all times obeyed with alacrity, and their conduct throughout the whole engagement merits my approbation.

The loss sustained was 21 killed, 74 wounded, and 10 missing; total, 105.* Of the number reported to be missing 6 are known now to have been captured and paroled.

I am, sir, very respectfully, your obedient servant,

F. J. LOCK,
Major, Commanding.

Lieut. G. A. VANDEGRIFT, *Acting Assistant Adjutant-General.*

No. 9.

Report of Col. Joseph W. Frizell, Ninety-fourth Ohio Infantry.

ARMY OF THE OHIO,
In the Field, October 10, 1862.

SIR: I have the honor to make the following report as to the part my command (Ninety-fourth Ohio Regiment) took in the action of the 8th instant at Chaplin Hills:

I formed my regiment, by order of General Rousseau, as a reserve, on the left and in the rear of Simonson's battery, but before it became necessary for me to go directly to the support of the battery I was ordered up by an aide of General McCook to the support of Terrill's battery. I moved up by my left flank, in double-quick, about 800 yards, some 200 yards to the left of the battery, where I found the enemy in great force, and where our forces had given way. I had scarcely halted my command and fronted when a most murderous and incessant fire from infantry was opened upon me. My men stood their ground for about three-quarters of an hour, when the enemy began gradually to fall back. Fresh troops at this moment came up and took our position, but was informed that I again must take the front. Knowing that I was almost out of ammunition, my only alternative was to resort to the bayonet. I moved forward with the expectation of using cold steel, but was satisfied to find that the enemy had promptly left when they saw us mak-

---

* But see revised statement, p. 1033.

ing toward them. They gave way entirely in front of us, and after advancing some 125 yards and not being supported I did not feel authorized to proceed farther.

My regiment remained in this position some half an hour, nothing occurring of note except that a rebel colonel came a little too close to us to make observations, when one of Company F's men shot him off his horse. He was brought inside of our lines and expired a few moments afterward. My attention was diverted to my rear, when I saw that a portion of Terrill's battery was going past me in hot haste, and heavy volleys of infantry to the right and rear of me. I immediately formed my men so as to meet the enemy's right, who appeared to be driving our men down the ridge we first occupied. The enemy, however, was checked before they reached our last line. I remained until I received your order to take another position about dark.

The numerous dead bodies found upon the ground in front of the position I occupied showed that the enemy were severely punished. In the early part of the engagement Capt. John C. Drury, of Company B, fell shot through the heart. A finer officer or a braver man fell not that day. In the death of Captain Drury the company lost a gallant leader, the regiment an officer whose place I am fearful will never be filled.

The officers and men of the regiment behaved most gallantly, going into action under a fire almost unprecedented in the annals of war for severity. It was astonishing to see the line stand as steadily as if in mere practice. Lieutenant-Colonel Bassford and Major King displayed great coolness and bravery, and these gentlemen are entitled to great credit for the successful action of my command on this occasion. James E. Edmunds, acting adjutant, rendered great aid. I commend him for his activity and gallantry. Sergt. Maj. William D. Putnam, during the hottest of the fire, attracted the attentive admiration of the officers of the regiment and incited the men by his great courage and daring. Our chaplain, Rev. William Arlington, gave ample proof of a Christian and kind-hearted gentleman by his incessant care to our wounded men.

I went into action with 500 men. My loss, in killed, 8; wounded, 25; prisoners, 2; missing, 5. Total, 40.*

Respectfully, your obedient servant,

J. W. FRIZELL,
Colonel Ninety-fourth Regiment Ohio Volunteer Infantry.

Lieut. G. A. VANDEGRIFT.

No. 10.

Report of Col. Alfred R. Chapin, Tenth Wisconsin Infantry.

HDQRS. TENTH REGIMENT WISCONSIN VOLUNTEERS,
Chaplin Hills, Ky., October 11, 1862.

SIR: I would most respectfully report that on October 8, at the battle of Chaplin Hills, by your order my regiment was sent to support Simonson's battery.

I took into the fight 360 enlisted men and 16 commissioned officers. in about three hours after taking our position we were attacked by a very large body of infantry, which charged over the ridge directly in

---

* But see revised statement, p. 1033.

our front. Three volleys from my regiment sent them back over the ridge, where we held them until support came from the Thirty-eighth Indiana Regiment, Colonel Scribner.

The battery having retired, the Thirty-eighth Indiana and my own regiment sustained the attack over one hour and thirty minutes, when, having expended all the cartridges, together with all in the boxes of the dead and wounded, by your order we retired for ammunition, which was done in good order.

Our loss is as follows: Killed, 36; wounded, 109; missing, 4. Total, 149.*

Much credit is due to all the officers and soldiers of the regiment for their courage and coolness under a terrible fire of musketry and artillery ; but to the soldiers in the ranks is the most credit due, as the nature of the fight was such as to require no military science, but simply brave men.

Very respectfully, your obedient servant,

A. R. CHAPIN,
Colonel Tenth Wisconsin Volunteers.

Col. L. A. HARRIS, *Commanding Ninth Brigade.*

No. 11.

Report of Capt. Peter Simonson, Fifth Indiana Battery.

CAMP NEAR HARRODSBURG, KY.,
October 12, 1862.

The colonel's order of this date was just received. I have to report in the action of Chaplin Hills a loss of 2 men killed, 16 wounded, and 3 missing;* also 16 horses killed on the field and 4 horses so badly disabled that I was obliged to leave them. My loss in material was one limber blown up by a shell striking it, the caisson of which we secured in the morning, but left behind for want of limber and horses. We also lost eight sets of artillery harness and several other small articles of artillery equipments not essential to the working of the guns.

The part taken by my battery during the action was as follows:

We were first ordered to take position by Colonel Harris some 400 yards east of the white hospital, and to the left of the road, in a corn field. After the order was partly executed General Rousseau ordered the battery forward to support Loomis on his left. We then, at about 1 p. m., opened fire on the enemy's batteries on the opposite hills, distance, respectively, one directly in front, say 1,600 yards; another, a little to our right, about the same, and another, still farther to the right, about 1,000 yards.

About 2 p. m. Loomis' battery fell back, and the enemy's battery on our extreme right advanced to a position about 800 yards distant on our right flank, under cover of thick woods. Our firing up to this time and until about 3 o'clock was directed principally against the two batteries in our front, up to which time we had suffered but little.

About 3 o'clock the fire of the battery on our right began to tell on us. At the same time large bodies of infantry appeared about 400 yards, directly in front and on our left and right flanks. I informed Colonels Chapin and Burke, of the Tenth Wisconsin and Tenth Ohio Volunteers,

----

* But see revised statement, p. 1033.

of these facts, who came to my support in the most prompt and gallant manner, the Thirty-eighth Indiana at this time occupying ground some 200 yards in the rear of the battery.

From this time until 3.30 p. m. we fired canister as rapidly as the men were able to work the guns, when we were ordered by Major Cotter, chief of artillery on General McCook's staff, to find a new position, where we could use the balance of our canister with effect. We would have been unable to execute this order but for the gallant support of the Tenth Wisconsin, Tenth Ohio, and the Thirty-eighth Indiana. Major Cotter placed us in position on the right of the road, near the old straw-stack, where one of the enemy's shells struck one of the limber chests.

Abandoned this position by order of Major Cotter at 4 p. m. and took position a little in rear of the white house, next to the woods, in which the brigade was formed the next morning. Finding we could not reach the enemy from this point, we then took position on the crown of the hill, across and in the road, about 100 yards in rear of the white house. At this point we fired away the remainder of our canister and then withdrew.

At about dark we took position in battery and went into camp for the night on the slope of the next hill about 500 yards in rear of the headquarters of the Ninth Brigade.

We fired during the action 755 rounds. The command was composed on entering the fight of 90 men. We brought from the field all our wounded.

Respectfully, yours,

PETER SIMONSON,
Captain, Commanding.

Lieut. G. A. VANDEGRIFT, Actg. Assist. Adjt. Gen.

No. 12.

Report of Col. George Humphrey, Eighty-eighth Indiana Infantry, Seventeenth Brigade.

HDQRS. EIGHTY-EIGHTH REGIMENT INDIANA VOLS.,
Camp near Harrodsburg, Ky., October 12, 1862.

SIR : I have the honor to make the following report of the part taken by the regiment under my command in the battle of Chaplin Hills on the 8th instant :

The regiment took up its line of march from the camp near Mackville at 5.30 a. m. and arrived at 10 a. m., after a fatiguing march of 7 miles without water, on the ground which was afterward the battle-field. I placed my regiment in line of battle on the left of the main road in a thick woods on the crest of a hill commanding the valley in front, the Third Ohio Volunteers on my left and the Fifteenth Kentucky on my right at right angles. After remaining in this position two hours I was ordered to move my regiment, by Major-General Rousseau, down to a position about 400 feet in front of the house on the hill. After remaining in this position under fire I moved back the regiment while under a severe fire in admirable order to a position on the right of the main road, commanding the cleared fields in front, my left resting on the house on the hill and my right resting in a valley at about an angle of 45° to the road. I remained in this position under a heavy fire of artillery and musketry. I ordered my men to lie on their faces. I waited patiently for an order to advance, which was received at 3 p. m., when I was ordered by Captain Grover, your acting assistant adjutant-general, to take a position in front in a ravine about parallel to our last position and 300 feet in advance. I lay in this position for an hour, when, finding that the enemy were about turning my left flank, I fell back without orders to the right of Loomis' battery, which was posted on the hill about 400 feet to the rear of the house on the hill. This movement was made under the most terrible fire of musketry and artillery. At this time the firing was the fiercest of the day. After remaining in this position about five minutes I ordered an advance to a position behind a fence and poured in about 20 rounds of ammunition upon the advancing enemy, which drove them back in about thirty minutes. By order of Major-General McCook, at 6 p. m. I was ordered to take position in the woods on the right of the cleared fields, where I bivouacked for the night. Finding my regiment in General Steedman's lines I reported to him, and being nearly out of ammunition, I made requisition for a supply and received it.

The loss in my regiment was 2 killed and 20 wounded and 6 taken prisoners while carrying the wounded from the field of battle after night. I also took 1 lieutenant and 5 privates prisoners, whom I turned over to General Steedman.

I take pleasure in saying that all of my officers and men behaved gallantly during the action, and particularly so my adjutant, H. B. Du Barry.

Very respectfully, your obedient servant,

GEO. HUMPHREY,
Colonel Eighty-eighth Indiana Volunteers.

Colonel POPE,
Comdg. Seventeenth Brig., Third Div., Army of the Ohio.

No. 13.

Report of Col. John Beatty, Third Ohio Infantry.

SIR : I herewith present a report of the operations of the regiment which I have the honor to command during the engagement of the 8th instant :

At 11 o'clock a. m. my regiment was ordered to take the advance of the brigade to which it belongs, and proceeded to the crest of the hill overlooking a branch of Chaplin Creek, when the enemy in front opened upon us from a battery and we were ordered to retire to the foot of the hill, some hundreds of yards in the rear. There we formed in line of battle and remained for more than an hour while the batteries were replying to those of the enemy.

About 2 p. m. the enemy were seen advancing toward our position, and my regiment was ordered to the crest of the hill. A battery, known as the Washington Battery, at once opened upon us, and I ordered my men to lie down and wait the approach of the enemy's infantry. The latter advanced under cover of a house upon the other side of the hill, and reaching a point 150 yards distant, deployed behind a stone fence, which was hidden from us by standing corn.

At this time my left wing rested upon a lane known as the ——

road, my line of battle extending along the crest of the hill and passing near to and somewhat beyond a large barn filled with hay.   In this position, with a well-handled battery playing upon us, our first fire was delivered, the enemy replying with destructive effect.   Capt. H. E. Cunard, Company I, was one of the first to fall, shot through the head, while gallantly performing his duty.   A little later Capt. Leonidas McDougal, Company H, while waving his sword and cheering his men, fell pierced by a ball through the breast.   Later still First Lieutenant Starr, Company K, died like a soldier in the midst of his men.   About 175 of my regiment were killed and wounded upon the crest of the hill.   Our line was steadfastly maintained until the barn on our right was fired by a shell from the enemy's batteries, and in a few minutes the heat became so intense that my right was compelled to fall back.   After rallying we were relieved by the Fifteenth Kentucky, Col. Curran Pope, and our ammunition being nearly exhausted, we retired to the bottom of the hill.   Soon after I sent Companies A, D, and F to act in conjunction with two companies of the Fifteenth Kentucky in endeavoring to hold a fence which ran along the side of a field in which we had been fighting and perpendicular to our former line, but the fire of the enemy's battery, combined with that of his infantry, was so deadly that these men were again ordered to retire.   The Fifteenth Kentucky having by this time left the crest of the hill and the enemy opening from a new battery on our right a fire which completely enfiladed our line, I concluded, after consultation with Colonel Pope, to leave the ravine, filed off into the ———— road and was marching toward the rear, when I perceived the enemy emerging from the woods upon our right and coming in great force toward the ground we had just been holding.   I immediately ordered my regiment to face about and advanced to meet the enemy, intending, in the absence of ammunition, to charge him with the bayonet.   I was met here, however, by Lieutenant Grover, of Colonel Lytle's staff, with an order from him to retire.   Accordingly we turned into a ravine on the right of the road and were supplying ourselves with ammunition when, hearing that Colonel Lytle, my brigade commander, was killed, and being separated from the other regiments of the brigade, I reported to Colonel Harris, commanding the Ninth Brigade, for further duty.   Night soon came on, however, and the engagement ceased.

During the battle the flag presented by the people of Ohio to the Third Regiment was gallantly upheld.   It never once touched the earth, although the color-sergeant, Macoubrie, was killed; and after him five others who successively bore it were shot down.

My regiment went into action with 500 men.   Our loss was 45 killed, 144 wounded, and 15 missing, a list of whom is hereunto annexed.* Fully appreciating the valor of my own officers and men, I desire to bear testimony to the gallant conduct of the Fifteenth Kentucky, whose members fought side by side with ourselves.

JOHN BEATTY,

Colonel, Comdg. Third Regiment Ohio Volunteer Infantry.

Col. CURRAN POPE, *Commanding Seventeenth Brigade.*

---

* But see revised statement, p. 1033.

No. 14.

Report of Capt. Percival P. Oldershaw, U. S. Army, Assistant Adjutant-General, Tenth Division.

HDQRS. 10TH DIV., 1ST CORPS, ARMY OF THE OHIO,
In Camp near Crab Orchard, Ky., October 15, 1862.

I have the honor to submit the following report of the part taken by this division in the action near Perryville, on Chaplin Heights, on the 8th instant:

At 8 a. m. the division, under the command of Brig. Gen. James S. Jackson, consisting of the Thirty-third Brigade, Brig. Gen. William R. Terrill commanding, viz: One hundred and fifth Ohio, Colonel Hall, 645 enlisted men; Eightieth Illinois, Colonel Allen, 659 enlisted men; One hundred and twenty-third Illinois, Colonel Monroe, 772 enlisted men; detachment, Colonel Garrard's, 194 enlisted men; light battery, Lieut. C. C. Parsons, 136 enlisted men, making a total of 2,406; and the Thirty-fourth Brigade, Col. George Webster commanding, viz: Ninety-eighth Ohio, Lieutenant-Colonel Poorman, 822 enlisted men; One hundred and twenty-first Ohio, Col. W. P. Reid, 814 enlisted men; Fiftieth Ohio, Col. J. R. Taylor, 655 enlisted men; Eightieth Indiana, Lieutenant-Colonel Brooks, 738 enlisted men; Nineteenth Indiana Battery, Capt. S. J. Harris, 142 enlisted men, making a total of 3,171, and a grand total of 5,577 enlisted men, left Mackville, on the road to Perryville, distant about 9 miles.

The One hundred and first Indiana, Colonel Garver, also belonging to the Thirty-third Brigade, was detached as guard to the train ordered that morning to Springfield, and consequently did not participate in the action.

We had not proceeded far before we heard the booming of cannon in the distance, and when about 3 miles on the road Captain Bartlett, of the artillery, and for the day acting as aide to General Terrill, met our front, with orders from General McCook to move up without delay, and to throw one regiment as skirmishers to the left of our line of march. Having to keep our column in rear of skirmishers, who were traveling on a very rough and broken country, we were delayed in our progress nearly an hour. The general, with his staff, rode forward to where temporary headquarters for the corps was established, and which afterward proved to be about the center of the scene of action.

At this time some batteries, I believe of General Rousseau's, were in action at long range on the right, and General Jackson, not then contemplating a general engagement, ordered me back to bring up the troops and to place the two brigades at rest on the right and left of the road. The Thirty-fourth Brigade, Colonel Webster, soon came up, and in my absence and delay in clearing the road of ambulances and ammunition wagons, to enable the Thirty-third Brigade to come up, the battery of Captain Harris was moved across the main road to the left and put in position on the right of a high, level ridge. It soon opened fire at long range, no enemy then being visible, and the regiments belonging to the same brigade were placed in position in the rear and left of the battery under the crest of the hill, as will be seen by the report of Lieut. E. E. Kennon, acting assistant adjutant-general, herewith submitted. Here I rejoined General Jackson. A few rounds having opened the enemy's batteries, a 12-pounder shot came within a foot of anticipating the fatal stroke our general received soon afterward.

Riding toward our left and a little in advance of Harris' battery we came upon an open knob, where we found General McCook and all his staff watching some beautiful artillery practice by Stone's battery farther on our left, which was firing up a wide ravine upon the enemy's cavalry moving up a road to our front.

Here Captain Parsons was located soon after, and by 2 p. m. opened with round shot and shell. The One hundred and twenty-third Illinois had been previously brought on the field forming our extreme left and angling toward the rear of the battery. Soon after the battery was in position the One hundred and fifth Ohio, Colonel Hall, came up and took position to the left and rear of the battery, and the Eightieth Illinois, Colonel Allen, through misdirection of the guide, came up later and formed in the valley near the edge of the woods, as will be seen by the report of Capt. William P. Anderson, assistant adjutant-general, herewith submitted.

This battery had fired but a few shots when we heard rifle-shots below in the woods, when the enemy soon advanced and came in sight in the edge of the woods fronting our troops. No sooner was this seen by General Terrill and Lieutenant Parsons, then directing the fire of the guns, than they changed the direction of the fire, and opened at short range (about 90 yards) on the flank of the enemy with grape with deadly accuracy. It checked the advance of the enemy, and after a few more rounds they changed front and faced the battery, which then flanked our left. General Terrill, seeing this, ordered the advance of the One hundred and twenty-third Illinois, Colonel Monroe, and to charge bayonets. It advanced bravely, but unfortunately the enemy had not then left the woods, and there was a rail fence on its edge, which prevented their advancing promptly. The regiment fired a volley and fell back, when almost immediately afterward General Jackson, who was standing on the left of the battery, was killed, two bullets entering his right breast. At the moment I was standing on the right of the battery, watching the gallant defense then being made by the troops on our left. Returning to the general to report the same, I found him on his back, struggling to speak, but unable to do so. He died in a few moments. His staff officers at once removed his body from the crest of the hill some 50 yards. Mr. Wing, one of the general's volunteer aides, went for an ambulance, and while I was absent, notifying General Terrill and Colonel Webster of the general's death, instructing the latter to take command of his entire brigade until he received further orders from General Terrill or myself, the battery had been taken by the enemy and the troops driven back from the open ground on the knob to the skirt of the woods, thus extending our left, and it was impossible to recover the body of our fallen general.

From this time up to 5 p. m. the battle raged with great fury and varied success on both sides. Two regiments, the Second and Ninety-fourth Ohio, belonging to General Rousseau's division, had come into our lines between the two batteries and behaved most gallantly.

Finding no enemy in front of Colonel Webster's brigade, which never lost a foot of ground up to this time, Colonel Webster rode off with me a little to the rear, where we found General McCook. He rode with us up to Colonel Webster's command and reported that his right was being heavily pressed and falling back. He and all of us then saw the progress of the enemy on Colonel Webster's right, as evidenced by the steady approach through the corn of a flag with a black ball in the center of a white ground, and he had hardly time to change the front of Colonel Webster's command (which was then all on exposed ground) when the enemy's infantry, arriving on the edge of the corn, opened fire upon them. The regiments moved down at a double-quick to the right face and formed in the woods, where they opened a deadly volley on the enemy, who were found in large numbers on the ground the next morning. They were killed mostly by the rifles of the Ninety-eighth Ohio. The enemy, however, still advanced, preventing Captain Harris from getting the whole of his battery off. Heavy firing all along this changed front still continued. The line, so far as was observable from this division, was then at a right angle with the main road instead of parallel with it as before, when fresh troops from the extreme right rushed in with rapidity and gallantry, checking the farther advance of the enemy and closing the fight at dark.

At 5.30 p. m. Col. George Webster fell from his horse mortally wounded. No man on that battle-field displayed more of the characteristics of the soldier than he did. He fully understood and most faithfully discharged his duty.

Of General Terrill's fatal wound I was not apprised until the battle closed, when I found him lying prostrate and receiving every aid and comfort from his devoted staff.

Up to the time of the loss of Lieutenant Parsons' battery both he and his adjutant-general, Capt. William P. Anderson, displayed such courage and persistent energy as is not to be surpassed. Lieutenant Parsons, whom I met passing through our lines after the loss of his battery, appeared perfectly unmanned and broken-hearted. His only remark was, " I could not help it, captain ; it was not my fault."

Captain Harris, commanding the battery on the right, is, with his men, entitled to all praise for their steady fire, continued for three and a half hours. I cannot conceive a battery to be better served than his was.

Too high praise cannot be given to Lieut. E. E. Kennon, acting adjutant to the Thirty-fourth Brigade, and to Lieut. John Collins, of the Ninety-eighth Ohio, aide to Colonel Webster. It would be hard to conceive of two young officers discharging their duties with more unflinching courage than they showed.

With the exception of Capt. S. M. Starling, inspector-general of infantry and ordnance, all the staff officers left me and I believe reported to General McCook on the decease of our general. Capt. B. D. Williams, division quartermaster, knowing well the topography of the country, was detailed before the engagement on General McCook's staff, and of him and of the other staff officers I have no doubt high praise will be awarded by the general commanding the corps. At one time I found Lewis Craig, a volunteer aide, bravely rallying a regiment then in disorder.

Captain Starling, who staid with me during the whole engagement, rendered most valuable assistance. He joined the service only when the division was formed at Louisville, yet appreciated at a glance the importance of many positions and aided personally in maintaining them. His coolness and courage were unsurpassed. Nor was the courage of the troops at all at fault. It must be remembered that the position of the two batteries forming our right and left was taken without regard to the line of infantry battle. Yet our entire force, with the exception of two regiments, was formed between the two, and from the contracted space and from the fact that all the men and most of the officers, being of the last and recent call, were without experience in such matters, they many times went up in line of battle four, five, and six deep, and delivered their fire. Many of the officers, whose names I never knew, did their whole duty. Some failed, and among them I regret to report Col. J. R. Taylor, of the Fiftieth Ohio. He, though on the field and in sight of his men, was of no service to them. The first position that I saw him in was lying on his face, crouching behind a stump, and twice subsequently I saw him far to the rear of his regiment, while his men were in line of battle, apparently trying to rally some half a dozen stragglers.

I annex a statement of killed, wounded, and missing, amounting to near twenty per cent. of the force engaged.*

The loss of our general, crushing as it is to this young division, and falling as he did so early in the fight, will be felt more deeply by many of his brother commanders, whose friend he had been and whose friends they were. But none will miss him more or mourn his death more sincerely than I, who have been so near him during this unhappy war.

Very respectfully, your obedient servant,

PERCIVAL P. OLDERSHAW,
Assistant Adjutant-General and Chief of Staff.

Capt. JOHN A. CAMPBELL, *A. A. A. G., First Army Corps.*

No. 15.

Report of Capt. William P. Anderson, U. S. Army, Assistant Adjutant-General, Thirty-third Brigade.

HDQRS. THIRTY-THIRD BRIGADE, TENTH DIVISION,
FIRST CORPS, ARMY OF THE OHIO,
October 10, 1862.

SIR: I have the honor to submit the following report of the part taken in the action of the 8th instant by the Thirty-third Brigade, commanded by the late Brig. Gen. W. R. Terrill:

The One hundred and fifth Ohio Volunteers, Eightieth and One hundred and twenty-third Illinois, a detachment of the Seventh and Thirty-second Kentucky Volunteers and Third Tennessee Volunteers, under command of Colonel Garrard, of the Third Kentucky Volunteers, and Parsons' eight-gun battery (made up of detachments from the regiments of the brigade), arrived upon the scene of action about 3 o'clock in the afternoon of the 8th instant. The One hundred and first Indiana Volunteers was not present, having been sent that morning as a guard to a train to Springfield.

A short time after its arrival General Terrill was ordered by General Jackson to occupy a hill upon the extreme left of the line. General Terrill immediately rode forward to survey the position, directing the brigade to follow. During the time occupied in marching from the place where the general left the brigade to the position we occupied several messages were sent me by him to push forward with it as rapidly as possible. The distance was probably three-quarters of a mile. The One hundred and twenty-third Illinois Volunteers, being the advance regiment, arrived upon the ground first. It was marching by the flank right in front, and the rebels at the time could be seen within 200 yards advancing to occupy the same ground. The One hundred and twenty-third was immediately brought to face the enemy. The position of the parties unluckily threw the rear rank in front, which produced much

---

* Embodied in revised statement, p. 1034.

confusion, the regiment being a new one. For 100 yards in front of them the ground was clear. The rebels were advancing in and protected by the woods beyond. They commenced pouring a heavy fire into the ranks of the One hundred and twenty-third, to which they nobly responded. Parsons' battery immediately took position in the rear of the One hundred and twenty-third. Six of his guns were brought to bear upon the enemy and drove them back. At this instant General Jackson was shot dead. He, with General Terrill, had been standing to the left of Parsons' battery, encouraging the men to stand to their places.

A heavy force of the enemy was now seen advancing upon both of our flanks. The One hundred and fifth Ohio Volunteers was ordered to meet them upon the left and the Eightieth Illinois Volunteers, with Colonel Garrard's detachment, upon the right. The One hundred and fifth were marching unfortunately like and thrown into line in the same form as the One hundred and twenty-third Illinois Volunteers, viz, rear rank in front. They at once opened fire upon the enemy, but did not succeed in stopping their advance. They moved up to within 100 yards of our line without discharging a musket. They then opened a deadly fire. In spite of the efforts of the officers most of our men broke and fell back in great confusion. Lieutenant Parsons at the time was placing his seventh gun into position, when every man at the piece deserted him. He was then ordered by General Terrill to withdraw his battery. He succeeded in bringing away but one gun, four caissons, and two limbers, the horses in the other carriages being killed or disabled.

General Terrill, assisted by some of the officers, succeeded in rallying about 200 men of the One hundred and fifth Ohio Volunteers and One hundred and twenty-third Illinois Volunteers at a fence about 100 yards in the rear of our first position. Here the conduct of some of the officers, I am sorry to report, was disgraceful. The Eightieth Illinois and Colonel Garrard's detachment behaved well. When the left gave way they were obliged to fall back, which they did in good order. The general ordered the fragment of the One hundred and fifth and One hundred and twenty-third to fall back, which they did in good order. He ordered me to find General McCook and to tell him his position and to ask for re-enforcements. General McCook informed me every regiment he had was in the hottest of the fight, but that he had asked for re-enforcements from General Gilbert, and as soon as they arrived General Terrill should be supplied.

Had the enemy pursued his advantage at this crisis the most disastrous results must have followed his vigor. Nothing but a very small, disorganized fragment of the division remained to dispute his possession of the Mackville road, upon which lay our ammunition train, ambulances, and such supplies as had accompanied us. Trusting that re-enforcements might yet reach him, General Terrill rallied the few troops he had left near the place where Bush's battery had taken position. While thus engaged he fell mortally wounded and was carried from the field. Although the command of the division devolved upon General Terrill after the death of General Jackson he fell before he assumed the command.

The brigade was in action less than an hour. Its loss during this time was very severe, as will be seen by the report of Colonel Hall, who assumed command upon the fall of General Terrill.

The conduct of First Lieut. C. C. Parsons, Fourth Artillery, who commanded an eight-gun battery manned by volunteers, cannot be too highly praised. He fought his guns nobly and drove back the advancing enemy, and not until overpowered by numbers did his men give way. Even then Lieutenant Parsons, deserted though he was, remained bravely at his post and had to be removed by force.

The conduct of Colonel Hall, commanding One hundred and fifth Ohio Volunteers; Colonel Allen, commanding Eightieth Illinois Volunteers, and Colonel Monroe, commanding One hundred and twenty-third Illinois Volunteers, is worthy of notice on account of their personal bravery and their efforts to rally their men, as is also that of Colonel Garrard, of the Third Kentucky Infantry.

Lieutenant Nichols, of the Tenth Kentucky Cavalry, and Lieutenant Tuttle, of the One hundred and fifth Ohio Volunteers, aides-de-camp, for the first time under fire, were of great assistance, manfully doing their duty.

Very respectfully, yours,

W. P. ANDERSON,
Assistant Adjutant-General.

Capt. P. P. OLDERSHAW, *Assistant Adjutant-General.*

No. 16.

Report of Col. Albert S. Hall, One hundred and fifth Ohio Infantry.

HDQRS. TENTH DIVISION, FIRST ARMY CORPS,
Perryville Battle-field, Ky., October 10, 1862.

SIR : Having commanded the One hundred and fifth Regiment Ohio Volunteer Infantry in the engagement of the 8th instant near Perryville, Ky., it becomes my duty, although now commanding the Tenth Division, to report the part taken by said regiment in the battle. The regiment was on the march from Mackville to Perryville as part of the Thirty-third Brigade, commanded by General W. R. Terrill, in the Tenth Division, commanded by Brig. Gen. James S. Jackson, in the First Army Corps, commanded by Major-General McCook.

The Thirty-fourth Brigade, commanded by Colonel Webster, of the Ninety-eighth Regiment Ohio Volunteer Infantry, was in the advance and engaged the enemy about 2.30 p. m. On hearing the fire of the skirmishers General Terrill ordered forward the Thirty-third Brigade with all possible dispatch and reached the field about 3 p. m.

My regiment was marching in rear of Parsons' battery, and at the moment of reaching the field was ordered to form on the left of the road in reserve. This point was occupied but for a few moments when the order of General Terrill was given to file to the left through the timber to the extreme left of the Union forces. Upon reaching my position I found the One hundred and twenty-third Regiment Illinois Volunteer Infantry, Colonel Monroe, hotly engaging the enemy to the right and rear of Parsons' battery, then in position.

At the moment of coming into position on the left and rear of Parsons' battery it was apparent that the enemy were determined to charge through the left of the One hundred and twenty-third Illinois Volunteers and cut off the battery.

This movement was immediately and effectually repulsed by the destructive fire of Parsons' battery and the charge of that wing of my regiment, most gallantly led by Major Perkins, executed by order of General Terrill, who was personally present.

The fire at this moment was terrific beyond description, and the running through my line of a six-horse team drawing a caisson created some disorder in my center. At almost the same moment of this repulse of the enemy a determined assault was made by them on our left. A battery opened on us from the enemy's right, and from the form of the ground nearly enfiladed my line. Parsons' battery was stationed on a sharp crest of open ground about 80 yards from a wood occupied by the enemy. From this crest the ground descended to the woods and then ascended, so that the enemy delivered us the fire of consecutive battalions in rear of each other. The battery was also on a crest which abruptly terminated on the left a few yards from the guns, exposing the support to a cross-fire from the enemy's extreme right, of which the enemy, as before described, promptly availed themselves.

Thus at the distance of 80 yards, in an open field, did Parsons' battery and the One hundred and fifth Regiment Ohio Volunteer Infantry deliver to the enemy a most terrible and destructive fire, receiving in return the fire of an enfilading battery and of a rebel brigade concealed in the woods. The battery becoming disabled, and the rebel battery on our flank making our position untenable, by the order of General Terrill in person I moved my regiment 60 yards to the rear and formed on the line of an old fence, then much broken down. The enemy followed the movement, and when he reached the crest (our former position) received a fire that opened their ranks with the wildest havoc. But the position of the ground was such that we were still under the fire of their battery, and the quick eye of General Terrill discovering a movement of the enemy in a ravine to turn our left, again ordered the regiment to retire into a corn field in our rear, which was done in good order and promptly formed. In this field, being much exposed to the artillery and musketry of the enemy and hidden from each other by the corn, some irregularity occurred in the line, while a movement by the flank, then ordered by General Terrill, who could not be seen or heard distinctly by the command, tended still more to divide and scatter the regiment. The most of the living, however, followed the movement promptly, and formed in the rear of Bush's battery, by General Terrill's order, and there remained in its support until the close of the engagement. At this last position, in the rear of Bush's battery, our brave and beloved Terrill, who had stood by my side and moved with my regiment from the moment it was engaged, fell mortally wounded by the fragment of a shell. At this moment the disability of the general threw the command of the Thirty-third Brigade upon me. Turning over the command of the One hundred and fifth Regiment Ohio Volunteer Infantry to Lieutenant-Colonel Tolles I proceeded to collect the brigade.

In the early part of the engagement and before the Thirty-third Brigade became engaged Lieutenant-Colonel Tolles with eight companies, by order of General Terrill, was sent to the left of the road a mile in rear of the line of battle to protect the rear. He joined me at Bush's battery, having come forward and joined in the engagement with the Eightieth Illinois Regiment. Of the bravery manifested by the officers and enlisted men of the One hundred and fifth Regiment Ohio Volunteer Infantry I can speak with the highest satisfaction. Not an officer and but few of the enlisted men flinched from the hail of death or left their positions until ordered by their proper officers. In the engagement at Perryville they have covered themselves with imperishable honor. Citizen soldiers, with not twenty days' drill, they have exhibited the coolness and efficiency of veterans. Of the mortality and of our wounded I speak with choking sorrow. Capt. L. D. Kee, Company I, and Robert Wilson, of Company H, are no more; they fell upon that fatal crest by Parsons' battery—the former dead, the latter mortally wounded. Braver or better men never lived; truer patriots never offered a holier sacrifice to their country's cause. On the same spot 29 enlisted men of my regiment gave their lives to the cause of constitutional liberty—each a precious offering on freedom's altar. God of the true and brave! these are thine; their country calls them no more. There too on that fatal spot were wounded no less than 130 of their gallant comrades.*

A. S. HALL,
One hundred and fifth Regiment Ohio Volunteer Infantry,
Comdg. Tenth Div., First A. C., Army of the Ohio.

Captain CAMPBELL, *A. A. A. G., First Army Corps.*

No. 17.

Report of Lieut. Ellis E. Kennon, Ninety-eighth Ohio Infantry, Acting Assistant Adjutant-General, Thirty-fourth Brigade.

NEAR CRAB ORCHARD, KY., *October* 18, 1862.

SIR: Owing to the death of Col. George Webster, commanding the Thirty-fourth Brigade of the Tenth Division of the Army of the Ohio, on the 8th instant, at Chaplin Heights, it becomes my duty to report to you the position and conduct of the brigade in that engagement.

The brigade arrived upon the battle-field about 1 p. m. and were by Colonel Webster immediately assigned position. The Nineteenth Indiana Battery, commanded by Captain Harris, occupied the crest of a hill. The country to the right and front of the battery being open, the enemy could not approach without being observed and receiving the fire of their guns. The Ninety-eighth Ohio, being under the command of Lieutenant-Colonel Poorman, was ordered to move into position to the right of the Nineteenth Indiana Battery to assist in sustaining it, but owing to the nature of the ground it was found impossible for them to form in line of battle. The order was then modified, and the left wing was formed in the rear of the right wing, to be used as the peculiar circumstances of the attack might require. The Eightieth Indiana, commanded by Lieutenant-Colonel Brooks, occupied a position immediately to the rear and left of the Nineteenth Indiana Battery and to the left of the Ninety-eighth Ohio. The Fiftieth Ohio was first formed in the rear and to the left of the Nineteenth Indiana Battery, but remained in that position a very short time, and was, by order of Colonel Webster, reformed about 300 yards farther to the left, advancing to the crest of the hill in the woods near a small log cabin, with the exception, however, of two companies, which remained during the engagement lying to the left of the Ninety-eighth Ohio. These companies were under command of Captain Cook, and the officers and men deserve credit for the bravery and gallantry they exhibited upon the field.

The Fiftieth Ohio, for some reason, was not under the immediate supervision of its colonel, but was under the command of Lieutenant-Colonel Strickland, assisted by Major Defrees, and continued to be under their command during the day. They both deserve credit.

The One hundred and twenty first Ohio was, by order of Colonel Webster, first formed in the rear of the Nineteenth Indiana Battery, to the

---

* See revised statement, p. 1034.

left of the Ninety-eighth Ohio, but was subsequently ordered to support Parsons' battery; but owing to some considerable delay in arriving at the point designated they failed to be of any material assistance in defending the battery. Indeed, before the regiment had been formed in line upon the hill the battery had been taken and the enemy were approaching in very considerable force. The One hundred and twenty-first abandoned their position in bad order, but were subsequently partially reformed some distance to the rear and fought in a creditable manner. I deem it due to Colonel Reid to here state that he acted bravely and used his utmost exertions to rally his men, as also did the officers of his command; and I would further state that I believe it to be no fault of Colonel Reid's that his regiment did not reach the point assigned them in sufficient time, but it was owing to a misconception of the position on the part of the guide.

About 3 p. m. the left wing of the Ninety-eighth Ohio was ordered to the left to support Parsons' battery; but upon arriving at the point designated were ordered back to their original position.

The cannonading and fire of musketry had been for some time and continued to be until the close of the engagement exceedingly severe and destructive. A rebel battery, posted on a hill half a mile distant to the right of Harris' battery, occupying a position nearly enfilading the Ninety-eighth Ohio and Eightieth Indiana Regiments, caused considerable loss in both of these regiments.

In justice to Captain Harris I would state that a well-directed shot from his battery (the shell exploding directly over the rebel battery) silenced it effectively; at least no more shots were fired from that position. The Fiftieth Ohio, with a few exceptions, perhaps 50 men, behaved gallantly, and drove the enemy back as they attempted to gain the summit of the hill and the woods to the left of the Nineteenth Battery, and those men who ran were rallied by their field officers and fought well afterward. The Eightieth Indiana, while occupying the position on the hill to the left of the Nineteenth Battery, and pouring in a steady deadly fire upon the enemy, was marched over by the Second Ohio, which had fallen back upon their line. By order of Colonel Webster the Eightieth changed from front to right flank, the left resting where the right had rested on the battery. They were subsequently ordered to take a new position some 200 yards in the rear of the position they first occupied. This regiment changed position several times under heavy fire, and both officers and men acted gallantly and well throughout. Lieutenant-Colonel Brooks took command of the Second Ohio, which remained with the Eightieth Indiana, and acted with him until nearly the close of the engagement.

After the return of the left wing of the Ninety-eighth Ohio from the position it had been assigned to take in support of Parsons' battery they formed in line to meet the enemy, who had already gained a position to the right of the Nineteenth Battery in a corn field. They were opened upon by the Ninety-eighth Ohio, assisted for a time by the Eightieth Indiana, and in a very few moments that field was covered with the rebel dead. The Ninety-eighth changed position several times under a most murderous fire. For the coolness and steadiness with which these evolutions were performed the service is much indebted to Lieutenant-Colonel Poorman, commanding the Ninety-eighth, who acted as a brave and gallant officer and deserves especial notice. In the mean time two of the guns of the Nineteenth Battery had been taken off the field by the artillerists; four were left. These four guns were fired a number of times by members of the Ninety-eighth after they had been abandoned.

At this time I was ordered to take the Eightieth Indiana to the rear and left upon a hill some 400 yards distant and form them in line, which was done. I then returned (the battle was virtually over) and found that our gallant commander, who had acted so gallantly, had been mortally wounded; and in his loss the country is bereft of the valuable services of as brave and gallant a soldier as ever stood upon a battle-field. Too much cannot be said of him. He was everywhere in the line of battle of his brigade, encouraging by his example his men to deeds of heroism. The affections of his brigade were centered upon Colonel Webster, their heroic leader.

The officers and men of the Ninety-eighth and Fiftieth Ohio and Eightieth Indiana behaved gallantly and well, as did the officers of the One hundred and twenty-first Ohio, and as I believe their men will, if an opportunity is again presented. It was not cowardice but want of discipline and the unfortunate position to which they were assigned that caused disorder in their ranks. The officers and men of the Nineteenth Battery did their duty well, and were of invaluable service.

Lieut. J. T. Collins, Company E, Ninety-eighth Regiment, aide to Colonel Webster, acted with great bravery. The brigade is in good condition and ready to perform any service which its commander may assign it.

The casualties of the brigade were as follows:

Command.	Killed.	Wounded.	Missing.	Total.
98th Ohio	35	162	32	229
50th Ohio	22	32	79	133
80th Indiana	25	116	16	157
121st Ohio	3	23	16	42
19th Indiana Battery	2	13	3	18
Total brigade	87	346	146	579

A considerable number of the wounded have since died, and many marked missing were wounded and taken prisoners, but the number I cannot now ascertain.

All of which is respectfully submitted.

E. E. KENNON,
Lieut. and A. A. A. G., 34th Brig., 10th Div., Army of the Ohio.

Capt. P. P. OLDERSHAW, *Assistant Adjutant-General.*

No. 18.

Report of Lieut. Col. Silas A. Strickland, Fiftieth Ohio Infantry.

HDQRS. FIFTIETH REGIMENT OHIO VOLUNTEERS,
Camp near Perryville, October 10, 1862.

SIR: I have the honor to submit the following brief report of the part taken by the Fiftieth Regiment Ohio Volunteers in the battle near Perryville on the 8th instant:

The regiment was thrown into line of battle, by order of Colonel Webster, commanding Thirty-fourth Brigade, Tenth Division, the regiment in command of Col. J. R. Taylor, in the ravine to the left and rear of the Nineteenth Indiana Battery, at 2.30 p. m.   At 3 p. m. Colonel Webster commanded Colonel Taylor to change position to the left, about a regiment and a half distance, on the crest of the hill, to support the same battery at this point.   Finding myself the ranking officer present of the regiment, I assumed command and ordered it to the front and commenced firing to resist the enemy, who was closely and rapidly marching on us.   The movement was successful, and the steady and continuous fire of the Fiftieth Regiment drove the enemy back.   I was then ordered by Colonel Webster to make a charge directly to the front over a fence and through a corn field down a ravine, which was done so promptly and successfully that the enemy fled in great disorder.

The regiment continued to hold this position, at which point I was ordered by Colonel Webster to halt it until about 5 o'clock p. m., when, not having seen nor heard from Colonel Webster for some fifteen minutes' time. an aide rode up and reported Colonel Webster mortally wounded and that the order was to move by the left flank.   At this moment I saw the Nineteenth Indiana Battery moving to the rear. Without having any further orders I moved the regiment to the left about 200 yards.   I then filed the regiment to the left about battalion distance, where I was met by General Rousseau.   He ordered me to move to the front to support a battery, which I promptly did.   I must here mention that Company A, Captain Cook, and Company F, Captain Clark, by order of Colonel Webster, from the first were left to the immediate support of the Nineteenth Indiana Battery, and remained in that position, under the command of Captain Cook, during a continuous and heavy fire of musketry, which was effectually returned until the moving to the rear of the battery, when the two companies moved off, supporting the battery, in perfect order.

The officers and men under my command behaved coolly and bravely through the entire engagement.   It would be injustice to make any distinction.   Captain Carr, of Company D, fell in the charge while boldly leading his men on.   Captain Carter, of Company I, fell as gloriously, with his face to the foe, as a soldier should.   Lieutenant Key, of Company I, after the fall of Captain Carter, while bravely leading his boys in the charge, was seriously wounded in the knee.   I must acknowledge in grateful terms the invaluable services throughout the day of the gallant soldier Maj. Thomas L. P. Defrees.   I also take great pleasure in bearing testimony to the promptness and bravery of Adjt. George R. Elstner in his constant assistance throughout the engagement.

Although out of the ordinary course of a report of this kind, still I hope you will permit me to make honorable mention of the bravery and timely assistance rendered me at a critical point of the engagement by Lieut. J. T. Collins, of Company E, Ninety-eighth Ohio Regiment, acting aide to Colonel Webster.   The Fiftieth Ohio went into action with 597 and came off the field with 467; lost in killed, wounded, and missing, 130; now present and returned fit for duty, 513.

Recapitulation.—Known to have been killed, 19; wounded, 32; missing, 79.*

I am, sir, your obedient servant,

SILAS A. STRICKLAND,
Lieutenant-Colonel, Comdg. Fiftieth Regiment Ohio Vols.
Colonel HALL, *Commanding Tenth Division.*

---

* But see revised statement, p. 1034.

No. 19.

Report of Col. William B. Hazen, Forty-first Ohio Infantry, commanding Nineteenth Brigade, Fourth Division, Second Army Corps.

HDQRS. NINETEENTH BRIGADE, ARMY OF THE OHIO,
October —, 1862.

At daylight on the morning of the 8th of October, 1862, the Nineteenth Brigade, Army of the Ohio, under my command, consisting of the Forty-first Regiment Ohio Volunteers, Ninth Regiment Indiana Volunteers, Sixth Regiment Kentucky Volunteers, Twenty-seventh Regiment Kentucky Volunteers, One hundred and tenth Regiment Illinois Volunteers, and Battery F, First Regiment Ohio Volunteers—artillery, under command of Captain Cockerill, the whole numbering 2,350 men, moved forward from camp on Rolling Fork, 2 miles from Haysville, toward Perryville. About 9.30 a. m. we arrived at a point within 3 miles of Perryville, where we were halted and ordered to deploy in line of battle. At 10 o'clock the deployment of my brigade was completed in the following order: The Forty-first Regiment Ohio Volunteers, Twenty-seventh Regiment Kentucky Volunteers, and Ninth Indiana Volunteers, covered by skirmishers from their respective commands, formed the first line. The One hundred and tenth Illinois Volunteers, 150 yards in rear, formed the second line. The Sixth Kentucky Volunteers was held in reserve 150 yards distant from the second line. The battery occupied the high ground upon my right near the Tenth Brigade. Upon my left was formed the Twenty-second Brigade, under command of General Cruft.

My command remained in its position with little of note transpiring save occasional shots by my skirmishers till about 1 o'clock p. m., when a party of the enemy's dismounted cavalry having advanced and taken possession of a farm-house and out-buildings and opened a brisk fire therefrom, my skirmishers of the Forty-first Ohio Regiment and a detachment of Colonel Wolford's cavalry advanced and dislodged them. A section of Captain Cockerill's battery was then brought forward and opened on the enemy's cavalry. They soon disappeared in the woods.

At sunset my brigade was moved to the right sufficiently to occupy the high ground previously occupied by the Tenth Brigade. Here my command bivouacked in line of battle.

About 9 a. m. of the following morning the Nineteenth Brigade was ordered forward in line of battle. It advanced to Walker's Springs, in the suburbs of Perryville, where we encamped, the enemy having retreated the night previous.

It is proper to express the keen disappointment of the members of the brigade at not having had an opportunity to engage the enemy at this point.

I am, very respectfully, your obedient servant,

W. B. HAZEN,
Colonel Forty-first Ohio Volunteers, Commanding Brigade.

Capt. H. ATKINSON,
Assistant Adjutant-General.

No. 20.

Report of Col. George D. Wagner, Fifteenth Indiana Infantry, command-ing Twenty-first Brigade, Sixth Division.

HEADQUARTERS TWENTY-FIRST BRIGADE,
In Camp near Perryville, Ky., October 11, 1862.

SIR: I have the honor to report that, in obedience to orders from General Wood, at about 3 o'clock I marched to the support of General Sheridan, whose right was being turned by the enemy, at the same time engaging him in front. My advance, under command of Lieutenant-Colonel Neff, Fortieth Indiana Volunteers, attacked their extreme right, while Cox's (Tenth Indiana) battery opened on them an enfilading fire with fearful effect, which brought them to right-about, march. At this time a battery, which was about one-half mile to my front, opened on us, their shell bursting with great precision within my lines. I ordered Captain Cox to concentrate his fire upon this battery, which was soon driven off to a respectful distance. I immediately advanced, the enemy falling back in the direction of Perryville, which position they held until dark. By this time Colonel Harker, of the Twentieth Brigade, had come up to my support.

The troops lay on their arms, in order of battle, without fires. This position was about one-half a mile from the town of Perryville and at least 1 mile in advance of where I first became engaged and as far in advance of the remainder of our corps (General Crittenden's).

The next morning at daylight, seeing the enemy in retreat, I ordered an advance upon the town, where they had planted a battery to protect their rear. Cox's battery soon drove them off. The troops entered the town, capturing a few prisoners. At this time a column of troops came from the left in order to gain the Danville road. This force might have been captured but for the reason that we had no support on the right, where it was said a large force of the rebels were posted, which afterward proved to be nothing but cavalry. Cox's battery was advanced so as to completely enfilade the road, causing them to scatter in every direction.

Both officers and men acted as cool as if on parade. My force consisted of the Fifteenth Indiana Volunteers, Lieutenant-Colonel Wood; Fortieth Indiana Volunteers, Colonel Blake; Fifty-seventh Indiana Volunteers, Colonel Hines; Twenty-fourth Kentucky Volunteers, Colonel Grigsby; Ninety-seventh Ohio Volunteers, Colonel Lane, and the Tenth Indiana Battery, Captain Cox, to all of whom I am much indebted for the prompt and efficient manner in which they handled their troops, as well as to my personal staff, Captain Tinney, Captain McCutcheon, Lieutenants Casterline and Tharp, and Surgeon Glick, who did their duty well.

All of which is respectfully submitted.

Your obedient servant,

G. D. WAGNER,
Colonel, Commanding.

Capt. M. P. BESTOW,
Acting Assistant Adjutant-General.

No. 21.

Report of Maj. Gen. Charles C. Gilbert, U. S. Army, commanding Third Army Corps.

HDQRS. THIRD CORPS, ARMY OF THE OHIO,
Near Crab Orchard, October 18, 1862.

SIR: Herewith I respectfully submit a report of the operations of the Third Corps pertaining to the conflict which took place near Perryville, Ky., on the 8th of this month:

On the 7th instant the Third Corps moved along the turnpike from Springfield toward Perryville. On approaching within 5 miles of the latter place it became apparent that the enemy was there in force. The head of the column at once halted, and the leading division (Mitchell's) was drawn up in line of battle across the road. The Eleventh Division (General Sheridan's) was shortly after brought up and passed to the front and established on some heights to the right of the road and not far from Doctor's Creek. The First Division (Schoepf's) was established in reserve.

By the time these dispositions were effected it was dark. During the night I directed General Sheridan to pass Doctor's Creek, take up a position, and hold it, as that stream contained the nearest water in sufficient quantity for my command. This movement brought McCook's brigade of Sheridan's division within 2½ miles of the place, and early in the morning the enemy testified his dissatisfaction at our presence there by an attempt to dislodge the brigade, but he was repulsed handsomely.

Toward the middle of the day the indications pointed toward a general engagement, and I ordered General Mitchell to establish himself on the right of Sheridan, and directed both commanders to call up their respective commands and establish them on the heights between Doctor's Creek and Perryville. When on that line Sheridan's left rested on the road, and Mitchell's right stretched off toward the Lebanon and Perryville turnpike, on which Crittenden's corps was hourly expected. Schoepf's division was moved along the road to the crossing of Doctor's Creek, where the leading brigade was established. Pending these movements the arrival of the First Corps (Major-General McCook's) was announced on my left, and the sound of artillery indicated that its appearance had attracted the serious attention of the enemy.

· I also received an officer from Major-General Crittenden, who had been dispatched to seek out our lines that he might make the junction with me. I gave him the position, and, being near general headquarters, I repaired thither and made a report in person of the disposition of my forces and of the operations of the day and then returned to my headquarters near the crossing of Doctor's Creek. On my way thither I was met by a message from Major-General McCook to the effect that his corps was upon the point of being overpowered, the enemy having attacked him in overwhelming numbers. About the same time I received from General Sheridan a warning that he could not hold his position if not supported with re-enforcements immediately and confirming the unfavorable intelligence concerning the First Corps. I at once ordered Schoepf to close more to the left to support Sheridan, and also to cover the movement of the First Corps, which was gradually swinging around toward our rear under the strong pressure brought to bear upon it. To support Sheridan's right I ordered Mitchell to close in to the left and co-operate closely with him.

These orders given, I continued on toward the left, and shortly was met by Captain Hoblitzell with an urgent demand for support for the First Corps. He was furnished with a brigade and battery from Mitchell's division, though at the time my own lines were assailed in the most lively and vigorous manner. Shortly after Major Wright brought an order to send two brigades from Schoepf's division to support the First Corps, but as one brigade had already gone and my own lines were undergoing a dangerous assault I dispatched only one of Schoepf's brigades. That moved toward the right of the First Corps. The enemy's columns, as they followed up their success, came now to present their left flank to Sheridan's batteries, and he at once turned his guns upon them and disposed his infantry to demand their further attention if they should presume to continue their progress. This, with the movement of the brigade from Schoepf's division, brought to a stand the left of the enemy's attack. At the same time Mitchell threw forward his right upon the repulsed and broken lines which had attacked Sheridan and himself, and, with gallant Carlin in the lead, drove them beyond Perryville and occupied the town with his skirmishers. Sheridan could not venture to join in following up the successful repulse of the enemy from his front, as his entire attention was directed to the columns then threatening to continue their progress toward my left and rear. It was about one hour before sunset that the enemy was repulsed from the front of my lines.

In disposing my troops for battle I had the timely advice of the major-general commanding, whose presence in the midst of my corps inspired all, from the highest to the lowest, with complete confidence.

The Third Corps presented itself on the field in an orderly and compact style, and I am indebted to Capt. O. L. Baldwin, of the Second Kentucky Volunteers, assistant inspector general, for his energy in clearing the road of the wagons, which on the 7th had under some mistake become involved among the troops and lined the road all the way back to Lick Creek, and were materially impeding the progress of the troops, especially of the artillery.

The other members of my staff, Capt. J. Edward Stacy, acting assistant adjutant-general, my two aides-de-camp, Lieut. George K. Speed and Lieut. John Speed, and Capt. George S. Roper, commissary of subsistence, were active and efficient in transmitting my orders.

Surg. George R. Weeks was active and ready in the duties pertaining to his office as medical director.

The officers of the Signal Corps rendered ready and useful service all day on the 7th and 8th.

Brigadier-General Mitchell this day sustained fully the reputation which he won at an early period of this war for energy and daring.

Brigadier-General Sheridan I commend to notice as an officer of much gallantry and of high professional ability. He held the key of our position with tenacity and used the point to its utmost advantage.

Colonel McCook, of the Fifty-second Ohio Volunteers, was at this point, and I can bear testimony to the fine discipline and excellent fighting qualities of his brigade.

Colonel Carlin, of Mitchell's division, is spoken of in terms of high praise, which I can most safely indorse.

Inspector-General Gay, in charge of the cavalry in my front, was active and highly efficient. His thorough professional training gave me confidence in all of his reports, and enabled me to prepare in time and at a proper distance for a more cautious and methodical advance upon the point at which the enemy had taken up his position.

I feel it my duty to report Col. George Ryan, of the Seventy-fifth Illinois Volunteers. He deferred reporting his regiment deficient in ammunition until the division to which he belonged was on the point of going into battle. He was arrested on the spot. Thanks to the efficiency of my ordnance officer, Lieut. Benjamin J. Horton, of the Twenty-fourth Ohio Volunteers, the regiment was supplied, and was put in position with full cartridge boxes before the fight became general.

During the night my dispositions were completed for the general attack ordered at daylight, but the withdrawal of the enemy in the mean time brought to a termination the encounter begun the previous day.

Of the two brigades sent to re-enforce the First Corps General McCook I presume will make a report. The Thirtieth Brigade lost more than the Third. It was sent toward the left when the battle was raging the most furiously. The Third Brigade was sent toward the right of the First Corps, and had the close support of Sheridan's left and the remaining brigades of Schoepf's division still held in reserve.

Casualties of the Third Corps, as far as ascertained at this date, are as follows: Killed, 250; wounded, 800; and missing, 60. Total, 1,110.*

C. C. GILBERT,
Major-General Volunteers, Commanding Third Corps.

Col. J. B. FRY, *Chief of Staff.*

No. 22.

Report of Col. William C. Kise, Tenth Indiana Infantry, Second Brigade, First Division.

CAMP NEAR CRAB ORCHARD, KY., *October* 10, 1862.

I have the honor to report to you that on the evening of the 7th instant, according to your order, I sent my regiment on picket duty, under command of Lieutenant-Colonel Carroll, and had it posted 1½ miles in advance of our camp, on the road leading to Perryville, in front of where the enemy was said to be in force.

About 12 midnight Lieutenant-Colonel Carroll sent out Companies A and E, Captains Hamilton and Johnssen, as skirmishers, to feel after and ascertain, if possible, if the enemy was in the vicinity. Captain Johnssen proceeded about a mile, when he came upon a considerable force of the enemy and engaged them. After exchanging a number of shots and finding a superior number of the enemy opposed to him he fell back, according to orders, on the regiment, Captain Hamilton taking position as outpost picket.

Nothing further occurred until 5 a. m., when the regiment was formed in line of battle and moved across an open field about one-half mile, when the skirmishers under Captain Johnssen were again fired upon by those of the enemy. I arrived on the field at 7 a. m. and took command. Soon after I relieved Captain Johnssen's company of skirmishers by sending forward Company B, Captain Goben, to take their place, which position Captain Goben maintained, skirmishing with the enemy occasionally until about 12 noon, when by your order I moved the regiment out of the wood across an open field under fire of shot and shell from a battery of the enemy, crossing a rail and also a stone fence, and ascending a steep hill, followed to our left, and somewhat in our rear, by the Eighty-sixth Illinois, under command of Colonel Irons.

---

* But see revised statement, p. 1036.

We came upon a force of the enemy outnumbering us, who at once opened a galling fire upon us, which was returned by my regiment in splendid order. Company B, Captain Goben, being the left flanking company, and near where the enemy was in heavy force, under cover of a rail fence and under the slope of a hill, sustained the brunt of the battle, suffering a loss of 4 killed and 3 wounded; but the captain, leading his men, stood up resolutely, and, after my regiment had obstinately contested the ground for twenty minutes, the enemy gave way and fled in confusion, leaving their dead and wounded on the field.

After remaining on the field of our success until 3 p. m., when a general line of battle was formed by General Sheridan's division, the Tenth Indiana being the only regiment on the field from your brigade or from the First Division, I was ordered by General Sheridan to the rear as a support, which order I promptly but reluctantly obeyed. Shortly after I received an order from you to rejoin the brigade, which I did about sunset.

My regiment lost 4 killed and 7 wounded. The list is herewith appended.

In closing this brief report I would be doing injustice to the officers and men of my command were I not to speak of the promptness with which my every order was obeyed and executed and the gallantry of officers and men of the regiment. Every line officer on the field was at his post. Lieut. Col. William B. Carroll, Maj. Marsh B. Taylor, and Adjt. John W. Harden, rendered me invaluable assistance by their energy, coolness, and courage on the field.

The movements of the regiment having been made under your immediate observation, this report is respectfully submitted, hoping that the day is not far distant when the Tenth Indiana will again have an opportunity of going to battle under your generalship, to assist in crushing out a rebellion raised by ambitious men and disappointed office-seekers.

I am, very respectfully, your obedient servant,

W. C. KISE,
Colonel, Commanding Tenth Indiana Volunteers.

Brig. Gen. S. S. FRY, *Comdg. Second Brig., First Div.*

No. 23.

Report of Brig. Gen. James B. Steedman, U. S. Army, commanding Third Brigade.

HDQRS. THIRD BRIG., FIRST DIV., ARMY OF THE OHIO,
Camp near Crab Orchard, Ky., October 19, 1862.

CAPTAIN: I have the honor to report, pursuant to Special Orders, No. 14, from corps headquarters, that late in the afternoon of the 8th instant, having been ordered with my brigade to support Major-General McCook, my command, in obedience to the orders of that officer, took position on the right of the division commanded by Brigadier-General Rousseau, where it was exposed to a quite severe fire of shot and shell and some musketry without being able to reply, except with the artillery attached (Company I, Fourth U. S. Artillery, commanded by Lieut. Frank G. Smith), which opened and fired with effect for about forty-five minutes, dismounting two guns, exploding one caisson, and effectually silencing the battery against which its fire was directed.

The casualties of this command were: Thirty-fifth Ohio Volunteers, Col. F. Van Derveer commanding—Lieut. Joseph S. Claypoole and 3 men taken prisoners (since paroled for exchange); Ninth Ohio Volunteers, Lieut. Col. Charles Joseph, commanding—1 man severely wounded and 2 men taken prisoners (since paroled); Eighty-seventh Indiana Volunteers, Col. K. G. Shryock commanding—2 men wounded, 1 severely; Eighteenth U. S. Infantry, Maj. F. Townsend commanding—3 men wounded, 1 severely; Second Minnesota Volunteers, Col. James George commanding—1 man taken prisoner; Company I, Fourth U. S. Artillery, Lieut. F. G. Smith commanding—1 man severely wounded and 1 man taken prisoner (since paroled); Lieut. Richard Schneider, serving on my staff, captured while conveying orders on the field (since paroled for exchange).

I avail myself of this opportunity to reassure you of my entire confidence in the officers and men of my command.

With esteem, respectfully, yours,

JAMES B. STEEDMAN,
Brigadier-General, Commanding Third Brigade.

Capt. J. EDWARD STACY, *A. A. G., Third Corps, Army of the Ohio.*

No. 24.

Report of Brig. Gen. Robert B. Mitchell, U. S. Army, commanding Ninth Division, including skirmish October 7.

HDQRS. NINTH DIVISION, ARMY OF THE OHIO,
Goodnight Spring, 2½ miles from Perryville, Ky., October 9, 1862.

CAPTAIN: I have the honor to submit the following report of the part taken by the Ninth Division in the engagement of the 7th and 8th instant, near Perryville, Ky.:

Upon the arrival of my column, about 2 p. m. of the 7th, at a point on the Springfield and Perryville turnpike about 5 miles from Perryville, I formed my brigades, under the direction of General Buell, on the right and left of the road, with the batteries in position and the men under cover. The Eighth Kansas, Lieutenant-Colonel Martin, and the Thirty-fifth Illinois, Lieutenant-Colonel Chandler, were advanced to the front in rear of a section of Captain Pinney's Fifth Wisconsin Battery, which, with the cavalry advance, had come upon the rebel outposts, and was then engaging a battery of the enemy. A little before sunset these regiments were advanced to the front of the battery and engaged the enemy till dark, when they fell back to their former position. The Eighty-first Indiana Volunteers, Major Woodbury, and Twenty-fifth Illinois, Lieutenant-Colonel McClelland, were thrown out as pickets upon the left and front.

At daylight on the morning of the 8th I sent forward a section of Captain Hotchkiss' Second Minnesota Battery to relieve the section of Captain Pinney's battery, which, under Lieutenant Hill, did such brilliant work the day before.

At 2 p. m. of the 8th, in obedience to orders received from Major-General Gilbert, commanding corps, I advanced my division on the road to a point designated by General Gilbert, where I formed my brigades as follows:

The Thirtieth Brigade, Colonel Gooding, Twenty-second Indiana Volunteers, commanding, composed of the Twenty-second Indiana Volunteers, Lieutenant-Colonel Keith; Fifty-ninth Illinois Volunteers, Maj. J. C. Winters; Seventy-fourth and Seventy-fifth Illinois Volunteers, commanded respectively by Lieutenant-Colonel Kerr and Lieutenant-Colonel Bennett, and the Fifth Wisconsin Battery, Capt. O. F. Pinney, on the left of the road.

The Thirty-first Brigade, Colonel Carlin, Thirty-eighth Illinois Volunteers, commanding, composed of the Twenty-first and Thirty-eighth Illinois Volunteers, commanded respectively by Colonel Alexander and Major Gilmer; the Fifteenth Wisconsin Volunteers, Colonel Heg; the One hundred and first Ohio Volunteers, Colonel Stem, and two sections of Captain Hotchkiss' Second Minnesota Battery, commanded by Lieutenant Dawley (Captain Hotchkiss, with one section, being engaged with General McCook on the left), I formed on the right of the road, on a wooded eminence, the men under cover, this brigade being in rear and within supporting distance of General Sheridan's division, which was then engaging the enemy in front.

The Thirty-second Brigade, Colonel Caldwell, Eighty-first Indiana Volunteers, commanding, was formed in rear of the Thirty-first Brigade, Colonel Caldwell's brigade comprising the following regiments and battery: Twenty-fifth and Thirty-fifth Illinois Volunteers, commanded by Lieutenant-Colonels McClelland and Chandler; the Eighth Kansas, Lieutenant-Colonel Martin; the Eighty-first Indiana Volunteers, Lieutenant-Colonel Timberlake, and the Eighth Wisconsin Battery, Captain Carpenter.

Almost immediately upon the formation of my lines the enemy appeared, advancing in force upon the right of Colonel Carlin's line, with the evident intention of charging upon his battery, which was upon his extreme right. I directed him to open fire upon them as soon as he could do so effectually, but they retired under cover at the advance of Colonel Carlin's skirmishers.

At this time I received a message from General Sheridan, stating that he was hardly pressed on his right and front and needed re-enforcements. I ordered Colonel Carlin to advance with his brigade rapidly to General Sheridan's right and aid his division. Colonel Carlin immediately advanced, leading his brigade through a skirt of timber to the open field on the right, and upon ascending the brow of the hill discovered the enemy rapidly advancing in great force upon General Sheridan's right. Colonel Carlin immediately formed his brigade, and at the double-quick charged upon the enemy, who after a moment's stand gave way to the impetuosity of the charge, and breaking in disorder ran precipitately to and through the town of Perryville a distance of nearly 2 miles. Colonel Carlin pressed them closely till they reached the bluff on the other side and formed under the protection of two batteries, which were in position there. The gallant Carlin charged with his brigade through the enemy's lines, completely piercing their center; but finding his ardor had outstripped all support, and having the enemy's artillery and infantry on both flanks, he fell back during the confusion of the enemy to a position immediately adjoining the town, and placed his battery in position on the west side of the town, the rebel batteries and our own firing directly over the town till darkness made further action impossible. This charge gave the officers and men of the Thirty-first Brigade a splendid opportunity to evince the intrepid, gallant, and soldierly qualities which the occasion showed they possessed. The manner in which they stood the subsequent severe artillery fire was worthy of high praise.

In Colonel Carlin's advance the Thirty-eighth Illinois Volunteers overtook and captured on the edge of the town a heavily loaded ammunition train of 15 wagons, 2 caissons, with their horses, belonging to the Washington Light Artillery, and the train guard of 138 men, with 3 officers. Major Gilmer, Thirty-eighth Illinois, deserves great credit for the skill and activity he displayed in this capture.

The Thirty-second Brigade, Colonel Caldwell, was advanced at different times to the positions vacated by Colonel Carlin. The officers and men of this brigade did not have the opportunity to gratify the desire for a chance at the enemy that their looks, language, and actions showed they possessed.

At the time Colonel Carlin's brigade advanced Colonel Gooding, Thirtieth Brigade, was ordered by General Gilbert to advance to the aid of General McCook, upon whom the enemy had massed a large force with the evident intention of turning his position. Colonel Gooding proceeded with his brigade to General McCook's position, and, under General McCook's direction, formed upon his left, and there remained, with some slight variations of the position of his regiments, till dark, receiving a most deadly fire from the enemy, who were possessed of great advantages of position.

The appearance of the field the next day showed, however, that the brave heroes of Pea Ridge (the Twenty-second Indiana and Fifty-ninth Illinois Volunteers) had returned the fire with terrible effect and had won new and bright laurels to add to their former fame.

The Seventy-fifth Illinois Volunteers, under Lieutenant-Colonel Bennett, were upon this line, and, having a reputation to gain as soldiers, nobly did the work before them. Their loss was heavy, including Major Kilgour, wounded severely. Colonel Gooding, during the temporary confusion produced by a heavy flank fire of the concealed enemy, became involved in the enemy's lines, was slightly wounded and taken prisoner. By his address and cool bravery, however, he succeeded in deceiving the commander of the rebel forces till his brigade had withdrawn to a position where it was less exposed to cross-fires. Lieutenant-Colonel Keith, Twenty-second Indiana Volunteers, and Lieutenant West, acting assistant adjutant-general of the Thirtieth Brigade, both fell here; the former killed, the latter severely wounded. Both were gallant officers and fell while discharging their duties.

Captain Pinney's Fifth Wisconsin Battery was placed in position under the orders of General McCook, and for nearly three hours (almost unsupported) defended itself against the terrible numbers and charges of the enemy, piling the ground in front of his guns with their slain. This brigade continued in position till, darkness rendering their position (the enemy being concealed) too much exposed, they withdrew to their position on the road, fatigued, terribly depleted in numbers, and mourning the loss of so many brave comrades, but still preserving their organizations intact, and anxious for the next day's opportunity to go again into the fight. Colonel Gooding's brigade operated more directly under the command of General McCook, and I presume his report will contain a more detailed account of their positions and operations.

The casualties in my command were as follows: The Thirtieth Brigade: Killed, 121; wounded, 314; prisoners, 35; missing, 29; total, 499. The Thirty-first Brigade: Wounded, 10. The Thirty-second Brigade, none. Grand total, 509.

I have already spoken of the gallant conduct and skillful management of Colonel Carlin, commanding the Thirty-first Brigade, but cannot refrain from again calling your attention to the eminent services and brave actions of this modest and efficient officer in this engagement.

By his courage and skill the enemy's center, a strong position, was broken and the rebels thrown into confusion. Colonel Gooding did his whole duty as the commander of one of the best brigades in the service of the Government. Indiana may well feel proud of his conduct in that bloody conflict.

I cannot refrain from expressing my gratitude to my staff, including Lieutenant Pratt, acting assistant adjutant-general; Lieutenant Lines, aide-de-camp; Lieutenant Rankin, of the Second Kansas Regiment; Lieutenant Andrews, Forty-second Illinois Volunteers, and Lieutenant Wood, of the Signal Corps, for the able, gallant, and heroic manner in which they discharged their respective duties during the engagement, always ready and willing to take any risk or make any sacrifice for the good of their country's cause.

Surgeon Hazlett, of the Fifty-ninth Illinois Volunteers; Lieutenant-Colonel Keith, Twenty-second Indiana; Lieutenant Johnson, Fifty-ninth Illinois; Lieutenants Tolbert and Ridlen and Capt. R. K. Smith, of the Twenty-second Indiana, and Lieutenants Blean and Eels, of the Seventy-fifth Illinois, died gallantly defending the honor of their country's flag. They will never be forgotten by a grateful country.

On the morning of the 9th a force of rebel cavalry was seen winding from the enemy's left and evidently proceeding toward the Harrodsburg turnpike. I directed Hotchkiss' battery to fire upon them, which was done with good effect, the enemy rapidly retreating. I then advanced with my division to this point, seeing on every side indications of the enemy's precipitate retreat. I discovered about 1,500 small-arms, which I have turned over to Lieutenant Horton, ordnance officer, staff of Major-General Gilbert.

I am, captain, very respectfully, your obedient servant,

ROBT. B. MITCHELL,
Brigadier-General, Commanding.

Capt. J. EDWARD STACY,
Acting Assistant Adjutant-General.

No. 25.

Report of Col. Michael Gooding, Twenty-second Indiana Infantry, commanding Thirtieth Brigade.

HEADQUARTERS THIRTIETH BRIGADE,
NINTH DIVISION, ARMY OF THE OHIO,
Danville, Ky., October 14, 1862.

SIR: In obedience to your orders, requiring me to furnish a report of the part taken by my brigade in the late battle of Perryville, I have the honor herewith to submit the following:

As ordered, I had massed my brigade in the edge of a dense wood, joining General Rousseau's right, to await your orders. Precisely at 3.30 o'clock p. m. I received orders directly from Major-General Gilbert, commanding Third *Corps d'Armée*, to proceed immediately to the support of General McCook, on my left.

I then proceeded at double-quick in the direction where General Mc-Cook's forces were engaged. On reaching the field I found the forces badly cut up and retreating (they then having fallen back nearly 1 mile) and were being hotly pressed by the enemy. After receiving instructions from General McCook I ordered my brigade forward into the fight, the Twenty-second Indiana taking position on the right, the Fifty-ninth Illinois on the left, and the Seventy-fifth Illinois in the center, and the battery took position on an eminence in our rear, which was bordered by a dense wood. I again ordered the brigade to the support of the brigade fighting on my left, which, as soon as I had become engaged, retreated and fell back in confusion.

The battle now raged furiously; one after one my men were cut down, but still, with unyielding hearts, they severely pressed the enemy, and in many instances forced them to give way. Here we fought alone and unsupported for two hours and twenty minutes, opposed to the rebel General Wood's entire division, composed of fifteen regiments and a battery of ten guns. Fiercer and fiercer grew the contest and more dreadful became the onslaught. Almost hand-to-hand they fought at least five times their own number, often charging upon them with such fearlessness and impetuosity as would force them to reel and give way, but as fast as they were cut down their ranks were filled with fresh ones. At one time the Twenty-second Indiana charged on them with fixed bayonets and succeeded in completely routing and throwing them from their position on our right, but at the same time they brought in a reserve force on our left. I now ordered the Twenty-second Indiana as quickly as possible to the aid of the Fifty-ninth Illinois on the left, which order was promptly obeyed.

The impetuosity of the firing now ceased for a moment, and I advanced to ascertain if possible the position of the enemy. As I advanced down the line we were greeted with a heavy volley of musketry, which plainly enough told me the direction of the enemy. With shouts and exclamations my men again rallied to the onset. Here it was that fell the gallant Lieutenant-Colonel Keith, while at the head of his regiment and in the act of flourishing his sword and urging his men onward to victory. At this time my horse was shot from under me, and before I could escape through the darkness I was taken prisoner and conveyed from the field. Although my men fought desperately it was of no avail, for being overwhelmed by vastly superior numbers they were compelled to withdraw from the field.

Retreating under cover of a hill the brigade was again formed in line of battle by the senior officer of the brigade, when, after consultation and learning that we had no support within 1 mile distant, it was deemed advisable to withdraw from the field and fall back upon our lines, which they did.

I cannot speak too highly of the officers and men generally of my command, but they deserve the highest honor for their patriotism and courage. I would here again mention the name of Lieutenant-Colonel Keith, of the Twenty-second Indiana. Until he fell from his horse he was everywhere in the thickest of the fight. Where the battle raged hottest he was to be found animating and cheering his men by his lofty words and noble example. He was universally loved by all who knew him and his loss is much regretted. In his example there is everything worthy of imitation. Major Winters, of the Fifty-ninth Illinois, has my grateful thanks for the coolness and courage which he displayed during the entire engagement. He displayed a patriotism and courage that is highly worthy of imitation. Lieutenant West, of the Fifty-ninth Illinois, and acting assistant adjutant-general, is entitled to great credit for the timely aid he afforded me and for the energy and promptness with which he delivered my orders. During the action he was wounded in five different places, but did not quit the field until entirely disabled.

Lieutenant Adams, acting adjutant of the Twenty-second Indiana, is also a worthy young officer. He had his horse shot from under him, and though wounded himself he remained on the field, preserving great coolness and calmness of mind and constantly urging his men forward. Also much praise is due to Orderly Gray for his courage, promptness, and energy in delivering my orders. Captain Pinney, of the Fifth Wisconsin Battery, cannot be spoken of too highly in this report. He delivered his orders with great coolness and deliberation, and his battery did great execution in forcing the rebels from their position.

The following is a list of casualties:

Of the Twenty-second Indiana there were engaged 300; killed, 55; wounded, 98; missing, 19. Total loss, 172.*

Of the Fifty-ninth Illinois there were engaged 325; killed, 43; wounded, 98; missing, 12. Total loss, 153.*

Of the Seventy-fifth Illinois there were engaged 700; killed, 47; wounded, 162; missing, 12. Total loss, 221.*

Of the Fifth Wisconsin Battery there were engaged 68; killed, 1; wounded, 2. Total loss, 3.*

Of the brigade there were engaged 1,423; killed, 141; wounded, 360; missing, 43. Total loss of the brigade, 549.*

Very respectfully, I am, general, your obedient servant,

M. GOODING,
Colonel, Commanding Thirtieth Brigade.

Brig. Gen. R. B. MITCHELL, *Commanding Division.*

No. 26.

Report of Brig. Gen. Philip H. Sheridan, U. S. Army, commanding Eleventh Division.

HDQRS. ELEVENTH DIV., ARMY OF THE OHIO,
CAMP ON THE ROLLING FORK,
Six miles south of Lebanon, Ky., October 23, 1862.

CAPTAIN: I have the honor to make the following report of the operations of my division in the action of the 8th instant, near Perryville, Ky.:

In accordance with the instructions of the general commanding I directed Col. Daniel McCook, with his brigade and Barnett's battery, to occupy the heights in front of Doctor's Creek, so as to secure that water for our men. This was done very handsomely after a sharp skirmish at daylight in the morning, giving us full possession of the heights.

In about two hours afterward the enemy advanced in considerable force through a line of heavy timber on the eastern slope to drive us from this position. I had however in the mean time ordered forward Colonel Laiboldt's brigade and Hescock's battery, so that I felt myself well prepared and strong enough to receive them. I then directed Colonel Laiboldt to advance two of his old regiments and drive the enemy from the timber, at the same time putting the batteries into position. Colonel Laiboldt succeeded in driving the enemy back down the hill and across Chaplin Creek after an obstinate contest, in which the loss was severe on both sides, Captain Barnett, with one section

---

* But see revised statement, p. 1035.

of his battery, and Lieutenant Taliaferro, with one section of Hescock's battery, driving the enemy from every position he took. About this time General McCook, with his corps, made his appearance on my left, the enemy opening on him. I then advanced Captain Hescock's battery to a very good position in front of this belt of timber, where he had an enfilading fire on the enemy's batteries on the opposite side of the valley of Chaplin Creek, advancing at the same time six regiments to support him. The fire of Captain Hescock was here very severely felt by the enemy, who attempted to dislodge him by establishing a battery at short range. But the firing of Hescock's battery was still so severe and his shots so well directed and effective as to force the enemy's battery from its new position in ten minutes.

The enemy then placed two batteries on my right flank and commenced massing troops behind them, with the apparent intention of making an attack on that point. I then, by direction of Major-General Gilbert, reoccupied the crest of the hill. I had no sooner got into position than the enemy attacked me fiercely, advancing with great determination almost to my very line, notwithstanding a large portion of the ground over which they were advancing was exposed to a heavy fire of canister from both of my batteries. I then directed a general advance of my whole line, bringing up the reserve regiments to occupy the crest of the hill.

On our advance the enemy commenced retiring rapidly but in good order. I could not follow up this advantage to any great extent, as the enemy were advancing on our left, General McCook's right having been driven back some distance. I then directed the fire of my artillery across the valley on this advance of the enemy, forcing them to retire, thus very much relieving General McCook. This ended the operations of the day, it being then dark and the enemy having retired from the field.

I cannot speak with too much praise of the good conduct of the officers and men of my whole division, all of whom were engaged. The new troops vied with the old troops of the division in their coolness and steadiness. My brigade commanders, Colonel Greusel, Col. Daniel McCook, and Lieutenant-Colonel Laiboldt, behaved with great gallantry, leading their troops at all times. Neither can I speak too highly of Captains Hescock and Barnett and the officers and men of their batteries.

I respectfully bring to the notice of the general commanding the excellent conduct of Surgeon Griffiths, medical director of this division, who was untiring in his care for the wounded on all parts of the field; also the following officers of my staff: Captain Beck, aide-de-camp; Lieut. George Lee, acting assistant adjutant-general; Lieut. Van Pelt, division commissary, and Lieutenants Denning and Burton, for their alacrity in bearing orders and other valuable assistance rendered me during the day.

The total casualties in my division were as follows: Killed, 44; wounded, 274, and missing, 12—total, 330.* I inclose herewith a list of same, giving names, rank, company, and regiment.

This report is also accompanied by the reports of brigade and battery commanders.

I am, sir, very respectfully, your obedient servant,

P. H. SHERIDAN,
Brigadier-General, Commanding.

Capt. J. EDWARD STACY, *A. A. A. G., Third Corps.*

---

* But see revised statement, p. 1036.

No. 27.

Report of Col. Daniel McCook, Fifty-second Ohio Infantry, commanding Thirty-sixth Brigade.

HDQRS. THIRTY-SIXTH BRIG., ELEVENTH DIV.,
THIRD ARMY CORPS, ARMY OF THE OHIO,
Battle-field Chaplin Hills, October 9, 1862.

SIR : In obedience to the orders of General Buell, conveyed through you, at 2 a. m. of the 8th instant I moved three regiments of my brigade, viz, the Eighty-fifth Illinois, the Fifty-second Ohio, and the One hundred and twenty-fifth Illinois, to the foot of Peters' Hill, the position I was ordered to carry. At this point, discovering the enemy's force upon the hill above, I deployed the Eighty-fifth Regiment Illinois upon the right of the Perryville road and the Fifty-second Regiment upon the left, throwing skirmishers to the front, enveloping my flanks. The skirmishers had scarcely taken intervals when a severe and galling fire was opened on them. As soon as sufficient ground was gained to the front I deployed the One hundred and twenty-fifth Regiment Illinois upon both sides of the road as a reserve. Although all my regiments were fresh from their homes they moved steadily up the hill driving the enemy, who contested warmly every step, and occupied the crest of the heights, which gave us a commanding position over the surrounding country and one of vast importance at a subsequent part of the day. There I halted my battalions in a favorable position, keeping the One hundred and twenty-fifth Regiment well in reserve under the crest of the hill and throwing skirmishers at such a distance from my line as to keep the enemy's sharpshooters, who still occupied a skirt of woods on the slope of the hill to the front, from annoying my regiments lying in position. About this time Captain Barnett's battery arrived and was put into position upon the left of the road. Two of his pieces he could not use on account of the inexperience of the men detailed to man them. With the remaining four he did good service during the day. The enemy, knowing the importance of the position he had lost, being re-enforced, advanced to retake it. He opened a battery upon the Eighty-fifth Illinois and began using spherical case. I ordered a section of Captain Barnett's battery upon the extreme right of the position to reply to this and ordered the right wing of the One hundred and twenty-fifth Illinois to take position to the right of the battery to support it. The enemy's fire for about fifty minutes was very severe, but Captain Barnett, after compelling him to change position three times, finally drove him off. The steadiness with which the Eighty-fifth and One hundred and twenty-fifth Illinois withstood the fire was admirable, as they were unable to reply and had during it a considerable number wounded. After this the firing almost ceased, with here and there a straggling shot aimed at mounted men. At this juncture General Sheridan arrived upon the field.

The enemy under Buckner soon began massing troops in the skirt of woods into the edge of which I had thrown my skirmishers. General Gay, commanding cavalry, came up and attempted to go toward Perryville, when his further advance was checked by the enemy in the woods. He dismounted a portion of his cavalry, and, supported by the skirmishers of the Fifty-second Ohio Regiment, advanced into the woods, where we afterward learned there were two rebel brigades.

The action quickly became sharp, when the Second Missouri Infantry, and soon the Forty-fourth Illinois to support it, were ordered into the woods. They drove the enemy from there across the open fields in front and took possession of a wooded hill beyond the Bottom House, upon which the rebels afterward planted their batteries, most destructive to the right of General McCook's corps. In the mean time we had observed the head of General Rousseau's division debouching into the field to our left from the Mackville road. At about the same time the Second Missouri attacked the woods. The Eighty-sixth Regiment Illinois, belonging to my brigade but being upon picket, was ordered to advance over the open fields to the left and seize the extreme left of the wood. This they did in gallant style at a double-quick, driving the enemy before them, and in doing which 1 private was killed and 11 wounded. General Sheridan then ordered that the Fifty-second Ohio go forward to relieve the Second Missouri. I met this regiment coming back, having been ordered to leave the advanced position it occupied.

The Fifty-second was halted in the woods so hotly contested. You soon ordered my brigade forward to form line of battle on the farther edge of the woods so often mentioned. Captain Hescock's battery, supported by the Eighty-sixth Illinois, had been here doing good service for some time by enfilading a battery planted upon the hill abandoned by the Second Missouri, and playing upon General Rousseau's division, just getting in position. The line General Sheridan selected was an admirable one, and General Rousseau formed his division upon a continuation of it, his right being separated from General Sheridan's left by the dry rocky bed of a stream which wound off toward Perryville.

The last regiment of my brigade was getting into position and the enemy's batteries had begun to play upon General Rousseau's division upon our left when we were ordered to fall back at least half a mile and assume the position carried in the morning, leaving General Rousseau without support on the right, exposing his flank. The enemy was not disturbed any longer by the batteries of our division ——— began to tell with effect upon General Rousseau. The enemy, assured by our retrograde movement, began to show themselves upon our right. A portion of Colonel Greusel's brigade got out of position, and the line, as formed with respect to my brigade, was as follows: The Thirty-sixth Illinois was on my left; the Fifty-second Ohio immediately upon its right, supporting a part of Captain Barnett's and Hescock's batteries. The Eighty-fifth Regiment was upon the right of these batteries. The One hundred and twenty-fifth acted under your orders in the last action. I am happy to learn it behaved finely, and I must trust to your report to do it full justice. The Eighty-sixth Regiment was held in reserve upon the pike, with orders to watch the woods to our left and resist any attempt to turn our flank. The enemy made two determined attacks to carry the position, and at one time was repelled by the bayonet, in which charge the Eighty-fifth and One hundred and twenty-fifth Illinois Regiments gallantly took part. The enemy reformed and advanced again. The Thirty-sixth Illinois being out of ammunitions I ordered the Fifty-second Regiment into line, and after an engagement of thirty minutes the enemy was driven from the field.

Too much praise cannot be given to the coolness, bravery, and steadiness of the troops of the brigade. To Col. R. S. Moore, of the Eighty-fifth Regiment Illinois, I call your special attention for his coolness, experience, and bravery on the field. Colonels Irons, Harmon, and Lieutenant-Colonel Cowen all deserve honorable mention for conspicuous bravery and judgment in action. Lieutenant-Colonels Dilworth, Magee, and Langley ably assisted their respective colonels, and were everywhere present where duty called them. Majors Cummings, Bean, and Lee, and Captain Clark, acting major of the Fifty-second Regiment, all performed well and ably their respective duties. A very large share of the honor of the day is due the respective regimental officers. Many instances of gallantry in line officers came under my notice, but regimental reports must suffice for these. With great pleasure I can call your attention to the conduct of my staff. Dr. Moore, brigade surgeon, coolly dressed wounds under the hottest fire and personally superintended the removal of the wounded. Captain Viemont was conspicuous through the day for his cool daring and assistance he offered me. Lieut. J. A. Mallory, acting assistant adjutant-general; Lieut. E. L. Anderson, Lieut. J. J. McCook, and Lieutenant Ashley all bore themselves with commendable gallantry and distinguished themselves by the intelligent manner in which they conveyed and executed my orders.

With the sincerest pleasure imaginable I call your attention to the signal bravery and daring heroism of Charles Common and Samuel J. Marsh, privates of Company A, Fifty-second Ohio. Their conduct was the admiration of all who saw them.

The casualties in my brigade are as follows: Six killed, 43 wounded, 6 missing.*

I am, very respectfully, your obedient servant,

DANIEL McCOOK,
Colonel, Commanding Brigade.

Captain LEE, *Assistant Adjutant-General, Eleventh Division.*

No. 28.

Report of Lieut. Col. Daniel D. T. Cowen, Fifty-second Ohio Infantry.

HDQRS. 52D REGT. OHIO VOLS., 36TH BRIG.,
11TH DIV., ARMY OF THE OHIO,
Battle-field near Perryville, Ky., October 9, 1862.

SIR: I have the honor to submit the following report of the part taken by the Fifty-second Regiment in the battle of yesterday:

In pursuance of the order of Col. Daniel McCook, commanding the brigade, the Fifty-second, Regiment on the left of the brigade, moved forward at 3.30 o'clock yesterday morning from its position 3 miles west of Perryville toward that village. After advancing about 1½ miles and crossing a bridge spanning a small stream the regiment was formed in line of battle, and being ordered to advance to and hold the crest of the hill some 500 yards in front, Company A, in command of Lieutenant Bucke, and Company H, under command of Lieutenant Summers, both companies under command of Captain Clark, acting major, were deployed as skirmishers and our line advanced to the position named.

Some 300 yards from the run, at five minutes past 4 o'clock a. m., the skirmishers were fired upon by the rebel pickets. They promptly returned the fire and drove the pickets over the crest of the hill into and through the field and wood beyond and took their position some 400 yards in front of the regiment.

I am thus particular in detailing these items because to the Thirty-sixth Brigade and to the Fifty-second Regiment thus attaches the honor of opening the great and decisive battle of Perryville.

---

* But see revised statement, p. 1036.

Our skirmishers were almost constantly exchanging shots with the rebel skirmishers, and the regiment retained its position on the crest of the hill till 10.30 o'clock, when, in pursuance of Colonel McCook's order, it moved forward about one-half of a mile, where we remained without material change of position until 4 o'clock p. m., when the regiment moved forward a short distance with Company D, under command of Captain Morrow, and Company I, under command of Captain Schneider, deployed as skirmishers. While thus advancing the regiment was ordered by Colonel McCook to move to the right some 500 yards to assist in supporting Captain Barnett's Second Illinois Battery, which was being threatened by a heavy force.

The regiment moved rapidly to its position immediately on the left of the battery and in the rear of the Thirty-sixth Illinois, and remained in line behind the crest of the hill until the ammunition of the regiment in our front was exhausted, when the Fifty-second, at 5 p. m., moved forward over the crest of the hill in fine order and became immediately engaged with the enemy. The regiment continued to fire steadily and effectively about thirty minutes, when at sundown the rebel line with which we were engaged broke and fled in confusion.

I cannot speak in too high terms of praise of the conduct of the officers and men under my command during the whole of this memorable day. When all did their whole duty it would seem unjust to make any apparent discrimination by specially naming any. Yet circumstances and the varied incidents of the day brought under my special observation the conduct of some whom I therefore name. Capt. I. D. Clark, of Company A, acting major, from the time the first shot was fired on the skirmishers under his command in the early morning until the battle was over and the victory won, discharged his varied and arduous duties with skill, courage, and promptness. Adjutant Blackburn and the officers of the skirmishing companies also attracted my special notice while the regiment was in its position behind the crest of the hill on the left of Barnett's battery, and before it relieved the Thirty-sixth Illinois and became actually engaged with the enemy at that point.

Sergeant Rudolph, of Company H, was conspicuous among others of the regiment in assisting at the battery. At 10 a. m. the Second Missouri Regiment charged past the right of our line of skirmishers upon a force of rebel infantry, and Private Samuel J. Marsh, of Company A, joined them in the pursuit. Charley Common, a little drummer-boy, having lost his drum, took a musket and fought manfully in the line.

The following is a list of our losses, and it seems impossible to credit our apparent miraculous escape. I take the liberty to say that I ascribe it to a very great extent to the consummate skill with which the regiment was handled by our brigade and division commanders.

Killed: None.

Wounded: Private James Moneysmith, Company I, shoulder, dangerously; Private Edward Grimes, Company H, arm, severely; Private George Wilson, Company E, shoulder, slightly. Total wounded, 3; missing, none.

I have the honor to be, very respectfully, your obedient servant.

D. D. T. COWEN,

Lieut. Col., Comdg. Fifty-second Regiment Ohio Vol. Infantry.

Lieut. J. A. MALLORY, *A. A. A. G., Thirty-sixth Brigade.*

No. 29.

Reports of General Braxton Bragg, C. S. Army, commanding Department No. 2, with orders and correspondence, and including operations August 28–October 24.

HEADQUARTERS DEPARTMENT NO. 2,
Bryantsville, Ky., October 12, 1862.

SIR : By a great pressure of active engagements I have been unable to communicate since my last dispatch until now. My rapid tour of inspection was suddenly terminated at Frankfort just at the close of the ceremony of installing the Provisional Governor into office, a heavy advance of the enemy on that point rendering it necessary for me to concentrate my forces. General Polk was about the same time heavily pressed at Bardstown, and he, in accordance with previous orders, fell back toward Harrodsburg.

Not having succeeded in getting my supplies from Lexington to my new depot near Bryantsville, it was necessary to hold a large portion of General Smith's forces in that direction. Finding the enemy pressing heavily in his rear near Perryville, Major-General Hardee, of Polk's command, was obliged to halt and check him at that point. Having arrived at Harrodsburg from Frankfort I determined to give him battle there, and accordingly concentrated three divisions of my old command (the Army of the Mississippi, now under Major-General Polk)—Cheatham's, Buckner's, and Anderson's—and directed General Polk to take the command on the 7th and attack the enemy next morning. Withers' division had gone the day before to support Smith.

Having on the night of the 7th learned that the force in front of Smith had rapidly retreated, I moved early next morning to be present at the operations of Polk's forces. The two armies were formed confronting each other on opposite sides of the town of Perryville. After consulting with the general and reconnoitering the ground and examining his dispositions I declined to assume the command, but suggested some changes and modifications of his arrangements, which he promptly adopted.

The action opened at 12.30 p. m. between the skirmishers and artillery on both sides. Finding the enemy indisposed to advance upon us, and knowing he was receiving heavy re-enforcements, I deemed it best to assail him vigorously and so directed. The engagement became general soon thereafter, and was continued furiously from that time until dark, our troops never faltering and never failing in their efforts.

For the time engaged it was the severest and most desperately contested engagement within my knowledge. Fearfully outnumbered, our troops did not hesitate to engage at any odds, and though checked at times, they eventually carried every position and drove the enemy about 2 miles. But for the intervention of night we should have completed the work. We had captured 15 pieces of artillery by the most daring charges, killed 1 and wounded 2 brigadier-generals and a very large number of inferior officers and men, estimated at no less than 4,000, and captured 400 prisoners, including 3 staff officers, with servants, carriage, and baggage of Major-General McCook. The ground was literally covered with his dead and wounded.

In such a contest our own loss was necessarily severe, probably not less than 2,500 killed, wounded, and missing. Included in the wounded are Brigadier-Generals Wood, Cleburne, and Brown, gallant and noble soldiers, whose loss will be severely felt by their commands.

To Major-General Polk, commanding the forces; Major-General Hardee, commanding the left wing (two divisions), and Major-Generals Cheatham, Buckner, and Anderson, commanding divisions, is mainly due the brilliant achievements on this memorable field. Nobler troops were never more gallantly led. The country owes them a debt of gratitude which I am sure will be acknowledged.

Ascertaining that the enemy was heavily re-enforced during the night, I withdrew my force early the next morning to Harrodsburg and thence to this point. Major-General Smith arrived at Harrodsburg with most of his forces and Withers' division the next day (10th), and yesterday I withdrew the whole to this point, the enemy following slowly but not pressing us. My future movements cannot be indicated, as they will depend in a great measure on those of the enemy.

The campaign here was predicated on a belief and the most positive assurances that the people of this country would rise in mass to assert their independence. No people ever had so favorable an opportunity, but I am distressed to add there is little or no disposition to avail of it. Willing perhaps to accept their independence, they are neither disposed nor willing to risk their lives or their property in its achievement. With ample means to arm 20,000 men and a force with that to fully redeem the State we have not yet issued half the arms left us by casualties incident to the campaign.

I am, sir, very respectfully, your obedient servant,

BRAXTON BRAGG,
General, Commanding.

The ADJUTANT-GENERAL, *Richmond, Va.*

—

GENERAL ORDERS, }   HEADQUARTERS ARMY OF TENNESSEE,
No. 1.   }   *Tullahoma, Tenn., November 23, 1862.*

I. The several regiments, battalions, and independent companies engaged in the ever-memorable battle at Perryville, Ky., on October 8, in which they achieved a signal victory over the enemy, numbering three to their one, and drove him from the field with terrible slaughter and the loss of his artillery, will inscribe the name of that field on their colors. The corps of Cheatham's division which made the gallant and desperate charge resulting in the capture of three of the enemy's batteries will, in addition to the name, place the cross cannon inverted.

*   *   *   *   *   *   *

By command of General Bragg:

GEORGE WM. BRENT,
Assistant Adjutant-General.

—

HEADQUARTERS ARMY OF TENNESSEE,
May 20, 1863.

SIR: Constant occupation and the absence of my records during the active service in this quarter have prevented until now a full narrative of the events incident to the campaign of this army last autumn in Tennessee and Kentucky.

Early in July, 1862, under instructions, a division of troops under Major-General McCown was sent from my headquarters, at Tupelo, Miss., to the Department of East Tennessee. In the latter part of that month it became evident we were being pressed there by a heavy corps of the enemy sent from Corinth under Major-General Buell. This movement threatened the very heart of our country, and was destined, unless checked immediately, to sever our main line of connection between the East and West. At this time the army in Mississippi had much improved in health and strength, and had progressed rapidly in discipline, organization, and instruction. Leaving a sufficient force, I determined to move to Chattanooga, oppose this dangerous combination of the enemy, and, if practicable, drive him from our important provision country in Western Alabama, Middle Tennessee, and Kentucky.

Early in August the infantry force for this purpose (four divisions) was concentrated near Chattanooga and awaited the arrival of the artillery, cavalry, and baggage train, which necessarily moved across the country by land. Maj. Gen. E. Kirby Smith, commanding the Department of East Tennessee, met me by invitation in Chattanooga, and most generously placed his whole command at my disposal. It was soon determined, upon his suggestion, that all his force should be used to operate upon the enemy's left at Cumberland Gap, and he was requested to confer with Brig. Gen. Humphrey Marshall, commanding in Southwestern Virginia, with whom he was already in correspondence, to secure his co-operation also in the movement. After returning to Knoxville General Smith asked for further assistance, and two fine brigades, under Brig. Gen. P. R. Cleburne and Col. Preston Smith, were sent to him in addition to the division which had gone from Tupelo. The balance of my immediate command, the Army of the Mississippi, divided between Major-Generals Polk and Hardee, made every preparation and awaited only its baggage train and artillery to cross the Tennessee River and enter upon its arduous and perilous campaign over the mountains dividing East and Middle Tennessee. The movement of the artillery and wagons across the mountain region of North Alabama having been successfully accomplished, late in August we commenced crossing the river at Chattanooga with very limited means. The enemy with a largely superior force occupied the lines of the railroads from Decatur to Bridgeport, Ala., from Decatur to Nashville, and from Nashville to Stevenson, with large detached commands at McMinnville and Cumberland Gap.

Having crossed the river at Chattanooga the column took up its march on August 28 over Walden's Ridge and the Cumberland Mountains for Middle Tennessee. Major-General Smith had already successfully passed through Northeastern Tennessee and gained the rear of Cumberland Gap, held by the enemy in strong force, well fortified. Leaving a sufficient force to hold the enemy in observation, his dislodgment being considered impracticable, he moved, as authorized, with the balance of his command on Lexington, Ky. This rich country, full of supplies so necessary to us, was represented to be occupied by a force which could make but feeble resistance. How well and successfully that duty was performed has already been reported by General Smith. His complete victory over the enemy at Richmond, Ky., and his occupation of Lexington rendered it necessary for me to intercept General Buell, now rapidly moving toward Nashville, or to move toward the right, so as to secure a junction with General Smith when necessary.

On reaching Middle Tennessee it was found that the enemy's main force, by use of railroads and good turnpikes, had concentrated in Nashville and was strongly fortified. With a heavy demonstration against this position my force was thrown rapidly to Glasgow, Ky., and to my great satisfaction reached that point September 13, before any portion of the enemy passed Bowling Green. As soon as my object was discovered they moved in haste by railroad and turnpike, but reached Bowling Green only in time to find we had seized and now held both roads near Cave City. An assault on the enemy's superior force, well fortified at Nashville, gave no promise of success, while any movement for that purpose would have enabled him to throw his whole force to his rear rapidly, thus rendering certain the capture or destruction of General Smith's small command at Lexington, whereas by the flank movement adopted the enemy's communications were severed and his forces separated, while my own communications were secured. Without firing a gun we had also compelled the evacuation of Northern Alabama and Middle Tennessee south of the Cumberland. Prepared to assail Buell's forces should he attempt to pass north, I determined to rest my jaded troops at Glasgow, where some subsistence was to be had. While thus engaged I learned that the commander of my outpost brigade at Cave City had advanced upon and assailed the enemy's fortified position at Munfordville (the railroad and pike crossing the Green River), and after a gallant fight against largely superior numbers had been repulsed with considerable loss. Unwilling to allow the impression of a disaster to rest on the minds of my men, the force was rapidly prepared and our march renewed on the evening of the 15th, with a very scanty supply of provisions. Hardee's wing moved by Cave City direct upon Munfordville, and Polk, by the Bear Wallow road, crossed the river some miles to the right and gained the enemy's rear in the afternoon of the 16th. An immediate demand for the surrender of the garrison was made, and after a few hours' negotiation an unconditional submission was obtained. We secured 4,267 prisoners, 10 pieces of artillery, 5,000 small-arms, and a proportional quantity of ammunition, horses, mules, and military stores.

This surrender having been received and completed on September 17, dispositions were made for an attack from General Buell's main force, supposed to be advancing on our rear from Bowling Green. Efforts were made to draw him to an attack by maneuvering a division in his front, while our main force held position south of the intrenchments on Green River. I failed to accomplish this object. With my effective force present, reduced by sickness, exhaustion, and the recent affair before the intrenchments at Munfordville, to half that of the enemy, I could not prudently afford to attack him there in his selected position. Should I pursue him farther toward Bowling Green he might fall back to that place and behind his fortifications. Reduced at the end of four days to three days' rations, and in a hostile country, utterly destitute of supplies, a serious engagement brought on anywhere in that direction could not fail (whatever its results) to materially cripple me. The loss of a battle would be eminently disastrous. I was well aware also that he had a practicable route by way of Morgantown or Brownsville to the Ohio River and thence to Louisville. We were therefore compelled to give up the object and seek for subsistence. Orders were sent for a supply train from our depot at Lexington to meet us in Bardstown, and the march was commenced for the latter place. Instructions had been given General Smith for a simultaneous movement of the column at Lexington to Shelbyville, that combined operations might be immediately undertaken against Louisville. Orders had also been given for a close observation on the enemy at Cumberland Gap, and that he should be intercepted in any attempt to escape.

On my arrival at Bardstown I learned from Major-General Smith, then at Lexington, that the enemy was moving from Cumberland Gap, endeavoring to escape by the valley of Sandy River, in Eastern Kentucky, and that he had sent his whole available force in pursuit. A sufficient force to prevent this escape and to hold the enemy in check there and compel his surrender had been ordered and was confidently expected from another quarter to have followed General Smith's movement in time for this purpose. Circumstances unknown to me in our then isolated position, and over which I could not exercise control, had prevented this consummation so confidently relied on and so necessary to our success. The delay necessarily resulting from this pursuit of the enemy by General Smith prevented a junction of our forces, and enabled General Buell to reach Louisville before the assault could be made upon that city.

The troops at Bardstown, much jaded and foot-sore from the long and arduous march, were placed in position for rest and recuperation during the absence of the column from Lexington. Having made all needful arrangements for them, ordered our supplies at Lexington transferred to a position selected as a general depot near Bryantsville, and provided for opening a line of communication through Cumberland Gap, I left Bardstown on the 28th for Lexington to confer with General Smith and inform myself fully as to our condition and the resources of the country. Major-General Polk, left at Bardstown in command, was directed, if pressed by a force too large to justify his giving battle, to fall back in the direction of the new depot near Bryantsville, in front of which I propose to concentrate for action.

Arriving in Lexington on October 1, I met the Provisional Governor of the State, who had previously been invited to accompany me, and arranged for his installation at the capital on the 4th. The available forces of General Smith, just returned to Lexington, were ordered immediately to Frankfort.

Finding but little progress had been made in the transfer of our accumulated stores from Lexington, and learning of a heavy movement of the enemy from Louisville, I ordered Major-General Polk in writing, dated Lexington, 1 p. m., October 2, and sent it by two routes, to move from Bardstown with his whole available force by way of Bloomfield toward Frankfort, to strike the enemy in flank and rear, and informed him that Major-General Smith would attack in front. When received at Bardstown on the 3d the general submitted this order, which is not mentioned in his report (see Exhibit No. 1), to a council of wing and division commanders, and determined to move as originally instructed by me on leaving Bardstown. Fortunately notice of this determination reached me at Frankfort in time to prevent the movement against the enemy's front by General Smith, but it necessitated an entire change in my plans, the abandonment of the capital, and the partial uncovering and ultimate loss of our stores at Lexington. Not doubting but that some imperative necessity unknown to me existed with the general for this departure from instructions I conformed at once to his movements, and put General Smith's command in motion to form the junction farther south, still covering the supplies at Lexington as far as practicable.

Proceeding rapidly to Harrodsburg myself, I was met there by Major-General Polk on October 6, with the head of the column, which had marched from Bardstown on the 3d. After a full and free conference with the general my first views remained unchanged, and as he reported to me at midnight of October 6, when inclosing a written report from

Major-General Hardee that he did not regard the enemy in large strength near there (see Exhibit No. 2), I renewed early on the morning of the 7th the orders to concentrate all the forces in front of the depot at Lexington. (See Exhibit No. 3.) But before this order was put in full operation information was received that the enemy in limited force was pressing upon General Hardee at Perryville; that he was nowhere concentrated against us, but was moving by separate columns; his right (see map herewith, marked A*) was near Lebanon, a corps in front of Perryville, and his left (two entire corps) extending by way of Mackville to Frankfort, a line of at least 60 miles. This presented an opportunity which I promptly seized of striking him in detail. Accordingly written orders were given to Major-General Polk, dated Harrodsburg, October 7, 5.40 p. m. (see Exhibit No. 4), to move Cheatham's division, now at Harrodsburg, back to Perryville, and to proceed to that point himself, attack the enemy immediately, rout him, and then move rapidly to join Major-General Smith, as before ordered, and, it was added, "no time should be lost in this movement."

Meanwhile, during the same day, I had received repeated and urgent applications from General Smith (near Frankfort) by express, representing the enemy to be in strong force in his immediate front and earnestly asking for re-enforcements. Accordingly Withers' division had been detached and sent to him (before receipt by me of the information from Perryville), and was already far on the way thither at the time when the movement to Perryville was ordered, and this will account for my being without the benefit of this division in the battle which ensued next day at the latter place. Major-General Polk arrived at Perryville with Cheatham's division before midnight of the 7th and the troops were placed by General Hardee in the line of battle previously established.

Our forces now in this position consisted of three divisions of infantry (about 14,500) and two small brigades of cavalry (about 1,500). To this the enemy opposed one corps (Gilbert's), about 18,000 strong. Information reached me during the evening and night of the 7th at Harrodsburg which indicated that no attack could be made on General Smith's command the next day, and I immediately changed my purpose to join him and determined to go to Perryville. From unofficial sources I was led to fear the existence of serious misapprehension in regard to the position and strength of the enemy's forces near Perryville, as well as to the location of our supplies, supposed to be at Bryantsville, when in truth but two days' rations for the army had yet reached that point.

Having ordered the attack and that no time should be lost, I was concerned at not hearing the commencement of the engagement early in the morning, but was much relieved for the time by receiving from General Polk a note, dated Perryville, 6 a. m., October 8, informing me that the enemy's pickets commenced firing at daybreak and that he should bring on the engagement vigorously. (See Exhibit No. 5.) To my surprise, however, no gun was heard, and on my arrival, about 10 a. m., I was informed that it was determined not to attack, but to assume the " defensive-offensive." After a hasty reconnaissance and consultation orders were given for some changes deemed necessary in the line of battle; a portion of it being withdrawn was restored, and Major-General Polk was ordered to bring on the engagement. Impatient at the delay after this order I dispatched a staff officer to repeat it to the general, and soon thereafter I followed in person and put the troops in motion.

Major-General Buell, commanding the forces there in our immediate

---

* To appear in Atlas.

front, in his official report says, "I had somewhat expected an attack early in the morning on Gilbert's corps while it was isolated." These delays had postponed the action until it was now past noon and a second corps of the enemy (18,000) had reached the field. The general officers at the meeting about daylight (see General Polk's report) who resolved on this delay must have acted without correct information and in ignorance that my orders were urgent and imperative for the attack; moreover I was within one hour's ride and was not consulted or informed.

The action, having at length commenced, was fought by our troops with a gallantry and persistent determination to conquer which the enemy could not resist; and though he was largely more than two to our one he was driven from the field with terrible loss. Night closed the operations just as a third corps of the enemy threw the head of its column against our left flank. We had entire possession of the battle-field, with thousands of the enemy's killed and wounded, several batteries of artillery, and 600 prisoners. For the details of this action, so creditable to our arms, I refer to the reports of subordinate commanders, herewith forwarded. In the progress of the engagement we had advanced so far as to expose our left flank to the third corps, just arrived from the direction of Lebanon. I therefore caused our line, which rested upon the field until midnight, to fall back to its original position. Assured that the enemy had concentrated his three corps against us, and finding that our loss had already been quite heavy in the unequal contest against two, I gave the orders to fall back at daylight on Harrodsburg, and sent instructions to Major-General Smith to move his command to form a junction with me at that place. There I again offered the enemy battle, which he declined, and moved to possess himself of my line toward Cumberland Gap.

My whole force was accordingly retired on the 11th upon Bryantsville. Here the enemy again declined to advance upon me, but occupied himself in the destruction of the numerous mills and other sources from which we drew our only supply of breadstuffs. There was no accumulation of this essential article at any point except Lexington which had been now lost, though the country afforded an immensity of grain. The necessary concentration of my forces rendered accumulation from the small country mills impracticable, and our supply was reduced to only four days' rations. To attack and rout an enemy largely superior in numbers (for simply to cripple him would not suffice) or to evacuate the country in which we could no longer subsist became now an imperative necessity. Moreover I was informed that still another force was moving on my right flank from Cincinnati in addition to the overwhelming one with which I was already contending. The season of autumnal rains was approaching; the rough and uneven roads leading over the stupendous mountains of Eastern Tennessee and Kentucky to and through Cumberland Gap would then become utterly impassable to an army. Should I remain till then and meet with a reverse the army would be lost. Had the foregoing considerations permitted a doubt to remain in my mind as to the course of duty it would have been entirely removed upon receipt of the intelligence of our disasters in North Mississippi, by which the whole country in our rear was left open to the enemy's victorious forces there.

Accordingly all necessary arrangements were made and the troops put in motion by two columns, under Major-Generals Polk and Smith, on October 13, for Cumberland Gap. After a rapid march, with some privations in the absence of baggage trains, which had been sent ahead, we passed the Gap with immaterial loss from October 19 to 24. The column of Major-General Polk was vigorously pursued by the enemy for several days, but was so successfully protected by the cavalry, under the admirable management of Colonels Wheeler and Wharton, that but little annoyance was felt.

Though compelled to yield to largely superior numbers and fortuitous circumstances a portion of the valuable territory from which we had driven the enemy the fruits of the campaign were very large and have had a most important bearing upon our subsequent military operations here and elsewhere. With a force enabling us at no time to put more than 40,000 men of all arms and in all places in battle we had redeemed North Alabama and Middle Tennessee and recovered possession of Cumberland Gap, the gate-way to the heart of the Confederacy. We had killed, wounded, and captured no less than 25,000 of the enemy; taken over 30 pieces of artillery, 17,000 small-arms, some 2,000,000 cartridges for the same; destroyed some hundreds of wagons and brought off several hundreds more with their teams and harness complete; replaced our jaded horses by a fine mount; lived two months upon supplies wrested from the enemy's possession; secured material to clothe the army, and finally secured subsistence from the redeemed country to support not only the army but also a large force of the Confederacy to the present time.

In four weeks after passing Cumberland Gap on this memorable and arduous campaign, jaded, hungry, and ragged (as necessarily incidental to that service), this noble army was found with serried ranks in front of the enemy at Nashville better organized, better disciplined, better clothed and fed, in better health and tone, and in larger numbers than when it entered on the campaign, though it had made a march at least three times as long as that of the enemy in reaching the same point, and was moreover entirely self-sustained. Too high an estimate cannot be placed upon officers and men capable of such fortitude, resolution, courage, and self-denial. Nothing short of the patriotism which pervaded our ranks, and the intelligence, zeal, and gallantry displayed on all occasions and by all grades, can account for such results.

I am, sir, very respectfully, your obedient servant,

BRAXTON BRAGG,
General, Commanding.

General S. COOPER, *Adjutant and Inspector General.*

[Indorsement.]

JANUARY 5, 1863.

Respectfully submitted to the President. I see very little objection to this report, and believe the effect will be on the whole to vindicate rather than diminish the reputation of the commander in the Kentucky campaign.

J. A. SEDDON,
Secretary of War.

[Exhibit No. 1.]

HEADQUARTERS ARMY OF THE MISSISSIPPI,
Bardstown, Ky., October 3, 1862—3 p. m.

General BRAXTON BRAGG,*
Commanding Department No. 2, Frankfort, Ky.:

GENERAL: I am in receipt of your note of the 2d, 1 p. m., directing me to move with all my available force via Bloomfield to Frankfort to

---

*See correspondence relating to the battle of Perryville, or Chaplin Hills, pp. 1097–1107.

strike the enemy in his flank and rear. The last twenty-four hours have developed a condition of things on my front and left flank which I shadowed forth in my last note to you, which makes compliance with this order not only eminently inexpedient, but impracticable. I have called a council of wing and division commanders, to whom I have submitted the matter, and find that they unanimously indorse my views. I shall therefore pursue a different course, assured that when the facts are submitted to you you will justify my decision. I move on the route indicated by you toward Camp Breckinridge. The head of my column moves this afternoon. I will keep you advised. I send this by a relay of couriers I have established at intervals of 10 miles from here to Lexington via Danville.

I remain, general, your obedient servant,

L. POLK,
Major-General, Commanding Army of the Mississippi.

[Exhibit No. 2.]

HEADQUARTERS ARMY OF THE MISSISSIPPI,
Harrodsburg, Ky., October 6, 1862—11 p. m.
General BRAGG:

GENERAL: I send you some dispatches just received. I have ordered General Anderson to move at 3 a. m. to-morrow morning to join General Hardee at Perryville and General Cleburne to follow him at 4 a. m. I have ordered both to have two days' cooked rations in the haversacks. Wood's rations will be sent him in the morning. I have ordered Wharton to report to General Hardee with his own and Wade's cavalry and the regiment of infantry now at Lebanon. This force, I think, will be sufficient for the general's purposes. I have directed General Cheatham not to leave his present camp near town for that under General Withers, 4 miles out, until further orders. I have directed General Hardee to ascertain, if possible, the strength of the enemy which may be covered by his advance. I cannot think it large.

I am, general, respectfully, your obedient servant,

L. POLK,
Major-General, Commanding Army of the Mississippi.

P. S.—I have had two companies of cavalry posted on the road leading to Mackville.

[Exhibit No. 3.]

CIRCULAR.]   HEADQUARTERS DEPARTMENT No. 2,
Harrodsburg, Ky., October 7, 1862.
Major-General POLK,
    Commanding Army of the Mississippi:

I. Cheatham's division will move forward to-night to Withers' position, and both divisions of the right wing (Withers' and Cheatham's) will move to-morrow to Lawrenceburg, thence to Versailles, and to follow General E. Kirby Smith's command.

II. General E. Kirby Smith's command will move to-morrow to Versailles, throwing a division toward Frankfort. Allston's cavalry, now at Salvisa, will cover Cheatham's movement, reporting to Major-General Cheatham.

III. Major-General Hardee, commanding left wing, Army of the Mississippi, will follow these movements as circumstances allow, notifying these headquarters of his move. Colonel Wade's infantry will join the guard at the depot at Bryantsville, reporting to the commanding officer there, and his cavalry will report to Colonel Wheeler, commanding cavalry of Hardee's wing.

By command of General Bragg:

GEORGE WM. BRENT,
Chief of Staff and Assistant Adjutant-General.

[Exhibit No. 4.]

HEADQUARTERS DEPARTMENT No. 2,
Harrodsburg, Ky., October 7, 1862—5.40 p. m.

General POLK:

GENERAL: In view of the news from Hardee you had better move with Cheatham's division to his support and give the enemy battle immediately; rout him, and then move to our support at Versailles. Smith moves forward to-day in that direction, and I wish Withers to march to-night toward Lawrenceburg, crossing thence to-morrow to Versailles, and follow up Smith and report to him. His wagon train, except the ammunition and ordnance, had better cross at McCown's, turning off at Salvisa. No time should be lost in these movements. I shall follow Smith.

Respectfully and truly, yours,

BRAXTON BRAGG,
General, Commanding.

[Exhibit No. 5.]

HEADQUARTERS ARMY OF THE MISSISSIPPI,
Perryville, Ky., October 8, 1862—6 a. m.

General BRAGG, *Commanding Department No. 2:*

GENERAL: The enemy seem disposed to press this morning. Their pickets commenced firing at daylight. Understanding it to be your wish to give them battle we shall do so vigorously. Should we succeed we will pass to the right, with the view of joining General Kirby Smith. If it should become necessary to fall back we will do so on Danville and Bryantsville, with a view of uniting with General Smith at that point. I have directed General Preston Smith to have all the trains belonging to this army now at Harrodsburg collected and moved out on the road to Bryantsville, and to be ready to move, when it should become expedient, on that place.

Respectfully, yours, &c.,

L. POLK,
Major-General, Commanding Army of the Mississippi.

P. S.—General Smith should cover and protect these wagons should it become necessary.

[Inclosure.]

List of ordnance and other articles captured and of men killed, wounded, and taken prisoners by General Bragg's army from August 27, 1862, to January 2, 1863.

	Artillery.	Muskets.	Wagons.	Mules.	Killed.	Wounded.	Prisoners.	Date.
Richmond, Ky	10	11,000	200	1,000	200	1,000	7,000	August 31 [30], 1862.
Munfordville, Ky	10	4,000	20	200	......	......	4,300	September 17, 1862.
Perryville, Ky	15	......	......	......	2,000	8,000	500	October 8, 1862.
Salvisa, Ky	......	......	10	50	......	......	700	October 8, 1862.
Morgan in Kentucky	......	......	100	500	200	500	2,000	September and October, 1862.
Bridgeport, &c	......	......	......	......	30	100	......	August 27, 1862.
Hartsville, Tenn	2	2,000	20	100	100	400	1,800	December 6, 1862.
Murfreesborough, Tenn	40	6,000	800	4,000	5,000	16,000	6,103	December 31, 1862, to January 2, 1863.
Morgan in Kentucky	......	2,500	50	250	100	400	2,000	December 26-30, 1862.
Forrest in West Tennessee	4	2,000	50	250	300	700	1,500	December, 1862.
Total	81	27,500	1,250	6,350	7,930	27,100	25,903	

Kentucky Campaign, August 27 to October 12, 1862.

Artillery	35
Muskets	15,000
Wagons	330
Mules	1,750
Killed	2,430
Wounded	9,600
Prisoners	14,500
Total killed, wounded, and prisoners	26,530

Campaign in Tennessee, December 1, 1862, to January 2, 1863.

Artillery	46
Muskets	12,500
Wagons	920
Mules	4,600
Killed	5,500
Wounded	17,500
Prisoners	11,403
Total killed, wounded, and prisoners	34,403

—

CORRESPONDENCE RELATING TO THE BATTLE OF PERRYVILLE, OR CHAPLIN HILLS.

HEADQUARTERS ARMY OF TENNESSEE,
Tullahoma, Tenn., April 13, 1863.

Lieut. Gen. W. J. HARDEE, *Commanding Corps :* *

GENERAL: In a communication from Major-General Polk, commanding Army of the Mississippi, dated Bardstown, October 3, 1862, addressed to me, he says:

---

*This seems to have been a circular-letter to the several division and other commanders. Copies are on file addressed to Patton Anderson, Donelson, B. R. Johnson, and A. P Stewart, and Buckner's letter of April 26, 1863, indicates receipt of copy by him.

I am in receipt of your note of the 2d, 1 p. m., directing me to move with all my available force via Bloomfield to Frankfort to strike the enemy on his flank and rear. * * * I have called a council of wing and division commanders, to whom I have submitted the matter, and find that they unanimously indorse my views. I shall therefore pursue a different course assured that when the facts are submitted to you you will justify my decision.

In the official report of the battle of Perryville by the general, after stating that he was ordered to attack the enemy early in the morning, he says:

At a meeting of general officers held about daylight it was resolved, in view of the great disparity of our forces, to adopt the "defensive-offensive;" to await the movements of the enemy, and to be guided by events as they were developed.

As these councils (usually regarded as sacred among military men) are now publicly disclosed, and in a manner compromising you as advising a disobedience to my orders, the facts are laid before you, and I beg, if consistent with your sense of duty, you will inform me to what extent you sustained the general in his acknowledged disobedience. For your information I inclose a copy of my order directing him to give the enemy battle at Perryville "immediately," and request to be informed whether, in asking your advice, he informed you of the existence of this order.

I am, general, very respectfully, your obedient servant,

BRAXTON BRAGG,
General, Commanding.

[Indorsement.]

General POLK, *Commanding, &c.* :

DEAR GENERAL : I send you this paper, received yesterday, as I fear you may not have received it from headquarters, and I think it right you should have it. My impression now is to decline answering it. First, because your "acknowledged disobedience" may lead to a court-martial, and, second, because I cannot well do so without opening up the Kentucky campaign, which would lead to controversy, which at this time ought to be avoided. These are my present convictions. The paper has been sent to Cleburne and Wood, and I suppose to all the general officers who were under your command. If you choose to rip up the Kentucky campaign you can tear Bragg into tatters.

Truly, yours,

W. J. HARDEE,
Lieutenant-General.

[Inclosure.]

HEADQUARTERS ARMY OF KENTUCKY,
Harrodsburg, Ky., October 7, 1862—5.40 p. m.

General POLK :

GENERAL : In view of the news from Hardee you had better move with Cheatham's division to his support and give the enemy battle immediately. Rout him, and then move to our support at Versailles. * * * No time should be lost in these movements.

Respectfully and truly, yours,

BRAXTON BRAGG,
General, Commanding.

PERRYVILLE, KY., *October* 7, 1862—7.30 p m.

General BRAGG, *Commanding Army:*

MY DEAR GENERAL: I am receipt of your "confidential circular" of this date, also your letter of instructions to General Polk. From the tenor of the letter of instructions to General Polk I presume that this is later than the confidential circular. Both are in the same inclosure and of the same date. Permit me, from the friendly relations so long existing between us, to write you plainly. Do not scatter your forces. There is one rule in our profession which should never be forgotten; it is to throw the masses of your troops on the fractions of the enemy. The movement last proposed will divide your army and each may be defeated, whereas by keeping them united success is certain. If it be your policy to strike the enemy at Versailles, take your whole force with you and make the blow effective; if, on the contrary, you should decide to strike the army in front of me, first let that be done with a force which will make success certain. Strike with your whole strength first to the right then to the left. I could not sleep quietly to-night without giving expression to these views. Whatever you decide to do will meet my hearty co-operation.

Your sincere friend,

W. J. HARDEE,
Major-General.

N. B.—If you wish my opinion, it is that in view of the position of your depots you ought to strike this force first.

I have no envelope, but I send this by an officer.

—

SHELBYVILLE, TENN., *April* 15, 1863.

General BRAXTON BRAGG, *Commanding Department No. 2:*

GENERAL: I am this day in receipt of yours of the 13th instant,* in which reference is made to action had in council of wing and division commanders held at Bardstown, Ky., on the 3d and at Perryville on October 8, 1862. After quoting extracts from General Polk's reports of these deliberations you remark that—

As these councils (usually regarded as sacred among military men) are now publicly disclosed, and in a manner compromising you as advising a disobedience of my orders, the facts are laid before you, and I beg, if consistent with your sense of duty, you will inform me to what extent you sustained the general in his acknowledged disobedience.

As I can see no way in which detriment to the public interest might now arise from such a course I do not hesitate to comply with your request.

On October 3, 1862, I was present at General Polk's headquarters in Bardstown at a council composed, as well as I now remember, of Major-Generals Polk, Hardee, and Cheatham, and Brig. Gen. S. A. M. Wood and myself. Your dispatch from Frankfort, of date 1 p. m. October 2, was read, and after an interchange of views in regard to our military condition, as junior officer present I was called upon by General Polk to give my views as to what was best to be done. I hesitated to do so, whereupon General Polk inquired as to the cause of my reluctance to advise a course which seemed to be so clear, and I replied that your order just read did not seem to admit of any other course than that of

---

* See Bragg to Hardee of that date, p. 1097.

compliance, and that if any other alternative than that of obedience to the order was adopted it might involve you and the forces with you near Frankfort in embarrassment, if not defeat; that in your dispatch you definitely stated that General Kirby Smith would attack the enemy then in your front, and that we must move through Bloomfield upon him and "strike him in flank and rear;" that in your contemplated attack you evidently relied upon co-operation, and that if we failed in that co-operation disaster might be the consequence. After other conversations, not now remembered, General Polk, again addressing me as the junior present, inquired what would be my advice in case there was no such order as the one referred to, remarking at the same time that you could not have had the lights before you at the time you issued the order which we had at that time, and that therefore the order should not be taken into consideration in making up our judgment as to what should be done. I replied promptly:

In that case, were there no order to the contrary, I should unhesitatingly recommend that we fall back to a more favorable position, to cover our depots at Danville and Bryantsville.

I understood that all of the other officers present concurred in that opinion. General Polk at once announced his intention to move in the direction of Danville. It is proper that I should state that he subsequently told me that he had received a dispatch from you the purport of which indicated the wisdom of the move he had determined on; remarked that it was fortunate that he had not obeyed the letter of your order. Of course at this late day, speaking from memory only, I cannot give more than the substance of conversations.

In regard to the action that was had at a meeting of general officers held about daylight near Perryville, on October 8, in which the "defensive-offensive" was adopted, I have no recollection at all. I cannot remember that I was present at any council at or near Perryville, except an informal one, composed of Major-General Hardee, Brigadier-General Wood, and myself, improvised on the evening of October 7, at which General Hardee, of his own motion, addressed you the note which I suppose is referred to in your communication to General Polk, dated Harrodsburg, October 7, 5.40 p. m. In that note General Hardee advised the policy of concentrating our forces before we made an attack. He read me the note after it was written and I fully concurred in the policy it advised. Your note just referred to I did not see nor was I made acquainted with its contents. Had I been present at a council on the occasion referred to, in the absence of orders to the contrary I think it quite probable I should have advised the "defensive-offensive" policy; but at this lapse of time I would not undertake to censure a different course.

Believing that throughout the Kentucky campaign, with the lights then before us, the best was done which could have been done under the circumstances, and having no disposition to cast censure now upon those whom I failed to find fault with at the time, I can only hope that the same army under its tried leaders may soon be permitted to repeat the experiments with better facilities and under more favorable circumstances.

I am, general, very respectfully, your obedient servant,

PATTON ANDERSON,
Brigadier-General.

HEADQUARTERS HARDEE'S CORPS,
Tullahoma, Tenn., April 16, 1863.

General BRAXTON BRAGG:

GENERAL : I have the honor to acknowledge the receipt of your letter of the 13th instant, containing extracts from official communications
made by Lieutenant-General Polk to you in regard to the operations in
Kentucky in October last.   You refer to an order issued by you on
October 2, directing Lieutenant-General Polk to move his forces to
Frankfort and strike the enemy on his flank and rear, which order you
say was disobeyed by the general after a council of war and at which I
was present.   You also refer to the official report of Lieutenant-General
Polk of the battle of Perryville, and state that after another meeting of
general officers he disobeyed your orders of October 7, a copy of which
you inclose.   After referring to these topics you censure the disclosure
of these facts, which you assert are in a manner compromising to me
[and begged me], if consistent with my sense of duty, to inform you to
what extent I sustained the general in his acknowledged disobedience.

In answer I have the honor to say that while I do not desire to shrink
from any responsibility incurred by me in the part I took in the councils of war called by Lieutenant-General Polk, I do not consider it
proper, in answer to a communication such as you have addressed, to
enter into details of what occurred on the occasions referred to.

I am, general, very respectfully, your obedient servant,

W. J. HARDEE,
Lieutenant-General.

—

HDQRS. POLK'S CORPS, ARMY OF TENNESSEE,
April 17, 1863.

Lieutenant-General HARDEE, *C. S. Army :*

DEAR GENERAL : I am in receipt of the letter addressed you on the
subject of the alleged disobedience of orders, and thank you for the
prompt indication of what was brewing.   I am compelled to say it does
not at all surprise me ; so that when I said to you I felt it to be quite
as necessary to watch Tullahoma as Murfreesborough you will see I
was not mistaken in my estimate of the necessities of my position or
of the character of others.   As to the specific acts for which the arrest
and trial are to be had (for I am satisfied that an arrest and trial are
deliberately determined upon), I have to say I feel quite easy.   There
was certainly no disobedience of orders in either case.   In that of Bardstown I was ordered to take all my available force and move, &c. · As
to what portion of my force was in that condition the general did not
undertake to judge himself nor did he require me to be guided by the
judgment of others.   By the terms of the order I was to be the judge
myself.   I did judge, and, in view of the fact that I knew I had the
largest part of Buell's army in my immediate front on the Elizabethtown, Shepherdsville, Mount Washington, and Taylorsville roads, and
that if I moved from my position at Bardstown to strike the column
moving upon Shelbyville in flank and rear I should not only cease to hold
four columns in check but would expose my own flank to be assailed
by them all while I was moving to assault one, I thought it quite plain
I had no troops at my command which were available for the execution
of such an order.   That was the precise point submitted by me to the
council of officers I summoned for consultation, to wit : Whether I had
any force which in the circumstances before me might be regarded as
available for the purpose indicated.   I thought not, and every officer in

the council approved the soundness of my decision. We were all clearly satisfied as to the position of the troops of the enemy, which information we were sure the general commanding the forces could not have, or he would not have issued such an order. It was this view of the case that caused General Anderson, as he admits and as all may remember, to see his way to vote for declining the movement indicated and to counsel the retreat on Harrodsburg.

As to the Perryville affair, if I am to be tried for disobedience of orders there the question arises, What orders? Surely not what purports to be orders in the paper sent you and by you to me. That paper is not mandatory, but simply suggestive and advisory:

In view of the news from Hardee you had better move with Cheatham's division to his support and give the enemy battle immediately, &c. No time should be lost in these movements.

The order was not "you will move upon Perryville and attack the enemy early the next morning," as the paper sent you charges. The writing sent me was not an order at all, but counsel or advice to do a certain thing in view of information received from Hardee. It does not help the matter to say that I was advised to do it immediately and that it was added that no time should be lost in profiting by the advice to rout him, &c. The language was clearly not peremptory, but suggestive and advisory, and left me the use of my discretion as to the details of the attack, it being understood that I accepted the advice and proceeded to carry the operations into execution as judiciously and promptly as a willing mind and sound discretion would allow. It will be observed also that I was advised to act in view of the news from Hardee. If that remark meant anything to an officer who was counseled to move to the support of Hardee it was that he should put himself in communication with Hardee and to take that news into his account in any movement to be made. This was done, as you know, in the council held, and the result was a confirmation of what I already knew—that four-fifths of Buell's army was before me, and consequently with my small force great caution must be observed.

I am said to have acknowledged a disobedience of orders. I have done no such thing. In regard to the paper sent me for my guidance I quoted from memory. I said I was ordered to attack the enemy in the morning, and on looking at the language of the paper it appears that the word "morning" was not used at all nor is the word "attack" used, but I was to give him "battle immediately." But supposing it to have been mandatory instead of advisory, which the face of the paper denies, what is understood by immediately? I could have attacked him the night of my arrival and before I had the benefit of daylight. Would I have been justified in this? Certainly not. Why? Because in the nature of things and in view of the news from Hardee, to which I was referred as the inspiration prompting the order or counsel, it would not have been judicious. I was, I conceived, left at liberty to exercise such discretion as sound sense and the facts before me demanded, and I felt that I was acting on the inside of the instructions given me, and under the deep and painful conviction that the force at my disposal was totally inadequate to perform the duty assigned it; and while I must attempt that duty I should do it in such a way as to prevent the wreck and destruction of the little army with whose conduct and safety I was charged. I took counsel of the general officers with me, frankly stating the whole case as I understood it. I expressed my opinion as to what my duty required me to do in view of all the facts. They unanimously agreed with me so far as I remember, and I proceeded to execute the suggestions, or orders, if you will, of the general as promptly and yet as wisely as the condition of affairs before me would allow.

While I was thus engaged the general came upon the field. I was engaging the enemy with my skirmishers, but thus far on the defensive-offensive. This was about the middle of the morning. Shortly after he gave me positive orders to attack the enemy and it was done. As to my being held responsible for disobedience of orders in this matter, it never entered my head until the reception of your note; however, I shall endeavor to bear the matter with becoming moderation, and although I cannot claim to have "a talent for quarreling," I trust I shall not be found wanting either in a capacity or willingness to take care of my reputation so far as it can be vindicated by the truth. The passage in reference to the sacred character of military councils in the connection in which it is introduced is unfortunate. What transpires in council is sacred, truly; that is, not to be disclosed so long as there is a military necessity or expediency for its being kept secret. When that necessity or expediency which affects the public welfare only has passed there can be no reason why the opinion or language of any officer upon any topic should not be the subject of remark. It is to be supposed that every officer, when expressing his opinion in a council, does so independently and honestly in the face of the facts before him and for patriotic objects only; that he has no by-ends to answer, nothing to conceal of which he might be ashamed, and therefore that, so far as his opinions or counsel are concerned, the only measure of concealment of importance to him is the extent to which the public interests would be affected by the disclosure. The implied censure therefore lacks a foundation and fails. Besides, if the general would reflect he would see that in that passage itself he is committing the very offense which he has unsuccessfully charged upon me. The report of the battle of Perryville which I sent to him, and through him to the Senate beyond him, it is not allowable for him or any other person to use for public purposes until its contents have been "publicly disclosed" by order of the Senate to print. This is a trifle, but it belongs to the same family with that to which he invites attention. How far you may feel obliged for the protection he is affording you against the indiscretion or treachery by which you have been exposed, or whether that piece of service has won his way into your confidence far enough to lay you under obligations to join me in acknowledging disobedience to your duty, is a matter I am not competent to determine.

I note what you say of the campaign. There is a time for all things, and I agree with you the time for dealing with that has not arrived.

I am, general, very truly, yours,

L. POLK,
Lieutenant-General.

—

NEAR SHELBYVILLE, TENN., *April* 17, 1863.
Lieut. Gen. LEONIDAS POLK, *Shelbyville, Tenn.:*

GENERAL: I have the honor to inclose herewith a copy of a note I have this day addressed to General Bragg, which will explain why I have not sooner complied with my promise to furnish you with a copy of my former communication touching the same subject.

Hoping I may soon have it in my power to do so and that you may suffer no inconvenience by the delay, I am, general, very respectfully, your obedient servant,

PATTON ANDERSON.

[Inclosure.]

SHELBYVILLE, TENN., *April* 17, 1863.

General BRAXTON BRAGG, *Tullahoma, Tenn.*:

GENERAL: On yesterday Lieutenant-General Polk requested an interview with me, for the purpose of comparing our recollections of the councils at Bardstown and Perryville, referred to in his official report of the battle of Perryville and of which you had inquired in your communication of the 13th instant. In that interview I promised to furnish the lieutenant-general with a copy of my reply to your communication just alluded to; but on returning to my quarters I find that I did not preserve a fair copy, but instead only rough notes, in which verbal corrections and interlineations occur so frequently that I must beg you will supply me with a copy to enable me to comply with my promise. In talking over with General Polk what transpired at the Bardstown council each was enabled to refresh the memory of the other to some extent, and in this way I now recollect that in combating my scruples in regard to any other movement than that indicated in your dispatch from Frankfort the general called my attention to the word "available," made use of in that dispatch, and proceeded to show that he had no available forces at Bardstown for a move of the kind. Again, my impression was that in that Frankfort dispatch you had expressed a purpose of attacking the enemy in your front at an early moment, if not the next day. The general's recollection is that such intention on your part was expressed in a different communication. I have not spoken with any of the other officers composing that council in regard to its deliberations, but the result of my interview with Lieutenant-General Polk discloses no discrepancy between our recollections of what transpired, at least on material points. The point upon which I was embarrassed was this: I feared you would move out with the forces at and near Frankfort and give the enemy battle, relying upon our co-operation upon his flank and rear, and of this trouble I felt entirely relieved when I found that you had not done so.

I am, general, very respectfully, your obedient servant,

PATTON ANDERSON,
Brigadier-General, &c.

—

HEADQUARTERS McCOWN'S DIVISION,
April 24, 1863.

Lieutenant-General POLK, *Shelbyville, Tenn.*:

GENERAL: Herewith I inclose to you copies of the correspondence between General Bragg and myself which was the subject of our conversation on the 22d instant.* I had an honest doubt of the propriety of mentioning the matter to you myself. You alluded to it, informed me you had received a copy of General Bragg's letter from another source, and I deem it but right and fair to forward to you a copy of the letter which I received and of my reply.

I am, general, very truly and respectfully, your obedient servant,

A. P. STEWART,
Brigadier-General.

---

* The first inclosure is a copy (addressed to Stewart) of Bragg to Hardee, April 13. See p. 1097.

HEADQUARTERS McCOWN'S DIVISION,
Shellyville, Tenn., April 14, 1863.

General BRAXTON BRAGG, *Commanding Army of Tennessee:*

GENERAL: Your communication of 13th instant, inclosing a copy of your order to General Polk, dated Headquarters Department No. 2, Harrodsburg, October 7, 1862, 5.40 p. m., has just been received. In reply I have to state that I was not present at either of the councils alluded to in your communication, and was not aware until informed of the fact by your letter that a council or meeting of general officers was held by General Polk on the morning of October 8, 1862, nor that he had received orders from you to attack the enemy early that morning When the council was held at Bardstown I was on outpost some 9 miles from Bardstown, on the Louisville road. In short, the only council called by General Polk to which I was ever summoned or ever attended was held in Columbus, Ky., in November or December, 1861. I have been present at one or two other assemblages of officers called by him, but they were not of the nature of advisory councils nor was I called upon to express an opinion.

I am, general, very respectfully, your obedient servant,

A. P. STEWART,
Brigadier-General, C. S. Army.

HEADQUARTERS DEPARTMENT OF THE GULF,
Mobile, Ala., April 26, 1863.

General BRAXTON BRAGG,
Commanding Army of Tennessee, Tullahoma, Tenn.:

GENERAL: Your letter of the 13th instant has been received. You ask me, if I deem it consistent with my sense of duty, to inform you how far I may have sustained Lieutenant-General Polk in his acknowledged disobedience of orders in his conduct at Bardstown and Perryville, Ky., as based upon the opinions of certain councils assembled by his orders at those points. At the first council alluded to in your note I was not present, but was with you at Lexington and Frankfort. My views of that portion of the campaign you can probably recall, as in interviews at each of those cities I gave my opinion, when sought by you, with the candor I have ever used toward my superiors. I was present at the consultation of general officers at Perryville, and at the request of Lieutenant-General Polk, who was my commander, gave my views of what, in my opinion, was the proper course to be adopted under the circumstances in which that portion of the army found itself at the time, without obtruding my opinion upon him more than I had done at other times upon yourself. I expressed it when called upon to do so with the same sincerity I have ever shown toward you.

With a desire to act in accordance with my duty and with proper deference to yourself I have considered for several days the course I should pursue in replying to your letter. While I have never sought responsibility I have certainly never shrunk from any which appropriately belonged to me, and I desire to avoid none which may now attach to any opinions held or expressed by me on the occasion to which you direct my attention; but I cannot, consistently with my sense of propriety and self-respect and my regard for the public interests, reply to your questions. My regard for you personally induces me to assign a few reasons for my action :

1st. It is improper for me to reply categorically to your questions, because my views were given as a matter of duty on the requirement of Lieutenant-General Polk. They were used or rejected by him at the time on his own responsibility, and therefore any official demand for information in regard to them should be sought through that channel.

2d. It is inconsistent with my feelings of self-respect to reply, because the subject may become one of legal investigation, and I consider it unworthy the commission I hold to make myself in advance a party either to aid the prosecution of an officer on the one hand or to defend a subordinate against the legitimate authority of his superior on the other. All the facts within my knowledge can be elicited before the proper tribunal.

3d. It would be hurtful to the public interests for me to reply, because whatever statements I may make to you in reference to the action of Lieutenant-General Polk I must, as an officer and a gentleman, make equally to him, together with the occasion which calls upon me to respond. Such a result would not tend to promote that degree of harmony which should always exist between the first and second in command, and in my opinion the public interest has suffered sufficiently in consequence of the unfortunate differences which have prevailed in the Army of Tennessee.

Such are the chief reasons which have influenced the character of my reply. It has been made in no unkind spirit, but with a sense of what I think is due to you, to myself, and to the public interests.

I cannot close this letter, general, without incurring the risk of appearing perhaps obtrusive. Our acquaintance has been brief, and neither my military position nor personal relations justify me in advising you ; but the latter, though they have never been intimate, have not been unkind ; and as your military subordinate, even when I may have differed with you officially, I have received every consideration at your hands and have ever found you sensitive to the public good. It is therefore with a confidence that you will review what I say in the kind spirit in which it is urged when I venture upon giving unsought advice. It was the remark of Turenne, when acknowledging a military fault, that " He must have made war but a short time indeed who had not committed errors." The remark is applicable now as it was then, and every officer in his distinct sphere of duty must expect the legitimate criticism of the public and of military men. It is true that these criticisms may sometimes be urged with intemperance, but that should not the less prevent us from awaiting the matured verdict of public opinion and of history.

As to what may have occurred since the Kentucky campaign I am not fully advised, but from my associations with the general officers of your army in Kentucky I feel warranted in stating that while there were essential differences of opinion in regard to the general conduct of the campaign you were sustained in your authority by the whole weight of their character. There was a disposition among all with whom I was thrown to lend their ability and their zeal to carry out successfully the determinations at which you arrived. I think they were alive to the difficulties which surrounded you, and did not view your actions in a critical or censorious spirit even when their views may have differed from yours. From my knowledge of these gentlemen as soldiers of ability and distinction I think I do not hazard too much in saying that you can without difficulty still secure their earnest co-operation and support.

In this view I would consider it most unfortunate if I should take any step which might tend to aggravate the feeling which public rumor imputes as existing between you and some of your subordinate commanders. I think the public interests, which with every patriot should be superior to individual preferences or favor, are deeply concerned in harmonious action between you and them. You have been sustained in your position, I understand, by the Government. You therefore better than any one else can afford to abide the judgment which history may pronounce on your actions. Whatever may be the asperities of feeling existing between you and your generals, I feel assured from my personal knowledge of them that they are as little disposed as you are to set their own interests above the good of the country. I believe that a frank personal explanation with them will be the means of removing any cause of dissatisfaction which may naturally exist, will harmonize the discordant elements which may now be present in your army, and at the expense of little personal pride on either part result in great public good.

Though I have no claims to your intimacy I profess to be sufficiently a patriot and sufficiently your friend to advise a course which would in my opinion, without any sacrifice of your personal dignity, redound so much to the advantage of the Republic.

Believing that you will appreciate the motives which have induced me reluctantly to urge upon you these views and that you will justify me in the candid manner in which I have conveyed them, I am, general, very respectfully, your obedient servant,

S. B. BUCKNER.

[Indorsement No. 1.]

KNOXVILLE, TENN., *May* 24, 1863.

This copy is confidentially communicated to Lieutenant-General Hardee, who, after perusing it, will please transmit to Lieutenant-General Polk, who informs me that he desires to retain it as part of the history of the events connected with the campaign.

Truly,

S. B. BUCKNER.

[Indorsement No. 2.]

MAY 28, 1863.

Respectfully referred to General Polk, with the compliments of Lieutenant-General Hardee.

W. J. HARDEE.

———

SHELBYVILLE, *April* 20, 1863.

General BRAXTON BRAGG:

GENERAL: Your letter of the 13th, in reference to the councils of officers called by Lieutenant-General Polk at Bardstown and Perryville, was duly received. My sense of duty at least for the present, compels me to decline to answer what part I took in the councils referred to.

Yours, very respectfully,

B. F. CHEATHAM,
Major-General.

No. 30

Incomplete return of Casualties in the Confederate forces at the battle of Perryville, or Chaplin Hills, Ky., October 8, 1862.

[Compiled from the reports.]

Command.	Killed.	Wounded.	Missing.	Aggregate.
RIGHT WING.				
First Division.				
First Brigade:				
8th Tennessee	4	29	......	33
15th Tennessee	9	25	......	34
16th Tennessee	41	151	7	199
38th Tennessee	5	38	......	43
51st Tennessee	9	25	......	34
Carnes' battery	......	4	......	4
Total	68	272	7	347
Second Brigade:				
4th Tennessee	11	72	2	85
5th Tennessee	14	64	12	90
24th Tennessee	8	60	......	68
31st Tennessee	17	78	5	100
33d Tennessee	10	65	7	82
Stanford's battery	2	1	......	3
Total	62	340	26	428
Third Brigade:				
41st Georgia	23	125	3	151
1st Tennessee	49	129	1	179
6th Tennessee	16	64	11	91
9th Tennessee	32	114	8	154
27th Tennessee	16	81	11	108
Smith's battery	......	4	......	4
Total	136	517	34	687
Fourth Brigade:				
3d Tennessee Cavalry.*	1	1	......	2
13th Tennessee	......	1	......	1
9th Texas	1	......	......	1
Total	2	2	......	4
Total First Division	268	1,131	67	1,466
LEFT WING.				
Second Division.				
Second Brigade	6	78	68	152
Third Division.				
Third Brigade:				
5th Confederate	5	34	6	45
17th Tennessee	4	20	......	24
23d Tennessee	7	43	3	53
25th Tennessee	......	8	......	8
37th Tennessee	1	28	......	29
44th Tennessee	13	30	......	43
Darden's battery	......	2	......	2
Total†	30	165	9	204
Grand total reported	304	1,374	144	1,822

* Escort.   † See also Polk's and Hardee's reports.

No. 31.

Report of Maj. Gen. Leonidas Polk, C. S. Army, commanding Army of the Mississippi.

HEADQUARTERS ARMY OF THE MISSISSIPPI,
Knoxville, Tenn., November —, 1862.

SIR : I have the honor to submit the following as my official report of the battle of Perryville :

At Bardstown, on September 28, the Army of the Mississippi, by order from General Bragg, was placed under my command. Up to that time I had command of the right wing only, General Hardee having command of the left. My orders from the general commanding, who was called on public duty to the capital at Frankfort, were to press in the enemy's pickets upon Louisville and to maintain my position. If the enemy advanced upon me in moderate force, to attack him ; if in large force, I was to fall back upon Harrodsburg, marching in two columns via Perryville and Mackville respectively. The enemy having made a general advance, I moved upon Harrodsburg, and in consequence of the state of the roads marched the whole column by the Springfield and Perryville pike. The object of this movement was to form a junction with the Army of the Kentucky under General Kirby Smith, who was to move for that purpose upon Harrodsburg also from the north side of the Kentucky River. Another object was to cover our base, which after the evacuation of Cumberland Gap by the enemy was established at Camp Dick Robinson, in the forks of the Dick and Kentucky Rivers. On arriving at Perryville I communicated with the general commanding the forces then at Harrodsburg, informing him that the right wing, under command of General Cheatham, had been ordered forward to take a position on the farther side of that town, and as there was a scarcity of water I had ordered General Hardee to halt Buckner's division near Perryville and to post Anderson's on Salt River between the two towns. These dispositions were carried into effect and I reported to the general commanding in person.

The enemy had been held in check along the whole line of march from in front of Louisville up to our present position by those gallant cavalry commanders Colonels Wharton and Wheeler, and we were constantly advised of his position and movements. He left Louisville in five columns on as many different routes, extending from the road to Elizabethtown around to that to Shelbyville, and we had reason to believe that much the larger portion of this force was concentrated upon Bardstown and followed our retiring army in the march to Perryville. The rest of his force pursued a route farther north to threaten General Kirby Smith.

Information having been received through General Hardee that the enemy was pressing with heavy force upon his position it was resolved by the general commanding the forces to attack him at that point. He accordingly directed me on the evening of the 7th to order Anderson's division, of Hardee's wing, to return to Perryville and also to order General Cheatham, with Donelson's division of his wing, to follow it immediately, and to return myself to that place, to take charge of the forces and attack the enemy next morning. I urged the strong expediency of concentrating all our forces upon the point to be attacked, and at all events the necessity of having the remaining division of the Army of the Mississippi (Withers') placed at my disposal. To this the general objected, upon the ground that General Kirby Smith had informed him that the enemy was in force in his front and that his troops could not be spared from that part of the field, nor could the division of Withers be spared, as he thought the force in front of Smith made it necessary for him to be re-enforced. He therefore proposed to order Withers to the support of Smith and to take charge of those combined forces himself in person. Generals Anderson and Cheatham proceeded to Perryville and reported to General Hardee as ordered, and on arriving were posted by that officer in a line of battle which he had selected. I followed as soon as practicable, arrived during the night, and reconnoitered the line of battle early on the following morning.

At a meeting of the general officers, held about daylight, it was resolved, in view of the great disparity of our forces, to adopt the defensive-offensive, to await the movements of the enemy, and to be guided by events as they were developed. The line of battle selected was that indicated by the course of Chaplin Fork of Salt River, on the banks of which our troops were posted. The division of General Buckner, of the left wing, occupied the extreme right; that of General Anderson the center; that of General Donelson, of the right wing, under General Cheatham, the left. General Wharton's brigade of cavalry covered the right wing, General Wheeler the left. General McCown, who reached the field by a forced march with a cavalry force at an early hour, was directed, by order of General Bragg, to turn over his command to Colonel Wheeler and to report to him for orders. The whole of our force, including all arms, did not exceed 15,000. We have good reason to believe that the force of General Buell immediately in front of us, consisting of the corps of Generals McCook and Gilbert, each about 18,000 strong, and that General Crittenden, with a corps of about the same number, was within 8 miles of the field at the opening of the attack. General Liddell's brigade of General Buckner's division was thrown forward in observation about one mile in front of Perryville between the Springfield and Mackville roads. Light skirmishing opened the operation of the morning, which grew heavier as the day advanced.

About 10 o'clock Liddell became hotly engaged and it became evident that the enemy was disposed to press upon our right. I directed General Buckner to retire Liddell's brigade and let it fall back upon our general line, and ordered General Cheatham to move the whole of his command from the left to the right of our line. These orders were promptly executed and Cheatham's command was held in column of brigades. It was now near 1 o'clock and the movements of the enemy were not continued. It was then determined by General Bragg, commander of the forces, who had arrived on the field some hours before, to assume the offensive, and by his direction orders were given for a general movement throughout our whole line. General Cheatham's column of brigades was deployed into line and ordered, with Wharton's cavalry still upon its right, to attack. At this juncture I was informed by Colonel Wharton that a column of the enemy's infantry was seen approaching by the Mackville road in a direction to support the enemy's left. This column I discovered was still quite distant, but concluding that our chances of success were greater against the line in my front even when re-enforced than it would be by attacking it as it stood and exposing my flank to the approaching force, I awaited until the re-enforcements got into position. The attack was then ordered. Wharton charged the enemy's extreme left with great fury, passing on over stone walls and ravines and driving back the enemy's infantry several hundred yards. This movement placed in our possession a skirt of woods and an eminence of great importance to our success on our right. It was quickly followed by the brigades of General Cheatham, under

Brigadier-Generals Donelson, Stewart, and Maney. These mounted the steep and difficult cliffs of Chaplin River in gallant style and moved forward upon the enemy's position with a most determined courage. Their approach was met by a storm of shot, shell, and musketry from several batteries strongly posted and supported by heavy masses of infantry. Their progress was nevertheless steadily onward, and although mowed down by well-directed volleys of musketry and well-served artillery the gaps thus produced in our lines were promptly filled and our troops pressed forward with resistless energy, driving the enemy before them and capturing three of his batteries. In this movement the enemy's left was forced back about a mile until his three lines were pressed into one. Here, being heavily re-enforced, he recovered one of his batteries, but did not attempt to regain any of the ground he had lost. This charge of these brigades was one of the most heroic and brilliant movements of the war. Considering the disparity of the numbers of the troops engaged, the strength of the enemy's position, the murderous character of the fire under which they had to advance, the steadiness with which they endured the havoc which was being made in their ranks, their knowledge that they were without any supporting force, the firmness with which they moved upon the enemy's masses of infantry and artillery, it will compare favorably with the most brilliant achievements of historic valor. In this charge General James S. Jackson, who commanded a division of the enemy, was killed amid the guns of one of the batteries that was taken.

While directing the operations in this part of the field I received a message from General Bragg, informing me that the right center, occupied by a portion of the troops of General Hardee, was hard pressed, and suggesting the sending re-enforcements to its relief. This was done at the earliest moment, the brigades of Generals Stewart and Donelson being detached for that purpose. These generals advanced their brigades in gallant style on the right of that of General Cleburne, and in conjunction with that efficient officer drove the enemy with great slaughter from his successive positions a full mile and a half.

As the enemy was yielding toward the close of the day the brigade of Brigadier-General Liddell approached from my left and rear and halted on the crest of a hill to determine the point at which to offer its support. It was directed to the place where it was most wanted and moved upon it with deafening cheers. Here, owing to the fading twilight, it was for a few moments difficult to determine whether the firing in our front was from our own or the enemy's troops. This difficulty, however, was speedily removed; it was the enemy, and in obedience to orders that veteran brigade, under its gallant commander, closed the operations of the day in that part of the field with a succession of the most deadly volleys I have witnessed. The enemy's command in their immediate front was well-nigh annihilated.

At this point a number of prisoners were taken, and among them several corps, division, and brigade staff officers; and, darkness closing in, I ordered the troops to cease firing and to bivouac for the night.

The operations of the left wing, which were under the immediate superintendence of Major-General Hardee, were not less satisfactory or successful. His combinations for the attack were judiciously made, and immediately after the onset of the right wing, under Major-General Cheatham, had been fully developed, he ordered General Buckner to move forward his division and unite in the assault. This order was executed with promptness and vigor. The position assailed—one of great strength and the key of that part of the field—was carried, and by a combined movement with two of the brigades of General Anderson's division and a skillful handling of his artillery, the whole of the enemy's line, reaching to Cheatham's left, was driven in confusion near a mile to the rear, and night put an end to farther pursuit. The gallantry of these troops and of their able and skillful commanders in that desperate struggle was in keeping with that of their comrades of the right wing, and the part they bore in the bloody conflict of the field of Perryville entitles them to a distinguished place in the records of that eventful day.

For further details I beg leave to refer to the reports of wing, division, brigade, and regimental commanders, herewith transmitted.

To Major-Generals Hardee and Cheatham I feel under obligations for the judgment and skill manifested in conducting the operations of their respective commands and for the energy and vigor with which they directed their movements. Few instances are on record where such successes have been obtained against such disparity of numbers.

My thanks are due also to the division and brigade commanders and their subordinates for the fidelity and gallantry with which they supervised and directed the operations of their commands; also to the soldiers for the zeal and alacrity with which they obeyed the orders of their several commanders and the active energy and dauntless courage with which they moved to the performance of the most difficult and perilous enterprises. No troops on any field have ever exhibited higher qualities of the soldier, as no troops at any time have ever had higher motives to inspire them with a contempt for danger and of death.

I am indebted likewise to Colonels Wheeler and Wharton, commanding the cavalry brigades, for their vigilance and activity in protecting our flanks and for the vigorous assaults made by them upon the enemy's lines. Of Colonel Wharton's charge on the enemy's left flank I have already spoken. Colonel Wheeler and the brave officers and men under his command exhibited the same dauntless energy and courage for which they have become distinguished. He kept a very large force of the enemy at bay and made a most brilliant charge, driving the enemy before him and capturing a battery. For particulars of the operations of the commands of these deservedly distinguished officers I beg leave to refer you to their reports, herewith transmitted.

To my staff, general and personal, I am under obligations for the promptitude and zeal with which they discharged the duties of their several offices.

I desire to return thanks to Almighty God for the persistent energy, determination, and courage with which He has inspired the hearts of our troops in the prosecution of this unrighteous war and for shielding our heads in the day of battle.

Respectfully, your obedient servant,

L. POLK,
Major-General, Commanding.

Col. GEORGE WILLIAM BRENT, *Assistant Adjutant-General.*

[Inclosure.]

List of Casualties in the Army of the Mississippi at the battle of Perryville, October 8, 1862.

	Killed.	Wounded.	Missing.	Total.
Right wing (commanded by Major-General Cheatham)....	268	1,131	67	1,466
Left wing (commanded by Major-General Hardee)........	242	1,504	184	1,930
Grand total...	510	2,635	251	3,396

No. 32.

Report of Maj. John Knight, Forty-first Georgia Infantry, Maney's Brigade, Cheatham's Division, Right Wing.

KNOXVILLE, TENN., *October* —, 1862.

On the 8th instant this regiment participated in a battle with the Federals at Perryville, Ky. Being on the right of General Maney's brigade, was led into the battle by a flank movement across a creek in the direction of the battle guided by the sound, and brought into line of battle by filing to the right through a brush-wood under heavy cannonading, being protected by an eminence in front where the line was formed, composed of the Forty-first Georgia, Sixth and Ninth Tennessee Regiments, and moved forward. As it emerged from the woods it came in view of the enemy's battery, situated on an eminence in a cleared field, supported by a heavy force, where it instinctively halted. In an instant the brigade was ordered forward by the brigade commander, and as it moved forward, owing to the situation of the enemy, the Forty-first Regiment was first exposed to the fire, and as soon as it was in view the enemy opened upon them a most terrific and deadly fire, when our regiment responded and halted for several minutes. It was a fearful time. At this critical moment General Maney passed down our line, encouraging the men by his personal presence and urging them forward. Just at this place our regiment sustained one-half, if not two-thirds, of their entire loss during the battle. Finally this suspense was relieved by the enemy's lines giving way, which was closely followed up by our troops, who seemed to vie with each other in seeing who could do the most to drive the enemy from the field. Never perhaps did troops fight more desperately than did these on this occasion.

Our regiment lost 6 men bearing aloft the colors (2 killed and 4 wounded). Our colors had six holes shot through them. Our noble colonel (Charles A. McDaniel) fell late in the evening, severely wounded, in the corn field beyond the belt of woods we passed through after going out of the old field.

We feel proud to be associated with the Tennesseeans who composed General Maney's brigade, and feel assured should danger threaten none would more readily come to our assistance and rescue.

I am, sir, yours, truly, &c.,

JNO. KNIGHT,
Major, Comdg. Forty-first Regiment Georgia Volunteers.
Capt. THOMAS H. MALONE, *Assistant Adjutant-General.*

No. 33.

Report of Col. H. R. Feild, First Tennessee Infantry.

CAMP NEAR BRYANTSVILLE, KY.,
October 12, 1862.

My regiment went into the action of the 8th instant in rear and on the left of the brigade at the field where we captured the eight-gun battery. I lost only some 3 or 4 men killed and wounded at that place. The brigade was ordered immediately forward to take another battery about a half mile in advance, planted on a very steep hill, commanding a large corn field, through which we had to advance. This battery and its support was making terrible havoc with the right wing of the brigade, so reported by the field officers of the Forty-first Georgia to me, whereupon I sent Captain Malone to General Maney asking for my regiment to be sent to the right, which request was granted. After deploying the regiment to the extreme right it was ordered to charge, which it did in splendid style, with close, compact ranks, killing all the horses and men of the battery and driving its support away. In this charge the brigade became very much disorganized, and after taking the battery by some mistake fell back in confusion. My regiment lost in that charge its gallant lieutenant-colonel (John Patterson) and some 40 or 50 men and officers. I rallied the regiment at the foot of the hill, no other regiment forming but mine, some 30 or 40 men of the other regiments falling into the ranks. In the mean time the enemy came back to the guns behind the battery, and also marched two regiments on our left on a wooded hill which lay at right angles with the hill that we charged up. I led the regiment up the hill alone, without any support, under a heavy fire of musketry, driving the enemy back and taking his guns again. The regiments on our left then opened their fire upon us, killing and wounding a dozen officers and men at each discharge. Just then I discovered Hardee's battle-flag coming up on our left about 500 yards in rear. Expecting that the regiment that carried the flag would engage the enemy that were cross-firing upon us I determined to hold the hill at every cost, thinking they would drive the enemy before them; they failed to do so and fell back before they had arrived in 200 yards of my position; whereupon I ordered my regiment to retire, which it did in much better order than could have been expected, leaving half their number dead and wounded on the top of the hill.

My whole loss amounts to 181 killed, wounded, and missing.

Respectfully submitted.

H. R. FEILD,
Colonel, Commanding First Tennessee Regiment.

Capt. Thomas H. Malone, *Assistant Adjutant-General.*

No. 34.

Report of Col. George C. Porter, Sixth Tennessee Infantry.

October 16, 1862.

Sir: According to instructions I beg leave to submit this my report of the Sixth Regiment Tennessee Volunteers in the action of the 8th ultimo at Perryville, Ky.:

About 1 p. m. the brigade, under the command of Brig. Gen. George Maney, was in line of battle immediately in rear of General Stewart's brigade. The position of this regiment was second from the right, between the Forty-first Georgia and Ninth Tennessee Regiments. Having proceeded in this manner for about half a mile the right of the brigade rested upon the bank of a creek, the opposite of which was rocky and precipitous. It was ordered by the flank farther to the right across said creek, under the cover of a bluff about 200 yards in front. Having moved in this new direction several hundred yards around this impassable ascent sufficiently far for three regiments (the Forty-first Georgia, Sixth Tennessee, and Ninth Tennessee) to be fronted and to move in its old direction a forward movement was again ordered. The nature of the ground was badly suited for this maneuver, the topography of which you are well acquainted with, hence it is not necessary for me to describe it minutely. It was a thick wood, covered with brush and undergrowth. These regiments were then ordered to move forward in line of battle. They had gone but a short distance when one of the most deadly and destructive fires that can possibly be imagined was poured in their whole line by the enemy, who occupied a strong and well-chosen position on an eminence in an open field about 300 yards to the front. Here had a battery of eight guns, strongly supported by infantry. This command still pressing steadily forward, all the time having the contents of this battery, consisting of grape, canister, and shell, together with the small-arms of the strong supporting force, it came to a high fence at the edge of the wood, at which time it seemed impossible for humanity to go farther, such was the havoc and destruction that had taken place in their ranks. A temporary halt was the inevitable result. Here, at this critical juncture, General Maney passed along the line from the right of the Georgia regiment to the left of the Ninth Tennessee, ordering and encouraging us to still press forward, as it was our last and only chance of safety and success. His presence and manner having imparted fresh vigor and courage among the troops the fence was crossed, the ascent gained, the battery taken, and the infantry, with terrible slaughter, driven from the field. It was here at the fence and between the fence and the point where this battery was in position that this regiment sustained its greatest loss. Here was the hottest part of the engagement. It was near the fence on entering the field that Capt. Thomas B. Rains, Company C, and First Lieut. Ed. Seabrook were killed, while acting nobly at the head of their respective companies. No truer and braver men fell that day. The color-bearer, John Andrews, was here too badly wounded to proceed farther and had to be carried to the rear. They were then seized by John Ayeres, one of the color guard, who carried them gallantly for a short distance and was killed. A. M. Pegues then carried them to the summit where the first battery was placed, where he was badly wounded, being shot in three places. They were then seized by Ed. Quin, private, Company H, who bore them in advance of the regiment across the field into the wood, where he was killed. At a lane about 200 yards in rear of the battery Lieut. N. A. Butler, Company C, was killed while nobly discharging his duty.

The brigade still continued to press forward across the woods into an adjoining field of corn, when part of Stewart's command came up. We, together with a portion of the Fourth Tennessee, were driven from the summit of this hill in the corn field, but were again rallied in a ravine near a stone fence and ordered back by General Maney to dislodge, if possible, certain sharpshooters and to fire upon a battery that was engaged with one of ours a short distance to the front. The order was again obeyed and the summit was again reached, but owing to a strong and destructive cross-fire it was deemed useless to endeavor to hold it. The rest of the day was consumed in gathering together the scattering ones that remained, and a line of battle was formed in this ravine near the edge of the corn field. What followed is not necessary for me to make special mention of.

In this fight there were so many instances of individual prowess and bravery that I find it no easy task to make proper discrimination in the matter. As far as I could judge they all did their duty well and deserve the highest praise; but, as ordered by the general, I beg leave to make special mention of Thomas Estes, private, Company A; Orderly Sergt. B. F. Collinsworth, Company I; John Lanier, private, Company E;

R. S. Cole, private, Company H; Lieut. [S. A.] Mason, Company B, and Capt. E. [C.] Harbert, Company K, who were certainly not remiss in any part of their duty. I should not fail to make special note of Lieut. C. M. Carter, who throughout the whole fight was most conspicuous in the extraordinary gallantry and courage displayed in front of his company and regiment. He unfortunately, however, fell in the last charge in the corn field so badly wounded that he died the next day. Maj. J. L. Harris and Adjt. T. H. Henderson conducted themselves with credit and gallantry during the whole action.

It may be necessary to mention that the center of the Sixth Regiment passed over the right gun of the battery on the hill.

Hoping that this will in part subserve the purpose for which it is intended, I beg leave to subscribe myself, your obedient, humble servant,

GEO. C. PORTER,
Colonel, Commanding Sixth Regiment Tennessee Vols.

Capt. THOMAS H. MALONE, *Assistant Adjutant-General.*

No. 35.

Report of Maj. George W. Kelsoe, Ninth Tennessee Infantry.

CAMP NEAR DICK'S RIVER, KY.,
October 12, 1862.

SIR : I have the honor to submit the following report of the conduct of my regiment in the action of the 8th instant :

When drawn up in line near the hospital established for our brigade my command was harassed by the cannonading of the enemy, and here 1 private was killed and several wounded by the explosion of a bombshell. We were ordered forward, passing up a steep declivity by the flank, and took our position under a most galling fire. Immediately after getting under fire we were ordered to charge a battery of seven guns immediately in our front, the three left guns of the enemy covering our right wing. It was carried at once, the men all seemingly determined not to halt for any obstacle.

Here the color-bearer, Robert Gibbs, of Company C, fell while gallantly rushing on, and Corpl. M. C. Hooks, of the color guard, seized the flag and kept in front of the lines throughout the entire action, although severely bruised. At this point Lieut. [P. J.] Fitzpatrick, commanding Company K, and Lieut. [W. T.] Lawler, commanding Company G, were both killed while gallantly leading their companies. They did their duty nobly to the last. Lieut. Col. [John W] Buford was wounded here, and the command devolved on me.

After the enemy abandoned these guns they formed a new line in rear of a lane fence, having the additional protection of being on the opposite side of the lane from us. From this fence they poured into our ranks such a destructive fire as to momentarily check our advance, but my men, determined to die rather than to waver, pressed on, in many cases bayoneting the more dogged of our opponents. The few who escaped fell behind a second line of the enemy drawn up behind the brink of a hill on which were planted four guns. Here every company had its commander struck down. The bravery of these officers had so far carried everything before us. Capt. [J. W.] McDonald, First Lieuts. [James I.] Hall, [J. M.] Matthews, and [D. M.] Bell were mortally wounded, and Capts. [J. W.] Hubbard, [C. B.] Simonton, [H. C.] Irby, [J. L.] Hall, and [H. A.] Rogers left the field severely wounded, Captain Rogers, however, returning and doing good service throughout the action. The conduct of all these officers cannot be too highly mentioned.

My horse being shot at this point I was compelled to leave the lines for a few minutes. In the mean time the regiment carried this four-gun battery, and advancing through the open wood lot in which it was planted, under a fire of grape and canister which our oldest veterans had never seen equaled, they pressed on all unmindful of the carnage surrounding them, and gained the crest of an elevation in a corn field, where, in addition to the musketry fire in our front and the grape and canister shots that fell like hail from a third battery to our right, planted on a hill in an old stubble field, a most murderous fire was poured into our flank from a thicket on our left. Our line pressed on, being within 50 yards of the last-named battery, when we were ordered to fall back, being relieved by General Stewart's (Second) brigade, which then advanced. It was impossible to communicate the order to all of my men, and a large majority continued to fight with the relieving brigade, remaining in the advanced line until the fire on the right wing entirely ceased.

Throughout the action the men behaved themselves as became the heroes of Shiloh, ever advancing, ever cheering, and the command forward was entirely unnecessary, as at all times the men in the line repeated the command without orders. It was an exception to see any of the men taking advantage of trees or other kind of shelter; the majority never lying down, but erect, advanced with the determination to carry the field or never leave it. Their conduct and that of the officers of my command was most gallant, and it would be invidious to make distinctions where credit justly belongs to so many.

We lost, killed dead on the field, 30; wounded, 120 (10 or 12 of whom have since died), and 8 missing.

Respectfully submitted.

GEO. W. KELSOE,
Major, Commanding Ninth Tennessee Regiment.

Capt. THOMAS H. MALONE, *Assistant Adjutant-General.*

No. 36.

Report of Lieut. Col. W. Frierson, Twenty-seventh Tennessee Infantry.

OCTOBER 26, 1862.

SIR: In accordance with orders from Brigadier-General Maney I hereby beg leave to submit the following report of the part taken by the regiment (Twenty-seventh Tennessee) under my command during the late engagement with the enemy near Perryville, Ky.:

I regret that it was not my fortune to observe in person the movement of the regiment and conduct of the men during the entire engagement, but the effects of the explosion of a shell near my head incapacitated me entirely for duty after the expulsion of the enemy from the open field in which the first battery was planted and the lane beyond. I will therefore complete the report with information received from Major Allen, in command.

About 11 a. m., it becoming apparent that the enemy were endeavoring to turn our extreme right, this regiment was ordered, together with the remainder of General Cheatham's division, to leave the position it then occupied on the extreme left and to hasten by the right flank to the point where the enemy had commenced to concentrate his forces. The distance marched was near 2 miles, under a very hot sun, and a portion of the time at a double-quick, and for a mile before the engagement commenced the men were continually exposed to the fire of the enemy's batteries. Tired and heated, the men were ordered to load and prepare for battle. The enemy's batteries had been planted upon a high bluff which it was impossible to ascend save in a few places, and in point of position the enemy had every advantage; but notwithstanding all these odds my men moved eagerly forward at the command. In ascending the bluff I was compelled, for want of room to preserve my position (second to the left) in line of battle, to move by the right flank, until coming in rear of the Sixth Tennessee Regiment I again moved by the left flank. Upon reaching the top of the bluff we found a strip of woods to pass through before coming to the field in which the battery was planted and separated from the field by a fence. During the whole time of passing through the woods the battery was playing upon us with terrible effect; but as soon as the fence was reached, in full view of the battery, such a storm of shell, grape, canister, and Minie balls was turned loose upon us as no troops scarcely ever before encountered. Large boughs were torn from the trees, the trees themselves shattered as if by lightning, and the ground plowed in deep furrows. Still my men hesitated but a moment. Although many had fallen, and almost certain death seemed to be the fate of the remainder if they advanced, I had only to command "Forward," when they as one man leaped the fence and most gallantly charged at a double-quick, firing at every opportunity. Upon arriving within a few feet of the battery the enemy opened a most murderous fire with their small-arms, which caused the men to hesitate for a moment, when they commenced to return the fire with effect. After witnessing the gallant example set by yourself, sir, the men awaited no second command to charge, but continued to move forward until the enemy was driven entirely from the field, leaving the battery, seven guns, I believe, in our possession. It was a complete triumph of resolute courage and determined fighting over every odds. The enemy had every advantage of position, and were superior to us in point of numbers by at least two, and probably three, to one. His battery was composed of large Napoleon guns, and still the Third Brigade, tired and alone, with a bright sun shining in their eyes to bewilder them, overcame all these obstacles and took the battery; but the battle is not yet closed. Upon reaching the fence on the opposite side of the field we met with stout resistance while crossing the lane that separated the battery field from a second battery and a largely superior force of infantry ; but even these odds were overcome by the determined spirit of our troops, the Twenty-seventh Tennessee always holding her position in line, and the enemy driven through the woods and an adjoining corn field in the direction of their battery. At this second battery the enemy made a desperate and successful stand. Our men, after charging it most bravely twice, were finally drawn off on account of very heavy cross-firing on the left, which, owing to our fewness of numbers, we were unable to prevent. My regiment was then reformed and moved in the vicinity of the first battery and afterward to the Harrodsburg pike. Such, sir, as well as I can remember and learn, were the principal movements made by the Twenty-seventh Regiment during the bloody battle near Perryville.

The long list of killed and wounded speaks in language more powerful than aught I can say of the gallant part taken by the men under my command in that engagement. We had out of 210 men carried into action 16 killed dead on the field, 84 wounded, and 12 missing, several of whom are supposed to be dead or wounded. We had 2 color-bearers killed and a third fell mortally wounded, but held on to the colors until told it would fall into the hands of the enemy, when he agreed to give it up. The flag-staff was shot off near the flag. Still another one of the color guard was wounded. At no time did the men or officers under me hesitate to obey most cheerfully every command they might receive, and none can be condemned for improper conduct. Please assure the general that if the regiment did not deport itself so well as he expected it was the fault of their commander and not of the company officers and men.

Although all did their duty so well, yet I feel that it is due a few others who exhibited more than ordinary coolness and daring to mention their names with this report : Capt. John M. Taylor, Company K; Lieut. [E. E.] Pate, Company H; Capt. John W. Carroll, Company I, and Lieut. [James] Stinnett, of Company B, were always foremost to lead their men to the charge and rendered me much assistance by their ready commands and brave examples. The first two named I fear were mortally wounded.

I desire also to mention the name of John Olive, private, Company B, who, though under military age, displayed the coolness and courage of a veteran. He carried the colors for some time, never ceasing to use his rifle all the while.

I am much indebted to Maj. [A. C.] Allen and Adjt. [S. M.] Howard for gallant services rendered me while in command and for still more gallant and efficient services when the command devolved upon them. The horses of both were shot under them, nor did they leave their posts until the engagement closed.

The regiment, sir, is not forgetful of the skill and gallantry of their chief of brigade and his efficient staff.

Respectfully,

W. FRIERSON,
Lieutenant-Colonel, Comdg. Twenty-seventh Tennessee Regt.
Capt. THOMAS H. MALONE, *Assistant Adjutant-General.*

No. 37.

Report of Maj. Gen. William J. Hardee, C. S. Army, commanding Left Wing.

HEADQUARTERS HARDEE'S CORPS,
Shelbyville, Tenn., December 1, 1862.

MAJOR : I have the honor to transmit the following report of the operations of my command on October 8 last against the forces of the United States in the battle of Perryville :

For several days before the engagement the enemy had advanced strong columns from Bardstown in the direction of Perryville and Danville. My troops occupied the village of Perryville, and on October 6 and 7 some skirmishing occurred between my cavalry under Colonel

Wheeler and the advanced forces of the Federal army, which were brilliantly managed by that brave and able officer.

On the 7th I informed General Bragg, who was at Harrodsburg, that the enemy was moving in heavy force against my position. With the view of inflicting a decisive defeat, or at least of pressing him back from any farther advance against our line of communications in the direction of Danville and Cumberland Gap, I urged the concentration of our whole army at Perryville.

On the evening of the 7th, my wing of the army having been re-enforced by the division of Cheatham and orders having been issued to engage the enemy on the following morning, I again earnestly urged upon General Bragg the necessity of massing his forces on that important point. That night Major-General Polk arrived and assumed command.

The country near Perryville is boldly undulating and varied with farm-houses, corn fields, and plantations, bordered by native forests. A creek called Chaplin Fork flows northwardly through the village and unites 4 or 5 miles beyond it with another little stream called Doctor's Fork. The space between the two from east to west is about 1½ miles. A good road running a little south of east from Mackville to Perryville crosses this stream, and a turnpike from Springfield running nearly east and west passes through Perryville to Danville. Another fine macadamized highway traverses the village from the south in a northwardly direction toward Harrodsburg and Lexington and another southwardly in the direction of Lebanon. The position at Perryville is strong, and offered many tactical and strategical advantages. The key of the enemy's position was at a point where the Mackville road crosses Doctor's Fork, about 1½ miles from the village, near a barn and white farm-house on the hill west of the creek. The autumnal drought left the streams almost dry, only pools of water being found here and there along their channels.

The forces under my command were two divisions, constituting the left wing of the army, commanded respectively by Major-General Buckner and Brig. Gen. J. Patton Anderson. Each consisted of four brigades, with a battery attached to each brigade. Thinned by battle and reduced by long and arduous service, my effective force did not exceed 10,000 men. No means exist for ascertaining accurately the strength of the Federal forces, but from information derived from prisoners captured from five of their divisions it is believed that the enemy displayed not less than 35,000 men, under the command of Major-Generals McCook, Rousseau, Jackson, and other generals.

My line of battle was originally established between the Harrodsburg turnpike and Chaplin's, its general direction being nearly north and south, with the left resting near the village and the right extending down the stream. The line was subsequently advanced about noon, by order of General Bragg, who arrived about 10 o'clock in the morning, westwardly, so as to take position on the space between the two streams on the west of the town, extending across the Mackville road, with its left toward the Springfield turnpike. An interval between the left and the Springfield road was swept and protected by a fine battery of 12-pounders, under Captain Semple, posted on the Seminary Hill, near the eastern side of the village. Brigadier-General Anderson, with two brigades, under command of Brigadier-General Adams and Colonel Powell, covered the extreme left on the Springfield road to protect our communications with Danville and Harrodsburg. The enemy occupied the western or left bank of Doctor's Fork, extending across both sides of the Mackville road and across the Springfield road. The left of the enemy north of the Mackville road was thrown back in a northwesterly direction, forming an obtuse angle deflected about 30° along broken heights from their center and right, the angle being near the point where the Mackville road crosses Doctor's Fork. About 1 o'clock in the afternoon General Cheatham's division crossed Doctor's Fork on our extreme right and engaged the enemy's left on the heights with great vigor. Immediately I ordered General Buckner to advance his division and attack the salient angle of the enemy's line where the Mackville road crosses Doctor's Fork. The position was a strong one. The enemy was posted behind a natural parapet afforded by the character of the ground and some stone fences, which were enfiladed by their batteries on their right and swept by another strong battery posted in their rear.

The brigade of Brigadier-General Johnson gallantly led the advance, with Brigadier-General Cleburne's as a support, while the brigade of General St. John R. Liddell was held as a reserve. The brigades of [John C.] Brown and Jones, of Anderson's, and [S. A. M.] Wood, of Buckner's division, had been detached to occupy the interval between the right of Buckner and the left of Cheatham, and the two remaining brigades of Anderson's division, under command of General [D. W.] Adams and Col. [Sam.] Powell, [Twenty-ninth Tennessee], covered the extreme left of our line. By this time, Cheatham being hotly engaged, the brigades of Johnson and Cleburne attacked the angle of the enemy's line with great impetuosity near the burnt barn, while those of Wood, Brown, and Jones dashed against their line more to the right, on the left of Cheatham. Simultaneously the brigades of Adams and Powell, on the left of Cleburne and Johnson, assailed the enemy in front, while Adams', diverging to the right, united with Buckner's left. The whole force thus united then advanced, aided by a crushing fire from the artillery, which partially enfiladed their lines. This combined attack was irresistible, and drove the enemy in wild disorder from the position nearly a mile to the rear. Cheatham and Wood captured the enemy's battery in front of Wood, and among the pieces and amid the dead and dying was found the body of General James S. Jackson, who commanded a division of the enemy at that point.

As evening closed in I ordered forward Liddell's brigade to re-enforce Cheatham. Arriving near twilight, it was difficult in the *mêlée* to distinguish friend from foe. Major-General Polk first discovered the enemy, in whose ranks he found himself by chance, and escaped by his coolness and address. Returning rapidly he gave Liddell the order to fire, and a deadly volley was poured in that completed the rout. By this brigade, so gallantly led and directed by General Liddell, arms, prisoners, and colors were captured, together with the papers and baggage of Major-General McCook. Night closing in our camp-fires were lighted upon the ground so obstinately contested by the enemy, so bravely won by the valor of our troops.

The loss sustained in the battle was severe—242 killed and 1,504 wounded from my command—attest the severity of the conflict. Brigadier-General Cleburne, who led his brigade with his usual courage and judgment, was wounded, but remained in command until the close of the day. Brigadier-General Wood was severely wounded in the head by the fragment of a shell; his quartermaster, commissary, and assistant adjutant-general were killed, and the three colonels next in rank, on whom the command successively devolved, were wounded. Brigadier-

General Brown was severely wounded while rendering efficient service on the right with his command. Many other valuable officers were killed or wounded in the battle.

To Major-General Buckner I am indebted for the skillful management of his troops, the judicious use of his artillery, and for the opportune services of himself and the veteran division under his command.

To Brigadier-General Anderson the defense of the extreme left in the direction of Danville was intrusted. His operations were not under my immediate supervision. Two of his brigades were detached and advanced boldly, but one brigade was compelled by greatly superior numbers to resume its original ground, from which, under the cool direction of General Anderson, it subsequently withdrew in good order. Both brigades were gallantly conducted by General Adams and Colonel Powell, the latter having suffered severely in the unequal contest.

To my staff I am under obligations for promptitude displayed by them in the execution of my orders and for the intelligence and zeal shown in the discharge of their respective duties. I refer to the reports of division and brigade commanders for details of the operations of their commands.

To the officers and men I tender my thanks for the daring courage and fine discipline exhibited by them on the field of Perryville. When advancing none shrank nor lingered in the attack; when engaged no Southern standard was abandoned. Our path was marked by the crushed lines and disorderly battalions of the enemy. Our troops displayed higher qualities than mere discipline can confer. The fervor of freemen and the enthusiasm of patriots animated their valor. Whenever they advanced the enemy recoiled before the shock; when they retired he dare not venture to pursue.

Very respectfully, your obedient servant,

W. J. HARDEE,
Lieutenant-General.

Maj. GEORGE WILLIAMSON, *Chief of Staff.*

No. 38.

Reports of Brig. Gen. Daniel W. Adams, C. S. Army, commanding Second Brigade, Second Division.

HDQRS. SECOND BRIGADE, SECOND DIVISION, A. MISS.,
Bryantsville, Ky., October 12, 1862.

SIR: I have the honor respectfully to report that on the 8th instant, about 11 o'clock a. m., in obedience to orders received through Brigadier-General Anderson, I formed the brigade under my command, composed of the Thirteenth, Sixteenth, Twentieth, and Twenty-fifth Louisiana Regiments, with the Battalion of Sharpshooters, and Fifth Company Washington Artillery, under Capt. C. H. Slocomb, in line of battle, and moved from our position near Perryville, Ky., obliquing to the right to attack the enemy.

At about 11.30 a. m., when advancing, I received an order from Brigadier-General Anderson, commanding the division, to halt or move slowly until the Third Brigade, commanded by Colonel Powell, arrived opposite my line. In obedience to this order I halted the brigade several times and moved very slowly until I came near the enemy at the foot of a hill on Beech Fork Creek. Before reaching this point I sent several messengers to Colonel Powell to move up as rapidly as possible. On reaching the point above designated I halted the command, had the artillery put in position so as to command that of the enemy, and again sent a messenger to Colonel Powell by my aide-de-camp, Lieut. E. M. Scott. Receiving no answer, and as it was then getting late in the day, I ordered the artillery to open fire, and after a very brisk, well-directed, and effective fire for a half or three-quarters of an hour, by direction of General Buckner I moved the infantry forward on the enemy's right at and near a very strong position on a hill. After a short but spirited contest we dislodged and drove them before us. They fled in great disorder, panic, and confusion, throwing their arms and equipments away as they fled. We followed them about a mile, the Washington Artillery coming up and halting at two positions, as directed, where they again opened fire with great accuracy and effect.

Finding my brigade in the advance and entirely unsupported on the right or left except by General Cleburne's brigade, which was in our rear to the right, and inactive from being out of ammunition, as I was informed, I halted my command under a very heavy and rapid fire from this point, when I was soon opened upon from the left and rather to the rear by a well-directed battery of artillery. Using my glass, I discerned the enemy moving their forces and forming line of battle at a distance of 600 or 800 yards to my left. Deeming this position untenable I ordered the brigade to fall back, which they did in perfect order. I communicated this intention to General Cleburne, with my reasons for doing it. After passing the first hill which we drove the enemy from I met General Hardee, who ordered the command to return and take position on that hill. This was promptly executed, and the Washington Artillery again opened fire with great force and effect and continued it until 7.30 o'clock p. m. My brigade remained at this position until 2 o'clock a. m. of the 9th instant, when, the balance of the command having moved in obedience to General Buckner's orders, I moved in, bringing up the rear, and reached our position near Perryville about 3.30 o'clock a. m.

The killed, wounded, and missing from my brigade amounted to 152, of whom 6 are known to be killed, 78 wounded, and 68 missing. Fortunately we had no officers killed that I am aware of. Lieut. Philip Sayne, whilst coming up in the rear in charge of the ammunition train, was captured by the enemy, with the train and its guard, consisting of 12 or 15 men, and at the same time and place Lieut. Thomas M. Blair, of the Washington Artillery, with 14 men and 2 caissons, returning for ammunition, were captured by the enemy.

My aide-de-camp, Lieut. Edward M. Scott, whom I sent with a message to Colonel Powell, commanding the Third Brigade, is missing; supposed to be captured by the enemy.

All the officers and men of my command behaved with coolness and gallantry, and whilst it would be invidious to make special mention of any names, yet I feel that it is due to mention Maj. J. E. Austin, of the Battalion of Sharpshooters; Maj. Charles Guillet, Twentieth; Capt. H. Brummerstadt, Lieut. E. P. Guillet, adjutant; Lieutenant Schaedel, of the Twentieth Louisiana; Capt. M. O. Tracy, of the Thirteenth Louisiana, and Lieutenant McCall, of the C. S. Army, and Maj. R. G. Higgins, volunteer aide-de-camp, as having been conspicuous for their gallantry and courage. Lieutenant Eichholz and Lieutenant Stewart, of the Twentieth Louisiana, were both severely wounded.

The Washington Artillery did most essential and valuable service and deserve particular notice of praise, and I would especially recommend that they be allowed to have Perryville inscribed on their banner.

Very respectfully,

DANL. W. ADAMS,
Brig. Gen., Comdg. 2d Brig., 2d Div., Left Wing, A. Miss.

Capt. W. G. BARTH, *A. A. G., Second Division, A. Miss.*

—

KNOXVILLE, TENN., *October* 25, 1862.

SIR: In making up yesterday hurriedly the report of the part taken by the Second Brigade under my command in the battle of Perryville, Ky., I omitted to mention the names of the officers in command of the different regiments, which I desire now to state.

The Thirteenth Louisiana was commanded by its colonel, Col. R. L. Gibson; the Sixteenth by its commanding officer, Col. D. C. Gober; the Twentieth, in the forepart of the action, by its commanding officer, Col. Aug. Reichard, who for some time previous had been suffering from bronchitis, and during the engagement, from loss of voice, and having his horse severely wounded, had to relinquish the command to Lieut. Col. Leon von Zinken; the Twenty-fifth Louisiana by Col. S. W. Fisk, its commanding officer, and the Battalion of Sharpshooters by Major Austin. The praises bestowed in my report for gallant service on the field fell under my immediate observation in the cases of Col. R. L. Gibson, Major Austin, and Captain Tracy, and the staff officers named, that is, Major Higgins and Captain McCall. The report of the others named was derived from the regimental reports. The regimental commanders named deserve credit for the manner in which they moved and kept their commands together, the Thirteenth Louisiana, Colonel Gibson, deserve special [mention] for the promptness with which they moved forward, the alacrity and rapidity with which they pressed the enemy until halted by my command. I will recommend Colonel Gibson for skill and valor to be brigadier-general in a separate communication.

Hoping that this may be received as a part of the report forwarded on yesterday, I remain, very respectfully,

DANL. W. ADAMS.

Capt. W. G. BARTH, *Assistant-Adjutant General.*

———

No. 39.

Report of Brig. Gen. Bushrod R. Johnson, C. S. Army, commanding Third Brigade, Third Division.

HDQRS. THIRD BRIG., THIRD DIV., ARMY OF THE MISS.,
Camp near Knoxville, Tenn., October 23, 1862.

SIR: I have the honor to submit the following report of the part taken by the Third Brigade, Third Division, Army of the Mississippi, under my command, at the battle near Perryville, Ky., on the 8th instant:

The Third Brigade on that day consisted of the Fifth Confederate Regiment, commanded by Col. [J. A.] Smith; Seventeenth Tennessee, commanded by Colonel Marks; Twenty-third Tennessee, commanded by Lieutenant-Colonel Keeble; Twenty-fifth Tennessee, commanded by Colonel Hughs; Thirty-seventh Tennessee, commanded by Colonel White; Forty-fourth Tennessee, commanded by Colonel Fulton.

Under orders from the major-general commanding the division I moved the brigade at about 11 a. m. to a position east of Perryville, on the brow of a hill which slopes westwardly for about 600 yards down to the Doctor's Fork. The two sections of Capt. [P.] Darden's battery (the Jefferson Artillery) were placed in position on spurs of this hill, the one supported by the right and the other by the left wing of my brigade. The brigade of Brig. Gen. John C. Brown (Brigadier-General Cleburne?) followed up the movements of my command with a view to support it.

The position which the Third Brigade occupied commanded a fine view of the cleared land on both slopes on the margins of the Doctor's Fork and of the open fields beyond, which were partly occupied by the enemy. The slope in front of my brigade was broken by slight spurs and by an undulation running nearly parallel with the general direction of the brow of the hill. In front of the right wing of the brigade and just below the crest of the undulation was a farm-house, with out-houses, orchard, and inclosed grounds. A rail fence ran nearly parallel with the crest of the undulation and to the left of the farm-house. Below this fence about 200 yards was the east bank of the Doctor's Fork, along a portion of which in front of my brigade was a stone fence, and the bank itself was nearly vertical, of solid rock, and from 3 to 5 feet high. Behind this bank the enemy were in position, with skirmishers advanced to the rail fence and farm-house on the undulation above. On the opposite or west bank and running parallel to the general direction of the stream was another stone fence, inclosing in part the yard of a farm-house, and a fence on the west side of this yard was also of stone. Beyond this last fence was the house or barn which was burned during the conflict of my brigade with the enemy. The Mackville and Perryville road descended the slope on the north side of the farm-house, leaving a yard in its front partly inclosed on that side by a stone fence and partly by a rail one. On the north side of the Mackville road and to the right of the farm-house last referred to was an elevation commanding the open fields and grounds on the west, south, and north, and much of the slope on the east of the creek. This height, the three stone walls (each commanding the one more advanced toward our position), and the crest of the hill above them all were occupied by the enemy or held within their lines. The position was a very strong one. There was perhaps none stronger in the enemy's lines.

While the Third Brigade was in position, as just described, the right section of Captain Darden's battery kept up a fire on the enemy in front, and Capt. [W. W.] Carnes' battery on our right, posted on a spur of the same hill, and a battery of the enemy on our left, kept a very brisk fire on each other and on the infantry within their reach. Their shots passed immediately in front of the Third Brigade in a direction very nearly parallel to its line of battle, so that an advance from our position upon the enemy in front seemed likely to expose the brigade to an enfilading fire from the enemy's battery on our left. Some of the enemy's shots fell among the men of the Thirty-seventh Tennessee Regiment without injury to the men.

Between the hours of 1 and 2 p. m., when the troops of the right wing of our army were seen advancing to the attack on my right and in a line of battle approaching a perpendicular to that on which we were formed, I was ordered to move my brigade in conjunction with the right wing by changing my front obliquely to the left. By this means the enfilading fire of the enemy's battery was avoided and my right moved forward until it came under the fire of the enemy's skirmishers near the first farm-house. It was at the same time under the fire of two of the enemy's batteries, one enfilading from the right, the other on the left, which was throwing balls and spherical-case shot. The Thirty-seventh Tennessee Regiment responded to the fire of the enemy's skirmishers and drove them beyond the creek. The Forty-fourth Regiment here suffered from these batteries and from sharpshooters behind the stone wall at the creek.

The first casualties in the brigade occurred here in the Thirty-seventh and Forty-fourth Tennessee Regiments. The Forty-fourth Regiment lost several men by shells from the enemy's batteries on our left. Under the conviction that the change of front first ordered in my brigade was for the object of moving on this battery, three of my regiments, the Fifth Confederate, Twenty-fifth and Forty-fourth Tennessee Regiments, continued to wheel rapidly to the left and speedily advanced to the height the enemy appeared to occupy, fixing their bayonets for a charge. Upon reaching that height it was found that General Adams had occupied that position. The Fifth Confederate Regiment was then promptly moved by Col. J. A. Smith upon the enemy behind the stone fences. The Twenty-fifth and Forty-fourth Regiments took a position, at the request of General Adams, in support of the battery placed in position on the height to which they advanced. Colonel Fulton, of the Forty-fourth, reports to me that when he moved with a view to unite his regiment with the brigade which had been advanced and driven the enemy from the stone fence beyond the creek, General Adams found his position so threatened by a column of the enemy that he thought it necessary to detain these regiments. He also reports that they were afterward put in position under cover of woods and in support of a battery by the major-general commanding the division. The remaining four regiments, the Thirty-seventh, Seventeenth, Twenty-third, and Fifth Confederate Regiments, advanced down the slope of the hill and under fire from artillery and infantry, driving the enemy from their strong defensive positions behind the stone walls and into the open field beyond the farm-houses on the north of the Doctor's Fork. These regiments then occupied the stone wall above the farm-house. A portion of the Thirty-seventh Regiment took position along the Mackville road, partly flanking the position of the enemy in the field and protected by the side slope of rock. The Twenty-third Regiment moved to a position to the left of the farm-house and in the open field.

The conflict continued here for about two hours, and was maintained with remarkable vigor and stubbornness on both sides and with heavy loss on the part of the enemy, who for a long time maintained their position in the open field exposed to the deadly aim of the regiment behind the stone fence. Early in this part of the conflict the houses in advance of the upper stone fence took fire and were consumed. The fire of the Fifth Confederate Regiment was particularly destructive, plainly thinning the enemy's ranks at every volley. Three times the flag of the enemy was cut down, and finally they were beaten back, utterly whipped.

The command of the enemy opposed to my brigade was that of Colonel Lytle, of the Tenth Ohio Regiment commanding the Seventeenth Brigade, which consisted of the Tenth Ohio, the Fifteenth Kentucky, the Thirty-second Indiana, and perhaps the Third Ohio.

Two of the four regiments of my command opposed to the enemy at this point (the Twenty-third and Thirty-seventh Tennessee Regiments) were very small, averaging only about 230 effective strength. Three of these regiments now, at about 5 p. m., reported their ammunition exhausted, and not knowing what fresh troops we might encounter by advancing beyond the stone wall and seeing Brigadier-General Cleburne advancing to our support, I directed them to wait until their cartridges could be replenished and reported to General Cleburne the condition of my command, suggesting the propriety of an advance upon the enemy. I immediately sent to the rear to have some ammunition brought up. About this time Colonel Lytle, the commander of the enemy's forces opposed to my brigade, was reported to me as prisoner by a soldier in charge of him and by whom Colonel Lytle was brought back from the field. The colonel was wounded in the head, and I sent him to my brigade surgeon, under charge of Private Perkins, a clerk in the office of my assistant adjutant-general.

My attention was now called to the fire of the left section of Captain Darden's battery, which had twice changed its position, advancing both times and opening from each position upon the enemy in front of the brigade. I now found it posted to the right of the Perryville and Mackville road, still on the western slope of the hill and supported by the Forty-fourth and Twenty-fifth Tennessee Regiments. Finding the fire of this section likely to damage my own men I caused its fire to cease, and an order having arrived to move this artillery to the height beyond the Doctor's Fork, to the right of the Mackville road, I ordered these regiments to move forward and to advance up the hill to the west of Doctor's Fork and on the left of the farm-house. Returning immediately to the four regiments in advance I found the Seventeenth and Thirty-seventh Tennessee Regiments had been ordered to advance up to the eminence above and to the right of the farm-house and support the artillery just ordered to that position. I also was directed by Major-General Buckner to go to that eminence in order to give my personal attention to the action at that point. On this eminence was now posted the whole of Captains Darden's and [C. H.] Slocomb's batteries, each four pieces, and one section of Calvert's battery, all of which were actively engaged, while they were exposed to a direct and enfilading fire from the enemy's batteries. Balls and shells here continued to fall thick and fast from the enemy's guns, while our own batteries replied with great rapidity until after dark and the ammunition of our batteries was exhausted, when they were withdrawn, and the Thirty-seventh and Forty-fourth Tennessee Regiments rested on the eminence until ordered to withdraw, at about 12 o'clock at night.

The Forty-fourth and Twenty-fifth Tennessee Regiments, which I had ordered to advance and pass the Doctor's Creek on the left of the farm-house, report to me that they advanced about 250 yards to the left and front of the burnt house to the foot of a small hill, where they remained under a heavy fire of the enemy's artillery and small-arms until General Adams' brigade fell back behind them and suggested that they had better fall back also. They then took post at a rail fence, where they received orders from General Hardee to advance and hold their former position, which they did, supported for a time by General Adams' command. They remained in this position until the firing ceased, at 12 o'clock. They fell back with the brigade.

[B. R. JOHNSON,
Brigadier-General, Commanding.]

Lieut. Col. GEORGE B. COSBY, *Chief of Staff.*

No. 40.

Report of Col. A. S. Marks, Seventeenth Tennessee Infantry.

CAMP NEAR BRYANTSVILLE, Ky.,
October 12, 1862.

GENERAL : In compliance with your order I have the honor to submit the following report relative to the part taken by my command in the battle of Perryville on the 8th instant :

By your order I moved forward from the position occupied by your brigade in rear of the White House, and advanced cautiously, with skirmishers thrown forward, to the crest of the hill overlooking the Doctor's Branch. At this point a section of Darden's battery was placed in battery, and I was ordered by Major-General Buckner to support it, and in a short time after the pieces were placed in battery the enemy directed his fire upon it from a battery in front and one from the left. The shelling from the enemy's batteries was well directed, but having my command behind the crest of the hill no casualties occurred. In the mean time you had moved all of your command forward save my regiment and the Twenty-third Tennessee. When the engagement became general upon the right I was ordered to move forward and join my brigade. I immediately began my advance, and not knowing the position occupied by you I directed my march toward the hill immediately beyond the Doctor's Branch. From a battery in my front the enemy kept up a continual shelling during my advance, but I found no difficulty in preserving perfect order and coolness. Our line upon the right had already forced the enemy to retire from his position, and it was my purpose in the absence of orders to move up the hill upon the right of the house beyond the Doctor's Branch and assail the enemy upon his right, but when I reached the branch I found the Fifth Confederate moving out from under the bluff by the left flank, and finding the bluff difficult of ascension I determined to move farther up the branch by the left flank, where the ascent would be easier, and also where I could act in conjunction with the Fifth Confederate. The Fifth Confederate had passed the house referred to when the enemy opened fire from beyond the house. There was a stone fence running parallel with the branch which gave entire protection to my command, and I did not suffer from the first fire of the enemy. There was a second stone fence about 40 paces beyond and parallel with the one upon the branch and also beyond the house. I immediately threw six companies forward and occupied it. I then ordered a company to move around to the right and turn the enemy's left, but at that conjuncture Colonel White came up with his command and took position upon my right, which prevented the move upon my part. The enemy's fire upon my regiment was heavy and incessant, but being well protected it suffered but little, while it delivered its fire with coolness and precision. The engagement was thus continued until the enemy abandoned his position and our ammunition was exhausted. By your order I then detached a company and sent it back for ammunition, but before its return I was ordered by a staff officer, unknown to me, to move forward over the hill upon which one of our batteries was afterward placed. I had bayonets fixed and moved forward. When I had arrived near the crest of the hill the same officer ordered me to have my bayonets taken off. I protested against this, as I had no ammunition. When he ascertained that fact he ordered me to retire, but immediately Major-General Buckner came up at that time and ordered me to hold the hill at all hazards.

In a short time several pieces were placed in battery upon the crest of the hill and General Buckner ordered me to remain and support them. The shelling upon us was terrific and continued until night closed the conflict. By your order I advanced skirmishers about half a mile in front of my position and held the field until midnight, at which time we were withdrawn and retired to our original position.

My whole command, both officers and men, displayed great coolness and courage and obeyed every order with alacrity during the entire engagement. I sent out details and collected 150 stand of arms, which I had carried off the field and deposited at our encampment upon this side of the creek.

Below you will find a statement* of killed and wounded : Killed, 4 ; wounded, 19. Total, 23.

All of which is respectfully submitted.

A. S. MARKS,
Colonel, Commanding Seventeenth Tennessee Regiment.

Brig. Gen. B. R. JOHNSON,
    Comdg. Third Brig., Third Div., Army of the Mississippi.

No. 41.

Report of Lieut. Col. R. H. Keeble, Twenty-third Tennessee Infantry.

OCTOBER 12, 1862.

The following report of the action at Perryville on the 8th instant is respectfully submitted :

The Twenty-third Tennessee, having advanced under orders from its original position, took a new position in a field upon the brow of a hill, with orders to hold it at all hazards. At this place it remained about two hours under fire of the enemy's batteries, without however any casualties, until orders were given to unite with the brigade and advance upon the enemy. We accordingly did so, marching over rough ground and having several fences to pull down and climb. Having advanced down the hill and across the ravine we marched by the left flank into another field and orchard for the purpose of being unmasked by the Fifth Confederate, which had moved by the left flank in front of us. Being thus unmasked we again marched to the front, and here we received the first heavy fire from the enemy, who were concealed within an inclosure to our right and behind a stone wall. It was during this fire that Capt. [W. A.] Ott, of Company H, fell mortally wounded. The regiment remained here for a while under shelter of the fence and stone wall until I ordered it to move forward to the next fence, to gain which it had to march across an open field under a heavy and galling fire from the enemy. Having gained the latter position we came upon the enemy, and now commenced a heavy and terrific fire on both sides, we engaging at the same time a regiment of the enemy in our front and another to our right behind a fence forming a right angle to the one occupied by us. The engagement lasted from one and a half to two hours, the enemy in the mean time having been twice beaten from the field. The enemy it seems had heavy reserves to bring upon the field as soon as one line would give way. Having driven the enemy from the field and exhausted our ammunition, acting in concert with

---

*Nominal list omitted.

the Fifth Confederate, I ordered the regiment to fall back under the brow of the hill for a new supply. Our position was soon occupied by the Forty-fourth Tennessee, under command of Maj [H. C.] Ewin, who advanced beyond the position occupied by the Twenty-third, the enemy having retired from the field. Having received our ammunition we again advanced.

Night had, however, set in, the enemy yielded the field, and the firing all ceased. We took our position upon and occupied the field, threw forward skirmishers beyond where the enemy's lines were in the evening, and there remained until late at night, when we were ordered to change our position.

I carried into action 201 men, officers and privates. Lost in killed, wounded, and missing 52, 7 of the number being killed upon the field. The loss of the enemy upon the portion of the field where we were engaged was much heavier, all who visited the spot concurring that there was not less than 100 killed left upon the field.

It would be doing injustice in such a small regiment as I had, where all, both officers and men, were so prompt to obey any order and eager to do their whole duty, to make any discrimination. The company officers were of great assistance to me in cheering and encouraging their men and the men of great assistance in encouraging and cheering each other.

Most respectfully submitted.

R. H. KEEBLE,
Lieut. Col., Comdg. Twenty-third Tennessee Regiment.

Brigadier-General JOHNSON,
Commanding Third Division, Army of the Mississippi.

No. 42.

Report of Col. John M. Hughs, Twenty-fifth Tennessee Infantry.

BRYANTSVILLE, KY., *October* 12, 1862.

My regiment was ordered to move from Lebanon, Ky., on the evening of the 6th instant, but after marching 5 miles we were ordered back to Lebanon. As soon as rations were cooked orders were received to move again in the direction of Perryville, at which place we arrived about 4 o'clock on the morning of the 7th. For the day we took a position in rear of the brigade, being much fatigued by our lengthy march of the previous evening and night, and also hungry and without rations.

Early on the morning of the 8th we took our place in line of battle and advanced between the Forty-fourth Tennessee on the right and the Fifth Confederate on the left. When the brigade moved forward the second time my line of skirmishers, commanded by Lieutenant Walker, moved forward half a mile to the front and took position on the hill in sight of the enemy. After a time the brigade advanced to the position occupied by my skirmishers and waited for the attack to begin on the right. In a short time the battery on our left, supported by this regiment and the Fifth Confederate, opened upon the enemy's main position. This caused the enemy to open fire upon our position. When the fight became general on the right the whole brigade was ordered forward to the attack. As soon as we advanced from under cover of the hill and timber a charge was ordered. I never witnessed a more gallant charge than that made by my regiment. I did not see any man flinch from duty, and although we crossed several fences a good line was kept. The enemy retired before us and many were shot as they went up the hill after leaving their place behind the rock fences in the creek bottom. Having orders to move in concert with the regiments on my right and left I was compelled to change my course more to the left than I thought we ought to go. However, the enemy had retired over the hill out of sight and ceased firing upon us. The Forty-fourth having passed entirely around us and the Fifth Confederate having disappeared, I do not know where, I was left on the extreme left of the brigade, and meeting General Adams, was advised by him to advance by the left flank and take position on the left of his batteries, then firing upon the enemy. This I did, and had just formed when I discovered the enemy advancing toward the battery, but discovering us between him and the battery he retired, except the pickets, which were seen all the time we held this position. In a short time the batteries advanced and I supported them, keeping just in rear, and forming in a little hollow just below where a house was burned, according to your own instructions. This position I held until the batteries ceased firing. I then marched by the left flank, unmasking the other regiment, and, leaving the low ground, again sent out skirmishers. Not finding the enemy on the left and seeing the batteries retire I marched back on the hill and took position on the hill. Nearly at night I again advanced and took position behind a rock fence and sent out pickets to the left. They soon reported that the enemy was placing batteries on the hill above us and sent a report of the same to you. The regiment was next ordered toward Perryville on picket. Two companies were sent to the woods 300 or 400 yards to the front. I then rested until ordered to take the position occupied by my command the day before.

My command only lost 8 men wounded and 1 missing, who was sent to the hospital in charge of a prisoner picked up by him, said prisoner being slightly wounded.

I am gratified to be able to report to you that not an officer or soldier of my regiment failed to do his whole duty. I think the men deserve great applause for the spirit with which they obeyed orders, being as they were very sore and tired from the effects of our late march from Sparta via Gainesborough, Livingston, and Burkesville without stopping a day and marching several nights.

Respectfully,

J. M. HUGHS,
Colonel, Commanding Twenty-fifth Tennessee Regiment.

Brig. Gen. B. R. JOHNSON.

No. 43.

Report of Col. Moses White, Thirty-seventh Tennessee Infantry.

OCTOBER 18, 1862.

SIR: On the 7th instant the Thirty-seventh Tennessee was in position near a creek in the vicinity of Perryville. We slept there that night. On the morning of the 8th, after considerable maneuvering, the regiment was advanced to a hill several hundred yards to the front and remained there until about 1 o'clock in support of [C.] Swett's and some other battery. Between the hours of 1 and 2 p. m. we were ordered to advance in line with General Cheatham's command, which was moving upon the enemy on our right. We advanced about 200 yards, when from the brow of a hill we had reached we saw the enemy in line below and received a heavy volley from them; simultaneously my men fired upon the enemy, who immediately fell back. Several of my men were wounded on the first fire by the small-arms of the enemy, shells and grape from their batteries, which swept around us in perfect showers. I commanded my men to reload immediately, and they continued to load and fire until we discovered that we were separated from the brigade, which was to us a matter of no little surprise, as we had received no command but forward. A house, outhouses, and orchard were situated immediately to our right, which obstructed the view and prevented us from observing the movements of the left of the brigade. Ascertaining that it had moved in the direction of the woods to the left, I commanded my men to march by the left flank in that direction. After passing the orchard we discovered a regiment emerging from the woods in the rear in the direction from which the brigade first moved; we wheeled into line on the right of what turned out to be the Seventeenth Tennessee and advanced to a stone wall in the hollow below, which inclosed a house, &c., several hundred yards to the left of the house first alluded to. Colonel Marks took his position behind a wall running parallel with the hollow. I filed right and took my position behind a post-and-rail fence running diagonally to the wall; here we were met with an almost overwhelming storm of lead from a corn or cane field near by. I commanded my men to mount the fence and take position behind a stone wall which separated the yard from the field, running parallel with and about 50 yards distant from the wall behind which the Seventeenth was stationed. They promptly and cheerfully obeyed the order and immediately opened upon the enemy, I hope with some effect. The fire raged with unabated fury for about one hour and a half, when, our ammunition being exhausted, we were compelled to cease firing, but were soon relieved by General Cleburne, but not until the enemy had almost ceased to fire. I had several officers and men wounded in the fight at the wall. After the regiment was withdrawn a sufficient detail was dispatched for ammunition and we were soon supplied. Meanwhile we had moved to the right and advanced near the brow of the hill on which Calvert's battery was planted. Late in the afternoon (the Seventeenth Tennessee was again on my left) General Buckner ordered us to advance, when I gave the command "Fix bayonets," and advanced to the summit. The Seventeenth did not advance, as I afterward learned the order was countermanded so far as that regiment was concerned. A battalion from the Sixteenth Alabama was soon after ordered to form on my left and we advanced about half a mile in the field, but took no further part in the battle, as night soon set in and the firing gradually ceased.

Maj. [J. T.] McReynolds and most of my company officers acted with great gallantry. Individual instances of both officers and men might be mentioned of the exhibition of the most gallant and desperate conduct.

I had 27 men wounded and some killed in the action. Their names have been furnished by the adjutant.

Respectfully submitted.

MOSES WHITE,
Colonel Thirty-seventh Tennessee Regiment.

Brigadier-General JOHNSON.

No. 44.

Report of Col. John S. Fulton, Forty-fourth Tennessee Infantry.

OCTOBER 11, 1862.

I have to report that the Forty-fourth Regiment Tennessee Volunteers was placed in position on the bluff of the creek on the morning of the 7th instant; that they remained there during the day and night, and on the next day the regiment was advanced toward a skirt of woods along our front about 11.30 a. m. After remaining there an hour we were advanced into the woods in front. Here we remained an hour. The enemy engaged in the mean time one of our batteries immediately on our right.

We were again ordered forward and occupied a ravine, and there remained until General Cheatham's division on our right made a charge, when we were ordered to advance upon the enemy and oblique to the left of our then present position.

The regiment was promptly in motion and charged rapidly over the hill and forward through a corn field and over a large meadow, where we were exposed to an enfilading fire coming from the enemy on our right and a battery upon our left. Obliquing to the left here we suffered terribly from the fire of the batteries right and left of us and the sharpshooters of the enemy posted in the orchard and behind the rock fence on our right. We charged rapidly up the hill with fixed bayonets to silence and take the battery on our left, and having gained the top of the hill we found it to be the Washington Artillery, and immediately reported to them that they had been playing upon their own men, when the firing ceased. This battery was supported by Brigadier-General Adams' brigade, who ordered the Forty-fourth and Twenty-fifth Tennessee Regiments to remain there to assist him, as the enemy was reported to be advancing on him to the left in heavy force.

We remained there some twenty minutes and then moved in direction of our brigade and were met by General Buckner, who ordered us to advance to the woods and form line of battle and wait further orders. This done, we remained there some twenty-five minutes and we again received orders to advance. We advanced up to the left of the burning house and occupied position there for some time, and again advanced some 250 yards to a gully at the foot of a small hill. Here we remained under a heavy fire of the enemy's small-arms and artillery.

General Adams' entire brigade fell back behind us with a battery, leaving no one in front of us or any other support. He suggested that we had better fall back. We fell back to a rail fence, where we received orders from General Hardee to advance and hold our former position so long as possible. This was done immediately. Shortly after General Adams' command (or a portion) returned to our support in our rear. They suffered from the fire of the enemy and again retired, leaving us in our position, where we remained until the musketry firing ceased. We then retired a few hundred yards to a rail fence running nearly north and south.

At 12 m. we received orders to fall back from this position and occupy the same position occupied two nights previously.

I am glad to be able to report that both officers and men of this regiment stood well under the heaviest fire of the enemy, evincing courage equal to the occasion.

Herewith you have a list* of the killed [14], and I refer you to the surgeon's report for other casualties.

All of which is respectfully submitted.

I am, sir, your obedient servant,

JNO. S. FULTON,
Colonel Forty-fourth Tennessee Regiment.

R. B. SNOWDEN, Acting Assistant Adjutant-General.

OCTOBER 9, 1862.—Action at Dry Ridge, Dog Walk, or Chesser's Store, near Salt River, Ky.

REPORTS.

No. 1.—Brig. Gen. Joshua W. Sill, U. S. Army, commanding Second Division, First Corps, Army of the Ohio, including skirmish, October 8, at Lawrenceburg.
No. 2.—Col. Edwin A. Parrott, First Ohio Infantry.

No. 1.

Report of Brig. Gen. Joshua W. Sill, U. S. Army, commanding Second Division, First Corps, Army of the Ohio, including skirmish, October 8, at Lawrenceburg.

THREE MILES NORTHEAST OF CHAPLINTOWN,
October 9, 1862—6 p. m.

GENERAL: Left Frankfort 1 a. m. yesterday. By arriving at Lawrenceburg the rebel cavalry appeared in front and a smart skirmish ensued, owing to an imprudent advance of Jacob's cavalry. The leading company lost 3 killed, 12 wounded, 13 missing. Several of the enemy killed and wounded I doubt not.

Our march from Lawrenceburg was closely watched by the enemy's cavalry, and at daybreak of to-day they appeared in force and attempted to drive in the pickets. They exhibited three regiments of infantry and one of cavalry. Our pickets were re-enforced and a sharp firing was kept up for three or four hours. On our side the Thirty-second Indiana, First Ohio, Fifteenth and Nineteenth Regulars were engaged, and a section of Guenther's battery. Their loss respectively was: Thirty-second Indiana, 1 killed; First Ohio, 3 killed and 8 wounded; Sixteenth[?] Regiment, 1 killed. The enemy must have suffered very severely. Many of their men were seen to fall.

I presume they picked up some of our stragglers, and I fear they have captured a train of sixteen wagons sent after me unadvisedly, and which contained articles for the Fifth Brigade. I know nothing of General Dumont's column, but I suppose he has moved on Frankfort.

Respectfully, your obedient servant,

J. W. SILL,
Brigadier-General, Commanding.

General BUELL.

Will move to Willisburg to-morrow via Chaplintown.

---

* Nominal omitted.

No. 2.

Report of Col. Edwin A. Parrott, First Ohio Infantry.

HDQRS. FIRST REGT. OHIO VOLUNTEER INFANTRY,
In Camp, October 9, 1862.

CAPTAIN: I have the honor to submit the following report of the skirmish had with the enemy this morning by the troops under my command at Dog Walk:

As my regiment left camp the general commanding apprised me that our rear was threatened by the enemy and ordered me to march back on the road until I overtook the Nineteenth U. S. Infantry, previously sent out. About half a mile from camp I came up with our troops on the road to Lawrenceburg. Major King, Fifteenth U. S. Infantry, had his battalion drawn up in an open field, where he commanded the road; Major Carpenter, Nineteenth U. S. Infantry, was to his left and in the road, which at that point makes an abrupt turn. Being the ranking officer present, I posted the First Ohio behind the crest of a ridge in the skirt of woods to the rear of the open ground and ordered the battalions of regulars to fall back across the field and form on the same line and to the right of the First Ohio. In the mean time Lieutenant Guenther had come up with a section of Battery H, Fifth U. S. Artillery.

Just as our line was formed the enemy appeared, marching by the flank up the hill in front of where I had found Major King's command. Lieutenant Guenther, having got one of his pieces in position, opened with such effect as to check the progress of the enemy and cause him to fall back under cover of the hill. From this position the enemy advanced a strong line of skirmishers. To oppose these I deployed forward a company from each battalion of the regulars; Company C, Captain Thruston, and part of Company B, Lieutenant Kuhlmann, First Ohio. The skirmishers became engaged at once and very warmly.

Major Drake at this time reported to me with the Forty-ninth Ohio Volunteers, and was sent to a position on the right and deflected at nearly a right angle to Major King, and was ordered to cover his front and right flank with skirmishers. I have no report from him, but believe there was no firing on his part of the line.

The guns of Lieutenant Guenther commanded the road in front of our center so as to check any advance along it, and the enemy's main attack was directed against our left.

The skirmish line in front of the First Ohio was strongly attacked and at one time driven a short distance from the hill on which it was posted, but being re-enforced, rallied and in turn drove the enemy back. For nearly four hours the firing here was strong and steady, and when the enemy had been driven from here he appears to have fallen back altogether and to have given up the attack, as the firing was not resumed until our troops had again taken up the march toward Mackville.

The section of Lieutenant Guenther's battery was handled with the usual vigor and skill of that accomplished officer, and was very effective in checking the advance of the enemy and in driving him from a dwelling-house, under cover of which he was making the most severe fire on our line of skirmishers.

I must particularly commend Captain Thruston and Lieutenant Kuhlmann, of the First Ohio, who bore the brunt of the enemy's attack.

The firing began a little after 8 a. m. and the enemy was finally repulsed about 1 p. m. I did not attempt to do more than hold our position and keep the enemy at bay, because I had been ordered to act strictly on the defensive.

The attacking force, I have learned from citizens and others who saw the enemy marching up, was about 2,500 to 3,000 strong, mixed infantry and cavalry, with two howitzers, which latter were not used on us. Eleven of his dead and 2 mortally wounded were found on the field, but many other bodies were seen to be carried off by him. We got from him three Springfield muskets and one Harper's Ferry rifle.*

I am, your obedient servant,

ED. A. PARROTT,
Colonel First Regiment Ohio Volunteer Infantry.

OCTOBER 10–22, 1862.—Pursuit of the Confederate forces from Perryville to London, Ky.

SUMMARY OF THE PRINCIPAL EVENTS.

Oct.   11, 1862.—Harrodsburg reoccupied by Union forces.
               Skirmish at Danville.
       13, 1862.—Skirmish at Harrodsburg.
       14, 1862.—Skirmish at Stanford,
               Skirmish at Lancaster.
   14–16, 1862.—Skirmishes near Mountain Gap.
       16, [15?], 1862.—Skirmish near Crab Orchard.
       16, 1862.—Skirmishes near Mount Vernon, at Wild Cat Mountain, and Big Rockcastle Creek.
       17, 1862.—Skirmishes about Camp Wild Cat.
       18, 1862.—Skirmish at Rockcastle River.
               Skirmish at Nelson's Cross-Roads.
       19, 1862.—Skirmish at Pitman's Cross-Roads.
               Reconnaissance on Madison Road.
   19–24, 1862.—Confederate forces retire through Cumberland Gap.
       20, 1862.—Skirmish at Pitman's Cross-Roads.
       21, 1862.—Expedition from Crab Orchard to Big Hill and Richmond.
       22, 1862.—Pursuit discontinued.

REPORTS.†

No. 1.—Col. William B. Hazen, Forty-first Ohio Infantry, commanding Nineteenth Brigade, Army of the Ohio.

No. 2.—Brig. Gen. W. Sooy Smith, U. S. Army, commanding Fourth Division, of skirmishes about Camp Wild Cat, October 17.

No. 3.—Col. Stanley Matthews, Fifty-first Ohio Infantry, commanding Twenty-third Brigade, of reconnaissance on the Madison Road.

No. 4.—Col. Edward M. McCook, Second Indiana Cavalry, commanding First Cavalry Brigade, of expedition from Crab Orchard to Big Hill and Richmond, October 21.

No. 5.—Col. James R. Howard, Third Confederate Cavalry, of skirmishes near Mountain Gap, October 14–16.

---

* Return of casualties shows 5 men killed and 1 officer and 5 men wounded in First Ohio Infantry and 1 man killed and 2 wounded in Fifteenth U. S. Infantry. Total, 6 killed and 8 wounded.

† See also Buell's and Bragg's reports of the battle of Perryville, and Wheeler's report of operations August 27–October 22.

No. 1.

Report of Col. William B. Hazen, Forty-first Ohio Infantry, commanding Nineteenth Brigade, Army of the Ohio.

COLUMBIA, KY., *November* 1, 1862.

SIR: In compliance with orders received from Headquarters Fourth Division, Army of the Ohio, I have the honor to submit the following report of the part taken by my brigade in the advance of the army from Perryville to London, at which point the van-guard retraced its steps:

On the 10th of October the brigade, consisting of the Ninth Indiana Volunteers, Col. W. H. Blake; the Forty-first Ohio Volunteers, Lieut. Col. George S. Mygatt; the Sixth Kentucky Volunteers, Col. Walter C. Whitaker; the Twenty-seventh Kentucky Volunteers, Col. C. D. Pennebaker; the One hundred and tenth Illinois Volunteers, Col. T. S. Casey, and Captain Cockerill's battery of the First Ohio Artillery, in all 2,530 effective men, was put *en route* with the division in the direction of Danville, encamping 3 miles from that place in line of battle.

On the morning of the 11th, agreeably with orders, I moved forward to Danville to reconnoiter the position of the enemy. I was accompanied by Wolford's cavalry and Throckmorton's battery of artillery. My orders were explicit and prevented my moving in any manner that would bring on a general engagement. The Ninth Indiana Volunteers was deployed as skirmishers and supported by the Sixth Kentucky and Forty-first Ohio, marching through the fields in double column, with the cavalry disposed on the flanks as effectively as their limited acquaintance with military maneuvers would admit.

The enemy was found drawn up in line of battle at the Fair Grounds, 1 mile from Danville, with cavalry and artillery. The latter opened without effect upon the skirmishers, who, pushing forward persistently, had no difficulty in driving the enemy through the town. My artillery and cavalry were both used in the skirmish, which at times was quite brisk, the enemy dismounting his cavalry and posting them as infantry. The Ninth Indiana pushed through the town and about 2 miles beyond, skirmishing with cavalry and artillery all the way, when they were recalled, and the brigade in obedience to orders returned to the encampment of the division.

I would mention the universal good conduct of all the troops of the command, except the cavalry companies of Captains Coppage and Fishback, of Wolford's regiment, who at the first discharge of the enemy retreated in disorder some half mile to a piece of wood and were with difficulty found by one of my staff officers. The entire regiment seemed greatly deficient in anything approaching military drill, and it was with difficulty that my orders, given in the simplest military language, were understood.

We found nearly 400 rebels sick in hospitals and captured 30 ablebodied. The enthusiasm of the people upon our entrance was beyond anything I ever before witnessed. Several of the enemy were killed and wounded. Our own casualties were 4 slightly wounded.

On the 12th the brigade, with the division, was moved forward near Camp Dick Robinson, returning to the Harrodsburg pike 3 miles from Danville, where it bivouacked until the morning of the 14th, when it took up its march on the Stanford road, bivouacking near that place until 12 o'clock at night, when it was again put in march in the direction of Crab Orchard, reaching that place about midday of the 15th, and passing to within 2 miles of Mount Vernon. On the morning of the 16th the brigade was put in march at daybreak at the head of the division, which had the advance of the Second Army Corps. On passing about 2 miles beyond that place the rear of the enemy was seen drawn up in line of battle. The Sixth Kentucky was advanced rapidly as skirmishers, which, with a few shots from Cockerill's battery, soon dispersed them.

On moving forward some 4 miles farther the enemy was found strongly posted, with his cavalry dismounted and acting as infantry and artillery. A brisk fire was opened by them upon a company of the Second Indiana Cavalry, commanded by Lieutenant ———, which was reconnoitering on foot. They met the fire gallantly, and were immediately relieved by the Sixth Kentucky, which moved forward splendidly, and after a brisk skirmish of thirty minutes the enemy retired precipitately. In this skirmish the Sixth Kentucky lost 1 killed and 2 slightly wounded. The enemy lost 11 killed and several wounded.

The Ninth Indiana now relieved the Sixth Kentucky as skirmishers, and pushing forward about 2 miles found the enemy again posted, with dismounted cavalry and artillery, in their favorite position, being upon the hill-sides opposite an open valley. One wing of this regiment, under Lieutenant-Colonel Suman, by a rapid movement succeeded in flanking the enemy and came near capturing his artillery, which was lost only by the rapidity of its retreat. A sharp skirmish was kept up during this movement, resulting in the killing and wounding of several of the enemy and the capture of several more, including a captain.

In moving forward the remainder of the day an almost uninterrupted skirmish was kept up, the enemy impeding our progress by felling timber. The brigade bivouacked at Big Rockcastle Creek. The prisoners of this day amounted to between 30 and 40.

On the 17th the command moved only to Camp Wild Cat, a distance of 4 miles, the Nineteenth Brigade being in rear of the division.

On the 18th, it being reported that the enemy were posted in strong force a few miles in our front, I was ordered forward to drive him from his position. This was effected after a sharp skirmish, in which the Ninth Indiana and the Forty-first Ohio took part, the enemy losing several officers and men, without casualty to our own arms. In obedience with orders the command was marched back to Camp Wild Cat and bivouacked for the night.

On the 19th I received orders to march to Pitman's Cross-Roads, but no farther without orders. The Forty-first Ohio was deployed as skirmishers, and the command moved forward without coming upon the enemy until within 5 miles of Pitman's. The roads had been blocked with fallen timber almost continuously, but by the hard labor of the pioneer party we were enabled to reach within one-half mile of Pitman's by night-fall, a sharp skirmish taking place about sundown, in which Lieutenant Hardy, adjutant of the Forty-first Ohio, had his horse shot and one man of the same regiment was slightly wounded.

The enemy posted himself with artillery at the cross-roads, throwing shot over my lines, but doing no damage. The Forty-first Ohio was pushed forward under cover of the darkness to examine their position, the people of the country reporting that a strong force of all arms was strongly posted there for an engagement. The women and children of the neighborhood had been sent away, which gave color to the report. The reconnaissance was pushed within 50 yards of the artillery, when the regiment was withdrawn some 400 yards and posted for the night behind a spur of the hill. Disposition was then made for an attack at dawn. At 10 p. m. the artillery of the enemy took up its march, followed by his other troops, the rear getting under way at 4 o'clock a. m.

On the morning of the 20th a patrol was sent through the town of London. On returning they brought some 25 prisoners, reporting the enemy 6 miles from that place.

On the 22d the command in obedience to orders marched back to Camp Wild Cat, carrying with it 75 prisoners.

In summing up this advance it appears that in eight days the brigade engaged in six skirmishes, killing some 20 of the enemy, wounding many more, and capturing, including many sick, between 500 and 600 prisoners. Our own loss was 1 killed and 5 or 6 wounded.

The conduct of the entire brigade could not have been better. Lieutenant Colonel Suman, of the Ninth Indiana Volunteers, deserves the warm thanks of his commander. I was an eye-witness to all that occurred on the entire march. The course of the road over which we passed after leaving Mount Vernon was through narrow gorges, occasionally debouching into narrow valleys, and of such a character as to render our movements necessarily cautious and affording opportunities for an energetic foe to have stopped our progress at almost any point. It is doubtful if the rear of the army proper was ever reached, but merely a light force of from 1,500 to 3,000 held back against our advance to feel our progress. It always yielded when closely pressed.

It is proper to add that during the entire campaign, although destitute of many of the comforts even of life on the march, without tents, often with an insufficiency of food, through inclemencies of weather, and marches of almost unprecedented length, I have never heard a murmur, and have now to report a good condition of health never before known in the brigade and a state of thorough discipline of which the command has reason to be proud.

My staff, as follows: Capt. R. L. Kimberly, Forty-first Ohio, acting assistant adjutant-general; Capt. H. W. Johnson, Forty-first Ohio, acting assistant quartermaster; Capt. James McCleery, Forty-first Ohio, assistant inspector-general; Dr. M. G. Sherman, Ninth Indiana, brigade surgeon; Lieut. C. D. Gaylord, Forty-first Ohio, aide-de-camp; Lieut. William M. Beebe, Forty-first Ohio, aide-de-camp, permitted no opportunity to escape of renewing the constant evidence since being in the service of brigade headquarters of ability, efficiency, and a desire to do their duty properly. They, with my entire command, have my warmest thanks.

I am, very respectfully, your obedient servant,

W. B. HAZEN,
Colonel, Commanding Nineteenth Brigade.

Capt. H. ATKINSON, *A. A. G., Fourth Division.*

No. 2.

Reports of Brig. Gen. William Sooy Smith, U. S. Army, commanding Fourth Division, of skirmishes about Camp Wild Cat, October 17.

ROCKCASTLE RIVER, *October* 17, 1862—9 a. m.

SIR: I have pressed a reconnaissance nearly up to Camp Wild Cat this morning. The enemy has passed on, leaving the road badly blockaded in his rear. There is no forage whatever in this neighborhood and none ahead.   Our animals are now suffering, and it will virtually sacrifice our train to move it any farther to the front.   Tne same may be said of our artillery.   Our infantry can go as far as rations will last which they can carry on their persons.

Kirby Smith encamped on the Madison road, 16 miles back from Pitman's, last night.   If Gay could have crossed over this morning into that road he might have intercepted stragglers, &c., but his horses were suffering to an extent that would not permit such movement, and there is no forage in that direction.

We have 50 prisoners, which I have paroled, and I send them to the rear this morning.   Many of them are deserters and beg that they may not be exchanged.   Shall I press forward with my infantry, leaving trains and artillery ?

Very respectfully, your obedient servant,

W. S. SMITH,
Brigadier-General, Commanding Fourth Division.

Maj. Gen. THOMAS L. CRITTENDEN, *Commanding Second Corps.*

—

ONE MILE FROM WILD CAT, *October* 17, 1862—12 m.

SIR : My advanced brigade has passed Camp Wild Cat.   We are pressing the rebel cavalry back, skirmishing with them at every turn of the road ; have killed one of their men and wounded several.   Three of our men wounded.   They have so obstructed the road by felling timber that our progress is very slow.   A cavalry force could prevent this, but our infantry cannot get ahead fast enough.   They fell trees until we come up to them, then fall back rapidly and chop away again. We push them as closely as possible.

Very respectfully, your obedient servant,

W. S. SMITH,
Brigadier-General, Commanding Fourth Division.

Major-General CRITTENDEN.

—

CAMP WILD CAT, *October* 17, 1862—8 p. m.

SIR : A colored man whom I sent over to the Madison road this fore-noon has returned, bringing me information to the effect that a rebel brigade encamped at the cross-roads skedaddled precipitately, leaving their rations cooking behind them, on Cruft's approach.   He says they did not retire toward London, but proceeded on the prolongation of the Winding Glade road (the one taken from this point by General Cruft) toward Goose Creek.   He says they left a drove of mules and some 20 cattle behind them.   He came back by a very circuitous route and missed our forces.   I have sent him with all haste, well mounted, to General Cruft's, to give him this information and to serve him as guide. We have just heard a cannon-shot in that direction, and hope Cruft has intercepted some of them.   I informed him in a note sent by the colored man that you had sent two brigades over to the Madison road— one from Van Cleve's division and one from Wood's.   I think I have reliable information that there is but one brigade of infantry and one of cavalry between this point and London on our road.

Very respectfully, your obedient servant,

W. S. SMITH,
Brigadier-General, Commanding Fourth Division.

GENERAL: Lieutenant Beeler, Cruft's quartermaster, has just returned from his command, which he left at the cross-roads at 6.30 this evening, shortly after it reached that point. He says Cruft had a pretty sharp skirmish with the rebels, in which he wounded several of them and took them prisoners; one officer. Only 2 of our men hurt. He has taken 11 prisoners. Cruft holds the road, and if there is anything back it will have to fight its way through.

Yours, truly,

W. S. SMITH,
Brigadier-General, Commanding Fourth Division.

—

CAMP WILD CAT, *October* 18, 1862—8 a. m.

SIR: Captain Wheeler, of our First Kentucky Infantry, captured near Crab Orchard, has just returned, bringing a citizen with him. They inform me that the accounts received yesterday with reference to the enemy's force in my front are correct. A force of one or two divisions has taken a strong position near Little Rockcastle River, to cover the retirement of their main army trains, artillery, &c. They report a very heavy force on the Madison road, and say that it is moving off toward Manchester. There is a practicable road leading over from the Madison road into the one upon which we are located, intersecting it 3 miles to my rear. Please have it closely watched.

We have no forage at all and our poor animals are suffering terribly.

Please inform me of the disposition of our forces to my rear and upon my flanks, that I may know what scouting is necessary. I should have some cavalry for scouting purposes.

Very respectfully, your most obedient servant,

W. S. SMITH,
Brigadier-General, Commanding Fourth Division.

Major-General CRITTENDEN.

P. S.—A colored man from Widow Baugh's, 1 mile from the point of intersection of the Winding Glade road with the Madison road and 10 miles from London, has just come in, stating that the rear of the rebel forces on the Madison road is stated by the rebels to be at Big Hill. Their troops are passing toward Manchester. He says that he heard one of their officers ordered to Goose Creek headquarters, and heard them say that that was the headquarters of their army. I send this for what it is worth.

[Indorsement.]

OCTOBER 18, 1862—9.20 a. m.

I was within 3 miles of General Smith's position when I received this. Will let General Van Cleve move up to the intersection of the Winding Glade road with this. General Van Cleve is now on the road and within 2 miles of me. Unless I get further information I will let General Wood come up to the place General Thomas and myself stopped at yesterday, which will be to within 3 miles of General Van Cleve.

By order of General Crittenden:

R. LODER,
Captain and Aide-de-Camp.

No. 3.

*Report of Col. Stanley Matthews, Fifty-first Ohio Infantry, command-
ing Twenty-third Brigade, of reconnaissance on the Madison road.*

HDQRS. TWENTY-THIRD BRIGADE, *October* 19, 1862.

GENERAL: I have the honor to report that in obedience to your
orders I marched the Twenty-third Brigade from the Crab Orchard
road to the Madison road by the old road along Roundstone Creek,
reaching the designated point about 4 p. m. The advance, consisting
of two companies of the Eighth Kentucky Regiment, under the command
of Lieutenant-Colonel May, on reaching the road captured several small
squads of straggling rebel soldiers, belonging principally, as they stated,
to Leadbetter's brigade, some to Gillespie's, and two or three to Chenault's cavalry regiment, recently organized in Madison County, Ky.

I sent a party on the road across Rockcastle River to Cruesis', where
6 prisoners were captured. I ascertained that Chenault's cavalry had
passed the same day, some hours before my arrival, and a portion at
least had remained at Cruesis' until about an hour before sunset, engaged in slaughtering beef, when on receipt of a dispatch from Scovill's
Cross-Roads they left in haste, without cooking their meat. A negro
captured there stated that he had come from Scovill's; that the last of
the troops encamped there had left at 3 o'clock that afternoon for Manchester, he escaping in the hurry of their departure. The cavalry at
Chenault's could take the same direction, without going as far as Scovill's. The Madison road was covered with tracks of cattle and sheep,
which had obliterated all other, and seemed to be the last made. From
the best information I could gather from prisoners and citizens I believe all the trains and cattle of the enemy had passed.

I was told by one of the prisoners that 500 of Morgan's cavalry left
Richmond on the night of the 17th instant, going toward Lexington,
but the understanding was that on their return they were to go out by
the way of Irvine, though it was also stated that Morgan had sent word
to Major Coffee, residing on the Madison road near the foot of the Big
Hill, that he would be with him last night and exchange him.

About dusk a party of 4 horsemen, riding toward us from the north,
were hailed by the pickets, and not answering the challenge, were fired
upon. One was taken prisoner (his horse being shot), but the rest
escaped. The prisoner is a citizen; the others it is likely belonged to
Morgan's cavalry.

The result of the reconnaissance, besides the information just detailed,
was the capture of between 25 and 30 prisoners and 10 or 12 horses, a
particular account of which will be hereafter furnished.

Respectfully,

STANLEY MATTHEWS,
Colonel, Commanding Twenty-third Brigade.

Brig. Gen. H. P. VAN CLEVE, *Commanding Fifth Division.*

No. 4.

*Report of Col. Edward M. McCook, Second Indiana Cavalry, commanding
First Cavalry Brigade, of expedition from Crab Orchard to Big Hill
and Richmond, October 21.*

LEBANON, KY., *October* 24, 1862.

SIR: I have the honor to report that in pursuance to your order I left

Crab Orchard on the morning of the 21st and arrived at Paint Lick Bridge that afternoon. On my arrival, finding no enemy there, I divided my forces, and sent one portion to Big Hill, where I was informed some of the enemy still remained, and another to Richmond, leaving a third portion at Paint Lick Bridge, to which point I had been notified in writing support would march.

The detachment under Captain Crosby sent to Big Hill found a wagon loaded with telegraph wires and a battery, which they destroyed, pouring acid on the wires and breaking up the battery. They also found 60 rounds of 10-pounder spherical-case and a caisson, which was turned over to the commander of the Home Guards to bury, as we had no wagons.

The Richmond detachment found some 200 or 300 sick and wounded rebels there, which they did not parole, not having time or facilities for paroling so large a number.

I have the honor to inclose a list of prisoners captured and paroled by me during the march, and also to report the capture of 11 horses, which were turned over to the Third Kentucky, Colonel Murray, and Seventh Pennsylvania, Major Wynkoop, the only troops of my brigade accompanying me.

The infantry supports arrived twenty-eight hours after we reached Paint Lick Bridge. I feel satisfied that none of the enemy except unarmed stragglers, sick and wounded, are in that part of Kentucky.

EDWARD M. McCOOK,
Colonel, Commanding Brigade.

Maj. GEORGE E. FLYNT.

No. 5.

Report of Col. James R. Howard, Third Confederate Cavalry, of skirmishes near Mountain Gap, October 14–16.

JAMESTOWN, TENN.,
October 17, 1862—8 a. m.

GENERAL : Your dispatch under the caption of 13th instant was received last evening. Wolford's brigade (Federal) has been skirmishing with me for three days and nights. I have engaged him to the best of my ability every time. It was his purpose to cut me off. I outmanaged him, and have secured all my wagons as far as this point. In a short skirmish yesterday with about 500 of his cavalry I lost 2 men killed and 4 missing. His whole force is still after me. His force is about 5,000 strong, and are now in ambush at the old cattle trail up the mountain. As I had led the citizens to believe I was going, I started up the mountain by the way of Poplar Cove at night and I got to this point at 4 a. m. There was not a particle of subsistence or forage near here. Will make my headquarters, according to instructions, as near here as practicable where I can subsist.

At crossing of Cumberland the enemy routed Colonels Scott's and Starnes' cavalry. My pickets heard the firing, and I took my command to the rear to assist him, but they had gone and the enemy in full pursuit. I made a very narrow escape from being cut off. Clift's forces, or rather a portion of his command, are acting with this Federal force, as are all the bushwhackers that are left. I have thinned them in

Fentress, Clinton, and Wayne Counties, and trust soon to exterminate them all.

I have the honor, general, with much regard, to be, very respectfully, your obedient servant,

JAMES R. HOWARD,
Colonel, Commanding Cavalry, C. S. Army.

General E. KIRBY SMITH.

OCTOBER 15–20, 1862.—Operations against guerrillas in the counties of Henry, Owen, and Gallatin, Ky.

No. 1.

Report of Col. Orlando H. Moore, Twenty-fifth Michigan Infantry.

HEADQUARTERS TWENTY-FIFTH MICHIGAN INFANTRY,
Louisville, October 22, 1862.

CAPTAIN : I have the honor to report that in compliance with orders I moved with seven companies of my command on the morning of the 15th instant, and in consequence of railroad detention did not arrive at Eminence until 10 o'clock a. m.   Captain Gore furnished a detachment of 8 men, under command of Lieutenant Armstrong, to act as scouts, and we proceeded to Bethlehem ; were re-enforced by Captain Sewell with 8 or 10 men, and then marched to Gratz, on the Kentucky River, in the night, where we expected to attack a force of the enemy by daybreak reported in that vicinity.   When we arrived the enemy had fled, and we proceeded to Owenton ; found a guerrilla force, which fled on the first appearance of our advance guard.   In the night I sent a detachment of soldiers mounted to Monterey, where they surprised and took prisoners 5 rebel soldiers of the First Florida Cavalry, together with their horses and equipments.   Three of them were paroled in consequence of ill-health.   On Saturday, 18th instant, I proceeded with two companies of infantry and 15 infantry soldiers mounted to attack a band of guerrillas in the hills, who proved as ambitious to get out of our way as we were to pursue and attack.   That same night we captured a rebel soldier in the hills and took into custody 5 rebel soldiers.   We arrested and paroled many rebels in and about Owenton.

On Monday, the 20th instant, we marched to Warsaw, on the Ohio River, where steamboat transportation was in waiting for the command ; but owing to a report of a large rebel force having arrived in that vicinity to attack us, we waited until the next morning before embarking on board the boat.   We kept the towns we occupied under strong guard and dispersed or arrested all parties after 10 o'clock at night. Our efforts in dispersing rebels in the counties of Henry, Owen, and Gallatin were successful, but the Union inhabitants are apprehensive of future depredations and annoyance from rebels and guerrilla parties in the absence of troops.

I have the honor to be, very respectfully, your obedient servant,

ORLANDO H. MOORE,
Colonel Twenty-fifth Michigan Infantry.

Capt. N. C. SEMPLE, *A. A. G., Louisville, Ky.*

OCTOBER 16–25, 1862.—Operations in Bath, Powell, Estill, Clark, Montgomery, and Bourbon Counties, Kentucky.

Report of W. H. Wadsworth.

MAYSVILLE, KY., *October* 29, 1862.

GENERAL: I arrived here yesterday evening from Mount Sterling, having left there Monday night last at 9 o'clock.

On Thursday, the 16th of this month, I left this place with 381 men, recruited for the Fourteenth Kentucky Cavalry, all but 70 unmounted, and one piece of artillery, an iron 6-pounder, the property of citizens of this place, and in charge of a volunteer squad of citizens under Mr. Gilmore.

We reached Sharpsburg, 11 miles from Mount Sterling, Friday evening, and there learned that Humphrey Marshall, with 6,000 men, fifteen pieces of artillery, and a train of 200 wagons, was at Ticktown, 7 miles from Mount Sterling, on the Hazle Green road, in full retreat. He had come from Camp Dick Robinson through Richmond, Red River Iron Works, &c., to that place.

Saturday morning early I marched to Mount Sterling and captured 17 of Marshall's men in the town. I immediately pushed out my small squad of horsemen with some mounted Lewis County and Fleming County Home Guards, under Jeff. Walker and Isaac Keely, and a few citizens of Montgomery, Bath, and Clark, on the Ticktown road. These brave men drove up Marshall's stragglers and captured altogether 49 almost in sight of his headquarters.

Learning Saturday night that 900 rebel horsemen, under Trigg and Camron, were at Owingsville, 15 miles on my left, and that John H. Morgan had captured Lexington that morning, and having received a letter from Major Bracht from Paris, dated Friday, saying he had but 125 men there and could not help me harass the retreat of Marshall, I fell back with my command and prisoners to Paris; there I telegraphed you Monday for help. You ordered Colonel Wisner, of the Twenty-second Michigan, to go with me at once to Mount Sterling, and we started off that night, our forces consisting of that regiment and one section of artillery, my lads, and one piece and two companies of the Tenth Kentucky Cavalry, under Major Doniphan. We reached Mount Sterling Tuesday evening. Next morning, under orders from Colonel Wisner, I took all the mounted men in camp that could be spared, 210 in number, and scouted the country for 80 miles through Bath, Powell, Estill, and Clark, capturing a number of prisoners, horses, and arms.

As I was returning from Winchester on Friday afternoon to Mount Sterling I met Colonel Wisner, with all his forces, marching toward Winchester and thence to Lexington. He was ordered to proceed cautiously by General G. C. Smith, as he had learned there was a large body of rebels there. These rebels (7 white men and 1 negro) had captured a picket of some 140 horsemen, sent to Winchester by General Smith the Tuesday before; whereupon the horsemen went back to Paris and made that report, I presume. These 7 whites and 1 negro I came on at Red River; captured 5 and shot 1, and that was all the rebel force in 30 miles of Winchester.

I went on to Mount Sterling again to endeavor to protect my district with 382 recruits, not in the service of the United States, against Humphrey Marshall's horsemen. Marshall, with his train and artillery, and such of his infantry as did not desert, has easily escaped, without any pursuit except such as I have detailed, through Prestonburg and on his way to Abingdon, Va. I should say 1,000 or 1,200 of his men had deserted him. I captured 150 and 50 horses, besides muskets, pistols, &c. His horsemen remain behind in Kentucky to plunder and ruin the people. On Saturday I heard of 600 under Witcher and 400 under Camron in Morgan and Bath Counties, and 150 in Powell, beyond Staunton, under Gay, Bradshaw, and other thugs, murdering, plundering, and burning.

General, my district has sent six infantry regiments to the Federal Army, and in addition the Tenth Kentucky Cavalry was principally raised in that district. The Government has never sent us the least assistance except the Twenty-second Michigan, ordered away before it could serve us an hour. After our whole State was evacuated, except Covington and Louisville, you ordered away the Tenth Kentucky Cavalry from this place, just raised and mounted hereabouts, and left us naked to bands of mounted rebels. These bands yonder around and beyond Mount Sterling still ruin the people. Smith, Bragg, and Marshall retreat beyond pursuit and no help comes.

Unless you order a force of mounted men, supported by some infantry, to clear out the region beyond Mount Sterling and Owingsville all this part of the State will be infested and plundered all fall and winter.

I find here Colonel Lucy and part of the One hundred and fifteenth Ohio. There are 400 cavalry at Ripley. The balance of the One hundred and fifteenth is at Cincinnati. Colonel Lucy is anxious to go on this duty. We have no use for a soldier at this point now, not one. I beg you will send him with these forces at once to Mount Sterling, with orders to clear away these rebel robbers. I do hope you will also support him with some of the Tenth Kentucky Cavalry or some other mounted force. They should also have some pieces of mountain howitzers. Troops at Mount Sterling, Owingsville, and West Liberty will protect and relieve a third of this State.

General, if you could see my ruined people and their desolate homes you would move up the brigades under your command and excuse the feeling I show in their behalf. I have done all I could for them without help from State or nation, and will not give it up. The President has shown himself friendly toward me, and I will beg him for protection against the damned villains.

Respectfully, your obedient, &c.,

W. H. WADSWORTH.

Maj. Gen. HORATIO G. WRIGHT.

OCTOBER 18, 1862.—Action at Lexington, Ky.

REPORTS.

No. 1.—Maj. Gen. Horatio G. Wright, U. S. Army, of the capture of Lexington
No. 2.—Maj. Charles B. Seidel, Third Ohio Cavalry, of skirmish near Lexington.

No. 1.

Report of Maj. Gen. Horatio G. Wright, U. S. Army, commanding Department of the Ohio.

CINCINNATI, OHIO, *October* 19, 1862—12.5 a. m.

John Morgan took Lexington yesterday morning (18th) and captured some of the Fourth Ohio Cavalry (report says 500 strong). General

Granger's command is moving in two columns, one by the Lexington pike, and is to-night not far from Big Eagle; the other by the road near the railroad, and has one regiment of infantry, 300 cavalry, and a section of artillery at Paris; two regiments at Cynthiana, and the rest at Falmouth. Both columns are being pushed forward as fast as transportation will permit, and the division you suggest will be in Lexington as soon as it can be got there. Remember they are all raw troops. Bridge at Cynthiana and Paris safe. Falmouth Bridge completed by Tuesday night.

H. G. WRIGHT,
Major-General, Commanding.

General D. C. BUELL, .
  Louisville, Ky., care General J. T. Boyle.

No. 2.

Report of Maj. Charles B. Seidel, Third Ohio Cavalry, of skirmish near Lexington.

DANVILLE, *October* 19, 1862.

SIR: In compliance to orders I received from your headquarters to go to Camp Dick Robinson and take charge of the provisions left there by the rebel forces I left camp on the 16th of October at 2 p. m. and arrived at Camp Dick Robinson at 5 p. m., finding Colonel Hoskins in charge of those stores, consisting of 2,600 barrels of pork and 2,000 bushels of wheat. Went into camp at Dick Robinson with intention to return the following morning to Danville. At 11 o'clock of same night I received a message from Colonel Hoskins of the approach of General Morgan with 500 men strong toward Hickman Bridge with intention to burn said bridge, and recommending one battalion of my forces to be immediately dispatched to Hickman Bridge to prevent it from being burned by General Morgan's forces. This I complied with, by sending one battalion of the Fourth Ohio Volunteer Cavalry under command of Captain Robie.

The next morning (October 17) at 5 o'clock I started with the balance of my command, consisting of one battalion Third Ohio Volunteer Cavalry, to join Captain Robie at said bridge. On my arrival here I learned that Captain Gotwald, commanding four companies of Fourth Ohio Volunteer Cavalry, had left Nicholasville for Lexington to drive a portion of Morgan's cavalry forces from that vicinity to prevent their pillage and burning of bridges. I then, knowing that Captain Gotwald could not accomplish his object with the force under his command, went with all the force under my command, numbering in all 260 men, to re-enforce him, which I accomplished by 3 o'clock of same day. Finding Captain Gotwald with his force stationed in town, I then went into camp 1½ miles from Lexington on the Richmond pike.

At 1 o'clock the same night two citizens living about 7 miles from Lexington came in with the following statement, viz: Morgan's forces of about 500 or 600 men were advancing on the Richmond pike. I immediately sent out a scouting party of 22 men, under command of Lieutenant Hall, Company K, Third Ohio Volunteer Cavalry, to procure all possible information. At about 3 o'clock 1 corporal and 2 privates returned with 2 rebel prisoners in charge, captured about 5 miles from Lexington on the Richmond pike. The balance of the scouting party marched on. On questioning said prisoners I became satisfied that a heavy force was coming upon us. I therefore called out my command immediately and formed in line, when we were attacked by General Morgan's forces of about 3,000 strong and six pieces of artillery pouring in most deadly volleys of musketry and grape on all sides. My command most manfully and gallantly returned their fire and fought them hand to hand until overpowered by an overwhelming force, when we were compelled to surrender. Our loss was 4 killed and 24 wounded.

The loss of the enemy I was unable to ascertain, but saw 3 wagons of killed and wounded leave the battle ground. Major Morgan, of General Morgan's cavalry, was mortally wounded. The scouting party have not been heard from. As a large rebel force left the scene of action in pursuit of them fears are entertained that all have been captured.

Much credit is due to Captain Robie, of the Fourth Ohio Volunteer Cavalry, for his cool and gallant behavior during the fight. Capt. P. H. Warner, Company D; Lieut. H. Hamilton, Company A, and Lieut. W. E. Crane, Company C, [Fourth] Ohio Volunteer Cavalry, having left the command on the evening previous without permission and remained in town all night, and have not reported themselves yet.

The greatest credit is due to all officers and men.

Most respectfully, your obedient servant,

CHAS. B. SEIDEL,
Major, Commanding Third Ohio Volunteer Cavalry.

Colonel ZAHM.

[Indorsement.]

Respectfully forwarded, with the addition that the four companies of the Fourth Ohio Volunteer Cavalry stationed at Lexington, under command of Captain Gotwald, have surrendered likewise. Have had no official reports from him.

LEWIS ZAHM,
Colonel, Commanding Second Cavalry Brigade.

OCTOBER 23-24, 1862.—Destruction of Goose Creek Salt-Works, near Manchester, Ky.

REPORTS.

No. 1.—Maj. Gen. Thomas L. Crittenden, U. S. Army.
No. 2.—Brig. Gen. William Sooy Smith, U. S. Army.
No. 3.—Brig. Gen. Charles Cruft, U. S. Army.
No. 4.—The Board of Officers.

No. 1.

Report of Maj. Gen. Thomas L. Crittenden, U. S. Army.

HDQRS. LEFT WING, FOURTEENTH ARMY CORPS,
November 17, 1862.

COLONEL: I herewith inclose reports of Brigadier-General Smith, of Brigadier-General Cruft, of Colonel Enyart, of Colonel Hanson, and of Lieutenant-Colonel Spencer of the destruction of the Goose Creek Salt-Works, in obedience to the order of Major-General Buell. These reports are exceedingly intelligent and complete, and do great credit to the authors of them.

I commend this matter to the prompt attention of the general commanding, and earnestly and urgently entreat that some plan be adopted to afford prompt and adequate compensation to the good and loyal citizens who have suffered.

Most respectfully, your obedient servant,

T. L. CRITTENDEN,
Major-General, Commanding.

Col. J. P. GARESCHÉ, *Chief of Staff.*

No. 2.

Report of Brig. Gen. William Sooy Smith, U. S. Army.

HEADQUARTERS FOURTH DIVISION,
Silver Spring, Tenn., November 16, 1862.

SIR : In obedience to your order of the 21st ultimo, a copy of which is hereto appended, marked A, I directed the Twenty-second Brigade, Brig. Gen. Charles Cruft commanding, to proceed to the Goose Creek Salt-Works and destroy them. This was as fully done as the time allowed by subsequent orders, directing the return of the brigade, would permit. The manner in which it was accomplished and the extent of the damage done are fully set forth in the accompanying reports of General Cruft and the board of officers appointed by him to look to the destruction of the works and to report their action in full. The want of familiarity with salt manufacture experienced by the officers constituting this board has deterred them from fixing any money value upon the damages done, present and prospective; and I concur in the recommendation contained in General Cruft's report that a competent commission be appointed immediately to take the necessary testimony and assess the damages.

The Salt-Works are situated in the midst of a population whose loyalty and patriotism are not excelled in any portion of our country. Much suffering must result to the poor people of the surrounding region from lack of the salt they have heretofore obtained at the works destroyed, and the length of time during which the proprietors should be required to suspend operations, leaving the works in their present crippled condition, is a matter that deserves careful consideration. This, of course, will depend very much upon the plan of the campaign and the movements of the United States troops in Southeastern Kentucky, and hence no direction could be given except that the manufacture of salt should be discontinued until further orders.

The noble conduct of some of those interested in the works, especially of Mrs. Garrard, who expressed her entire willingness that not only that valuable property, but all else that she and her husband (a colonel in our service) owned, might be destroyed if such destruction would help to restore the Union, constrains an earnest recommendation that prompt restitution be made for the damage done.

W. S. SMITH,
Brigadier-General, Commanding Fourth Division.

Major STARLING,
Assistant Adjutant-General.

[Inclosure A.]

HEADQUARTERS SECOND ARMY CORPS,
October 21, 1862.

Brigadier-General SMITH, *Commanding Fourth Division:*

GENERAL : You will immediately send forward a brigade to destroy the Salt-Works at Manchester.   Order them to return promptly as soon as that object has been accomplished, reporting their position at least every day to these headquarters.

By order of Major-General Crittenden :

LYNE STARLING,
Assistant Adjutant-General.

(Referred to General Cruft October 22.)

No. 3.

Report of Brig. Gen. Charles Cruft, U. S. Army.

HDQRS. TWENTY-SECOND BRIGADE, FOURTH DIVISION,
Rockcastle Ford, October 25, 1862.

CAPTAIN : On the morning of the 22d instant, in pursuance of a written order from Brigadier-General Smith, commanding division (a copy of which is hereto attached,*) I marched this brigade from camp at Mershon's Cross-Roads to the Salt-Works, five in number, situated upon Goose Creek (see plat hereto appended), near Manchester, Ky., a distance of 26 miles.

On the 23d and 24th instant these Salt-Works were so far destroyed as to render them ineffective for the future manufacture of salt, without the lapse of considerable time, large expense, and most probably the boring of new wells.   The manufactured salt on hand at the various works was destroyed as effectually as possible.   The manner in which the works and salt were destroyed is set forth in the written report of Colonel Enyart (First Kentucky Volunteers), Lieutenant-Colonel Hanson (Twentieth Kentucky Volunteers), and Lieutenant-Colonel Spencer (Second Kentucky Volunteers), acting as a commission under Special Orders, No. 3, from headquarters of this brigade.   A copy of this report and the special order on which it is based are hereto appended.†

The time allowed me (by subsequent communication from General Smith) for the destruction of the works was too limited to thoroughly complete the job.   Over 1,000 men were worked in details for one night and a day and a half in handling the salt and dismantling the works.

I recommend that a special commission or commissioners be appointed by the Government of the United States to repair to the works and take evidence as to the quantity and price of the salt destroyed, the permanent damage to the works, and the amount of any remote or consequential damage that may ensue to the owners or lessees from the stoppage of their manufactories.   This appears to be the only proper means to do even-handed justice between the parties interested and the Government.

In regard to the propriety of the destruction of these works as a military necessity, a matter that is, I am aware, the special province of my superiors to decide, I may still be pardoned to remark that everything

---

* See above.   † See No. 4.

conspired to show its wisdom. An army sufficient to protect them could not be subsisted from the country in the vicinity of the works. The condition of the mountain roads and the usual severity of the winter thereabouts would have rendered it nearly impossible to supply rations by hauling from the rear. At least as a matter of economy the destruction of the works seemed a wise movement. The Confederates had carried away not exceeding perhaps from 3,500 to 4,000 bushels of manufactured salt, but every circumstance led to the belief that the quantity on hand would have been shortly taken, as soon as their means of transportation would permit, and that the leaders of the rebellion calculated on their supply of salt to come from these works. In addition to the destruction of the Salt-Works my expedition to Manchester threatened a body of 2,100 Confederate cavalry lying in camp at Paine's farm, 12 miles beyond the town, in direction of Cumberland Gap; so much so that it broke camp and left in great confusion during the night of my arrival. The country about the Salt-Works was thoroughly patrolled and reconnoitered. Fifty-six straggling prisoners were captured and sent back to the cross-roads and there paroled. There were 35 beef cattle captured from the enemy, which were driven in and used to subsist my command. There is a considerable amount of Government property scattered about in the hands of the citizens in vicinity of the Salt-Works. As many as 20 or 30 Government wagons, only slightly injured by fire, were seen by my patrols, and the number of such could have been increased to one hundred and more (if the statement of apparently credible men could be relied on) in that neighborhood. Government harness, mules, horses, and boots of various kinds were heard of constantly. This property was a portion of trains partially destroyed and abandoned by General Morgan (U. S. Volunteers) on his retreat from Cumberland Gap. I had no time to hunt up the property and no means to transport it away, and can simply make report of it as being there. While at the Salt-Works and *en route* there many of the members of Home Guard associations had interviews with me, and were stimulated to watch the mountain roads and tracks for stragglers and to complete and render effective their associations. At the time of my leaving they had already begun to spread terror among stragglers and to make it dangerous for small bodies of the enemy's cavalry to attempt incursions into their neighborhoods. The people in the mountain districts in direction of Manchester are loyal and true to the Government. They have been robbed by the rebel army of nearly all of their available personal property—cattle, horses, and crops—and are left generally in a destitute condition.

I am, captain, very truly, yours, &c.,

CHARLES CRUFT,
Brig. Gen., Comdg. Twenty-second Brigade, Fourth Division.

Captain ATKINSON, *A. A. G., Fourth Div., Army of the Ohio.*

[Inclosure.]

SPECIAL ORDERS, }   HDQRS. TWENTY-SECOND BRIGADE,
  No. 3.   }   *Goose Creek Salt-Works, Ky., October* 23, 1862.

Colonel Enyart, First Kentucky Volunteers; Lieutenant-Colonel Hanson, Twentieth Kentucky Volunteers, and Lieutenant-Colonel Spencer, Second Kentucky Volunteers, are hereby appointed a board to destroy the Salt-Works near Manchester, Ky., and the manufactured salt on hand as speedily as practicable. They will take such measures as will most effectively destroy the works and prevent the future manufacture of salt and prevent that on hand from falling into the hands of the enemy. For this purpose they will use the force of their own commands as may be necessary, but if insufficient, details will be made from other regiments of this brigade.

They will make a full report in writing to these headquarters of their action under this order.

By order of Brigadier-General Cruft:

W. H. FAIRBANKS,
Captain and Assistant Adjutant-General.

No. 4.

Report of the Board of Officers.

HEADQUARTERS FIRST KENTUCKY VOLUNTEERS,
Camp near Columbia, Ky., November 1, 1862.

CAPTAIN: In obedience to Special Orders, No. —, that issued from the headquarters of the Twenty-second Brigade of the Army of the Ohio on the 23d day of October last (a copy of which order is here inclosed), directing the undersigned to destroy the Salt-Works near Manchester, Ky., including the product on hand, and to report to you our proceedings under said order, availing ourselves of the first opportunity, we tender the following statement of what we did in carrying out said order:

The works, consisting of five in number, are situated and are owned and occupied as follows:

The first, owned and occupied by Col. T. T. Garrard, is situated about 2 miles from Manchester, on the main fork of Goose Creek. The second, third, and fourth are situated on Collins' Fork of that creek, within 3 miles of Manchester, and are owned and occupied as follows: The second one, by Mrs. J. T. Woodward and her daughter, Mrs. Mollie Shackelford, and rented by James W. Reid for the years 1862 and 1863, and were occupied by him. The third, owned by A. T. White, Michael Horton, and Daniel Gara, sr. The fourth, owned by Alexander White and Mrs. J. T. Woodward and her daughter, Mrs. Mollie Shackelford, and was occupied by Stephen Gibson and A. Chastain. The fifth works, owned and occupied by J. and D. White, situated on the east fork of Goose Creek, 5 miles from Manchester.

These works were furnished with water from bored wells from 500 to 600 feet deep, and were in complete order and full operation, making from 50 to 100 bushels of salt a day each.

We proceeded to render these works useless and unfit for service by destroying the pumps and wells and the pipes conveying the water also. In each case the pumps, or portions of them where they all could not be gotten out, were taken out of the wells, broken to pieces, and the pieces forced back into the wells into and upon the pipes; and in the case of those of White, Horton, and Gara a piece of iron grate was driven into that portion of the pump which could not be gotten out of the well; and in the case of Chastain and Gibson an iron bar was forced down into the well and into the well pipe, and 300 feet of the surface pipe and all the wood work of the pans were destroyed. The pumps used by J. and D. White, except small portions of them, could not be drawn out of the well. Therefore, after forcing back into the well portions of the pump, we forced into them cannon balls and in that way rendered the wells useless. We also destroyed the scaffolding and a large portion of the wood work of the pans and all the surface pipe.

We found at all these works large quantities of salt. The amount at the several works, in our judgment, from a hasty examination, without the means of measuring it, and from the statements of the persons using them respectively, were about as follows :

At Works No. 1 (Garrard), 5,840 bushels; at Works No. 2 (Reid), 5,000 bushels; at Works No 3 (White, Horton and Gara), 2,000 bushels; at Works No. 4 (Gibson and Chastain), 8,000 bushels; at Works No. 5 (J. and D. White), 9,000 bushels.

This estimate of the salt may be very inaccurate. We had no experience in estimating salt, and had to guess at it and take the statement of the parties interested and such persons as happened to be present. The true amount can be obtained when necessary from the testimony of those experienced in such matters and familiar with the works and competent to judge of such matters.

By the verbal permission of Brigadier-General Cruft we permitted the loyal citizens around and in the neighborhood of the works to remove enough salt to supply the neighborhood and country around, binding them by oath not to permit any of it to go to the benefit of the Southern Confederacy. This privilege was necessary in order to prevent great suffering among the citizens. In this way a considerable quantity of salt was appropriated, and the remainder we destroyed by turning the water from the cisterns upon it and as far as practicable throwing the remainder into the pools and streams of water convenient.

This destruction of these works and their products was not as complete as we desired, but was as thorough as practicable, considering the time allowed and the want of facilities for doing the work. We worked 500 men—as many as could be employed at it—continuously for thirty-six hours, doing in that time a vast deal of work. The wells and pumps upon which the works depended for supplies of water to manufacture the salt, although not entirely destroyed, were rendered useless and totally unfit for service and the most of them damaged beyond repair, and if any of them can be repaired it will be at nearly as heavy an expense of time and labor as boring a new well.

The salt was so effectually appropriated by the neighbors and destroyed and scattered as stated that no considerable amount of it can ever fall into the hands of the enemies of the country.

The buildings and other machinery not referred to were very common and of little value and could have been easily replaced if destroyed, and having no way of effectually destroying them, and believing that the works were already rendered useless for making salt, and, further, not being willing to commit any wanton waste of private property, they were all left untouched as we found them.

We regret delay in sending in this report, but owing to having been constantly engaged in heavy marches we could not present it at an earlier hour.

Very respectfully submitted.

D. A. ENYART,
Colonel First Kentucky Regiment.
CHARLES S. HANSON,
Lieutenant-Colonel Twentieth Kentucky Regiment.
WARNER SPENCER,
Lieutenant-Colonel Second Kentucky Regiment.

Capt. W. H. FAIRBANKS,
Assistant Adjutant-General, Twenty-second Brigade.

APPENDIX.

Embracing documents received too late for insertion in proper sequence.

OCTOBER 8, 1862.—Battle of Perryville, or Chaplin Hills, Ky.

Report of Col. John C. Starkweather, First Wisconsin Infantry, commanding Twenty-eighth Brigade, Third Division.

ON BATTLE-FIELD,
Chaplin Hills, October 11, 1862.

SIR: I have the honor to report that the Twenty-eighth Brigade, composed of the Seventy-ninth Pennsylvania Volunteers, Twenty-fourth Illinois Volunteers, First and Twenty-first Wisconsin Volunteer Infantry, commanded, respectively, by Col. H. A. Hambright, Captain [August] Mauff (Colonel Mihalotzy being absent, sick), Lieut. Col. George B. Bingham, and Col. Benjamin J. Sweet; First Kentucky Artillery, Capt. D. C. Stone, and Fourth Indiana Artillery, Capt. A. K. Bush, left Maxville [Mackville], under orders, on the 8th instant, the Twenty-first Wisconsin marching in the rear as guard to the division ammunition train, the Seventeenth Kentucky Volunteer Infantry, Col. John H. McHenry, jr., having been sent to Springfield as guard to division supply train, and arrived on the field of battle at about 1.30 p. m., having marched 12 miles, about 3 miles thereof being through fields, woods, &c. Finding the troops already engaged well on the right, center, and left, and thinking the extreme left position most accessible, and, from appearances, one that should be held at all hazards, I placed my command at once in position facing the enemy's right (countermarching a portion of my brigade for such purpose), the Twenty-fourth Illinois and Seventy-ninth Pennsylvania forming the right wing, to be supported by the First Wisconsin and Twenty-first Wisconsin, when the last-mentioned regiment should arrive, and holding my two batteries to act as the disposition of the enemy might require. General [D. S.] Donelson's brigade at this moment engaged the Twenty-fourth Illinois and Seventy-ninth Pennsylvania on the right, but were driven from the field, after most desperate fighting. While this engagement was progressing, I placed, by your order, Bush's battery on the extreme left, Stone's battery next on its right, the First Wisconsin to the rear of Bush, to support him, and the Twenty-first Wisconsin, which had arrived (excepting two companies acting as flankers to the ammunition train), to the front of the two batteries, in a corn-field at the foot of the hill, upon which artillery was placed, forming it at once in line of battle. This disposition of my forces was hardly complete before General Maney's brigade attacked me in front, assisted by a battery, and General Donelson's brigade again attacked on the extreme right, the enemy at the same time placing a battery on my extreme left, upon a well-chosen position, to flank me. The flank movement on the left was prevented by Stone's battery shelling the position chosen, and Donelson's brigade was again forced to retire by the well-directed and continuous fire of the Twenty-fourth Illinois and Seventy-ninth Pennsylvania. I then ordered the Twenty-first Wisconsin to fire and charge the front, but, being a new regiment, their colonel being severely wounded and their major killed at about the time such order was given, no field officer was left to carry the command into execution, although several companies, hearing the order, attempted to obey it, but being sorely pressed by the brigade and battery in front, it retired in some disorder and confusion. I immediately advanced the First Wisconsin to the front, supported by an oblique fire from the Seventy-ninth and with canister from my artillery, and held such position until many of the artillery horses were killed and the balance became unmanageable, creating such confusion that proper discharges could not be continued. Other regiments on my right at this time were retiring, and being unable to obtain any support from them, I ordered the Seventy-ninth, Twenty-fourth, and First to hold their positions, while Stone's battery, of four guns, and Bush's battery, of two (all that was manageable), were retired to a new and safer position. The retirement was made in good order, and the fire from the artillery again opened. A part of the First Wisconsin then charged to the front, capturing the colors of the First Tennessee. The fire from the Seventy-ninth and Twenty-fourth held the enemy in check, while the balance of the First Wisconsin took by hand every remaining gun and caisson from the field. The enemy by this time was completely routed, the firing ceased on our front and flank, and the regiments were retired to the support of the batteries in their new position, which was occupied until 12 o'clock at night, when a change was made by your order.

My loss in officers and men was terrible indeed.

Where all did so nobly and well, one cannot be mentioned without doing injustice to others; but I must acknowledge the great service rendered me by my staff officers, Lieutenants Franklin, Searles, and Bingham, in carrying orders to and fro in the midst of the terrible fire surrounding them.

Trusting that the brigade will receive at your hands the proper mention which it deserves for its bravery, good conduct, and magnificent fighting, I subscribe myself, yours, to command,

JOHN C. STARKWEATHER,
Colonel First Wisconsin, Commanding Twenty-eighth Brigade.
Capt. W. P. McDOWELL,
Assistant Adjutant-General, Third Division.

Report of Lieut. William B. Turner, Smith's (Mississippi) Battery.

IN CAMP NEAR BRYANTSVILLE,
October 12, 1862.

SIR: I have the honor to report that, on the afternoon of the 8th instant, while accompanying the Third Brigade, which was advancing on the enemy, I received orders from General Maney, through Lieutenant [James M.] Keeble, to halt on the ascent of the hill, which the brigade had ascended, and immediately afterward I received orders from General Maney, through Captain [E.] Cockrill, to advance. I had not reached the top of the hill, when orders were brought to me from General Cheatham, by Capt. M. Smith, chief of artillery, to advance rapidly, and was conducted by the latter to a position on the hill to the extreme right, and overlooking the enemy, who was then in a fighting attitude before our forces. I immediately opened an enfilading fire on them, at the distance of 250 or 300 yards, with canister, and continued it with shell and spherical case as the enemy retired. This continued until our forces had so far advanced as to be between our battery and the enemy's infantry, when we commenced replying to a battery of the enemy, which had annoyed us considerably, opening upon us with guns of heavier caliber than ours as soon as we commenced our firing. I continued this until I received orders from General Cheatham to cease firing, and our infantry advanced and took the battery opposing us. I then advanced the battery to a position farther to the front, to open on a battery which was firing on Captain Carnes' battery, when I received orders from General Cheatham to withdraw my battery to the rear.

After night, I received orders from Capt. M. Smith to send my horses and limbers to the front, and withdraw some of the enemy's guns which had been captured, the enemy having taken off most of their limbers with their horses. I brought off all I could find (excepting two caissons, which were disabled), amounting to five 12-pounder Napoleon guns (brass), one 12-pounder howitzer gun (brass), and one 6-pounder Parrott gun (steel), with two limbers and two caissons, without limbers, filled with ammunition for the Napoleon guns. During the night, I exchanged my two 6-pounder guns for two of the Napoleon guns, together with the ammunition, and the next morning, on our leaving for Harrodsburg, my men, by order of Capt. M. Smith, dismantled the guns which we were unable to take with us.

Our casualties consisted of 4 men wounded and 1 missing, and 1 horse killed and 3 wounded.

I take pleasure in bearing testimony to the zeal and gallantry displayed by the officers and men of the battery on the occasion.

Respectfully, your obedient servant,

WM. B. TURNER,
First Lieutenant, Commanding Battery.

Capt. T. H. MALONE,
Assistant Adjutant-General.

Report of Brig. Gen. St. John R. Liddell, C. S. Army, commanding First Brigade, Third Division.

HEADQUARTERS FIRST BRIGADE, THIRD DIVISION,
Knoxville, Tenn., October 24, 1862.

COLONEL : In obedience to the order of Major-General Hardee, on the morning of the 7th instant, I placed my brigade 1 mile in advance of our lines, on the right of the Springfield road leading from Perryville, on the crest of a hill, covered with some open woods, with ground rapidly sloping to the front and facing a skirt of woods on the opposite hill, beyond which the enemy were actively engaged with Colonel Wheeler's cavalry, and at the same time taking position. The interval between the woodlands of these hills was hardly exceeding 200 yards, with a small corn-field next to the road opposite my left and open ground on my right. At the base of the hills was a dry bed of a branch of Doctor's Fork. During the day the cavalry were skirmishing with the enemy, and the shells fell constantly within and beyond my lines.

Perceiving the necessity of holding the woodland in front, to make my own position tenable, I threw forward, as skirmishers, the Seventh Arkansas Regiment, then under the command of Lieutenant-Colonel [Peter] Snyder, who occupied the position in my advance with but little interruption for the rest of the day and the night following. At nightfall Colonel Wheeler fell back on the road past my lines, after contesting his ground most obstinately until dusk. As my left flank rested on the Springfield road, all on that side, having no support, was exposed to a flank movement of the enemy; but feeling satisfied that he must be in need of water, and that he would push for that point whence it could be obtained from pools lower down on Doctor's Fork, on my right, I separated my battery, and placed one section on a high hill on my right, commanding the woods opposite and open valley below. The other section I retained in advance of my left, as it commanded the field before us, and, to some extent, the fields to the left of the Springfield road. Early on the following morning (8th instant), the enemy began a brisk fire upon my advanced line of skirmishers, and with superior numbers drove them from the woods. Colonel [D. A.] Gillespie having assumed command of his regiment, the Seventh Arkansas, I directed him to try to regain the position; and for that purpose I ordered forward the second line of skirmishers, Fifth Arkansas Regiment, Colonel [L.] Featherston commanding, with Lieutenant-Colonel [John E.] Murray and Major [P. V.] Green, of the same, gallantly assisting. The attempt was promptly and cheerfully made, but the force of the enemy had been increased so largely and suddenly as to force back both lines, the officers and men contesting the ground with resolute determination, unwilling to yield it to even the great odds against them. Whilst this was going on, the enemy pushed a regiment of cavalry around the point of woods and down the valley of Doctor's Fork in front of my right, against which I had directed a few shots from the section of artillery on the hill, causing it to retire under cover of the woods in great confusion. Both sections of artillery now began firing upon the moving lines in the woods from which my skirmishers had been driven, whilst, with rapidly increasing numbers, the enemy was fast nearing my line of battle. All this time his artillery was assuming new positions, and throwing grape and shell among us from many points. Fearing the effect upon my artillery, the sharpshooters now getting in close proximity, I ordered both sections to withdraw from their advanced position, and to unite upon the right of my line of battle. This was done with the loss of but one horse, and I now became interested in getting in my skirmishers, when an order came to me from Major-General Buckner to withdraw my brigade in good order to the rear. This was done without confusion across the Chaplin Fork, about 11 a. m. In this morning occurred my principal loss, being chiefly confined to the lines of skirmishers, of which the Fifth Arkansas suffered most. In this action Captain [H. W.] Robinson, of the Fifth, fell, bravely doing his duty. The gallantry of officers and men was conspicuous, rendering comment superfluous. The loss of the enemy must have been great, as they were exposed in double lines to a well-directed fire from both sections of artillery at short range, as well as the heavy firing of the Seventh and Fifth Regiments as skirmishers. I was now ordered to hold my command in reserve, and for that purpose was directed by Major-General Buckner to recross the Chaplin Fork at a point some half a mile lower down, and take position on an eminence about 1 mile from the field of battle and nearly in rear of the center. Whilst in this place a shell from the enemy's extreme left fatally wounded Adjutant [S.] Harris and a private of the Sixth Arkansas. The fight was going on vigorously in our front and on the right of the advanced position I held in the morning, and almost at right angles to it. About 5 p. m. I received an order from Major-General Hardee to move forward to the crest of the hills surrounding, amphitheater-like, the field of battle, where the action was progressing in full view in the valley and on the lower ranges of hills below us. While here, a shell fell in the ranks of the Second and Eighth Arkansas Regiments, disabling 6 privates in the former and killing 1 in the latter. About 5.30 p. m., Colonel [S. H.] Perkins, of General Hardee's staff, directed me to follow him with my brigade to the valley, and after reaching Doctor's Fork said to me, "General Hardee wishes you now to move upon the enemy where the firing is hottest." Some latitude being here given me, which was fully appreciated, I thought proper to continue my movement toward the enemy's extreme left, as indicated by the heavy firing apparently moving in that direction on the Nashville road. As soon as I had reached the place where I desired to form my line of battle, I moved forward at once. Here I met with Major-General Cheatham, who urged me anxiously to push on and relieve his troops from the heavy pressure upon them. In pressing on, I caused the battery to open fire from high points upon the enemy beyond our lines as chance offered. After passing through and overlapping the right of Major-General Cheatham's lines, I soon found myself in the immediate presence of the enemy. I commenced firing. It being twilight, however, with a bright full moon shining, and dress not clearly distinguishable, my men mistook the enemy for friends; at the same time the cry came from the enemy's lines, "You are killing your friends," which serving to strengthen the impression, I gave the signal to cease firing, intending to push up the line; but at this moment Major-General Polk, who had joined me a few moments before, ordered the ranks to be opened for him to pass, and riding hastily up to the lines in front of us, distant not more than 25 paces, quickly returned, exclaiming, "They are enemies; fire upon them." Heavy volleys were at once rapidly poured into this mass of men, and after the lapse of some ten minutes I again ordered the firing to cease, and when the smoke had cleared away nothing was visible of the enemy but their wounded, dying, and dead. It was at this place that the brave young Captain [W. H.] Grissom, of the Second Arkansas, fell, regretted by all the command. I now forthwith ordered my battery to the top of the hill, in advance of our forces, and placed it in position to fire upon the woods, some 200 yards distant and directly opposite. When I felt satisfied that the enemy had hastily retired in confusion, I was about to recommence firing, fully intending to follow up without delay our success, when General Polk ordered me to desist, and to keep my command near by to await further instructions. Meanwhile some skirmishers, pushing forward to the edge of these woods, reported a battery of the enemy there, under protection of some cavalry; but my orders to remain stationary being imperative, I could do nothing toward its capture, and in a short time it was heard rapidly moving away. My time was now taken up in receiving and disposing of the prisoners who were being constantly brought in. Two fine ambulances, now in possession of General Bragg, were captured by the Second Arkansas Regiment and by the battery, one of which contained the personal baggage of General McCook; the other was supposed to belong to General Rosecrans, both of which officers were reported by the prisoners to have been near by at the close of the action. Two flags are now in my possession, taken by the Second Arkansas Regiment. Two others were taken by this regiment and one by the Sixth, but, not being valued by the captors, were torn to pieces, and the fragments retained as trophies of the day's work. The fields and woods in front and around us on every side were strewn with the enemy's dead and wounded; their loss could hardly have been less than 500 killed and wounded in the space of four to five acres. My own wounded having been cared for, I directed a detail to assist the infirmary corps in removing the wounded of the enemy to a white house not far off on our left, which was soon filled with them, leaving large numbers unprovided for. Though this occupied our attention up to the moment of leaving, I also ordered the arms to be collected; but after attempting to get together those immediately around the position occupied by my battery, and finding the task greater than I expected, I ordered the men to desist, and to take some rest. There must have been several thousand stand lying closely around us. This place seemed to have been selected by the commanding general of the enemy, as it overlooked the field from his side, and was easily accessible to his reserves from the Springfield and Mackville roads, to be thrown on any desired part during the action. This, possibly, may account for the accumulation of the dead and arms at this place. I held my place here, as ordered by General Polk, until about midnight, when I withdrew my command, by order of Major-General Buckner, beyond the Chaplin Fork, in our rear. This was done in silence, with manifest surprise and regret by the whole command. Colonel [John H.] Kelly, of the Sixth [Eighth] Arkansas, personally captured Colonel Goode, of the Twenty-third Indiana [Colonel Gooding, Twenty-second Indiana], commanding brigade. This regiment was said to have caused great havoc in Arkansas, and it seems as if retributive justice had at last been meted out to it by the very men most injured by it. I take the greatest pleasure in stating that not a single instance of lack of gallantry amongst officers or privates came under my personal observation throughout the day; on the contrary, all were fearless in doing their duty, and obeyed orders with alacrity. Captain [George A.] Williams, adjutant-general; Lieutenant [J. L.] Bostick, aide-de-camp, and Lieutenant [J. M.] Dulin, brigade inspector, cheerfully and fearlessly assisted me in the conveyance of all necessary instructions, regardless of all exposure. In forming my line of battle, just before passing through General Cheatham's lines, I discovered that Colonel Kelly's regiment, Sixth [Eighth] Arkansas, which held the left wing, was not in its place. I forthwith sent my aide-de-camp, Lieutenant Bostick, to look after it, and in his absence the adjutant of his regiment reported to me, by order of his colonel, that Major [W. K.] Beard, of General Bragg's staff, some distance back, had ordered the regiment detached, and moved directly forward. Having no time to lose, I moved on in line of battle without it, and, on reaching the front of the enemy, I was gratified to find that the colonel had, by a rapid right-oblique movement, rejoined the brigade at the very time needed. I afterward understood that the order was intended for the whole brigade, but luckily it did not reach me, as its execution would not have enabled me to flank the enemy, and results not so fortunate might have followed. In the entire day's work, the total loss of my brigade, in killed, wounded, and missing, was 71. For names and particulars, I refer to adjutant-general's report.

I humbly thank God for our preservation, and that we have been the means in His hands of destroying so many of the enemies of our country with so little fatality to ourselves.

I am, colonel, respectfully, your obedient,

ST. JOHN R. LIDDELL,
Brigadier-General.

Col. W. D. PICKETT,
Assistant Adjutant-General, Hardee's Corps.

Report of Maj. Frederick Townsend, Eighteenth U. S. Infantry.

HDQRS. DETACHMENT EIGHTEENTH U. S. INFANTRY,
Camp near Crab Orchard, Ky., October 17, 1862.

Brig. Gen. JAMES B. STEEDMAN,
Comdg. *Third Brigade, First Division, Third Army Corps :*

GENERAL : I have the honor, pursuant to Special Orders, No. 13, of October 17, 1862, Headquarters Third Brigade, First Division, to report that on the evening of the 8th instant, about 6 o'clock, this detachment, at the head of the brigade, was ordered to re-enforce Major-General McCook, took position on the right of Lieutenant Smith's battery, and was under severe fire, without the opportunity of replying, for perhaps an hour and a half, during which time 3 men were wounded—one private (Isaac Linn) in Capt. Robert Hull's company (G), First Battalion, slightly in the breast, and Corpl. Bernard [C.] Connelly and Private Dennis Brannon, of Capt. Henry Belknap's company (D), Third Battalion, attached to Second Battalion; the first severely in the leg by a shell, whose leg has since been amputated, and the second slightly in the leg.

I take great pleasure in stating that all the officers and men of the detachment, in the performance of their duties, met my fullest expectation.

I am, sir, very respectfully, your obedient servant,

FRED. TOWNSEND,
Major Eighteenth U. S. Infantry, Commanding.

AUGUST 30, 1862.—Battle of Richmond, Ky.

JOINT RESOLUTION OF CONFEDERATE CONGRESS.

Resolved by the Congress of the Confederate States of America, That the thanks of Congress are due, and are hereby tendered, to General E. Kirby Smith for the signal victory achieved by him in the battle of Richmond, Ky., on the 30th of August, 1861 [1862], and to all the officers and soldiers of his command engaged in that battle, and especially to General Churchill, General Cleburne, and Col. Preston Smith, of whom he says, " I almost fear to particularize, lest I do not full justice to all. But I cannot close without expressing my admiration at the promptness and intelligence with which Generals Churchill, Cleburne, and Col. Preston Smith executed the orders given to them."

SEC. 2. *Resolved,* That special acknowledgments and commendation are declared for that highest order of generalship with which this victory was followed up, utterly annihilating with 5,000 an army of 10,000, of whom full 5,000 were actually captured, besides the slain in battle; and for the brilliant campaign, in which the speed, vigor, and constancy of a rapid advance resulted in planting the Confederate flag upon the capitol of Kentucky, and upon the shores of the Ohio River, in front of the great city of Cincinnati.

SEC. 3. *Resolved,* That the superior generalship displayed in rapidly gathering the immediate fruits of a victory, and in following it promptly with a campaign of activity, enterprise, and unwearied constancy, renders it worthy of the applause of the Government and the emulation of the army.

SEC. 4. *Resolved*, That the President is requested, in appropriate general orders, to make public the sense of Congress in the premises, and to cause the same to be communicated to General E. Kirby Smith and the officers named, and to be read at the head of each regiment engaged in that battle.

Approved February 17, 1864.

ALTERNATE DESIGNATIONS OF ORGANIZATIONS MENTIONED IN THIS *VOLUME.**

Adrian's (T. W.) Cavalry. (See *Tennessee Troops, Confederate*, 12th *Battalion*.)

Alexander's (John W. S.) Infantry. (See *Illinois Troops*, 21st *Regiment*.)

Allen's (Thomas G.) Infantry. (See *Illinois Troops*, 80th *Regiment*.)

Allen's (W. W.) Cavalry. (See *Alabama Troops*, 1st *Regiment*.)

Anderson's (John D.) Artillery. (See *Wisconsin Troops*, 1st *Battery*.)

Anderson Troop Cavalry. (See *Pennsylvania Troops*.)

Andrews' (John S.) Artillery. (See *Michigan Troops*, 6th *Battery*.)

Andrews' (Norman S.) Artillery. (See *John S. Andrews' Artillery*.)

Ashby's (H. M.) Cavalry. (See *Tennessee Troops, Confederate*.)

Austin's (J. E.) Sharpshooters. (See *Louisiana Troops*, 14th *Battalion*.)

Ayres' Command. (See *Ohio Troops*.)

Bacot's Cavalry. (See *N. B. Forrest's Cavalry*.)

Baird's (John F.) Infantry. (See *Indiana Troops*, 66th *Regiment*.)

Barnes' (Sidney M.) Infantry. (See *Kentucky Troops, Union*, 8th *Regiment*.)

Barnett's (C. M.) Artillery. (See *Illinois Troops*, 2d *Regiment, Battery I*.)

Barteau's Cavalry. (See *Tennessee Troops, Confederate*.)

Beatty's (John) Infantry. (See *Ohio Troops*, 3d *Regiment*.)

Bennett's (J. D.) Cavalry. (See *Tennessee Troops, Confederate*.)

Bennett's (John E.) Infantry. (See *Illinois Troops*, 75th *Regiment*.)

Berry's (G. W.) Home Guards. (See *Kentucky Troops, Union*.)

Biddle's (James) Infantry. (See *Union Troops, Regulars*, 16th *Regiment*.)

Bingham's (George B.) Infantry. (See *Wisconsin Troops*, 1st *Regiment*.)

Bishop's (W. H.) Infantry. (See *Mississippi Troops*, 7th *Regiment*.)

Blair's (Thomas M.) Artillery. (See *Washington Artillery*, 5th *Battery*.)

Blake's (John W.) Infantry. (See *Indiana Troops*, 40th *Regiment*.)

Blake's (William H.) Infantry. (See *Indiana Troops*, 9th *Regiment*.)

Blalock's (J. M.) Cavalry. (See *Georgia Troops*, 1st *Regiment*.)

Bledsoe's (Captain) Cavalry. (See *Tennessee Troops, Confederate*.)

Blythe's Infantry. (See *Mississippi Troops*, 44th *Regiment*.)

Board's (B.) Cavalry. (See *Kentucky Troops, Union*, 2d *Regiment*.)

Boone's (William P.) Infantry. (See *Kentucky Troops, Union*, 28th *Regiment*.)

Boyle's (John) Cavalry. (See *Kentucky Troops, Union*, 9th *Regiment*.)

Boyl's (James H.) Infantry. (See *Indiana Troops*, 10th *Regiment*.)

Bracht's (Frederick G.) Infantry. (See *Kentucky Troops, Union*, 18th *Regiment*.)

Bracken County Home Guards. (See *Kentucky Troops, Union*.)

Bradford's Command, Home Guards. (See *Kentucky Troops, Union*.)

Bradley's (Luther P.) Infantry. (See *Illinois Troops*, 51st *Regiment*.)

Bristow's (Benjamin H.) Cavalry. (See *Kentucky Troops, Union*, 8th *Regiment*.)

Brooks' (Lewis) Infantry. (See *Indiana Troops*, 80th *Regiment*.)

Buckner Guards, Cavalry. (See *Kentucky Troops, Confederate*.)

Buell's George P.) Infantry. (See *Indiana Troops*, 58th *Regiment*.)

---

* References are to index following.

Bullard's (J. G.) **Infantry.** (See *Mississippi Troops*, 10th *Regiment.*)
Burke's (Joseph W.) **Infantry.** (See *Ohio Troops*, 10th *Regiment.*)
Burks' (J. C.) **Cavalry.** (See *Texas Troops*, 11th *Regiment.*)
Bush's (Asahel K.) **Artillery.** (See *Indiana Troops*, 4th *Battery.*)
Byrd's (Robert K.) **Infantry.** (See *Tennessee Troops, Union*, 1st *Regiment.*)
Caldwell's (J. W.) **Cavalry.** (See *Kentucky Troops, Confederate*, 1st *Regiment.*)
Calvert's Artillery. (See *Helena Artillery.*)
Campbell's (Archibald P.) **Cavalry.** (See *Michigan Troops*, 2d *Regiment.*)
Campbell's (Lewis D.) **Infantry.** (See *Ohio Troops*, 69th *Regiment.*)
Campbell's (William P.) **Infantry.** (See *Kentucky Troops, Union*, 15th *Regiment.*)
Camron's (O. G.) **Mounted Rifles.** (See *Kentucky Troops, Confederate.*)
Carnes' (W. W.) **Artillery.** (See *Tennessee Troops, Confederate.*)
Carpenter's (Stephen D.) **Infantry.** (See *Union Troops, Regulars*, 19th *Regiment.*)
Carpenter's (Stephen J.) **Artillery.** (See *Wisconsin Troops*, 8th *Battery.*)
Casey's (Thomas S.) **Infantry.** (See *Illinois Troops*, 110th *Regiment.*)
Chandler's (Robert G.) **Artillery.** (See *Loomis'* (Cyrus O.) *Artillery.*)
Chandler's (William P.) **Infantry.** (See *Illinois Troops*, 35th *Regiment.*)
Chapin's (Alfred R.) **Infantry.** (See *Wisconsin Troops*, 10th *Regiment.*)
Chenault's (D. W.) **Cavalry.** (See *Kentucky Troops, Confederate*, 11th *Regiment.*)
Chiles' (John C.) **Infantry.** (See *Tennessee Troops, Union*, 3d *Regiment.*)
Chilson's (Levi) **Cavalry.** (See *Kentucky Troops, Union*, 4th *Regiment.*)
Cincinnati Police. (See *Ohio Troops.*)
Clark's (J. W.) **Infantry.** (See *Arkansas Troops*, 31st *Regiment.*)
Clift's (William) **Infantry.** (See *Tennessee Troops, Union*, 7th *Regiment.*)
Cluke's (R. S.) **Cavalry.** (See *Kentucky Troops, Confederate*, 8th *Regiment.*)
Cochran's (Thomas B.) **Cavalry.** (See *Kentucky Troops, Union*, 2d *Regiment.*)
Cockerill's (Daniel T.) **Artillery.** (See *Ohio Troops*, 1st *Regiment, Battery F.*)
Connell's (John M.) **Infantry.** (See *Ohio Troops*, 17th *Regiment.*)
Cooper's (Joseph A.) **Infantry.** (See *Tennessee Troops, Union*, 6th *Regiment.*)
Corbett's (C. C.) **Artillery.** (See *Kentucky Troops, Confederate.*)
Cowen's (D. D. T.) **Infantry.** (See *Ohio Troops*, 52d *Regiment.*)
Cox's (Jerome B.) **Artillery.** (See *Indiana Troops*, 10th *Battery.*)
Crawford's (M. J.) **Cavalry.** (See *Georgia Troops*, 3d *Regiment.*)
Cross' (Bill) **Infantry.** (See *Tennessee Troops, Union*, 3d *Regiment.*)
Croxton's (John T.) **Infantry.** (See *Kentucky Troops, Union*, 4th *Regiment.*)
Cruft's (Charles) **Infantry.** (See *Indiana Troops*, 31st *Regiment.*)
Darden's (P.) **Artillery.** (See *Jefferson Artillery.*)
Davidson's (Henry G.) **Infantry.** (See *Kentucky Troops, Union*, 10th *Regiment.*)
Degenfeld's (Christopher M.) **Infantry.** (See *Ohio Troops*, 26th *Regiment.*)
Douglas' (J. P.) **Artillery.** (See *Texas Troops.*)
Drake's (Levi) **Infantry.** (See *Ohio Troops*, 49th *Regiment.*)
Duffield's (W. W.) **Infantry.** (See *Michigan Troops*, 9th *Regiment.*)
Duke's (B. W.) **Cavalry.** (See *Kentucky Troops, Confederate*, 2d *Regiment.*)
Dunham's (Cyrus L.) **Infantry.** (See *Indiana Troops*, 50th *Regiment.*)
Dunlop's (James E.) **Cavalry.** (See *Georgia Troops*, 2d *Regiment.*)
Dure's (G. A.) **Artillery.** (See *Jackson Artillery.*)
Earp's (C. R.) **Cavalry.** (See *Texas Troops*, 10th *Regiment.*)
Ector's (M. D.) **Cavalry.** (See *Texas Troops*, 14th *Regiment.*)
Edgarton's (Warren P.) **Artillery.** (See *Ohio Troops*, 1st *Regiment, Battery E.*)
Eggleston's (B. B.) **Cavalry.** (See *Ohio Troops*, 1st *Regiment.*)
Estep's (George) **Artillery.** (See *Indiana Troops*, 8th *Battery.*)
Featherston's (L.) **Infantry.** (See *Arkansas Troops*, 5th *Regiment.*)
Feild's (H. R.) **Infantry.** (See *Tennessee Troops, Confederate*, 1st *Regiment.*)
Finley's (James L.) **Infantry.** (See *Mississippi Troops*, 10th *Regiment.*)
Fisk's (S. W.) **Infantry.** (See *Louisiana Troops*, 25th *Regiment.*)

Fleming County Home Guards. (See *Kentucky Troops, Union.*)

Flood's (James P.) **Artillery.** (See *Illinois Troops, 2d Regiment, Battery C.*)

Forrest's (N. B.) **Cavalry, Regiment.** (See *Tennessee Troops, Confederate.*)

Foster's (J. T.) **Artillery.** (See *Wisconsin Troops, 1st Battery.*)

Frazer's (John W.) **Infantry.** (See *Alabama Troops, 28th Regiment.*)

Freeman's (S. L.) **Artillery.** (See *Tennessee Troops, Confederate.*)

Frierson's (W.) **Infantry.** (See *Tennessee Troops, Confederate, 27th Regiment.*)

Frizell's (Joseph W.) **Infantry.** (See *Ohio Troops, 94th Regiment.*)

Fulton's (John S.) **Infantry.** (See *Tennessee Troops, Confederate, 44th Regiment.*)

Fyffe's (Edward P.) **Infantry.** (See *Ohio Troops, 26th Regiment.*)

Gano's (R. M.) **Cavalry.** (See *Texas Troops.*)

Garnett's Cavalry. (See *Buckner Guards.*)

Garrard County Home Guards. (See *Kentucky Troops, Union.*)

Garrard's (Theophilus T.) **Infantry.** (See *Kentucky Troops, Union, 7th Regiment.*)

Garrity's (James) **Artillery.** (See *Ketchum's Artillery.*)

Garver's (William) **Infantry.** (See *Indiana Troops, 101st Regiment.*)

George's (James) **Infantry.** (See *Minnesota Troops, 2d Regiment.*)

Gibson's (R. L.) **Infantry.** (See *Louisiana Troops, 13th Regiment.*)

Gillem's (Alvin C.) **Infantry.** (See *Tennessee Troops, Union, 10th Regiment.*)

Gillespie's (D. A.) **Infantry.** (See *Arkansas Troops, 7th Regiment.*)

Gillespie's (J. W.) **Infantry.** (See *Tennessee Troops, Confederate, 43d Regiment.*)

Gilmer's (Daniel H.) **Infantry.** (See *Illinois Troops, 38th Regiment.*)

Goben's (Frank) **Infantry.** (See *Indiana Troops, 10th Regiment.*)

Gober's (D.) **Infantry.** (See *Louisiana Troops, 16th Regiment.*)

Goins' Home Guards. (See *Kentucky Troops, Union.*)

Gorman's (George W.) **Infantry.** (See *Indiana Troops, 17th Regiment.*)

Grigsby's (J. Warren) **Cavalry.** (See *Kentucky Troops, Confederate, 6th Regiment.*)

Grigsby's (Lewis B.) **Infantry.** (See *Kentucky Troops, Union, 24th Regiment.*)

Grose's (William) **Infantry.** (See *Indiana Troops, 36th Regiment.*)

Guenther's (Francis L.) **Artillery.** (See *Union Troops, 5th Regiment, Battery H.*)

Hagan's (James) **Cavalry.** (See *Alabama Troops, 3d Regiment.*)

Haggard's (David R.) **Cavalry.** (See *Kentucky Troops, Union, 5th Regiment.*)

Hale's (Luther F.) **Artillery.** (See *John S. Andrews' Artillery.*)

Hall's (Albert S.) **Infantry.** (See *Ohio Troops, 105th Regiment.*)

Hambright's (Henry A.) **Infantry.** (See *Pennsylvania Troops, 79th Regiment.*)

Hamilton's (O. P.) **Cavalry.** (See *Tennessee Troops, Confederate.*)

Harlan's (J. M.) **Infantry.** (See *Kentucky Troops, Union, 10th Regiment.*)

Harmon's (M. B. W.) **Infantry.** (See *Ohio Troops, 31st Regiment.*)

Harmon's (Oscar F.) **Infantry.** (See *Illinois Troops, 125th Regiment.*)

Harper's (A. R.) **Cavalry.** (See *Georgia Troops, 1st Regiment.*)

Harper's (R. W.) **Mounted Rifles.** (See *Arkansas Troops, 1st Rifles.*)

Harris' (Joseph E.) **Artillery.** (See *Corbett's Artillery.*)

Harris' (Leonard A.) **Infantry.** (See *Ohio Troops, 2d Regiment.*)

Harris' (Samuel J.) **Artillery.** (See *Indiana Troops, 19th Battery.*)

Harrison County Home Guards. (See *Kentucky Troops, Union.*)

Heg's (Hans C.) **Infantry.** (See *Wisconsin Troops, 15th Regiment.*)

Helena Artillery. (See *Arkansas Troops.*)

Hescock's (Henry) **Artillery.** (See *Missouri Troops, Union, 1st Regiment, Battery G.*)

Hewett's (John M.) **Artillery.** (See *Kentucky Troops, Union, Battery B.*)

Hilliard's Legion. (See *Alabama Troops.*)

Hill's (L. E.) **Cavalry.** (See *Mississippi Troops.*)

Hines' (Cyrus C.) **Infantry.** (See *Indiana Troops, 57th Regiment.*)

Hopkins' (Enos) **Engineers.** (See *Michigan Troops, 1st Regiment.*)

Hotchkiss' (William A.) **Artillery.** (See *Minnesota Troops, 2d Battery.*)

Houk's (Leonidas C.) **Infantry.** (See *Tennessee Troops, Union, 3d Regiment.*)
Howard's (J. R.) **Cavalry.** (See *Confederate Troops, Regulars, 3d Regiment.*)
Huffman's (J. M.) **Cavalry.** (See *Gano's Cavalry.*)
Hugh's (John M.) **Infantry.** (See *Tennessee Troops, Confederate, 25th Regiment.*)
Humphrey's (George) **Infantry.** (See *Indiana Troops, 88th Regiment.*)
Humphreys' (John T.) **Artillery.** (See *Arkansas Troops.*)
Hunton's (Kinsman A.) **Engineers.** (See *Michigan Troops, 1st Regiment.*)
Hunt's (A. A.) **Cavalry.** (See *Georgia Troops, 2d Partisan Rangers.*)
Hutcheson's (J. B.) **Cavalry.** (See *Kentucky Troops, Confederate, 2d Regiment.*)
Innes' (William P.) **Engineers.** (See *Michigan Troops, 1st Regiment.*)
Irons' (David D.) **Infantry.** (See *Illinois Troops, 86th Regiment.*)
Jackson Artillery. (See *Georgia Troops.*)
Jacob's (Richard T.) **Cavalry.** (See *Kentucky Troops, Union, 9th Regiment.*)
James' (Thomas C.) **Cavalry.** (See *Pennsylvania Troops, 9th Regiment.*)
Jefferson Artillery. (See *Mississippi Troops.*)
Jessee's (George M.) **Cavalry.** (See *Kentucky Troops, Confederate.*)
Jordan's (Thomas J.) **Cavalry.** (See *Pennsylvania Troops, 9th Regiment.*)
Joseph's (Charles) **Infantry.** (See *Ohio Troops, 9th Regiment.*)
Keeble's (R. H.) **Infantry.** (See *Tennessee Troops, Confederate, 23d Regiment.*)
Keith's (Squire I.) **Infantry.** (See *Indiana Troops, 22d Regiment.*)
Kelley's (D. C.) **Cavalry.** (See *N. B. Forrest's Cavalry.*)
Kell's (John) **Infantry.** (See *Ohio Troops, 2d Regiment.*)
Kelly's (John H.) **Infantry.** (See *Arkansas Troops, 8th Regiment.*)
Kelsoe's (George W.) **Infantry.** (See *Tennessee Troops, Confederate, 9th Regiment.*)
Kennett's (John) **Cavalry.** (See *Ohio Troops, 4th Regiment.*)
Kennon's (Ellis E.) **Infantry.** (See *Ohio Troops, 98th Regiment.*)
Kentucky Squadron, Cavalry. (See *Kentucky Troops, Confederate, 1st Regiment.*)
Kerr's (James B.) **Infantry.** (See *Illinois Troops, 74th Regiment.*)
Ketchum's (W. H.) **Artillery.** (See *Alabama Troops.*)
King's (John H.) **Infantry.** (See *Union Troops, Regulars, 15th Regiment.*)
Kise's (W. C.) **Infantry.** (See *Indiana Troops, 10th Regiment.*)
Knight's (John) **Infantry.** (See *Georgia Troops, 41st Regiment.*)
Konkle's (Andrew J.) **Artillery.** (See *Ohio Troops, 1st Regiment, Battery D.*)
Korff's (Herman J.) **Infantry.*** (See *Indiana Troops, 69th Regiment.*)
Landram's (John J.) **Infantry.** (See *Kentucky Troops, Union, 18th Regiment.*)
Lane's (John Q.) **Infantry.** (See *Ohio Troops, 97th Regiment.*)
Lanphere's (Edwin O.) **Artillery.†** (See *Lanphere, Edwin O.*)
Lawton's (W. J.) **Cavalry.** (See *Georgia Troops, 2d Regiment.*)
Lay's (J. F.) **Cavalry.** (See *Confederate Troops, Regulars, 6th Regiment.*)
Lester's (Henry C.) **Infantry.** (See *Minnesota Troops, 3d Regiment.*)
Lewis County Home Guards. (See *Kentucky Troops, Union.*)
Link's (W. H.) **Infantry.** (See *Indiana Troops, 12th Regiment.*)
Lock's (Frederick J.) **Infantry.** (See *Ohio Troops, 33d Regiment.*)
Loomis' (Cyrus O.) **Artillery.** (See *Michigan Troops, 1st Battery.*)
Louisville Provost Guard, Infantry. (See *Kentucky Troops, Union, 34th Regiment.*)
Lucas' (Thomas J.) **Infantry.** (See *Indiana Troops, 16th Regiment.*)
Lythgoe's (A. J.) **Infantry.** (See *South Carolina Troops, 19th Regiment.*)
Lytle's (W. H.) **Infantry.** (See *Ohio Troops, 10th Regiment.*)
McAfee's (A. L.) **Cavalry.** (See *Kentucky Troops, Confederate.*)
McClelland's (James S.) **Infantry.** (See *Illinois Troops, 25th Regiment.*)
McClintock's Home Guards. (See *Kentucky Troops, Union.*)
McCook's (Daniel) **Infantry.** (See *Ohio Troops, 52d Regiment.*)
McCook's (Edward M.) **Cavalry.** (See *Indiana Troops, 2d Regiment.*)

---

* Temporarily commanding. † Improvised.

McCray's (T. H.) **Infantry.** (See *Arkansas Troops*, 31st *Regiment*.)
McCulloch's (Robert) **Cavalry.** (See *Missouri Troops, Confederate*.)
McDaniel's (C. A.) **Infantry.** (See *Georgia Troops*, 41st *Regiment*.)
McHenry's (John H., jr.) **Infantry.** (See *Kentucky Troops, Union*, 17th *Regiment*.)
McKinstry's (Alexander) **Infantry.** (See *Alabama Troops*, 32d *Regiment*.)
McLin's (J. B.) **Cavalry.** (See *Tennessee Troops, Confederate*.)
McMillen's (William L.) **Infantry.** (See *Ohio Troops*, 95th *Regiment*.)
McMillin's (J. M.) **Cavalry.** (See *Tennessee Troops, Confederate*.)
Mahan's (John R.) **Infantry.** (See *Indiana Troops*, 55th *Regiment*.)
Marion Artillery. (See *Florida Troops*.)
Marks' (A. S.) **Infantry.** (See *Tennessee Troops, Confederate*, 17th *Regiment*.)
Martin's (James C.) **Cavalry.** (See *Kentucky Troops, Union*, 6th *Regiment*.)
Martin's (J. M.) **Artillery.** (See *Marion Artillery*.)
Martin's (John A.) **Infantry.** (See *Kansas Troops*, 8th *Regiment*.)
Mason's (Rodney) **Infantry.** (See *Ohio Troops*, 71st *Regiment*.)
Mason's (Tyler A.) **Artillery.** (See *Indiana Troops*, 13th *Battery*.)
Mauff's (August) **Infantry.** (See *Illinois Troops*, 24th *Regiment*.)
Maury's (Henry) **Infantry.** (See *Alabama Troops*, 32d *Regiment*.)
Megowan's (W. S. D.) **Cavalry.** (See *Kentucky Troops, Union*, 3d *Regiment*.)
Mendenhall's (J.) **Artillery.** (See *Union Troops, Regulars*, 4th *Regiment, Battery M*.)
Metcalfe's (Leonidas) **Cavalry.** (See *Kentucky Troops, Union*, 7th *Regiment*)
Milliken's (Minor) **Cavalry.** (See *Ohio Troops*, 1st *Regiment*.)
Mims' (A. L.) **Cavalry.** (See *J. B. McLin's Cavalry*.)
Monroe's (James) **Infantry.** (See *Illinois Troops*, 123d *Regiment*.)
Moody's (Granville) **Infantry.** (See *Ohio Troops*, 74th *Regiment*.)
Moore's (James) **Infantry.** (See *Mississippi Troops*, 44th *Regiment*.)
Moore's (Oscar F.) **Infantry.** (See *Ohio Troops*, 33d *Regiment*.)
Moore's (Robert S.) **Infantry.** (See *Illinois Troops*, 85th *Regiment*.)
Morgan's (John H.) **Cavalry Regt.** (See *Kentucky Troops, Confederate*, 2d *Regt*.)
Morgan's (John T.) **Partisans.** (See *Alabama Troops*, 51st *Regiment*.)
Morrison's (J. J.) **Cavalry.** (See *Georgia Troops*, 1st *Regiment*.)
Morrison's (Thomas G.) **Infantry.** (See *Indiana Troops*, 66th *Regiment*.)
Mount Sterling Home Guards. (See *Kentucky Troops, Union*.)
Moyers' (G.) **Cavalry.** (See *Michigan Troops*, 3d *Regiment*.)
Munday's (Reuben) **Cavalry.** (See *Kentucky Troops, Union*, 6th *Regiment*.)
Mundy's (Marcellus) **Infantry.** (See *Kentucky Troops, Union*, 23d *Regiment*.)
Murray's (Douglas A.) **Cavalry.** (See *Ohio Troops*, 3d *Regiment*.)
Murray's (Eli H.) **Cavalry.** (See *Kentucky Troops, Union*, 3d *Regiment*.)
Mygatt's (George S.) **Infantry.** (See *Ohio Troops*, 41st *Regiment*.)
Nelson's (T. M.) **Partisans.** (See *Georgia Troops*.)
Newsom's (John E.) **Cavalry.** (See *Alabama Troops*.)
Newport Home Guards. (See *Kentucky Troops, Union*.)
Nicklin's (Benjamin S.) **Artillery.** (See *Indiana Troops*, 13th *Battery*.)
Nixon's (J. O.) **Cavalry.** (See *Louisiana Troops*, 1st *Regiment*.)
Nix's (F. M.) **Partisans.** (See *Georgia Troops*, 16th *Cavalry Battalion*.)
Owen County Home Guards. (See *Kentucky Troops, Union*.)
Owen's (Richard) **Infantry.** (See *Indiana Troops*, 60th *Regiment*.)
Paramore's (James W.) **Cavalry.** (See *Ohio Troops*, 3d *Regiment*.)
Paris Home Guards. (See *Kentucky Troops, Union*.)
Parkhurst's (John G.) **Infantry.** (See *Michigan Troops*, 9th *Regiment*.)
Parrott's (Edwin A.) **Infantry.** (See *Ohio Troops*, 1st *Regiment*.)
Parsons' (Charles C.) **Artillery.** * (See *Charles C. Parsons*.)
Pennebaker's (Charles D.) **Infantry.** (See *Kentucky Troops, Union*, 27th *Regiment*.)

---

* Improvised.

Pinney's (Oscar F.) **Artillery.** (See *Wisconsin Troops,* 5*th Battery.*)
Poorman's (Christian L.) **Infantry.** (See *Ohio Troops,* 98*th Regiment.*)
Pope's (Curran) **Infantry.** (See *Kentucky Troops, Union,* 15*th Regiment.*)
Porter's (George C.) **Infantry.** (See *Tennessee Troops, Confederate,* 6*th Regiment*)
Pugh's (John L.) **Cavalry.** (See *Ohio Troops,* 4*th Regiment.*)
Reichard's (Aug.) **Infantry.** (See *Louisiana Troops,* 20*th Regiment.*)
Reid's (William P.) **Infantry.** (See *Ohio Troops,* 121*st Regiment.*)
Rhodes' (Clark) **Cavalry.** (See *Tennessee Troops, Confederate, Ashby's Regiment.*)
Rice's (P. H.) **Cavalry.** (See *J. R. Howard's Cavalry.*)
Richards' (W. C.) **Sharpshooters.** (See *Mississippi Troops,* 9*th Battalion.*)
Ridgell's (Joel W.) **Infantry.** (See *Kentucky Troops, Union,* 7*th Regiment.*)
Roberts' (George W.) **Infantry.** (See *Illinois Troops,* 42*d Regiment.*)
Robertson's (C. S.) **Cavalry.** (See *Confederate Troops, Regulars,* 1*st Regiment.*)
Rock Creek Home Guards. (See *Kentucky Troops, Union.*)
Roddey's (P. D.) **Cavalry.** (See *Mississippi Troops.*)
Rodman's (Jasper N.) **Infantry.** (See *Indiana Troops,* 66*th Regiment.*)
Rogers' (H. C.) **Cavalry.** (See *Ohio Troops,* 4*th Regiment.*)
Ryon's (George) **Infantry.** (See *Illinois Troops,* 75*th Regiment.*)
Sanders' (E. J.) **Cavalry.** (See *Tennessee Troops, Confederate.*)
Scott's (John S.) **Cavalry.** (See *Louisiana Troops,* 1*st Regiment.*)
Scribner's (Benjamin F.) **Infantry.** (See *Indiana Troops,* 38*th Regiment.*)
Seibert's Cavalry. (See *Pennsylvania Troops,* 7*th Regiment.*)
Seidel's (Charles B.) **Cavalry.** (See *Ohio Troops,* 3*d Regiment.*)
Semple's (H. C.) **Artillery.** (See *Alabama Troops.*)
Shelley's (James T.) **Infantry.** (See *Tennessee Troops, Union,* 5*th Regiment.*)
Shoemaker's (Michael) **Infantry.** (See *Michigan Troops,* 13*th Regiment.*)
Shryock's (Kline G.) **Infantry.** (See *Indiana Troops,* 87*th Regiment.*)
Simonson's (Peter) **Artillery.** (See *Indiana Troops,* 5*th Battery.*)
Slocomb's (C. H.) **Artillery.** (See *Washington Artillery,* 5*th Battery.*)
Smith's (Baxter) **Cavalry.** (See *Tennessee Troops, Confederate.*)
Smith's (J. A.) **Infantry.** (See *Confederate Troops, Regulars,* 5*th Regiment.*)
Smith's (M.) **Artillery.** (See *Mississippi Troops.*)
Smith's (R. A.) **Infantry.** (See *Mississippi Troops,* 10*th Regiment.*)
Snyder's (Peter) **Infantry.** (See *Arkansas Troops,* 7*th Regiment.*)
Spaulding's (John) **Infantry.** (See *Kentucky Troops, Union,* 15*th Regiment.*)
Speer's (Robert) **Cavalry.** (See *Gano's Cavalry.*)
Spiller's (C. C.) **Cavalry.** (See *Tennessee Troops, Confederate.*)
Stanford's (T. J.) **Artillery.** (See *Mississippi Troops.*)
Starnes' (J. W.) **Cavalry.** (See *Tennessee Troops, Confederate.*)
Stem's (Leander) **Infantry.** (See *Ohio Troops,* 101*st Regiment.*)
Stenbeck's (Andrew) **Artillery.** (See *Illinois Troops,* 2*d Regiment, Battery H.*)
Stewart's (Robert R.) **Cavalry.** (See *Indiana Troops,* 2*d Regiment.*)
Stokes' (William B.) **Cavalry.** (See *Tennessee Troops, Union,* 5*th Regiment.*)
Stone's (David C.) **Artillery.** (See *Kentucky Troops, Union, Battery A.*)
Stoughton's (William L.) **Infantry.** (See *Michigan Troops,* 11*th Regiment.*)
Streight's (Abel D.) **Infantry.** (See *Indiana Troops,* 51*st Regiment.*)
Strickland's (Silas A.) **Infantry.** (See *Ohio Troops,* 50*th Regiment.*)
Suman's (Isaac C. B.) **Infantry.** (See *Indiana Troops,* 9*th Regiment.*)
Sweet's (Benjamin J.) **Infantry.** (See *Wisconsin Troops,* 21*st Regiment.*)
Swett's (C.) **Artillery.** (See *Warren Light Artillery.*)
Taylor's (Captain) **Cavalry.** (See *Kentucky Squadron, Cavalry.*)
Taylor's (Jonah R.) **Infantry.** (See *Ohio Troops,* 50*th Regiment.*)
Texas Rangers (Wharton's) **Cavalry.** (See *Texas Troops,* 8*th Regiment.*)
Texas Squadron, Cavalry. (See *R. M. Gano's Cavalry.*)
Thompson's (John C.) **Infantry** (See *Mississippi Troops,* 44*th Regiment.*)

Throckmorton's (C. B.) Artillery.   (See *Union Troops, Regulars, 4th Regt, Batty. H.*).
Timberlake's (John) Infantry.   (See *Indiana Troops, 81st Regiment.*)
Tinker's (Stephen R.) Infantry.   (See *Indiana Troops, 54th Regiment.*)
Tolles' (William R.) Infantry.   (See *Ohio Troops, 105th Regiment.*)
Topping's (Melville D.) Infantry.   (See *Indiana Troops, 71st Regiment.*)
Townsend's (Frederick) Infantry.   (See *Union Troops, Regulars, 18th Regiment.*)
Turner's (W. B.) Artillery.   (See *M. Smith's Artillery.*)
Van Derveer's (Ferdinand) Infantry.   (See *Ohio Troops, 35th Regiment.*)
Voris' (Jeremiah) Artillery.   (See *Indiana Troops, 8th Battery.*)
Wade's (W. B.) Cavalry.   (See *Confederate Troops, Regulars, 8th Regiment.*)
Wadsworth's Home Guards.   (See *Kentucky Troops, Union.*)
Wagner's (George D.) Infantry.   (See *Indiana Troops, 15th Regiment.*)
Walker's (John C.) Infantry.   (See *Indiana Troops, 35th Regiment.*)
Walker's (John G.) Cavalry.   (See *Texas Troops, 8th Regiment.*)
Walker's (Moses B.) Infantry.   (See *Ohio Troops, 31st Regiment.*)
Walthall's (E. C.) Infantry.   (See *Mississippi Troops, 29th Regiment.*)
Waltham's ? (Captain) Cavalry.   (See *Kentucky Squadron, Cavalry.*)
Warner's (William A.) Infantry.   (See *Kentucky Troops, Union, 18th Regiment.*)
Warren Light Artillery.   (See *Mississippi Troops.*)
Washington Artillery.   (See *Louisiana Troops.*)
Waters' (D. D.) Artillery.   (See *Alabama Troops.*)
Weaver's (James A.) Cavalry.   (See *Texas Troops, 15th [32d?] Regiment.*)
Webb's (Junius Y.) Cavalry.   (See *Louisiana Troops.*)
West's (O. F.) Sharpshooters.   (See *Mississippi Troops, 9th Battalion.*)
Wharton's (John A.) Cavalry.   (See *Texas Troops, 8th Regiment.*)
Whitaker's (Walter C.) Infantry.   (See *Kentucky Troops, Union, 6th Regiment.*)
White's (Moses) Infantry.   (See *Tennessee Troops, Confederate, 37th Regiment.*)
White's (T. W.) Infantry.   (See *Mississippi Troops, 9th Regiment.*)
Whittlesey's Company.   (See *Ohio Troops.*)
Williams' (Edward C.) Cavalry.   (See *Pennsylvania Troops, 9th Regiment.*)
Williamson's (J. A.) Mounted Rifles.   (See *Arkansas Troops, 2d Rifles.*)
Wilson's (H. Blair) Infantry.   (See *Ohio Troops, 44th Regiment.*)
Wilson's (Lafe) Home Guards.   (See *Kentucky Troops, Union.*)
Winfrey's (Thomas C.) Cavalry.   (See *Kentucky Troops, Union, 5th Regiment.*)
Winn's (S. J.) Cavalry.   (See *Georgia Troops, 16th Battalion.*)
Winters' (Joshua C.) Infantry.   (See *Illinois Troops, 59th Regiment.*)
Wisner's (Moses) Infantry.   (See *Michigan Troops, 22d Regiment.*)
Wolford's (Frank) Cavalry.   (See *Kentucky Troops, Union, 1st Regiment.*)
Woodbury's (Horatio) Infantry.   (See *Indiana Troops, 81st Regiment.*)
Wood's (Gustavus A.) Infantry.   (See *Indiana Troops, 15th Regiment.*)
Worthington's Home Guards.   (See *Kentucky Troops, Union.*)
Wright's (J. J.) Company.   (See *Ohio Troops.*)
Writer's (Stephen C.) Cavalry.   (See *Ohio Troops, 1st Regiment.*)
Wynkoop's (George C.) Cavalry.   (See *Pennsylvania Troops, 7th Regiment.*)
Wynkoop's (John E.) Cavalry.   (See *Pennsylvania Troops, 7th Regiment.*)
Young's (William H.) Infantry.   (See *Ohio Troops, 26th Regiment.*)
Zahm's (Lewis) Cavalry.   (See *Ohio Troops, 3d Regiment.*)
Zinken's (Leon von) Infantry.   (See *Louisiana Troops, 20th Regiment.*)

INDEX.

Brigades, Divisions, Corps, Armies, and improvised organizations are "Mentioned" under name of commanding officer; State and other organizations under their official designation. (See Alternate Designations, pp. 1162–1168.)

Page.

Page.

Page.

Buell Commission—Continued.

Testimony of

Hazen, W. B.. 271–275
Hieronymus, H. W... 588–591
Huston [Houston], Russell... 496–505
Innes, W. P... 247–252
Johnson, Andrew.. 697, 698
Johnson, R. W... 265–267
Jones, Frank J... 91, 92
Jones, Stephen E.. 302–314
Kennett, John.. 513–515
Lane, George W.. 472–485
Lytle, W. H... 67–75
McCook, Alexander McD.............................. 15, 87–91, 98–127
McCook, Daniel.. 238–241
McCook, Edward M... 325–333
McElwee, James B... 671–673
Macfeely, Robert.. 333–338
Mack, O. A... 275–278
Merrill, Jesse.. 505–513
Miller, John F... 267–271
Mitchell, Robert B.. 92–98
Morton, J. St. C.. 666, 720–723
Mundy, Marcellus... 631–644
Negley, James S... 257–265
Oldershaw, P. P... 293–296
Pratt, J. T... 82–86
Rapier, M. A... 320–325
Roper, George S... 283–285
Rousseau, Lovell H... 15, 343–360
Shoemaker, Michael.. 127–130
Sidell, W. H... 252–257
Slocum, Joseph J.. 492–496
Smith, F. A.. 290–293
Smith, W. S.. 386–417
Steedman, J. B... 15, 130–146
Streight, A. D... 15, 147–149
Symonds, H. C... 339–342
Taylor, George R.. 317–319
Thomas, George H... 182–204
Todd, Harry I... 367–369
Wagner, G. D.. 235–238
Wilder, John T.. 204–215
Wilson, Tancred R... 591, 592
Wood, Gustavus A... 360–366
Wood, Thomas J.. 15, 149–182
Wright, H. G.. 692, 693
Wright, J. M.. 650–666
Yates, John B... 485–492

Witnesses, evidence, etc. Communications from

Buell Commission.. 690, 691, 721
Buell, Don Carlos........... 21, 66, 598, 600, 601, 690, 691, 723, 724
Judge-Advocate-General's Office, U. S. A......................... 21, 66
Rosecrans, W. S.. 417

(See also *Proceedings*, pp. 417–426.)

Page.

Page

* Also known as 16th Battalion P. R.

Page.

Page.

Page

* Designation changed to 6th Cavalry in February, 1863.

---

* Attached to Morgan's command. † Sometimes called 1st Battalion. ‡ Also called 3d Regiment.

---

*Afterward Company E, 18th Battalion Tennessee Cavalry.

---

* Emergency troops in service in defense of Cincinnati.
† Includes skirmish near Lusby's Mill, June 20.

*Also called Chaplin Hills.

Page.

---

* Also called Spiller's battallion.
† Also called 1st Middle Tennessee.
‡ Merged into 7th Kentucky Cavalry in September, 1862.